The Birdwatcher's Companion to North American Birdlife

American Birding
ASSOCIATION

The American Birding Association
aims to inspire all people
to enjoy and protect wild birds.

The Birdwatcher's Companion to North American Birdlife

CHRISTOPHER W. LEAHY

Illustrations by Gordon Morrison

PRINCETON UNIVERSITY PRESS
Princeton and Oxford

Copyright © 2004 by Princeton University Press
Published by Princeton University Press, 41 William Street, Princeton,
    New Jersey 08540
In the United Kingdom: Princeton University Press, 3 Market Place,
    Woodstock, Oxfordshire OX20 1SY
All Rights Reserved

LIBRARY OF CONGRESS CATALOGING-IN-PUBLICATION DATA

Leahy, Christopher W.
    The birdwatcher's companion to North American birdlife /
Christopher W. Leahy; illustrations by Gordon Morrison.
        p. cm.
    Includes bibliographical references (p.).
    ISBN: 0-691-09297-4 (cl : alk. paper)
        1. Bird watching—North America. 2. Birds—North America. I. Morrison,
Gordon. II. Title.
QL681.L35 2004
598'.07'2347—dc22   2003066383

British Library Cataloging-in-Publication Data is available

This book has been composed in Utopia, Type Embellishment One,
    Dorchester Script

Printed on acid-free paper. ∞

nathist.princeton.edu

Printed in the United States of America

10   9   8   7   6   5   4   3   2   1

FOR DOROTHY E. SNYDER

CONTENTS

ILLUSTRATIONS

FOREWORD

I admit that I do not recall how my copy of *The Birdwatcher's Companion* appeared on my shelves in the early 1980s. Like many other birders, then as now, my acquisition of books on birds and birding outstripped my ability to digest them at leisure. I do, however, clearly remember my first perusal of *The Birdwatcher's Companion*. It was in a moment of fiddling distraction at my office, in between interviews with students, that I reached for the nearest tome and seized the *Companion*. In a sort of *sortes vergilianae*, I let the book open itself, and I read the first passage my eyes fell upon. It so happened that the section was entitled "Identification."

When I reached the third paragraph of that section, I had no doubt: here is a living writer who possesses the charm and depth of a William Beebe or a Robert Cushman Murphy, a writer capable of conveying the complexity of our emotional investment in birds in a few, brief conversational sentences, a writer able to shift registers effortlessly without losing continuity. It was immediately clear, on reading another several dozen pages, that Mr. Leahy has at his command a staggering breadth of human learning—cultural history and science, hobby and profession are given equal and thorough weight in the *Companion,* and the sections on "Birds in Human Culture" and "Birds in Imagination" are as refreshing as they are original. Yet nowhere does this erudition feel intimidating or ponderous; rather, it invites, clarifies, and delights. Here is an encyclopedia writer, I thought, who gives countenance to birding's rich local vernacular ("a wobbla wave"), who welcomes a well-placed alliteration, and who even allows himself wry remarks *sotto voce*. One reads the entries in the *Companion* as much for their informative aspects as for their stylistic merits. As I read and re-read further that first time, I could not believe my good fortune. Even the very brief accounts of minor figures in the early Army Corps left a smile. Alongside occasional pearls of gossip from the early centuries of American ornithology, we find a poem on ectoparasites, the etymology of the word "jacana," and a brief history of the use of decoys. No stone seems unturned.

Over a lifetime, people who batten on birds take in words that a "nonbirder" might never have occasion to use—not just words for birds ("parula" or "murrelet") or their modifiers ("hepatic" or "flammulated") or even their parts ("pileum" or "alula"), all of which are found in a good English dictionary—but words that distance us culturally from nonbirders: "jizz," "lumping," "scansorial." It was only years after I had first read the

Companion that I realized the value in this book for nonbirders: here was the perfect gift for a puzzled friend, spouse, or family member seeking to understand more about the life—and language—of the birder close to him or her. No matter what the word or phrase, from "accidental" to Princess Zénaide," the new birder or curious bystander will find it here glossed, with nuance and aplomb. I have purchased a half-dozen copies for family and friends over the years; the reviews have been rave.

The pleasures of reading are very personal, but I confess I find no comparable endeavor in the literature of ornithology and of birdwatching that engages so consistently as the *Companion.* Even moments of critique and reflection in the *Companion* are light and unencumbered, never descending into deprecation; the text abounds with good will and humor for its subjects. Perhaps the greatest achievement in this enormous undertaking has been to maintain this fair, open, consistently fresh and readable tone throughout. I am relieved to see that in this marvelous second edition, in which much of the scientific material was revised, Mr. Leahy has left his unerring, pioneering accounts on "Identification" and "Birdwatching" largely intact. If there were an agenda detectable in this book, it might be the author's clear conviction, always eloquently advanced, that the joy we take from the lives of birds should have as its consequence a natural predisposition for equally passionate work on birds' behalf, in the ethics and activities of bird conservation. And the appreciate reader, if not already so, will be swiftly won over.

EDWARD S. BRINKLEY,
Editor, *North American Birds*

INTRODUCTION

Authors of books that aim to be "encyclopedic" are assailed by two unreasonable exhortations as they write. On the one hand, a perfectionist instinct insists that *everything* be included; on the other, the ego whispers that the author's own interests should be fully elaborated and short shrift given to topics he or she considers obscure or boring. I have done my best to resist both of these errant urges in the present instance, but the reader may still be curious about the premises on which the information in this book has been selected and presented.

The inspiration for the *Companion,* which first appeared in 1982, was rooted in two desires that, as a veteran reader and writer about birds, I had expected someone else to fulfill. One was the practical wish to own a single reference book that I could hold in one hand but that would tell me, for example, whether birds have a well-developed sense of taste; what "agonistic" means; what color a dipper's eggs are; how to pronounce "parula"; who Bendire was; how many species of woodpeckers there are in the world; what aspect of a jaeger "pomarine" refers to; what kind of bird a "hagdon" is; what special birds I might hope to see in the Pribilof Islands; how to measure a bird's bill; whether I should subscribe to *The Condor;* how to cook a scoter . . . and other such information, from the critical to the trivial.

The other worthy objective involved my longing for readable, nontechnical (yet pithy and accurate) accounts of the basic elements of birdlife—accounts that can be read for pleasure as well as information after a thought-provoking day in the field or simply for the fun of discovering some of the more bizarre peripheries of the bird world. These still seem to me to be worthwhile goals, and so, when the American Birding Association and Princeton University Press asked me to undertake a revised edition, I readily agreed.

I soon discovered that this commitment entailed a good deal more than a little updating. In the two decades since the *Companion* was written both ornithological knowledge and the world of birding have experienced vastly expanded horizons. This is excellent news, of course. It means that birds apparently really are—as I have always thought—infinitely fascinating, worthy of ever-deeper scientific investigation as well as the boundless enthusiasm now being lavished on them by birders reaching nearly every tiny island of avian endemism on the planet. It also meant that I needed to take a crash course in two decades worth of significant

discoveries in major realms such as migration, avian physiology, and the evolution of birdlife, not to mention the advent of the technologically savvy robo-birder. This is not, therefore, merely a tweaked version of the old *Companion.* Many major entries have been completely rewritten to reflect present knowledge; many new entries have been added and the bibliography and appendixes have been thoroughly updated. To make these additions without making this tome even more useful as a doorstop than it already was, I have had to make some cuts. I have been guided in this painful surgery by my original premise of minimizing the technical and emphasizing the fascinating while retaining—in my sometimes not too humble opinion—what the twenty-first-century birdwatcher wants and needs to know.

It could be said that a love of birds manifests itself in three fundamentals ways: (1) as pure pleasure—that first Blackburnian Warbler, the cry of the Whimbrel over the marsh; (2) as an intense curiosity that leads to the acquisition of a new body of knowledge, perhaps even to wisdom; and (3) as concern for the fate of the world's avifauna—now gravely threatened by human recklessness—and a willingness to take action, however modest, to conserve it. My fondest hope for this new edition of *The Birdwatchers' Companion* is that it might serve all three.

ACKNOWLEDGMENTS

No work of this kind can claim to be "original" in the sense that a novel or a scientific paper documenting new discoveries may be. It is essentially a collection of other people's work, and the author's creativity is seen mainly in the selection of information, the organization of the material, and the words he chooses to summarize his sources. My main debt then is to the hundreds of ornithologists and other biologists and naturalists from whose work I derived the *Companion.* Many of these men and women are cited directly in the main text, particularly where verbatim quotations or summaries of original assertions demand this courtesy, and the names of the rest appear in the Bibliography. I am especially indebted to the authors of some of the major modern secondary sources on birdlife whose admirable works I virtually inhaled during the course of this project. They gave me an invaluable perspective, guided me to many crucial primary sources, and kept me humble.

The individual to whom I am most and immeasurably beholden is James Baird, former director of the Conservation Department of the Massachusetts Audubon Society and a fount of ornithological wisdom, who read through the entire original typescript making countless critical contributions relating both to profound issues and to minute details. Anyone tempted to underestimate Mr. Baird's resolve and good humor should try reading even the shortest alphabetical reference book through from A to Z.

Walter Ellison performed this Herculean labor for the second edition, identifying the many areas that required updating, suggesting new entries, pointing out the most important new references in the scientific literature and diplomatically questioning my rhetorical excesses.

Roger F. Pasquier also read the original typescript through—at astonishing speed—and furnished numerous valuable suggestions; he also provided an elegant Preface to the first edition.

Arthur Wang of Hill & Wang, who inspired and edited the first edition, unfailingly displayed a high degree of literacy and taste, infinite patience, and the ability to apply pressure gracefully.

Robert Kirk of Princeton University Press, editor of the second edition, has proven to be a worthy successor to Mr. Wang in all respects.

Gerard A. Bertrand, former President of the Massachusetts Audubon Society, provided both time and support, without which I never could have written such a long book.

Paul Baicich of the American Birding Association and Wayne Petersen of the Massachusetts Audubon Society, were instrumental in promoting the idea of a second edition and supported the project through a number of unusual circumstances.

Gordon Morrison worked many hours of overtime without compensation on the *Companion*'s original illustrations as well as a series of new ones for this second edition. He cheerfully made dozens of revisions in his work right up through its final stages and seemed to thrive on frank appraisals, evincing character traits not exhibited by all artists of his competence and reputation.

The late Jim Lane cast his expert eye over the BIRD FINDING entries, thereby improving them significantly.

Jack Lynch took on the onerous task of copyediting the first edition of the *Companion* with its multiple subheadings, eccentric features, and ornithological obscurities. He did so with uncommon thoroughness, allowing me to correct a number of substantive points as well as compensating for my abundant lapses in matters of punctuation and the like. Virginia Dunn edited the second edition at a similar high level of competence and good humor.

Others who freely contributed their time and expertise to the crucial details or broad philosophical aspects of this book are Peter Alden, Arthur Argue, Gabriel Behringer, Dr. Robert Buchsbaum, Shawn Carey, Linda Cocca, Thomas Davis, Alan Feduccia, Richard Forster, Thomas French, Norman Hill, David Larsen, Kathryn Leahy, Trevor Lloyd-Evans, Simon Perkins, John Peterson, Raymond Paynter, William Satterfield, Art Smith, Norman Smith, Paul Spitzer, Julian Taverner, Barry Van Dusen, and Peter Vickery.

Since I was not always wise enough to heed the advice of the generous people named above, all errors noted in the *Companion* can be attributed to my own ignorance and/or carelessness.

HOW TO USE THIS BOOK

Most readers will not feel the need for elaborate instructions on how to use a book with an alphabetical format—ALBATROSS will surely be found under A somewhere between ACCIPITER and ALCID; M is clearly the likely place to look for MIGRATION; and so forth all the way to ZYGODACTYL. However, anyone who has ever used an encyclopedia knows that a subject is not always treated under its own name and that a considerable exercise of wits and an extended expedition within the uncharted archipelago of the cross-references are sometimes necessary to find the required information in what the author or editor considers the proper location. This common frustration results from the necessity, in compendiums such as this one, of striking a balance between excessive consolidation and excessive repetition. On the one hand, it is galling for readers to have to scan a long entry called CARE OF PLUMAGE when all they are interested in is ANTING. On the other hand, it is not practical for the author to repeat the same information about down under FEATHER, PLUMAGE, MOLT, and YOUNG, DEVELOPMENT OF as well as under DOWN itself. There is no perfect solution to this problem—the author's subjective judgment regarding the organization of material can never coincide precisely with the reader's—but confusion and fruitless labor can perhaps be minimized. I have tried in this book to include brief definitive entries for the great majority of specific subjects as well as to provide the appropriate cross-references when necessary, so that readers will find at least some information (perhaps all they require) where they first think to look. Further effort has been expended to purge the *Companion* of excessively broad or extraneous headings, again to minimize entries that offer nothing but a command to look elsewhere (AIR, BIRDS IN: see FLIGHT!).

The following summary of the book's organization, contents, and features will help users of the *Companion* understand what is included and what is omitted, where to look first for specialized information, and how the author has approached the presentation of various subjects.

SCOPE. The geographical scope of the *Companion* is the continental United States and Canada, i.e. the same as that of the American Birding Association checklist area and *nearly* equivalent to the Nearctic region, but excluding Baja California and the northern plateau of Mexico, Bermuda, and Greenland.

Wherever possible, North American birds are used in examples of avian phenomena. However, many broad subjects and those dealing with

various extremes of birdlife cannot be adequately treated without alluding to other avifaunas. No one hoping to learn about INCUBATION, for example, should be cheated of an awareness of megapodes simply because no member of this fascinating family occurs in North America. Likewise the Ostrich is essential to any comprehensive discussion of size variation among birds.

LONG ENTRIES. Broad subjects are treated in essay form with the aim of summarizing present knowledge or current practice in a particular field. Though subheadings are freely used to allow the information seeker to find facts readily, the longest entries are also meant to be read through at leisure as one might read a chapter of a book or a magazine article. Major entries on general subjects are listed immediately below, except for those dealing with parts, systems, and functions of a bird's body, which are given separately in the next section.

ABUNDANCE	FOOD/FEEDING
AGE	HUMAN CULTURE, BIRDS IN
AGGRESSION	HYBRIDIZATION
BANDING	ILLUSTRATION
BATHING	IMAGINATION, BIRDS IN
BIRD CLUB	INCUBATION
BIRD FEEDING	INTELLIGENCE
BIRD FINDING	INTRODUCED BIRDS
BIRDHOUSE	LAWS PROTECTING BIRDLIFE
BIRDWATCHING	LISTING
CAPTIVITY, BIRDS IN	MIGRATION
CARE OF DISTRESSED BIRDS	MOLT
CENSUS	NAVIGATION
COLOR AND PATTERN	NEST
CONSERVATION	NOMENCLATURE
DISEASE	OPTICAL EQUIPMENT
DISPLAY	ORNITHOLOGY
DISTRIBUTION	PARENTAL CARE
DOMESTICATED BIRDS	PHOTOGRAPHY
DOMINANCE	PLUMAGE
ECTOPARASITE	POPULATION
EGG	PREDATION
ENDANGERED BIRDS	PREENING
ENDOPARASITE	PROBLEMS INVOLVING BIRDS
EVOLUTION OF BIRDLIFE	RECORDING OF BIRD SOUNDS
EXTINCT BIRDS	SIZE
FALCONRY	SLEEP
FEATHER	SONG
FLIGHT	SPECIATION
FLOCK	SPEED

SWIMMING/DIVING   THREATS TO BIRDLIFE
SYSTEMATICS   YOUNG, DEVELOPMENT OF
TERRITORY

One of the inherent inadequacies of reference books containing many entries is that they inevitably include a wealth of information from which
the reader never benefits because she doesn't know it exists and therefore
has neither the occasion nor the ability to look it up. Entries from the
Companion that may fit this description include

ANTING   IRRUPTION
ATLAS, BREEDING-BIRD   MARKING
BIRD CALLS (made by humans)   MATING SYSTEMS
BIRDING EVENTS   MEASUREMENTS
BIRDING TOURS   MOBBING
BIRDSMANSHIP   MOON WATCHING
CANNIBALISM   MORTALITY
CANOPY FEEDING   MUSEUMS
CAPTURE (of wild birds)   NAMES, COLLOQUIAL
CATS   NAMES, SCIENTIFIC
CHUMMING   NAMES, VERNACULAR
CITIZEN SCIENCE   NEST FAUNA
CLIMBING   NOMADISM
COFFEE   NOUNS OF ASSEMBLAGE
COLLECTING (bird specimens)   OBSERVATORY
COMFORT MOVEMENTS   ODOR
DAWN CHORUS   OWLING
DISPERSAL   PAIR FORMATION
DRINKING   PIRACY
DRUNKENNESS   PLAY
DUCK STAMPS   POLITICS, BIRDS IN
DUETTING   POLLINATION
DUSTING   RADAR
EDIBILITY   RARE BIRD ALERT
ESCAPES   RELIGION, BIRDS IN
ETIQUETTE FOR BIRDWATCHERS   SCRATCHING
EXOTIC SPECIES   SMOKE/FIRE
FLIGHTLESSNESS   SUNNING
FOLLOWING SHIPS   TAMENESS
GAP ANALYSIS   TECHNOLOGY FOR BIRDERS
GUANO   TELEMETRY
HANDEDNESS/FOOTEDNESS   VAGRANCY
HAWKWATCHING   VERIFICATION OF RECORDS
HIBERNATION   WALKING/RUNNING
HOMOSEXUALITY   WEATHER
HOPPING

PHYSIOLOGY AND ANATOMY. For the most part, the principal components of a bird's body are treated within long entries describing the body systems, functions, or regions. Organs and other structures or physiological phenomena that are unique to or highly specialized in birds are defined briefly under their own headings and then (in most cases) cross-referenced to the appropriate longer entry. Main headings are allotted to basic organs common to most or all vertebrates for the convenience of the reader, but these are followed only by a cross-reference to the applicable system (EYE: see VISION; or BRAIN: see NERVOUS SYSTEM). No attempt has been made to be anatomically exhaustive: the avian gall bladder (some birds have one, others do not) is not mentioned in the main text. A few body parts, e.g., TONGUE, are treated with thoroughness apart from their systems. These, along with all longer entries covering systems, functions, and body regions, are listed below.

BILL	MUSCLES
BROOD PATCH	NERVOUS SYSTEM
BULLA	NOSTRILS
BURSA OF FABRICIUS	OIL GLAND
CIRCULATORY SYSTEM	OSSIFICATION
COLOR AND PATTERN	PELLET
CROP MILK	PLUMAGE
DIGESTIVE SYSTEM	REPRODUCTIVE SYSTEM
ECHOLOCATION	RESPIRATORY SYSTEM
EMBRYO	SALT GLAND
ENDOCRINE SYSTEM	SEX, CHANGE OF
ENERGY	SKELETON
EXCRETORY SYSTEM	SKIN
FAT	SMELL
FEATHER	STOMACH OIL
FECAL SAC	SYRINX
FLIGHT	TAIL
FRIGHT MOLT	TASTE
GRANDRY'S CORPUSCLES	TEETH
GYNANDROMORPHISM	TEMPERATURE, BODY
HEARING	TONGUE
HERBST'S CORPUSCLES	TORPIDITY
KERATIN	TOUCH
LEG/FOOT	VISION
MOLT	WING

TERMS. In addition to exclusively ornithological terms (e.g., NIDIFUGOUS) and birdwatching jargon (e.g., JIZZ), the *Companion* contains a number of widely used biological terms relating to habitat, anatomy, be-

havior, etc. In general, these are words that occur frequently in ornithological/birdwatching contexts but may not be well understood by the general reader. All such terms used within the text of the *Companion* are defined under their own headings. Again, I have not attempted to be exhaustive and fulfill the function of a biological dictionary.

FAMILY ACCOUNTS. The *Companion* does not attempt to treat comprehensively taxonomic groupings below the family level—that is, the reader can expect to find an entry on thrushes in general under THRUSH, but will find no entry such as THRUSH, GRAY-CHEEKED that gives a full account of an individual species. The exceptions to this general rule are those families that contain only a single North American species. In such cases, e.g., DIPPER, the family account refers particularly to the native form and thus becomes hardly distinguishable from a species account. When one of these sole North American family representatives does not bear its collective family name, the comprehensive entry will be found under the generic or species name rather than that of the family. For example, the lone North American babbler is described in detail under WRENTIT, not BABBLER, and our only cracid is covered under CHACHA-LACA, not CURASSOW.

The family accounts are written in a standardized format giving in sequence the following information: taxonomic definition; number of species contained in the family both worldwide and in North America (world totals follow the Monroe and Sibley checklist, 1993; North American totals are consistent with the *ABA Checklist*, 6th ed., 2002), characteristic morphological and behavior traits, nest, eggs, voice, distribution, and derivation of the English family name.

A few groups within large, varied families are so distinct from other members of their family (if only superficially) that they have been accorded full family treatments as described above. The family-type entries are listed below; those marked with asterisks are sole North American representatives or distinctive subgroups of larger families (noted in parentheses).

ALBATROSS
ANHINGA   CHACHALACA* (curassow)
ANI* (cuckoo)   CORMORANT
AUK   COWBIRD* (blackbird)
AVOCET   CRANE
BARN OWL   CROW
BECARD* (tyrant flycatcher)   CUCKOO
BLACKBIRD   DIPPER
BOOBY   DUCK
BUSHTIT* (long-tailed tit)   EMBERIZID
CARACARA* (falcon)   FALCON
CARDINAL-GROSBEAK   FLAMINGO

FRIGATEBIRD

FRINGILLID FINCH
    (incl. Cardueline finches)

GNATCATCHER*
    (Old World warbler or Certhiidae)

GOOSE* (duck/goose/swan)

GREBE

GROUSE

GULL* (gull/tern)

HAWK

HUMMINGBIRD

IBIS

JACANA

JAEGER

JAY* (crow)

KINGFISHER

KINGLET* (Old World warbler)

LARK

LIMPKIN

LOON

MEADOWLARK* (blackbird)

MIMIC THRUSH

NIGHTJAR

NUTHATCH

OLD WORLD WARBLER

OLD WORLD SPARROW

ORIOLE* (blackbird)

OSPREY* (hawk)

OWL

OYSTERCATCHER

PARROT

PELICAN

PHAINOPEPLA* (silky-flycatcher)

PHALAROPE* (sandpiper)

PHEASANT

PIGEON

PIPIT

PLOVER

QUAILRAIL

ROADRUNNER* (cuckoo)

SANDPIPER

SHEARWATER

SHRIKE

SKIMMER

SOLITAIRE* (thrush)

SPARROW-BUNTING

SPOONBILL* (ibis)

STARLING

STILT* (avocet)

STORK

STORM-PETREL

SWALLOW

SWAN* (duck/goose/swan)

SWIFT

TANAGER

TERN* (gull/tern)

TIT

TREECREEPER

TROGON

TROPICBIRD

TURKEY

TYRANT FLYCATCHER

VERDIN* (penduline tit or
    gnatcatcher)

VIREO

VULTURE

WAGTAIL* (pipit)

WAXWING

WOODPECKER

WOOD WARBLER

WREN

WRENTIT* (babbler)

STANDARD ENGLISH BIRD NAMES. The *Companion* contains an entry for all North American English generic bird names. Some of these (e.g., AUK and WOODPECKER) are also family names and are followed by comprehensive family accounts. Others (e.g., RAZORBILL and FLICKER) pertain to only a single species or a small group and are accorded only brief taxonomic and etymological definitions and perhaps a sentence or two on unique characteristics when these exist.

The phrase "standard English name" is used consistently in the text to refer to the "official" vernacular (common) English names recognized by the American Ornithologists' Union or (in a few cases) other nomenclatural authorities.

NAME DEFINITIONS AND ETYMOLOGY. The meaning and origin of standard English generic bird names are noted under the appropriate headings, unless they are obvious: the derivation of WOODPECKER does not require lengthy explication. When these are family names (e.g., FALCON), the etymology is given at the end of the entry.

Unusual adjectives used in standard English names, e.g., POMARINE or HEPATIC, are also defined under their own headings, but obvious modifiers, such as "Common" or "White-throated," are omitted.

Etymology of Latin (scientific) bird names is not attempted in the *Companion*, but some excellent sources for this information are noted in the Bibliography under BIOGRAPHY (Gruson 1972 and Choate and Paynter 1985) and under NAMES (Borror 1985 and Jobling 1991).

BIOGRAPHIES. The lives of all the men and women whose names appear in current Latin or English species names of birds that occur regularly in North America have been sketched briefly. Also included are accounts of a number of men who, though uncommemorated in ornithological nomenclature at the species level, were responsible for describing and/or naming a significant number of North American species. And a few entries are devoted to men with neither of the above qualifications but of such towering reputation in American ornithology/birdwatching that they demand inclusion. Towers, of course, are perceived to be of different heights depending on the perspective of the viewer and many prominent names will inevitably be missed as a result of the author's slant.

All men and women profiled are deceased and only a few can be said to belong to the modern era.

For further discussion of biographical subject matter and a list of useful references, see BIOGRAPHY.

COLLOQUIAL BIRD NAMES. Over a hundred of the best-known and most colorful "local" or "folk" names for birds are listed alphabetically and briefly defined under NAMES, COLLOQUIAL. Even widely used colloquialisms such as "shag" and "chewink" are to be found in this collective entry and not as separate headings in the text.

NOUNS OF ASSEMBLAGE, or collective nouns relating to birdlife, e.g., "gaggle of geese," are listed alphabetically under NOUNS OF ASSEMBLAGE rather than scattered as main headings throughout the text.

FALCONRY TERMS, such as eyass and ostringer, are defined at the end of FALCONRY and not under headings of their own in the main text. A few exceptions are made for terms that have gained a broader usage, e.g., HACKING.

BIRD-FINDING LOCALITIES. The *Companion* contains brief descriptive entries on a selection of the best-known birdwatching hot spots of North America. Bird finding is now a major segment of the ecotourism industry, and descriptions of all the "best-known" birding spots on the continent would fill a bookshelf. The loose selection premises I have used involve superstar quality and the general notion that if you skillfully bird all of the places noted, you will have a pretty good start on a high-quality North American list. A few localities were added so that some regions of the country do not seem (erroneously) devoid of ornithological interest. I have lumped some localities under broader regions as noted below. The Bibliography contains a comprehensive listing of bird-finding guides currently (2003) available.

ALASKA
ANHINGA TRAIL (see FLORIDA)
ATTU (see ALASKA)
BAXTER STATE PARK (see BOREAL BIRDING)
BEAR RIVER MARSH NATIONAL WILDLIFE REFUGE
BIG BEND
BONAVENTURE ISLAND
BRIGANTINE
BROWNSVILLE (see RIO GRANDE VALLEY)
CAPE MAY
CHIRICAHUA MOUNTAINS (see SOUTHEASTERN ARIZONA)
CHISOS MOUNTAINS (see BIG BEND)
CHURCHILL
CORKSCREW SWAMP (see FLORIDA)
DELTA MARSHES
DRY TORTUGAS (see FLORIDA)
EDWARDS PLATEAU
EVERGLADES NATIONAL PARK (see FLORIDA)
FALCON DAM (see RIO GRANDE VALLEY)
FLORIDA KEYS (see FLORIDA)
GALVESTON ISLAND
GAMBELL (see ALASKA)
HAWK MOUNTAIN
HIGH ISLAND
HORICON MARSH
JAMAICA BAY
LOXAHATCHEE NATIONAL WILDLIFE REFUGE (see FLORIDA)
MACHIAS SEAL ISLAND
MADERA CANYON (see SOUTHEASTERN ARIZONA)
MALHEUR NATIONAL WILDLIFE REFUGE
MILE-HI (see SOUTHEASTERN ARIZONA)
MONOMOY NATIONAL WILDLIFE REFUGE

PERIODICAL LITERATURE. Major North American ornithological and birdwatching periodicals, as well as a few foreign journals published in English, are listed in the Bibliography under PERIODICALS along with contact information.

The best-known ornithological and birdwatching periodicals are also described briefly in entries of their own. See PERIODICALS in the main text for a listing of these.

DEFINITIONS OF LATIN TAXA. Rather than crowd the main text with repetitive entries defining each of the North American orders, suborders, families, etc., a taxonomic list of the North American avifauna is included as Appendix I. The list makes the relationship of a given taxon to all others apparent at a glance: *Dendroica,* for example, is immediately seen to be a genus in the family Parulidae, order Passeriformes, containing numerous species and subspecies. In addition, the list has been annotated to show pertinent facts about the various taxa, e.g., extinct species and number of species in a given family worldwide and in North America.

For easy reference, alphabetical listings of all North American orders, suborders, and families with the pages on which they appear are given under ORDER, SUBORDER, and FAMILY. For further details of this system, see the introduction to Appendix I.

Appendix I follows the 7th edition of the *AOU Checklist* (1998). Appendix III shows the alternative phylogeny proposed by Sibley and Monroe (1990, 1993–SYSTEMATICS) as far as the tribe level.

CLASSIFICATION AND NOMENCLATURE. The taxonomy and nomenclature of the *Companion* generally follow the *AOU Check-list of North American Birds,* 7th edition (1998) and the 42nd Supplement (2000). Alternative relationships proposed by Sibley and Ahlquist (1990–SYSTEMATICS), Sibley and Monroe (1990, 1993–SYSTEMATICS), and Monroe and Sibley (1993–CHECKLIST) are noted where relevant, e.g., in the family accounts in the main text, and the Sibley/Ahlquist/Monroe phylogeny is given to the tribe level as Appendix III.

PRONUNCIATION. Guides to pronunciation are provided only when the word in question is likely to be unfamiliar to the general reader, when the pronunciation is not obvious, or when two or more pronunciations are popular. In the last case, all widely used pronunciations are given and no attempt is made to dictate correct usage.

Pronunciations are indicated not by phonetic symbols but by substituting words or syllables with familiar, relatively unambiguous pronunciations for potentially problematic ones. Syllables to be emphasized are set in capital letters, and if two emphases occur in a word, they are shown as having equal weight, though they will usually be unequal in reality.

This system is not intended to convey phonetic niceties, but merely to allow the reader to say a word with which he is unfamiliar.

For other sources on pronunciation of both English and Latin names, see the Bibliography under NAMES.

BIBLIOGRAPHY. The Bibliography includes not only works cited in the text but also a selection of books and papers deemed to be of particular interest or pertinence to the various entry subjects. The arrangement of the Bibliography parallels the format of the main text, with all references appearing under headings that correspond to major entry headings in the body of the *Companion.* (Not all entries, of course, have corresponding bibliographies.) Under the subject headings in the Bibliography, individual works are arranged alphabetically by author. The reader wanting to look up the citation "(Emlen 1967)" from the entry headed NAVIGATION will turn to the NAVIGATION heading in the Bibliography and will then locate the author's name alphabetically. The reader who wishes a comprehensive work on navigation by birds or who wants to review principal references on the subject can turn directly to the Bibliography without referring to the NAVIGATION entry in the main text.

To avoid excessive duplication of references that are relevant under two or more headings (applies particularly to major secondary sources), many textual citations are cross-referenced to bibliographical headings different from the entry headings under which they appear. The citation "(Fisher and Peterson 1964–BIRD)" appearing in the entry on ABUNDANCE means that this particular reference is given not under ABUNDANCE in the Bibliography (as would usually be the case), but under BIRD, where various general titles are listed.

Comprehensive references on individual bird species are best sought under ATLAS, FIELD GUIDE, ORNITHOLOGY (see especially Poole, et al.) and STATE/PROVICIAL BOOKS.

APPENDIXES

Appendix I: *Checklist of North American Birds* is a coded phylogenetic list of all bird species that occur regularly in North America.

Appendix II: *Checklist of Casual and Accidental Species* lists all bird species that have occurred as casual visitors or "vagrants" in North America and whose occurrence has been convincingly documented per the *ABA Checklist,* 6th edition (2002).

Appendix III: *Alternative Phylogeny of North America Bird Families* shows taxonomic revisions as suggested by Sibley and Ahlquist (1990– SYSTEMATICS) and Sibley and Monroe (1990, 1993–SYSTEMATICS).

Appendix IV: *Classification of Extinct Birds* shows proposed relationships among early forms following Feduccia (1996, 1999–EVOLUTION OF BIRDLIFE).

Appendix V: *Exotic Species* lists non-native bird species that may be encountered in the wild but that are not naturalized or only marginally so.

Appendix VI: *Birdwatcher's Calendar* gives dates for a selection of North America's principal birdwatching events, places, and species.

The use and special features of the appendixes are detailed where necessary in introductions to each.

ILLUSTRATIONS. Eighty-four species representing forty-four living bird families are depicted in the *Companion's* illustrations. The figures illustrate avian phenomena treated in the text and in most cases are associated with specific entries, e.g., MOBBING (Fig. 19) or DISPLAY (Fig. 7). However, captions are also provided to describe the details of each illustration.

The thirty black-and-white figures were executed on Strathmore Bristol board (3-ply, medium surface), using 2H, HB, and 2B pencils for the line and tone work throughout.

The Birdwatcher's Companion to North American Birdlife

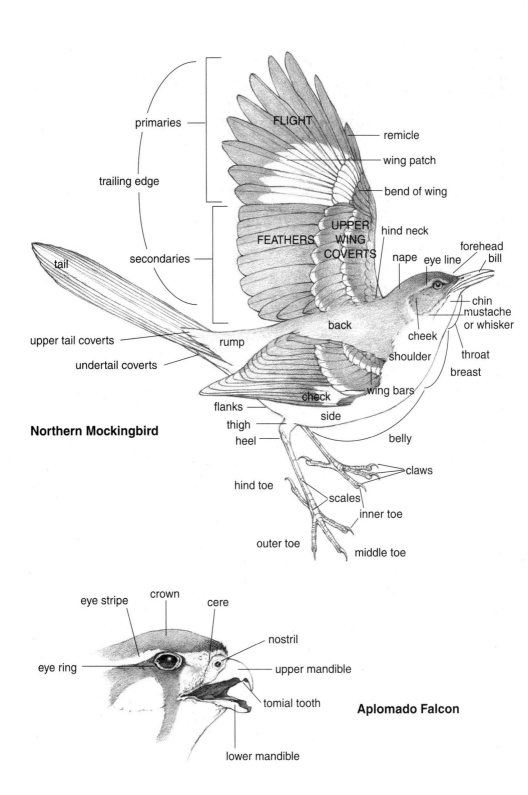

Northern Mockingbird

primaries

trailing edge

secondaries

FLIGHT

remicle

wing patch

bend of wing

UPPER WING COVERTS

FEATHERS

hind neck

nape

eye line

forehead

bill

chin

mustache or whisker

cheek

throat

breast

shoulder

back

tail

upper tail coverts

undertail coverts

rump

check

wing bars

flanks

side

thigh

heel

belly

hind toe

scales

inner toe

outer toe

middle toe

claws

Aplomado Falcon

eye stripe

crown

cere

nostril

eye ring

upper mandible

tomial tooth

lower mandible

A

ABBREVIATIONS. Like other major fields, ornithology and birdwatching are immersed in an alphabet soup made from the initial letters of organizations that it has engendered. The following is a selected list of frequently used abbreviations and acronyms for prominent bird-related institutions, many of which have entries of their own in this volume.

ABA See AMERICAN BIRDING ASSOCIATION
ABC See AMERICAN BIRD CONSERVANCY
AOU See AMERICAN ORNITHOLOGISTS' UNION
BBS See BREEDING BIRD SURVEY
BNA See *BIRDS OF NORTH AMERICA* PROJECT
CITES See LAWS PROTECTING BIRDLIFE, CITES
DVOC See DELAWARE VALLEY ORNITHOLOGICAL CLUB
GAP See GAP ANALYSIS (PROGRAM)
HMANA Hawk Migration Association of North America
ICBP See BIRDLIFE INTERNATIONAL
ICF See INTERNATIONAL CRANE FOUNDATION
IOC See INTERNATIONAL ORNITHOLOGICAL CONGRESS
NARBA North American Rare Bird Alert
NAS See NATIONAL AUDUBON SOCIETY
NORAC North American Bird Atlas Committee
WHSRN See WESTERN HEMISPHERE SHOREBIRD RESERVE NETWORK

ABERRANT (ab-AIR-ent). Abnormal; deviant. Sometimes used to describe untypical plumages or structural malformations in birds. See ABNORMALITY; PLUMAGE.

ABERT (AY-bert), James William, 1820–97 (Abert's Towhee: *Pipilo aberti*). One of a number of officers in the Army Corps of Engineers who collected birds for Spencer BAIRD while on duty in the West. Baird repaid this service by naming one of Abert's New Mexico specimens for its collector.

Fig. 1. *Topography of a bird.* Mostly field terms; for technical terms, see Fig. 35.

ABNORMALITY. It is not unusual for banders and feeder owners to encounter birds with physical handicaps or deformations. Some of these—e.g., lost or broken wings and legs or damaged eyes, resulting from accidents, encounters with predators, frostbite, etc.—reflect the inherent hardship of avian life. And the resiliency of apparently fragile and vulnerable organisms is also exemplified in the fact that many birds survive such handicaps with surprising adaptability. Other abnormalities due to disease or genetic defects are noted less frequently, possibly because they often prove fatal shortly after birth. However, even some avian "monsters" with extra legs or wings or bizarrely deformed mandibles are sometimes able to function satisfactorily.

For reviews of various abnormalities recorded in birds, see, Michener (1936), Nickell (1965), Pomeroy (1962; illustrations of bill deformations), and Ellegren et al. (1997). For plumage abnormalities, see ALBINISM; MELANISM; ERYTHRISM; LEUCISM; XANTHOCHROISM; PLUMAGE. See also DISEASE.

ABRASION. In an ornithological context, the wearing away by normal friction of the edges of a feather. In many species, marked plumage changes result from abrasion. The speckled basic (winter) plumage of adult European Starlings, for example, is produced by the pale tips of body feathers acquired in the pre-basic (post-nuptial) molt. Most of these tips wear off by spring, leaving a nearly spotless alternate (breeding) plumage.

Individual feathers may become worn "to the bone"—i.e., down to a nearly vaneless shaft—thus altering the protective and insulation capacity of the plumage (see TEMPERATURE, BODY).

Abrasion can also be a significant factor in identification. For example, many sandpipers seem particularly "scaly" when freshly molted, because of body feathers with dark centers and broad, pale edges; such birds appear darker and more uniformly colored as the feather margins become abraded.

Some feathers are subject to more abrasion than others. Feathers of the upperparts typically get more wear than those of underparts, as do flight and tail feathers, especially at the tips. These wear-prone areas are often black or dark in color, reflecting the fact that melanin, the dark pigment in feathers, is stronger structurally than white or carotenoid pigments (Burtt 1986—COLOR AND PATTERN). Thus, the color patterns of birds can have physical functions as well as signaling identity and intent as in display.

ABUNDANCE (of individual birds/species). It should surprise no one that the question of how many individual birds are alive on this planet at any given moment has yet to be answered with any degree of certainty. True, there are a few species, e.g., Whooping Crane, whose distributions

have been fully discovered and whose total populations are so small that we know precisely how many individuals presently exist (see ENDANGERED BIRDS). But even estimates for scarce and well-studied species may have large error factors either because it is difficult to distinguish individuals in populations of wide ranging species, such as raptors, or because population numbers are extrapolated based on counts of singing males (e.g., Kirtland's Warbler). The *breeding* populations of certain seabirds, e.g., Laysan Albatross, Greater Shearwater, Northern Fulmar, Northern Gannet, Atlantic Puffin, and Roseate Tern, that nest locally in compact colonies—most of which are known—can be estimated with a high degree of accuracy simply by counting nest sites (though these counts do not included prebreeding or "vacationing" birds). But when we consider even so limited a goal as calculating the number of Black-capped Chickadees in Massachusetts during a given month—not to mention the number of songbirds in Canada or the planet's total avian population—we begin to appreciate the difficulty of the task. To begin with, simply counting accurately the number of small woodland birds in a 10-acre plot involves much patience and labor (see CENSUS) and leaves the counter with little confidence that absolute accuracy has been achieved. Once there are reasonably reliable counts for a range of species and habitats, one can begin to make some tentative extrapolation—but consider some of the variables involved:

- The populations of all birds fluctuate greatly in the course of the year, hitting a low before birds of the year have hatched—when only individuals that have survived the ravages of age, winter, and predation exist—and peaking at the end of the breeding season, when in most cases juvenile birds outnumber adults by at least severalfold.

- Even small-scale censuses show that some habitats support many more birds than others—from as few as 13 birds (adults of all species) per 10 acres of woods or farmland to over 1000 individuals in the same amount of exceptionally rich habitat (Lack 1966—POPULATION).

- Bird populations in a given locality change drastically during the year not only due to seasonal fluctuations effected by reproduction but also due to bird movements. Areas of arctic tundra that teem with breeding shorebirds and other birds are nearly (or totally) barren of birdlife for 6 or more months of the year. And the already rich resident avifauna of Central America is increased no-one-knows-how-many times by the flood of North American migrants that arrive on their wintering grounds there each fall.

- Population densities of different species vary greatly, making it impossible to extrapolate total bird populations from what is known about one or a few species.

- Bird populations increase and decrease in cycles and according to ecological variations (see POPULATION). Northern finches and raptors experience alternating "booms" and "busts"—continually shifting pattern brought about by fluctuations in the amount of food available to the potential consumers.

Some "Guesstimates." Despite the inherent difficulty in counting birds, the question of "how many" exerts a powerful fascination, partly, no doubt, because there are obviously so many and partly because it would be very useful in judging the health of a given species (as well as of the whole environment) to know whether bird populations are declining drastically (as many earnestly contend), holding their own, or even (certainly true in some cases) increasing. Readers wanting more detail or insights than can be included here should refer to the references cited in the bibliography under ABUNDANCE; ATLAS, BREEDING BIRD; and CENSUS, from which the following figures are taken:

- The world's total avian population has been reckoned (by broad extrapolation) at around 100 billion birds (Fisher 1951—BIRD-WATCHING)—give or take some hundreds of millions!
- The total population of wild land birds in the contiguous United States at the beginning of the breeding season has been estimated (Fisher and Peterson 1964–BIRD) at 5–6 billion birds, jumping to perhaps 20 billion with the addition of birds of the year.
- In a notably careful survey running the length of Finland and considering all habitats, Merikallio (1958) came up with a total of 64 million adult breeding birds, with the two commonest species (Chaffinch and Willow Warbler) making up 10% of the whole.
- There are about 44 species of birds (scarce, local and/or conspicuous, colonial seabirds; see above) whose total populations are accurately known (Fisher and Peterson 1964–BIRD).
- The Red-billed Dioch or Quelea, a tiny African waxbill finch (family Estrildidae), is arguably the most abundant bird species in the world. It occurs in locust-like plagues in the dry savannas south of the Sahara, where it wreaks havoc on grain crops. Single invasions of a particular region have been estimated to be 100 million birds strong and the total population has been estimated at about 10 billion.
- The Wilson's Storm-Petrel is another candidate for the most numerous bird in the world, not according to any census but in view of its enormous colonies, large (antarctic-subantarctic) breeding distribution, and wide oceanic range, over much of which it is (seasonally) abundant (Fisher 1951–BIRDWTACHING)
- The European Starling and the House Sparrow have been nominated as the world's most abundant land birds (Fisher 1951–BIRDWATCHING), but other authorities point out that while their distribution is wide, their occurrence is relatively localized.

- The domestic chicken population is said to be roughly equal to that of our own species, 6.1 billion as of 2001.
- The most abundant species of wild North American bird known was the Passenger Pigeon; about 3 billion are thought to have been alive at the time of Columbus.
- Based on its extremely broad distribution, local population densities, and vast wintering roosts, the Red-winged Blackbird has been judged the most numerous of living native North American land birds (Pettingill 1970–ORNITHOLOGY).
- The Red-eyed Vireo might be the most abundant of eastern North American deciduous-woodland birds (Peterson 1948– BIRDWATCHING). Of course, any land-bird species with high population density and broad distribution (e.g., Yellow and Yellow-rumped Warblers, House Wren, Black-capped Chickadee, American Robin, Brown-headed Cowbird, or Chipping Sparrow) can enter this contest without fear of being too badly defeated.

For rarest North American birds, see ENDANGERED BIRDS. For numbers of species, see SPECIES and Appendix I.

ACADIAN (uh-KAY-dee-un) (Flycatcher). Acadia was a French colony consisting of present-day Nova Scotia, Prince Edward Island, and parts of neighboring New Brunswick and Maine; in 1755 its inhabitants were forced by the British to flee and many settled in coastal Louisiana (see H. W. Longfellow's *Evangeline*). It would be gratifying to report that the Acadian Flycatcher breeds in eastern Canada and winters along the Gulf coast. In fact, however, it is a rare vagrant in Nova Scotia and winters from Costa Rica to northern South America. Its type was collected "near Philadelphia," and it is commonest as a breeding bird in southeastern North America.

ACCIDENTAL. A term used to describe bird species that occur in a given place only very infrequently and irregularly. The *ABA Checklist*, 6th edition (2002), defines this as five or fewer records total in the ABA area or "fewer than three records in the past 30 years." For a discussion of the phenomenon, see VAGRANT, VAGRANCY; see also Appendix II.

ACCIPITER (ak-SIP-ih-ter). A genus of hawks characterized by short, rounded wings, long tails, and long legs. There are about 50 species of accipiters worldwide, of which three—northern Goshawk, Cooper's Hawk, and Sharp-shinned Hawk—occur in North America. The accipiters are forest raptors that feed mainly on birds and are superbly adapted for the speed and agility required to follow fast-moving prey amidst a maze of tree trunks. Except for the adult goshawk, plumages in this group are very similar and the three species can be difficult to identify in the field. Added challenge comes from the fact that females are normally larger than males and therefore females of the smaller species approach males of the larger

species is size. It is common to hear honest birdwatchers report that they have seen "an accipiter" or "a medium-sized accipiter."

The word derives from a Latin verb meaning "to seize" and was used by Pliny to refer to the hunting habits of a species of hawk.

For family characteristics, see HAWK.

ADAMS, Edward, 1824–55 (Yellow-billed Loon: *Gavia adamsii*). A British naval doctor and naturalist who accompanied several exploratory expeditions to the American Arctic. Not least of these was the voyage of the *Enterprise* (1850–55) during which the Northwest Passage was discovered. In addition to dispensing medical services, Adams collected numerous natural history specimens, including several species that proved new to science. One of these, the Yellow-billed Loon, was named for him.

ADAPTATION. Adjustment by an organism, through natural selection, to a particular way of life. A widely applicable term that may relate to structure, function, and/or behavior. Cryptic coloration, night vision, and canopy feeding, for example, are all adaptive characteristics of certain groups of birds. See also RADIATION.

ADDLE (or addled). An addle egg is one that has become rotten or one in which the living contents of which have died or been destroyed. "Addled" has become the popular adjective form.

ADULT. Used loosely in avian contexts to refer to birds that have acquired their definitive plumage (see MOLT, Sequence and Terminology). In zoology the term is restricted to sexual maturity, and since neither condition consistently defines the other, adult *plumage* should be distinguished from adult *status*.

AFTERFEATHER. A secondary, usually much smaller feather that branches from the shaft of the body feathers of most birds below the beginning of the vane (see Fig. 13). In a few cases, almost as prominent as the main feather or entirely absent; presumably provides additional insulation.

AFTERSHAFT. The shaft of the AFTERFEATHER and sometimes used (imprecisely) as a synonym for it; also called the hyporachis.

AGE. *Longevity* in birds can be determined with precision in two ways: (1) by recording the life spans of birds that are born and die in captivity, and (2) by banding birds of known age (e.g., nestlings) and recovering the bands upon their deaths. These two methods yield two different kinds of information on the ages of birds. The first tells us something of a bird's *po-*

tential life span; i.e., the greatest age a given species may achieve under ideal circumstances. The champions in this category are often cited. The longest reliably recorded avian life was that of a male Andean Condor *(Vultur gryphus)* named Kuzya, which took up residence in the Moscow Zoo as an adult in captivity in 1892 and died 72 years later. An Eagle Owl *(Bubo bubo)* lived in captivity for 68 years, and a Siberian Crane for 62. Other families with representatives surviving 50 years or longer in captivity are the hawks and eagles, the pelicans, the corvids (a raven), and the parrots. The last are renowned for long life and there are many apocryphal (or at least unsubstantiated) accounts of psittacine Methuselahs. For example, *The Guinness Book of World Records* (1980) noted (with reservations) the assertion of Bella Ludford of Liverpool, England, that her pet parrot, Jimmy (genus *Amazona*), was born in captivity in 1870 and survived for 104 years.

Certain conditions of captivity that are not encountered in the wild—e.g., lack of exercise, an artificial diet, and air pollution in city zoos—may, of course, prevent a long life from being even longer, but, in general, hazards to life in the wild are far greater and the chances of recording extreme natural ages are therefore much smaller.

Banding records give good indications of average life spans of birds as well as providing a few record ages under natural conditions. The albatrosses hold the present record for longevity in the wild. The current champions in this category are a Laysan Albatross (42 years 5 months) and a Black-footed Albatross (40 years 8 months), and it has been suggested (e.g., Tickell 1968) that albatrosses may routinely reach 70 or 80 years. Seabirds in general seem to attain long spans, with several species of terns and at least one Great Frigatebird still going at 35+ years and an ancient Atlantic Puffin hanging on at 31 years 11 months. The only small land bird known to pass 30 in the wild is a Mourning Dove now at 31 years 4 months. Other groups with members surviving to over 25 years in nature include herons, hawks, cranes, waterfowl, and New World vultures. The longest wild passerine life span on record is that of a European Starling banded as an adult 20 years before its death (Rydzewski 1962), but at least two corvids (a Blue Jay and a Clark's Nutcracker) are now over 17. Most songbirds seem to reach their limit in the wild at 8–12 years, though a *captive* Northern Cardinal is reported to have lasted to 28½ (Terres 1980–BIRD). For an up-to-date comprehensive list of North American avian longevity records based on banding records, see Klimkiewicz (2000) or visit the U.S. Bird Banding Laboratory's website at www.pwrc.gov/bbl.

It should be emphasized that the *natural* age limits of many birds that have proven to be long-lived in captivity (e.g., owls, parrots) are so far unknown, and new data will doubtless continue to break existing records. Conversely, the records cited above for wild *songbirds* are probably close to extremes of old age. This highlights the distinction between longevity

and *life expectancy,* which for most small birds is very short. From 2 to 5 years is probably close to the average life span of most adult songbirds.

Life expectancy increases greatly after the highly perilous period between egg and fully functional adult when predation, disease, accidents, and vulnerability to exposure take a high toll. It then tends to level off, since wild birds normally meet their end in sudden death, and old age is reached so infrequently as to be a negligible factor in avian actuarial tables.

AGE DETERMINATION. For methods of aging bird species in which plumage characters are not reliable for this purpose, see BURSA OF FABRICIUS; OSSIFICATION.

AGGRESSION. Aggressive behavior is common among birds and occurs in a variety of contexts. While acts of avian aggression probably never originate in malice as human aggression sometimes does, it is a mistake to think of birds as innately gentle creatures that resort to violence only with inherent reluctance and restraint. Most aggressive acts by birds occur in several utilitarian categories.

Obtaining Food. As with most other groups of organisms, many bird species kill and eat other species, including other birds. Whether we choose to view this activity as "aggressive" depends a lot on our feelings about the choice of prey. Most people probably don't think of flycatchers as attackers of the innocent, but many of us react to the Sharp-shinned Hawk that stalks the chickadees at our feeder as a ruthless murderer. (A better analogy is probably the pre-Thanksgiving visitor to the turkey farm). See PREDATION.

It is characteristic of gulls and especially jaegers and skuas to "bully" other birds until they are forced to drop or regurgitate food (see KLEP-TOPARASITISM).

Territorial Aggression is essentially defensive in nature and is most evident among birds during the breeding season (see TERRITORY); a functional link has been established between levels of testosterone (the male sex hormone) and an aggressive urge toward other males of the same species. Even territorial song can be considered aggressive behavior to the extent that it acts as a warning to other members of the singer's species to "stay out or else!" When this warning is ignored, the trespasser is often chased "off the property" but only seldom touched physically. In colonial situations, where constant territorial conflict is routine because of the "close quarters," extended squabbles are more common. Gulls, for example, may grab each other's bills or wings and play tug-of-war for many minutes or even hours. But again, such animosities rarely result in serious injury. It is, of course, the innate territorial aggressive urge of roosters that is exploited in organized cockfights, though wild roosters, unaided by steel spurs, rarely fight to the finish. Certain bird species also

defend *feeding* territories. You don't have to watch a flock of feeding sand-pipers, blackbirds, or finches for long without witnessing an "angry" bill thrust by a bird whose neighbor has infringed on the former's innately perceived feeding space (see FLOCK). Solitary species can also be defensive of their food supply: your neighborhood mockingbird probably has a favorite fruiting bush that it defends (aggressively!) against your dog and the papergirl, as well as any frugivorous avian rivals.

Competition. Cavity nesters often face tough real estate markets, because the number of natural cavities typically falls short of demand. If nest sites are already occupied by relatively docile species such as Tree Swallows or bluebirds, more aggressive species (especially House Wrens and House Sparrows) will not hesitate to destroy eggs or kill young nestlings and move in. Larger species routinely chase smaller ones from prime feeding areas, a phenomenon known as *interference competition.* Even among parents and siblings, things can get nasty, especially when food is scarce. There are many accounts in the literature (see, especially, Mock 1984–CANNIBALISM), of a parent or a stronger brother or sister killing (and eating) a smaller, weaker nestling (see CANNIBALISM; PARENTAL CARE).

Courtship Rituals also involve acting out of aggressive urges. This tendency is perhaps most conspicuous among "lek" species such as the Ruff and many grouse. The involved rituals enacted by companies of males of such species on their "dancing grounds" usually include aggressive gestures and even innocuous contact (see DISPLAY; LEK; DOMINANCE). Even the more common male/female courtship ritual often begins aggressively with the male treating a prospective mate as a rival. The female must gradually encourage a more benign approach by behaving in a way that "defuses" the male's attack response (see COURTSHIP).

Nest Defense is the circumstance in which birds regularly punish each other (and other animals) physically. As in territorial defense, threatening behavior usually precedes actual contact, but the aggression level is much more likely to escalate in the case of nest defenders. The degree of punishment likely to be inflicted in defense of eggs or young varies widely according to species and circumstance. Many hawks, eagles, falcons, and owls will unhesitatingly kill an avian intruder large enough to be deemed a threat and do as much damage as possible to a human one. Gulls, terns, jaegers, and skuas typically "dive-bomb" and "splash" humans invading a colony, and may make actual contact with bill or wing if these warnings are ignored. While most small birds will flee before human intrusion, many species—notably the larger tyrant flycatchers—will follow and physically abuse raptors or nest-robbing birds, even ones many times their own size.

Bird Conspiracies. The avian animosity engineered by Alfred Hitchcock for his film *The Birds* with the aid of a lot of trained crows and

drugged gulls is, of course, pure fantasy as well as a clever exploitation of our atavistic fear of all nonhuman, nondomesticated animals. Though it is hard to fathom why crows and gulls would want to attack their chief benefactors, it must be admitted that many bird species do have reason enough to hate us (see THREATS (OF HUMAN ORIGIN) TO BIRDLIFE). But birds lack the intellectual equipment to launch a concerted attack on humankind even if they possessed sufficient emotional equipment to perceive injustice or feel resentment.

AGONISTIC. Relating to aggressive behavior between members of the same species. The threat displays of male birds defending their territories or the antagonistic gestures of lek displays are examples of agonistic behavior. See AGGRESSION; LEK; DISPLAY; and Fig. 7.

AIGRETTE (AY-gret or ay-GRET) (also spelled aigret and egret). The long, delicate, and particularly beautiful plumes acquired by various species of herons during the breeding season. Around the turn of the century, these feathers were in such demand as ornamentation for hats, fans, and other items of apparel that Great, Snowy, and Reddish Egrets were brought to the brink of extinction by commercial plume hunters. It was also (presuffrage) women who raised the cry against this industry, in the process pioneering some of the nation's earliest conservation laws and giving birth to the Audubon movement (see CONSERVATION).

AIR SACS. Thin-walled extensions from the bronchi of the lungs, which fill most of the space of the body cavity not occupied by the viscera (see RESPIRATORY SYSTEM). The term is also used to refer to the inflatable pouches on the necks of some birds, which function in courtship display and temperature control (see DISPLAY; TEMPERATURE, BODY).

ALAR (AY-lar). From *ala*, the Latin noun for "wing." Used as a technical adjective meaning "of the wing." A wing stripe is an alar characteristic of many sandpipers.

ALASKA. For North American birders, Alaska offers a unique combination of ornithological thrills, including superb arctic and subarctic breeding species; fabulous concentrations of colonial and migratory seabirds (including the greatest diversity of alcid species in the world), by far the best opportunity on the continent to find rare Palearctic species, and some fine examples of Pacific coast rain forest. Among regularly occurring Alaskan specialties that set birders heart's racing are Yellow-billed Loon, Emperor Goose, Steller's and Spectacled Eiders, Steller's Sea-Eagle (irregular recently), Mongolian Plover, Bristle-thighed Curlew, Bar-tailed Godwit, Red-necked Stint, Sharp-tailed Sandpiper, Slaty-backed and Ross's Gulls,

Aleutian Tern, Kittlitz's and Ancient Murrelets, Parakeet, Least, Whiskered, and Crested Auklets, Horned Puffin, Gray-headed Chickadee, Arctic Warbler, Bluethroat, Yellow, White and Black-backed Wagtails, Red-throated Pipit, and Brambling and McKay's Bunting. And for the hardiest of the hard core willing to put up with primitive living conditions, foul weather, and irregular travel schedules, opportunities abound in the extremities of the Bering Sea to find mind-altering rarities such as Spoon-billed Sandpiper, Middendorff's Grasshopper Warbler, or Red-flanked Bluetail.

In addition to world-class birding, Alaska offers many spectacular mammals (Wolf, Arctic Fox, Sea Otter, Walrus, sea lions and many seal species, Black, Brown and Polar Bears, Hump-backed Whale and other cetaceans, Muskox, Dall's Sheep, and Mountain Goat), not to mention stunning wildflower displays and some of the planet's most photogenic wilderness scenery. Alaska is also extraordinarily rich in the culture of native peoples.

Only a few of our largest state's best-known birding areas can be noted here.

The Southeastern Panhandle carries the northern tail of the great Pacific rain forest, sadly devastated, alas, by aggressive timbering in many places. The mixed conifer forests around Ketchikan, Sitka, Juneau, Skagway, and other localities hold "southern" birds typical of the whole Pacific Northwest, such as Blue Grouse, Marbled Murrelet, Rufous Hummingbird, Red-breasted Sapsucker, Varied Thrush, Chestnut-backed Chickadee, and Townsend's Warbler, as well as many more widely distributed forest birds. Birders not obsessed with ticking off Alaskan specialties should consider sampling the *Inside Passage* ferry routes, which can be good for coastal waterbirds and (if you get out into the Gulf of Alaska) pelagics. *Glacier Bay* (best accessed in smaller tour boats, which allow more mobility) holds 60% of the Alaskan breeding population of Kittlitz's Murrelets, and the glaciers aren't too shabby either.

Copper River Delta is the largest continuous estuarine wetland on the Pacific coast and from late April to mid May millions of Dunlins and Western Sandpipers (most of the latter's world population) stop to rest and feed in the vast mudflats and other coastal habitats. Access is from Cordoba, which can be reached only by air or ferry, and birders should be prepared for bad weather and the fact that small planes or fishing boats must be hired to see the greatest concentrations of birds. But most participants in the Copper River Delta birding festival are quite happy about what they can see from the road.

Denali National Park. This 6-million-acre preserve combines some of interior Alaska's most spectacular scenery with easy viewing of large mammals (Caribou, Moose, Dall's Sheep, and, with luck, Wolf) and excellent boreal and alpine birding (e.g., Gyrfalcon, 3 ptarmigan species, breeding shorebirds, Hawk Owl, Northern Wheatear, Arctic Warbler, Bohemian

Waxwing, crossbills, and Gray-crowned Rosy Finch). Less reliable (10% shot) is a clear view of the peak of Mt. McKinley (Denali), the highest in North America (20,320 feet). Unlike many Alaskan locales, it is easy to get to (by car or tour bus). Campsites are available or you can stay in near luxury (or just simple comfort) in one of the lodges near the park entrance. The best birding month is June.

Nome and the Seward Peninsula. This is a no-miss locality for Alaskan specialties, especially if you are not going to Gambell or the Pribilof's (see below). By simply exploring the gravel road system and stopping in what are now well-documented hot spots for 4–5 days in late spring/early summer, you are likely to find a satisfying assortment of widespread arctic species (loons, gyrfalcon, ptarmigan, shorebirds, jaegers, etc.), some Alaskan specialties, such as Emperor Goose, Steller's and Spectacled Eiders, Bar-tailed Godwit, Bristle-thighed Curlew, Arctic Warbler, Bluethroat, and wagtails, and, with luck, an Asian vagrant or two. Late summer and fall can also be good. There is also a nice variety of big, beautiful, dangerous mammals in the Nome region.

Gambell is a settlement on the northwestern extremity of 90-mile-long St. Lawrence Island in the Bering Sea. The island is characterized by its barrenness, bad weather, "simple" accommodations, and annual (mainly spring, but increasingly fall) visits by a large number of North American birdwatchers. One explanation for the last, apparently anomalous, characteristic is that, while St. Lawrence is a U.S. possession and thus officially part of North America, it lies closer to the Siberian Chukotski Peninsula than to the Alaskan mainland and is now the most reliable accessible spot on our continent to see Palearctic bird species that rarely or never occur farther east. It also home to one of the most spectacular seabird shows on earth—Paul Lehman writes of "a blizzard of alcids" (in West 2002)–BIRD FINDING, Alaska—with millions of birds passing The Point in late May and early June and 10 nesting auk species. Seeing 4 loons and 4 eiders is not unusual (though not guaranteed) and there is a healthy smattering of more widespread arctic species and Alaskan specialties. But for the keenest twitchers the main draw is the chance of "mega-ticks" such as Great Knot, Dusky Warbler, or Pallas' Bunting. Access is by several daily round-trip flights from Nome and in the high spring season the major bird tour companies all have contingents led by experts on Palearctic and Asian birds. (See Appendix II for Alaskan-Palearctic vagrants.)

Pribilof Islands. Four islands in the Bering Sea about 250 miles north of the Aleutian chain and 285 miles off the west coast of Alaska. The two largest islands, St. Paul and St. George, are most notable for their spectacular seabird colonies (the steep cliffs of St. George hold the largest populations in Alaska), and avian waifs from Siberia are regular if uncommon. A major attraction in the Pribilofs is the opportunity to see and photograph the seabirds at very close range (within a few feet), including, espe-

cially, Red-faced Cormorant, Tufted and Horned Puffins, Parakeet, Crested, and Least Auklets, and Red-legged Kittiwake. The two big islands are also home to most of the world's Northern Fur Seals and there are impressive wildflower displays in summer. St. Paul has decent accommodations (the King Eider Hotel!), and (sometimes) trucks to rent. St. George is much wilder and less visited, with more limited amenities. There is regular airline service from Anchorage, weather permitting. Many birding and nature tours to Alaska include St. Paul, but it is also possible to make your own bookings, keeping in mind that reservations will be tight in the high season (mid-May to mid-June).

Barrow is the northernmost point in Alaska and is best known to birders for its high arctic tundra nesters, such as three species of loons (including Yellow-billed), all four eiders, many other species of waterfowl (including Snow and Greater White-fronted Geese and Tundra Swan), and lots of breeding shorebirds (including occasional "Asiatics"). Barrow's other claim to birding fame is the fall (late September through October) flights of Ross's and Ivory Gulls. Songbirds are thin. The peak season for spring birding in Barrow is the first three weeks of June. Daily flights reach Barrow from Anchorage and Fairbanks. There are several hotels in town but it is advisable to book early if you're not with a tour group. Vehicles can be rented and are near-essential in the spring due to road conditions. All the hot stuff can be seen near the town, but there are also options for exploring further afield. Beware of Polar Bears.

Other options for North Slope and Brooks Range birding include the Dalton Highway ending at Deadhorse and the Arctic National Wildlife Refuge (accessible only by plane and wilderness camping, but a decent shot at Gray-headed Chickadee!).

Alaska Peninsula and Aleutian Islands. While there are a number of good birding options on the Alaska Peninsula and adjacent Kodiak Island, the standout experience is the weeklong *Alaska Marine Highway ferry trip* from Homer to Dutch Harbor and back. Sea birding from the deck is superb, with great variety and sometimes large numbers of tubenoses and alcids, including the possibility of rarities such as Short-tailed Albatross and Whiskered Auklet. The scenery and ports of call are additional attractions. There are three round-trips each summer, which need to be booked the previous January; the itinerary varies with the weather and seas can be rough.

For many years the westernmost Aleutian Island of Attu was the stuff of legends for North American birders seeking Asian rarities. During the decade that Larry Balch's Attour, Inc. arranged passage and spartan accommodation for the hardiest of the hard core, tales of *Locustella*'s that got away and other forms of suffering were told at many a bird club meeting. Alas, today, your only chance of getting to Attu is on a cruise ship, whose landings are not necessarily timed to coincide with the best

birding. However, see Balch's chapter in West (2002)–BIRD FINDING, Alaska for tips on how to make the most of such a visit.

If You Go . . . Birding Alaska requires more planning, gear, fortitude, and patience than a trip to your local sanctuary. It's wicked big, so you may want to take advantage of a well-planned tour (see BIRDING TOURS for the best national operators) or pick out one or two destinations for one trip and then go back. Some of the best birding areas have limited accommodations so it's often necessary to book months in advance. The weather is predictably unpredictable and often poor to foul (fog, snow, cold, and high winds even during the summer). This makes plane and ferry schedules subject to change without notice, and multiday waits in remote airports are not uncommon. It also demands that you bring adequate cold weather clothes and rugged waterproof footwear. Biting flies are ubiquitous and voracious. At the other end of the size spectrum are a number of large, spectacular, but potentially dangerous mammals (Moose, Brown Bear, Polar Bear) that are locally common and can outrun any human. In many places permits are required to visit sensitive areas or native lands. If all of that (plus thoughts of Spectacled Eiders and Parakeet Auklets) turns you on rather than off, then Alaska is bound to exceed your expectations.

In 2002 The American Birding Association published *A Birder's Guide to Alaska* by George C. West. It is an exceptionally well-organized, detailed, and well-written volume, filled with helpful features and was immensely useful in writing this entry. Buying it is the first intelligent step in planning a birding trip to Alaska.

ALBATROSS (pl.: albatross or albatrosses). Standard English name for all members of the family Diomedeidae (order Procellariiformes). There are 14 species of albatrosses worldwide, 2 of which, Black-footed and Laysan, occur regularly off our Pacific coast (Laysan has bred on islands off Baja California since 1986), while 5 or 6 others have occurred as accidental stragglers in either the Atlantic or the Pacific (see Appendix II). The Short-tailed Albatross was once a regular visitor to the western Pacific from northeast Asian breeding colonies but has since been exploited to the brink of extinction (see ENDANGERED BIRDS); there are a few recent records from California, Washington, and Oregon.

Albatrosses are among the largest and most graceful of seabirds, with heavy bodies and extraordinarily long, narrow wings, adapted to soaring on strong oceanic winds (see FLIGHT, Dynamic Soaring). They measure from about 2½ to 4½ feet in length, and the wingspan of Wandering and Royal Albatrosses is probably the greatest of any living bird, averaging over 10 and possibly reaching 13 feet in extreme individuals (see SIZE). Their general coloration runs to combinations of black, white, and various shades of brown with touches of yellow and pink on bill and legs. As with the other tubenoses, the hind toe (hallux) of the albatrosses is tiny or

absent, and the front three toes are webbed. Their nasal "tubes" are located on either side of the bill ridge (culmen), rather than on top as in the SHEARWATERS and STORM-PETRELS, and they walk erect on land, another point of distinction from those two families, whose members must shuffle along on their tarsi. Despite their ethereal bearing, albatrosses are the most ravenous of marine carnivores and scavengers, known for their gluttonous consumption of squid, fish, crustaceans, ships' wastes, and whale carcasses. Some species follow ships for days or even weeks and they figure in many marine legends (see, for example, Coleridge's "The Rime of the Ancient Mariner").

Albatrosses nest in colonies on remote oceanic islands or desolate coasts; their courtship rituals are elaborate and often comical (see DISPLAY). The nest may be simply an unlined scrape in the earth, sometimes with dirt or vegetation pulled up by the sitting birds, or a high (to one foot) mud cup (Black-browed). They lay a single egg that is white in most species, brown-spotted in a few.

The voices of albatrosses are heard mainly on the breeding grounds or when flocks are feeding at sea. Squeaks, brayings, moans, and clucks are standard sounds in the repertoires of most species. They also make hollow "woody" noises by snapping or "fencing" with their long bills.

The 2 species that visit North American waters regularly breed on islands in the tropical and subtropical Pacific Ocean and range widely over those warm seas and to the food-rich waters of the North Pacific. Most albatrosses, however, are birds of the cold antarctic and subantarctic oceans, breeding during the southern summer (our winter) and dispersing around the high latitudes of the South.

"Albatross" evolved from an Arabic word for "bucket." The Spanish version was *alcatraz* and referred to the bucket-like gular pouch of the pelicans. The term was then applied indiscriminately to other large seabirds and finally settled in its present form on the distinctive Diomedeids.

ALBINISM (AL-buh-nizm). An abnormal lack of pigment resulting in white or whitish external features. Total albinos have pink irises (and other parts), because blood vessels at the surface become visible in the absence of other pigmentation. The feathers of totally albino birds are uniformly and completely white. More common, however, is partial albinism, in which only some features are white. Birds in this condition may appear splotchy or have a symmetrical pattern. Nero (1954) documents "albinistic" male Red-winged Blackbirds in which the absence of melanin leaves a pinkish or reddish (salmon) coloration instead of white; this carotenoid-based coloration is present in normal birds as well but is masked by the melanin of the typical black plumage.

Though often due to the emergence of a recessive genetic character and therefore present at birth and transmitted to offspring, albinism can also appear in individuals born with normal coloration. In this case the

cause is a malfunction in body chemistry, which may in some cases be related to dietary deficiencies or physical trauma. For example, albinism in Barn Swallows living near Chernobyl (Russia) has been correlated with the infamous nuclear accident (Ellegren et al., 1997–ABNORMALITY). Albinism is recorded in certain groups of birds more often than in others—notably waterfowl, raptors, quail and pheasants, crows, thrushes, swallows, New World blackbirds, and fringillid finches—whereas it is unrecorded in many other families. See also LEUCISM; SCHIZOCHROISM.

ALBUMEN (al-BYU-men). The egg white. A gelatinous or semiliquid substance surrounding and protecting the yolk. See EGG; EMBRYO.

ALCID (AL-sid). A member of the bird family Alcidae. The name by which the murres, murrelets, guillemots, puffins, auks, auklets, and dovekies are referred to collectively, e.g., "a small alcid" or "an alcid flight." See AUK.

ALEXANDRE, M. M. (Black-chinned Hummingbird: *Archilochus alexandri*). A little-known French physician who sent biological specimens home from Mexico during the mid-nineteenth century.

ALIMENTARY SYSTEM. See DIGESTIVE SYSTEM.

ALLANTOIS (al-LAN-toh-iss). A membranous sac that develops from the hind gut of embryonic birds and other animals. It receives the urinary waste products and supplies oxygen to the embryo through connecting blood vessels. At its greatest development during incubation, the allantois lines almost the entire inside of the egg, surrounding the embryo and yolk sac, but it dries up before hatching time and is left behind together with its connective tissue. See EMBRYO and Fig. 11.

ALLEN, Arthur A., 1885–1964. One of four distinguished American ornithologists with the same surname (see following entries). Arthur A. Allen is perhaps best remembered as a founder of the CORNELL LAB OF ORNITHOLOGY, as a pioneer of bird photography, and as the author of many popular (as well as scientific) books and articles about birdlife. An important educator, Allen's graduate students were among the first and most influential of true twentieth century ornithologists and established the specialty as a biological profession in North America. Cornell offered the first pure ornithology degrees in the United States.

ALLEN, Charles A., 1841–1930 (Allen's Hummingbird: *Selasphorus sasin*). An amateur ornithologist from Milton, Massachusetts, who moved to California for his health. There he collected specimens for professional east-

ern naturalists. One of these, a hummingbird that he recognized as distinct from the similar Rufous, was eventually named for him by H. W. Henshaw.

ALLEN, Joel A., 1838–1921. One of the supporting pillars of American ornithology, whose death heralded the passing of the generation of great nineteenth-century bird men that included BAIRD, BREWSTER, and COUES. J. A. Allen is generally acknowledged as the "father of the American Ornithologists' Union" and served as its president for its first seven years. His professional life was devoted mainly to curatorships of mammals and birds, first at the Museum of Comparative Zoology at Harvard and then at the American Museum of Natural History, where he ultimately assumed the role of "Dean of the Scientific Staff." Allen served as editor for 8 volumes of the *Bulletin of the Nuttall Ornithological Club* (the club was the predecessor of the AOU), 28 volumes of *The Auk,* 3 editions of the *AOU Check-list of North American Birds,* and 22 volumes of the *Bulletin of the American Museum of Natural History.* His own bibliography comprises some 1,450 technical papers, mainly dealing with birds and mammals but also including important work on reptiles and evolution. He was a major influence in the stabilization of American scientific nomenclature and formulated ALLEN'S RULE.

Allen began as a boy naturalist from a strict Puritan New England family and became a protegé of Louis Agassiz. He was a shy man with no talent for public speaking and little inclination to popular writing. Consequently, he was little recognized outside the scientific community and today tends to be confused with the small host of other ornithological Allens (see preceding and following entries). But his influence in nearly all realms of our ornithology was immense and, as noted by one of his eulogists (Witmer Stone), his peers regarded his death as "a calamity."

ALLEN, Robert Porter, 1905–63. Ornithologist, National Audubon Society conservationist, early student of raptor migration, and author of several definitive studies of North American wading birds (e.g., see the Bibliography–FLAMINGO) and widely read natural history classics (e.g., *On the Trail of Vanishing Birds*).

ALLEN'S RULE. The generalization (formulated by J. A. Allen) that representatives of bird and mammal species living permanently in warmer climates tend to have larger external appendages (e.g., bills) than their counterparts living in cooler climates. The ecological significance of this formula is that heat loss from external appendages has been minimized through adaptive size reduction of these parts in populations constantly subjected to lower temperatures. Many other factors, e.g., preferred food items in different regions, influence the evolution of features such as bill,

producing many exceptions to this "rule" (see James 1983). For example, the bills of Clapper Rails of the Atlantic coast become shorter on average as one moves south (Ripley 1977–RAIL).

For a related concept, see BERGMANN'S RULE. See also SPECIATION.

ALLOPATRIC (al-loh-PAT-rick). Separated geographically; usually refers to closely related species or subspecies whose breeding ranges, although adjacent, do not overlap. In this situation the possibility of interbreeding cannot be tested because the two forms do not normally meet. See SYM-PATRIC; SPECIATION.

ALLOPREENING. The preening of one bird by another; also referred to as "mutual preening." It has been recorded in at least 19 orders of birds, including, among other families, the albatrosses, shearwaters, storm-petrels, boobies, cormorants, herons, storks, ibises, waterfowl, New World vultures, hawks and eagles, pheasants and quail, rails, gulls, auks, pigeons, cuckoos, parrots, owls, swifts, wrens, New World blackbirds and orioles, weaver finches, starlings, and crows and jays.

The activity is usually performed by two birds of the same species (often mated pairs), but it may involve a group of birds or two birds of different species. In the latter case, it is thought by some authorities to involve redirection of aggressive urges. See PREENING and Harrison (1965).

ALPINE. In natural history, refers to the habitat above the tree line of the highest mountains. Though the word derives from a European mountain range (the Alps), the concept applies worldwide. The characteristic vegetation of such areas is typically low and creeping, often sparse, and has much in common both in form and in species composition with that in arctic regions: low creeping growth forms and frequency of sedges, willows, and shrubs of the heath family (Ericaceae) . The term "arctic-alpine" is often used to imply this relationship between high altitude and high latitude. The rosy-finches of the Rocky Mountains and Alaska are typical alpine birds. They breed on the stony barrens near the snowfields and descend to lower elevations during the winter. See ARCTIC; TUNDRA; LIFE ZONES. See also BIOME; DISTRIBUTION; and Figs. 8 and 9.

ALTERNATE PLUMAGE. Generally synonymous with "nuptial," "breeding," or "summer" plumage. See MOLT, Sequence and Terminology.

ALTITUDE. Our perception of the relative height of bird flight is strongly subject to distortions of circumstance. We are impressed (as we should be) when we watch an eagle disappear from view somewhere between 8,000 and 9,000 feet above us and when we hear of nocturnal land-bird and shorebird migrants routinely traveling at 5,000 to 10,000 feet (see

MIGRATION). Yet many small birds that live above the tree line on our highest mountains double or triple these altitudes as they flit from one lichen-encrusted stone to another. Of course, in terms of energy expenditure, there is a great difference between the minor exertions of alpine songbirds and the heroic effort required to flap over the Himalayas. And it is no coincidence that the holders of the altitude records listed below are all strong-flying or soaring birds, most of which either inhabit mountainous regions or must traverse them in migration.

Some Record Altitudes Attained by Birds
- 37,000 feet: The highest documented bird flight—Ruppell's Griffon Vulture *(Gyps rueppelli)* in collision with an airplane over the Ivory Coast (West Africa), November 29, 1973 (Laybourne 1974).
- Approximately 28,000 feet: A flock of Bar-headed Geese *(Anser indicus)* heard calling above the Himalayan peak Makalu (elev. 27,842 feet) (Swan 1970).
- 27,000+ feet: Flock of 30 Whooper Swans reported by a commercial airline pilot over the Outer Hebrides, Scotland, December 9, 1967 (Footman 2001).
- 26,000 feet: Alpine Choughs *(Pyrrhocorax graculus)*—highest known altitude for a songbird, recorded by the British expedition to Mount Everest in 1924. The birds followed the climbers' camp as it ascended, probably scavenging leftovers, as is typical of this species, which habitually forages above the snow line. A good candidate for highest nesting record as well, but data are lacking.
- 21,000 feet: Highest recorded altitude for small land-bird migrants; detected by radar over Norfolk, England (Lack 1960–MIGRATION).
- 21,000 feet: North American altitude record; a Mallard *(Anas platyrhynchos)* collided with a commercial airliner, July 9, 1963, over Nevada (Terres 1980–BIRD).

How Do They Do It? No human being can engage in strenuous exertions above 20,000 feet without supplementary oxygen. How do birds, especially those that normally live near sea level, fly in the rarefied atmosphere prevailing at the altitudes listed above? According to Tucker (1968), birds can hyperventilate when circumstances demand it, thereby increasing oxygenation of the blood and availability of oxygen to the lungs. However, this reduces the flow of oxygen to the brain to a degree that is fatal in mammals; high altitude birds apparently have an altered structure in the protein hemoglobin that increases its already considerable affinity for oxygen. (Oberthur et al. 1982).

ALTRICIAL (al-TRISH-ul). Refers to young birds and mammals that are helpless—usually naked, with eyes closed, and totally dependent on their parents—for a period after hatching. Contrast with PRECOCIAL. See YOUNG, DEVELOPMENT OF.

ALULA (al-YOU-la). A small group of feathers attached to the first "finger" of the wing. The number of feathers varies from 2 to 7 (3 or 4 in most passerines). It is used as a braking and steering mechanism both in flight and underwater. Also called the "bastard wing." See WING; FLIGHT; SWIMMING/DIVING; and Fig. 35.

AMERICAN BIRD CONSERVANCY (ABC). A not-for-profit membership organization dedicated to the conservation of wild birds and their habitats in the Americas. To quote from its mission statement, "The fundamental role of ABC is to build coalitions of conservation groups, scientists, and members of the public, to tackle key bird priorities using the best resources available." ABC is a leader in the Partners in Flight (PIF) coalition and in the North American Bird Conservation Initiative (NABCI) and has also created its own Policy Council composed of 85 organizations that work collaboratively on bird conservation strategies; the council publishes a newsletter *(Bird Calls)* on current issues three times a year. Through its International Program ABC provides linkages among conservation groups throughout the Western Hemisphere and currently (2003) supports more than a dozen field projects. ABC has also created its own Important Bird Areas (IBA) Program in which scientists have identified more than 500 New World sites of global significance to bird conservation. Among the policy issues that ABC has chosen to focus on are the roles of cats (Cats Indoors! program), pesticides, tall towers, and climate change in bird mortality. The organization issues a quarterly magazine *(Bird Conservation)* and has recently published a "revolutionary" field guide called *All the Birds.* For more detail go to http://www.abcbirds.org. See also IMPORTANT BIRD AREAS; PARTNERS IN FLIGHT; NORTH AMERICAN BIRD CONSERVATION INITIATIVE; CATS.

AMERICAN BIRDING ASSOCIATION (ABA). North America's largest birdwatching organization with a current (2003) membership of more than 22,000 enthusiasts. Founded in 1968, the ABA was initially focused on recreational birding and especially the "lure of the list." As it has grown with the burgeoning popularity of birding, its purview has broadened, but it continues to emphasize the fun of birding. The organization's present mission is "to provide leadership to field birders by increasing their knowledge, skills and enjoyment of birding and by contributing to bird conservation." It now publishes a full color magazine *(Birding)* six times a year, a monthly newsletter *(Winging It),* a quarterly journal with comprehensive records and analysis of trends in North American birdlife *(North American Birds),* and a student newsletter *(Bird's Eye View).* It also publishes an authoritative series of North American bird finding guides pioneered by Jim Lane. Its website (see below) is a clearing house of birding information, such as lists of birding hotlines and a directory of birding tours. In addition to publications the ABA holds workshops and conven-

tions, promotes bird conservation and the economic and environmental value of birding, advocates a code of birdwatching ethics, offers bird-watching tours worldwide, and dispenses all manner of birding parapher-nalia through The Birder's Catalogue/ABA Sales. True to its roots, ABA continues to publish a "compilation of birding achievements and member life lists" in an annual *Supplement.* For more on the numbers game, see LISTING. See also ORNITHOLOGICAL SOCIETIES OF NORTH AMERICA; BIRD CLUB. For further information, go to www.americanbirding.org.

AMERICAN ORNITHOLOGISTS' UNION (AOU). The preeminent sci-entific ornithological organization of North America and the oldest and largest such organization in the New World. The AOU was founded in 1883 largely under the auspices of the ornithological elite of the day in the form of the NUTTALL ORNITHOLOGICAL CLUB of Harvard University, Cam-bridge, Massachusetts. It currently has about 2000 members. The AOU publishes the authoritative *AOU Checklist of North American Birds; The Auk,* a quarterly scientific journal of ornithology; and *Ornithological Monographs,* a series of longer research papers.

This organization has always represented the cutting edge of scien-tific bird study not only on this continent but worldwide. Accordingly, it is now possible to trace the course of modern ornithology over the last cen-tury by examining a sequence of issues of *The Auk* from the early numbers to the latest. In the beginning they contained many articles with titles such as "The Birds of Southeastern Dakota" (Agersborg, *Auk* [1885], 2:276–89), reflecting the descriptive, phenological, and conservation-oriented emphasis in the ornithology of the day. While important articles of this kind still appear in *The Auk,* they are now likely to be outnumbered by pa-pers such as "Molecular phylogeny of jacanas and its implications for morphologic and biogeographic evolution" (Whittingham et al., *Auk* [2000], 117:22–32) and other documents of the most meticulous research. Reflective of the academic thrust of the AOU is the fact that its member-ship is largely drawn from colleges and universities rather than from the ranks of birdwatchers, though many serious amateurs belong.

Serious birdwatchers of the older generation can still be heard to complain of what they consider a shift of emphasis in this venerable jour-nal away from their subjects of interest, though, of course, the annals of field ornithology—from the trivial to the scientific—are increasing recorded in many other periodicals (for which see the Bibliography).

For more detail on this venerable organization go to www.nmnh.si.edu/BIRDNET/.

For more on the history of the AOU, see Barrow (1998).

AMNION. In birds, a fluid-filled sac within the eggshell that encloses the embryo. See EGG.

ANATID (an-AT-id). A term of convenience for any member of the Anatidae, the family of birds containing the swans, geese, and ducks. In the plural, refers to these species collectively—e.g., "Sixteen species of anatids were recorded, including Tundra Swan and Greater White-fronted Goose." See DUCK; GOOSE; SWAN; and Appendix I.

ANATOMY. For details of bird anatomy, see individual systems: MUSCLES; RESPIRATORY SYSTEM; SKELETON; etc. and body parts: OIL GLAND, TAIL, etc. For a complete listing of such entries, see p. xx.

ANHINGA (an-HING-guh). Standard English name for a single American species, *Anhinga anhinga,* and a collective term for all members of the family Anhingidae (order Pelecaniformes), known in most of the English-speaking world as darters. There are 4 species of anhingas worldwide, all in the genus *Anhinga,* only one of which occurs in the New World.

Anhingas, which average about 32 inches in length, resemble cormorants that have fallen into the "skinny mirror" at the carnival, with almost absurdly elongated wings, tail, neck, and bill. Like the other members of the order Pelecaniformes, they have webs between all four toes and reduced nostril openings in the bill—both adaptations to underwater habits. An unusually elaborate system of neck muscles and a sharply pointed bill enable anhingas to spear fish underwater with extraordinary agility.

Anhingas are birds of wooded rivers, bayous, and swamps. Characteristic activities are swimming with all but head and neck submerged, perching singly or in groups with wings outspread, and soaring high in the air.

Anhingas eat frogs and aquatic crustaceans and insects in addition to fish.

The nest of the New World anhinga is a surprisingly small stick platform in an arboreal colony. Alternatively, these birds will adopt an abandoned heron nest. The 3–5 (rarely, 2) eggs are blue with a white, chalky coating covering the surface.

Anhingas are normally silent but can make guttural croaks if the occasion arises.

The distribution of the anhingas is essentially pantropical and they tend to be migratory in Temperate Zone extremities of their range.

The name anhinga derives from Tupi, a common language of native tribes of the Amazon Basin.

ANHINGA TRAIL. See FLORIDA

ANI (AH-nee). Standard English name for 3 of the 4 members of the subfamily Crotophaginae (family Cuculidae [cuckoos]; order Cuculiformes), 2 of which breed in North America.

Anis are medium-sized (11–14 inches), uniformly shiny and black, loose-plumaged birds with uniquely arched upper mandibles. The only obvious clues to their membership in the cuckoo family are their long, highly mobile tail and their hunchbacked manner of perching; a less obvious clue is the arrangement of their toes (ZYGODACTYL). They are birds of hot, open, scrubby country and feed mainly on insects. They sometimes follow grazing livestock and catch the insects that are flushed by the foraging animals, and are even known to pick ticks from the backs of cattle. Unlike the "true" cuckoos, they are often gregarious.

Both of the North American species build a communal nest, a rather large, messy cup of sticks, lined with fresh leaves and placed in a low tree or shrub, usually in a tangle of branches and foliage. Several females contribute eggs to this one nest and alternate incubation duties. A single female may lay 4–7 (Smooth-billed) or 3–5 (Groove-billed) eggs and one nest may contain up to 29 or 15 eggs, respectively. The eggs are light greenish to bluish and covered (except rarely) with a thin, white, chalky coating, which becomes scratched and stained to some degree during incubation.

Ani calls are a "surprised" or "inquisitive" whining whistle—*wooo leeek!* (Smooth-billed); a sharp, abrupt, metallic *whleenk*, often uttered in a staccato, flicker-like series (Groove-billed); and other assorted calls.

All three anis are birds of the New World tropical lowlands; the North American range of our two look-alike species is normally restricted to southern Florida (Smooth-billed) and southern Texas (Groove-billed), though the former has wandered up the east coast as far as New Jersey and the latter has a broad vagrancy record to both coasts and as far north as Manitoba.

The name "ani" was coined by the indigenous tribes of Brazil.

See references in the Bibliography under CUCKOO.

ANISODACTYL (AN-ih-so-DAK-til). Describes the commonest form (invariable in passerines) of a bird's foot, with three toes directed forward and one behind. See LEG/FOOT; SKELETON, Bones of the Leg.

ANNA de Belle Massena, Princess Anna D'Essling, 1806–c.1896 (Anna's Hummingbird: *Calypte anna*). The wife of the François Victor Masséna, Duc de Rivoli of France was a noted beauty of her day, and therefore aptly immortalized by one of her countrymen, the great naturalist Lesson, in the name of this spectacular species. The Duc, who inherited his title from his father, one of Napoleon's greatest marshals, was a patron of natural history, introduced Audubon to French society, and assembled one of the largest private collections of bird specimens of his time. He also had his own hummingbird for a time until the monotypic Neotropical highland species that bore his name *(Eugenes fulgens)* officially became Magnificent Hummingbird in the 1970s.

ANTICRYPTIC. See CRYPTIC.

ANTING. The application by birds of the body fluids of ants (or other substances) to their plumage. In "passive anting" a bird squats on an ant nest and allows the insects to crawl over its plumage (see Fig. 24), sometimes while anting "actively" or going through the motions.

In "active anting" a bird crushes an ant in its bill and rubs it vigorously on parts of its plumage, particularly the underside of the wing tips, the undertail coverts, and the base of the tail feathers. The ant fluid may be spread on the head and other parts from the wing tips, but certain parts of the body—e.g., the belly—are anted directly only infrequently.

More than 200 species of birds (worldwide) have been observed anting. It is practiced chiefly by passerines but a few nonpasserines are known to engage in anting—or at least anting-like behavior.

The purpose of anting is not fully understood. Ants that emit chemicals (especially formic acid) as a defense technique are favored over ants whose main defense is stinging. It has also been demonstrated that formic acid kills feather mites. The consensus theory is, therefore, that anting is an avian form of delousing. The activity is often followed by preening and bathing.

In the absence of ants, birds will use mothballs, citrus fruits, vinegar, still-glowing embers, and other substances, most of which produce a burning sensation, as does formic acid. This kind of stimulation apparently "releases" the anting impulse, and since individual birds must discover the effect for themselves, some members of a species ant regularly while others seldom or never learn the behavior.

An alarming side effect of certain birds' fondness for a burning sensation is a propensity for picking up flaming tinder and transporting it elsewhere—in some cases to nests constructed in buildings (Mayfield 1966).

ANTIPHONAL (an-TIFF-uh-null) **SONG.** Song composed of closely spaced phrases sung alternately by the male and female of a pair of birds. In "classic" antiphonal song, each bird sings a characteristic *different* phrase and the phrases are so closely spaced that the effect is of a single song. In North America, male and female Plain Chachalacas, Northern Bobwhite, and California and Gambel's Quail are recorded as responding to one another with similar calls at brief intervals; this appears to be the nearest any North American bird approaches true antiphonal song. See also DUETTING; SONG, Multiple Vocalizations.

APATORNIS (AY-pah-tor-niss or AP-ah-tor-niss). An extinct genus of toothed birds (order Apatornithiformes; family Apatornithidae), two species of which have been described from fossils found in Upper Creta-

ceous deposits in Kansas and Wyoming. Similar to *Ichthyornis,* but apparently not as strong a flier. See EVOLUTION OF BIRDLIFE.

APICAL (APE-ih-cul or AP-ih-cul). At or near the tip. The bill of a Sandwich Tern has a yellow apex or apical area. Opposite of BASAL.

APLOMADO (ah-pluh-MAH-doh) (Falcon). Spanish for "lead-colored," referring to the mantle color of this largely Neotropical species.

APOSEMATIC (AP-uh-seh-MAT-ic). Protective, especially in the context of color or pattern. There are various forms of aposematic plumage types in birds. Species such as most nightjars, many rails, and gallinaceous birds are protected by mimicry of their habitat; other species may escape predators by flashing a momentarily disconcerting patch of bright color (e.g., the white rump of many woodpeckers). The kind of conspicuous aposematic coloration that warns of a bad-tasting meal, well-known in insects, has now been documented in several New Guinean bird species with bright plumage combined with toxic skin and feathers (Dumbacher et al., 1992–COLOR AND PATTERN). The phenomenon may also apply to some egg patterns and colors. See TASTE.

APTERIA (app-TEER-ee-uh) (sing.: apterium). Areas of a bird's skin from which no contour feathers grow; they are sometimes down-covered. The apteria vary in size and shape among different types of birds. For a more detailed description, see FEATHER TRACTS.

ARANSAS (uh-RAN-zuss) National Wildlife Refuge (Texas). A 54,289-acre federal reserve located on the Blackjack Peninsula of the Texas coast near Tivoli. Its principal claim to fame is as the wintering ground of the rare Whooping Crane (see ENDANGERED BIRDS), but it also is host to a good selection of regional breeding birds and (especially) migrant and wintering water birds.

ARCHAEOPTERYX (arky-OP-tuh-ricks) *(A. lithographica).* A genus of extinct birds, Subclass Sauriurae, Infraclass Archaeornithes, Order Archaeopterygiformes. Despite recent rivals, *Archaeopteryx* remains the most important of avian fossils. Fossil remains including exquisite complete skeletons with feather impressions dating from the late Jurassic/early Cretaceous periods 135–155 million years ago were first found in fine limestone deposits in Bavaria, Germany during the mid-1800s. The earliest of these were originally identified as reptiles and indeed the skeleton is still considered more reptile-like than bird-like; yet the fossils clearly show that quintessentially avian characteristic—feathers. For more on the anatomy, taxonomy, and significance of *Archaeopteryx,* see EVOLUTION OF BIRDLIFE.

ARCTIC (Arctic Loon, Arctic Tern, Arctic Warbler). Geographically, the Arctic extends from the North Pole south to 66° 33' N latitude, north of which the sun does not rise above the horizon on midwinter day (December 22) and remains above the horizon on midsummer day (June 22). Biologically, however, the Arctic is better delineated by a climatological boundary, the 10°C. (50°F) isotherm, i.e., that part of the Northern Hemisphere in which the mean temperature for the hottest month of the year (July) does not exceed 10°C. Because of variations in temperature over the earth's surface, this line is very irregular, extending south more than 10° of latitude below the Arctic Circle in the Bering Sea and to above 70°N in northern Scandinavia. It roughly coincides with the line above which standing trees will not grow, i.e., the line above which tundra prevails.

Though only a very few bird species (Common Raven, Gyrfalcon, ptarmigan species, Snowy Owl)) are equal to the arctic winter, the avian *breeding* fauna of the Arctic is surprisingly rich. Loons, grebes, waterfowl, hawks and eagles, falcons, plovers, sandpipers, jaegers, gulls, auks, owls, warblers, sparrows and buntings, and finches are all well represented north of the Arctic Circle during the brief (about 6-week) nesting season, taking advantage of prodigious summer insect populations and the marine life that thrives in cold arctic oceans. The brevity of the breeding season is mitigated to some degree by the fact that birds can forage in daylight for nearly 24 hours during much of June and July.

While Arctic Loon, Tern, and Warbler all nest above the Arctic circle, they also nest well below it and none are quintessentially arctic birds in the sense of breeding exclusively in the tundra.

For discussion of particular arctic habitats and the bird species that occupy them, see MUSKEG; TAIGA; TUNDRA; and accounts of the families noted above. See also SUBARCTIC; BIOME; DISTRIBUTION; and Figs. 8 and 9.

ART, BIRDS IN. See HUMAN CULTURE, BIRDS IN and ILLUSTRATION.

ASPECT RATIO. The ratio of wing length to breadth; more specifically, the figure obtained by dividing a wing's length by its average width. Birds with a notably high aspect ratio—i.e., those with long, narrow wings (e.g., albatrosses and other seabirds)—are well equipped to glide long distances without flapping and to "sail" on (and even into) strong winds. Species with an especially low aspect ratio are often soaring birds with broad wings, such as eagles and storks, which make use of thermals and updrafts to gain altitude. See FLIGHT and Figs. 28 and 32.

ASPERGILLOSIS (ASS-pur-jill-OH-siss). A respiratory disease contracted by birds and other animals by eating or inhaling the spores of a fungus *(Aspergillus fumigatus)* that grows on decaying plant material. Its rare human victims are mainly breeders of chickens and other domestic birds. See DISEASE.

ASSOCIATION OF FIELD ORNITHOLOGISTS (AFO). Founded in 1922 as the New England Bird-Banding Association (changed for a period to the Northeastern Bird-Banding Association), the AFO is "dedicated to the scientific study and conservation of birds and their natural habitats. Its geographical focus is the Western Hemisphere and it actively promotes contributions to Neotropical ornithology. This venerable organization has traditionally served as a bridge between professional and amateur ornithologists and continues to emphasize bird banding and the development of field techniques. It publishes the quarterly *Journal of Field Ornithology,* the bimonthly *Ornithological Newsletter,* and an occasional newsletter, *AFO Afield.* For membership information and other details, go to: www.afonet.org.

ATLAS, BREEDING-BIRD. A system for mapping the distribution of breeding-bird *species* in a given area, as distinct from a breeding-bird census, which attempts to determine numbers of pairs of nesting birds in such an area to derive an estimate of *abundance.* An atlas amounts to a "snapshot" of species distribution during a specified period of time. Its conservation value lies in creating a picture of how species are distributed across a landscape and in providing a baseline against which the results subsequent atlas surveys can be compared to reveal distributional change.

The biological atlas concept was pioneered in Great Britain in the 1950s where the first comprehensive breeding bird atlas on a national scale was published in 1976 (Sharrock 1976). The British model was an instant hit among field birders elsewhere in Europe and in North America, and by the late 1980s over 30 states and provinces had atlases in progress on this side of the Atlantic (Davis 1997). Great Britain has already completed its second round atlas (Gibbons et al., 1993) and New York's follow-up effort is underway at this writing (2002).

Details of the many atlases that have now been completed vary, but the basic system works as follows. A given state or other geographical area is divided into a grid of blocks of similar area. The "standard" size for an atlas block has been 5 × 5 km or 10 × 10 km. Larger than this and the value of the distributional data begins to diminish, while a finer grid tends to challenge the ability of a relatively small number of people to effectively cover a relatively large area competently. In the United States many atlases have used the U.S. Geological Survey topographic grid divided into 6 equal blocks, each of which measures approximately 5 × 5 km. This has the added advantage of giving atlas workers a readily accessible map of their assigned territory. However, New York State used the 5-km-square transverse mercator grid, and any standard grid of appropriate dimensions will work.

Species are recorded according to specified criteria, such as *possible breeding* (e.g., a bird present in suitable habitat during the breeding season), *probable breeding* (e.g., a single male apparently on territory in

suitable habitat for an extended period of time), and *confirmed breeding* (e.g., the finding of an active nest or unambiguous evidence, such as a bird carrying a fecal sac). Most atlases allow 5 breeding seasons in which to gather the requisite data, sometimes with a start-up and/or cleanup season tacked on to either end. The data are collected on standardized forms and entered into a computerized data base capable of printing out a map that shows at a glance the possible, probable, or (ideally) confirmed nesting distribution of each species that breeds in the atlas area.

The beauty of the system is that it requires only a single confirmation for each species in each block without regard for the species' abundance. Thus, experienced birdwatchers at the peak of breeding activity can verify nesting of a number of species in a single morning's work; and the resulting data do not require any strained extrapolations. The central problem is getting adequate coverage (a likelihood of confirming the majority of breeding species present) for all blocks, and therefore places with a small area, large population, and high density of birders (e.g., Britain and Massachusetts) lend themselves better to "atlasing" than places where the coverage area exceeds the coverage capacity, such as many western states. States in such circumstances have sometimes found it more practical to use a larger grid system, e.g., one record required per topographical quadrangle, perhaps adding more concentrated coverage in areas of localized habitats or as spot surveys in more widespread representative habitats.

Another factor that may have contributed to what seems in retrospect to have been something like an "atlas boom" is that the work turns out to be fun—at least some of the time. The competitive camaraderie involved in "block bashing," for example, in which a group of hard-core birders try to cover a block (competently) in a single 24-hour period, may to some degree make up for hours spent on a blistering summer day in a mosquito-infested bog waiting for some local specialty to emerge with a fecal sac. (Or perhaps atlasing simply induces a form of euphoric dementia.)

The atlas volumes that present the results of the data collection have also tended to follow the British model, with a species map on one page and a species account summarizing breeding status on the facing page. Some of these books are elaborate hardcover affairs providing detailed analyses and acetate overlay sheets so that factors such as vegetation cover and elevation can be related to species distribution, while others are little more than a stapled sheaf of maps. If the data are sound, such discrepancies in production value are of little consequence. In an atlas, after all, it's the maps that count.

The North American Ornithological Atlas Committee (NORAC) maintains a *Handbook for Atlasing American Breeding Birds* (1990), a list of published atlases, and a directory of atlas contacts at the American Birding Association website: www.americanbirding.org. For atlases, see the Bibliography; see also Davis (1997) for an excellent overview of North American atlases. See also STATE/PROVINCIAL BOOKS in Bibliography.

ATTU. See ALASKA.

AUDUBON (in English, AW-duh-bonn), John James, c. 1785–1851 (Audubon's Oriole, *Icterus graduacauda*; Audubon's Shearwater: *Puffinus Iherminieri*). The name the world associates inextricably with birds belonged to an artistic genius who, like many of his kind, was as eccentric as he was brilliant. He was born at Les Cayes, Santo Domingo (now Haiti), the acknowledged bastard of a well-to-do French merchant-slaver, Jean Audubon. The artist once described the mother he never knew as being "a lady of Spanish extraction . . . as beautiful as she was wealthy," but this appears to be another example of the autobiographical imagination that encouraged him to let it be rumored that he might just be the lost Dauphin of France. Who exactly his mother was remains a matter of speculation. She may have been Jeanne Rabin, a French chambermaid, or "a free . . . Creole woman." In addition to the name by which history knows him, Audubon was also called Jean Rabin and various combinations of Jean Jacques La Foret (La Forest) Audubon.

Like many another genius (one thinks of his near-contemporary U. S. Grant), Audubon was a failure at workaday occupations such as family and business; even his early labors as an itinerant portraitist amounted to little except, probably, to hone his drafting skills. To the world's immeasurable benefit, his *raison d'etre*, the double elephant folio edition of *The Birds of America* announced in 1827, consumed Audubon body and soul until its completion in 1838. These plates, engraved largely by Robert Havell, Jr. of London from Audubon's original watercolors and hand-colored under the artist's direction, comprise 497 bird forms (many of Audubon's "species" have been "lumped") painted life-size. They also contain a wealth of carefully rendered plants (especially those by the teen-age Joseph Mason), mammals, reptiles, insects, and other life-forms plus a fine series of period landscapes and townscapes. A small selection of the original watercolors, including a series showing one of the copper engravings and a hand-painted print therefrom, is on permanent exhibition at the New York Historical Society (New York City), which owns the collected originals and occasionally mounts a comprehensive show.

As was common practice at the time, *The Birds of America* was sold by subscription and published serially. Thus, while between 175 and 200 complete, bound sets of the 27 × 40-inch double-elephant folio edition are thought to have once existed, an unknown number of incomplete sets were also published. Many of the complete sets have since been broken up and the individual leaves sold for increasingly impressive sums. The original subscribers paid $1,000 for the four huge volumes containing 435 plates—a grand enough sum in the 1830s. However, today a single plate can command as much as $150,000 (game birds typically bringing the highest prices) and a complete elephant folio sold at auction for $8.2 million in 2000 (up from $440,000 in the early 1980s).

After completing *The Birds of America,* which brought its creator fame and a measure of financial security, Audubon embarked in 1859 on a smaller, octavo edition in collaboration with the Philadelphia lithographer J. T. Bowen. The rapid completion of this project could not be matched in the production of another famous edition, the chromolithographs in the original double-elephant size begun by Julius Bien just before the Civil War. Unscrupulous business partners and the war halted publication when only 15 numbers containing 105 plates (150 species) had been issued. A plethora of popular editions (in all sizes, price ranges, and degrees of quality) have appeared since. Most notable are the so-called Amsterdam edition, full-sized plates issued by the Teyler Art Museum in 1972 at about $12,000 initially (now hard to find and worth in the neighborhood of $50,000) and a 1985 full-sized printing by the Abbeville Press (New York), which originally sold for $8,500 complete, but is now also closer to $50,000. For popular editions, catalogues of the oevre, and Audubon biographies, see the Bibliography.

Also begun right after the publication of the elephant folio was Audubon's collaboration with his friend the Reverend John BACHMAN on *The Viviparous Quadrupeds of North America*: but the master's eyesight and energy were beginning to fail, and many of the paintings for this work were done by his son John Woodhouse Audubon. He grew senile in the last two years of his life and died at Minniesland, his home overlooking the Hudson in upper Manhattan.

Though Audubon represented himself abroad as a colorful frontier character, "an American woodsman," acting and dressing the part with long flowing tresses and rustic, fur-trimmed attire, he was not the naive, rude "natural genius" he sometimes pretended to be. He studied in Paris before coming to his father's farm in Pennsylvania at the age of seventeen, and his shrewdness in promoting himself and his paintings in the highest circles of European society is verified by the publicity he quickly generated and his success at peddling such an expensive work. His wit and intelligence came through in many of his dramatic (some think overdramatic) compositions and in his writings. Both his *Ornithological Biographies,* written (with William MACGILLIVRAY supplying the scientific detail) to accompany *The Birds of America,* and his journals, edited by his granddaughter, Maria A. Audubon, contain many passages that are movingly evocative of the early-nineteenth-century American wilderness and its inhabitants. Audubon was among the first to lament the sad destruction of the former.

AUDUBON SOCIETIES. The Audubon movement began in the late nineteenth century as a lobby for bird preservation, responding to the largely unheeded slaughter of the continent's avifauna that continued well into this century (see CONSERVATION). Until this new conservation

ethic awakened, birdlife—and indeed all wildlife—was being annihilated with ruthless abandon for the game market, for products such as decorative feathers and just for the fun of it. By the 1870s it had become clear that a number of bird species, including the Eskimo Curlew, Passenger Pigeon, and Carolina Parakeet, were at the brink of extinction as a direct result of decimation by men with guns. And the largely unregulated felling of America's forests was also being remarked—though this was not yet thought of as bird habitat.

History of the Audubon Movement. One of the first American heroes of bird conservation was George Bird Grinnell, editor of *Forest and Stream* magazine. A well-educated outdoorsman of vision, Grinnell saw what was happening to the nation's wild resources and in 1886 invited his readers to join the first organization dedicated to the protection of birdlife. He called the new organization the Audubon Society after the man whose name no less then than now was inextricably associated in the public's mind with birds. Within a few months, the Society had attracted more than 38,000 members. Unable to manage this sudden success Grinnell was forced to disband the organization in 1888. But public sympathy for the plight of wild birds had been aroused and the Audubon movement quickly reinvented itself. In 1896 two well-to-do Boston women, Harriet Hemenway and Minna Hall, appalled at a newspaper account of the slaughter of egrets in Florida for use in fashionable millinery, assembled a group of 900 of their peers in Boston society—many of whom would themselves have worn egret plumes on their hats—and got them to agree "to work to discourage the buying or wearing of feathers and to otherwise further the protection of native birds." They sought and won the support of the Boston scientific community, convincing William Brewster, cofounder of the AMERICAN ORNITHOLOGISTS' UNION, to be the first president of the Massachusetts Audubon Society. From the beginning, these founding mothers had determined that this movement needed to be national in scope. The greatest persecution, after all, was taking place in Florida and other southern states where most of the plume birds nested, and feathered hats were fashionable nationwide. An early goal, therefore, was to establish Audubon Societies in other states, and by 1897, Pennsylvania, New York, Maine, Colorado, and the District of Columbia had Audubon Societies of their own, many of which have promoted bird conservation in their own states and beyond continuously into the present. Another early goal was the passage of the nation's first legislation prohibiting the killing of wildlife. In 1897 Massachusetts passed a law prohibiting trade in wild bird feathers and strong wildlife protection bills were soon passed in other states. In 1900 the U.S. Congress passed the Lacey Act, outlawing interstate shipment of animals killed in violation of state laws. This was the beginning of the end for the plume trade and other of the most egregious practices of the trade in wild animals in the United States. It is notable that

this first successful wildlife protection movement was founded and largely driven by women fully 24 years before they were granted the right to vote; and that a parallel bird conservation organization, the Royal Society for the Protection of Birds (RSPB), was founded in Britain—also by women— in the same year that the Massachusetts Audubon Society began.

In 1899 Frank Chapman, ornithologist and conservationist based at the American Museum of Natural History in New York, started *Bird-Lore* magazine, which became a unifying forum for the state Audubon societies and published the results of the first annual Christmas Birds Counts beginning in 1900. In 1905 of some of the state organizations incorporated as the National Association of Audubon Societies for the Protection of Wild Birds and Animals, with William Dutcher as President. This alliance evolved gradually into today's NATIONAL AUDUBON SOCIETY.

The powerful advocacy movement that motivated Audubon's founders and early leaders has continued to the present with the enactment of many effective wildlife and habitat protection laws (see LAWS PROTECTING BIRDLIFE). However, Audubon also broadened the battlefront early on to include active protection of important bird colonies, the acquisition of wildlife sanctuaries, and a broad-based effort to educate the public about birds and bird conservation through outdoor programs, school curricula, camps, and dissemination of information through all available media. To protect the colonies of the plume birds Audubon societies hired wardens, three of whom were killed by poachers in the line of duty. The Massachusetts Audubon Society established its first sanctuary in 1916 and the National Audubon Society now manages thousands of acres of protected land across the country. As early as the 1930s Audubon recognized the importance of scientific research to effective conservation action, not only as the means of understanding the true nature of conservation issues but also to give credibility to advocacy initiatives. Using data developed by Audubon scientists, advocates have been able to draft model legislation promoting clean air and water, the protection of wetlands and endangered species, and the banning of chemicals such as DDT, which eventually became some of our strongest federal environmental laws. These experiences also revealed the necessity of having effective environmental lobbyists in the state and national capitals to counter the powerful interests that are still bent on exploiting natural resources for the sake of short-term profits.

Today the Audubon movement remains one of the most vital forces for the environment in North America encompassing both a strong national organization with 600,000 members, 500 chapters, and offices in 27 states (see NATIONAL AUDUBON SOCIETY) and effective independent Audubon societies in many states. For example, the Massachusetts Audubon Society has continued to grow since its founding and as of 2003 had 69,000 member households, 30,000 acres of wildlife sanctuaries, and

20 staffed nature centers, which offer thousands of programs to hundreds of thousands of visitors each year. While most of its conservation efforts are now concentrated in Massachusetts, in recent years it took the lead in protecting a quarter of a million acres of habitat in Belize, where many Massachusetts breeding birds spend the winter.

The history of the Audubon movement shows that love of birdlife has enormous power to influence the national environment agenda and that the most effective conservation efforts benefit from a combination of approaches, including advocacy, scientific research, habitat protection, hands-on conservation, and education. See also CONSERVATION.

For a detailed, well-written history of the Audubon movement, see Graham (1990–CONSERVATION).

AUK. Standard English collective name for the family Alcidae (order Charadriiformes), though no living species is currently known by the name "auk" in North America. There are 23 species of auks worldwide, 19 of which breed in North America; in addition, Craveri's Murrelet occurs as a visitor to southern California in fall and the Long-tailed Murrelet, recently re-elevated to species rank, is now known to be a vagrant of nearly annual occurrence. Not included in these totals is the Great Auk, which was eradicated for food and feathers by 1844 (see EXTINCT BIRDS).

The auks are small to medium-sized birds (62–14 inches; the Great Auk measured about 30 inches) with narrow wings, short to medium-length bills, and the front three toes fully webbed. Excepting the puffins, they hobble awkwardly on their tarsi when on shore (which they visit only to breed) rather than walk upright. Their plumage is generally patterned in black (or sooty brown) and white, though two western species have a rusty-brown alternate (breeding) plumage. Their legs, mouth linings, and bills are often brightly colored, and a number of species have elaborate bill modifications and facial plumes (see Fig. 7).

Auks occur exclusively in the marine environment except (in a few cases) while nesting. Most nest in dense colonies, building no nest but laying their eggs on rocky ledges, in crevices, or under rocks. A few species (e.g., puffins) excavate burrows in the earth and provide a sparse lining of vegetation, feathers, and/or other debris. The great majority of auks nest within feet of the sea, but the Kittlitz's Murrelet nests on talus slopes near the tops of mountains above the tree line. Most remarkable of all is the preferred site of the Marbled Murrelet, which nests in coniferous trees, laying its egg on a pad of moss up to 148 feet from the ground (see NEST for details of discovery). The size, shape, color, and markings of auk eggs are all remarkably variable—even among individuals in the case of the last two characteristics. The eggs of the two murre species are long and strongly pyriform, an adaptation usually supposed to have evolved in conjunction with their predilection for nesting on narrow cliffside ledges:

when the eggs are kicked by parent birds, they tend to roll in a circle rather than over the edge. Murre eggs are also noted for their impressive variation in color and markings (see Fig. 10). Auk eggs may be white, yellowish, buff, green, or olive; unmarked, finely speckled, heavily splotched, and/or scrawled in gray, buff, reddish, purplish, brown, or blackish, and the markings may be well defined or fuzzy, evenly distributed, concentrated at the large end, or cover the surface so thoroughly that the egg appears almost wholly dark. Most auks lay a single egg as a rule; the Ancient Murrelet and the guillemots *(Cepphus)* are exceptional in regularly laying two and the latter unique in sometimes producing three.

Auks are seldom heard at sea, but on the breeding grounds they utter low moans, guttural growls, quacks, and croaks; a few species give piping cries and shrills.

The auks are the quintessential birds of the northern seas, just as penguins are of the Antarctic. Most species breed in the Arctic and disperse to sea—but not far south—after nesting; a few species breed as far south as Baja California and a couple regularly cross the Tropic of Cancer in winter. The group reaches its greatest diversity by far on the west coast of North America and a number of species are endemic to this region. Several species have a circumpolar arctic breeding distribution.

According to Lockwood (1993–NAMES) "auk" derives from the Old Norse word *alka,* which means "neck" and refers to the Razorbill's habit of stretching its neck when it lands at its nest site. The term may be used synonymously with ALCID.

See also AUKLET; DOVEKIE; GUILLEMOT; MURRE; MURRELET; PUFFIN.

AUKLET. Standard English name for 6 species of auks (family Alcidae; order Charadriiformes), all of which breed along the North Pacific coasts of North America. Except for the three congeneric species, the name has no taxonomic integrity and is not even a reliable diminutive, since one species (Rhinoceros) averages larger than several of the medium-sized auks (the other auklets are under 10 inches). All of the auklets, except Cassin's, have unusual bill modifications and/or head plumes in alternate (breeding) plumage. All nest in rocky crevices (most species) or burrows excavated in earth (Cassin's and Rhinoceros).

For family characteristics, see AUK.

AURICULARS (awe-RIK-yeh-lerz). The ear coverts. The area of feathers covering the ear openings near the center of the "cheeks." Often visible in the field as a distinctly outlined patch below and behind the eye. Male Golden-winged Warblers have black auriculars. See Fig. 35.

AUSTRAL (AWE-strull). Southern. Sometimes seen in older ornithological works especially in reference to the superceded Life Zones system of Merriam.

AVIAN (AY-vee-un). Referring to birds, e.g., "Feathers are a uniquely avian characteristic."

AVIARY (AY-vee-air-ee). A place where birds are kept in captivity. The term often implies a relatively large, but enclosed area in which a variety of species are able to fly freely. A "bird house" at a zoo could also be called an aviary, but a small cage housing a canary generally would not. See AVICULTURE.

AVIATION (birds as hazards to). See PROBLEMS INVOLVING BIRDS, Hazards to Aircraft.

AVICULTURE. The breeding and rearing of wild bird species in captivity for pleasure, profit, and (sometimes) noble purposes. For a more complete description see CAPTIVITY, BIRDS IN. See also COCKFIGHTING; DOMESTICATED BIRDS; FALCONRY; ENDANGERED BIRDS.

AVIFAUNA. The birdlife of any given place or era, e.g., North American avifauna, urban avifauna, backyard avifauna, and Pleistocene avifauna.

AVIS (pl.: Aves) (AY-viss [veez] or AH-viss [veez/vaze]). The Latin word for "bird"; and in the plural, the name of the class of animals that consists exclusively of birds. For a definitive description of the class, see BIRD. See also RARA AVIS.

AVOCET (AV-uh-set). Standard English name for 4 members of the family Recurvirostridae (order Charadriiformes), which also includes the STILTS. The American Avocet is the sole species of avocet recorded in North America.

Avocets are tall (average about 15 inches), gracefully proportioned shorebirds with stilt-like legs, upturned bills, and elegantly patterned plumage. Like the stilts, avocets are colonial nesters and often feed together in flocks, "swishing" their bills in bottom muck to disturb small vertebrates (fish, frogs) and large invertebrates (shrimp, insects). They are good swimmers (front three toes almost fully webbed) and even dive occasionally.

A sparsely lined depression in sand or mud in shortgrass marsh or in the open is the typical avocet nest. The 2–5 (usually 4) eggs are brownish yellow, normally rather densely covered with distinct, dark brown spots.

The call of the American Avocet is a loud, high *klee-eep* or *plee-eek*.

Avocets occur in all the major zoogeographic regions of the world, usually breeding in neither the warmest nor the coldest climates. The

North American species is distributed mainly in the West, where it nests along lakeshores and marsh edges and migrates to the coast for the winter.

The significance of the lovely name is lost, though Lockwood (1993–NAMES) says that it first appears in the ornithological literature as *avosetta*, describing the Venetian habitat of the Eurasian or Pied Avocet; he also notes that had this graceful Italian name not been preferred over the years to the early English names in common usage, we might be calling these long-legged shorebirds "clinkers", "yelpers" or "crooked-bills."

AXILLARS (or axillaries). A small group of stiffened feathers in the "armpit." The black axillars of the Black-bellied Plover, which stand out strikingly against the pale gray of the basic (winter) plumage, are a classic field mark, used by birdwatchers worldwide.

BABBLER. Standard English name for about 150 species of birds in the essentially Old World family Timaliidae (order Passeriformes), which also includes the lladopses, jeries, chatterers, babaxes, laughing thrushes, mesias, barwings, minlas, fulvettas, sibias, yuhinas, oxylabes, and several other forms. All of these are known collectively as "babblers." There is only one North American babbler: the Wrentit *(Chamaea fasciata)*, long an ornithological puzzle and, until recently, placed in a family of its own, the Chamaeidae (see WRENTIT). Sibley and Monroe (1990–SYSTEMATICS) give it its own tribe and locate it taxonomically between the parrotbills and the *Sylvia* "warblers."

"Babbler" refers to the raucous, varied, and long-winded vocal habits of many members of the family.

BACHMAN (BOCK-mun), Rev. John, 1790–1874 (*Haematopus bachmani*: Black Oystercatcher; Bachman's Warbler: *Vermivora bachmanii*; Bachman's Sparrow: *Aimophila aestivalis*). A Lutheran minister born in Rhinebeck, New York, but residing in gentlemanly comfort for most of his life in Charleston, South Carolina. Over his long career as a prominent naturalist he knew both Wilson and Agassiz, but he is best remembered for his complex and intimate association with AUDUBON. They first met in 1831 when the pastor put Audubon up for a few weeks during one of the latter's collecting expeditions. Bachman's sister-in-law, Maria Martin, did some botanical and entomological details, such as the flame azalea and

the Florida atala and buckeye butterflies, which rather overwhelm Audubon's drab Swainson's Warbler in Havell's Plate CXCVIII. Audubon's two sons married Bachman's two (alas, short-lived) daughters. And Audubon and Bachman collaborated on a number of natural history projects, of which the greatest was their *Viviparous Quadrupeds of North America.* Audubon named the oystercatcher and the warbler (now probably extinct) for his friend. It was Bachman who discovered the warbler and his sparrow near Charleston. Maria Martin painted the *Franklinia* tree in which the pair of warblers in Havell's Plate CLXXXV are placed. The tree, named for Benjamin Franklin by the Bartram brothers, is almost as rare as the warbler; it is now widely cultivated, but was found in the wild only recently in one locality after having been "lost" since 1790.

BAIRD, Spencer Fullerton, 1823–87 (Baird's Sandpiper: *Calidris bairdii*; Baird's Sparrow: *Ammodramus bairdii*). A central figure in American ornithology in the latter half of the nineteenth century (see also BREWER; CASSIN; COUES; RIDGWAY; George Newbold LAWRENCE) and, perhaps more than any other single person, responsible for bringing knowledge of the North American avifauna from the pioneering stages of Wilson and Audubon to the comprehensiveness and meticulous classification of the modern era. In the Historical Preface to his *Key . . .* (1890), Elliott Coues outlines the "Bairdian Epoch" in American ornithology and at Baird's death, J. A. ALLEN called him the "Nestor of American Ornithology."

Baird began as a boy naturalist in Pennsylvania, took his first degree in natural history, made friends before he was twenty with the aging Audubon, and rapidly developed talents as a linguist, administrator, politician, and writer. He published extensively not only on birds but on mammals, reptiles, and fishes. He became the secretary of the Smithsonian Institution in Washington, DC, and persuaded Congress to build the National Museum of Natural History to house the collections he accumulated so assiduously. He created and headed the U.S. Commission of Fish and Fisheries and founded the marine science laboratory at Woods Hole, Massachusetts. Through his connections in the government and his relationship by marriage (son-in-law) to the Inspector General of the Army, he was responsible for the remarkable involvement of government surgeons (see BIOGRAPHY) in the collecting of zoological specimens in the West. These collections along with his own field work provided the basis for a government report (part of the survey for the railroad route to the Pacific) on birds of the United States. Later reissued as *The Birds of North America* (1859), this work included 738 forms, constituting the first truly comprehensive, scientifically organized checklist of the avifauna. Baird's other major ornithological works are noted in the Bibliography. In addition to his achievements, he was remembered as a friend and supporter of other naturalists. For a full biography see Rivinius and Youssef (1992).

BALDPATE. An alternative name, still in wide usage, to the standard English name American Wigeon. The pate (crown) of this duck is not bald in the sense of showing bare skin, but merely covered in white feathers.

BANDING. The placement of a numbered metal band on the leg of a bird in an effort to individualize the bird and thereby discover certain facts of its life history. In Britain the practice is called "ringing."

 ORIGINS. History does not record when the first curious naturalist tried to keep tabs on a bird by tying a bit of colored yarn to its leg. We know that early falconers attached metal "identification bracelets" to their (valuable) birds' legs and that England's King Henry IV inadvertently collected some interesting data about the traveling ability of Peregrines when one of his birds excused itself from a bustard hunt; it was next seen 24 hours later and 1,350 miles away in Malta! We also know that John James Audubon tied silver strands on the legs of young Eastern Phoebes near Philadelphia in 1803 and observed their return the following spring—so it is entirely fitting that the title of First North American Bird Bander go to him.

 More organized efforts began in Western Europe in the 1890s, with the first serious banding operation, generally credited to Hans Christian Mortensen of Viborg, Denmark in 1899, and the first banding station, established in 1903 at Rossitten on the Baltic coast of Germany. Some small individual operations began in America about the same time and by 1909 there were enough of these to inspire the formation of the American Bird Banding Association. In 1920 the coordination of North American banding efforts was assumed jointly by the U.S. Bureau of Biological Survey (now the U.S. Geological Survey) and the Canadian Wildlife Service. Like nearly everything else relating to birds, banding has expanded in recent decades, though its appeal and most of its energy still reside largely in countries of the developed world.

 PURPOSES. In essence, the value of bird banding lies in allowing us to keep track of an individual bird (or many individual birds) in more than one time and place during the course of its life. If we band a nestling Herring Gull in 1981 and it is found dead in the summer of 2001, we have proven that Herring Gulls live to be *at least* 20 years old. If we band a Manx Shearwater in Boston and retrap it on its arrival back at its breeding hole in England, we get a fair idea of the speed at which the species travels, its navigational skills, and its homing instincts. If a Blackpoll Warbler is banded in Canada, retrapped along the New England coast, and found dead in South America, we begin to discover the migration route of at least some members of this species. In all these cases, the more individuals of a species that are both banded and recovered, the clearer their behavior patterns become. If we band nestlings from a colony of cormorants, for a period of years we can not only reckon average life span,

Fig. 2. *Bird banding and marking.* Much of what we have learned about migration and other aspects of birdlife has depended on being able to recognize individual birds and track their movements over time. The illustration shows some of the basic tools and techniques that allow us to do this efficiently without harming the birds. Mist nets of fine, strong silk or nylon (1 and 2) are set strategically where target species are likely to concentrate; they are tended constantly to ensure that birds—such as the Carolina Wren (4)—are removed, banded, and released as quickly as possible. The lightweight aluminum bands (7) come in all sizes (swan to hummingbird shown) and are fitted carefully using special pliers (8). Before the birds are banded they are measured, and relevant information is noted on a data sheet (6)—probably the most important tool of all. When it is desirable to be able to distinguish individual birds on sight rather than re-capturing them to read the band numbers, other types of marking devices are used, such as the illustrated *patagial* wing tag (3) and neck collar (5; on Canada Goose). Using different colored bands placed according to a standard formula, scientists can give shorebirds such as this Red Knot (9) their own easily read code denoting specific nesting or wintering areas. For a full description of these techniques and their value, see **BANDING.**

homing abilities, migration routes, and wintering grounds, but also assemble data on dispersal, mortality rates, social behaviors such as territorial patterns and mating systems, and other characteristics of that particular population. In addition to being of intrinsic scientific interest, such information is crucial to the formulation of sound conservation strategies. Banding has also proven useful in tracking the incidence of diseases that affect people, such as West Nile virus.

PROCEDURES. The collection and analysis of large amounts of reliable information requires centralized organization and regulated standards as well as the skill, care, and enthusiasm of individuals.

Permission to band birds must be obtained from the North American Bird Banding Program administered jointly by the United States Department of the Interior (Bird Banding Laboratory [BBL] of the Patuxent Wildlife Research Center) and the Canadian Wildlife Service (see contact information, below) and also in many cases from the appropriate state or provincial fish and game or conservation agency. Applicants must be eighteen or older and have requisite bird identification skills and the demonstrable ability to keep accurate records and handle birds without harming them; they must also supply the names of three professional ornithologists or licensed banders as personal references. Would-be banders must educate themselves, often by apprenticing with a veteran bander or taking a course at a bird observatory. Novice banders typically hold subpermits under a Master Bander. Currently (2002), there are 2000 Master Banders and 2000 subpermitees in the United States. The majority (59%) of permits here are held by universities and government agencies with bird research programs.

Banding in the United States falls under the jurisdiction of the federal migratory Bird Treaty Act, and licensed banders are subject to all federal and state regulations governing keeping, breeding, collecting, or transporting wild birds, their nests, or their eggs (see LAWS PROTECTING BIRDLIFE).

Paraphernalia and Techniques. Once banding permits are obtained from the appropriate government agencies, the Bird Banding Laboratory supplies the bander with bands, reporting procedures, and the official procedural guide, the *Bird Banding Manual,* all without charge. Banders are responsible for supplying their own bird-capturing equipment and other accessories. In most countries, they must also purchase the bands from the controlling agency; in the United States and Canada these are licensed to the bander free of charge.

The typical bird band is a short cylinder of light metal (usually aluminum alloy) ranging from less than 2 to 30 mm in diameter to accommodate the varying leg sizes of different species (hummingbird to swan). Of critical concern is that the band not encumber or in any way harm the bird. The standard "butt-end" band is split lengthwise so that it can be opened and then reclosed by pliers around a bird's leg (usually the tarsus).

Each band is inscribed with an 8 or 9-digit number and an indication of where reports should be sent (see below). Plastic color bands are used when field recognition is important, and various types of plastic or metal wing clips, neck rings, and bill markers—all harmless to the birds—are used in special situations (see also MARKING).

Numerous trapping devices have been developed over the years to catch birds (see CAPTURE and Bub [1991]) and very infrequently birds may be "tranquilized" by "treated" bait for banding purposes. By far the most widely used method of catching birds up to the size of a Sharp-shinned Hawk is the setting of mist nets. These nets consist of a relatively open mesh made of fine but strong black silk or nylon. Different strengths and mesh sizes are used depending on the size of the birds to be captured. A typical mist-net setup is 30–40 feet long and consists of five "trammels" strung horizontally about a foot apart one above the other between the poles. The netting is made to hang loosely so that a long pocket is formed along the lower margin of each trammel. The effect is not unlike a series of flimsy, sagging badminton nets, except that against vegetation the mesh is all but invisible. A bird crossing a trail along which a net has been strung blunders into the net, falls into the pouch area, and becomes enveloped in the fine mesh. The bander carefully untangles the captive, records its vital statistics (see below), affixes the right-sized band to its leg, and releases it. Normally this is a quick and completely painless (though no doubt somewhat stressful) experience for the birds involved. Banders are obligated to check their nets frequently to prevent birds from becoming too badly entangled and to make sure they are not running more nets than they can humanely handle when many birds are likely to be caught, e.g., during migration.

Perhaps the commonest and certainly the most convenient method of banding *large* birds is to concentrate on nestlings. The dangers risked in trying to band juvenile goshawks in their treetop nests or young gannets on a precipitous cliff face are not inconsiderable, but they are trivial compared to grappling with adults of such powerful, "well-armed" species.

Collecting and Processing Data. The minimum information a bander must record includes the identity of the species, sex and age (when known), the place of its banding, and the band number. Other information, such as a bird's degree of fat accumulation or its subspecies and various key measurements, results in more precise deductions if the bird is recaptured or found dead. Some of these things may be obvious from superficial examination; others require knowing what to look for where, e.g., the bursa of Fabricius and ossification of the skull (age) and a cloacal protuberance (sex).

The unusual closeness to the bird, the difference in perspective, and the impossibility of judging physical attitude and gesture (see JIZZ) can

make identification of birds "in the hand" surprisingly difficult, even for those who consider themselves proficient at field identification. And, of course, some species, such as certain *Empidonax* flycatchers, are hard to label under any circumstances. A compensating factor is the ability of the bander to examine a captive bird minutely from every angle, take measurements, and observe clues, such as wing formula, that are at best subtle and very difficult to see and interpret correctly in the field. The *Bird Banding Manual* (now on-line) and banding journals (see below) record a broad spectrum of minute but definitive characters, and perceptive banders continue to discover new ones. The current standard identification guide for banders endorsed by the Bird Banding Laboratory is Peter Pyle's *Identification Guide to North American Birds.*

Obviously, the more information that is recorded about an individual bird, the greater the possibility of learning something useful. However, banders must resist any temptation to record data that they are "almost" sure of, since a mistake could lead to completely false conclusions about a species or individual's behavior.

All of the information collected by the bander is recorded in standardized format supplied by the Bird Banding Laboratory, where all data are sent for computer storage, retrieval, and analysis. This information center makes it possible for researchers to use not only the data that they collect but also that of hundreds of other banders across the continent. Currently (2002) the BBL is undergoing a major conversion of its computer systems and shifting to a strongly electronically oriented mode of communication with banders.

RESULTS. Although much can be learned by the analysis of initial bandings, the greatest rewards come when a bird falls into human hands at least twice—once when it is trapped and banded and again when it is captured, killed, or found dead. In the case of larger birds (e.g., gulls), which take larger bands, it is sometimes possible to read band numbers through a spotting scope, obviating the need for a dead or captive bird. Color marking improves the odds of identifying distant birds, though typically it provides less detailed data, since normally it is populations or other groupings rather than individuals that are so marked. A disparity in the dates and/or places of the successive contacts with the bird often yields the most dramatic insights, especially in the case of long-distance migrants. However, recapture of individuals from resident populations or as returning migrants also provides important ecological insights.

It is easy enough to band a lot of birds, but a number of factors work against a second recorded recovery. The sheer abundance of birdlife is one limitation. Since only a tiny percentage of birds can be banded, the chances of banded birds being reported a second time are slight. Furthermore, many thousands of banded birds doubtless end up at the bottom of the sea, in the digestive system of a raptor, or buried in the leaf litter of a

Central American rain forest. The uneven distribution of bird banders and people who are likely to return a band also limits the percentage of interesting returns and distorts the data that are collected. Many of the people most likely to hold a banded bird in their hands in Latin America would be unlikely to guess its significance correctly, even if they could read the inscription on the band. The true explanation, after all, is as strange as almost any invented one, and countless bands probably end up as ceremonial jewelry or mementos of supposed religious significance. If our perception of world bird distribution were limited to banding records, we would be given to assume that most birds occur in heavily populated regions of the Western world, particularly those where bird banders are numerous.

It is probably obvious that it is *accumulated* recoveries of a given species in a given place, at a given time, etc., that yield credible theories, not isolated returns. If a Canada Warbler banded in Ontario is recovered a year later in Mexico, we have no way of knowing whether it is a migrant, winter resident, or vagrant there, whether it is common or not, its time of arrival or departure, its rate of travel, or the mortality rate of the species. If, however, *numerous* banded Canada Warblers are netted and renetted during a certain period of the winter over successive years in a particular locality in Peru, we can make reasonable assumptions about all of these things and even shed some light on the single Mexican record. Unfortunately, banding stations are scarce (though increasing) in Mexico and Peru, as they are throughout the wintering grounds of most Northern Hemisphere migrants, and data from these tropical regions are proportionately scarce.

In spite of these formidable limitations, bird banding has been one of our principal sources of facts about birdlife. And as the number of competent banders increases, our insight expands. In 1995, 1,148,151 birds were banded in North America and 58,342 recoveries (c. 5%) were reported. Sixty-five percent of these were nongame species, but for obvious reasons, recovery rates of game birds were much higher (c. 12%) than for nongame species (less than 1%). Approximately 57 million birds have been banded in North America to date (c. 2000) and roughly 3 million (5.3%) recoveries have been reported.

Some short-term, "flashy" data are yielded by bird banding, e.g., prodigious speeds or journeys of which some birds are capable. But a great deal of the valuable information about birdlife derived from banding is attributable to patient, long-term efforts and the great advantage of a collective information system—aided immensely these days by what used to be called "electronic brains." Governments and philanthropic institutions may be unlikely to deem the plumage sequence of the Cape May Warbler or the life span of the Red-legged Kittiwake worthy of a grant or a scientist's time. But over the years—with a class of graduate students working here, a

retired backyard bander there—such worthwhile minutiae accumulate in data bases and the banding literature, where they wait to take their place in a work of grander ornithological or ecological significance.

Banding Associations, Observatories, Publications, and the Internet provide the easiest access to more information about bird banding. If you are lucky enough to live near a bird observatory, you have the opportunity to witness a large-scale banding of migratory birds. There are now more than 30 such major banding operations across the United States and Canada. During peak periods these stations often need to recruit capable volunteers. Many also offer programs and classes on bird banding, as do various colleges and conservation organizations. For a listing of bird observatories, see the Bird Banding Laboratory website, cited below).

There are four regional bird banding associations in North America (Eastern, Inland, Western, and Ontario) plus the national North American Bird Banding Council. The three U.S. regional associations publish the *North American Bird Bander* quarterly; see also *The Journal of Field Ornithology* (formerly *Bird-Banding*), a national quarterly published by the Association of Field Ornithologists (formerly the Northeastern Bird-Banding Association).

If You Find a Banded (Wild) Bird, the number of the band should be reported to the proper authorities. In addition to the number, all official bird bands carry an address (BIRD BAND LAUREL MD 20708; older bands say AVISE BIRD BAND WASH DC)) and telephone number (1-800-327-BAND) and reports can also be submitted electronically in Spanish as well as English through the Bird Banding Laboratory's website (see below). If the bird is dead you can remove and mail the band itself; release live birds after carefully noting the band numbers. You need not worry about identifying the bird since the band number is unique to the bird wearing it and the bander will have recorded its species. In return for your effort, the banding office will send you the bird's basic data.

Pigeons are banded by pigeon racers for identification rather than scientific purposes. You can discover the owner of a racing pigeon that strays into your life by looking up the letter code on the band on the websites of the International Federation of American Homing Pigeon Fanciers, Inc. (IF), www.americanpigeon.org, or the American Racing Pigeon Union (AU), www.pigeon.org. The IF site includes a band list; people who find AU birds must send the band information to an e-mail address to get the name and address of the bird's owner. Be warned, however, that pigeons that have wandered from their appointed course are usually of little interest to their owners.

Owners of private waterfowl collections also usually band their birds, which not infrequently escape when their clipped flight feathers are replaced in the next molt. Finding the source of these strays may involve more research and long-distance charges than it is worth.

For more details about all aspects of bird banding, contact:

USGS Patuxent Wildlife Research Center
Bird Banding Laboratory
12100 Beech Forest Road
Laurel, MD 20708-4037
Tel.: 301-497-5790
E-mail: BBL@usgs.gov
Website: www.pwrc.usgs.gov/bbl/

Bird Banding Office
National Wildlife Research Center
Canadian Wildlife Service
Hull, Quebec, Canada K1A 0H3
Tel.: 819-994-6176
E-mail: BBO_CWS@ec.gc.ca

To report a recovery on the Internet: bandreport@patuxent.usgs.gov

BANNER MARKS. See FLASH MARKS.

BAPTORNIS. A fossil genus containing a single described species, *B. advenus* (Subclass Ornithurae, Order Hesperornithiformes), described from remains found in the famous Upper (late) Cretaceous Niobrara chalk beds of Kansas in the 1870s. Closely related to *Hesperornis, Baptornis* was a toothed (probably fish-eating), flightless, loon-like bird about 3 feet in length. See EVOLUTION OF BIRDLIFE.

BARB. One of the main branches that project laterally from the rachis of a feather. In contour feathers, the barbs interlock by means of the barbules and barbicels to form a smooth, continuous vane. Less frequently called the ramus. For more detail, see FEATHER and Fig. 13.

BARBICEL. A projection extending laterally from the barbule of a contour feather. Sometimes the term is used to include the hooked projections (hamuli) borne on the forward-pointing barbules and sometimes it is confined to the shorter, straight projections borne by both forward- and rearward-pointing barbules. For more detail, see FEATHER and Fig. 13.

BARBULE. One of the branches that project laterally from the shafts of the barbs, the main branches of the rachis of a feather. In contour feathers, the barbules that project forward toward the feather tip clasp by

means of hooks (hamuli) onto the ridged edges of the rearward-pointing barbules, thus forming a smooth, continuous vane. Less frequently called the radius. For more detail, see FEATHER and Fig. 13.

BARN OWL. Standard English name for the single North American representative of the family Tytonidae (order Strigiformes). Sometimes used as a collective name for the family as a whole, which contains 17 species worldwide, all but two in the genus *Tyto*.

Many of the characters by which taxonomists separate barn owls from "true" owls are either internal (e.g., structure of the pectoral girdle; see SKELETON) or inconspicuous (the pectinate, i.e., the comb-like-middle claw, like that of the nightjars). However, even a casual observer of a barn owl would remark the heart-shaped facial disk (which gives the bird a slightly creepy expression), the long legs and toes, and the rather uniform, lightly speckled (rather than heavily streaked or barred) plumage—all characters lacking (or nearly so) in true owls.

Differences notwithstanding, barn owls are closely related to true owls and have much in common with them: nocturnal habits; a taste for live vertebrate prey, especially small rodents; eyes placed in the front of the head; unusually soft plumage; silent flight; the practice of swallowing prey whole and regurgitating indigestible parts in compact pellets; and a reversible outer toe.

Barn owls nest in cavities in either banks or trees or on the ground as well as in barns and other man-made structures. They add nothing but owl pellets to these "nests." The 3–11 (usually 4–7) white, unmarked eggs are not as round as the eggs of the true owls.

The barn owls' dry scream has been likened to the sound of ripping canvas.

The family as a whole and *the* Barn Owl *(Tyto alba)* are both cosmopolitan in distribution, though they are absent from the colder regions and higher mountains. Thus, in North America the species barely reaches southern Canada and does not occur in much of the Rockies. See the Bibliography under OWL.

BARROW, Sir John, 1764–1848 (Barrow's Goldeneye: *Bucephala islandica*). A highly competent British administrator and sometime mathematician, teacher, explorer, engineer, geographer, and diplomat, who rose from relatively humble origins to become Second Secretary of the British Admiralty. Much of his long career was spent in South Africa. He visited the Arctic in his youth, but his lasting contribution to that region was his encouragement of the Admiralty's efforts to find the Northwest Passage.

BARROW (Alaska). See ALASKA.

BARTRAM, William, 1739–1823 (*Bartramia longicauda*: Upland Sandpiper). Son of John Bartram (1699–1777), who was botanist to King George III and whose scientific prestige and botanical garden attracted ambitious and eminent naturalists from far and wide, making Philadelphia a kind of Athens of early American biology. William, like many other young men with his interests, was a failure at practical forms of livelihood. In addition to being a devoted naturalist, however, he was a skillful artist and writer and by this combination of gifts attained a fame equal to or greater than his father's. Though he illustrated Bartram's early *Elements of Botany* (1803), he had wider interests than his father, and during his travels noted details on many "new" life-forms. He recorded 215 species of birds in eastern North America, the most comprehensive listing to that time, and set down details of life history in many cases. One of his most interesting avian anecdotes is a detailed description of a King Vulture he encountered in Florida, a record that remains the best argument for including this Neotropical species in our avifauna. The younger Bartram recorded his adventures in *Travels through North and South Carolina, Georgia, East and West Florida,* a highly readable account of his four-year ramble in the wilderness, which was acclaimed by European (as well as American) readers, including Wordsworth and Coleridge. William Bartram is often credited with giving Alexander Wilson the encouragement he needed to tackle his groundbreaking *American Ornithology.*

BASAL (BAY-sul). In a biological context, the region nearest the main body. For example, the base or basal area of the bill of a bird is the part of the bill nearest the skull. A field mark of the Glaucous Gull is the pale bill base or basal area. Opposite of APICAL.

BASIC PLUMAGE. Generally synonymous with "nonbreeding" or winter plumage. See MOLT, Sequence and Terminology.

BASTARD WING. The ALULA.

BATHING. Almost all birds wet their feathers in some manner on a regular basis as part of their ritual of plumage maintenance. Some desert birds seldom or never take water baths, and gallinaceous birds substitute dust baths in most instances. Most authorities seem to agree that birds bathe not as a direct cleaning process as humans do, but more as preparation for preening and oiling the feathers. As is true of most other forms of bird behavior, bathing is not done haphazardly but rather in a sequence of characteristic gestures that vary consistently among different types of birds. Observations of both captive and wild young birds suggest that the urge to bathe is innate, though some of the particular gestures of the

wetting and drying process may be learned or at least triggered by watching older individuals.

Most songbirds bathe while standing in shallow water (e.g., in a birdbath), and waterbirds dunk and flutter in their preferred element. But birds are also known to bathe by fluttering in wet vegetation (leaf bathing and dew bathing) and by simply exposing their plumage to the rain (Larks may use only this method). Highly aerial birds bathe on the wing: swallows and many species of flycatchers wet themselves by flying over water and splashing themselves by touching the water surface; and hummingbirds will hover under natural drips or even lawn sprinklers.

As noted, the specific gestures that accompany bathing vary. Songbirds tend to dip the head while standing in the water to flip water onto the back and then splash on the water by shaking the bill in it and by fluttering the wings rapidly, thus wetting the flight feathers; the tail is also immersed and fluttered (see Fig. 24). Swimming birds usually dip their head and neck while sitting on the water, allowing the water to roll down onto their backs; this is alternated with beating the wings on the surface. Some species practice various combinations of these basic gestures. In all cases the body feathers are "fluffed," i.e., raised.

The object is not to soak the feathers, though Berger (Van Tyne and Berger 1 976–ORNITHOLOGY) mentions young Blue-winged Warblers that did just this and were unskilled at drying themselves; a bathing bird is already more than usually vulnerable to predators and one unable to fly because of sodden plumage would be easy prey indeed. Waterbirds depend on the air trapped in their feathers to stay afloat and would sink if soaked "to the skin."

Both during and after the wetting procedure, birds flap, shake their body, and vibrate their wings and tail to throw off excess water. Following the bath, they typically do a thorough preening job, which eliminates the rest of the water, arranges the ruffled feathers, and spreads the preen oil over the plumage. It is thought that wetting and preening permits the efficient removal of old oil and facilitates the smooth and even distribution of fresh oil by the bill from the preen gland. Vultures, hawks, cormorants, and anhingas characteristically hold out their wings "spread-eagle" to the sun. Though it has long been assumed to be a means of drying, this posture may also be means of regulating body temperature and aiding pest control.

See also PREENING; OIL GLAND; SUNNING; DUSTING; TEMPERATURE, BODY.

BAY DUCK. Collective term for the ducks in the genus *Aythya* (family Anatidae; order Anseriformes), of which 5 species (the scaups, Canvasback, Redhead, and Ring-necked Duck) (breed in North America and 2 others (Common Pochard and Tufted Duck) occur as migrants in the Aleutians.

The term is an apt one, for while the bay ducks breed in a variety of habitats—from tundra to prairie marsh to wooded pond—they all favor sheltered coastal waters as their wintering grounds.

BEAK. Essentially synonymous with BILL. In more restrictive usage, refers particularly to larger bills, especially the hooked beaks (or bills) of birds of prey. In general, "bill" is the preferred term in ornithological/bird-watching contexts.

BEARDLESS. The smallest North American flycatcher (4½ inches) is "beardless" in that it lacks the bristles that line the upper margin of the gape in most members of its family (Tyrannidae). These so-called "rictal" bristles are widely supposed to aid flycatchers in capturing their prey and, if so, it may be significant that the Northern Beardless Tyrannulet (Beardless Flycatcher) feeds at least partially on fruit and picks insects from leaves and branches in the manner of a warbler, rather than snatching flies from the air.

BEAR RIVER National Wildlife Refuge (Utah). One of the most spectacular concentrations and important stopover habitats in North America for migratory waterbirds, consisting of over 100 square miles (74,000 acres) of diked wetlands on the eastern edge of the Great Basin near Brigham City, Utah. Excellent birding prevails throughout the year, accessible via a 10-mile-long "auto loop." The greatest spectacle occurs in the fall when up to half a million ducks and geese may be present during the peak in September on their way south from northern breeding grounds; over 40,000 Tundra Swans are present mid-October through December. The fall migration also brings a great diversity of other migrants, such as shorebirds (peak in mid-August). Breeding specialties include Eared, Western, and Clark's Grebes, White Pelican, White-faced Ibis, Cinnamon Teal, Long-billed Curlew, American Avocet, Wilson's Phalarope, Franklin's Gull, and Yellow-headed Blackbird. Winter highlights include Bald and Golden Eagles. Extensive flooding in the 1980s, including inundation by saltwater from Great Salt Lake, destroyed the refuge headquarters and much of the water management infrastructure. While most of this has been restored, visitor services were still limited as of 2003. See also MALHEUR National Wildlife Refuge.

BECARD (see below for pronunciation). Standard English name for 16 species of Neotropical passerines, only one of which, the Rose-throated Becard, breeds in North America. The closely related (same tribe) Masked Tityra has been recorded once in the lower Rio Grande Valley of Texas. These and a number of other species that were once placed in a separate family,

the cotingas, are now considered by the AOU to belong with the tyrant fly-catchers (family Tyrannidae), but with their more specific taxonomic relationships still uncertain. Sibley and Monroe (1990–SYSTEMATICS) consider them a tribe (Tityrini) of the subfamily Tyranninae.

The 6-inch Rose-throated *(Pachyramphus aglaiae),* reaches North America as a summer resident of southeastern Arizona, southwestern New Mexico, and (rarely) the lower Rio Grande Valley of Texas. It eats both fruit and insects, as befits its ambiguous status; builds a large, untidy, globular nest woven of coarse plant fibers and wool, lined with fine plant down and bark strips, and suspended from the end of a branch; and lays 4–6 white, lavender, or buff-colored eggs marked with rather fine brownish, reddish, or gray speckles, blotches, and scrawls.

The becard "song" is a distinctive (in North America), rather quiet, descending two-syllable whistle, sometimes accompanied by some unmusical "conversational" sounds.

The French *bécarde* means "shrike," and while becards are totally unshrike-like in behavior and unrelated taxonomically, many species are gray and white and (like other tyrant flycatchers) have heavy, hooked bills. Of the two pronunciations heard commonly in North America, BECK-erd is the closest to the sound of the French name noted above, but buh-KARD is heard more frequently.

BEGGING (by young birds). See YOUNG, DEVELOPMENT OF.

BEHAVIOR. See listings under "Long Entries" in the "How to Use This Book" section, pp. xviii–xix.

BELL, John Graham, 1812–89 (Bell's Vireo: *Vireo bellii; Amphispiza belli*: Sage Sparrow). A well-known collector and taxidermist from New York State who accompanied his friend John James Audubon on the latter's expedition up the Missouri River in 1843. He was also known and liked by eminent ornithologists of the next generation, e.g., BAIRD, RIDGWAY, CASSIN, and LE CONTE. Audubon named the vireo for him, Ridgway the sparrow, and an ornithologist named Giraud added a Mexican warbler species now known as the Golden-browed Warbler *(Basileuteris belli).*

BENDIRE (BEN-dye-er), Charles Emil (born Karl Emil Bender), 1836–97 (Bendire's Thrasher: *Toxostoma bendirei*). After abandoning ecclesiastical studies in Germany, Bendire emigrated with his brother to the United States while still in his teens. He joined the army, serving competently and bravely in the Civil and Indian wars, eventually attaining the rank of major. He was part of the group of army ornithologists who corresponded with and were encouraged by Spencer BAIRD. Bendire's specialty was eggs, of which he amassed a large collection (8,000 specimens), and he

was eventually considered a ranking oologist of his day. On giving his collection to the National Museum, he was made Honorary Curator of the Department of Oology by Baird. Late in his life he began chronicling the *Life Histories of North American Birds* (*U.S. Natl. Mus. Bull.*, vol. 1, no. 1, Washington, DC, 1892). Even Mr. BENT, on whose shoulders the completion of this Herculean labor ultimately fell, did not live to see its completion. Bendire's friend Elliott Coues named the southwestern thrasher for him.

BENT, Arthur Cleveland, 1866–1954. The chief biographer of North American birds in his well-known volumes of *Life Histories* (see family categories throughout the Bibliography), published by the Smithsonian as National Museum Bulletins between 1919 and 1968. From a "frail youth" of modest circumstances Bent transformed himself through hard work into a highly successful businessman of apparently limitless energy. His interest in birds began during his childhood in Massachusetts, and in 1910 he decided to complete the monumental task Charles BENDIRE had made a slim start on in 1892. Between 1901 and 1930, Bent traveled extensively throughout North America, acquiring a comprehensive perception of the avifauna. In 1948 he partially retired to give more time to the project. He lived to see the nineteenth volume (Wood Warblers) published in 1953, having completed the manuscript of the twentieth (Blackbirds, Orioles, and Tanagers). The last volume of the series (Finches) was completed by a number of ornithologists under the editorship of O. L. Austin, Jr.

It does not diminish Bent's great achievement to note that the known details of North American birdlife now exceed the capacity of even the most accomplished ornithologist to describe single-handedly. The *Life Histories* can now be seen as a broad foundation on which the multi-authored *BIRDS OF NORTH AMERICA* now rests.

BERGMANN'S RULE. The observation (formulated by a nineteenth-century German zoologist) that overall body size tends to be greater in representatives of bird and mammal species living permanently in cooler climates than in those living in warmer climates. Put simply, American Kestrels in Maine *(Falco sparverius sparverius)* are larger on the average than those in Florida *(F. s. paulus)*. The ecological principle followed is that large bodies retain heat more efficiently than small ones, and that there is therefore an adaptive size increase in populations constantly subjected to lower temperatures. James (1983), switched eggs of Florida Red-winged Blackbirds into Minnesota nests and vice versa. Despite their origins, the changelings ended up larger in the North and smaller in the South, suggesting an environmental, rather than a genetic basis for Bergmann's rule.

BEWICK (BYOO-ik), Thomas, 1753–1828 (Bewick's Wren: *Thryomanes bewickii*). English naturalist and master wood engraver commemorated by his friend and fellow artist-naturalist John James Audubon. Though Bewick's artistic competence was broad, he is best known for two books of engravings on natural history subjects: *The General History of Quadrupeds* and *History of British Birds*.

BIBLE, BIRDS IN. See RELIGION, BIRDS IN.

BICKNELL, Eugene P., 1859–1925 (Bicknell's Thrush: *Catharus bicknelli*). According to his biographer, Maunsell Crosby (*Auk*, 1926), Eugene Bicknell was "interested in natural history from his early youth" and "one of the very few ornithologists of his time who used the field glass more than the gun." In 1878, when he was 19 years old, Bicknell was one of the ten original organizers of the Linnaean Society of New York and served as its president from 1879 to 1887. Six years later he became the youngest founder of the American Ornithologists Union. A banker, by profession, Bicknell was an active amateur field naturalist throughout his life, publishing works on the presence of "the Carolinian fauna" (i.e., birds of southern affinity) in the Hudson and Connecticut river valleys and on the breeding birds of the Catskills, one of which proved to be a "new" thrush. Described by Robert RIDGWAY in 1882 as a subspecies of the Gray-cheeked Thrush, Bicknell's Thrush was recognized as a distinct species in the 7th edition of the *AOU Checklist* (1998). Bicknell was also an accomplished botanist, discovering a number of new plant species and publishing a seminal series of papers on the flora of Nantucket.

BIG BEND National Park (Texas). 708,281 acres of desert, canyon country, and mountain woodland located in the great curve in the Rio Grande that forms the southwestern border of Texas. Access via Alpine (west) or Marathon (east). The avian superstar here is the Colima Warbler, whose North American breeding range is restricted to the Chisos Mountains in

Fig. 3. *Specialized bills and feeding techniques.* The crossbills have evolved a unique and complex technique for prizing open the scales of unripe cones. It involves insertion of the long, sharp upper mandible between the cone scales; a twisting head motion in which the opposed crossed mandible tips pry the scales apart; and *lateral* play of the mandibles, which also acts to separate the scales. Once the pine seed is revealed, a cartilaginous cutting "tool" on the tip of the thick crossbill tongue detaches it at its base. The laterally flattened oystercatcher bill is in effect an oyster knife that is inserted between the shells of a closed bivalve to sever the adductor muscle(s) holding the shells together. The Black Skimmer "slices" calm shallows with its knife-thin lower mandible until it encounters a prey item, such as the luckless killifish illustrated. It then snaps the shorter upper mandible closed on its prey with a characteristic downward/backward jerk of the head before raising it out of the water to be swallowed. For more detail on these techniques and other specialized feeding methods, see FOOD/FEEDING.

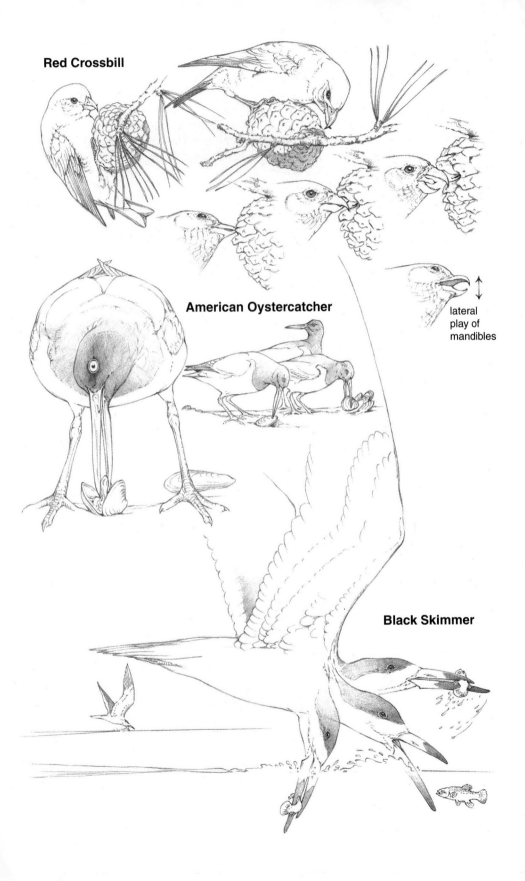

Red Crossbill

American Oystercatcher

lateral play of mandibles

Black Skimmer

the park. The deciduous (oak/maple) woodland at Boot Springs (6,500 feet) is the locality for this specialty. The habitat and avifauna are similar to that of SOUTHEASTERN ARIZONA, noted for a large variety of Mexican bird species, some of which—notably Lucifer Hummingbird and Black-chinned Sparrow, are most readily found at Big Bend. The nearby Davis Mountains harbor additional southwestern specialties and are a natural side trip to a Big Bend expedition.

BIG DAY. See BIRDING EVENTS.

BILL. A bird's bill (or "beak") is analogous to our jaws, though it is used differently in many respects and bears little obvious resemblance in form. It consists of two bony frontward extensions of the skull—one above and one below the mouth—covered with a horny or leathery sheath made of keratin, which, like our fingernails, is a product of the upper layer of the skin (epidermis). In most animals the upper jaw is called the maxilla and the lower the mandible, but in birds the two parts of the bill are known as the upper and lower mandibles. The upper mandible is of a single piece in most birds, though in a few (e.g., tubenoses, frigatebirds, jaegers) it is divided into sections. The lower mandible is made up of two identical pieces (*rami*), which extend outward from the skull, meet usually at the midpoint of the bill's length or beyond, and are fused at the tip. This meeting place is called the *gonys* (see Fig. 35) and is conspicuous as a distinct angle in the profile of the lower mandible of the larger gulls. Both mandibles have two sharp edges, called the *tomia,* often equipped with some form of serration for holding food securely. In most birds the upper mandible is slightly longer, deeper, and wider than the lower mandible, so that there is a slight overlap from above. Nostril holes (*nares*) are evident in all but a few species and in all North American birds occur nearer the base of the bill than the tip. (For nostril structure, shape, and variation, see NOSTRILS.)

Bill wear is compensated for by formation of new keratin much in the way our outer skin layer flakes away and is imperceptibly replaced; and broken bills can also "grow out" in some cases.

The young of species with unusually long or peculiarly shaped bills (e.g., curlews and spoonbills) begin life with these features much reduced and inconspicuous; the modifications emerge as the birds mature. Bill length is subject to age and sexual dimorphism; sandpiper bills, for example, are, as a rule, longer in older females and shorter in younger males of the same species. In the extinct Huia (one of 3 species of the endemic New Zealand wattlebird family) this sexual dimorphism was expressed to a unique extreme. The male had a relatively short, sharp, bill which it used to excavate decayed wood for insect larvae, while the female had a much longer, thin, sickle-shaped bill with which she probed in holes for the

same prey. Apparently they never worked together with their different tools.

LENGTH. Mandibles, like fingernails, grow continuously, so that if the tips don't meet, they fail to be worn down to their normal size and shape through constant use. Bills vary greatly in length, from a few millimeters in swifts to a foot and a half in the largest male pelicans. The longest bill (culmen chord) in the world is that of the Great White Pelican (*Pelecanus onocrotalus*) at 47.1 cm (18.5 inches); in North America this distinction belongs to the American White Pelican (*P. erythrorhynchos*: 36.5 cm/14.4 inches) the largest of Old World storks are close runners-up, several species bearing beaks in the 35-cm (13.5-inch) range. The Long-billed Curlew, whose bill sometimes appears almost grotesque, actually measures "only" 8.6 inches at its longest (maximum females); the fact that this appendage belongs to a large sandpiper rather than a stork accounts, of course, for our perception that its bill is gigantic.

SHAPE. Bills also come in a wide range of shapes adapted to various feeding habits (see Use, below). In addition to obvious adjectives, such as "short," "long," "straight," "curved," "broad," "narrow," and "pointed," a few specialized terms are used to describe certain bill types: *recurved* = curved upward, e.g., godwits, avocets; *decurved* = curved downward, e.g., curlews, ibises, many wrens; *serrate* = having rows of tooth-like modifications along the edges of the bill, e.g., mergansers; *lamellate* = having seine-like ridges across the inside of the mandibles, e.g., dabbling ducks, geese, and swans; *hooked* = bending at the tip into a sharp point, e.g., raptors; *toothed* = having one or more serrations in the upper mandible, e.g., falcons, trogons; *conical* = pointed at the tip and expanding evenly to a more or less round base, e.g., many seedeaters; *compressed* = flattened on the sides, e.g., Razorbill, kingfishers; *depressed* = flattened from top and bottom, e.g., many ducks and flycatchers; *spatulate* = wide and flat at the tip, e.g., spoonbills; *terete* = round in cross section, e.g., hummingbirds, and *beveled* = chisel-shaped at the tip, characteristic of woodpeckers. A number of bizarre bill shapes, e.g., pelican, flamingo, skimmer, and crossbill, are not adequately described by single adjectives. Some of these are discussed below.

APPENDAGES, MODIFICATIONS. The bills of some birds have special features added onto their basic bill structure (as distinct from modifications of shape). Some of these seem to be simply ornamental, others have clear-cut functions, and the purpose of a few remains mysterious.

Nails. Ducks, geese, and swans have a hard, sharp-edged tip to the upper mandible, which contrasts with the leathery texture of the rest of the bill. This "nail" is used in cropping vegetation. A superficially similar but unrelated structure is the "egg tooth," a calcium deposit that develops on the tips of the upper mandibles before hatching and is used to break through the eggshell at hatching; it drops off soon afterward.

Knobs and Shields. Adult coots and gallinules of both sexes develop flat, rather hard, colored appendages of the bill, which extend up onto the forehead (frontal shields). According to Bellrose (1976–WATERFOWL), the brightly colored frontal shield of the drake King Eider is largely fat and is prized as a delicacy among Hudson Bay Inuit; the yellow knob at the bill base of the drake Black Scoter is of similar construction, but its esculence is unvouched for. The American White Pelican develops a knob near the center of the upper mandible during the breeding season and sheds it thereafter.

Ceres are leathery, sometimes brightly colored "saddles" that form the base of the upper mandible in hawks, eagles, and falcons. A similar structure occurs in parrots but is feathered and therefore less conspicuous. In both cases the nostrils open through the cere, but the function of the latter is unknown. Pigeons also have a naked cere at the base of the bill, which in some species (e.g., Rock Dove) develops into a soft prominence, called an *operculum* by some authorities.

Seasonal Sheaths are developed as part of the breeding "plumage" of many alcids, notably the puffins. It is typically larger and more brightly colored than the "winter" bill and is shed and reacquired annually.

Throat Pouches made of leathery skin and hanging from the forked portion of the lower mandible are conspicuous among cormorants but reach their highest development in the pelicans. When the pelican enters the water headfirst, the flexible lower mandible and attached sac is forced open like a wide-necked pouch into which the fish are scooped; when the pelican surfaces the pouch is contracted and the water seined out through the sides of the mandibles.

Malformations of the bill, including crossed mandibles (in species other than crossbills) and abnormal extensions of one mandible or the other, are seen occasionally in wild birds. This is usually the result of an accident that prevents proper occlusion of the mandibles.

USE. Because a bird's bill is inevitably associated with its mouth and because birds spend a great deal of time eating, it is natural to associate bill functions with food. Perhaps, therefore, it should be emphasized that many of the things birds do with their bills—including catching and preparing food, but also carrying, digging, and nest building—are things we would do with our fingers and hands. The most generalized bill function is a pliers-like grasping, performed to some extent by all birds. No modern birds have true teeth or chewing capacity and must therefore either swallow their food whole or pull or break it into manageable pieces. However, gripping of slippery prey such as fish is aided in many cases by tooth-like serrations of the mandible edges. These are highly developed and conspicuous in the mergansers but also appear on the bills of herons and a few other birds.

Another widespread bill action, for which a *pointed* bill is handy but not essential, is pecking, used to hack up nuts and other hard-shelled

foods, to chop large pieces of food into manageable bits, to dig in the earth or tree trunks, and to repel enemies; ground-feeding birds (e.g., grouse, quail, sparrows) use a sharp pecking motion as they pick up grain and seeds. Many birds, members of the crow family, for example, survive very well with simple bills adapted for grasping and pecking but without highly specialized catching or feeding modifications. Others use one or a combination of other basic bill actions, which follow.

Tearing large prey into pieces small enough to be swallowed is typical of birds with strong hooked bills, such as day-flying raptors (including shrikes), owls, and to some extent tubenoses, jaegers, and gulls.

Probing is most highly developed among shorebirds (including woodcocks and snipes), many of which have sensitive, relatively soft bill tips for "feeling" and grasping subterranean life forms. The great variety of bill shapes and lengths in this group shows adaptation to feeding "niches" at different depths. Ibises probe in a similar manner. Hummingbirds practice another kind of probing, penetrating deep calyxes of flowers with their long bills to sip nectar with their even longer tongues; hummingbird bills are also ideal "forceps" for picking insects off plants and out of the air.

Stabbing at prey is favored by many waterbirds with long, sharp bills, e.g., anhingas, herons, and cranes. In many cases what seems to be a spearing motion is in fact a fast grab, but fish eaten by Western Grebes are apparently all pierced by that species' very sharp bill before being swallowed (Palmer 1962–ORNITHOLOGY).

Husking seeds has been perfected by finches, some of which have a specially reinforced skull structure to withstand the strain of crushing very hard fruit pits.

The interior of a seedeater's bill is adapted to facilitate the husking/crushing process. The edges of the lower mandible fit into grooves along the inside of the upper mandible when the bill is closed. A seed to be husked is maneuvered into one of these grooves (i.e., right or left side) by the tongue. The sharp edge of the lower mandible is then brought up to bear on the seed's husk. After the outer husk is pierced, the tongue revolves the seed and the husk is "shorn" from the kernel by the same sharp mandibular edge. This procedure is performed very rapidly, and larger-billed finches can hold more than one seed in their mouths at once and husk each sequentially. The size and hardness of seeds that a species can deal with depend on the size of its bill and the development of its jaw muscles, cranial structure, etc. Since large-billed species can eat small, soft seeds as well as large, hard ones, they have a wider choice of food in general than do smaller finches.

The massive bill of the Eurasian Hawfinch can exert a pressure of up to 100 pounds per square inch, and the similar "nutcracker" borne by our Evening Grosbeak may be comparable.

Straining animal and vegetable matter out of water or mud is achieved with the aid of a series of ridges (lamellae) running across the

interior of the bill. This adaptation is found in ducks, geese, and swans and flamingoes.

Some bills are peculiarly adapted to highly specific feeding methods. For details of these, see FOOD/FEEDING. See also Fig. 3.

Display. Most bills are "horn-colored," which ranges from pinkish brown to blackish gray. However, bright bill color, including the various appendages noted above, occurs in many families and in some cases becomes heightened during the breeding season. Bill noises are also included in some courtship rituals. Black-browed Albatrosses, for example, accompany one of their nuptial "dances" with loud bill snapping.

BILLING. A courtship ritual involving "affectionate" bill gestures between a pair of birds. Such caresses accompanied by vocalizations are practiced with apparent relish in public by feral Rock Doves and give rise to the human lovemaking metaphor, "billing and cooing." The more aggressive bill-whacking gestures performed by some albatross species, among others, are not normally referred to as billing.

BILL NOISES. See SONG, Nonvocal Sounds.

BINOCULARS. See OPTICAL EQUIPMENT.

BINOMIAL (or binominal). Literally, a name consisting of two words. In the Linnaean system of biological nomenclature, all species are referred to by a Latin binomial, the first word being the name of the genus and the second the name of the specific members of that genus. Thus, the Common Goldeneye is scientifically labeled *Bucephala clangula.* See NOMENCLATURE, ZOOLOGICAL; SYSTEMATICS; TRINOMIAL.

"BINS." Nickname for "binoculars." For other variations see OPTICAL EQUIPMENT, Terminology.

BIOGEOGRAPHY. The distribution of living plant and animal life; or the study thereof. Compare ZOOGEOGRAPHY, See DISTRIBUTION.

BIOGRAPHY. Numerous fascinating human stories are related to the progress of American ornithology—far more, indeed, than can be included in the present book. However, there are two good reasons to learn about the most prominent ones: (1) Curiosity. It is natural when contemplating, for example, Lucy's Warbler to wonder who Lucy was. Sometimes the fruits of such inquiry are meager, as when the person commemorated is little known or unexceptional. But in other cases the life of a bird's namesake proves to be one of the most fascinating attributes of the species. (2) The names, both Latin and English, of North American birds

embody to a great extent the history of the discovery, classification, description, and illustration of the native avifauna.

In a time when interest in birds has reached an all-time high and nearly every family owns an illustrated field guide, we may be tempted to imagine Adam and Eve recognizing Prothonotary Warblers and Calliope Hummingbirds as they strolled around their garden. It is good to remember, therefore, that the scientific differentiation and systematic arrangement of birdlife has been accomplished almost entirely within the last 250 years. This is not to slight indigenous taxonomies—usually based on the utility of the species in question—many of which were (and are) quite sophisticated, but only to point out the degree to which science has in a real sense sharpened our perception of natural detail. Furthermore, as with other aspects of American history, the pioneering period of ornithological investigation is a particularly fascinating one. Though not very distant in years, the eighteenth and much of the nineteenth centuries are distantly removed from us by the rapid changes in the way we live. Many of the exploits of the early naturalists bring those times to life with greater verisimilitude than the deeds of the legendary public figures that crowd the textbooks.

Information about the people of American ornithology is given here in three ways: (1) People for whom species are currently named or who named a significant number of species or who fit neither of these categories but whose reputation merits inclusion (in the admittedly subjective judgment of the author) are listed as entries in the main text. All such entries describe persons now dead. (2) Modern ornithologists are increasingly tied to the lab and the library, so their contributions tend to be better reflected in their writing than in recountings of their adventures in the field. Therefore, prominent *modern* ornithologists, living and dead, are recorded here (with a few exceptions) only in the Bibliography. (3) The bibliography for the present entry provides a list of references that chronicle the doings of the whole range of American bird men, in many cases far more thoroughly than it has been possible to do here.

In reviewing the range of people for whom North American birds have been named a few facts stand out.

- Except for Anna Blackburne, the only women commemorated are those we might call "loved ones"—the daughters, wives, or beautiful aristocratic patronesses of the men who did the naming. These women are commemorated exclusively by their *first* names, and even this was not always considered flattering. At least once Audubon was rebuffed when he offered to name a pretty bird after a pretty lady of his acquaintance; having one's name associated with a bird was "not quite nice" in some circles. There is not a single woman among the *authors* of North American bird species.

- In contrast to the general scarcity of women is the plethora of doctors. Of the 90-odd people whose names are used for North American

bird species, over 20% were closely connected to medicine—of which the great majority at least completed medical school, and one, William HAMMOND (flycatcher), was a U.S. Surgeon General. Not a few of the doctors were also in the army; for an explanation and account of this circumstance see BAIRD in the main text and Hume (1942). For what it is worth, doctors are today very well represented in birdwatching circles; without supporting statistics (but with extensive field experience) the author ventures that doctors far outnumber birders of other professions, e.g., lawyers. (One birder-doctor has offered the explanation that birding allows doctors to exercise their passion for diagnosis without burdening them with the obligation to treat.)

- Finally, it is impossible not to be impressed with the haphazardness with which fame-by-bird descends and is withdrawn. An obscure English lady botanist (Ms. Blackburne) is remembered in the name of one of the most exquisite North American wood warblers because she was known by a German systematist (Gmelin); while poor John Selby, the English ornithological illustrator, is cast into nomenclatural limbo because what Audubon thought was Selby's Flycatcher was really an immature Hooded Warbler.

This kind of injustice is mitigated somewhat by the fact that it falls with almost equal cruelty on the great as on the slight. Mark CATESBY has no memorial bird and even the giant Audubon has lost much ground at the species level. Audubon's Caracara, Audubon's Woodpecker, and Audubon's Warbler are now mere subspecies or less. True, his shearwater remains (though some would call it "Dusky"!), and he recently regained an eponym when Black-headed Oriole was renamed.

BIOLOGY. All forms of life, now divided among five kingdoms: Animalia (animals), Plantae (plants), Fungi (mushrooms, molds, yeasts, lichens, etc.), Protoctista (eukaryotic microorganisms, seaweeds, slime molds, protozoa), and Monera (bacteria); also the science of same. The concept is divisible in space and time, e.g., the biology of the earth of North America or the Cretaceous period. For the ultimate description, see Mayr (1997).

BIOMASS. The total *weight* of organisms in a specified area. Biomass may be measured by land unit, e.g., weight per acre or cubic foot; by habitat; and by groups of organisms, e.g., insect mass per acre of rain forest. The measure is useful in comparing fundamental differences in biological structures and functions. We know, for example, that the number of species of terrestrial birds tends to increase as one moves into the tropics, but in many instances biomass—the total weight of birds—remains the same as in equivalent habitats in the Temperate Zone. In these instances we can deduce that there must be fewer individuals in relation to the number of species in parts of the tropics.

BIOME (BY-ome). One of the main types of biological community, characterized by soil conditions and climate that produce a distinctive form of vegetation, which, in turn, is inhabited by characteristic animal forms. The major North American terrestrial biomes are tundra, coniferous forest, deciduous forest, grassland, southwestern (U.S.) pine/oak woodland, pinyon/juniper woodland (and hills and mountain slopes of the western United States), chaparral (southwestern United States), and desert. Each of the biomes may be subdivided on the basis of geography, e.g., arctic tundra vs. alpine tundra, or differences in plant associates, e.g., sagebrush desert vs. creosote scrub desert.

Many species of birds are characteristic of or confined to one of the various biomes, while others span two or more: Wrentits and chaparral are almost inseparable in North America, while the American Crow occurs to some extent in most biomes. Compare HABITAT; NICHE; LIFE ZONES; see also DISTRIBUTION and Fig. 8.

BIOTA. All the living organisms of any given place, e.g., the marine biota or the biota of your backyard.

BIRD. Collective name for all members of the vertebrate animal class Aves. Though there are many traits that we strongly associate with birds— e.g., wings, bills, nest building, egg laying, and song—only one character is unique to them: feathers. This does not mean that birds—both as a class and within the great variation of avian forms—have not evolved many unique adaptations to particular lifestyles. For example, the modification of the avian forelimb for flight is very different from the homologous bat wing (see WING). Furthermore, birds can be characterized by a *combination* of features that typifies no other class, viz. (1) endothermy ("warm-bloodedness"; birds and mammals only); (2) a four-chambered heart (also in mammals; crocodiles similar); (3) feet and lower leg usually scaled and featherless; (4) teeth lacking (in modern birds; also in turtles); (5) mandibles covered with a horny sheath (bill); (6) a large breastbone usually with prominent keel (see FLIGHT); (7) an air sac system filling spaces of body cavity (see RESPIRATORY SYSTEM); (8) pneumatized bones; (9) the absence of a bladder; (10) hard-shelled (calcareous) eggs with large yolk, incubated externally. For the cladistically oriented, characters 5–9 are clear morphological synapomorphies as probably is 4, though it is shared with turtles.

Birds evolved either from theropod dinosaurs in the Jurassic Period (the prevailing theory as of 2002) or some 90 million years earlier from thecodont reptiles in the mid-Triassic Period (see EVOLUTION OF BIRDLIFE). Just over 9,700 bird species are living at present (Sibley and Monroe 1990), though this number is both rising (due to new studies of species phylogeny) and falling (due to an increasing extinction rate). Birds are among the most ubiquitous organisms. Representatives breed on all

of the continents, occupy a full range of ecological niches, and are variously adapted for existence on land, water (including the open ocean), ice, and air, with a majority of species adapted for perching and feeding in trees and/or shrubs. Birds presently achieve greatest diversity in South America, where over 3,000 species have been recorded. About 747 bird species occur regularly in North America (as defined on p. xvii); about 175 others have been recorded as vagrants (see Appendix II).

The deepest roots of the word "bird" have disappeared, but the Old English form was *brid,* first seen in literature around AD 800. According to etymologists this was at first a generic term for *young* birds (and other animals), a usage that survives to the present, e.g. "a hen and her birds" (Lockwood 1993–NAMES). The meaning was expanded to refer to all small birds around 1300 (op. cit.).

For entries treating broad aspects of birdlife, see "How to Use This Book," pp. xvii–xxvii.

BIRD BANDING. See BANDING.

BIRD CALLS (made by humans). Sound, sometimes made with the aid of a mechanical device, to attract wild birds. Hunters have long used instruments made of wood or metal, which, when blown into, reproduce the call of their intended victims. Crows, for example, may be attracted by imitating their distress call. The effect of wooden decoys is enhanced by signaling flocks of waterfowl with enticing quacking sounds; turkey hunters traditionally make use of calls both vocal and mechanical; and in the past shorebird shooters used a variety of tin whistles, which, with some practice, could be made to imitate the calls of yellowlegs, godwits, various plovers, and the like.

Birdwatchers also make noises to attract birds. A metal plug inserted into a small wooden cylinder (patented as the "Audubon Bird Call") makes a squeaking noise when twisted, which seems to provoke curiosity in some birds. Squeaking sounds can also be made orally or by kissing the back of the hand in hopes of the same effect. By far the most widely used and effective of oral bird calls is "pishing" or "spishing," a hissing or "shushing" sound uttered in a pulsating rhythm. That a wide variety of birds respond to this technique in many instances cannot be disputed. *Why* they respond is less clear. Simple curiosity may be a factor, and it has also been suggested that pishing sounds resemble alarm calls of many species and therefore elicit a mobbing response from birds within hearing range. Birds thus attracted often add their own alarm calls, intensifying the general excitement and enhancing the cumulative effect. Sustained and somewhat aggressive pishing seems to work best, and it is not unusual during migration to be able to attract dozens of individuals of many species. Certain families and species are particularly responsive. Chick-

adees, nuthatches, and kinglets are usually among the first to arrive. Woodpeckers, flycatchers, jays, wrens, mimics (especially Gray Catbird), thrushes, vireos, warblers, and sparrows are also susceptible. Effectiveness varies dramatically and there is still a great deal of myth and mystery connected with the phenomenon. For example, in the Neotropics, North American migrants respond much more readily than resident species—an experience that can be demonstrated but is difficult to explain; however, if one imitates a common resident flocking species, e.g., Common Bush-Tanager, results improve somewhat. Pishing is not practiced by European birdwatchers and is viewed with a mixture of suspicion and derision by many of them. The fact that it is seldom tried there with any enthusiasm reinforces the belief that it doesn't work. Casual experiments show, however, that shy woodland birds *will* respond well to the "irate jay" form of pish in at least some parts of Europe.

Like peering with an (apparently) vacant expression into the air or wading about in fetid marshland, pishing may direct a certain amount of not altogether approving human attention to the birdwatcher. But the effect of the technique depends on a certain emotional commitment and unembarrassed vigor, and fainthearted birders will do as well to remain silent.

Another version of this technique is to imitate the call of a small owl, preferably one native to the region in which one is birding. Pygmy and screech owl calls sometimes produce amazing results (see Fig.19) and are often quite easy to mimic. Quite often the imitated owl will show up to check out his presumed rival and the mobbers go wild.

See also RECORDING OF BIRD SOUNDS.

BIRD CHAT GROUPS. On-line state and provincial chat groups and listservs dedicated to birds and birding now exist throughout North America with many subsets for specific demographics (e.g., Teen Bird Chat). There is also a national service called BIRDCHAT. Each of these groups has guidelines regarding content and specific instructions for logging on. The American Birding Association publishes a comprehensive listing of chat groups and listservs on its website: www.americanbirding.org. See also BIRDNET; LISTSERVS; RARE BIRD ALERTS.

BIRD CLUB. In the broadest sense, any organization that promotes the study and/or enjoyment of birdlife among a group of people. The range is from the venerable Nuttall Ornithological Club of Cambridge, Massachusetts, which gave birth to the American Ornithologists' Union in 1888 and continues to present programs and publish work of scientific value; to the National Audubon Society, a conservation organization with a membership of about 600,000; to the American Birding Association (22,000); to the smallest neighborhood birding group, which meets, as the spirit moves its

members, for birding and chitchat. Many clubs publish local checklists, organize field trips, and give programs. They are a great resource for beginning birdwatchers, newcomers to an area who want to learn some of the region's "hot spots," and anyone seeking a little sociable fun in the field.

In his 1978 guide, Rickert listed more than 820 bird clubs in North America. Like all other numbers associated with birding, this one has undoubtedly grown substantially. Though no similar comprehensive guide has been published recently, the American Birding Association gives contact information on their website (www.americanbirding.org/) for more than 50 of the best established clubs and those that have chosen to provide information to ABA.

BIRDER (birding). A relatively new term that has become popular as an alternative to "birdwatcher" with its unflattering (to some) overtones of passivity, eccentricity, frivolity, and even effeminacy. A birder is one who "birds" or "goes birding" in a serious and energetic manner, whether to hone his or her field-identification skills or to amass an impressive list.

The strong identification of "birding" with "listing" has recently forced the hippest of field ornithologists to resort to the anti-snobbery of calling themselves "birdwatchers."

For another interpretation and some discussion of the term's history, see J. A. Tucker, *Birding* (1981), 13:38 (editorial; also responses in subsequent issues).

See also BIRDWATCHING; LISTING.

BIRDER'S EXCHANGE. A brilliant concept to promote conservation by collecting used (or new) equipment—binoculars, telescopes, field guides, etc.—useful in bird-related field work and distributing it—free of charge—to researchers, conservationists, and educators in neotropical countries. Founded in 1990 at the Manomet Center for Conservation Science in Massachusetts, it is now being runs by the American Birding Association. The program has distributed thousands of items to more than 350 conservation programs in over 30 Latin American countries. Contributors to the program can donate equipment, make a financial contribution, or act as couriers. *Contact information*: Birder's Exchange, 720 West Monument Street, Colorado Springs, CO 80904; tel. 719/578-9707; e-mail: bex@aba.org. For a more detailed description of the program, go to www.americanbirding. org/programs/consbex.

BIRD FEEDING. Humans have been feeding birds, at least inadvertently, for at least as long as they have had agriculture. Flemish genre paintings of the fifteenth century, for example, show magpies and sparrows nibbling at kernels spilled from grain barrows and crusts in dooryards. But it is only since about the 1930s that bird feeding has become a highly organized

pastime complete with specialized (and expensive) merchandise and written guides dealing with the growing technology in the field. Polls have revealed that about 70 million Americans are engaged in some form of bird feeding. In some cases, this amounts to nothing more than throwing the stale bread out the kitchen window, but increasingly it is a full-fledged hobby that involves dispensing over a billion pounds of birdseed annually in the United States alone.

The appeal of bird feeding is easy to understand. Birds are attractive, amusing, companionable, and provide a contact with the natural world that is generally lacking in the lives of many urban and suburban dwellers. Dealing with the intricacies of feeder placement, catering to special tastes, dispensing different consistencies of feed, and discouraging pests can keep a dedicated gadgeteer in nearly perpetual motion for life. And, for many, there is a sense of helping fellow creatures to survive life's cruelties. Many full-length books have now been devoted totally to the skills and pleasures of this new pastime. What follows is but a skeletal outline.

EFFECTS ON BIRDLIFE. Given the explosive increase in bird feeding, it is reasonable to speculate that there have been correspondingly enormous effects on bird populations. That there have been effects, no one would deny. What kinds of effects and their magnitude are matters still principally addressed by guesswork, educated and otherwise. Some of the most popular speculations together with our best-documented responses are as follows:

1. Feeding has increased bird populations. This has been used to rationalize the conservation benefit of feeding birds and as negative argument that feeding favors predator and parasitic species such as jays and cowbirds that prey on less common, "more desirable" songbirds. *Response:* Feeders may increase the survival rate of weaker individuals, thereby adding somewhat to the total population of a given species. But there are other pressures, potentially fatal, on birds besides finding an adequate food supply and there is no scientific evidence as yet that feeder bird species as a whole in particular segments are increasing. Given the present magnitude of bird feeding, however, the matter merits serious study.

2. Feeding is responsible for the northward extension of the range of the Red-bellied Woodpecker, Tufted Titmouse, Northern Cardinal, and other species. *Response:* Changes in habitat and climate have probably been more important to the recent northward movement of these species than the assisted living provided by feeders. Northern Mockingbirds and Blue-gray Gnatcatchers after all, which generally stay clear of feeders, have undergone an analogous increase during roughly the same period.

3. Birds are forsaking their normal habitat and becoming hooked on store-bought millet in suburbia. *Response:* Except for inherently weak individuals, birds do not *depend* on your feeder or *forget* how

to find food for themselves; they simply take advantage of the easiest supply of food available. If you stop feeding, the healthy members of your clientele will resort to wild food sources (or to your neighbor's feeder) without hesitation. Only those that need a "crutch" to survive are likely to fall prey to real life.

4. Feeding makes smaller birds more vulnerable to predation because it promotes unnatural concentrations of individuals. *Response:* Dunn and Tessaglia-Hymes (1999) conclude that the risk of predation from species such as Cooper's and Sharp-shinned Hawks was not significantly higher around feeders.

5. Feeder birds are especially susceptible to communicable diseases. Feeding stations—especially poorly maintained ones—probably create increased potential for spreading naturally occurring pathogens. A recent epidemic of mycoplasmal conjunctivitis in House Finches, which reduced the population of this common species by 40–50%, may have been more virulent due to the togetherness fostered by feeders. For the full range of possibilities, see DISEASE; for remediation, see below.

If part of your pleasure from feeding birds depends on the Florence Nightingale rationale, you can take solace from the probability that migrants such as hummingbirds, thrushes, warblers, tanagers, and orioles, which have remained in winter climes "by mistake," doubtless owe their survival, in many cases, to the emergency rations to be found at feeders. When spring arrives they will probably return to breeding grounds near their birthplace but may also come back to your orange slices on schedule each winter—undeniably beneficiaries of bird feeding.

Finally, some have noted that the phenomenon of well-off Americans supplying birds unnecessarily with tons of grain—possibly grown at the expense of forest habitats abroad—costing billions of dollars that might go to truly starving *people* is morally ambiguous at best.

WHICH BIRDS TO EXPECT. This depends on a variety of factors, such as where you live and what kind of food you put out. One of the intriguing things about feeding birds is the knowledge that virtually anything is possible. If you think this is hyperbole, note the record of an Ivory Gull that dropped in on a suet feeder in Saratoga Springs, NY. It would only be risking contradiction by a resident of Key West to announce that you can rule out frigatebirds. Having acknowledged the *possible*, however, it is doubtless wise to recognize that of the avifauna as a whole, typical feeder birds are a modest subset. A colleague notes that of the 142 species on his upstate New York yard list, only 36% (51 species—actually pretty impressive!) ever visited his feeder. However, it is possible to narrow the field in a general way.

True "feeder birds" are land birds. Among these, the species that are least likely to put in an appearance at your feeder are the migratory insect

eaters, such as cuckoos, swifts, nightjars, flycatchers, swallows, wrens, pip-its, gnatcatchers, vireos, and warblers. Many of these will visit feeders if faced with starvation, and a few (e.g., Carolina Wren, Yellow-rumped War-bler) are even regular customers, but others would literally die amidst plenty because they don't recognize a sunflower seed or suet as food. Owls and most large diurnal raptors are also unlikely, though a number of suet providers have Red-shouldered Hawks as regular customers and some small predators (see below) feed on the fed. This leaves grouse, quail and pheasants, doves, hummingbirds, woodpeckers, larks, corvids, titmice, nuthatches, mimic thrushes, true thrushes, starlings, blackbirds and ori-oles, tanagers, and finches. Not all of the species in these families come reg-ularly to feeders, and some families are far better represented than others or are more frequent in particular regions of the country, but the remaining possibilities are still very wide. Some species seem particularly susceptible to the temptation of artificially proffered goodies. One species or another of dove, woodpecker, chickadee, nuthatch, jay, and several finches are almost certain to appear very promptly if you live where they are fairly common.

REGIONAL DIFFERENCES. The area of the country in which you live will largely determine the dramatis personae of your avian groaning boards. In the northern United States and southern Canada, influxes of winter finches such as Pine Siskin, redpolls, Evening Grosbeak, and (rarely) crossbills, which have exhausted supplies in their native coniferous forests, eat feeder owners to the doorstep of the poorhouse one year and are ill-represented or totally absent the next (see IRRUPTION/ERUPTION). The Southwest is unparalleled for hummingbirds. Denverites get rosy-finches when the snow drives them (the rosy-finches) from their high-altitude breeding areas; and southern Floridians can expect anything from a bulbul to a macaw.

WHEN TO FEED. When they're not sleeping birds spend by far the greatest proportion of their time searching for food and they are quick to spot an opportunity for easy regular meals. Once a bird discovers that a copious and inexhaustible banquet is to be had at your feeder, it will re-turn regularly, and this behavior will, in time, attract other birds. Since your food source is likely to be more reliable than any "natural" one, you can count on good attendance even in the warmer months when "wild" food is abundant.

On the other hand, there is no doubt that a cover of snow or other en-vironmental effect that makes food scarce or hard to get at will increase feeder activity. Some people feel that they "ought" to feed birds in the win-ter lest they starve, but this is a moral obligation with which no one need be burdened.

KINDS OF FOOD. There are probably few edible substances that feeder birds have not been offered by experiment-minded "station man-agers" (e.g., spaghetti!). The staples, however, are as follows.

Seed and Grain. Sunflower seeds, with and without hulls, black oil and striped, millets, seeds of several species of *Setaria* grasses, and Niger/Nyjer thistle seeds are among the most attractive food to doves, finches, tits, jays, and other regular feeder birds. Some seeds are in special demand by certain species (Evening Grosbeaks, for example, are mad for sunflower seeds). Some, e.g., thistles, are more expensive than others. Cracked corn and other coarse grains (usually in the form of chicken scratch feed) are especially popular with grouse, pheasants, quail, doves, jays, and blackbirds. Mixtures that include most or all of the above are sold in grocery stores as well as feed stores. However, it has recently been demonstrated (Geis 1980) that these mixtures contain ingredients such as sorghum, wheat, oats, and rice to which the majority of feeder birds are indifferent. The same study revealed that white *proso* millet and black oil-type sunflower seeds are outstanding favorites and that peanut hearts are gobbled by starlings but little else. This U.S. Fish and Wildlife report also contains a list of food preferences species by species and many other details of interest for the serious bird feeder.

Fruit. Oranges, bananas, pears, apples, grapes, and raisins are frequently offered on bird tables and any other soft fruit is probably equally effective. Not surprisingly, they are particularly attractive to species that normally feed on fruit, such as thrushes, Yellow-breasted Chat, tanagers, orioles, and certain finches. Migrant fruit eaters that remain up North when most of their kind have left for tropical wintering grounds are more likely to be drawn to feeders offering their preferred food. Such birds are often celebrities of the winter birding scene and may (if the word gets out) attract a flock of avid human fans. Here again there are obvious regional variations: Fruit eaters may be present year-round in southern states while in the frigid zones the fruit almost invariably freezes before it can be consumed.

Suet and Cooking Fats. Both of these are appealing to most species but particularly to tits, woodpeckers, starlings, and insect eaters, including lingerers.

Sugar Water. Primarily used to attract hummingbirds, but also appealing to orioles, warblers, and a surprising assortment of other species (even woodpeckers!). It is important that these substances be used with some care to ensure the health of the birds they attract. (See Hazards, below, for proper "formula" and other considerations pertaining to this specialized type of feeding.) "Instant nectar" can now be purchased ready-made in your local "bird store."

Bread. A staple of human charity toward birds and a symbol of the days before bird feeding became an industry. It still works, fresh or stale, and apparently the least nutritious type of white bread is the most popular. However, other bakery products, from Danish pastry to dog biscuits, will not be scorned. *Caution:* This class of food is especially popular with

avian lowlife such as pigeons and House Sparrows, not to mention mammalian undesirables such as rats. Furthermore, bread is nutritionally bad for birds and thus not appropriate if you truly care about your "guests."

Peanut Butter. Immediately popular with titmice, nuthatches, woodpeckers, starlings, and many other species; for rumored ill effects, see Hazards, below.

Water. For drinking and bathing, water may bring a greater variety of birds to your yard than your feeder. It is best made available in the shade and near cover, into which bathers can duck when the local Sharpshinned Hawk makes a pass. A drip fountain seems to increase popularity, and if you can continue to offer open water when the temperature drops below freezing your yard will virtually throb with avian gratitude. Birdbath heating elements are available commercially. Glycerin, sometimes touted as a means of keeping birdbaths "open" in winter, has one major drawback—it doesn't work. Cleaning birdbaths thoroughly and often is crucial, as they are an ideal medium for bacterial growth to which the birds might be susceptible. Then, too, in warm weather, a stagnant "bath" may well add to your yard's mosquito population.

FEEDERS. You can now spend almost any amount of money you desire on elaborate feeding apparatus. Feeders come equipped with the latest technology in squirrel baffles, intricate compartmentalization, which excludes certain species to the benefit of others, and convenient gizmos for cleaning and filling. Other recent "improvements" include two-way mirrors for window-mounted feeders that can intrude into the human living space slightly, and mechanized squirrel tossers. Architecturally, some are so grand that one's house may suffer by comparison. The thrifty and lovers of simplicity will recognize, of course, that feeding birds does not require a feeder. Simply throwing your offerings on the ground is likely to be highly effective; however, it does deprive you of the measure of control that feeders provide. For example, food spread on the ground is vulnerable to waste from the effects of weather and the depredations of less desirable guests such as squirrels. Furthermore, not all birds prefer to feed on the ground, and certain substances, such as suet and peanut butter, are most conveniently offered in some kind of container. By raising a feeder on a pole, nailing it to a tree trunk, or suspending it on a wire, you can minimize waste, exclude uninvited visitors, and make your offering more attractive to certain species. Feeders may also enhance your enjoyment. The kind of window feeders described above, for example, allow almost intimate contact between observer and bird, and some feeders are designed to force titmice and other agile species to perform acrobatic stunts for their supper. All of this may be achieved with minimum expense by the application of a little ingenuity and effort. The chief considerations in making a homemade feeder are (1) keeping food dry in wet weather with drainage holes and/or roof; (2) stability—platforms poorly

suspended will dump their contents onto the ground when the first star-ling lands on the edge; and (3) convenient refilling—climbing trees or poles in a blizzard with a bucket of seed can be tiresome. Everything else is a matter of taste and ingenuity. Suet can be suspended in mesh fruit bags, placed in simple "cages" of folded hardware cloth nailed to a tree, or spread onto pine cones or into bark crevices; effective seed dispensers can be made from milk cartons, cans, plastic bottles, or any other con-tainer; and a feeding tray or table need be nothing more than a piece of wood with drainage holes and raised edges to minimize scattering of feed.

Hummingbird feeders are also available in elaborate and expensive designs, but, again, homemade versions (e.g., a test tube wired at an angle to a branch) are just as effective. To help hummers find your feeder, adorn it with something red and, if possible, position it near flowers that you have seen hummingbirds visiting. Once they have found the feeder and realize that it is a consistent food source, hummers will visit it regularly and remember it from year to year. The most important precaution in hummingbird feeding is keeping the syrup clean. It ferments rapidly and soon becomes poison rather than nourishment. Water for the solution should be boiled and residues in feeders removed frequently. When start-ing out, you may have to dump several untouched solutions before the lo-cal hummers discover your feeder. For a discussion of the correct syrup formula and more detail on potential health problems, see Hummingbird Formulas, below.

Location. Once you have made (or bought) your feeder you should give some thought to where you're going to put it: (1) Having several feed-ers in different situations will appeal to a greater variety of birds, make it more convenient to watch the activity from your house, and make possi-ble a kind of segregation if necessary (see Pests, below). (2) Place feeders where you can see them easily from inside. (3) Sunny spots, sheltered from the wind, are preferred. (4) Some birds prefer to feed closer to the cover of vegetation, which, however, makes handy hiding places for cats; other birds want to have an open view. If possible, provide both.

Pests. Gluttony and covetousness are the characteristic sins of most feeder pests. Some gobble more expensive provisions than, so to speak, they are worth; others aggressively hog feeder space, keeping the more genteel clientele away; quite a few do both. The best solutions lie in sepa-ration of offerings, placement of feeders, and the odd mechanical device.

Rats. Sometimes attracted to food spread on the ground. If you have reason to believe that your rat population is a small one, you can try to trap them (not always as easy as it sounds). However, you may discover some alarming facts about you neighborhood rat population. Selective poisoning is also possible, but, of course, should be undertaken with the utmost caution. Needless to say, the best solution is simply to stop feed-ing on the ground.

Squirrels. Though regarded by most as "nicer" than rats, squirrels are far worse pests at feeders. The eastern gray squirrel is probably enemy No. 1. It has an apparently bottomless appetite for almost anything, and is so agile that only a feeder hovering unattached in midair with no climbable surface within 20 feet can be considered truly squirrel-proof. A more practical solution, called a "squirrel baffle," comes in various forms. Slippery metal collars with no graspable edges can be placed around poles that support standing feeders; slippery, tippy baffles, placed along the suspension wires of hanging feeders, are also popular; and there are some ingenious inventions on the market, which, for example, close off the food supply when a heavy squirrel steps on the platform but remain open under the modest weight of small birds; a more aggressive device actually flips the marauders into space. When all your baffles are in place, sit back and prepare to enjoy watching the squirrels get around them all.

Trash birds. This term is defined in the eye of the beholder. To some bird lovers there is no such thing; many feeder owners, however, include at least pigeons, starlings, and House Sparrows; and not a few include doves, jays and crows, and all blackbirds. Their "faults" are the same as squirrels', but the corrective measures differ. (1) All the birds named above prefer coarser foods; therefore, separate the gross stuff—cracked corn, bread, Froot Loops, etc.—from the *haute cuisine* and the pests will tend to feed with their own kind, leaving the classier types largely unmolested. (2) Most of the pests are relatively large species and not sufficiently agile to negotiate cylindrical hanging feeders with short perches. (3) Some pest species seem to feel more secure feeding away from human habitation. Place a diversionary feeder with favorite foods in a location remote from your main operation.

Predators. Some "bird lovers" categorize Sharp-shinned and Cooper's Hawks, small falcons, and shrikes as pests and worse—avian malefactors that ruthlessly destroy innocent chickadees. This view is humane in origin but grievously flawed as an interpretation of the relationships among living organisms. It is simply a hard fact of life that most animals serve partly as food for other animals. Prolific species such as chickadees can and do withstand high mortality rates and thereby sustain a variety of other life forms. If chickadees were not checked, they would become intolerably abundant. One of the natural checks on chickadee fecundity is the Sharp-shinned Hawk, and the grace and skill with which it performs its ecologically essential service is one of nature's most elegant achievements. The feeder with a small predator in attendance is a feeder of distinction. The compulsive vigilante who refuses to be enlightened should then be warned: the predacious species are all protected by laws that impose heavy fines for killing birds of prey (see LAWS PROTECTING BIRDLIFE).

The real villain on the bird feeder scene is that most efficient of mammalian predators, the domestic cat. Right-thinking citizens keep their cats

indoors at all times, of course, and feeder owners have a particular incentive to harangue miscreant neighbors on this issue. If your problem is a feral cat, town animal control officers will sometimes trap and dispose of these dangerous beasts. For more on this major bird conservation issue, see CATS.

HAZARDS. Some feeding practices have proven detrimental rather than beneficial to the birds they attract. They are avoided by observing simple precautions.

Disease. It has been suggested that ASPERGILLOSIS, a bacterial infection that originates in decaying plant matter and is common among birds, may on occasion be picked up from fruits left to rot at feeding stations. Salmonellosis and other bacterial diseases may infect stagnant water in birdbaths, and recent outbreaks among siskins and other seedeaters has spread in part simply from large numbers of birds defecating at feeders during invasion winters. The communality that feeders encourage also exacerbates potential for mycoplasmosis, such as the recent conjunctivitis epizootic among House Finches populations. A partial solution to all of these potential health threats is frequent cleaning of receptacles and changing of food and water.

Choking and Bloating. It is alleged that undiluted and especially frost-congealed peanut butter and certain large seeds sometimes choke birds at feeders. The alarm has also been sounded regarding the unwholesome effect on the avian tummy of "inflatable" foods such as oatmeal. It is probably safe to say that birds exercise much more control over how they eat than do most humans and therefore show a correspondingly low incidence of food-related deaths. Furthermore, many choking records originate in imaginative autopsies rather than eyewitness accounts of strangling chickadees. Peanut butter and oatmeal can probably be offered without undue concern, but peanut butter is easily "thinned" with cornmeal or mixed seed if you wish to be extra cautious.

Cold Metal Surfaces. Birds' eyes and tongues may freeze to feeder parts made of iron (e.g., suet dispensers); greasing such surfaces will prevent this kind of accident. Commercially available suet feeders are vinyl coated.

Hummingbird Formulas. Particularly in the Southwest, where hummers are abundant and their species varied, providing them with artificial nectar has long been one of the most popular feeding practices. With experience it became clear that the most attractive potion consisted of two parts water, one part sugar, and enough red food coloring to make the transparent feeder glow like a flower. Leery of feeding refined sugar to their hummers, some people suggested honey as a more "natural" alternative. Over the years the salubriousness of all three of these items has been questioned: the 2:1 solution as being too rich for bird livers; the red dye as a carcinogen; and the honey as the cause of a fatal disease that at-

tacks the tongue. Only the charge against honey has been thoroughly documented; it is best avoided. Most commercial feeders now come equipped with red trim, eliminating the needs for dye, and, of course, this is easy enough to add to a homemade nectar dispenser. A strong sugar solution also helps in the initial attraction problem but is not essential in the long run; a 4:1 water/sugar ratio is the accepted industry standard.

Summer Suet. In warm weather suet tends to liquefy and can dangerously mat birds' plumage. Woodpeckers seem particularly vulnerable. Best reserved as a winter offering.

Cutting Off the Supply. As noted, most birds would return to finding "wild" food without difficulty if you suddenly stopped feeding. However, if you have built up a large dependent flock over months of feeding, you could at least be accused of a certain callousness if you abandon your operation abruptly during the harshest season. Having a feeder is not unlike taking on a number of pets—your responsibility will inevitably impinge somewhat on your freedom.

ORGANIC BIRD FEEDING. You can combine bird feeding and horticulture by planting your property with trees, shrubs, and herbs that bear edible nectar, fruits, or seeds as well as providing cover and nesting materials.

Most of the plant species listed here are widespread and many are cultivated as garden ornamentals in the Temperate Zone. A host of others occur in subtropical and arid regions of North America and the lists below are by no means complete. They can easily be expanded by watching what birds eat in the field and bringing seeds or cuttings into your yard. A nice tangle of catbriar or poison ivy, in addition to fulfilling several avian needs, has the added advantage of deterring trespassers. The following trees, shrubs, and vines are highly attractive to fruit-eating birds. *Caution:* Note that certain *invasive shrubs,* such as Multiflora Rose, Russian and Autumn Olives (*Eleagnus,* spp.), Japanese Barberry, Tartarian Honeysuckle, and species of buckthorn, once touted as ideal bird food plants, should be *avoided* at all costs. As the list shows there are many native and noninvasive alternatives.

Apples, pears, chokeberries, crab apples *(Malus [Pyrus])*
Bayberry *(Myrica pennsylvanica)*
Blueberries *(Vaccinium)*
Cherries *(Prunus)*
Curlewberry *(Empetrum nigrum)*
Currants *(Ribes)*
Dewberries, blackberries, raspberries' etc. *(Rubus,*spp.)
Dogwoods *(Cornus)*
Elderberry *(Sambucus)*
Firethorn *(Cotoneaster pyracantha)*

Grapes (*Vitis,* spp.)
Greenbrier *(Smilax)*
Hawthorns *(Crataegus)*
Hollies *(Ilex)*
Huckleberries *(Gaylussaccia)*
Mountain ash *(Sorbus)*
Poison ivy *(Rhus radicans)*
Red cedar *(Juniperus virginiana)*
Shads (Juneberries or serviceberries) *(Amelanchier)*
Viburnums *(Viburnum)*
Woodbine (Virginia creeper) *(Parthenocissus quinquefolia)*
Yew *(Taxus canadensis)*

Trees and shrubs visited frequently by seed-eating birds include:

Alders *(Alnus)*
Birches *(Betula)*
Firs *(Abies and Pseudotsuga)*
Hemlocks *(Tsuga)*
Larch (*Larix*)
Maples (*Acer*) (except the invasive Norway)
Mast trees: beech (*Fagus*), oak (*Quercus*), and hickories (*Carya*)
Pines *(Pinus)*
Spirea *(Spirea)*
Spruces *(Picea)*

The following common plants (both wild and cultivated) bear flowers attractive to hummingbirds. Experiments have shown that red flowers are most attractive to hummers, followed by yellow; blue flowers are less appealing, though some species, e.g., delphiniums, are quite popular. Where only one name is given the common name and scientific name are the same.

Azaleas *(Rhododendron)*
Bee balms *(Monarda)*
Bellflowers *(Campanula)*
Bouncing bet *(Saponaria)*
Butterfly bush *(Buddleia)*
Cannas
Cardinal flower *(Lobelia cardinalis)*
Century plants *(Agave)*
Columbines *(Aquilegia)*
Coralbean (*Erythrina*) (flowering tree)
Coralbells *(Heuchera sanguinea)*
Flowering tobacco *(Nicotiana)*
Four-o'clock *(Mirabilis)*

Foxgloves *(Digitalis)*
Fuchsias
Gladiolus
Hamelia
Hollyhock *(Althaea)*
Impatiens, garden variety
Iris
Jasmines *(Jasminicum)*
Jewelweed *(Impatiens)*
Larkspur *(Delphinium)*
Lilac *(Syringa)*
Lilies *(Lilium)*
Louseworts *(Pedicularis)*
Matrimony vine *(Lycium)*
Milkweeds *(Asclepias)*
Mints *(Mentha,* etc.*)*
Monkey flower *(Mimulus)*
Morning glories *(Ipomoea)*
Nasturtium *(Tropaeolum)*
Oriental poppy *(Papaver orientale)*
Painted cup *(Castilleja)*
Pelargonium
Penstemon
Petunia
Phlox
Poinciana
Ragged robin *(Lychnis)*
Rattlesnake root *(Prenanthes)*
Red-hot poker or torch lily *(Kniphofia)*
Scabious *(Scabiosa)*
Scarlet runner bean *(Phaseolus coccineus)*
Scarlet sage *(Salvia splendens)* and other *Salvias*
Snapdragon *(Antirrhinum)*
Solomon's seal *(Polygonatum)*
Spiderflower *(Cleome)*
Sweet William *(Dianthus barbatus)*
Tritoma
Virginia bluebell *(Mertensia)*

A well-planned weed patch made up of local species can be more attractive to both birds and humans than a sterile lawn and borders of cultivated flowers. Composites such as thistles, asters, and goldenrods, have showy flowers and an abundance of seed in the fall and winter. Slightly less attractive species—e.g., pokeweed *(Phytolacca americana)*, various

knotweeds *(Polygonum)*, amaranth *(Amaranthus)*, and large grasses such as foxtails *(Setaria)*, panic grass *(Panicum)*, and barnyard grass *(Echinochloa crusgalli)*—can be made to look quite presentable if planted carefully.

The literature on bird feeding is now oceanic in scope and unavoidable in any store catering to the needs of the burgeoning bird lover market. For more statistics on who feeds birds and why and for how much, etc., see the Cornell Lab's FeederWatch at http://birds.cornell.edu/ and the National Bird Feeding Society at www.birdfeeding.org.

BIRD FINDING. With the recent "explosion" of the North American birdwatcher population (see BIRDWATCHING) and the great mobility its members enjoy, it is now commonplace to encounter birders in the farthest corners of the continent—or the world—in search of new ornithological adventures. This has sparked a new service industry in both print and electronic bird-finding guides. It is no longer possible to give a comprehensive listing of these services, but some of the most prominent resources are given in the Bibliography.

Of course, bird finding is not the exclusive province of ornithological jet-setters. In fact, anyone who has not honed his finding skills in seeking the avian specialties of his yard, hometown, county, state, and region is unlikely to be very successful at ferreting out the feathered denizens of rain forests and other exotic habitats beyond. The key to seeing the greatest possible number of species is the same whether you are listing the birds of your neighborhood or the world—namely, to examine all ecological niches in as many habitats and as many geographical regions as possible (see DISTRIBUTION). And, of course, it helps to learn as much as you can about the habits of the birds you seek. Many species are highly specific in their feeding, breeding, and migratory behavior and quite a few are inordinately secretive—presenting what some birders consider an "unfair" advantage. It is finding these "tough birds" that brings the greatest rewards to the serious "lister," "twitcher," or "tick hunter." Anyone can buy a ticket to Africa or South America and come home with an enormous list of relatively common birds. But the birders who know what to look for, along with how, when, and where to look for it, in their own region are the types who play the sport best and get the most satisfying thrills.

Most beginning birders reading this book probably entertain the goal—however vaguely—of seeing as much of the splendidly diverse North American avifauna as possible. Having practiced the above dictum about learning one's backyard birds first, they will eventually want to explore the following major geographical/biotic regions of the continent: (1) the northeast coast (Maritime Provinces, New England) for exclusively Atlantic tubenoses, gulls, and alcids; (2) the northern coniferous forest (northern New England, southern Canada, central and northern Rockies,

Cascades) for specialties of this biome such as Spruce Grouse, Three-toed and Black-backed Woodpeckers, Bohemian Waxwing, Gray Jay, and a variety of breeding thrushes, wood warblers, and northern finches; (3) the south-eastern woodlands (pine *and* hardwood) for the likes of Red-cockaded Woodpecker, Carolina Chickadee, Brown-headed Nuthatch, Carolina Wren, Swainson's and other wood warblers, and Bachman's Sparrow; (4) south-ern Florida for great waterbird concentrations and Caribbean specialties (both breeding and vagrant) in the Keys; superlisters will also want to check out the numerous officially "listable" exotics in the Miami area; (5) southern Texas for Mexican land-bird specialties and a great wealth of birdlife generally; (6) southwestern deserts for such dry country birds as Gila Woodpecker, Le Conte's Thrasher, Cactus Wren, Verdin, Phainopepla, and Black-throated Sparrow; (7) southeastern Arizona and West Texas for species of largely Mexican distribution, especially highland ones, e.g., hummingbirds, Elegant Trogon, and Red-faced Warbler; (8) the western mountains (Rockies, Sierra Nevada, Cascades, etc.) for montane en-demics, e.g., White-headed Woodpecker, Williamson's Sapsucker, Moun-tain Chickadee, Hammond's Flycatcher, Clark's Nutcracker, Cassin's Finch, and rosy-finches; (9) the central prairies for grouse species, Dick-cissel, Le Conte's and Baird's Sparrows, Lark Bunting, Clay-colored Spar-row, and McCown's and Chestnut-collared Longspurs; (10) the Pacific coast for numerous waterbird species, especially pelagics, shorebirds, gulls, and alcids; (11) Alaska for its endemic specialties (alcids, McKay's Bunting, etc.) as well as myriad coastal, coniferous forest, and arctic species; and (12) the Arctic for breeding shorebirds, jaegers, ptarmigan, raptors, and a few passerine specialties such as Hoary Redpoll. The mobile bird seeker will also want to visit areas where great concentrations of birdlife occur, such as coastlines, swamps and marshes, and places where migrat-ing birds pass or stop. And if truly serious, he or she will have to make pil-grimages (some definitely out of the way) to look for very local species, such as Yellow-billed Magpie and Colima, Golden-cheeked, and Kirtland's Warblers. Of course, these regions and localities overlap at their margins and each contains many species other than their avian "highlights." Fur-thermore, with the aid of the migration phenomenon, birders can see a large percentage of American bird species in their own backyard, as it were, especially if they live near the coast. But for a comprehensive view of North American birdlife, a bird finder must, like many of his quarry, be-come a bird of passage.

The pioneer of North American bird-finding guides was Olin Sewell PETTINGILL, whose seminal *Finding the Birds East of the Mississippi* and its western counterpart appeared respectively in 1951 and 1953. The other Ur-bird finder that should be mentioned is Jim Lane, whose series of very detailed guides to the nation's hottest birding regions are now edited and being expanded by the American Birding Association. These and other

guides listed in the Bibliography give highly specific details not only on what birds are where ("The wide shoulders along Farm Road 2004 are particularly good for Sprague's Pipits"—Jim Lane on the Texas coast) but on how and when to look for them, whom to ask for advice in a given area, and (occasionally) where to stay; the best guides even mention nonavian specialties. In addition to electronic analogs to written guides, the internet now contains a wealth of "contacts", who can tell you what was seen in your destination of choice just this morning.

The present book does not attempt to compete with these comprehensive and meticulous bird-finding sources. However, the neophyte birder unfamiliar with the names of North American birding meccas ("Patagonia" in American birdspeak usually refers to southeastern Arizona, not Argentina) will find a selection of more than 50 such famous localities included as entries here with brief descriptions of the habitat(s) they comprise and their bird specialties. For a list of these hot spots, see pp. xxiv–xxv. For timing your birding expeditions, see the Birdwatcher's Calendar, Appendix VI. See also references in the Bibliography under SANCTUARY.

BIRDHOUSE (or nest box). Attracting cavity-nesting birds by setting out homemade nesting sites is an ancient tradition. Native Americans hung hollowed-out gourds to attract Purple Martins. In Europe the practice of putting out specially made clay or wooden flasks for birds to nest in can be traced at least as far back as the Middle Ages.

The custom did not originate from altogether altruistic impulses. The medieval Europeans ate the first broods of the birds that used their birdhouses (usually House Sparrows and Common Starlings), and the early Americans were motivated (according to Audubon) by the territorial aggressiveness of the martins, which kept the vultures away from their deer kills. Even today, many people erect martin houses not solely for the company of the birds but for their (alas, highly exaggerated) taste for mosquitoes (see below). But if the practice was initially self-serving, there can be no doubt that putting up nest boxes near one's home for the simple pleasure of it has also appealed to us for a long time. And for those whose pleasure depends on the notion that they are providing quarters for birds that would otherwise be homeless, there is some experimental evidence that this is indeed the case. The majority of cavity nesters depend upon the abandoned holes of woodpeckers (which generally excavate a new site each year), and these sites are, of course, much scarcer than those used by species that construct their own nests in trees or on the ground. In a number of forest localities the number of birds seeking cavity sites far exceeds their availability and almost as many birdhouses as are erected are occupied. This is not true everywhere, but it is a reliable indication that you can expect to have a fair degree of success in redressing the avian housing shortage.

WHAT KIND OF BIRDS. More than 50 species of North American birds have been reported nesting in "artificial situations," and over 35

species are known to do so with some degree of regularity. In any given place, the variety will, of course, be considerably less. The construction chart below includes the species you are most likely to attract.

SOME BASIC GUIDELINES. There is nothing complicated or tricky about making and locating a successful birdhouse, and specific construction details are given below, accompanied by Fig. 4. However, naturalists have learned a few things since they began putting out nest boxes in a methodical way (in nineteenth-century England), which both encourage occupancy and enhance your tenants' welfare.

- The young of most cavity nesters are born naked (see YOUNG, DEVELOPMENT OF) and are therefore particularly sensitive to extremes of heat and cold. Accordingly, it is important that the materials, plans, and location of your nest box do not increase the birds' vulnerability to the elements. These considerations are incorporated in the more specific guidelines given below.

- Even if there is a housing shortage (as described above) in your area, most birds have strong territorial instincts, which will normally deter them from nesting too close to other birds, especially ones of their own species. Recent studies have revealed that even Purple Martins, which we encourage to live together in homemade apartment houses, would not nest in such density given their preference. Other studies indicate that 4–5 cavity nesters per acre seem to be average for many localities and this may be a reasonable guideline to follow on your property. Except for the martins, make "single dwelling units" and space them widely.

- In addition to the location suggestions for particular species given under Construction, below, pay attention to just where you put your bird box. Try to allow for a fairly clear flight path to the entrance. Place it so that the entrance hole is not exposed to the prevailing direction of wind-driven rainstorms or other prevailing winds of your region. In most cases, this will mean that the preferred direction will be south, southwest, or west. Make sure the box rests vertically or slanted toward the ground; if tilted toward the sky, it is more vulnerable to precipitation.

- Cavity nests can provide easy prey for cats; if you have one or live in the suburbs, make sure your birdhouse is cat-proof. A metal pole or "cat guard" of some kind (see, for example, under Construction) will discourage Felix as well as raccoons, snakes, and other potential molesters. Many nestling birds normally leave the nest before they are able to fly another potential bonanza for free range cats in your neighborhood.

- To reduce nest parasites, some of which winter over in old nests, remove the contents of your nest boxes at the end of the breeding season. If you do this conspicuously, it may also win you housekeeping points with your neighbors (Audubon said that he could

BIRDHOUSE SPECIFICATIONS

Type of Bird	Interior Floor Dimensions (Inches)	Depth of Cavity (Inches)	Diameter of Hole (Inches)	Distance— Hole to Floor (Inches)	Box Placement Height (Feet)	Site/Remarks
Wood Duck	10 × 10	15–18	4	8–12	4–20	On pole or tree trunk over quiet water, near cover; sawdust lining and predator guard; see above and Fig. 4
American Kestrel	8 × 8	12–15	3	9–12	10–30	On tree in open country or woodland edge or high on a building
Barn Owl	10 × 18	15–18	6	4	12–18	Near open fields on building or tree trunk
Saw-whet Owl	6 × 6	10–12	2½	8–10	12–20	Tree trunk in dense woods; prefers conifers and low wet areas; 2" of sawdust on floor
Screech Owl	8 × 10	16–18	3¾	11–13	12–20	Tree trunk in woods or at edge; 2" of sawdust on floor
Common Flicker	7 × 7	16–18	3¾	11–13	12–20	Tree trunk in woods or at edge; 2" of sawdust on floor
Red-headed Woodpecker	6 × 6	12–15	2	9–12	12–20	Tree trunk in open woods, wood edge, or even in open
Hairy Woodpecker	6 × 6	12–15	1½	9–12	12–20	Tree trunk in woods

BIRDHOUSE SPECIFICATIONS (*continued*)

Great Crested Flycatcher	6 × 6	8–10	2	6–8	8–20	Tree trunk in woods
Bluebirds, Tree and Violet-green Swallows, Prothonotary Warbler	5 × 5	6–8	1½	5–6	4–12	In open or near wood edge; warbler in swampy woods, usually low; see Fig. 4
Purple Martin	6 × 6	6	2½	1	15–20	On pole in open field; near water; see above and Fig. 4
Chickadees and other tits, nut-hatches, and Downy Woodpecker	4 × 4	8–10	1¼	6–8	8–15	Tree trunk in or at edge of woods; line with sphagnum, sawdust, and/or wood chips for best results with tits
House and Bewick's Wrens	4 × 4	6–8	1	4–6	5–10	Wood edge or open woods
Carolina Wren	4 × 4	6–8	1¼	4–6	5–10	Wood edge or open woods

judge the quality of country inns by the state of the martin houses traditionally erected on the hostelry signboards). The construction plans below provide for easy cleaning.

Though it is possible to encourage certain species and discourage others by methods of construction and location, it can be very difficult to keep out some "undesirable" birds. This is especially true of the usual species so termed-the House Sparrow and European Starling. Both of these introduced pests are extraordinarily uncritical in judging the suitability of a nest site; often occupy a box very early in the season before native migratory birds have arrived; usually prevail in contests with more desirable species over a suitable site; and of course are very common in many areas. The only solution to this problem is to actively discourage the unwanted tenants. You can block the entrance holes until the species you want to encourage have returned in the spring. And if starlings or House Sparrows begin to build, simply remove nest material as the birds collect it. If eggs or young are present, only your personal code of ethics prevent you from destroying them since neither the law nor responsible conservation organizations advocate the protection of these aliens.

CONSTRUCTION OF A SIMPLE NEST BOX. The design and building instructions that follow are adapted from the Massachusetts Audubon Society's Public Service Information Sheet, "Nest Boxes for Birds." They result in a well-tested, easy-to-make birdhouse that can be modified or "fancied up" according to the taste of the builder. The instructions are numbered to correspond with the plans in Fig. 4.

1. This *bluebird box* is made from a single board, $1 \times 6 \times 48$ inches; pine or spruce is recommended. Measure and cut the pieces as shown one at a time to allow for the width of the saw cut. *Then:* Drill four $\frac{1}{4}$-inch ventilation holes in each side, 1 inch below the roof line; cut off the corners of the floor board as drainage holes; drill an entrance hole of the desired diameter in the front board, making sure the distance from the center of the hole to the bottom of the front board is that given in the chart (below) under "Distance-Hole to Floor" for the species you are aiming to attract.

2. Nail one of the three $5\frac{1}{2}$-inch strips as shown on each of the side boards, 1 inch (or the *thickness* of the front board) in from the edge.

3. Nail the back to the floor, then attach the sides to the back and floor. Note that the sides are supposed to extend beyond the front edge of the floor board, as this is where the front board will lie. Attach the roof so that it will be flush in back but overhang in front, providing shade and shelter from rain.

4. Nail the last strip across the top of the box just below the roof overhang and cut it flush with the sides.

Fig. 4. *Birdhouses.* See building instructions in text.

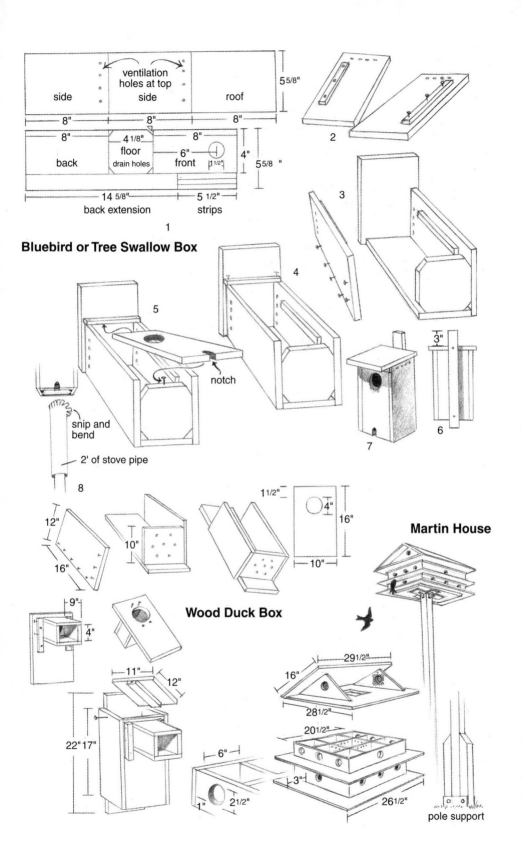

Bluebird or Tree Swallow Box

ventilation holes at top

side
side
roof

5 5/8"

8"
8"
8"

back
floor
front
drain holes

4 1/8"
6"
1 1/2"
4"
5 5/8"

8"
8"

14 5/8"
back extension
5 1/2"
strips

1
2
3
4
5

notch

snip and bend

2' of stove pipe

8

3"

6

7

12"
16"

10"

1 1/2"
4"
16"
10"

Wood Duck Box

Martin House

9"
4"

11"
12"

22" 17"

6"
1"
2 1/2"

29 1/2"
16"
28 1/2"

20 1/2"
3"
26 1/2"

pole support

5. Cut a ⅜-inch notch at the center of the bottom edge of the front board. Then slip the front board into position under the roof strip and resting on the two side strips. Make a pencil mark on the front edge of the floorboard where the *top* of the notch meets it. Then remove the front and drive a front-support nail in (to the depth shown) at the pencil mark.

6. Attach the extension board to the back *with screws* so that it projects 3 inches above the roof.

7. Note that the finished box does *not* include a perching peg below the entrance hole as called for in some plans. Such pegs are not only unnecessary but actually encourage predation by giving the nest robber a place to sit while it goes about its unseemly business. If the wood used is smooth-planed you should score or roughen the interior surface to avoid trapping young birds and adults (especially swallows) in the box. A screwdriver or file is a good tool for this. If you wish to stain the house, use a non-insecticide stain and coat only the outside. Houses placed in the open should be light-colored or painted with reflective paint to obviate the danger of overheating.

8. Shows how a simple cat/raccoon baffle can be attached to a pole mount.

Wood Duck boxes are built on the same principle (see Fig. 4, lower left), but with a few specific modifications to accommodate the requirements of the species.

- A tunnel entrance should be provided for protection from predators, especially raccoons.
- Top rather than front is removable (as shown).
- Ventilation holes in *bottom.*
- Use unplaned boards; roughen the inside of the front board from floor to hole or put screen or hardware cloth in this area so that ducklings can climb out of the box after hatching.
- Line the bottom of the box with about 4 inches of wood shavings and sawdust—*not* leaves, grass, or other "nesting material."
- Boxes to be sited over water should be affixed to wooden poles (preferably cedar) no less than 4 inches in diameter or on metal pipes (require U-bolt clamps).
- The best location for Wood Duck boxes is over open water at least 20 feet from shore and out of reach of any overhanging limbs. Such locations are naturally safeguarded against predators and provide efficient, safe access to open water for ducklings. Quiet, open water with good marshy or wooded cover nearby is ideal Wood Duck habitat. Boxes are best placed in such sites in winter when the ice is solid. Be sure that the pole is set deep enough in the bottom of the pond or marsh to withstand flood or ice movements, and that the

box is at least above spring flood line. Do not place the pole in the path of a strong current.

- Boxes fixed to trees are more vulnerable to predators but are workable provided: the trees are near water and no less than 10–12 inches in diameter; the boxes are placed 8–10 feet from the ground (where prospecting ducks look for them); tunnel entrances are provided; and the top cover is secured. (The above guidelines are adapted from the recommendations of the Massachusetts Division of Fisheries and Wildlife.)
- *Caution:* Recent studies (see, especially, Semel et al. 1988) have found that overzealous duck box programs can lead to local overpopulations and problems with intraspecific brood parasitism.

Martin houses are also essentially a variation on the principles governing the construction of the "basic house" above. See Fig. 4, lower right, for details. Note especially the ventilation holes in the central cubicle and roof. All tiers, including the roof, should be fastened with hooks and eyes for easy removal and cleaning.

Because martin houses are most attractive (to the birds) when raised 15–20 feet off the ground, the "support system" for the structure is very important for both the birds' safety and the landlords' convenience. The foundation on which the bottom floor of the house rests should be 20½ inches square and 2½ inches thick. Centered on its underside, attach a cross made of a double thickness of 3 × 6-inch boards. Attach four heavy angle irons (one to each spoke of the cross) spaced to meet the 4 × 4-inch center pole. The pole itself can be hollow—i.e., made from ¾-inch-thick hard-pine boards. The base is the other essential point of security. This consists of two 8-foot-long 4-by-4s buried in the ground to a depth of 4 ft and held apart by another 4-by-4 buried between them. The house pole is fitted between the two support poles and metal plates are bolted across the opening between the support poles and across the base of the house pole. In addition, a pipe or large bolt runs through the tops of the support poles and the house pole, holding the latter at another point. This bolt serves as a hinge or lever in lowering the martin house for cleaning at the end of the season.

Purple Martins, like other swallows, are "aerial insectivores," meaning they feed exclusively on the wing on flying insects. The ideal site for a martin house, therefore, is in the middle of a large open field-not in or near woods or other shelter. Nearby bodies of water and additional open perching places also increase real estate value from the martin point of view. *Note:* Store-bought aluminum martin houses with telescoping poles now provide relatively easy manipulation and maintenance.

A Word About Martins and Mosquitoes. It is widely claimed that Purple Martins are man's best hope in winning the war against mosquitoes. Since martins do indeed eat a great quantity of flying insects, the assumption is

not illogical, and since its adherents are advocating biological rather than chemical control of pest insects, the motives are essentially noble ones. Unfortunately, martins and mosquitoes are generally not abroad at the same time of day. Martins are mainly diurnal, mosquitoes mainly crepuscular and nocturnal. (For more on this sad truth, see Kale [1968].) One should be particularly wary of extravagant claims made by those offering martin houses for sale. None of this should diminish anyone's enthusiasm for Purple Martins one iota. They are beautiful, interesting, and charming birds well worth attracting.

BIRD SHELVES. Phoebes, American Robins, Barn Swallows build partly with mud and prefer flat, level surfaces on which to nest. House Finches may use shelves too, though they seem to prefer old wreaths and hanging plants. In nature, a rocky shelf or broad horizontal branch may fill this requirement but man-made structures are often ideal. These species occupy sheltered eaves or similar shelves on houses or barns. A simple 6 × 8-inch platform, sheltered from the weather and otherwise oriented favorably as described in the instructions for the basic nest box, may attract these birds. For attracting birds with plantings and offering food, see BIRD FEEDING.

OR HELP THE ECONOMY. Not all of us have the time or "handiness" to undertake even so simple a carpentry task as a birdhouse. There is no shame in this and there is now an astonishing variety of bird dwellings— from the classic forms described above to the technologically sophisticated and the architecturally magnificent—available in the birding market place. Hints on birdhouse shopping are given in the Bibliography.

BIRDING EVENTS. Given the recent explosion of interest in birds and all forms of birdwatching, it should surprise no one that our enterprising species has continued to invent new ways to channel this wholesome passion. There are now events catering to every interest from the sheer competitive fun of racking up more species than your buddies during a limited time period to contributing to the ornithological record and/or raising money for bird conservation. What follows is a brief summary of organized bird-focused activities currently on offer throughout North America and, increasingly, the world.

The Big Day A birdwatching game invented (or at least made famous) by Ludlow GRISCOM in which a single party of birders tries to record as many species as possible during a 24-hour period. There is no limit to the size of the area covered or the methods of transportation used—a Texas Big Day using airplanes and a neighborhood Big Day on foot are equally valid—but a standardized itinerary usually evolves so that totals for succeeding years can be fairly compared. One-man Big Days are theoretically possible but credibility (and efficiency in finding the most birds) is enhanced if two or more participate; on the other hand, more than five

probably cramps efficiency. A notable limiting factor for any Big Day total is that team members must stay together ("within direct voice contact distance" per ABA rules). The traditional Big Day begins and ends at midnight, but revisionists have instituted the "Singapore Big Day" starting and ending at noon, and other schedules are also possible; ABA Big Days must take place within a single calendar day. This game has become so popular that ABA has created a set of rules so that competing teams can be fairly judged. The ultimate North American Big Day is the World Series of Birding, which combines pure sport with fund raising for bird conservation (see below). For detailed rules see the ABA and WSOB websites.

In addition to field competence and indefatigability, a successful Big Day depends on reasonably favorable weather, visiting the widest possible variety of habitats, timing stops to coincide with factors such as tides and species habits, a good score on local "stakeouts," and good migration. The best timing for a Big Day—that period during which the largest number of species are likely to be in a given area—varies of course from region to region, though classically it is a spring event.

Griscom's first Big Days took place in May in Duchess County, New York, but there are now over a hundred such events of various scales across the continent and around the world that are reported to the ABA each year and doubtless as many more casual efforts. Results of Big Days following ABA rules are published in an annual supplement to *Birding* along with annual list reports (see listing). Some of the most notable current Big Day statistics from the 2002 ABA Big Day Report include

258 species, Texas, April 24, 2001. This is the current high count for North America.

231 species, California, April 29, 1978. This early high count remained the champion until it was superceded by a total of 233 in Texas, April 18, 2001.

225 species, Kansas, May 13, 2002. Highest count in a noncoastal state or province

200 species, Ontario, May 29, 1999. Highest Canadian count.

331 species, Peru, September 5, 1982. Highest non-North American total (w. Ted Parker as one of two participants).

308 species, Costa Rica, April 2, 2000. Highest recent non-North American total.

17 species, Antarctica, December 19, 1987 and January 29, 1998. Lowest total ever recorded.

Needless to say, because of great variation in handicaps, resources, weather and other factors in different places these top numbers do not necessarily reflect the most brilliant birding techniques.

See Jaques, *Birds Across the Sky* (1942), Chapter 1, for an "outsider's" description of one of the early Griscom efforts and Dunne

(1992–BIRDWATCHING) and Kaufmann (1997–BIRDWATCHING) for more recent accounts.

Bird-a-thons build upon the Big Day concept by adding a fund-raising component. Subscribers sponsor teams or individuals either by donating a lump sum or by agreeing to pay a designated amount of money for each species seen during the 24-hour period. Someone who agrees to contribute 25 cents per bird species, for example, has to contribute 25 dollars if the birders under contract finds 100 species. In many places and even within organizations teams compete against each other, thus raising the stakes. This has proven to be a fun and reliable way to raise money for bird conservation.

The World Series of Birding is the ultimate synthesis of the Big Day and Bird-a-thon traditions. Founded in 1984 by Pete Dunne of the New Jersey Audubon Society, the event is now indisputably the nation's most prominent birding event, attracting hundreds of participants from all over the world and raising hundreds of thousands of dollars annually for conservation. It is a purely mission-driven event with goals of promoting awareness of bird conservation issues, raising money for conservation organizations and promoting birdwatching especially among young people. Corporate sponsors can underwrite teams in exchange for the high media profile the WSB creates, but the independent New Jersey Audubon Society realizes only operational costs through registration fees aside from the fruits of its own team's efforts and the positive publicity. All income from pledges goes to the organizations for which the teams are birding.

The event is held annually on the second (sometimes third) weekend in May and is now governed by a detailed set of rules. In 2002, 67 teams participated the winning team was the Cornell Laboratory of Ornithology Sapsuckers sponsored by Swarovski Optik . It recorded an all-time high total of 224 species in the prescribed 24-hour period and raised $150,000 for its Golden-winged Warbler Research project. For a comprehensive description of this extraordinary event see www.worldseriesof-birding.org.

Birding Festivals are community-based events designed to attract large numbers birders to spend time—typically a weekend—enjoying the bird specialties and other natural highlights of particular localities. They are not fund-raising or conservation events per se, however they can generate significant income for local businesses such as hotels, restaurants and other enterprises that cater to birders' needs and are often organized by the local chamber of commerce. In addition they inevitably offer opportunities for local conservation groups to publicize their issues to a large, sympathetic audience The core program typically consists of a schedule of field trips focusing on birding and (increasingly) other natural phenomena, e.g., butterflies. In addition there may be workshops, guest lecturers, live bird exhibits and, especially at the larger festivals, retail booths demonstrating and selling major brands of birding related prod-

ucts such as optical equipment. In 1997 there were approximately 70 birding festivals throughout North America, up from 12 in 1993. For an annotated listing of festivals and instructions on starting your own, go to the ABA website at http://americanbirding.org/.

Christmas Bird Count (aka Christmas Count or CBC). A popular census of birdlife taken each year by a growing number of enthusiastic birdwatchers between December 14 and January 5. The tradition was started by Frank CHAPMAN on December 25, 1900 as a modest affair to draw attention to the plight of the nation's birdlife at a time when a day's birding usually meant a day's shooting. On that first Christmas Bird Count 27 participants counted 18,500 individual birds of 90 in 25 localities. Today more than 52,000 birders conduct more than 1,800 individual counts, recording hundreds of millions of individual birds of more than 650 species. The event is sponsored by the National Audubon Society in cooperation with the Cornell Laboratory of Ornithology and as of this writing the results are published in a phonebook-sized publication, *American Birds* as well as on-line (see URL, below).

Though the great majority of participants still take part in Christmas Counts for the fun of it, the sheer scope that the phenomenon has attained has made the data collected of some scientific significance. To make the count as useful in this regard as possible, it is carried out under specific guidelines. Each local census is restricted to a circle with a diameter of fifteen miles that does not overlap another count circle. Numbers of individual birds as well as species are recorded and the habitats, weather, number of counters, and miles traveled by car and foot are noted. Fed into a computer, these data can give a rough approximation of densities of wintering bird populations on any selected scale and clearly point out cyclical movements of birds such as invasions of winter finches and their extent. See, for example, Terry Root's *Atlas of Wintering North American Birds* (1988), based on CBC data.

The variation in "styles" of Christmas Counts throughout the vast and varied continent (not to mention counts now being conducted in Hawaii and the Neotropics) can be imagined. In frozen interior Alaska or Newfoundland a couple of hardy souls may be responsible for an entire circle, braving the harsh climate for the sake of reporting a few individual birds of even fewer species. Other counts, especially those in the warmer (hence "birdier") parts of California, Texas, and Florida, have become star events, attracting hundreds of participants and top birding talent. The competition among these supercounts to record the highest number of bird species doubtless improves the thoroughness with which habitats are investigated in the regions involved. The count traditionally ends with a convivial gathering at the end of the long birding day, during which an official tally for one or more circles is compiled orally from the lists of individual teams, bird tales are swapped, field competence impugned, old counts relived, and much warming refreshment consumed.

For a detailed history of the Christmas Count, see Gill and LeBaron (2000), *American Birds: One-hundredth Christmas Bird Count* issue; also Dunne (1992–BIRDWATCHING) and Kaufman (1997–BIRDWATCHING).

For current information including records and how to participate go to www.audubon.org/bird/cbc/ho.html.

See also ATLAS; BREEDING BIRD CENSUS; BREEDING BIRD SURVEY; CENSUS; LISTING.

BIRDING FESTIVAL. See under BIRDING EVENTS, above.

BIRDING TOURS. An unmistakable signal that birding was becoming a mainstream activity was that relatively sane people began paying good money (sometimes quite a lot of it) to travel with expert field ornithologists on custom-designed birdwatching tours around the world. Tour programs put together by early entrepreneurs like Orville Crowder, Peter Alden, and Joel Abramson in the 1960s were the precursors of today's thriving international "ecotourism" industry. The potential educational and conservation value of exploring the world's most significant bird habitats with clients who were inevitably well-educated, well-off and well-disposed toward conservation soon became evident to the foresightful, and in the early 1970s the Massachusetts Audubon Society launched an international natural history travel program (with a strong emphasis on birds), which has operated continuously ever since. Eco-travel has become so popular that a few negative phenomena began to surface (tourist waste in Antarctica, profits going to tour operators rather than to help conservation and local people in developing countries, etc.). But the response has been the development of a code of ethics for ecotourism, and on balance, birding and other nature tours, often bring significant resources to struggling economies and conservation efforts with little negative impact on the destinations. The largest of the for-profit tour operators specializing in birding tours worldwide (including many North American programs) are Limosa, Sunbird, Victor Emmanuel Nature Tours (VENT), and Wings, but birding magazines are crammed with ads for smaller companies, e.g. 39 in ABA's *Winging It* in 1996. Many of the larger conservation organizations (including state Audubon societies and the like) run natural history based travel programs as do various museums and universities. There is also now a burgeoning cottage industry in local bird guiding, so that visitors to birding hot spots worldwide often have a choice between several native guides who have their backyard birds "nailed down." There are, of course, many different styles of tours—Do you calculate the success of your trip on a birds-per-dollar basis and cathedrals be damned? Or do your prefer a bit of culture with your nature?—reflecting both the philosophies of the organizations and the personalities of the leaders. For a clearinghouse of the most reputable birding tour operators with links to their websites, go to the ABA website at www.americanbirding.org.

BIRD LICE. Chewing lice in the insect order Mallophaga, which live their entire life cycles on the bodies of mammals and (mainly) birds, eating bits of skin, fur, feathers, and some body fluids. For more detail, see ECTOPARASITE.

BIRDLIFE INTERNATIONAL. Founded in 1922 as the International Council for Bird Preservation, BirdLife International is the oldest international conservation organization in the world and the leading advocate for the conservation of birds and their habitats worldwide. It consists of a "global partnership of nongovernmental conservation organizations with a focus on birds that works together on shared priorities, exchanging skills, achievements and information, and so growing in ability, authority and influence." Its mission is "to conserve birds, their habitats and global biodiversity, working with people towards sustainability in the use of natural resources." BirdLife is currently (2003) working in more than 100 countries and territories throughout the world with a membership of over 2.5 million, a staff of more than 4,000 and an annual budget of $263 million.

In 1981 BirdLife initiated a program to identify the most Important Bird Areas in Europe. This has grown into a program of global scope with more than 20,000 IBAs identified worldwide and the creation of a World Bird Database, which has become the most important single source of information on the status of the world's birds, their habitats, and their conservation. In addition to its computerized database, BirdLife shares its information through a variety of high-quality publications including regional catalogues of IBAs, accounts of the threatened birds of the world, atlases of endemic bird areas, species monographs and two periodicals: a popular magazine, *World Birdwatch*, and a quarterly journal, *Bird Conservation International.*

The world headquarters of Birdlife International are located at Wellbrook Court, Girton Road, Cambridge, UK CB3 0NA with regional offices in Tokyo, Quito, Brussels, and Amsterdam For more information, go to www.birdlife.net. See also IMPORTANT BIRD AREAS.

BIRDLIME. See LIME.

BIRDNET. An on-line ornithological information source provided by the ORNITHOLOGICAL COUNCIL and its ten constituent ornithological societies. It provides a broad spectrum of information on ornithology and birding, issues relating to birdlife, professional meetings, recent research, grants and awards and recent ornithological literature, and publishes guidelines for bird monitoring and a manual for the humane study of birds *(Guidelines to the Use of Wild Birds in Research).* To visit the site go to www.nmnh.si.edu/BIRDNET/. See also BIRD CHAT GROUPS; LISTSERVS; RARE BIRD ALERTS.

BIRD OF PREY. Generally understood to refer to hawks, eagles, falcons, and their relatives (except perhaps for the vultures) and owls. Often defined as birds that hunt, kill, and eat other animals or other vertebrates or other "warm-blooded" animals, but there are too many exceptions to this formula to sustain the validity of it. Many herons, corvids, and specialized species of other families (e.g., roadrunners!) fit this definition but are not thought of as birds of prey. Both Ospreys and mergansers hunt, kill, and eat fish, yet the former is certainly a bird of prey, while the latter is certainly not. A better definition is birds equipped with talons and/or hooked bills adapted for holding and tearing meat; this would admit the shrikes and vultures, which might be disputed, but would exclude other carnivores. Essentially synonymous with "raptor." See PREDATION.

BIRD SKIN. The usual form in which specimens of birds are preserved in museum collections for a variety of purposes vital to the study of birdlife. Novice birdwatchers and those with a particularly deep empathy for living things of all kinds are often dismayed the first time they see a large scientific collection—drawer upon drawer filling cabinet after cabinet sometimes occupying room after room, all filled with stuffed bird carcasses, most of which were intentionally collected. Most soon realize, however, that the number of birds sacrificed to science is barely discernible next to the carnage of migrant birds produced by a single skyscraper or TV tower during a single night or the annual toll from the continent's population of domestic and feral cats. And that what has been learned from the systematic collection and preservation of specimens is of incalculable scientific value. For a detailed discussion of the function of skin collections, see Parkes (1963–MUSEUMS); see also Mark Barrow's *A Passion for Birds,* (1998–ORNITHOLOGY).

The usual method of preparing a bird skin is (very briefly) as follows: The bird is laid on its back and the feathers parted manually down the center of the breast and belly. An incision is made through the skin running from the top of the breastbone to just above the vent. The skin is then worked back with fingers and scalpel from the muscular body to which it adheres. This internal carcass is detached at the knee and shoulder joints and at the base of the tail, and the skin is inverted over the neck and head to the base of the bill. The carcass is then detached from the base of the skull, so that only the skull and lower wing and leg bones remain attached to the feathered skin. These and the inside of the skin itself are now cleaned of any remaining muscle, fat, and other perishable tissue, and the whole interior is treated with a drying agent. The skin is then turned "right side to," with the cleaned skull remaining in the head. Finally, a "body" composed of cotton or other stuffing substance is made in proportion to the original one, fitted into the cavity, and the incision is sewn up. The specimen is laid on its back, its bill pointing forward (in short-necked

birds), its wings folded, its legs crossed, its plumage arranged, and—a crucial step without which all effort would be wasted—a label is attached giving as much information as is known about the specimen, e.g., place and date of collection, age, state of sexual organs, colors of soft parts, stomach contents, weight before skinning, measurements of various parts, species and subspecies, and the name of the collector. Few specimens, in fact, are labeled this thoroughly, but any ornithologist will affirm that a specimen's value is proportionate to the thoroughness with which it is labeled.

All of this may sound simple enough—especially if you are not squeamish about entrails—but the preparation of a good bird skin is a minor art, as you will quickly discover if you ever have the opportunity to try it. In the old days when collecting and preparing 50 birds in a weekend was routine for the serious amateur collector, a skilled hand was said to be able to turn out a "passable" skin in 10 or 15 minutes (for hard cases). These gentlemen typically omitted to sew up the incision in small birds, however, and how passable they were in fact is a matter of highly subjective judgment.

For a lengthy and often entertaining account of how bird skins were made in the old days, see Coues (1890). For detailed modern technique, see Anderson (1965), Johnson, et al. (1984), and Longmore and Boles (1990). See also MUSEUMS; COLLECTING.

BIRDSMANSHIP. A matter of style. Conducting oneself to the best advantage in birding and ornithological situations. Encompasses all aspects of the birdperson's world, e.g., dress, comportment in the field, public speaking, and dinner conversation. For the seminal work on the subject, including many instructive anecdotes, see Bruce Campbell's definitive essay reprinted in Peterson (1957–BIRDWATCHING). See also Oddie (1980, 1995–BIRDWATCHING), and Dunne (1992–BIRDWATCHING). A single example must serve here. A birdsman of repute was scoping the sea one breezy November morning when another birder, scanning nearby, called out with that crisp air of infallibility that only second-rate field persons seem able to master: "Red Phalaropes, moving right, two o'clock, about halfway to the horizon."

"Excellent," said the birdsman, shifting his scope to the flock in question and managing to convey both enthusiasm and regret over not having found the birds himself: "Where exactly from the Sanderlings?"

BIRD'S NEST SOUP. An expensive Asian delicacy made from the nests of several species of Old World swifts in the genus *Collocalia*. The nests are made of viscous, solidifying saliva, secreted by the swifts for this purpose. The saliva itself is relatively tasteless and is improved in most soup recipes by the addition of vegetables and condiments. Swift spittle is considered an aphrodisiac by the Chinese. See EDIBILITY for other avian delicacies.

BIRDS OF NORTH AMERICA PROJECT. Now the standard—and quite magnificent—comprehensive reference on North America birds with authoritative scientific accounts by leading ornithologists on all of the 700+ species of birds that breed in North America. In addition to complete descriptions and life histories the work contains distribution maps, discussion of conservation and management issues, color photographs and line drawings, extensive bibliographies and many other useful features. It has replaced A.C. Bent's *Life Histories of North American Birds* as the indispensable source of information on the continent's birdlife.

Edited by Frank Gill and Alan Poole, the *BNA* has been published over a number of year in a series of single species profiles in a standardized format collected in 18 "volumes" of 40 fascicles each. The nonprofit project was supported by the American Ornithologists' Union, the Cornell Lab of Ornithology and the Academy of Natural Sciences of Philadelphia. For a more detailed description sample profiles, reviews and ordering information, go to http://www.birdsofna.org/.

BIRDWATCHING. Usually refers to the regular, somewhat methodical seeking out and observation of birds, whether for pure aesthetic pleasure or recreation or out of a more serious, scientific motive. That is, the term usually does *not* apply either to people who may feed birds but are not particularly interested in which species they attract or to professional ornithologists, most of whom spend at least as much (usually much more) time in the laboratory and library as they do observing birds in the field. The relatively new, but rapidly evolving behavioral branch of ornithology intrinsically involves long hours of watching birds, yet the practitioners of this discipline are known as bird behaviorists, or behavioral ecologists implying the specialized education that birdwatchers usually lack.

The semantics, history, and social implications of "birdwatcher"/ "birder"/"ornithologist" are rather complex and sometimes amusing. It should be noted first that many serious birdwatchers of today could easily instruct an ornithologist of 100 years ago—due, of course, to the accumulation of knowledge that the early ornithologists helped to discover. Nevertheless, modern "birders" should neither feel nor be disparaged by modern ornithologists; their contributions have been significant and are increasing with the rise of CITIZEN SCIENCE.

In North America an interest in birds has traditionally been associated with somewhat different values than it has in Europe and especially England, where birds and man meet on a more nearly equal footing than in any other country. Until after World War II, birdwatching in America was regarded as a pursuit of (1) the rich (perhaps because many early conservationists, e.g., Teddy Roosevelt, were American aristocrats); (2) the eccentric (because of field clothes? because only a crazy would spend time peering up into trees at tiny, flitting forms?); and in males (3) the some-

what effeminate (not enough physical contact for a proper sport!). In spite of the dramatic increase in environmental education and the popularity of environmental causes here since the 1970s, there is still some stigma felt by any boy over ten who would just as soon watch birds as play baseball. In much of Europe, these negative values attached to an interest in natural history are not so apparent—the idea of a father and son going birdwatching in the morning and to a soccer match in the afternoon surprises no one (mothers and daughters are a different case). Pretentious analyses of this difference, involving Americans' relatively recent subjugation of their "wilderness," will not be indulged in here.

Another interesting difference between American and European birdwatchers involves how each perceives his/her avocation. In a book aimed at British birdwatchers, Alan Richards (1980) observed: "In the early 1950s ornithologists tended to believe that all birdwatching should yield some scientific return; in more recent years this attitude has disappeared and birdwatching is usually done for sheer pleasure and interest." With some notable exceptions the situation in America has been just the reverse. In the 1950s (and later) most ornithologists here expected nothing whatever of birdwatchers, and most birdwatchers expected nothing of scientific value of themselves-only fun. Only recently have young American birdwatchers in any numbers begun "watching" (rather than simply identifying and listing) birds and carrying notebooks into the field to record their observations. This trend has accelerated over the last 20 years, with the popularity of Breeding Bird ATLAS projects, and academic ornithology now actively promotes contributions by birders. Furthermore, as has long been realized in Europe, effective bird conservation must involve a constituency of committed people if it is to have any political leverage, and engaging troops of volunteers in bird censuses and other useful efforts has proven to be an excellent means of promoting conservation action (see CITIZEN SCIENCE).

Then there is the matter of what one *calls* oneself and one's interest. Twenty years ago British field ornithologists called themselves "birdwatchers," a no-nonsense, reasonably descriptive term, and distained the Americaism "birder" as a bit frivolous or trendy. For their part, Americans have long thought "birdwatcher" rather stodgy and smacking of some of the unwholesome traits noted above. "Birder" by contrast seemed to imply a more serious, aggressive approach to the activity.

Someone wishing to emphasize transatlantic differences in birding styles might say that American birdwatching (birding) has typically been a form of competitive sport involving how many species of birds one can see in a day, year, life, state, or the world; a great deal of driving and talking are usually involved in a day's birding and relatively little attention is paid to numbers, behavior and the like. European birders (birdwatchers) have tended to concentrate more on honing field identification skills to

the level of microcopy and to think of their activities as worthwhile *obser-vations* ; they tend to walk (and slog) more, write and sketch a great deal in notebooks (field marks, behavior, phenological data), are not very tolerant of idle conversation while "watching," and are usually suspicious of "twitchers" (i.e., listers); they consider good notes on a particular species better evidence of a good day in the field than a long species list. Obviously there are distinct advantages to both of these approaches to birdwatching and, as was probably inevitable, they seem to be merging into an activity of global popularity that is both fun and of conservation value. "Birder/birding" are now the accepted terms of art in the United Kingdom, while birdwatcher/-ing is uttered more frequently and without embarrassment here. There are many more twitchers in Britain now and apparently fewer (or at least less mindless) listers here than previously, and keeping records and supporting bird conservation is, wholesomely, far more prevalent among American birders than was once the case.

For a particularly acerbic British expatriate's account of North American birders, see Jack Connor's *Season at the Point* (1991). Bill Oddie (1980) also gets off some good lines on the subject in a chapter titled, "What am I? What are you?" See also LISTING; TWITCHING.

SOME DEMOGRAPHICS

Popularity. Birding is near the top of the list of most popular outdoor recreational activities in North America and its popularity continues to grow. As of 2000–01, 70.4 million Americans identified themselves as birdwatchers, an increase of 232% over 1983. The number of "hard-core" birders is, of course, much smaller (but is also growing).

Gender. Birdwatching was once a strongly male-dominated activity, the most adept and ardent birders often beginning as obsessive preadolescent boys. In 1975 78% of ABA members were male; by 1994 the number was down to 65% (*fide* ABA membership poll, 1994; see Butcher, 1996). In the general population, women now make up 56% of all U.S. birdwatchers, though the hard-core element is probably still male dominated.

Age. In America, the largest age segment of the birding community is the 40–59 group (37%). Children and teens were once quite rare in gatherings of birdwatchers here in contrast to northern Europe, where birdwatching hot spots are often dominated by younger people. However, this is changing with the 16–24 age group increasing here by 5% (from 10.5 to 15.5%) between 1994–95 and 2000–01.

Wealth. The old stereotype of the well-to-do birdwatcher is still valid to some extent. To successfully pursue a respectable life list, a certain minimum of leisure and mobility are necessary, and as of 2000–01, 46.7% of birders earned more than $50,000 a year. It is interesting that this number is significantly down (from 58.6% in 1994–95) apparently indicating that the sport is becoming more appealing to the less affluent. Birders

have become known to chambers of commerce as a highly desirable demographic who often patronize high-end stores and services and are "well-behaved." The rise of Birding Festivals (see BIRDING EVENTS) and trade magazines pitched at "bird merchants" is a response to proliferation of birder-consumers. The professions are well represented among birders, particularly doctors, who have always figured prominently in American ornithology (see BIOGRAPHY).

Education. More than 28% of birders held college degrees as of 2001 (against 21.5% in the general population) and 55.1% had graduated from high school. The education level of members of the American Birding Association is even higher: 98% with high school diplomas, 80% with bachelor's degrees, and 43% with a master's degree or PhD (*fide* ABA membership poll, 1994; see Butcher 1996). An interesting trend in this category is that the percentage of birders without high school diplomas has more than doubled since 1995 from 7.6 to 16.7%, while the college-educated group dropped from 34.7 to 28.3%.

Ethnicity. White people still make up the majority of the American birdwatching community (77.4%). But this is down from 86.3% in 1995 largely as a result of an almost tenfold increase in the percentage of Hispanic birders from 1.9% of the total in 1995 to 10.8% in 2001. Only the percentage of whites in the birding population exceeds their percentage in the total population (77.4/68.6%). By comparison the percentage of blacks in the birding community was 8.2% as of 1995 versus 12.6% in the general population. For Asians those percentages are 2.9 versus 3.6%.

Global distribution. While birdwatching is pursued mainly in "developed" countries of the Temperate Zones—especially North America, northern and Western Europe, Japan, South Africa, and Australia and New Zealand—it is growing steadily in the developing world as ecotourism and conservation programs are creating economic opportunities there.

Other statistics (from ABA/Butcher 1996 and Kerlinger and Wiedner (1990):

- 24.7 million people take trips every year to watch birds.
- 85% of ABA members travel outside their state to bird; 49% travel outside their country to bird.
- 70 million Americans feed birds at home.
- In 1997 there were about 70 birding festivals in North America.
- *WildBird* magazine had a distribution of 160,000 in 1996.
- "Avid" birders spend over $200 million per year on birding related travel, optics, and other retail items (not including bird feeding).
- 19% of ABA members and 7% of females identify themselves as experts in their home area; 8% of males and 21% of females call themselves beginners.

Based on the above figures it seems fair to say that birding is not only growing dramatically as a popular pastime, but also appealing to a more

diverse audience. It has also become a major market segment. These trends are all the more striking in view of the fact that participation in other popular outdoor activities involving wildlife, e.g., hunting and fishing, is actually declining.

For more detail on birding demographics see the Cordell and Herbert (2002), Kerlinger (1990) and the Economics of Birding section of the ABA website (http://american birding.org) from which many of the figures above were gleaned.

For cross-references to this entry, see . . . the rest of the book.

One great boon of the birding boom is that birding literature has increased in volume and (more importantly) in quality. See the Bibliography for the works of Pete Dunne and other masters of this new genre as well as a selection how-to books.

BITTERN. Standard English name for all members of the Tribe Botaurini (family Ardeidae [herons]; order Ciconiiformes). There are 13 species of true bitterns worldwide, though the name is also applied to a few other herons not in the bittern tribe. Two species of bitterns, the American and the Least, breed in North America and the Yellow Bittern of Asia has been recorded once as a vagrant in the Aleutians.

The bitterns are secretive, semicrepuscular marsh birds, more often heard than seen. The American Bittern is widespread in wetlands from subarctic Canada to Central America. The Least Bittern barely crosses the Canadian border and is essentially absent from the Great Plains but reaches South America as a breeding bird.

The Least Bittern has a dark (melanistic or erythristic) color morph once thought to be a separate species, called Cory's Least Bittern.

"Bittern" goes back at least to Latin and relates to the remarkable sound that the Eurasian Bittern makes; Lockwood (1993–NAMES,VERNACULAR) notes the Latin verb Butire meaning "to boom like a bittern." This sound resembles the lowing of an ox, a fact that inspired the Latin bittern genus *Botaurus*—from *Bos taurus,* the European wild white ox or aurochs. The characteristic sound of the American *(Botaurus)* Bittern is less bovine but even more remarkable and has given rise to nicknames such as "dunk-a-doo," "stake driver," and "thunderpump."

For family characteristics, see HERON.

BLACKBIRD. Standard English name for about 24 of the approximately 97 members of the family Icteridae (order Passeriformes). The name is often used to refer to all of the largely black members of the family, i.e., the cowbirds and grackles, as well as the species actually called blackbirds. It has also been applied to the family as a whole, as the New World Blackbirds, encompassing the New World orioles, the Troupial, oropendolas, caciques, meadowlarks, and Bobolink. The icterids are so diverse in form,

coloration, and behavior that it is almost impossible to discuss them in terms of their common traits. Therefore, the "black blackbirds," including the grackles, are considered together in this entry and the others under ORIOLE, MEADOWLARK, and BOBOLINK.

Ten species of "black blackbirds" breed in North America, including 5 that are called blackbirds, 3 species of grackles, and 2 of cowbirds. Two additional species, the Tawny-shouldered Blackbird and the Shiny Cowbird, have been recorded as vagrants (see Appendix II).

The blackbirds range in size from 6½ inches (Brown-headed Cowbird) to 18 inches (Great-tailed Grackle). In most species the bill tapers to a sharp point; in some species this is used to pry into various objects (e.g., cattail stems) and soil. The males of all species are largely black, most are "shiny," several have strong green and purple iridescence, and three have areas of brilliant red or yellow feathering. Except in the Common Grackle, females are mainly dull grayish or brownish and are streaked in some species. The blackbirds are essentially ground feeders, walking deliberately over fields, lawns, and the margins of marshes or lakes, picking up virtually any form of animal or plant life that they are capable of swallowing, including worms, insects, mussels, snails, crayfish, frogs, lizards, bird's eggs, and nestlings. Several species (especially the grackles) wade in shallow water and catch small fish. All blackbirds also have great appetites for seeds, especially grain, and Red-winged Blackbirds and Brown-headed Cowbirds eat more vegetable than animal food. The blackbirds are very (many people would say excessively) gregarious, gathering in wintering flocks of mixed species that sometimes number in the millions of birds. These blackbird armies can be serious pests at stockyards, in grain fields, and occasionally in their vast noisy night roosts (see PROBLEMS INVOLVING BIRDS).

Most of the blackbirds nest in loose to rather crowded (Tricolored Blackbird) colonies. The tree-nesting species (grackles, Rusty Blackbird) make rather bulky cups of twigs and coarser grasses. The marsh nesters usually weave cup-shaped baskets around upright cattail or rush stems, in some cases using soggy dead materials which tighten into a neat structure as they dry. Many blackbird nests are cemented with mud or dung and all have an inner lining of finer plant fibers, fresh grasses, and/or hair. The cowbirds never make nests, the females of both species laying their eggs in the nests of a wide variety of land-bird and (less usually) waterbird species (see COWBIRD). Blackbirds lay 3–7 (usually 4–5) eggs, except for the cowbirds, which may lay 10–12 eggs (or perhaps as many as 30) in a given season. Blackbird eggs are rather glossy and extremely variable, even within one species (e.g., Red-winged Blackbird). The ground color varies from white to pale blue, green, pinkish, purplish, or brown. They may be immaculate (Bronzed Cowbird) or sparsely or densely speckled, spotted, or scrawled with what look like letters of the old Arabic alphabet.

Blackbird songs are generally rather harsh with loud squeaks, whistles, and clarion calls, yet some (e.g., Red-winged Blackbird) are pleasantly exuberant and the cowbirds' odd liquid sounds border on the subtle.

Blackbirds are restricted to the New World and range from the Arctic to the Straits of Magellan, achieving their greatest diversity in South America. Several of the North American species breed from coast to coast. Most are migratory from the northern parts of their range but winter largely in the warm southern United States, where a majority of native species is resident year round.

"Blackbird" is, of course, perfectly apt for a few members of the Icteridae, but hardly appropriate with regard to species like the meadowlarks and orioles. A further complication is the name of the abundant and widespread Eurasian thrush that replaces the American Robin in much of the Palearctic. This species is called simply Blackbird in Britain, where (according to Mother Goose) four and twenty of them were once baked in a pie and set before the king.

BLACKBURNE, Anna (Blackburnian Warbler: *Dendroica fusca*). An eighteenth-century botanist and keeper of a natural history museum in her native Lancashire, England. Her brother, Ashton, collected birds for her while visiting New York, New Jersey, and Connecticut. The exquisite wood warbler was named for her twice, first in Latin by Johann Gmelin (*Motacilla blackburniae,* a name soon discarded) and then in English by the zoologist Thomas Pennant.

BLACKPOLL (Warbler). Standard English name for a single species of wood warbler, *Dendroica striata* (family Parulidae), which breeds exclusively in coniferous forests continent wide in boreal North America and winters in South America (see Fig. 18). The "poll" is the top and back of the head including the nape; this region is black only in male Blackpoll Warblers in alternate (breeding) plumage. See WOOD WARBLER.

BLIND. A small building, tent, wall, or other structure with narrow "windows" behind which hunters, birdwatchers, or photographers can conceal themselves and thereby get close to birds or other animals without alarming them. In Britain usually called a "hide." See PHOTOGRAPHY.

BLUEBIRD. Standard English name for the 3 small, cavity-nesting thrushes in the genus *Sialia* (family Turdidae; order Passeriformes); also used for the 2 species of leafbirds in the genus *Irena* (family Irenidae; order Passeriformes)—the fairy bluebirds of Asia.

The American bluebirds are among our most popular songbirds, owing to their colorful plumage, pleasant song, and fondness for man-made

habitats, especially agricultural lands, suburban landscapes and structures. There is even a North American Bluebird Society (The Wilderness
Center, Box 244, Wilmot, OH 44689-0244; www.nabluebirdsociety.org),
which promotes the erection of nest boxes and relates the adventures of
dedicated bluebirders in its quarterly journal, *Sialia.*

Bluebirds are readily attracted to birdhouses, though care must be
taken to keep potential bluebird sites from being occupied by starlings or
House Sparrows (see below and BIRDHOUSE). The Eastern Bluebird suffered a severe decline recently in the Northeast, which reached a low
point in the 1950s and 1960s. This has been attributed to a combination of
severe winters and competition from two invasive Eurasian cavity nesting
birds the European Starling and the House Sparrow. As of this writing
(2002) the species has rebounded significantly apparently due to a warming winter climate, a decline in its alien competitors and the efforts of
bluebird lovers who have provided vast numbers of additional housing
units throughout a national "bluebird trail" (see Sauer and Droege 1990).

In the northern parts of its breeding range, the Eastern Bluebird is
among the earliest birds to return in the spring and has therefore become
a traditional herald of that season.

The range of the Mountain Bluebird reaches beyond the Arctic Circle
and that of the Eastern Bluebird to Nicaragua. Among them the three
bluebirds are distributed continent wide.

For family characteristics, see THRUSH.

BLUETHROAT. Standard English name for a single species of small
thrush, *Luscinia (Erithacus) svecicus* (family Turdidae) that breeds across
the northern Palearctic region and just reaches the Nearctic in western
and northern Alaska. The Alaskan population winters in southern Asia.
The name is apt for adult males in alternate (breeding) plumage. For family characteristics, see THRUSH.

BOBOLINK. Standard English name for a single species in the New World
blackbird family (Icteridae), *Dolichonyx oryzivorus.* It undertakes the
longest migration of any North American land-bird species, its greatest
mileage being from southern Canada to the grasslands of northern Argentina. Along with the meadowlarks, the Bobolink is the quintessential
songbird of North American grasslands. It was once widely known as
"ricebird" for its habit of gobbling rice crops in the southeastern states
during its southbound migration causing losses estimated at $2 million in
1886 dollars; later it was itself "harvested" for the game market, 60,000
dozen being shipped from South Carolina alone in 1912. The species is
presently declining due mainly to the succession and developments of
its grassland habitat. The name is a shortened form of a folk name, "Bob

Lincoln," and echoes the species' bubbling song. Thoreau recorded a Cape Cod boy's reaction to a singing Bobolink: "What makes he sing so sweet, Mama? Do he eat flowers?" See BLACKBIRD.

BOBWHITE. Standard English name in North America for a single species of New World quail, the Northern Bobwhite, *Colinus virginianus.* The two or other *Colinus* quails of Latin America are also called bobwhites. The name is a close approximation of the surprisingly loud whistled call of the Northern Bobwhite. See QUAIL.

BOHEMIAN (Waxwing). Bohemia is a region (once a kingdom) in western Czechoslovakia, where *Bombycilla garrulus* occurs only as a winter visitor. It is the alleged home of the gypsies and the name may refer to this species' habit of wandering unpredictably and at irregular intervals south of its normal wintering range. See IRRUPTION/ERUPTION; WAXING.

BONAPARTE, Charles Lucien, 1803–57 (Bonaparte's Gull: *Larus philadelphia*). A nephew of Napoleon I, he tackled the description of the North American avifauna in his *American Ornithology* during an eight-year stay in America. He was well educated in science and is generally acknowledged to have been one of the foremost ornithologists of his time. His American reputation is eclipsed somewhat due to his appearance on the scene between the two giants of early American ornithology, WILSON and AUDUBON. He continued to study and write about birds and other zoological subjects on returning to Europe, but much of his later life was consumed by politics, especially the independence of Italy. Bonaparte's Gull was described and named by George ORD, one of Wilson's chief patrons. For a recent biography see *The Emperor of Nature* by Patricia Stroud (2000, University of Pennsylvania Press).

BONAVENTURE ISLAND (Québec). One of the most famous seabird colony of eastern North America, located 2.2 miles (3.5 km) off the east coast of the Gaspé Peninsula. Bonaventure is a small (1.6 square miles/4.16 sq km) circular island, with a spectacular cliff face to the north and east. It holds the second largest colony of Northern Gannets in the world (25,000 pairs) as well as Leach's Storm-Petrel, Common Murre, Atlantic Puffins (a few), Razorbills, and Black-legged Kittiwakes. The island is now a reserve of the Ministère du Loisir, de la Chasse et de la Pêche of Québec and of the Canadian Wildlife Service, and the breeding birds are protected from disturbance by visitors. An interpretive center in the adjacent mainland village of Percé highlights Bonaventure's fascinating flora as well as the avifauna. Day tours of Bonaventure begin by boat from Percé. Visitors can take naturalist-led tours or hike on their own around and across the roughly circular island. Overnight stays on Bonaventure

are not permitted. The Gaspé mainland is an excellent place to find boreal birds, e.g. Bicknell's Thrushes breed on Mt. St.-Anne just west of Percé. See also BOREAL BIRDING (Northeast).

BONES. See SKELETON.

BOOBY. Standard English name for 6 or 7 members of the family Sulidae (order Pelecaniformes), all but one in the genus *Sula.* The other 3 species of the family are called gannets and are usually distinguished in the genus *Morus.* The Masked Booby nests occasionally in the Dry Tortugas (Florida Keys) and the three other species of boobies visit the southernmost coasts of North America with varying degrees of regularity. The Northern Gannet breeds on islands along the northeast coast from the Gasper to Newfoundland and winters offshore in the Atlantic and Gulf of Mexico.

The boobies and gannets are large (30–40 inches) pelagic seabirds, most of them boldly patterned in white, black, and shades of brown and often with brightly colored feet and facial skin. Like the other members of their order, they have webs between all four toes (totipalmate); they lack external nostril openings in the bill.

Sulids are strong fliers that soar over the ocean and plunge dive intermittently on fish and squid from heights of up to 100 feet (Northern Gannet).

All boobies and gannets are colonial. All, except for the Red-footed Booby, some populations of Masked Boobies, and the gannets, nest on bare ground, sand, or rock with only a ring of guano deposited by the sitting birds for a "structure" and no lining. The exceptional boobies make stick nests in the tops of bushes or trees (to 35 feet). Gannets make a mound of seaweed and other flotsam on bare rock. All boobies and gannets typically lay 1 or 2 (or up to 4 if food is plentiful) pale blue to green eggs, covered at laying with a white, chalky coating, perhaps a protection against the hot sun to which the nests are often exposed. The latter is soft at first but dries quickly and becomes stained and scratched off in places. During incubation the eggs rest at under the wide webs of the feet and then are moved to the top of the feet when the chicks begin to hatch.

These birds are not often heard except on the breeding grounds. There is a marked sexual dimorphism in the structure of the trachea and syrinx in the Masked and Blue-footed Boobies, so that the males give a whistling call and the females a "resonant trumpeting" (Palmer 1962–ORNITHOLOGY). The other species make only harsh quacks, squeaks, screeches, and hisses.

The boobies are pantropical in distribution, whereas the gannets are restricted to colder waters of the Northern and Southern hemispheres (see GANNET).

Boobies are named for their naiveté in dealing with mankind. Having little experience with human behavior on their remote breeding islands,

they reacted with curiosity rather than alarm at the approach of hungry mariners. For their innocence they were clubbed on the head for immediate consumption or thrown alive into the "booby hatch," a small hold under the poop deck where a supply of fresh meat was customarily stored.

BOOMING (booming ground). The wild, somewhat mournful sound produced by male prairie-chickens on their spring courtship "dancing" (or booming) grounds (see LEK). The birds create a resonating chamber for the sound by blocking the nasal passages with their tongue and inflating their esophagus, which connects to their bright orange neck pouches. The low-frequency sound carries farther at the same volume than a higher frequency call, and can be heard by human ears from 3–4 kilometers away. The booming is often likened to the sound of blowing across the top of a small empty bottle; while not inaccurate, this description leaves out the eerie plaintiveness of the sound, especially when uttered in random chorus and echoed by a dozen or more birds. Forbush (1925–1929–STATE PROVINCIAL BOOKS, Massachusetts) says of the now extinct eastern race (Heath Hen) that it "ends in the air like a Scotch ballad." One of the fine wild sounds of the North American prairies, now, alas, all too seldom heard. Compare GOBBLING GROUND.

BOREAL (BOR-ee-yul) (Owl, Chickadee). In the most general sense, simply "northern," deriving from Boreas, the Greek god of the north wind. In technical usage, it refers to the circumpolar zones that contain the coniferous forest (taiga) of Canada and northern Eurasia as well as the similar zones of our higher mountains; sometimes called the "spruce-moose biome." The ranges of the Boreal Owl and the Boreal Chickadee in North America are essentially coextensive with the Boreal Zone. Other bird species typical of the boreal forest and associated habitats such as bogs and alder and willow thickets are Merlin, Spruce Grouse, Yellow Rail, Greater and Lesser Yellowlegs, Solitary Sandpiper, Common Snipe, Bonaparte's Gull, Great Gray, Boreal, Saw-whet and Hawk Owls, Black-backed and Three-toed Woodpeckers, Olive-sided, Yellow-bellied and Alder Flycatchers, Northern Shrike, Gray Jay, Boreal Chickadee, Red-breasted Nuthatch, Ruby-crowned and Golden-crowned Kinglets, Swainson's, Bicknell's, and Gray-cheeked Thrushes, Bohemian Waxwing, Orange-crowned, Tennessee, Magnolia, Cape May, Blackburnian, Townsend's, Black-throated Green, Palm, Bay-breasted, Blackpoll, Connecticut, Mourning and Wilson's Warblers, Pine Grosbeak, White-throated, White-crowned, Fox, and Lincoln's Sparrows, Dark-eyed Junco, Rusty Blackbird, Pine Grosbeak, Red and White-winged Crossbills and Pine Siskin. See also TAIGA; MUSKEG; SUBARCTIC. For boreal birding see the following entry and associated cross-references.

BOREAL BIRDING (Northeast). Some of the best boreal birding localities readily accessible by road to easterners include Cape Breton Highlands National Park (Nova Scotia), Gros Morne National Park (Newfoundland), Baxter State Park (Maine), Mount Mansfield State Forest (Vermont), White Mountain National Forest (New Hampshire), Adirondack Forest Preserve Park (New York). These contain many species that are either permanent residents in northern or mountain spruce zone or are somewhat inconspicuous on their southward migrations in the East, e.g., Spruce Grouse, Black-backed and Three-toed Woodpeckers, Yellow-bellied Flycatcher, Gray Jay, Boreal Chickadee, Gray-cheeked and Bicknell's Thrushes, Mourning Warbler, Fox and Lincoln's Sparrows, Pine Grosbeak and Red and White-winged Crossbills. See also preceding entry.

BOTTERI (BOT-er-ee), Matteo, 1808–77 (Botteri's Sparrow: *Aimophila botterii*). A well-known Dalmatian (now Croatian) professional collector who worked principally in southeastern Europe and Mexico. He eventually founded a natural history museum and became a professor of natural history at Orizaba in the Mexican state of Veracruz. The sparrow, the range of which is largely in Mexico, was named for him by one of the systematists, William L. Sclater, to whom he sent specimens.

BOTULISM (BOT-chew-lizm). A virulent and deadly bacterial infection that occasionally kills large numbers of waterfowl; it is also a source of human food poisoning. See DISEASE.

BRACE. A hunting term meaning two dead game birds of the same species. For example, six grouse, regardless of sex, are referred to as "three brace of grouse." See NOUNS OF ASSEMBLAGE.

BRAIN. See NERVOUS SYSTEM.

BRANDT, Johann Friedrich von, 1802–79 (Brandt's Cormorant: *Phalacrocorax penicillatus*). A prolific zoologist, paleontologist, and geographer who made his reputation in St. Petersburg (Russia), though a native of Germany. He described and gave the Latin name to the cormorant that now memorializes him.

BRANT. Standard English name in North America for a species of small goose, *Branta bernicla,* which breeds in the High Arctic and winters along the Atlantic and Pacific coasts. The dark race of western North America *(B. b. nigricans)* was once considered a distinct species called Black Brant. Brant were once largely dependant on a subtidal flowering plant called eelgrass *(Zostera marina)* as a principal food source. This preference almost doomed eastern populations of the species during the eelgrass

blight of the 1930s, but nonspecialist individuals survived and eastern brant now graze happily on Sea Lettuce *Ulva lactua,* a marine algae, as well as cultivated grasses. However, the Atlantic brant population never recovered its former abundance. The species is esteemed as a table bird and is therefore widely hunted. According to Lockwood (1993–NAMES, VERNACULAR), the name derives from the Old Norse *brandgas,* meaning burnt or black goose, quite evocative of the species scorched look. Though the standard English name for this goose in Europe is *Brent* Goose, brant is actually an earlier usage. For family characteristics, see GOOSE.

BREEDING BIRD CENSUS (BBC). An extensive long-term data set of habitat-based breeding bird populations in North America. Initiated in 1914 by the U.S. Bureau of Biological Survey, the program was sponsored by the National Audubon Society from 1937 to 1984 and since then has been under the auspices of the Cornell Laboratory of Ornithology. The methodology was designed to provide scientifically valid information on trends in breeding bird populations using a methodology that could be employed by skilled birdwatchers. In essence it involves recording the location of singing male birds or pairs during a minimum of 8 visits per breeding season to a chosen plot of a single habitat type. This allows a reasonably accurate estimate of the number of breeding pairs present in a given plot each year, and since the data is recorded according to a consistent methodology, it is possible to compare results over the period during which any single census has been conducted. The size, dimension and location of the plots are determined by the volunteer census takers, though a minimum of 10 hectares (24.7 acres) is recommended for closed habitat such as forest and 40 hectares (98.8 acres) for open habitats such as grasslands. When a new census is initiated a quantitative survey of the vegetative structure and species composition of the plot is completed and may be repeated at intervals to assess changes in successional habitats. Of the hundreds of BBC plots now in existence most are located in forest habitats on protected (therefore relatively undisturbed) land.

The BBC was published by the National Audubon Society (*American Birds,* etc.) and most recently as a supplement to the *Journal of Field Ornithology.* Some of the data are now accessible through ftp files. Given the size and potential value of this database, it is notable that (according to the administrators of the program) it is, so far, underutilized.

For more information or to participate, contact Cornell Laboratory of Ornithology, 159 Sapsucker Woods Rd., Ithaca, NY 14850 or visit the BBC website at http://www.mp1-pwrc.usgs.gov/birds/bbc.html.

See also CENSUS and the following entry.

BREEDING BIRD SURVEY (BBS). North America's most important program to monitor and assess the status and trends of bird populations on a continentwide basis. Founded in 1966 by Chandler Robbins and others at

the Patuxent Wildlife Research Center in response to the threat of wide-spread bird population declines related to indiscriminate use of DDT and other pesticides, the BBS is now jointly coordinated by U.S. Geological Survey and the Canadian Wildlife Service (National Wildlife Research Center). The survey sites consist of 24.5-mile roadside routes covered each year during the breeding season (mainly June) by volunteers with good bird identification skills. Starting half an hour before sunrise, participants move along the designated route stopping at half-mile intervals to count every bird that can be seen or heard in 3 minutes at that point; in addition, every bird heard from the survey route or seen within a quarter-mile radius is recorded. There are now more than 4,100 survey routes across the United States and Canada, and population trend estimates are now available for more than 420 bird species. The BBS has proven to be an invaluable stimulus and resource for avian research and has been crucial in setting priorities for North American bird conservation.

For participation instructions, results and analysis, a bibliography and other details, see the BBS website: http://www.pwrc.usgs.gov/bbs.

BREEDING CYCLE. See COURTSHIP; DISPLAY; PAIR FORMATION; MATING SYSTEMS, REPRODUCTIVE SYSTEM; SONG; TERRITORY; NEST; LAYING; EGG; EMBRYO; INCUBATION; HATCHING; PARENTAL CARE.

BREEDING IN CAPTIVITY. See AVICULTURE.

BREEDING PLUMAGE. The plumage that results from either feather wear or a preceding molt in the spring of the year, as the breeding season approaches. In many species it is much gaudier, especially in males, than the basic or winter plumage. Also called "nuptial" plumage in some instances, though "alternate" plumage is probably the most apt term avoiding—as the others do not—the implication that this plumage is a *result* of the breeding cycle. For more detail on the process and the terminology, see MOLT.

BREEDING SEASON. The time period (weeks or months) during which birds mate, lay eggs, and rear young in any given locality. Though a few tropical species seem to breed according to no discernible schedule, the great majority of birds have fixed breeding seasons (or at least patterns), which are ultimately related to some environmental factor(s) affecting reproductive success. The fact that the majority of temperate zone birds breed during the warmer months reflects the advantages which longer days, abundant food, dense cover, and simple warmth offer in rearing young. Of course, the relationship between the season and the calendar is different in the North Temperate Zone from that in the South, and while Greater Shearwaters and Wilson's Storm-Petrels are experiencing the very height of their breeding seasons in South Atlantic and subantarctic islands, northern breeding grounds are deep in the silence of winter.

Exceptions to the warm weather breeding season rule are some seedeating birds, e.g., crossbills, and Mourning Dove, which feed their young mainly on seeds. Because they can obtain food for nestlings year round, these species are freed from bondage to the seasons and have been recorded breeding in every month of the year; other species in this category include Gray Jay, Common Raven, and many owls.

In the tropics, where the temperatures remain mild and the days of about equal length year round, wet and dry seasons often govern the abundance of food and cover, and tropical birds too tend to have fixed breeding seasons based on these variables. In tropical rain forests, where rainfall is uniform at all seasons, different species will breed at different times throughout the year but most individual species still follow a characteristic breeding calendar. This seems mysterious, but obviously depends on factors perceived by birds, e.g., fruiting seasons, but not as yet by humans.

It is important to make the distinction between the breeding season in a particular *place*—e.g., roughly April through August in Massachusetts—and the usually much shorter breeding season for any given *species*: Louisiana Waterthrushes in Massachusetts breed between mid-April and about mid-June. Of course, multiple-brooded populations (see BROOD; NEST) have longer breeding seasons than those that rear only a single brood.

The time of the full breeding season is divied-up by some species occupying the same niche, one species breeding early, another late, perhaps a third still later (see DISTRIBUTION, Temporal Effects), and the breeding season may vary (usually by only a few days) from year to year depending on whether the season is "early" or "late." There is considerable evidence that in recent decades breeding seasons in North America and northern Europe are earlier on average in response to global warming.

BREWER, Thomas Mayo, 1814–80 Brewer's Sparrow: *Spizella breweri*); (Brewer's Blackbird: *Euphagus cyanocephalu.* Though he was interested in birds from boyhood until his death, Brewer's capabilities could never be contained in a single field. He was a medical doctor (Harvard), a newspaperman (Boston *Atlas*), an influential figure in the Whig Party, a partner in a successful publishing house, and an electee of the Boston School Committee. In addition to all this, he kept active in ornithological circles. He was a friend of Nuttall's and won Audubon's praise for data and specimens tendered. His chief interest was eggs, but his great work on the subject was never completely published due to the cost of printing the plates. He wrote most of the text of his joint ventures with Baird and Ridgway (see the Bibliography under BAIRD). Gruson (1972–BIOGRAPHY) notes that he was something of a "curmudgeon," and among the younger generation of field ornithologists, could tolerate only William BREWSTER.

BREWSTER, William, 1851–1919 (Brewster's Warbler, originally described as a full species; now recognized as the "dominant" hybrid form of
Blue-winged and Golden-winged Warbler parentage; see HYBRIDIZA-
TION). Perhaps the most prominent of New England naturalists around
the turn of the century Brewster's chief interest was birds, of which he
amassed a significant collection and about which he wrote a number of
faunal works. He was one of the founders (and president for 40 years) of
the Nuttall Ornithological Club at Harvard. This organization was the
progenitor of the American Ornithologists' Union, of which he was also a
founder and president. In addition, he became the first president of the
Massachusetts Audubon Society a seminal organization founded at dawn
of the bird conservation movement. Brewster's father was a successful
banker, a circumstance that allowed the son—after giving "business" a
year's trial—to live his life as a gentleman farmer and devote his energies
to birds. Brewster was admired but also liked by his associates—reputedly
the only member of the younger generation who could get along with the
cranky Thomas BREWER. Though Brewster did some collecting in the
South and in the American tropics, his reputation is strongly tied to New
England, on account of both his faunal studies and his literary evocations
of New England country life (see the Bibliography).

BRIDLED (Tern, Titmouse). In most cases refers to dark linear head
markings which suggest a horse's bridle. In both the Bridled Tern and the
Bridled Titmouse, the line runs from the gape through the eye. Also used
to describe the white eye ring and line that characterize the "ringed" (or
"bridled") phase of the Common Murre in breeding plumage.

BRIGANTINE. Now officially known as the Brigantine Division of the Ed-
win B. Forsythe National Wildlife Refuge. Together with the Barnegat Division, the refuge consists of more than 43,000 acres of tidal marshes (80%),
barrier beaches, several forest types and fields, located just north of Atlantic City. Within the tidal marshes a 1,415-acre impoundment has been
created to combine both fresh, brackish, and salt water habitats and improve bird diversity; water levels are adjusted seasonally, e.g., drawn down
to provide mudflats for feeding shorebirds. The road atop the dike surrounding this managed wetland is ideal for surveying the avian highlights.
"Brigantine" is principally known for concentrations of water birds and
especially for rare migrants such as Ruff, Curlew Sandpiper, Spotted Redshank, Bar-tailed Godwit, and Gyrfalcon (winter); Piping Plover, Osprey,
and Peregrine Falcon nest. The variety of accessible habitats, avian wealth
and drivable dikes, make Brigantine a magnet for birdwatchers nationwide. For more detail including maps, bird lists and a month-by-month
listing of natural highlights, go to http://forsythe.fws.gov/.

BRISTLE (Bristle-thighed Curlew). In birds, a more or less stiff, hair-like feather, lacking a vane and sometimes completely barbless (see Stettenheim 1973–FEATHER, and Fig. 13). A number of the flank feathers of the Bristle-thighed Curlew bear only a few barbs at the base and extend downward an inch or more beyond the contour of the belly plumage. Though certainly no field mark, these bristles are visible in the wild at very close range or with the aid of a telescope.

BROKEN-WING ACT. Describes the characteristic gestures of certain forms of distraction display, especially among the shorebirds, e.g., Killdeer. For evolution and other details, see DISPLAY.

BROOD. A brood consists of all the young hatched from a single clutch of eggs, e.g., Northern Pintails normally rear broods of 7–9 ducklings. "Brooding" is the practice by parent birds of "sitting on" nestlings to maintain sufficient body temperature in the latter as well as to shade them and prevent overheating in direct sunlight, shield them from precipitation, and conceal them from predators. The term is sometimes used loosely to mean INCUBATION, i.e., "brooding of eggs," but is probably more useful if restricted to the narrower definition.

Parent birds that are "in the mood" to sit on nestlings—an innate response that normally follows the laying and subsequent hatching of the eggs—are said to be "broody."

Birds that rear only one "family" in a season are said to be "single-brooded"; those rearing two, "double-brooded"; etc. The brood pattern varies from species to species and among populations of the same species according to climate (length of season). Single and double broods are the rule among the majority of North American birds and more than three broods in a season (treble-brooded) is rare. For more detail on brooding rhythms, see NEST, Pattern and Timing. See also PARENTAL CARE.

BROOD PARASITISM. Describes the laying of eggs by one bird species in the nest of another, "host" species, which rears the changeling(s), often at the expense of some or all of its own young. This behavior has also been called "nest parasitism," but this term is easily mistaken to mean nest piracy—the appropriation of one species' nest by another (e.g., by the Piratic Flycatcher of the Neotropics)—or the infestation of a nest by arthropod parasites (see NEST FAUNA, ECTOPARASITE); "social parasitism" is yet another synonym. See PARASITISM for general definitions.

Intraspecific Brood Parasitism. Laying eggs in the nests of neighboring members of the same species is now known to be a common practice among songbirds and certain other groups of birds including grebes, waterfowl, gallinaceous birds, gulls, and pigeons. It tends to be especially

prevalent when population density is high (e.g., in colonial species) and when good nest sites are scarce. In some cases as many as a quarter (colonial swallows) to three-quarters or more (ducks) of nests have been found to contain the eggs of another pair. European Starling females actually prospect for host nests of their own species and remove an egg from the clutch before laying a replacement. Because such parasitic eggs are virtually identical to those of the host, they are usually accepted (unless the receiving female has not yet laid any of her own eggs) and the unrelated young reared along with the host's own. This model has little or no detrimental effect on the host's reproductive success and gives the parasite's genes an additional survival option. It has been suggested that such parasitism within species may have been an early stage in the evolution of obligate brood parasitism described below.

Facultative Brood Parasitism describes cases in which birds *occasionally* lay eggs in nests of different (usually closely related) species. In North America several ducks practice this casual form of parasitism, and the Redhead and Ruddy Duck avail themselves of the alternative regularly. In the species studied the parasite's eggs typically outnumbered the host's own in completed clutches conferring a reproductive disadvantage on the foster parents. Black-billed and Yellow-billed Cuckoos also parasitize each other occasionally, especially in years when good food supplies permit high egg production (Nolan and Thompson 1975).

Obligate Brood Parasitism refers to species that never build a nest of their own or care for their own eggs or young, including a few taxa of (mainly social) insects and fishes as well as birds. It is characteristic of only about 1% of all bird species in 6 families worldwide, including 1 duck species, the majority of Old World cuckoos in the family Cuculidae (as defined by Sibley and Ahlquist 1990–SYSTEMATICS), 3 species of New World cuckoos (family Neomorphidae); probably all 17 species of honeyguides (Indicatoridae), 5 of 6 cowbird species (Icteridae); 1 species of African weaver, and the whydahs and indigobirds in the genus *Vidua* (Passeridae).

Behavioral Variations. Brood parasitism has evolved independently in the families noted, and its practice varies significantly among them. The Black-headed Duck of South America, the only precocial species in this category, will use virtually any nest it can find (including that of at least one raptor), does not displace eggs or young from the host's nest, takes no food from the host parents, and becomes fully independent within 2 days of hatching; it has therefore been called "the most perfect of avian parasites" (Weller 1968). Even more "virtuous" perhaps is the Giant Cowbird, which according to Smith (1968), actually benefits its host oropendolas in some circumstances by removing botfly larvae from its step-siblings. All of the other obligate brood parasites inflict some degree of harm on their hosts by removal of host eggs or young (by parent or

nestling parasites) by consuming food intended for a nest's rightful inhabitants and/or by taking up inordinate amounts of the parent birds'
time and energy.

The response of the host also varies from apparently complete obliv-
iousness of the deception and sacrifice of its own young to the needs of
the (often much larger) parasite; to rearing the parasite *along with* some
of its own young; evicting the parasitic egg; covering over a parasitized
nest with successive "floors" (an often-recorded response by Yellow Warblers to Brown-headed Cowbird parasitism); or abandonment of the parasitized nest.

No summary of brood parasitism is complete without mentioning
the well-studied case of the Common Cuckoo of Eurasia *(Cuculus
canorus)*. The habits of this common and widespread Old World parasite
have been familiar in a general way for centuries, providing a common
metaphor for sexual insults and many a verse, both good and bad. Only in
this century, however, have the subtleties of the cuckoo's deception been
fully appreciated. One of the most intriguing facts of this (and some other
cuckoo) species is the degree to which it has perfected *egg mimicry.* Since
it generally parasitizes hosts much smaller than itself, it has evolved the
ability to lay small eggs, which are also shaped, colored, and patterned to
match those of the species victimized. This adaptation has led to the evolution of "clans" (gentes) of cuckoos, which specialize in particular host
species. It is a form of polymorphism in which, for example, "wren cuckoos" consistently lay remarkably wren-like eggs exclusively in wren's
nests. In some brood parasites the gape color/pattern of nestlings and
their food-begging calls also mimic those of the host nestlings, further enhancing anonymity and discouraging rejection by host parents. Adult
cuckoos also employ mimicry to facilitate their deception. Many males in
the genus *Cuculus* strongly resemble small hawks (accipiters) in form,
coloration, and manner of flight. When host pair "mobs" the supposed
predator, the female cuckoo, waiting near the nest, plants her egg with
maximum efficiency, actually dropping it in many cases from a perch
above; cuckoo eggs have unusually thick shells which not only protect the
parasite's egg, but in some cases also damages those of the host.

Parasite chicks may be anatomically adapted to eliminate their competition. The concave backs of nestling cuckoos allow them to cradle eggs
or chicks from below and then tip them over the side of the nest. Nestling
honeyguides have strongly hooked bills and simply kill their nest mates
outright.

Identity Crisis? How does a young cuckoo know it is not a warbler and
how to find an appropriate mate? In cuckoos and cowbirds the answer lies
at least partially in their genetically inherited ability to sing, recognize and
respond to the songs of their own species. The African indigobirds by contrast adopt much of their host's identity throughout their lives. In addition

to mimicking the appearance and behaviors of the host nestlings—species of firefinches in the same waxbill family—both males and females learn the song of their host fathers and will mate only with indigobirds that sing or respond to the right firefinch song, including the correct local inflection (Payne 1973–SONG). On the one hand, this improves the odds of cuckolding the right host species and maintaining this remarkable identity bond. However, if an oddball female indigobird places eggs in the "wrong" waxbill nest and the hosts do not reject them, the misplaced young are programmed to learn the ways of their foster parents, and the foundation is laid for the evolution of a new species of indigobird (see SPECIATION; INTELLIGENCE; IMPRINTING). While female cuckoos are also linked to their hosts' identities through genetic lineages, male cuckoo genes have no such constraints and therefore prevent the formation of new cuckoo species based on host fidelity.

For an account of the habits of North America's most successful brood parasites, see COWBIRD.

Brood Parasitism and Bird Conservation. A potential catch-22 in the brood parasite model is that theoretically if the parasite is too "successful," it could put its hosts—and therefore itself—out of business. Under normal circumstances, this unhappiest of endings is avoided by (1) the imperfection of deceptive adaptations, facilitating (2) the ability of many hosts to recognize and reject parasite eggs; (3) asynchrony between parasite laying season and host nesting season allowing some potential host species to successfully rear at least one brood without danger of parasitism; and (4) the ability of many hosts to rear one or more of its own young along with that of a brood parasite. However, where small isolated populations of birds coexist with generalist parasites, local extinctions can occur. Sadly, there are already examples of the worst-case scenario, partly created by human agency. Cowbird populations and distribution have expanded greatly due to habitat alteration and an increase in food sources. This has enabled Brown-headed, Shiny, and other cowbirds to reach hosts from which they were once barred by ecological barriers. Were it not for muscular efforts to control Brown-headed Cowbirds in and around the Huron-Manistee National Forest in northern Michigan, the world's only population of Kirtland's Warbler would probably have vanished forever decades ago. And the endemic Yellow-shouldered Blackbird of Puerto Rico faces a similar threat from the rapidly increasing Shiny Cowbird (Post and Wiley 1977). Furthermore, due to fragmentation of forest habitats, cowbirds can now reach the nests of many more widespread songbird species that were once protected by their preference for the forest interior. The final chapters chronicling the long-term effects on hosts species of the continuing cowbird expansion have yet to be written.

See also PARASITISM; DUMP NEST; COWBIRD; CUCKOO.

BROOD PATCH. Also called "incubation patch." An area of skin on the belly of a bird modified during the breeding season to facilitate incubation of the eggs. It is located for the most part in the area(s) of the abdomen which lack(s) feather tracts (apteria), but down and/or some contour feathers are usually lost or plucked. The resulting area of bare skin becomes somewhat thickened due to an increase in blood vessels as the patch develops. There may be from one (all passerines) to three discrete patches, the number and location varying among different groups of birds. Development begins a few days to a week before laying begins, and lost feathers return with the following pre-basic (post-breeding season) molt. As would seem logical, it is usually only the parent with incubating responsibilities that develops a brood patch, but there are exceptions.

All North American species, except pelicans, tropicbirds, frigatebirds, gannets and boobies, cormorants and anhingas (i.e., the Pelecaniformes), and Crested Auklet, develop brood patches.

See also INCUBATION and R. E. Bailey, *Condor* (1952), 54:121–36.

BROWNSVILLE (Texas). See RIO GRANDE VALLEY.

BUDGERIGAR (or Budgerygah, in Australia; budgie) (BUDGE-uh-ree GAR or GAH). Standard English name for a small (7–8 inches) parrot, *Melopsittacus undulatus,* abundant throughout most of the drier regions of Australia and a very popular "talking" cage bird in Europe and North America. Its natural coloration is largely vivid grass green with a yellow, partially barred head, a blue-green tail, and a brown, scaly back, but pigments have been manipulated in captive bred birds to produce entirely white, blue, or yellow individuals. See AVICULTURE; SONG, Vocal Mimicry. Small naturalized population of budgies in Florida are declining.

BUFFLEHEAD. Standard English name for a single species of sea duck, *Bucephala albeola,* which breeds exclusively and winters largely in North America (continentwide). The name comes from "buffalo head," though not, apparently, from our round-headed American bison but rather from the European wild ox or buffalo. The Latin genus name of this species and the goldeneyes *(Bucephala)* has the same origin. See DUCK.

BULBUL. Standard English name for most of the approximately 120 members of the family Pycnonotidae (order Passeriformes), one of which, the Red-whiskered Bulbul, was accidentally introduced near Miami, Florida, in 1960 and continues to maintain a small population there.

The bulbuls are cut from a "standard" passerine pattern with few remarkable characteristics, but with a wide assortment of color patterns-some quite striking. Many species are gregarious; most are birds of the forest and forest edge. They have broad tastes in small invertebrates and fruits. Their songs are often rather noisy, with some tuneful themes but

little musical distinction. As a family, bulbuls are essentially restricted to Asia and Africa.

The Red-whiskered Bulbul is a medium-sized (8 inches), surpassingly abundant species of India, Southeast Asia and southern China. It builds a cup nest of small sticks, dead leaves, and debris bound with spider silk and lined with finer fibers. The site is a shrub or low tree. The 2 or (usually) 3 eggs are white or pink to light purple, profusely but often finely marked with various shades of brownish-purple speckles and blotches.

According to Newton (1893–96–ORNITHOLOGY), the name bulbul probably originated in Persia, where it referred to a songbird with a reputation similar to the nightingale's; this species may or may not have been what we now call a bulbul; most bulbuls have conspicuous but not notably beautiful songs. Later the name may have echoed the call of a particular pycnonotid species and then been adopted for all of its relatives.

BULLA. Generally, a blister-like structure in bone or other tissue. Many male ducks have such an enlargement in the syrinx at the base of the windpipe (trachea). It may function in the production of characteristic whistling calls, which bulla-less female ducks never utter.

BULLER, Sir Walter Lawry, 1838–1906 (New Zealand Shearwater: *Puffinus bulleri*). A native of New Zealand who practiced law and bird study both in his homeland and in England. He published *A History of the Birds of New Zealand* in England in 1871–74 and *A Manual of the Birds of New Zealand* in 1882.

BUNTING. Standard English name for a large, heterogeneous assortment of birds in two families. In British terminology, bunting refers to seed-eating birds in the family Emberizidae (or tribe Emberizini), which includes the New World sparrows and longspurs. In North America only three emberizids, the Lark, Snow, and McKay's Buntings, are so named, but the term is also used here for the smaller, brightly colored species in the family Cardinalidae, e.g., Indigo and Painted Buntings. For further untangling of the confusing taxonomy and nomenclature of seed eating birds, see FINCH. See also EMBERIZID, CARDINAL-GROSBEAK and SPARROW-BUNTING.

Lockwood (1993–NAMES) says that "bunting" literally means (or *meant*) "a plump or thickset person or creature" and its first recorded use in a bird name c. 1300 referred specifically to the prototypically plump (Emberizid) Corn Bunting of Europe. The Cardinalid buntings are also on the plump side and one can see how all of this confusion might have begun.

BURSA OF FABRICIUS. A sac or pocket which opens via a duct from the upper (dorsal) wall of the last section of the cloaca (proctodeum). All young birds have such a sac, but it gradually shrivels, and its opening to

the cloaca disappears as a bird reaches sexual maturity. Its function in a bird's system is not completely understood. The fact that, like the thymus, it is best developed in youth suggests that it may have an influence on growth or it may function as part of the immune system. Its usefulness to the ornithologists is more clear-cut: it is a means of determining age, especially in large birds, e.g., waterfowl. The investigator spreads open the bird's vent and examines the dorsal wall of the cloaca. If the opening to the bursa is present, the bird is immature. It is even possible by measuring the degree to which the sac is involuted to fix age within a year. As may be imagined, the delicacy of the procedure makes it impractical with small birds.

BUSHTIT. Standard English name for a single species, *Psaltriparus minimus,* family Aegithalidae (which also includes the long-tailed tits); order Passeriformes). Recent analyses (Sheldon and Gill 1996 *Syst. Biol.* 45:471–493) suggest that this species is more closely related to the Old World warblers (family Sylviidae) than to the tits and penduline tits with which they have traditionally been associated. The black-eared "morph," or color phase, of the species, which predominates from the mountains of west Texas to Guatemala, was once considered a distinct species, Black-eared Bushtit.

In general form and coloration, Bushtits are indeed tit-like with small pointed bills, short but strong legs, and generally grayish coloration. However, at less than 4 inches they have proportionally longer tails. Bushtits are birds of scrub oaks, chaparral, and riparian brush. They are highly gregarious, often traveling in feeding flocks of 50 or more individuals, sometimes in company with kinglets and other small songbirds. Such flocks move rapidly through brush or copses, nervously but deftly probing bark crevices and gleaning leaves in search of insect food. They also eat some berries.

The presence of Bushtits is often first detected by the faint lisping twitter produced by the flock as a whole; it is the only sound the species makes.

The Bushtit nest is typically located in a bush or tree 4–50 feet from the ground. It consists of a distinctive, rather untidy, pendulous sack, which may be a foot long, though it is often only half as long; the entrance is near the top. The nest is made with grasses, mosses, lichens, leaves, and a great variety of other materials, bound with spider silk and heavily lined with feathers, fur, and plant down. Bushtits may lay as many as 15 immaculate white eggs per clutch (usually 5–7).

The Bushtit occurs from southwestern British Columbia south into Baja California and Guatemala and east in North America to western Colorado and Texas. It is non-migratory. Of the seven other species in this family, one ranges from western Europe across the Paleartic region and all the others are residents of Asia.

BUTEO (BOO-tee-oh [Latin genus] or BYOO-tee-oh [vernacular English collective term]). A genus of broad-winged, short-tailed hawks. In a broader sense, any hawk with these characteristics, whether or not it belongs to that genus. Thus, the Common Black Hawk *(Buteogallus anthracinus)* may be included among North American "buteos." This broader usage is analogous to the British term "buzzard" (see below).

BUZZARD. In North America this is a slang term for the New World VULTURES. In British terminology it is more usefully employed to distinguish broad winged, short-tailed raptors in the genus *Buteo* and similar forms. In this system our Red-tailed Hawk would be Red-tailed Buzzard and the term HAWK would be reserved for the Accipiters, as falconers have long done. The vernacular name derives from the Latin verb *buteo,* meant to suggest the shrill call of these raptors.

CACHING. The practice of storing food for future use, practiced by jays, tits, and other species. For more detail see under FOOD/FEEDING.

CAECUM (SEE-kum) (pl.: caeca). A narrow sack or, as frequently described, "a blind tube" that opens onto the digestive tract where the small intestine meets the large. Sometimes in pairs; notably present in species that feed largely on plant tissue (e.g., grouse). See DIGESTIVE SYSTEM.

CAGE BIRD. Avian house pet. For favored species and other details, see CAPTIVITY, BIRDS IN.

CAHOW (kuh-HOW). A traditional name for the Bermuda Petrel, a species of gadfly petrel *(Pterodroma cahow)*. Once considered a subspecies of the Black-capped Petrel *(Pterodroma hasitata),* current analysis based on call (Bretagnole 1995–GADFLY PETREL), postulates that the two species are not closely related. Once ranging to the Bahamas, this rare tubenose is now restricted to a few small islands in Bermuda where it is slowly being pulled back from the brink of extinction by strenuous conservation efforts. Still considered globally endangered, with a total population estimated at 180 individuals. Now seen rarely but with some consistency on pelagic trips off North Carolina. "Cahow" echoes one of this species' calls.

CALAMUS (KAL-uh-mus) (pl.: calami). The lower, hollow portion of the shaft of a feather before the beginning of the vane. See FEATHER and Fig. 13.

CALL (or call note). A vocal sound, often brief, uttered by a bird on a regular basis and distinct from its "song." A given species usually has a repertoire of different call notes that convey a variety of behavioral information within a migratory or feeding flock or between parents and young birds. Many species have highly distinctive call notes by which they can be readily identified. See SONG, Calls; also BIRD CALLS; GOOD CALL/BAD CALL.

CAMOUFLAGE. See COLOR AND PATTERN, Concealment.

CANARY. In its wild form, *Serinus canaria* is closely related to the widespread European Serin *(Serinus serinus)* but is restricted to Madeira, the Azores, and, of course, the Canaries. It was first introduced as a cage bird in Europe in the sixteenth century and has become popular worldwide for its loud, musical, and varied song. In its natural state its plumage is streaky with grayish back, wings, crown, and tail but it has been artificially bred to produce a pure-yellow strain as well as an astonishing number of variations involving color, song, and even feather structure. In the wild the famous song is often given accompanying a courtship flight. See CAPTIVITY, BIRDS IN.

CANNIBALISM. The eating of an individual of a given species by another individual of the same species. With reference to birds, most often applied to the eating of "extra" young birds in the nest by the parent birds or other nestlings (see SIBLICIDE). This is recorded in a number of families (e.g., boobies, pelicans, storks, eagles, owls), especially when hatching is staggered and the earliest hatchling dominates in size and parental attention. In seasons of short food supply, the youngest/weakest birds of a brood are often allowed to languish in favor of the survival of the older/stronger birds and cannibalism may serve as an even more "efficient" means to the same end. For a comprehensive treatment see Mock (1984, 1987–YOUNG, DEVELOPMENT OF).

In another context, certain rapacious species (e.g., gulls) may kill and eat young, sick, or injured members of their own species.

CANNON NET. A device for trapping flocks of medium-sized to large ground-feeding birds such as waterfowl or shorebirds; the net is attached to rockets that propel the net over the flock, enclosing it before the birds have time to take flight. The simultaneous firing of the rockets is achieved by electric remote control. The technique requires a situation where birds are feeding or roosting at close quarters or a place to which they can be lured by bait.

CANOPY FEEDING. A practice peculiar to several species of herons in which the wings are spread forward to shade the area of water in which a feeding bird is standing, presumably affording some advantage in catching prey. It has been suggested that the canopy acts as a trap of sorts, with fish attracted to a suddenly available patch of shade. It also seems plausible that the gesture may act as a simple sun shade for herons feeding in the open, where glare off the water obstructs a clear view of activity below the surface. It is not yet clear to what extent either or both of these possibilities explain this distinctive behavior.

Fig. 5. *Canopy feeding* is characteristic feeding behavior for the Reddish Egret. The shadow cast apparently acts not only as a sunshade but also serves to attract prey such as these silversides.

Canopy feeding is most highly developed in the Black Heron (*Egretta ardesiaca*) of Africa, but it is also characteristic of the Reddish Egret (see Fig. 5), and a less elaborate form of wing shading is occasionally practiced by the Tricolored Heron and the Snowy Egret. See Hancock and Elliott (1978–HERON). Not to be confused with birds feeding in the top foliage layer of a tree.

CANVASBACK. Standard English name for a single species of bay duck, *Aythya valisineria,* which breeds exclusively in North America. It was praised by Audubon and has been praised by many other epicures before and since for its excellent flavor. The light color and mottling of the back plumage give it a resemblance to canvas. See DUCK and A. H. Hochbaum's classic 1944 monograph, *The Canvasback on a Prairie Marsh.*

CAP. An area of contrasting color on the crown, e.g., the black "cap" of the male Wilson's Warbler; or including the entire top of the head from the bill through the nape, e.g., the Black-capped Chickadee (see Fig. 19) or Black-capped Vireo.

CAPE MAY (New Jersey). One of the oldest and best-known migratory bird localities in North America, this peninsula projects into Delaware Bay south of Atlantic City. It comprises barrier beach, dunes, salt marsh, freshwater ponds, pastureland, scrubby copses, and coastal pine/oak woodland. This diversity of habitats, its coastal location, and the cul-de-sac that the point forms to concentrate southward-bound migrants make Cape May a magnet for a superb variety of bird species, especially raptors, shorebirds (including a notable woodcock flight in early November), and frequently spectacular numbers of passerines of many species. The peak of popularity among birdwatchers is in the fall (late August–early November), but the area is also interesting for wintering water birds and is far from boring during spring migration. For detailed and readable account of this locality's birdlife, see works by Stone, Connor, Dunne, and Sibley referenced in the bibliography.

The place also gives its name to one of our handsomest wood warblers, which nests in the spruce-fir forests of Canada and winters largely in the West Indies. Audubon noted in his journals that "I never met a single bird of this kind on my rambles," but gave it this name on one of his "mixed bag" plates of warblers. The specimens he painted from came from his friend Edward HARRIS, who shot them near Moorestown, New Jersey, which is just northeast of Camden.

CAPON (KAY-pon). A rooster that has been castrated and then fattened for the dinner table.

CAPTIVITY, BIRDS IN. The reasons for and circumstances in which people keep wild bird species in captivity are surprisingly varied. Some examples follow.

Cage Birds. A great many people who have little or no interest in observing birdlife in nature keep birds in captivity mainly for the simple amusement and company that a pet bird can provide. Originally, of course, native birds—especially those with fine songs—were trapped for this purpose. And while this is now illegal in Europe and North America, it remains a common custom throughout much of the world. The species most commonly kept as pets in the developed world are now bred in captivity especially for the pet market and can be bought cheaply in an astonishing array of color variations, which may include little trace of the original plumage characteristics of their species. The best-known pet cage birds are the Canary, derived originally from the wild Serin *(Serinus canaria)* of the Canary Islands, the Azores, and Madeira and justly famed for its voice, which, along with its plumage characteristics, has been "improved" in captivity; the Budgerigar *(Melopsittacus undulatus)*, or "parakeet" as it is often called in America, native of arid regions of Australia and capable of making some word-like sounds with training; the Cockatiel *(Nymphicus hollandicus)*, another native of the Australian interior; the Hill or Talking Mynah *(Gracula religiosa)*, a resident of humid forest in southern Asia, and a truly remarkable vocal mimic, which not only enunciates words but copies the tone of the imitated sound; and several species of strikingly patterned waxbill finches (family Estrildidae), e.g., the Zebra Finch *(Taeniopygia guttata)* of Africa and Australasia. In many American families having a caged budgie is part of the child rearing ritual, falling between the goldfish and the puppy as a means of instilling youthful responsibility.

Among rural peoples wild songbirds are often captured and kept for their spectacular plumage, rich song, and/or some reputed spiritual powers. Typically, these captives in their (sometimes ornate) cages are hung in house or garden much as one would place wind chimes, a decorative ornament or a good luck charm. In China, various species of laughing thrushes (among the most operatic of songbirds) are taken by their owners on regular outings to neighborhood parks to enjoy the company of— and even compete with—their fellow prisoners.

Yet a different ethos prevails among keepers of some of the larger parrots, which have become increasingly popular in North America for their exotic quality and brilliant plumage as well as the ability (of a few species) to "talk." These birds, some of which cost thousands of dollars fall more into the category of grandiose decorations (e.g., in the gardens of luxury hotels), status symbols or trappings of "cool," and in some cases are worn, like boa constrictors, around college campuses and elsewhere as personal adornments. It is in this last category that some of the most serious conservation issues arise (see below).

Collections. Some aviculturists collect birds more or less in the way that a philatelist collects stamps, i.e., with a taste for the beauty and the rarity of particular species and a desire to have "a full set" of a particular group, e.g., certain colorful waxbills or small Australasian parrots. Most birdwatchers and other North Americans think of cage birds as tending to the exotic and may be surprised to find that there is a thriving and perfectly legal trade in songbirds in which a collector in Desmoines can legally buy and keep a European Song Thrush and many other "soft-billed species" as long as they have been bred in captivity. Awareness of this other sort of bird lover has given fits to more than one Bird Record Committee trying to sort out the provenance of, say, a July Brambling (see Escapes, below, and VAGRANT, VAGRANCY). Apart from cage birds there is a tradition among aristocratic (or at least financially well-heeled) landowners with some acres of parkland of assembling private synoptic collections of waterfowl or pheasants, both of which families of birds offer great diversity, attractive plumage, and relative ease of keeping and breeding. While this hobby doubtless arose from the frivolous tradition of the royal aviary, many collectors of these birds now add the virtue of rearing rare species for conservation purposes to the aesthetic pleasure of gazing on pretty feathers. Perhaps the most famous of such collections is the Severn Wildfowl Trust in Slimbridge, England (Gloucestershire), founded by Sir Peter Scott in 1946. Though it is open to the public, Slimbridge (and many other large waterfowl collections today) is more than a zoo of odd ducks. It serves as a base for research into breeding biology and other aspects of behavior, population dynamics, hybridization, disease, and the like and also acts as a gene reserve and breeding center for rare and endangered species. In North America many much smaller collections are kept by hobbyists, and this sometimes plays havoc with authentication of anatid records (see under Escapes, below).

The ultimate live wild bird collection is of course the zoo aviary. Like most zoo exhibits of yore, these tended to be dreary enclosures inhabited by a random assortment of maimed raptors, out-of-favor peacocks, some local gulls crashing the aviary for the free eats, and the odd Crowned Crane traded as surplus from another zoo. Alas, such places still exist, mainly in the developing world and as small town "petting zoos" or "wildlife parks." Happily, however, most modern metropolitan zoos, responding to their patrons' increasingly humane attitudes and consequent falling attendance have cleaned up these eyesores, provided at least a semblance of appropriate habitat for their charges (most of which are unreleasable due to injury or other factors) and in some cases dedicated themselves to the captive-rearing of endangered species (see below).

Conservation Issues. While most exotic-bird collectors are scrupulous with regard to dealing in rare species and do not try to evade import-export laws, it is nonetheless a fact that a lucrative trade in some of the

world's rarest and most beautiful birds, such as certain parrots and wax-bills, continues to thrive. The critical conundrum is that the rarer a species is (or becomes), the more desirable it is to certain collectors, raising its price in the black market. In tropical countries where most illegal bird trade activity occurs, the economic structure is also tilted against the birds. Macaws, for example, bring such high prices that a poor nest robber can make a year's wages stealing a few nestlings, while one or more middlemen as well as the retailer also make substantial profits. This ugly partnership between poverty and the exploitation of exotic animals has decimated populations of once common species and driven some of the rarer ones, e.g., the surpassingly beautiful Glaucous and Lear's Macaws, over the brink of extinction in the wild.

Legality. Until relatively recently there were few laws preventing capture, sale, or possession of rare birds and no conventions prohibiting international trade in such living commodities. This situation has improved, especially with the enactment and increasingly rigorous enforcement of the Convention on International Trade in Endangered Species of Wild Fauna and Flora (see CITIES under LAWS PROTECTING BIRDLIFE for details of its provisions), but due to the high profitability of the illegal trade, abuses are still common. Some states have also done their part in stemming the exploitation of wild bird populations. New York, for example, requires that all birds sold as pets be bred in captivity. Unfortunately, laws restricting capture, sale, and importation of wild birds are based on lists of species perceived to be vulnerable at present. The door remains open both in countries of origin and in North America for international trade in more common species, e.g., many species of South American tanagers.

Captive Breeding. Breeding birds in captivity is an inherent part of the aviculturist's craft and a number of journals (see Bibliography) serve a substantial clientele who rear birds simply for pleasure and in some cases (entirely legal) profit. There is also a clear conservation benefit if rarer species can be bred in captivity for the pet and exotic species trades, eliminating the need for decimating wild populations and the extortionate cost of illegal trade. It is only fairly recently, however, that avicultural skills have been adapted to the rearing of endangered bird species in captivity for eventual release back into an appropriate habitat in the wild. Species exploited for the pet trade are only one group of rare birds benefiting from captive breeding. Peregrine Falcons ended up on the endangered species list because of pesticide poisoning (see THREATS OF HUMAN ORIGIN TO BIRDLIFE) and have just been removed from the list due in no small measure to successful captive breeding and release programs. And similar success stories can now be told about the Whooping Crane and the California Condor (see CRANE and CONDOR), each threatened with extinction for different reasons. Unfortunately, not all such breeding and release

programs have been so successful—witness the recent failure of Thick-billed Parrots to "take" in their former range in Arizona. This underscores not only the difficulty of rearing wild birds in captivity but also the problems associated with finding suitable habitat in which to release rare species—many of which have become rare as a result of habitat loss.

Escapes. Inherent in the concept of captivity—as every prison drama emphasizes—is the possibility of escape. Wing-clipped birds in waterfowl collections that regain their ability to fly, for example, may depart and take up with nearby free-living populations of similar species. Florida and California support a diverse exotic avifauna, including more than 20 species in the parrot family. These may be fugitives from "jungle garden" zoos or cage birds, which are frequently released because the owner becomes bored with them or for more understandable, if misplaced, humanitarian reasons.

Escaped birds cause at least two kinds of problems: (1) If they are able to breed successfully and proliferate, they may compete for habitat with native species and/or become pests. The most of obvious examples here are the European Starling and House Sparrow (see EXOTIC SPECIES and INTRODUCED BIRDS), but similar issues arise with the House Finch, which is native to North America but not to the Northeast, which it has now populated extensively as the resulted of the escape of illegal caged birds. (2) Records of species that might plausibly reach North America under their own steam are made ambiguous by birds that have escaped from some form of captivity. This difficulty arises most often in the case of Palearctic waterfowl, many species of which are kept in collections in North America. But many Bird Record Committees are now becoming aware that there is a thriving North American trade in Palearctic songbirds, including species of cardueline finches and thrushes, which might well arrive here aided only by a westerly gale. In a few cases the origins of escaped individuals can be established by inquiring of known collectors about recent losses. However, a negative response doesn't always eliminate doubt.

If suspected escaped birds are evaluated according to the following criteria, it is usually possible to see where the burden of proof should be: (1) Is the species frequently kept in captivity in North America? (2) Is it a migratory species or a permanent resident within its normal range? (3) Is it particularly susceptible to weather patterns (e.g., hurricanes) that might explain its occurrence outside its normal limits, and has any such weather pattern occurred recently? (4) Is the species abundant within its normal range or comparatively scarce? (5) Does the individual bird show any signs of having been in captivity, i.e., unusual tameness or (in the hand) callused feet, broken feathers, or other symptoms common among captive birds?

Even such an analysis will not resolve all such quandaries. For example, Barnacle Geese have occurred both in well-documented cases of natural vagrancy and equally proven escapes from waterfowl collections.

In such cases the only credible solution for bird record committees may be to do as much research as is practical, record all details of the occurrence, and publish the findings with a consensus opinion (if one exists) without making a (by definition arbitrary) judgment on the quality of the record.

For another perspective on this problem, see Ryan (1972–ESCAPES). See also EXOTIC SPECIES; VAGRANT, VAGRANCY; VERIFICATION OF RECORDS.

CAPTURE (of wild birds). Men have always caught and killed birds for food. In many large seabird colonies or on remote islands where large predators were unknown to the native birds, this required no more effort or ingenuity than it takes to club a tame bird over the head and haul it back to the campfire or ship's galley. Boobies are so named for what sailors perceived as their foolish innocence, and the "booby hatch" was originally the opening to a hold under the poop deck of a ship where live boobies were stored to provision extended stays at sea. In most cases, however, birds were too wary (or became so) to be simply picked up or subdued on the spot, and over time a number of techniques and devices—from the rudimentary to the sophisticated—have been invented to trick birds into captivity.

Fire and other forms of bright light have long been known to both attract birds and render them helpless in certain circumstances. Natives of Central America have caught hundreds of songbird and shorebird migrants by lighting bonfires on high mountain peaks at the proper season; and both primitive hunters and bird banders are aware that roosting birds can often be captured easily in large numbers at night with the aid of a torch or flashlight. Even nocturnal birds such as nightjars may be dazzled by light and allow themselves to be approached and even picked up, and banders use this effect to net resting shorebirds at night.

Several cultures have concocted substances from plants that are so sticky that birds perching on branches thus "limed" are held fast. And putting soporific chemicals in drinking water has also proven effective for capturing certain types of birds.

A major breakthrough in game-catching of all kinds was the invention of snares and nets, once made out of animal hair, more recently out of fine synthetic fibers. Inconspicuous slip loops placed where birds walk, for example, catch birds well, though setting such snares and recovering them consumes much time and effort. Variations are, of course, practically innumerable. Greenland Inuit catch Dovekies out of the air above their nesting colonies using long-handled dip nets, and similar methods have been widely adapted to catch both flying and sitting birds. More ingenuity but less physical exertion is required in using devices such as "clap" or "bow" nets, which consist of a furled net fixed to the ground at one edge and attached to a pole hinged to a peg or bow along the opposite

edge. A pull cord is then tied to the bow or pole and held by the would-be trapper concealed nearby. When the bird is lured to the baited catching area, the furled net is pulled over it. A rocket-powered modification of this principle is used to capture whole flocks of large birds (see CANNON NET for details). Probably the most widely used bird-trapping device today is the exceedingly fine nylon mist net, which, when properly set, is virtually invisible and effectively entangles most small to medium-sized birds that fly into it (see BANDING for details of operation).

In addition to nets are what might be termed "structural" traps, all of which require some initiative on the part of the victim, usually elicited by means of bait or a lure. Perhaps the simplest of such traps is a box propped up over a baited area with a stick. A string is attached to the stick and held by the trapper, who watches from his hiding place until a bird comes to feed on the bait and then pulls out the peg, letting the box fall over the quarry. Some very elaborate structural bird traps have been invented, most of them relying on a funnel or lobster-trap principle, whereby the birds are lured or encouraged to wander into a wide "mouth" and soon find themselves unable to return or unable to perceive the narrow escape route (see HELIGOLAND TRAP and DECOY for more detail on such traps).

It should be emphasized that, except for a few introduced and pest species, it is illegal to trap birds in North America without a federal permit, and these are granted only for such legitimate purposes as BANDING, FALCONRY, and emergency control of bird pests. See LAWS PROTECTING BIRDLIFE for particulars.

For a comprehensive account of this subject, see Bub (1991–BANDING).

CARACARA (CAH-ruh-CAH-ruh). Standard English name for all 10 members (1 extinct) of the subfamily Caracarinae (family Falconidae; order Falconiformes), 1 of which breeds in North America.

Taxonomists assure us that the caracaras are so closely related anatomically to the falcons that they should be placed in the same family. Superficially, however, they seem to be made up of equal parts of hawk and vulture. The single North American species, Crested Caracara *(Caracara plancus)*, is typical, with long legs, a heavy bill for tearing flesh, and a broad area of bare skin over the face and base of the bill; this, like the vultures' naked heads, probably evolved in conjunction with the eating of greasy, decomposing carrion. Caracaras are nearly omnivorous, taking in all kinds of waste matter and small animals (alive as well as dead), including insects; they have even been known to eat some vegetable matter and wade in shallow water to catch fish.

The nests of caracaras are bulky, messy accumulations of sticks and other plant matter placed in trees, in cacti, on ledges, or on open ground and lined (if at all) with dung, bits of carrion, and other organic debris.

The 2–3 (rarely, 4) eggs are white to buff or lavender, usually densely speckled, the whole overlaid with heavy dark splotching covering almost the entire surface.

The vocal repertoire of the caracara subfamily as a whole contains a broad selection of croaks, squeaks, and screams as well as some rather haunting "well-articulated" phrases. The subfamily name, a Tupian word, is derived from the common call of the Crested Caracara, which is usually described as a rattle.

The caracaras are restricted to the New World and are most diverse in South America, whence one species reaches Antarctica. The Guadalupe Caracara, once endemic to Guadalupe Island off Baja California, became extinct about 1900. Our one handsome species is a permanent resident in southern Florida, Texas, Arizona, and New Mexico; the 42nd *AOU Checklist Supplement* (2000) has recently adopted the assertion (Dove and Banks 1999) that our northern form is a distinct species *(Polyborus cheriway)* to be distinguished from the Neotropical *P. plancus* (Southern Caracara).

CARDINAL. Standard English name for 8 species of finches in several genera, 7 in the family Emberizidae and 2 in the Cardinalidae. One of these, the Northern Cardinal *(Cardinalis cardinalis),* is common virtually throughout eastern North America as well as in the extreme Southwest. It is one of the most familiar and best-loved of American songbirds, not least, perhaps, because it seems to prefer man-made habitat such as hedgerows and suburban plantings and visits bird feeders readily. A measure of this affection is the fact that more states (7!) have adopted it as the state bird than any other species (see STATE/PROVINCIAL BIRDS). Within the last 25 years it has undergone a marked northward extension of its range (see DISTRIBUTION). Though not called a cardinal, the Pyrrhuloxia of the arid southwest is one of the three members of the genus *Cardinalis.*

The Latin derivation of "cardinal" refers to the high station of the Roman Catholic official of that name, i.e., a "cardinal bishop"; the association with red comes from the cardinal's garb, especially the red hat bestowed on cardinals by the Pope. However, in the illogical way of the coining of vernacular names, the 6 species of South American emberizid cardinals are neither all red nor all crested and one of them is accurately named Yellow Cardinal!

CARDINAL-GROSBEAK. Collective name for the 42 species of fruit- and seed-eating birds in the Family Cardinalidae (Order Passeriformes) 10 of which breed in North America; another 3 species occur as vagrants from Mexico. Sibley and Monroe (1990–CHECKLIST) classify this group as a tribe (Cardinalini) in the subfamily (Emberizinae) of the family Fringillidae. The Cardinalids include the *Pheucticus* grosbeaks (including Rose-

breasted and Black-headed), the *Cardinalis* cardinals (including Pyrrhuloxia), the *Passerina* buntings (including Blue Grosbeak), the saltators and Dickcissel.

These birds all have fairly heavy to very heavy bills, and in most species the males are very colorful at least in alternate (summer) plumage. The male Painted Bunting, for example, is arguably the gaudiest North American bird.

Most species of cardinal-grosbeaks forage with equal facility on the ground or in shrubbery and trees (depending, of course, on preferred habitat), where they feed on a wide variety of insects (e.g., moth larvae, grasshoppers, beetles), fruits, and seeds. Most come readily to feeders. Their songs are typically loud whistles or gentler, protracted warbles, except for the Dickcissel's, which is buzzy and sparrow-like.

The nests of these finches are comparatively small, loose, or compact cups made of thin twigs, coarse grasses, dead leaves, and often bits of paper, cotton, snakeskin, or other miscellaneous debris and lined with finer grasses, plant fibers, and hair. The 2–5 (average varies) eggs vary widely among species: ground color white to pale blue or green; immaculate to heavily blotched, speckled, and streaked with brown or reddish.

The cardinal-grosbeaks are confined to the New World and achieve their greatest diversity in the Neotropics. As a whole, this group is widely distributed south of the coniferous forest zone in North America, though only one species (Blue Grosbeak) has a continuous continentwide distribution here. The closely related Rose-breasted/Black-headed Grosbeaks replace each other east/west and hybridize to some degree where they overlap in the Great Plains. One is tempted to see a similar relationship between the eastern Indigo Bunting and the western Lazuli Bunting, but recent research (Klicka et al. 2001) shows that the closest relative of the latter is the Blue Grosbeak. All members of this family except Northern Cardinal, Pyrrhuloxia, and the southern Florida population of Painted Bunting migrate from their North American breeding ranges to winter in Latin America.

For the family Emberizidae, see SPARROW-BUNTING; for Fringillidae, see FRINGILLID FINCHES.

For name derivations, see CARDINAL; PYRRHULOXIA; BUNTING; DICKCISSEL.

CARDIOVASCULAR SYSTEM. See CIRCULATORY SYSTEM.

CARDUELINE FINCHES. See FRINGILLID FINCHES.

CARE OF DISTRESSED BIRDS (young, sick, injured, oiled). It is a credit to our species that the word "human" carries a strong connotation of sympathy for our fellow creatures. This is nowhere more clearly manifested

than in the common inclination to try to "nurse" birds or other wild animals on which some misfortune has fallen. Though understandable and praiseworthy this is almost always a mistake. Here are some reasons why.

NATURE IS A HARSH MOTHER and puts enormous pressure on most organisms, including birds, to be nearly perfect in function. Injuries to which humans can readily adjust—a limp or blindness in one eye—may put a bird at a fatal disadvantage in surviving the threats of predation that it meets daily. A bird that has truly been "cured" or successfully reared must be able to participate fully in the role characteristic of its species in the wild, to find enough to eat, to reproduce, and to avoid predators. This goal may be simply impossible for human nurses to achieve in cases in which birds have suffered some form of physical damage.

Mortality rates in birds are also much higher than in humans. For example, only about 50% of young songbirds survive to adulthood. This fact is one way of explaining to children that people and birds are fundamentally different in many ways.

THE ODDS of a nonspecialist saving (in the above sense) a bird with a serious problem may be reckoned at about 10 to 1 *against* success, and in many cases, e.g., unfledged nestlings, the success rate is substantially lower. This grim statistic is stated not to discourage would-be Florence Nightingales, but to make clear the difficulty of the task and the frustration of possible failure. Children, who are often injured animals' best friends, are especially likely to embark on a salvation project with overly high hopes and to be badly disappointed by the death of their charge.

LONG HOURS AND CONSIDERABLE PATIENCE are necessary in treating many bird patients. Very young birds, for example, must be fed almost constantly and in most cases—not understanding the benevolent intentions of their keepers—birds make feeding and dressing of wounds as difficult as possible. Administering effective animal care, even to a single individual, is not unlike taking on a part-time (or even full-time) job. Putting a sick or injured bird in a box with a dish of water and a piece of lettuce or a dog biscuit, though well-intentioned, is just not good enough. Inadequate care may simply prolong suffering or be worse for the bird than leaving it in the wild.

HUMANS ARE INADEQUATE PARENTS for young birds despite the best of intentions. We tend to think of the natural "cruelties" from which we can protect helpless baby birds, but forget that we are incapable of giving them an introduction to the ways of their species in the wild. This puts human-reared birds at some disadvantage (at least initially), even if we wean them as soon as possible.

STATE AND FEDERAL LAWS now prohibit keeping wild birds (except for the non-native Rock Doves, European Starlings, and House Sparrows), even for the bird's own good, unless a special permit has been issued. The nearest office of your state fish and wildlife department can tell you what

permits are required if you are interested in becoming a licensed animal rehabilitator.

THE BEST OPTIONS. The implications of the above are that in general people encountering birds in some form of distress should avail themselves of one of the following options:

1. Leave the bird where you find it or if it has been removed from this location take it back. In many cases the bird either does not require help (see under "Baby" Birds, below) or its suffering will be prolonged by trying to help it. If the bird is in imminent danger (e.g., in traffic or being stalked by a cat), you can try to remove it to a safer location. In the case of large birds, e.g., a heron, gull, or raptor, be extremely cautious; they are not aware that you are trying to help them, are experienced in defending themselves, and can inflict serious injuries with their sharp bills and claws.

2. Seek professional help. Call you local animal control office or your nearest conservation organization (e.g., Audubon society), humane organization, or state wildlife agency. These contacts may be able to direct you to a local licensed wildlife rehabilitator or, if not, they can tell you what your options are. Keep in mind that most of these agencies receive hundreds of calls in a season about distressed animals and do not have sufficient staff to retrieve them or care for all of them. Sadly, in a great many cases, the animal in question will have to be euthanized (put down).

What follows are some common situations and further information on dealing with them.

"BABY" BIRDS. The first and most frequent mistake made by saviors of bird "orphans" is coming to the rescue prematurely. Young songbirds leave the nest before they can fly or find food for themselves and are fed and defended by their parents until they are independent—usually in about three weeks. Such birds will have a full coat of feathers, though these will not be fully grown. If you find such a bird, it is best to leave it where it is and assume the parents are off fetching it food or waiting for you to go away. If someone brings you such a bird, tell her to take it back to where it was found. *Touching young birds does not discourage parent birds from caring for them.*

FALLEN NESTS. Not infrequently nests containing young birds are blown or otherwise dislodged from their places in trees. Here again the best solution is to leave the birds in the wild. Find the original nest site and replace the nest; tie it in place with string, if necessary. If the nest has been destroyed, any reasonable substitute—e.g., a small basket—that will hold the young securely will do. Both active fledglings and fallen nestlings are vulnerable to cats and dogs (see CATS); anything you can do to minimize this hazard will greatly improve a young suburban bird's chances for survival. If you can't stand leaving a "helpless" youngster on an open lawn,

you can move it into some *nearby* cover, to set your (or your child's) mind at ease.

SICK, INJURED, AND OILED BIRDS. Distressed adult birds that you encounter may be only slightly injured and capable of a rapid recovery or be suffering from a condition that is beyond your ability to remedy. The following guidelines may be helpful in dealing with such situations while you contact a wildlife professional.

Assess the Problem. Birds that have been struck by a car or have hit a window may be only temporarily stunned, and protecting them from predators for a few hours or days may indeed increase their life spans significantly. Problems such as broken wings, internal injuries, or advanced diseases may already be beyond the stage at which the best of care can be expected to return the bird to the wild. In such cases leave the bird in the wild and/or seek professional help.

WDQ. If the bird is in your possession, the best thing to do for it while you are seeking help is to keep it Warm, in the Dark, and Quiet. Many distressed birds regardless of the extent of their injuries are in shock and it is best to make them secure and then leave them alone for at least several hours. Do not handle them more than absolutely necessary. Do not try to give them food or water; this can actually be fatal to a traumatized bird.

Oiled Birds. Water birds are very vulnerable to even small amounts of petroleum in their plumage. It mats the feathers, destroying the natural insulation that allows them to maintain body temperature while swimming and diving in cold water (see THREATS OF HUMAN ORIGIN TO BIRDLIFE). If the oiling is extensive, even professional treatment will probably not suffice to save a bird's life. If the amount of oil is small, it may be possible to clean the feathers and allow the bird's natural insulation system to repair itself. But this requires at least several days, and the bird's recovery is much more likely if this time is spent under the care of someone experienced with rehabilitating oiled birds.

Euthanasia. Despite the best of intentions and meticulous care, many birds will not respond to the "first responder" treatments described above and will become clearly moribund. Rather than prolong probable suffering you may wish to "euthanize" the bird. A painless method for small birds is to soak several balls of cotton in motor ether (available at auto supply stores; chloroform is not obtainable without prescription) and place them with the bird in a container with an airtight lid for at least 15 minutes. The bird will "go to sleep" painlessly. (Do not allow the cotton or ether to come in contact with the bird, as this might be painful.)

Hygiene. Transmission of salmonella and other conditions is possible from handling birds, so you should follow the basic sanitary precautions of covering any cuts you may have on your hands and washing your hands thoroughly after handling a bird, whether or not it seems sick. Many wild birds (especially sick ones) are host to a variety of small

invertebrates on their bodies (see ECTOPARASITE), which, while mostly not transmittable to human beings, can make contact with an avian patient unpleasant.

CARINA (kuh-RYE-nuh) (carinate [KAIR-uh-nate]). A keel-like ridge, a basic form found on parts of many species of plants and animals. In birds it usually refers to the keel of the breastbone (sternum) found to some degree in all nonratite birds (see RATITE); "carinate"—literally, having a carina—is sometimes used as a synonym for nonratite.

CARNIVOROUS. Flesh-eating; generally reserved for those animals (and a few plants) that catch and eat live prey, usually to the exclusion of other food. Thus, vultures, which prefer carrion, may be excluded from classification as true avian carnivores. Members of the hawk, owl, and shrike families usually spring to mind at the mention of carnivorous birds, but herons, some ducks, and a variety of other waterbirds are equally carnivorous, as in the broadest sense are insectivores. Compare HERBIVOROUS.

CARPAL(S). Small bones of the wrist. The bend of a bird's wing is sometimes referred to as the carpal joint or simply the carpal. Distinctive plumage markings near this wrist joint, e.g., the dark spot on the underside of the wings of Rough-legged Hawk, are sometimes called carpal spots or carpal bars.

CASPIAN (Tern). The Caspian Tern was originally described from a specimen collected from the Caspian Sea. The species is not, of course, restricted to the Caspian Sea; in fact, it is one of the few nearly cosmopolitan species of birds. For other geographical vernacular names, see NAMES, VERNACULAR.

CASSIN, John, 1813–69 (Cassin's Auklet: *Ptychoramphus aleuticus;* Cassin's Kingbird: *Tyrannus vociferans;* Cassin's Vireo: *Vireo cassinii;* Cassin's Sparrow: *Aimophila cassinii*); Cassin's Finch: *Carpodacus cassinii.* One of the prominent Philadelphia bird men who along Wilson and Audubon helped shape American ornithology. Cassin was a businessman by profession but pursued his interest in birds with the avidity and competence of a full-time ornithologist. Coues comments on his "bookishness," by which he apparently meant his meticulous scholarship manifested in his curatorship of the bird-skin collection of the Philadelphia Academy of Natural Sciences—the largest then in existence—and in his numerous publications. He was ornithologist on Admiral Perry's "opening" voyage to Japan in 1853–54. Cassin named a number of bird species after colleagues and was certainly well commemorated in turn.

See the Bibliography under BAIRD.

CASTINGS. In some organisms, used as a synonym for droppings, i.e., feces; in birds generally refers to regurgitated wastes and is synonymous with PELLET.

CASUAL. Of infrequent and (perhaps) irregular occurrence; a necessarily subjective term used in field guides and in studies of bird distribution to describe the status of a species that occurs too frequently to be termed "accidental" but appears at unpredictable intervals. Sometimes considered synonymous with vagrant, although vagrant is usually defined as inclusive of accidental and casual. *The ABA Checklist,* 6th edition (2002) places this category between Rare and Accidental and defines it as "reflecting some pattern of occurrence." Another term in this general category that is gaining in popularity is "low-density migrant"—demonstrating perhaps the increasing subtlety of the birding "dialect."

CATBIRD. Standard English name for 2 species of mimic thrushes (family Mimidae), each in its own genus. The Gray Catbird, *Dumetella carolinensis,* breeds exclusively in North America; one of its many calls suggests a cat's meow. The Black Catbird, *Melanoptila glabrirostris,* is a permanent resident of the Yucatan Peninsula and adjacent islands, ranging south to northern Guatemala. The name catbird is also applied to a species of Australian bowerbird, and to an African babbler/flycatcher. For family characteristics, see MIMIC THRUSH.

CATESBY (KATES-bee), Mark, c. 1680–c. 1750. Author and illustrator of *Natural History of Carolina, Florida and the Bahama Islands,* a large-format work in two volumes and an appendix consisting of 220 plates comprising 109 bird species as well as many species of plants, mammals, reptiles, fish, and insects: the first comprehensive, illustrated (engraved by Catesby himself and hand-colored), accurate (given the pre-Linnaean state of early-eighteenth-century biology) work on the natural history of North America. All of the three early editions (1743/48, 1754, 1771) are now exceedingly rare. Almost nothing is known of Catesby's life. He was English, apparently relatively well-to-do (his sister was the wife of the secretary of the governor of the Virginia colony); he was well connected in London scientific circles; his chief field of expertise was botany; he was self-taught as an artist; and he visited the New World twice between 1712 and 1726 for a total of 11 years.

CATS. Free-ranging cats—whether pampered pets or feral animals living semi-independently—are highly efficient predators of small birds and mammals and are therefore one of the greatest threats that humanity has imposed on wild birdlife. Scientifically based estimates put the number of birds killed annually by cats in United States in the hundreds of millions.

In some of the worst instances, feral cat populations on remote islands where there are no large predators have devastated populations of seabirds and other species, some of them endangered. In the worst of these cases, massive cat eradication programs have been necessary. None of this, of course, is the cats' fault. Domestic tabbies are descendants of the wild cats of Europe, Africa, and Asia and are simply following their natural instincts in stalking and catching small live prey. The large populations of feral cats that now live around most towns result from (1) abandonment by their human owners and (2) failure of pet owners to neuter their animals to prevent unwanted reproduction. To give some sense of the magnitude of the problem, the Massachusetts Society for the Prevention of Cruelty to Animals estimates that there are more than 700,000 unowned, free-ranging cats in Massachusetts alone. Many home owners believe that if their cats get enough to eat or wear bells, they will not be a threat to birds, but, in fact, well-fed cats will kill simply as an instinctual reaction to available prey and can learn to stalk their quarry without shaking their bells; in any case birds do not associate the sound of a bell with an approaching predator.

The solution to the problem is to neuter domestic cats and to keep them indoors. This is not only highly beneficial to native birds and other small animals such as chipmunks, it is also greatly improves life for cats. Research has proven that keeping cats indoors more than triples their average life expectancy. It also protects them from a host of factors that kill and maim millions of cats every year, such as exposure to diseases (some of which, such as rabies, are transmissible to people); getting hit by cars; infestation by worms, fleas, ticks, and other parasites; attacks by wild and feral animals; falling victim to traps and poisons set for other species; an astonishing variety of cruel treatment by people; and euthanization by animal control officers who are forced to put down millions of homeless cats each year.

The American Bird Conservancy working in partnerships with national humane organizations has created a program called Cats Indoors! designed to improve life for both birds and cats. To find out how you can participate go to http://www.abcbirds.org/cats/.

CENSUS. People count birds for three basic reasons: (1) scientific inquiry, (2) wildlife management, and (3) fun. In studying the animal communities of a particular habitat, for example, a census of the total population of breeding and/or wintering birds of all species might be desirable. Or in studying a particular species it is often useful to know how many pairs occupy a given unit (acre, square mile, etc.) of their preferred habitat. Simply by recording numbers of birds at a particular place and time and comparing totals over a period of time, patterns of abundance for species, seasons, weather conditions, changes in habitat, or other contributing factors can

be discovered. Finally, spending a day in the field trying to see as many species and individuals as possible can be great sport and is recognized as such by a growing number of North Americans (see BIRDING EVENTS). Birding a particular area regularly, keeping careful notes and comparing results of successive visits, can have scientific value if methods (time spent, distances traveled, habitats visited, etc.) are consistent and recorded carefully enough to permit valid comparisons; CHRISTMAS BIRD COUNTS are examples of this kind of census. Increasingly, such data are being collected and analyzed to aid the conservation of species.

Several census methods have become standard for counting birds. The most straightforward, of course, is to simply count all individual birds in a population. Though virtually impossible in censusing most birds—especially small species in large areas of dense habitat—this method is sometimes workable in counting species (e.g., seabirds) that nest colonially in the open. In such situations, aerial photographs can be taken and occupied nests counted at leisure, or census teams can walk through the colony counting according to a prescribed method that minimizes omission and duplications. Similarly, arboreal "rookeries" of large species such as herons can be accurately censused by determining the number of occupied nests.

Spot Mapping is used when absolute numbers of pairs of breeding land birds is desired. The counter maps the study area and route then makes separate maps for each species present, noting its location and behavior. When maps from a series of visits are combined the locations of individuals of a given species tend to be clustered, giving a rough map of a bird's territory. This is a labor-intensive methodology but involves no extrapolation; it has been greatly facilitated by field applications of GPS and GIS techniques (see TECHNOLOGY FOR BIRDERS).

The procedure for counting small birds in large areas of dense habitats is usually some form of sampling method, whereby the number of birds in a specified area is determined. When this is repeated on a regular basis statistically significant population trends can be detected or estimates for a broader area or an entire population can be extrapolated.

Plot Samples involve a square section of uniform habitat marked off by grid lines or a marked circle. In the former, counters walk along the grid lines, attempting to count all birds (or all of a particular species) on their assigned route; in the latter an attempt is made to count all of the targeted birds within the circle. To maximize accuracy, the procedure is repeated a number of times and counts are typically taken when birds are most conspicuous (usually early morning).

Transects or strip samples follow a similar basic procedure but are taken along a longitudinal section of uniform habitat (or through a cross section of different habitats), often, for example, along a road. The census taker counts birds seen or heard within a given distance (usually 100 feet)

of his route. Again standardization (of date, time of day, weather, etc.) and repetition are critical in yielding reliable data. The BREEDING BIRD SURVEY conducted largely by amateur field ornithologists uses this technique. With many counts now having been repeated over many years, this census is now the best baseline we have from which to measure trends in North American breeding bird populations.

Point Counts. In this technique the counter typically selects a number of points in a given study area and records all the birds that can be seen and heard in a certain time period (e.g., 10 or 20 minutes) from that point. The points should be far enough apart that individuals are not counted more than once. Again, consistency of conditions and repetition are important.

Mark-and-Recapture. Rarely, an attempt is made to trap and mark or band all individuals in a designated area to reduce the error factor inherent in sight-and-sound censuses. Or, by marking as many individuals as possible and then counting how many marked birds are recaptured in a similar time period, the size of the population can be estimated. In this case the labor involved must be weighed against the degree of improvement in accuracy. Some extrapolation techniques attempt to compensate for how difficult it is to see or hear a particular species.

Stationary Counts. Though the most precise data consist of absolute numbers, much can be learned by careful comparisons of *relative abundance.* Sea (or lake) watches and hawk watches, during which migrating birds passing a given point over a given time are counted and meteorological conditions noted, can yield valuable information about population fluctuations as well as bird movements. Such counts also involve the thrill of seeing lots of birds, often including some rarities.

Frequently more than one form of census is conducted in a given study to detect the biases of the operative technique. An International Bird Census Committee has created standards for conducting various types of census.

For a comprehensive description of techniques for estimating numbers of land birds see Ralph and Scott (1981).

See also ATLAS; BREEDING BIRD CENSUS; BREEDING BIRD SURVEY; BIRDING EVENTS; HAWK-WATCHING; SEA-WATCHING.

CENTURY RUN. Synonym for Big Day; see BIRDING EVENTS.

CERE (seer). The raised, fleshy base of the upper mandible in the members of the Falconiformes (hawks, eagles, falcons, etc.), through which the nostrils open. A similar, but feathered, structure is typical of the parrots and owls. Among members of the hawk and falcon families, the cere is often bright yellow or orange, though in juvenile birds it may be duller. Its function, if any, is unclear.

CERULEAN (suh-ROO-lee-un) (Warbler). A shade of relatively pale blue, as the clear blue of a cloudless sky or the softer, grayer tone on the head and neck of *Dendroica cerulea.*

CHACHALACA (CHA-chuh-lah-kuh). Standard English name for all 12 members of the genus *Ortalis*, one of which, the Plain Chachalaca *(O. ve-tula)*, is the sole North American representative of the guan family (Cracidae; order Galliformes). Like all of the guans, chachalacas are fairly large (to 2 feet), long-tailed, partially arboreal gallinaceous birds that feed mostly on fruits, buds, and other plant matter. *Unlike* most of their relations, the chachalacas are typically birds of shrubby brushlands rather than forest.

Chachalacas construct a surprisingly small, flimsy, stick platform nest, sparsely lined with fresh leaves and placed near the end of a branch but within the densest foliage of a small tree. They normally lay 3 immaculate white eggs.

Natural populations of the Plain Chachalaca in North America are restricted to the acacia scrublands of the southern Rio Grande Valley of Texas, the northern edge of their largely Mexican range. They are also established by introduction on three coastal islands off Georgia.

The name is from a Nahuatl (indigenous Mexican) word via Spanish and echoes the insistent raucous "songs" of these birds (see SONG, Multiple Vocalizations).

See Delacour and Amadon (1973–GALLINACEOUS BIRDS).

CHALAZA (kuh-LAY-zuh). Two fibrous cords of albumen that connect a developing embryo, yolk, etc., to the egg membrane (see Fig. 10). Its basic function is to stabilize the embryo as it passes through the oviduct. Since the developing embryo must remain at the top of the egg mass as it tumbles down, the chalaza becomes twisted as the egg turns. For more detail, see EGG.

CHAPARRAL (chap-uh-RAL or SHAP-uh-ral). In the broadest sense, seasonally dry, dense, evergreen shrublands such as occur in the western and southwestern United States and northwestern Mexico. The chamisal scrubland on the dry western slope of southern California and northern Baja California has been described as the "coastal chaparral biome."

The term derives from *chaparro*, a Spanish word for the dwarf scrubby oaks that are characteristic of the habitat. It is generally agreed that rainfall in typical chaparral is between 10 and 30 inches a year—too little for forest and too much for desert—but neither the plant nor the animal communities are closely defined. Most authorities agree that scrub oaks, mountain mahogany *(Cerocarpus betuloides)*, manzanita *(Arctostaphylos, spp.)*, and chamisal *(Adenostoma fasciculatum)* are typical chaparral

plants, but sagebrush, mesquite, madrone, and even the pinyon/juniper association of arid mountain slopes may be included. Bird species most closely associated with California coastal chaparral are California Gnatcatcher, Wrentit, and California Thrasher and California Towhee. Others that might reasonably be called "chaparral birds" (though by no means restricted to this habitat) are California Quail, Mountain Quail, Dusky Flycatcher, Bushtit, Green-tailed Towhee, Rufous-crowned Sparrow, Black-chinned Sparrow, and Sage Sparrow (Bell's or Pacific subspecies).

CHAPMAN, Frank M., 1864–1945. Curator of Birds at the American Museum of Natural History for 54 years and a founder of the National Audubon Society. Chapman's outstanding career was described by Robert Cushman Murphy as follows: "He was a creative museum-builder, a life-long conservationist, a taxonomist and biogeographer, a student of bird behavior and always an educator" (*Auk*, 67:312). Chapman's best-known published works are the several editions of his *Handbook* (see the Bibliography), and his distributional studies of the birds of Colombia (1917) and Ecuador (1926) continue to support his reputation as a scientist. His total output comprised 17 books and 225 articles.

He was born into a well-to-do New Jersey family and spent 6 years of "servitude" as a banker before becoming J. A. ALLEN's assistant at the American Museum. Though he was reserved with some people and in later life, Chapman's personality was essentially robust (Murphy compares his temperament to the "Latin" one); he was an athlete when young, a keen businessman—despite his preference for birds—and a man of strongly held opinions. He was an early popularizer of the concept of bird conservation. Among his achievements in this realm were the creation and editorship of *Bird Lore*, the most significant early popular bird periodical in 1899, and the organization of the first Christmas Bird Count 1, 1900 (see BIRDING EVENTS).

CHARACTER DISPLACEMENT. When two similar species come into contact in either breeding or nonbreeding ranges and compete for similar resources, this can lead to changes in body size, or the size of body parts— e.g., bill size and shape in birds—reflecting lifestyle, especially feeding behavior. A well-documented example is that of Darwin's finches, which show convergent bill size on islands where one or the other is absent but divergent bill sizes when both species occur on the same island (see Grant 1999–SPECIATION; Wiens 1989–SPECIATION).

CHAT. Standard English generic name for a variety of passerine bird species in several families, including the Australian chats (Meliphagidae), a number of small Palearctic and African thrushes (Turdidae), and a few species of atypical wood warblers (Parulidae). The name is often used to

comprise the generally small "saxicoline" thrushes, including the Old World redstarts, wheatears, various robins, and chats in several genera. A unique wood warbler, the Yellow-breasted Chat *(Icteria virens)*, is the only North American bird to bear this name.

The name seems to have derived from "stone chack," first used to describe the habitat and call respectively of the Northern Wheatear, but was then also used in the same way for the Eurasian Stonechat and Whinchat, both in the thrush genus *Saxicola* (Lockwood 1993–NAMES).

CHECK. A pale (usually white) area usually at the base of the primary feathers of certain birds, which appears as a squarish mark on the folded wing of a bird at rest (see Fig. 1). A "classic" field mark for female and immature Black-throated Blue Warblers, but present in a number of other North American species, e.g., the shrikes.

"CHECK!" An exclamation of delight at being able to add a bird to one's life list; in Britain "tick!" is preferred, and it is reported that some Texas associates of the late Edgar Kincaid exulted, "Yip, yip, yip!" See TICK; LISTING.

CHECKLIST. In a biological context a very broad term that includes everything from a simple listing of vernacular names of species in a particular region to lengthy, technical, profusely detailed taxonomic works. Many local bird clubs print small cards entitled, for example, "Birds of the Genesee Valley," with spaces for "checking" species seen on a particular day, month, year, etc.; state or regional faunal lists are often in the form of "annotated checklists," which document in detail the status and abundance of species and subspecies that have occurred therein, e.g., *The Birds of Massachusetts,* subtitled "An Annotated and Revised Checklist" (Griscom and Snyder 1955, 295 pp.). The *AOU Checklist of North American Birds,* now in its 7th edition is an 829-page work (plus Supplements) listing in phylogenetic order all of the species and subspecies of birds for which there are substantiated records for the United States, Canada, Mexico, Central America, the West Indies, and (from political rather than ornithological logic) the Hawaiian Islands, including the habitat and distribution of each form and appropriate taxonomic notes; it is the standard reference for taxonomy and nomenclature of North American birds.

A Checklist of the Birds of the World, by J. L. Peters et al. (1931–86) consists of 15 volumes and lists the species and subspecies of all the birds of the world and their ranges. More current one-volume checklists of global scope are *Distribution and Taxonomy of Birds of the World,* C. G. Sibley and Burt L. Monroe, Jr. (1990, and 1993 supplement), and the same authors' *A World Checklist of Birds* (1993). Perhaps the most popular checklists among birders, both of which follow current scholarship are *Birds of*

the World: A Checklist by J. F. Clements (2000) and the *ABA Checklist,* 6th edition (2002).

CHICK. A downy, relatively independent (precocial) young bird, during the period between hatching and flying. The young of ducks, gulls, shorebirds, gallinaceous birds, and others are usually called "chicks," as distinguished from the largely naked, helpless (altricial) young typical of songbirds, which are called NESTLINGS.

CHICKADEE. Standard English name for the 7 North American members of the genus *Poecile* (until recently, *Parus*) (family Paridae; order Passeriformes) that have black caps and black throats. In British usage, these and all other members of their family are known as "tits"; the of Alaskan and Canadian tundra edge is mainly a Palearctic species and its English name in Europe is Siberian Tit (though note the British spelling of gray that is preferred in the *AOU Checklist.*

The chickadees range almost throughout the continent (absent from treeless habitats), with the ranges of two species overlapping in several regions. They are among the most common, familiar, and adored of native songbirds due to their expressive-seeming "faces," their active, acrobatic feeding behavior, their tolerance of humans, and their "cheerful" calls. They are invariably among the first birds to appear at a new feeding station and with a little patience can be coaxed to take seeds from the hand. They are also among the most responsive species to human BIRD CALLS such as pishing and squeaking.

Most species have a call that (with a little imagination) can be heard as *chick-a-dee;* most also have a clear whistled "song."

For general characteristics of the family, see TIT.

CHICKEN. General name for the domestic barnyard fowl, especially the young and hens. Most of our chicken breeds are presumed descendants of the Red Jungle Fowl of Asia, *Gallus gallus* (Phasianidae), which has been kept by man for thousands of years. See DOMESTICATED BIRDS.

CHICKEN HAWK. Pejorative colloquial name used, in its broadest sense, to refer to any of the medium-sized to large hawks, all of which are presumed by the ignorant to ravage poultry yards habitually. The Cooper's Hawk is the only species to which the name can be applied with any justification, since it feeds principally on medium-sized birds and knows an easy kill when it sees one. The other accipiters and several species of buteos are known to take chickens only very infrequently.

CHIRICAHUA MOUNTAINS (Arizona). See SOUTHEASTERN ARIZONA.

CHISOS (CHEE-sose) **MOUNTAINS** (Texas). Sole breeding area in North America for the Colima Warbler; see BIG BEND.

CHLAMYDIOSIS (kluh-MID-ee-OH-sis). A group of bacterial diseases certain strains of which occasionally produce severe epidemics in a wide range of bird species and may cause a form of pneumonia in people who handle a lot of birds, e.g., poultrymen and aviculturists. For further detail, see DISEASE, Ornithosis and Psittacosis.

CHRISTMAS COUNT. See BIRDING EVENTS

CHUCK-WILL'S-WIDOW. Standard English name for a single species of nightjar, *Caprimulgus carolinensis,* which breeds exclusively in eastern North America. The name is a literal approximation of its call. See NIGHTJAR.

CHUKAR (CHUCK-er). Standard English name for a single species of southern Eurasian partridge, *Alectoris chukar,* which has been introduced and established as a game bird in its preferred dry, rocky, barren habitat in the western United States. The name "chukar" derives from the species' chicken-like clucks (or "chucks").

For family characteristics, see PHEASANT or QUAIL. See also PARTRIDGE.

CHUMMING. In birdwatching parlance, the ladling of a loathsome concoction of putrid fish entrails upon offshore waters in the hope of attracting interesting pelagic birds. Though "chum" in an advanced stage of decomposition is preferred, the oily livers of freshly caught fish will serve. Heating the brew is said, by a few who have tried it, to increase its volatility, thus improving its effectiveness, since tubenoses are attracted by the odor (see SMELL).

Chumming is a worthwhile technique, but even the most seaworthy birders often find themselves nearer the rails than the petrels when it is used in rough weather.

CHURCHILL (Manitoba). A justly famous low arctic birding locality consisting of wet tundra, rocky shore, and boreal forest habitats at the mouth of the Churchill River, on the western shore of Hudson Bay; accessible by plane and train from Winnipeg. With reasonable accommodations and transportation available and catering to birdwatchers. Though situated below the Arctic Circle, Churchill's vegetation and birdlife and other fauna are authentically arctic due to the climatic effects of Hudson's Bay. It is especially famed for its diversity of breeding shorebirds and since 1980 as a dependable place to find Ross's Gull, which nests there sporadically.

However, its broad, flat, marshy expanses also hold loons, waterfowl, Yellow Rail, terns, and Smith's Longspur; its willow and alder copses provide nesting localities for Harris's Sparrow, Gray-cheeked Thrush, Common and Hoary Redpolls; its islands of spruce forest contain Spruce Grouse, Gray Jay, Boreal Chickadee, Blackpoll Warbler, Pine Grosbeak, Fox Sparrow, and other typical passerines; and the area also hosts almost the entire spectrum of high arctic species that pass through in migration. Mammalian attractions include beluga (white) whales in the Churchill River and polar bears (September–November). For further detail, see Bonnie Chartier's *A Birder's Guide to Churchill* (revised 1994) in the ABA/Lane series. See also ARCTIC; TUNDRA; MUSKEG; and the Bibliography under ARCTIC.

CHYME (kyme). Food that has been reduced to a semiliquid state by the digestive processes in the stomach of a bird. This unpleasant substance is sometimes vomited forth—notably by the tubenoses and vultures—as a defense technique.

CIRCADIAN (sur-KAY-dee-un) **RHYTHM.** Changes occuring within an organism that are synchronized with the progression of a natural day (approximately 24 hours), regardless of proximate external stimuli, such as changes in light or temperature. The concept is related to the question of an intrinsic "time sense" in birds and other life forms, and there is some experimental evidence to indicate that organisms do indeed function partially according to an "internal clock," though little is known about how the mechanism works. See Gwinner and Hau (2000).

CIRCULATORY SYSTEM. As in humans, the means of supplying nutriment and oxygen and transporting hormones through the bloodstream to all the tissues of the body and of removing wastes. Blood is pumped from the heart through the arteries into ever more narrow and finely divided vessels, eventually reaching the network of minute "hair-like" capillaries through which the tissue takes sustenance and returns impurities. The "dirty" blood passes from the capillaries to the veins, is purified by various organs, returns to the heart, is reoxygenated by the lungs, and returns once again to the heart.

There are a number of anatomical details in the more intricate reaches of this system that are peculiar to birds. On the whole, however, the avian circulatory system functions essentially like our own and only a few differences stand out in a nontechnical context.

The Heart. A bird's heart is located in the center of the chest (thoracic) cavity. As in man, it is the muscular organ that pumps blood continuously throughout the circulatory system. Though they evolved separately, the hearts of both birds and men have four chambers, two each for "incoming" and "outgoing" blood. The route the blood takes through a bird's

body is also similar to that in man: out left ventricle of heart > arteries > capillaries in all parts of the body > veins > in right atrium of heart > out right ventricle > lungs > in left atrium, etc.

Heart Size. The weight of the heart in proportion to body weight tends to be greater in birds than in mammals and has been found to vary significantly among different types of birds: (1) Fast fliers and those capable of long-sustained flight tend to have larger hearts than do weak fliers; here, size of heart is apparently more significant than development of wing muscles. (2) Residents of high altitude tend to have larger hearts than those of low. (3) Residents of cold climates tend to have larger hearts than those of warm, even if of the same species. (4) Males tend to have larger hearts than females. (5) Species with louder songs tend to have larger hearts. (6) Heart size tends to increase slightly in winter.

Rate of Heartbeat in resting birds is about half that of mammals of comparable size, However, it varies over a much greater range both among individuals (as much as hundreds of beats per minute) and among species. Though rates lower than the human average of 72 beats per minute are known in larger birds (Ostrich as low as 38 beats per minute), the average for passerines tends to be between 300 and 500 beats per minute and hummingbirds routinely exceed 1,000. Heartbeat varies according to circumstances: (1) Not surprisingly, it increases under stress and exertion. (2) It is greater in smaller birds than in larger in parallel with metabolic rate. (3) It increases in cold weather. (4) It tends to be higher in an incubating bird than in one simply perched.

Blood. Compared to animals below them on the phylogenetic tree, birds' blood is rich in red blood cells (erythrocytes) at between 1.5 and 5.5 million per cubic millimeter, which is in the lower range of that for mammals. Richness varies among species and among individuals, depending on circumstances, such as size, sex, and temperature.

The Lymphatic System. A bird's lymphatic system is as inscrutable to the layman as the human one. Among myriad other functions, it produces a type of white blood cells (lymphocytes), transports fats and proteins, and combats harmful bacteria. Only a few species of birds—some waterfowl, coots, Herring Gull—have the lymph glands that are prominent in humans and other mammals.

Certain details of the circulatory system have been used in making taxonomic judgments.

CIRCUMBOREAL. Refers to the distribution of organisms that occur worldwide within the Boreal Zone north of 45–50 N latitude. Pine Grosbeak is an example of a bird with a circumboreal breeding distribution. Compare CIRCUMPOLAR; HOLARCTIC REGION.

CIRCUMPOLAR. In a distributional context, ranging continuously around the earth near the North or South Pole. Many antarctic seabirds are

circumpolar in distribution. The breeding range of the Snow Bunting may be described as "circumpolar arctic." Compare CIRCUMBOREAL; HOL-ARCTIC REGION.

CITES. The Convention on International Trade in Endangered Species of Wild Flora and Fauna. An international agreement between governments with the purpose of ensuring "that international trade in specimens of wild animals and plants does not threaten their survival." For further detail, see LAWS PROTECTING BIRDLIFE, CITES.

CITIZEN SCIENCE. A relatively new term for a venerable tradition, the critical role of the amateur in scientific endeavor. "Amateur" is sometimes used as a pejorative term implying a lack of expertise, but in this context it typically refers to passionate dedicated often highly educated and knowledgeable people who happen to lack *academic* credentials in their area of interest. It is to these people that we owe much of what we know about avian natural history and the bird species of North America, many of which are named for such amateurs (see BIOGRAPHY). Bird studies such as breeding bird atlas projects that involve the gathering of large amounts of data over a broad geographic area would simply be impossible without cadres of "citizen scientists." The concept is currently enjoying broad popularity within conservation (and other) institutions for several reasons: (1) many people are strongly attracted to participating in scientifically based programs generating data that serve a worthy cause; (2) it serves the interests of science to have large numbers of people learning the value of scientific research and how it is practiced; (3) there is no better way to educate people about a subject (e.g., bird conservation) than by involving them in a challenging project in which they must acquire and use specialized knowledge; and (4) as noted, large numbers of trained, conscientious data gatherers are invaluable in certain kinds of studies.

In recent court cases involving the protection of endangered species on private property, the argument was made that the data used to support the importance of the habitat in question was invalid because it was gathered by "amateurs." Had the court found for the plaintiffs, the decision could have had a profound negative impact on the utility of projects such as breeding bird atlases in devising sound conservation strategies. Fortunately, the court rejected this challenge to the validity of citizen science.

For an institution that specializes in citizen science programs and offers many options, see CORNELL LAB OF ORNITHOLOGY.

CLADISTICS (Clade, Cladogram). (kluh-DIS-ticks; KLADE; KLAY-duh-gram or KLAD-uh-gram). A system of biological classification originally articulated by the German entomologist and systematist Willi Hennig (1913–76) in his *Phylogenetic Systematics* (1966). In essence, cladistics fo-

cuses on establishing the closest possible evolutionary relationships between species based on "shared derived characters" (synapomorphies) inherited from a common ancestor. Such groups of "monophyletic" species, including the ancestral species, are called "clades." The concept may be applied to groups of any size, e.g., the jaegers and skuas—which uniquely share certain bill characteristics—or the entire order of perching birds (Passeriformes), which also share characters that derive from a single source. More primitive traits (symplesiomorphies), e.g., hard-shelled eggs with yolks, shared by all birds, but also various reptile groups, are not relevant to the cladistics methodology, which is concerned only with building the evolutionary tree outward from well-documented branchings. The branched diagram that represents this form of genealogy is called a cladogram. Cladistics is the prevailing modern approach to phylogenetic classification. For another methodology see PHENETIC CLASSIFICATION.

CLARK, Lt. John Henry, 1830?–? (Clark's Grebe, *Aechmophorus clarkii*). One of Spencer BAIRD's many protégés at Dickinson College, Pennsylvania, Clark became a surveyor/zoologist with the United States Army's Mexican Boundary Survey in the 1850s.Together with fellow surveyor Arthur C. V. Schott, he made notably fine zoological collections in the Rio Grande Valley of Texas and elsewhere that included as many as 100 species new to science. Baird named several southwestern reptiles for him in addition to what was then assumed to be a subspecies of Western Grebe. As the question marks in his dates imply, little else is recorded of his life.

CLARK, William, 1770–1838 (Clark's Nutcracker: *Nucifraga columbiana*). Frontiersman, surveyor, naturalist, Indian fighter, gentleman farmer, and friend (from the army) of Meriwether LEWIS, with whom he made the first overland crossing of the United States to the Pacific coast. Following this successful adventure, Clark was appointed Superintendent of Indian Affairs, and became governor of the Missouri Territory and a hero of the War of 1812.

CLASS. The major taxonomic category between the Phylum and the ORDER, i.e., a subdivision of a phylum and a grouping of orders. All birds, living, extinct, and fossil, belong to the class Aves. For a definition of this class, see BIRD. For a phylogenetic breakdown of a single bird species, see SYSTEMATICS. For a phylogenetic listing of all North American species in the class Aves, see Appendix I.

CLASSIFICATION. See SYSTEMATICS; NOMENCLATURE, ZOOLOGICAL; and Appendix I.

CLAW. A modified scale present at the ends of the toes of all species of birds and adapted for a variety of functions according to the habits of the species. See LEG/FOOT.

CLEMENCIA. Clémence Lesson (Blue-throated Hummingbird: *Lampornis clemenciae*). Wife of the preeminent French naturalist René P. Lesson (1794–1849), the author of many species and subspecies of New World birds, one of which—a very elegant one—bears the name of his wife.

CLIMBING. Though many species of birds that live and/or feed in trees "climb" in the sense of hopping upward with the aid of a wing beat or two, only a few families have evolved special adaptations for climbing. Woodpeckers have relatively large feet and heavy claws, with two toes placed forward and two behind (except for the two species of three-toed woodpeckers, which have only a single hind toe). The stiffened, wedge-shaped woodpecker tail is also well suited to vertical climbing and is used for support and to stabilize the body in its jerky progress up a tree trunk.

Woodpeckers ascend and descend in a series of hops with the body held vertically, though the hop itself may take them to one side as well as upward/downward. They will, on occasion, perch on a thin horizontal branch or even a wire—though they always look awkward doing so.

Flickers, which spend most of their time on the ground feeding on ants, nevertheless retain their climbing "gear" and in effect "climb" (i.e., hop) over the earth in the same manner used to ascend trees.

Like woodpeckers, the treecreepers (family Certhiidae)—including the North American Brown Creeper—hop vertically up tree trunks and have a specially modified supporting tail. But their feet are more like those of typical perching birds, with three forward toes and one behind—all, however, equipped with long curved claws adapted for clinging. In contrast to the more or less random ascent route of most woodpeckers, treecreepers characteristically take a spiral course beginning at the base of a trunk; when they have reached a certain height they fly down to the base of another trunk and repeat the pattern.

Nuthatches have long toes and claws but do not have a propping type of tail—indeed, they hardly have a tail at all. Their climbing technique is different from that of the treecreepers or woodpeckers and allows more versatile movement. One foot is always placed higher than the other, so that no matter which way a nuthatch moves, one foot is always clinging from above and the other supporting from below. This allows it to move with the head up, down, or sideways.

The Black-and-white Warbler climbs and gleans tree trunks and branches in a manner essentially similar to that of the nuthatches. The foot and leg musculature modifications that accommodate this feeding behavior were the basis for putting this otherwise typical *Dendroica* war-

bler in a genus of its own *(Mniotilta)* See also LEG/FOOT; TAIL; WOOD-PECKER; TREECREEPER; NUTHATCH.

CLINE. Also termed "character gradient." In species with ranges spanning broad geographical areas or climatic zones, it is often possible to trace a *gradual* change in mensural and/or morphological characteristics—e.g., from smaller to larger or darker to lighter. Populations of birds at either end of this cline may be strikingly different though linked by populations that grade imperceptibly one into the other. The extremes may be taxonomically differentiated as subspecies, but the precise racial boundaries may be difficult or impossible to define.

CLIPPING (of wing). Severing of the primary feathers of one wing to keep captive birds flightless so that they need not be enclosed in cages. The procedure is painless and not permanently damaging since the feathers grow back with the next molt. Compare PINIONing.

CLOACA (klo-AY-kuh); pl. cloacae (klo-AY-see). In birds, reptiles, amphibians, and many fish, the terminal enlargement of the digestive tract through which solid wastes, urine, and the products of the reproductive system all pass prior to excretion, egg laying, or copulation. In mammals, of course, the digestive passage is completely separate from the urinary and genital passages. "Cloaca" is sometimes used as a synonym for the cloacal opening or "vent." The word derives from a Latin verb meaning to cleanse and the nonzoological meaning in English is sewer or toilet.

CLUBS, BIRD. See BIRD CLUB; ORNITHOLOGICAL SOCIETIES OF NORTH AMERICA.

CLUTCH. All of the eggs laid and brooded by a given bird (or birds, in the case of communal nests) during a single incubation period. Also known as a "set." For number of clutches per season and eggs per clutch, see EGG; NEST.

COB. A male swan of any species.

COCK. In the broadest, earliest sense used in combination with a modifier to denote simply "bird" as in "woodcock." Later narrowed to refer to the *male* of any bird, and in Britain still widely used in this way, e.g., "a cock siskin." In North America, usually reserved for the male chicken, i.e., a rooster; complementing "hen" for the female.

COCKADED (Red-cockaded Woodpecker). A cockade is an emblem or badge, often of a bright color, worn in the hat as a symbol of office or other

affiliation. In the case of the endangered woodpecker (Fig. 31), it refers to the tiny (frequently invisible) wisp of red feathers on the side of the male's head.

COCKFIGHTING. A "sport" in which two roosters, bred and trained with the aim of developing their natural sexual aggressiveness, are fitted with razor-sharp steel spurs and set to fight each other in a ring or pit. Illegal now in all parts of the United States and Canada, but still widely practiced in clandestine meetings.

COCK NEST. Synonymous with DUMMY NEST.

COFFEE. Derived from an understory shrub or small tree *(Coffea arabica)* native to the southwestern highlands of Ethiopia (where it still grows wild), coffee did not become popular in Europe until the seventeenth century and was not grown in the Neotropics until the eighteenth century. When it was first cultivated, it was typically planted in the understory of native forests, leaving much of the biota, including the birdlife, intact. As demand grew, farmers found it more efficient to clear the forest and plant fast-growing nonnative trees such as the Australian *Gravillea*, the assumption being that shade was essential for producing a quality product. While this had a far worse impact on the avifauna, many species of songbirds were still able to use cafetal as feeding habitat. More recently, Latin American growers realized they could cut costs and improve yields by dispensing with shade trees and increasing fertilizers and pesticide, As a result, coffee plantations in many areas became sterile monocultures and avian deserts. Coffee is one of the world's most lucrative crops, consuming millions of acres of tropical habitat at moderately humid middle elevations where many species of Neotropical migrants from North America winter. Alarmed by the potential effects of the new farming methods, conservationists have created a campaign to encourage customers to purchase more expensive, but bird-friendly, shade-grown coffee. This movement has also sought to improve the lot of coffee workers (often exploited indigenous populations) and to see that they receive a greater share of coffee profits. The effort has achieved some success and a number of organizations promote shade-grown coffee with their constituents and even market their own brand. See, for example, The American Birding Association's Songbird Coffee at www.americanbirding.org/abasales/.

For other bird conservation issues, see THREATS (OF HUMAN ORIGIN) TO BIRDLIFE.

COHORT. A little-used tertiary taxonomic division between SUBCLASS and SUPERORDER. Also used to designate age groups in populations: the 1980 "crop" of Song Sparrows is the 1980 "cohort." See SYSTEMATICS.

COLIMA (coh-LEE-muh) (Warbler). A small state on the Pacific slope of Mexico that lies within the wintering range of *Vermivora crissalis* and is the TYPE LOCALITY for this species.

COLLECTING (bird specimens). The killing, by shotgun or other means, of birds, which are then prepared as "study skins" and preserved as a record of occurrence in a given place and time. In the previous century, before the advent of modern field guides and optical equipment, professional and amateur bird students alike pursued their interest by collecting and preserving as many specimens as they could. For an excellent account of the nineteenth-century approach to the subject, see Part I, "Field Ornithology," of Coues's *Key to North American Birds* (1890).

Until very recently, a specimen was considered the only acceptable scientific documentation of a species' occurrence, and it is still necessary and desirable in the case of species and subspecies that cannot be identified with certainty from obvious characters. However, federal and state laws and regulations require thorough review of any proposal for the scientific collecting of birds before permits are issued. Though millions of birds are killed each year by hunters without great ado, the scientific collecting of birds has come under critical scrutiny in recent years. In fact, birds collected under scientific collecting permits in any given year represent an insignificant fraction of the number killed by cats, picture windows, TV towers, or automobiles each year.

For the greatest North American museum collections of bird skins, see MUSEUM. See also BIRD SKIN.

COLLECTIONS (of live birds). See AVICULTURE; MUSEUM.

COLLOQUIAL BIRD NAMES. See NAMES, COLLOQUIAL.

COLONY (colonial birds). The broadest collective term (see NOUNS OF ASSEMBLAGE) for birds that breed in close association with other members of their own (and sometimes other) species. Most conspicuously colonial birds are waterbirds: many tubenoses (albatrosses, shearwaters, petrels, storm-petrels), Pelecaniformes (pelicans, cormorants, boobies, etc.), herons, ibises, storks, some waterfowl, stilts and avocets, gulls and terns, skimmers, and alcids. But some swifts, swallows, and blackbirds are strongly colonial and not a few other passerines (e.g., Pinyon Jay, Kirtland's Warbler) breed in close association with a few other birds of their species and are sometimes said to be "semi-colonial" or "loosely colonial."

Colonial birds are afforded a measure of nest security because they can mount a collective alarm and defense against predators and as a consequence many such species lay fewer eggs than do solitary nesters without diminishing breeding success. Colonies may also improve the feeding

success of their less adept members by providing an "information exchange center" and by directing members to widely and randomly dispersed food patches. See Ward and Zahavi (1973) and Brown and Brown (1996).

Not to be confused with communal nesters (see NEST; ANI).

COLOR AND PATTERN. Including the nature of avian color—both of feathers and of "soft parts"—and the adaptive significance of color and pattern among some North American species.

WHAT IS COLOR? The colors of birds (and everything else) are different wavelengths of light selectively reflected from different substances. White light consists of all wavelengths together and therefore a substance that reflects them all appears white. A substance that reflects *none* of them, i.e., that *absorbs* all light, lacks all color and appears pure black. When some but not all of the wavelengths are reflected, we see one of the colors in our visible spectrum—red, yellow, blue, and all possible combinations thereof. The color we see in a given object or substance may be simply the result of the light-absorbing and light-reflecting properties of its chemical makeup. This is called chemical, pigmentary, or biochromatic color (pigments or biochromes). Our perception of color is also affected by the structural composition of the material from which light is reflected, which may, for example, scatter the light in such a way as to make certain wavelengths visible to us while others are diverted out of the line of our perception. This effect is called structural or schemochromatic color (schemochromes).

Both pigmentary and structural colors occur in many different forms and may exist alone or in combination to produce a particular chromatic effect. The breadth of possibilities thus implied is amply demonstrated in the spectacular variety of bird coloration.

Pigments account for most of the colors we see in the plumage and irises of birds. (Blues and greens in the skin are produced by collagen arrays reflecting in the shorter wavelengths [fide Prum et al. 1994]). Most pigments belong to one of three groups of organic compounds: the melanins, the carotenoids, and the porphyrins, all of which occur very commonly throughout the animal kingdom. Some specific pigmentary compounds (e.g., eumelanin and carotene) have been identified and may be responsible for only very particular areas of coloration.

Melanins are the commonest pigments in birds. They are almost insoluble, and occur as minute granules on both feathers and "soft parts." They are responsible for most of the "earth tones" exhibited by birds— especially blacks, grays, and shades of brown, but also including some "off pinks" and yellows. Melanins are also the chief pigments in human hair and skin.

Carotenoids are the most widespread of organic pigments, occurring throughout the plant as well as the animal kingdom. Unlike the other pig-

ments noted here, the carotenoids must be ingested by birds in plant food, for they are not synthesized by the body. The carotenoids give most of the yellows, oranges, and reds seen in birds, including the yellow of egg yolk (carotene). Variations in diet can produce color variations in individual birds, e.g., the terminal tail band in Cedar Waxwings, which can vary along the yellow-orange spectrum depending on what the birds are eating (Hudon and Brush 1989).

Porphyrins are also very common throughout the animal kingdom, as well as in birds. They are responsible for some greens, reds, and a range of browns (especially pinkish buffs).

Dietary deficiencies and metabolic imbalances may upset the pigment-producing process in a bird's system. For instances of both excesses and insufficiencies, see ALBINISM; MELANISM; LEUCISM; SCHIZOCHROISM; ERYTHRISM; XANTHOCHROISM.

Structural Color produces all whites and blues in birds' plumage and the various forms of iridescence—the now-you-see-it/now-you-don't head colors of most male hummingbirds as well as the multicolored oil-on-water iridescence of the European Starling, the grackles, and others. Recent research by Prum and others (1994) has shown that many "soft part" colors result from reflections from ordered collagen (fibrous protein) arrays in a bird's skin.

White results from an absence of pigment in the feathers, allowing the reflection of all wavelengths of sunlight from a colorless surface. The quality of the whites, whether dull or glossy, depends on the structural details of individual feathers and the texture of the plumage as a whole (see below).

The romantically inclined will be pleased to learn that the blue of bird feathers owes its existence to the same phenomenon that makes the sky blue; the technically inclined may prefer a brief description of the "Tyndall phenomenon" by which it is achieved: White light falling through a perfectly clear atmosphere would produce no color. But the upper atmosphere is filled with minute particles that pick up and scatter (i.e., reflect) the shortest (blue) light waves; when larger particles are encountered nearer the earth, the longer yellow and red waves are scattered, giving us brilliant sunsets. In bird feathers the light-scattering elements are not particles but tiny air pockets (vacuoles) in a layer of cells in the feather barbs (see FEATHER). This layer lies beneath the outer transparent covering and above a core of cells darkened by melanin granules. The blue light is scattered by the vacuoles and the rest of the spectrum is absorbed by the melanin beneath. Most noniridescent greens in feathers appear in the same way except that the outer covering of the barb contains yellow pigment instead of being transparent, so that the blue light is reflected through a yellow medium, giving green. When a Blue Jay's feather is dipped in alcohol and the air in the vacuoles is displaced by the liquid, the feather appears a dull blackish.

Iridescent Colors result from the structure of the barbules and are produced according to the principle of "interference" of light waves, the mutual change that occurs when two light waves intersect. The barbules are twisted and flattened in such a way as to reflect light only at certain angles and sometimes, as in the case of hummingbirds, with spectacular intensity. The colors originate in the microstructure of the surface of the barbules. In hummingbirds, at least, this consists of extraordinarily thin successive films of minute elliptical "platelets" arranged mosaic-like in a dark matrix. Interference of light waves occurs by reflection and refraction in these films in a manner similar to that produced by a film of oil on water or soapy water over air (e.g., soap bubbles). In the multicolored iridescent neck feathers of pigeons the interference occurs between the light reflected from transparent surface carotene and a layer of granular melanin immediately below. Other kinds of birds showing different iridescent effects produce them by variations of the basic principle. The details of this complex phenomenon are too numerous to give here, but are explicated *and illustrated* with admirable lucidity and at the length they deserve in Greenewalt (1960–HUMMINGBIRD).

In many if not all cases, the iridescent feathers lack the interlocking structure of the barbules of "normal" feathers; they are, therefore, relatively weak and tend to occur as body feathers rather than flight feathers.

Texture. The appearance of plumage coloration is strongly influenced by the size of feathers and the angle at which feathers and their constituent barbs lie. Short feathers projecting vertically, as from the heads of many ducks, give a soft velvety effect. When feathers, barbs, and/or barbules are arranged with flat surface facing outward, the effect is increased shininess—not to be confused with iridescence. The brightly colored (red or yellow) crown feathers of woodpeckers show this quality on close inspection.

While a number of bird species are unicolored and clear primary hues are not infrequent in avian coloration, the plumages of most species are to some degree combinations of the effects described above. Variations of hue and intensity of color, for example, are often the result of mixtures of pigments present in individual feathers. Dark melanin granules among a carotenoid pigment result in a range of dull olive greens and browns or dull reds. Structural blue combined with biochromal red yields purple. Melanin forms a part of the structure of at least some forms of iridescence, serving as a refraction and/or absorption medium as well as providing background color as in the "iridescent black" granules.

And striking plumage patterns are often the results of mixed effects—iridescence next to "matt" color; primary hues next to muted tones; dark patterns against light—as exemplified by males of many species of ducks.

Special Effects also modify coloration in a few cases. Particles of powder down, for example, covering the surface of the plumage soften tones

slightly and make them less glossy. The roseate bloom that appears on the breasts of some species of gulls and terns early in the breeding season may be a pigment produced seasonally from the oil gland and applied with the bill like "rouge." The "soft parts" and irises of many heron species vivify dramatically during the very acme of breeding season excitement. This effect is at least in part due to a hormonally triggered expansion of the blood vessels via increased blood supply to the surface of the affected areas. This color has been seen to change in response to an immediate stimulus, so that when the legs of a Green Heron or the loral skin of a Snowy Egret intensifies it seems, in essence, to be "blushing." However, it has been shown that an increase in pigments is also involved, which may help to explain how a Tricolored Heron's bill base changes in the breeding season from dull yellow to bright blue.

COLOR SPECIFICATION. Redheads, Ruby-throated Hummingbirds, Vermilion Flycatchers, American Robins, Orchard Orioles, Scarlet Tanagers, Northern Cardinals, and Rose-breasted Grosbeaks all display "red" in some plumage. An observer can attempt to describe the shade of red with adjectives such as dark, light, brownish, scarlet, etc., but will be understood only if these names apply to an accepted standard, however arbitrary. It doesn't really matter if a given shade is *truly* "rufous" as long as it is always labeled as such. Two widely used standards are the Villalobos system, which is represented in abbreviated form in the introduction to Palmer (1962–ORNITHOLOGY), and the more recent Smithe's (1975–1981), based on the Munsell System.

PURPOSES OF COLOR AND PATTERN. One should always exercise caution when attempting to explain striking natural phenomena. Clearly adaptive plumage characteristics, such as the cryptic forest-floor coloration of most nightjars, encourage us to look for similar "reasons" for all eye-catching colors or designs, when, in fact, many may have evolved simply in the absence of any selective pressure *against* them. However, the stunning variety in plumage color and pattern inevitably excites our curiosity, especially when certain "motifs" seem to be repeated consistently in correlation with factors of habitat or behavior. A few of the better-known "functions" of color and pattern are therefore described briefly below.

Physiological Benefit. It has been suggested that species with dark plumage may benefit from superior heat absorption and that the pale coloration of many desert birds may aid temperature control, in addition to providing a measure of concealment against pale arid landscapes (see below and DESERT). Due to the chemical composition of melanin, black feathers are stronger than pale feathers and a glance through a modern field guide reveals that wing tips or all flight feathers are frequently darker (often black) than other body feathers. See Burtt (1986).

Recognition. A great many distinctive plumage colors and patterns in male birds seem to be related to the ability of females to recognize the

best potential mates of their own species (see Savalli 1995; Greene et al. 2000); some displays involving conspicuous feathers may release appropriate breeding behavior, e.g., the urge to copulate. These same characteristic species colors and patterns can serve as warning to territorial trespassers. Other recognitive functions are as follows:

- Brightly colored/patterned bills and gapes release begging and feeding responses in young and parent birds, respectively, and feeding nestlings in cavities or other dark locations is doubtless facilitated by the white or bright yellow gape margins seen in many species.
- The white or pale gray coloration of gulls, terns, and gannets congregated at a food source may act as a signal—visible for miles against the dark sea—to other seabirds in the area, making food seeking more efficient; likewise "kettles" of dark vultures against a pale sky may alert other scavengers to a kill (or a dump).
- Species, such as shorebirds, that maintain tight flocking formations may be aided in their synchronous movements by contrasting "flags" in wings and tail that release "following" instincts.
- Conspicuous coloration as a warning to potential predators of unpalatability or toxicity is common among insects, and has now been documented for several bird species (see Dumbacher et al. 1992, 2000–EDIBILITY).

For mimetic coloration, rare among birds, see MIMICRY.

Distraction. Many birds have bright (often white) flashes or "banner marks," which are concealed when the birds are at rest but instantly revealed when the bird spreads its feathers in flight. The white rumps of woodpeckers, the white outer tail feathers of pipits, juncos, and other passerines, and the spots on the tail corners of *Dendroica* warblers are familiar examples. These may serve to momentarily startle a predator, allowing crucial seconds for escape, and/or induce an attacker to strike at expendable parts of the body. Some of the "flash patterns" probably function mainly by aiding insectivorous birds in the flushing of prey (see Jablonski 1999).

Concealment. Many birds are so colored/patterned as to blend with their characteristic habitat. Some animals (e.g., toads, anglerfish) use such "camouflage" to capture prey that wander unsuspectingly within reach (anticryptic). But cryptic coloration in birds largely serves the opposite function, that of concealing them from potential predators (procryptic).

Perhaps the most interesting thing about this phenomenon is the many ways in which near-invisibility is achieved. To begin with, one should recognize that brilliant color and bold patterns may be as cryptic against the proper background as somber colors and uniform patterns. Gerald Thayer (1909) taxes our credulity when he suggests that the salmon pink of American Flamingoes is adapted to conceal flocks of this species against brilliant Caribbean sunsets, but an adult male Scarlet Tan-

ager in nuptial plumage moving amidst the vivid contrast and moving shadows of its treetop habitat is not nearly as conspicuous as the inexperienced observer might expect. Conversely, even the most highly evolved cryptic coloration stands out like the proverbial sore thumb against the "wrong" background.

The *extent* of concealing color/pattern among birds ranges from the not-as-obvious-as-you-might-think (Scarlet Tanager) to the impossible-to-find-even-when-you-know-where-to-look (nightjars). A great many species, e.g., ducks (females), sandpipers, vireos, and sparrows, match in a very general way the colors and textures of the habitats in which they are normally found. In a few species (the American Bittern is the favorite example, followed closely by the nightjars and the woodcocks) the background mimicry reaches a high degree of fidelity, providing (1) that the species in question is in the appropriate habitat at the appropriate season—bitterns are much more conspicuous against green cattails than against brown; and (2) that appropriate behavior reinforces coloration: a bird trying to be invisible must remain motionless; many species crouch low to the ground to minimize giveaway shadows; and a few have a concealment "display," such as the vertical freeze posture of the American Bittern, which has been called "bitterning."

A number of species whose habitat tends to be snow-covered for at least part of the year have evolved white plumage, and in some cases the concealing elements must change according to the season and/or the habits of the species. Snowy Owls do not alter their plumage seasonally, but Snow Buntings, which winter somewhat farther south and on a more regular basis, become mottled with brown following the breeding season. The ptarmigan, by contrast, which do not migrate, change with the seasons in an unusual sequence of molts (see MOLT): their plumage is at its whitest in winter, brownest at midsummer, and patchy (like the snow cover) between times.

Concealing coloration may also change with age. Most precocial chicks are clothed in a highly cryptic natal down whether their parents make use of the same phenomenon (gallinaceous birds, sandpipers, etc.) or not (gulls, terns).

Countershading or obliterative shading takes advantage of the fact that under normal circumstances a bird's upper surface will be under direct light while the undersurface remains in shadow. The shading of many plumages reverses this, being darkest above and palest below, thus neutralizing the contrast and "flattening" the bird's form to blend more easily with background patterns. An adult Herring Gull in full sun demonstrates this effect, though in many passerines the gradation from darkest to palest is more gradual.

Disruptive patterning juxtaposes contrasting patches of color of irregular shape, making the outline of a bird ambiguous and encouraging the eye to relate parts of the bird's coloration to elements of the background

rather than bringing them together in the shape of a bird. The *Charadrius* plovers against their stony or shell-strewn habitats are excellent examples of disruptive patterning.

A few species seem to combine most of the cryptic elements in a single "act." The waterthrushes, for example, have a general resemblance to their background color, are countershaded, have disruptive eye and breast stripes, and heighten the last effect by adding a bobbing motion that seems to mimic the motion and play of light of their preferred aquatic habitats.

For birds that seem to mimic other birds rather than habitat, see MIMICRY.

Sighting Lines. The prevalence in birds' facial patterns of lines that pass through the eye or from eye to gape is undeniable. It has been suggested (Ficken et al. 1971) that such marks help a bird coordinate its bill movement with the movements of its prey.

Perception. Finally it should be emphasized that people can see only a portion of the colors and patterns visible to birds. For example, because birds can see in the ultraviolet wavelength invisible to humans they can perceive clear distinctions, such as patterns of iridescence, to which we are blind. Thus, Fish Crows and American Crows, which appear nearly identical to us, may appear strikingly different to each other. See Finger and Burkhardt (1994) and Bennet et al. (1996).

For aberrant color/pattern, see ALBINISM; MELANISM; LEUCISM; SCHIZOCHROISM; ERYTHRISM; XANTHOCHROISM.

See also DISPLAY; PLUMAGE.

COMB. A fleshy, featherless, usually brightly colored, serrated crest adorning the heads of some gallinaceous birds from the base of the bill to the rear of the crown. In addition, male grouse have seasonally engorged pectinate brow combs over the eyes. Combs undoubtedly function in sexual display and are usually more prominent in the male than the female. In North America, only cock domestic fowl are adorned with full head combs.

COMFORT MOVEMENTS. Collective term for a variety of actions and gestures made by birds, usually in association with PREENING or resting. The commonest comfort movements are shaking of the body or parts thereof, notably the head and tail; ruffling and resettling of the body feathers; "shuffling" of the wings, a distinctive motion in which the folded wings are "sawed" alternately back and forth over the back; yawning; and stretching. The last type of movement has several standard variations, especially (1) stretching both wings upward simultaneously; (2) stretching both wings downward simultaneously; (3) stretching one wing and the leg of the same side outward and downward, usually with the same side of the tail fanned; and (4) stretching both legs while lowering head and neck and arching the back. Closely related species of birds tend to practice similar stretching gestures.

For a detailed account of comfort movements in the duck family, see McKinney, *Behavior* (1965), 25:120–220. See also Campbell and Lack (1985–ORNITHOLOGY).

COMIC (COMMIC) TERN. Combination of "Common" and "Arctic" (Tern), used by birdwatchers to refer to birds that belong to one of these two similar species but that cannot be identified with certainty as one or the other.

COMMENSALISM. Close association between two or more organisms of different species that is detrimental to neither. Insects that live in a bird's nest without any direct contact with its owner share a commensalistic (or commensal) relationship with the bird. The most frequently cited commensals are those in which one species derives a distinct benefit without either harming or aiding the other. For example, it has been documented (Rand 1955–ANI) that Groove-billed Anis that follow grazing cattle catch the insects that are flushed much more efficiently than they would in the absence of the cattle: the ani benefits the cow does not. In the case of anis picking ticks from a cow's back (Bolen 1974–ANI), both species benefit and the relationship is termed mutualistic or Symbiotic. See also PARASITISM.

COMMISSURE. In birds, the line along which the upper and lower mandibles close.

COMMUNICATION. See SONG.

CONDOR. Standard English name for the two largest living species of New World vultures (family Cathartidae), the Andean Condor *(Vultur gryphus)* and the California Condor *(Gyrnnogyps californianus)*. The name derives from the Peruvian (Quechua) word *cuntur,* which apparently refers to all vultures and which was corrupted by the Spanish to condor. For characteristics of the family, see VULTURE. For details of the nearly extinct California Condor, see ENDANGERED BIRDS.

CONDOR, THE. Quarterly journal of the COOPER ORNITHOLOGICAL SOCIETY, which see for details.

CONGENERIC. Belonging to the same genus. The three phoebes are all placed in the genus *Sayornis* and are thus congeneric.

CONJUNCTIVITIS. A type of eye infection characterized by inflammation and discharge. A recent epidemic among House Finches and other North American fringillids, caused by parasitic bacteria in the genus

Mycoplasma, severely reduced the population of eastern House Finches. For more detail, see DISEASE, Mycoplasmosis.

CONSERVATION. The protection of natural resources, including birds and other living organisms, whether for humanitarian reasons or to prevent the extinction of valuable and/or aesthetically desirable life forms.

The Conservation Impulse and the State of the Earth. Though it is possible to point to the hunting reserves of Chingiis Khan and the like as early manifestations of a conservation ethic, the conservation of wildlife or biodiversity as an influential social consensus is a relatively modern phenomenon. It has come to the fore simultaneously with a general realization that resources are finite and are dwindling due to exploitation by people. The impulse to conserve is rooted in three visions of humankind's relationship with the nature world: (1) *Self-interest:* a perception that the destruction of a particular species is a detriment to one's personal interests. These interests can be physical or spiritual, highfalutin or quite base. If we kill all the Passenger Pigeons there will be none left for us to eat. Or if we kill all the Carolina Parakeets *we* will be deprived of the transcendent aesthetic experience of these exquisite birds. It is a utilitarian vision: we protect things because they are useful—to *us.* (2) *Stewardship.* This notion tends to come to us through religious revelation: The earth and all its creatures belongs to us and since we are blessed to enjoy the benefits of God's creations, we have a responsibility to shepherd them—or at least not destroy them totally; some would-be stewards also believe that it is sinful *not* to utilize these "gifts" to some degree—the rationale behind the so-called "wise use" movement. (3) *Inherent worth of all aspects of the natural world.* This holds that all elements of nature have a right to exist, and we have no right to destroy them for our selfish pleasure or utilitarian purpose.

The emergence of the conservation ethic bespeaks two uniquely human characteristics (1) the ability to view the consequences of past actions and contemplate the effects on the future and (2) the capability, never before possessed by one species or even a group of species, to destroy other species entirely as well as their habitats and indeed the biosphere itself. Credible recent models estimate that the present rate of extinction on earth is at least 1,000 times more rapid than the "normal" extinction rate documented in the fossil record (including the known great extinctions, such as the demise of the dinosaurs and many of their contemporaries near the end of the Cretaceous Period); for the planet's imperiled rain forests the rate may be as much as 10,000 greater than the norm. For the construction of this model, see Wilson (1992) and the cause this time is not a colliding asteroid sending a cold pall over much of earthly life, but rather a single species: *us.*

History of Bird Conservation in North America. The earliest American bird conservation initiatives resulted from isolated cases in which it

was realized that "if we kill any more, there won't be any left to kill" (see Self-interest, above). Thus, as early as 1616 the government of Bermuda passed a law prohibiting the further destruction of the Bermuda Petrel or Cahow, whose abundance had recently been sacrificed to feed starving colonists during a severe winter.

Late in the seventeenth century a few citizens of the North American colonies began to notice a decline in some game birds and urged self-control, and in 1708 New York passed seasonal hunting restrictions on the Wild Turkey, Heath Hen, Ruffed Grouse, and Bobwhite, but only for those few counties where these species were already scarce.

In 1818 a Massachusetts law extended protection in a vague way to birds that ate "noxious" insects as well as those that were "useful" as food. In the 1850s and 1860s about a dozen states (northeastern and midwestern) passed laws protecting specific songbird species that passed muster as "friends of the farmer" or were at worst "small and harmless."

More significant than these early laws, which tended to be vague and enforced only near large cities, if at all, was the appearance, beginning before the middle of the nineteenth century, of illustrated bird books. Many of these, such as DeKay's *Birds of New York* (1844), covered regional avifaunas, and though they were not meant to be hauled along on outdoor excursions (see FIELD GUIDE), they contained descriptions of what we now call field marks and species "histories," aimed at both satisfying and encouraging a growing curiosity and enthusiasm in the public. By the 1870s and 1880s periodicals such as *The Atlantic, Harper's*, and *Scribner's* magazines regularly contained "nature" pieces, often about birds. *St. Nicholas* magazine encouraged young people (especially boys) to regard birds as their friends rather than as amusing targets, even going so far as to organize a club for young "Bird Defenders." The pious moralizing and shameless sentimentality and anthropomorphism ("old grandmother Towhee Bunting"—Samuels [1868]) would not go down well with current subscribers to *Ranger Rick*, but the popularity of this style of bird lore in the last century is beyond dispute.

Encouraging as this wave of "nature appreciation" may sound out of context, it in no way mitigated the slaughter of wagonloads of Passenger Pigeons, Eskimo Curlews, and other game species by market gunners and sportsmen, or the appetite for fresh game on the table (see EDIBILITY), or the enthusiasm of male adolescents for collecting songbirds, their nests and eggs. Even serious students of birdlife and most of the early conservationists did most of their birdwatching through the sights of a shotgun. Then around 1875 there arose a phenomenon that seemed to spell doom for many of the world's most decorative bird species—though it would ultimately prove their salvation—the desire of all ladies of fashion to wear birds on their hats!

The advertisements for feather fashions are more amusing than shocking to the modern sensibility: there stands a pretty young lady—

elegant, well corseted, with an air of self-conscious superiority—apparently unaware that there is a dead grebe squatting among the silk flowers of her bonnet. But what now seems a peculiar and callous fad reigned unhindered for 25 years and survived under fire for at least 10 more. It made the fortunes of many milliners, earned good livings for plume hunters, and decimated populations of the most popular species, especially the plumed egrets. If it is difficult to put in perspective the 5–20 million birds per year that ended as frills, consider Frank CHAPMAN recording 40 species of "hat birds" on an afternoon's stroll in New York City in 1886. To the hunters, clean, cured bird skins brought from a few cents apiece for small or less desirable species to five dollars for a Roseate Spoonbill. And the treasured nuptial plumes or "aigrettes" were sold separately. In addition to egrets, gulls and terns were much in demand for their graceful wings. Smaller, colorful species were also popular (an entire dress made from the iridescent throat feathers of 3,000 hummingbirds was admired in a society column), and even woodpeckers and owls found their niche in *haute couture.*

By the 1880s it was clear to those few who cared that the combination of millinery fashion, the appetite for bird flesh, and shooting for sport would inevitably lead to the extinction of some species (as indeed it did— see EXTINCT BIRDS) unless something was done. In 1883 the American Ornithologists' Union was founded and almost immediately organized a Committee for the Protection of North American Birds, which served to enlist the efforts of prominent ornithologists—many of them wellborn and influential—in the incipient conservation movement. In 1886 the first Audubon Society was founded in New York and almost immediately attracted nearly 40,000 supporters, among them such cultural "lights" as Oliver Wendell Holmes and a new breed of sportsman-naturalist whose prototype was President Theodore Roosevelt. Another enlightened patrician of this ilk, George Bird Grinnell, who owned and ran Forest and Stream Publishing Company, produced the first Audubon magazine in 1887.

In spite of all this pro-avian activity—accompanied by a continued proliferation of popular bird books and articles and even some natural history in public school curricula—the country at large was still opposed or at best indifferent to the idea of bird protection. This was made manifest by the failure of the Audubon Society and its magazine in 1889 and the declaration by conservationist William Dutcher that 1895 represented the "low tide of bird protection." In 1896, however, the Audubon movement rallied with the formation of the Massachusetts Audubon Society under the direction of William Brewster. Other states followed this example and at the turn of the century formed a national federation that included 20 local Audubon societies (see AUDUBON SOCIETIES). In 1899 Frank Chapman started *Bird-Lore* magazine, a comparatively no-nonsense publication dedicated exclusively to the "study and protection of birds," and a

voice for the bird conservation movement, which the milliners and shooters were unable to shout down.

The early years of the new century saw the enactment of the first bird
protection laws with teeth, mostly patterned after a "Model Law" proposed by the AOU in 1886. This document clarified the distinction between game birds (ducks and geese; rails and coots, Wild Turkey; grouse;
pheasants and quail; and in those days most sandpipers and plovers) and
"nongame"; recommended prohibitions against the destruction of nests
and eggs of nongame species (except the House Sparrow); and allowed
the necessity of licensing scientific collectors.

As continues to be the case today, emotions and rhetoric over conservation reached apoplectic intensity. In a display of congressional wisdom
still entirely familiar, United States Senator Reed of Missouri announced
on the floor of the Senate in August 1913 that he "really, honestly want[ed]
to know why there should be any sympathy or sentiment about a long-
legged, long-beaked, long-necked bird that lives in swamps and eats tadpoles and fish and crawfish and things of that kind; why should we worry
ourselves into a frenzy because some lady adorns her hat with one of its
feathers, which appears to be the only use it has."

The most pious of the conservationists replied to the likes of Senator
Reed by calling them "human fiends," "bloated epicures" "sensualists,"
and worse.

It is impossible to designate a single event that turned the tide in favor of the conservationists—though the shooting to death of Audubon
warden Guy Bradley by a plume hunter in Florida in 1905 doubtless converted many skeptics—but by the start of World War I, the milliners were
having to make do with game birds and illicit imports, and market gunning was largely history. The early conservationists had good reason to
congratulate themselves, and we owe them much, though we can smile in
hindsight at their innocence of what was to come.

Conservation Comes of Age. As the United States became a modern,
fully industrialized society and especially after World War II a broad spectrum of new conservation issues emerged along with a growing awareness that species and habitats are not isolated entities that can be fenced
off and preserved, but rather parts of an interconnected ecosystem of
which human beings are a part. There also began to appear incontrovert-
ible evidence that our species—unlike any that had ever lived—had the
capability to wreak wholesale environmental havoc on the planet. The
dropping of atomic bombs on Hiroshima and Nagasaki in 1945 may be
seen as a global proclamation that humanity had attained god-like powers, but after the war, it also became increasingly apparent that we often
exercised these new-found powers irresponsibly with little consideration
of their consequences. In 1962 Rachel Carson published *Silent Spring,*
which documented pervasive threats to natural systems and human

health due to the indiscriminate use of chemical pesiticides in agriculture and for mosquito control. While some of Carson's data were criticized by industry scientists, her main premise was sound, and the alarm she sounded created a new consciousness about our relationship to the environment even among people who never read the book. Among the many studies launched to verify or disprove Carson's assertions were investigations of the causes of the precipitous and increasingly obvious decline of many raptors, including such high-visibility species as the Osprey and the Bald Eagle. It was shown conclusively that pesticides, especially DDT, applied to agricultural fields were being flushed by natural precipitation into aquatic systems and then concentrated as they moved up the food chain until top predators either got a lethal dose or were made infertile (for more detail, see THREATS [OF HUMAN ORIGIN] TO BIRDLIFE). The implications of these and other scientifically documented effects of industrial phenomena for human well being were not lost on the general public and in 1972 the use of DDT was prohibited by law in the United States.

The 1960s and 1970s were a time of great turbulence across the entire horizon of social issues. A new generation of Americans that had grown up in relative prosperity were less preoccupied with economic concerns, felt more connected to the world than had their parents, and began to question the status quo in matters of war and peace, racial justice, and the environment. The idealistic young environmentalists of this activist period discovered issues such as the destruction of the rain forest and the decimation of the great whales and envisioned global eco-disaster. This passionate outcry culminated in the first Earth Day in New York City in 1970. Alas, the dire warnings issued by 1960s "rebels" have proven all too valid.

Bird Conservation Today. Originally bird protection amounted to simply prohibiting humans from killing non-game birds for whatever purpose. Though large numbers of North American migrants are still killed for food in Latin America each year despite the enactment of migratory bird treaties, direct destruction of birds by humans in the United States and Canada is a relatively minor concern of today's conservationists. The hunting of game birds is now restricted to relatively few species (see HUNTING) and is regulated by state and federal law as to season and bag limits and taxed; and many hunters consider themselves conservationists out of enlightened self-interest. Wearing birds and market gunning are gone, probably forever, and while some boys of all ages continue to shoot at birds for fun and the occasional songbird stew doubtless gets served in rural areas, these misdemeanors are not considered threatening to the population of any bird species. Most present-day conservationists, however, would probably trade the new problems for the old without a moment's thought. Overpopulation, draining and filling of wetlands, reckless lumbering practices, pesticides, and oil spills are just a few of the

by-products of the post-industrial age that threaten not only birds but all life forms, including ourselves (SEE THREATS [OF HUMAN ORIGIN] TO BIRDLIFE). Since today's life-threatening phenomena tend to affect entire habitats or ecosystems (including the world ecosystem), conservation efforts have had to become more holistic in approach. Because of the overwhelming dominance of human life on the planet, we have also had to try to deliberately manage the survival of particular species, rather than simply removing a threat and letting nature control the recovery.

Most conservationists' energies today are devoted to four basic approaches often used in concert:

1. *Direct conservation efforts,* which include such strategies as buying large tracts of critical habitats for permanent protection; managing successional habitats important for the survival of many species through prescribed burning and other techniques; intensive wardening of severely threatened species, such as barrier beach birds decimated by off-road vehicles; and captive breeding of endangered species for eventual release into appropriate habitat.

2. *Research* on many critical questions about how ecosystems work and what threatened bird populations need to survive over time. This category also includes long-term monitoring of populations of selected bird species, the status of which is poorly understood in many cases.

3. *Advocacy,* including drafting and lobbying for stronger environmental protection laws, maintaining existing legislation against the constant pressure to weaken it and creating grass roots support for the environment at the local level.

4. *Education.* A major focus of many conservation organizations involving in-school programs, field programs through nature centers, camps, and publications and other media vehicles. While such programs are designed to be fun—not difficult, considering the subject matter—their single-minded goal is (or should be) to stimulate conservation *action.*

How Are We Doing? While awareness of and concern for birdlife has made encouraging progress in the last 30 years, populations of many bird species continue to decline, including those of some of our best-loved birds that we are used to thinking of as common. BirdLife International calculates that 12% of the world's bird species are in serious danger of extinction within the next 100 years and fully 20% are considered at risk. This does not mean that 80% of bird species are doing fine; in fact, evidence continues to mount that many species, though apparently not in immediate danger are suffering precipitous declines in their populations. In Europe, for example, 255 of species have undergone a decrease of more than 20% in more than a third of their populations in the last 20 years. Similar patterns are occurring in the most heavily populated regions of

North America. In Massachusetts for example 15% of resident bird species are on the state endangered species list.

While the threats to birdlife have changed, the dynamics of the eco-battlefield would be entirely familiar to the early conservationists. Despite the inescapable logic of giving meticulous protection to the only habitable environment we know of, the current trend in the United States as this book goes to press (2003) is to lift the few safeguards we have managed to install in favor of transient short-term gains, to cut off funds for environmental research and repair work, and to condemn environmentalists as spoilsports and impeders of human progress. The good news is that environmentalism is here to stay. It has become more than a movement. Increasingly a healthy global ecosystem with its biodiversity intact if not whole is an inescapable component of any sane vision of a viable future for the planet, especially among young people. If we can get beyond a few monster issues—the looming population bulge, our dependence on fossil fuels, economic inequality, the society-crippling effects of AIDS—then the logic of preserving our environment, including its remarkable birdlife, can probably prevail.

What Can I Do? Traditionally, conservation has been a people's movement. Its life force has always come from individuals who care about the quality of the environment they live in or about the welfare of their fellow animals. By contrast, the "enemy" is usually a large collective entity made up of people who don't live near what they intend to destroy and can't see the forest *or* the trees for the profits. The experience of the last 30 years has shown that a majority of people feel strongly about maintaining the beauty and diversity of the continent even at some expense to their standard of living. There is also a reasonably encouraging track record of conservation-minded citizens defeating the most powerful economic interests when they make their views and feelings known within a political process. Unfortunately, we are often ill-informed on the issues and the ways of even local government and therefore are often absent when the votes are counted. *Therefore:*

- Become more knowledgeable about birds or other aspects of the natural world. Many excellent (and enjoyable!) programs are now offered by colleges and conservation organizations, and free nature walks are often advertised in local newspapers. Take the kids along.
- If you have specialized knowledge about nature be sure to share it, especially with younger people. Appreciation of the natural world does not necessarily come naturally these days.
- Bone up on the conservation issues in your city or town and learn how these maters are handled within your municipal government, e.g., who has the power to protect or develop open space.
- Become a conservation volunteer as a member of your local conservation commission at a local wildlife sanctuary or other venue.

- Don't hesitate to write to or call your representatives at all levels of government. Expressions of thoughtful concern about environmental issues are needed by officials to support issues they favor and counter the (often self-interested) parties who oppose conservation measures. Contrary to what you may think, public servants often hear little from their constituents, and a few letters, e-mails, or phone calls can have a big impact on decisions.
- Join a reputable conservation organization and support it as generously as you can. Choose one with a reputation for accomplishing concrete goals such as protecting significant amounts of habitat and taking courageous stands against powerful economic interests. If you already belong to one join another: perhaps the ideal if affordable would be to support local, state/provincial, national, and international conservation efforts.
- Live a little "greener." Sacrifice some lawn for a patch of weeds or other useful bird habitat. Eradicate invasive plants and replant with native species. Dozens of similar suggestions are readily available from many conservation organizations.

See also AUDUBON SOCIETIES; BIRDLIFE INTERNATIONAL; ENDANGERED SPECIES; THREATS (OF HUMAN ORIGIN) TO BIRDLIFE.

CONSPECIFIC. Belonging to the same species; frequently used in arguing the validity of species/subspecies: "Are Rose-breasted and Black-headed Grosbeaks conspecific?"

CONTOUR FEATHER(S). The outer layer of feathers including flight and tail feathers, which give a bird its characteristic form. See PLUMAGE.

CONURE. A generic English name sometimes used for most of the species of New World parakeets. The term is popular with aviculturists, much less so with ornithologists/birdwatchers; however, see in Forshaw (1973–PARROT).

CONVERGENCE (convergent evolution). The development of similar traits in unrelated groups of organisms due to adaptation to similar living conditions. In a broad context, the development of the forearm into a wing in both bats and birds is an example. In birds a number of uncanny look-alikes from different families have evolved in this manner. Two striking examples are the superficial resemblance between the Northern Hemisphere members of the auk family (Alcidae) and the phylogenetically distant penguins and diving petrels of southern oceans (see Fig. 6).

COOPER, William, 1798?–1864 (Cooper's Hawk: *Accipiter cooperii*; Olive-sided Flycatcher: *Contopus cooperi*). Independently wealthy, taken with

Fig. 6. *Adaptive convergence.* Evolution has produced similar physical traits in unrelated groups of birds as a result of the constraints and opportunities present in the cold, nutrient-rich oceans surrounding both poles. All of the birds shown are countershaded in patterns of black and white and are adapted for capturing marine organisms under water. The Dovekie (1), an Arctic alcid, is much more closely related to the gulls and terns than it is to its look-alike, the Magellanic Diving Petrel (2) of sub-Antarctic waters. The extinct Great Auk (3), also an alcid from the North Atlantic, stood at a similar phylogenetic distance from another large, flightless sea bird, the Magellanic Penguin (4) of the Patagonian coast. The Dovekie and the Great Auk demonstrate another phenomenon of evolution, *adaptive radiation,* which produces strikingly *different* forms within a single group of species to fill available ecological niches. For more on these phenomena, see SPECIATION.

natural history from boyhood, and schooled in zoology in Europe, Cooper was a founder of the New York Lyceum of Natural History and a man of substantial reputation in the scientific community of his day. He was a student of paleontology, malacology, botany, and herpetology as well as ornithology. His dwindling prominence results from his scanty bibliography. He edited the last two volumes of Lucien BONAPARTE'S *American Ornithology.* Bonaparte described as a new species a hawk that Cooper had collected and named it for him. In a recent reversal of fame-by-taxonomy, Cooper gained a species at Nuttall's expense when Olive-sided Flycatcher was moved from the monotypic genus *Nuttallornis* to the peewee genus *Contopus.* This is especially poignant (or at least ironic) in that it was Nut-

tall who originally named this species for Cooper. See also NUTTALL. Cooper is also commemorated by *Tringa cooperi*, a sandpiper collected and described by Spencer BAIRD; it has proved to be unique (a hybrid?), no one having seen its like before or since until the recent appearance of Cox's Sandpiper. William Cooper's son, James, also became a well-known naturalist, one of the surgeon-collectors whom Baird sent west with the army and railroad surveys. James was interested in everything, but his name is now most often heard in the context of the Cooper Ornithological Society of California (see following entry).

COOPERATIVE BREEDING. See PARENTAL CARE.

COOPER ORNITHOLOGICAL SOCIETY. A nonprofit organization based in California that promotes the scientific study of birds and has a special interest in the birds of Mexico, Central and South America, and the Pacific. It was founded in 1893 and its name commemorates Dr. James G. Cooper, an early California ornithologist, and son of William COOPER, for whom Cooper's Hawk was named. The society publishes a quarterly journal, *The Condor*, which contains scientific papers, bird notes of more general interest, book reviews, etc. Contact through BIRDNET at www.nmnh. si.edu/BIRDNET/.

COOT. Standard English name for 11 members of the rail family (Rallidae; order Gruiformes), all in the genus *Fulica*. One species, the American Coot, breeds continentwide and the Eurasian Coot *(Fulica atra)* has occurred as a vagrant to both coasts. It is now agreed that all "Caribbean" Coots reported in the United States (excluding Puerto Rico and Virgin Islands) have been morphological variants of American Coot.

All species of coots have a uniformly slaty-black plumage with yellow, red, or white bills and some form of frontal shield (an elaborate horny caruncle in one South American species). Their most distinctive external feature is their peculiarly lobed toes, which are adapted for swimming. Coots are equally at home swimming and diving like a duck and walking along lake margins like a rail. They appear to be weak fliers, but some populations undertake long migrations. Like the rails, coots feed on a wide variety of plant and animal foods.

The coots achieve their greatest diversity in South America, where 8 species are resident. However, at least 1 species of coot is abundant on every major landmass in the world, excluding Arctic islands and Antarctica. The American Coot is found south of the boreal forest throughout North America, though in much of the east it occurs as a migrant only. As a potential game bird, its continued abundance may be attributable in part to its unpalatability—it is said to be muddy-tasting.

As a bird name "coot" goes back at least to the mid-sixteenth century and is based on the bird's monosyllabic tooting calls. There is also an

etymological association with "scoter," and scoters are widely known as "coots" today by east coast hunters. The naive, comical "expression" of coots and their distinctive, awkward head-bobbing gesture when swimming have made "coot" a metaphorical term for a fool"; also a pejorative for the elderly, as in the Vermont phrase, "the old coot don't know enough to suck alum and drool." And to "coot along" implies slow, halting progress.

For family characteristics, see RAIL.

COPULATION. In birds, accomplished by contact of the everted cloacae of male and female of a species, aided in a few groups (e.g., waterfowl) by a penis-like structure. This act is sometimes referred to as a "cloacal kiss." See REPRODUCTIVE SYSTEM.

CORKSCREW SWAMP. See FLORIDA.

CORMORANT. Standard English name in North America for all members of the family Phalacrocoracidae (order Pelecaniformes). There are 37 species of cormorants worldwide, all in the genus *Phalacrocorax,* of which 6 breed in North America.

Cormorants are moderately large (2–3 feet), usually black, swimming and diving birds, with fairly long, cylindrical, hooked bills. Like the other members of their order, they have webbing between all four toes and no nostril openings in the bill. All species have throat pouches and brightly colored patches of facial skin at the base of the bill in breeding plumage.

Cormorants are gregarious by nature and are customarily seen standing in erect battalions on rocks or pilings—often with their wings spread (see BATHING)—or swimming, partially submerged, with only the head, neck, and part of the back showing above the surface. They feed mainly on fish but also take amphibians, marine/aquatic invertebrates, and even some plants. In migration cormorants fly in long V formations and are often mistaken for geese.

All cormorants are colonial breeders that prefer offshore islands or remote peninsulas, where they nest on the ground or in arboreal "shaggeries" (cormorantries), often in company with herons and other wading birds. Ground nesters assemble piles of seaweed; tree nests are made largely of sticks. The 2–4 (rarely, 6) eggs are pale blue or green and unmarked, with a white, chalky coating that typically becomes scratched and stained during incubation.

Cormorants are generally silent but are capable of some guttural croaks uttered in the various "emotional" incidents of the breeding season.

Some species of cormorants are strictly marine (e.g., Brandt's), others largely prefer fresh or brackish water (e.g., Neotropic), while a few (e.g., Double-crested) are apparently equally at home in fresh or salt water.

The family is distributed worldwide in coastal areas except for the islands of the central Pacific Ocean. In North America cormorants are familiar along all coasts except icebound arctic ones, as well as on many large lakes and rivers of the interior. Northern populations of some species are migratory, but few North American birds winter beyond coastal waters. Cormorant populations have increased dramatically along the northeast coast and in the Great Lakes within the last decade. The reason for the increase (upward fluctuation in food-fish supply? lack of persecution?) is as yet undetermined, but fishery authorities are beginning to worry about adverse effects of overabundant cormorants on threatened anadromous fish species such as salmon, and about predation at hatcheries and seines. It has also been documented that large inland cormorant colonies have caused declines in important sport fisheries in certain conditions, though, in general, cormorants' impact on food and game fish has proven to be negligible.

"Cormorant" is derived from one or more Romance-language variations of the Latin *corvus marinas,* i.e., "sea crow." "Shag" is the standard British name for all but one species of cormorant, and this name is widespread here as a colloquial name among east coast fishermen.

CORMORANTRY. A breeding colony of cormorants, also called a shaggery. Other specific names for bird colonies are given under NOUNS OF ASSEMBLAGE.

CORNELL LAB OF ORNITHOLOGY. The preeminent academically based North American institution focusing on the study and conservation of birdlife. The mission of this nonprofit, member organization is "to interpret and conserve the earth's biological diversity through research, education, and citizen science focused on birds."

According to Arthur A. Allen, the laboratory's first director, the Cornell Lab was named by the eminent entomologist James G. Needham to justify the appointment of an ornithologist to a zoology department renowned mainly for its work on insects. It became a separate department of the university in 1955 and was the first institution in North America to offer a doctorate in ornithology.

Long distinguished for its broad spectrum of scientifically based programs, the Lab continues to expand its efforts integrated under four broad categories.

Research programs focus on understanding "the causes and consequences in the distribution and abundance of North American birds." These form the foundation on which other programs of the Lab are built and encompass selected bird population studies, a Bioacoustics Research Program (BRP) and the Macaulay Library of Natural Sounds. Originally established by Peter Kellogg and Albert Brand, the Library now houses

one of the most comprehensive collection of bird and other animal sounds in the world and the BRP is a world leader in research on whales and elephants as well as birds.

Education. The Lab offers a range of classroom, home study, and school-based programs focusing on birds, and disseminates information on birds and other aspects of natural history though various media. For two decades starting in 1962, the Lab published *The Living Bird,* an annual ornithological journal that concentrated on field studies. In the early 1980s this was transformed into a glossy, popular (now award-winning) quarterly covering all aspects of bird life; the Lab also publishes *Birdscope,* a quarterly newsletter focusing on citizen science projects.

Citizen Science. The Cornell Lab has been a leader in the development of programs that involve the public in collecting data and other activities that contribute to bird research and conservation. Programs such as Project FeederWatch, the Birdhouse Network, and Citizen Science in the Schoolyard are designed to collect scientifically usable data, while giving participants an introduction to research and a role in helping native bird populations.

One of the Lab's most innovative concepts (developed in cooperation with the National Audubon Society) is BirdSource (http://birdsource. cornell.edu/), an interactive on-line database that collects information on backyard birds, hawk migration and many other bird phenomena.

The Lab now manages the databases for the Christmas Bird Count (see BIRDING EVENTS) and the BREEDING BIRD SURVEY. See also CITIZEN SCIENCE.

Conservation. The integrated programs noted above all contribute to the broader imperative of bird (and biodiversity) conservation. Among specific hands-on bird conservation projects are species atlases (e.g., Cerulean and Golden-winged Warblers), Project Tanager, Birds in Forested Landscapes, and leadership within cooperative efforts such as PARTNERS IN FLIGHT AND THE IMPORTANT BIRD AREAS program.

For full descriptions of the Lab's programs see their excellent website: http://birds.cornell.edu/.

See also SAPSUCKER WOODS.

CORNEOUS. Horny; having a hard texture such as that of a bird's bill.

CORNIPLUME. A horn-like tuft of feathers, such as the "ears" of several owl species, the "crests" of the Double-crested Cormorant, and the "horns" of the Horned Lark.

CORVID(S). Any member of the bird family Corvidae. In the plural, a name by which the crows, ravens, jays, magpies, and nutcrackers can be referred to collectively. Nineteen species of corvids breed in North America. See CROW (includes ravens); JAY; MAGPIE; NUTCRACKER.

CORY, Charles B., 1857–1921 (Cory's Shearwater: *Calonectris diomedea*). Wellborn, well educated, and independently wealthy (until ruined at the age of 46), Cory spent his life collecting bird specimens, especially in North America and the Caribbean, and writing faunal works on the areas he knew best. His vast accumulation of bird skins became the nucleus of the collection at the Field Museum of Natural History (Chicago Natural History Museum). On Cory's personal attributes, Gruson (1972– BIOGRAPHY) is eloquent: "Cory was the blithe spirit of American ornithology . . . A wit, raconteur, tireless ballroom dancer, sportsman, yachtsman, marksman, hypnotist, belletrist, writer of songs and light operas."

COSMOPOLITAN. Loosely defined: occurring worldwide, i.e., at least in the Northern, Southern, Eastern, and Western Hemispheres. In a more restrictive sense: occurring in all of the major zoogeographic regions (see DISTRIBUTION; ZOOGEOGRAPHY).

It can be stated as a truism that the broader the taxonomic grouping, the more likely it is to be cosmopolitan, i.e., most orders of birds are cosmopolitan, and *many families* of birds are so, whereas relatively few genera can claim the distinction and even fewer species. The Great Egret, Cattle Egret, Osprey, Peregrine Falcon, Common Moorhen,* Kentish (including Snowy) Plover,* Black-winged Stilt,* Gull-billed, Caspian, Sandwich, and Roseate Terns, and Barn Owl Barn Swallow have cosmopolitan breeding ranges; the Black-bellied Plover, Ruddy Turnstone, Red Knot, Sanderling, Red-necked Phalarope, Common Tern, and all three Jaeger species breed in the Temperate Zone worldwide (all but the Common Tern in the Arctic) and migrate to equally cosmopolitan wintering grounds; Barn Swallow and Sand Martin (Bank Swallow) follow a similar pattern, though both of these also have localized breeding populations in the Southern Hemisphere; the House Sparrow has become cosmopolitan by a combination of introduction and an ability to spread to nearly any place of human habitation.

COSTA, Louis Marie Pantaléon, Marquis de Beau-Regard, 1806–64 (Costa's Hummingbird: *Calypte costae*). A Sardinian (French Savoyard) military officer, diplomat, and historian. He owned a collection of hummingbird specimens.

COTINGA (kuh-TING-uh). Collective name for any member of the Neotropical family Cotingidae (order Passeriformes). The Rose-throated Becard, which breeds north to the extreme southwestern United States was once placed in this family, but is now considered to be a tyrant flycatcher (family Tyrannidae) of uncertain taxonomic affinities (see BECARD).

---

* Subject to a broad taxonomic interpretation.

COUES (cows), Elliott, 1842–99. Until recently Greater Pewee (*Contopus pertinax*) was known as Coues' Flycatcher. One of the foremost and easily the most interesting of the American ornithologists of the late nineteenth century. Coues was born in New Hampshire, graduated from the college and medical school of what is now Georgetown University in Washington, DC, and almost immediately began a writing career that eventually included almost 1,000 works, several of them major volumes. He was the most eminent of the army surgeons who collected specimens for Spencer BAIRD while on duty in the western states and became secretary and naturalist of the (U.S.-Canadian) Border Commission, out of which experience came two of his own ornithological works, *Birds of the Northwest* and *Birds of the Colorado Valley*. He also published extensively on western mammals. As secretary and naturalist for the Geological and Geographical Survey of the Territories, Coues added papers on the history of the exploration of the American West to his extensive bibliography. He was a founder of the American Ornithologists' Union and his 1882 *Check-list of North American Birds* was the basis for the AOU publication of the same name, the first edition of which appeared shortly thereafter. What set Coues apart from the other brilliant naturalists of his time was his personality, which has been described as "electrifying." He was physically handsome and had a highly developed sense of humor, boundless energy, and a greater than average taste for the eccentric. The most notable example of this characteristic was his passionate conversion late in his life to the cult of the infamous theosophical charlatan Madame Blavatsky. He took to spiritualism with the same zest he brought to his other interests but was eventually banished from the movement for publishing the details of a Blavatskian hoax. Coues has remained unchallenged as the best writer among American ornithologists and much of what was in his personality is evident in the eloquent, witty, and opinionated introductory chapters to his *Key to North American Birds*. Besides being a landmark in American ornithology, this volume contains a fine evocation of what being a nineteenth-century naturalist was like, from how to clean your collecting gun ("elbow grease"), to the wisdom (none) of taking "stimulation" when afield, to the perils of skinning a putrid bird (festering sores), to the excesses of the overzealous "splitters" who dominated taxonomic theory in Coues' time. The loss of his eponym is a pity.

COUNTERSINGING. The vocal response of a male bird on territory to another singing male on an adjacent territory. Also sometimes used in the sense of ANTIPHONAL SONG.

COUNTING. The ability to estimate accurately the number of birds in a passing flock is a useful skill for participants in sea watches and other kinds of censuses. By practicing with beans and other inanimate objects

of varying number and size, one can develop a high degree of precision in this perceptual technique. See Arbib in *American Birds,* 26:706. See also CENSUS. For counting ability *of birds,* see INTELLIGENCE.

COURTSHIP. An early stage in the breeding cycle, beginning with male and female birds of a given species coming together and leading to copulation. A few migratory species arrive in established pairs on the breeding ground (see PAIR FORMATION), but for most species courtship begins with the attraction of the female by the male's territorial song or display. Once he has attracted a potential mate to his territory, the male follows her around, displaying to her, and attempts to copulate. He is usually rejected at first, but if the female remains on his territory, pair formation is established, and the female will permit copulation within a few days. In the brief period of chaste betrothal, the male may let up on his song or even stop singing altogether. But once allowed his connubial privileges, he resumes his territorial behavior with renewed enthusiasm, which does not normally abate until the eggs hatch.

Display rituals are a crucial element of courtship. They take many forms, each with a special significance—e.g., attraction, enforcement of the pair bond, and preparation for copulation—and they may continue even after the young have hatched. For more detail, see DISPLAY. See also COURTSHIP FEEDING; LEK; PAIR FORMATION; SONG; TERRITORY.

COURTSHIP FEEDING. A ritual of the breeding cycle during which a male bird offers food to its mate. It has been recorded in some herons, gulls, doves, cuckoos, and many passerines. It has been observed preceding, during, and after copulation, but, contrary to the implication of its name, may take place even after the young have hatched. The female usually calls and begs in response to the offering of food by the male and the calls used are the same as those used by recently fledged young.

COVERTS (KUV-erts). Contour feathers that overlap the primary and secondary feathers of the wings and also the main tail feathers (rectrices) from above and below. The coverts are divided into several named sections, e.g., the greater secondary coverts (see WING; TAIL; and Fig. 35).

The feathers covering the ear holes are called the ear coverts or auriculars.

COVEY (KUV-ee). A widely used collective noun referring to a mother and young or a flock of small game birds, especially quail.

COWBIRD. Standard English name for 6 species of New World blackbirds (family Icteridae; order Passeriformes), all but 1 in the genus *Molothrus.*

Three species breed in North America; the rest are Neotropical in distribution.

All but one of the cowbirds are brood parasites, and the exception, the Bay-winged Cowbird of South America, often appropriates the nest of other songbirds. This antisocial behavior is biologically redressed by the Screaming Cowbird, which lays its eggs exclusively in the nests of its only nonparasitic congener.

The life history of the Brown-headed Cowbird has been well studied (see especially Hann 1941; Friedmann 1929, 1971; and Lowther 1993); it represents the most successful form of avian brood parasitism to have evolved in the New World.

Like other brood parasites, Brown-headed Cowbirds do not engage in any form of nest-building behavior or develop brood patches. But females do occupy a defined territory in which to parasitize; all individuals occupy restricted breeding and wintering ranges for life; and males erect their shiny plumage in nuptial display. However, both sexes are promiscuous. Fertilized females locate hosts by watching for nest-building activity, typically that of small to medium-sized songbirds. The species is known to have laid eggs in the nests of 220 bird species, including (possibly by accident) shorebirds and ducks. One hundred forty-four species have reared cowbird young, its most frequent hosts being small tyrant flycatchers, *Catharus* thrushes, vireos, wood warblers, tanagers, finches and sparrows; only rarely does it parasitize cavity nesters. As one might expect, the commonest species are the most frequent hosts. The Bronzed Cowbird is known to parasitize only 62 species of birds, mainly finch-like birds and members of its own family, but some of the Neotropical hosts of this species, which reaches its northernmost distribution in the southwestern United States may remain undiscovered.

Typically, the female cowbird waits until the host's nest is complete and a clutch is begun before slipping onto the nest before dawn—while both parent birds are away—and depositing a single egg (white speckled with brown) within a few seconds. Much variation is recorded in this sequence of events—some cowbird eggs being laid before the host nest is complete or after the host young are hatched—but the preceding is apparently the most successful strategy. Later in the day (or on the preceding or following day) the parasite removes one of the host's eggs, piercing it with its bill and eventually eating the contents; there are a few records of cowbirds removing nestlings of the host species as well. The best available evidence indicates that the female cowbird parasitizes additional nests until a "clutch" of up to 6 eggs is completed and that she usually produces 2–3 "clutches" a season, or a total of 10–15 eggs; however, Nice (1949) records a total of 25 eggs in 7 clutches for a single cowbird. It is unusual for the female cowbird to lay 2 (or even 3) eggs in a single nest, but a nest may be visited by several parasites and contain as many as 8 cowbird eggs (Byers 1950).

Unlike the avian brood parasites in other families (see BROOD PARA-
SITISM), cowbirds do not exhibit any form of egg or nestling mimicry, and
hostility by prospective hosts is seems to be limited or sporadic unless
they are perceived to be menacing the nest after incubation or brooding is
well established; however, harassment of the parasite by parent birds has
been observed in some species.

The responses of cowbird hosts vary among different species and individuals. About half of individuals parasitized accept the changeling
as one of their own and rear it faithfully even when it results in the starvation of other nestlings. The most frequent negative response to being
parasitized is to desert the nest, but certain species—Pettingill (1970–
ORNITHOLOGY) cites the American Robin and Gray Catbird—can recognize cowbird eggs and remove them. (Rejection behavior is now a cottage
industry in avian behavioral ecology, see Rothstein and Robinson (1998–
BROOD PARASITISM). A relatively rare solution—habitual with the Yellow
Warbler—is to build a new nest over the parasitized one, covering the
host's eggs as well as the cowbird's.

The cowbird incubation period is unusually short and the nestling
fast-growing and usually larger than its foster siblings, so that even if the
cowbird egg is laid after the host's young are hatched, the parasite has a
chance of survival. Cowbird nestlings do not instinctively push host eggs
out of the nest (as does that most famous of brood parasites, the Eurasian
Cuckoo) or kill the nestlings directly (as do the honeyguides), but it often
starves members of the normal brood by consuming more than its share
of the food brought by the parent and will sometimes deliberately evict a
rightful tenant. In most cases, however, the host is able to fledge some of
its own young as well as the cowbird.

The effect of brood parasites on their host and therefore their own
populations is a complex question, which ornithologists are still deliber-
ating. Logically, in "natural" situations the cowbird populations and their
effect on host species populations reach a natural equilibrium since the
extinction of the host in a host-specific parasite would put the parasite
out of business. But in cowbirds, where host-switching is common, it is
plausible that uncommon hosts could be driven to extinction with little
effect on the parasite's overall population. There can be no question that
abnormally high cowbird populations can be detrimental locally, notably
in the cases of Kirtland's Warbler and Least Bell's and Black-headed Vireos
(see ENDANGERED BIRDS). And it is also apparent that the Brown-
headed Cowbird is more widespread and numerous than it once was due
to human land clearing, agricultural and livestock-rearing practices and
that it may have access to more nests of forest interior species due to sub-
urbanization and other forms of habitat fragmentation.

The distribution of the Brown-headed Cowbird once coincided
largely with that of the plains Bison and the species was once known as

"buffalo bird." All of our cowbirds continue to seek bovine company, following cows as well as other livestock to catch the insects they flush while grazing and (at least in the case of the Bronzed Cowbird) picking ticks from the backs of their mammalian associates. However, cowbirds are largely granivorous and the pastoralization of the vast eastern forests (whether for livestock or crops) has enabled the Brown-headed Cowbird to expand its range to continent wide and into open habitats with and without cows. Their fecundity and fondness for grain have made them pests of feedlots and grain fields. This species now breeds throughout North America south of the Arctic and is a permanent resident in the southern part of its range. The Bronzed Cowbird is essentially a Middle American species. The Shiny Cowbird ranges through most of South America and is well established in the West Indies at least partly though human introduction; it has been established in southern Florida since the 1980s and it is casual west to Oklahoma and Texas and north to North Carolina and has been recorded once in Maine.

For other icterids, see BLACKBIRD; ORIOLE; GRACKLE; MEADOWLARK; BOBOLINK; see also PARASITISM; BROOD PARASITISM; and related references.

CRAKE. Name in wide usage worldwide for most species of small, short-billed rails. The Eurasian Corn Crake *(Crex crex)* is an accidental straggler to North America for which there are 20 records, mainly from the nineteenth century; the Paint-billed Crake *(Neocrex erythrops),* which nests no closer than western Panama, has shown up twice in winter in Texas and Virginia. Many species in the genera *Porzana, Laterallus,* and *Coturnicops,* to which our Sora, Black Rail, and Yellow Rail belong, respectively, are called "crakes." The name comes from the call, a loud rasping rendition of it scientific name.

CRANE. Standard English name for all 15 members of the family Gruidae (order Gruiformes), 2 of which breed in North America; a third species, the Common Crane of Eurasia, has occurred about 15 times as a vagrant.

The cranes range in size between 30 and 60 inches and are superficially much like the herons and storks, with very long legs and neck; fairly long (but not *very* long) bill; broad, powerful wings; and a short tail. Many crane species have patches of bare red skin on the forehead and elongated and/or curled secondary feathers that are used in display. Like the storks and unlike the herons (usually), they fly with necks extended. The cranes feed in uplands, including cultivated fields, more habitually than the other long-legged wading birds and are virtually omnivorous, with a strong taste for tuberous roots as well as small vertebrates and large invertebrates. They are renowned for their courtship dances and are regarded as sacred in the Orient, where they have proven inspirational for

many generations of traditional painters and poets (see HUMAN CUL-
TURE, BIRDS IN).

Cranes' nests consist of piles of plant material—a considerable heap
when built in shallow wetlands or merely a hollow with a sparse lining in
drier sites. The usually 2 (atypically 1 or 3) eggs are yellowish buff to olive
with reddish-brown splotches and speckles and similar but paler (lavender or grayish) subsurface markings.

Wild, bugling cries and less spectacular honking or grunting calls are
both typical.

Cranes range to the high Arctic in the Holarctic region and to the tropics in Africa, Asia, and Australia. They are absent from Central and South
America, the Malaysian and Polynesian archipelagos, and New Zealand.

The two North American species, Sandhill and Whooping Cranes, are
essentially North American endemics, though there is a breeding population of sandhills in northeastern Siberia and a few birds winter annually in
Japan. Sandhills range from arctic Alaska to Florida (resident population)
and winter mainly in the southwestern United States and northern Mexico. For more on Whooping Crane see ENDANGERED BIRDS.

"Crane" is recognizable as a name for these birds a long way back, as
in the Old English *cran*. Beyond this the word mavens find Indo-European
roots such as *gar* (to cry out), referring presumably to the distinctive ut-
terings produced in gruid courtship rituals. The name also has a long and
continuing history of colloquial use for any tall wading bird, especially the
larger herons.

CRAVERI, Federico, 1815–90 (Craveri's Murrelet: *Endomychura craveri*).
A native of Turin, Italy, Professor Craveri spent 20 years in Mexico, where
he taught chemistry in Mexico City. He also toured the country extensively, collecting rock and animal specimens, which he shipped back to
the Academy of Science in his hometown. While investigating Raza Island
in the Gulf of California (apparently to assess the guano potential), he collected a small alcid. It was eventually named for him by his countryman
Count Tommaso A. Salvadori, director of the Zoological Museum in Turin.

CRÈCHE (kraysh or kresh). In general usage the term means a nursery or
foundling home. Ornithologically it refers to the "pooling" of precocial
chicks of the same age from a number of nests in a colony. Among North
American species, Common Eiders and Royal and Sandwich Terns are
known to form crèches. See YOUNG, DEVELOPMENT OF.

CREEPER. Standard English generic name, alone or in combination, for
many species in several families of birds worldwide. In North America it
applies unambiguously to our only member of the treecreeper family
(Certhiidae), the Brown Creeper *(Certhia americana)*. For a discussion of

this problem of vernacular nomenclature and a family account, see TREE CREEPER.

CREPUSCULAR (cre-PUS-kya-ler). In the context of animal behavior, the term means active in low levels of light, especially at dusk. No North American bird species is *exclusively* crepuscular, but some species of owls, swifts, and nightjars are particularly active or conspicuous in the twilight hours before sunset and dawn. Some shorebirds (e.g., woodcock and snipe) and songbirds (e.g., Henslow's Sparrow) are especially active at these hours especially in the context of courtship. The Black Skimmer, which can feed best in calm water (see SKIMMER and Fig. 3), usually takes advantage of the low wind levels characteristic of dawn and dusk and is therefore largely crepuscular in its feeding habits.

CREST. An adornment of feathers, usually peaked, on the top of the head; not readily distinguishable from a "tuft," e.g., Tufted Titmouse, or very reliable as to general contour, e.g., Double-crested Cormorant. Only 7 North American species can claim to be "nomenclaturally crested": Double-crested Cormorant, Crested Auklet, Great Crested Flycatcher, Brown (Wied's) Crested Flycatcher, Crested Caracara, Crested Myna (introduced), and Blue Jay *(Cyanocitta cristata)*; Black-crested Titmouse is now widely considered a subspecies of Tufted Titmouse. Many other species, e.g., Scaled Quail, Royal Tern, Belted Kingfisher, are crested without acknowledgment. For a detailed analysis of the geographical distribution of crests and other appendages, see Pidler in the 1973 edition of *The Auklet*, p. 9.

CRISSUM (Crissal Thrasher). The undertail coverts; the area of feathers between the vent and the rectrices (see Fig. 35). On the Crissal Thrasher this area is dark chestnut, contrasting sharply with its generally gray-brown coloration; no other thrasher has a distinctive crissum, but a close relative, the Gray Catbird, does.

CROP. A sac-like appendage opening into the gullet (esophagus) where food is stored temporarily before digestion or regurgitation. Absent or poorly developed in most birds but well developed in species of doves and gallinaceous birds. More loosely, any enlargement of the gullet used for food storage. Also called the ingluvies. See DIGESTIVE SYSTEM.

CROP MILK. A "cheesy" secretion from the lining of the crop, regurgitated to feed nestlings during their early development. Like the milk of mammals, it is composed mainly of fat and protein, is rich in A and B vitamins, and its production is stimulated by the pituitary hormone prolactin. Though especially characteristic of members of the pigeon family, crop milk is also produced by the Greater Flamingo and Emperor Penguin.

Pigeons and doves have very well-developed crops, which, as in other birds, are used for storing food (see DIGESTIVE SYSTEM and Fig. 27). In the last week to 10 days of the incubation period, the interior lining (epithelium) of this sac becomes greatly thickened in both sexes. The "milk" is contained in the cells of this layer, which are progressively shed into the crop cavity ready for regurgitation. For the first 4 or 5 days after hatching, nestlings are fed exclusively on this crop milk, but gradually thereafter it is mixed with increasing amounts of seeds (pigeons do not feed their young any animal food). Milk production continues for up to 18 days, its cessation coinciding roughly with the young's departure from the nest.

CROSSBILL. Standard English name for a presently undetermined number species of cardueline finches (family Fringillidae; order Passeriformes). Traditionally 3 species have been recognized, including 2 in North America. Recent work on Red Crossbill (Groth 1993) distinguishes at least 9 species in this complex in North America alone, which can (sometimes) be identified by proportions and call.

The most striking distinction between the crossbills and the other "winter finches" that breed in northern coniferous forests is, of course, the former's peculiarly elongated and crossed mandibles. Though crossbills frequently eat seeds of fruit (after slicing the pulp in two with a scissorlike action), pick up seeds or insects in an unexceptional manner, and even take suet from feeders, the unique function of their unusual bills is to pry open the scales of *closed* cones. It has long been recognized that different geographical populations of crossbills have bills of varying size and strength, which correspond to the heaviness of the preferred cones to be "cracked." The relatively delicate-billed White-winged Crossbill prefers larch cones; the massive-billed Parrot Crossbill of Europe specializes in the toughest of green Scotch pine cones. Among the best distinguishing characters of the "new" species of Red Crossbills are the length and shape of their bills, which also reflects feeding preferences. For a detailed description of the cone-opening procedure, see FOOD/FEEDING and Fig. 3; see also Benkman (1992).

The crossing of the mandibles takes place gradually after hatching, the upper mandible beginning to lengthen by the 14th day, but no crossing is evident for about 4 weeks. At this time the lower mandible starts to bend to one side and soon sticks up beyond the upper. Only the horny sheath of the bill, not the bones beneath, is bent and curved. The feet of crossbills are also specially adapted—notably large with heavy claws—to hold cones while prying them open.

The lives of the crossbills are dictated to a large extent by northern (and montane) cone crops. Different populations time breeding so that hatching coincides with an abundance of ripe cones. Since cones provide easy meals at all seasons, both Red and White-winged Crossbills can

breed throughout the year. The young are altricial but unusually downy at hatching and can withstand being uncovered for brief periods in ambient temperatures at least as low as −35°C (−31° F).

Like other "winter finches," crossbills are given to periodic "irruptions," during which they appear (and even remain to breed) south of their "normal" winter range sometimes in large numbers. This phenomenon is also tied to the success of the northern cone crops in relation to the size of crossbill populations (see IRRUPTION/ERUPTION). Seasonal incursions of crossbills and the birds' fascinating feeding adaptation have long been observed. The English diarist R. Carew wrote in 1607: "there came a flocke of birds into Cornwall, about Harvest season, in bignesse not much exceeding a sparrow, which made a foule spoyle of the apples. Their bills were thwarted crosswise at the end, and with these they would cut an apple in two at one snap, eating onely the kernels."

Crossbills have largely circumboreal distributions. The White-winged breeds well beyond the Arctic Circle, but does not generally range south of northern forests except in irruption years (though there is a summer record for the mountains of New Mexico and a disjunct, nonmigratory population in Hispaniola). Members of the Red Crossbill complex do not nest so far north, but range south in the mountains until the pines run out in the Nicaraguan highlands.

For general family characteristics, see FINCH. For an interesting comparison with the recent taxonomic work by Groth, see Griscom's monograph on the Red Crossbill, *Proc. Boston Soc. Nat. Hist.* 41:77–210.

CROW. Standard English name for about 30 members of the family Corvidae (order Passeriformes). Also used in a broader collective sense to refer to the approximately 43 species of the genus *Corvus,* including the jackdaws, rooks, and ravens as well as the crows, and to refer to the family as a whole, including the jays, magpies, treepies, choughs, and nutcrackers as well as the above-named forms. Including the 2 ravens, 6 species of crows breed in North America.

The *Corvus* crows are among the largest songbirds, ranging in length from the comparatively diminutive Jackdaw (13 inches) to the Common Raven, which, excepting species with inordinately long tail feathers (e.g., the lyrebirds), can fairly claim to be the largest passerine bird in the world. All crows are husky birds, with stout (sometimes massive) bills; powerful, broad wings; sturdy legs and feet well adapted to walking; and short to moderately long tails. The plumage of most species of crows is entirely glossy black, but several have broad areas of gray feathering, one has extensive white on the nape and breast, and brown and iridescent blue overtones are not uncommon. It has recently been noticed that at least some crows have iridescent plumage patterns visible only in the ultraviolet portion of the color spectrum. These are presumably striking to other crows

but of no use to birders without special optics in distinguishing look-alike species.

Crows are virtually omnivorous except for green plants. Insects, crustaceans, shellfish, small vertebrates of all kinds (including nestling birds), eggs, carrion (including dead fish), garbage, fruit, and grain are all staple items of the crow diet. They tend to gather in large foraging flocks sometimes containing hundreds of individuals. Many crow species soar freely and engage in playful aerobatics.

Crows are typically gregarious and some species nest in colonies. They make large, bulky stick cups in trees and shrubs, on rock ledges (Common Raven), and in abandoned buildings. Most species plaster the cup with mud and/or dung and then provide an inner lining of bark strips and other fine plant material, wool, hair, etc. The 3–8 eggs (average 4–5 in most species) are pale or moderately dark green or blue (rarely white), sparsely to very densely speckled and splotched with olive and dark brown.

Crow calls are notably harsh and guttural for songbirds, but individual species tend to have a fairly wide repertoire of calls. Crows in captivity have proven themselves to be excellent vocal mimics of the human voice and other sounds (see SONG) but rarely exhibit this talent in the wild. The combination of their abundance and fondness for grain earns crows little love among farmers (see PROBLEMS INVOLVING BIRDS), and they are also traditional targets for sport shooting in many parts of the world.

To the extent that the term can be applied to any bird, the crows have a reputation for being "smart" (see INTELLIGENCE). There are many elaborate hunting tales recounting the cleverness of crows in avoiding decoys and recognizing the hunter's intent. And these casual observations are supported by experimenters who have found that crows are able to learn "tricks" more quickly than birds from other families. Heinrich's work (2000) indicates that ravens are capable of "insight learning" as well as the more rudimentary "reinforcement learning" (see INTELLIGENCE). Some taxonomists believe the crows to be the most highly evolved of all bird families, based on the charming (if self-serving) notion that mental development is proof of evolutionary "excellence." Their cleverness and "personality," in combination with their blackness, have made crows almost as ubiquitous as owls in folklore and superstition (see IMAGINATION, BIRDS IN).

Crows show broad habitat tolerances and are widely distributed, though they are absent in South America, New Zealand (except for the introduced Rook), and many oceanic islands. The American Crow and Common Raven range continentwide in North America; our other species are much more local. The northern populations of American Crow are migratory; otherwise, crows are relatively sedentary.

"Crow" comes straight from the call, though as Choate and Paynter (1985–NAMES) point out, "crowing" suggests more the sound of a rooster than a crow these days.

See also JAY; MAGPIE; NUTCRACKER.

CROWN. The top of the head, technically including the area above the eye between the forehead (front) and the nape. See Fig. 1.

CRUS (rhymes with "bus") (pl.: crura [KROOR-uh]). The part of the leg between the knee and the ankle. On a bird, the section above the "tarsus," called the "drumstick" on table birds. See LEG/FOOT.

CRYPTIC. In reference to birds, usually refers to plumage pattern and coloration that conceal a species from predators ("procryptic"), but can also refer to so-called "anticryptic" plumage or behavior that fools potential *prey.* Though the latter is little-studied in birds, it has been suggested that the Zone-tailed Hawk mimics the Turkey Vulture in form, coloration, and manner of flight to capture prey, which perceive the vulture as unthreatening. See also MIMICRY; COLOR AND PATTERN.

CRYPTIC SPECIES. Synonymous with SIBLING SPECIES.

CUCKOO. Standard English name (including hyphenated forms such as ground-cuckoo) for about 78 members of the family (order Cuculiformes); Sibley and Monroe (1990–CHECKLIST) divide these into 4 distinct families. In the broader interpretation the family also encompasses the North American ANIS and ROADRUNNER as well as a wide assortment of Old World couas, coucals, koels, and malkohas. Three species of cuckoos breed in North America and 2 others have occurred as accidental stragglers (see Appendix II).

Cuckoos are slender birds with long tails and slender, decurved bills. They exhibit great variation in form and color worldwide but all of the North American species measure about a foot in length, are brown above, paler below, and have colored fleshy eye rings and some form of spotting on the tips of the outer tail feathers. The feet of cuckoos have 2 toes (I and IV) pointing to rearward while the other 2 point forward (zygodactyl).

Our cuckoos are rather skulking in habits and therefore are not often seen by the casual observer. Their favorite food is hairy moth larvae such as those of the pestilent gypsy moths, tent caterpillars, and webworms, but they also eat other insects, spiders, small vertebrates, and fruit. The cuckoos are among the most solitary of birds, never flocking with members of their own or other species.

The American cuckoos do lay their eggs in the nests of other birds, but only occasionally rather than habitually as do some of their Old World relatives (see BROOD PARASITISM). Their own nests are loose stick plat-

forms or shallow cups lined with finer plant material and placed in low trees and shrubs. The 1–5 (usually 2–3) eggs are unmarked, light blue to green with a dull finish.

Our cuckoos make a series of low, unmusical, rather "woody" clucks as well as softer, shorter (3–4 notes) hooting or cooing. It is only the Common Cuckoo of Eurasia that "says" *CUCK-oo* and inhabits clocks.

Cuckoos are distributed almost worldwide except at the highest latitudes of both hemispheres and reach their greatest diversity in the tropics. The single North American genus *(Coccyzus)* is restricted to the New World, and Sibley and Monroe (1990–CHECKLIST) put all the New World cuckoos into their own family, the Coccyzidae). Two of our species are long-distance migrants that winter in the tropics, and the third is a local permanent resident in southern Florida, where its preferred habitat is mangroves.

The name, of course, comes from the song of the Common Cuckoo of Eurasia and first appears in English in the famous anonymous poem that begins: "Sumer is icumen in, Lhude sing cuccu." It is the origin of the word "cuckold" in reference to the species fame as a brood parasite, even though neither the male cuckoo nor the male of the host pair has been cuckolded.

CULMEN. The ridge of the upper mandible from base to tip. See Fig. 35.

CURLEW (KERR-loo or KERR-lyoo). Standard English name for all but one of 8 species of large, long-billed sandpipers in the genus *Numenius* (family Scolopacidae; order Charadriiformes). The exceptional curlew is the WHIMBREL *(N. phaeopus).*

Including the Whimbrel, 4 species of curlews breed in North America, though one, the Eskimo Curlew, may now be extinct due to overshooting in the last century (see ENDANGERED BIRDS). Four other species have occurred here as accidental stragglers (see Appendix II). All curlews have brownish plumage, varying in tone and marked with streaks and spots, and all have long (female Long-billed to 8.6 inches) decurved bills that they use for probing in mud or soil. Some curlews prefer upland habitats, including cultivated fields, while others prefer coastal dunes, marshes, and flats. They eat small organisms (insects, crabs, etc.), which they pick up from the surface of the ground, as well as subterranean fare, which requires probing; in the Arctic they also feed on fruits, e.g., Curlewberry *(Empetrum nigrum).*

Curlews breed throughout the Holarctic region (mainly in the Arctic) and migrate over or winter in most of the rest of the world.

"Curlew" echoes the splendid plaintive fluting of these birds (specifically the Eurasian Curlew)—a sound that has inspired more than one poet.

For family characteristics, see SANDPIPER.

CURSORIAL. Adapted for walking or running; particularly of species in which this is the preferred form of locomotion. Ostriches are quintessen-

tially cursorial, having no other choice; in North America, the Roadrunner and Wild Turkey fit the definition.

CYGNET (SIG-net). The young of any species of swan; applied to birds in immature plumage as well as downy chicks. It is a diminutive form of *cygnus,* the Latin word for swan.

DABBLING DUCK. Collective name for the ducks in the subfamily Anatinae ("true ducks") or the tribe Anatini ("surface-feeding ducks"), including the teal, pintails, shovelers, wigeons, Wood Duck, Muscovy, and Mallard. All are primarily freshwater ducks that feed from the surface of the water by "dabbling" with their flattened, lamellate bills after bits of vegetation and aquatic invertebrates. See also DUCK.

DAMAGE (caused by birds). See PROBLEMS INVOLVING BIRDS.

DARTER. Standard English name—except in North America—for members of the family Anhingidae, which are here called anhingas. The single American species, *Anhinga anhinga,* the Anhinga, has (by the perversely stubborn) been called the American Darter. The name refers to the fast fish-spearing motion of neck and bill. See ANHINGA.

DAWN CHORUS. Describes the notable din of birdsong that occurs before and just after first light; though there is a similar, less symphonic effort at the end of the day, no one refers to it as the "dusk chorus." The phenomenon is characteristic of the breeding season in the temperate zone, but occurs year round in the tropics, where it can be operatic in its intensity and volume. Different species begin to sing at different times, but—at least in some cases—on a fixed schedule, cued perhaps by light intensity. Why birds should sing more at dawn and dusk has been attributed to simple opportunity (it's hard to find food this early so might as well defend my territory) and to the fact that the still morning and evening atmosphere makes for better transmission; it also makes sense that activity, including song, should slacken off during the heat of the day, though some species (e.g., Red-eyed Vireo) seem to repeat their song ceaselessly during daylight hours. For additional thoughts, see Kacelnik (1979–ROOST).

DDT (dichlorodiphenyltrichloroethane). A "miracle" organochlorine insecticide formerly widely used in North America and eventually proven to have disastrous effects on the reproductive capability of large raptors (especially fish- and bird-eaters) and other organisms, including humans. Once hailed as a weapon against malaria in the tropics, its impact, like that of most pesticides, diminished as mosquitos became immune to its effects. It was banned in the United States in 1972 but is still being sold and used elsewhere, especially in "developing" nations. For more detail on its effects, see THREATS (OF HUMAN ORIGIN) TO BIRDLIFE, Pesticides.

DECOY. Originally (sixteenth-century Holland) a trapping method by which wild ducks were encouraged to "mob" a trained dog, which would lead them into a trap. Later the same term was applied to tame ducks that lured their kind to within gunshot range. Today in North America, usually applied to wooden, composition, or plastic replicas of waterfowl (also crows, pigeons, and formerly shorebirds) that are placed close to where shooters wait in concealment. An imitative call may be used to enhance the effect (see BIRD CALLS). Old painted wooden decoys have become valuable items of folk art, collected at considerable expense.

DEFECATION. See DIGESTIVE SYSTEM; EXCRETORY SYSTEM; GUANO; LIME; EXCREMENT.

DEFINITIVE (plumage). In Humphrey-Parkes' (1959–MOLT) molt terminology, a plumage that has ceased to change with age, though it continues to change seasonally according to a consistent sequence. See MOLT, Sequence and Terminology.

DELAWARE VALLEY ORNITHOLOGICAL CLUB (DVOC). One of the most venerable of North American bird clubs (founded in 1890), the DVOC meets twice a month at the Philadelphia Academy of Natural Sciences. Its mission is "The advancement and diffusion of ornithological knowledge." To this end, it publishes a newsletter, *Philadephia Larus,* and an annual scientific journal, *Cassinia,* and offers an ambitious field trip program and supports conservation efforts and birders in the Delaware Valley.

DELTA MARSHES (Manitoba). An impressive expanse of prairie marshland filled with associated birdlife at the mouth of the Assiniboine River, where it empties into Lake Winnipeg, northeast of the city of Winnipeg. The Delta Research Station is located here and has produced an extensive literature on prairie waterfowl. See, for example, *Life in a Prairie Marsh* and other titles by A. H. Hochbaum. Among local breeding birds of the marshes and nearby lakeshore and prairies of interest to birders are

Western, Red-necked, and Horned Grebes, Canvasback, Redhead, Lesser
Scaup, American Avocet, Willet, Upland Sandpiper, Marbled Godwit, Wilson's Phalarope, Franklin's Gull, Burrowing Owl, Sprague's Pipit, Western
Meadowlark, Yellow-headed Blackbird, Le Conte's and Clay-colored Sparrows, and Chestnut-collared Longspur.

DEME (deem). Once used (mainly in botany) to describe any group of organisms within a taxonomic category that has clearly definable characteristics. It is now used more specifically in the context of evolution to
describe a well-defined, local population of organisms in which interbreeding is theoretically random, i.e., a reproductively cohesive and genetically homogeneous population. Isolated subspecies of birds represent
separate demes. Larger demes are prone to genetic stability and smaller
ones to relatively rapid change. A deme is not a taxonomic category. See
SPECIATION.

DENALI (National Park, Alaska). See ALASKA.

DERTRUM. The tip of the upper mandible.

DESERT. Broadly defined, deserts are places of extreme dryness in which
plant and animal species are relatively few and often markedly adapted to
the harsh conditions of their habitat. Based on relatively predictable biological (especially vegetational) differences that coincide with differences
in moisture levels, deserts have been more specifically defined as regions
that receive 10 inches (250 mm) or less of rain per year (arid), and some
authorities extend the category to include areas that receive as much as 20
inches (500 mm) of rain annually (semiarid). Frequency of rainfall, evaporation rate, cloud cover, dew level, and other climatic factors apart from
the amount of annual rain also mitigate extreme aridity in some localities.

Deserts cover approximately one-fifth of the earth's land surface and
are concentrated mainly in the subtropical zone. In some places they are
extending themselves due to overgrazing, the destruction of moisture-retaining vegetation (forests, etc.), and possibly a fluctuation in the atmosphere of the planet.

Though the popular image of a desert includes a strong element of
pallid sand dunes, deserts in reality take a great variety of forms—flat or
rugged topography; rocky or sandy texture; and black, red, or varicolored
in hue. This diversity is reflected in the fact that the vocabularies of
Bedouins and other desert dwellers contain many words referring to different desert types, just as Inuit peoples have terms for all the different
kinds of snow and ice conditions.

The North American desert is largely confined to the southwestern
quarter of the continent. It is sometimes known as a whole as the Sonoran

Desert or divided into major subregions, viz.: Chihuahuan, Sonoran, Arizona, Mojave, and Great Basin deserts, all of which also have distinctive subdivisions.

As noted, desert animals (as well as plants) tend to be specialized to suit their extreme environment. Among the most notable characteristics of desert birds worldwide are marked adaptive coloration that blends cryptically with the local soil tones (arguably a protective adaptation in response to the desert's general scarcity of cover in which to escape predators) and some form of modification that enhances conservation of body moisture. Because North American desert birds seem to have few obvious adaptive features of the latter kind and also on the basis of certain botanical elements, our deserts are thought by some authorities to be relatively "young" as compared with Old World deserts.

Udvardy (1958–DISTRIBUTION) identifies 29 North American species as desert birds, of which 22 represent monotypic genera, and this taxonomic distinction is another characteristic of desert birds worldwide. Of course, many broadly adapted bird species (e.g., Turkey Vulture) occur in arid habitats in addition to those that are restricted to them. Among our best-known dry-country birds are White-tailed Hawk, Inca Dove, Greater Roadrunner, Elf Owl, Costa's Hummingbird, Gila Woodpecker, Vermilion Flycatcher, Verdin, Cactus Wren, Le Conte's Thrasher, Phainopepla, Lucy's Warbler, Pyrrhuloxia, Varied Bunting, Black-throated and Rufous-winged Sparrows, and Chihuahuan Raven. This last species exemplifies another—apparently anomalous—characteristic of many desert animals: blackness. Examined superficially, heat-absorptive black would seem to be the worst possible coloration for animals exposed to hours of scorching sunshine (see GLOGER'S RULE). But studies have confirmed that the solar energy accumulated most efficiently by black plumage may balance the high energy expenditure required to maintain adequate body temperature during the characteristically frigid desert night and fuel foraging activity in the still-cold desert morning. Black species can easily seek shade and remain inactive in the intense heat of midday when their color might otherwise work to their disadvantage. That desert "black birds" usually are not species that are vulnerable to large predators is consistent with the fact that they tend to be highly conspicuous against desert landscapes. For a comprehensive discussion, see Serventy (in Farner et al. 1971–75–ORNITHOLOGY, Vol. 1).

See TEMPERATURE, BODY; COLOR AND PATTERN. See also BIOME; DISTRIBUTION; and Figs. 8 and 9.

DETERMINATION. In comparative biology, a judgment about the identity of a given form. In the case of poorly defined subspecies of birds, for example, a taxonomist may compare a specimen with hundreds of others in a museum collection, as well as consider factors such as locality and

date of collection, to properly "determine" its identity or to make an accurate "determination."

DIAL-A-BIRD. See RARE BIRD ALERTS; VOICE OF AUBUBON.

DIATRYMA (dee-uh-TREE-muh or dye-uh-TRY-muh). A fossil genus of huge, flightless, long-legged birds with massive skulls and bills. At least 4 species have been described from skeletal remains from the Paleocene and Eocene epochs (65 million to 35 million years ago) in the Canadian Arctic, American West, New Jersey and Europe. A species that lived in what is now Wyoming *(D. steini)* stood over 7 feet tall. Long assumed to be predacious, *Diatryma* may actually have been a leaf browser, according to some authorities. See EVOLUTION OF BIRDLIFE.

DICKCISSEL (DIK-siss-ul or dik-SISS-ul). Standard English name for a single species of finch, *Spiza americana* (family Cardinalidae). It is an open-country species that breeds exclusively in North America and winters in South and Central America, where it is sometimes encountered in flocks of thousands. Its breeding distribution in North America fluctuates significantly (see NOMADISM). The name is a fairly close approximation of its song. For family description, see CARDINAL-GROSBEAK.

DIGESTIVE SYSTEM. The digestive apparatus, by which food is broken down into fuel for all bodily functions, is basically a flexible tube running from the mouth to the vent; it is enclosed and protected along most of its length by the sternum and rib cage (see SKELETON). The tube is enlarged and modified in several places to facilitate stages of the breakdown process. These modifications vary according to the eating habits of different species.

The breakdown of food is accomplished by both chemical and mechanical processes, and the raw material and wastes are pushed through the system by rhythmic, wave-like contractions of the muscles in the walls of the tube. All of the above is true of both birds and people. The differences between the avian and human digestive systems lie chiefly in the equipment that each has evolved to accomplish similar goals.

The first major step in human digestion takes place in the mouth, where solid food is tasted, chewed into small pieces, moistened with saliva, and passed through the gullet (esophagus) to the stomach. Lacking teeth and with comparatively little sense of taste, birds tend to swallow their food whole or, in the case of seed-eating birds, after crushing it with a heavy bill. Salivary glands are present in most birds but are reduced in number or totally lacking in many waterbirds, whose food is premoistened.

The Esophagus of a bird, rather than being simply a connecting passage to the stomach, as in humans, may also be used for temporary stor-

age of food. In most species the gullet simply expands as it becomes full, but in some cases there is a permanent enlargement in this part of the digestive tract. This "crop" or ingluvies may be just an expanded area of the gullet or a relatively elaborate, pouch-like *cul de sac.* The most developed crops are found in gallinaceous birds, pigeons and doves, and parrots. This mechanism allows birds to "gorge" when and where food is plentiful or to gobble a meal or two quickly in vulnerable situations and digest later at leisure. It is also a handy means of carrying fresh food back to the nest to be regurgitated for young birds.

The Stomach, a single pouch in humans, is divided into two sections in birds. In the first, the proventriculus, the same digestive juices that act in the human stomach (principally the enzyme pepsin in combination with hydrochloric acid) are secreted and the whole passes on to the second, large stomach—the ventriculus or gizzard. In birds that prefer soft foods, this organ is not very different from the proventriculus in function. But in birds that feed on solid substances such as seeds, the tough, hard muscular walls of the gizzard, aided by swallowed sand and gravel, serve a function similar to that of human teeth (see GRIT). Fur, bones, fish scales, and other substances that the gizzard cannot properly pulverize are separated out at this point in the digestive process to be regurgitated in a compact mass (see PELLET) and the now more or less liquefied remainder, called chyme, enters the small intestine.

The Intestines, small and large, of both birds and humans are responsible for the final stage of transforming food into usable fuel and releasing it to the rest of the body. This happens mainly in the small intestine, where bile from the liver and enzymes from the pancreas are added to the chyme, which is thereby transformed into proteins, fats, and carbohydrates. These are absorbed through the intestinal walls into the bloodstream, leaving little but water, to be absorbed from the relatively short large intestine, and waste products, to be expelled through the vent (see EXCRETORY SYSTEM).

In some species of birds that feed principally on vegetation (e.g., ptarmigan), the small intestine is larger than usual to accommodate the great quantity of material that must be digested to supply sufficient energy. These and other vegetarians usually have well-developed caeca (sing: caecum), narrow sacs that open where the small intestine meets the large. These hold concentrations of bacteria and secrete additional enzymes needed to break down plant tissue.

See also FOOD/FEEDING.

DIMORPHISM (dye-MORF-ism). Literally, the occurrence of two distinct forms or "morphs." Many species of birds are "sexually dimorphic," i.e., the males and females differ strikingly in plumage and/or mensural characteristics (e.g., the pair of Hooded Mergansers in Fig. 23). Seasonal

dimorphism is also common, as exemplified by the summer and winter plumages of the Black Guillemot, also shown in Fig. 23. Compare POLYMORPHISM; see PLUMAGE; COLOR AND PATTERN. See also the Bibliography.

DIPPER. Standard English name for all 5 members of the family Cinclidae (order Passeriformes), one of which breeds in North America.

Dippers superficially resemble large (average 6 inches), stocky wrens, with their compact form, short wings, and frequently "cocked-up" tail. Closer inspection, however, reveals a slightly hooked bill, which is laterally flattened; an unusually thick feather coat and underlying down; somewhat pointed wings; and rather large, strong feet with short, stout claws. All dippers are brown or gray, some with patches of white. Most of these features are adaptations to the dippers' unique life style. They are quintessentially birds of fast-water streams and rivers and make their living swimming and walking underwater on the stream bed, picking aquatic insect larvae, snails, small fish, and the like from among the submerged rocky crannies. They can dive to a depth of at least 20 feet. Periodically they rise to the surface, float buoyantly to a nearby rock, and preen their feathers, all the while bobbing in a characteristic abrupt "curtsy" quite different from the "teetering" of the Spotted Sandpiper and the waterthrushes. Dipper songs are also wren-like, i.e., "bubbly" and loud (audible above the splash of rushing water); they also make a variety of loud calls.

Dippers build domed nests of moss and other plant material, lined with dead leaves, with the entrance hole "aimed" toward the water. These may be tucked in streamside crevices, under a waterfall, or placed on a large rock in the midst of the torrent. The 3–6 (usually 4–5) eggs are glossy white and unmarked.

Dippers occur throughout much of the Holarctic area, though in most cases they are restricted to mountainous regions with permanent streams; they also range throughout the Neotropical highlands. The American Dipper occurs in our western mountains from arctic Alaska through Central America.

DISEASE. Birds are beset by a wide variety of health problems, brought on by equally diverse causes. Malnutrition, vitamin deficiency, accidental injury, poison, extreme weather conditions, internal and external parasites—alone or in combination—can bring on death or weaken the constitution, making a bird's system more vulnerable to disease. Many of these causal factors are discussed under separate headings (see, for example, WEATHER; ENDOPARASITE; ECTOPARASITE; THREATS [OF HUMAN ORIGIN] TO BIRDLIFE). The present entry is confined to a summary of common illnesses of birds that result from infections of microorganisms such as bacteria and viruses.

Though the immediate reaction to disease in any context tends to be a negative one, we should remember that it plays an important role in the complex business of population balance. Disease affects populations at high densities and keeps them at or below their carrying capacities, and it is a driving force behind adaptive evolution. The "Red Queen Hypothesis" states that all living things are "running" as fast as they can to keep abreast of the adaptations of their parasites to their own defenses.

Much of what we know about sickness in wild birds is a result of the study of diseases of poultry, pets, or other domestic or captive birds. However, in many cases the conditions under which such birds live (e.g., indoors, in great density, and/or with artificial food sources) produce health problems that are rare among free-living birds, and these are omitted here.

BACTERIAL DISEASES. Bacteria are an extremely important, vastly diverse group of microscopic single-celled organisms that lack nuclear membranes around their genes (prokaryotic). They are neither plants nor animals but are contained within a separate kingdom, Monera. They are abundant, ubiquitous, and crucial to such important processes as soil formation, plant growth, waste decomposition, and human health. They are also the "germs" or "microbes" that cause many important diseases in both plants and animals. The following bacterial diseases frequently afflict wild birds.

Tuberculosis. The microorganism *Mycobacterium tuberculosis avium* is frequently taken into birds' systems with their food and the bacilli are spread very effectively by excretion in the feces. Seabirds, gallinaceous birds and raptors seem to be particularly susceptible, but all birds can contract the disease and it is prevalent in many species of wild and domestic birds. At least some birds (e.g., parrots) can catch the disease from people. The organism spreads through the lymph and blood systems, forming tissue-destroying *tubercles* in intestines, liver, spleen, and other organs, often causing fever, emaciation, weakness, and death.

Erysipelas (err-uh-SIP-uh-lus). The bacterium *Erysipelothrix rhusopathiae* causes a form of septicemia (blood poisoning) that commonly affects young domestic pigs and other vertebrates as well as birds. It causes disease of the skin and subcutaneous tissue, which results in fever and red blotches on the body. The organism lives and is very persistent in soil and probably infects through open wounds. It can be a major problem in zoos.

Salmonellosis. Several of the many species of *Salmonella* bacterium are eaten in birds' food and spread through the diarrheal symptoms that develop. Liver, spleen, and lung disease and death may result or the disease may persist at a low level over a long period. Since it is ingested from droppings of other birds, heavily patronized feeding operations—especially ground-feeding areas or other flat surfaces—may become abnormally infected if not cleaned regularly. *Salmonella* causes many cases of "food

poisoning" and diarrhea in humans. It is the main reason that you should wash your hands thoroughly after handling birds and reptiles.

Botulism (Duck Sickness). The *Clostridium botulinum* bacterium causes another kind of "food poisoning" but is much more virulent and has a much more disastrous effect on bird populations than *Salmonella*. It thrives best in warm, stagnant, alkaline waters where large amounts of decaying vegetable or (especially) animal matter are present. Wildfowl are therefore particularly susceptible, especially during the summer, but it has been diagnosed in many other kinds of birds. As in humans, it causes violent, usually fatal symptoms and has occurred in a number of infamous outbreaks in western North America in which millions of ducks and other waterbirds perished. It also affects gulls and other species that scavenge in garbage dumps, shorebirds feeding on estuarine mudflats, and birds that feed on infected blowflies.

Ornithosis and Psittacosis (SIT-uh-CO-sis). Once thought to be caused by viruses, these ailments are now known to be forms of a bacterial disease, chlamydiosis (from the genus of the infecting organism, *Chlamydia psittaci*). Though responsible for fatal epidemics among a wide variety of bird species, external and even internal symptoms are often lacking or inconspicuous. Eventually, victims may show runny eyes and nose, lethargy, and bloody diarrhea. The disease is characteristically transmitted by inhalation of infected particles in breath, by ingestion of infected excretion, and by ectoparasites; it is often contracted in the nest. Petrels, gulls, pigeons, chickens, and a variety of cage birds are frequently cited hosts of the ornithosis form of the infection, and the psittacosis form is, as its name implies, restricted to members of the parrot family. See below for symptoms in humans. Not to be confused with the common human sexually transmitted disease organism of the same genus, *Chlamydia trachomatis*.

Chlamydiosis (cluh-midi-OH-sis). See above.

Mycoplasmosis. Mycoplasmas belong to a genus of parasitic bacteria that commonly cause chronic respiratory ailments in raptors, parrots, and gallinaceous birds as well as pneumonia in humans. Epidemics of economic significance have occurred in the poultry industry. Around 1993–94 an outbreak of a new strain of mycoplasmal conjunctivitis in House Finches reduced the eastern (introduced) population by 40–60% within a few years. The condition, which affected America Goldfinches and other fringillids to a lesser extent, causes crusted swollen eyes, which can lead to blindness and starvation due to the inability to find food. All of the avian mycolplasmas are most virulent where many birds come in close contact with each other, such as poultry rearing facilities, aviaries, and bird feeders as well as natural communal roosts.

VIRAL DISEASES. Viruses are submicroscopic agents of disease in plants and animals that can survive only within the particular tissue they

infect. Defining viruses—even to the extent of deciding whether they are living or nonliving—in order to control them is a chief aim of medical science. Viruses seem to be self-replicating packages of biochemicals that can exploit the reproductive machinery of cells. Though not exactly alive, they can pose a serious threat to the infected organism, but they are also proving very useful in studying at the fundamental chemical processes of the organisms they infect. The following viral diseases are common among birds.

West Nile Virus and Equine Encephalitis. These diseases are called "arboviruses" because they are **ar**thropod-**bo**rne, i.e., transmitted by a vector, such as a mosquito or tick. Encephalitis or brain inflammation is the condition that can result from infection and that may in the worst cases prove fatal. Many birds (as well as horses) serve as reservoirs for the Equine Encephalitis virus, but typically are not seriously affected by the disease. By contrast, thousands of birds of more than 140 species (as well as many other types of animals) have been killed by West Nile Virus since it was first discovered in North America in 1999. Corvids (crow and jays) and raptors (eagles, hawks, and owls) seem to be especially vulnerable— or their deaths may be more evident because of their size and conspicuous behavior. While most scientists believe that the virus will become less virulent within a few years as immunities to the new pathogen evolve, there is some concern that certain bird populations (e.g., very localized endangered species or those that depend on long lives to replace themselves effectively) could suffer serious losses. There is also some threat from people who mistakenly believe that killing birds is an effective way to combat the virus. For relationship between human and bird diseases, see below.

Fowl Pox (also Avian or Bird Pox). Infects only birds, and the common form, producing warts on head and feet, is nonfatal. An internal form can occur in epidemics where many (wild or domestic) birds roost together and may cause heavy mortality, especially among young birds.

Newcastle Disease. A highly contagious major killer of domestic fowl, much less apparent in wild birds (occasional cases in waterfowl); however, the causal virus (NDV) has been found to occur, apparently benignly, in a wide variety of wild species.

Duck Plague. Known mainly from northern Europe until 1969, when it was diagnosed in domestic ducks in northeastern United States. A major outbreak occurred in North Dakota in the winter of 1972–73, killing over 40,000 ducks and geese within a few weeks. Restricted to members of the Anatidae; survivors apparently retain an immunity (Leibovitz in Davis 1971).

Dermatitis. Blistering on the feet of a number of species of colonial seabirds is caused by several viruses that are transmitted from foot to ground to foot.

OTHER DISEASES. Common bird diseases that are neither bacterial nor viral in origin are the following.

Aspergillosis. (asper-jill-OH-sis) Transmitted by a fungus *(Aspergilla fumigatus)* that occurs as a mold on decaying plant material. Birds eat or inhale the spores, which destroy tissue in the respiratory system and many other parts of the body. The disease is known from many species of birds and occasionally occurs in large epidemics with heavy mortalities, particularly among waterfowl and gallinaceous species. It has been suggested that fruit or other vegetable matter left to rot in bird feeders could be a source of aspergillosis—one of many good reasons to keep feeders clean. For implications for humans, see below.

Trichomoniasis (trick-oh-muh-NY-uh-sis) is best known as a common sexually transmitted disease in humans, but it occurs in many forms that also affect other animal species. It is caused by species of one-celled protozoan parasite in the genus *Trichomonas.* One strain attacks pigeons and doves and raptors that prey upon them. Affected birds may develop mouth sores that make them unable to swallow; thus infected food may be dropped and ingested by other birds. Many other protozoan parasites, e.g., the blood parasite Haemoproteus, carried by louseflies (see EC-TOPARASITE); avian malaria; coccidia; and Sarcoplasma, commonly affect birds though they do not always cause sickness or death.

Colds (Coryza). Birds, like humans, are subject to the common cold, an inscrutable disease that can be caused by a variety of infective agents, including viruses. Its symptoms in birds (inflammation of the respiratory membranes with discharge of mucus, fever, and chills), the conditions under which it is contracted (cold/wet weather, close contact with other individuals, inhalation of infected mucus particles), and its course (usually short-lived, rarely becoming a more serious respiratory infection) will all be familiar to the reader.

BIRD DISEASES AFFECTING PEOPLE. Humans are susceptible to most of the "bird diseases" described above, but the risk of catching something from birds is very small in any case and practically nonexistent unless you are in close and prolonged contact with birds or places where they nest. For example it is not uncommon among people who handle a lot of birds, e.g., poultry farmers, aviculturists, and bird banders, to contract chlamydiosis (ornithosis/psittacosis). It typically produces a type of pneumonia in people, which, though potentially fatal, is effectively treated with antibacterial drugs such as tetracycline.

Similarly, bird colonies, poultry yards, and (especially) enclosed spaces where droppings collect are likely places to inhale spores from the fungus *Histoplasma capsulatum,* which grows on bird droppings. Symptoms of histoplasmosis include enlargement of the liver and spleen, fever, and anemia; however, 95% of people who are exposed develop immunity without suffering any symptoms.

Because there have been over 250 human deaths from West Nile Virus in the United States (as of 2003) and because birds are widely known to be reservoirs (and victims) of the disease, it may be tempting to make a causal link between the presence of birds and coming down with West Nile encephalitis, but the virus resides in a surprising number of species and the vectors that give us the virus, from whatever source, are always mosquitoes, never birds.

Considering the number of potential disease vectors that are destroyed by insect-eating birds and the amounts of carrion and organic waste matter that is neutralized by various avian scavengers, there can be little doubt that on balance birds are a net benefit to human health.

DISJUNCT. (dis-JUNKT) In reference to distribution or range, discontinuous, separate; existing in widely separated populations. The Sandhill Crane, for example, has a disjunct distribution in North America with unconnected breeding populations in arctic Canada and Alaska, north-central and western United States, and Florida; the cosmopolitan range of the Gull-billed Tern is made up of a series of disjunct populations. See DISTRIBUTION.

DISPERSAL. In a strict biological sense, refers to moving to a new breeding territory. In birds this applies to the characteristic wanderings of young birds in all directions from their natal areas to new breeding areas, i.e., *post-breeding dispersal.* Birds of the year typically disperse more widely than their elders after the breeding season, thus ensuring that individual birds find an unoccupied territory away from the parents' territory (see MIGRATION; DISTRIBUTION). The term also refers to *breeding dispersal* in which adult birds shift to a new breeding location after nesting at a site in a given year.

"Dispersal" is also used more loosely (less usefully) to refer to other types of bird movements, such as IRRUPTION, INVASION, and VAGRANCY, but such uses are valid only if the result of the movement is the establishment of a new breeding territory. For example, the case of Sooty Terns blown to Maine in a hurricane and then returning or perishing does not constitute true dispersal, whereas a flock of Fieldfares blown by gales from Europe to Greenland and remaining to breed does.

Also, not to be confused with DISPERSION.

DISPERSION. A spatial concept describing the density and configuration of birdlife or other organisms in a given area or habitat. The "dispersion" of feeding shorebirds—i.e., how closely they associate with one another in a marsh or on a mud flat—may depend on the density of the food source and also be governed by certain behavioral factors (see FLOCK

and V. C. Wynne-Edwards, *Animal Dispersion in Relation to Social Behaviour* [London, 1962]). Not to be confused with DISPERSAL.

DISPLACEMENT ACTIVITY. Birds respond in an innately prescribed way to certain signals or "releasers" (see INTELLIGENCE). When two conflicting signals are received—e.g., the presence of a perched owl in daytime, which provokes both fear (flee) and aggression (attack)—birds may respond to the ambiguity by doing something totally irrelevant, such as feeding or preening. These "inappropriate" gestures are called "displacement activities." See Fig. 19.

DISPLAY. See Fig. 7. In the broadest sense, any innate, stylized visual signal made by a bird, the function of which is to trigger or "release" appropriate behavior in the intended object of the signal. Under this definition, the gaping or pecking motions of juvenile birds can be called "begging display." The most conspicuous examples of bird display are complex, prolonged rituals in a sexual or defensive context. These frequently involve the actual "display" of some prominent plumage or other characteristic, but the gestures involved often give no hint of the intended outcome—at least to the human witness.

All birds engage in some form of display, though there is much variation both in size of repertoire and in intricacy of ritual. Certain kinds of

Fig. 7. *Display* serves many purposes as this figure shows. Many auks such as this Tufted Puffin (1; see also jacket photo) acquire bizarre head plumes and bill modifications at the start of the breeding season. These are worn by both sexes and presumably help the birds recognize their own species. Auks appear to communicate mainly with these "costumes," as their courtship rituals are not elaborate. By contrast the Ruby-throated Hummingbird (2) plunges back and forth in a great horseshoe arc, chirping ecstatically, its brilliant gorget flashing periodically when the light hits it at the right angle. Western and Clark's Grebes (3) dispense with color and turn courtship into a water ballet; the "race" shown here is only the most elaborate and energetic of half a dozen displays performed by these grebes during the breeding season. The Snowy Egret (4) performs a more elegant fan dance by erecting the "nuptial plumes" once sought at the birds' expense to adorn ladies' hats; in the brief period of peak excitement the yellow lores and feet blush to orange. Male Lesser Prairie Chickens (6) do not defend territories, but gather together early on spring mornings on flat display grounds called LEKS. Stamping and hooting, tail and nape plumes cocked up, pink neck pouches inflated, the effect somehow combines dignity and farce. Hens on the sidelines appear indifferent but in fact are checking out the best dancers with whom they will mate.

Courtship is not the only context in which birds display. The young Red-tailed Hawk (5), cornered on the ground unable to take off, sits back on its tail, raises its formidable talons and broad wings, and expands its body feathers in a *threat display* meant to be as intimidating as possible. The American Avocet (7), like other shorebirds, lures predators away from eggs or young using a *distraction display*. Dragging a limp wing and calling as if injured, it appears to be easy prey, but takes flight once the intruder's attention has been diverted.

For other examples see DISPLAY.

"choreography" may be characteristic of particular families of birds, e.g., the bowing and leaping courtship dances performed by members of the crane family. But each species has its stereotyped variation, which in turn may be modified slightly by individual birds.

ORIGINS. Some courtship displays are so theatrical and exuberant that it is tempting to interpret them as spontaneous expressions of sexual energy or even imaginative ballets inspired by avian affection. In reality, many displays seem to have evolved out of half-realized movements made by birds in ambivalent situations. In forming pair bonds, for example, birds are normally torn between attraction to a potential mate and aggression toward a potential rival, especially in cases in which the plumages of male and female are alike. Within the aggressive impulse is yet another ambivalence, namely, whether to stay and fight or to flee. Viewed as a series of discrete gestures, courtship dances can often be seen to consist of recognizable expressions of all these motivations, as well as apparently irrelevant gestures, such as presenting nesting material or preening—displacement activities that over time have become integrated into the courtship ceremony. Likewise, so-called distraction displays are amalgams of protective and escape movements, though they have come to function as distractions to nest predators.

INTERSEXUAL DISPLAY. The reproductive cycle, which necessitates frequent and varied interactions between two or more birds, is the richest source of specialized displays.

Function. Courtship displays performed by males alone serve not only to identify the displaying species and attract the attention of unmated females but also as "no trespassing" signs to other males. As the mating ritual proceeds, the genetically prescribed movements, usually accompanied by appropriate sounds, dissipate aggressive urges, thus permitting the successful completion of the many details of reproduction—copulation, nest building, feeding of young, etc.—that mated birds do together. In many cases, each of these is accompanied by its own specialized ritual—precopulatory display, postcopulatory display, food-bringing display, incubation-relief display—which, in effect, are simple operating instructions, allowing birds to fulfill their biological roles with a comparatively rudimentary mental capacity. "Displays of affection," such as mutual preening and "billing," may lack the emotional depth imputed to them by some humans, but they do serve to maintain pair bonds during the breeding season and in some species for life.

Sexual Roles. Many waterbird species in which the sexes look alike—e.g., loons, grebes, tubenoses, pelecaniforms, gulls, and terns—perform courtship displays in which the sexes are equally active. Such pairs may perform in tandem, like the Western Grebes "racing" in Fig. 7; or face each other in a mirror-image tableau, as in the gannets' "greeting" ceremony; or take different parts in a more or less fixed ritual and periodically change roles, as in the "dance" of the Black-footed Albatross.

The displays of most ducks, shorebirds, hummingbirds, and passerines, by contrast, are dominated by the male. While he engages in some form of plumage display accompanied by song and/or movements (sometimes including aerial maneuvers), the female remains composed: sometimes appearing completely indifferent or even impatient, sometimes expressing her reaction with displacement activities such as feeding or preening, and sometimes responding with ritualized gestures of submission alternating with solicitation. The gender roles are reversed, of course, in polyandrous species such as Spotted Sandpiper, jacanas, and the phalaropes.

Among North American grouse species (excluding the ptarmigan) and a few species of shorebirds, females are not "performers" in the courtship display—except, of course, for the finale of copulation. Cock Ruffed, Spruce, and Blue Grouse perform solos from carefully chosen perches or openings in the forest; the sounds accompanying these rituals carry well through the dense vegetation to be heard by other displaying males and the judgments of female auditors. Males of Sage and Sharp-tailed Grouse, the prairie-chickens, and a few species of shorebirds (most famously the Ruff) gather in the spring to "dance" *together* in communal "arenas" or "leks." As with the other grouse, the females play no part in the display itself, but visit the display area to observe the competition and be fertilized by the one or two cocks that emerge as the fittest mates. and the nest sites are chosen outside the "stage" area.

Forms of Courtship Display. The often bizarre and elaborate antics of birds engaged in sexual display are among the most fascinating and entertaining aspects of birdlife. The diversity of courtship rituals in any avifauna is always as great as the number of species it contains—more so, in fact, since many species have several acts in their repertoire. Virtually every avian attribute and external anatomical feature—plumage, bill, legs, eyes, flight, voice—is active in one ritual or another, and not a few adaptations apparently function solely in display. Many "breeding" or "nuptial" (alternate) plumages are in prime condition only long enough to complete the rituals that precede reproduction. In addition to more colorful or contrasting contour feathers, the display "costume" may include decorative features that irresistibly suggest makeup, jewelry, and fancy clothes to human observers. Egrets (of both sexes), for example, acquire exquisite back plumes; many alcids, like the Tufted Puffin in Fig. 7, develop facial tufts and colorful bill sheaths (again, in both sexes). The roseate bloom on the breasts of some species of gulls and terns may be applied as "rouge" provided by the oil gland only during the breeding season; and the color of so-called soft parts—bills, legs, fleshy eye rings, and facial skin—intensifies greatly (though sometimes very briefly) in a wide range of species during courtship. Other features—the colored air sacs of frigatebirds and some grouse, the brilliant crown tufts of the kingbirds, the epaulets of Red-winged and Tricolored Blackbirds—are present year

round but are revealed to full effect only in the ardor of sexual display (or the ire inspired by territorial transgression). Finally, much of any species' repertoire of songs, calls, mechanical sounds, and physical agility is reserved for performance during courtship.

Not all birds engage in extravagant displays. The most brilliantly colored passerine species (e.g., wood warblers, tanagers, orioles) find it sufficient simply to erect their most exciting feathers and dance a modest (though characteristic) jig accompanied by appropriate sound effects. Of course, bright feathers are not the only way to impress a potential mate. In many species of subtle (not to say drab) plumage—e.g., wrens, thrushes, mimids—it can be argued with some confidence that elaborate songs stands in for spectacular feathers. We should also recall that since the ultraviolet portion of the spectrum is invisible to us, some birds are doubtless wowing their audiences with plumage displays we can't see.

At the other extreme are courtship rites that are impossible to ignore. These frequently involve stylized movements that birds use in no other context (see above for origins) and in some cases are so unusual that the human observer is overcome with awe—or with laughter. The most distinctive rituals are categorized below; almost all are accompanied by some vocal and/or mechanical sound.

FLIGHT DISPLAYS

Soaring: Anhingas and the Roseate Spoonbill soar en masse over their colonies; many hawks and eagles do so over territory during the mate-attracting phase of the breeding cycle.

"Volplaning"—i.e., gliding down from a height with wings held motionless, outstretched: Loons, especially the Red-throated, volplane over territory with wings held stiffly upward, calling as they descend; pairs of Chimney Swifts perform a similar, if more buoyant version of this activity. Red-billed Tropicbird pairs volplane one above the other with the upper bird's wings held down, lower bird's up, so that they almost touch; some sandpipers volplane down from song flights and anhingas do so from communal soaring flights. Perhaps the most readily seen volplaning displays are those of the Mourning Dove and feral Rock Dove, both of which perform over a long breeding season and occur continentwide.

"Butterflying": Most North American plovers incorporate a very distinctive, slow, shallow wing beat in their flight displays, as do male Vermilion Flycatchers and American Goldfinches.

Hovering: This replaces a tall singing perch for many open-country species, e.g., Bobolink, larks, pipits, longspurs, tundra-breeding shorebirds. The singer may hover hundreds of feet in the air while delivering a full-throated aria.

Plummeting: The American Woodcock and Common Snipe descend from the top of their aerial displays in erratic swoops, making characteristic sounds as they do so (see SONG); Upland Sandpipers sometimes fold

their wings and drop from nuptial flights; and Common Nighthawks plummet and "pull out," making a characteristic noise with their wings.

"Sky dances": Male hummingbirds describe characteristic patterns in the air before mates (see Fig. 7), calling and in a few cases making feather noises as well; Leach's Storm-Petrels perform eerie circling (chasing?) flights accompanied by haunting calls over their nesting burrows at night.

Aerobatics: Perhaps the most thrilling of aerial displays are the stunt maneuvers performed by most species of hawks and eagles. A familiar variation is a series of continuous undulations (shallower in accipiters deeper in buteos and eagles). Some species will also fold their wings and plummet from as high as 1,000 feet, pulling out, sharply and rising to repeat the dive. The most remarkable display stunt of any North American bird may be the "tumbling" of Bald Eagle pairs: the male flies above the female, she turns on her back and presents her talons, which the male grasps in his; then they fall down through space in a tumbling roll.

Chasing: Many species from loons to passerines chase each other as part of the courtship ritual; "three- (or more) bird chases" are characteristic of many waterfowl.

DANCING

Pairs (and sometimes small groups) of albatrosses (including the Black-footed), cranes, some pelecaniforms, and many gulls and shorebirds engage in more or less conspicuous formalized earthbound displays. These involve a great diversity of actions, including bill fencing, gaping (to show color of mouth lining), wing posturing, "curtsying," pointing, stretching, and presentations of food or nest materials. Owing to their size and the exaggeration of many of their movements, the albatrosses and cranes are especially famous as "dancers."

As noted elsewhere, male Sage and Sharp-tailed Grouse and the two species of prairie-chickens gather in leks (called "strutting grounds," "gobbling grounds," or "booming grounds"—according to the characteristic sounds and gestures made) and perform a rather staid sequence of stamping motions, the culmination of which is the inflation of brightly colored air sacs at the neck or breast.

The Ruff, a largely Eurasian sandpiper as well as Pectoral and Buff-breasted Sandpipers, are also noted for elaborate lek displays, and males of some other North American shorebirds (e.g., Willet) gather in (less formal?) display grounds. See LEK.

The Great Blue Heron (including the Great White) and the Reddish and other egrets sometimes "dance" among members of their species early in their breeding cycle.

WATER DISPLAYS

Racing: Loons and grebes, with legs placed near the end of their bodies, are capable of standing nearly erect and paddling furiously across

their breeding lake or pond in this vertical posture. Pairs do this in tandem as one act of their courtship display (see Fig. 7). Fulvous and Black-bellied Whistling Ducks also do a tandem "race" as a postcopulatory ritual.

Other: The courtship displays of loons, grebes, and waterfowl are essentially aquatic dances. In the first two families, the sexes share equally in the ritual, while among the waterfowl the male dominates, and often many males display to a single female. The goldeneyes execute a very distinctive combination of head and neck motions involving "inflating" the head feathers until the head is nearly spherical, stretching the neck forward, and then wrenching the head violently over the back ("head throwing"); in one version, this is accompanied by splashing, which exposes the bright orange legs and feet. Other bay and sea ducks do less exaggerated forms of this display. The drake Ruddy Duck inflates a tracheal air sac and then slaps its enlarged chest with the bill near the waterline, making a distinctive sound (by hitting the air sac?) and simultaneously producing a cluster of bubbles. In another irresistible courtship maneuver of this species, the male races toward the female while clapping its long stiff tail on the water behind, leaving (briefly) a series of rings ("the ring rush").

DEFENSIVE DISPLAY. Called upon to defend themselves, their mates, young, eggs, or territory, birds, like other animals, may respond straightforwardly by attacking, harassing, sounding a vocal alarm, or fleeing. They may also, however, react with more complex and subtle behavior the result of which is to deceive the source of the threat. Like those connected with the breeding cycle, such defensive displays evolved out of ambivalent intentions in stressful situations, especially the quandary of whether to flee or remain and fight. That ambivalence is a major influence in display is nowhere clearer than in the frequent appearance of "defensive" gestures in courtship rituals. Defensive displays may be grouped for convenience under three headings.

Threat Display. Most if not all birds have characteristic threat postures, which they assume when confronting a member of their own species invading their territories and also perhaps in other threatening situations. Many passerines, for example, crouch and "flatten" themselves, compress their body feathers, and adopt "nervous" gestures like flipping the wings or tail or raising and lowering the crown feathers. The tendency to erect body feathers, with the effect of making the potential victim seem larger or otherwise more impressive, is also common. Blue-footed Boobies, for example, create an imposing presence by raising the head and neck feathers, making them "bristle like porcupine quills" (Palmer 1962–ORNITHOLOGY). Nestling hawks and owls and cornered adults (like the Red-tailed Hawk in Fig. 7) will often spread their wings and display their talons as well as raise feathers, all gestures aimed (often successfully) at intimidating would-be attackers. Several American blackbird species—e.g., Bronzed Cowbird, the grackles, and the Red-winged Black-

bird—"puff up" in displays that function effectively to deter predators as well as warn territorial rivals and attract mates.

Perhaps the most impressive achievement in the evolution of threat displays—at least in human terms—is the "snake display" performed by some species of titmice. When the hole nest is invaded, the sitting bird gapes wide, hissing and swaying in a serpent-like manner, and finally "strikes" upward, simultaneously hitting the nest wall with its wings. A few species—e.g., skuas and Northern Goshawk—do more than threaten and will actually draw blood from a human intruder to the nesting area, which is also very "impressive."

Distraction Display. This type of display by nesting adults diverts the attention of predators from eggs or young. It is most highly evolved (or at least most conspicuous) among open-country ground nesters, but it has been observed in some form in most bird families, including cavity nesters. The basic effect, performed with greater or lesser verisimilitude by different species, is of an injured or ill bird flopping helplessly over the ground and crying out in anguish. The Killdeer's "broken-wing act"—the epitome of brilliantly evoked pathos—is the best-known North American example of this form of display. Fig. 7 shows an American Avocet's version.

A variation is the "rodent run" practiced by small rails, shorebirds, and not a few songbirds. It consists of darting off the nest and running vole-like through the ground vegetation. The Green-tailed Towhee is said to have refined the technique by raising its long tail over its back in emulation of a ground squirrel (Van Tyne and Berger 1976–ORNITHOLOGY).

Freezing should perhaps be mentioned here, though in one sense it might be termed "anti-display." It involves simply remaining motionless in the face of perceived danger. It is innate in many juvenile birds, often released by a special parental call, and is reinforced in many cases by cryptic coloration. For more detail on this and other defensive adaptations related to plumage markings, see COLOR AND PATTERN, Concealment, and Fig. 23.

See also COURTSHIP; PAIR FORMATION; SONG; TERRITORY.

DISTAL. Farthest away from the main body. The white patch in the wing of a Yellow Rail is in the distal secondaries. Opposite of PROXIMAL.

DISTRACTION. In an avian context, a form of display in which a parent bird simulates injury or sickness, drawing the attention of a potential predator to itself and away from its eggs or young. Practiced to some degree among most birds, but most conspicuous among open-country species, e.g., shorebirds. See DISPLAY, above, and American Avocet in Fig. 7.

DISTRIBUTION. Where birds live and why—a very broad subject, ultimately touching on nearly every other entry in this book.

Anyone who remembers writing something like the following in his or her grade-school geography book—

Chris Leahy
15 Rockaway Street
Marblehead
Essex County
Massachusetts
USA
North America
Western Hemisphere
Earth
Solar System
Milky Way Galaxy
Universe
Infinity

—will probably appreciate the many levels of inquiry presented to the would-be student of bird distribution. Consider, for example, that

- Some species of birds are found only in small areas of very specialized habitats, while others are tolerant of many kinds of environment.
- Some species occur only on a single mountain peak, while others are distributed nearly worldwide.
- Some stay put year round, while others travel great distances between breeding and wintering grounds.
- Some never leave regions of constant high temperature and humidity, while others never breed beyond the isotherm that marks a mean annual temperature of 50° F or less (see ARCTIC).
- Some will not cross a narrow river or strait even when good habitat is clearly visible on the far side, while others spend their entire lives beyond the sight of land except for a few months every other year when they return to isolated oceanic islands to nest.
- Whole families of birds are restricted to certain regions of the globe, while other families are represented in all major regions.

These are only some of the readily observed facts of bird distribution. The questions of "how" and "why" that they pose are generated exponentially.

HISTORY OF BIRD DISTRIBUTION. Bird distribution began, of course, with the evolution of the first bird. The fossil evidence that we have uncovered so far suggests that this probably happened in what we now call the Old World (Eurasia and Africa) sometime during the 30 million years of the Jurassic Period, which ended about 135 million years ago (see EVOLUTION OF BIRDLIFE). If we could watch a time-lapse film showing how the first bird or birds evolved into the present worldwide avifauna of c. 9,700 species and the climatic and geological events that accompanied

that evolution, we could see quite clearly why bird species now live where they do. But we were only a gleam in the Creator's eye (as it were) during the greater portion of avian evolution and were not even making notes (much less movies) until about 5,000 years ago. Furthermore, we have paid scant attention to the details of world bird distribution until only the last 200 years or so. If, then, we wish to trace the course of bird distribution from its beginnings, we must try to unravel the crisscrossed trails of evolution *backward* from present distributions and a few fossil remains. Until very recently this has been a highly speculative undertaking. The meager fossil record does not even begin to describe the intricate vicissitudes of evolutionary history. Using carefully interpreted molecular relationships in conjunction with the fossil record, we now have a rough "molecular clock" to estimate the dates of origin for bird families (see Cooper and Penny 1997—EVOLUTION). But how a particular species has come to live where it does remains infinitely more mysterious in most cases than the birthplace of your great-great-great-great-grandfather (in most cases). The modern example of the Cattle Egret—which invaded Australia from Asia in historic times and then in the space of about a hundred years has expanded its range from Africa throughout the New World tropics and now thrives as far north as coastal Maine and Lake Champlain—shows that hundreds of thousands of overlapping population shifts have occurred within the earth's avifauna over the millennia. Hundreds of species, some no doubt common and widespread, have long since disappeared, leaving no trace of their existence and condemning us to puzzle over the relationship between their ancestors and descendants. Furthermore, our understanding of the phylogeny of living species is far from perfect, especially regarding the great order of perching birds (Passeriformes)—though, again, that picture has become clearer over the last 20 years due to molecular studies and refined analytic techniques provided by CLADISTICS. In tracing the Wrentit's ancestry, it makes a great difference, after all, whether it is taken to be a titmouse (as first supposed), a unique form in a family of its own (as it is defined in the 1957 *AOU Check-list*), or, as many authorities now agree, the sole New World member of the babbler family (Timaliidae).

MAJOR INFLUENCES ON BIRD DISTRIBUTION. It may be that we will never be able to completely untangle the long interwoven skeins of evolution, much less map the successive distributions of bird species past and present. However, there are a number of basic influences on distribution that are plainly evident today or can be reasonably inferred and which help us guess at the distribution patterns of the past.

In considering the nature of distribution it is important to realize that (1) it is a part of the evolutionary process and is thus always changing—rapidly in some cases (e.g., the Cattle Egret), imperceptibly in others; (2) the distribution of any given bird species is influenced by varying

combinations of some or all of the factors noted below; and (3) not all species respond in the same way to apparently identical distributive "opportunities"—i.e., "psychological" factors seem to predispose some species to expand their ranges and others to remain confined to a limited area despite a lack of physical inhibitions.

Physiographical Barriers. Many truly pelagic birds are ill disposed to come within sight of land, much less to attempt to cross a landmass in getting from one ocean to another; similarly, many land-bird species are inhibited from crossing bodies of water. (During the Pleistocene, expanses of inland seas, created during several interglacial periods, doubtless made such a barrier between birds of eastern and western North America.) These tolerances vary widely from species to species, some fearing to cross the narrowest barrier between similar habitats, while others seem oblivious to such inhibitions as long as other influences (see below) are not involved. Presumably, however, if North America and Europe "drifted" together again, their avifaunas would soon intermingle. And this is exactly what happened to the North American and South American avifaunas when the Isthmus of Panama arose.

High mountain ranges in themselves probably do not constitute barriers to bird movements, but crossing them usually means leaving a preferred environment and passing through several alien ones before again reaching suitable habitat (see *Adherence to Niche/Habitat,* below). Birds (e.g., the Brown-capped Rosy-Finch) can also be isolated on the tops of mountains—unwilling to travel to adjacent "islands" of alpine habitat.

Physical Capability. Flightless birds are obviously at a distinct disadvantage in undertaking large-scale shifts in distribution—although the penguins' swimming abilities have allowed them to colonize much of the Southern Hemisphere. Though there are no living flightless species in North America (see FLIGHTLESSNESS), the gallinaceous species are not equipped to make long-sustained flights; they are nearly all nonmigratory and (with the possible exception of Willow Ptarmigan) are unlikely to turn up as pioneers in areas very distant from their present ranges. At the opposite extreme are species such as the Black-headed and Little Gulls, Eurasian species, which have been recorded in North America only within the last 50 years and now breed locally in the northern United States and Canada. These species are strong fliers, well able to survive the rigors of an ocean crossing, regardless of where their travels take them. There are several theories as to precisely how they arrived in North America.

Adherence to Niche/Habitat. In the course of evolution, many species have become strongly adapted to fill a certain role (niche) in a highly specialized habitat, e.g., desert, coniferous forest, fast-moving rivers, to which they become essentially restricted. This kind of distributional enforcement is inextricably connected to variations in soil, temperature, and rainfall, which to a large extent dictate the vegetation (or lack of it).

The vegetation in turn influences the food, nest-site, and nest-building preferences of the birds in the habitat and in some species these preferences become exclusive. Thus, Cactus Wrens are never found in deciduous forest and Pileated Woodpeckers are not found in the desert, though no barriers or physical incapacities exist to prevent either species from going where it will.

Food. A factor of perhaps preeminent importance in niche/habitat adherence is food. Some species (e.g., many corvids) are practically omnivorous and their distribution is therefore unrestrained by their feeding habits, but many species have more restrictive tastes and tend to be found only in association with their principal food source. Birds such as flycatchers and warblers, which depend largely on insects, must shift their distribution southward in cold weather or perish from starvation. Crossbills sustain themselves mainly on conifer seeds and are seldom found away from cone-bearing trees. In years when northern cone crops fail or are insufficient to sustain crossbill populations, the birds move south seeking a new supply; occasionally some birds will remain south of their normal breeding range to nest. A few species are extremely fussy eaters, and their fate is therefore rather precariously tied to the welfare of another organism. The population of Brant that winters along the Atlantic coast of North America suffered a precipitous decline when its favorite food, eelgrass (*Zostera marina*—a saltwater submergent in the pondweed family, Majadaceae), was nearly wiped out by disease in 1931 and 1932; fortunately some of these geese switched to a common marine algae called sea lettuce, *Ulva lactua,* learned to graze fields, and made a recovery (as did the eelgrass). Snail Kites and Limpkins specialize on the large "apple" snails in the genus *Pomacea.* The fondness of Bald Eagles and Ospreys for fish was a significant factor in their recent decline due to the effects of waterborne DDT (see THREATS [OF HUMAN ORIGIN] TO BIRDLIFE). Some narrow eating habits, of course, are less precarious: the American Woodcock's strong preference for earthworms (75% of its diet) is probably indulged at low risk—except for early arrivals caught by late cold snaps and blizzards.

Dispersal. When breeding success surpasses the death rate in a given bird population, the competition for food and nest sites could in some cases increase to intolerable levels if some young birds did not move into new breeding areas. The population explosion of large gulls in the Northeast, for example (see Environmental Changes, below), has resulted in occupation of virtually all suitable nesting sites in many parts of their ancestral range and a pronounced expansion southward and inland.

There is a measure of "accident" in some distributional shifts. Wilson's Phalarope was, until recently, largely restricted to the central prairies of North America as a breeding bird, with only sporadic nesting records east of the Great Plains. Its migration route was also mainly west of the

Mississippi. It was traditionally known as an accidental or very rare spring and fall migrant along the Atlantic coast (Griscom and Snyder 1955–GRISCOM). Since the 1960s, records of the species during migration have increased dramatically, and it now nests very locally in New Brunswick (probable), in New York, and in a salt marsh on the north shore of Massachusetts. How to explain this apparently sudden range expansion? Increased breeding success in the West? The gradual reoccupation of a range that dwindled in prehistoric times? An increase in suitable open-country wetland habitats as eastern forests have been cut? All of the above?

Competition Among Bird Species. How a bird species is distributed within its preferred habitat (or the scope of its niche) is strongly influenced by the number of its avian competitors. A widely ranging species may share its habitat with only a few others in some areas and thus be able to exploit a greater variety of food sources, nest sites, singing perches, etc., than it could where rival species made stronger claims on some of these.

On a broader scale, pioneer males of a given species—of which there is often an excess—may be pressured by competition (see POPULATION) to spread to a new habitat or an unexploited niche in the species' traditional area, thus taking a first step toward becoming a distinct species with a "new" distribution and/or habitat preference.

Environmental Changes. When habitat is altered or destroyed, the birds that depend on it, experience an change in their distribution. There is evidence that Whooping Cranes were once widespread in the prairie and taiga wetlands of North America, for example, but were reduced to their present extremely limited distribution by drainage of marshes for agriculture and other encroachments of civilization (see ENDANGERED BIRDS). Beavers (one of humankind's few rivals in habitat altering ability) were once abundant in eastern North America, then they were extirpated by European colonists cashing in on the demand for beaver pelts, and now they have returned and are once again pursuing their genetic destiny of flooding the northeastern landscape. What does this have to do with bird distribution? When beavers flood woodlands, they often create dense stands of tree skeletons emerging from shallow lakes; these are preferred nest sites for Great Blue Herons, which have increased significantly following the return of the beavers.

Very often, of course, the narrowing of one species' range coincides with the broadening of another's. When a forest is cleared, open-country birds gain the ground that the forest birds lose. Some species, e.g., the misnamed Prairie Warbler, specialize in successional scrub habitats, which spring up after burns or logging. The distribution of such species therefore fluctuates to a much greater extent than those that live in more "long-lived" habitats.

Altering habitat is only one of the ways in which human society affects the distribution of birdlife. Open dumping of refuse and the enor-

mous increase in offshore fishing operations are credited with the spectacular range extensions of Herring and Great Black-backed Gulls, formerly northern species, which now breed as far south as the Carolinas. Their abundance along the New England coast and their ability as year round residents to claim preferred island nesting areas early in the season resulted in the altered distribution of less aggressive species, such as the Laughing Gull and some terns.

The unified suburban "green belt," which now accompanies the eastern megalopolis from southern cities to New England, is suspected of at least encouraging the recent northward spread of the Northern Mockingbird, Tufted Titmouse, and Northern Cardinal; a similar effect is probably responsible for drawing such "eastern" species as the Blue Jay and Baltimore Oriole westward across the once treeless Great Plains. And man's careless introduction of highly adaptable alien bird species, such as the European Starling and House Sparrow, which compete with native species (see INTRODUCED BIRDS), may drastically reduce populations to the extent of altering distribution—at least temporarily.

Temporal Effects on Distribution. The passage of time affects distribution of birdlife in at least three distinct ways. (1) As noted earlier, distribution is an ever-changing phenomenon. In many species, distribution changes significantly within a generation for a variety of reasons (see above) and the distribution of the world avifauna has been shown to alter radically within a few thousand years, especially with the intervention of a major geoclimatic event such as an ice age. (2) Bird distribution changes with the seasons, with the majority of species from the North Temperate Zone moving south during the winter months, many to the Neotropics. Obviously, this means that there are more or fewer of both species and individuals in a given area at different seasons. Except for northernmost regions, all parts of North America support (a) bird species that are present year round (permanent residents); (b) species that only breed in the region and migrate afterward (summer residents); (c) species that arrive from the north and are present only during the nonbreeding season (winter residents); and (d) those that neither breed nor winter but only pass through during migration (transients). There are also a few anomalies, such as pelagic species (e.g., Wilson's Storm-Petrel, Greater Shearwater), which arrive in the North Atlantic during our summer after their Southern Hemisphere breeding season. (3) Bird species that occupy the same habitat and overlapping niches may reduce competition by nesting on different schedules. Berger (1954) cites the Yellow Warbler (earliest), Willow Flycatcher (second), and American Goldfinch (latest) as exemplifying this phenomenon in southern Michigan.

Other Factors. The distribution of some species seems to be defined by none of the above factors. The limited breeding grounds of Kirtland's Warbler are *apparently* surrounded by ideal habitat, free of competitors, into which it could easily expand—yet it does not. And Henslow's Sparrow

is renowned for its tendency to form isolated colonies without occupying seemingly "good" intervening habitat. Perhaps they are innately maintaining an ancestral range that was once restricted by factors no longer present. Perhaps they continue to be restricted by factors we have yet to perceive.

DEFINING BIRD DISTRIBUTION. In an effort to analyze the complex patterns of bird distribution, scientists have proposed a number of schemes. These approach the problem in two basic ways: (1) by dividing the earth into distinctive areas—based on climate, vegetation, faunal homogeneity, or other factors—with which birds (and other life forms) are then categorically associated, e.g., tropical birds, coniferous-forest birds, and Nearctic birds (see below); and (2) by defining the distribution of individual species, again according to a number of factors—e.g., geographical and ecological. The main schemes are as follows.

Zoogeographic Regions. This concept divides the earth into 6 major regions, in each of which the animal life can be seen to have (in very general terms) an evolutionary identity distinct from all the others. The regions are the Palearctic, Ethiopian, Oriental, Australasian, Neotropical, and Nearctic. (The boundaries of the last closely coincide with those of North America.) An additional region, the Holarctic, was suggested by Heilprin in 1887; it combines the Nearctic and Palearctic, which share a large proportion of species. (See ZOOGEOGRAPHY for origins of the concept and Fig. 34 for location of the regions.) A number of faunas, such as those of isolated island groups (Galapagos, Hawaii, Madagascar, etc.), and oceanic organisms do not fit within the major regions, and the ranges of numerous species overlap two or more regions (indeed, some occur in all of them; see COSMOPOLITAN). Nevertheless, the concept embodies a significant measure of "distributional truth" and is much more realistic in making broad faunal comparisons than trying to compare "artificial" geographical entities such as countries or even continents. One way of demonstrating how the zoogeographic scheme works is to note that all but a few *orders* of birds occur in all the major regions (i.e., are cosmopolitan); that only about a quarter of bird *families* are cosmopolitan, while about a quarter are restricted to a single region; but that only a few *genera* and a *very* few *species* are distributed throughout, while a high proportion of both of those categories are regional endemics.

Zoogeography also provides a broad framework on which to consider the origins of animal groupings and their subsequent changes in distribution with evolution. And it is a handy way of referring to the elements of our own avifauna—the Plain Chachalaca is an essentially Neotropical species, wagtails are today largely Palearctic breeders, while vireos are likely of Nearctic origins (see Origins of North American Birdlife, below).

Latitudinal Zonation is another form of zoogeographical division, articulated by Darlington (1957), which recognizes affinities and differences

among animal groups in distinctive zones of latitude, which, of course, are closely related to climatic variation: the tropics, the North and South Temperate Zones, the Subarctic/Arctic, and the mainly oceanic Antarctic. Looked at from this perspective, we can see that some families of birds, e.g., trogons, are distributed mainly throughout the tropical regions of the earth (pantropical) and that sandpipers are conspicuously concentrated as breeding birds in the Arctic/Subarctic. It also becomes clear that whereas there is a relatively sharp distinction between tropical and north temperate avifaunas, south temperate birdlife seems to be a kind of avian outwash plain from the tropics with few distinct bird groups above species level. Another "latitudinal insight" is that the tropics contain a spectacularly greater diversity of bird species than any other zone and that numbers of *individuals* also have a tendency (far less pronounced) to diminish as one approaches the poles. A latitudinal perspective also allows recognition of many cases of evolutionary convergence.

Oceanic Zones. The distribution of pelagic birds does not fit into either the regional or the latitudinal concepts that apply to the landmasses, but is divisible into distinctive zones of its own, largely on the basis of water temperature. Marine organisms on which true seabirds depend are most abundant in cold water, with the result that arctic and (especially) Antarctic seas support a wide variety and impressive concentrations of such species. Movements of cold water, such as the Labrador and Humboldt currents, penetrate the lower latitudes here and there, bringing their rich plankton contents and avian dependents along, but, in general, the warm tropical seas are relatively barren of birdlife. The northern oceanic zone has nurtured the evolution of numerous alcid species (unique to the Northern Hemisphere), while the Antarctic seas are characterized by a wealth of penguins and tubenoses (Procellariiformes); both zones support species of cormorants, gannets, gulls, and skuas; and a few species (e.g., Wilson's Storm-Petrel, Greater, Sooty, and other shearwaters) migrate between the polar seas (see MIGRATION). Though comparatively depauperate as noted, the avifauna of tropical oceans does have a distinctive ornithological character, defined by the unique occurrence of the well-named tropicbirds, the frigatebirds, a proliferation of booby species, more than half the world's tern species, and a few tubenoses (e.g., Black-capped Petrel, Audubon's Shearwater).

Altitudinal Zones. Baron Alexander von Humboldt (1845–62) was the first to draw attention to certain similarities between moving northward (or southward) from the tropics to the poles and moving up the slopes of high mountains. In both cases the temperature drops as the elevation/ latitude rises and the forms of the vegetation and the animal life change accordingly. This is not a perfect analogy; precipitation or other moisture, cloud cover and wind often increase as one ascends in elevation, while this is not true of "climbing" in latitude. Another way of looking at this

phenomenon is to note that (very generally speaking) as one approaches the tropics from the poles the distinctive vegetational zones in effect "climb" the mountains—at 70° N tundra occurs at sea level, but at 30° N it is not encountered below 10,000 feet. In general, it would be misleading to cite similarities between the avifaunas of arctic and alpine tundra, but it can be noted that, for example, "northern" birds (e.g., Black-throated Green Warbler) breed *only* in the mountains in the southern extremities of their ranges.

Life Zones and the Holdridge System. Postulated by C. H. Merriam (1894), the concept of "life zones" was an attempt to prove a direct correlation between changes in temperature and plant and animal distribution. This early attempt to formulate scientific principles of distribution was widely accepted in the early part of this century, but the temperature correlation has proven to be a too simplistic solution to this complex phenomenon. In 1947 L. R. Holdridge published an extensive refinement of the life zone concept that incorporated precipitation and the ratio of potential evapotranspiration to precipitation displayed logarithmically in a pyramid of interlocking hexagons—the famous chicken-wire diagram—each representing a life zone. This system allows for a better definition of distinct vegetation communities—e.g., of a number of temperate coniferous forest communities that the Merriam system lumped as a vast "Canadian Zone"—as well as allowing for transitions between them. Much scientific work has been done in this realm since Holdridge, with the best current summary of North American vegetation communities to be found in Barbour and Billings (1988); see Fig. 9 for a map of this system.

Biomes and Ecotones. Biomes may be defined as distinctive, relatively stable communities of plants and animals, usually named for their characteristic ("climax") plant formations, e.g., tundra biome, chaparral biome. Since these plant communities and their associated animal life are products of diverse factors (e.g., soil, humidity, as well as temperature), the biome concept represents a more realistic approach to distribution than the earlier life zone classification (see above). The major North American biomes are listed under BIOME (see also Fig. 8). Of course, many species inhabit more than one biome.

Fig. 8. *Major North American biomes.* Because of the scale of the map and the complexity of the patterns depicted, some detail has been sacrificed: alpine tundra exists above tree line atop the highest peaks of the western mountains (usually over 10,000 feet) as well as on the highest peaks of the Northeast; the southwestern pine-oak woodland occurs at moderate elevations (5,000–8,000 feet) in the hills and mountains of Oregon, Colorado, Utah, and California, and in southern Arizona and New Mexico where it contains a variety of "Mexican" bird specialties. Many of the plant and animal associations of southern Florida and the southern-most end of the Rio Grande Valley of Texas do not fit neatly into any of the major North American biomes. Compare Fig. 9.

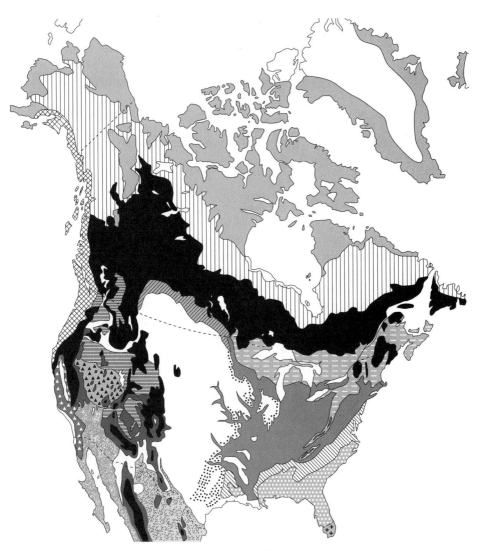

Arctic Tundra		Deciduous Forest	
Tundra–Coniferous Forest Ecotone		Oak–Pine Ecotone (subclimax)	
Creosote Scrub Desert		Southeastern Pinewoods (subclimax)	
Sagebrush		Deciduous Forest–Grassland Ecotone	
Coniferous Forest		Moist Coniferous Forest	
Coniferous–Deciduous Forest Ecotone		Grassland	
Coniferous Forest–Grassland Ecotone		Grass–Sage Ecotone (subclimax)	
Coniferous Forest–Sage Grass Ecotone		Desert (Mesquite) Scrub (subclimax)	
Coastal Chaparral		Mixed Subtropical	
Pinyon–Juniper Interior Chaparral			

The transition between one biome and another usually occurs over a zone in which aspects of both are represented as well as elements unique to the transition zone. These zones are called *ecotones* and sometimes contain richer faunas and floras than the "pure" communities they separate at least locally. The birdwatching cliché that "birds like edges" reflects this characteristic.

Range is the geographic distribution of a particular organism or grouping of organisms beyond which they are absent (except for vagrants). We can speak of the ovenbird family (Furnariidae) as ranging only within the New World tropics, but the term is applied most often to the distribution of species and subspecies. The Western Tanager ranges from southern Alaska and central Saskatchewan to Costa Rica: its total or "gross" range. Its breeding range is western North America from southern Alaska to central Saskatchewan, south to northern Baja California and western Texas, east to western South Dakota and Nebraska. Its winter range extends from southern Baja and central Mexico to Costa Rica; it normally occurs only as a transient in that part of its range between its breeding and wintering grounds. In the broadest sense eastern North America, where Western Tanager occurs with some frequency as a vagrant, might be included in the species range, and extension of its "normal range."

Note that "range" is a strictly geographical term. Most birds occupy only a particular habitat and ecological niche within the boundaries of their ranges. The ranges of hundreds of bird species overlap at any given point on the earth (except at sea and at the polar extremities), yet no two ranges are exactly alike.

Habitat, Niche, Community, and Ecosystem are additional terms commonly used to describe where birds (and other organisms) live. All are useful in describing specific phenomena, but can be confusing because of their overlapping interrelationships. Within a bird's *range* (see above), it lives in one or more *habitats,* which may be defined very broadly (seashore, woodland) or more narrowly (sandy beach, oak woodland) and which include the nonliving as well as living components. Habitat (in Latin, "it lives") is described from the perspective of the organism that occupies it. Rocky shores are the winter habitat of the Purple Sandpiper.

A natural *community* is an assemblage of organisms found together often enough to give them a distinct collective identity. The pine barrens community of the Northeast is characterized by Pitch Pine and Scrub Oak as its dominant tress species but also has other characteristic plants and animals or, some of which may be *endemic* to this community, occurring

Fig. 9. *Major vegetation formations of North America.* (After Barbour and Billings [2000–DISTRIBUTION]. Reprinted with the permission of Cambridge University Press.)

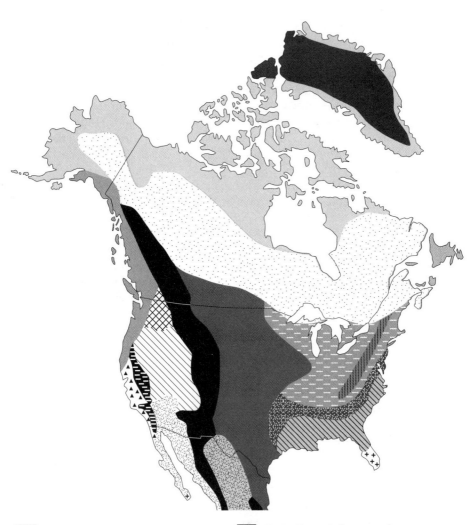

■ Ice		■ Rocky Mountain forests and alpine vegetation	
Arctic tundra		Central prairies and plains	
Taiga		Mixed deciduous forests	
Pacific coastal–Cascadian forests		Chihuahuan deserts and woodlands	
Palouse prairies		Appalachian forests	
Intermountain deserts, shrub-steppes, woodlands, and forests		Piedmont oak–pine forests	
California forests and alpine vegetation		Coastal plain forests, bogs, swamps, and strand	
Californian grasslands, chaparral, and woodlands		Tropical forests	
Mojave and Sonoran deserts			

no where else (e.g., the Barrens Buckmoth); other species may be *characteristic* of pine barrens, but also occur in other community types (e.g., the Prairie Warbler). Some communities (e.g., salt marsh) are easier to define sharply than others (e.g., some forest types) because they have more *obligate* species and share few species with other communities; boundaries between communities are often (and naturally) blurred.

The collective interrelations of plant and animal communities together with the nonorganic elements of habitat (rock, water, temperature, etc.) make up a functional unit of the environment called an *ecosystem.* This can be described at any scale from the global ecosystem to the sphagnum bog ecosystem.

Each species occupies a unique ecological *niche,* which is not a place but more like its role: what it eats, where it nests, how it uses and modifies both living and nonliving entities with which it comes in contact, or the total combination of factors that allows an organism to occupy its place in nature; niche is inclusive of habitat.

It might be said in summary that these concepts attempt to describe essentially the same thing—how organisms live on the planet—from different perspectives: habitat, a *place* where a species lives; community, an definable *assemblage* of species; ecosystem, a *system* of interacting species and physical elements; niche, the *role* defined as the sum of its interactions in nature.

The details of bird distribution within a niche, ecosystem, community, or habitat—e.g., how a bird recognizes its proper nesting habitat; how it utilizes its niche in competition with other members of its community; the relative numbers of species/individuals a given habitat can support— these and many other fascinating aspects of distribution are beyond the scope of the present book, but see the Bibliography, especially, Hutchinson (1957), Ricklefs (1966), MacArthur (1972), Milstead (1972), Cody (1985), Wiens (1989), Hengeveld (1990), and Myers and Giller (1988).

ISLANDS AND BIRD DISTRIBUTION. When a portion of a major landmass becomes separated from the mainland, there is a tendency for the diversity of plant and animal species to diminish. Bird species on a small island, for example, that are unwilling or unable to cross to and from the mainland may not have a sufficient "gene pool" among the island population to permit survival. Species that *do* survive tend to expand into the empty niches.

Remote islands (Galápagos, Hawaiian) tend to be colonized by wide-ranging pelagic birds and by strays from distant mainlands. Without competition for niches, the immigrant land birds (as well as the plant, insect, and other organisms that also arrive by wind and water) tend to evolve into distinct forms (eventually species) and to fill the wealth of niches. If the island has a wide range of habitats, the diversity of bird species may evolve to a comparable width. Such island life forms are, of course, unique—

"endemic"—to their particular island or island group—and eventually become incapable of interbreeding with (and distinct in appearance from) the mainland ancestor from which they originally evolved (see SPECIATION). Ocean islands, such as the Antilles, which are close but not too close to the mainland, usually have a combination of endemics and resident populations of strong-flying continental species. But on the Hawaiian Islands (for example)—more than 2,000 miles from any mainland coast—98% of the resident birds (excluding introductions) occur nowhere else in the world.

Since the publication in 1967 of Robert MacArthur and Edward O. Wilson's *The Theory of Island Biogeography,* the dynamics of island ecology and their implications for conservation have become hot topics for research. Many of the distinctive qualities of island biotas—e.g., small number of species (though relatively large number of individuals, tameness of animals, loss of dispersal ability (e.g., flightless birds), and a tendency to dwarfism or gigantism (Foster's rule)—tend to make them highly vulnerable to extinction. For an extensive popular description of this phenomenon, see David Quammen's *The Song of the Dodo* (1996).

See also SPECIATION.

ORIGINS OF NORTH AMERICAN BIRDLIFE. Despite the difficulties involved in tracing avian lineages, some highly educated guessers have speculated very convincingly about the origins of some bird families. Mayr and Short (1970) thought it impossible on the evidence available to postulate the origins of 29 families worldwide, including most waterbirds and some families of cosmopolitan distribution, such as hawks, nightjars, and swallows. Of the bird families that currently occur in North America, they believed that the American vultures, grouse,* turkeys, limpkins, wrens,* mimic thrushes, waxwings,* silky-flycatchers (e.g., Phainopepla), vireos, and wood warblers evolved in North America (including Mesoamerica and the Antilles in Mayr's definition); with recent insights in bird taxonomy, the gnatcatchers, American cuckoos, and American quail. Families with asterisks are the only ones that have reached the Old World—one species each in the case of the wrens and waxwings. The shallow sea bed of the Bering Strait that periodically bridges the watery gap between what are now Alaska and Siberia during times of low sea level is believed to have been a major route for interchange of New and Old World avifaunas. Excepting the grouse, all of the families listed above now occur in the Neotropical region as well.

Families believed to have originated in South America are the hummingbirds, guans (e.g., chachalacas), tyrant flycatchers, tanagers, and American blackbirds/orioles. None of these families occurs in the Old World; all reach greatest diversity in the Neotropics.

The pheasants and quail, cranes,* pigeons and doves, Old World cuckoos, barn owls, typical owls, kingfishers, larks,* crows and jays, tits,[†]

nuthatches,[†] treecreepers,[†] babblers,[*] thrushes, Old World warblers[*] (e.g., Arctic Warbler), kinglets,[†] pipits and wagtails,[*] and shrikes[*] originated in the Old World according to Mayr. Those marked with asterisks do not reach the Neotropics or only barely so; daggers mark families that reach only the highlands of Mexico and Central America. The only bird species in the New World considered to be a member of the large and diverse babbler family is the Wrentit, which occupies a narrow range in the chaparral of coastal Oregon and California and Baja California.

See also SPECIATION.

DIURNAL (dye-UR-nl). In the context of animal behavior, the term means "active by day," which describes the great majority of bird species. Contrast NOCTURNAL; see also CREPUSCULAR.

DIVING. See SWIMMING/DIVING.

DODO (doe-doe). One of at least 3 species of turkey-sized, flightless, pigeon-like birds endemic to islands of the Mascarene group in the Indian Ocean. The extirpation of these last members of the family Raphidae in the late seventeenth and early eighteenth centuries shortly followed the arrival of Europeans. The Dodo was a heavy, ungainly species with blue-gray plumage, short legs, a heavy hooked bill, and small, useless wings and was confined to the island of Mauritius. Little was recorded of its habits except its fearlessness of men, which gained it quick extinction and immortalization, on the one hand, as a symbol of stupidity and, on the other, of human fecklessness.

DOMESTICATED BIRDS. Restricted here to birds that have been bred in captivity for many generations for the sake of some product useful to human beings. For other instances of tamed and wild birds kept and bred in captivity, see CAPTIVITY; FALCONRY; COCKFIGHTING. The following domestic birds are familiar throughout North America. Only the species from which they originally derived, their range in the wild, and the principal use of the domestic breeds are given. In addition to their importance as food, most of these species are extensively bred in ornamental forms purely for show, many are also a source of feathers for decoration and stuffings, and a few are used in sport and ritual. For information on the nearly innumerable breeds that have been developed and other details, see the Bibliography.

BARNYARD GEESE AND DUCKS come in a great variety of shapes and colors but derive on the whole from a relatively few species. Chief among these are the following.

Greylag Goose *(Anser anser)* breeds from Europe through central Asia and winters in North Africa, through northern India and southern China;

still common as a wild bird throughout much of its range despite its popularity as a game bird. Delacour (1964–WATERFOWL) thinks that the Greylag is probably the oldest domesticated bird, as it appears in Egyptian
frescoes dated from about 4,000 years ago, but this opinion has been offered for most of the birds under discussion here. The many domestic versions may resemble the wild goose—i.e., largely brownish gray with white
lower belly and undertail—or be totally white or some combination of the
two. The legs and in some races the bills of wild greylags are pink; in domestic breeds both are usually bright orange; domestics also tend to be
larger than the wild birds, sometimes (e.g., Toulouse Goose) spectacularly
so; Greylags are used mainly for meat and down. Escaped barnyard gray-
lags and hybrid Greylag × Canada Geese are not infrequently found asso-
ciating with wild geese in North America.

Swan Goose *(Anser cygnoides)* breeds from central Siberia to Kamchatka in the north, to central Asia and Mongolia in the south; winters
eastward to northern China and Japan; a striking species of the Eurasian
steppe, now becoming scarce due to overhunting. Another species long in
domestic service, beginning at least 3,000 years ago in China. The usual
domestic incarnations are either all white or brown and white like the
"original" and have a very prominent knob at the forehead; they are often
called Chinese Geese, are kept for their meat, and are also useful—due to
their large size and loud voice—as "watch geese."

Greylag and Swan Geese are often interbred.

Mallard *(Anas platyrhynchos)* breeds throughout most of North America; once largely a western species, spreading rapidly throughout the east
in twentieth century, due largely to the establishment of feral population.

Also native to Europe, and Asia to above the Arctic Circle; winters
south to central Mexico, North Africa, and southern China; introduced to
Hawaii, the Virgin Islands, Australia, and New Zealand. Mallards, too,
were domesticated by the ancient Egyptians and the classical cultures,
whence to Europe and America. Domestic Mallards may be much larger
than wild ones, retain their normal colors or show varying degrees of albinism (e.g., Pekin Ducks) or melanism; a frequent melanistic variation is
nearly all black or iridescent green with a white breast. Many different
breeds are cultivated for meat, eggs, and ornamental characteristics.
Many "wild" populations are regularly augmented by domestic stock
(usually Easter ducklings) and it is not unusual to see birds with domestic
plumage characteristics and a huge size range in these populations.

Muscovy Duck *(Cairina moschata)* is resident from northeastern
Mexico to northern Argentina; birds of uncertain origin that show wild-
type plumage and wariness occur regularly along the Lower Rio Grande
in Texas. The conquistadors first brought Muscovies to Europe from
South America, where they had been domesticated by the natives of
Colombia and Peru—probably for centuries. The nearly all black and

metallic green (with white wing patch) plumage of the wild Muscovy is seldom seen in domestic birds, which may be all white, patchy black and white, tan, or blue-gray. It is a large species in its natural state and like other domestics is often selectively bred to near-monstrous proportions. Domestic drakes tend to develop great, hideous red facial caruncles. They will interbreed with other domestic species and when paired with female Mallards, for example, produce hybrids with good-quality meat. This is their principal use.

The name Muscovy is either (1) a corruption of a South American Indian name, (2) a corruption of the species epithet *moschata,* which refers to the species' strong odor, or (3) the result of a confusion about the species' origins by the namer (Linnaeus).

DOMESTIC TURKEYS all derive from a single species, the Wild Turkey of North America, *Meleagris gallopavo.* This species once ranged throughout the open deciduous forests of North America south to southern Florida and central Mexico; once scarce due to habitat destruction and overhunting it has been successfully reintroduced over much of its original wild distribution and even exceeds its historic limits in some places. It continues to be a popular game bird.

Our Thanksgiving turkeys arrived on our tables by a circuitous route. Turkeys were domesticated by the native peoples (e.g., Aztecs) of Mexico for an unknown period before the arrival of the Spanish conquistadors. The Spanish introduced the Mexican breeds into Europe in the sixteenth century, and these were eventually carried back to North America by early colonists, where—possibly together with northeastern wild birds—the domestic American stocks developed. There are 6 major domestic breeds, including the Bronze (similar in plumage to wild birds), the White Holland, the Narragansett, the Bourbon Red, the Black, and the Slate (gray). The present great popularity of turkey meat began only in about 1935, previous to which turkeys were bred here mainly for show. Today they represent a major (and still growing) segment of the poultry industry. For origin of the name, see TURKEY.

CHICKENS are descended from one of four forest-dwelling gallinaceous species in the genus *Gallus* (family Phasianidae), all from India and southern Asia. They may have been domesticated in India before 3000 BC, but they were certainly bred in China by 1400 BC, where they were described as "the domesticated animal that knows the time." They then moved westward via the Middle Eastern civilizations. Chickens reached North America during the earliest phases of colonization, but there is evidence that they were present in South America (via Asia and Polynesia) in pre-Columbian times. The raising of domestic poultry for both meat and eggs is, of course, a major industry today in North America. More than 100 breeds of chickens are recognized; perhaps only 30 of these are raised for food, the rest being of ornamental interest. Well-known American breeds

include Plymouth Rock (white or barred with black), Rhode Island Red (state bird of Rhode Island), and Wyandotte (usually white). The Leghorns, another familiar breed, originated in Europe; the Delaware Blue Hen, state bird of Delaware, no longer exists; it was a cockfighting breed.

In addition to their importance as food, chickens have long been and continue to be frequent victims of blood sport and animal sacrifice; the entrails have for millennia been perceived as a medium from which to divine the future (see COCKFIGHTING).

GUINEA FOWL belong to the strictly African family Numididae, which contains 6 species in 4 genera. Domestic guineas apparently all descend from the widespread species *Numida meleagris,* the Helmeted Guineafowl. Guineafowl were introduced several times into Europe and then to America, but have not "developed" and consequently look very much like their wild ancestors. They are used largely for food—and make a fearsome racket.

PIGEONS, now ubiquitous in a stunning assortment of color varieties throughout North American population centers, all come from the Eurasian Rock Dove (aka Common Pigeon) *(Columba livia),* which still breeds in scattered enclaves away from domestic stock in its original cliffside habitat throughout much of the Old World. Beginning as early as 3000 BC and perhaps long before, pigeons figured in Persian and Egyptian civilizations as sacred symbols as well as food sources. Uninspiring as it may be to contemplate from our present vantage point, the dove of Genesis was more likely a Common Pigeon than any more exotic columbid. Though young pigeons do occasionally grace gourmet menus as "squab," the species is more likely to be bred in ornamental show varieties, used in sport (pigeon racing), or kept as pets. Lamentably, they are also a significant nuisance, particularly in urban areas, where in addition to their general messiness they have been cited as carriers of histoplasmosis and chlamydiosis, both diseases that can affect humans. Pigeons are also agricultural pests, feeding on grains in storage and in the field.

DOMINANCE. Birds, mammals, and other animals that engage in social interaction set up natural hierarchies, based on an individual's ability to dominate others. The rank of a given individual within a particular group is typically established by means of a physical contest, though sometimes simple presence (e.g., a very large individual among small ones) or precedence in a location or social group is enough to establish dominance. In some species, notably the turkeys, grouse, and other gallinaceous birds, courtship displays are social events at which the "peck order" of a particular population of birds is reaffirmed or rearranged. Prolonged physical contests, such as those between rutting sheep or deer, are rare among birds, though elaborate ritualized fighting occurs in some species (e.g., Ruffs) and a sharp peck or blow with a spurred wing or leg to show a

subordinate bird its place is not uncommon. There tends to be a general correspondence between position in the peck order and sexual success, the alpha or top-ranked male getting to mate with more females and therefore having a greater likelihood of perpetuating his genes. The variance in mating success in species with social display is very high; many males do not breed at all in these species, though all males in a display situation are likely to be "primed" for copulation, and with numbers of available females present, it is by no means universal that the "winner takes all."

Dominance is not restricted to male sexual hierarchies. The original "peck order" is that among barnyard *hens*. And interspecific dominance contests are common where food is abundant. Anyone who has watched the interactions that take place at a bird feeding station knows that battles for preferred positions or even the entire feeder take place almost constantly and are not always won by the larger species. Though sheer size does often confer dominance, age, sex, hormonal levels, and location also affect who prevails over whom.

Even in stable flocks of a single species, disputes over dominance occur regularly, especially as younger generations overtake older. But a certain conservatism also prevails in such hierarchies once dominance has been clearly established. This inhibits constant challenges within the ranks and even allows the alpha individual to sustain a defeat or two without losing position.

For another form of individual dominance, see TERRITORY. For genetic dominance, see GENETICS, SPECIATION; HYBRIDIZATION.

DORSAL. Upper (surface); the dorsal aspects of a bird are principally those of the back or mantle but also include the top of the bill, head, tail, etc.; the lower or under portions are VENTRAL.

DOTTEREL (DOT-er-ul). Standard English name in North America and Europe for a single species of tundra-breeding, essentially Palearctic plover, *Charadrius (Eudromias) morinellus*. Four other species of plovers in as many genera—of Australian and South American distribution, are also called dotterels in their English names. *The* Eurasian Dotterel breeds locally in extreme northwestern Alaska; these birds presumably winter in Asia, although a few have appeared along the western coast of North America in fall and winter.

According to Lockwood (1993–NAMES), the name came originally from "dot plover" referring to "the distinctive note often heard at the end of the soft, fluting call." The name also refers to the species' alleged stupidity, as in dotard and dolt, though this meaning did not show up in print until 1440. Dotterels were once widely trapped in nets for food in Europe. The trappers believed that the birds imitated any action they made and, thus distracted, were easily caught. The belief was based on the "fact" that

when men stretched out their arms, the dotterels followed suit. In reality the trappers were mimicking the broken-wing distraction display typical of many plovers. Doubtless, the birds *were* easy enough to net, since they rely on cryptic coloration and "sitting tight" for protection and are reluctant to leave the vicinity of the nest, once flushed. Still, it seems there were "dotterels" among the hunters as well as the plovers. See also PLOVER.

DOVE. Standard English name for about 160 members of the family Columbidae (order Columbiformes), including hyphenated names such as ground-dove, quail-dove, and fruit-dove; 13 species of "doves" are recorded for North America, including native, vagrant, and introduced species. The doves share the family with the pigeons. There is no real (i.e., morphological/taxonomic) distinction between a dove and a pigeon; for such distinctions as exist and the general characteristics of the family, see PIGEON.

"Dove" may come from the German *dubo,* "dark-colored" (Gruson 1972–BIBLIOGRAPHY), a word that Lockwood (1993–NAMES) says refers to the cooing of one of the European *Columba* pigeons; Choat and Paynter (1985–BIOGRAPHY) prefer as origin the Anglo-Saxon *dufan,* meaning to dive, possibly in reference to the courtship flight.

DOVEKIE. Standard English name in North America for a single small auk, *Alle alle,* which breeds on arctic coasts and islands from northwestern Greenland east to Novaya Zemlya and south to Iceland; it is the smallest alcid of this region. Dovekies breed largely in teeming high arctic colonies and are a principal food source for other inhabitants of the barren lands, including some Inuit populations. In spite of their small size they are fully equal to the harsh conditions on their North Atlantic pelagic wintering grounds, but are vulnerable during migration to onshore storms and are sometimes driven onto coastal beaches and even far inland. Helpless to take off except from water, many become victims of gulls and other predators. Others are adopted by humans, glad to take a little "penguin" under their protection; Dovekies are often killed by this form of kindness and are much more likely to survive if released immediately in the ocean or another large body of water from which they can take off.

The standard English name in Europe is Little Auk. "Dovekie" is a Scandinavian whaler's name meaning "little dove," but it was originally applied to the Black Guillemot *(Cepphus grylle);* the smaller alcids were called *rotche* in that area. The switch was apparently made by New World seamen, many of whom today call Black Guillemots "sea pigeons." For family characteristics, see AUK.

DOWITCHER (DOW-itcher; like "dowager"). Standard English name for all 3 species of long-billed sandpipers in the genus *Limnodromus* (family

Scolopacidae; order Charadriiformes), 2 of which breed in North America. The dowitchers make up a monogeneric tribe, the Limnodromi.

The North American dowitchers (Long-billed and Short-billed) are comparatively short-legged shorebirds with "rusty" underparts in alternate (breeding) plumage, which is replaced by drab gray and dirty white in basic (winter) plumage. The two species are notoriously difficult to distinguish in the latter plumage.

"Dows" probe in mud and soft sand with a characteristic "sewing machine" motion duplicated only by the Stilt Sandpiper. The Long-billed Dowitcher nests in western Alaska and Siberia, and normally appears in eastern North America only during the fall passage; it shows a stronger preference for inland freshwater habitats than its sibling species. The Short-billed breeds in marshy tundra in the Low Arctic of central and eastern Canada as well as southern Alaska. Both dowitchers winter along the southern coasts of the United States and in the American tropics.

Two theories are commonly advanced on the origins of the name "dowitcher." It may be an anglicization of the Iroquois name for the birds or a corruption of *deutscher,* referring to the popularity of roast dowitchers among New York Dutchmen of an earlier age. The species must have enjoyed a much broader ethnic appeal than this analysis implies, for by 1909 dowitchers had been decimated by market gunners. With full protection they have recovered well.

For family characteristics, see SANDPIPER.

DOWN. Small, soft, tuft-like feathers with a short, often negligible rachis and free-branching barbs that form no vane (see FEATHER). Individual down feathers are technically known as plumules, plumulae, or plumaceous feathers. In all its forms, down serves mainly in the conservation of body heat. It is not confined to feather tracts.

The definition of the different types of down is a confusing business, made more so by a baroque terminology. Only a few undisputed generalizations will be hazarded here.

(1) There is a difference between natal down feathers (neossoptiles) and adult (teleoptile or definitive) down feathers. (2) Natal down does not occur in all species. (3) When it does occur, it may be scattered over the skin of a nestling or, as in precocial chicks (e.g., of ducks and shorebirds), form a dense continuous coat. (4) The barbs of the natal down feathers of many species emerge in a ring from the top of their calamus and have no rachis whatever; other neossoptiles (e.g., of ducks) have a well-developed rachis. (5) Many but not all natal down feathers are simply specialized tips connected to the incoming juvenal "pinfeathers" and are dropped as the vanes of these unfold from their sheaths. (6) The natal down coat of precocial chicks is often cryptically colored and patterned to resemble habitat near the nest, which conceals the chicks from predators. (7) Most owls

and many falconiforms have two successive coats of down as nestlings, followed by the "mature" feathers of the juvenal plumage. (8) Adult down feathers have a rachis that is shorter than the longest of its barbs and may be negligible. (9) Adult down is usually completely concealed. (10) Adult down is best developed in waterbirds and is used as nest lining by the overwhelming majority of North American swans, geese, and ducks (see NEST).

An interesting evolutionary note is that feather-like structures seen on undisputed theropod dinosaur fossils from China are structurally very similar to natal down: ontogeny recapitulating phylogeny.

Humans appreciate the highly effective insulating capacity of down and use it (as well as adult feathers and man-made down-like substances) in clothing, blankets, sleeping bags, and the like. In Nordic countries, down is "harvested" from the nests of the Common Eider. Female ducks have a quantity of easily detachable down beneath their breast feathers with which they line their nests. When "down pickers" remove the first lining, it is promptly replaced by the sitting bird and this too may be harvested and replaced without noticeably affecting breeding success or unduly depleting the female's store of down.

See also FEATHER; PLUMAGE; MOLT.

DRAKE. A male of any species of duck; "duck" then becomes specific for females. This terminology is still current in some hunting circles and in Britain, e.g., "two drake Gadwalls and a Pintail duck."

DRIFT. The phenomenon in which migrating birds, whether disoriented or "on course," are forced in a given direction by the prevailing wind. Seabird "wrecks," in which migrating alcids, phalaropes, petrels, and other species are blown far inland by onshore gales, could be considered one extreme form of drift; but the "piling up" of numbers of land-bird migrants along the coast of North America in fall when the prevailing winds are westerly is a better example of the term's usual import. See Baird and Nisbet, *Auk* (1960), 77:119–49. Not to be confused with the population genetic concept of genetic drift.

DRINKING. Water is essential to the survival of birds and all other organisms. A great many birds obtain sufficient water in the solid foods they eat and are seldom or never seen to drink. And the capacity of some species—even ones that live in a dry habitat—to go without drinking for long periods is well documented. This is in part explained by the fact that birds do not excrete quantities of liquid urine as mammals do, but reabsorb most fluids internally. Also, birds are able to metabolize water in their tissues even from apparently dry foods, such as seeds. Nevertheless, anyone who owns a birdbath knows that birds do drink from time to time, some species more often than others.

There are two basic avian drinking methods. By far the commoner is to take a mouthful of water and then tilt the head back, allowing the water to pass into the esophagus. When the head is tilted the glottis "automatically" closes, preventing the water from flowing into the windpipe (trachea); the same involuntary reflex ensures the safe swallowing of food. A few birds, notably the pigeons, can suck in water as mammals do without raising their heads. Other species, e.g., hummingbirds, are known to drink from wet vegetation, and aerial species such as swifts and swallows can snatch a mouthful of water from a pond or lake while on the wing.

See Bartholomew, *Proc. XVth Int. Ornithol. Congr.*, 1972, pp. 237–54.

DROPPINGS. Matter excreted through the vent consisting of both urine and feces. See DIGESTIVE SYSTEM; EXCREMENT; EXCRETORY SYSTEM; GUANO; PROBLEMS INVOLVING BIRDS.

DRUMMING. This term is applied to birds in two contexts: (1) A sequence of booms and "thunder rolls" that the Ruffed Grouse produces by beating its wings rapidly from a stationary perch. Precisely how the sound is produced was long in dispute, but it has now been demonstrated that the sound comes solely from the interaction of the cupped wings and the air. This drumming is most strongly associated with the courtship and territoriality of the cock grouse in spring and usually resumes for a brief period in fall; but the sound has been heard throughout the year, day and night, and, according to some sources, is at least occasionally performed by the hen. This is one of the great "voices" of the northern forests of North America, often described as more felt than heard and so pervasive that it is often difficult to judge the location of the drummer.

(2) The sounds woodpeckers make with their bill, especially the distinctive hammering performed by various species as part of their courtship and territorial displays. Ellison, has pointed out that the drum solos of different woodpecker species are quite distinctive and can be used (with caution) to identify even closely related species; he gives a useful and entertaining overview and species by species description in *Birding* (December 1992).

DRUNKENNESS. Birds occasionally become intoxicated from eating fermented fruit or nectar, and instances of fatalities occurring due to the resulting loss of control have been recorded. Robins, waxwings, and other frugivores that habitually depend on "old" fruits of mountain ash, crab apple, or other species in winter are sometimes killed outright by the alcoholic toxins contained in the fruit or fly into windows or other objects after becoming tipsy. Similarly, *Agave* blossoms, which are very popular with a wide range of nectivorous birds in warm climates, ferment rapidly when filled with rain and then "boiled" by the hot sun. In at least one case,

a highway near such an organic cocktail lounge was littered with squashed corpses of avian tipplers that apparently were rendered less sensitive to the danger of passing traffic and/or lost some motor coordination. See Phillips, *Audubon* (1959), 61:6.

DRY TORTUGAS. See FLORIDA.

DUCK. Standard English name for about 60 members of the family Anatidae (order Anseriformes), including combination names such as whistling-duck and Shelduck, but also a collective term for about 80 additional members of the family that do not include "duck" in their names. Though "duck" has little taxonomic integrity, various subgroups do, as with the "true ducks" classified in the subfamily Anatin226ae and the "bay ducks" (or pochards) making up the tribe Aythyini; see the cross references below for further definition.

There are 35 species of ducks (in the broadest sense) that breed in North America, and another 9 that have occurred as vagrants; a single species, the Labrador Duck, is extinct. Taxonomists have grouped members of the order Anserifomes and the family Anatidae in various ways. No attempt will be made to explicate the variations in this entry, but see Appendix I which follows the *AOU Checklist,* 7th edition (1998); Appendix III for the Sibley and Monroe order; and Livezy (1991–1996–WATERFOWL) for his cladistic phylogeny.

For some enlightenment on individual groups, see DABBLING DUCK; BAY DUCK; SEA DUCK; WHISTLING DUCK; STIFFTAIL DUCK; MALLARD; GADWALL; PINTAIL; SHOVELER; TEAL; WIGEON; POCHARD; BUFFLE-HEAD; GOLDENEYE; OLDSQUAW; EIDER; SCOTER; MERGANSER.

The ducks are a highly varied group of medium-sized (10–18 inches) waterbirds, mostly with a broad, flat bill (mergansers exceptional) ending in a small hook or "nail" and lined with sieve-like lamellae (see BILL); the front three toes are webbed. Coloration ranges from rather drab (e.g., Black Duck) to spectacular (e.g., male Wood Duck). Many ducks have a brightly colored patch in the secondaries, called the speculum. Most can be described as either diving or surface-feeding species, both types eating a wide variety of plant and animal foods.

Dabbling ducks, bay ducks, eiders, scoters, the Long-tailed Duck (formerly Oldsquaw), and the Harlequin Duck typically nest in a hollow on the ground near water, concealed in shore vegetation or (especially in tundra species) in the open. The Wood Duck, Bufflehead, goldeneyes, mergansers, and Black-bellied Whistling-Duck usually nest in tree cavities. The Fulvous Whistling-Duck deposits plant material on a flattened clump of swampland vegetation. And the stifftails (genus *Oxyura*) make floating nests anchored to emergent vegetation, heap up plant matter on the shore, or use the top of a muskrat lodge or an old nest of other duck

species. All but the whistling ducks and the stifftails line their nests with down from the female's breast and (in some species) some scraps of handy plant material. Many ducks (e.g., the Ruddy Duck and Hooded Merganser) occasionally lay eggs in the nests of other ducks (see DUMP NEST). Ducks typically lay large clutches of eggs; 3–21 is the range for North American species, but 6–12 is average for most. These vary considerably in size and shape, are often somewhat glossy with a waxy (waterproof?) coating. They may be white, yellowish, buff, olive, bluish, or greenish and are always unmarked (see Fig. 10).

Ducks produce many variations of the stereotypical "quack" (which is actually a vocalization of hens only), of course, but also make a wide range of cooing, whistling, grunting, and croaking sounds. Long-tailed Duck flocks are characteristically noisy, whence the old species' name, Oldsquaw; less sexist auditors have likened this wild sound to a distant kennel of hounds. The whistling ducks and wigeons give pleasant, somewhat plaintive, piping notes in flight or when alarmed.

Ducks occur worldwide in both salt and fresh water and the majority of species are migratory.

"Duck" comes from an Old English word, *duce* or *ducan,* meaning "diver" or "to dive" and this is also the root of our warning verb "duck!" For bibliography, see under WATERFOWL.

DUCKLING. The young of any species of duck until fully fledged. Analogous to "gosling" (goose) and "cygnet" (swan).

DUCK STAMPS. A stamp issued annually (on or about July 1) by the U.S. federal government to raise revenues for the conservation of waterfowl through the purchase of wetland. By law all wildfowl hunters over 16 years of age must buy a stamp and help support refuges and other efforts to maintain populations of ducks, geese, and swans. The Migratory Bird Hunting Stamp Act, passed by Congress in 1934, was a response to the precipitous decline in waterfowl numbers during the "dust bowl" period of the early 1930s. The stamp issue brings in millions of dollars annually to preserve wetland habitat. The design for each year's stamp is chosen from entries in a contest sponsored by the federal government and open to anyone. The stamps are invariably fine depictions of waterfowl themes and are popular with nonhunting collectors who make up an additional source of support for wildfowl conservation. Many states issue their own state duck (or conservation) stamps as well.

For more on hunting regulations, see LAWS PROTECTING BIRDLIFE.

DUCKS UNLIMITED was founded in 1937 by a small group of sportsmen in the United States who were alarmed about the destruction of prairie wetlands during the dust bowl drought of the 1930s. The initial effort raised funds to conserve the continent's most productive waterfowl

habitat across the border in Canada. Since then, DU has helped protect more than 10 million acres of wetland habitat, which, as their website points out, "also benefits other wildlife and people." DU continues to be an organization supported mainly by recreational waterfowl hunters with a mission to "conserve, restore and manage wetlands and associated habitats for North America's waterfowl." The organization publishes a magazine and sponsors a TV program and a daily radio show. For more information go to www.ducks.org.

DUETTING. A pair of birds (or members of an extended family) singing together: either the same song in unison or in closely synchronized, alternating phrases (ANTIPHONAL SONG). Duetting/antiphonal singing is mainly a tropical phenomenon, and is recorded in over 200 species in 44 families. Most duetters are monogamous species that defend breeding territories year-round. Presumably, duets help solidify the pair bond as well as maintaining territory; they also allow birds to locate each other in dense habitats. The phenomenon is not common in North America, but is practiced by Plain Chachalacas, several species of quail (Stokes and Williams 1968–SONG) and in Brown-headed Cowbirds (Brackbill 1961–SONG). See especially Farabaugh (1982–SONG). See also SONG, Multiple Vocalizations.

DUMMY NEST. A phenomenon, especially characteristic of wren species, in which the male, arriving on territory ahead of the female, constructs a series of shells (i.e., external nest structures). When the female arrives, she is taken on a songful tour of inspection, following which she selects a nest and lines it or makes more substantial improvements in preparation for egg laying. After the breeding season the dummy nests may be used by young and adult birds as "dormitories." In North America, House, Winter, and Marsh Wrens habitually make dummy nests, and the practice has also been recorded in the Prothonotary Warbler (Terres 1980–BIRD). "Cock nest" is a synonym.

DUMP NEST. A phenomenon, characteristic of some ducks and gallinaceous species and the South American rheas, in which several females lay eggs in a single nest that is ultimately abandoned. In at least some cases, dump layers are birds with no nest of their own, and also tend to be species that sometimes practice parasitism (nonobligate parasites). In a nest where only a few extra eggs are dumped, the owner may incubate the clutch, even if it includes eggs of a different species. However, when the egg pile reaches intimidating proportions—one Redhead nest was found with 87 eggs (Weller 1959)—the hen abandons it.

Dump nesting in the strictest sense differs from communal practices of ostriches, tinamous, anis and other birds that typically lay in a single nest and share incubation duties. See Semel et al. (1988) and NEST.

Intraspecific brood parasitism in which a female lays her eggs in the nest of another member of her own species is well documented in some species of swallows and also does not belong in this category.

DUNLIN. Standard English name for a species of small sandpiper, *Calidris alpina,* with a circumpolar breeding distribution. An early meaning of "dun" is chestnut brown, the color of a Dunlin's back in breeding plumage and the suffix -lin or -ling refers to a bird. Originally the name applied only to birds in spring, which were thought to be different from the gray dunlins that appeared in the fall. Later dun came to mean "dust-colored," which is not a bad description these sandpipers in winter plumage. In North America the species was once called Red-backed Sandpiper.

DUSTING (dust bathing). Some species of birds actively and regularly fill their plumage with fine dry soil or sand and then remove it by shaking and preening in a ritual known as "dusting" or dust bathing. The practice seems to be most prevalent among birds of open country, such as larks, gallinaceous birds, and some (emberizine) sparrows, but has also been recorded in some hawks, doves, owls, nightjars, wrens, Wrentit, Common Grackle, and House Sparrow. Some "dusters," e.g., gallinaceous birds, apparently never bathe in water, and larks bathe only by exposing themselves to the rain. But other birds both bathe and dust. According to Simmons (1985), dusting and ANTING are mutually exclusive as far as is known, except for one species of Australian songbird, the White-winged Chough (family Corvidae, subfamily Corcoracinae).

  While some dusting gestures—fluffing of feathers, shaking of bill in dust, flicking of wings—are similar to water-bathing gestures, the process is not truly analogous either in performance or in function. The ritual varies from species to species. Songbirds typically make a hollow in the dust by scratching with their feet and rotating their bodies, and the dust is applied by a combination of direct wallowing and the water-bathing gestures just described. Gallinaceous birds and others use bill and feet both to gather dirt around them and to "drive" it into or throw it onto their plumage. After a thorough dusting, birds shake and flap vigorously to rid themselves of the dirt. House Sparrows typically dust in small groups and groups of turkeys (hens with poults) have been seen bathing together in dusty roads, but for the majority of species it is a solitary activity.

  The purpose of all this is far from clear. Present evidence (e.g., Healy and Thomas 1973) suggests that dusting helps keep plumage fluffy (hence air-retentive for good insulation) by removing excess moisture and preen oil. It is also a means of flushing out ECTOPARASITES such as bird lice; it may also reduce the abundance of keratin-consuming bacteria.

  For related behavior, see BATHING; PREENING; SUNNING; ANTING; OIL GLAND.

EAGLE. Standard English name for about 60 members (including fish-eagles, hawk-eagles) of the family Accipitridae (order Falconiformes), which also includes the hawks. Two species of eagles, Bald and Golden breed regularly in North America; White-tailed Eagle bred briefly on Attu in the Aleutians in the 1980s and 1990s and both this and Steller's Sea-Eagle occur as vagrants from Asia.

Ornithologically, the term "eagle" refers to the largest of the diurnal birds of prey. These do not form a unified taxonomic group, however, and in some cases it would not be inaccurate to describe them as large or very large hawks (see HAWK for the confusing etymology of this term); furthermore, some "eagles" are smaller than some "hawks."

Like other members of their family, eagles have powerful wings and legs; a broad wing area; a heavy, hooked bill for tearing flesh; and long, sharp claws for dispatching and/or carrying prey.

The Golden Eagle is distributed throughout the Holarctic region and has been a symbol of majesty and might from the beginning of recorded history. It preys mainly on small animals (e.g., rabbits), but it is widely (and mistakenly) thought to be a major threat to livestock. In the past this has given rise to recreational shooting of eagles from airplanes and the like, and this and other raptors have also died from eating the flesh of poisoned mammalian "varmints." The Bald Eagle, our national emblem, has suffered from a different form of hubris, the indiscriminate use of pesticides, which it ingests with its preferred food, fish (see THREATS [OF HUMAN ORIGIN] TO BIRDLIFE); it was on the Federal Endangered Species List for many years, but due to the banning of DDT and the success of reintroduction programs, many populations have been substantially restored and the species was recently removed from the federal list with much fanfare. Both eagles continue to be protected by federal statutes (see LAWS PROTECTING BIRDLIFE), which carry stiff fines and jail sentences for violators.

Like hawks, eagles construct large stick nests to which they add materials each season. Old eagle nests consequently may attain almost ridiculous mass and weigh two or more tons (see NEST). For other details of nesting and voice, see HAWK.

Aquila, the Latin word for "eagle," connotes dark color and the north wind (Choate and Paynter 1985–BIOGRAPHY); this became *aigle* in French, from which it is but a short step to "eagle." This name came to England with the Normans and replaced the indigenous name "erne"; this, of course, is the answer to the crossword puzzle entry for which the clue is

"sea-eagle." All but two of the eagles in the genus *Haliaeetus* are called fish-eagles or sea-eagles, correctly reflecting their preferred habitat and/or food preference; the exceptions are the Bald Eagle and the White-tailed Eagle.

See references in the Bibliography under HAWK.

EAR. See HEARING.

EATING. See food/feeding.

ECDYSIS (EK-duh-sis). The shedding of old feathers in the molting process (Compare ENDYSIS and see MOLT).

ECHOLOCATION. Bats, marine mammals, and some amphibians and insects can navigate in total darkness, even in the presence of numerous obstacles, by making noises and judging the time taken for the sound waves to bounce off surrounding objects and return to their highly sensitive ears. The only bird species in which the use of echolocation has been confirmed are the Oilbird *(Steatornis caripensis)* of South America and Asian swiftlets in the genus *Collocalia*, all of which breed and roost in dark caves. It is suspected, but not proven, that the regular *peent's* uttered by Common Nighthawks while hunting on the wing may be a means of echolocating insect prey.

ECLIPSE (plumage). In the broadest sense, refers to a drab basic plumage acquired by male birds in a pre-basic (post-breeding) molt that makes a hiatus between the splendor of the preceding and following alternate (breeding) plumages. The term is usually directed more specifically to the unusually brief basic plumage that occurs in most male *duck* species. Typically, this is acquired in the midst of the breeding season but has been shed in favor of the alternate plumage by fall or early winter. See MOLT.

ECOLOGY. The study of the interrelationships of plants, animals, and all the factors that make up the environment in which we live. Ecological studies of birds, for example, include such factors as habitat preference, food sources, relative abundance, migration habits, details of the breeding cycle—how all these factors are shaped by the environment and how they, in turn, affect it.

ECOSYSTEM. All of the factors, including organisms, geology, climate, etc., that make up a particular environment or the earth's environment as a whole. Birds are, of course, a conspicuous and significant component of the global ecosystem and also of the smaller interlocking ecosystems that make up the whole. For further discussion of this and similar terms, see DISTRIBUTION.

ECOTONE (EE-koh-tone). A zone of transition between two major environments and their respective natural communities. Between forest and prairie, for example, there is likely to be an area that is neither one nor the other. An ecotone may have a fairly uniform character of its own with few apparent similarities with either extreme; or take the form of interlocking fingers of the two merging environments. In some instances ecotones are particularly rich in organisms, since they contain elements of the communities they bridge as well as ones unique to themselves.

The birdwatcher's truism that birds like "edges" is related to the ecotone concept.

ECOTOURISM. See BIRDING TOURS.

ECTOPARASITE. An organism that lives *on the surface* of the body of another organism to the detriment of the host. (For parasites that live internally, see ENDOPARASITE.)

Birds are host to an astonishingly populous and varied fauna of invertebrate ectoparasites. Thousands of species and subspecies of flies, fleas, lice, ticks, and mites have been identified as living to some degree and in various ways on the bodies of birds. A single small songbird may have an unwelcome guest list numbering dozens of individuals of several species, and in the breeding season, its nest is likely to contain several times more. This will confirm for some the prejudice that birds are "dirty" and dangerous, yet most birds are able to control these pests to a tolerable level (at least from the bird's viewpoint) and transmission of either parasites or parasite-borne diseases from birds to people are probably rare (however, see below).

A few of the more frequent parasite life styles are worth noting in a general way. Some bird parasites, notably the bird lice (order Mallophaga) and feather mites (Acarina), live out their entire life cycles on the bodies of their hosts. Others feed on the host only at intervals or during one stage of their development and live in the nest, in the ground, on another host, on flowers, or elsewhere during other stages. Consequently, how birds become infested also varies.

Parasites that live exclusively on bird hosts are passed directly from bird to bird by direct contact. This occurs, of course, between parent birds and their young and also between raptors and their avian prey (hawks and eagles, vultures, and owls usually accommodate an unusually rich variety of pests). Bird lice occasionally hitch rides from host to host on the bodies of larger and more mobile louse flies (Hippoboscidae). Parasites that live part of their lives "ex-avis" contact birds in diverse manners. The eggs of some flies are laid in birds' nests and progress through larval and pupal stages during a single breeding season, parasitizing nestlings as larvae

and quitting the nest as adults; other flies overwinter in the nest as larvae. Many parasites live in the nest but visit their hosts only at night. And most ticks fall off their host after a single blood meal and must find a new host for the next feeding.

A wide range of tolerances is exhibited by invertebrates that parasitize birds. Some adult chiggers are equally content to feed on the blood of birds, mammals, or reptiles. Bird lice and feather mites are restricted not only to birds but usually to certain types of birds (see below). Some are habitat-specific and may be attracted, for example, only to marsh-haunting birds or birds of arid scrub; the nest fly (family Neothopilidae) prefers nests made partly of mud such as those of many thrushes.

Families and species of bird lice tend to parasitize particular orders and families of birds exclusively and to parallel the phylogenetic relationships of their hosts. Thus, gull lice may be different from tern lice, but are likely to be more closely related to each other than to duck lice. The parallel has proved so consistent that comparison of lice has been used to argue taxonomic relationships.

Food preferences of ectoparasites also vary. Fleas, flies, ticks, chiggers, and some lice suck blood, but feather mites and certain lice attack feathers (both the webs and the core of the shaft), and skin debris, body grease, and other bodily fluids are specialties of a number of species.

It may seem that a bird's chances of surviving the onslaughts of this army of tiny attackers are slim, and there is no question that ectoparasites can cause debilitation and death. Some are vectors of diseases fatal to birds; the toxic saliva of some ticks can cause death; an unusually heavy burden of any type of blood-sucking parasite can readily kill nestlings and severely weaken adult birds, making them more vulnerable to larger predators and disease; and the feather-eaters and itch mites, which cause birds to scratch until raw, sometimes cause extensive feather loss resulting in impaired flying ability and exposure.

Still, birds are not totally defenseless. Preening appears to be crucial, and birds unable to preen through some disability are more vulnerable to parasites. Practices such as dusting, smoke bathing, sunning, and anting may be, at least in part, methods of pest control. And, finally, among the array of tiny creatures that inhabit birds and their nests are a number that feed not on birds but on bird parasites! One is reminded of that venerable lyric summary of invertebrate biology:

Big fleas have little fleas
Upon their backs to bite 'em.
Little fleas have smaller fleas,
And so, *ad infinitum.*

The principal ectoparasites are listed below with brief descriptions of their appearance, habits, and importance. All are arthropods (phylum

Arthropoda). Flies, fleas, and bird lice are insects (class Insecta); ticks and mites belong to the same class as spiders (Arachnida).

Flies (order Diptera)

Blowflies (family Calliphoridae). Adults are similar in appearance to greenbottle or bluebottle flies. The larvae of species in two genera (*Apaulina* and *Protocalliphora*) live in the nest and suck the blood of young birds at night. They prefer hole nesters, may occur by the hundreds and cause death.

Botflies (family Oestridae). Adults are large, hairy, and somewhat bee-like in appearance. The eggs are laid on nestlings; the larva hatches and burrows into skin, where it feeds until ready to pupate. Not a major pest in birds in the Temperate Zone.

Mosquitoes (family Culicidae). Females suck blood as adults, attack birds, and have some importance in transmitting disease among them and to other hosts, including people (see below). Avian malaria is of particular concern in the Hawaiian Islands because nonnative malaria is implicated there in the rarity and extinction of native Hawaiian birds. Mosquitoes also transmit arboviruses, most importantly those causing Equine and West Nile encephalitis.

Black Flies (family Simuliidae) and *Biting Midges* (Ceratopogonidae) also suck avian and human blood and transmit protozoan blood parasites, such as species of *Haemoproteus* and *Leucocytozoon*.

Louse Flies (family Hippoboscidae). These are the most important fly parasites on birds, and a few species (e.g., the wingless sheep ked) attack mammals. Adults are usually smaller than a housefly, flat and "leathery"-looking, winged or wingless, and feed on their hosts' blood. Wingless forms crawl through feathers and resemble crab lice. Adults remain on the host for life; the larva hatches and matures within the body of the female fly and pupates as soon as it is "born"; the pupa may overwinter in the nest or in the ground. Hippoboscids tend to be habitat- (i.e., species-) specific, but some are generalists and—logically enough—all species can be found on bird predators. There are about 150 bird-feeding species worldwide, and they have been recorded from at least 24 orders of birds. In birds that reuse nests year after year, Hippoboscid pupae overwinter in the nest and reinfest the following generation. These flies can occur in relatively large numbers on relatively small birds, e.g., 30–40 on species of swifts and swallows. They transmit trypanosomes and the blood parasite *Haemoproteus*, but, in general, do not seem to greatly injure their hosts.

True Bugs (order Hemiptera). Some 25 species of bedbugs (family Cimicidae) prey on birds. Their avian modus operandi will be familiar to anyone who has cohabited with these insects. They live and reproduce in the nest rather than on the host itself and emerge to feed—sometimes in large numbers—when the occupants have settled in.

Fleas (order Siphonaptera). Bird fleas resemble mammal fleas. About 20 species and subspecies attack North American birds. They are mainly habitat-specific and a few are host-specific. The larvae feed on debris in nest and adults suck blood of hosts. Raptors that eat mammals may acquire mammal fleas.

Bird Lice or Chewing Lice (order Mallophaga). Perhaps the most important bird ectoparasites, these are small, usually flattened, and wingless. There are more than 800 North American species in several families and they are known from more than 500 bird species; a few prefer mammal hosts. Most birds are host to a number of species in different body "niches": Head and neck lice are fat, rounded, and sluggish with clasping mouth parts. Wing and back lice are slender and agile to elude preening; these do not suck blood but bite off bits of skin or eat feathers and the pith of the rachis. A few specialist species live in throat pouches of cormorants and pelicans. Bird lice spend their entire life cycle on the bird, attaching eggs to feathers and dispersing by contact between birds. Heavy infestation may coincide with debilitation of the host and the lice may die with the host. They are highly host-specific and phylogeny parallels that of hosts; thus, they are useful as taxonomic characters. Prodigious "blooms" of lice sometimes occur on moribund birds, apparently as an effect rather than a cause of the individual's condition.

Ticks and Mites (order Acarina) include many important bird parasites in about a dozen families of this large order. Behavior patterns are very variable with regard to host specificity, and feeding and breeding habits and they may occur in nests in spectacular numbers. A few groups should be emphasized.

Hard and Soft Ticks (families Ixodidae and Argasidae). Typical ticks, which lay eggs away from host and feed on blood during two nymphal stages and the adult stage. Hard ticks gorge once during each stage, then drop off and find a new host for next meal. Soft ticks usually live in the nest and take successive meals at night. Species of both types may favor particular places of attachment, e.g., around eyes. Both can transmit disease or inject a toxic saliva that can cause fatal paralysis. *Ixodes scapularis* (synonym: *dammini*) transmits the bacterium *Borrelia burgdorferi*, the pathogenic agent of Lyme disease.

Chiggers (family Trombiculidae) are very small. Adults are tolerant of wide variety of prey, including birds, reptiles, man, and other mammals; the larval stage is usually more host-specific. Chiggers generally have blood-sucking habits similar to those of ticks and tend to cluster on areas of the head. A few species invade the respiratory system by way of the nostrils; other species are predatory on feather mites.

Itch Mites (family Sarcoptidae). These are mostly mammalian pests, but a few species attack birds. Some invade internal systems, others burrow beneath skin and cause severe irritation and mange, which is often aggravated by scratching of the host, causing feather loss and/or infection.

Feather Mites (Analgesidae and several other families) are important parasites, which, of course, are restricted to birds. Like bird lice, they spend their entire life cycle on their host, laying eggs on feathers or within quills. They are often host-specific and habitat-specific on individual birds, different species preferring different types of feathers and even different parts of particular feathers. Heavy infestation may severely damage plumage.

Bird Parasites Affecting People. The major issue here is the transmission of disease organisms to people via mosquitoes or ticks. Birds are known to host ticks carrying *Borrelia burgdorferi*, the Lyme disease bacterium, which is transmitted to people by *Ixodes* ticks, but it is still unclear whether birds are significant reservoirs of the disease, as are deer mice and white-tailed deer. Birds also carry West Nile and equine encephalitis viruses. These diseases affect both mammals and birds, and the latter is most virulent in birds. When transmitted to people by the bite of a mosquito they can be fatal, especially to the most vulnerable individuals, such as children and the elderly. See Friend et al. (2001–DISEASE), and Steele et al. (2000–DISEASE).

See also DISEASE and nest fauna.

EDIBILITY (of birds, eggs, nests). In the present era of Migratory Bird Acts, strict hunting seasons, and heightened "eco-consciousness," the notion of eating birds suggests to most North Americans the grocery store much more strongly than the wilderness. Yet as late as 1882, one O. A. Taft, proprietor of a hotel and restaurant at Point Shirley, Boston Harbor (famous for its "game" menu), could bet an assembled company of friends that they could not name an edible North American bird that he could not produce instantly. It is reported that he had no takers. Lest the reader have too narrow a conception of what Mr. Taft considered edible, a menu from his establishment that has been preserved (Garland 1978) includes the following species (translated where possible by the present author): Owls "from the North," Chicken Grouse (Prairie-Chickens) "from Ill.," Upland Plover (Sandpiper), Dough Birds (Eskimo Curlew), Brant Birds (Marbled Godwit?), Willet "from Jersey," Godwit, Jack Curlew (Whimbrel), Jack (Common) Snipe, Sand Snipe (Dowitcher?), Rock Snipe (Purple Sandpiper?), Golden-Plover, Beetle-head (Black-bellied) Plover, Redbreast Plover (Knot), "Seckel-bill" (Long-billed) Curlew, Chicken Plover (Ruddy Turnstone), Summer (Lesser) Yellowlegs, Winter (Greater) Yellowlegs, Reed Birds (Bobolinks) "from Del.," Ringneck (Killdeer?), Snipe, Rail (Clapper?) "from Del.," Brown Backs (Pectoral Sandpiper), Grassbirds (Baird's Sandpipers), and Peeps (small sandpipers). The pièce de résistance of this particular bill of fare is Hummingbirds Served in Walnut Shells! A good crowd easily—and apparently frequently—disposed of a thousand such "game birds" of an evening at Taft's. And though by the 1890s a few voices were being raised against the slaughter required to

stock such sumptuous larders (see CONSERVATION), one could still buy songbirds and shorebirds in market game stalls here in the first decade of the twentieth century. Even today, the occasional (illegal) deep-dish robin pie or other such fare finds its way to the table, especially in rural areas.

Feather hunting and "pure sport" have, of course, taken their toll of birds (see EXTINCT BIRDS), but the most important single encouragement to man's inclination to kill birds is that they are very good to eat. Some are better than others, of course; many—consider vultures, for example—do not recommend themselves because of their habits. Yet it is not unreasonable to suppose that every species of North American bird has been eaten at least once by someone.

Taste. It is gospel among some hunters that how a bird tastes depends on where it lives and what it eats. By this rule nearly all seabirds are despised by some as "fishy" and coots rejected as "muddy." Though there is some truth to this generalization—as most people who have sampled cormorant flesh will affirm—it is belied by certain ingenious methods of cleaning and preparing "strong" birds, which make them very tasty or at worst innocuous. The author has heard recipes for virtually every species of seabird in the North Atlantic from experienced gourmands of Newfoundland. Many of these involved immediate evisceration and "blooding" and often the use of marinades ("pickles") in which strips of breast meat are cured for weeks or longer before cooking.

Another recipe, this one for the notoriously unpalatable scoters (or "coots" as they are called along the coast of New England), was offered by R. W. Hatch in the December 1924 issue of *Field and Stream:*

> The easiest way is to place the coot in a pot to boil with a good flatiron or anvil. Let it boil long and merrily, and when you can stick a fork in the flat iron or the anvil, as the case may be, then the coot will be ready to eat. If that takes too much patience, take the goodly coot and nail it firmly to a hardwood board. Put the board in the sun for about a week. At the end of that time, carefully remove the coot from the board, throw away the coot, and cook the board.

Other New England coot fanciers allow that it is preferable to roast the coot with a brick in the cavity and when the latter becomes soft, it (the brick) is ready to eat.

In addition to insisting that birds are what they eat, common knowledge also holds that the bigger and/or older a bird, the tougher and "gamier" the meat. Here, again, there is both support and refutation from those who have dined on ancient swans and the like.

A more scientific note was sounded by Cott (1946, 1951) and Dumbacher et al. (1992, 2000), who show that there is some correspondence between cryptic coloration and palatability in birds (and eggs) and that some very conspicuous birds are notably distasteful.

Game Birds. Many species in the duck, turkey, grouse, pheasant, rail, and dove families are still shot legally in parts of North America (see LAWS PROTECTING BIRDLIFE for specifics). Though many sportsmen shoot for fun alone, all of these species are valued by at least a few for their flesh, and some are very tasty indeed. Most wildfowl eaters agree that Canvasback, teal, and Brant deserve special praise among waterfowl, provided, of course, they have fed in the right places and are prepared properly. The epicurean merits of sea ducks have been discussed above.

Shorebirds. The steep decline of shorebird populations by the turn of the last century is directly attributable to market gunning. With protection, many species have recovered well, others not at all. The Eskimo Curlew or Doughbird, once of "sky-darkening" abundance, may now be extinct, a consequence of its superb flavor (second, according to many, only to the Passenger Pigeon). By all accounts most of the sandpipers and plovers make excellent eating. Woodcock and snipe are the only shorebirds that may now be hunted legally in North America.

Songbirds. Larks, thrushes, "ortolans" (buntings), and many other passerines have been traditional food in civilized Europe for centuries and were legally trapped and eaten in large numbers in many countries until very recently. They are usually skinned, roasted on small spits, and eaten bones and all. There is no point in denying that they are delicious. Many southern European householders set window traps for House Sparrows, which some claim are only marginally inferior to ortolans. House Sparrows are not protected by law in North America.

In Latin America, people of all social strata who have never heard of migratory bird treaties shoot migrant warblers and other birds and prepare them by methods similar to those just described. There is no satisfactory way to estimate how many birds perish in this manner.

Museum curators, having skinned a bird for their collection, have been known on occasion to cook and sample the remains; in a statistically insignificant survey made by the author, they too have a generally high opinion of the flavor of small North American songbirds. Evidently Cott's "bright color/bad taste" hypothesis does not hold for breeding-plumaged wood warblers.

Eggs. "Egging" at seabird colonies was once widespread; it was at least partially responsible for the demise of the Great Auk and allegedly brought about the virtual absence of Herring Gulls along the New England coast early in the twentieth century. Innuit and other North American natives are still allowed by law to harvest the eggs from seabird colonies (as well as the birds themselves).

Seabird eggs, like their parents, are widely thought to be "fishy." This may be the case under certain circumstances, but in the experience of many, a fresh Herring Gull egg is superior in taste to a supermarket hen's egg.

Plover, gull, and quail eggs are familiar European delicacies—the latter, at least, being provided by domestically bred birds.

Cott (1954) says that eggs of larger colonial nesters taste better, in general, than those of smaller solitary nesters and that (as with birds) cryptically colored eggs tend to taste better than conspicuous ones. The latter (he says) are likely to be bitter.

Nests. Only the nests of a few species of Asian swiftlets in the genus *Collocalia* are eaten by man (see BIRD'S NEST SOUP). They are made almost entirely of the bird's sticky saliva. Since the amount of spittle used by some of our native swifts in cementing their nest materials together is comparatively small and the toil of removing it from the other nest materials comparatively great, savory bird's nests have remained an imported delicacy in North America.

EDWARDS PLATEAU (Texas). An approximately 20,000-square-mile elevated block of limestone in south-central Texas (the "hill country") pitted with sinkholes, traversed by cool, clear streams, and covered with pleasant juniper/scrub oak woodland. The breeding range of the Golden-cheeked Warbler is restricted to this region. Other specialties of the plateau, only slightly less restricted in North American range, are the Cave Swallow (breeds in caves and sinkholes) and Black-capped Vireo (oak/juniper scrub). The area also contains many species of both eastern and western affinity. Austin is situated at the eastern end of the plateau and San Antonio just off the southeastern edge.

EGG. In the broadest sense, simply the female reproductive cell or ovum. A bird's egg, however, consists of the ovum, including its attached food supply (yolk), surrounded by a mass of gelatinous and nearly liquid "egg white" (albumen), the whole enclosed in a hard calcium shell.

FORMATION AND STRUCTURE (see Fig. 10). A bird's egg originates as a germ cell within a small sac (follicle), many of which, together with "supportive tissue," make up the female reproductive organ or ovary (see REPRODUCTIVE SYSTEM for a different perspective on this process). In addition to germ cells, the lining of the follicles contains other types of cells, some of which develop into the egg yolk. As the yolk grows preceding ovulation, the follicles expand into a spherical shape, and the ovary as a whole takes on the appearance of a tiny whitish or yellowish cluster of grapes.

The Yolk when fully formed ranges in color from pale yellow to deep orange-red. It consists essentially of protein and fat granules arranged in concentric layers of white yolk (narrower layers; less fatty) and yellow yolk. The germ cell (the nucleus of the unfertilized ovum; also called the germinal spot or vesicle) remains on the surface of the yolk but is connected to its core (latebra) by a narrow column of white yolk of which the

core itself also consists. Once fertilized, the germ cell will divide—the first step in embryonic development—and as the EMBRYO continues to grow it will take most of its nourishment from the attached yolk.

Ovulation. When the ovum reaches full size it bursts the skin of the follicle and passes through the wide mouth (infundibulum) of the oviduct and into the uppermost reaches of this tube for fertilization by the male reproductive cell (spermatozoon). Whether fertilized or not, the ovum then passes into the magnum, an enlarged chamber of the oviduct with muscular walls containing mucous glands from which is secreted the albumen.

Albumen consists of protein and carbohydrate (i.e., a glycoprotein) dissolved in water and is secreted in four layers around the yolk. The layers are alternately thin (almost watery) and thick (more gelatinous) and together serve to cushion the developing embryo and its food supply, to retain essential water, and to provide an additional source of nutriment. The first (innermost) layer of albumen encloses the yolk closely and develops at opposite ends into fibrous cords of albumen, called the chalazae. These structures, unique to birds, hold the yolk in a stable position with the germ cell (later the embryo) on top as the developing egg tumbles through the spirally ridged walls of the oviduct. The outer ends of the chalazae are connected to an outer fibrous layer of albumen (which is ultimately linked at both ends to the shell membranes), so that in order to hold the yolk stationary the chalazae must twist as the rest of the egg revolves.

The Shell Membranes are acquired in the narrower chamber of the oviduct (following the magnum) called the isthmus. The inner shell membrane fuses with extensions of the outer fibrous albumen layer at what will become the "pointed" ends of the egg and encloses the outer layer of "thin" albumen. The outer shell membrane—in addition to being attached to the inner shell membrane—will in the next step become attached to the eggshell itself.

The Eggshell is secreted from the walls of the shell gland, the portion of the oviduct (in some respects analogous to the human uterus) that follows the isthmus. The suspended calcium carbonate salts that are secreted quickly harden into interlocking crystals (calcite), the cohesion of which is further reinforced by interconnecting protein fibers. The eggshell has thin, partially organic inner and outer layers but all but a small percentage of the whole is calcium carbonate, which is also the essence of chalk and limestone. The eggshell is porous rather than solid, allowing the contents to "breathe."

Egg colors and patterns are also secreted from the walls of the shell gland. Two types of pigment—blue/green and red/brown/black—are produced, possibly from bile and blood, respectively. The blue/green coloration is deposited throughout the shell and when it is present provides a uniform coloration, though varying in shade and intensity from species to species. The darker pigment is responsible for the patterns that decorate

many eggs and can be deposited at various stages in the shell production. On the surface of the egg these markings can range in color from pink to black and also may show through superficial layers of eggshell in muted tones. In some cases the red/brown/black pigment appears uniformly in the surface layers (cuticle) of the egg, altering the underlying color—white becomes yellow or brown; blue becomes olive. In a few species a chalky coating is secreted as a final icing on the finished egg. (See also Color and Texture, below, and Fig. 10.)

The Air Space. Immediately after laying, the contents of the eggshell cool and contract, causing a separation of the inner shell membrane from the outer in what in most species is the blunter end of the egg. It is in this air space that the full-grown embryo takes its first breath of air before beginning the hatching struggle. For internal development beyond the formation of the air space, see EMBRYO.

LAYING. The completion of the nest seems to "release" the egg-laying urge in many species. Some, however, delay laying for a day or more after the nest is finished, while others begin laying before completion.

Many species lay at a particular time of day. Dawn is characteristic of most songbirds, but pigeons and doves typically lay in early afternoon and at least a few species do so in the evening.

The commonest laying pattern is one egg every 24 hours, but 2- to 3-day intervals are not uncommon among falconiforms and intervals of up to 7 days are recorded for the Masked Booby. This, as is turns out, has a slightly ominous overtone, since hatching asynchrony has been found to be closely linked to siblicide, of which Masked Boobies have a high incidence. The female may sit on the nest for about an hour while depositing a given egg but otherwise tends to ignore the nest until the clutch is complete. The male usually continues to be songful during the laying period and copulation often occurs throughout it.

Some species will lay replacement eggs if their first clutch is removed or destroyed and will, in fact, continue to lay almost indefinitely if eggs continue to disappear. Mallards have been induced to lay up to 100 eggs in succession. Such birds are known as *indeterminate layers.* Some gulls, plovers, pigeons, and others, on the other hand, will lay only a fixed number and are therefore called *determinate layers.* See also INCUBATION and HATCH.

CLUTCH SIZE. The number of eggs laid varies mainly according to genetic determination, simple physical factors, and selective elements that optimize success. To begin with, particular species and families are "programmed" genetically to lay a certain number of eggs per clutch. A single egg per clutch is typical of the tubenoses, tropicbirds, gannets and boobies, frigatebirds, most alcids, some doves, and the odd species in other families. Most passerines average clutches of 3–6 eggs, but totals of 8 or more are not uncommon among tits, nuthatches, wrens, and kinglets. The

champion layers are the ducks and gallinaceous birds, among which clutches of 12–15 are not unusual; a Bobwhite clutch of 28 has been recorded. Other groups of birds fall between the extremes—for details, see egg identification references in the Bibliography.

The inherent breeding biology of a species also affects clutch size: colonial nesters whose chicks have high survival rates often lay only 1–2 eggs, while less "secure" species must lay more eggs to compensate for the high attrition rates among eggs, juveniles, and/or adults.

The fact that some small birds or those with small brood patches cannot incubate more than a few eggs successfully is an example of a simple physiological clutch-size determinant.

Modifying these deep-seated factors are environmental elements, such as geography, climate, and food supply. It has been shown, for example, that (1) northward-breeding passerines average larger clutches than their southern counterparts—compensating for the fact that their shorter season restricts them to fewer broods; (2) first nests of the season contain larger clutches on the average, maximizing the success of the brood during the optimal period when food supplies are most reliable; (3) island populations of some species lay consistently smaller clutches than their counterparts on the coast of the mainland at the same latitude (Crowell and Rothstein 1981)—perhaps caused by island environmental factors, such as lower quality food or the hormonal effects of a crowded population.

For number of clutches/broods per season, see NEST.

SUPERFICIAL CHARACTERISTICS OF EGGS

Size. In general, the larger the bird, the larger its egg (though smaller birds generally produce eggs that are larger *in proportion to the adult's body mass* than is the case with larger birds; however, there are some anomalies (e.g., the Ruddy Duck is much smaller than the Canvasback but lays a larger egg). The kiwis lay enormous eggs relative to body size (25% of the female's total mass compared to the average range of 2–11%). These large eggs represent a high percentage of female reproductive energy devoted to this stage of their offspring's life. The fossil eggs of the gigantic extinct Elephant Bird, *Aepyornis*, are as large as 14.5 × 9.5 inches (36.8 × 24.1 cm) and are thought to have weighed up to 27 pounds (12.27 kilos).

The largest egg of a living bird worldwide is that of the Ostrich (the largest bird), both in diameter—average 7 × 5.5 inches (17.8 × 14 cm)—and in weight—3 pounds (1,400 g). The largest native North American bird's egg is that of the Trumpeter Swan—4.3 × 2.8 inches (10.9 × 7.1 cm)—closely rivaled by the California Condor's—4.3 × 2.6 inches (10.9 × 6.6 cm). The egg of the Mute Swan is slightly larger than either—4.5 × 2.9 inches (11.43 × 7.37 cm).

Hummingbirds unquestionably lay the smallest eggs of any living birds, though which species holds the absolute world record is unresolved. The egg of the Bee Hummingbird (*Mellisuga helenae*—a Cuban

endemic and the world's smallest bird) is often cited: 0.45 × 0.32 inch (1.14 × 0.81 cm) or thereabouts, but lengths as short as 0.25 inch (0.64 cm) are reported for the family. In North America the competition for smallest egg may be too close to call, given normal variation. The egg of the Calliope Hummingbird (smallest North American bird) is recorded at 0.48 × 0.33 inch (1.22 × 0.84 cm); that of Costa's Hummingbird at 0.49 × 0.32 inch (1.25 × 0.81 cm); both may, however, be edged out by the slender egg of the White-eared Hummingbird, measured at 0.49 × 0.31 inch (1.25 × 0.79 cm). The smallest hummingbird eggs weigh in at about 0.5 gram (0.0176 ounce).

Because precocial young develop more fully in the egg, their eggs tend to be larger in relation to the size of adult birds than those of altricial species. The eggs of an American Wigeon, for example, are significantly larger than those of the similar-sized American Crow.

Egg size may also vary within a given species according to clutch size (more eggs = smaller ones); season (some songbirds lay slightly larger eggs in succeeding clutches during a given breeding season, while some seabirds' eggs are smaller on the average as the season advances); and age of the female (the eggs of some birds tend to be slightly larger as the female ages).

Shape. Most, but by no means all, eggs are "egg-shaped," i.e., with one end slightly more pointed than the other. But the range of variation even within this one, readily visualized shape is broad, and several terminologies have been used to describe different shapes with varying degrees of exactness. The account below is based on the now widely used system of Preston (1969) and attempts to sort out some of the ambiguity. Preston's terminology recognizes four basic shapes, each with a longer and shorter variation.

1. *Elliptical,* long elliptical, spherical (substituted for short elliptical). An ellipse is a geometric form widest at the middle of its long axis and with *equally rounded ends.* When this shape is "shortened" to the point of eliminating its longer dimension, it ceases to be an ellipse and becomes a circle or, in the case of a three-dimensional shape, a sphere; hence the substitution of "spherical" for "short elliptical." "Round" is another substitute for "spherical." Among North American birds only some owls lay eggs that approach spherical shape; most are better described as elliptical. Hummingbirds provide the best North American examples of long-elliptical eggs.

2. *Subelliptical,* long subelliptical, short subelliptical. Longer and more tapered toward both ends with greatest width not at the midpoint of the long axis. Cranes' and rails' eggs are typically subelliptical. Grebes' eggs exhibit an extreme of long subelliptical,

Fig. 10. *Eggs.*

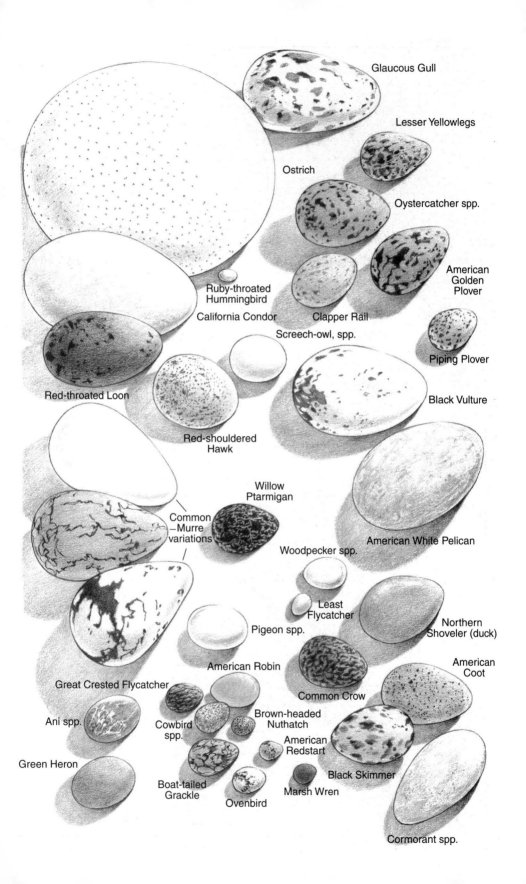

Glaucous Gull

Lesser Yellowlegs

Ostrich

Oystercatcher spp.

Ruby-throated
Hummingbird

California Condor

Clapper Rail

American
Golden
Plover

Screech-owl, spp.

Piping Plover

Red-throated Loon

Red-shouldered
Hawk

Black Vulture

Willow
Ptarmigan

Common
—Murre
variations

American White Pelican

Woodpecker spp.

Least
Flycatcher

Pigeon spp.

Northern
Shoveler (duck)

American Robin

American
Coot

Great Crested Flycatcher

Common Crow

Ani spp.

Cowbird
spp.

Brown-headed
Nuthatch

American
Redstart

Green Heron

Boat-tailed
Grackle

Ovenbird

Marsh Wren

Black Skimmer

Cormorant spp.

sometimes called "biconical" or "fusiform," with both ends somewhat pointed and widest about the midpoint.

3. *Oval,* long oval, short oval. In the strictest sense "oval" means explicitly "egg-shaped," i.e., broader, more rounded at one end, tapering gradually to a more pointed end. One source of confusion here is that elliptical shapes are often referred to as "oval" in popular usage. As noted, the majority of bird's eggs fit one of the three oval types. "Ovate" may give a technical ring to "oval" but adds nothing to the meaning.

4. *Pyriform,* long pyriform, short pyriform. Pyriform literally means "pear-shaped" and is essentially an extreme form of oval with one very broad end, one *very* pointed end, and a tendency for the strongly tapered sides to be relatively straight (or even slightly concave). This form has also been labeled "conical." Murres and many shorebirds lay distinctly pyriform eggs. It is often suggested that in the latter group this shape is an adaptation to efficient incubation, since the four pyriform eggs that sandpipers usually lay form a neat, tight circle when clustered with their pointed ends together; it has also been noted that pyriform objects roll in a circle, a useful adaptation for birds such as murres that lay their eggs on a bare, narrow cliff shelf.

On the whole, basic egg shapes tend to conform within bird families; however, there is also significant variation among members of the same species and even age and seasonal variation in shape among individuals.

Shape no less than structure (see Formation, above) contributes to the inherent strength of an egg. It has been estimated that a chicken's egg can withstand pressure of 10 tons per square inch *evenly applied.* This is demonstrated in the parlor trick in which the "volunteer" is challenged to crush a raw hen's egg between his hands along the long axis. The results are usually impressive but can also be messy if the pressure is not applied at the egg's "pointed" ends. Another proof of egg strength is the presence of uncracked starlings' eggs on suburban lawns in the spring. In most cases these are "laid" prematurely by inexperienced females or ejected by intraspecific brood parasites as they fly over.

Color and Pattern. The normal ground colors of North American bird's eggs are white (i.e., without visible pigment), blue to green, or brown. Depending on where in the shell the pigment occurs and the developing of different pigments (see Formation, above), a wide range of hues and shades is possible. In the palest forms, for example, brown can produce a dirty yellow or pink as well as dark umbers. Though many eggs are "plain," the majority show some kind of marking, again in a form of brown pigment. The markings are classified by oologists into categories such as scribbled, scrawled, speckled, spotted, and blotched and may occur in characteristic patterns. The eggs of many species, for example, are

"wreathed," i.e., have a concentrated circle of markings at the blunter end, which passes through the "shell gland" first and picks up the bulk of the pigment.

There is close color/pattern conformity in some bird families; for example, all North American owls have white or off-white, unmarked eggs. But there is also much variation, not only among species in a family but among individuals of a species. In fact, no two bird's eggs are exactly alike.

Because the eggs of birds' nearest phylogenetic ancestors, the reptiles, are white, it is generally assumed that bird's eggs were originally white and evolved color and pattern in accordance with various survival pressures. Birds, such as terns and plovers, that nest in the open usually lay eggs cryptically colored and patterned to blend with the ground, making them less obvious to predators. The fact that many cavity nesters have unmarked or sparsely marked eggs suggests a possible relationship between color and exposure to the sun or a predator's prying eyes—but such theories are hard to justify in view of the numerous exceptions. The great individual variation in the patterns of murres' eggs may have recognition value for individuals looking for their own eggs in a crowded colony. And some brightly colored eggs may advertise an unpleasant taste.

Texture. Loon, swan and goose, many hawk, alcid, chachalaca, stork, jaeger, and some gull eggs have a *granular* texture (mostly rather fine). Duck eggs have a *waxy* or *greasy* coating, which may be a kind of waterproofing. The California Condor's egg is finely *pitted*. Gannets, cormorants, Anhinga, pelicans, flamingoes, and anis lay eggs with a superficial white *chalky* coating, which tends to scratch or flake off at least partially during incubation. Except for the pelicans, the underlying shell color of these eggs is green/blue. Woodpeckers have notably smooth and *shiny* eggs.

Other North American species have smoothly textured eggs that vary from nonglossy (i.e., "eggshell" or matte) through various degrees of glossiness.

IDENTIFICATION. A number of field guides currently on the market, comprehensively illustrated in color (see the Bibliography under NEST) make it easy for anyone with a moderately well-developed critical faculty to identify bird's eggs at least to family if not to species.

On the other hand, the opportunity to practice one's oological expertise is now strictly limited by law and (one hopes) by personal ethics. Among wild bird species, only the eggs of the European Starling, Rock Dove or Common Pigeon, and House Sparrow are unprotected by federal law (see LAWS PROTECTING BIRDLIFE), and the risk of disturbing birds or attracting the attention of nest-molesting species will keep scrupulous naturalists from satisfying their curiosity about "live" eggs too zealously. See also EGG COLLECTING, below.

HUMANE CONCERNS. A popular "science" lesson among parents and teachers is to artificially incubate commercially purchased eggs, so that

the hatching can be watched by wide-eyed youngsters, who thereby derive firsthand experience with the wonders of life. Regrettably, once the hatchling has performed, it rapidly becomes less wonderful, and frequently suffers a lingering death from starvation or rough handling, or it may just be callously flushed down the toilet. There are two lessons in life in the above scenario—they cancel each other out.

For additional behaviors involving eggs, see INCUBATION and HATCH.

EGG BLOWING. The practice of emptying a bird's egg of its contents while keeping the eggshell essentially intact for the purpose of preserving it in a collection. This is best achieved, of course, when the embryo is in an early stage of development and the contents of the egg are largely liquid or gel. The simplest method is simply to carefully poke a smallish hole with any fine-pointed implement into both ends of the egg. Usually the hole in the blunter end is made somewhat larger and the mouth is applied to the sharper end. Serious oologists, however, are equipped with impressive kits of drills, tiny saws, and blowing tubes of different sizes to perform the task with maximum efficiency and end up with the best possible specimen. See EGG COLLECTING for restrictions.

EGG-BOUND. Refers to a condition in which a bird is unable to lay an egg that is in its oviduct, due, for example, to an obstruction or a malformation of the egg.

EGG COLLECTING. Before it was prohibited by law (see LAWS PROTECTING BIRDLIFE), collecting birds' eggs was a popular hobby among men and boys in northern Europe and America. Good collections not only included a large species representation (with as many rarities as possible) but also displayed the greatest possible range of variation in the eggs of a given species and often different-sized clutches of the same species. Clandestine egg collectors are still a bane to conservation authorities in parts of Europe (especially Britain), but on the whole the passion for the activity seems largely to have died out in North America. An exception was the theft in the 1970s of a nest and eggs of Ross's Gull from its then newly established breeding station at CHURCHILL, Manitoba. The culprit apparently cut the entire nest and the grassy tussock on which it was placed from the tundra with a sharp tool between 7 p.m. and 3 a.m., managing to elude a guard posted to protect the site. It is estimated that the eggs might bring as much as $10,000 to $20,000 in the oological underground.

Since the rarest birds inevitably lay the rarest eggs, we can be grateful that the thrill of risking jail and a stiff fine for stealing a bird's egg that can be admired by only a handful of other egg-loving criminals appeals only to a kinky few.

See L. F. Kiff, "Bird Egg Collections in North America" (1979), *Auk* 96:746–55.

EGGSHELL. See EGG.

EGG TOOTH. A small, hard (calcareous) protuberance on the tip of the bill, which develops in the embryos of all birds to help break through the eggshell. It is also present in reptiles and a few frogs (tadpoles). In birds, it is usually situated on the upper mandible, but may be on the lower (e.g., in oystercatchers, avocets, and plovers) or on both (a few species of auks and woodpeckers). The egg tooth usually falls off or is reabsorbed within the first week after hatching (sometimes during the first day) but may remain longer. All North American birds develop this structure; it is lacking only in the Ostrich and the megapodes of Australasia. See Clark, *Wilson Bull.* (1961), 73:268–78.

EGRET (ee-GRETT, EE-grett, even EGG-rett). Standard English name for 9–11 species of herons (family Ardeidae; order Ciconiiformes), most in the genus *Egretta*. Four species of egrets breed in North America and 2 others have occurred as accidental stragglers (3 if Western Reef *Egret* of some authors is followed (see Appendix II).

The plumage of all egrets is largely or totally white (the Reddish Egret has both white and dark color morphs and all but the Cattle Egret develop long, exceedingly delicate plumaceous feathers as part of their breeding plumage used in display. These graceful plumes or "aigrettes" were in great demand around the turn of the century as decorations for women's fashions. This taste created a thriving trade for plume hunters and nearly extirpated the egrets (see CONSERVATION for details of the feather trade).

Aside from their whiteness and inordinately decorative plumage, the egrets resemble the other HERONS.

"Egret" derives from a diminutive form of Old French words for "heron."

EIDER (EYE-der). Standard English name for 4 species of sea ducks (family Anatidae; order Anseriformes), all of which breed in North America. Together with the scoters, Harlequin Duck, Long-tailed Duck, Bufflehead, goldeneyes, and mergansers, they make up the tribe Mergini. All of the eiders have unusual head shapes and color patterns and the drakes are among the handsomest of sea ducks. All four species breed primarily in the Arctic (all but Common Eider exclusively so) and migrate relatively short distances south of pack ice in the winter. The eiders dive in shallow water, feeding on mollusks and other bottom life.

The down that the female Common Eider plucks from her breast to line her nest is harvested in Iceland and other Scandinavian countries for mattresses, pillow stuffing, and clothing linings. Harvesters usually take two linings and leave the third in place; the only ill effect on the birds seems to be inconvenience.

A Danish naturalist named Worm first described the (Common) Eider in the scientific literature; the name he gave it is the Danish transliteration of the Icelandic word for the species, which means "down bird" (Lockwood 1993–NAMES).

For family characteristics, see DUCK.

ELECTROPHORESIS (ee-LEK-tro-for-EE-sis). The movement of minute particles suspended in a liquid or gel under the influence of an electric field. The technique has been used to discover phylogenetic relationships of bird species. The size, shape, and electric charge of the proteins and the combinations in which they are present are unique in different forms of birds, and because these characters are genetically determined, they can provide more reliable clues to taxonomic affinities than superficial structural characters. See SYSTEMATICS, Biochemical Analysis.

EMARGINATE. In ornithological parlance, usually refers to the abrupt tapering of the outer web of a primary feather between its midpoint and tip (see Fig. 13). This character is occasionally used in identifying hard to distinguish species, such as the *Empidonax* flycatchers, in the hand. See WING FORMULA.

EMBERIZID (em-buh-REE-zid or em-buh-RYE-zid) or EMBERIZINE. Any member of the family Emberizidae (or subfamily Emberizinae; order Passeriformes), and in the plural, the family as a whole. The emberizids as defined by the *AOU Checlist*, 7th edition (1998) include the grassquits, seedeaters, Antillean bullfinches, flowerpiercers, *Paroaria* cardinals, brushfinches, New World sparrows, towhees, juncos, longspurs, Old World *(Emberiza)* buntings, snow buntings, and an assortment of Neotropical "finches" in many genera. Some authorities (Sibley and Ahlquist 1990–SYSTEMATICS) consider the seedeaters, Antillean bullfinches flowerpiercers, and a number of Neotropical finches to be tanagers rather than emberizids, and Sibley and Monroe (1990–SYSTEMATICS) place the emberizids in a subfamily (Emberizinae) under a very large Fringillidae, which includes the Cardueline finches, Hawaiian honeycreepers, wood warblers, tanagers, "cardinal-grosbeaks," and New World blackbirds and orioles. For a systematic breakdown of these closely related species, see Appendixes I and III.

For a family description of Emberizids as currently define by the AOU, see SPARROW-BUNTING.

EMBRYO (embryonic development). The embryonic development of a bird begins immediately after fertilization with the division of the nucleus (germinal vesicle) of the female reproductive cell (ovum). This nucleus is visible as a germinal spot (blastodisk) about ⅛ inch in diameter on the top

surface of the yolk of a newly laid egg (see EGG, Formation and Structure, and Fig. 11). Within the first 24 hours of incubation, this unimpressive spot shows vestiges of circulatory, nervous, and digestive systems and during the second day a head of sorts with eyes becomes visible. For the first few days, a bird embryo remains a large-headed, long-tailed, tad-pole-like creature hardly distinguishable, except by an embryologist, from a human fetus at a similar stage of development. But well before half the incubation period has elapsed, unmistakably avian features, such as a bill and feather tracts, can be discerned. And for the last few days before hatching, the embryo essentially resembles a full-grown chick crammed into much too small a space.

One of the first features to develop is a system of veins, through which the embryo draws nourishment from the fats and proteins that, together

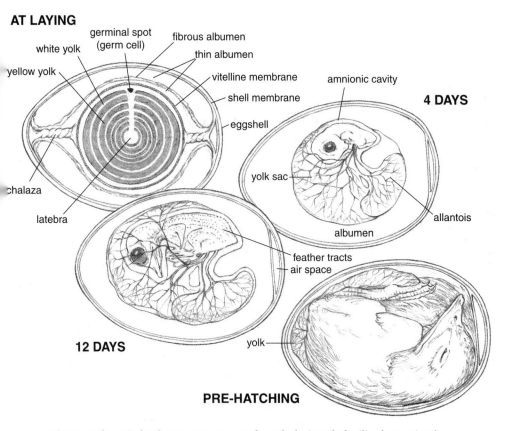

Fig. 11. *Embryonic development.* Four stages from the laying of a fertilized egg to just be-fore hatching.

with water (about 50%), make up the yolk. The percentage of the total egg volume taken up by this food supply at the start of incubation depends on the state of development at which hatching will take place. Most North American passerines have a relatively short incubation period of about 12–15 days, but at hatching the young are blind, naked, and helpless. In these species, the yolk takes up only about 20% of the egg. So-called precocial species, such as ducks, shorebirds, and gallinaceous birds, take longer to hatch (from 3 to 7 or more weeks; see INCUBATION), and require a larger yolk (about 35% of total volume), but emerge from the shell with a full coat of protective down and are almost immediately able to fend for themselves.

The yolk is gradually consumed by the developing embryo until, shortly before hatching, the yolk sac and what little of its contents is left pass into the body of the young bird through the umbilical opening. This yolk remnant can nourish the nestling for several days after hatching, allowing time for the parents or chick to establish the new feeding routine.

The egg white (albumen), which is 90% water, cushions the yolk and embryo, retains vital moisture, and provides an additional source of protein. It, too, is consumed during the incubation period.

The embryo takes its necessary oxygen through the porous walls of the eggshell until, just before hatching, the bill is poked through into the air space at the wider end of the egg (see Fig. 11) and the young bird takes its first real breath. Waste products in the form of crystalline, non-toxic, and relatively inert uric acid flow into a special sac, the allantois, a kind of external bladder that develops out of the hind gut of the embryo. The tissue of the allantois is also thickly threaded with blood vessels, which carry oxygen to the embryo. Eventually, of course, these excretory and respiratory functions are taken over by kidneys and lungs within the bird's body. Adult birds have no urinary bladder and by hatching time most of the allantois has dried up and remains in the shell.

Barring disease or accident, the success of the embryonic progress from germinal spot to bird—an enormously complex process barely hinted at here—requires only that the temperature of the embryo be kept close to that of the parents (see INCUBATION).

EMPIDONAX (em-PID-uh-nacks). A New World genus of 15 species of small (4–6 inches), famously nondescript tyrant flycatchers (family Tyrannidae; order Passeriformes), 11 of which breed in North America.

The "empis," as they are fondly called by birdwatchers who enjoy a challenge, present one of the great field identification problems in the North American avifauna. They are exceedingly similar in general shape, coloration, and jizz. All are drab with prominent wing bars and (almost always) eye rings. All are readily identifiable during the breeding season by song and habitat preference and some (notably the Buff-breasted, Yellow-

bellied and Gray Flycatchers) can be "called" with a high degree of certainty on color (together with distribution) alone. Several of the others are distinctive enough to the practiced eye as adults but remain inscrutable in immature plumage. Short of murder or the bird's suicide, there are two traditional ways to deal with the identification of "empis." One is to catch the bird in question (for which one needs a permit from the federal authorities; see BANDING) and compare the lengths of the primary feathers (see WING FORMULA), which vary distinctively among the different species—a careful (and optimistic) observer with good looks at the bird in question can use wing shape as a useful clue. The other approach is to study all members of the genus intensively, noting the minutest variations in plumage color (brownish olive or olive brown?), form of eye ring, mandible color, tone and extent of wing bars, and tail shape and gestures—for all ages and in all light conditions. The field ornithologist with this level of detailed expertise can, under good conditions, often make a highly educated guess about the identity of any given *Empidonax*.

For identification, see especially Whitney and Kaufman 1985–87.

ENCEPHALITIS. An inflammation of the brain. Birds and mammals harbor the equine encephalitis virus that is transmissible by mosquitoes to humans. See DISEASE.

ENDANGERED BIRDS. See Fig 31. The need for federal legislation to protect endangered species was perceived by the end of the nineteenth century and laws were passed giving some measure of protection to certain groups of birds, mainly those seen to be threatened by direct exploitation (see CONSERVATION and LAWS PROTECTING BIRDLIFE). By the 1960s it had become clear that native plant and animal species were declining dramatically due to a wide spectrum of manmade phenomena and early endangered species laws were passed in 1966 and 1969, but the legal foundation on which protection of our birds and other wildlife now depends is the Endangered Species Act of 1973. This powerful and comprehensive federal law incorporated provisions of the earlier laws but also refined and strengthened the ability of the federal government to protect species threatened with extinction. Among its key provisions are
- Explicit definitions of Endangered Species and Threatened Species (see below).
- Vesting power in the Secretary of the Interior to determine whether a given species is endangered or threatened because of habitat destruction or any of four other explicit causes "solely on the basis of the best scientific and commercial data available."
- The requirement that all federal agencies undertake programs for the conservation of endangered and threatened species and that they are likewise prohibited from taking any action that would

jeopardize and listed species of modify its "critical habitat," as defined in the act.

- The mandate that all federal agencies consult in cooperation with the Secretary of the interior to further the purposes of the act.
- The authorization for the Secretary of the Interior to acquire critical habitat as necessary.
- The requirement to respond promptly to petitions to add species the list of endangered species under the act, periodically publish updated lists, create recovery plans, and monitor the condition of listed species.
- The extension of protection to foreign species and a mandate for U.S. compliance in restrictions in international trade in endangered species (see LAWS PROTECTING BIRDLIFE, CITES).
- Providing matching funds to the states for the purpose of conserving and restoring listed species.

The law is administered within the regional system of the U.S. Fish and Wildlife Service, Department of Interior.

As with other powerful federal laws, the Endangered Species Act has been the source of great controversy and legal activity. The main sources of contention have been the responsibility implicit in the act to regulate commercial activity and acquire critical habitat to ensure the conservation of listed species. This has resulted in numerous court cases, often involving constitutional issues that basically pit the public's interests in the survival of species against competing property rights and economic interests. A sign of the act's effectives has been the apoplectic response of many commercial interests and the actions taken at the highest levels of government by sympathetic politicians to weaken the law's authority by withholding funding, imposing moratoria on new listings, and delaying the act's reauthorization. While conservationists have lost some significant battles in fighting for the vigorous application of this act, it remains an indispensable tool to ensure the identification, protection, and restoration of our rarest birds and other species and their habitats.

DEFINING RARITY. The Endangered Species Act of 1973 defines "Endangered" as "any species (including subspecies) which is in danger of extinction throughout all or a significant proportion of its range." It defines "Threatened" as "any species which is likely to become an endangered species within the foreseeable future." It is these two categories that mandate full enforcement of the law, but the act also defines a "rare" species or subspecies as "although not presently threatened with extinction . . . in such small numbers throughout its range that it may be endangered if its environment worsens. Close watch of its status is necessary."

ARE WE SAVING THE BIRDS? While there have been some notable success stories—such as the recovery and consequent delisting of the Bald Eagle and Peregrine Falcon (see below)—and some reasons for hope—

such as the recent hatching of a California Condor chick produced by captive reared parents in the wild—a glance at the general trend in the welfare of endangered bird species is far from heartening. When the first edition of this book was published in 1982, this entry listed 11 Endangered North American bird species, *no* Threatened species, and 15 subspecies listed as either Endangered or Threatened. Twenty years later the list below contains 14 Endangered species, 7 Threatened species, and 19 subspecies listed as either Endangered or Threatened. Examining the details of the record provides no consolation. For example, while the U.S. Fish and Wildlife Service maintains the optimistic position, credible 20 years ago, that the Eskimo Curlew and Bachman's Warbler are still with us, most ornithologists are convinced that they are extinct, with no credible sightings since the 1960s or 1970s; the Ivory-billed Woodpecker, despite a recent report from Louisiana and perhaps a few individuals hanging on in Cuba, is almost certainly doomed by its inadequate reproductive potential; and the remaining Dusky Seaside Sparrows, all males, died in captivity.

As of September 2002, The U.S. Fish and Wildlife Service listed 78 species and subspecies of birds as Endangered and 14 species and subspecies as Threatened. Because the geographical scope of this book is North America, the list below does not include the (many) Endangered and Threatened birds of Hawaii, Guam, and Puerto Rico that fall under the jurisdiction of the USFWS.

- First the good news: Two of our most spectacular birds of prey have been pulled back from the brink of extinction (to which of course *we* pushed them).

Bald Eagle *(Haliaeetus leucocephalus)*. Regardless of what one may think of its scavenging and piratical habits, the Bald Eagle certainly deserves its identification with the United States on the basis of its geographical distribution: it ranges continentwide from Alaska to Florida, Newfoundland to California and breeds no where else in the world. In the eighteenth century the Bald Eagle population in the lower 48 states is believed to have numbered at least 25,000 adult birds, with some estimates putting it as high as 75,000. By 1960 only 450 breeding pairs remained in the contiguous states. Perceiving a threat to our national bird's existence even earlier, Congress passed a special Bald Eagle Protection Act in 1940, and the species was declared Endangered in 1967. It has long suffered from illegal shooting and habitat destruction, but the main culprit in the Bald Eagle's most recent brush with extinction was poisoning with DDT consumed in concentrated form in the fish that make up most of its diet. The result was the inability to form hard eggshells, resulting in a rapidly declining reproduction rate, a fate shared with many other species of raptors and some seabirds. The eagle also suffered from ingesting lead shot from the carcasses of hunter-killed ducks, another favorite food item.

The heartening recovery of the Bald Eagle is attributable first to the banning of DDT in 1972 and second to a proactive nationwide effort to restore local populations using captive breeding and a reintroduction program. A key component of this effort was the breeding program organized by the U.S. Fish and Wildlife Service at its Patuxent Wildlife Research Center in Laurel, Maryland. The Center ultimately sent 125 captive-reared young eagles to restock depleted populations, and "extra" wild eaglets from nests with two young elsewhere in the country were also placed with foster parents. In some cases nestling eaglets were placed in towers in wilderness areas and "hacked" i.e., reared by unseen humans until they learned to fend for themselves in the wild. Fueled by the species' inherent popularity, this campaign to bring back the eagles was so successful that Bald Eagles now breed in many places where they had not nested for many years and have been restored to healthy population levels in old strongholds, e.g., Florida, the Great Lakes and Pacific Northwest; in some places breeding populations now exceed known historic levels. As has always been the case, the species is most common in coastal areas in the far north, especially Alaska. In 1995, the official status of the Bald Eagle in the lower 48 states under the Endangered species Act was changed from Endangered to Threatened and then in 1998 the species was, as the jargon has it, "delisted."

Peregrine Falcon *(Falco peregrinus anatum* and *F. p. tundrius)*. This majestic cosmopolitan species suffered from the same drastic population decline as the Bald Eagle due to the same reproductive failure caused by DDT poisoning (see preceding account). The species had been in decline even before this final indignity, due to the depredations of egg collectors and persecution by people who believed them to be a "bad" species that killed other "useful" birds. The two most widespread American subspecies were added to the federal endangered species list in 1970. Thanks to the banning of DDT and a heroic recovery program spearheaded by Tom Cade and his Peregrine Project (originally based at Cornell's Laboratory of Ornithology; now the PEREGRINE FUND/World Center for Birds of Prey in Idaho) in cooperation with the U.S. Fish and Wildlife Service and the National Audubon Society, peregrines are once again breeding in many ancestral localities in suitable mountainous habitat from the Arctic to Mexico and on both coasts. As with the Bald Eagle, recovery was based on a captive breeding program. Female peregrines were induced to lay eggs in captivity, which were then artificially incubated; the young were reared until they are about 30 days old, and then placed in artificial nest sites where unseen humans fed them until they fledged. In the spring of 1980 two pairs of captive-bred Peregrines successfully reared young in New Jersey—the first east of the Mississippi since the 1950s. Peregrines now nest in over 10 eastern states and in the Maritimes, Québec and Ontario and have recovered very well in the West as well. These captive-

reared birds are of "mixed genetic stock" and many are similar in appearance to the dark Peale's race of the Pacific Northwest and Alaska.

An interesting aspect of the peregrine saga is that ledges on skyscrapers in several cities have proven to be ideal nest sites, the urban habitat affording both security and a ready source of well-fed pigeon and rats. Web cams have been trained on several of these eyries so that the daily life of these spectacular birds can be viewed on-line by anyone with access to a computer.

The nominate race of peregrine, *F. p. peregrinus,* of Europe, was also endangered by DDT, but has recovered encouragingly in the British Isles.

- The following three species are *probably extinct* though the possibility that a few individual may continue to hang on is entertained by the *AOU Checklist,* 7th edition (1998) and the U.S. Fish and Wildlife Service. In this optimistic spirit two of them are retained here in the Endangered category.

Eskimo Curlew *(Numenius borealis). Former Range:* Bred in Northwest Territories west (probably) to western Alaska; migrated eastward in the fall to staging points near Ungava Bay, and perhaps James Bay, and the Maritime Provinces and then crossed the western Atlantic over the Lesser Antilles to winter quarters in southern Brazil, Paraguay, and Argentina. In the spring the preferred route passed up through the Mississippi drainage. *Present Range:* Unknown, but if any individuals remain they doubtless range within the vast boundaries of the species' historical range. *Habits:* Nested in a virtually unlined depression in barren tundra; wintered on short-grass pampa. In migration frequently associated with American Golden Plover and Whimbrel in close-cut or well-grazed pastures, plowed fields, coastal marshes, and dunes. *Main Reasons for Decline:* Though mention has been made of a conversion from grazed pastures to agriculture along its Midwestern migration route, it can be stated unequivocally that, like the Passenger Pigeon, the Eskimo Curlew was simply, thoughtlessly, shot out of existence. Before its decline it was renowned for its great abundance, delicious flavor, and fearlessness of man. Heavy hunting is recorded from the Ungava region; on South American wintering grounds; along the Atlantic coast of the United States, (when bad weather forced it to interrupt its transoceanic southern migrations); and in spring in the Midwestern United States, whence wagonloads were carted off to market. An abrupt decline was noted in the 1870s; large flocks had ceased to occur by the late 1880s; and by the turn of the century the possibility of extinction had been raised. Unlike most species of shorebirds that were wantonly killed for food and sport in the last century, the Eskimo Curlew never recovered. Since other shorebirds were persecuted to a similar degree, it seems that hunting or the disruption that this caused in the birds' critical migration stopovers and staging points may have triggered a collapse of the species population dynamics

similar to that experienced by the Passenger Pigeon (see EXTINCT BIRDS). It should also be noted, however, that while species such as American Golden Plover have "recovered" to the extent that they apparently can maintain stable populations, we have never again seen concentrations of the species of the magnitude recorded in some of the shooters' logs during the peak market gunning years. *Current Status:* Almost certainly extinct; extremely rare if still surviving. Recent reliable records since 1960 are as follows: April 3, 1960: Galveston Island, Texas (good sight record of single bird); March–April 1962: Galveston Island, Texas (3 or 4 seen and conclusively photographed); April 11, 1963: Rockport, Texas (sight record of 2 birds by experienced observers); September 4, 1963: Barbados, West Indies (bird shot; preserved at Philadelphia Academy of Natural Sciences); August 15, 1976: North Point (James Bay), Ontario (inconclusive but "reasonably convincing" sight record of 2 birds by experienced observers—Hagar and Anderson [1977]). Other sight records in the 1980s from Texas, New England, and elsewhere at the proper season are intriguing but lack the authority of the sightings noted above.

For a moving and well written account of this sad story see Bodsworth (1995).

Ivory-billed Woodpecker *(Campephilus principalis). Former Range:* The U.S. subspecies ranged from east Texas though the Gulf states to southeastern North Carolina and up Mississippi drainage to southern Illinois and Ohio. The Cuban race once ranged widely in mature pine and mixed forests throughout the main island, gradually becoming confined to vestiges of forest habitat on the eastern end. *Present Range:* If any birds remain they are most likely to be reported from mature lowland forest in the southeastern United States, especially Louisiana or in the Sierra de Moa, Oriente Province, Cuba. *Habits:* Ivory-bills occupied large territories (maximum density: 1 pair per 16 square miles) in mature and senescent river-bottom forests, feeding principally on the larvae of wood-boring beetles and excavating nest holes high in trees. *Main Reason for Decline:* Destruction of extensive southern hardwood forests for timber. *Current Status:* Probably extinct. The last pair photographed in the United States was found May 22, 1971. On April 1, 1999 there was (despite the date!) a credible report of a pair of birds from the Pearl River Wildlife Management Area in southeastern Louisiana, an area that at the time was still being logged. Since then the area has been searched intensively, including a 30-day expedition in January 2002 by a cooperative team from the Cornell Laboratory of Ornithology, the Louisiana Department of Wildlife and Fisheries, and Zeiss Sport Optics; though some intriguing sounds were heard, analysis proved that they were not of Ivory-bill origin. In Cuba 12–13 pairs survived up to 1956. As of 1974 it was estimated that no more than 6 pairs survived; the last credible reports were in 1987–88.

Bachman's Warbler *(Vermivora bachmanii)*. Designated as extinct by the *AOU Checklist* 7th edition (1998), though still listed as Endangered by the U.S. Fish and Wildlife Service. For an account of this lost wood warbler see EXTINCT BIRDS.

- The following 6 *Endangered* birds are *full species that breed exclusively in North America*. If they become extinct here they will have ceased to exist on the planet.

California Condor *(Gymnogyps californianus)*. *Former Range:* Permanent resident from Washington State south to northern Baja California and east at least as far as Texas. Though it has never been abundant or wide-ranging in historical times, it undoubtedly ranged much more widely prior to 1,000 years ago. It may have existed in Arizona and Utah as late as the 1880s and Pleistocene specimens range eastward to Florida and New York State. *Present Range:* Captive bred birds have been released in western Monterey, eastern San Luis Obispo, and eastern Santa Barbara counties, California and near the Grand Canyon in Arizona. *Habits:* Nests in caves or (rarely) in large tree cavities or stumps and lays its single egg on sand or litter on the ground. The species is somewhat sluggish and careless in reproductive matters. Egg breakage is frequent and wild pairs apparently did not always renest if the egg was lost. Parents normally reared only a single young every other year at best, though biologists successfully "double-clutched" some of the last wild nesters. Condors only sporadically return to same nest site in successive breeding years; they spend much time roosting in dead trees or rocks near nest sites and soaring over a wide range on sunny days in search of carrion—their only known source of food. *Main Reasons for Decline:* Tracking of individual birds using marking and telemetry indicates that lead poisoning and shooting seem to be the chief causes of the condor's decline. However, many other issues, including collisions with high-power lines; a shortage of food (carcasses), poisoning by DDT and Agent 1080 (used by ranchers for ground squirrel and coyote control), predation (Common Ravens), and undetermined habitat inadequacies, may have played a role. *Current Status:* A captive breeding program was established in 1981 as part of the USFWS Condor Recovery Plan; at that time only 21 individuals remained in existence. The last condor was removed from the wild in 1987 and reintroductions began in 1992; a number of the released birds were killed in contacts with powers lines. The present goal of the recovery plan is to establish two separate viable populations containing 150 birds each with at least 15 breeding pairs. As of spring 2002 there were 63 free-ranging condors in California and Arizona as well as 18 at hack sites being prepared for release and 104 birds remaining in captivity. On April 11, 2002 for the first time in 18 years, a condor chick, the offspring of captive-reared parents hatched in the wild in Ventura County, California. The recovery program has been a public-private partnership of state and federal wildlife

agencies, the Los Angeles Zoo, the San Diego Wild Animal Park, and the Peregrine Fund.

For a thorough history of this crisis-plagued experiment in endangered species management see Snyder and Snyder (2000).

Whooping Crane *(Grus americana). Former Range:* Bred from Hudson Bay to northern Mackenzie, NWT, in the north, south through the Great Plains to Iowa and Nebraska, and in Gulf coastal marshes (at least in Louisiana) in recent times; may once have ranged continentwide; wintered in the Gulf states from Florida to Texas and south into central Mexico. *Present Range:* A single wild population now breeds in Wood Buffalo National Park, a 17,300-square-mile wilderness reserve south of Great Slave Lake in Mackenzie and northern Alberta and winters on the Blackjack Peninsula, part of the Aransas National Wildlife Refuge near Rockport, Texas. A vestigal introduced population exists in Idaho and New Mexico (see below); there is a nonmigratory population on the Kissimmee Prairie in Florida and a new migratory population being established in Wisconsin/Florida (see below). *Habits:* Makes a large (4–5 feet in diameter) mound nest in open water in wilderness marshlands in subarctic plains or (formerly) coastland and lays 1–3 (usually 2) eggs. Main foods are plant tubers and a variety of large invertebrates and small vertebrates. *Main Reasons for Decline:* Like the condor, probably never abundant in historical times, and with a low reproductive rate. A large, conspicuous, and "meaty" bird, it was undoubtedly shot for food during the frontier period in the Midwest and continued to be a good target for slob hunters until well into this century. However, human settlement—dissipation of wilderness, draining of marshes for farmlands—and finally trophy shooting and egg collecting, were probably the major factors in the species' decline. *Current Status:* Following a low point in the winter of 1941–42, during which only 13 adults and 2 juvenile birds survived, the cranes have made steady gains due to intensive efforts by government agencies, conservation organizations and many dedicated individuals. In 1967 U.S. and Canadian wildlife authorities began removing single eggs from crane clutches at Wood Buffalo and hatching them at Patuxent Wildlife Research Center in Maryland (current captive breeding is conducted by the International Crane Foundation of Baraboo, Wisconsin). This effort resulted in a flock of 22 *captive* cranes capable of producing their own eggs. In 1975 biologists began placing these "extra" whooper eggs in the nests of incubating Sandhill Cranes on the Grays Lake National Wildlife Refuge in Idaho. Though this population reached a peak of 33 birds in 1984–85 and migrated with the Sandhills to Bosque del Apache National Wildlife Refuge in New Mexico, the young whoopers identified with their surrogate parents and never formed pair bonds with members of their own species. The current Whooping Crane Recovery Plan mandates building the Wood Buffalo/Aransas population to at least 40 breeding pairs

and establishing two additional, separate populations. Since 1993 about 20 captive-bred cranes a year have been released in the Kissimmee Prairie in Florida, which as of 2001 had resulted in a nonmigratory population of 75 birds; a few of these birds have managed to hatch chicks, but only a single bird has fledged so far (2002), due to heavy predation and incidence of disease. Perhaps the most remarkable adventure in the annals of endangered species recovery has been the ultralight migration program pioneered by Kent Clegg, an Idaho rancher who taught members of the Rockies population to follow his aircraft to New Mexico. In the fall of 2001, three ultralights led a small flock of whoopers from their "hack site" at the Necedah National Wildlife Refuge in Wisconsin to the Chassahowitzka National Wildlife Refuge in Florida, a new migration route of almost 1200 miles over seven states; five of these birds returned to Wisconsin in the spring of 2002.

Piping Plover *(Charadrius melodus). Former Range:* May once have occupied a continuous breeding range in appropriate habitat from the Great Plains and throughout the Great Lakes region to the eastern seaboard. *Present Range:* Still widely distributed, but populations increasingly localized, the species having disappeared from much former breeding territory. Now nests locally from Alberta to Manitoba south to eastern Colorado and Oklahoma. The Great Lakes population survives only in Northern Michigan. On the east coast the species breeds from Newfoundland to North Carolina. Winters along the Atlantic and Gulf coasts of the United States as well as Mexico and the Caribbean; the nonbreeding distribution is still incompletely defined. *Habits:* A classic sand plover, nesting in dune blowouts and shell just above the high tide line on lake shores and barrier beaches; forages for invertebrates over the intertidal zone at all seasons. *Main Reasons for Decline:* Shot to the brink of extinction for food by the mid-nineteenth century and never recovered to former levels. Recent declines are mainly attributable to human recreational uses of breeding habitat, especially the use of off-road vehicles; plover nests are also vulnerable to predation by foxes, skunks, gull, crows, etc. Other human-caused factors, such as rising or falling water tables and beach erosion, have also contributed to local extirpations. *Current Status:* Still highly threatened throughout its range and continuing to decline in many areas. A bright spot is that intensive management of human activities during Piping Plover nesting season on barrier beaches has proven highly successful in increasing the species' population in New England. The species is listed as Endangered on its inland breeding grounds and Threatened elsewhere.

Red-cockaded Woodpecker *(Picoides borealis). Former Range:* Northern Oklahoma, Tennessee, and southern Maryland south to eastern Texas, the Gulf coast, and southern Florida; recorded as far north as Pennsylvania and New Jersey. *Present Range:* Though this species has withdrawn from

its northernmost limits (e.g., Maryland and northern Oklahoma), it still occupies much of its former nesting range. However, it has become increasingly isolated in islands of habitat. *Habits:* The life cycle of this species is inextricably bound to aging (80–120 years), "unhealthy" pine woods, ideally open stands of Longleaf, Loblolly, Shortleaf, and Slash Pines. It feeds largely on wood-boring (pine-associated) insects, and nests 20–100 feet up in pines infected with "red heart," a fungus disease that attacks the core of older pines. The species forms extended family groups that share rearing responsibilities; these groups excavate of roosting cavities in "clusters" of trees in a 10-acre area. The main food source is forest insects, including wood-boring species and also fruit. *Main Reasons for Decline:* The commercial management of southern pine woods for timber and pulp, including removal of older diseased trees and the prevention of new infestations, deprives this woodpecker of suitable nesting and roosting habitat. Fire suppression in pine stands has promoted growth of a hardwood understory, which the species avoids. Chemical control of fire ants may also diminish food resources and affect the species' reproductive success. *Current Status:* As of the mid 1990s the population was estimated to consist of 4,500 groups containing a total of 10,000–12,000 birds. This is one of the most controversial endangered species with private landholders, especially timber interests, and a great deal of effort is going into management plans that balance the needs of the birds with competing commercial values. For a recent detailed monograph see Conner et al. (2001).

Golden-cheeked Warbler *(Dendroica chrysoparia). Former and Present Range:* Restricted as a breeder to the region of the Edward's Plateau in south central Texas; winters in Mexico and Central America. *Habits:* This is a typical *Dendroica* warbler except for its dependence on mature stands of Ashe Juniper mixed with scrub oak in which it nests exclusively; it requires strips of juniper bark for nesting material. Like its congeners, Golden-cheeks feed chiefly on insects, foraging mainly in the oak portion of their nesting habitat; in wintering areas, it travels in mixed species flocks mainly in highland pine and pine-oak woodlands, though it has also been found in cloud forest and lowland broadleaf forest. *Main Reasons for Decline:* Habitat destruction and degradation. Though tolerant of some degree of timbering and grazing, the species is vulnerable to extensive habitat alteration. It also heavily parasitized by cowbirds. This exquisite warbler's very limited range in the attractive Texas hill country borders the encroaching metropolitan sprawl of Austin, San Antonio, and Waco with the accompanying clearing and fragmentation of the juniper-oak community on which it depends. *Current Status:* Gradually declining. Perhaps as few as 2200–4600 individuals as of 1990 (Ehrlich et al. (1992); remaining suitable habitat has been estimated at 10,000–50,000 acres.

Kirtland's Warbler *(Dendroica kirtlandii)*. *Former Range:* Not known to have ranged far beyond its current distribution but may have occurred more widely in the extensive appropriate habitat in Canada. *Present Range:* Known to breed only in north-central Michigan (east of Grayling; see Fig. 25). Unmated males have been found singing in Ontario on the Lake Huron north shore, in northern Wisconsin, and the Upper Peninsula of Michigan but no disjunct nest sites have been found despite some educated looking. The species winters in the Bahamas and is very rarely seen on migration. *Habits:* Kirtland's Warbler nests in loose colonies, building a lined cup on the ground under cover of low, young Jack Pines between 5 and 20 feet tall. It requires extensive stands of this successional forest habitat and therefore must shift its breeding sites to areas where there have been forest fires or timbering in the recent past. The pines reach the ideal stage about 6 years after a fire and remain suitable—with healthy sheltering lower branches—for 6–12 years. The U.S. Forest Service now manages this habitat for the birds' protection in the 4,000+ acre Huron-Manistee National Forests and on adjacent state lands. The habits of Kirtland's Warbler are typical of wood warblers in other respects. *Main Reasons for Decline:* The most conspicuous threat to Kirtland's Warbler in recent decades has been parasitism by Brown-headed Cowbirds (see BROOD PARASITISM; COWBIRD), which did not occur in northern Michigan prior to European settlement. Cowbirds were probably the main culprits in the 60% decline (to 201 singing males) of the species over a 10-year period ending in 1971, though this period also coincided with heavy logging of the species wintering habitat in the Bahamas. Lest one underestimate the magnitude of the cowbird threat, more than 121,000 of these parasites have been trapped during the last 30 years during the warbler's nesting season. Due to the warbler's dependence on a particular stage of forest succession—a natural result of wild fires—fire suppression is another threat that arrived with modern human settlement. *Current Status:* Due to an intensive program to control cowbirds and provide suitable nesting habitat, this species is presently doing well. The goal of the federally mandated Kirtland's Warbler recovery plan is to establish a self-sustaining population of 1000 pairs. In the 2001 nesting season 1,085 singing males were counted, up from 891 in 2000. Continued success depends on ongoing cowbird control, an extensive timbering and replanting program to provide suitable habitat (prescribed burning is little used for reasons of cost and safety), and conservation partnerships with Bahamians to ensure the survival of winter habitat.

- The following 4 species are *Endangered* within all or part of the *North American* portion of their range.

Brown Pelican *(Pelecanus occidentalis):* Occurs in warm waters along Atlantic, Gulf, and Pacific coasts. Drastic declines, including the extirpation of the entire Louisiana population occurred in the 1960s due to the

effects of chemical poisoning by DDT and PCBs. As with many species of fish-eating birds, concentrated ingestion of these toxins inhibited the ability of the affected birds to produce eggshells, resulting in inability to reproduce. Following a ban on the use of DDT in 1972, populations began to recover, aided in Louisiana by a pelican reintroduction program. Brown retains its Endangered status where it occurs in the United States, except for the Atlantic coast, Florida, and Alabama, where populations are stable or increasing.

Wood Stork *(Mycteria americana):* Ranges throughout the New World tropics south to northern Argentina. In the United States Wood Storks breed only in South Carolina, Georgia, and (mainly) Florida. They are colonial, making bulky stick nests in tall cypresses or mangroves, and also feed together in flocks; their preferred prey is fish. From an estimated 20,000 pairs the United States in the 1930s, breeding population declined to c.11,000 adult birds by 1996. Though rookeries have been protected for decades, the Wood Stork remains Endangered due significantly to extensive alterations of natural water regimes, especially in southern Florida, which have eliminated as much as 35% of the species' feeding habitat. Continued survival in the United States is contingent on effective management of aquatic systems to meet all of its breeding and feeding requirements.

Roseate Tern *(Sterna dougallii):* A cosmopolitan species, the Roseate Tern is listed as Threatened throughout the Western Hemisphere and adjacent oceans, including its Florida populations, and Endangered in its North American populations from Quebec and Newfoundland to North Carolina. Factors affecting Roseate Tern populations over time have included hunting (for plumage and food), competition with gulls for optimal nesting sites, disturbance of breeding areas by humans, foxes, etc., predation by rats, owls, etc., and chemical poison ingested in food (fish). Intensive management of breeding colonies has maintained stability or allowed slight increases at some sites, but the population as a whole remains vulnerable. Relatively little is known about how and where this species spends the winter along the Caribbean and Atlantic coast of South America, though trapping of terns by protein-starved human residents has been documented.

Black-capped Vireo *(Vireo atricapillus):* This distinctive little vireo breeds from central Oklahoma through central Texas to the highlands of central Coahuila, Mexico (formerly in Kansas and elsewhere in Mexico); it winters mainly in west Mexico south as far as Oaxaca. It nests in scrub oak and other dense, early successional shrubbery in rocky hill country; winter habitat includes arid tropical scrub. Like other vireos, this one eats mainly terrestrial invertebrates and some fruit. Nearly 90% of the United States population was said to be threatened by residential development and associated highway construction in 1990 (Ehrlich 1992); parasitism

by Brown-headed Cowbirds is also a major threat locally, affecting 80–100% of nests in some areas. Less dire threats include fire suppression and (conversely) over-browsing by sheep and goats. The global population, mainly in Mexico, may be between 3,000 and 10,000 pairs, but in the United States there may be as few as 250–500 individuals.

- The following 5 species are listed as *Threatened* by the U.S. Fish and Wildlife Service throughout all or a part of their *global range,* which includes North America.

Spectacled Eider *(Somateira fischeri):* This is one of the world's most spectacular sea ducks with a very limited breeding and wintering range along the coast and islands of northern Alaska and adjacent Bering Sea and Arctic Ocean. It suffered a 96% breeding population decline in the Yukon-Kuskokwim Delta from 96,000 birds in the 1970s to fewer than 5,000 in 1992. Causes are uncertain; candidates are lead poisoning (from spent shot), hunting pressure, other forms of human disturbance, breeding ground predation by foxes, gulls, jaegers, and ravens (caused by increased food supply from human sources), or a combination of two or more of these factors. There is also a suspicion that this and other species may be affected by major changes now occurring in the Bering Sea ecosystem. In January 2001 the U.S. Fish and Wildlife Service designated 39,000 square miles of critical wintering, molting, and spring staging habitat in marine waters and 1,000 square miles of nesting habitat in the Yukon-Kuskokwim Delta.

Steller's Eider *(Polysticta stelleri):* This handsome northern sea duck breeds on tundra mainly in the Russian Arctic west perhaps as far as northern Norway and east to northern Alaska. Most of the world population (68% or more) winters in Alaskan waters from the eastern Aleutians to Lower Cook Inlet. The global population of this species may have declined by as much as 50% in the last 30 years, and the Alaskan breeding population has nose-dived since 1960 from c. 4,000 pairs in the Yukon-Kuskokwim Delta to a total of 1,000 pairs in the late 1990s. The main Alaskan nesting range is now on the central Alaskan coastal plain mainly around Barrow. As with the previous species the cause of this eider's decline has not been pinpointed, but there are numerous possibilities, including oil and gas development in Siberian breeding areas, marine contaminants and ecological changes in the Bering Sea, hunting pressure, lead poisoning (from spent shot), predation by foxes, gulls, jaegers, and ravens (caused by increased food supply from human sources, e.g., dumps), or a combination of two or more of these factors. In 2000, responding to a lawsuit filed by the Southwest Center for Biological Diversity and Christians Caring for Creation, the USFWS designated 3,682 square miles of marine, inland, and shoreline in five areas as critical habitat for Steller's Eider. Special permits are now required for projects undertaken within 200 meters of a nest site.

Least Tern *(Sterna antillarum):* Like the Piping Plover, the Least Tern prefers to nest on shores near the water's edge. Along lakeshores and barrier beaches it nests squarely in the "recreational zone" and is thus subject to constant disturbance during the nesting season. Coastal development has eliminated habitat and contributed to coastal pollution and loss of food sources. Nests of Least Terns are also subject to predation by gulls, crows, and a number of predacious mammals species. Inland populations have declined during the same time period that river flows were altered. This species is listed differentially, with the inland populations considered Threatened and the California subspecies listed as Endangered. Least Terns appear to be quite resilient and have responded well to intensive management of their breeding habitat, including symbolic fencing to minimize disturbance and predator "exclosures." Though in many cases greatly reduced from historic high points, all major populations at present seem to be stable or increasing.

Marbled Murrelet *(Bracyramphus marmoratus)*: This diminutive seabird breeds along the Pacific coast of North America from the Aleutians to central California. Its Threatened status is related to the remarkable fact that though it spends most of its life at sea, it nests in loose associations high in mature conifers as much as 50 miles from the coast. Sexually mature (2-year-old) adults lay a single egg and may not nest every year. Decline of the species' populations in Washington, Oregon, and California is attributed to the destruction and fragmentation of the murrelet's forest habitat. Current (2002) population in California is estimated at 2,000 birds. Aproximately 3.89 million acres of Federal and non-Federal lands in these states is considered critical habitat for the species.

Florida Scrub-Jay *(Aphelocoma coerulescens)*. Once considered a race of a species that ranged continentwide, this jay has been now distinguished from the Western and Island Scrub-Jays on the basis of structural features, voice, and behavior. It breeds almost exclusively on scrub oak sand ridges of central Florida. The species has declined by 90% over the last 100 years as the result of habitat destruction, specifically development and agricultural conversion of scrub habitat; fire suppression and competition with Blue Jays may have played a role locally. Florida Scrub-Jays have been extirpated from at least 6 counties. Total population may have exceeded 10,000 as of 1993 (Woolfenden and Fitzpatrick 1996), but most populations are small and isolated. The species continues to decline. Like many corvids, this jay has interesting social relations, with young birds remaining as helpers at the parental nest for as long as several years.

- The North American distribution of the following three *Endangered* species is presently *peripheral*, but all have (or had) a legitimate claim to be included in the North American avifauna.

Short-tailed Albatross *(Diomedea albatrus)*. Once occurred commonly off the Pacific coast of North America and bred by the millions mainly in the Isu Islands of Japan. Now reduced to colonies on two islands, Torishima and Minami-kojima, totaling 1,000–2000 birds, about half of which are of breeding age. The population has been steadily increasing over the last 20 years. The species now occurs annually off the Pacific coast of North America.

White-tailed Eagle *(Haliaeetus albicilla)*. This essentially Palearctic species has withdrawn from much of its world range with encroachment of human settlement and attendant threats. The Siberian subspecies nested on Attu Island in the Aleutians from the late 1970s until 1996 and vagrants—presumably from the West Greenland population—were recorded in New England in 1935 and 1945. The species seems to be slowly recovering in some regions, including the West Greenland population, which is presently estimated to contain 150–170 pairs.

Thick-billed Parrot *(Rhynchopsitta pachyrhyncha)*. Once occurred in southeastern Arizona and perhaps southwestern New Mexico, mainly as a winter irruptive species from Mexico. The last reliable Arizona record is of a flock in Rhyolite Canyon in the Chiricahua Mountains in 1938, though there are rumors of sightings as late as 1945. There is no evidence that the species ever bred in the United States and attempts to establish a population in Arizona using captive-bred birds ultimately failed due to predation by Northern Goshawks and other factors (Snyder et al. 1994). The species is severely endangered due to habitat destruction (timbering) and continues to decline in remnants of its old growth coniferous forest habitat in north-central Mexico.

- The following 21 *Endangered or Threatened* North American *subspecies* make up only a part of the population of their species, the rest of which, in many cases, is not presently considered endangered.

Everglade Snail Kite *(Rostrhamus sociabilis plumbeus)*. Endangered. Once occurred widely in marshlands of the Florida peninsula, but now restricted to areas of the southwest shore of Lake Okeechobee, the Loxahachee National Wildlife Refuge, and the north end of Everglades National Park. From a low of 10 individuals, the subspecies has increased to at least 500 birds, but remains vulnerable. The main cause of decline is the well-publicized, profit driven alteration of the Everglades ecosystem, which destroyed much marsh habitat. The kite feeds almost exclusively on the Apple Snail *(Pomacea paludosa)*, which it locates by sight. It is therefore further threatened by encroachment of the invasive Water Hyacinth, mats of which make the snails invisible. Shooting and loss of food supply due to pesticides and cultural eutrophication have been contributing threats. The species as a whole occurs in suitable habitat throughout the New World tropics to central Argentina where it is still locally common.

Audubon's Crested Caracara *(Polyborus plancus audubonii)*. Threatened. Once common in the prairie region of central Florida, this subspecies is now restricted to five counties north and west of Lake Okeechobee. As of the early 1980s, the population was estimated at 400–500 birds (Layne 1985). Its decline is due directly to destruction of its habitat due to agriculture and commercial and residential development. The population is scattered and isolated and nests occur mainly on private land.

Northern Aplomado Falcon *(Falco femoralis septentrionalis)*. Endangered. Fairly common from south Texas to southern Arizona until the beginning of the twentieth century. The last nest was recorded near Deming, New Mexico in 1952. Decline is attributed to habitat alteration for human use, shooting, egg collecting, and pesticide poisoning. In a cooperative international program the Peregrine Fund has reared and released 578 Aplomado Falcons in suitable habitat. In 1995 a pair successfully fledged young in Cameron County, Texas.

Attwater's Greater Prairie Chicken *(Tympanuchus cupido attwateri)*. Endangered. Very local resident of coastal prairies of Texas. Listed as merely rare by BirdLife International (ICBP) in 1981, the subspecies is now on the brink of extinction, with fewer than 20 birds in existence. This despite heroic efforts to save it, including the acquisition of an extensive refuge and a captive breeding program.

Masked Bobwhite *(Colinus virginianus ridgwayi)*. Endangered. Formerly resident in southern Arizona, as well as Sonora, Mexico, this quail has been extinct in the United States since the early twentieth century, and near extinction throughout its range, due mainly to the advent of cattle ranching and the resulting destruction of native grasslands. Efforts to reintroduce birds began in 1937, and are presently focused on restoring sufficient natural grassland habitat in the Buenos Aires National Wildlife Refuge in Arizona.

Mississippi Sandhill Crane *(Grus canadensis pulla)*. Endangered. A nonmigratory race with fewer than 100 birds surviving, most of them on the Mississippi Sandhill Crane National Wildlife Refuge in Jackson County. The population of this race has been low since at least 1929, following which large areas of its grassland habitat have succumbed to agricultural, commercial, and residential development. Pesticides, genetic weakness, and natural catastrophes have also caused mortalities. The population has been supplemented with captive-bred cranes and 26,000 acres of critical habitat have been designated. The Recovery Plan calls for a sustainable, free living, genetically viable population self-sustained for 10 years.

California Clapper Rail *(Rallus longirostris obsoletus)*. Endangered. Restricted to the salt marshes of the San Francisco estuary. This habitat has declined by 84% since 1850 to just over 30,000 acres. The rails are distributed in small, isolated populations in fragmented marsh. Bird and

mammal predators, including Norway Rats, and mercury poisoning are also a threat.

Light-footed Clapper Rail *(R. l. levipes)*. Endangered. Still inhabits its historic range in coastal salt marshes from Santa Barbara California to San Quentin Bay in northern Baja California, but in many fewer localities due to marsh fragmentation, and degradation, human disturbance, predators, and pesticide contamination. Perhaps 250 birds remain, 55% in the Upper Newport Bay Ecological Reserve.

Yuma Clapper Rail *(R. l. yumanensis)*. Endangered. Breeds locally in fresh and brackish marshes along the Colorado, Gila, and Salt rivers, Arizona and at Salton Sea, California; also south along Pacific coast of Mexico to Nayarit. At least 700 birds responded to tapes during counts up to 1991. Vulnerable to river channelization and water level manipulation.

Western Snowy Plover *(Charadrius alexandrinus nivosus)*. Threatened. The United States population of this subspecies is restricted to 28 areas of beaches, salt pans, and other coastal habitats between southern Washington and Baja California; it also ranges south to the tip of the Baja peninsula. Main threats consist of various forms of disturbance by people (see Piping Plover, above, for details).

California Least Tern *(Sterna antillarum)*. Endangered. See Least Tern, above.

Cactus Ferruginous Pygmy Owl *(Glaucidium brasilianum cactorum)*. Endangered. The U.S. population, once reaching north of Phoenix, is now confined between Tucson and the Mexican border. As of 2001 only 47 adult owls are believed to remain in Arizona. The bird inhabits riparian forest (especially ironwood) and desert, habitats that are threatened by development, lowering of water tables, firewood cutting, and overgrazing. The USFWS is currently reevaluating the owl's critical habitat requirements, which could result in doubling the present designated acreage.

Northern Spotted Owl *(Strix occidentalis caurina)*. Threatened. Infamous because its needs have been pitted against commercial logging interests, this owl prefers extensive tracts of old-growth forest from southwestern British Colombia to central California. Recent estimates (Thomas et al, 1993) total 6,090 pairs. There are (controversial) studies showing declining survival and productivity in recent years. There may also be competition from closely related Barred Owls that seem to be invading Northern Spotted Owl habitat. Due to the complexities of modeling population changes in an area of rapidly changing habitat and the highly charged political atmosphere, creating a credible management plan for this owl is challenging.

Southwestern Willow Flycatcher *(Empidonax traillii extimus)*. Endangered. Breeds (in Arizona) in dense riverine thickets of willow, tamarisk, and cottonwood thickets. Also occurs in California and New Mexico with much smaller populations in Nevada, Utah, Colorado, and Texas;

winters from central Mexico to northern South America. Extensive declines apparently occurred as early as the 1880s as a consequence of riverine habitat destruction. A more recent threat is high incidence of parasitism by Brown-headed Cowbirds. Recent Arizona surveys documented 160 occupied territories.

San Clemente Loggerhead Shrike *(Lanius ludovicianus mearnsi).* Endangered. Restricted to one small island off the coast of southern California. As recently as 1998 there were only 13 shrikes alive in the wild. The primary reason for the bird's decline was severe habitat degradation as a result of overgrazing by feral sheep, goats, and pigs. Even after these animals were removed the shrikes continued to be impacted by feral cats, rats, ravens, and (ironically) another endangered species, the Channel Island Fox. Under threat of law suits by the Defenders of Wildlife and others, the U.S. Navy, which manages the island, began to take conservation of the shrike seriously, including building a captive breeding facility, implementing predator control measures, and employing fire management techniques. In 2001 the maximum number of San Clemente Shrikes (including captive-bred releases) in the wild was 160 birds.

Least Bell's Vireo *(Vireo bellii pusillus).* Endangered. Once abundant from northern California to northern Baja, this subspecies had disappeared from the heart of its range by 1985, with only 300 pairs remaining, mainly in San Diego County. The principal causes of the decline were destruction of 90% of the vireo's riparian habitat (willow thickets with a dense shrub understory of wild rose and Coastal Live Oak) through water diversions and withdrawals and parasitism by Brown-headed Cowbirds. As a result of habitat restoration and cowbird-trapping programs the population was up to about 2,000 pairs by 1998.

Coastal California Gnatcatcher *(Polioptila californica californica).* Threatened. The flagship species for California coastal sage scrub habitat, aka soft chaparral. Once the dominant coastal habitat, 85% has been lost to agricultural and residential development. In addition to the gnatcatcher it harbors about 100 other endangered or threatened species, but because of the development value of the land, a bitter battle has been waged in the courts between conservationists and developers. An initial plan, once touted as a "win-win solution," allowed developers to eliminate a certain numbers of gnatcatchers and other rare species along with their habitat (called "incidental taking" in the trade) in exchange for the preservation and management of sufficient coastal scrub to maintain the endemic species. The Department of Interior agreed not to designate critical habitat as part of the bargain and without this legal restraint, the developers (including the Walt Disney Corporation) proceeded at full tilt. Following a lawsuit by conservationists, 513,650 acres of critical habitat were designated, but this was challenged by the Building Industry Association of Southern California. As of 2002, the presumption is that the next

"solution" will favor developers, not gnatcatchers. A further threat to 50,000 of the habitat on military bases may be declared exempt from the Endangered Species Act. The U.S. population of the gnatcatcher may be under 2,000 pairs.

Inyo California Towhee *(Pipilo crissalis eremophilus)*. Restricted to riparian willow patches in the Argus Ranges in the Mojave Desert, Inyo County California. The decline of the species is due destruction of habitat by mining, grazing, off-road vehicles and water diversion. Only 200–300 individuals remain.

San Clemente Sage Sparrow *(Amphispiza belli clementeae)*. Restricted to San Clemente Island off the coast of southern California. The population was once down to 20–30 birds due to habitat destruction by feral goats and other causes, but recent mitigation has resulted in some increases. See under San Clemente Loggerhead Shrike above for more detail.

Florida Grasshopper Sparrow *(Ammodramus savannarum)*. Endangered. Restricted to the prairies of south central Florida, with about 250 pairs inhabiting 9 sites as of the mid 1980s. This represents a substantial decline in the sparrow's population, which is said to have been "large and widespread" in the early twentieth century. This race prefers an early successional stage of saw palmetto and dwarf oak scrub mixed with bluestems and wiregrass that is burned every few years. The main cause of decline is conversion of the native scrubby grasslands to improved pastureland for cattle. Remaining populations occur on private land, several wildlife management areas, and the Avon Park Bombing range owned by the U.S. Air Force. Prescribed burns have been applied to the Air Force land in an attempt to protect a portion of the sparrow's habitat.

Cape Sable Seaside Sparrow *(Ammospiza maritime mirabilis)*. Endangered. Continues to occupy much of its historic range in Collier, Dade, and Monroe Counties in southern Florida. The subspecies strongly prefers seasonally flooded subtropical marshes dominated by grasses and sedges without brush. The populations of this sparrow are typically ephemeral because of their sensitivity to coastal flooding. The race was nearly wiped out by the hurricane of 1935 and was severely reduced (from 6,450 to 2,800 birds) by hurricane Andrew in 1992. In addition to flooding, the habitat is also maintained by periodic fires. So far the sparrow has been able to hang on in two core populations near Taylor Slough and in Big Cypress swamp.

- The following full species has been officially *proposed by* the Secretary of the Interior to be included on the federal endangered species list as *Threatened.*

Mountain Plover *(Charadrius montanus)*. A Great Plains endemic that once ranged abundantly from Canada to Mexico. Since the beginning of the twentieth century, the species has declined 50–89%. The main

breeding strongholds are patches of native prairie in Colorado and Montana. Most of these birds winter in the heavily developed San Joaquin Valley of California. Mountain Plovers were heavily hunted during the market-gunning era, but a more pervasive factor in its decline was the destruction of its native short grass prairie habitat for agriculture; pesticides may also have played a role. The species seems to find ideal habitat in association with prairie dog colonies; this is more bad news since prairie dog "control" is popular in Mountain Plover country. Federal listing will result in more research, a mandate to seek cooperative agreements with landowners and funding for habitat conservation and other measures.

- The following are *candidate,* species and subspecies (as of 2002), meaning that their case has been accepted for consideration, but their listing has not yet been proposed by the Secretary of the Interior.

Gunnison Sage-Grouse *(Centrocercus minimus)*
Western Sage-Grouse *(Centrocercus urophasianus phaios)*
Lesser Prairie-Chicken *(Tympanuchus palliicinctus)*
Yellow-billed Cuckoo *(Coccyzus americanus)*
Streaked Horned Lark *(Eremophila alpestris strigata)*

Selected facts for this entry taken from NatureServe.2003.

For more detail on the species and subspecies described above, see *The Birds of North America* accounts (Poole et al. 1990–ORNITHOLOGY) for the full species. For on-line accounts, go to http://www.natureserve. org/explorer.

THE SCORE KEEPERS. The U.S. Fish and Wildlife Service periodically publishes a register of species and subspecies of plants and animals of the world that have been identified as endangered. An "Endangered Species Technical Bulletin" is published monthly to report the latest news on particular species. Up-to-date information on species status and life histories, as well as the full text of the Endangered species Act of 1973, is available at the USFWS website: http://endangered.fws.gov. For additional life history and status information on these species go to http:// natureserv.org. BirdLife International's also produces its own thoroughly annotated lists of endangered bird species of the world, especially Collar and Andrew (1988) and Collar et al. (1992), as well as the BirdLife website: www.birdlife.net.

Most states and provinces have some form of endangered species list, usually administered by the state or provincial wildlife agency. All federally listed species must, of course, be included on such lists and the states may not reduce the level of protection provided in the Endangered Species Act of 1973. They may, however, pass stronger laws and provide legal protection for species that are Endangered or Threatened in the state

but are not listed nationally. Many state endangered species lists are available on-line through state government websites.

See also EXTINCT BIRDS; CONSERVATION; LAWS PROTECTING BIRD-LIFE; THREATS (OF HUMAN ORIGIN) TO BIRDLIFE.

ENDEMIC (en-DEM-ik) (endemism). In a biological context, "endemic" means restricted in distribution to a given area. The term can be applied to any taxon and to an area of any size. The bird family Parulidae (wood warblers) is endemic to the New World but not to North America. The Bay-breasted Warbler is a breeding endemic of North America or the Nearctic region but winters in the Neotropics. Brown-capped Rosy-Finch is endemic to a few peaks of the central Rocky Mountains above timberline. The medical meaning of "endemic," most often used in describing the occurrence of disease, is quite different: that bilharzia is "endemic" in Venezuela does not mean that the parasitic condition is restricted to that country, but that it is constantly present there.

ENDOCRINE SYSTEM. Endocrine glands produce chemicals called hormones and secrete them directly into the bloodstream; exocrine glands produce substances other than hormones and secrete them (usually by means of a duct) externally or to other parts of the body: the liver, which secretes bile to the intestines for digestion, and the oil gland, which secretes oil from a bird's rump, are both exocrine glands. Another key distinction between these two types of glands is distance to target: exocrine glands dump their secretions directly into the target tissue/region, whereas endocrine glands have a distant target tissue or system.

The endocrine system is linked by function rather than tissue. It works in close conjunction with the nervous system to stimulate and balance a great diversity of bodily functions. Many of these are subtle and therefore little understood or undiscovered. The following brief description of these glands gives the name, location, characteristic hormones, and some of the main functions of a bird's endocrine glands. Those familiar with the human endocrine system will recognize many similarities.

The Pituitary Gland is suspended on a stalk from the hypothalamus at the base of the brain. It secretes several hormones that act specifically on other endocrine glands, as well as oxytocin, prolactin (see CROP MILK), antidiuretic hormone (ADH), follicle-stimulating hormone, luteinizing hormone, somatotropin or growth hormone, thyroid-stimulating hormone, adrenocorticotropic hormone, and melanocyte-stimulationg hormone. This gland is actually composed of two parts: the anterior part is glandular and produces seven hormones, whereas the posterior part is a hybrid structure that shares tissue with the brain and secretes ADH, and oxytocin. The pituitary is a kind of master gland that stimulates activities in many of the other glands and is regulated by them in return. It plays a

significant role in the breeding cycle: stimulating sexual function, e.g., the development of a brood patch, promoting behavioral characteristics such as courtship rituals, and regulating circadian rhythms. It is also known to be responsible for more mundane necessities, such as water retention and the muscular contractions required for egg laying. Many pituitary functions known in mammals have yet to be confirmed in birds.

The **Thyroid Gland** rests at the base of the neck. It secretes thyroxin when stimulated by the pituitary gland. The thyroid has many general metabolic functions, e.g., blood production, pulse rate, and physical growth. It also controls feather development and coloration and molt sequences and may influence the urge to migrate.

The **Parathyroid Glands** are very small and are located near the thyroid, though precise location and number vary (usually 2 or 3); they produce parathyroid hormone (PTH), which monitors calcium and phosphate levels in the blood and is therefore crucial to bone and eggshell development.

The **Ultimobranchial Glands** are also tiny, lie near the parathyroids, and secrete a hormone called calcitonin. This lowers blood calcium levels in mammals, but its function is less clear in birds and other vertebrates.

The **Adrenal Glands** come in pairs (sometimes joined) near the top of the kidneys. In birds, as in humans, adrenaline (epinephrine) is the "emergency" hormone. It can rapidly raise the amount of sugar in the blood, supplying extra fuel for the muscles, and increase heart rate and blood pressure. The adrenal medulla also produces the epinephrine antagonist norepinephrine. The adrenal cortex produces corticosterone and aldosterone. Known as the "stress hormone" corticosterone is now being studied as a critical element in reproductive and migratory biology of birds because it is important in fat deposition and must be suppressed when adults are feeding nestlings (Wingfield et al. 1990; Wingfield 1991).

The **Pancreas** is a large gland that rests in a loop of the small intestine. It serves both an exocrine function—the secretion of digestive enzymes—and an endocrine function—the secretion of insulin and glucagon. Insulin and glucagon are instrumental in maintaining blood sugar levels within necessary limits.

The **Gonads** (testes and ovaries) are the sex glands and also have both exocrine and endocrine roles. As exocrine glands they produce the male and female reproductive cells (see REPRODUCTIVE SYSTEM). As endocrines they produce male and female sex hormones (testosterone, estrogen, and progesterone). These work in close association with the pituitary gland and, like it, have a wide influence throughout the body, affecting growth, behavior, blood chemistry, and changes in internal and external structures, particularly those associated with breeding conditions. (See chapters on endocrinology in Whittow [2000].)

ENDOPARASITE. An organism that lives inside the body of another organism to the detriment of the host. (For parasites that live on the surface of the body, see ECTOPARASITE.)

For obvious reasons, endoparasites in birds are far less conspicuous than ectoparasites; nevertheless, they occur in great variety and sometimes in great numbers, and are occasionally responsible for significant mortalities.

Internal parasites usually enter the body of the host via one of three routes widely used by different types of organisms: (1) filarial worms (a type of roundworm—phylum Nematoda) and a variety of single-celled organisms are transmitted from the bloodstream of an infected bird by mosquitoes or other biting insects. (2) Other types of roundworms and tapeworms (subclass Cestoda) and intestinal protists, e.g., *Entamoeba* & *Eimeria* (the agent of coccidiosis), have a more or less dormant infective stage, e.g., an egg or in protists a cyst that is eaten inadvertently by a feeding bird and develops in its preferred site in the host's body. Gallinaceous birds and other ground foragers ingest parasites in this way. (3) Many endoparasites, including some roundworms, some tapeworms, and all flukes (class Trematoda) infect an intermediate host, which is then eaten by a bird. A typical fluke life cycle runs as follows: All flukes have snails as their first intermediate host. In some cases, the snails themselves are ingested by birds, which then become infected with the fluke. Schistosome flukes transform into an infective stage in the snail, become free-swimming in the water, and enter a bird's body directly through the skin. Most flukes, however, require a second intermediate host, such as a fish or aquatic insect, which must be eaten by a bird (or other predator) in order to develop into its final stage. Fluke eggs deposited in the digestive tract of the bird are excreted into the water, hatch, and find their appropriate host snail to complete the cycle.

Virtually all organs and spaces in the body are vulnerable to attack by endoparasites, though the digestive tract is especially popular.

Wild birds apparently have a high tolerance for internal parasites and are known, in some cases, to support thousands of them with no noticeable ill effects. Paradoxically, there are also instances in which death seems to have been caused by a relatively minor infestation. Poultry yards seem to be more vulnerable to certain common endoparasites than wild bird populations.

For a more detailed, but still highly readable review of the commoner avian endoparasites, see Soulsby's revised review in Campbell and Lack (1985–ORNITHOLOGY).

ENDYSIS (EN-duh-sis). The acquisition of new feathers, replacing those being dropped in the molting process. Compare ECDYSIS, and see MOLT.

ENERGY (expenditure and storage). Attempts have been made to calculate energy expended by birds in flight. There are many variables, such as flying conditions, wing shape, and manner of flight, that make such calculations tricky at best. Some of the data can be interpreted to show that birds cannot possibly produce sufficient energy to fly any distance. Other figures, seemingly closer to reality, indicate energy expenditure in birds to be many times (perhaps 30 times) greater in some cases than that of mammals of comparable weight.

Obviously, small, nonsoaring migrants that travel thousands of miles must expend great amounts of energy, even under the most favorable conditions, and it has been proven that they store fat prior to their journeys from which to draw the necessary energy (see Nisbet et al.,1963–FAT; Blem 1990; Blem [in Whittow] 2000; Gannes 2001–FAT).

In addition to flight, energetics is concerned with phenomena such as resting metabolism and environmental drivers such as temperature and moisture; for example, see Holmes and Sawyer's studies of *Catharus* thrush metabolism; also see Calder and King (1974).

The data on bird energy expenditure that exist are expressed in formulas involving ergs per unit of time per unit of muscle or total body weight and often by other technical means, beyond the scope of this book. However, see the Bibliography.

See also FAT; METABOLISM; TEMPERATURE, BODY.

EPIGAMIC (EP-ih-GAM-ik). Characters or behavior patterns that promote reproduction are said to be epigamic. The inflated neck pouches of various grouse species (see Fig. 7) are epigamic characters; ritualized precopulatory calls and gestures between mated birds are epigamic behavior patterns.

ERNE. An eagle or sea-eagle; see Eagle.

ERYTHRISM (eh-RITH-rizm). In birds, refers to the conspicuous presence of reddish (rufous) pigment in the plumage. The phenomenon is most often seen in normal color variations, such as the erythristic (red) morph of the Eastern Screech-Owl and the so-called Cory's Least Bittern. However, abnormal erythrism (akin to MELANISM or ALBINISM) has also been recorded, for example, in prairie-chickens and in Rufous-sided Towhees. Dietary erythrism also occurs, e.g., by Cedar Waxwings with orange tail tips, and in reddish Baltimore Orioles (see Hudon and Brush 1989–COLOR).

ESCAPES. See CAPTIVITY, BIRDS IN, Escapes. See also EXOTIC SPECIES; VERIFICATION OF RECORDS.

ESTUARY. The region within the tidal zone at the mouth of a river where salt and fresh water meet. Saline water tends to sink below fresh water, forming a salt wedge that runs up the bottom water layer of an estuary for some distance. However, tides and topography effect mixing close to a river's mouth, and fresh water dilutes the surface salinity of the adjacent ocean. Estuaries are physiologically stressful, but also nutrient rich, so that species, such as anadromous fish and many invertebrates with wide salinity tolerances, can become abundant within them. Such places are therefore enormously rich feeding areas for waterbirds, especially herons, certain ducks, shorebirds, gulls, and terns. Estuarine areas also give rise to unique habitats, e.g., salt marsh and mangrove swamp, defined by plant species that have evolved to thrive in the tidal zone where fresh and salt water meet. See also MANGROVE; SALT MARSH.

ETHOLOGY (ee-THOLL-uh-jee). The study of behavior in an adaptive context, i.e., examining behavior as a genetically induced adaptation that can be dissected through observation and experimental analysis. This can be distinguished from *behavioral ecology*, which looks at the behavior of a bird or other organism as a tuned response to environmental conditions within the context of its natural environment. In his definitive essay on ethology (1969), Niko Tinbergen quotes Julian Huxley's nomination of Konrad Lorenz as "the father of modern ethology." Some of the most significant ethological studies of Lorenz and Tinbergen were based on bird species, Greylag Geese and gulls, respectively.

ETIQUETTE FOR BIRDWATCHERS. It is always surprising to find birdwatchers and other naturalists abusing the very resources from which they derive pleasure, but it happens. There have been all too many nest desertions by rare birds that are directly and unequivocally attributable to harassment by birders either directly or by the use of tapes that drive off territorial males (see RECORDING OF BIRD SOUNDS). It probably must be taken for granted that there will be a few yahoos in any interest group, and the slob birders are doubtless best checked by the responsible majority of the birding community in combination with diligent wardening of rare bird localities.

A knottier problem has arisen with the vastly increased popularity of bird listing. These days, property owners must think twice before alerting the public about a rarity on their land, lest they find their privacy invaded and their acreage trashed by battalions of birders laying siege for as long as the avian celebrity remains on the premises. In many such cases, damage and inconvenience are less the result of individual callousness than simply by-products of large numbers of people in a limited space. Birders have always had to endure being thought a little odd. Far worse would be to gain a reputation as destructive. This would not only reduce access to

good birding areas, but perhaps more importantly, give credibility to anti-environmentalist sentiments.

A "Country Code" of conduct for outdoor recreation is a time-honored tradition in Britain. One always has the feeling that those who most need such standards either never become aware of them or choose to ignore them. However, there needs to be a standard, and the following *Code of Birding Ethics,* refined over the last 20 years or so by the American Birding Association and published in all its bird finding guides, is reprinted below, with permission of ABA.

RESPECT WILDLIFE, ITS ENVIRONMENT, AND THE RIGHTS OF OTHERS.

Promote the welfare of birds and their environment.
> Support the protection of important bird habitat.
> Avoid stressing birds or exposing then to danger.
> Limit methods of attracting birds.
> Remain well back from nests, roosts, display areas, and feeding sites.
> Keep habitat disturbance to a minimum.

Respect the law and the rights of others.

Ensure that feeders, nest structures, and other artificial bird environments are safe.
> Maintain and clean feeders and nest structures regularly.
> Keep birds safe from predation from cats and other domestic animals.

Group birding, whether organized or impromptu, requires special care.
> Respect fellow birders. Share your knowledge, especially with beginners.
> Document unethical birding behavior, intervene if prudent, and notify appropriate individuals or organizations.
> Leaders should teach ethics by word and example.
> Limit group impact on birds and their environment and on others using the same areas.

To supplement these guidelines here are a few more specific suggestions gleaned from codes published by conservation organizations in Britain and elsewhere.

1. Ask permission before entering private property and abide by what you are told. If part of a large group looking for a rarity on someone's land, be an active part of the group's conscience about impact on the land and the owner's privacy.
2. Leave gates, chains, etc., as you found them.
3. Keep to paths, especially on active croplands.
4. Don't disturb livestock.
5. Leave no litter.

6. Respect other life-forms:
   - Don't flush birds unnecessarily.
   - Don't approach active nests too closely.
   - Don't use tapes to excess when disturbance of breeding birds is in question.
   - Don't pursue your bird at the expense of other organisms, e.g., plants underfoot.
7. Respect other birdwatchers and naturalists:
   - Keep talk to a minimum or at least at low volume—a particularly tough one for American birders. If you are obliged to lead a group, keep your lectures brief and dulcet while you are in the field.
   - Don't flush birds for a photo or a better look when others are present.
   - Don't assume that all birders benefit from the sounds issuing from your tape recorder; many prefer to pursue their quarry without resorting to mechanical trickery; naturalists and hikers trying to capture a semblance of wilderness are likely to be even less sympathetic to taped bird calls.
   - Don't slam car doors.
   - Leave your dog at home.

EURASIA. Europe and Asia combined. Though we sometimes speak of the "continents" of Europe and Asia, the boundaries between the two are more ethnic and political than physiographical. Therefore, many species of animals are common to both and may be said, for example, to have a Eurasian breeding distribution.

The term also provides one solution to the problem of synonymy in vernacular names. Thus, the American Woodcock, *Scolopax minor,* is distinguished in the vernacular from its near relative the *Eurasian* Woodcock, *S. rusticola,* which in European field guides in English sometimes still appears simply as Woodcock.

EVERGLADES National Park. See FLORIDA.

EVOLUTION. In biology, the process by which organisms change through time by alteration of the patterns of their cumulative inherited (genetic) traits through mutation, often in response to environmental pressures. That all species, including ourselves, are descended from other life-forms and have a common ancestor in the first simple organism to appear on earth is inherent in the concept of evolution. The evolutionary scenario suggested by Charles Darwin in his *On the Origin of Species by Means of Natural Selection* (London, 1859; many current reprints) depicts gradual, continual change taking place in minute, increments over tens of millions of years, but some evolutionary biologists believe that organisms

are more likely to change in relatively rapid (i.e., *two* million years) bursts of adaptation followed by long periods during which they change little if at all. The latter theory, known as "punctuated equilibrium," was propounded by Stephen Jay Gould and Niles Eldridge.

Evolutionary theory has been from its inception and continues to be at odds with the theological notion of special creation, wherein all species are believed to be unrelated and immutable works of a deity.

For a highly readable recent overview of this fascinating and complex subject see Ernst Mayr's *What Evolution Is* (2002).

For examples of evolutionary theory relating to birdlife see the following entry; see also SPECIATION; NATURAL SELECTION.

EVOLUTION OF BIRDLIFE. Even a cursory inspection of our planet's present day birdlife reveals an astonishing diversity of avian forms: albatrosses and penguins, condors and ibises, kingfishers and nightjars, dippers and hummingbirds—roughly 9,700 species, each highly adapted to a specialized role in the earthly ecosystem. It is even more of a wonder then that this represents at most a tenth of the bird species that have soared, waded, and flitted though habitats that no human eyes ever saw and that entire ancient avifaunas arose and disappeared before our species emerged from apedom a mere 6 million years ago. We owe our ever-increasing knowledge of these previous worlds (1) to the lucky natural accident that extinct animal forms are preserved in stone and asphalt; (2) to the ingenuity of the scientists who have figured out how to date rocks accurately and even tell time using molecular clocks; and (3) to Mr. Darwin and others who showed us how these fossils could be related to each other.

Doubtless many more insights about prehistoric birdlife lie buried than we have yet unearthed. Yet the fragments that we have managed to discover and fit into their places in the evolutionary puzzle have proven sufficiently fascinating, including some remarkable discoveries within the last decade. This entry can do no more that sketch the contours of early birdlife and its origins. Fortunately, excellent comprehensive texts on the subject (see especially Feduccia 1999) are now readily available.

READING THE ROCKS

Perspective. Since our only physical evidence of prehistoric birdlife is fossilized remains, we should remember that this source of data does not present anything like a thorough and balanced overview of the past. For one thing, there isn't very much of it. Then, as now, the fragile bird skeletons that evolved as concomitants to flight were pulverized in predators' digestive tracts or scattered and broken by scavengers and moving water far more often than they fell intact into preservative sediment or tar pits. Furthermore, fossils tend to present a habitat bias. Lake-bed sediments, after all, can be expected to contain a certain number of fossilized lake birds, but not to yield many clues as to what kinds of birds inhabited the lakeside forests. Finally, it should be noted that paleo-ornithologists are

themselves *rarae aves*, with the result that old bird bones have been looked for and studied less than either modern birds or extinct lizards. However exciting new fossils are to our imaginations, we must keep in mind that our present picture of prehistory is like an obliterated fresco in which we have managed to replace a few randomly unearthed fragments.

Sites. North America boasts some of the world's most productive known fossil repositories. During the Cretaceous Period, 50% of the continent was submerged below sea level, so that much of the surface rock of what is now the western United States is limestone formed by the accumulation of the calcareous skeletons of hard-shelled protozoans called foraminifera. The Niobrara chalk beds, a part of this inland ocean floor in western Kansas, yielded admirably whole skeletons of the famous Cretaceous toothed birds (see below) late in the nineteenth century. The Lower Eocene Green River and Willwood formations in Wyoming are one of the principal sources of early Tertiary fossils of modern bird forms.

Another exemplary fossil boneyard is the great asphalt deposit or tar pits at the 23-acre Rancho La Brea (= tar in Spanish) near Los Angeles, which was first excavated in 1906–13. Along with mastodons, saber-toothed cats (*Smilodon*), and other Pleistocene mammals, 400,000 bird fossils comprising at least 135 species, including the great vulture-like *TERATORNIS,* have been recovered from this mire. California is also rich in sedimentary fossil beds, and other sites important to ornithology have been excavated in Oregon (especially Fossil Lake), New Mexico, Texas, Florida, and New Jersey.

THE ANCESTRY OF BIRDS. That birds evolved from reptiles has not been disputed by science since the time of Darwin; birds and reptiles share many traits (see list, below) and their relationship is literally embodied in the famous "lizard bird," *Archaeopteryx* (see below). But this is where the really interesting questions begin rather than end. For example, what is a "reptile"? As systematists have refined phylogenetic relationships recently, they no longer posit a single reptile class alongside similar discrete classes for birds and mammals. A modern family tree of vertebrates shows the main trunk emerging from Paleozoic forms called "base reptiles." From here spring separate branches in sequence for mammals (through therapsid reptiles), for turtles, for snakes and lizards, and for birds (via thecodonts and dinosaurs), with crocodiles emerging from the same thecodont limb as birds. In other words, birds are more closely related to crocodiles than either is to turtles.

The big question about the descent of birds concerns their *immediate* ancestors. The current (2002) consensus among scientists holds that based on a cladistic analysis of similar traits, birds evolved directly from theropod dinosaurs, which include not only the fearsome *Tyrannosaurus,* but more pertinently, the small, agile, fast-running predators, such as *Velociraptor.* The fact that theropods and *Archaeopteryx* fossils share the same geological strata seems to support this view. However, Alan Feduccia

(1999) and others argue credibly that the apparent similarities between early birds and the theropods are either nonexistent when examined closely (e.g., the perceived similarity in bird and theropod 3-digit "hands") or result from convergent evolution. This camp holds that birds sprang directly from thecodont reptiles lower on the crocodile branch of the vertebrate tree and cite many "pre-avian" traits in support of this theory. Why, then, the theropodists ask, is there no lizard-bird in the fossil record for another 90 million years? It is a classic scientific debate replete with both brilliant argument and personal insults, which will probably be resolved only with the discovery of new fossils.

Reptile Characteristics Shared by Birds
- The presence of a *single occipital condyle,* an oval bone process that connects the base of the skull to the first cervical vertebra; mammals, including humans, have two occipital condyles.
- The presence of a *single* small bone, the *columella or stapes,* in the middle ear (tympanum); humans have 3.
- An *ambiens muscle* attached to the pelvis, its tendon facilitating grasping or perching with the toes.
- *Ankles located in the tarsal bones,* not between tibia and tarsi as in mammals.
- *Uncinate processes* uniting the rib cage (see SKELETON and Fig. 27) found only in birds and extinct or primitive reptiles.
- The presence of *5–6 bones in the lower jaw* (mandible); mammals have a single mandible bone.
- Eggs with large *yolks* and an *egg tooth* on the bills of embryos.

Of course, modern birds have evolved away from many reptilian features such as toothed jaws and long bony tails; they have established characters unique to their class, especially feathers; and they possess some features, such as warm-bloodedness and a four-chambered heart, that are associated with "higher" animals, i.e., mammals, and are lacking in reptiles.

EVOLUTION OF FEATHERS AND FLIGHT. The close relationships between reptilian scales and feathers and between modern bird feathers and flight are undisputed. The scales of some of the fossil thecodonts seem to bear the pattern of a feather impressed on their surface, and the processes of scale and feather formation are very similar in modern reptiles and birds (see FEATHER, Formation). Likewise, the adaptive elegance with which feathers suit flight in present-day birds seems obvious, though it is equally clear that feathers also serve other functions. However, reconstructing the step-by-step transition from scale to feather and earthbound to airborne remains an even more speculative—and controversial—undertaking than exploring the roots of the avian family tree.

If you think of the typical reptilian scale, a basic body-armoring device, it isn't difficult to imagine potential evolutionary improvements: If

the scale is split at angles along the midrib, it becomes more flexible; if it is frayed, it could provide more insulation and therefore the ability to be active in extremes of heat and cold; if the structure becomes thinner and more open, weight is reduced and agility increased; if limb, tail, or back scales are elongated, they can improve balance and maneuverability and permit parachuting or gliding; and all of the preceding modifications could also function as mechanism for display, making sounds or other

Fig. 12. *Evolution of flight.* Did avian flight develop from the ground up as fast-running theropod dinosaurs such as the 7-foot tall *Struthiomimus* (1) leaped into the air to catch prey? Or did it evolve from the trees down as the remarkable gliding apparatus of the 2-inch *Longisquamma* (2) or other, earlier thecodont reptiles gradually morphed into feathers. The quintessential reptile bird *Archyopteryx* (3) has been used to defend both theories. For more on this debate see EVOLUTION OF BIRDLIFE.

secondary uses. All of these are, of course, speculative mutations that would have conferred selective advantages on scaly animals on their way to being feathered ones. But was flight the irresistible advantage that turned scales into feathers or, as herpetologists tend to think, were feathers initially a more sophisticated means of controlling body temperature that later came in handy as reptiles began taking to the air?

The debate about the origins of powered avian flight breaks out pretty much along thecodont/theropod lines into "trees-down" and "ground-up" camps. The thecodonts took many forms, and we know from fossils that some were small, light, arboreal species with greatly elongated scales; some also gave rise eventually to flying reptiles such as *Pteranodon*. These might have begun their evolution toward flight with just enough extra scale extension to slow a nervy leap from one tree to another, called "parachuting." The next stage for an "avimorph thecodont" would have been the development of a broader airfoil giving the ability to glide some distance after launching from a perch and to control the quality of the ride. The 2-inch-long *Longisquama* ("long-scale") is the only reptile known so far to have scales that may be intermediate with feathers; it had a remarkable double fan of scales extending from its back that it could apparently unfold like a butterfly's wings and glide—though not flap—around the Triassic forests.

The so-called "cursorial" or ground-up theory evokes the image of the nimble theropod racing around the desert on its hind legs catching whatever it can grab with its forelegs. Elongation and fraying of these forelimbs would have nothing to do with flight initially, but would simply allow higher leaps after prey with better control and/or also the ability to catch more prey with greater ease using the wing-like arms (Ostrum's "insect net theory" [1974]). As the wings and tail broadened, leaps could become glides, followed eventually by powered (flapping) flight. One thecodontian objection to this scenario is that the fossil theropods that we know of so far do not show any tendency toward the elongation of the forelimbs and shifting of weight forward that are required by aerodynamic principles to get a running dinosaur into the air.

So perfectly does *Archaeopteryx* embody the emergence of a reptile into birddom, that it is claimed as evidence by both sides in the origins-of-feathered-flight controversy. Tree-downers say its ancestors were arboreal reptiles that evolved feathered wings and tails as gliding devices; they cite its pronounced backward pointing toe (hallux) as proof of its tree-perching proclivity. Ground-uppers argue that it supplies the necessary link between the running, leaping, bug-catching theropods and the birds they became and that it climbed into the trees from its original terrestrial habitat.

The detailed arguments evinced in the debates summarized above make for more than a century's worth of fascinating reading. See especially Marsh (1880), Osborn (1900), Nopsca (1923), Ostrum (1974), Chatterjee (1997), and Feduccia (1999).

THE FOSSIL RECORD. The following overview attempts to sketch the broad shape of the fossil record to date and includes brief descriptions of those extinct bird species whose skeletons have excited the most wonder. (For an excellent series of photos and artistic reconstructions of many of the birds mentioned here, see Feduccia [1999]).

Archaeopteryx and Its Rivals. Though many significant discoveries have been made in recent years, it is probably still fair to say that the most important bird fossil that has yet been found is that of *Archaeopteryx lithographica,* seven specimens of which, including complete skeletons, have been liberated from late (Upper) Jurassic limestone sediments in Bavaria, the first of them in 1861. In addition to being the first-known feathered animal, the significance of *Archaeopteryx* lies in the fact that its skeleton is more that of a reptile than a modern bird. It has, in fact, been described by more than one authority as a small (crow-sized) dinosaur. And while it now resides officially in an Infraclass (or Subclass) of its own, Archaeornithes ("ancient birds"), it is described by many authorities as a feathered reptile. Coming as it did just two years after the publication of Darwin's *On the Origin of Species by Means of Natural Selection* (1859), this "missing link" was celebrated not just as the earliest known bird, but for many as conclusive proof of the validity of Darwin's theory. For here was an organism clearly in transition between two well-defined groups of animals, reptiles and birds.

The *Archaeopteryx* fossils are dated at 135–155 million years before the present, in the middle of the Mesozoic era, the so-called Age of Reptiles. Its habitat appears to have been a dry tropical shore with highly saline lagoons not unlike the present day coast of northeastern Venezuela (Feduccia 1999). The vegetation was probably dominated by cycads, including palm-like tree species, and the air was apparently filled with several species of flying reptiles (pterosaurs). Regardless of whether *Archaeopteryx* was descended from arboreal or terrestrial ancestors, authorities generally agree that it lived in trees and possibly behaved rather like modern guans, walking along branches, and gliding from tree to tree; the structure of its skeleton and feathers suggest that it may have been capable of some degree of powered flight. It also bore long claws at the bend of the wing, which it presumably used for crawling around the tropical canopies.

The fame and detail of the *Archaeopteryx* fossils make them, as it were, the mark to beat among paleontologists in search of a new "ur-bird." In 1978 "Dinosaur Jim" Jensen of Brigham Young University unearthed fossil bones in a Colorado quarry that were contemporaneous with and, he claimed, more bird-like than *Archaeopteryx.* However, the main evidence for the avian character the species he named *Paleopteryx thomsoni* was a femur that his colleagues were not convinced could be distinguished from that of a a nonavian reptile.

The most sensational of recent bird fossil discoveries is Sankar Chatterjee's *Protoavis texensis* found in 1986 in the Dockum Formation of west

Texas, which dates from the late Triassic. If truly a bird, this species would set the dawn of birdlife back 75 million years and demolish the current orthodoxy that birds are descended from theropod dinosaurs. Though *Protoavis* ("first bird") has no feathers, Chatterjee points to knobs to which he believes quill feathers were attached and he describes a number of other bird-like traits. Because of both the nature of the evidence and issues of scholarly protocol, the announcement of Protoavis ignited a heated exchange of scientific views, but there is as yet no consensus on the true identity of this intriguing find.

Perhaps the most credible rival to *Archaeopteryx* is the wonderfully named *Confusiusornis sanctus* described in 1995 among many other bird fossils from lake bed sediments in northern and eastern China by Hou Lian-Hai and Zhou Zhonge of the Academia Sinica in Beijing. Plausibly dated as contemporaneous with *Archaeopteryx* in the late Jurassic, *Confusiusornis* combines many of the former's primitive traits with more modern features. It is toothless and one of its fossils shows evidence of a feathered body.

Cretaceous Birds. Leaving the Jurassic we enter a period of geological time during which life on earth and indeed the surface of the earth itself underwent a sequence of remarkable changes. During the 80 million years of the Cretaceous Period from 146 to 65 million years before the present, existing continental land masses moved apart significantly—a major influence on species distribution; flowering plants appeared and broadleaved forests gained dominance as early conifers declined; the great dinosaurs flourished worldwide and then declined and marsupial and early placental mammals evolved. At the end of the Cretaceous a meteorite (or perhaps several meteorites) smashing into the earth at 50,000 miles per hour and/or a series of volcanic eruptions created a global cataclysm involving fires and tidal waves and an encompassing cloud of dust that either cooled the planet by blocking the sun's rays or warmed it by creating a greenhouse effect. The result was a period of mass extinctions during which the dinosaurs and many other species that prospered during the Cretaceous disappeared altogether from the earth's biota. The event or series of events that changed the world is detectable in the geological strata as a thin line of dust that settled out of the atmosphere as it cleared. Known as the K-T boundary, it marks the border between the Cretaceous Period and the Tertiary Period that followed and also an invisible wall in time between two biologically different worlds.

THE OPPOSITE BIRDS.

Undoubtedly the greatest breakthrough in the study of early bird evolution since *Archaeopteryx* has been the recent and rapid discovery and description of a whole fauna of landbirds that emerged, diversified to become the dominant land birds of their time, and then went extinct within the 80 million years of the Cretaceous Period. These are the so-called "opposite birds," named for the fact that their leg bones are fused in the op-

posite direction from those of modern birds. They combine anatomical characters found in *Archaeopteryx*—such as the structure of the pelvic girdle and hind legs—with traits typical of more recent forms, such as features of the pectoral girdle and wings that favor powered flight. Far from being an isolated discovery represented by a few bones, the opposite bird remains including complete skeletons have been unearthed worldwide and belong to a wide range of types, including predators, shore inhabitants, and arboreal perchers and climbers. The following are some of the stars of this "new" avifauna.

Enantiornis leali, one of many bird fossils found in northwestern Argentina in 1975 and the first to be described as part of a new suborder (Enantiornithes) erected to define the opposite birds.

Alexornis antecedens a small landbird described from Baja California in 1976, before the opposite birds had been conceptualized as a group.

Gobipteryx. Described in 1974 by a Polish paleontologist from excavations in Mongolia and initially believed to be related to the ostriches. Among the remains were fossil eggs that showed the young of this species to be well-developed (precocial) at hatching; unusual among Mesozoic birds for its lack of teeth.

Avisaurus species. Originally described as members of a new family of small theropod dinosaurs (the Avisauridae), examples of which have been found in Montana, Utah, and Argentina.

Iberomesornis romerali. Less than 4 inches long, this species has feet strongly adapted for perching; it is one of a number of opposite birds recently described from sites in Spain.

Sinornis santensis. The best known of at least 20 birds found in northern and eastern China in the 1990s. A small bird with claws resembling those of modern nuthatches, this species was described from an unusually complete, articulated fossil skeleton found by a farmer in lakebed sediments in northeastern China. It dates from the early Cretaceous and is a mere 10–15 million years younger than *Archaeopteryx.*

Not surprisingly, the revelation of a diverse, wide-ranging, and previously unknown assortment of closely related bird species prompted some revisions in the prevailing classification. Not long ago the Class Aves (birds) was divided into only two subclasses, the Archaeornithes, with its single genus, *Archaeopteryx,* and the Neornithes, which encompassed all modern birds, including the extinct orders of the Cretaceous. Martin (1983) suggested a revision in which many of the unique fossils described above have been placed in their own orders under a new Infraclass of opposite birds. For a general sense of how the major groups of extinct birds are related to each other in time and a sense of where some of the most significant fossils have been unearthed, see the table in Appendix III.

EARLY MODERN BIRDS.

Before the opposite birds stole the show, the main focus of Cretaceous birdlife was two groups of toothed seabirds represented most

prominently by loon-like species in the genus *Hesperornis* ("western bird") and other genera and the tern-like members of the genus *Ichthyornis* ("fish bird"). Both types appear to have ranged worldwide or nearly so and to have evolved into a variety of species. The Hesperornids of which 13 species are known were large (up to 5 feet long), heavy-bodied diving birds with only vestigial wings and large swimming feet located at the extreme stern end as in present day loons and grebes; they had lobed toes not unlike those of modern coots and phalaropes; closely related species in the genus Baptornis ("dunking bird") were similar. We know from coprolites (fossil feces) found with some Baptornis remains that these birds were fish eaters.

Judging from skeletal features, *Ichthyornis*—and the similar *Apatornis*—were strong-flying predacious species that foraged over the great inland seas of North America and beyond during the late Cretaceous. *Ambiortus dementjevi* recovered from Mongolian lakebed sediments is very similar anatomically to *Icthyornis* and *Apatornis,* but was a land bird and, dated in the early Cretaceous, is presently the oldest known Ornithurine (modern) bird. *Gansus yumenensis* from China, also a modern-type bird from the early Cretaceous, is judged on the basis of an incomplete left leg fossil to have been shorebird-like, though possibly with a toothed bill.

There are four things to remember about these birds: (1) They are structurally much closer to modern birds than to *Archaeopteryx* or the opposite birds; (2) despite this they do retain one distinctly reptilian feature, rooted teeth set in sockets; (3) though "modern" and "loon-like" (or "tern-like"), they are not phylogenetically related to the loons and terns that evolved in the Tertiary; and (4) they were diverse, very common and widespread during much of the Cretaceous, declined gradually toward the end of the period (because the inland seas were shrinking?) and then disappeared completely along with the dinosaurs in the K-T extinction.

THE TRANSITIONAL SHOREBIRDS.

Since no toothed birds, opposite birds, or early modern (ornithurine) birds are known to have survived the Cretaceous extinctions and since no representative of a modern family is known for certain from the Cretaceous, we have a problem: Where did the hugely diverse tertiary avifauna come from? What was the genetic base on which it was built? One way to answer this is simply to say we don't know yet and encourage the paleornithologists to keep digging. Using the DNA of recent birds as a "molecular clock" Cooper and Penny (1997) have concluded that more than 20 orders that evolved much earlier in the Cretaceous than any fossil evidence confirms made it across the K-T boundary. While these findings have been disputed on a number of grounds, it is certainly possible that the discovery of more fossils will change our mind about extinction and survival at the end of the Cretaceous. For now the main working hypothesis for this conundrum involves a few known fossil species that *may* have

slipped through the K-T barrier. Among these "transitional shorebirds" are species once identified with modern loons, tubenoses, cormorants, flamingoes, rails, and sandpipers, but now thought to belong in the Charadriiformes, the order containing modern sandpipers, gulls, and related forms. Unfortunately, these fossils are either extremely fragmentary or uncertainly dated or both, and no authority is comfortable making such an important call until there is better evidence. An intriguing argument put forth in favor of the shorebird hypothesis is that these birds might have been comparatively well adapted to survive the effects of the K-T catastrophe (Janzen 1995). If the earth passed through a period when photosynthesis was impaired because sunlight was occluded, many plant-dependent species and their predators would have rapidly perished, while species like sandpipers and sandgrouse that can make do with seeds and invertebrate eggs, would have been better able to squeak through.

The Tertiary "Explosion." If the Cretaceous can be said to have ended with a bang, the early Tertiary had a certain explosive quality as well, albeit of a different kind. We tend to think of evolution as an almost painfully gradual process with small incremental changes taking place over millions of years. But the fossil record shows that at least in some instances an evolutionary "opportunity" allows certain groups of organisms to diversify rapidly (by geological standards) to fill newly available ecological niches. The dawn that eventually came following the long night of the K-T transition revealed a world with many fewer species, waiting, as it were, to be reinhabited by new assemblages of animal life. The gap left by the dinosaurs made room for the rise of some intimidating giant birds (see below) and, eventually, a new fauna of large mammals. And whatever smaller "transitional" birds made it into the Tertiary had the place to themselves and underwent what is invariably referred to in the literature as an *explosive radiation* that "invented" the modern avifauna in only a few million years. By the Eocene Epoch just 10 million years into the new period all modern orders of birds except the perching birds (passerines) had evolved—and left sample skeletons to prove it. The passerines which were still nowhere to be seen in the Oligocene 30–40 million years into the Tertiary, experienced their own dynamic radiation in the Miocene, resulting in the advent of more than 50% of the modern avifauna. Almost as fascinating as this Tertiary burst of evolutionary creativity is the fact that once the modern genera of birds had emerged, the expansion all but stopped, nature confining herself to fine tuning at the species level up to the present day. Time-traveling birdwatchers finding themselves 10 million years back in the Miocene would recognize the great majority of genera they encountered, though a lot of the species might be puzzling. (Birders should note that when this option becomes available the destination to book is the Pliocene just 5 million years or so back when the earth's birdlife probably reached its greatest diversity, perhaps with as many as 150,000 potential "ticks."

AVIAN GIANTS.

Among the most impressive birds that ever lived were the species of *Diatryma*, the largest of which reached nearly 7 feet in height and weighed close to 400 pounds. The remains of these and similar flightless giants have been found in Paleocene and early Eocene deposits in New Mexico, Colorado, Wyoming, New Jersey, and the Canadian high Arctic as well as Europe and may be relatives of cranes or geese. Because of their massive bills and powerful build the prevailing view has been that *Diatrymas* were ferocious predators that ran down their prey in open country. However, a recent alternate theory (Andors 1991) suggests that the great bill was a cropping device and that the great birds wandered flood plain shrublands eating bushes. The similar but more agile phorusrhacids of South America are still believed to have been swift running predators. These feathered monsters went extinct along with much of the rest of the South American fauna when the Panamanian land bridge permitted the southward invasion of North American mammalian predators. Before this happened, however, a 10-foot-tall phorusrhacids, *Titanis walleri*, found its way north to Florida, where it probably fed on prey up to the size of small deer.

Another gigantic avian relic from this period is a seabird from California with a wingspan as great as 16 feet (modern-day Wandering and Royal Albatrosses have a maximum documented wingspan of between 11 and 12 feet, the greatest of any *living* bird species); of more interest to ornithologists are the tooth-like structures that arise out of the jawbones, giving the species its Latin name, *Osteodontornis*. ("bonetooth bird"). A smaller but hardly less interesting species of which we have a clear image is *Neocathartes*, a long-legged vulture and another gift of Eocene rock from Wyoming. Though it was capable of flight, its proportions indicate that it probably foraged largely on foot with intermittent short glides.

Of Ice and Men. In the Quaternary Period (from the beginning of the Pleistocene epoch to the present), the gradual cooling of the earth's climate begun in the Tertiary culminated in a series of glacial advances and retreats across the Northern Hemisphere. The advent of a bipolar, strongly seasonal climate subject to periodic "ice ages" had a pervasive influence on the distribution of the earth's biota, including its birdlife. Among other effects it created zones of extreme heat and cold, and dryness and wetness that in many cases acted as ecological isolating mechanisms promoting speciation. As glaciers advanced they pushed tropical habitats and their resident species toward the equator, marooned species on mountaintops and were probably a major factor in the evolution of migratory patterns. While it is reasonable to suspect that these inexorable ice sheets hastened the doom of the many bird species that vanished during the Pleistocene, one of the glaciers' most significant impacts on Pleistocene life-forms may have been an indirect one. During the periods of maximum glaciation, much of the planet's water turned to ice, resulting in a drop in sea level

amounting to hundreds of feet. This created land bridges spanning continents that had formerly been isolated from each other. About 14,000 years
ago human beings walked from what is now Siberia across the Bering land
bridge and into the New World for the first time. It took us only 2,000 years
more to reach the tip of South America. We arrived on a continent populated by the so-called Pleistocene megafauna, vast numbers of elephants,
horses, and other herbivores, many predators, such as the saber-toothed
cat (*Smilodon*) and the dire wolf (*Canus dirus*), and a large community of
scavengers. Among the last were the great vulturine teratorns, including
the North American *Teratornis incredibilis*, which had a 17- to 19-foot
wingspan and weighed over 40 pounds; its cousin from Argentina, *Argen-
tavis magnificens*, weighing nearly 160 pounds with a wingspan of up to 25
feet, was the largest flying bird we know of. Another—relatively puny—
scavenger that prospered during the Pleistocene was the California Condor. Some students of the Pleistocene megafauna and its demise, have
recently argued persuasively that the collapse of this ecological community not long after the arrival of people in its midst may not be simply co-
incidental. Alas, this would be consistent with the fate of large animals and
especially large birds—elephant birds, moas, dodos, Great Auks—that
quickly follows their first meeting with our species.

No new species of birds are thought to have evolved since the end of
the Pleistocene and since about 80 have become extinct within the last
300 years, the decline of bird diversity begun around the time of the last
glacial interval continues—largely under human auspices.

EXANTHROPIC (EX-an-THRO-pik). Preferring to live apart from humanity. We can all think of species that we consider especially "wild" (e.g.,
many raptors) or "reclusive" (e.g., rails), but it is doubtful whether such
species are avoiding man so much as they are adhering to inherent habitat requirements (e.g., extensive forest tracts, dense marshlands) where a
human presence is by definition excluded. Therefore, this is not the opposite of *eusyanthropic* in which birds or other organisms seek the "company" of people because we provide them with optimal living conditions
(e.g., Peregrines nesting on city skyscrapers). Furthermore, many putative
exanthropic species (e.g., Pileated Woodpecker, Cooper's Hawk) have
proven not be be particularly "shy," and have come to reside quite happily
in our suburbs, provided their basic requiremenst are met.

EXCREMENT. In birds, urine and feces are voided together through a single anal opening, or vent. Bird droppings, therefore, usually consist of
solid, dark wastes (feces) in a white, chalky, semisolid material (urine in
the form of uric acid). The excreta of the nestlings of many passerine birds
are enclosed in a gelatinous membrane or fecal sac for easy disposal by
the parents.

The excrement of certain seabirds is commercially exploited (see GUANO); where bird droppings collect in enclosed spaces, they may present a health hazard (see DISEASE).

The presence of certain groups of birds, e.g., grouse and geese, may be reliably confirmed by the unique forms of their droppings.

EXCRETORY SYSTEM. Excretion of solid waste in the form of feces is the final stage of the digestive process, for which see DIGESTIVE SYSTEM. The processing of birds' blood-borne wastes in the form of urine, on the other hand, has evolved as with us in conjunction with the reproductive system, and the two functions are often discussed together as the urogenital system. Unlike mammals, however, birds have only a single opening, the cloacal vent, through which pass both solid and liquid wastes, as well as the products of the reproductive system.

A bird's urinary system consists of a pair of kidneys each connected by a narrow tube or ureter to the cloaca. The kidneys lie protected within the pelvic region close to the backbone; birds have no urinary bladder.

Urinary systems, in general, remove excess water, salts, and nitrogen wastes from the body. But birds reabsorb almost all of the water in the kidneys and ureters, leaving a white, nearly solid substance very different in appearance and chemical composition from human urine. This is voided, together with the feces, through the vent.

For another method of salt excretion, see SALT GLAND.

EXOTIC SPECIES (exotics). A term used to describe birds or other organisms that are not native to a given geographical locality or ecosystem. It almost invariably implies human agency, either through accident or design. For example, a Fork-tailed Flycatcher straying to Maine may be "exotic," but in birding/ornithological jargon, it would be described as a "vagrant" or an "accidental straggler" rather than as an exotic. For such species with a claim to inclusion on the North American checklist, see Appendix II.

Other discriminations need to be made with regard to exotics. An *invasive* exotic is a species that proliferates abundantly in its new home and cause some form of ecological damage. It is one of the most critical issues facing conservationists and wildlife managers today. Avian examples would be European Starling and House Sparrows, both exotics and both cavity nesters that compete with native species, such as Eastern Bluebirds, to the detriment of that species. Mute Swans, though beloved by most people, have been shown to damage aquatic habitat to the disadvantage of native waterfowl. Native birds may also be adversely affected by invasive plant species such as *Phragmites,* which in North America often replaces native marsh plants and renders the habitat much less useful to indigenous marsh birds. It is important to note that it is not the "foreignness" of invasive species that is objectionable, but rather their negative ef-

fect of reducing native biodiversity. Fortunately, invasive exotics tend to be be far less common than noninvasive ones; Ring-necked Pheasant and many of our commonest grasses and field wildflowers in eastern North America would be examples of the latter.

A *naturalized* species is one that has successfully adapted to a habitat in a place outside its normal range, e.g., Spot-breasted Oriole, a native of Mexico and Central America, has reproduced successfully in southeastern Florida for about 40 years (without apparent harm to the native ecosystem). A term used more frequently in ornithological parlance is *established,* which simply means that the species in question is maintaining a stable breeding population. This can, of course, be true of both invasive and noninvasive species, but excludes exotics such as Cockatiels, which escape frequently but have never established breeding population in the wild. Species do not need to be from other continents in order to be exotic, naturalized, established, and invasive. The resident Canada Geese that have become a pest species in northeastern North America derive mainly from a race of this species native to the Midwest. These birds were originally kept in captivity and used by hunters as live decoys until that practice was outlawed, following which the birds were released and became established where no Canada Geese had previously nested or wintered.

A few species, e.g.,the Red-crowned Parrot of northeastern Mexico, may have occurred here both as exotics and as vagrants.

Some of the better-known and most successful North American exotics—many living in the warm climate and cage-bird paradise of southern Florida and most having nested at least once—are listed with annotation in Appendix V. Many are illustrated in Sibley (2000–FIELD GUIDE). For other perspectives on nonnative species, see CAPTIVITY, BIRDS IN; INTRODUCED BIRDS; VAGRANT, VAGRANCY; VERIFICATION OF RECORDS.

EXTINCT BIRDS. It is probably a healthy exercise, when considering the extinction of species in this age, to remember that many thousands of life forms have ceased to exist from wholly natural causes—dinosaurs spring inevitably to mind—and, further, that some organisms—especially ancient forms, which, as it were, are "past their prime"—will pass into oblivion both without human assistance and in spite of it. At the same time it should be noted that we are presently witnessing extinction of species on an unprecedented scale due to the rapid and widespread destruction of the planet's tropical rain forest (which contains about 50% of the species of living organisms) and other manifestations of the recent quantum leap in human technology and the consequent ability to alter the planet in fundamental ways. We should also not kid ourselves about the implications of such losses. Extinctions to date can be dismissed by the callous as marginal aesthetic deprivations, but if the extinction rate accelerates to the degree now predicted by many biologists, there can be no doubt that the potential for human food, medical, and other vital (economically

calculable) resources will be measurably diminished and the prospects for our own survival possibly made problematical (see Ehrlich and Ehrlich 1981; Wilson 1992; see also discussion under CONSERVATION.

That said, this entry will simply present the facts of recent bird extinctions in North America leaving the moral/ethical issues of human responsibility to be pondered by the reader.

More than 80 full species and over 50 subspecies of birds have ceased to exist on the planet since the beginning of the eighteenth century, the greatest proportion of them (about 35%) taking their final bow between 1850 and 1900. This is about 40 times the historical extinction rate predicted by the fossil record—and the pace of extinction is accelerating. BirdLife International estimates that 1,200 bird species now faced a real risk of extinction in the next 100 years and another 630 come close to qualifying for this grim category (www.birdlife.net). A significant proportion of the extinct and near-extinct were/are island forms, which evolved in the absence of human and other predators and therefore succumbed all too quickly when man arrived with his usual contingent of rats and domestic animals—not to mention clubs and guns. For example, the islands of Hawaii have lost 13 full species of endemic birds since 1825, as opposed to 5 to date in all of North America (7 if Ivory-billed Woodpecker and Eskimo Curlew are counted; see ENDANGERED BIRDS). While declines in mainland areas are masked by their greater diversity of species and higher bird populations, current surveys reveal shocking declines, especially in areas with high rates of endemism, especially forested habitats in the tropics. And the cause of the decline is always the same: habitat destruction by people.

A brief account of the 5 full species and 2 that have become extinct in North America in the historical period follows.

Labrador Duck *(Camptorhynchus labradorius). Former Range and Status:* Apparently ranged from the southern coast of Labrador, where it bred, as far south as Chesapeake Bay in winter. It was known to science for less than 100 years, so that its distribution is known only where it was hunted, and nothing at all was discovered of its breeding biology. Early accounts indicate that it was never abundant but was common enough so that "a fair number" made it to the New York market in the years from 1840 to 1860; it has also been stated that it was not uncommon along the coasts of New England and Long Island in winter. *Main Causes of Extinction:* Unknown. There is no doubt that it was shot for sport and meat, and there is also a suspicion that colonies may have been raided in the St. Lawrence for meat and eggs. However, the bird's rapid demise will probably never be accounted for completely. *Date(s) of Extinction:* The last verifiable specimen was taken in 1875, with a lost specimen reported as shot in 1878.

Great Auk *(Pinguinus impennis). Former Range and Status:* Bred in Norway, Iceland, southern Greenland, and down the east coast of North America at least as far as the St. Lawrence; wintered regularly to Cape Cod and was recorded as a straggler as far south as Florida. The species was

abundant within its normal range until the late eighteenth century. The largest North American colony, on the Funk Islands off the east coast of Newfoundland, was decimated between 1830 and 1841. *Main Causes of Extinction:* There is no ambiguity about the disappearance of the Great Auk. It was extirpated by white men for food and commercial gain. The species had long been traditional food on fishing and other vessels in Britain and Scandinavia. The adults and young were killed and salted down or kept alive on board as a source of fresh meat, and the eggs were also collected. Another widespread use of the birds was as bait. This kind of depredation alone was responsible for the extinction of the auk in the British Isles long before the discovery of the American colonies. But the inevitability of its doom was probably not settled until the late 1700s, when commercial hunters began to systematically devastate the colonies, not only for marketable game but for oil and feathers for mattress stuffing. These operations were carried out indiscriminately throughout the breeding season, and continued unabated well after the threat of extinction was obvious. The Great Auk was flightless, awkward on land, and unafraid of men and could be herded and clubbed with a minimum of inconvenience. *Date(s) of Extinction:* The last record of the species is from Iceland in 1844; the last North American record is from the Funks in 1841.

Passenger Pigeon *(Ectopistes migratorius). Former Range and Status:* Bred throughout the northern forests from Manitoba to Nova Scotia, south to Kansas and West Virginia; wintered from Arkansas and North Carolina south to central Texas and northern Florida. Its abundance is legendary, numerous reliable sources reporting migrating flocks in excess of one or even two billion birds and nesting colonies miles in extent with a hundred or more nests to a single tree. *Main Causes of Extinction:* Like the Great Auk, the Passenger Pigeon was killed unmercifully for food, for the market, and for the hell of it. In addition, its forest habitat was being converted to farmland. The species was so numerous that its extirpation, and particularly the suddenness with which it occurred, was probably impossible for men to imagine at the time. Even modern authorities suggest that disease or a migratory "wreck" may have played a part in the disappearance of the last millions, which took place in a mere 20 years. Most now agree, however, that the bird's breeding success depended on its gregarious habits and that the reproductive rate dropped precipitously once the population dropped below a (seemingly still high) number of individuals. This would explain in part the suddenness of the final exit. *Date(s) of Extinction:* The last well-verified shooting of a wild Passenger Pigeon took place in Wisconsin in 1899. "Martha Washington," hatched at the Cincinnati Zoo, was the last survivor. She succumbed on September 1, 1914, at the age of 29.

Carolina Parakeet *(Conuropsis carolinensis). Former Range and Status:* Once occurred throughout most of the eastern United States from the Great Plains to the eastern seaboard and from the tip of the Great Lakes and western New York south to the Gulf coast and southern Florida.

Before it declined, it occurred regularly in flocks of 200–300. *Main Causes of Extinction:* Probably a combination of habitat destruction and decimation by shotgun, but there is little documentation from the period. The favored nesting sites were tree hollows in forested swamps and river bottoms, much of which was cleared by the ax in the eighteenth and nineteenth centuries. The bird was also, and with some justification, regarded as a pest on grain and fruit crops and was, as Audubon put it, the victim of "severe retaliation on the part of the planters." However, the species was never shot on a large scale for food, sport, or ornamentation and dwindling habitat may have been the dominant cause of extinction. *Date(s) of Extinction:* The last specimen reportedly shot in the wild is from Kansas (!) in August 1904; the last known survivor died in the Cincinnati Zoo on February 21, 1918. There were numerous sight records and rumors until at least 1936; a few from the 1920s sound convincing, but Nicholson (1948) has noted that, even then, exotic parrots were escaping from their cages in Florida (see EXOTIC SPECIES)

Bachman's Warbler *(Vermivora bachmanii).* Sadly, since the last edition of this book, this species has been listed as extinct by the AOU and has therefore been moved from the ENDANGERED BIRDS entry to this one. *Former Range and Status:* Southern Indiana and southern Missouri east to Virginia, south to northern Arkansas and Alabama; nesting was proved in five states; wintered in Cuba, and the Isla de la Juventud (formerly Isla de Pinos); migrants recorded in the Bahamas. A bird of mature swamp woodlands, breeding in marginal thickets of "cane," i.e., bamboo, Bachman's Warbler was probably never abundant or widespread, though it could be locally common (150–200 in migration, Key West, July–August 1887–1889), *Main Cause(s) of Extinction:* Shot by late-nineteenth-century collectors in large numbers (e.g., 46 in one area in 1890) in migration. However, the most plausible explanation for the loss of this species appears to be destruction of the native bamboo stands (canebrakes) on which this warbler depended for nesting (Remsen 1986). There have been intimations (Shuler 1977) that the National Forest Service, which managed the I'on Swamp when it was one of the last strongholds of the species, traditionally acted in the interests of the lumber industry rather than those of Bachman's Warbler in discharging its responsibility. *Dates of Extinction:* No more than 6 per year were recorded anywhere after the 1950s, with records decreasing rapidly thereafter. The last conclusive record is from the vicinity of Charleston, South Carolina in 1962; the last report was of a female from Cuba in April 1980.

Heath Hen *(Tympanuchus cupido cupido),* the eastern race of the Greater Prairie-Chicken. *Former Range and Status:* From southern New England (southern New Hampshire) south along the coast probably as far as Virginia. Originally common albeit rather local due to the scarcity of its preferred heathland/grassland habitat except along the coast. *Main Causes of Extinction:* It has been suggested that this subspecies may ini-

tially have increased with the clearing of forest that came with European colonization. But this gain (if it occurred) was soon counterbalanced by shooting, the depredations of domestic animals, and settlement. A bill passed by the Massachusetts legislature in 1831 to protect the bird (during the breeding season only) was inspired by its obvious decline. *Date(s) of Extinction:* The Heath Hen may have been extinct on the mainland by 1850 (though there was a report from New Jersey in 1869). It was officially reported extinct in 1876 except for an estimated 120–200 birds left on the "great plain" of Martha's Vineyard, Massachusetts. This population fluctuated violently during the early twentieth century, perhaps reaching a high of 2,000 birds in 1916 but repeatedly reduced by fires. There was a final rally in 1921, with over 400 birds estimated, but two wet and cold breeding seasons reduced them to a mere 54 by 1924. In spite of renewed protection efforts, the population continued to decline. A single bird appeared on the "booming field" until March 11, 1932, and none was seen thereafter. From the perspective of the present, the extinction of the Heath Hen may be viewed as precursor of the fate of the species as a whole. The Atwater's race of the Greater Prairie Chicken endemic to the Texas coast is expected to expire any minute and the prognosis for other scattered populations of the species is unfavorable.

Dusky Seaside Sparrow *(Ammodramus maritimus nigrescens). Former Range and Status:* Once a locally common resident in salt marshes of central eastern coast of Florida (Brevard County near Merritt Island). *Main Cause(s) of Extinction:* The initial decline resulted from draining of marshes for pasturage and flooding for mosquito control; by 1980 only 6 individual remained and all were males. In an effort to preserve a genetic vestige of the subspecies, biologists bred 5 of the males with females of a different race of Seaside Sparrow from the Gulf coast; the plan was then to backbreed the offspring to maximize Dusky genes and then reintroduce the "almost-Duskies," Unfortunately, the Gulf race proved too distant a relative and the hybridization attempt failed (see Avise and Nelson 1988). *Dates of Extinction:* The last pure Dusky Seaside Sparrow died on June 16, 1987.

Although the editors have chosen to withhold the little dagger that signifies extinction in the 7th edition of the *AOU Checklist,* they describe two other species, Eskimo Curlew and Ivory-billed Woodpecker, as "probably extinct." Following this gesture of optimism, I have continued to include these species under ENDANGERED BIRDS. However, scientific consensus consigns them to eternity. See also CONSERVATION; THREATS (OF HUMAN ORIGIN) TO BIRDLIFE.

EXTIRPATE (EKS-tur-pate or eks-TUR-pate). To exterminate or eradicate. Used in biological contexts to describe the man-made elimination of a species, e.g., "The Passenger Pigeon was extirpated by wanton overshooting." It also refers to local or regional loss of a species that is not extinct in the global sense, e.g., "The Loggerhead Shrike is extirpated in New England."

EYE. See VISION.

EYE LINE/EYE STRIPE. A linear mark (light or dark) running through or behind the eye; loosely synonymous with eye stripe and even more loosely with *supercilium,* which properly refers to the area of feathers *above* the eye (the eye *brow).* Eye lines/eye stripes and eye brows often occur together as field marks on a single species (e.g., Red-eyed Vireo). These terms are used inconsistently in popular guides with some referring to the supercilium as an eye stripe. See Figs. 1 and 35.

EYE RING. An area of contrasting feathers (e.g., Ruby-crowned Kinglet) or unfeathered skin (e.g., Black-billed Cuckoo) encircling the eye of a bird; cited as a field mark for many species of birds. See Fig. 1.

EYESHINE. A reflection of colored light from an animal's eye. Most nightjars show a brilliant eyeshine when fixed by headlight or flashlight beams and some species can often be located in this manner by walking or driving along little-used country roads after dark. The phenomenon can also be seen when using a headlamp or a flashlight held at temple height when owling or visiting a nocturnal roost. For physiology of eyeshine in general, see VISION, Eyeshine.

EYRIE (or eerie, many alternate spellings) (EYE-ree). The nest of a large bird of prey, generally with an implication of remoteness and inaccessibility, such as the cliffside sites preferred by Gyrfalcons, Peregrines, and Golden Eagles. In a broader sense could also be used to describe the redoubts of other solitary cliff-nesting birds, such as Great Horned Owl or Common Raven.

FALCON (FAL-kun or FALL-kun. Standard English name for about 30 members of the family Falconidae (order Falconiformes), including the forest-falcons and falconets. Also, in a general sense, referring to all members of this family worldwide (c. 63 species worldwide), including the kestrel, hobbies, and Merlin. Five species of falcons (all in the genus *Falco)* currently breed in North America; a sixth, the Aplomado Falcon, bred historically and is now being reintroduced; and 3 others—Collared Forest-Falcon, Eurasian Kestrel, and Eurasian Hobby—have been recorded as vagrants. The falcon family also includes 8 living species of CARACARAS,

which are usually not called falcons in general usage, and are described in a separate entry.

Falcons range in size from the tiny (6 inches) falconets of the Old World to the 20-inch Gyrfalcon. They are usually boldly patterned and in some cases (e.g., American Kestrel) highly colored. Like their close relatives, the hawks and eagles (family Accipitridae), falcons have powerful wings and legs, a short, heavy, hooked bill for tearing flesh, long, sharp claws for holding prey, and a fleshy cere and eye ring—both usually bright yellow or orange in adult birds. In general form, all falcons are characterized by long, powerful wings and long tails. All are predators on other animals, though specific food preferences and manner of hunting vary among species. Some (especially the Peregrine) are famed for the incredible velocity of their "stoop"; however, see SPEED.

A falcon's nest consists of a scrape on open ground, a hollow on a rocky ledge, the ledge of a city office building, the abandoned stick nest of a corvid, hawk, or eagle, or in a few cases (e.g., American Kestrel) a tree (or other) cavity. No nest material is added. The 2–8 (usually 3–5) eggs have a white to pale buff or yellowish ground color, which, however, is normally obscured by fine speckling of reddish/brownish that in turn may be heavily overlaid with dark brown splotching sometimes covering almost the entire surface.

Falcon calls are staccato piping notes, high-pitched in smaller species, more "throaty" in larger; also various harsh cackles.

Falcons have captured the human imagination at least since the time of the ancient Egyptians, and the swift and graceful hunting techniques of the larger species inspired the development of the ancient, aristocratic sport of FALCONRY.

Because of their susceptibility to DDT (see THREATS (OF HUMAN ORIGIN) TO BIRDLIFE) Peregrines recently approached the brink of extinction throughout much of the world. But thanks to the efforts of dedicated falconers and scientists (and, of course, the banning of DDT), the species has made an impressive comeback and was removed from endangered and threatened status by the USFWS in 1998 (see ENDANGERED BIRDS).

The falcons are truly cosmopolitan as a family, ranging from the Arctic to the Antarctic and finding a niche in every major biome. Most of our North American species (American Kestrel, Merlin, and Peregrine) range throughout the continent as residents, migrants, or winterers, with the Gyrfalcon largely restricted to arctic barrens and the Prairie Falcon to open country in the West.

"Falcon" comes from the same root as the Latin word *falx*, "sickle," the connotation being the curved talons and/or bill of these raptors. See Cade (1982).

FALCON DAM (Texas). See RIO GRANDE VALLEY.

FALCONRY. The ancient sport of flying falcons, hawks, and eagles at live prey. Often called the "sport of kings" because of its immense popularity with the medieval aristocracy. Though game killed by falcons has often found its way to someone's table, the practice of falconry has always been mainly a source of pleasure rather than food.

History. Falconry is recorded in ancient texts, paintings, and sculpture from at least 2000 BC in China and from the seventh century BC in the Middle East, where legend attributes its origins to a prehistoric Persian king. The sport was also practiced within the first millennium BC in Japan and perhaps in North Africa. Though falconry has never been proven to have existed in any New World culture until the modern era, there is some evidence that the inhabitants of what is now Latin America may have trained birds to hunt. Aristotle and Pliny confirm the practice of falconry in classical times, and it is believed to have reached England by way of France around AD 860. It flourished as a sport among the higher social orders in Europe and was employed on a more practical level by those of a lower station, who were allowed to use accipiters (Northern Goshawk and Eurasian Sparrowhawk) to provide game for the table. With the decline of feudalism and (especially) the advent of readily available firearms in the seventeenth century, the popularity of falconry waned greatly, but the tradition has been maintained locally in Western societies by a few dedicated sportsmen of all classes. And in the oil-rich sheikdoms of the Middle East it thrives today as it always has—to the detriment, alas, of the world's falcon and bustard populations (see below).

Species Used and Prey. The large falcons have historically been thought of as the greatest sporting birds, with the Peregrine generally preferred above all others for its flying style, gentle behavior, and capacity to be trained. The Gyrfalcon, traditionally reserved for kings or sheiks, has always been appreciated for its size and majesty, but south of its native arctic tundra habitat, its heartiness declines, and its far-ranging hunting style becomes impractical, especially for the modern falconer. Among the less tractable (though very agile and exciting) accipiters, the Northern Goshawk is favored for its ability to catch small game (e.g., rabbits, grouse) for the table; it is the "falcon" of choice in Japan and the subject of many paintings. Smaller falcons, such as Merlin and the hobbies, and the sparrowhawks *(Accipiter)* put on a good show but are not capable generally of capturing prey that humans care to eat. On the whole, the species most popular in a given region are those best adapted to the prevailing habitat. For example, Saker Falcons, native to the arid wastes of the Palearctic region, are favored for chasing bustards in the deserts of North Africa.

The prey at which falcons are flown also varies with the fauna and traditions of the region. "Coursing" the diminutive Dorcas Gazelle with large falcons and salukis (the highly bred, greyhound-like Arab dog) was the fa-

vorite sport in the Middle East until the gazelles became scarce, due to overhunting. In Europe and America medium-sized to large birds, such as ducks, pheasants, partridges, herons, and crows, and smaller mammalian game such as rabbits were and are the chief targets of falconers hunting for both meat and sport. Smaller hawks were flown on songbirds and shorebirds, though "larking"—as setting hobbies or Merlins on high-flying Skylarks was called—was not considered "serious" falconry. Eagles have always been prized for their inherent grandeur and trained to take jack-rabbits and even larger game. On the Asian steppes, Golden Eagles are still used, especially among the Kazakhs, to capture foxes and wolves, the pelts of which are a source of livelihood for subsistence falconer-hunters. Eagles and their smaller cousins, the buteos or broad-winged hawks, are generally deemed to be less exciting to watch than the falcons and accipiters, though they are equally efficient hunters using their own methods. However, because of the characteristic docility and relative abundance of some species, the buteos have come to be among the birds most frequently used by American falconers (see below).

Capture, Training, and Flying. Normally hawks are either caught as immatures during their first fall migration or taken from the nest before they are able to fly. Once captured, wild birds are traditionally (but no longer invariably) fitted with a leather hood that covers their eyes; kept in a special building called a "mews"; and gradually accustomed to the falconer's glove, the sights and sounds of humanity, the touch of the "master," and the habit of being fed on the glove at the sound of a whistled signal. The bird is then trained to fly to the falconer's gloved fist to be fed, to fly at a lure that is swung on a cord, and finally flown free after live quarry in the field.

Whereas the first part of a wild bird's training involves acclimating it to captivity, the chief aim in raising birds taken from the nest is to attempt to teach them as many of the lessons they would learn naturally in the wild while at the same time preserving their "tameness." These "eyasses" are cared for in the first month with minimal human contact. Once able to fly well, they are given their freedom for a period, during which they are said to be "at hack." As soon as they are able to catch prey on their own, they are recaptured (if possible) for further training. This consists mainly of releasing live birds (usually pigeons) for the falcon to stoop on, in the process learning to "wait on" (i.e., fly above) the falconer in anticipation of stooping.

Because wild-caught birds tend to have the greatest determination to hunt, some falconers are of the opinion that birds trained from infancy are never as satisfactory as those reared initially among their own kind. Bedouin falconers captured passage hawks, trained them quickly and hunted with them, and then released them to complete their migration to their wintering grounds. This practice reflected an unwillingness to keep

birds regarded as invested with supernatural powers in prolonged captivity, but it also freed the nomadic captors from the chores of feeding and caring for the birds year round. American falconers often use Merlins in this way and the Kazakhs release their resident Golden Eagles during the breeding season and then recapture them for hunting during the winter months.

In the old days, once a bird was trained, it was usually carried into the field hooded and released when prey was spotted or flushed. Today birds are usually released in appropriate habitat to "wait on"—in the case of falcons at a height of 200–300 feet, or with accipiters to take up perches and scan for prey as they would on their own. European falconers of yore normally went afield on horseback, allowing them to reach a bird with prey quickly. This permitted the falconer to retrieve the falcon before it ate too much of its victim and thereby dulled its appetite for another stoop; in some cases the falconer was able to release larger game to be chased another day. Falcons thus deprived are always rewarded with a morsel of food. The Arabs still ride to the hunt but nowadays in jeeps modified to carry and protect their falcons. Western falconers generally go on foot, though they may use dogs to point up and flush game for their birds.

Modern Falconry in North America. Though a few falconers may have practiced their sport here since colonial times, the birth of modern North American falconry can be dated for convenience in the 1920s when the first continentwide organization was founded. Today there are perhaps as many as 2,500 licensed falconers in the United States and Canada, though perhaps as few as half this number is active. They are distributed fairly evenly over all regions, except for the minority of states and provinces where this method of taking game is not permitted. For more information contact the North American Falconers' Association at http://www.n–a–f–a.org.

Modern falconry is defined as "the pursuit of wild game with a raptor" and, though one courts inaccuracy to generalize about a group made up of self-avowed individualists, it is probably safe to say that most falconers come from the ranks of the traditional hunting community. The typical falconer (if such exists) is fiercely dedicated to his sport and his birds, committed to sound conservation practices, and is something of an elitist. He tends to consider himself a more highly skilled, dedicated, and "natural" sportsman than the rifle (or even bow) hunter and a far more knowledgeable, realistic, and unsentimental naturalist than the average birdwatcher. One need not subscribe to every detail of this flattering self-image to believe that falconers today are as deeply in thrall to the powerful beauty and romance of their sport as they always have been.

No one becomes a falconer casually. Those who begin with a mild interest are soon discouraged by the great difficulties and expenditure of time involved in acquiring, training, and keeping a bird and the burden of

legal stipulations that must be satisfied. All falconers are bound by federal regulations, which in many cases are made more restrictive—never less— by state laws. Though state regulations vary, qualification as a licensed falconer is basically achieved through comprehensive written examinations and a sponsor/apprentice system. There are three levels of falconers: apprentice, intermediate, and master, each with its own specified duration requirements and prescribed species. At each level, written tests must be passed, and some states require field trials as well. Would-be falconers must also acquire (or make for themselves) a minimum of essential equipment (e.g., jesses, hoods, perches, hawk house) and satisfy a strict standard of housing and maintenance for their bird(s). A master falconer is permitted to keep up to three birds at a time, but keeping so many fit is so time-consuming that many falconers limit themselves to a single bird. In addition to earning state and federal licenses, the falconer must also satisfy any applicable hunting regulations. If he intends to fly his bird at waterfowl, for example, a falconer must buy whatever licenses and duck stamps are required by his country and state and is restricted to the legal mandated season. In many cases gun and falconry seasons are identical, a situation falconers generally deplore, since they sometimes lose birds to gunners unable to resist potting an unwary raptor that has been trained to hunt with man.

Falconers are allowed to trap any species of hawk or falcon that is neither on the endangered species list (see ENDANGERED BIRDS) nor under special protection locally, and even protected species may be taken under special circumstances, as when a permit is issued to capture a particular Golden Eagle that habitually kills livestock. They may also capture Great Horned Owls. There are provisions for taking young birds from the nest (leaving the majority of the brood), trapping birds of the year (passage hawks) during the fall migration, or receiving captive-bred birds from licensed breeders.

According to both the law and the falconer's code, hawks are always "slipped" at specific prey, but once a bird has left the fist, there is always the chance that it will be diverted from its intended victim and take a nongame species or one that is out of season. To cover this contingency, most states have adopted "let it lay" regulations, which provide that the hawk be allowed to feed on such kills and that whatever remains then be left for other animals and to decompose—just as would happen in a natural raptor/prey encounter. For other regulatory details, see LAWS PROTECTING BIRDLIFE.

By far the most popular species among modern North American falconers is the docile, yet spirited, Red-tailed Hawk, whose abundance also favors its widespread use. Next in popularity is an essentially Neotropical, dry-country species, the Harris's Hawk, which reputedly combines the Red-tail's even temperament with the agility of a large accipiter. Another

reason for this bird's popularity is the ease with which it is bred in captivity and thus its ready availability. Accipiters are very exciting to fly but commensurably difficult to train (see White [1951] for a vivid confirmation). Apprentice falconers often cut their teeth on the small, colorful American Kestrel.

Falconry probably will always remain drenched in ancient tradition—it is part of the mystique of the art. But today's falconers also reap both the rewards and the detriments of the modern world. Techniques of rearing and caring for birds in captivity have improved immeasurably since the Middle Ages (especially in the last 10 years), and some ancient rituals practiced out of superstition, rather than for their effectiveness, have been winnowed out. Falconers can now recover many of their lost birds by attaching tiny radio transmitters to legs or plumage and thereby tracking birds that stray. On the other hand, early falconers did not have to contend with slob hunters, low-flying aircraft, power lines, pesticides, and all the other hazards that a free-flying hawk must now suffer.

Falconers themselves are also under some pressure, mainly from the humane element of the wildlife protection movement, which sees his sport as a kind of organized cruelty, comparable to cockfighting. The falconer's defense is that, unlike gun or bow hunting, falconry is a nonconsumptive sport, the falconer simply modifying a natural process, so that he can observe its beauty and share in the experience. Of course, some people are simply uncomfortable with the fact that some animals kill others as a way of life; they shudder to think that anyone could possibly enjoy the natural beauty of this predatory behavior. But the falconer—unlike the cockfighter—does not gamble on his birds and is not interested in the bloody and competitive aspects of his birds' behavior. His pleasure comes as much from the ability of prey species frequently to avoid the falcon's talons as from the performance of his own bird; he exults in the evolutionary beauty of the predator/prey equilibrium. Furthermore, all of us can be grateful for the crucial contribution of American falconers to the highly successful Peregrine recovery program. The captive breeding and reintroduction of this magnificent species might still be in its infancy were it not for the hawkers' expertise. Of course, like all groups, falconers are not without their "bad eggs." There is no denying that Peregrine and other nests have been robbed by unscrupulous hawkers. And the avidity of Arab falconers has contributed to the perilous present status of some desert wildlife, notably the Dorcas Gazelle and species of bustards, as well as to populations of wild falcons that have pillaged worldwide. The immense wealth of the richest sheiks allows them to buy off reserve wardens in places they wish to hunt and decimate entire populations of bustards in a season (Weaver 2002). The literature of falconry is extensive and contains medieval classics as well as modern texts, "how to" books as well as more evocative experiential prose. Beebe (1984) is a highly regarded cur-

rent work on North American falconry, and other books and articles are given in the Bibliography.

Anyone wishing to watch falconry in action must exert some initiative. Falconers are generally not interested in public audiences at their occasional meets and couldn't care less about encouraging the popularity of their obsession. Most would tell you that falconers are born, not made.

Falconers' Jargon. Like many venerable practices, falconry has evolved its own special language, unintelligible to the uninitiated. Some of the commonest falconry terms are defined below. Terms relating to specialized gear are omitted.

Austringer: One who flies accipiters, especially Northern Goshawks, as differentiated from hawkers who use only falcons.

Bate, bating: An attempt by a hawk to fly from a perch to which it is tethered. As a display of fright or temper this behavior is characteristic of birds in the early stages of training, but seasoned hawks also bate in a fit of pique or out of simple boredom.

Brancher: A juvenile hawk sufficiently mature to perch (e.g., on a branch) near its nest, but not yet fully independent.

Cadge: Formerly a frame or box with padded perches for transporting birds of prey. This contraption was carried by a "cadgeman" in the old days, and the birds thus given a free ride. This may be the source of the current "cadge," meaning to get for nothing, e.g., to cadge or "bum" a cigarette. Today, usually means simply a portable perch used to carry birds into the field.

Eyass (EYE-US) (also spelled eyes and eyess): A juvenile hawk that is captured from the nest, as opposed to a bird captured after fledging and on the wing. Birds captured in the former manner continue to be called eyasses even after reaching adulthood.

Hacking: See entry in main text.

Haggard: A hawk captured from the wild after it has completed at least one molt (first pre-basic); i.e., an adult; more loosely, any wild adult hawk.

Imping: See entry in main text.

Intermewed: Refers to a hawk that has undergone a molt in captivity.

Jack: A male Merlin.

Jerkin: A male Gyrfalcon.

Mantle: To mantle is to stretch the wing and leg simultaneously to one side; reputedly a sign of contentment. Or the instinctive spreading of the wings and tail over freshly caught prey or when something threatens removal of partly consumed prey.

Mews: Traditionally, the place where hawks were kept while they molted. Now simply the "hawk house," where the birds live permanently.

Mutes: Hawk droppings.

Passage hawk: A bird of the year captured during its first fall migration or "passage."

Stoop: See entry in main text.

Tiercel (or tercel): Originally the mate of a "falcon" when the latter term was reserved for the female. Now a male hawk of any species that is used in falconry. The term derives from male Peregrines and accipiters being characteristically smaller than their mates, usually by about a *third.*

Yarak: A hawk's state of readiness to hunt, detectable in certain bodily gestures, particularly among accipiters, buteos, and eagles.

For more on the birds used in falconry, see FALCON; HAWK; PEREGRINE; etc.

FALLOUT. Birders' jargon for the sudden landing of migratory birds typically as the result of weather condition, such as the arrival of a front from the opposite direction or fog. The overnight appearance of a "wave" of warblers and other Neotropical migrants typical of the Gulf and Atlantic coast in spring is a form of fallout. But the appearance of a small number of rarities becoming disoriented in bad weather, overshooting their destination, and making an "emergency landfall together also qualifies."

FALL WARBLERS. Species of wood warblers in juvenal plumage or after the pre-basic (first-winter) molt, many of which are notoriously difficult for the tyro birdwatcher to distinguish. A male Hooded Warbler is, therefore, never a "fall warbler," even though it may be seen during the autumn migration.

FAMILY. The major taxonomic category between ORDER and GENUS; orders may be divided into suborders and families; families into subfamilies, tribes, and genera (see SYSTEMATICS and Appendix I). A family may also be defined as a grouping of phylogenetically related genera. All Latin family names of birds and other animals end in *-idae.* There are about 145–170 families of birds worldwide, the precise number being a matter of taxonomic opinion. Authorities tend to agree on the composition—if not the phylogenetic order—of most nonpasserine families. There is, for example, no dispute over what species belong in the loon family or the flamingo family, but the familial breakdown of the huge order of perching birds (Passeriformes) has been the subject of wide ranging speculation. The use of DNA analysis by Sibley and Ahlquist (1990–SYSTEMATICS) and others has started to bring a new authority and clarity to these relationships.

The families of birds that occur regularly in North America are listed below in alphabetical order following the taxonomy of the 7th edition of *The AOU Checklist of North American Birds* (1998). For a "definition" of these families—which orders they belong to; which and how many genera and species they contain—note the page number given after each family in the first list below, which refers to the full taxonomic list in Appendix I.

Each family has its own descriptive entry, which occurs alphabetically by the English family name—ALBATROSS; BABBLER; etc. in the main text. To compare the Sibley and Monroe taxonomy (1990 and 1993–SYSTEMAT-ICS), see Appendix III.

"New" families erected in the 7th edition of the *A.O.U. Checklist* (1998) are noted below. Former families reduced to subfamilies include the Ryncopidae/-nae (skimmers) and Stercorariidae/-nae (jaegers and skuas) now both in Laridae; and the Tetraonidae/-nae (grouse) now in Phasianidae).

Accipitridae, p. 907
Aegithalidae, p. 924
Alaudidae, p. 923
Alcedinidae, p. 920
Alcidae, p. 915
Anatidae, p. 905
Anhingidae, p. 904
Apodidae, p. 919
Aramidae, p. 910
Ardeidae, p. 904
Bombycillidae, p. 928
Caprimulgidae, p. 918
Cardinalidae (Cardinal-Grosbeaks; elevated to full family from subfamily of Fringillidae), p. 932
Cathartidae, p. 905
Certhiidae, p. 925
Charadriidae, p. 911
Ciconiidae, p. 905
Cinclidae, p. 925
Columbidae, p. 916
Corvidae, p. 923
Cracidae, p. 909
Cuculidae, p. 917
Diomedeidae, p. 902
Emberizidae, p. 930
Estrildidae (Estrildid Finches; no native species; included in the AOU list based on introductions in Hawaiian Islands, Puerto Rico, and elsewhere), p. 934
Falconidae, p. 908
Fregatidae, p. 904
Fringillidae, p. 933

Gaviidae, p. 901–2
Gruidae, p. 910
Haematopodidae, p. 911
Hirundinidae, p. 924
Hydrobatidae, p. 903
Icteridae, p. 932
Jacanidae, p. 911
Laniidae, p. 922
Laridae, p. 913
Mimidae, p. 927
Motacillidae, p. 927
Muscicapidae, p. 926
Odontophoridae (New World Quails; elevated to full family from subfamily of Phasianidae), p. 909
Paridae, p. 924
Parulidae, p. 928
Passeridae (Old World Sparrows; elevated to full family from sub-family of Ploceidae), p. 934
Pelecanidae, p. 903
Peucedramidae (Olive Warbler; moved from Parulidae and placed in new monotypic family), p. 928
Phaethontidae, p. 903
Phalacrocoracidae, p. 903
Phasianidae, p. 909
Phoenicopteridae, p. 905
Picidae, p. 920
Ploceidae (Typical Weavers; included in the AOU list on the basis of two introduced African bishops), p. 934

Except for the Passeridae (Old World Sparrows), the Pycnonotidae (Bulbuls), and the Sturnidae (Starlings and Mynas), which together contribute 6 introduced species to the North American avifauna, all of the above families are native, although the parrot family (Psittacidae) now comprises only one extinct species and one to three natural vagrants in North America.

Representatives of 6 additional families have occurred in North America as accidental stragglers. These families are the Burhinidae (thick-knees); Glareolidae (pratincoles), the Upupidae (hoopoes); the Prunellidae (accentors); the Muscicapidae (Old World Flycatchers); and the Coerebidae (honeycreepers). These vagrant species are listed in Appendix II.

For illustrations and descriptions of the bird families of the world, see references in the Bibliography under BIRD, e.g., Austin and Singer (1985).

FAT. Migratory birds typically acquire a heavy layer of subcutaneous fat in a bout of voracious feeding before their journeys. These reserves are essential fuel during long, uninterrupted flights, which last more than 24 hours and span vast stretches of open ocean in many instances. The amount of fat laid down varies from species to species, with short-distance migrants usually putting on considerably less than half their "normal" weight as fat (e.g., White-throated Sparrow: 23–28 grams "normal" weight vs. 24–33 grams premigratory [fat] weight), while a long-distance migrant such as the Blackpoll Warbler more than doubles its "normal" weight (from 11–12 grams to 27 grams). In birds resident in temperate and cold climes average fat content increases seasonally in autumn followed by a spring decrease, and fat fluctuates daily in response to cold in the winter. See Nisbet et al. (1963), Blem (1990–ENERGY), and Blem in Whittow (2000–ENERGY). See also ENERGY and MIGRATION.

FAUNA. The animal life of any given place or time. Fauna + flora = BIOTA. Avifauna is the birdlife of any given place or time.

FEAR OF MAN. See TAMENESS.

FEATHER. See Fig. 13. A very elaborate modification of the outer layer (epidermis) of a bird's skin, made almost entirely of a light, strong, horny protein called keratin, which also forms the covering of a bird's bill, feet, and skin. Feathers are unique to birds, are variously modified in form to serve different functions (e.g., flight, temperature control, display), and in the aggregate make up a bird's PLUMAGE, which covers nearly the entire surface of its body.

   Evolution of the Feather. Authorities differ as to how feathers evolved from reptilian features. Some believe that the first feathers were elongated scales adapted for flight; others think that down evolved first from filaments found among the scales of some reptiles and paralleled development of "warm-bloodedness." In either case, it is clear that the first phase of feather formation in the skin is identical to that of scale formation (see Formation, below). For evolution of feathers from reptilian scales, see EVOLUTION OF BIRDLIFE.

   Basic Structure. A typical wing, tail, or body feather consists, when fully formed, of a central spine or shaft, from each side of which a thin, relatively soft *vane* or web emerges along its upper length. The lower, hollow portion of the shaft before the beginning of the vane is called the *calamus* and is round in cross section. The calamus has a hole *(umbilicus)* at its lower tip and another on its underside at the point where the vanes begin. At this point, the shaft begins to taper, contains a pithy core *(medulla)*, and becomes more or less square in cross section. This part of the shaft, which continues to the feather tip and holds the full length of both vanes, is called the *rachis*. The two vanes, which may be of different width in certain feathers (e.g., primaries), consist of a continuous series of narrow, closely interlocked branches, called *barbs*, which diverge from the rachis angled toward the feather tip. The barbs in turn branch on both sides into a close-set continuous series of much shorter *barbules*, which have a different shape on either side of the barb. Those emerging from the front of the barb (i.e., the side nearest the feather tip) bear a row of hooks *(hamuli)*; those emerging from the rear of the barb are flattened and curled or flanged along the upper edge. The hooks of the forward-projecting barbules grip the ridged edge of backward-projecting barbules to maintain the smooth, even surface of the vane. Both the forward-pointing (hooked) barbules and the rearward-pointing (flanged) barbules also bear short, straight, pointed projections called *barbicels,* which probably serve to increase the Velcro-like adhesiveness of the mesh. (Some sources refer to the hamuli as barbicels as well and the barbules can then be said to bear

both hooked and straight barbicels.) This intricate but precise intermeshing of hooks and edges explains why it is so easy to "repair the vane of a feather that has been pulled apart (see PREENING), but the delicacy of the vane "fabric" can only be appreciated by looking at it under a microscope.

At the base of the rachis of most feathers are a few rows of soft barbs, the barbules of which have no hooks and do not therefore interlock into a vane. Down feathers (see Formation, below, and DOWN) and specially modified feathers, such as SEMIPLUME and FILOPLUME, also lack vanes.

Formation. The first external sign of feather formation is the appearance of small bumps on the skin of an embryo during incubation. These result from the formation in the lower skin layer (dermis) of pimple or nipple-like structures called *feather papillae,* which push up the outer skin layer (epidermis). This is identical to the beginnings of reptilian scales, which, however, take a different course at this point. In birds, each papilla continues to grow outward, taking the shape of a pointed cylinder, and at the same time it recedes into the skin, forming a cavity, the *feather follicle.* As the cylinder grows it hardens (keratinizes) into a feather sheath. It eventually pushes through the surface of the skin and the central dermal pulp is reabsorbed, leaving in essence a hollow tube. Along the inner wall of this hollow sheath a lining of straight longitudinal ridges develops within which the barbs of the first (natal) down feathers (if any) are formed. Eventually the top of the sheath splits open, releasing the barbs, each of which emerges separately from around the top edge of the calamus of this first feather like a fringe around a cuff. Meanwhile from the same follicle, a second dermal papilla is developing into another sheath just below the first down feather. The barb ridges of this second feather, however, rather than growing straight and vertical as before, grow in descending half-spirals along either wall of the sheath and finally meet and fuse with a central ridge that has formed along the (interior) upper surface. The ridge will be the rachis of a feather of the first full (juvenal) plumage. As before, the top of the feather sheath splits and the new barbs emerge, bearing the down feather at their tip. The barbs of the new feather having been fully formed within the sheath, the vane simply unfurls once it has emerged and the down feather quickly drops off. Succeeding feathers begin, as before, but are not connected to the preceding feather as was the initial down feather. In molt, the worn feathers are dropped before the new sheath emerges from the surface of the skin.

Fig. 13. *Feather form and structure.* The Cooper's Hawk primary at center is magnified to three different levels to demonstrate how the vane of contour feathers achieves its smooth cohesion. The other drawings show different types of feathers (as labeled), and at the top, the rictal bristles that fringe the gapes of most nightjars are shown "in action."

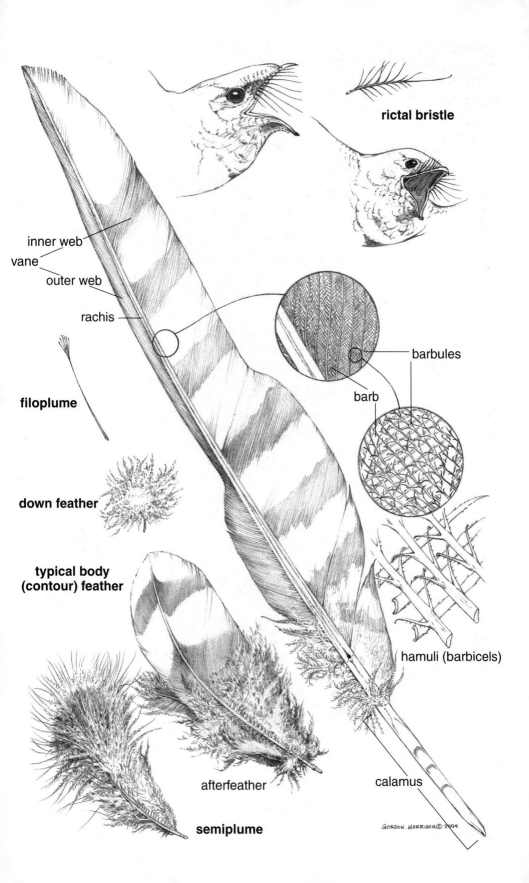

rictal bristle

inner web

vane

outer web

rachis

filoplume

down feather

typical body
(contour) feather

barbules

barb

hamuli (barbicels)

afterfeather

calamus

semiplume

GORDON MORRISON© 2004

The somewhat complex subject of adult down feathers as opposed to the natal (neossoptile) down is discussed under DOWN. See also PLUMAGE and specific feather types, e.g., PRIMARY, FILOPLUME, etc., and MOLT.

For good illustrations of the formation process, see 'Espinasse–FEATHER in Campbell and Lack–(1985–ORNITHOLOGY) and Prum (1999).

FEATHER MITES. Important arachnid parasites belonging to several families of the order Acarina. Feather mites spend their entire life cycle on the bodies of birds, eating feather parts and sometimes causing severe damage to plumage. For further details, see ECTOPARASITE.

FEATHER TRACTS (and apteria). Except for the ratites, penguins, and toucans, which have feathers evenly distributed over the surface of the skin, birds' feathers grow in discrete tracts or *pterylae* separated by featherless areas called *apteria* (see PLUMAGE). Because the feathers normally overlap the apteria, the arrangement is not visible unless a bird is examined in the hand. The number of tracts/apteria and their respective sizes and shapes have proven to conform more or less among closely related species and are thus of significance as taxonomic characters.

The major feather tracts and apteria are as follows.

Capital tract: Top of the head from bill base to beginning of neck and over the face to the "jawline."

Spinal or dorsal tract: From the top of the neck (where capital tract leaves off) down across the back to the beginning of the upper tail coverts (caudal tract).

Ventral tract: From the chin (base of lower mandible) down the underside of the neck to the breast, where it forks (around the midventral apterium) and continues to just above the vent.

Cervical apteria: The sides of the neck, separating the capital and spinal tracts from the ventral.

Lateral apterium: Covering much of a bird's sides from the outer margins of the spinal (dorsal) tract around to the outer margins of the ventral tract.

Midventral apterium: The space enclosed by the fork in the ventral tract from the breast or even neck to somewhere on the lower belly. The form of the spinal and ventral tracts relative to the lateral and midventral apteria varies widely among different groups of birds.

Humeral tract: A narrow strip running across the wing bases above (dorsally); the tract from which the scapulars arise (see Fig. 35).

Alar tract: The margins of both surfaces of the wings from which the flight feathers and coverts arise. Alar apteria sometimes occur in the center (or elsewhere) of both of the wings, separating the alar and humeral tracts.

Femoral tract: A narrow strip running along the thigh separated from the lower portion of the spinal tract by the lateral apteria.

Crural tract: Covering most of the feathered portion of the legs (variable); separated from the femoral tract by a narrow apterium.

Caudal tract: From the end of the spinal tract/uropygium/upper tail coverts around the tail to the base of the undertail coverts; it includes the circle of feathers (anal ring) surrounding the vent and gives rise to the rectrices as well as the tail coverts.

An accurately labeled diagram of the feather tracts and apteria is much clearer than a verbal description. For such a diagram, see Gill (1994–ORNITHOLOGY), p. 75.

FECAL (FEE-kl) **SAC.** A gelatinous pouch into which the feces of nestling (mainly passerine) birds are excreted. The adaptation would seem to be an aid to nest sanitation. Adult birds remove the sacs from the cloacae of their young and usually eat them or carry them away from the nest, at least during the early stages of the brooding period. See PARENTAL CARE.

FEEDER. A contraption for dispensing seeds, fruit, syrup, or other substances to attract wild birds. It may be a simple shelf or platform on which to place food, but these days it is much more likely to be an elaborate structure providing shelter, a variety of perches, food-dispensing mechanisms, and baffles to discourage nonavian visitors or birds of insufficient beauty or charm. See BIRD FEEDING.

FEEDING (of birds by humans). See BIRD FEEDING.

FEEDING HABITS. See FOOD/FEEDING.

FEEDING OF YOUNG. See PARENTAL CARE, Feeding.

FERAL. In general, wild or untamed; but usually refers to domesticated animals that have "gone wild." Feral birds such as barnyard Mallards and pigeons seem to retain more of the characteristics of domestication, e.g., trust of man, than do feral cats and dogs.

FERRUGINOUS (fuh-ROO-juh-nuss) (Hawk, Pygmy-Owl). Literally, iron-colored; rusty, e.g., the Ferruginous (Pygmy) Owl or (in breeding plumage) the Curlew Sandpiper, *Calidris (Erolia) ferruginea.* Ideally, the shade should be darker and duller than "rufous."

FERTILIZATION. In birds, as in humans, the conjunction of male and female reproductive cells (sperm and ova); in birds this takes place in the upper end of the female's oviduct, following copulation. See REPRODUCTIVE SYSTEM.

FIELD GUIDE. A book designed to be carried outdoors and used to identify species of birds or other particulars of natural history. A field guide is typically portable, if not "pocket-sized"—though recent versions of the genre are becoming ever heftier to accommodate the ever-expanding amount of information deemed essential for bird identification. Key components are diagnostic paintings or photos of the forms under consideration; concise descriptions of physical details, habits, voice, and other facts pertinent to identification and distribution maps.

Birds inspired the composition of the first field guides, though early works were not so named. The prototype of the genre may be Thomas Nuttall's *A Manual of the Ornithology of the United States and Canada,* first published in two smallish volumes in 1832–34. Among the earliest efforts to aid the general public with the identification of birds afield were several pamphlets published in the late 1880s by Florence Merriam, particularly "Birds Through an Opera Glass" (1889); in this context, Barrow (1998–AOU) indicates that some of the early antipathy of practicing ornithologists to field identification may have been that many of its advocates were enthusiastic women.

More recognizable progenitors of modern identification aids were Ralph Hoffman's *A Guide to the Birds of New England and Eastern New York* (1902) and especially Chester Reed's *Bird Guides,* first published in 1906. These handy 3½ by 6-inch volumes (Roger Peterson described them as "the size of a fat checkbook"), illustrated by the author, showed and described one species per page. The paintings are more than passable, even by current standards, and the pithy texts cram description, habits, song, nest, and range into about 6 square inches, and they were very popular. Frank Chapman's *Handbook of Birds of Eastern North America,* published in 1930 and (ultimately) illustrated by Louis Agassiz Fuertes, incorporated much more specific detail in the species accounts, consistent with the increasing sophistication of field ornithology. It need hardly be explained that these worthy volumes were eclipsed in 1934 by the appearance of *the* field guide (the first so named)—Roger Tory Peterson's *A Field Guide to the Birds* (Eastern North America). This seminal work combined clear, diagrammatic illustrations with a unique system, which uses arrows on the plates to point to diagnostic field marks and a concise text that emphasizes differences among similar species. In spite of predictions that sales of the guide would not repay the costs of printing it, it eventually sold over 2 million copies. At this writing (2003) the Peterson Field Guide Series contains nearly 50 titles with new titles continuing to emerge. These cover almost all aspects of natural history and include seven bird guides. The last guide illustrated by Peterson himself was the second edition of the Western bird guide published in 1990.

In 1966 *Birds of North America,* by Chandler Robbins, Bertel Bruun, and Herbert Zim and illustrated by Arthur Singer, posed the first serious challenge to the preeminence of the Peterson guides. It offered a new for-

mat and fewer diagrammatic illustrations, covered all North American species in one small volume, and was as indispensable to the dedicated American birdwatcher as *the* field guide. Another North American bird guide series (now, alas, long out of print) that attained richly deserved popularity was Richard H. Pough's *Audubon Bird Guides* (three volumes: Land Birds, Water Birds, and Western Birds); illustrated in a lifelike style by Don Eckleberry, these guides contained more life history information than their contemporaries. The two-volume *Audubon Society Field Guide to North American Birds* (Eastern Region, by John Bull and John Farrand, Jr.; Western Region, by Miklos D. F. Udvardy), was the first authoritative guide to use color photographs in place of painted illustrations; these proved to be popular with the public, but were scorned by some of the cognoscenti as far less useful than painted illustrations for field identification. The current (2003) state-of-the-art guides are The National Geographic Society's *Field Guide to the Birds of North America* (2002), illustrated (rather unevenly) by 13 artists; Kenn Kaufman's new *Birds of North America* (2000), which pioneers a technique that attempts (with considerable success) to combine the best attributes of photography and painting; and *The Sibley Guide to Birds* (2000), written and illustrated by David Allen Sibley.

In 1983 Peter Harrison published his *Seabirds*, which ushered in a new generation of guides focusing on particular groups of birds and fine points of identification gleaned from the literature and extensive personal experience. Hayman, Marchant, and Prater's *Shorebirds* (1986) was next and there are now many titles in the genre. Because of their "depth," these guides had to abandon any illusion of being "pocketable," but they are now essential to the practice of serious field ornithology. These and other bird guides (including some classics as well as those currently in print) pertinent to the North American avifauna are listed in the Bibliography.

FIELD IDENTIFICATION. The art of recognizing species of live birds in the wild—as opposed to identifying birds "in the hand," e.g., those trapped in a mist nest or museum specimens. Field identification is the essence of one kind of interest in birds. See IDENTIFICATION; BIRDWATCHING.

FIELD MARK. A characteristic, such as color, shape, or specific feature (eye ring, wing bars, breast stripes, etc.), by which a species can be distinguished in the field from similar species. In many cases, a number of field marks taken together are necessary for a conclusive identification. The black "armpits" of the Prairie Falcon are a field mark that serves to distinguish that species from the other large falcons. Compare JIZZ.

FIELD PROBLEM. Refers to an inherent difficulty in identifying certain species of birds. To novice birdwatchers, most of the sparrows and the "confusing fall warblers" often present frustrating field problems. However,

some field problems—e.g., separating, basic plumaged dowitchers, immature jaegers, *Empidonax* flycatchers or Gray-cheeked and Bicknell's Thrushes—can tax or defeat the expertise (and patience) of even the most brilliant field ornithologist.

See FIELD IDENTIFICATION; BIRDWATCHING; JIZZ.

FIGHTING. See aggression; territory; population.

FILOPLUME (FYE-low-ploom). A soft (not stiff), hair-like feather, i.e., one that lacks a vane or whose vane is insignificant. Two types of filoplumes are recognized. The first typically emerges in small groups from around the base of the body feathers and is normally completely concealed by them; this type usually has a tuft of vane at the tip and is present in nearly all birds. The second type has no vane at all and extends beyond the body feathers, most often in the head and neck region; these are present in many species but are difficult to see except on close inspection. Other hair-like feathers are sometimes called filoplumes but usually have more or less extensive vaning, e.g., bristles or certain long, narrow display plumes. Exposed filoplumes act as indicators of feathers ruffled in out-of-the-way parts of the plumage and also serve a sensory function similar to that of the vibrissae of mammals (Clark and de Cruz 1989–FEATHER).

See FEATHER and Fig. 13.

FINCH. In its broadest usage, "finch" has been used to refer generically to virtually all bird species with conical, "seed-eating" bills as well as a number without. This great finch umbrella sheltered such diverse forms as the seedeaters, New World sparrows, towhees, both Old and New World buntings, juncos, longspurs, grosbeaks, crossbills, siskins, redpolls, weavers, and waxbills in addition to various species bearing the name finch in combination (goldfinch) or by itself (Purple Finch). In the past the term also figured in a number of family names, again referring to birds with (vaguely) similar bill and feeding characteristics, e.g., emberizid *finches,* weaver *finches,* waxbill *finches,* and the word has retained some taxonomic integrity in the latest *AOU Checklist* (7th ed., 1998), where the family Fringillidae is described as containing two subfamilies, the Fringilline and Cardueline finches—and allies!

With the advent of molecular analysis taxonomists have been able to define relationships among groups of songbirds with much greater clarity than previously with the result that some "finches" are now classified with birds that until recently were not deemed to be particularly close relatives, while at the same time "finches" once thought to be allies have been moved to a more distant family tree. At one extreme, Sibley and Monroe (1990–SYSTEMATICS) have placed all of the birds previous thought of as "finches" into two large families, the Passeridae and the Fringillidae, and

have also included in these megafamilies subfamilies and tribes of birds—once given full family status—that no one has ever thought of as containing finches. For example, the Sibley/Monroe Passeridae, in addition to comprising the Old World sparrows, weavers, and waxbills, also encompasses the wagtails and accentors, while their truly gargantuan Frigillidae (with 995 species, largest in the world) envelops not only goldfinches, Old and New World buntings, and different types of grosbeaks, but also the tanagers, wood warblers, New World blackbirds and orioles, and Hawaiian honeycreepers.

The latest *AOU Checklist* has taken a more conservative approach and preserved more traditional family definitions. However, we can expect many of the affinities recently detected by DNA analysis and shaped by a cladistic approach to taxonomy to be codified in standard checklists.

It is important to realize that the "confusion" just described is not the result of scientists tampering with traditional "sensible" classification system. The scientists are in fact engaged in one of the great clarifying periods in the history of taxonomy. Rather it is our dated terminology—trying to make the venerable "finch" serve as a description of many different unrelated birds—that needs to yield. Accordingly, the groups of birds once lumped in this rubric will be described in separate family entries following the *AOU Checklist,* 7th edition (1998). See, therefore, BUNTING; CARDINAL-GROSBEAK (Cardinalidae); SPARROW-BUNTING (Emberizidae); FRINGILLID FINCH (Fringillidae); OLD WORLD SPARROW (Passeridae); WEAVER (Ploceidae); WAXBILL (Estrildidae).

"Finch" goes back 3,000 years (!) to an "echoic" name for the Chaffinch of Eurasia whose call was rendered (accurately enough) as "ping"(hard "g"), thence to German "fink" and Old English "finc" (Lockwood 1993– NAMES).

FISCHER von Waldheim, Johann Gotthelf, 1771–1853 (*Somateria fischeri:* Spectacled Eider). A German polymath-geologist, physician, paleontologist, zoologist, and authority on the history of printing. Though of humble origins, he became a protégé of Humboldt and Cuvier and eventually became prominent in the natural science establishment of Moscow. The spectacular duck that commemorates him was named by Johann BRANDT, another Russified German scientist.

FISHING. The majority of birds that wade, swim, and/or dive and not a few land birds (including, occasionally, some owls, flycatchers, corvids, warblers, and blackbirds) eat at least some fish. For specific fishing techniques, see SWIMMING/DIVING; BILL; CANOPY FEEDING (and Fig. 5).

FIXED ACTION PATTERN (FAP). The ethologist's term for the instinctive, highly stereotyped patterns of stimulus and response that govern the

rituals of daily life of birds and other animals. A bird that, so to speak, is "in the mood" to eat, court, copulate, fight, etc., must receive the correct sound, gesture, or color signal that acts as a "releaser" of the intended behavior. See INTELLIGENCE.

FLAMINGO. Standard English name for all 5 (or 6 depending on taxonomy) members of the family Phoenicopteridae. The taxonomic home of the flamingoes is still under discussion, with various authorities arguing plausibly that they should remain near the storks where they have traditionally been located (Sibley and Ahlquist 1990–SYSTEMATICS), or with the ducks and geese (Hagey et al. 1990), or, on the basis of fossil evidence, in the suborder Charadrii with the plovers and oystercatchers. The *AOU Checklist* 7th edition, keeps them in an order of their own (Phoenicopteriformes) between the storks and the ducks and geese.

All flamingoes are pink with black wing tips and have almost absurdly long legs with neck to match and (unlike herons and storks) full webs between the three front toes. They stand almost 5 feet tall with neck extended normally. Perhaps their most extraordinary characteristic is their odd, thick bill, which is bent sharply downward at the middle. The interior of this device is lined with rows of lamellae, which act as a sieve as the birds strain bottom mud in shallow water with their heads upside down. Their principal diet is diatoms, fly larvae and pupae, algae, and bacteria, as well as some small fish, shrimps, etc. Their pink color is derived from a pigment in their normal food sources and fades when these are unavailable, e.g., in captivity. So bizarre are flamingoes in reality that their appearance as organic croquet mallets in *Alice in Wonderland* by Lewis Carroll hardly stretches one's credulity further. They seem to inspire the imagination. The American naturalists Abbott and Thayer believed that the red plumage of flamingoes was cryptically adaptive, providing cover for the birds against flaming tropical dawns and sunsets; this notion is illustrated—perhaps not wholly convincingly—in the Thayer's wonderful book on cryptic coloration (Thayer 1918–COLOR AND PATTERN).

Colonial nesters, flamingoes build a unique nest in—or at least surrounded by—shallow saltwater. It consists of a mud cone with the top hollowed out to accommodate the single (rarely, 2) egg, which is pale greenish with a white chalky coating.

To quote Palmer (1962–ORNITHOLOGY), Greater Flamingo flocks engage in a convivial "fowl-like gabble," and individual birds give a honk reminiscent of a Greylag Goose. The flocking flight call is likened to "a chorus of frogs" and a courtship call is rendered as *eep-eep cak-cak, eep-eep cak-cak.*

Flamingoes are generally associated with the tropics, though they range well into the Temperate Zone in Patagonia and to lakes in the high puna zone of the Andes. The Greater Flamingo *(Phoenicopterus ruber),* may possibly have bred in "the old days" in the Florida Keys but there are

only anecdotes to support this speculation. They undoubtedly once occurred on the Gulf coast as stragglers from Caribbean colonies, and they
may still do so, but it is now hard to distinguish these from birds that have
escaped from Hialeah Park and elsewhere in Florida.

The origin of "flamingo" is widely described as deriving simply from a
Latin root as in the French *flammant* (flaming) referring, of course, to the
birds' color. However, Lockwood (1984–NAMES) says that the name derives from "Fleming," an epithet created by the Spanish because the birds'
rose wing coverts against their whitish body plumage reminded them of
the pale complexions and pink cheeks of the Flemish merchants with
whom they were trading as early as the fourteenth century. Spanish fla-
menco dancers are so named because their strutting movements resemble those of courting and "marching" flamingoes.

FLAMMULATED (FLAM-you-lay-ted) (Owl). Literally, "inflamed" or perhaps "tinged with flame" (color). This vivid adjective can only (barely!) apply to the rarer red morph of this little western scops-owl.

FLASH MARKS (aka banner marks). Bright, pale (often white) areas or
"flashes" in a bird's plumage, normally concealed when a bird is in repose
but revealed when it takes flight or otherwise displays the area. Examples
are the white rump patches in many woodpeckers and other birds, the
white spot in the tips of the tail feathers of many warblers, and the bold
striping that becomes apparent in the spread wings of a Willet. Some of
these markings may play a part in a species' courtship display, but they
are also thought to surprise and momentarily distract potential predators
and/or to direct their attention to parts of the body, which, if seized, will
not cause mortal injury. Flash marks such as the tail spots of redstarts and
wing flashes of mockingbirds may also aid in foraging as a means of flushing insect prey. See, for example, Jablonski (1999–COLOR AND PATTERN)
on Painted Redstart foraging behavior.

FLEDGE (fledged, fledgling). To grow feathers and, therefore, a verb
unique to birds; does not include the downy covering with which some
species are born. A young songbird confined to the nest is a "nestling";
once out of the nest it is a "fledgling" until it is independent of its parents.
When it has acquired its first true feather coat (juvenal plumage) or makes
its first flight, it is said to be "fledged." The term fledgling is problematic in
the case of precocial birds such as waterfowl, gallinaceous birds, and
shorebirds, which leave the nest before acquiring adult feathers. See
MOLT; YOUNG, DEVELOPMENT OF; FEATHER.

FLICKER. Standard English name for 6 species of woodpeckers in the
genus *Colaptes* (family Picidae; order Piciformes), two of which, the
Northern and Gilded Flickers, breed in North America. In 1973 the AOU

"lumped" three forms of North American flickers—Red-shafted, Yellow-shafted, and Gilded—into a single species, Northern Flicker. However, recent studies, including molecular research, while affirming the close relationship of the extensively hybridizing "red-shafted" and "yellow-shafted" flickers, also clearly showed a deep genetic divide between Northern Flicker and the seemingly intermediate, southwestern Gilded Flicker (see SPECIATION; HYBRIDIZATION).

The flickers build their nests by digging tree cavities, as do other woodpeckers, but they forage mainly on the ground, pursuing their preferred food, ants.

The Northern Flicker is among the most familiar of birds and has acquired a very long list of colloquial names. Ironically, the one that became official is of uncertain origin. Gruson (1972–BIOGRAPHY) associates the name with striking, i.e., pecking; Choate and Paynter (1985–BIOGRAPHY) suggests a connection with an old Anglo-Saxon usage meaning a "fluttering of birds." Without too much imagination, the call can be rendered as "flicka, flicka, flicka . . ."

For family characteristics, see WOODPECKER.

FLIGHT. Although all bats and a great many insects are skillful fliers—and a few birds are hopelessly earthbound—the words "bird" and "flight" are almost inextricably associated in the human mind. And for good reason. There can be no question that in the evolution of birdlife the power of flight has reached its greatest natural refinement and versatility.

EVOLUTION OF FLIGHT. The earliest adaptations among vertebrate animals to traveling through the air were kite-like modifications consisting of webs of skin stretched across the angles of front and/or hind limbs. This model is still with us in the form of flying squirrels, flying fish, and a few species of reptiles and amphibians. It allows these animals to "glide" or "sail" over much greater distances than can be traversed by simply jumping, but the duration of their flight is largely dependent on the height from which they launch themselves and the initial power they expend in takeoff.

Sustained flight, powered by a greatly modified forearm or wing, first evolved among reptiles such as the various pterodactyls familiar from the painted skies in museum reconstructions of the Jurassic and Cretaceous periods. Structurally, the reptilian wing was very different from the modern bird wing (for comparative anatomy of insect, reptile, bird, and bat wings, see WING). It still made use of the "stretched-skin kite" design but it did provide what only the lowly insects had by then achieved: the ability, once launched upon the air, to stay there.

The first *feathered* wing we know about belonged to *Archaeopteryx*, a very reptile-like bird of the Upper Jurassic, which may have been a far weaker flier than some of its fully reptilian contemporaries (see EVOLU-

TION OF BIRDLIFE). Its wing was an early experiment in what has proven to be the earth's most efficient flying mechanism.

DEFYING GRAVITY. The wings of flying birds, though widely variable, are all adapted in structure and shape to take advantage of a physical phenomenon called "lift." When air passes over a convex surface, such as an inverted saucer or a bird's wing in a normal, outstretched position, it travels faster across the top than across the hollow undersurface. This creates differential pressure, with low pressure in the smooth flow atop the airfoil of the wing and high pressure from below pushing it upward, which will raise the object in question if it is not too heavy. An inverted saucer exposed to a strong wind will be "lifted"—briefly. But a bird's wing, with its rigid, blunt but rounded leading edge, its smoothly curving convex surface (camber), and its tapered, flexible trailing edge, is adapted to "catch" lift and then control it in precise opposition to the downward pull of gravity. Adaptations to lightness in a bird's body, such as a fused and simplified skeleton and the hollowness of some of its larger bones (see SKELETON, Pneumatization), complement the force of lift in making a bird airborne.

Lift will not occur, of course, unless there is a continuous stream of air passing across the surfaces of a bird's extended wing. Gulls on a beach can sometimes be seen to simply raise their wings and be borne aloft by a strong wind. But in most cases birds must propel themselves into the air until the airspeed they encounter is great enough to raise their weight. This explains why we see birds "taxi" over the surface of the water or the ground and also why it is expeditious for them to "fall" off a high cliff or leap from the top of a tree. The alternative to these launching techniques is a powerful, rapid flapping of the wings, requiring a great expenditure of energy (see Taking Off, below).

Conquering gravity is only the first step in the complex art of flying. Once aloft, a bird must be able to move through the air, to maintain stability while moving, and to execute certain basic maneuvers efficiently and safely in a manner appropriate to the proportions of its body.

MOVING THROUGH THE AIR. Just as lift balances weight in getting a bird off the ground, another opposing force is needed if a bird is to overcome inertia and the resistance the air puts up against any body moving through it (drag). Evolution has provided all modern flying birds with an aerodynamically efficient form and a smoothness of surface, which minimizes drag to a great degree. And we shall eventually see that some birds are capable of using natural air movements such as thermals and updrafts to assist their efforts. But all birds must provide their own source of propulsion (or thrust) at least intermittently or on certain occasions, and many birds must do this more or less constantly when in the air. They do this by flapping their wings.

Whereas lift is managed largely by the broad, curved, relatively inflexible *inner* part of the wing (from the bend of the wing to the base, includ-

ing the secondary feathers), the forward motion produced by flapping is accomplished mainly by the flexible primary feathers that form the wing tip.

The mechanical details of how a bird achieves forward motion by flapping its wings are surprisingly complex. Common sense and a casual inspection of a passing cormorant lead us to the conclusion that birds more or less row or swim through the air, pushing the air below and behind them with their wings. But slow-motion and stop-action photography have revealed that neither the nature of the motion nor the details of wing action support this common sense hypothesis.

The basic physical components of a typical wing beat are clear enough (Fig. 14). When the main flight muscle (pectoralis major) contracts, pulling the wing down for the power stroke (see MUSCLES), the wing tip moves down *and forward* simultaneously. The primaries are held closed together so that air does not pass through them, and the resulting pressure bends them up and back. The power stroke ends with the wing tips swept far forward. Then the pectoralis major relaxes and the supracoracoideus muscle contracts, pulling the wing upward, the primaries open "like Venetian blinds," and, aided by the force of the air, the wing returns

Fig. 14. *Mechanics of flight.* The diagram at the upper right shows how the breast muscles act in conjunction with the skeleton to raise and lower a bird's wings. Some of the details have been simplified or stylized for the sake of clarity. Our model is flying directly at us and is raising one wing while it lowers the other—something birds *never* do in actual flight. To the let of the dotted divider, the *supracoracoideus* muscle (or *pectoralis minor*) has just contracted, pulling on the tendon that passes through a hole formed at the juncture of the scapula, coracoid, and clavicle bones (the last not shown) and is ultimately attached to the base of the humerus. The wing, in effect, is hoisted by a rope (tendon) and pulley (bone) powered by the supracoracoideus. To the right of the dotted divider, it is the *pectoralis* (major) that is contracting, hauling the humerus down in the powerful downstroke. The two breast muscles work in synchronized opposition, the pectoralis relaxing as the supracoracoideus contracts, and vice versa.

The "cutaway" loon shows the form of the pectoralis major muscle as it lies attached to and covering the breastbone (sternum). Note that the supracoracoideus muscle is completely obscured below the pectoralis from this view, as is the "rope-and-pulley" mechanism shown at upper right. Of course, birds move their wings in many subtle ways in addition to the up-and-down strokes of flight, but (except for two prominent tendons) the complex musculature that powers these wing movements has been omitted here.

A Bufflehead is shown in stop-action poses depicting the configuration of a single wingbeat. The top line shows the downstroke and the bottom the upstroke. Note that the wing tip moves down and forward and then up and back, inscribing a narrow, diagonal figure 8.

Another detail of the flying process is demonstrated by the meadowlark at bottom. To gain maximum lift from air pressure, the primary feathers are held tightly closed in the downstroke and then opened, like Venetian blinds, allowing less air resistance as they return to the top of the upstroke. Especially in larger birds, the wing tips are also curved upward in the midst of both strokes (as shown in the 4th and 5th "frames" in the top row of Buffleheads), creating a propeller-like action that pulls the bird along.

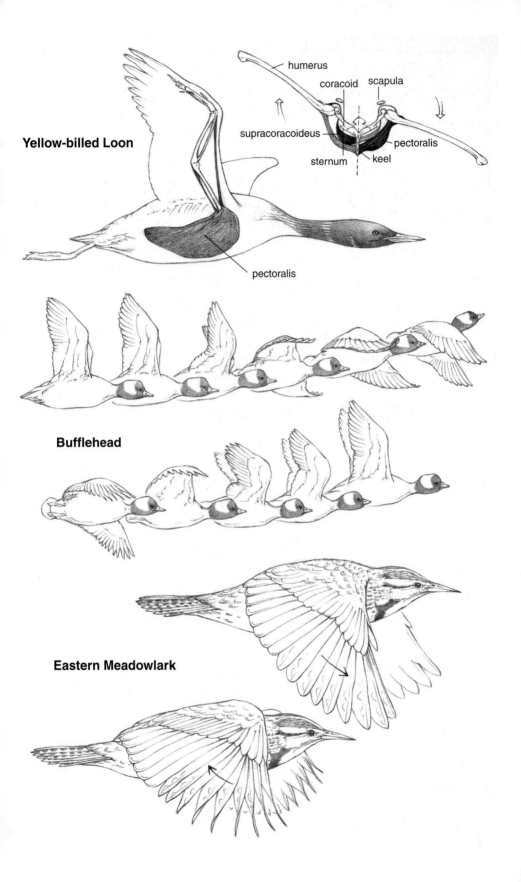

Yellow-billed Loon

humerus

coracoid   scapula

supracoracoideus

sternum   keel

pectoralis

pectoralis

Bufflehead

Eastern Meadowlark

to the top of the stroke. The pattern described by the wing tip is a diagonal figure eight. The supracoracoideus is unnecessary for maintaining flight once takeoff is achieved. Pigeons with the supracoracoideus tendon surgically cut cannot lift off from a standstill but can fly quite well if given a boost (Sy 1936, cit. in Gill 1994).

The way the wing tips and in some cases the individual primary feathers are twisted by the force of the air on the downstroke (and to a lesser extent on the return stroke) is thought to simulate the shape and motion of a propeller blade and in effect *to pull* the bird through the air. Other details of the wingbeat and of a bird's stabilizing systems remain inscrutable.

STABILITY. The airstream, which keeps a bird aloft and through which it travels, must pass smoothly over a bird's entire body. If the stream becomes turbulent, then uneven and counterproductive stresses on the body will disrupt the balance of speed and lift and if uncorrected will lead to a loss of control and a rapid loss of altitude. Again, there are some built-in antiturbulence feathers on a bird's body, but the individual must also exercise certain controls. As mentioned, the contours of the avian form have evolved to permit a smooth, even flow of air over all surfaces, and a bird can adjust its form by muscular control of the feather coat—becoming "sleeker" if necessary.

Crucial to stable flight is controlling the "angle of attack," i.e., the angle at which the wing meets the oncoming air. As the angle of attack increases, so does lift, but so also does turbulence. If the angle is increased too much, turbulence overcomes lift and the bird "stalls." To prevent stalling at a high angle of attack, a bird may raise its alula, the small group of feathers at the bend of the wing; this forms a "slot" that, in effect, corrects the flow of air, stabilizing the stream as it passes through the opening and over the wing surface. In some birds, notably broad-winged soaring birds, additional "slots" are apparent between the emarginate tips of the outer primaries.

Another constant source of turbulence is the eddies of air created along the trailing edges and tips of the wings in flapping flight. These "wing-tip vortexes" drag against forward motion and also swirl up onto the upper wing surfaces, disrupting the smooth flow of air over them. In wings that are long in proportion to their width, such as those of an albatross, such turbulence is minimized by the shorter surface over which the air must travel. In broad-winged birds, the problem is again corrected by the wing "slots," which "cut" the air into fast, uniform streams.

FORM AND FUNCTION. Though basic principles of flight must be obeyed by all birds, and mastery of basic maneuvers, such as landing and taking off (see below), are necessary for all, it is clear, if we compare warblers, woodpeckers, eagles, and albatrosses, that the *manner* in which basic principles are followed and maneuvers executed varies widely ac-

cording to a bird's particular "equipment" and the demands of its lifestyle. Length, breadth, and shape of body, wings, and tail, body weight, development of muscles, form of bill and feet—all in proportion to one another—determine the characteristic way different birds move in the air and their relative competence in various situations. Several of these physical relationships are essential in discussing the many flight styles that have evolved.

Aspect Ratio is the wingspan divided by average breadth. Albatrosses and other birds with long, narrow wings have *high* aspect ratios, which permit maximum lift with minimum drag and turbulence. This arrangement allows long-distance gliding with little necessity for flapping, which these birds cannot do with any force. This technique is greatly assisted by winds over the sea (see Dynamic Soaring, below). Most birds with low aspect ratios (e.g., songbirds) are incapable of gliding for any distance without rapidly losing altitude and must flap almost constantly. Soaring birds such as eagles have *low* aspect ratios but can catch maximum lift with their broad, strongly cambered wings with additional help from rising air currents (see Soaring, below). They are thus able to hold flapping energy in reserve.

Wing Loading is the proportion of wing area to body mass expressed as mass/unit area. Birds with low wing loading (lower mass/greater wing area)—vultures are good examples—tend to be more buoyant and capable of slow reconnaissance flight with little flapping, again aided by thermals. Loons, with massive bodies and smaller wing areas, have heavy wing loads and also a relatively low aspect ratio because of their short (though narrow) wings and so have to propel themselves by constant, rapid wing beats. This apparent shortcoming in flying apparatus is compensated by the benefits of a loon's small "retractable" wings and a heavy body in deep diving, an activity that would prove futile to an albatross and fatal to a vulture. The auks, by comparison, are "designed" to use their wings both above the waves and beneath them, in effect flying through the water.

Muscles. Not nearly as apparent as aspect ratio or wing loading is muscle development. The size and shape of a hummingbird's wings do not suggest great aerial competence. But hummers have enormously developed pectoral muscles (the greatest, proportionally, of any bird), and also highly developed supracoracoideus, which allows them to use a powered upstroke as well as a powered downstroke. This makes their wings uniquely powerful propellers.

Basic Maneuvers. All birds must be able to perform the following operations if they are to be successful fliers. Once again, method and competence are married to physical equipment. In addition, many commonplace actions, whether routine (e.g., landing) or subtle (e.g., pursuing prey through dense woods), are not entirely instinctive but rather are skills that must be learned and perfected for the sake of survival.

Taking Off. Birds with high aspect ratios, e.g., shearwaters, are masters of flight once airborne, but their long, narrow wings are not designed for flapping; they depend on "taxiing" over the sea surface on powerful legs until they can catch enough lift. Heavy birds with comparatively small wings, such as alcids, also have trouble taking off from a level surface and tend to perch or nest where they can simply drop off into the air.

Most birds, however, begin their takeoff at a more nearly vertical angle to the ground, thrusting downward with their legs for a boost and beating their wings powerfully in a horizontal plane back and forth to initiate the necessary airstream. This is a very different motion from the figure eight of normal flapping flight and is controlled by different muscles (mainly the supracoracoideus).

Altitude. To rise, a bird can shift its wings (and thus its center of gravity) forward, raising its head and lowering its tail. Ordinarily, though, it will raise its angle of attack as described above. Soaring birds are often assisted in gaining altitude by a variety of atmospheric aids (see Soaring, below). Losing altitude requires less effort, of course, but must be controlled by the mechanisms of speed and direction described below. (For height records, see ALTITUDE.)

Speed. A bird can accelerate by simply flapping faster and/or by streamlining its body to minimize drag. Depending on its needs, it can fold back the wing tips only, leaving the base of the wing extended for lift to maintain altitude. Or, like a Peregrine stooping, it can fold its entire wing close to its body and drop, gaining great speed through inertia and minimal drag. In slowing down, a bird applies an appropriate amount of drag by raising its angle of attack, putting wings, tail, and body before the wind (see Landing, below).

Turning. Altering body symmetry, e.g., folding one wing or twisting the tail to one side, will effect a turn, because the air then strikes part of the body with greater force than other parts. Birds soaring in the slipstreams of ships are easily seen making continual adjustments to fluctuating updrafts in this manner. More abrupt, directed changes of course require a shift in body weight and the twisting of the tail in a rudder-like action in addition to the appropriate wing movements to control stability and speed as well as direction.

Landing. Birds begin to lose speed in preparation for landing by increasing drag. They may, for example, tilt the trailing edge of the wing into the wind—the original "flaps"—or spread the tail to the same effect. If aiming for an elevated perch rather than a level surface, most birds will approach from below, raise their angle of attack, and then swoop up to the stalling point with wings fully extended and tail held vertically and spread. Simultaneously, the alula is extended to break the stall, the legs are thrust forward to meet the branch or perching surface, and the wings flap rapidly forward, halting all forward momentum. Anyone who has

watched a young bird overshoot a perch and crash into the adjacent shrubbery will appreciate the muscle coordination and skill required for a successful landing. Coming to rest on water or land usually is accomplished by a similar method, minus, of course, the upswoop. Waterbirds can afford less precise landings because their final contact is somewhat cushioned—grebes and alcids, for example, often bounce several times on choppy seas or aquaplane for several feet on calm water. Other aquatic birds, e.g., cormorants and ducks, extend their webbed feet forward and "water-ski" in as they make their stopping flaps.

Birds that are well adapted for soaring, when landing into the wind—e.g., a hawk on a treetop or a gull on a parking lot—may be able to maintain lift without forward motion and then simply drop gracefully into place. Less buoyant birds can do the same thing by hovering briefly before dropping onto their perch.

SPECIAL FLYING TECHNIQUES

Soaring might be defined as maintaining altitude without self-propulsion (flapping). By the laws of aerodynamics, then, it requires some other source of lift. One source is air currents diverted upward after meeting a surface. Winds hitting a cliff face, for example, are deflected upward and birds can sail along the edge of a precipice effortlessly suspended by these updrafts. Winds blowing out over a cliff face, i.e., offshore, can create upward-curling eddies below the edge that can also be used for support. A coastal or offshore gull or gannet colony is a good place to watch this method of soaring. Another is a ridge of mountains during a hawk migration. Similar updrafts over sea waves are also exploited. Pelicans are expert at sailing in formation along the crest of the wave line at tropical beaches, and shearwaters ply the air in the troughs of swells so skillfully that their wings do actually "shear" the surface occasionally with no loss of stability. Another variation is practiced by the gulls that ride the slipstream along the gunwales of large boats, flapping only to drop on a proffered potato chip.

Thermal Soaring (Fig. 28) depends on columns of rising warm air (thermals) that are generated at irregular intervals from the earth's surface via solar heat convection. As the column rises it expands toward the top and is finally set free by surrounding cold air. (Picture a bubble of air rising from the bottom of a glass container of boiling water.) Within the bubble there is a revolving circle of warm air with a continual updraft of cold air through the center. Finding one of these thermals, some birds can "ride" the rising ring of moving air to the desired height and then drift off in the desired direction, finding another thermal when they get too low. Vultures, eagles, and buteos depend on thermals in searching wide areas for prey without expending too much energy. These and other raptors as well as pelicans, cranes, and storks also need them to efficiently cover the long distances they travel during migration.

Since thermals are not generated over water, migrating soaring birds must skirt large lakes or other bodies that lie along their route, which explains why migrating raptors become concentrated along shorelines and especially in bottlenecks with water on both sides. When a large group of birds enters a thermal it swirls upward with it, showing the actual form and movement of the air mass. They may rise out of sight into the clouds, but at a given moment a single bird leaves the spiral and heads off in the appropriate direction, followed by the rest of the birds in a line, like a string unwinding from a top. Such whirlpools of birds are called "kettles" in North America.

Dynamic Soaring (Fig. 32) exploits the fact that winds blowing over the surface of the sea are slowed by the waves at the surface and gradually increase in velocity with altitude. Relatively heavy birds such as albatrosses, fulmars, and shearwaters with high aspect ratios (best for control and stability) can gain speed high in the fastest air and then plunge downwind; when they reach the slower air near the sea surface they then use their momentum to head up again, simultaneously turning into the wind, which blows them back aloft. The entire sophisticated maneuver is performed without a single flap. A variation of this technique is used in flying across the wind. One of the great spectacles of birdwatching along the coast is a flight of pelagic birds executing these dynamic arcs across the horizon in a gale.

Hovering is essentially flying in place. A number of bird species have developed the technique as a way of watching for and lining up on their prey from above. In a strong wind, gulls, jaegers, and certain raptors, such as Rough-legged Hawks, White-tailed Kites, and American Kestrels, can simply glide into the wind, flapping only often enough to keep their airspeed equal to the wind speed. Most hovering, however, is powered by a rapid horizontal beating of the wings with the body held more or less vertically; this is simply an extended version of the taking-off motion (see above) and requires a tremendous investment of muscular energy. Warblers and other insectivorous birds may hover momentarily while chasing an insect or during indecisive moments before perching. A few species—kingfishers, terns, American Kestrel, Osprey—have evolved the extra muscular stamina to sustain the action longer. Hummingbirds, of course, are the master hoverers. As noted above, they have the largest flight muscles in relation to body size of any bird and their flight feathers take up almost their entire wing—all flap and little lift. Their precision maneuverability is achieved with the aid of their broad tails. Even with this special design, hummingbirds must feed constantly and often become torpid during the night to conserve energy for such high-power hovering.

V Formation is standard travel procedure for pelicans, cormorants, cranes, ducks, geese, and swans and is practiced less habitually by gulls. The same destabilizing eddies that rise up over the trailing edge of a bird's

wing as it flaps (see Stability, above) can give a bird flying in its wake added lift, saving energy on long journeys. The lead bird, of course, misses the advantage, which perhaps explains why we often see the leadership shift in migrating flocks. The fact that we see no small birds in V formations suggests that they do not generate enough helpful ascending air to encourage the evolution of the pattern. See Weimerskirch et al. (2001) for a recent study of the phenomenon in pelicans.

See also EVOLUTION; FEATHER; WING.

FLIGHTLESSNESS. It is tempting to liken a bird that can't fly to a fish that can't swim, but this is not really a very good analogy. With very few exceptions, such as the swifts, birds tend to be at least as well adapted to life on the ground or in the water as they are to an aerial existence. Some birds, e.g., gulls, seem equally adept at all three. It is not very surprising therefore to find that there have always been and continue to be birds that have evolved terrestrial lifestyles at the expense of their power of flight. And it is now generally believed (Feduccia 1999–EVOLUTION) that *all* flightless birds descended from flying ancestors.

Though doubtless a precursor of a stronger-flying form, the first known bird, *Archaeopteryx,* was a poor flier whose wings mastered the air only to the extent that they enabled their owner to glide from tree to tree, much as a flying squirrel does today. Later diving birds in the genus *Hesperornis* of the Cretaceous Period, had only the tiniest of vestigial wings and passed its life on and under the water while strong-flying reptiles flapped and soared overhead. Terrestrial flightless birds often show a conspicuous protective adaptation that compensates for their inability to escape into the air. In many cases this adaptation takes the form of great size. The giant *Diatryrnas* of the Paleocene and Eocene epochs stood to 7 feet and had powerful legs and massive heads and bills to offset the uselessness of their puny wings. The much more recent Elephant Bird of Madagascar is thought to have weighed half a ton, and the largest of the giant moas of Australasia to have stood as tall as 13 feet—proportions that would inhibit most predators, though there was a moa-eating eagle in New Zealand (Atkinson and Millener 1991). Most of the living ratite birds, the Ostrich, Emu, cassowaries, and rheas, are also very large, though the kiwis of New Zealand rely on secretive nocturnal behavior rather than size for protection.

On isolated islands or lakes, species of flightless grebes, cormorants, ducks, and rails evolved in the absence of predators and consequently lacked any effective defense when man and his attendant rats, pigs, cats, and dogs disembarked in their domains. Many unique species, e.g., the Dodo and Great Auk, have ceased to exist through a combination of human callousness and their inability to fly from it, and almost without exception those that survive are severely threatened. Given its obvious

disadvantages, one is compelled to ask what the compensations of flightlessness might be. In addition to the circumstance that the ability to fly simply became unnecessary for nonmigratory species on predator-free islands, it has also been suggested, beginning with Darwin, that flightlessness (in insects as well as birds) might decrease the risk of getting blown out to sea.

Unique among modern flightless birds are the penguins, which, unlike the Ostrich and other ratites, did not lose the power of flight but rather adapted it to swimming. The term "ratite" implies the lack of a keel on the breastbone, to which the flight (pectoral) muscles of flying birds attach (see Figs. 14 and 27). Penguins have both keel and flight muscles, but their wings have become flippers, and they fly through the water rather than in the air.

If we survey the present world avifauna, it becomes clear that the ability to fly is not represented in a simple "have" or "have not" fashion but is highly variable among different species. Some birds, e.g., albatrosses, vultures, alcids, are powerful fliers under the proper conditions but are unable to get off the ground in others. Many species fly well enough but do so relatively infrequently, spending most of their energy in the water (grebes) or on the ground (many gallinaceous birds). Even within a single family, great variation in flying ability may be apparent. Many cuckoo species are graceful fliers and long-distance migrants, yet the anis seem barely able to cross a road despite a furious flapping of their short wings followed by a long *Archaeopteryx*-like glide; and the roadrunners, though apparently more capable than the anis, almost never take to the air, but prefer to run—even for their lives.

The only passerine bird species suspected of being flightless was the Stephen Island Wren, a member of a small family of birds (Acanthisittidae) endemic to New Zealand. It reputedly ran around on the ground like a mouse, but its habits were little known and it became extinct soon after it was discovered in 1894; its wing structure suggests that it may have been capable of weak flight.

Since the demise of the Great Auk (see EXTINCT BIRDS) no flightless bird species have occurred in North America.

FLIGHT PATTERN. The manner in which birds fly, often highly distinctive among different families of birds and even diagnostic at the species level. For example, almost all woodpeckers travel in a series of regular swooping undulations, alternating bursts of flapping with a glide of about equal length. The Spotted Sandpiper can be distinguished in flight from any other North American species from as far away as it can be seen by its highly distinctive flight pattern, consisting of a furious "whir" of shallow beats with wings held stiffly, interspersed with periods of glide. Only small shearwaters fly in a similar manner in North America.

Flight pattern is an element of JIZZ and is crucial to skillful field identification.

FLIGHT YEAR. A year in which unusually large numbers of a species occur in a given locality. The phenomenon is associated mostly with northern species—e.g., Great Gray, Hawk, and Boreal Owls, alcids, winter finches, Bohemian Waxwings—due to inadequate food supplies, overpopulation, or the like. See IRRUPTION/ERUPTION.

FLOCK (flocking). "Flock" is a broad collective term that applies to groups of any kind of bird, as well as to certain other animals, e.g., sheep; for more specific and less conventional collectives referring to birds, see NOUNS OF ASSEMBLAGE.

Flocking as a pattern of behavior may be practiced by normally solitary species under certain circumstances—e.g., Downy Woodpeckers often travel with mixed feeding flocks of titmice, nuthatches, kinglets, etc. Or it may be characteristic of at least one major phase in the life of a species. For example, Snow Buntings, not notably gregarious when nesting, migrate and feed in flocks before and after the breeding season; even more dramatic is the flocking of kingbirds in winter when they switch from an insect diet and become frugivores. Many colonial waterbirds—e.g., Double-crested Cormorants—tend to spend much of their entire life cycle in close association with others of their own kind, though not necessarily with the same individuals. Other species—e.g., Merlin, Yellow-billed Cuckoo—are just as determinedly solitary and are seldom found in even small groups.

Leaving aside colonial nesting (for which, see COLONY), flocking is associated with three basic activities: feeding, travel, and defense.

Feeding Flocks of foraging birds, such as blackbirds, move in a systematic "leapfrogging" progress across fields; birds at the rear of the flock pass over the heads of their fellows when they have gleaned a certain area of ground and land at the front rank. These flocks are normally silent or nearly so. Other species (e.g., many finches, waxwings) will arrive at a feeding site—a fruiting tree or seed-bearing conifer—en masse but feed individually (though closely) without following any apparent group dynamic. Such flocks tend to be noisier. Mixed flocks of forest birds, which often include titmice, creepers, nuthatches, kinglets, vireos, warblers, and representatives of other families, move noisily through the trees, feeding according to preference, seemingly oblivious to each other, and sometimes at some distance from their companions yet connected by the common goal of finding food efficiently while maintaining vigilance against predators. Seabirds of several species frequently congregate to exploit abundant food sources, such as fish schools or landfills. Groups of Double-crested Cormorants and American White Pelicans appear to have taken

this one step further when they engage in cooperative fish drives (see FOOD/FEEDING, Feeding Flocks).

Traveling Flocks include flights of birds (e.g., crows, herons) to feeding grounds and back to communal roosts, but reach greatest development during migration. A noteworthy feature of migratory flocks is the degree to which their membership may be "exclusive." In the great majority of cases, birds migrate only with their own species, though mixed flocks of closely related species (e.g., cormorants, scoters, swallows, waxwings)—usually with one species clearly predominating—are not unusual. Arctic shorebirds flock in different age groups, the adults leaving the breeding grounds a month or more before the birds of the year. Especially in spring, many passerine species (e.g., Red-winged Blackbirds) travel only with their own sex, a fact that may be related to the males' need to establish a territory on the breeding grounds before the females arrive. Canada Geese and other anatids migrate in congregations that are subdivided into family groups; the composition of the larger flocks may change but the family units (parents and offspring of the year) leave, winter, and return together.

Despite the tendency of most species to some form of segregation, migratory flocks containing mixed ages, sexes, and relationships also occur and, as noted, certain species are fundamentally solitary, even in migration.

Defensive Flocks are formed quickly in response to a common threat and usually consist of birds that are gregarious in another context. Mixed colonies of seabirds, for example, will rise together to harass an eagle, and foraging flocks of forest birds (described above) join forces to "mob" owls and jays for the same reason (see Fig. 19). Starlings and small sandpipers often arise in unison and form dense flocks, to thwart the intentions of predators such as Merlins and Sharp-shinned Hawks, which are confused by a mass of shifting forms and must "cut out" an individual bird in order to follow and kill it successfully. Indeed, some behaviorists hypothesize that the main impetus for feeding in groups is defense, since it combines the advantages of improved awareness, more effective response to threats, and statistical dilution of risk.

FLOCK DYNAMICS. No one who has seen moving aggregations of birds can fail to be impressed with the high degree of cohesion and simultaneity of motion. Though some behaviorists (e.g., Tinbergen 1951–INTELLIGENCE) have theorized that flocking is merely a by-product of instinctive activities such as feeding and migration, it is now widely believed that there is also a separate "flocking instinct." This is not to deny that certain details of flocking behavior (e.g., appropriate calls) need to be learned by individual birds.

A few specific flocking phenomena deserve emphasis.

"Following" describes an action initiated by one or a few birds in a flock and immediately imitated by the rest. This is best seen in flocks as

they cease one activity, e.g., feeding or resting, and begin another, e.g., drinking or preening.

Communication is a major element of cohesion in most flocks, though there are exceptions (see Feeding Flocks, above). Individuals in migratory and some feeding flocks often keep up a steady utterance of short notes; and alarm notes, warning of danger, are heeded in unison even when issued by a different species.

Spacing of precise dimensions is strictly observed in most flocks, each bird having in effect a tiny territory or "individual distance," which it will not permit to be transgressed. This is easily observed in sparrows feeding on the ground, swallows on a wire, or shorebirds working a beach or mud flat. At the other extreme, birds on the edge of a flock may allow themselves to lag or to wander some distance, but only to certain (apparently instinctual) limits. Except for aggressive encounters or where heat conservation is at stake (e.g., swallows or titmice huddling in a roosting cavity for warmth), birds rarely make physical contact with other members of a flock.

"Schooling" movements, such as the sharp, split-second turns executed in apparent perfect harmony by flocks of sandpipers, may be under the control of the central nervous system instead of (or as well as) being simply an unusually precise "following" action.

BENEFITS OF FLOCKING. The prevalence of flocking among birds is an indication that the practice has advantages that favor survival. A few obvious ones are as follows.

- Large numbers of birds congregated at an abundant food source (e.g., at sea) serve as a conspicuous signal to other birds searching for food within visual range.
- Flocks have increased sensitivity (multiple eyes, ears) to potential dangers, such as predators.
- Aggressive flocks discourage predation by mobbing raptors, nest robbers, or other "enemies."
- Close cohesion and rapid "schooling" movements frustrate falcons, accipiters, and other predators that take prey on the wing.
- Migrants that travel in V formation save energy by taking advantage of air currents created by the preceding birds (see FLIGHT).
- Navigational accuracy is improved in flocks where a "consensus" orientation is maintained, and presumably young birds benefit from traveling in flocks of experienced individuals (see NAVIGATION).

FLORIDA (South). The tip of Florida is the southernmost point in the United States and extends to within less than a hundred miles of the Tropic of Cancer. Its subtropical habitats, West Indian affinities, and remnants of one of the world's great wetland ecosystems result in the presence of bird species that occur regularly nowhere else in North America—which, in

turn, are a magnet for birdwatchers. A few of southern Florida's best-known birding areas are described below.

Sanibel Island. A once pristine, now extensively developed barrier island-cum-causeway off the Gulf coast of Florida near Fort Myers. The beaches and wetlands still contain numbers of shorebirds and wading birds, and the 7000-acre mangrove estuary of the J. N. "Ding" Darling National Wildlife Refuge is famous for its impressive population of herons, egrets, and Roseate Spoonbills that come (spectacularly) home to roost in the evening. Mangrove Cuckoo, Gray Kingbird, and Black-whiskered Vireo are present during the breeding season and White Pelicans winter in numbers. Unlike most barrier islands, Sanibel runs east-west, making it a kind of catchment area for marine mollusks and therefore a shell collector's treasure trove.

Corkscrew Swamp. An 11,000-acre National Audubon Society Sanctuary near Immokalee, northeast of Naples, Corkscrew contains the largest remaining stand of old growth Bald Cypress in North America. It is all that remains of the once extensive forest of the Big Cypress Swamp that succumbed to logging and fire. It was a major source of birds for the plume hunters (see CONSERVATION; AUDUBON SOCIETIES) and, as a result, became a major focal point of the early conservation movement, which managed its salvation. The sanctuary is noted among birders and thousands of other visitors for its raised boardwalk, which traverses 2.25 miles of the swamp and allows excellent studies of swampland birdlife (e.g., Limpkin, Wood Stork-major population of this endangered species, Pileated Woodpecker, Barred Owl, and more than 200 other species). It is also of great interest to birder-*botanists*. For a virtual tour and species lists, go to http://wwwaudubon.org/local/sanctuary/corkscrew.

Loxahatchee National Wildlife Refuge. A 147,392-acre (221 square mile) wetland just west of Palm Beach. The refuge now encompasses the last viable remnant of the northern Everglades ecosystem (see below). Florida wetland birds (e.g., herons Limpkin, rails) abound, but the refuge is probably best known for nesting Snail Kites and the occasional presence of the extremely local and retiring Masked Duck; it is a reliable south Florida locality for Fulvous Whistling-Duck, and Smooth-billed Anis may also be seen. For more detail, go to http://loxahatchee.fws.gov/Refuge/.

Tamiami Trail. Nearly 50 miles of scenic highway (U.S. 41) that crosses southern Florida between Naples and Miami. En route, it traverses an extensive mosaic of Everglades habitats (see below) in which thousands of herons, egrets, storks, and ibises can be seen with great ease along with other Florida specialties, such as Anhinga, Limpkin, Swallow-tailed and Snail Kites, and Short-tailed Hawk (uncommon, winter).

Everglades National Park. The everglades was once an immense "river of grass" flowing from Lake Okeechobee south through vast saw-grass prairies and freshwater sloughs to the mangrove estuaries of the

Gulf of Mexico. At over 1.5 million acres the present national park is the largest designated wilderness east of the Rockies and the only subtropical reserve in North America. It has been declared an International Biosphere Reserve and a World Heritage Site. Scattered throughout the grass (actually sedge) marshes are areas of open water, bald cypress swamps, and islands ("hammocks") of tropical hardwoods and pinelands composed of slash pine with a palmetto understory and more than 200 species of tropical plants. The birdlife of the park encompasses all the specialties of Southern Florida, including great concentrations and variety of waterbirds such as Anhinga, Purple Gallinule, herons, Roseate Spoonbill, Limpkin and Mottled Duck, raptors such as Snail and Swallow-tailed Kites and Short-tailed Hawk, the Cape Sable race of the Seaside Sparrow, and most of the land bird specialties noted for the Keys below. It is also, of course, rich in other forms of tropical wildlife, including many species that in North America occur only here; it is the only place in the world where alligators and crocodiles occur together.

Sadly, due to the development of the region for human use, Everglades has become one of the most threatened of our national parks. Populations of waterbirds have declined by 93% over the last 60 years and toxic levels of mercury are found throughout the food web. A key issue in the degradation of the system is disruption of the water cycle due to draining and water withdrawals for human use, but air pollution, chemical runoff from agricultural fields, and encroachment by the burgeoning population of the region have also contributed to this sad decline. In recent decades there has been strong popular mandate to restore the everglades and some progress has been made, but at present (2003) powerful economic lobbies have succeeded in stalling restoration momentum. For a famously evocative description of the Everglades, see *The River of Grass* by Marjory Stoneman Douglas, a conservation hero who founded the Friends of the Everglades when she was 79 years old.

Among the trails created by the U.S. Park Service to accommodate the million-plus tourists that visit Everglades annually is the boardwalk called *Anhinga Trail* not far from the park's Homestead entrance. It is particularly noted for the tameness of its birdlife (as well as its alligators). For extensive descriptions of the everglades ecosystems, its conservation, species lists and visitor logistics, go to http://www.nps.gov/ever/.

The Keys. A string of coral islands stretching southwestward from the southeastern tip of Florida and connected by the remarkable 165-mile Overseas Highway (the tail end of U.S. 1). The Keys are noted for a number of tropical (especially West Indian) bird species, most of which occur regularly in North America only in southern Florida: Magnificent Frigatebird, Great White Heron (white morph of Great Blue Heron), Reddish Egret, White-crowned Pigeon, Mangrove Cuckoo, Antillean Nighthawk, Gray Kingbird, Black-whiskered Vireo, and Shiny Cowbird. Many more

widespread species (especially waterbirds) are also present, and West Indian rarities such as LaSagra's Flycatcher and Western Spindalis are encountered regularly (see Appendix II).

The Dry Tortugas. The outermost of the Florida Keys, 68 miles west of Key West, and the best place in North America to see Sooty Tern and Brown Noddy, which nest on Bush Key. The waters around the Tortugas are good hunting grounds for other tropical seabirds, such as Audubon's Shearwater, Band-rumped Storm-Petrel, Magnificent Frigatebird, Brown, Masked, and Red-footed Boobies, White-tailed Tropicbird, and Black Noddy. During migration, windblown migrants seek safe haven on these barren, coral semi-deserts and occasionally spectacular concentrations of exhausted birds occur; West Indian land-bird vagrants are also recorded. Access is by commercial or charter flights or by boat from Key West. The destination point is historic Fort Jefferson and landings on Bush Key are prohibited during tern nesting season (March–September). However, the birds are a feature of most boat trips, including inexpensive 1-day ferry excursions or more costly 3-day birding tours that concentrate on the area's specialties. There are no hotels in the Tortugas, but campsites are available. Prime birding season is April through early May.

The current indispensable guide to Florida birding is Bill Pranty's *A Birder's Guide to Florida* in the ABA/Lane series (1996–BIRD FINDING).

FLYCATCHER. See TYRANT FLYCATCHER for New World flycatchers (Tyrannidae); OLD WORLD FLYCATCHER for Muscicapidae.

FLYWAY. A relatively narrow route along a prominent topographical feature, such as a large river valley or seacoast, which migratory birds follow to their destinations. It was once thought that most migration was concentrated in major flyways, e.g., the Mississippi Flyway, the Atlantic Flyway, but recent studies using RADAR and other techniques (see MOON WATCHING) have revealed that, on the whole, migration takes place over much broader areas of airspace. This is not to say that migrating birds do not make use of prominent landmarks for navigation, but rather that the once popular mental picture of masses of birds funneling down from northern breeding grounds into narrow travel corridors separated by vast areas of empty sky is a distorted view of the phenomenon. The concept continues to bear the federal government's stamp of approval due to the convenience it lends to regional waterfowl management programs. See MIGRATION.

FOLKLORE (birds in). See IMAGINATION, BIRDS IN.

FOLLOWING SHIPS. Many species of seabirds associate with boats of all sizes. Gulls have learned from long association the advantage to be gained by visiting even a small rowboat where fish are being caught and cleaned.

And the incredible largesse offered by modern fishing operations has proven so attractive to seabirds that it is given much of the credit/blame for the enormous increase and range expansion of several North Atlantic gull species (though open landfills associated with major coastal cities were also a major factor). The albatrosses, shearwaters, and gulls that follow larger, relatively high-speed vessels, such as large fishing boats or liners, not only profit from the refuse that is disposed of overboard but can also take advantage of the updrafts of air that are pushed up along the sides and stern of a moving ship to get a little free lift (see FLIGHT) and save energy. Fulmars seem to ride the side currents for the sheer joy of it (see PLAY) and will race along the rails, sometimes within reach of the passengers, and then cut sharply across the bow as if seeing how close they can come before allowing themselves to be blown astern for another run. Albatrosses, which are particularly adept at exploiting air currents in various ways (see FLIGHT, Dynamic Soaring, and Fig. 32), have been known to follow liners for weeks at a time over hundreds of miles of ocean. Gulls, too, are devoted followers, sometimes making transatlantic crossings in the company of ships, which may explain why European Lesser Black-backed Gulls are found with unusual frequency at outlying landfalls such as Bermuda, Nantucket Island (Massachusetts), and centers of shipping activity such as New York Harbor (though this species' recent great increase in Iceland is an alternative explanation).

It is interesting, though problematical, that the urge to follow ships occurs in varying intensity even among closely related species. Wilson's Storm-Petrels, for example, are inveterate ship followers, while Leach's Storm-Petrels will never fly in the wake for any distance, though it comes readily enough to feed on refuse. Some species, e.g., jaegers, will follow for short distances, but typically seem to lose interest quickly and move off.

A tangential phenomenon is the transportation of small land-bird migrants, which frequently wander (or are blown) out of their prescribed migratory routes and take refuge on ships at sea. A majority of these birds perish due to starvation or an excess of salt ingested with food they find on deck, but it has been proven that a few "hitchhike" all the way to the British Isles, explaining, in part, why so many North American land-bird vagrants occur in the Scilly Isles, the first land encountered on the southwest approach to England. Of course, some of these landbirds "belong" out there, e.g., Blackpoll and Cape May Warblers, and Northern Waterthrushes bound in fall from northeastern North America to the West Indies. It is therefore not surprising that Blackpoll is the most frequent parulid vagrant to Britain with 26 records as of 1991.

FOOD (birds, eggs, nests as). See EDIBILITY.

FOOD CHAIN/FOOD WEB. A way of describing interrelationships among life-forms and, especially, the transfer of energy from one organism

to another. The "classic" food chain begins with green plants, which manufacture energy from sunlight by means of photosynthesis. The next link in the chain is a leaf beetle (for example), which eats and derives energy from the plant; a Sulphur-bellied Flycatcher eats the beetle; a Cooper's Hawk catches and devours the flycatcher. The hawk, which is the ultimate benefactor of the combined energy of the organisms "below" it on the chain and is not likely to be consumed by a larger organism, is said to be "at the top of the food chain." It has been estimated that 99% or so of the original solar energy is lost to respiration and general "waste" through physiological inefficiency, a major reason why food chains peter out at three or four "links" (Lindeman 1942).

The cumulative effect of a food chain can be harmful as well as beneficial if there is something amiss in the lower links. Pesticides entering aquatic food chains after being washed out of croplands reach ever higher levels as increasing amounts pass from microorganisms to aquatic invertebrate larvae to small fish to big fish and finally to Ospreys or Bald Eagles or Brown Pelicans, which may be poisoned outright or rendered incapable of reproduction (see THREATS [OF HUMAN ORIGIN] TO BIRDLIFE).

"Food web" is a metaphor for the "interconnectedness" of the innumerable food chains that make up a particular system, whether a microhabitat or the world ecosystem. If we return to our original example, it is obvious that there are thousands of plant species and even more plant-eating insects, that both plants and insects are eaten not only by many species of birds but by an awesome variety of other organisms as well, and that even the corpse of the hawk at the top of many food chains is a juncture in the web, providing sustenance for blowfly maggots, carrion beetles, and perhaps vultures, as well as returning nutrients to the soil that will eventually be absorbed by green plants, and so ad infinitum.

FOOD/FEEDING. Birds, like all other animals, must eat to live, and if we analyze what most birds do during an average day, we would be justified in concluding that they live to eat. Food is the reason that the falcon stoops, the dipper dips, the woodpecker pecks, and the turnstone turns stones. Only the rituals of the breeding cycle even begin to claim a bird's time and attention to the extent that the activities associated with feeding do—and much of the breeding cycle involves harvesting food for voracious offspring! Having largely replaced hunting and gathering with fast food, most postindustrial humans forget that such an all-consuming obsession with food is the norm in the animal kingdom—even for the majority of their own species. To most of us, a meal is an event, like writing a letter. To a bird, however, the urge to feed is instinctual and nearly continuous; it is more a function—like breathing or reproduction—than a series of events.

BORN TO EAT. All birds come into the world with certain anatomical "tools" that are characteristic of their species and serve their particular

feeding priorities—e.g., specialized bills (see Techniques of Finding and Obtaining Food, below). And they are also born with a knowledge of specific ways of feeding that are triggered by stimuli in their normal surroundings (see INTELLIGENCE; FIXED ACTION PATTERN). For example, when chicks of gallinaceous birds, ducks, or sandpipers hatch, they almost immediately begin pecking or dabbing at small objects. Experiments indicate that at least in some cases this action is "released" merely by the size of the object and its degree of contrast with its background. By trial and error and parental example, the instinctive pecking eventually provides a meal, which, of course, reinforces the urge to peck. At the same time, we now know through field studies that much foraging behavior is learned and that individual birds hone their feeding technique and are capable of developing "specialty" feeding behaviors. Birds also learn—e.g., the location of reliable food sources—from other birds, including their parents (see INTELLIGENCE.).

WHAT BIRDS EAT. The record of what birds eat is far from complete—think of the effort involved in identifying the minutest plant and animal forms that birds doubtless ingest. But present evidence points to the conclusion that birds eat pretty much everything. Since sand, pebbles, shell, salt, and/or water are included in most species' "diets," their menu is not even restricted to organic substances. Only some of man's improbable concoctions, such as plastic, seem to be totally lacking in appeal.

One way to demonstrate the catholicity of animal tastes in food is to try to think of feeding opportunities they *don't* exploit. After all, we find birds taking food from deep in mud (godwits); from the upper layers of soil (American Robin); from ground surfaces (raptors, sandpipers, gallinaceous birds, doves, many finches); from rock surfaces (Purple Sandpiper, dippers); from leaf litter (Wood Thrush, towhees); from grasses (many sparrows); from tree trunks (woodpeckers, Brown Creeper, Black-and-white Warbler); from foliage at all levels (wide range of passerines); from lake and ocean bottoms (swans, Brant, some ducks); from stream beds (dippers); from deep waters (penguins, loons, auks, some ducks; see SWIMMING/DIVING); from the water's surface (many ducks, tubenoses, phalaropes); from crevices, including those in man-made structures (wrens, tits); and from the air (falcons, swifts, nightiars, swallows, and flycatchers). Of course, many species exploit two or more of these major feeding realms.

A similar comprehensiveness is revealed if we enumerate broad classes of matter that birdlife takes for food: seeds (gallinaceous birds, doves, many finches); leaves of flowering plants (doves, grouse); coniferous foliage (some grouse); lichens (ptarmigan); seaweed (sea ducks, Brant, Glaucous Gull); freshwater algae (ducks); flowers (parrots, waxwings); nectar (hummingbirds, orioles, some wood warblers); fruits (grouse, thrushes, waxwings, Phainopepla, wood warblers, tanagers, orioles, many finches); sap (sapsuckers and a variety of passerines); wax (Myrtle War-

bler); macrozooplankton (storm-petrels and other seabirds); jellyfish (gulls, other seabirds); annelids, e.g., earthworms and sea worms (woodcock, many other long-billed shorebirds, American Robin); an enormous range of crustaceans, e.g., amphipods, barnacles, shrimp, isopods (many water birds), and crabs (gulls); spiders (wrens, many other "insectivores"); ticks (anis); insects (the majority of birds eat some, many feed on them almost exclusively); mollusks (loons, grebes, ducks, geese, gulls, shorebirds, thrushes [snails]); starfish and sea urchins (gulls); fish (most water birds, Osprey, kingfishers, occasionally flycatchers, grackles, dippers, etc.); amphibians (herons, some hawks, some ducks, kingfishers, crows); reptiles (hawks, some owls, herons, cormorants, ducks, turkeys, cranes, rails, roadrunners, crows, and even small passerines—albatrosses are known to eat an occasional sea snake); birds (hawks, falcons, owls, shrikes, and occasionally herons, gulls, corvids, and other large omnivores); bird eggs (turnstones, gulls, skuas, corvids, wrens); other eggs—e.g., fish and horseshoe crab, etc. (sandpipers, gulls, probably corvids); mammals (hawks, falcons, jaegers, owls, shrikes, occasionally herons, gulls, corvids, and other large omnivores—the largest live prey taken by any North American bird are young deer and antelope, which are occasionally attacked by Golden Eagles); carrion (vultures, some hawks, gulls, corvids); animal blood, fat, and oils (many tubenoses, in addition to raptors and carrion eaters); garbage (vultures, some eagles, gulls, and some corvids); and even excrement (vultures, petrels, gulls, and alcids).

This is by no means an exhaustive account of what birds eat, but it hints at the range. Of life-forms with which most people are familiar, only the fungi are apparently little eaten by birds. Another generality that emerges from this overview is that, though many species of birds are essentially vegetarians, most are sustained primarily by animal food and virtually all at least occasionally balance their diets with some high-protein invertebrates.

VARIATION IN DIET. Birds eat different things according to the habit of their species, their age, where they live, and the availability of acceptable food.

Some bird species are notably fussy eaters. Limpkins and Everglade Kites, for example, prefer large freshwater snails to other foods and tend to live only where these flourish. Of course, such narrow tastes can be dangerous if the favorite food disappears for some reason. When the eelgrass beds of the east coast suffered a plague in the 1930s, the Brant populations, which were sustained almost exclusively by this one plant species, also declined drastically. The survival risk implicit in such narrow diets probably explains why most species have more flexible tastes; some individual Brant figured out that sea lettuce (*Ulva lactua*) wasn't too bad and the species is still with us.

At the other extreme, some species and/or families (e.g., gulls, many

corvids) are nearly omnivorous and will eat plant material, live vertebrates and invertebrates of all kinds, as well as carrion and waste products. Though it might balk at a dead skunk, the Ruffed Grouse is known to
have eaten parts of at least 414 species of plants and 580 species of animals (Van Tyne and Berger 1976–ORNITHOLOGY).

Most birds have characteristic but not severely restrictive food preferences. Ospreys prefer fish, hummingbirds nectar, and a great many
species are partial to insects or seeds. But Ospreys will eat any of a wide
variety of fish *species*, depending on what is available, and faced with a
general dearth of fish will take small mammals or birds—or even a small
alligator (Poole et al. BNA, 2002, #683). A Magnolia Warbler would quickly
starve if it demanded the same species of insects on its Mexican wintering
grounds that it habitually consumes in Canada, where it breeds. Therefore, its tastes must encompass hundreds of species of many families of
insects, not to mention spiders and other invertebrates and even occasional sips of nectar. On the other hand, Magnolia Warblers are still slaves
to their food preferences to a large extent. Since both invertebrates and nectar are in short supply during the Canadian winter, birds that feed on them
must move south to warmer climes (see MIGRATION; DISTRIBUTION).

Other birds have solved this problem by staying put and adapting
their feeding habits to prevailing conditions. Some woodpeckers, for example, shift from a largely insect to a largely fruit and seed diet as the season changes. Almost universally, nestlings are fed "meat," even in species
whose mature tastes run to plant food. Pigeons and doves, which nourish
their nestlings on a high-protein crop secretion (see CROP MILK), and
crossbills, which often rear young during the winter months and feed
them exclusively conifer seeds, are among the few exceptions. Some authorities believe this supports the theory that the earliest birds fed on
animal substances exclusively (as do most modern reptiles) and only
gradually evolved vegetarian forms.

ROLES OF THE SENSES IN FINDING FOOD. Indisputably, the sense
most crucial to finding food for the majority of birds is sight, but there are
important exceptions. After debates going back 200 years, it has finally
been proven that the Turkey Vulture can locate at least some types of carrion by its odor (see SMELL), but this talent is apparently less developed in
its near relative, the Black Vulture. Owls, hunting at night, depend to a
large extent on their sense of hearing to zero in on their prey, and Barn
Owls are known (Payne 1962–HEARING) to be able to capture a mouse in
total darkness, guided only by the sounds made by the animal, a feat
made possible by the owls' acute hearing and asymmetrical ear apparatus; harriers also use hearing to capture prey (see HEARING).

The range of certain birds' hearing and certain gestures they make
while foraging have led some authorities to infer that woodpeckers,
woodcock, and American Robin (for example) locate their quarry under-

ground or in a tree trunk by hearing its movements. Woodcock and many other mud-probing shorebirds with sensitized bill tips find their prey by touch.

TECHNIQUES OF FINDING AND OBTAINING FOOD. So great is the extent to which birds' lives are occupied in finding food that the evolution of avian anatomy can be read as the development of a variety of food trapping, harvesting, and processing machines. Any mutation that inhibited food getting would obviously reduce its bearer's odds for survival and therefore its own likelihood of being perpetuated. It can also be fairly stated that most well-established avian features can be shown to assist the nearly perpetual search for a meal, however indirectly. It might be argued that birds do not catch food or eat with their feathers, but, of course, without them, many raptors and insect-eaters could not catch their respective prey.

The feet of a Northern Goshawk (see Fig. 17) are well adapted to grasping branches and are even useful in walking in the few circumstances in which a goshawk needs to do so. But their most important function is to catch and kill food.

Given its proximity to the mouth, it is perhaps not surprising that a bird's bill—as with a mammal's teeth—reflects its owner's specific feeding habits more vividly than any other obvious physical character: an ibis's bill is a probe, a duck's bill a strainer, a phalarope's bill a forceps, a hawk's bill shears, an anhinga's bill a lance, a nightjar's gape a funnel, a nutcracker's bill a hammer, and so forth—the specialized tools of master food getters. The uses of many bills are easily guessed at—long, slender bills are clearly designed for probing, whether in mud (snipe) or flowers (hummingbird); while a grosbeak's bill is obviously ineffective as a probe but it is an ideal crushing mechanism. Some bills have evolved as all-purpose tools. A gull's beak is a kind of avian Swiss Army knife, capable of shearing an eel in two, tearing flesh, hammering into a crab's carapace, grasping a purloined cormorant egg, and picking dainty morsels from a raft of floating garbage. For a more comprehensive discussion of some of these self-evident functions, see BILL.

Some of the methods and "tools" by which birds search out and obtain their food are more complex and/or less obvious to the casual observer and merit a brief description.

Flight Mannerisms. An unusually slow flight has evolved in the harriers and the Turkey Vulture as a means of effectively scanning large areas for their preferred prey. Some seabirds, most buteos, and vultures soar on rising air currents for a similar purpose. And the American Kestrel, some hawks, and kingfishers hover in midair, keeping their heads stationary to watch for movements of small, quick prey below. See FLIGHT, Soaring and Hovering, and Fig. 28.

Nightjars have small bills but enormous gapes (2 inches fully opened in Chuck-will's-widow; see Fig. 13) and fly through the air with their

mouths open, swallowing numbers of insects (from tiny flies to large bee-tles) and even an occasional small bird tree frog or bat! (Lentino 1978 in BNA, 2000, #499). It has been widely suggested—but not conclu-sively shown—that the long, stiff, modified feathers (rictal bristles; see FEATHER) that border the upper half of the gape in most nightjar species serve to enlarge their effective "funnel" and also detect the presence of in-sects flying nearby in the dark. The latter hypothesis gains some support in the fact that the nighthawks (genus *Chordeiles*), which on the average fly during daylight hours more frequently than other nightjars, lack rictal bristles.

Canopy Feeding is practiced by some heron species and consists of raising the wings to create a shadow over shallow water. This may serve the dual purpose of attracting fish and cutting surface glare for the heron. See CANOPY FEEDING and Fig. 5.

Foot Movements are used in several bird families to flush prey within reach. Herons and some shorebirds stir the bottom in shallow pools and pick up any disturbed invertebrates. The characteristic "spinning" of phalaropes is an elaboration of this technique. Some gulls are reputed (Meyerriecks 1966) to "paddle" the earth with their feet to bring earth-worms to the surface. And "foot flushing" is also recorded in some ground-feeding songbirds.

Tongues. Many woodpecker and hummingbird species have unusu-ally long tongues that can be extended into a tree cavity or flower calyx as much as several inches aided by the HYOID APPARATUS, an extendible bone and muscle structure present in all birds (and in reptiles). This mechanism is attached at the base of the tongue, coils around the back and top of the skull, and is anchored at the nostrils. The tongues of these birds bear a variety of specializations—barbs, brushes, grooves, saliva—that help to capture and/or swallow particular food types (see TONGUE for details).

Wing/Tail Flashing, i.e., lifting the wings suddenly, is apparently used by species of herons and mockingbirds to startle aquatic life and insects into motion, so that they can be seen and eaten. Mockingbirds also use this gesture (see Fig. 1) in confrontations with snakes and other threaten-ing situations. Tail flashing by gnatcatchers, fantails, and redstarts ap-pears to have a similar function.

The Bills of Avocets are strongly recurved toward the tip and vertically flattened. When a bird lowers its bill into the water, the upturned third of the bill becomes parallel to the surface and is swept rapidly back and forth amidst the surface algae or in bottom sediment, flushing invertebrates to be caught and eaten. This action is analogous to the foot motions of other shorebirds (see above).

The Bills of Spoonbills are strongly flattened vertically and widened into a spatula shape at the tip. The interior of the "spoon" is lined with sen-sitized tissue. Spoonbills feed by wading in shallow water and sweeping

their partially opened bills from side to side in bottom sediment and vegetation. When live organisms (small fish, mollusks, crustaceans, etc.) are
felt by the bill, the mandibles close on the prey.

Skimmers are unique in having a lower mandible that is significantly
longer than the upper—an adaptation to an equally unique method of
feeding. The birds fly low over calm water (often at dawn and dusk and in
flocks) and "shear" the surface with the tip of the lower mandible, which
is laterally flattened to nearly razor sharpness. When a fish or other edible
object is encountered by this blade, the upper mandible closes down on it
instantaneously. (The action is pictured in Fig. 3.) Skimmers will often re-
trace a stretch of water they have just "plowed," apparently to take advantage of fish that rise to investigate the initial disturbance.

See also INTELLIGENCE, Tool Use.

Feeding Flocks. Flocks of cormorants, sometimes containing hundreds of birds, will form a line at the edge of a school of fish swimming
near the surface and systematically advance on their prey. The flock
members do some "leapfrogging," such as that practiced by foraging
blackbird flocks (see FLOCK), but they also dive continuously so that a
large proportion of the flock is always beneath the surface.

American White Pelicans, which do not dive for fish from the air as do
Brown Pelicans, form semicircles of half a dozen birds, surround a school
of fish, and by splashing and beating their wings drive them into shallow
water where they are readily caught. Flocks of American Avocets and
Black-necked Stilts also engage in fish drives.

Seabirds of several families (e.g., gulls, terns, jaegers, shearwaters,
storm-petrels, gannets) are sensitive to the sight of congregations of birds
over the ocean, which indicate the presence of food, in the form of either
a school of small fish driven to the surface by marine predators or a fishing boat cleaning its catch. It has been theorized that the light color of
many seabirds against the dark sea contributes to the success of this form
of cooperation. A white under surface may also make these birds less visible against the pale sky to potential prey looking up from the water. A
similar practice is followed by vultures and other scavengers that are
alerted to the presence of carrion by a conspicuous column of their kind
marking a distant carcass.

Mixed flocks of small forest birds may stir up more live food as they
move through vegetation than would a single bird, and thus benefit all
participating individuals. This advantage may also explain the flock feeding of American Avocets, which flush food by agitating bottom sediment
with their bills (see above).

Secondary Feeding, i.e., taking advantage of a food source generated
by another animal.

- Anis, Bronzed Cowbirds, and Fish Crows reportedly pick ticks and
  other ectoparasites off cows and other ungulates.

- Frigatebirds, jaegers and skuas, and some gulls and eagles habitually steal food caught or found by other birds, though all such "kleptoparasites" can and frequently do obtain food on their own. Other forms of kleptoparasitism include pilfering from caches by tits, jays, etc., food stealing in mixed-species foraging flocks, and eelgrass theft by wigeon from diving bay ducks. (For further detail, see PIRACY.)
- Many species of birds, including herons, ducks, phalaropes, and kingfishers, have been observed following other bird species that stir up edible plants and animals while foraging for themselves. Swans, for example, which can reach bottom vegetation in deep water with long necks, are sometimes attended by dabbling ducks, which pick up floating plant parts dislodged by the swans.
- Numerous small birds (e.g., hummingbirds, vireos, warblers, kinglets) sip sap from the holes made by sapsuckers.
- Cattle Egrets, anis, and gulls follow feeding livestock to catch the insects flushed by the larger animals. Cattle Egrets have, of course, made a "profession" of this practice. In Europe small songbirds have been observed to use small mammals in a similar way (e.g., Eurasian Robins and moles), and elsewhere various insectivorous birds have been seen to "use" trains and automobile traffic with similar motives. In the tropic flocks of forest birds will follow beneath with troops of monkeys that shake insects out of the canopy as they move through it.
- Humans have inadvertently created many new food sources for birds, the most copious of which, e.g., open garbage dumps and the refuse of a burgeoning fishing industry, have been credited with (or blamed for) increasing populations of birds such as fulmars and (especially) gulls. A number of our labor-saving machines dispense bird food as by-products. Gulls, American Robins, and other birds frequently follow plows to pick up grubs and the like from the turned soil, and gulls and crows take advantage of mowing machines, which expose nests of voles and hayfield-nesting birds. Many seabirds follow ships—even in the absence of fish spoils or garbage—to pick up marine tidbits churned to the surface by the screws. Pelagic birds follow pods of whales and dolphins and schools of tuna and other large fish to take advantage of small prey driven to the surface as well as "leftovers." Some insectivorous birds have learned to wait along busy roadsides and pick up insects disabled by passing cars; this, in turn, sometimes results in dead birds, which may attract crows, whose corpses invite vultures, and so on. Chickadees and nuthatches have been observed feeding on hickory nuts cracked by passing cars along a back road. (W. Ellison and N. Ellison 2001, personal communication).

How Much Birds Eat. The quantity of food ingested by birds is directly related to how much energy they can store and the level of energy required by a species' particular lifestyle. As anyone would guess, large birds eat more in absolute quantity than small birds. However, in general, the smaller the bird, the more it eats *in proportion to its body weight.* This is because small birds have a higher metabolism, i.e., "burn fuel" faster than large birds. Therefore, while an eagle may eat 2 pounds (1 kg) of meat a day and a pelican 4 pounds (2 kg) of fish (Terres 1980–BIRD), these amounts constitute only about a quarter and a half of body weight, respectively. By contrast, a hummingbird that consumes twice its weight or more per day in nectar and insects may have taken in under half an ounce (12 g) of food. Within this generality based on size, there are many exceptions because of differing lifestyles. Small, but comparatively sedentary birds, such as doves, may consume less in relation to body weight, for example, than eagles do. Another generality about avian food consumption is that birds eat more in cold weather and less in hot. This, too, is related to expenditure of energy, which is greater when low temperatures require more energy to maintain sufficient body heat.

A more vivid way of conveying how much birds eat is to report what is likely to be found in a bird's stomach at any given moment during a normal day. It is not unusual for a dabbling duck's stomach to contain between 50,000 and 100,000 seeds or plant parts, and 185 blue mussels have been taken from the digestive tract of a single Common Eider.

The stomachs of insectivorous birds may contain hundreds of caterpillars or 5,000 or more small insects, such as ants or mosquitoes. These totals are all the more impressive when we consider that birds can pass food through their digestive tracts in 30–90 minutes, so that the above totals represent only a fraction of a day's consumption.

When and How Often Birds Feed. The feeding schedules of species and individual birds differ markedly according to a number of variables. Obviously, hummingbirds and small songbirds, which must consume a large proportion of (or more than) their body weight per day, must feed almost constantly during daylight hours. Observers of such species maintain that this is indeed the case, and it has been proven that at least some hummingbirds occasionally go into a kind of coma after dark to lower their metabolism during the nightly fast (see TORPIDITY). As with the amount of food needed, there is a general reverse correlation between the size of a bird and the number of meals. It should be remembered, however, that birds such as eagles or vultures must spend much more time hunting and/or killing their food than, for example, insect or seed eaters, and, therefore, food-associated activities may take up a large proportion of their day, despite the fact that relatively little time is spent actually eating.

Obviously, food availability affects how often birds eat (though it does not usually reduce time spent searching for food). Many birds can gorge

themselves when food is available and hold it for a short period undigested in their crops (see DIGESTIVE SYSTEM) for use when snow covers food supplies or, in the case of vultures, when no carrion can be located. A few birds (penguins, chicks of many tubenoses) can accumulate vast fat stores and live for weeks or even months without a meal.

Under normal circumstances, the majority of bird species have some kind of regular feeding routine. Most feed only during daylight, but, of course, owls and nightjars have evolved nocturnal feeding schedules, and a few species prefer the twilight periods near sunrise and sunset. Some routines are based on environmental factors: shorebirds tend to feed on exposed flats at low tide and roost in marshes, fields, or dunes at high water; vultures must wait for thermals to be generated to begin their hunting day (see FLIGHT); plankton tends to rise toward the surface of the sea during the night and is followed by the many larger marine organisms that feed on it, so that many pelagic birds feed most actively in the dark or in the early morning hours; earthworms also rise to the surface at night, encouraging American Robins and woodcock to seek them mainly near dawn and dusk; at midday, robins usually seek other fare.

Every birdwatcher and feeder owner is aware that early morning and late afternoon are periods of increased feeding activity for most diurnal birds and has probably also noticed other apparent peaks of activity during the middle of the day. Small birds that must forage constantly nonetheless tend to adhere to a fairly fixed routine, especially when the food source is dependable—feeder birds show great regularity in their visits even though they may hunt food elsewhere throughout the day. Another phenomenon noticed by feeder owners is the apparent sensitivity of birds to approaching bad weather, which results in unscheduled—often frenzied—visits to the seed and suet bins.

PREPARATION OF FOOD. With no teeth and a poorly developed sense of taste, most birds swallow their food whole, leaving hard substances to be pulverized by the powerful muscles and grit reserves in the gizzard (see DIGESTIVE SYSTEM). Indigestible substances, such as shell, bone, feathers, and hair, are then regurgitated in a consolidated mass (see PELLET).

There are, however, some conspicuous exceptions to this general rule. Hawks, eagles, and falcons usually pluck feathers or areas of fur and pull small pieces of meat from their prey. They also tend to eat somewhat selectively, often discarding or ignoring the entrails, for example. Owls, by contrast, tend to bolt prey whole or, in the case of large animals, tear off and swallow large pieces.

The versatile gulls will gulp their food when possible and in many cases manage to swallow fish that clearly stretch their flexible esophagi to the limit. But they will also hack and tear pieces out of very large items, e.g., a seal carcass, as will skuas and some of the larger tubenoses.

Some gulls learn the effectiveness of dropping hard-shelled items (mollusks, crabs, sea urchins) from the air to crack their shells, but com-

petence in the technique varies: certain individuals show poor judgment as to the surface on which they drop their prey, while others habitually fly to suitably hard "cracking grounds." Crows are also known to use this system and some have figured out that items dropped on roads will be "prepared" by passing traffic.

Birds that take large insects sometimes remove struggling legs that would impede consumption and are frequently seen to whack their prey against a branch or rock to kill it, remove hairs (e.g. from caterpillars), or otherwise improve its consistency.

Some seed-eating birds habitually crack the hard outer husks of seeds either by holding them between their toes or wedging them in a crevice and hacking at them with their bill (tits, nuthatches [= "nuthacks"], jays) or crushing them under the pressure of their heavy, specially modified bills (e.g., grosbeaks; see BILL for a description of the process).

A few unusually sophisticated preparation methods deserve emphasis:

The ability of some birds to avoid toxic chemicals deposited in the exoskeletons of certain insects from their food plants has been proven in at least one instance. Bullock's Orioles have been recorded as squeezing out the "uncontaminated" insides of monarch butterflies, thus avoiding the cardiac glycocides concentrated in their wings and "skin." The origin of the poison is the milkweed plants (*Asclepius* spp.) on which the butterflies' larval stage feeds. In many if not most cases the effect of the toxin is to discourage birds from eating monarchs after an encounter or two with the bad-tasting cathartic. See Brower and Brower (1964). A similar fastidiousness is demonstrated by birds that wipe irritating spines off caterpillars and the toxic slime from slugs.

The bills of oystercatchers are laterally flattened toward the tip. This thin, sharp tool is inserted chisel-like between the shells of live bivalves and then shears the powerful adductor muscle(s), which otherwise would hold the shells closed "as tight as a clam" (see Fig. 3). Anyone who has tried to open an oyster or hard-shelled clam without proper tools will appreciate the finesse in this evolutionary achievement. Occasionally a bivalve gets the better of the bird by closing tightly on its bill before the muscle is severed and while the mollusk is still anchored in the sand; when the tide comes in, the oystercatcher drowns.

The bills and feet of Everglade (Snail) Kites are specially adapted for extracting from their shells the large snails on which they feed exclusively. Their long toes and claws are ideal for holding the round, slippery shells and the long, slender, strongly decurved upper mandible serves to penetrate the columellar muscle by which gastropods hold on to their shells. Lang (1924) reported that Snail Kites in Guyana wait until a captured snail raises its hard operculum of its own accord before stabbing their bills into the soft muscle and then wait again for the pierced muscle to relax so that the shell can be shaken free. But Snyder and Snyder (1969) observed a

more active procedure in Florida whereby the bill is inserted under the closed operculum and severs the columellar muscle.

Crossbills have evolved the most interesting bill modification of any North American bird species; its precise workings have been debated in print at least since the eighteenth century. A description of the crossbills' unique means of extracting cone seeds should perhaps begin by noting that they do not always need to employ all of the several aspects of their technique. They are, for example, perfectly willing simply to pick seeds out of a fully opened pine cone, munch spruce buds, or even gobble suet from a feeder, as do seedeaters with less elaborate equipment. The full play of a crossbill's talents is exercised only in extracting seeds from *green, tightly closed, unripe cones.* In attacking such a cone, the crossbill plucks it and takes it to a horizontal perch, where it holds it down firmly with one of its unusually large, powerful feet so that the long axis of the cone lies slightly at an angle to the long axis of the bird. The tip of the longer upper mandible (which curves downward) is then wedged between two of the cone scales so that the curve of the lower mandible rests on the surface of the cone and the tip of the upper mandible is fixed on the inside surface of a scale. The bird then twists its head in such a way that the force exerted against the stable lower mandible forces the scale apart on the tip of the upper mandible. Simultaneously, the two mandibles are forced apart by special jaw muscles—not in the usual vertical plane of birds opening their bills, but in a horizontal (lateral) motion that contributes essential force to the separating process. Once the scales have been forced apart, the unusually large, protrusible tongue reaches into the cavity and detaches the firmly anchored, unripe seed with the aid of a special cartilaginous cutting tool that forms the tongue tip. Needless to say, this procedure is very difficult to observe in wild (or even captive) crossbills, and is not easily illustrated. Figure 3 shows the dynamics of the head/bill maneuver in relation to the already opened pine scales. Watching crossbills feed at close range, one is most aware of the head-twisting motion, which is very vigorous and rapid and accompanied by loud cracking noises as the pine scales give. It is also possible to see the fat, parrot-type tongue come into play, but the lateral motion of the mandibles and the cutting action of the tongue tip are normally invisible. The crossbill's unique mandibles are also used as shears to slice through soft fruits such as apples to get at the pips.

STORING FOOD. Woodpeckers, tits, nuthatches, and members of the crow family habitually store food. The degree to which it is retrieved by the storers apparently varies and has been thoroughly studied in only a few species. Eurasian Nutcrackers are known to recover a majority of the nuts they bury in caches in the ground both for sustenance during the winter and to feed young in the spring. And the North American Clark's Nutcracker stores food in communal caches and displays an uncanny

ability to relocate these sites even when they become obscured by heavy snow cover (See MEMORY). Acorn and Lewis's Woodpeckers store huge quantities of acorns and other nuts in the trunks of trees, telephone poles, and the like—the former drilling shallow holes into which the acorns are riveted. These species are known to retrieve stored items and to defend their caches against theft by other birds, indicating that such reserves are at least a hedge against starvation. In Acorn Woodpeckers this is a communal activity.

Several species of carnivorous birds occasionally store carcasses to which they return. The shrikes do this most conspicuously, hanging small mammals and birds on thorns or in crotches and feeding on them over a period of days. There are instances of them revisiting these "larders" after a period of months, but whether this qualifies as true storage in the sense of laying by crucial food reserves has not been clearly documented.

That many stored materials go unrecovered is demonstrated, for example, by the sprouting of oak trees where jays were known to have buried acorns (see SEED DISPERSAL). Tits, nuthatches, and treecreepers have also been seen eating the stores secreted in bark crevices by other tits and nuthatches. To explain why birds would store food to which they did not "intend" to return, some authorities hold that it satisfies the urge to forage and feed after a bird's appetite has been sated. However, though food-storing birds may not be showing true "forethought," recent research makes it clear the behavior has evolved as a mechanism for creating food supplies for lean times.

See also DRINKING; GRIT.

FOOD PASS. A habit of some species of raptors, especially the harriers, in which an item of food is transferred from the talons of one bird to those of another. The receiving bird sometimes turns upside down in the air, as in the tumbling nuptial display of some eagles (see DISPLAY), and, indeed, food passing is part of the courtship ritual of the harriers; however, it has also been observed between adult and young birds. It is probably the raptorial equivalent of the courtship feeding seen in passerines, a precursor to male parental care.

FOOT. See LEG/FOOT.

FOREST. A plant formation consisting of an extended area of tall, relatively closely spaced trees. The presence of forest implies a certain degree of warmth, humidity, and/or soil fertility, as demonstrated by the absence of large or dense stands of trees in tundra, desert, and savanna. In some contexts, "forest" is used to mean only stands of tall, mature tree formations and less statuesque or secondary tree formations or those in which the trees are relatively widely spaced are distinguished as "woodland," but this distinction is not made consistently.

Forest birds are, of course, those that inhabit (especially breed in) forest. Thus, it is possible to speak of both Pine and Kentucky Warblers as "forest species," though the former typically occupies the upper stories of coniferous forest and the latter prefers the deciduous forest floor. There are many different types of forest, and these are often designated as characteristic habitat for specific bird species and groups of species. For example, Gray Jays and nesting Cape May Warblers typically inhabit spruce-fir forest. Wood Thrushes nest in deciduous forest and winter in tropical rain forest. For a comprehensive and accessible overview of North American forests, including their birdlife, see Kricher (1993, 1998).

FORM. In a strict nomenclatural sense, a variation below subspecific rank, a "variety," e.g., the "blue form" of the Lesser Snow Goose. But also widely used to refer to species/subspecies/varieties of uncertain nature: "Authorities disagree on the taxonomic status of these forms." Also a collective for all entities below genus rank, e.g.: "That genus contains a great diversity of forms." In technical circles the words "taxon" and "taxa" are commonly used in the latter context.

FORMULA MUSCLES. Muscles of the pelvis and legs used in classification. See MUSCLES.

FORSTER, Johann Reinhold, 1729–1798 (Forster's Tern: *Sterna forsteri*). A talented German clergyman who gave up the church for natural history (see also BENDIRE). He worked as a teacher, natural historian, and translator in England and ended as a professor of mineralogy at the University of Halle in Germany. The central event in his life was a disastrous sailing as a naturalist on Cook's second voyage around the world (for details, see Gruson 1972–BIOGRAPHY). Forster was the first to attempt to catalogue the American avifauna (as well as the rest of its animal life) in *A Catalogue of the Animals of North America* (1771); he listed 302 species of birds. The tern was named for him by Thomas NUTTALL.

FOSSORIAL (fah-SORE-ee-ul). Adapted for digging or burrowing in the earth. The Burrowing Owl, which digs its own nest chambers as well as taking over those made by prairie dogs and other mammals, and the Belted Kingfisher and Bank Swallow, which excavate cavities in the sides of earth banks, are all birds of fossorial habits.

FOWL. Once a general term for any kind of bird (e.g., Chaucer's "Parlement of Foules"). Now usually refers to birds that are used for food (e.g., wildfowl or waterfowl) and especially gallinaceous species, e.g., guinea fowl or barnyard fowl, or for chicken-*like* birds species, e.g., the Australasian scrubfowl.

"Fowl" originates from Germanic *vogel* (bird) and refers to the ability to fly.

FRANKLIN, Sir John, 1786–1847 (Franklin's Gull: *Larus pipixcan*). British naval commander best known for his terribly arduous and vain attempts to reach the North Pole and navigate a Northwest Passage. He came within a few miles of achieving the latter with the *Erebus* and *Terror* before becoming hopelessly trapped in the ice and perishing along with the entire expedition. Franklin's travels resulted in a vastly improved knowledge of the geography of the American Arctic. He and his companion, Sir John Richardson, traced the coast of the Arctic Ocean from Coppermine to 149° 37' W on the Alaskan coast in 1829, and the more than 40 expeditions sent to search for his ill-fated final expedition accumulated much new data over the 10 years before the mystery was solved. It is one of the ironies of commemorative zoological nomenclature that the great arctic explorer's name should be given to a gull that breeds in the American prairies and winters largely in tropical seas.

FRIGATEBIRD. Standard English name for all members of the family Fregatidae (order Pelecaniformes). There are 5 species of Frigatebirds worldwide, one of which, the Magnificent Frigatebird, visits southernmost coasts of Atlantic and Pacific North America and breeds in the Dry Tortugas, Florida. The Great Frigatebird has occurred as a vagrant in Oklahoma (1975) and California (1992), and the Lesser Frigatebird was recorded in 1960—from Maine! Both of the latter species range mainly in the tropical Pacific Ocean, though both are also present in colonies on Trinidade Island and Martín Vas Rocks, Brazil in the South Atlantic.

In appearance, frigatebirds are unique. They are among the largest seabirds (length about 3 feet), with long, pointed wings (wingspan 7½ feet), long, forked tail, and a long, prominently hooked bill. They carry the lightest wing loads (mass in proportion to wing area) of all birds, allowing them to soar slowly over vast areas of ocean and expend minimal energy in search of food. Their feet are small, weak, and (as in the other Pelecaniformes) webbed between all four toes—but only at the base. Frigatebirds never alight at sea, and their feet are used only to grasp perches on roosts or breeding grounds. There are no external nostril openings in the bill. Male frigatebirds have an extendible red throat pouch, which they inflate in courtship like a great balloon.

Frigatebirds breed in colonies, placing stick platforms in trees and shrubs (when available), on the ground, and in rocky niches on barren islands. The single egg (rarely, 2) is white and unmarked.

They are usually silent at sea, but the adults utter a strange, far-carrying guttural/whistling sound on the breeding grounds, and the cackling and whining of nestling birds can create a respectable din. Males also

make a drumming sound that may be a product of their inflated throat sacs.

Frigatebirds range over tropical seas worldwide. They are essentially nonmigratory, but undertake lengthy peregrinations, especially when immature. The name is, of course, a metaphorical evocation of their graceful sailing before the wind.

FRIGHT MOLT. The shedding of feathers as a result of extreme stress— usually fright, but perhaps also occasionally out of frustration. Apparently, the muscles that control the feathers are relaxed and the feather tip itself may be forcibly released from its follicle. The tail feathers (rectrices) are those most regularly lost in this manner, but breast and back feathers may also be shed. In the case of a predator grasping a bird by its tail, there would, of course, be survival value in being able to leave the tail behind as efficiently as possible. But birds are also known to undergo a fright molt from nonextremities while being gently handled. Some types of birds, e.g., some pigeons and gallinaceous species, seem to "jump out of their feathers" more routinely than others.

For a detailed review and discussion of this phenomenon, see Juhn, *Wilson Bull.* (1957), 69:108.

FRINGILLID FINCH (frin-JILL-id). Collective name for a family of songbirds the taxonomic "boundaries" of which are still under discussion. As defined by the *AOU Checklist,* 7th edition (1998), which is followed here, the Fringillidae comprises about 162 living species worldwide (not including the newly expanded interpretation of the Red Crossbill), classified in 3 subfamilies: the Fringillinae (Fringilline Finches), the Carduelinae (Cardueline Finches), and the Drapanidinae (Hawaiian Honeycreepers). Sibley and Monroe (1990–SYSTEMATICS) define the Fringillidae to encompass all of the nine-primaried oscines, including not only the fringilline and cardueline finches and Hawaiian honeycreepers but also a very broad interpretation of the subfamily Emberizinae that includes the sparrow-buntings, the wood warblers, the tanagers, the seedeaters, the flowerpiercers, the cardinal-grosbeaks, and the New World blackbirds and orioles and many other "finches"; they also include the Olive Warbler in its own subfamily of the Fringillidae. This mega-Fringillidae contains 988 species. For additional sorting out of this complexity see FINCH and Appendixes I and III.

Fringilline Finches. This subfamily contains only 3 species worldwide, all of them normally of Palearctic distribution. Two of these, Common Chaffinch *(Fringilla coelebs)* and Brambling *(F. montifringilla),* have occurred in North America as vagrants. Since both of these species are kept as cage birds, some North American records are suspects, but most are believed to have been wild birds (see CAPTIVITY, BIRDS IN). Brambling

is also a regular migrant through the western Aleutians and is known to have bred there once.

Cardueline Finches. This subfamily contains 138 species worldwide (not including the "new" Red Crossbills, and includes the rosy-finches (genus *Leucosticte*), Grosbeaks, rosefinches (genus *Carpodacus*), crossbills, redpolls, siskins, goldfinches, canary-seedeaters (genus *Serinus*), linnets, Eurasian bullfinches, and several genera of grosbeaks. Sixteen of these breed in North America and 6 others have been recorded as vagrants (see Appendix II).

Except for the crossbills, the cardueline finches have conical bills that vary in form from the relatively narrow, thin bills of the siskins to the massive crushing mechanism borne by the hawfinches and Evening Grosbeak (see BILL). The birds themselves range in size from the 4½-inch (11-cm) Lesser Goldfinch to the 9-inch (23-cm) Pine Grosbeak. Many male carduelines are brightly colored as adults.

Most of these finches are essentially arboreal (the alpine rosy-finches exceptional), though they all feed readily on the ground when that is where the food is, e.g., at a feeding station. The main content (up to 97% in some species) of the cardueline diet is seeds, though all are known to take some insects during the warm seasons; while berries are also eaten by some species, the pulp is normally discarded and just the seed is consumed. In contrast to many seedeaters, which normally forage for seeds on the ground, the carduelines usually extract seeds from their source in cones, catkins, or flower heads. The bills of the various species are adapted for dealing with preferred seed types: the crossbills have evolved a highly specialized apparatus for prizing apart cone scales and extracting the seeds—described in detail under FOOD and illustrated in Fig. 3. A number of the carduelines (e.g., rosy-finches, Pine Grosbeak) have throat pouches in which to temporarily store food for feeding of young or eventual digestion.

Most carduelines have rich, melodious, if somewhat chaotic-sounding songs, though some (e.g., redpolls) make more "tinkling" and sparrow-like noises and the rosy-finches produce no sound that deserves to be labeled anything but a "call."

The cardueline nest is typically placed off the ground (except rosy-finches)—from the barely elevated weed clumps tenanted by some pairs of Lesser Goldfinches to the 70- to 80-foot-high treetop sites occasionally favored by the grosbeaks and rosefinches. A relatively bulky cup nest is the rule, made loosely with sticks (Evening Grosbeak) or more compactly of grasses, stems, bark strips, dead leaves, etc., lined with finer plant fibers, hair, fur, feathers, moss. The rosy-finches build mainly of mosses and coarse grasses and place the nest in a rock crevice. Many northern carduelines use a lot of lichens, and the American Goldfinch is strongly partial to thistle and other plant down. The House Finch often (but not al-

ways) nests in a cavity, which, as its name implies, is frequently an opening in a man-made structure; it also shows a special fondness for hanging
planters and undiscarded Christmas wreaths adorning urban and suburban homes. The 2–6 (average 4–5) eggs are white or pale blue, immaculate
or sparsely spotted and/or scrawled in brownish/purplish, the markings
typically concentrated at the large end.

The carduelines are well represented in North and South America and
Eurasia and several European species have been successfully introduced
in Australasia. They are particularly prevalent in the Temperate Zones—
both of latitude and of altitude. In North America, these finches breed
throughout the continent except for the lowlands of the Southeast. The
Hoary Redpoll is one of the few passerines to breed in high arctic barrens
and one of the few birds of any kind to routinely endure arctic winters.
The rosy-finches show a similar hardiness in their preferred alpine habitat
and are sometimes called "mountain finches." Most species are at least
partially migratory, though most North American populations winter
within the continent. The so-called WINTER FINCHES are subject to periodic IRRUPTIONS south of their "normal" range.

See also SISKIN; ROSY-FINCH; GOLDFINCH; ROSEFINCH; CROSS-
BILL; GROSBEAK. See FINCH for etymology.

FRONT. The forehead; the area on a bird's head between the base of the
upper mandible and the crown. Beginning birdwatchers often assume the
term refers to the breast and are therefore puzzled by names such as
White-fronted Goose. See Fig. 35. For "front" in the meteorological sense,
see WEATHER.

FRONTAL SHIELD. A relatively hard (horny or leathery), often brightly
colored extension of the bill onto the forehead (front) present in a few
species of birds, e.g., King Eider drakes, Common Moorhen, and American Coot. See BILL.

FRUGIVOROUS (froo-JIV-er-us; *not* froo-GIV-er-us). Fruit-eating. Tanagers, for example, are largely frugivorous. An animal that habitually eats
fruit is a "frugivore."

FUERTES (FWAIR-teez), Louis Agassiz, 1874–1927. The greatest American bird portraitist with the *possible* exception of Audubon. A native of
New York State, Fuertes was instinctively drawn to both birds and art as a
child. His talent was skillfully nurtured by Elliott COUES, the artist Abbott
Thayer, and Frank CHAPMAN. He had a long association with Cornell
University, as had his father, and eventually became a lecturer there on
birds. Fuertes was a highly skilled technician, but his greatest gift was generally acknowledged to be his ability to capture a bird's "jizz," i.e., to paint

the living essence of a given species, rather than simply its color, pattern, and form. He was also admired by all who knew him for his personal warmth, his intelligence, his enthusiasm for nature and his work, and his generosity with his talents. Fuertes was killed in an automobile collision at a railroad crossing when only fifty-three, thus depriving the world of untold works by a great artist in his prime. For some of the many works illustrated by Fuertes, see the Bibliography under ILLUSTRATION and STATE/PROVINCIAL BOOKS.

FULMAR. Standard English name for 2 species of petrels in the genus *Fulmarus,* one of which, the Northern Fulmar *(F. glacialis),* occurs throughout the coldest waters of the Holarctic region. The 2 Giant Petrels in the genus *Macronectes* are sometimes called Giant Fulmars. Darwin once opined that the Northern Fulmar was the most abundant bird in the world. Anyone who has been at sea in the midst of a fulmar migration or on a fishing boat in the heart of its pelagic range can understand how he might have formed that opinion—though, almost certainly, it has never been the case.

The Atlantic population of the species has undergone a dramatic increase within the present century, particularly on the eastern side, where it has markedly extended its range southward. Some authorities have speculated that this phenomenon is related to increases in fishing activity, but if so it is hard to explain the relatively slight increase and range extension in the western Atlantic.

Fulmar is a Viking word meaning "foul gull," referring to the obnoxious (but effective!) procellariiform practice of vomiting foul-smelling STOMACH OIL onto molesters.

For family characteristics, see SHEARWATER; see also Fisher (1952–SHEARWATER).

FULVOUS (FULL-vuss) (Whistling-Duck). Yellowish brown; tawny.

FURCULA (FER-kew-luh) (pl.: furculae). The fused clavicles (collarbones) typical of birds; also known as the wishbone or merrythought. See SKELETON, Pectoral Girdle, and Fig. 27.

GADFLY PETREL. Collective name for 34 species of petrels that make up the genus *Pterodroma* (family Procellariidae), most of which breed on islands in south temperate seas and range within the Southern Hemisphere. No gadfly petrel breeds in North America; the endangered Ber-

muda Petrel or Cahow (*P. cahow*) nests exclusively in Bermuda, and at least 8 other species in the genus have been recorded as vagrants or visitors.

A gadfly is, first, a fly (family Tabanidae, Oestridae, or Muscidae), which bites or buzzes in the ears of cattle, making them "gad," i.e., dash about wildly; second, a person who annoys other people (as a gadfly annoys cattle). The petrel doubtless takes its name from the notion of rushing about aimlessly (gadabout petrel might be better), from either its far-flung oceanic wanderings or more likely the fast, erratic, swooping, careening flight characteristic of *Pterodroma*.

For family characteristics, see PETREL.

GADWALL. Standard English name for a single widespread species of dabbling duck, *Anas strepera*. No one has yet been able to suggest a credible origin for this name. Lockwood (1993–NAMES) says the name is onomatopoeic and relates it to the scientific name *Anas stepera*, which means "noisy duck." Whether Gadwalls are especially noisy is open to debate. See DUCK.

GALLINACEOUS. Chicken-like. The members of the order Galliformes— which includes the chachalacas, grouse, quail, pheasants, and turkeys— are commonly referred to collectively as gallinaceous birds.

GALLINULE (GAL-uh-nool or GAL-uh-nyool). Standard English name for 4 members of the rail family (Rallidae; order Gruiformes), only one of which, the Purple Gallinule (*Porphyrio martinicus*) breeds or otherwise regularly occurs in North America; there is a 1986 record of the South American Azure Gallinule from Saratoga New York. Most of the species in the genus *Gallinula* are now known as moorhens, including the Common Moorhen, once known in North America as Common Gallinule.

To North Americans, the gallinules (and coots) seem rather distinct from our species of rails, with a different type of coloration in adult birds and a more duck-like "jizz," due in large measure to the fact that they are more often seen swimming in the open than are the rails. Placed in context with the rails of the world, however, they do not represent an extreme variation. Like the other rails, gallinules eat a combination of plant and small invertebrate animal foods. The Purple Gallinule is essentially a bird of the New World tropics and is restricted in North America to the southeastern region.

"Gallinule" is an anglicization of a Latin word meaning "little hen," referring to the gallinules' walk-and-peck method of feeding when on land; They are known in some languages as "water chickens."

For family characteristics, see RAIL; see also MOORHEN.

GALVESTON ISLAND (Texas). The northernmost of a string of barrier islands that line the southern coast of Texas southeast of Houston. Most of

the east end of the island is occupied by the city of Galveston (Kempner Park in the center is a notable haven for landbird migrants during the storied spring migrations of the Texas coast; see HIGH ISLAND and ROCKPORT), but the west end is largely composed of beach, pastures, sloughs, marshes, and flats, which abound in all kinds of waterbirds. In addition to the impressive fact that more than 300 bird species have been observed on the island over the years, Galveston's greatest claim to ornithological fame is that it hosted some of the latest reliable occurrences of the Eskimo Curlew (1959–63); see, however, ENDANGERED BIRDS.

GAMBEL, William, 1819–49 (Gambel's Quail: *Lophortyx gambelii; Parus gambeli:* Mountain Chickadee). A doctor/bird collector of the mid-nineteenth century and sometime colleague of BAIRD, CASSIN, and NUTTALL. Remembered particularly for his collections in California and northern Mexico. He died at 30 of typhoid while crossing the Sierra Nevada. For a summary of some of Gambel's frontier adventures, including Indian raids and a sojourn as surgeon on an ox train led by Daniel Boone, see Gruson (1972–BIOGRAPHY). Gambel described his own quail, but it was his mentor Nuttall who named it for him. RIDGWAY added the chickadee.

GAMBELL (Alaska). See ALASKA.

GAME BIRD. In the broadest sense, any bird that is hunted for sport or food. Two more specific definitions are used in the following contexts. (1) *Sporting:* There is a hunter's tradition, that excludes ducks and geese from the strictest usage of "game bird"; they are instead "waterfowl." This leaves the gallinaceous birds, the shorebirds (now protected except for woodcock and snipe), the rails, and the pigeons and doves as "true" game birds. (2) *Legal:* Those species of birds for which there is a hunting season or which are not protected: ducks and geese, gallinaceous birds (many of them introduced for this purpose), woodcock and snipe, rails, pigeons and doves, and crows. Many other birds, including small land birds, were of course hunted for food and sport before protection, and this tradition doubtless continues in remoter parts of North America where the "pioneer spirit" still prevails. See LAWS PROTECTING BIRDLIFE.

GANDER. A male goose of any species.

GANNET. Standard English name for 3 species of seabirds in the family Sulidae (also including the boobies), one of which, the Northern Gannet, breeds and winters in coastal and offshore waters in eastern North America. The three gannets are very similar in appearance (they constitute a superspecies) and occupy separate ranges, one in the North Atlantic and two in south temperate seas (South African region and Tasmania/New

Zealand). Their preference for cold waters sets them apart from the boobies, all of which normally occur only in tropical seas.

Their large size and striking plumage, together with their habit of nesting colonially on picturesque wilderness isles and of plunging into the sea for fish from heights of up to 100 feet, make the Northern Gannet one of our most striking seabirds.

Gannets were once thought to be related to geese, whence the present name, which arises from the same root as "gander."

For family characteristics, see BOOBY.

GAP ANALYSIS. A scientific method for assessing the effectiveness of landscape-based conservation strategies in protecting the broadest possible spectrum of biodiversity. The concept was pioneered in the early 1980s by J. Michael Scott, who was assessing the conservation of endemic Hawaiian forest bird species. He first mapped the distribution of each species, then overlaid the maps to show those areas of habitat that had the greatest diversity of the rare birds. When this map was compared to then protected areas of Hawaii, it emerged that less than 10% of the ranges of the endangered birds was protected. This turns out to be a common phenomenon, since many national parks and other "conservation" lands are chosen for their scenic beauty or the presence of a few charismatic species rather than for their importance as reservoirs of biological diversity. The "gap" refers to that which often occurs between biodiversity hotspots and lands ostensibly managed for conservation. Capitalized, GAP is an acronym for the Gap Analysis Programs that Scott went on to create at the University of Idaho Cooperative Fish and Wildlife Research Unit, which evolved into a national GAP program now under the U.S. Geological Survey. For more detail go to http://www.gap.uidaho.edu.

GAPE (gaping, gaper). Sometimes used synonymously with COMMISSURE or to refer to the softer rictal region at the corners of the mouth. Usually the gape is associated with the *open* mouth, especially of nestling birds begging for food. This gaping gesture, together with a distinctive color pattern of the mouth lining in at least some species and the calls of the young birds, stimulates a feeding response in the parent birds. Juvenile birds, even when fully fledged and out of the nest, can often be recognized by the enlarged, fleshy, often brightly colored corners of the mouth; such birds are sometimes called "gapers."

GASTRULATION. A complex process that occurs early in embryonic development (following the blastula) and consists of movement of cells to their appropriate positions in the embryo. It is at this point that cells begin to differentiate into broad tissue types, e.g., the mesoderm.

GAUSE'S RULE. The principle that no two (or more) organisms with exactly the same ecological requirements can coexist in the same environment permanently, since the inevitable competition will always favor one species over the other. Therefore one normally finds birds and other animals occupying different ecological "niches" in any given habitat. Also called the "principle of competitive exclusion." See DISTRIBUTION and G. F. Gause, *The Struggle for Existence* (Baltimore, 1934).

GENERA (JEN-er-uh). Plural of GENUS.

GENETICS (jeh-NET-iks). A major facet of biology, dealing with the nature of heredity; the means by which the traits of any organism persevere or vary through succeeding generations.

All of the traits that we can identify in an organism are the product of the interaction of environmental conditions with the genetic "program" of that individual. In the study of birds and other living things it is important—as well as fascinating— to understand how these phenomena interact.

This is not the place to attempt a summary of such a vast subject matter, single facets of which have generated many books even fatter than this one. One aspect of basic Mendelian genetics that is distinctive in birds is the fact that the two members of the female pair of sex chromosomes are different. This female chromosome pair is represented as WZ; the male's pair as ZZ. The small W chromosome bears fewer genes and is largely inactive *but determines the sex of the offspring*. In mammals and most other vertebrates, the sex chromosome is carried by the male. The W chromosome also carries genes that control traits other than sexual determination, but because they are borne on the sex chromosomes, these traits are said to be "sex-linked." For more detail see Buckley in Cooke and Buckley (1987).

For an admirably clear primer in Mendelian genetics using avian examples see Parkin in Campbell and Lack (1985–ORNITHOLOGY).

For aspects of bird study to which genetics is relevant, see DISTRIBUTION; HYBRIDIZATION; INTELLIGENCE; PARENTAL CARE; SONG; SPECIATION; SYSTEMATICS.

GENITALIA. Birds lack external sexual organs, though in a few cases, notably ostriches, some gallinaceous birds, most waterfowl, and a few others, males have a penis-like organ (in some cases quite large and "ornate") that is extruded during copulation; females of these species have a rudimentary clitoris. All sexual as well as excretory functions take place through a single anal opening, the vent or cloacal aperture. See especially McCracken (2000–REPRODUCTIVE SYSTEM), Briskie 1998–REPRODUCTIVE SYSTEM, and Briskie and Montgomerie (1997–REPRODUCTIVE SYSTEM.)

GENOTYPE (JEE-no-type). All of the genetic variation found in an individual, including hidden traits (e.g., recessive traits) apparently not expressed in the external appearance and behavior (the phenotype) of that individual. Genotype can also be defined as all of an individual's DNA. For further discussion, see PHENOTYPE.

GENUS (JEE-nuss) (pl.: genera [JEN-er-uh]). The major taxonomic category between the FAMILY and the SPECIES. Families may be divided into subfamilies and genera; genera into subgenera and species. A genus can also be defined as a grouping of phylogenetically related species. In a scientific name, the species name always includes the name of the genus followed by the species name, e.g. *Turdus* (genus) *migratorius* (species) is the scientific name of American Robin. The 300+ genera of birds that occur regularly in North America appear in phylogenetic order in Appendix I. See SYSTEMATICS.

GEOGRAPHICAL VARIATION. Differences that have evolved in animal forms living in different places. The Savannah Sparrow exhibits marked geographical variation over its broad North American range in color, size, and bill size and shape. See SPECIATION; DISTRIBUTION.

GILA (HEE-luh) (Woodpecker). Possibly of native American origin, this name seems to refer simply to the Gila River valley of Arizona, where the type specimen of this species of woodpecker was collected.

GIS or **GIZZ.** See JIZZ. For Geographical Information Systems, see TECHNOLOGY FOR BIRDERS.

GIZZARD. The second of two enlargements in a bird's digestive tract, which together function like the human stomach; it could also be described as the lower of a bird's two stomachs. Also called the ventriculus. See DIGESTIVE SYSTEM and Fig. 27.

GLAUCOUS (GLAW-kuss) (Gull, -winged Gull). From a Greek word originally meaning "gleaming," but in biological nomenclature evolving to mean bluish, gray, or silvery, e.g., the mantle color of adult Glaucous, Glaucous-winged, and other "white-winged" gulls.

GLOGER'S RULE. The generalization that representatives of bird or mammal species that breed in warmer, more humid climates tend to be darker in color than those breeding in cooler, drier climates. For example, the pale plumage of the desert-dwelling races of the Horned Lark (e.g., *Eremophila alpestris leucansiptila*) contrasts strikingly with that of races such as *E. a. merrilli* and *E. a. strigata* from the humid Northwest. The

implications of Gloger's rule are not well understood (Mayr [1963–SPECIATION] says that its "physiological basis is not clear.") And, of course, some desert-inhabiting species are partially or totally black (see DESERT). It is probable that some color traits in desert organisms may be adaptive in nature while others are functions of developmental biochemistry influenced by ambient moisture.

The rule was first articulated by C. W. L. Gloger in *The Variation of Birds Under the Influence of Climate* (1833). Compare ALLEN'S, BERGMANN'S, and KELSO'S RULES.

GNATCATCHER. Standard English name for the 10–13 members (depending on taxonomy) of the genus *Polioptila*. The gnatcatchers have traditioinally been classified with the Old World warblers (family Sylviidae) or kinglets (Regulidae), but recent molecular studies (Sheldon and Gill 1996–BUSHTIT) suggest that they are most closely related to the wrens (Trolodytidae). Sibley and Ahlquist (1990–SYSTEMATICS) put them in a subfamily (Polioptilinae) together with the gnatwrens and Verdin in the family Certhiidae, which also contains the treecreepers and wrens. Three species of gnatcatchers breed regularly in North America and a fourth has bred in southeastern Arizona.

The gnatcatchers are all small (average 4 inches), with a comparatively long, slender bill and a long, mobile tail, frequently held in a "cocked-up" position. All are colored in combinations of black, slate, and/or blue-gray and white. See Fig. 31.

They feed in the hyperactive manner common to tits and warblers, gleaning the interstices of tree trunks and the undersides of leaves; they also do a lot of gleaning while hovering and frequently chase prey they have flushed, but seldom sally after already flying insects. Their diet consists almost entirely of insects, but like most insectivores, they occasionally partake of a berry or seed.

Several gnatcatcher species have soft warbling songs, but, in general, they are not very songful, and their nasal buzzy calls are heard far more frequently.

The tiny (2–2½ inches) gnatcatcher nest is sited on a limb or in the fork of a tree or shrub 2–80 feet from the ground. It is a neat, rather deep cup made of plant fibers, bark strips, grasses, etc., bound with spider silk and "shingled" on the outside with lichen flakes (Blue-gray Gnatcatcher); it is lined with plant down, fur, and/or feathers. The 3–5 (usually 4) eggs are pale blue and variably marked (lightly/heavily; densely/sparsely) with reddish or purplish.

The gnatcatchers are restricted to the New World, most species occurring in the tropics. Of the North American species, the Blue-gray Gnatcatcher breeds across the continent north to southern Oregon and Idaho in the west, and north to Ontario, Québec, and Maine in the east; it has recently become more common northward; it winters southward, including

the southern extremities of the United States as far as Central America. The Black-tailed is resident in the arid lowlands of the Southwest. The California Gnatcatcher breeds along the coast of southern California where it is a threatened (and controversial) species, and southward through much of Baja California.

While gnatcatchers doubtless catch their share of gnats, the name is no more definitive than warbler or sandpiper.

GOATSUCKER. Widely used English name, especially in North America, for the nightjar family, Caprimulgidae (literally "goat milkers"); perhaps excluding the nighthawks. The superstition that members of this family (e.g., Whip-poor-wills) suck at the teats of goats and other livestock during the night goes back at least to Aristotle and is prevalent in many cultures. See NIGHTJAR.

GOBBLING GROUND. Dry, grassy fields where males of the Lesser Prairie-Chicken come early on spring mornings to perform their distinctive courtship displays; the "dances" involve a characteristic cackle or "gobbling" sound, which, according to Pough (1957–FIELD GUIDE), lacks the "resonance and volume" of the Greater Prairie-Chicken's "booming."

GODWIT. Standard English name for all 4 species of large, long-billed sandpipers in the genus *Limosa* (family Scolopacidae; order Charadriiformes). Three of these breed in North America and the remaining species has occurred with relative frequency as an accidental straggler (see Appendix II).

Godwits are statuesque shorebirds cryptically patterned with splotches and streaks and colored in rich earth tones. The godwits tend to probe much more deeply with their long bills than do the curlews, frequently working them down to the base into mud or soil in search of worms, shellfish, crustaceans, and the like.

Hudsonian and Bar-tailed Godwits breed in arctic tundra and their migrations are among the longest of any birds (see Fig. 18). The Marbled Godwit nests wholly on the central prairies of southern Canada and the northern United States and migrates to the coasts for the winter, reaching New England and the Pacific Northwest in small numbers and occurring as far south as northern South America.

The name originated with the call of the Black-tailed Godwit of Eurasia but is also a fair transcription of both Hudsonian and Marbled Godwit's cries.

For family characteristics, see SANDPIPER.

GOLDENEYE. Standard English name for 2 of the 3 members of the sea duck genus *Bucephala* (family Anatidae; order Anseriformes). Both of these—the Common Goldeneye *(B. clangula)* and Barrow's Goldeneye

(B. islandica)—nest in tree cavities in coniferous forest, the Common preferring boreal lowlands and Barrow's adapted to western alpine forests as well as the rocky barrens of Greenland and Iceland. The latter has also recently (1998) been confirmed breeding in Québec north of the St. Lawrence River and east of Ville de Québec, and it probably also nests in Labrador, although proof is lacking. The distribution of the Common Goldeneye is Holarctic, that of Barrow's essentially Nearctic, though it is a permanent resident in Iceland. North American populations of both winter along Atlantic and Pacific coasts.

Barrow's Goldeneye favors streams on its breeding grounds, where it dives for the larvae of aquatic insects. The Common Goldeneye prefers crustaceans, insects, and other invertebrate life of still northern waters. Both species feed heavily on mollusks on their marine wintering grounds.

The eyes of all adult goldeneyes are bright yellow and are discernible from a surprising distance.

GOLDFINCH. Standard English name for 4 species of cardueline finches (family Fringillidae; order Passeriformes), all in the genus *Carduelis.* Three species of goldfinches breed in North America and the European Goldfinch has been introduced here unsuccessfully a number of times and in a number of localities.

The goldfinches eat mainly small seeds, but also a few insects and berries. They make notably thick-walled nests with much soft fibrous material, such as plant down and feathers. Lawrence's Goldfinch of the Southwest tends to breed in loose colonies. The American Goldfinch is one of the most familiar and appreciated of American songbirds, as reflected in the fact that it has been honored with three state birdships (Iowa, New Jersey, and Washington). In some regions, this species delays its nesting until late summer to coincide with the availability of thistle seeds for feeding its young and thistle down for nest lining. At 4½ inches (11 cm), the Lesser Goldfinch is one of the smallest North American songbirds.

Though the yellow wing stripe of the "original" (European) goldfinch is striking, the male American Goldfinch is the only species in this group that truly merits its name.

GONADS. The sexual glands, testes (male) and ovaries (female), which produce reproductive cells, spermatozoa (male) and ova (female), as well as sexual hormones, which stimulate other phenomena of the reproductive cycle. In female birds, only the left ovary and its companion oviduct usually develop. See REPRODUCTIVE SYSTEM.

GONYS (GO-niss). The ridge formed where the two rami of the lower mandible come together, making a conspicuous angle in the outline of

the lower margin of the bill in some birds, e.g., the larger gulls, Razorbill. See Fig. 35.

GOOD CALL / BAD CALL. Birdwatching terminology referring to quick, accurate identification or lack thereof. Ludlow GRISCOM may have pioneered the concept. He was always "calling" an anonymous speck on a distant phone wire or a grayish waterbird in a distant bay from a speeding car. He is said to have once accurately "audioed" (called by call) a Bridled Tern flying overhead along the coast of Massachusetts. An appropriate response from an admiring companion would have been: "Good call, Ludlow!"

Bad calls are rarely announced but give off an odor of embarrassment for several minutes after they are revealed. You are standing at the bow during a pelagic trip in the North Atlantic in late September. You pick up a buoyant white form on the horizon and as it comes into focus you detect a bold pattern of contrasting triangles emblazoned across its wings and mantle. ''Sabine's!'' you cry triumphantly to the assembled bird clubs of six states. "Sabine's Gull!" The bird turns and heads straight for the boat and just as you are beginning to feel some unease about your snap call, your archrival—an insufferable fool whose reputation in the field rests solely on his arrogant posturing and uncanny luck—says calmly but loudly, "Immature kittiwake." Silence.

See also IDENTIFICATION.

GOOSANDER (GOO-san-der or goo-SAN-der). Standard English name, except in North America, for *Mergus merganser,* which we call Common Merganser. The name Goosander is obscure but may be of Scandinavian origin and probably implies something like "goose-duck"; it is indeed a large duck (22–27 inches), measuring about an inch longer on the average than a Brant.

GOOSE. Standard English name for 27 members of the family Anatidae (order Anseriformes), including the so-called South American "sheld-geese" in the genus *Chloephaga* and such oddities as the Spur-winged Goose of Africa, the Egyptian Goose of Africa and Asia Minor, and the three very un-goose-like species of pygmy geese distributed from Africa through Asia to Australasia. The Magpie Goose of Australia and New Guinea is now isolated in a family of its own the Anseranatidae. Fourteen of the 15 so-called "true geese" in the tribe Anserini, including the Brant, have occurred in North America in one form or another: 6 as breeders, 4 as vagrants, and 4 as escapes from captivity. The fifteenth, the Hawaiian Goose or Nene, is endemic to the Hawaiian Islands.

Geese are medium-sized to large, essentially vegetarian waterbirds, many of which spend as much time (or more) "grazing" in wild and

cultivated fields as they do in the water. Like the other members of their family, geese have lamellate bills, flattened in some cases like ducks' bills (Canada Goose, Brant) or somewhat arched and narrow (e.g., Snow Goose). All geese are relatively stout-bodied and long-necked. Honking V formations of Canada Geese are familiar sights throughout North America, heralding the change of seasons. These and the Brant are popular game birds.

Most goose species are solitary nesters, but some (e.g., Snow and Ross's) are loosely colonial. The nest is a scrape in the open, lined with down and small contour feathers from the female's breast and bits of handy vegetation; sometimes a low rim is scraped up from the sides by the sitting bird. Canada Geese are also known to use the tops of beaver and muskrat lodges, stumps, and even abandoned raptor nests 10–20 feet off the ground. The 2–11 (usually 3–6) eggs are white to yellowish and unmarked.

High, usually quavered, bugling or honking notes are typical goose sounds, characteristically uttered in chorus from flocks on the wing. Geese also make defensive hisses and low "conversational" mutterings.

The geese are distributed worldwide, but largely restricted to the Temperate Zones, north and south. All North American geese breed in the Arctic or subarctic, all but Canada Goose exclusively so. And all—except the large, problematic, semidomesticated population of Canada Geese—are migratory.

Lockwood (1993–NAMES) says that "goose" is "arguably the most ancient bird name in our vocabulary"—going back to an Indo-European root from at 3000 BC and referring to swans and ducks as well as geese.

For bibliography see under WATERFOWL.

GORGET (GOR-jet). An area of brightly colored feathers covering the throat; often used to refer to the brilliantly iridescent throats of hummingbirds; originally the part of a suit of armor that protected the throat.

GOSHAWK (GOSS-hawk). Standard English name for 21 of the larger members of the genus *Accipiter,* one of which, the Northern Goshawk *(A. gentilis),* has a Holarctic distribution and ranges throughout much of the northern and mountainous regions of North America; 7 other goshawks occupy 4 additional genera. The "gos" is famed for its magisterial bearing, its deft capture and dispatch of birds and mammals, and its ferocious defense of its nesting territory. Its skill and panache as a hunter make this species a favorite of falconers.

"Goshawk" means "goose hawk," originally a falconer's term, with the implication that it was flown after geese. This seems unlikely and the name may have been "transferred" from the Peregrine.

For family characteristics, see HAWK.

GOSLING. A young goose of any species; applied to birds in immature plumage as well as downy chicks.

GRACE Coues (Grace's Warbler: *Dendroica graciae*). Miss Coues (eventually Grace Darling) was the sister of Elliott COUES, the brilliant ornithologist of the later nineteenth century. Spencer BAIRD named this western warbler species for her.

GRACKLE. Standard English name for 11 species of New World blackbirds (family Icteridae; order Passeriformes), 3 of which breed in North America.

The grackles are black birds with a multicolored iridescence and moderately long, distinctively shaped tails.

Together the North American species occur throughout the continent south of the boreal forest except for the Far West. They winter in staggering multitudes in the Southeast, where they are justly regarded in some cases as significant pests (see PROBLEMS INVOLVING BIRDS).

"Grackle" comes from the Latin *graculus,* which has referred to several black birds as diverse as the Jackdaw (the call of which it was meant to echo) and the cormorant.

GRAMINIVOROUS (GRAM-ih-NIV-er-us). Refers to eaters of grass, e.g., sheep and the grazing species of geese.

GRANDRY'S CORPUSCLES. Ovoid masses of nerve endings of about 1.5 hundredths of a millimeter in length in the lower layer of skin (dermis). Known so far only in birds, they apparently function as receivers of tactile sensation. According to Necker (2000–HEARING), Grandry's corpuscles are limited to aquatic birds, particularly waterfowl, and are largely found near the tip of the bill. See TOUCH; HERBST'S CORPUSCLES.

GRANIVOROUS (gran-IV-er-us). Feeding on grains and/or other seeds. Some ducks, geese, gallinaceous birds, doves, blackbirds, sparrows, and finches are largely granivorous, at least for part of the year or in situations where this form of food is readily available.

GRASSLAND. Any upland habitat in which the principal vegetation is grasses. A number of bird species are partial to grassland as a breeding habitat, e.g., Upland Sandpiper, Sprague's Pipit, Horned Lark, Grasshopper, Vesper and other sparrows, Lark Bunting, McCown's and Chestnut-collared Longspurs, Dickcissel, Bobolink, and the meadowlarks. Wetlands dominated by grasses, e.g., salt marshes and stands of *Phragmites* reed, are not usually called grasslands, though, strictly defined, they are. See also PRAIRIE; SAVANNA.

GREBE (greeb). Standard English name for all members of the family Podicipedidae, the sole family in the order Podicipediformes. There are 21 species of grebes worldwide, 7 of which breed in North America.

The grebe family is a varied one, containing small (9 inches), drab, and short-billed species as well as large (29 inches) species with long, sharp bills and ones with a colorful breeding plumage. Shared characteristics include peculiarly lobed toes (see Fig. 17) with flattened claws adapted for strong swimming at the surface and underwater (see SWIMMING/DIVING), a dense glossy plumage, short wings, and a negligible tail.

Because of their peculiarly adapted legs/feet, grebes are most at home in the water, and extremely awkward on land, which they visit, if at all, only to nest. They fly little except during migration; several Latin American species, isolated on highland lakes, are flightless. Grebes have the unusual ability to reduce their buoyancy and sink below the surface by "squeezing" the air from their plumage. Once underwater, they can swim surprising distances, often seeming to disappear altogether, a practice that has generated superstitious names such as "water witch" and "helldiver." Grebes are said to submerge for "divers" reasons and return to the surface for "sundry" reasons; for more detail, see SWIMMING/DIVING.

Grebe's nests are heaps of wet, dead plant material piled up at the margin of a lake or pond or floating and anchored to emergent vegetation. The 2–10 (most species average 3–5) eggs are notably long and "biconical" (see Fig. 10); they are white and unmarked when laid, but become stained from the soggy plant material of the nest. Grebes are among the few birds that cover their eggs when they leave the nest, and it has been suggested that the rotting plant material used may generate enough heat to aid incubation.

Grebes are seldom heard except on their breeding grounds, where most species give extended, sometimes tremulous braying, whinnying, or crooning "songs" as well as shorter whistles, squeaks, and wheezes.

"Grebe" may be another of the many bird names to have arisen out of a generalized term for a seabird, or it may be a corruption of the Breton word *krib,* meaning "crest" and probably referring to the Great Crested Grebe of the Old World.

GREGARIOUS. Characteristically found in flocks; Evening Grosbeaks, European Starlings, and many shorebirds, for example, are normally gregarious; Peregrine Falcons and Belted Kingfishers are not. See FLOCK.

GRIFFIN (Griffon, Gryphon). An ancient imaginary beast, perhaps originating with the Hittites. A lion with an eagle's beak, wings, and talons (on the forelegs) and, occasionally, a serpent's tail; in some accounts, eight times as large as a lion. Among various ancient cultures (Greek, Syrian, Roman) it was thought to range throughout Asiatic Scythia; to be a guardian

of gold mines and other treasures; to pull the chariot of the sun; and to be the enemy of horses.

One of the Gryphon's most recent appearances is in Lewis Carroll's *Alice in Wonderland,* where it plays straight man to the Mock Turtle.

Also standard English name for Old World vultures in the genus *Gyps,* especially *Gyps fulvus,* the Griffon Vulture.

For other fantastic "birds" see IMAGINATION, BIRDS IN.

GRINNELL, Joseph, 1877–1939. Joseph Grinnell's scientific achievements are inextricably associated with the fauna of California, but his influence in elevating ornithology to a "full-fledged" science was nationwide. He was the director of the Museum of Vertebrate Zoology at the University of California at Berkeley, long-time editor of *The Condor,* and president of the American Ornithologists' Union, 1929–32. His bibliography comprises 554 titles, mostly on avian subject matter but not a few on mammals. Despite this prolific output and his heavy administrative load, he was also an ardent and able field man. A number of subspecies of North American birds and mammals are named for Grinnell, e.g., Grinnell's Waterthrush *(Seiurus noveboracensis notabilis)* and a Baja California race of Loggerhead Shrike *(Lanius ludovicianus grinnelli).* He may have been the first authority to use the term "niche" to describe the ecological position of an organism in its environment.

Not to be confused with George Bird Grinnell (no relation), 1849–1938, the patrician outdoorsman, Indian authority, and early conservationist, who greatly influenced the establishment of the National Parks system, the early Audubon movement, and early bird protection laws.

GRISCOM, Ludlow, 1890–1959. The patron saint of modern American birdwatching. As an ornithologist at the American Museum of Natural History in New York and at Harvard, Griscom's main professional contribution was the elucidation of the Mexican and Central American avifaunas. But the achievement of his life was to show that "birding" did not need to be practiced with a gun—except in cases where field identification is impossible and a specimen is required for the record—and that the great majority of birds can be identified with absolute accuracy by a practiced and intelligent observer. Griscom's brilliance in the field, his eloquent enthusiasm for the "sport" of field ornithology, and his large circle of protégés (including Roger Tory Peterson) were responsible to a large degree for spawning the legions of present-day birdwatchers and their need for good optical equipment and comprehensive field guides. Griscom's love of field work is reflected in his best-known works, which were mainly distributional in nature (see the Bibliography). For a full account of Griscom's life, see Davis (1994).

GRIT. Small pieces of rock, shell, or other hard substance ingested by birds to assist the digestion process in the gizzard (ventriculus) (see DI-GESTIVE SYSTEM). Seeds, buds, and other coarse vegetable matter are pulverized by contractions of the powerful muscles of the stomach walls aided by digestive "juices." The grit acts in combination with rhythmic contractions of the tough, coarse muscles that line the stomach walls to pulverize the seeds, buds, and other coarse vegetable matter. Relatively little grit is ever excreted with waste products and, therefore, it accumulates in the stomach throughout a bird's life.

Gallinaceous birds, doves, and seed-eating finches are perhaps most readily associated with this digestion technique, but grit of varying coarseness has been found in a wide variety of both land and water birds. Birds take in certain types of grit as an antidote to the biochemical defenses of some of their plant foods. Examples of this include intake of clay (kaolin) by some parrots to neutralize poisons in fruits they eat, and by crossbills to counteract conifer resins. The practice of picking up grit contributes to the susceptibility of birds in ingesting lead shot pellets, with serious consequences to many game birds, especially ducks (see FOOD/FEEDING; THREATS [OF HUMAN ORIGIN] TO BIRDLIFE, Lead Poisoning).

GROSBEAK. Standard English name for about 32 species of large-billed Cardinalid and Fringillid (cardueline) finches. Three "cardinal-grosbeaks" (Rose-breasted, Black-headed, and Blue) and 2 "finch-grosbeaks" (Evening and Pine) breed in North America.

The name is largely one of convenience, referring to the large seed-crushing bill, and has little taxonomic significance.

For general family characteristics, see CARDINAL-GROSBEAK and FRINGILLID FINCH.

GROUND-DOVE. Standard English name for 29 species of relatively small (6–10 inches), short-tailed members of the family Columbidae (order Columbiformes). These are divided between closely related Neotropical species in 3 genera and doves of the tropical Pacific in the genus *Gallicolumba*. One species, the Common Ground-Dove, breeds in southeastern and southwestern North America, and another, the Ruddy Ground-Dove, occurs as a rare, but regular visitor from Mexico (see Appendix II).

Like many other doves and pigeons, ground-doves habitually feed on the ground; unlike most others, they also often nest on the ground.

For general characteristics of the family, see PIGEON; for provenance of "dove," see DOVE.

GROUSE. Standard English name for 11 of 17 members of the subfamily Tetraoninae (Family Phasianidae; order Galliformes), which also includes

the ptarmigan, capercaillies, and prairie-chickens. Eleven species of grouse (including 3 ptarmigan and 2 prairie-chickens) breed and winter in North America. Rock and Willow Ptarmigan are Holarctic in distribution, but all of the other species are North American endemics. The Gunnison Sage-Grouse isolated in the Gunnison Basin of Colorado was defined as a distinct species in the 1990s.

Members of the grouse family are mostly medium-sized (average 15 inches), chicken-like birds with a short bill and short legs and wings. They often have elaborate or strikingly patterned tails as well as facial wattles and inflatable colored sacs on the neck—all of which are used in nuptial display. Many species of grouse have evolved foot adaptations for coping with walking and scratching in snow. The tarsi and feet are heavily feathered in some cases (ptarmigan), making them resemble rabbits' feet; other species develop little comb-like projections (pectinations) from the sides of the toes, which act as "snowshoes" (see LEG/FOOT and Fig. 17).

Grouse inhabit both forest and open country. They feed mainly on seeds, buds, shoots, fruit, and other vegetable matter and in most cases have unusual courtship rituals involving "dances" and strange sounds.

The typical grouse nest is a shallow scrape on the ground lined sparsely (if at all) with handy plant fragments. Large clutches of eggs are characteristic of grouse, and nests with as many as 17 eggs have been found, though 6–12 is the norm. The eggs may be whitish, yellowish buff-brown, or pinkish, with markings highly variable among different species: immaculate, very finely speckled, spotted, or heavily splotched with pale brown to black.

Everyday grouse vocalizations are mostly variations on chicken-like cluckings and gobblings with some squeaks and rattles given in alarm; a female Ruffed Grouse defending a brood hisses like a steam train and squeals like tires on wet pavement. Displaying males produce unique "instrumental" (i.e., nonvocal) sounds using their wings and inflatable neck pouches (see SONG; DISPLAY; BOOMING; DRUMMING; GOBBLING GROUND; STRUTTING GROUNDS).

The grouse family as a whole is restricted to the Holarctic region. Our grouse occupy the northern forests (coniferous and mixed), the prairies, and western sagebrush plains.

The origins of "grouse" have so far remained obscure; possibly imitative at first of the call of the Black Grouse of northern Eurasia.

See references in the Bibliography under GALLINACEOUS BIRDS.

GUANO. Originally, the excrement of the Guanay Cormorant *(Phalacrocorax bougainvillii)* and other island-nesting seabirds of the west coast of South America. Guano, which accumulates to great heights at the largest colonies, is commercially "mined" for fertilizer and gunpowder and was once Peru's chief export and source of income. By the end of the

nineteenth century, however, reckless exploitation had depleted supplies of guano built up over the centuries (see pp. 286–295 of Murphy 1936–SEABIRD). Presently an attempt is being made to extract guano in equilibrium with its accumulation.

The excrement of other species of colonial birds has been exploited elsewhere in the world, but the food preferences of the seabirds and the aridity of the west coast of South America are ideal for the production of nitrogen-rich guano.

The term is now also used more broadly for other kinds of excrement, e.g., "bat guano."

GUILD. In a zoological context refers to groups of organisms that share a particular ecological niche and the resources it contains, e.g., forest songbirds such as titmice, nuthatches, and kinglets. The concept appears in discussions of competition among ecologically similar species. See Wiens (1989).

GUILLEMOT (Eng.: GILL-uh-mott; French: GEE-mo). Standard English name for the 3 species of auks in the genus *Cepphus* (family Alcidae; order Charadriiformes), 2 of which breed and winter in North America; also Standard name in British usage for the 2 species of alcids in the genus *Uria*, which are called "murres" in North America.

All of the *Cepphus* guillemots are largely black in alternate (breeding) plumage, becoming substantially white after the breeding season. They breed on rocky islets and remote rocky coasts and winter more inshore than other alcids. The Pigeon Guillemot inhabits the North Pacific, and is replaced in the North Atlantic and most of the north coast of the USSR by the Black Guillemot. For characteristics of the *Uria* guillemots, see MURRE. For family characteristics, see AUK.

The name is a diminutive of the French name Guillaume, which might be translated roughly as "Will." Lockwood (1993–NAMES) says that this derives from the call of the juvenile Common Guillemot, the first species to which this name was applied.

GUINEAFOWL (also guinea hen). Standard English name for 6 species of gallinaceous birds in the exclusively African family Numididae. Widely domesticated in meat and eggs, the Helmeted Guineafowl is sometimes found in small feral populations in parts of North America. See DOMESTICATED BIRDS.

GULAR (GYOU-ler). Referring to the throat. The red inflatable pouch on the throat of a male frigatebird, for example, may be called a gular sac.

GULL. Standard English name for all but 2 of the 50 members of the subfamily Larinae (family Laridae [gulls and terns]; order Charadriiformes).

All but 6 gull species belong to the genus *Larus*. Two species are known as
KITTIWAKES.

Twenty-two species of gulls breed in North America, not including a
single breeding record for Slaty-backed Gull in Alaska), 3 are regular visitors, and at least 3 (possibly 5) others have occurred as vagrants.

Gulls range in size from 10 to 30 inches, though most are medium
sized to large. Their plumage is invariably in tones of black, white, and
gray (brown in immatures). Their bills and legs are often bright red or

Fig. 15. *Appearance changes with age (Herring Gull).* Large gulls take four years to become fully mature, passing through a baffling sequence of plumage variations. (1) Juvenile and 1st Winter birds are a fairly uniform dark brown with paler areas developing
through feather wear; (2) 1st Summer birds are notably blotchy tan and gray with some
fathers bleaching with age enhancing this motley look; (3) 2nd Winter birds (often) begin to show some gray on back and in primaries and tail feathers can be all dark or paler
with wear; (4) By the 3rd Winter the adult plumage predominates but there remain
many brown feathers, giving an "unfinished" appearance. (5) In breeding plumage
adults the remaining brown coloration is lost through molt and wear, giving these birds
a crisp black, gray, and white look. The bill also changes dramatically with age from
black to pinkish with a dark tip to yellow with red spot at the tip. Though basic types are
described here, the reality is more of a continuum with every imaginable variation typically present in a large flock of gulls.

yellow and some species acquire a rosy "bloom" during the breeding season (see COLOR AND PATTERN). A large proportion of gull species also acquire dark (gray, brown, black) head feathers in the alternate (nuptial) plumage. Gulls' bills are relatively short but vary from rather thin and delicate to fairly massive. The first three toes are fully webbed and the hind toe (hallux) is small or vestigial.

Gulls are among the most successful birds in the modern world. They are strong fliers and swimmers, and some species make shallow dives from the air. Their diet tends to be nearly all-encompassing. They seek food not only over the world's oceans, lakes, and rivers, but also inland, where some species follow the farmer's plow and consume the grubs of crop-eating beetles, not to mention nests of mice exposed behind haying equipment; Ring-billed Gulls "hawk" in aerial ant swarms. A statue to the California Gull in Salt Lake City, Utah, commemorates that species' "heroic" efforts in stemming the plagues of large grasshoppers that threatened Mormon crops in 1848 and 1855.

Gulls nest colonially, different species preferring a wide variety of breeding habitats: marshes, beaches, tundra, and cliffs are typical locations and islands are often favored. The nest itself may be a fairly well-shaped cup of grasses, seaweed, and/or other available material, a simple pile of the same material on which the eggs are laid; or a plover-type scrape with a sparse lining of debris. Franklin's Gull builds a floating raft of marsh vegetation anchored to emergent plants, and Bonaparte's Gull makes a loose cup of sticks lined with grass, moss, and lichens, placed in a spruce tree in the boreal forest. The color and markings of the 2–5 eggs (usually 3 in most species) are variable among both species and individuals. Many are some shade of olive or buff with fairly profuse dark brown splotches and many paler subsurface markings, but they can also be nearly white, unmarked, sparsely marked, or finely speckled.

Gulls make a great variety of loud, penetrating sounds, from extended buglings and mewings to short nasal ejaculations.

The gulls provide a striking example of man's potential effect on animal populations. At the turn of the last century, Herring Gulls bred mainly in the Arctic and taiga and visited the New England coast only in winter. Though summering birds may have attempted to breed farther south before the mid-nineteenth-century, shooting and egg hunting inhibited such range expansion. In the 1920s, Herring Gulls established a few small breeding colonies as far south as Massachusetts, and owing at least in part to commercial fishing practices and the open dumping of human refuse, these pioneers have replicated themselves exponentially into the burgeoning gull population that currently clogs our harbors, beaches, lakes, and sanitary landfills and occupies breeding habitat at the expense of other bird species, especially terns. Herring Gulls and Great Black-backed Gulls (another "arctic" species) now breed well down the Atlantic coast to

the Carolinas and beyond. Other species of gulls have shown similar spectacular recent increases.

Gulls breed worldwide from the Arctic to the Antarctic, and inhabit most watery ecological niches from the high seas (some species strictly pelagic) to Andean lakes above 10,000 feet. They tend to be especially numerous along shorelines and near human habitation, where they are useful (if now often overabundant) scavengers.

"Gull" derives from Celtic names for these birds. These may originally have described the wailing noises made by gulls or their gluttonous appetites.

GYNANDROMORPHISM (guh[orjuh]-NAN-droh-MORF-izm). A genetic abnormality in which characteristics of both sexes are combined in a single individual. Avian gynandromorphs are very rare, but birds showing normal male plumage on one side of the body and normal female plumage on the other (bilateral gynandromorphism) have been recorded.

GYRFALCON (JURR-fall-kun). Standard English name for a single species of falcon *(Falco rusticolus)* that breeds, usually on cliffs, throughout much of the Arctic; a few individuals occasionally wander south as far as northern Europe, Russia, and the United States. Occurs in a range of color variations from nearly black to ivory white. It is a more robust and powerful bird than the Peregrine and is widely and justly regarded as the most splendid of the falcons.

In medieval falconry, it was reserved for kings (Khubilai Khan is said to have owned 200), and Arab princes will still pay exorbitant sums for them, their royal worthiness being enhanced today by increasing scarcity and strict protection throughout most of the breeding range. In spite of their distinguished reputation, modern falconers find them harder to train and less spectacular in action than the Peregrine.

Gruson (1972–BIOGRAPHY) traces the name to Old High German *gir-valke*, which means (O regal moniker!) "greedy falcon." Lockwood (1993–NAMES) is kinder and links the name to *geir,* literally spear and implying excellence as a weapon.

For family characteristics, see FALCON.

H

HABITAT. A flexible term for a restricted part of the environment in which a given plant or animal prefers to live; the perspective is that of the

inhabitant. Often (but by no means always) associated with a broad plant community; e.g., coniferous forest is the preferred habitat of the Gray Jay. Surf-washed rocks are the characteristic habitat of the Purple Sandpiper for most of the year, though its breeding habitat, upland tundra, is quite different. Semipalmated Sandpipers have broader feeding habitat specifications; though they prefer mudflats, they are likely found feeding in almost watery situations with an invertebrate food supply and a safe place to roost, e.g., marsh and pond edges, riverbanks, sandy beaches or even coastal rocks. The term can also refer to groups of organisms: Mudflats are ideal shorebird habitat. For related ecological concepts, see NICHE; BIOME; DISTRIBUTION.

HACKING. In falconry, the practice of setting young, captive, fledged falcons free for a period of weeks to allow them to develop full powers of flight and a wild spirit. During the hacking period (when birds are said to be "at hack") they are sometimes equipped with bells on their legs to hinder any efforts to capture their own food and to force them to come back to the food set out by the falconer at a fixed perch.

The term is also used today in the broader sense of reintroducing birds into the wild after a period of captivity. Injured birds, for example, rapidly grow accustomed to kindly human benefactors and "free" meals and must therefore be "hacked back" into the wild if they are to survive. Endangered species, reared in captivity, need be acclimated to wild conditions to be successfully reintroduced into their native habitat.

HACKLES. Long, narrow feathers of the neck; especially those of domestic roosters, which are key components in certain fishermen's flies. The golden nape of adult Golden Eagles, which contrasts with the dark body feathers, is made up of hackle-like feathers. The throat hackles of the ravens give them their bearded appearance versus the "clean shaven" crows.

HALCYON (HAL-see-on). A literary word for kingfisher and, by a combination of fanciful metaphor and bad ornithology, an adjective meaning calm, peaceful, e.g., "halcyon days."

A minor Greek goddess, Halcyone, threw herself into the sea out of grief for her drowned husband, Ceyx (both *Halcyon* and *Ceyx* have been adopted as names of kingfisher genera). Taking pity, the gods turned them both into kingfishers. From this legend arose the belief that kingfishers nest on the surface of the sea for a period of two weeks near the winter solstice and have the power to calm the waves to facilitate the incubation process.

HALLUX (HAL-iks) (pl.: halluces). The first digit or "big toe" of a bird's foot. In most species, the hallux is the hind toe, opposed to three others

pointing forward. Several other arrangements also exist, however, and not a few birds (e.g., many shorebirds) typically lack a hallux altogether or bear only a vestigial one. See LEG/FOOT and Fig. 35 or SKELETON and Fig. 27.

HAMMOCK. A land form/plant community typical of the southeastern United States, especially Florida. Sprunt (1954–STATE/PROVINCIAL BOOKS) defines a hammock as "a wooded island in a sea of grass," and quotes another definition: "a dense growth of trees other than pines in comparatively dry soil . . . in a region where open pine forests predominate" (Roland Harper). The botanical composition of hammocks varies and the term is modified accordingly, e.g., "palm hammock." The hammocks of the Everglades are dominated by tropical hardwoods. Hammocks are likely to contain woodland bird species, e.g., Red-bellied Woodpecker, Barred Owl, which are not typical of the surrounding open country. White-crowned Pigeons are characteristic of hammocks in the Everglades north of the mangrove habitats they generally occupy closer to saltwater.

HAMMOND, William A., 1828–1900 (Hammond's Flycatcher: *Empidonax hammondii*). In the legion of army doctor-birders (see BIOGRAPHY) Hammond was unquestionably the most eminent in his profession. He was a distinguished neurologist, professor of medicine, and an active and innovative (though underappreciated; see Gruson [1972–BIOGRAPHY]), U.S. Surgeon General. As with many other amateur ornithologists of his day, Hammond's interest was fostered through his army service and Spencer BAIRD. It was the exotic John XANTUS, befriended by Hammond, who described and named the western highland "empi" for him.

HAMULUS (HAM-yuh-luss). A hook, e.g., those on the barbicel of a feather. See FEATHER.

HANDEDNESS/FOOTEDNESS. Perhaps it is not surprising that few studies have been undertaken to determine to what degree birds are left-handed or right-handed (or to be precise in this case, left- or right-*footed*). There is some evidence that a majority of individuals of at least some parrot, hawk, and owl species are lefties; the Feral Pigeon, on the other hand, may be largely right-footed. It has also been shown that in some instances the preferred foot is actually slightly longer than the other and that some individual birds appear to be ambidextrous. For a concise overview with such references as exist see McNeil in Campbell and Lack (Footedness) (1985–ORNITHOLOGY).

HARD CORE (pronunciation in New England: "hahd coah"). Indefatigable in the pursuit of a "good bird"; also, such birders as an elite, "the hard

core." The quintessence of this state of being is embodied by those hardy souls who spend thousands of dollars in transportation costs and guide fees, camp in an execrable environment with inadequate sanitation and hostile natives in arctic Alaska, driven by the hope of adding an immature Scarlet Rosefinch (or other species abundant throughout the Palearctic region) to their "North American" lists. Norman Hill, author of *The Birds of Cape Cod*, deems these folk and their kind "the flinty haht (heart) of the hahd coah."

HARLEQUIN (Duck, Quail). Standard English name for a single Holarctic species of sea duck *(Histrionicus histrionicus)*. The Harlequin, a traditional clown character of the Italian commedia dell'arte, always appears in varicolored tights. His name is therefore an apt metaphor for the plumage of the male Harlequin Duck, arguably the most strikingly patterned duck in existence. Older references also refer to Harlequin *Quail (Cyrtonyx montezumae)*, now known officially as Montezuma Quail. The males of both the duck and the quail are decidedly "clown-faced."

HARRIER. Standard English name for the 13 species of hawks in the genus *Circus* (family Accipitridae; order Falconiformes), 1 of which, the Northern Harrier, *C. cyaneus* (formerly called the Marsh Hawk here and still known as the Hen Harrier in the Old World), breeds in North America.

The harriers are among the most graceful of raptors, all with exceptionally long wings, tails, and legs and a characteristic slow "tippy" manner of flight. They course over marsh, prairie, and tundra, periodically dropping suddenly to catch a small mammal, reptile, amphibian, or bird on the ground or in shallow water. The harriers also nest on the ground and sometimes form communal roosts in marshlands or other open-country cover after the breeding season. The harriers are notably "owl-faced" and are apparently unique among the hawks in their ability to hunt prey by sounds as do owls.

The genus *Circus* is distributed worldwide except (as usual) for the oceanic islands and frigid antipodes, and the Northern Harrier breeds throughout most of the Holarctic region.

"Harrier" means simply "hunter," though it derives from "harry," originally a military term meaning to plunder or harass.

For family characteristics, see HAWK; see also Simmons (2000).

HARRIS, Edward, 1799–1863 (Harris's Hawk: *Parabuteo unicinctus*; Harris's Sparrow: *Zonotrichia querula*). An amateur naturalist and gentleman horse breeder of New Jersey who accompanied his friend John James Audubon on his expeditions to the Florida Keys and up the Missouri River. On more than one occasion he provided Audubon with crucial financial support, for which we all have reason to be grateful to him. He also "ob-

tained" in New Jersey the pair of Cape May Warblers that Audubon used as models for *The Birds of America,* a species that the artist never saw alive. Audubon called Harris "one of the finest men of God's creation" and wished that "he was my brother." He also named the hawk after him (originally *Buteo harrisi*); Nuttall named the sparrow.

HATCH. To break through and emerge from an eggshell, as: "All the chicks (were) hatched (out) yesterday." Also, speaking of the egg, to break open as a result of the efforts of the embryo, as: "All the eggs hatched yesterday."

Hatching may be described as the final act of a bird embryo or the first act of a young bird, and preparation for this major transition begins early in the incubation period. As embryonic moisture evaporates through the porous eggshell, an air space is created between the inner and outer shell membranes at the blunt end of the egg. The embryo itself develops two temporary structures, the egg tooth and the hatching muscle, that aid the final escape from the egg. And the eggshell becomes weaker through the transfer of minerals to the embryonic skeleton.

Two or three days before hatching, the chick-to-be thrusts its bill into the air space and begins taking air into the lungs—though it continues to depend for part of its oxygen exchange on the allantois (see EMBRYO). In this first act of the hatching process, the embryo realigns its body from the crosswise to lie along the long axis of the egg, the most favorable position for forcing an exit from the blunt end. Aided principally by the leg and neck muscles and by the special hatching muscle attached to the back of the skull, the embryo's body soon begins to make convulsive thrusting motions that end in forcing the bird's bill against the inside of the shell. With the help of the horny egg tooth (located at the tip of the upper mandible in most species), the egg is eventually cracked or "pipped." The chick rotates its body counterclockwise with its legs during the process to produce a circular series of cracks around the blunt end of the egg. The internal hammering continues until enough of the shell is cracked to cause the end of the egg to fall away and to allow the chick to emerge exhausted on the floor of the nest. Having fulfilled their function, the hatching muscle and the egg tooth soon disappear, the latter dropping off or in some species being reabsorbed into the bill proper (see EGG TOOTH for more detail on this structure).

From pipping to full emergence the hatching process may take from as little as a half hour (small passerines) to as much as 6 days (albatross), but among small to medium-sized birds it consumes a few hours to most of a day on average. In most cases, eggs in a clutch do not hatch simultaneously but in sequence, reflecting the intervals in laying and the subsequent start of incubation.

Parent birds of some species may pick bits of shell away or poke into the initial cracks as the embryo struggles from within, and Ostriches are

said to crack their eggs with their breastbones and pull the chicks out with their bills but in most cases, chicks must make their way into the world unassisted.

After the embryo has broken into the air space, but well before it has hatched, it often begins "peeping," a sound that may trigger the shift in parental behavior from the "incubation mode" to the "brooding/feeding mode." Such vocalizations also serve to coordinate the near synchronous hatching of many precocial birds, e.g., waterfowl. Some parents will even bring food to these noisy eggs before they have been pipped.

For egg formation and prehatching development, see EGG; EMBRYO; INCUBATION; for posthatching behavior and development, see YOUNG, DEVELOPMENT OF; PARENTAL CARE.

HATCHLING. A bird that has just emerged from its egg. See CHICK; NESTLING.

HAWK. Standard English name in North America for about 50 members of the family Accipitridae (order Falconiformes) and used in combination in the names of a number of other birds of prey, e.g., Northern Goshawk. Worldwide more than 100 species of day-flying raptors include "hawk" alone or in combination form (e.g. "harrier-hawk," "sparrowhawk," hawk-eagle") in their name. "Hawk" is also popularly used to refer to any member of the Accipitridae except the vultures, condors, and eagles and even to the members of the Falconidae; i.e., in a loose context it is possible to say that Swallow-tailed Kites and Peregrine Falcons are both types of "hawks." In a slightly more restricted usage, the family Accipitridae is referred to as the hawk family, including the accipiters, buteos, eagles, kites, harriers, and Osprey, but not the falcons and caracaras or cathartid vultures, which are in different families. There are currently 15 species of resident North American birds of prey called "hawks" (including Northern Goshawk), all either "buteos" or "accipiters"; 2 other hawks have occurred as vagrants from the Neotropics; other native members of the hawk family (Accipitridae) include 5 kites, 1 harrier (formerly Marsh Hawk), and 3 eagles.

Hawks vary greatly in size (11–23 inches in length, not including the eagles), but all have powerful wings and legs and a short, stout, hooked bill for tearing flesh and long, sharp claws for grasping and killing prey. All species have a fleshy eye ring, and a "saddle" of skin at the base of the bill (cere) through which the nostrils open (see Fig. 1); both of these are often bright yellow or orange in adult birds. Members of the Accipitridae (and Falconidae) have a bony ridge over the eye, the supraorbital ridge, that lends them a perpetual fierce scowl. Many hawks are boldly patterned and handsomely colored and in action often display admirable agility and grace.

Hawks and eagles are all predatory on other animals, though the choice of prey (ailing antelopes to insects) and methods of hunting vary widely among different species. They never take plant food.

The typical hawk's nest is a large, bulky, sometimes carefully constructed cup of sticks, lined with moss, roots, grasses, and finer plant material. Nests are often decorated with fresh sprigs of conifers or other evergreen plants, possibly to discourage nest parasites. The site varies with the habitat of species and populations: on the ground, in marshland, on rocky cliffs, in trees, or atop a utility tower. Nests are often reused and "improved" with additional materials year after year and sometimes become massive structures over time (see EAGLE; NEST). The 1–8 eggs (average 2–4 in most species) are notably round (short, subelliptical; see Fig. 10). Color and marking very variable among both species and individuals: whitish to pale buff to pale bluish; unmarked to fine, pale speckling to very heavy, dark brown splotching covering almost the entire surface.

Vocalizations of hawks and eagles include harsh screams, plaintive fluted whistles, whinnies, and chatters.

Hawks are distributed worldwide except for Antarctica and throughout all North American biomes. Except for the Northern Goshawk and the Rough-legged Hawk, all our species are endemic to the New World; most are migratory.

"Hawk" goes back to Old Norse as a general term for diurnal birds of prey as described above; Lockwood (1993–NAMES) speculates on a possible root in the Latin verb *capere,* meaning "to seize."

Gradually British naturalists and especially falconers evolved a more precise usage in which "hawk" was reserved for the bird hunters in the genus *Accipiter;* "falcon" referred strictly to the members of the Falconidae (swift raptors with pointed wings and distinctive species names such as Peregrine, Merlin, and kestrel); "harrier" described only the long-winged, long-tailed open-country raptors of the genus *Circus*; and broad-winged soaring raptors, mostly in the genus *Buteo*, were called "buzzards." In America this nomenclature deteriorated again. "Hawk" was again substituted for all these more precise names and, of course, "buzzard" was reassigned as slang for the New World vultures (Cathartidae). More recently the official nomenclatures have restored many of the useful distinctions. North American birdwatchers no longer speak of Sparrow Hawks when they mean American Kestrels or Marsh Hawks when they mean Northern Harriers. But it is doubtful that buteos will ever be called "buzzards" here. See also KITE.

HAWKING. Another name for falconry. Also, flying over an area, eyeing the ground or water carefully in search of prey. Some hawks (e.g., Northern Harrier) do this habitually, but so do many other birds. Gull-billed Terns, for example, characteristically "hawk" over marshes and mudflats.

The term, along with "sallying," is also used by ornithologists studying feeding behavior of passerines to mean snatching prey out of the air while on the wing. Papers on foraging never speak of this as "flycatching," though that would seem to be a more apt description of the activity.

HAWK MOUNTAIN Sanctuary (Pennsylvania). A narrow spur of the Kittatinny Ridge in the eastern Appalachians, along which tens of thousands of day-flying raptors—mostly Broad-winged (c. 47%) and Sharp-shinned (c. 25%) Hawks—pass between late August and mid-November (see Appendix VI for peak dates). This famous flyway was once the site of an annual "varmint shoot" by misguided farmers and "sportsmen" of the region, but it is now a protected area visited by thousands of hawk watchers annually. It is located about 17 miles north of Reading, Pennsylvania, and is reached via the town of Hamburg. For more details on Hawk Mountain birds and the saga of raptor preservation, see Broun (1949), Harwood (1973), and Bildstein's excellent short account of the mountain and Broad-winged Hawk migration in "Gatherings of Angels" (1999).

HAWKWATCHING. This form of birdwatching has taken on a life of its own in the last 30 years, owing its popularity, no doubt, to the inherent glamour of birds of prey and the impressive concentrations in which they can be seen during migration. These aerial rivers and eddies of raptors occur due to the fact that migratory soaring birds depend on air currents such as thermals and updrafts to facilitate their journeys (see FLIGHT) and seek out these conditions where they occur in nature. These birds also migrate by day in large numbers and during a narrow window of time. The birdwatcher who visits the right mountain top, ridge, lake shore, or geographical cul-de-sac (think Cape May, New Jersey) in the right day in spring or fall will witness one of nature's most thrilling spectacles. The ur-hawkwatching locale in North America is Hawk Mountain, Pennsylvania (see preceding entry), and a few other traditional spots have attracted birders in season for decades. Fairly recently, however, a new breed of hawkwatcher has actively sought out undiscovered watch points—finding hundreds of "new" ones throughout North America—and also started counting raptors in a methodical way (see CENSUS, Stationary Counts) to foster their conservation. *Hawks in Flight* by Dunne, Sibley, and Sutton is perhaps the one "must-have" guide, but there is now a small library of books on the subject (see Bibliography). Founded in 1974, the Hawk Migration Association of North America (HMANA)—with its mission "to conserve raptor populations through scientific study, enjoyment, and appreciation of raptor migration" is the place to go for all your hawkwatching needs, including finding the best sights near you. See its website at http://www.hmana.org/.

HAZARDS TO AVIATION. See PROBLEMS INVOLVING BIRDS.

HEARING. Birds are among the most vocal of animals, and it is therefore not surprising that they possess good hearing, at least within their species' vocal range. Courtship and territorial songs, vocal signals between parents and young, alarm notes, threat sounds, calls among flocking birds, and sounds made by predators are important elements in the lives of birds and would be useless, of course, unless they could be heard.

The Avian Ear. Bird ears are similar in general to human ones, but simpler in structure; for example, like reptiles they have only a single bone—the columella or stapes—in the middle ear, where humans have three. Avian ears, like ours, are located in the sides of the head and have three interconnected chambers: the outer, middle, and inner ears. Birds lack the fleshy external sound-catching appendages so prominent in mammals, and their ear holes are usually totally concealed under the feathers called ear coverts (auriculars) (see Fig. 35); these feathers lack barbules and apparently serve to protect the inner ear from wind disturbance in flight while permitting the passage of sound; they can be erected from the sides of the head—though this is rarely witnessed. In penguins and other diving birds the feathers covering the ears are thickened and act as earplugs. The skin and muscle that surrounds the outer ear is adapted for specialized functions in different groups of birds. Deep divers can close a flap extending from the rear rim of the ear. And owls have flaps of skin (opercula) in front of and behind the ear holes that can alter the size and orientation of the opening to focus and enhance sound perception. Owl ears are also unique (as far as known) in being asymmetrical both in position (one higher than the other) and in internal structure, adaptations for finding prey in the dark. The processing of sounds in a bird's brain occurs mainly in the hindbrain (medulla); in nocturnal birds that must locate their prey by sound the ganglia that serve this function are greatly enlarged.

What Birds Can Hear. To understand the useful comparison between human hearing and that of birds, the reader will recall that sound is recorded as the rate at which sound vibrations pass through the air, called cycles per second (cps or hertz). The more vibrations or cycles per second, the higher the frequency or pitch. The normal human ear hears sounds between about 20 and 17,000 hertz (20,000 maximum). The known hearing range for all birds is between 34 and 29,000 hertz. *However,* the range of any single bird species is significantly less than ours: we hear about nine octaves; birds average about five. Nor is the hearing ability of birds especially acute; humans can generally pick up fainter sounds than birds across the frequency spectrum.

As logic suggests, bird species tend to hear about the same range of sounds they can produce. Many small songbird species can sing and hear sounds of higher frequency than we are capable of hearing. However, these same birds miss several lower octaves that we hear easily. For

example, these avian tenors and sopranos often cannot hear the relatively low-frequency human voice, so that loquacious birdwatchers usually disturb their fellow birders more than their quarry.

At least some birds can hear "faster" than we can. Slowing down a recorded bird song often reveals notes we couldn't hear at normal speed, though birds that mimic other birds (see SONG) have been shown to include these fast notes in their imitations.

Birds use their hearing not only in communicating but also in locating food. Payne (1962) revealed how Barn Owls can zero in on mice in the dark by precisely locating the position of their squeaks and scuffles; and there is some evidence that robins, plovers, and other birds that hunt over the ground for invertebrates can *hear* their prey as it moves under the surface; and that woodpeckers can hear grubs and other wood-inhabiting insects moving in bark and trunks.

It has been shown (Kreithen and Quine 1979) that domestic pigeons can detect "infrasounds" (frequencies below 20 hertz), which include vibrations made by tectonic disturbances and more mundane sounds like the rumble of waves breaking along a coast—possibly at great distances. This would explain instances of birds "predicting" earthquakes, e.g., chickens that crow in alarm before people are able to feel earth tremors. Birds cannot, however, hear the ultrasonic (very high frequency) sounds on which bats depend.

Echolocation, highly developed in bats, has been verified in a few species of cave-dwelling birds in South America (Oilbird) and Asia (swiftlets). However, the clicks that these birds bounce off their home caves to keep from bumping into the walls are well within normal hearing frequencies and thus much cruder than the ultrasonic signals used by bats.

For more detail on avian ear anatomy and hearing mechanics, see, especially, Necker in Sturkie (2000) and Dooling (1982).

HEART. See CIRCULATORY SYSTEM.

HEAT (regulation of). See TEMPERATURE, BODY.

HEATH HEN. Standard English name for the extinct eastern subspecies of the Greater Prairie-Chicken, *Tympanuchus cupido cupido*. Today the species is associated with undisturbed grasslands of central North America, but in colonial times the Heath Hen thrived in ericaceous (blueberry, huckleberry, etc.) barrens, characteristic of burned-over areas in the East. The destruction of the eastern population is directly attributable to overshooting, which was essentially accomplished by the early 1800s, when hunting the species for the market ceased to be profitable in the East. After this period, only a few remnant populations remained. The last of these was on the glacial outwash plains near the south shore of the island

of Martha's Vineyard, Massachusetts, near present-day Katama. The last bird here succumbed sometime after March 11, 1932.

For other details, see EXTINCT BIRDS; also PRAIRIE-CHICKEN.

HEERMANN (HAIR-mahn in German; HERE-mun in North American), Adolphus L., c. 1827–65 (Heermann's Gull: *Larus heermanni*). Heermann was a boy naturalist and grew to attain all the characteristics of the successful nineteenth-century bird man; he was a doctor, a member of the Philadelphia Academy of Arts and Sciences, and an officer in the U.S. Army. These circumstances inevitably brought him into contact with Spencer BAIRD, with whom he worked on the zoological portions of the Pacific Railway Survey. He collected birds and eggs in Florida, Mexico, and California and, according to Gruson (1972–BIOGRAPHY), died by the cruel (but intriguing) combination of advanced syphilis and an accidental self-inflicted gunshot wound. He collected the beautiful Pacific coast gull that commemorates him, which was named by his contemporary John CASSIN. He also coined the term "oology," the study of birds' eggs. For a fuller biography, see Stone, *Cassinia* (1907), 9:1–6.

HELIGOLAND (HELL-ih-goh-LAND) **TRAP.** A famous, rather elaborate trap for land-bird migrants, which takes its name from the tiny German island in the North Sea where the contraption was pioneered as a banding tool in the early part of the twentieth century. It is essentially an enormous funnel made of chicken wire or other mesh fencing material. The mouth is 20 or more feet high and once birds have entered they are driven up into a box fitted with devices to facilitate getting hold of the trapped birds so that they can be banded. Heligoland traps are usually placed near low, dense vegetation so that birds can be flushed from one side into the trap on the other. Bait in the mouth of the funnel is also used.

Mist nets have replaced trapping methods such as this one at most bird-banding stations. See MIST NET; CANNON NET; BANDING; CAPTURE.

HEN. The female of any species of bird, especially of the gallinaceous birds (grouse, quail, pheasants, etc.) and more especially of the domestic chicken. The corresponding term for the male is "cock." It is not uncommon in Britain to hear expressions such as "a hen Reed Bunting" or "a cock siskin." But this usage is rare at best in North America.

HENSLOW, John S., 1796–1861 (Henslow's Sparrow: *Passerherbulus henslowii*). English botanist, geologist, clergyman, and teacher. He was a principal in the establishment of Kew Gardens. Perhaps most notably, he was one of Charles Darwin's teachers and recommended him as a young naturalist for a post on the *Beagle*. He was also a friend of Audubon, who named the sparrow for him.

HEPATIC (Tanager). Pertaining to the liver. The liver is normally dark, dull red or purplish brown; the male Hepatic Tanager in breeding plumage is brick orange—with some dusky shading on back, wings, and cheek. It would be surprising to find a truly liver-colored Hepatic Tanager and alarming to find a Hepatic Tanager-colored liver. Perhaps the coiner of this name was thinking of the yellow female or immature male and the jaundice produced by a malfunction of the liver.

HERBIVOROUS (her-BIH-ver-us). Describes a preference for plant food. Plant-eating animals are known as "herbivores." Ptarmigan and other grouse are examples of herbivorous birds.

HERBST'S CORPUSCLES. Ovoid masses of nerve endings about 1.5 hundredths of a millimeter in length in the lower layer of skin (dermis), so far known only in birds. They serve as receivers of tactile sensation. See TOUCH; GRANDRY'S CORPUSCLES. See Necker in Sturkie (2000–HEARING).

HERON. Standard English name for about 40 members (including pond-herons, night-herons, and tiger-herons) of the family Ardeidae (order Ciconiiformes), which also includes the egrets and bitterns. Twelve members of this family breed in North America, and 5 others have occurred here as vagrants (see Appendix II).

The herons are relatively small (13 inches) to large (4½ feet) wading birds characterized, in general, by long legs and neck, long, pointed bill, broad wings, a short tail, and, in many species, long, beautiful plumes on head, back, and/or chest, which develop during the breeding season (see Fig. 5). They consistently feed in shallow water or marshland, perhaps preferring fish, but by no means eschewing frogs, snakes, small birds and mammals, and any invertebrate large enough to be worth the trouble.

Most heron species nest in colonies, usually placing their stick platforms in trees or bushes but also on rocky ledges or clumps of wetland vegetation. The structure is a notably flimsy affair when first built but becomes larger and more substantial in succeeding years. If any lining is added it usually consists of a few leaves and other plant debris. Herons lay 2–7 (usually 3–4) pale to fairly deep greenish blue (American Bittern) to olive brown, unmarked eggs.

Herons are mostly silent, except in the social atmosphere of the breeding colony. Their repertoire consists mainly of throaty croaks, squawks, and the occasional hiss. The Green Heron and the night-herons call more often, the first giving a distinctive, sharp *kuke* when disturbed and the latter uttering its familiar *quok* en route to and from feeding grounds. For the most unusual of heron sounds, see BITTERN.

The heron family is distributed worldwide except for the barrens above tree line and they reach their greatest North American diversity in the Southeast, but occur continentwide wherever there is water. A num-

ber of "southern" species (Snowy and Great Egrets, Little Blue and Tricolored Herons) have extended their range markedly northward in the last half-century. The recent phenomenal range expansion of the Cattle Egret is in a class by itself (see DISTRIBUTION).

Herons are popular as characters in fables and fairy tales due to their distinctive, somewhat humanoid form and their manner, which, in turn, is now dignified, now stealthy, now relaxed. And their delicate plumage and graceful movement both in the air and on the ground doubtless explain their prominence in the ancient tradition of Oriental brush painting (see HUMAN CULTURE, BIRDS IN). The species with the most beautiful plumes (egrets) were hunted to the brink of extinction around the turn of the century for the sake of millinery fashion (see AUDUBON SOCIETIES and CONSERVATION). Most species have rebounded strongly with protection.

"Heron" may be traced back through various ancient words, all referring specifically to the birds themselves and perhaps some call of the Grey Heron of Eurasia. Local versions of the name in sixteenth-century England included "hern," "hernshaw" (a young heron), and "harnsaw." This, it is widely supposed, is what Hamlet is talking about when, feigning madness, he tells Guildenstern (Act II, scene 2): "I am but mad north-northwest. When the wind is southerly I know a hawk from a handsaw." However, some critics note that a "hawk" was a common plasterer's tool and that the prince may have been talking carpentry not ornithology.

HESPERORNIS (HESS-purr-OR-niss). Literally, "western bird." A genus of extinct birds (order Hesperornithiformes; family Hesperornithidae), 4 species of which were first described from fossils uncovered in Upper Cretaceous chalk beds in Kansas and Montana. The order is now known to have been nearly cosmopolitan in distribution and to have contained up to 7 genera and 13 species. All were large (4–5 feet), flightless, swimming and diving birds, superficially resembling (but not related to) modern loons. O. C. Marsh, the famous paleontologist who described the first *Hesperornis,* erected a new subclass (Odontoholcae) defined by the presence of this bird's most distinctive feature: teeth set in grooves in the jaws; but it is now placed in the Infraclass Odontornithes. See also EVOLUTION OF BIRDLIFE.

HETEROCHROISM. Technical term for abnormal color differences. See ALBINISM; MELANISM; LEUCISM; ERYTHRISM; XANTHOCHROISM.

HIBERNATION. In the sense of a prolonged, regular, seasonal period of dormancy in which life functions are dramatically reduced, hibernation has been claimed for only one bird species, the Poor-will *(Phalaenoptilus nuttallii),* though doubt has been cast about whether this nightjar is a *true* hibernator. For a similar metabolic phenomena in this and other species see TORPIDITY.

HIGH ISLAND (Texas). A knoll of high ground with live oaks along the predominantly marshy Texas coast northeast of Galveston. Such copses, known locally as "hummocks" (or "cheniers" in nearby coastal Louisiana), form the only satisfactory sanctuary for migrant woodland birds arriving from the long spring journey across the Gulf of Mexico. In good weather the migrants disperse inland, but when bad weather forces them to put down on the nearest land, High Island (as well as other localities along the Gulf coast) occasionally becomes deluged with millions of exhausted birds. See Appendix VI for prime dates. For a discussion of the import of such layover sites see Moore *in Gatherings of Angels* (1999). The economic impact of birders on this small Upper Texas Coast community has been documented in an article in *Birding* (Eubanks et al. 1993–BIRDWATCHING).

HINCKLEY, Ohio. Site of an annual celebration on March 15, the approximate date of the spring return of hundreds of Turkey Vultures (or "buzzards" as they are known locally) to an area of breeding cliffs about 20 miles south of Cleveland.

HIPPOBOSCID (flies) (hippo-BOSS-id). A family of parasitic flies that live externally on the bodies of birds and mammals; c. 200 species have been identified worldwide. For details, see ECTOPARASITE, Louseflies.

HISTOPLASMOSIS (HIS-toh-plaz-MO-sis). An ailment rarely contracted by people by inhaling the spores of a fungus that grows on bird droppings. For more detail see DISEASE.

HOARY (Redpoll). Whitish, especially with age. Redpolls of both sexes do become paler than the preceding age class as they get older. However, the point of the name is that the Hoary Redpoll is generally paler than the Common Redpoll, especially with regard to the rump and undertail coverts, which are nearly to completely unstreaked in the Hoary and usually appear streaked in the Common.

HOLARCTIC REGION. The Nearctic and Palearctic zoogeographic regions combined. A bird species such as the Northern Shrike (called Great Grey Shrike in the Old World), the range of which is continuous (except for current ocean barriers) around the world north of the tropics, is said to have a Holarctic distribution. See ZOOGEOGRAPHY; DISTRIBUTION and Fig. 34.

HOLOTYPE. When the author of a new species (or other taxon) designates a particular specimen as the basis for his description at the time of publication, that specimen is called the holotype. Compare LECTOTYPE; see also NOMENCLATURE, Types.

HOME RANGE. The total area that a bird inhabits while resident in a given place. The home range may be essentially the same as the breeding territory (in species with large territories in which they feed, gather nesting material, etc., as well as nest); or contain the breeding territory but extend far beyond it (many colonial nesters); or be totally separate from the breeding area, e.g., on wintering grounds.

Though species of raptors may avoid hunting within another individual's home range, the latter differs from a territory mainly in not being vigilantly defended (see TERRITORY).

On the average, the home range is larger than the territory and may be very large indeed (28 square miles [72.5 square kilometers] recorded for one Golden Eagle), but size varies among both species and individuals.

HOMOIOTHERMAL (HO-moy-o-THERM-ul) (or homoiothermic or homoiothermous). "Warm-blooded"; i.e., capable of maintaining a high body temperature independent of the environment. While mammals and birds are the most broadly homoeothermic, tuna and crocodiles also fit the criteria. Furthermore, the young of bird species that are born naked are in fact "cold-blooded" and therefore dependent on their parents for maintenance of body temperature until at least partially fledged. Compare POIKILOTHERMAL. See TEMPERATURE, BODY.

HOMOSEXUALITY. In bird populations in which one sex greatly outnumbers the other, homosexual pairing sometimes occurs. The phenomenon is particularly prevalent among captive birds. During the mating season in a colony of birds such as gulls, in which males and females are superficially similar, a certain amount of sexual confusion—females mounting males, males mounting other males—is not very unusual. Hunt et al. (1980) have recorded a high incidence of female-female pairing among Western Gulls on Santa Barbara Island, California (again, probably due to a skewed sex ratio). When members of such pairs are fertilized by promiscuous males, both females may contribute to a clutch and successfully rear broods by sharing responsibilities. This is probably more in the category of "same-sex parenting" than "homosexuality" in the human psychosexual sense. See also POLYANDRY; POLYGAMY; POLYGYNY; MATING SYSTEMS.

HOOD. Either a feathered crest, e.g., Hooded Merganser, or an area of distinctly colored feathers covering part of the head and neck, e.g., Hooded Warbler, Hooded Oriole. A Laughing Gull may be said to have a black "hood" in breeding plumage.

In falconer's parlance, a leather headpiece of varying design, which covers the eyes of hawks to keep them docile.

HOOTING. A general term for the "song" of all owls; some, e.g., Great Horned Owls, actually "hoot"; others screech, wail, howl, and even ululate.

HOPPING. The manner in which most perching birds (order Passeriformes) move when on the ground. By contrast, most nonpasserines walk (see WALKING/RUNNING). Notable exceptions (i.e., passerines that usually walk rather than hop) in North America include Horned Lark, ravens, crows, and magpies (jays regularly both hop and walk), pipits and wagtails, starlings, meadowlarks, grackles, cowbirds, blackbirds, and the Savannah Sparrow. Of course, a great many arboreal or aerial species, e.g., warblers or swallows, do not normally spend any time on the ground and so rarely hop or walk. Other species, e.g., American Robin, Northern Mockingbird, though normally hoppers, will occasionally run. It is generally supposed that ground-haunting birds evolved the habit of hopping in order to move efficiently among small obstructions, such as rocks, encountered frequently in their preferred habitat.

HORICON MARSH (Wisconsin). 35,000 acres of freshwater marsh in southeastern Wisconsin (near Waupun) protected as a waterbird refuge by both state and federal governments. The greatest avian event at Horicon is the concentrations of waterfowl, especially when Canada and Snow Geese occur in March and April (peak: first two weeks in April); the fall flight, late September to early November (peak: mid-October), is less spectacular. The refuge also contains a heronry and an interesting assortment of midwestern marsh birds, e.g., Sedge Wren and Yellow-headed Blackbird.

HORMONES. See ENDOCRINE SYSTEM.

HORNED LARK. Standard English name for the 2 members of the lark genus *Eremophila* (family Alaudidae; order Passeriformes). One of these, the Horned Lark *(E. alpestris),* is widespread in the Holarctic region, occurring in virtually every open-country habitat: some 20 subspecies have been distinguished in North America alone.

The name derives from the species' characteristic *corniplumes—* small, pointed tufts of feathers projecting from the top of the head above and behind the eyes in adult birds.

For family characteristics, see LARK.

HORNEMANN, Jens Wilken, 1770–1841 *(Acanthis hornemanni*: Hoary Redpoll). Eminent Danish botanist, co-author (with eight others) of the 14-volume *Flora Danica.* The redpoll was named by the Dutch ornithologist C. P. Hoelboll, a contemporary of Hornemann's and for a time governor of Greenland. Mr. Hoelboll's name is attached to a subspecies of the

Common Redpoll *(Acanthis flammea hoelbolli)* and was once used as the accepted common name for the Red-necked Grebe. Unfortunately, the governor's name was long misspelled by taxonomists as Holboell, but the error has now been officially corrected.

HOST. In a biological context, an organism that is parasitized by another. Many songbird species are "hosts" to the brood parasitism of the Brown-headed Cowbird. See PARASITISM; COWBIRD.

HOVERING. Remaining stationary in midair, usually by rapid beating of the wings. A flight technique used for hunting terrestrial animals by a number of raptors, including the shrikes, kestrels, and some kites and buteos and by some fish-eating birds, including terns, kingfishers, and Osprey. Also characteristic of the flight of hummingbirds. See FLIGHT, Special Techniques.

HUMAN CULTURE, BIRDS IN. It is far beyond the scope of the present book to treat this vast and fascinating subject with anything like thoroughness. All the subtopics below merit full-length books of their own, and in most cases such books already exist. The aim here is to sketch a broad outline and to prick readers' curiosity; the Bibliography lists some sources in which they may find satisfaction.

The ubiquity, variety, and abundance of birds have always made them familiar to human beings. They are more universal even than trees (for many Eskimos have lived and died without ever seeing a full-sized tree) or mountains (for inhabitants of coral atolls never see mountains) or even the sea (which many inland cultures know only from legend). Since birds are also good to eat, are decorative, and can be trained to participate in several sports, it is hardly surprising that birdlife figures prominently in the whole spectrum of human activities. But that bird themes should be so pervasive in our *cultural* life—in our painting, music, literature, religion, and folklore—requires further explanations, of which I think there are essentially five: (1) Birds lend themselves very readily to anthropomorphic characterization—the wise owl, the vain peacock, the noble eagle—much more so even than most of our nearer relatives the mammals. Perhaps the fact that birds walk erect on two legs as we do is partly responsible for our tendency to "humanize" them. (2) Only birds among the other animals are as vocal as ourselves and often *seem*, at least, to sing for pleasure as we do, as well as for communicating (see SONG). (3) Birds lead a conspicuous family life with many habits—elaborate and silly courtship rites, nest building, food bringing, family "outings"—that remind us of ourselves. Many mammals have these habits, but one sees them less often. (4) Birds have an intrinsic, almost otherworldly beauty—rather like angels—that is manifested in spectacular plumage, ethereal

song, and an apparently ephemeral nature; these qualities provide a rich source of poetic metaphor. (5) Birds can fly—the one nonhuman attribute that we unreservedly and universally envy.

These speculations about the prominence of avian themes in human culture apply to all the categories below and so will not be emphasized again in each case.

PAINTING. There are two discernible kinds of "bird painting": (1) bird portraiture in which birds are treated for their own sake as the main objective of a painting and (2) works of art by acknowledged masters in which birds figure—sometimes very prominently—in the composition. (The Swedish impressionist Bruno Liljefors may be the only painter who managed to be both a brilliant bird portraitist and an acknowledged mainstream artist.) The best examples of the former may exhibit exquisite draftsmanship together with fine perceptions of light, texture, composition, and other values. But their *intent* is altogether different from that of the latter and so this form of bird painting is treated separately under ILLUSTRATION.

There is little exaggeration if any in the statement that you can find birds wherever you look in the history of art. They occur most often as genre elements included, so to speak, to show the world as it is (or was). Some of the most realistic depictions of birds (i.e., those in which the species or at least the family is recognizable) appear in hunting scenes, the first of which are Paleolithic cave paintings—about 17,000 years old—among the oldest works of art we know of. Herons and kingfishers are clearly portrayed in the limestone relief of a hippopotamus hunt in the tomb of Ti (c. 2400 BC) of the Old Kingdom of Egypt; and one of the treasures of Tutankhamen's tomb (c. 1360 BC) is a painted chest showing the young king hunting bustards (among many other animals) and attended by two Griffon Vultures. Hunting scenes with birds also show up in classical Etruscan, Greek, and Roman wall paintings and in medieval tapestries and illuminated texts (falconry was a very popular genre subject in the Middle Ages), and continue to appear in serious works of art until nearly the present day (e.g., Winslow Homer's *Right and Left,* showing a pair of Common Goldeneyes in the foreground being dispatched from a distant boat on a wintry sea). The hunt continues to be a central theme in the "primitive" art of African, Australian, South American, and Inuit cultures. In the fifteenth century common dooryard birds such as crows, magpies, and sparrows became prominent in carefully drawn scenes of daily life, such as the Limbourgs' *Les Très Riches Heures du Duc de Berry* and later in the town-and-country-scapes of Brueghel. Though recognizable species occasionally appear in later landscapes (e.g., Rubens's *Landscape with the Château of Steen*), birds are more likely to be used as vague evocations of nature, e.g., the anonymous avian shapes in flight added with a few strokes of the brush by Claude, Constable, and the Impressionists. The

American Luminist Movement (1850–75) made liberal use in its seascapes of the kind of little wide-V "sea gull" that all schoolchildren learn to make and stick picturesquely in their skies. A grisly variation on the obligatory seascape gulls depicts black-and-white birds (Cape Petrels?) hovering over the carnage in Turner's *The Slave Ship.*

The purely decorative qualities of birds also appealed to some of the earliest-known artists, e.g., Greek seventh-century BC perfume vases in the shape of an owl or motifs on painted black-figure Attic kylikes (sixth century BC). The highly formalized garden scenes in late-fourteenth- and early-fifteenth-century tapestries and frescoes made good use of the forms and bright colors of such birds as peacocks and Golden Orioles *(Oriolus).* And these "ideal" birds were also popular in sensual Arcadian scenes in the Renaissance (e.g., Titian's *Bacchanal,* 1518) and in the romantic eighteenth-century nymph-scapes of Watteau and Fragonard. On Baroque ceiling frescoes, cupids and angels usually outnumber birds, but not infrequently a flight of swallows or some other suitably idyllic avian phenomenon is included, as in Guercino's ceiling fresco *Aurora* (1620s) in the Villa Ludovisi in Rome. Somewhat ironically, some of the most detailed depictions of birds in art are found in Dutch still lifes of the seventeenth century. Like the sumptuous flower and food arrangements of the same Baroque tradition, birds of many species, carefully chosen for the variety of their colors and patterns, are shown to exquisite advantage— except that they are all dead.

A few painters have recognized the potential of birds in enhancing fantastic themes. The unrivaled master of feathered fantasy is Hieronymus Bosch, who, to judge by the precision with which he painted actual species and the variety of them he uses, seems to have been more than a little interested in birdlife. Birds appear in many of his paintings as elements of genre (see above), but in his famous *Garden of Delights* triptych he uses a staggering variety of birds—real and imaginary—in three of art's most fantastic landscapes. In the Eden and Hell side panels, he gives us fairly standard idyllic (egrets, peacocks) and horrific (owls and other night birds) avian images, respectively. But in the center panel, showing either an Adamite heaven on earth or (much more probably) "man in sin," the birds are far more than peripheral decorations. Giant goldfinches, woodpeckers, hoopoes, jays, and owls wade about in crowded pools with the same spirit of frolicsome liberation that their human brethren display; a smiling duck drops fruits into a man's mouth, spoonbills squawk in delight at riding on a goat's back, a robin *(Erithacus)* is entirely content to carry a man with a huge seed pod on his head. To a modern eye this scene (though somewhat overcrowded) might be seen as representing some eco-paradise in which birds and people (and a great many other things) seem to be living together in perfect contentment. But most art historians agree that, despite the innocent expressions of the creatures in the Garden

of Delights, they represent the consequences of the Fall depicted in the left-hand panel of the triptych and the precursor to the eternal damnation shown to the right. Like virtually every other animal and shape in the painting the birds all have an allegorical meaning relating to one or more specific vices that a contemporary viewer would have recognized.

Before leaving fantasy, we should probably give a respectful nod to the twentieth-century fantast Henri Rousseau, whose haunting jungle scenes (e.g., *The Dream*) often include a bird or two of imaginary species that help to evoke an aura of primitive innocence.

Finally, it should be emphasized that, especially in early painting, birds in are often symbols for concrete entities, e.g., saints or Satan, or for emotions or phenomena, e.g., the volatility of the spirit or spring. Bosch's owls, for example, stand specifically for evil/the underworld, omnipresent but often unnoticed in the human sphere, and his eggs, which bear surprising contents in many of his works, are alchemistic devices. Birds in early ecclesiastic paintings are also included in many cases to represent a specific aspect of Christianity, e.g., the bleeding pelican, which appears in painted crucifixions (see IMAGINATION, Religion). The less literal form of symbolism is exemplified Brancusi's gleaming abstract bronze, *Bird in Space* (1919), which embodies the sleek grace that man admires in the flight of birds.

Arguably the most exquisite of painted birds are those done in the tradition of the Northern Sung Dynasty painter-emperor Hui Tsung of eleventh-century China. The graceful egrets among lotuses and fierce goshawks perched in flowering plum trees also stand for qualities that they suggest to human observers, though no one can deny their decorative appeal. The elegant lines and harmonious forms are meant to express Buddhist teachings, such as transmigration of the soul and the insubstantiality of the ego, as well as simply delighting the eye.

MUSIC. The songs of some of the famous European songbirds, e.g., Common Cuckoo and Nightingale, have been incorporated now and then as themes in classical music. These species plus the European Quail *(Coturnix)* can be heard in the second movement of Beethoven's Pastoral Symphony (see Howes [1964] for other birdsong motifs). Plaintive calls such as those of various plover species and the Eurasian Curlew have purportedly inspired music intended to evoke the mood of a lonely landscape or the like, much in the way the "emotional" qualities of birdsong are often used in poetry (see below). On the whole, however, bird "music" does not correspond very closely to the characteristic range of melodies and rhythms of Western music and therefore is seldom transposed successfully or at least recognizably. A major exception is the work of Olivier Messiaen who composed several works directly inspired by specific bird sounds. His "The Quartet for the End of Time," written while the composer was imprisoned in a German concentration camp, clearly features the cadences and tonal qualities of the Common Nightingale.

Other musical traditions, e.g., Oriental flute music, seem to lend themselves much more naturally to the use of birdsong than do western forms.

The occurrence of birds in musical *lyrics* is, of course, an altogether different matter. As with recording avian appearances in poetry (see below), noting instances of birds in human song would require the lifetime services of a professional bibliographer. Suffice to say that bird lyrics may be found throughout all (or very nearly all) musical traditions, from the oldest folk songs to Gilbert and Sullivan's tit-willow (not to be confused with the Willow Tit, *Parus montanus*), to "Listen to the Mockingbird," to the Beatles' "Blackbird" *(Turdus merula)* on the White Album.

The most famous "musical bird" is undoubtedly Mozart's starling *(Sturnus vulgarus)*, which Mozart purchased on May 27, 1784. A snatch of song sung by starling may have inspired a passage in Mozart's Piano Concerto in G major, K453, and, in any case, the bird could imitate the phase so accurately (only substituting a G sharp for a G natural) that the composer wrote in the starling's version under his own with the note: "Das war schön" (That was beautiful).

LITERATURE. Here distinguished from both ornithological "literature," i.e., technical writing, and "nature writing" on the subject of birds; also from fairy tales and other fanciful writings about birds, which are discussed under IMAGINATION, BIRDS IN. The present subject matter is "real" birds in fiction and poetry.

Fiction. Excepting the odd parrot on a sea captain's shoulder or caged canary used as a prop, birds in fiction usually serve as background scenery and mood-setting devices. Novelists with an eye for nature or a fondness for outdoor action frequently conjure the seacoast with some gulls wheeling and crying; it is very difficult to describe spring without a certain amount of exuberant birdsong; and some ecstatic avian caroling from field or forest is as indispensable as the perfume of wildflowers to love alfresco. There is also, evidently, a strong compunction, when writing about tropical landscapes, to include some "strange" and/or colorful birds for the sake of verisimilitude.

Such use of birds, if well done, may enhance a reading experience for someone who knows something about birdlife or it may hand him a laugh if the author has skipped his ornithological homework. But overall the impact of birds in English and American fiction must be accounted negligible.

A few oddities where birds assume a more prominent role than usual may be mentioned.

Gulliver's Travels by Jonathan Swift. The hero is "boxed" by a Brobding-
    nagian "Linnet somewhat larger than an English Swan" and in the
    same country narrowly escapes a "kite," which sounds suspiciously
    like a kestrel.
The Narrative of Arthur Gordon Pym by Edgar Allan Poe. Includes some
    fairly detailed and (on the whole) accurate accounts of south polar

oceanic birds, which add a suitably bizarre touch to the later chapters. Poe also invents a few species of his own, e.g., a "Black Gannet."

Green Mansions by W. H. Hudson. Some touches involving tropical forest birds help the reader pass through the soggy romantic wilderness; Hudson's reminiscences of his naturalist boyhood on the Argentine pampa (especially *Far Away and Long Ago*) are far superior, from both an ornithological and a literary perspective.

An American Tragedy by Theodore Dreiser. The Adirondack wilderness setting of the famous drowning scene (Book II, Chapter 47) is alive with birds that either call ominously or provide a counterpoint to the grim occasion with their fine songs or bright plumage. Though Dreiser uses his avian images to good effect, he is an indifferent ornithologist. But his inclusion of a Caribbean endemic (Yellow-shouldered Blackbird) in the avifauna of upstate New York is more than compensated by that sinister corvid, the "weir-weir," which hops about the branches of dead trees during the murder, going "Kit, kit, kit Ca-a-a-ah!"

Birds of America by Mary McCarthy. The central character is a young birdwatcher (= sensitive) and the novel is about a phase of his late adolescence. It gets some good mileage out of the "personalities" and habits of a number of bird species.

Peter Mathiessen, a keen birdwatcher and brilliant chronicler of the natural world often includes avian images in his fiction, including the recent *Killing Mr. Watson.*

J.R.R. Tolkien makes excellent use of magisterial eagles and venerable, watchful ravens, not to mention the wise old thrush in "The Hobbit."

The literate ornithologist-birdwatcher can only lament that Vladimir Nabokov, the only great naturalist who was also a great novelist, was fascinated with lepidoptera, not with birds. See, however, under Poetry. The above does not, of course, pretend to be a comprehensive survey of birds in fiction. Perhaps this may inspire someone to make one. The subject seems to be that rarest of phenomena, an unexplored facet of English literature.

Poetry. It is in poetry that birds and literature seem to form a natural alliance. The poet's need to conjure place and express emotion concisely but vividly finds a ready answer in birds' deep and varied symbolic (as well as real) presence in human experience. There is also a nice kinship between verse and birdsong that blends effectively with the poet's anthropomorphic metaphor in a poem such as Hardy's "The Darkling Thrush." Song may also be used to good effect in devising a poem's structure, as in the onomatopoeic lines in Whitman's "Out of the Cradle Endlessly Rocking," cited below. Finally, poets, as the ultimate wordsmiths, must appre-

ciate the ample selection of useful and telling "sounds" present in the names of any avifauna. Words such as loon, albatross, fulmar, shag, harrier, falcon, plover, curlew, thrush, and sparrow serve the poet at least as well as they serve the taxonomist or birdwatcher.

Birds have been part of the tradition of Western poetry from its beginning. They appear in the lyrics of Homer (before 800 BC) and Catullus (first century BC), are mentioned in *Beowulf,* the first English epic (early eighth century), and by the end of the thirteenth century had fully assumed their archetypal function as symbols of renewal and the joy of nature in the famous anonymous rondel that begins

> Sumer is icumen in,
> Lhude sing cuccu!

From this point on, the English avifauna—particularly the Skylark *(Alauda arvensis),* the (Barn) Swallow *(Hirundo rustica),* the Eurasian Robin *(Erithacus rubecula),* the Common Nightingale *(Luscinia megarhynchos),* the Eurasian Blackbird *(Turdus merula),* and the Song Thrush *(Turdus philomelos),* as well as the Common Cuckoo *(Cuculus canorus)*—is generously represented in every period, form, poetic usage, and in every length and quality of verse in the English language. From Chaucer to contemporary poets in England and America, the challenge is to find one who has not included a bird at least once.

Until well into the eighteenth century, the ornithological versatility of Shakespeare remained unchallenged—in fact, it may remain so today. At least one scholar (Gelkie 1916) has taken the trouble to confirm that more than 60 species are distributed throughout the plays and many of the sonnets. But more impressive than Shakespeare's "list" is the resourcefulness with which he makes use of his considerable knowledge of both the habits of common species and the folklore and superstition that surrounded them. He works dozens of changes on the familiar spring/love/birdsong theme, but also has birds appear as omens, jokes, character analogues, in genre scenes, and in examples of nature's simple wisdom.

Without doubt, the greatest literary bird refuge of all was the age of Romantic poetry, beginning with Blake's outrage at a caged Robin Redbreast (in "Auguries of Innocence") and ending (perhaps) with Thomas Hardy's pathetic darkling thrush. The Romantics are characterized by their love of nature's rich, wild imagery and a strong sense of "song," so it is hardly surprising to find birdlife generally abundant in their poetry or that the period produced the best-known (and perhaps best) "bird poems" of all time: Shelley's "To a Skylark" and Keats's "Ode to a Nightingale." Also hatched between the late eighteenth century and the death of Queen Victoria were Coleridge's deliverance-bearing albatross (in "The Rime of the Ancient Mariner"), Burns's "green-crested Lapwing" ("Afton Water"), a well-stocked and songful (but largely unlabeled) variety from

Wordsworth, Tennyson's "Throstle," Browning's unlikely Gannet, Swinburne's "sister swallow" ("Itylus"), Gerard Manley Hopkins' kestrel ("Windhover"), to name a very few.

In modern poetry, man seems to take precedence over nature, but this is due more to a change of context than to any marked shift in theme. After all, Shelley's Skylark and Keats's Nightingale are never glimpsed. They are simply metaphors for an unblemished—totally anthropomorphic—ecstasy, which is contrasted with the melancholy that inevitably tempers man's joy. The tendency among many modern poets is to omit nature and look at man in contexts of his own making—contexts such as war and cities, which are generally inhospitable to birdlife.

Nature is hard for a poet to ignore, however, and so we have Yeats's exquisite "The Wild Swans at Coole"; the very rich and frequent avian imagery in Dylan Thomas (e.g., "Over Sir John's Hill"), T. S. Eliot's Sweeney placed ironically among Keats's Nightingales, and many other examples.

In examining American "bird poetry" it is hard to disagree with Welker (1955), who found little to praise. Most is sentimental doggerel—the kind of "ladies' verse" sometimes published in newspapers: "Our merry friend the chickadee/Chirps his song from the tall pine tree / Chick-a-dee-dee-dee, Chick-a-dee-dee-dee," etc.

It is only respectful to remember that Alexander Wilson was a poet before he was an ornithologist and left us several stanzas on the Osprey:

> True to the season, o'er our sea-beat shore,
> The sailing osprey high is seen to soar
> . . . . .
>
> She rears her young on yonder tree,
> She leaves her faithful mate to mind 'em;
> Like us, for fish, she sails to sea,
> And, plunging, shews us where to find 'em . . .

And Poe's "The Raven" must be noted in passing, though the bird of the title is a pet and a literary device, not the subject of the poem.

Admirers of Emerson and Longfellow are bound to bring up the former's "The Titmouse" and various avian musings of the latter, e.g., "Birds of Passage": "I hear the beat / Of their pinions fleet."

But there is really only one nineteenth-century bird poem worth the name, Walt Whitman's "Out of the Cradle Endlessly Rocking." Whitman was both a serious student of natural history and (much more importantly in this context) a serious poet. And the mockingbird in "Out of the Cradle . . ." is not "nature observed" or a banal metaphor for some transcendental human quality. It is a voice of knowledge calling a boy out of his innocence:

> O solitary me, listening—nevermore shall I cease perpetuating
> you . . .

And Whitman uses the rhythmic repetitions of the mocker's song in his lyric. *Leaves of Grass* contains many birds, used skillfully to evoke the wilderness, but there is only one "Out of the Cradle Endlessly Rocking."

Other first-rate American poets have used avian themes or images, but few are cited among their makers' best work. The poetry-reading naturalist may want to look up the following, if he does not know them; these are not, with a few exceptions, poems *about* birds, but serious poetry that use bird imagery in a variety of ways.

Emily Dickinson: "At Half Past Three a Single Bird"; "The Robin Is the One"; "To Hear an Oriole Sing"; "I Dreaded That First Robin So"; "A Bird Came Down the Walk"; and many other poems with bird themes.

T. S. Eliot: "Cape Ann" (the last part of *Landscapes*).

Robert Frost: "The Oven Bird"; "Looking for a Sunset Bird in Winter"; "A Minor Bird"; "On a Bird Singing in Its Sleep."

Vladimir Nabokov: "Pale Fire" (first stanza) in *Pale Fire*; not, of course, a "bird poem."

Robert Penn Warren: *Audubon* and "Ornithology in a World of Flux" in *Some Quiet, Plain Poems.*

Wallace Stevens: "Thirteen Ways of Looking at a Blackbird" and "The Bird with the Coppery, Keen Claws."

See the Bibliography for works on the subject of birds in art, literature, and other manifestations of human culture. See also IMAGINATION, BIRDS IN.

For natural history writing with birds as a principal theme, see the Bibliography under BIRDWATCHING.

HUMMINGBIRD. Standard English collective name for the approximately 320 members of the family Trochilidae (order Apodiformes, or Trochiliformes), of which 15 species breed in North America, another is a regular visitor, and 7 others have been recorded here as vagrants (see Appendix II).

The world's largest hummingbird measures 8½ inches in length, but most members of this family are small or very small—including the world's smallest bird, the 2¼-inch Bee Hummingbird *(Melisuga helenae)*. The size range of North American species is 3¼ inches (Calliope) to 5¼ inches (Magnificent). The Rufous Hummingbird breeds in southern Alaska and is therefore the member of its largely tropical family that ranges farthest north.

Most of the hummingbirds' most striking physical adaptations are related to their mode of feeding, which consists of hovering in midair while probing the calyxes of flowers for nectar or picking insects off vegetation or out of the air.

Hummingbirds' bills are exceedingly thin and pointed and come in a wide range of lengths and variations in shape, though the bills of North American hummers are of medium length and slightly to fairly strongly decurved. Their tongues are exceptionally long, extensible, and grooved, becoming tubular toward the tip with an apical brush. Thus the nectar is not sucked through the bill (as with a soda straw) but "pumped" along the tongue with the aid of capillary action.

Hummers have long, narrow wings and highly developed flight muscles that take up a quarter to a third of total body weight and power a wing beat as fast as 80 beats per second in the case of smaller species. (Oddly enough, this is *slower* than the wing beats of most birds when measured in relation to body weight!) Due to hummingbirds' small size and low body weight, "their twin propellers" give them extraordinary maneuverability: they can remain stationary as they probe blossoms for nectar; they can move backward if necessary; and they are capable of precision aerobatics in courtship displays and fly-catching forays. Some species attain speeds of at least 27 mph (43 kph) and perhaps up to 50 mph (80 kph) or more.

The broad, stiff tails of hummingbirds act as a rudder, crucial in fast changes of direction. Many tropical species have elaborately modified rectrices used in courtship and other displays, but the tails of North American hummers are slightly rounded to modestly forked. The legs and feet are so small as to be practically nonexistent—one of the few visible characters hummers share with their order-mates, the swifts.

Every schoolchild knows that hummingbirds "drink" nectar, but even many birdwatchers are unaware that a substantial part of all hummers' diet consists of insects and spiders that they catch in the bill without the aid of the tongue.

Hummingbirds have the highest metabolism of any warm-blooded vertebrate, with the possible exception of the shrews. So high is their rate of energy consumption that they must feed almost continuously during the day, store a supply of food in their tiny crops, and not infrequently (perhaps on days when food has been scarce) lapse into a state of torpidity for the night.

Tropical hummingbirds come in a spectacular variety of plumage variations. There are a few dull species, and females are usually drab in comparison with their resplendent mates, but the spectrum of brilliant, metallic-iridescent colors represented in the family as a whole is nearly complete, and the assortment of feathered tufts, puffs, frills, streamers, and spangles exhibited would be the envy of a Hollywood costumer. As befits the temperate climate in which they live, North American species depart only in a few cases from the basic hummer design, consisting of bright, metallic-green upperparts and an electric-iridescent gorget and/or crown. This male finery is displayed in courtship flights characteristic of each species. Hummingbird voices are also used in courtship, but song is

one of the few avian gifts denied the family. To the human ear, hummer voices are no more than combinations of high-pitched twitters or squeaks, occasionally assembled into a phrase that approaches one of the more insipid wood warbler songs.

Hummingbirds build cup nests of plant or lichen flakes bound together with spider silk and lined with plant down. These are placed on a branch in the open. They lay 2 (rarely, 1 or 3) white, unmarked, notably elongate eggs (see Fig. 10), which are tiny compared to those of most other birds (see EGG) but large in relation to the size of the layers.

In spite of their small size, hummingbirds are very aggressive, always ready to attack rival members of their own species, much larger birds of other species, the family dog, or even a full-grown human if any of these are perceived to be invading breeding territory or competing for food.

The distribution of the hummingbird family is strictly confined to the New World and extends from southwestern Alaska (Rufous) to the Straits of Magellan (Green-backed Firecrown). However, diversity diminishes in proportion to distance from the Equator. In North America only a single species (Ruby-throated) breeds east of the Mississippi, the other 14 residents being concentrated in the West and particularly in the mountains of the Southwest, where several Neotropical species reach the northern extremity of their range. No hummer breeds on the prairies of the Great Plains. Hummers occur in most major biomes, including the desert, and their seasonal distribution is governed in part by the presence of blooming flowers; sapsucker "wells" also are important, especially in the Northeast and in the Rockies. Most of our species are migratory and the Ruby-throat undertakes the crossing of the Gulf of Mexico and continues to wintering grounds in Central America.

The name comes not from the voice but from the audible whir of the wings. North Americans may be surprised to learn that only a little over a quarter of hummingbird species are called "hummingbirds." Various ornithologists have revealed their sentimental side by giving the rest such whimsical monikers as brilliant, coquette, comet, fairy, hermit, mango, mountain gem, plumeleteer, sun angel, sunbeam, sylph, trainbearer, wood nymph, and woodstar.

Two recent guides focus on North American hummers; see Howell (2002) and Williamson (2002).

HUNTING (of birds). Before prohibited by law, the taking of a wide variety of bird species—including large numbers of songbirds—for food, feathers, and decoration was commonplace in North America. Bird shooting as a sport is now restricted to upland game species (turkeys, grouse, quail, pheasant), waterfowl, most rails, one race of Sandhill Crane, woodcock and snipe, and some dove and crow species. Some of the most popular species in the first category are introduced from the Old World

(e.g., Ring-necked Pheasant), and their populations are artificially maintained by stocking in regions where they have not become naturally self-sustaining.

Present-day hunters generally acknowledge that at least minimal conservation practices—e.g., ensuring that bag limits are consistent with the ability of a given species to maintain its population—are in the best interests of their sport. And any excesses committed by the unconvinced are redressed by both state and federal hunting laws. This is not to imply that few birds fall to the gun these days. For example, hundreds of thousands of hunters collectively bag tens of millions of Mourning Doves annually in the United States; hundreds of thousands of woodcock and tens of thousands of rails are also taken. See periodic Special Science Reports (Wildlife), available from the U.S. Fish and Wildlife Service, Washington, DC.

See also LAWS PROTECTING BIRDLIFE; CONSERVATION; THREATS (OF HUMAN ORIGIN) TO BIRDLIFE; ENDANGERED BIRDS; EXTINCT BIRDS; EDIBILITY; INTRODUCED BIRDS.

HUTTON, William, mid-nineteenth century (Hutton's Vireo: *Vireo huttoni*). Except for the vireo, which he collected in California and which was named for him by CASSIN, Hutton has left few traces. He was one of the many enthusiastic and talented young naturalists who collected specimens for the National Museum in the nineteenth century, particularly in the West.

HYBRIDIZATION. The interbreeding of two taxonomically distinct forms, usually species or well-defined subspecies. The resulting offspring (if any), which shares the characteristics of both parents, is called a "hybrid" or "cross" between the two forms involved. The interbreeding of a male Mallard and a female Northern Pintail would, if successful, produce young that would be designated as Mallard × Northern Pintail or *Anas platyrhynchos* × *Anas rubripes* hybrids. Hybridization occurs when the so-called isolating mechanisms, which normally inhibit interbreeding between unlike forms, break down or when topographical or ecological barriers are eliminated, allowing distinct but closely related populations to meet and interact. Both of these phenomena occur only infrequently (on a human timescale) or very locally, so that hybrids are relatively rare in natural circumstances (see SPECIATION). They are much more frequent among captive birds, where choosing the "right" mate may be impossible or choice is limited and where closely related species normally of separate distribution are brought together.

Certain families or orders of birds are more prone to hybridization than others. Ducks and geese are by far the most "ambitious" hybridizers, with more than 400 different crosses to their credit—though a high percentage of anatid hybrid records come from waterfowl collections. Other

families with a high incidence of hybridization—e.g., grouse and hummingbirds—share the characteristic of a brief and/or weak pair bond, which, of course, allows "freer" selection of a mate.

Forms that are closely related (phylogenetically) are more likely to interbreed than distant relatives. For example, hybrids between different orders of birds—e.g., between hawks and owls—are unknown, and inter-family hybrids are extremely rare (recorded in gallinaceous birds). By comparison, intergeneric and interspecific hybrids are relatively frequent. This does not mean, however, that closely related forms are *likely* to hybridize. It is the strength/weakness of the isolating factors that chiefly determines the likelihood of interbreeding, not genetic similarity.

A variety of possible results can follow the interbreeding of unlike forms. If the genetic difference is too great (i.e., the relationship too distant) the eggs may be sterile or the embryos may be defective and die before hatching. When healthy offspring do result they are often sterile, i.e., incapable of reproducing themselves. On the other hand, it is also possible for a hybrid to be "better" than either parent, owing to inheritance of dominant strong characteristics that overshadow weaknesses. This phenomenon is called "hybrid vigor" or "heterosis" and is, of course, the goal in artificially interbreeding domestic fowl. The resulting hybrids, for example, may be larger and faster-growing than their progenitors, obvious merits for the poultry farmer. This has also been demonstrated in nature with closely related species of Galapagos ground-finches (*Geospiza* spp.) (Grant and Grant 1992, 1997–SPECIATION).

A hybrid can look more like one of its parents, or share superficial characters equally, or in rare instances show features that are not present in either parent. Audubon's "Bimaculated" Duck—a presumed Mallard × Gadwall hybrid with a bright tawny cheek patch not characteristic of either species—was probably such a case. These traits have been explained hypothetically as atavistic—i.e., "throwback" characters from an ancient ancestor—and have been recorded more recently.

Apart from this rare phenomenon, the appearance of a hybrid that results from the interbreeding of two "pure" forms is usually predictable according to a fixed pattern of gene dominance within the chromosomes of each bird. When a pure Golden-winged Warbler interbreeds with a pure Blue-winged Warbler, for example, the first-generation hybrids (so-called Brewster's Warblers) are largely white below but lack a black cheek mark and throat. This is because the color-of-underparts gene is "dominant," in Golden-winged, and masks the "recessive," color-of-underparts gene of Blue-winged. The reverse is true in the case of the face and throat markings. The first-generation Brewster's hybrids may then interbreed with other hybrids or with pure Blue-wings or Golden-wings, resulting in offspring that can be typically Golden-winged, typically Blue-winged, or various hybrid mixtures. It is only when two hybrid birds interbreed that the two sets of recessive genes can combine in one individual to produce

the so-called Lawrence's Warbler with black facial and throat markings and yellow underparts. It is therefore easy to understand why Brewster's type of hybrids are much commoner in nature than Lawrence's type.

Succeeding hybrid generations need not always be confined within the genes of *two* pure forms. Hybrid ducks involving at least 5 different species are known and crosses involving many more components are theoretically possible, though, of course, very unlikely except in captivity.

Male bird hybrids are recorded more often than female, and there is a theoretical basis for believing that they are in fact more frequent; however, it is also true that male plumages are more likely to be noticed and that females with impaired sexual function are sometimes "cock plumaged" (see SEX, CHANGE OF).

The hybrids most frequently encountered in the wild involve forms with a close common origin that have evolved separately on either side of some ecological or topographical barrier. When the barrier is bridged or removed, and the forms have an opportunity to mingle, they may ignore each other sexually, indicating complete differentiation into distinct species; or they may engage in an orgy of interbreeding that results in the two once distinct forms melding into one; or a relatively stable "zone of secondary hybridization" may develop in which hybrid birds, distinct from either "pure" form, are common. The last situation occurs in North America in the case of "Myrtle" and "Audubon's" Warblers; "Red-shafted," and "Yellow-shafted," (but not Gilded) Flickers and "Slate-colored," "White-winged," "Oregon," and "Grayheaded" Juncos. By definition such hybrids are of local occurrence and are, like other hybrids, rarely encountered except in the restricted zones of overlap. Since a species is defined by its reproductive isolation from other species, this manifestation of hybridization is important in taxonomy.

Bullock's and Baltimore Orioles make the same point with an opposite example. These two forms were (memorably for many birdwatchers) "lumped" and named (unimaginatively—adding insult to injury) "Northern Oriole." Subsequent studies demonstrated that within the hybrid zone of Bullock's and Baltimore intergrades did not outnumber the parental types nor did they spread and the forms were "re-split." If, as in this case, hybrid zones are narrow and don't move, it is a sign that "good" species are involved (see SPECIES; SPECIATION).

For a listing of known hybrids, see Gray (1958). See also Grant and Grant (1992).

HYOID APPARATUS. A specialized system of bones and muscles of the avian tongue. See TONGUE.

HYPERPHAGIA (HY-per-FAY-gee-uh). A technical term for overeating; in humans usually neurotic and unhealthful, but normal in some avian con-

texts. Perhaps the best example is the eating binge in which many migrants indulge, preceding their departure, to store energy in the form of fat to fuel their long flights. See Nisbet et al. (1963–FAT) and MIGRATION.

HYPERSTRIATUM (HY-per-stree-AY-tum). Part of the basal ganglia of the brain; unique to birds. It is the main headquarters of avian intelligence and capacity to learn and is most highly developed in parrots, as well as crows and other passerines. See NERVOUS SYSTEM, Brain; INTELLIGENCE.

HYPORACHIS (HY-po-RAY-kiss). Technical term for the shaft of the afterfeather, a smaller, subsidiary feather stemming from the calamus of a main body feather. See AFTERFEATHER; FEATHER; and Fig. 13.

IBIS. Standard English name for 26 members of the family Threskiornithidae (order Ciconiiformes), which also includes the SPOONBILLS. Also formerly a misnomer for the single native North American STORK, once officially designated as Wood Ibis (now Wood Stork). Three species of ibis breed in North America, and another is an accidental visitor.

Ibises are large (20–40 inches) wading birds with long legs, a long, decurved bill, broad, strong wings, and a short tail. Except for the Scarlet Ibis of South America, they tend to be uniformly dark or white but often with some black in the primaries, iridescent highlights in the plumage, and/or brightly colored "soft parts." They feed on small fish, shrimp, insects, the occasional small frog or snake, and some plant material by probing in marshland muck with their specially adapted bill.

An ibis nest is a bulky stick platform in low trees, shrubs, or (less typically) on the ground in wetlands; marsh nests tend to be of cattails, sedges, etc.; two Old World species in the genus *Geronticus* are cliff nesters. Ibises lay 2–4 eggs: moderately dark blue and unmarked in the Glossy Ibis; yellowish buff to olive with irregular light to dark brown blotches and speckles in the White Ibis.

Ibises have only a rudimentary vocal apparatus, but are capable of some harsh grunts (*urnk*), cooing sounds, and hisses.

Ibises are distributed worldwide, mostly in warmer climates. They have traditionally been thought of as "southern" birds in North America as well, but the Glossy Ibis has extended its range dramatically in recent years and now breeds north to the coast of Maine and the similar White-faced Ibis reaches Oregon, Idaho, and Montana.

"Ibis" can apparently be traced to ancient Egypt, where the Sacred Ibis of the Nile *(Threskiornis aethiopicus)* was revered as the animal form of Thoth, the god of wisdom and magic.

ICHTHYORNIS (IK-thee-OR-niss). Literally "fish bird" an extinct genus of toothed birds (order Ichthyornithiformes; family Ichthyornithidae), at least 9 species of which have been described from fossils found in Upper (late) Cretaceous deposits in Alberta, Kansas, Manitoba, Montana, New Mexico, and Texas as well as Antarctica and Russia. The species of *Ichthyornis* are thought to have resembled small (8 inches in height) gulls or terns, hence their name, referring to presumed feeding habits. Their pronounced keel suggests they were strong fliers. See EVOLUTION OF BIRDLIFE.

ICTERID (IK-tuh-rid). Any member of the New World family Icteridae (order Passeriformes), including the blackbirds, cowbirds, grackles, orioles, oropendolas, caciques, meadowlarks, Bobolink, and Troupial, and a useful collective term for this heterogeneous family as a whole. See ALSO TROUPIAL.

General descriptions of the icterids are given under BLACKBIRD; COWBIRD; GRACKLE; ORIOLE; MEADOWLARK; BOBOLINK.

IDENTIFICATION. Well into the twentieth century bird identification was something that a "field ornithologist" did in his study at the end of a day or when foul weather kept him indoors. Having spent the day exploring the woods and wetland borders, shotgun under arm, eager to live up to Dr. COUES's injunction to bag "all you can get," the first "birders" returned home, measured their specimens, noted the color of their "soft" parts, plugged their mouths with cotton, and then set about preparing them as "bird skins." This done, if the collector was puzzled by any of his new acquisitions, he took the specimen in question in one hand, Coues's *Key to North American Birds* (or other reliable reference) in the other, and proceeded to identify his bird. Did the long-tailed flycatcher in hand have "three or four primaries emarginate; crown spot yellow in black cap" or merely "one primary emarginate; crown spot flaming in ashy cap"? If the former, it must be a Fork-tailed Flycatcher; if the latter, a Scissor-tailed.

Birds are still identified "in the hand" by ornithologists and bird banders using keys that systematize measurements or combinations of obscure plumage details. And there are still a few instances in which taking a specimen may be necessary (if not exactly desirable). However, with the amazing quality of optical and photographic equipment now available it is increasingly possible to perceive even minute details of plumage to identify birds and their age and sex without having the bird "in the hand." It is also true that all masters of field identification have probably put in

their time at a banding station or poring over museum trays to gain an accurate sense of what they are looking for. But before the 1920s identifying birds—especially "obscure" species such as sparrows and "fall warblers"—on sight was seldom attempted. About that time Ludlow GRISCOM and a rapidly expanding group of his proteges began to prove that the great majority of bird species could be positively identified in life with the aid of a pair of "field glasses" and a comprehensive knowledge of field marks. This insight, aided by the appearance of illustrated FIELD GUIDES and ever-improving optical equipment, gave rise to a new era in field ornithology now known (with fewer elitist overtones) as "birdwatching."

Birdwatching and its sportier variation, "birding," suggest many things to many people (see BIRDWATCHING), but identifying species is

Fig. 16. *Beyond field marks.* Novice birders tend to look for "silver bullet" field marks: If it's red with a crest it *must* be a Northern Cardinal. But they quickly discover that one of the fascinating challenges of bird identification is that the same bird can look very different under different circumstances, as demonstrated in these drawings of Broad-winged Hawks. Against a dark background and well lit on the underside the broad-wing at far left seems colored and patterned differently from the backlit individual to its right. JIZZ is all-important in raptor identification: with its wings half folded and tail closed in a glide, a Broad-wing can look remarkably like an accipiter (far right). Posture can also be deceptive—an alert Broad-wing looks quite different from one "fluffed out" after a rain.

central to everyone's notion of the activity. Many now-obsessive birders can remember a particular bird—a Magnolia Warbler glimpsed at scout camp or a spoonbill noticed on a business trip to Florida—that unaccountably inflamed a dormant curiosity about nature and made them desperate to find a book that would tell them what they had seen. Once you have identified your first bird, it is difficult to stop wondering about this world of hitherto unnoticed beauty that has suddenly materialized or to resist the satisfaction derived from the possession of arcane knowledge and the ease with which herons and ducks, woodpeckers and orioles yield their identities to your increasingly sophisticated scrutiny in the early months. But the hook of addiction is not firmly set until the reddest of Northern Cardinals, the most radiant of Yellow Warblers have become just the slightest bit boring and you find yourself scanning the sparrow pages of your field guide, or concluding that all sandpipers suddenly look intriguingly different rather than depressingly alike, or taking an interest in those tiny moving objects near the horizon that some show-off is presuming to name. For the animus that drives the serious modern birdwatcher is not a yearning for aesthetic thrills or scientific discovery; it is not even the "lure of the list" (though all these may be important ancillary rewards). Rather, it is the evolutionary accident that many birds look a great deal like many other birds.

This truth soon appears in rudimentary form to the novice birder in the realization that mockingbirds and shrikes, for example, are superficially similar. But the paragon among today's birders is one who holds in mind every field mark, every call note, every nuance of gesture and posture (see JIZZ), every fact of distribution, seasonality, and extralimital occurrence of every species that could possibly paddle, flap, or hop into his line of vision. She knows where, when, and how to look for birds; he sees them and hears them with an acuity astounding to the uninitiated; they identify them at a distance or in motion confidently, rapidly, and (it usually proves) accurately. There is often a degree of swagger in the manner of such paragons, but they readily and humbly admit their infrequent errors.

A unique pleasure of being a birdwatcher in the first decades of the phenomenon's existence was to watch the horizons of field identification pushed back. The legendary Griscom died puzzling over field problems now routinely solved by dedicated adolescent birders. This casts no disgrace on Griscom's reputation; it is the logical result of an increased number of sharp eyes, ears, and brains scrutinizing birds in the field with the kind of systematic fervor that Griscom pioneered. One effect of the continual breaking of identification barriers is that rarities become less rare: Have the Eurasian stints suddenly become more frequent visitors to North America? Probably not, but there are certainly more people around who recognize one when they see it. Another mark of advancing sophistication is the growing obsolescence of the standard field guides among birders of the upper echelons of birdernity. Members of this airy realm

now take their instruction from journals of field ornithology (see PERIOD-ICALS in the Bibliography) and "postgraduate" field guides (see Kaufman 1990; Grant and Mullarney 1989; Pyle 1997; and others) that unlock almost all the mysteries of unsongful *Empidonax* flycatchers and immature gulls and "peeps," and largely ignore "fall warblers," most of which have long since ceased to be confusing to them.

There is a grumpiness in some quarters about the alleged snobbery of so-called "professional birders." "We," say the self-styled amateurs, "bird for fun," the implication being that the better you play the game, the less enjoyable it becomes. This is nonsense, of course, and the goal of total identifiability—however unattainable—is a healthy one, both intellectually and spiritually. If the hyperbirder is exceptionally liable to any character flaws, they are hubris (e.g., listing no unidentified alcids or jaegers for a day's sea watch) and humorlessness (e.g., discussing the possibility of a hybrid Kumlien's × Thayer's Gull with a straight face for more than a minute).

Those scanning this entry for the "how to" section will be disappointed, for, in the author's opinion, bird identification skills cannot be taught. There is undeniably a knack to the business, but there are no tricks that can be transferred verbally from one who knows them to one who does not in the way that, say, magicians can share expertise. Everyone must start from scratch, though, in fact, some begin before scratch by being born with keen eyesight and hearing, the most useful of birding faculties, which, unfortunately, are not dispensed equably or available on demand. Making the best of inherited traits, the would-be bird identifier should (1) Buy the best pair of binoculars and the best telescope affordable, learn how to use them as if they were essential prostheses, and keep them in the best condition. (2) Memorize—no, inhale—all available bird guides and all other literature relevant to identification (omitting books that purport to explain how to watch birds). (3) Spend every available minute of your life out looking for birds and examining them critically for their distinctive qualities. (4) Form an intimate friendship with someone as intelligent, as enthusiastic, and approximately as knowledgeable about bird identification as you are. If, after five years of following these guidelines faithfully, you are still saying things like "That Swamp Sparrow is much browner than the one in the book," you may have to resign yourself to remaining a novice birder for life. Happily, there is no shame in this; looking at birds seems to yield equal pleasure at all levels of expertise.

For additional analysis see especially Griscom (1976) and Svensson (1994). See also BIRDWATCHING; LISTING; FIELD GUIDE; OPTICAL EQUIPMENT.

ILLUSTRATION (of birdlife). Defined here as the depiction of birdlife for its own sake—in an attempt to distinguish ornithological painting from birds that appear for a variety of reasons in works in the mainstream of the

ILLUSTRATION   410

painting tradition (see HUMAN CULTURE, BIRDS IN) and also from symbolic depictions, e.g., the thunderbird/eagles, painted for eons by native
Americans (see IMAGINATION, BIRDS IN). The unfortunate but inevitable
implication of this definition is that paintings of birds (i.e., *about* birds)
can never aspire to be more than minor works of art. For a fascinating
tour—but no convincing way out—of this labyrinthine problem, compare
Sutton (1962), Eckelberry (1963), Mengel (1980), and Jonsson (2002).

Leaving "What is art?" "Why won't curators hang Fuertes next to Ma-
tisse?" and other vexed questions to these articulate bird painters—artists
all—it may yet be possible in the limited space afforded here to suggest an
approach to evaluating the qualities to be found in "bird art," a genre that
has never been more popular. We might begin by examining the abilities
and probable intentions of the artist-craftsman. Some people learn to
draw birds out of devotion to their subject matter, knowing and caring little about "art" and acquiring only as much knowledge of light, composition, draftsmanship, and atmospherics as is necessary to produce a
comment such as: "Now *that's* a Blue Jay!" or "Why, you can see every
feather!" Many such "bird artists" produce admirable—often much
prized—work, which, however, does not aspire to be more than a "lifelike"
and decorative depiction of an attractive animal. Other people are artists
first—schooled in the traditions and techniques of painting—but also
have a deep understanding of the natural world and are committed to using their gifts and experience to express their acute perceptions.

The line just drawn is not a sharp one. Any trained artist who sets out
to make a living painting birds will invariably spend at least his or her
early years doing illustrations, which, because of their purpose (field
identification, scientific description), allow for little interpretation. Such
work cannot be expected to show an artist's depth or range no matter how
fine his sensibilities or sophisticated his technique. Contrariwise, the
most talented of bird portraitists sometimes produce works of some
depth and subtlety out of fortuitous combining of raw talent and their
feeling for their subject. As a general guideline, however, we can expect
even the most straightforward field sketches of the artist-who-paints-
birds to contain a difficult-to-define quality (artistic imagination, aesthetic insight?) that is usually lacking in the grandest, most colorful
designs of the bird painter.

Sadly, the public, and particularly the American public, is severely
handicapped in its ability to develop any subtle discernment regarding
bird painting. The best bird guides and the most magnificent of illustrated
monographs can show only one aspect of an artist's ability and very little of
his "vision." The sentimental animal prints now hawked in airports and in
nature magazines at exorbitant prices do little to educate the public taste.
And the most expressive works of our best natural history artists are mostly
sealed from our view in the homes of the few who can afford to buy them
as originals, because, justly or not, few art museums will hang a painting of

a bird even alongside a minor artist in a mainstream tradition. So what we tend to see in infinite succession are bird portraits, some very fine, many incompetent or excruciatingly dull, but all of them too limited in concept truly to measure up to the term "bird art." Fortunately, a few fine arts books have begun to be published in this realm, which illuminate the European tradition of the artist of nature. Preeminent in this tradition is the Swedish impressionist Bruno Liljefors (1860–1939), who has influenced virtually every would-be painter of nature that followed. After decades of near obscurity in North America his work can finally be seen (though, alas, poorly reproduced in many cases) in Martha Hill's *The Peerless Eye* (1987). Aficionados of this genre should also seek out the published work of Liljefors most brilliant modern heir, Lars Jonsson, who has managed to be both an unsurpassed field guide illustrator as well as gallery artist of international stature; see especially *Birds and Light* (2002), which provides an historical overview as well as many example of the artists' work. Many images of North American birds by Jonsson can be seen in Leahy et al. (1996). Other good surveys of current natural history art are catalogues from the Lee Yawkey Woodson Art Museum in Wausau, Wisconsin (including sculpture and other media as well as painting) and the series of books published in the Netherlands by the Artists for Nature Foundation.

Offering a list of the "essential" bird artist/illustrators is of course a dangerous business both because of the incipient (or underappreciated) geniuses that may be left out but also for the inevitable range of talents that may be lumped uncomfortably together. Such risky gambits are the prerogative of authors, however, so here is my list of not-to-be-missed "bird artists" (in strictly alphabetical order!) with apologies to those inadvertently omitted whose reputation is not yet the equal of their talent:

John James Audubon	Robert Hainard
Robert Bateman	Charley Harper
Major Allan Brooks	Francis Lee Jaques ("Jakes")
Gunnar Brusewitz	Lars Jonsson
John Busby	Ron Kingswood
Mark Catesby	J. Fenwick Lansdowne
Raymond Harris Ching	Bruno Liljefors
Robert Verrity Clem	Don Malick
James Coe	George McLean
Guy Coheleach	Larry McQueen
Barry Van Dusen	Robert M. Mengel
Don R. Eckelberry	Gordon Morrison
Eric Ennion	Killian Mullarney
Louis Agassiz Fuertes	John O'Neill
(the father of modern	Roger Tory Peterson
American bird painting)	Keith Shackleton
A. E. Gilbert	Guy Tudor

Charles Tunnicliffe   Arthur Singer
Terry M. Shortt   George Miksch Sutton
David Sibley   Alexander Wilson
John Sill

The work of some of those noted above may be continually before you in the form of their popular field guide illustrations; some of the best-known examples of bird art are noted in the Bibliography for this entry, which also contains sources on the history of bird art; see also the finely illustrated volumes noted in the Bibliography under STATE/PROVINCIAL BOOKS and BIRD.

Wildlife art is not of course restricted to painting. Whether one takes the dawn of this tradition to be Summerian lions carved in relief in the fourth millennium BC or nature red-in-tooth-and-claw animal groupings in bronze by Antoine-Louis Barye (1795–1875), it is alive and thriving in the hands of modern masters such as Larry Barth.

Those with a budding interest in this subject should be aware that several North American museums specialize in art of the natural world, e.g., the Leigh Yawkey Woodson Art Museum, Wausaw, Wisconsin; the National Museum of Wildlife Art, Jackson Hole, Wyoming; and The Massachusetts Audubon Society's Visual Arts Center, Canton, Massachusetts.

For another perspective birds and art, see HUMAN CULTURE, BIRDS IN.

IMAGINATION, BIRDS IN. An astonishing variety of fanciful bird imagery permeates human culture. It has occurred throughout our history and crops up in almost all societies, both primitive and modern. And it enlivens human endeavors from the most frivolous amusements to practical matters of daily life to the most solemn rituals. On the whole, this imagery owes very little to ornithological truth; rather its integrity tends to lie in ancient cultural traditions, and this, in turn, explains why it is impossible to make clear-cut distinctions between the bird images we find in religion, mythology, fairy tales, heraldry, superstition, and so forth. Often they all have their roots in man's primordial striving to explain his world and his touching need to invest his surroundings with a complex animism.

PRIMITIVE BELIEFS AND RITUALS. When we can't perceive the reason for something, we tend to attribute it to some force or power that is "supernatural" or at least more powerful than ourselves. Often, we also try to associate it with things we do know that seem to have some connection. Birds lend themselves very well to association with the supernatural. We have watched them soar out of sight into the "heavens" or "space" or "never-never land." They live in ways that until very recently were mysterious to us—disappearing (or perhaps transforming themselves) for parts of the year. And both their physical and behavioral characteristics—

seemingly as varied as human personalities—beg to be invested with the animism—the "souls"—that we long to give them.

The Great Spirit is thought of among many native American tribes as a "sky father" or as being embodied in the sun, both of which lend themselves to strong association with birds, especially powerful, high-soaring species such as eagles. A more concrete figure among these people is a hero of sorts commonly referred to as a "trickster." He is usually the creator of the universe and of people and acts as their protector, but he is also the source of great mischief, such as bringing on the flood and inventing death. For the Indians of the northwest coast, this being was embodied in Yetl, the raven (or, rarely, crow), which would seem logical in many cultures since the "tricky" or "clever" nature of corvids is well known wherever they occur. For many northeastern tribes, the Gray Jay or "wiskedjak" was the trickster's animal form.

The best-known of North American bird spirits is the thunderbird, which occurs in the beliefs of tribes virtually throughout the continent. It is seen as the embodiment of the life force, which engages in continuous battle with a man-eating serpent. The thunderbird is therefore the protector of humanity and also the guardian of fire, and, like those other thunderers, Zeus and Thor, it is also the spirit of war.

The Micmacs and other tribes of northeastern North America have a legend of a huge bird that once made great winds with its wings so that the people could not venture onto the sea to catch food. A young brave discovers the source of the trouble and contrives to break the bird's wing "by accident." This results in a total lack of wind, which brings on the stagnation of the ocean, a fate as bad as the original one. Finally, the people fix the broken wing and, when the great bird has healed, set it free but exhort it to flap more gently.

A common means of exhorting or appeasing powerful bird deities is to dance, adorned, in the case of the thunderbird, in eagle feathers and imitating many of that bird's mannerisms.

Courtship dances in many "primitive" cultures throughout the world also have strong avian themes. In New Guinea and elsewhere brilliant feathers are worn—as they are by the birds themselves—to attract a mate and in some instances the elaborate courtship rituals of birds such as cranes are mimed by their human counterparts.

RELIGION. With the development of civilization, animal deities are gradually replaced by gods with human forms. The early Egyptians believed that the figures in their pantheon were originally animals but evolved human bodies over time. Therefore, these gods are usually represented with human bodies and the heads of particular sacred animals. Ra, one of Egypt's chief deities, the great god of the sun, often appears with a falcon's head, as does Horus, another sun god. The Sacred Ibis *(Threskiornis aethiopicus)* was the animal of Thoth, the time measurer and inventor

of numbers–hence the god of wisdom and magic (also the moon god)—and Thoth appears in hieroglyphs and paintings with the head of an ibis.

The deities of classical Greece and Rome are even more fully evolved into (idealized) human form, and most of the bird-man creatures (e.g., the Harpies) as well as assorted monsters with some bird features (e.g., the Griffin) principally appear in more secular mythical contexts (see below). However, Pallas Athene, one of the most important of the Greek deities, was associated with the owl (*Athene* is used as the genus name of Burrowing Owl) and is sometimes represented as winged; so is her daughter, Nike, the goddess of victory, portrayed in the famous statue Nike of Samothrace (c. 200 BC). Like the thunderbird, Athene is associated with thunder and lightning and war, but was also the goddess of wisdom and the protector of cities.

The major Greek and Roman gods would on occasion transform themselves into animals, as Zeus did when he visited Leda, queen of Sparta, in the guise of a swan. As a result of these avian attentions, Leda bore two prodigious eggs: out of one hatched the immortal Helen and Pollux and from the other came the mortal Castor and Clytemenestra. The classical tradition is also full of people or lesser gods being transformed into birds or other animals (see Myth, p. 415).

Among the "modern" religions widely practiced today, the main holy figures have human forms. However, there is one prominent vestige of the superhuman bird-man tradition in Judeo-Christian belief, namely, the angels. Some of the creatures that came to be identified in post biblical times as part of the heavenly choirs of celestial beings started out as the kind of hybrid beasts typical of classical myth. We tend to think of Cherubs, for example, as chubby baby angels, but the Cherubim that appear in the bible were enormous "lion-bulls" with a man's face and the wings of an eagle or griffon vulture. Similarly, the biblical Seraphim (which appear only once, in Isaiah, Chapter 6) were some sort of fiery serpent-bird with three sets of wings. These dreadful beasts were transformed in medieval angelology into the highest of the nine ranks of angels and assumed human form except for their wings. They are normally thought of as beautiful "winged creatures" rather than "part bird," which would be considered an unsatisfactory description of God's messengers. Nevertheless, their wings are always painted and described as bird-like—rather than butterfly-like, for example—and the feature seems to inspire artistic invention. The upper-echelon angels in Milton's *Paradise Lost* are given multiple sets of wings of many gorgeous colors, and angels' wings in ecclesiastical painting (see, for example, the angel in Fra Angelico's Annunciation fresco in the monastery of San Marco in Florence) are also often spectacular, doubtless reflecting (at least in part) the artists' perception of the beauty of birds' wings. For actual birds that appear in scripture, see RELIGION, BIRDS IN.

MYTH. Though religions invariably take their substance from a body of myths, myths are also generated in secular contexts, though the line between religious and secular myth is often hard to draw. The thunderbird is both an attempt to explain inscrutable natural phenomena (thunder is a huge eagle flapping its wings) and a deity that influences the fate of humanity. As has been shown, these mythical forces appear under different names again and again throughout time and all over the world in religious ritual, and the same is true of secular myths. An enormous bird of prey, usually with gorgeous plumage, has been associated for ages with the workings of the heavens, especially the movements of the sun. The first of these to achieve mythical prominence was the Garuda, the bearer of the Hindu sun god Vishnu; it became known by different names throughout Asia and was believed to feed on elephants, among other prey. The Simurgh, a similar creature of Persia, also shared behavioral traits (e.g., elephant eating) with the Rukh (Roc). And the fire-bird tradition has its most splendid culmination in the storied Phoenix and its Chinese incarnation, the Fung-whang, which is a popular motif in Chinese and Japanese art.

The best-known mythical birds are further described under PHOENIX, ROC, GRIFFIN, and HALCYON, and those that are important in religious myth are discussed above. A few other bird myths are briefly accounted for below.

Harpies, literally "snatchers" (Greek), were originally wind or death spirits *(Odyssey)* but evolved into loathsome, predatory birds, with the faces of ugly women, which figure malevolently in the saga of the Argonauts, and in the Aeneid. The world's largest raptor, the Harpy Eagle *(Harpia harpyja),* takes its names from this myth.

Sirens were creatures from Greek mythology, not unlike the Harpies, sometimes depicted as birds with narrow heads, or women with birds' legs and/or wings. Two or three of this species were supposed to live on an island between that of Circe and the rock of Scylla *(Odyssey)* in the Strait of Messina and to have lured sailors to their death by their sweet songs. Odysseus (warned by Circe) foiled them by having his men plug their ears with wax. Orpheus saved the Argonauts from them by singing more beautifully than they.

Stymphalian Birds. The sixth labor of Hercules was to rid marshlands at Arkadian Stymphalos of man-eating birds, part eagle, part stork, which had lethal arrow-like feathers. This he did by banging brass cymbals supplied by Athene (see above) which flushed the birds, enabling him to shoot them. (Compare control methods under PROBLEMS INVOLVING BIRDS.) The Stymphalian birds may have been a metaphor for pestilence thought to emanate from stagnant marshland.

The Tengus. These mischievous creatures, half man, half eagle, with long red bills and eyes like lightning, are still familiar in Japanese legend.

The tengus are the protectors of all remote and lonely places on earth and delight in promoting war. They dance to the music of the thunder and are extremely skillful with weapons, a talent they occasionally teach to a human captive. Originally considered the natural enemies of Buddhism, tengus were said to transform themselves into priests and to play other tricks in order to thwart Buddha's pacifist ideals.

Quetzalcoatl, the feathered serpent, is a widespread figure in Middle American pre-Columbian mythology, originating with the Toltecs of Mexico. He discovered corn, art, science, and the calendar and was symbolized in Aztec and Mayan rituals by the wearing of the long plumes of the Resplendent Quetzal *(Pharomachrus mocinno)*. To their everlasting grief, the Aztecs at first confused the Spanish conquistadors with the predicted return of the power of this benign figure.

The Caladrius. An avian phenomenon of the Middle Ages, the caladrius was said to be totally white and capable of predicting whether a sick person would live or die. Faced with the patient, the bird would turn its back on him/her if doomed, but if curable would take the disease on itself fly up to the sun, and vomit the poison forth. White (1954) notes the similarity of this name with the current plover genus *Charadrius,* but also that the species, or even family, of this useful bird seems always to have been vague. This leads us to speculate that a caladrius may have been an albino of any (or many) species. The birds were apparently sought out in shops for diagnostic purposes. Unless the shopkeeper demanded money down, the customer would find out which bird was the caladrius, obtain his diagnosis, and walk out without having made a purchase.

FOLKLORE AND SUPERSTITION. As we have seen, many fanciful ideas about birds have arisen out of attempts to understand natural phenomena, whether as awesome as creation and the sun or as relatively mundane (though crucial) as crop fertility. Because birds have been known for ages as having seasonal comings and goings among peoples of the Temperate Zone, because many species adapted well and quickly to human agricultural practices, and because they seemed to embody "sky powers," birds have always been a source of various degrees of folk wisdom. Some was truly observed and retains validity to this day, while the rest has proven to be wholly imaginary. It is instructive that the lore of uneducated, simple rural "folk" has often been closer to fact than the elaborate divinations and "scientific" hypotheses of more sophisticated thinkers. A sampling of bird beliefs both wise and wonderfully inaccurate follows.

Predicting the future by observing birdlife is a fixture in many primitive traditions and was an accepted branch of science/magic (ornithomancy) in classical times. An augur divided the sky into four quadrants and would then predict, say, the outcome of a battle based on how many birds of what species appeared in the different quadrants and what they were doing. Reading other bird signs was simply a matter of common

sense, as when Shakespeare's Cassius notes that the eagles that had followed his legions and fed from his soldiers' hands had been replaced
on the eve of the confrontation at Philippi by ravens, crows, and kites,
which "downward look on us, as we were sickly prey" (*Julius Caesar,* Act V,
Scene I). In Western cultures, older people may still remember telling fortunes by seeing a number of crows or other birds and repeating the
rhyme: "One for sorrow, two for mirth, three for a wedding, four for a
birth." A more specific superstition holds that upon hearing the first call
of the dove in spring, you will find a hair the color of your future mate's if
you step back three paces.

Similarly complex divination rituals involving particular species of
birds and their actions are still practiced locally in Southeast Asia. And
some of our common superstitions involving birds are predictive (see
below).

Certain types of birds have long been associated with forces of good
and evil, especially the latter. Owls are still widely believed to presage
death or disaster. And ravens, crows, jays, and magpies are also associated
frequently with misfortune or mischief. Owl and raven gods have the
most ancient lineage (see Primitive Beliefs and Rituals, p. 412); both owls
and corvids seem to embody more human-like spirits than most birds;
and owls' nocturnal habits and the blackness of ravens and crows doubtless contribute to their dark reputations.

Similarly, luck or the lack of it is perceived in the presence, actions, or
numbers of birds. A bird (like a black cat) crossing one's path to the left or
right is lucky or unlucky depending on the bent of one's superstition. It's
good luck to see a red bird (Northern Cardinal) fly up, bad luck if it flies
down. Wrens nesting near a house are good luck. It's bad luck to break a
bird's egg (or to bring eggs into the house after sunset), but good luck to
break off the larger piece of a wishbone. Owls hooting in the daytime (or
any time) are bad luck; to drive away a screech-owl, take off your right
shoe and turn it upside down. A bird flying against a house is an ill omen.
Putting salt on a bird's tail is lucky (!) as well as a means of catching it. The
first bluebird of spring is lucky and three birds flying in a line is good for
business. If you wish for luck when you see three birds on a wire, it will
come true if the birds don't fly away; a similar advantage is attached to
throwing three kisses to the first robin of spring.

Particular birds have long been thought to influence or at least predict the weather and seasons. Farming activities have been scheduled to
coincide with the return of certain birds from their wintering grounds
and, of course, the notion has considerable validity because of the rather
precise timing of migratory movements (see MIGRATION); geese, cranes,
and swallows were especially useful in this way.

A number of North American species have been known as "rain
birds." The word "plover" and the plover genus *Pluvialis* are sometimes

said to imply a connection (now inscrutable) with rain, though Lockwood (1993–NAMES) scoffs at this and (as usual) finds the origin of the name in the plovers' calls. The Red-throated and other loons are known as "rain geese" in cultures as disparate as those of the Indians of the northwestern United States and Scottish Highlanders: both contend these birds are especially noisy before a rain. Black-billed and Yellow-billed Cuckoos are said to do the same and are widely known, therefore, as "rain crows." Swallows feeding low are said to precede rain. There is nothing intrinsically suspicious in these observations as long as one sorts out proper cause and effect. No doubt swallows often do fly low preceding a storm, reflecting the movement of aerial insects down from the wet or turbulent upper air. Most rain birds seem to make their "predictions" as the impending weather change has become only too clear, though it has been demonstrated that birds can sense changes in atmospheric pressure (Kreithen and Keeton 1974).

Fertility, both human and agricultural, has also been associated with birds. Cranes, for example, are thought by some to be good for crops, while dangling and waving a bird or image thereof over the belly of a barren woman is only one of a number of bizarre solutions that have evolved to rectify that situation.

That spirits of human dead inhabit the bodies of birds is another venerable folk belief, stemming no doubt from birds' ethereal qualities, their association with the heavens, and their great variety. Some cultures believe that all or most birds serve this purpose, while others think it to be true of only particular species. It is a common maritime tradition that storm-petrels represent the souls of drowned seamen.

The notion that nightjars suck the teats of goats or other milk-giving domestic animals was accepted as fact by Aristotle and has persisted in rural areas in many cultures to the present. The teats are said to whiten and the animal to gradually waste away when visited by a Whip-poor-will or other bird in this family. This superstition is utterly without foundation, and except for the nocturnal habits and generally odd appearance and calls of nightjars, it is hard to imagine what can have lent this belief credence for so long; perhaps it is thought too strange not to be true.

SYMBOL. In addition to evoking certain powers, events, or particular figures in religion, folklore, and art, birds have also been widely used as concrete symbols, as in the heraldry of a family or nation, and this custom often relies on the perceived characters of certain species. The eagle is the favorite symbol of nations wishing to project an image of both nobility and might.

Symbols are by nature superficial and rely on appearance and inference rather than fact. Benjamin Franklin's naive suggestion that we adopt the Wild Turkey—a beautiful, gentle species that stands for plenty rather than war—as our national emblem would never have been approved by

the Congress in any era. The Bald Eagle, by contrast, is an ideal national bird, as long as we are careful to overlook the fact that it is fond of carrion and is a compulsive kleptoparasite and that we very nearly accomplished its extermination by the indiscriminate use of DDT. Certainly it is an *opportunistic* species, which can be seen in both the good and bad sense as emblematic of the nature of the various human settlers of this continent.

FANTASY. Encouraged by all the traditions sketched above and the seemingly endless and often bizarre variations in bird form, inventors of tales have created fanciful avifaunas of their own, related in some cases to recognizable legendary birds or wholly produced out of the mind of the human creator. These tale makers have been so prolific that it is impossible to give a concise account that conveys the richness of make-believe birdlife in the various languages. Talking birds, birds that come to the aid of princes, birds that cause trouble, birds that lay golden eggs, the Simurgh-like Nunda in Swahili tales, the witty storks of Aesop, the vain crow of La Fontaine, Andersen's ugly duckling (cygnet), the Grimm brothers' *Fundvogel,* Disney's Donald Duck, Hitchcock's avian uprising, *Sesame Street*'s Big Bird, and Snoopy's feathered pal Woodstock—these and the rest of their kind probably make up a fanciful class of animal life with more forms and of greater taxonomic complexity than the world's actual current avifauna of c. 9,700 species.

See also HUMAN CULTURE, BIRDS IN.

IMMATURE. Not fully adult, either generally or in some specific aspect of development. Some species of birds, for example, may acquire adult plumage while they are still sexually immature. Used in field guides to describe the plumage or plumages between juvenile and adult plumage. Because plumage sequence varies widely among species, it is not a very precise term and is often misused by birdwatchers to refer to any individual bird not in full alternate plumage. See PLUMAGE; MOLT.

IMPING. Chiefly a method of mending damaged flight feathers, especially in birds of prey. The technique was first developed among falconers and involved the use of metal pins (imping needles) on which a broken feather could be rejoined. Today, imping is used not only by falconers but by animal care specialists to rehabilitate a wide range of damaged birds.

In the modern method, the base of the feather shaft (calamus) remaining attached to the bird is cleanly cut and glue placed in the hollow center. A replacement feather (perhaps taken from a dead individual of the same species or even a different species) is cut to the right length and its sharpened end inserted into the glue-filled hollow of the basal section.

Imping has also been used as a marking technique; dyed feathers have been imped into the tails of ducks, for example, so that they can be identified on sight. See MARKING.

IMPORTANT BIRD AREAS (IBAs). Launched in Europe in 1981 by BirdLife International, the Important Bird Areas program has proven to be an immensely effective mechanism for conserving bird habitat worldwide. The process begins by identifying specific sites of critical importance to birds according to a set of standard criteria. The sites may be among the few viable breeding sites for a particular rare species, or represent a rare bird habitat type, or harbor unusual concentrations of birds of many species. Merely identifying the site, though it carries no force of law, tends to give the place and its birds increased visibility to local people, to governments, and to the world conservation community. In an ideal scenario an identified IBA will be studied with the goal of determining what kind of management might be required to protect the habitat and its birdlife; the site will become a focus for local education efforts; and ultimately it will be afforded legal protection and the means to carry out ongoing monitoring and management. At present (2003) BirdLife International has identified more than 20,000 IBAs in more than 60 countries worldwide and has published descriptive atlases for Europe, the Middle East, and Africa, with an Asian atlas nearing completion. In addition to producing crucial documentation, the IBA program is a catalyst for active involvement by local residents, birdwatchers, educators, and conservation advocates.

In the United States there are two distinct IBA programs, one operated on the standard BirdLife model in affiliation with the National Audubon Society and other partners in individual states and another administered by the American Bird Conservancy— using different criteria— in which ABC scientists have identified more than 500 IBAs of global significance in the United States.

For more information about IBAs worldwide, go to www.birdlife.net where you can search for regional, territorial, or state programs and find listings of publications. For Canadian IBAs, go to www.ibacanada.com. For U.S. programs, go to www.audubon.org/bird/iba for the BirdLife model program or to www.abcbirds.org/iba for the American Bird Conservancy Program. In addition, many states also have their own IBA websites.

IMPRINTING. A form of rapid learning that occurs soon after hatching, during which a bird normally attaches its own identity to that of the parent birds. In abnormal or experimental situations, chicks may attach themselves to the wrong bird species, humans, or even inanimate objects. See INTELLIGENCE.

INCERTAE SEDIS. Literally, "doubtful place"; a Latin taxonomic term applied to families, genera, or species of uncertain phylogeny. Several genera of Neotropical perching birds, once placed in the cotinga family, are now lodged "above" the cotingas and "below" the tyrant flycatchers and

labeled "Genera INSERTAE SEDIS" in the *AOU Checklist,* 7th edition (1998). See SYSTEMATICS.

INCUBATION. The embryos of birds are "warm-blooded" and, therefore, once they leave their mother's body, they must still be kept at a constant, relatively high temperature (see below)—unlike the eggs of insects, for example, or amphibians, which are laid in a suitable site and left to mature on their own. The term for this egg-warming process is "incubation." Except for the "ingenious" megapodes (see below), and brood parasites such as cowbirds, which let other birds incubate their eggs for them, all bird species keep their own eggs at the proper temperature by covering them in such a way that their body heat is transferred more or less directly to the developing embryo. On occasion (e.g., early in the egg-laying period) birds will "sit on" (cover) their eggs but not apply full body heat; this is not true incubation.

Physical Preparation. As with copulation, nest building, and food gathering, the instinct to incubate is initiated by hormonal changes triggered by external stimuli (e.g., increased daylight) associated with the onset of the breeding season—and by specific behavior "releasers" (see INTELLIGENCE), such as the appearance and feel of the actual eggs. The most significant physiological adaptation to incubation is the development of a *brood patch* (incubation patch)—an area (or up to three adjacent areas) at the center of a bird's abdomen in which the skin becomes slightly thickened and the tissue markedly vascularized (density of blood vessels increases) and generally more edematous (filled with fluid), allowing more body warmth to pass directly to the embryos. The region where the brood patch develops—the midventral apteria (see FEATHER TRACTS)—is normally relatively free of feathers year round, but any down that normally occurs there in some species and perhaps some marginal contour feathers are shed with the development of the patch (see BROOD PATCH for further specifics). A few birds, notably members of the order Pelecaniformes (pelicans, boobies and gannets, cormorants, etc.), ratites, penguins, and some alcids, do not develop brood patches. The pelicaniforms compensate for this lack by applying their large webbed feet to the eggs.

Both male and female birds may develop brood patches, though this varies from species to species. While it would satisfy our sense of logic to find that males or females that develop patches incubate and those that don't, don't, Skutch (1957) presents evidence that this is far from the case, at least among passerines: males without patches are known to incubate in some cases, whereas some *with* patches do not! Although this incubation patch is widely called a brood patch and the patch does remain while nestlings are being brooded, it is clear that its greatest development coincides with the incubation period, after which the tissue involved returns to normal.

Another physiological phenomenon that occurs in this phase of the breeding cycle is the production of a milk-like secretion from the walls of the esophagus stimulated by the pituitary hormone prolactin. This occurs in all members of the pigeon family and in at least one species each of penguin and flamingo. For more detail see CROP MILK.

Timing. The incubation period is usually timed from the laying of the last egg in a clutch to the hatching of that same egg (usually, but not always, the last to hatch), though this method of measurement is considered less than ideal when precise heat transfer/development rate data are wanted (Kendeigh 1963; Ricklefs 1993).

The incubation period varies widely—from 80 or more days (the largest albatrosses) to as little as 10.5 days recorded for some small passerines—the period for most of the latter is under 16 days. The Black-footed Albatross has the longest incubation period of any "North American" species (to 67 days); many native passerines incubate for as little as 11 days. The time required for incubation is subject to many variables, but a few broad generalities have been hazarded:

- Larger species, even within the same families, tend to have longer incubation periods; it takes more time to develop a bigger chick.
- Cavity nesters tend to have longer incubation periods than species that nest in the open; cavity nests are less prone to predation and their occupants appear to "take their time" relative to this selection pressure.
- Fully altricial species (see YOUNG, DEVELOPMENT OF) tend to have shorter incubation periods than other (semi-altricial, precocial) types, correlated with the fact that they are less developed at hatching.
- Longer-lived birds have longer incubation periods (Ricklefs 1993).

The onset of true incubation is also variable. It may begin after the first egg is laid or not until several days after the last egg is laid; the norm lies in between. In most cases incubation begins with the completion of the clutch.

Some birds (e.g., pigeons) seem to have an innate sense of the "correct" length of the incubation period and will stop sitting if the eggs do not hatch on schedule. However, Skutch (1962) has shown that birds in a wide range of families will incubate for twice the normal period (on average) in an effort to hatch defective eggs.

The percentage of the total incubation period during which the eggs are covered is another variable, but comes to between 60 and 80% in most birds. The rhythm of coverage often changes according to atmospheric conditions, since eggs can be left more often or for longer periods when the ambient temperature is high; birds tend to sit tighter and more continuously at night and in bad weather. At least in some birds, the incubation period decreases as the season advances, possibly due to warmer air temperatures.

Incubation Behavior. As noted, the principal duty of an incubating parent is to keep the developing embryos at a constant temperature. The "proper" temperature for the majority (about 75%) has proven to be 35°C (95°F) (Irving and Krog 1956), i.e., slightly lower than the body temperature of the parent bird (see TEMPERATURE, BODY).

We tend to think of incubation as a warming process, but especially with nests in the open in warm climates, shading the eggs is also crucial. It has been shown that, in general, embryos are much better able to withstand extremes of cold than of heat.

In addition to sitting, parent birds of most species *turn* their eggs regularly—in some cases several (up to 11) times an hour. The internal structure of the egg is so "designed" that no matter how many times the egg is turned, the embryo remains uppermost; shifting prevents adhesion of the allantois (see EMBRYO and Fig. 11).

Sitting birds usually do a fair amount of fidgeting while in the nest—adjusting their posture, shaking their feathers, picking at their nest, and in dense colonies taking a poke at a neighboring bird. "Off-duty" birds behave much as they do at other seasons—feeding, sleeping, etc. Males sing enthusiastically during this period and many continue certain "programmed" rituals of courtship, such as bringing nesting material or food to the sitting mate. As would seem prudent, incubating birds are normally silent; however, grosbeaks, vireos, and other species not infrequently sing their version of "The Incubation Blues" while on the nest.

A very few species cover their eggs when leaving the nest: ducks and other anatids with down, grebes with the wet vegetation of their nests, and one species of *Charadrius* plover with sand. Obviously, this provides a measure of concealment and helps keep the eggs at a constant temperature.

Division of Labor and Work Rhythm. Bird species have evolved virtually all possible variations in the manner in which they discharge their incubation duties. One analysis (Van Tyne and Berger 1976–ORNITHOLOGY) based on the available data shows that on a worldwide basis male and female birds share incubation in 54% of species; the female alone incubates in 25%; the male alone in 6%; and it varies between male, female, and both in about 15% of species. However, Pettingill (1970–ORNITHOLOGY) states that among North American species incubation by the female alone is far commoner than incubation shared by both sexes. Verner and Willson (1969) found that male incubation is the norm in a third of North American species.

When incubation is shared, the parents may switch off relatively frequently (several times a day) or do long stints (to several days—e.g., many tubenoses). Often the schedule is on some form of day shift/night shift basis.

When only a single parent incubates, it may remain on the nest almost continuously—fasting or being fed by the partner; or take fairly long recesses to feed, etc., at fairly long intervals; or take a great number of

shorter recesses. It stands to reason that eggs attended by both parents would get better coverage than those attended by a single parent, would therefore hatch faster, and would perhaps aid species survivability—but once again nature sets reason on its ear. Skutch (1962) showed that some species in which both parents incubate spend *less* total time on the eggs than others in which only one parent does. He concluded that the number of incubators bears little if any intrinsic relationship to breeding success.

The above is by no means a complete analysis of incubation rhythms. Among Sanderlings, only one parent incubates a given clutch—but it may be either one (Parmelee 1970). Some *Alectoris* partridges (including the Chukar) sometimes incubate two nests simultaneously, the male sitting on one, the female on the other. The eggs laid by a single Bushtit may be incubated by other adult Bushtits in addition to the parents. And anis and Acorn Woodpeckers have communal nests with a number of females laying and a number of adults (male and female) sharing incubation.

For a schematic outline of the various incubation patterns, see Skutch (1957) or Van Tyne and Berger (1976–ORNITHOLOGY, pp. 492–493).

The Megapode Method. The superficially chicken-like members of the Australasian/Polynesian family Megapodiidae (megapodes, Mallee Fowl, Brush Turkeys, etc.) bury their eggs in the warm ash of active volcanoes or sun-warmed sand or sizable mounds of decaying vegetation and avoid the ennui of sitting on eggs altogether— though they do daily temperature checks and adjust the "thermostat" regularly. The adults gauge the incubation temperature—with their ultrasensitive tongues (!)—and make adjustments by airing the fermenting plant material when it is too hot and building up more insulation or allowing more sun exposure when the air becomes cooler.

The Worst Job in the World possibly belongs to the male Emperor Penguin, condemned by evolution to take the first incubation shift after the female has laid the egg and promptly taken off to go fishing. This is the only species that nests during the dark, frigid Antarctic winter when the temperature may reach –60°F and the wind 200 km/h. While mom is at sea, dad sits on the egg and the sea ice without food for 90–120 days, losing up to 45% of his body weight. When he is relieved just after the chick has hatched, he must then walk—in some cases many miles— to the open sea and start chasing a meal through the near freezing water.

For related aspects of the nesting period, see NEST; EMBRYO; YOUNG, DEVELOPMENT OF.

INCUBATION PATCH. Same as BROOD PATCH.

INCURSION. Sometimes used as a synonym for IRRUPTION, e.g., an "incursion" of Great Gray Owls.

INDIVIDUAL VARIATION. Differences that may occur between two members of the same population of a given species, as opposed to racial or geographical variation in which whole populations or many populations share common differences that distinguish them from other populations. Individual variation is crucial to the biological selection process. Genetically transmitted variations that help an individual survive tend to perpetuate themselves, as they give advantage to one successful generation after another. Variations that are detrimental to an individual's survival tend to be "weeded out" because of the disadvantaged individual's diminished capacity to reproduce itself. See SPECIATION. Individual variation can complicate life for birders because it produces birds that don't appear in any field guide ("It can't be a Sanderling; it's much smaller than the others!"). In extreme cases it has a tendency, with the help of birders' characteristic "optimism," to turn common birds into rarities.

INFRAORDER. A taxonomic category between suborder and superfamily. Previously little used, but deployed by Sibley and Monroe (1990–SYSTEMATICS) to categorize their conception of the phylogeny of the Ciconiiformes. To accurately depict the genetic "distance" between the taxa involved, this system also calls upon the Parvorder, so that the sequence runs as follows:

Order
  Suborder
    Infraorder
      Parvorder
        Superfamily
         Family

INGLUVIES (in-GLOO-veez). The crop. See DIGESTIVE SYSTEM.

INJURY FEIGNING. See DISPLAY, Distraction Display.

INSECTIVOROUS (IN-sek-TIV-er-uss). Insect-eating; feeding mainly on insects. Not surprisingly, most flycatchers are largely insectivorous; humrningbirds and kestrels are partially insectivorous.

INSTINCT. A very broad, general term, used in nontechnical contexts to describe behavior that is inherited, rather than learned by an individual bird or other organism. For relevance to birdlife, see INTELLIGENCE.

INSTRUMENTAL SOUNDS. Nonvocal sounds, such as bill noises. For a breakdown of those made by North American birds, see SONG.

INTELLIGENCE. Terms such as "booby," "dodo," and "birdbrain" carry the unmistakable implication that birds are not very smart. And until about 20 years ago science seemed to corroborate this assumption. The cerebral cortex—that great wrinkly mass of "gray matter" that dominates the appearance of the human brain and is known to be the source of our subtler tricks of ratiocination—is at best a smooth, thin, covering layer in birds. For early investigators, that pretty much settled the matter of avian intelligence. It has since been discovered, however, that a bird's "mind," originates in the relatively well-developed *corpus striatum,* on which the vestigial cortex rests. More specifically, avian intelligence has been located in a part of the corpus striatum called the *hyperstriatum* and learning centered in the bulge on the hyperstriatum called the *wulst.* In other words, in the evolution of intelligence birds have taken an alternative anatomical path from that of mammals with different parts of the brain developing to provide the physiological basis for intelligence. Another relatively recent insight is that while bird and mammal brains are both significantly more sophisticated than the brains of reptiles, there is great variation in the degree and nature of intelligence in these "smarter" classes. For example, members of some bird families do much better at certain mental tasks, such as counting and problem solving, than even relatively intelligent mammals, such as monkeys. Other kinds of birds—such as pigeons, on which many early assumptions about bird intelligence were based—are dunces at the same tests. As avian IQs are more thoroughly investigated and compared, it interesting to note that many of the birds that we intuitively think of as "smart," e.g., members of the parrot and crow families, are indeed the whiz kids of the bird world.

Another factor that delayed the recognition that at least some birds are quite brainy was the once dominant influence of animal behaviorists who theorized that almost everything a bird does is "programmed," so to speak, into the genes it inherited from its parents and that its behavior throughout its life is essentially a combination of innate abilities (e.g., the ability to fly) and a series of unchanging, highly predictable responses to objects and events. In a famous series of experiments, the Dutch ethologist Niko Tinbergen showed (1953–ETHOLOGY) that nestling Herring Gull chicks apparently responded mainly to their parents' bills while being fed—or rather to a long, thin object with a contrasting red spot pointing downward. Chicks that had never seen adult Herring Gulls responded to such objects, showing that the reaction is innate. When the chick sees the bill-like object, it "begs" and pecks at the red spot. When the parent bird is pecked on the bill it regurgitates food. No red spot, no pecking; no pecking, no food. Herring Gull chicks do not respond to *blue* bills nor would an adult gull respond to "unconventional" pleas for food, no matter how pathetic. Such instinctual exchanges are known in the behaviorist school as *fixed action patterns,* and stimuli that, like a gull's red bill spot, provoke a

predictable response are called *releasers*. These concepts are both valid and useful and the early behaviorists erred only in insisting that virtually *all* avian activity could be explained as complexes of mechanical responses to genetically programmed signals. More recent experiments have shown that while birds (like humans) arrive in the world with many genetic predispositions and do indeed respond robot-like to key cues characteristic of their species, the responses are increasingly informed and enhanced by learning and some degree of deduction.

So how smart are they? The trap inherent in defining the intelligence of other animals is that we inevitably tend to use our own species as a kind of norm or, even more misleading, as the highest expression of evolution to date. As with the structure of the avian brain, it is more accurate to think of bird intelligence not as inferior or superior to the human version, but profoundly *different*. Birds experience the world very differently than people—in many instances with superior equipment— and their needs, the driving force behind the adaptations of their brains, require different uses of intelligence.

One way of gaining an understanding of how bird intelligence functions is to observe how they use various well-defined forms of *learning*, the interface where instinct may be modified by experience. A very basic form of learning is known as *habituation*, in which young birds (and most other organisms) begin to distinguish shapes and actions that are harmless—e.g. the movements leaves—from those that are threatening. Many birds have learned that if approached nimbly and according to certain guidelines, fast-moving motor vehicles are not a threat and in fact can be a reliable source of food.

Imprinting is another fundamental form of learning. It has been shown that young birds begin to recognize familiar external sounds while still in the egg. Immediately after hatching, they tend to become strongly attached to the first moving object of a certain size that they see and hear. Normally, this is one of the parent birds, and the fixation initiates the chicks into a sense of identity with their own species and leads them into their characteristic life patterns as exemplified by their parents. But if, instead of first seeing their parents, young birds are immediately exposed to a different bird species, a person, or even a beach ball, their attachment to such unlikely "parents" is no less ardent. If such chicks continue to be encouraged in their devotion to a beach ball and are deprived of any contradictory learning experiences, they may develop a permanent attachment and even, as they mature, direct sexual behavior to the stand-in, though this kind of prolonged attachment to the wrong parent is very rare. The initial gross association with one's (presumed) own species associated with the first hours after hatching, rapidly advances to more refined forms of discrimination with important implications such as choosing an appropriate mate and habitat selection in later life.

Another kind of perceptual learning involves imitation and practice. Experiments have shown, for example, that, though born with an innate knowledge of their song, at least some species never learn to sing it correctly unless they hear it "properly" sung and try to repeat it (see SONG). It is often difficult to tell where innate abilities leave off and learned skills begin. Watching young birds "learning" to fly, it is easy to assume that the process is a textbook example of "practice makes perfect." However, captive young pigeons have been denied this practice, as well as the opportunity to watch other birds, and when they were of the age when their siblings were flying skillfully, they were released and found to do just as well. In other words, the clumsiness of juvenile birds may have more to do with immaturity of muscle coordination than with lack of experience. In similar situations, parental "teaching" may consist mainly of stimulating young birds in an instinctual "following response" (see FLOCK), akin to the human propensity to yawn when others do. Whatever the origin, there can be little doubt that such experience increases proficiency to some degree.

Birds also learn by *trial and error*—the ability, for example, to recognize and avoid eating certain kinds of caterpillars that once (or repeatedly) made them violently ill. This can be seen simply as a form of *conditioning*, which "rewards" an animal for doing the "right" thing and "punishes" it for doing the "wrong" thing, thereby forming habitual patterns of behavior. However, Blue Jays can learn to avoid Monarch Butterflies by just watching other birds get sick (Brower et al. 1970), which properly belongs in the next category.

Insight learning is, so to speak, the ability to put 2 and 2 together without any previous experience with 4. It is in this realm of intelligence that bird performance is most impressive to people, since it approaches the deductive reasoning on which our own technologies and societies are based. And recent studies in this area have greatly enhanced our appreciation of bird brains.

Some of the most intriguing examples of insight learning in birds involve the *use of "tools"* to obtain food. Perhaps the best-publicized example of this is the practice among some African populations of Egyptian Vultures of breaking Ostrich eggs by dropping rocks on them—documented and photographed for *National Geographic* in 1969 by the van Lawick-Goodalls. Equally famous is the Galápagos Woodpecker Finch, which habitually uses cactus thorns to probe for grubs burrowed in holes beyond the reach of its short finch bill. Other instances of tool use include the use of bark scales by Brown-headed Nuthatches to pry off other bits of bark under which invertebrate prey are expected (Morse 1968); and the tearing off of bits of newspaper by laboratory Blue Jays to rake food pellets into their cages (Jones and Kamil 1973). Alcock (1970) and others have made the case that these "innovations" arise by accident rather than intu-

ition: the vulture, unable to pick up the huge Ostrich egg in its bill, picks up a nearby rock instead in a redirection of its frustration; on rare occasions the rock is dropped on an egg, yielding a meal and conditioning the vulture to drop rocks on eggs. But this does not detract from the "innovator's" ability to grasp the significance of the event and repeat it, or from the "cultural transmission" of such bright ideas among whole populations of birds. In another famous instance involving insight without tools, British Great Tits learned to pick open the caps of milk bottles to get at the cream at the top; this became so popular in Great Tit society that the milk company made stronger caps— which the tits soon mastered.

Arguably the most remarkable of recent breakthroughs in our knowledge of avian intelligence have come from Irene Pepperberg's research on the African Grey Parrot, especially an individual named Alex who now has his own foundation and website (www.alexfoundation.org). Some of Alex's cognitive and communicative achievements are comparable to or exceed those documented for the brighter apes. He can, for example, with more than 80% accuracy identify and describe an object by a character not mentioned in the question: "Which object (of a varied assortment) is yellow, Alex?" Alex: "Key." He also grasps sophisticated concepts such as absence and same/different. He converses and expresses desires spontaneously using an extensive English vocabulary and is currently studying phonics with the goal of learning to read.

For a comparison of the avian and human brains, see NERVOUS SYSTEM.

INTERNATIONAL COUNCIL FOR BIRD PRESERVATION (ICBP). See BIRDLIFE INTERNATIONAL.

INTERNATIONAL CRANE FOUNDATION (ICF). Founded in 1973 by George Archibald in Baraboo, Wisconsin, the ICF "works worldwide to conserve cranes and the wetland and grassland habitat on which they depend." Its headquarters are now indisputably the world center for the study and conservation of cranes. There ICF staff manages a captive breeding and reintroduction program, works to protect crane habitat throughout the world, hosts international conferences, and encourages the public to see and learn about the live cranes on the site. Its many successes result in part from the compelling beauty of cranes and the fact that they embody positive human values— peace, long-life, happy marriage, good luck— in many cultures worldwide. For more information, go to http://www.savingcranes.org/ or write to ICF, P.O. Box 447, Baraboo, WI 53913-0447.

INTERNATIONAL ORNITHOLOGICAL CONGRESS (IOC). An official gathering of ornithologists from all over the world held in a different city

and country on each occasion, at intervals of four years. The first congress was held in Vienna in 1884; the 2006 congress will take place in Hamburg, Germany. The institution is governed by a committee of about 200 members and each meeting is chaired by a distinguished ornithologist. Like other conventions, the IOC serves social as well as professional functions. Papers are given (and later published in some form of *Proceedings*), ideas exchanged, job opportunities advertised, and field trips taken. Occasionally, positions are taken on international ornithological issues. Contact through BIRDNET.

INTRODUCED BIRDS. Defined here as birds that have been released— for the most part intentionally—by man in a locality outside their present native range for a specific purpose and that have become established—at least locally—for a significant length of time (at least a few decades). For the much larger number of species that have escaped from captivity or domestication and in some cases established "wild" populations, see EX- OTIC SPECIES; CAPTIVITY, BIRDS IN, Escapes; DOMESTICATED BIRDS.

Bird introductions are generally made for one of four reasons: for sport (upland game shooting); to control alien pests; as an aesthetic improvement; or for conservation purposes.

Those responsible for pursuing any of these purposes have tended to keep their narrow gaze fixed steadfastly on the benefits they believed would accrue from introducing nonnative species without considering the possible detrimental consequences both to native birds and other wildlife and to people (see PROBLEMS INVOLVING BIRDS). Though some of the effects of introducing alien species have become obvious, the subject ("invasion ecology") is just beginning to get the attention it deserves, e.g., in studies of the many bird species introduced into Hawaii (see Pimm et al. 1988–EXTINCT BIRDS) and work on the eastern House Finch population (see below).

Introduction for Sport. A number of alien upland-game-bird species have been released in North America in an attempt to enliven the hunting "potential" of a township, state, or the country as a whole. In addition to importing species from other parts of the world, state and federal game authorities have transplanted species native to one part of the continent to another part (e.g., Sharp-tailed Grouse). Most attempted introductions fail to establish themselves because their new habitat lacks some essential characteristic of their native one. Those documented below, however, have adapted well, and are apparently able to maintain their population levels without further introductions. A striking exception to these generalities is the Ring-necked Pheasant, arguably the world's most popular game bird, hundreds of thousands of which are raised annually by government fish and game agencies as well as privately—for release in designated hunting areas where the local (i.e., previously introduced)

Species	Natural Range	Established in North America
Plain Chachalaca *Ortalis vetula*	Rio Grande Valley, south to northern Nicaragua	Sapelo and Blackbeard Island, Georgia
Chukar *Alectoris chukar*	Rocky, arid areas, southeastern Europe through Middle East	Southern British Columbia through Great Basin to southern California and New Mexico
Himalayan Snowcock *Tetraogallus himalayensis*	Arid mountains above tree line in the Himalayan region from Afghanistan to northern India and western China	Introduced in 1963 and subsequently in the Ruby and East Humboldt mountains of north-eastern Nevada
Ring-necked Pheasant *Phasianus colchicus*	Ukraine through central Asia to southern China	Fairly common continent-wide between c. 35°N and 50°N latitude, esp. in farmland; local in southern regions and elsewhere; declining over much of its former introduced range (see above).
Gray Partridge *Perdix perdix*	Most of Europe to central Siberia	Common to abundant locally in farmland, Nova Scotia to British Columbia south to northern California and Michigan

population cannot sustain itself. Reasons for low survival rates among both adults and juveniles include absence of essential habitat requirements, reforestation, extreme cold in the north, incompatible agricultural practices, and, of course, constant hunting pressure. Many wildlife agencies no longer promote pheasant introduction and the species is dying out over much of its former introduced range.

Introduction as Biological Pest Controls. Without doubt, the two most "successful" introduced birds in North America are the House (English) Sparrow and the European Starling. While the people who released these two avian pests on the continent found them pleasing birds, most of them also made great claims for the beneficial habits of the birds. The House Sparrow, which was introduced more than 100 times, mostly in the

northeastern United States and Canada in the 1850s and 1860s, was, among other benefits, meant to save eastern shade trees from the ravages of the larvae of two species of geometer moths—the spring cankerworm *(Paleacrita vernata)* and the elm spanworm *(Ennomos subsignarius)*. The sparrows did eat a lot of these inchworms in New York and Philadelphia, but they also apparently displaced the native bird species that normally checked the numbers of another pest, the white-marked tussock moth *(Hemerocampa leucostigma)*. The tussock moths rapidly increased to equal or surpass the ill effects achieved by the geometers. All of these lepidopterous pests are still with us, but to them has been added a pernicious destroyer of grain and fruit crops. Perhaps the most serious effect of the introduction of the House Sparrow, however, was the decline of a number of hole-nesting native bird species. House Wrens, Purple Martins, and Cliff Swallows, among others, were extirpated by the aggressive sparrows in some regions; and, though reduced from the plague proportions their populations reached around the turn of the century, House Sparrows are still major competitors of hole-nesting birds. Needless to say, their aesthetic appeal has dwindled—even many fervent bird lovers revile them as the cockroaches of the avifauna. Their decrease is attributed to the passing of the horse as transportation, since they found a principal source of food in the undigested grain in "road apples." According to Breeding Bird Survey data, the species continues to slowly decline due to the dwindling of small-scale, family-based agriculture, reductions in livestock, and cleaner more efficient farm practices, and perhaps in some measure to competition from other alien birds, notably the starling and House Finch. However, House Sparrows remain common enough in certain urban and agricultural settings to be in no serious danger of disappearing at least in the near-term. The species is unquestionably the most widespread introduced bird in the world (domesticated species excepted), ranging virtually throughout the New World south of the Arctic, except for the Amazon Basin, and well established in Australia, New Zealand, and Asia as well as its native Europe. The House Sparrow shows clearly the multiple folly of introducing alien species: (1) They rarely (if ever) work the miraculous cures promised. (2) They are apt to produce an upset in the ecological balance that will cause more trouble than the original problem. (3) They may turn out to be pests themselves. (4) They are likely to compete with native species. These caveats apply to all introduced organisms, not just to birds.

The European Starling was introduced from the 1870s to about 1900 but not as often as the House Sparrow (the 1890 and 1891 attempts are usually cited as the ones that "took"), nor did it spread as rapidly and widely. Its song and plumage, both once regarded as very fine, had more to do with the starling's introduction than those of the House Sparrow, but its alleged "value" in devouring legions of crop pests (beetle larvae, etc.) was also advertised. Alas, in North America about 50% of its diet consists

of vegetable matter and, with the increase in its numbers, it has become a serious vineyard and orchard pest. Because starlings assemble for the night (after the breeding season) in prodigious roosts in cities and suburbs, the species surpasses the House Sparrow in two forms of pollution: noise and "guano." It is also a cavity nester and, along with the House Sparrow, is a major nest-site competitor of the Eastern Bluebird. In the East, starlings are no longer seen in the massive flocks of 50 years ago, and it would appear that their populations have declined markedly after the initial "explosion" characteristic of introduced species freed for a time of limiting factors (see POPULATION). The causes of this apparent stabilization are not clear, but a combination of newly adapted ecological constraints is probably responsible. These did not take effect in time to slow the spread of the species westward, and the starling has now established strongholds across the entire continent north to Alaska and south through Baja California.

The Eurasian Tree Sparrow, close relative of the House Sparrow, may also have been introduced at least partly with "beneficial" rationales. It arrived in St. Louis in 1870. Though a potential pest, it has not increased (except initially) or spread very far.

Introduction for Aesthetic Reasons. One of the minor aberrations of Western civilization is the passion for introducing all the birds of the Bible, Shakespeare, or one's native land (usually England) onto some hapless distant shore. This curious notion has attained its apogee in New Zealand, where 13 species native to Great Britain are now the dominant

Species	Natural Range	Established in North America
House Sparrow *Passer domesticius*	Europe, Asia, and North Africa	Virtually throughout to about 50°N (sporadically northward), esp. near human habitation
Eurasian Tree Sparrow *Passer montanus*	Europe and most of Asia	St. Louis, Missouri, and adjacent Illinois
European Starling *Sturnus vulgaris*	Europe, western Asia, and North Africa	Throughout North America from above the Arctic Circle in the West south into Mexico
Crested Mynah *Acridotheres cristatellus*	Widespread southern Asia	Vancouver, British Columbia, and vicinity

Species	Natural Range	Established in North America
Mute Swan *Cygnus olor*	Throughout most of Eurasia	Central New England and south along the coastal plain to Chesapeake Bay; also locally in the Great Lakes
Rock Dove *Columba livia*	Britain, southern Europe, and North Africa to China	Throughout, near human habitation
Spotted Dove *Streptopelia chinensis*	Southeast Asia	Los Angeles and Orange counties, California
Eurasian Collared Dove *Streptopelia decaocto*	Eurasia from the British Isles and Morocco east to Burma	Established in Florida and Gulf and southeastern Atlantic states and spreading rapidly north-ward and eastward apparently re-peating its invasion of western Europe from Asia (see Hengeveld [1993] and Romagosa and McEneaney [1999])

songbirds throughout the man-made agricultural habitats of that country, to the great detriment of the vastly more interesting native species. North Americans have largely been spared the effects of this whimsical presumption, primarily because our well-entrenched and adapted continental avifauna is a lot less prone to entry by invading species. Though hundreds (probably thousands) of attempts have been made to add "nice" species to the native avifauna, only a small population of Skylarks (*Alauda arvensis*, native throughout the Palearctic region south of the Arctic Circle) has become established—at the southern end of Vancouver Island, British Columbia. The European Goldfinch *(Carduelis carduelis)* may also have been widely introduced and reproduced briefly on Long Island, but no longer survives there.

There remain a few species that were introduced for a combination of reasons and might as well be called escapes, exotics, and/or domestic birds as introduced birds. However, since they were more or less deliberately "feralized," they are included here.

Introductions (and Reintroductions) for Conservation Purposes. While introducing alien organisms into "new" ecosystems has on the whole proven to be a terrible idea that creates many more problems than

it solves, there are a few instances in which it may be considered beneficial. One is the *reintroduction* of indigenous species such as Peregrine Falcon, California Condor, and Wild Turkey and into areas where they had
been extirpated by hunting, habitat destruction, or other man-made phenomena. While this has proven successful in some cases and offers some
hope for restoring native endangered species, the consequences need to
be carefully monitored, especially when species are introduced to new regions where they are not known to have occurred in the past. There is evidence, for example, that the introduction of "native" Trumpeter Swans
to presumptive old haunts may prove as pernicious for other wetland
species as have alien Mute Swans in the Northeast.

Another concept that is being tested with species of rare antelopes
and a few other large mammals, but not so far with birds, is to introduce
species endangered in other parts of the world to appropriate North
American habitats. For example, rare species of bustards might be established in deserts or arid grasslands on this continent, as a temporary measure until the species could be reintroduced within their native range or
even as a permanent alternative to extinction in the wild. Either case
raises many questions, but given the current state of the world's birdlife,
especially in developing countries, all potentially viable conservation options should be considered.

INVASION. Often used as a synonym for IRRUPTION, but perhaps more
properly restricted to more or less permanent range extensions, such as
the recent "invasion" of North America by the Cattle Egret. The term is
also used for the process of range expansion by introduced species.

IRIDESCENCE. See COLOR AND PATTERN.

IRIS (pl.: irises or irides [EYE-ruh-deez]). The pigmented part of the eye
surrounding the dark pupil; used as a field mark for some species of birds.
The *yellow* iris of Bendire's Thrasher, for example, is helpful in distinguishing it from the similar Curve-billed Thrasher, which has an *orange*
iris. It is, of course, the iris that is referred to in names such as Red-*eyed*
Vireo. As a rule, juvenile birds have dark irises, which become more colorful or paler in some species as they mature.

For the function of the iris and more detail on eye color, see VISION.

IRRUPTION/ERUPTION. "Irruption" denotes movement of large numbers of birds following the breeding season *into* areas beyond their normal range, as distinct from "eruption," which refers movement *out of* the
areas from which the birds came. These are the orthodox terms for this
phenomenon, but such movements have also been called invasions, incursions, and influxes. Partly because the species involved tend to erupt
out of relatively remote regions, irruptions are typically more remarked by

birders. Years in which irruptions of a particular species occur are commonly known as "flight years." Irruptions, as described below, are a fairly well-defined phenomenon and should not be confused with other movements and fluctuations in the numbers of certain species as a result of bad weather (Dovekie "wrecks," flocks of hurricane-driven Sooty Terns); intermittent range expansions (Carolina Wren); local breeding population increases not related to food scarcity (Black- and Yellow-billed Cuckoo populations tend to increase in areas where outbreaks of gypsy moths and/or tent caterpillars are occurring); or the characteristically erratic behavior of certain species (Dickcissel; see NOMADISM).

A list of the most frequently irruptive of North American species is given below. Most are birds of the tundra or boreal (coniferous) forest; however, some species that inhabit deciduous or mixed forest (e.g., Blue Jay) also fit the pattern, and irruptions from mountain coniferous habitats to lower elevations are undertaken by Clark's Nutcracker and Pinyon Jay. The families best represented among "irruptives" are the hawks, owls, and especially the cardueline finches (Fringillidae); however, 8 other families are represented in the list below.

The characteristic that these species share, aside from the irruptions themselves, is a fairly restricted food preference, which is subject to sharp fluctuations—irregular or cyclical—in abundance. For example, the biology of many northern raptors is strongly influenced by the population cycles of the small rodents (e.g., lemmings and voles) with which they feed themselves and their young. Similarly, crossbills are dependent on cone crops in their native boreal forests. When rodents and conifer seeds are abundant, populations of raptors and crossbills increase, but when the food source declines precipitously, the birds cannot find enough to eat within their usual range and must seek new supplies beyond it. When food supplies are abundant for a period of years, populations of dependent species tend to increase and when the food source declines significantly, more birds are left with less to eat. This forces the starvlings to vacate their normal range, with young birds usually predominating among erupters. Because rodent populations rise and fall with some regularity—typically building up gradually over several years and then "crashing" precipitously—the irruptions of rodent-dependent species are somewhat predictable; e.g., Snowy Owls winter southward in large numbers about every 4 years. Cone crops also follow cycles; e.g., boreal trees follow 2- or 3-year masting rhythms (Koenig and Knops 2001), but these are greatly influenced by variables such as rainfall and temperature and the irruptions of crossbills and other "winter finches" are therefore less predictable and can be much more dramatic. What makes individual birds "decide" to irrupt is more difficult to determine. Lack (1954–POPULATION) has suggested that the unusually high density of birds triggers an innate urge to move.

Birdwatchers who live south of the ranges of irruptive species logically tend to perceive these movements as proceeding from north to south. But this is not always the case. Many birds of the boreal forest (e.g., Red Crossbill) are somewhat nomadic within that continentwide belt of conifers, so that there is often much east-to-west exploration before the depleted reserves of a whole region compel an advance southward. Similarly, in the last century, poor cone crops in the mountain pine forests of Mexico forced irruptions of Thick-billed Parrots *northward* into southeastern Arizona (though owing to habitat destruction on the birds' breeding grounds, they have not appeared north of the border in any numbers since the winter of 1917–18). It is also plausible that periodic *northward* irruptions by Tufted Titmice and Red-bellied Woodpeckers may have contributed to their range expansions.

The details of irruptive behavior vary from species to species. In some cases the participants have been shown to be nearly all immature birds, which conforms with a tendency in birds of the year to wander farther afield than adults after they leave the breeding grounds (see MIGRATION); however, in other instances adults predominate. There is no doubt that a large percentage of some irruptive hordes fail to find an adequate supply of food and die of starvation. Yet many also survive to return to their normal area of residence. Crossbills and some other finches not infrequently will stay on well south of their usual breeding grounds to breed for a year or more. Irruptions may also be implicated in more lasting population shifts. Evening Grosbeaks were virtually unknown in New England and the Maritime Provinces of Canada until the winter of 1889–90, during which the first of a series of irruptions from the west arrived in the region. Though its abundance still varies from winter to winter, the species is now regular at that season and nests regularly (if sporadically) throughout the Northeast.

The following list includes those North American species whose populations are subject to the most conspicuous irruptions. Populations of other species also fluctuate and move according to the availability of food, but on a small scale that does not justify the use of the term "irruption."

Northern Goshawk	Steller's Jay
Rough-legged Hawk	Pinyon Jay
Willow Ptarmigan	Clark's Nutcracker
Snowy Owl	Black-capped Chickadee
Northern Hawk Owl	Boreal Chickadee
Great Gray Owl	Red-breasted Nuthatch
Boreal Owl	Bohemian Waxwing
Thick-billed Parrot	Northern Shrike
Three-toed Woodpecker	Evening Grosbeak
Black-backed Woodpecker	Purple Finch
Blue Jay	Cassin's Finch

Pine Grosbeak   Red Crossbill
Common Redpoll   White-winged Crossbill
Pine Siskin

ISOCHRONAL (eye-SOCK-ruh-nl) **LINE.** A line on a map connecting points at which a given event happened at a given time. If the average arrival dates of a migrant bird species are plotted on a map for different regions of North America and all the marks representing the same dates are connected, the rate of movement of the species and the "shape of its progress" across the continent are revealed.

ISOLATING MECHANISM. A characteristic that limits the possibility of interbreeding among species. This may take the form of a functional incompatibility, as when two animals are physiologically unable to copulate, or, between more closely related forms, a distinctive signal. Familiar isolating mechanisms in birds are plumage colors and patterns, song, and courtship displays. The development of reliable isolating mechanisms is crucial to the process of SPECIATION, and closely related species that share a habitat or breeding range tend to have the most strongly marked differentiating features. See SPECIATION.

ISOPHENE (EYE-suh-feen). In an ornithological context, an imaginary line that connects similar forms in a cline of a variable species. Visualize, for example, a hypothetical species that occurs throughout North America but becomes gradually darker the farther south it occurs. A line drawn between the points where the darkest individuals occur from west to east is an isophene. The same, of course, would apply to lines connecting the occurrences of the lightest or any equivalent individuals.

JACANA (see below for pronunciation). Standard English name for all 8 members of the family Jacanidae (order Charadriiformes), 1 of which, the Northern Jacana, has bred sporadically in southern Texas.

Jacanas look like a cross between a shorebird and a rail. Most species are generally dark with contrasting frontal shields and/or wattles near the base of the bill. Several species, including the American one, have vividly contrasting "flashes" in the webs of the primaries. The most striking characteristic of the family is enormously elongated toes, adapted for walking

easily over the leaves of floating vegetation and giving rise to the apt nick-name "lily trotter" (see Fig. 17). Jacanas eat a broad assortment of foods, including small fish, invertebrates, and some seeds.

The jacana nest is a rather flimsy layer of water weeds laid on top of floating aquatic plants, e.g., water lettuce *(Pistia)*. The 3–4 yellowish-brown eggs are heavily inscribed with fine and/or heavy, irregular scrawls. The Wattled Jacana, closely related to the Northern, is polyandrous, and females will resort to infanticide against the chicks of competitor females of lower social rank (Emlen et al. 1989).

Jacanas break into a mirthful cackle when flushed or interacting with their fellows, and can also make a sharp whistle.

The distribution of the jacanas is essentially pantropical, and they are notably intolerant of low temperatures. Even winters near the southern Texas coast periodically prove too harsh for the small populations of Northern Jacanas that establish residence there in mild years.

"Jacana" is indisputably derived from a name given the bird by South American natives and entered our language via the Portuguese. There all agreement ends. The Tupi-Guarani word was apparently something like *jassana,* probably with little or no emphasis on any syllable. The "official" Portuguese rendition is close to ZHA-seh-nah. Southwestern birders, pre-suming it to be a Spanish word, often say hah-KAH-nuh, and eastern elit-ist bird-tour leaders insist upon jah-KAH-nuh (or jah-KAH-ner, as in "Cuber"). The variations are limited only by imagination; jah-KAY-nuh is popular locally, and from some eccentric corner has come the refreshing JACK-a-naw. All of this makes a strong case for "lily trotter."

JAEGER (YAY-ger). Standard English name in North America for all 3 members of the genus *Stercorarius* (subfamily Stercorariinae; family Lari-dae; order Charadriiformes), all of which breed in North America. The subfamily also includes the skuas (genus *Catharacta*).

The jaegers are rather elegant, gull-like birds with aggressive, raptor-ial feeding habits. All have a horny cere-like "saddle" on the upper mandible (referred to in the name POMARINE Jaeger) and adults in breed-ing plumage all have elongated and modified central rectrices that are distinctive in each species. If these tail feathers are included, jaegers range in size between 16 and 24 inches. Their front three toes are fully webbed and the hind toe (hallux) is minute.

On their arctic breeding grounds, jaegers catch and eat lemmings and other rodents and small songbirds and shorebirds; they take eggs and nestlings of other species; and they also pick up insects and other inverte-brates, feed on carrion, and eat arctic berries. At sea, where jaegers spend most of their lives, they habitually harass gulls, terns, and other sea-birds, forcing them to drop or disgorge food, which the jaegers then re-trieve for themselves. The smallest species (Long-tailed Jaeger) does this

less frequently than the others. All species also feed on fish, marine invertebrates, floating carrion, and ships' refuse.

The Latin name *Stercorarius* means "excrement eater," and there are many less delicate mariner's terms (e.g., "jiddy" hawk) that similarly characterize the jaegers. Birds being harassed by jaegers frequently defecate in the air, and unquestionably jaegers do occasionally follow and retrieve the falling excrement, but whether they do this "on purpose" or mistake the excrement for dropped food is open to argument; it is also true that many observers have mistaken vomited food for feces and assumed that this was the dietary preference.

The jaegers are among the aerial masters of the bird world; their agility in pursuing a tern or gull with piratic intent is rivaled only by some of the falcons.

A Jaeger nest consists of a shallow hollow in the tundra with little or no lining. It contains 1–3 (usually 2) eggs, which may be tan, olive, or brown, rather sparsely and erratically splotched with dark brown. Jaegers are solitary nesters or sometimes loosely colonial.

Jaegers are seldom heard at sea; on the breeding grounds they make high-pitched gull-like or hawk-like whistles as well as dry clicks and sharp squeals.

The breeding distribution of all three jaegers is circumpolar arctic; after the brief arctic nesting season they disperse over the oceans of the world regularly reaching subanarctic waters; they are seldom seen from land at this time except during onshore storms.

"Jaeger" means "hunter" in modern German and Dutch and can be traced back to Old Norse roots with the same meaning. In British usage all of the jaegers are called "skuas." See Olsen and Larsson (1997), and O'Donald (1983). See also SKUA; POMARINE.

JAMAICA BAY Wildlife Refuge (New York City; a unit of Gateway National Recreation Area). One of the county's most important urban water-birding hot spot, accessible by subway from Manhattan and by road only a few miles southeast of Kennedy Airport. More than 325 species of birds have been recorded from the refuge. It is particularly noted for breeding herons, egrets, and Glossy Ibis and for migrant waterfowl and shorebirds. Interesting in all seasons, but perhaps most exciting for birders April–October, especially after July when "fall" shorebird migration begins. The visitor center and parking lots are open every day except Thanksgiving, Christmas, and New Year's Day, 8:30 AM–5 PM. For a detailed site description with birding and other natural highlights, go to http://www.brooklynbirdclub.org/.

JAY. Standard English name for about 47 (including the 5 species of Central Asian ground-jays) members of the family Corvidae (order Passeriformes), 10 of which breed in North America.

Jays are medium-sized to moderately large (7–28 inches) songbirds with sturdy, nutcracking bills, strong legs and feet, and (Pinyon Jay excepted) long (or *very* long) tails. A number of species are crested and most have a conspicuous—often predominant—area of blue feathering.

Jays are widely, and justly, famed for handsome plumage, a fearless nature (though many species are retiring, even skulking), incessant noisiness, and omnivorousness. They gobble seeds, fruits, insects, small reptiles, young birds, and eggs with equal relish, though overall they consume more plant than animal food. The Gray Jay of the boreal forest is notorious as a camp robber that will not only steal bacon from your plate but also make off with your favorite fishing lure or your baby's pacifier and then "cache" it in the crotch of a tree. Jays customarily travel in feeding flocks when not nesting. Many species of Temperate Zone and highland jays are associated with pine-oak habitats, reflecting a feeding preference for acorns and pine seeds.

The typical jay nest is a bulky cup of twigs, sometimes lined with mud (Steller's and Blue Jays), always with an inner lining of moss, plant down, grasses, roots, feathers, and/or hair. The site may be fairly low in a shrub or high in a tree. The 2–7 (usually 3–5) eggs vary in color and markings among different species and individuals: pale to dark buff, greenish, bluish, or olive; unmarked (eastern subspecies of Mexican Jay, occasionally) or sparsely to densely speckled and/or splotched with buff to dark brown.

Jays are well known for their harsh, raucous, frequently uttered screams, but they also make mewing noises, clicking sounds, and resonant whistles and are accomplished mimics, especially of hawk calls.

Jays are distributed throughout the Holarctic and Neotropical regions and reach by far their greatest diversity in the latter; they are notably absent from the Old World tropics. Except for Gray Jay, American jays belong to exclusively New World genera and are sometimes distinguished taxonomically from "typical" jays of the Old World.

"Jay" seems to be no more than the off-spring of "jai," the Old French name for the Eurasian Jay via the Latin "gaius"—which, Lockwood (1993–NAMES) instructs us, "has nothing to do with the proper name, Gaius, as has often been suggested."

JIZZ. A distinctive physical "attitude," totally apart from any specific field mark, which may help in certain critical field identifications. It is essentially an amalgam of shape, posture, and behavior. Knowledge of a species' "jizz" comes only after long experience with it and that of similar species in the field. In some cases, it is more reliable than rote observation of detail. The use of jizz is crucial, for example, to the skillful discrimination of diurnal raptors in flight, especially at a distance; it is also helpful in sorting out shorebirds. The most likely origin of the term is "GIS" (General Impression and Shape), a concept created by British plane spotters in

World War II to distinguish friendly from enemy aircraft. It has also been suggested that jizz is a corruption of "gestalt," which denotes a whole that cannot be adequately derived from the sum of its parts. See also Oddie (1980–BIRDWATCHING) and Svensson (1994–IDENTIFICATION).

JOURNALS, ORNITHOLOGICAL. See PERIODICALS in the bibliography.

JUNCO. Standard English name (and Latin genus) for 4 species of ember-izine finches (family Emberizidae; order Passeriformes), 2 of which breed in North America. Our Dark-eyed and Yellow-eyed Juncos occur in 10 readily recognizable geographic races, some which (e.g., "Oregon" Junco, "White-winged" Junco) were until recently considered distinct species.

The juncos are easily recognized as a group by their uniform gray and/or brown upperparts, paler (usually clear white) belly, and pink (at least partly so) bill. Two species have pale irises. All but one (Central American) species have white outer tail feathers.

Juncos are widespread, often abundant birds that breed largely in bo-real or montane coniferous forests and winter at lower altitudes and lati-tudes in woodland edges and brush. They are frequent visitors to winter feeders.

"Junco" comes from the same root as *Juncus,* the Latin generic name for members of the rush family (Juncaceae). *Junco* was apparently a Span-ish bird name implying "bird of the rushes" (perhaps the Reed Bunting of Europe?), and then found its corrupt way to the present birds, which sometimes feed in grasses, but rarely if ever in rushes or reeds.

For general family characteristics, see SPARROW-BUNTINGS.

JUNGLE FOWL. Any of 4 species of forest-dwelling, chicken-like birds in the genus *Gallus* (family Phasianidae) native to India, China, and parts of Southeast Asia. It is from one or several of these species that all our breeds of domestic chickens are descended. See DOMESTICATED BIRDS.

JUVENAL, JUVENILE (both: JOO-vuh-nl). Originally, perhaps, alternate spellings (American and British, respectively) of a general term relating to youth. They have evolved distinct ornithological usages, which, however, are frequently confused.

"Juvenal" plumage refers specifically to the first coat of teleoptile feathers acquired by a young bird. It supplants the natal down (if any) in the pre-juvenal (post-natal) molt and, in turn, is replaced (in many species almost immediately) by the first basic (first winter) plumage in a first pre-basic (post-juvenal) molt. The juvenal plumage differs from all other adult plumages in texture and in the shape of the remiges and rec-trices; usually it is also different in pattern and colouration.

A "juvenile" bird is one that is older than a nestling or chick but has not yet achieved sexual maturity or its first basic (first winter) plumage, i.e., a "juvenile" bird wears "juvenal" plumage.

Birdwatchers often use "juvenile" (or "juve") to refer to a bird in a distinctive juvenal plumage and sometimes (mistakenly) to one in first basic or other immature plumages. See also MOLT; MATURITY.

K

KEEL. The narrow median process of the breastbone that provides additional surface area for the attachment of breast (pectoral) muscles; most prominent in strong-flying species; absent in ratite birds. See SKELETON; FLIGHT; and Figs. 14 and 27.

KELSO'S RULE. The generalization that the ear openings and the flaps of skin that cover them in owls are larger among members of northern populations, smaller in southern. See Kelso, *Wilson Bull.* (1940), 52:24–29.

KERATIN (KAIR-uh-tin). The tough protein of which the outer layer of human skin, hair, and nails and birds' bills, legs , and feathers are largely composed. It is highly insoluble and contains much sulfur.

KESTREL. Standard English name for 13 members of the genus *Falco* (family Falconidae; order Falconiformes), 1 of which, the American Kestrel *(F. sparverius),* is a New World endemic and a common resident throughout North America. The Eurasian Kestrel *(F. tinnunculus)* has been recorded five times as an accidental straggler to the east coast and northwest.

Our native kestrel is an exquisite little raptor that hovers gracefully over open spaces (including highway medians) as it searches for the small rodents and large insects that it prefers to eat. Unlike most members of its family, it nests habitually in cavities and can be induced to inhabit a nest box (see BIRDHOUSE).

"Kestrel" may have come down through centuries of corruption from the Latin verb *crepitare,* "to rattle or crackle," which is suggestive of the distinctive kestrel call.

KETTLE. A flock of migrating hawks or other soaring birds spiraling upward on warm air currents. Because of the form of the rising "thermals," the birds riding them take on the form of an inverted cone and suggest the

whirlpool effect created when one vigorously stirs a kettle of liquid (see FLIGHT, Thermal Soaring, and Fig. 28). In parts of Europe the formation is called a "screw."

KILLDEER. Standard English name for a single species of plover, *Charadrius vociferus,* which is common at some season nearly throughout North America; local breeding populations occur south to northwestern Chile. This plover is fond of man-made habitats has the habit of nesting in "inconvenient" places, such as driveways and baseball diamonds The name is a close approximation of the species' call, not a description of unlikely predatory habits. For general family characteristics, see PLOVER.

KIN SELECTION. A genetic concept in which organisms enhance their own reproductive success by assisting in the development of related individuals. Classic examples are found among social insects in which nonreproductive members of a colony assist the queen in the rearing of their siblings. For avian examples see PARENTAL CARE.

KINGBIRD. Standard English name for 13 species of tyrant flycatchers in the genus *Tyrannus* (family Tyrannidae; order Passeriformes), 7 of which breed in North America. An additional species, the Loggerhead Kingbird of the West Indies, has been reported as a casual visitor to southern Florida, but all such records have been analyzed and doubted in print (Smith et al. 2000. *North American Birds* 54:235–240). Most kingbirds are of exclusively Neotropical distribution.

Kingbirds are relatively large (c. 9 inches), open-country flycatchers with broad, heavy bills, a dark "mask" through the eye, and a bright red or orange crown patch (usually concealed). Of all the members of their family, the kingbirds best deserve the name "tyrant." They usually choose conspicuous perches from which to chase flying insects and this serves double duty as a sentinel post. When potential nest robbers, such as crows or hawks, approach, kingbirds typically sound a loud alarm and fly at the intruder remorselessly until it has been "escorted" to a safe distance.

"Kingbird," of course, carries the same implication of dominance as "tyrant flycatcher."

For family characteristics, see TYRANT FLYCATCHER.

KINGDOM. The highest category in scientific classification. Five kingdoms are generally recognized today: Monera: bacteria and relatives; Protoctista (or Protista): algae, protozoa and other "eukaryotic" microorganisms; Fungi: mushrooms and relatives; Animalia: multicelled animals; and Plantae: plants. See also SYSTEMATICS; TAXONOMY; NOMENCLATURE.

KINGFISHER. Standard English name for most of the 95 members of the family Alcedinidae (order Coraciiformes), as well as a collective name for the family as a whole. Sibley and Monroe (1993–SYSTEMATICS) split the kingfishers into 3 families: (1) Alcedinidae, 25 small, fish-eating kingfishers, mainly of the Old World tropics, but including the Common Kingfisher of Eurasia; (2) the Halcyonidae, 61 Old World species, including the kookaburras and paradise kingfishers of Austalasia and other largely terrestrial feeding species; and (3) the Cerylidae, 9 fish-eating species, including all of the New World kingfishers plus one Asian and two African species. Three species of kingfishers breed in North America.

Kingfishers range in size from 4 to 18 inches (North American species: 8¾ to 16½ inches). The most striking physical characteristic of kingfishers is a long, straight, pointed—sometimes massive—bill connected to a head of the same scale. The rest of the body often looks disproportionately small. The legs and feet are particularly small and oddly modified: toes III and IV are fused for most of their length and IV and III are fused at the base (syndactyl); these three toes point forward (II is lacking in some species) and toe I (hallux) points rearward. Some species are dull-plumaged, but most are boldly patterned in bright, sometimes brilliantly metallic colors. The plumage of North American species is sexually dimorphic, with the female wearing the gaudier version. Many species are crested. Their wings are short, rounded, and strong, though as a rule kingfishers fly only short distances between perches.

Despite their name, kingfishers are not true waterbirds, but land birds (related to bee-eaters and motmots), many of which have evolved the habit of diving into shallow water after fish. Though all 3 North American species are strongly piscivorous, the majority of species worldwide are not, many living, for example, in arid or forested habitats and feeding mainly on large insects, small reptiles, and the like. A typical manner of catching prey (of whatever kind) involves hovering above a prospective victim and then diving down to snatch it, though the smaller species (e.g., Green Kingfisher) seldom hover but plunge directly from a perch overhanging the water. The Belted Kingfisher is known to take shellfish, small mammals, frogs, young birds, and even fruit in addition to fish. Food is swallowed whole and indigestible items regurgitated in pellet form.

Kingfishers are solitary and nest in holes in earthen banks, which they excavate themselves and which are notable for the loathsome accumulation of excrement and putrifying food scraps they contain by the time the young are grown. These unsanitary habits do not seem to have any negative effect on reproductive success. The 3–8 (usually 4–6) eggs are white, glossy, and unmarked.

Kingfisher calls consist of harsh chatters or rattles.

The family is distributed worldwide, being most diverse in warmer climates. In North America, the Belted Kingfisher ranges throughout the

continent and even breeds in the Arctic (Alaska/Yukon); the other two native kingfishers (Green and Ringed) are essentially Neotropical species that reach the northern limits of their range along our southwestern border.

The name, of course, connotes fishing expertise and, as noted above, does not suit most members of the family.

See also HALCYON.

KINGLET. Standard English name for 3 of the 5 members of the genus *Regulus* (family Regulidae; order Passeriformes), 2 of which breed in North America. The monogeneric family contains 3 additional Old World species. Once considered to be Old World Warblers (familiy Sylviidae), the kinglets are now placed by Sibley and Monroe (1993–SYSTEMATICS) between the swallows and the bulbuls. Audubon's attempt to give us an additional kinglet and name it for Baron Cuvier (see Havell Plate LV) is discounted as an error of memory by most authorities.

Kinglets (including the Old World *Regulus* species) are tiny (3½ to 4½ inches), but rotund songbirds with short, slender bills and rather short tails. Their plumage is largely olive green with prominent wing bars, and the males of all species (and females of some) have bright, erectile crown patches of red and/or yellow feathers. Kinglets are hyperactive gleaners of vegetation and live largely on small insects, though they occasionally take fruit, seeds, and sap. They are among the regular constituents of mixed forest flocks of foraging chickadees, nuthatches, warblers, woodpeckers, etc.

Kinglet songs are surprisingly loud and mellifluous considering the size of the resonating chamber. Their calls are high and lisping or "dry" and wren-like.

The kinglet nest is usually suspended from a fork but may also rest on top of a branch. It is a small (3–4 inches in diameter), fairly deep cup, almost spherical in shape, made of mosses, *Usnea* lichen, pine needles, grasses, hair, fibers, etc., bound with spider silk and lined with fine plant fibers, hair, and feathers.

The 5–11 (usually 7–9) eggs are white or yellowish-buffy with ill-defined, rather pale brownish or reddish speckles often forming a "wreath" at the larger end.

The kinglets range throughout much of the Palearctic region and North America and penetrate the Neotropics as far as the Guatemalan highlands. Both North American species breed in coniferous forest, mostly in Alaska, Canada, New England, and the Rockies, and migrate through or winter in the rest of the continent. The Ruby-crowned Kinglet breeds well above the Arctic Circle in the Northwest.

Like the Latin generic name *Regulus*, "kinglet" is literally "little king," and refers to the bright "crown."

KIRTLAND, Jared P., 1793–1877 (Kirtland's Warbler: *Dendroica kirtlandii*). A productive and prestigious physician, zoologist, and legislator,

born in Connecticut, but active for much of his adult life in Ohio. He was a founder of the Cleveland Medical College and *the* founder of the Cleveland Academy of Natural Sciences. He found a surprising amount of time to collect and mount birds and correspond with Spencer BAIRD, who named the warbler for him. Gruson (1972–BIOGRAPHY) quotes Kirtland's biographer as opining that this pillar of society led "the happiest [life] of which I have any knowledge."

KISKADEE. Standard English name for 2 species of tyrant flycatchers in the genus *Pitangus*. Both are largely Neotropical in distribution, but one, the Great Kiskadee, *P. sulphuratus,* breeds commonly in the Rio Grande Valley of Texas and has been introduced *all too successfully* in Bermuda. The name is a good imitation of this species' loud, frequently uttered call. See TYRANT FLYCATCHER.

KITE. Standard English name for 22 members of the family Accipitridae (order Falconiformes), 5 of which breed in North America. The kites are a heterogeneous lot (the 5 North American species are all in different genera) that are phylogenetically closely related to the sea-eagles (e.g., our Bald Eagle). In form and habits, some species of kites are accipiter-like, some falcon-like, some almost buteo-like, and others, e.g., the splendid Swallow-tailed Kite, are unique. Physical characteristics and general habits of the kites are like those of the other members of their family (see HAWK). The kites are distributed worldwide, except for the coldest regions, but in North America are found mainly in the southern half of the United States. Several North American kites have suffered severe declines in the last century and the native race of the Snail Kite, the Everglade Kite, is officially endangered (see ENDANGERED BIRDS).

"Kite" is one of many pleasing bird names whose etymology is rather obscure. It is widely repeated that it may come from an old Indo-European word meaning "to shoot," referring to the "swooping" action characteristic of some kites when hunting. Lockwood (1993–NAMES) relies, as usual in such cases, on onomatopoeia, which anyone who has heard the Eurasian kites or buzzard may be permitted to doubt. The name was applied first to the Eurasian Buzzard *(Butoe buteo),* then broadened to include the Red "glede," then narrowed again to specify just the *(Milvus)* kites. The use of name for the toy paper kite emerged about the same time it was being applied to the Red Kite (mid-1600s); the toy was named for the bird rather than the reverse.

KITTIWAKE. Standard English name for 2 species of marine gulls traditionally distinguished from other gulls in the genus *Rissa*. One of these (Black-legged Kittiwake) occurs throughout the world's northern oceans, while the other (Red-legged) breeds only on islands in the Bering Sea,

including the Aleutians and Pribilofs. Both kittiwakes are particularly graceful in form and flight and both nest on narrow ledges of precipitous cliffs.

The name approximates both species' calls, which can be described
as high pitched titter or giggle. In the same vein, many North Atlantic fishermen still call this gull "tickle-arse" as in "tickle-your-arse-with-a-feather."

For general family characteristics, see GULL.

KITTLITZ, Friedrich H., 1799–1874 (Kittlitz's Murrelet: *Brachyramphus brevirostris*). A German soldier-naturalist who traveled widely, collected specimens, and wrote ornithological treatises on such widely separated places
as Chile and the Philippines. According to Gruson (1972–BIOGRAPHY), ill
health and the resulting delays in publication denied him the recognition
that he may have deserved. He collected his alcid on a Russian expedition
to Kamchatka; it was named for him by his fellow German-Russian zoologist Johann Friedrich von BRANDT.

KLEPTOPARASITISM. A technical term for stealing food by one animal
from another. This can be direct, as when a jaeger forces a tern to drop or
regurgitate its catch, or indirect, for example, raiding recent food caches
of other species or individuals. Of course, there is no moral fault as in human stealing, since birds neither own property nor recognize any rights to
it. For examples among birds, see PIRACY.

KNOT. Standard English name for 2 of 18 species of relatively small
sandpipers in the genus *Calidris* (family Scolopacidae; order Charadriiformes), one of which, the Red Knot, breeds in North America. The Great
Knot, which breeds in the mountains of Siberia and winters from India to
Australasia, is a casual migrant in western Alaska, and has occurred once
in Oregon as a vagrant.

The Red Knot is the largest of the North American *Calidris* sandpipers, in basic (winter) plumage more resembling a Black-bellied Plover
than any species of "peep." In alternate "breeding" plumage its breast is
dowitcher "red." Knots prefer sandy beaches and rocky shorelines to
marshy situations, though they appear occasionally on mudflats. This
taste may reflect their breeding preferences, for they are among the few
shorebird species (Sanderling and Ruddy Turnstone are the others) to tolerate the stony barrens of northernmost Greenland and similar ultrahigh
arctic habitat. This species has been studied intensively for more than
30 years (Harrington 1996–SHOREBIRD) and has demonstrated the importance to long-distance migrants of regular stopover points where an
abundant food supply can be expected. For example, on its migration between the high arctic and the southern extremities of South America the
Red Knot arrives in numbers in Delaware Bay in spring coincident with
the prodigious hatch of horseshoe crab eggs. Without these reliable food

sources and the absence of disturbance at such critical points, it is doubt-ful that this and similar great migratory journeys could be sustained.

The Red Knot has a circumpolar breeding range and migrates and winters over the remainder of the planet, including the New Zealand and Fuegian antipodes. The population that nests in northern Greenland and adjacent Canadian islands winters in Europe, making a routine stop in Iceland to rest and feed.

The charming notion that "knot" comes from King Canute (or Cnut) of Denmark, whence knots were once thought to come, has, alas, been au-thoritatively dismissed. The Oxford English Dictionary suggests an associ-ation with "gnat." The call note of the Red Knot might be rendered as *knut*.

LAB OF ORNITHOLOGY. See CORNELL LAB OF ORNITHOLOGY.

LAMELLAE (luh-MELL-ee) (sing.: lamella). In reference to birds, trans-verse ridges along the inside edges of the bill that act as a sieve in aquatic feeding situations. Characteristic of swans, geese, and ducks (family Anatidae) and a few other waterbirds. Bills with lamellae are described as "lamellate" (LAM-uh-late).

LAND BIRD. A term of convenience without taxonomic or other scientific significance for birds that do not habitually frequent aquatic or marine habitats except by chance or to bathe and/or drink. The Osprey, kingfish-ers, dippers, and waterthrushes are generally considered "land birds" despite their close association with watery habitats. North American wa-terbird families are listed under WATERBIRD; all other families consist of land birds. See also WALKING/RUNNING; PASSERINE; SONGBIRD.

LARID (LAR-id). Any member of the bird family Laridae. In the plural, a name by which all jaegers, skuas, gulls, skimmers, and terns can be re-ferred to collectively; e.g., "We saw seven species of larids, including Para-sitic Jaeger, Heermann's Gull, and Elegant Tern."

LARK. Standard English name for the 91 members of the family Alaudi-dae (order Passeriformes), only 1 of which, the Horned Lark, is native to North America. An Old World species, the Sky Lark, has been successfully

introduced on Vancouver Island, British Columbia and has occurred as a natural vagrant from eastern Asia on the west coast.

Most larks are relatively small (average 7 inches), open-country, ground-haunting birds with drab grayish or brownish upperparts that blend cryptically with their preferred habitat. Many species have streaked breasts, and not a few have bold areas of black on face, breast, wings, and/or tail. A very long, straight, sharp claw on the hind toe (hallux) is typical of many larks and other terrestrial songbirds. Leg length and bill shape are quite variable within the family. They often occur in flocks after the breeding season and forage over the ground for seeds, insects, and the occasional snail. They walk, rather than hop, as most passerines do. As if to compensate for their drab plumage, larks are accomplished songsters, in many cases performing lengthy arias while hovering or circling high in the air. The Sky Lark is such an excellent musician that it inspired one of the most famous poems in English literature (see HUMAN CULTURE, BIRDS IN); and it has been widely introduced in British colonies because of its cheerful evocation of the British countryside.

Larks make a grass cup in a depression on the ground, usually near a clump of vegetation or a rock and lined with finer grasses, hair, and plant down. The 2–7 (usually 3–4) eggs are pale gray, buff, or greenish, very densely speckled or splotched with buff, olive, or dark brown. "A lark's nest" is also one of the many polite elimination euphemisms, such as "rest stop" or "call of nature." The British are to blame for "I'm off to look for a lark's nest," the connection presumably being that the errand is one preferably accomplished alone.

The larks occur on all continents and achieve considerable diversity in the steppes, deserts, and farmlands of the Old World.

For distribution and other particulars of North American species, see HORNED LARK; SKYLARK.

LATIN NAMES. See NAMES, SCIENTIFIC.

LAWRENCE, George Newbold, 1806–1895 (Lawrence's Goldfinch: *Carduelis lawrencei*). Coues put Lawrence as one of the "peers" of the mid-nineteenth-century ornithologists, along with BAIRD, BREWER, and CASSIN. His present reputation results mainly from his early descriptions of species of the Neotropical avifauna. Lawrence began collecting birds early in his life, and had the good fortune to be the son of a successful businessman, so that he could pursue bird study unencumbered by the need to make a living. He eventually was able to donate more than 8,000 specimens to the American Museum of Natural History. He was one of Baird's collaborators on the ornithological volume of the *Pacific Railroad Reports* (see BAIRD). The uncle of the Lawrence of warbler fame; see following entry.

LAWRENCE, Newbold Trotter, 1855–1928 (Lawrence's Warbler—originally described as a full species, now known as the rare recessive hybrid of Golden-winged × Blue-winged Warbler parentage). An amateur New York ornithologist, honored by a college classmate, Harold H. Herrick (another amateur New York ornithologist), who shot and described the first-known of these striking anomalies. The nephew of George Newbold Lawrence; see preceding entry.

LAWS PROTECTING BIRDLIFE. North American bird protection laws resulted from public concern about the devastation cause by killing birds for the plume trade and unregulated market hunting beginning in the late nineteenth century (see CONSERVATION; AUDUBON SOCIETIES).

FEDERAL LAW. The key piece of federal legislation was and remains the Migratory Bird Treaty Act (MBTA) of 1918. The initial Act included a treaty with Canada and was amended in 1936, 1972, and 1976 to include treaties with Mexico, Japan, and the former Soviet Union, respectively. The MBTA provides varying levels of protection to all migratory bird species, which are listed in the Act's regulations (50 CFR, section 10.13), and all of the listed species are provided a basic level of regulatory protection. The Act prohibits the "take" of these species, meaning that citizens may not engage in certain activities, including to hunt, capture, kill, possess, sell, purchase, import, export, or transport listed birds, their parts (including feathers), nests, eggs, or products made from their materials—*except as allowed by a permit or license.* Some of the major activities that are governed by federal permits or licenses are as follows:

Hunting. Many of the bird species covered by the MBTA can be legally hunted. These "migratory game birds" include species of ducks, geese, swans, cranes, rails, coots, woodcock, snipe, doves, and native pigeons and crows. The hunting of these species is highly regulated at the federal level and the rules are reviewed and amended every year. These regulations control such details as which species may be hunted in a given year, how many (by species and sometimes by sex) may be killed in a day (the daily bag limit) or may be accumulated from more than one day of hunting (the possession limit), what days of the year and times of the day they can be hunted, what kind of weapon can be used, what size (gauge) ammunition can be used, what size shot can be loaded into the ammunition, and what material can be used to make the shot (see THREATS [OF HUMAN ORIGIN] TO BIRDLIFE, Lead Poisoning). Federal law also forbids certain hunting methods, e.g., the use of live decoys, poisons, explosives, bait, or chasing game birds in motor vehicles. The intent of all these regulations is to ensure that hunting, when added to all of the other causes of bird mortality, will not harm the health of the populations of any of these species. A number of federal licensing requirements need to be met before a person can legally hunt migratory birds, including a Federal Migra-

tory Bird Stamp for waterfowl species (see DUCK STAMPS), and a Harvest Information Program (HIP) number for all migratory birds. The HIP number provides the U.S. Fish and Wildlife Service with a hunter survey sampling database that can be used to assess how much time hunters spend hunting each species, how much success they have, and other information related to hunting activities. The fees collected from hunting licenses are used for wetlands restoration and other conservation measures that ensure the replenishment of the resource that is tapped by hunting. In addition to the federal rules, the states impose their own hunting regulations and licenses (see below).

Falconry. Federal and state permits may be issued to persons who have passed written examinations in falconry to keep native species of hawks, falcons, owls, and Golden Eagle. The most highly qualified falconers may keep threatened and endangered species of raptors that have come from captive breeding, but Bald Eagles may not be kept by any class of falconer. A federal Falconry Permit is *not* required to keep raptor species that are not native to North America, such as Lanner Falcon, Saker Falcon, Tawny Eagle, or Eurasian Eagle Owl. Falconers quarry is limited to game species and unprotected species (e.g., European Starling and Rock Dove), and can be pursued only during prescribed seasons (see FALCONRY for more detail).

Raptor Breeding. A federal Raptor Breeding Permit allows for a person to possess and breed all of the same species that can be kept by a Master Falconer. There are no limits on how many birds or eggs that can be kept under a Raptor Breeding Permit and the offspring can be kept, sold, traded, given away, or (with the permission of state authorities) released.

Banding. Marking birds for scientific purposes, such as migration studies, requires both a federal and state permit (see BANDING; MARKING).

Scientific Collecting. A permit for this can allow activities such as capturing birds alive to collect parasites, stomach contents, or blood, tissue, or feather samples before releasing them or to maintain them for study of behavior or physiology or killing them for tissue samples or for museum specimens. It may also apply to eggs and nests. Both federal and state permits are required.

Salvage. Birds that are found dead may be salvaged for legitimate educational or scientific uses. Salvaged birds are most often found dead-on-the-road (DOR), washed up on a beach, under a radio or television transmission tower, or beneath a window. Both a federal and a state permit are required.

Rehabilitation. The intent of rehabilitation is to care for sick, injured, or orphaned birds just long enough that they can be released back into the wild with a good chance of survival. If a bird cannot be released it must be euthanized or placed with an authorized educational or research facility (see CARE OF DISTRESSED BIRDS). Both a federal and a state permit are required.

Education. This permit allows wild species of birds to be kept and used in educational programs or for public display. These birds are often nonreleasable injured birds but may also come from captive-bred sources. Both a federal and a state permit are required.

Depredation. Birds that are causing damage to property or are creating a public health or safety hazard may be killed under the conditions of a depredation permit. Most depredation permits allow birds to be killed only as reinforcement for an overall harassment program. Permit conditions identify the species that may be killed, the total number that may be killed in a year and during any single day, and the method that may be used, usually shooting or avicides (bird poisons). Sometimes permits may allow raptors to be trapped and relocated (e.g., from an airport).

Taxidermy. Taxidermists need no permits to mount legally killed game birds or nonnative unprotected species. However, they must be reasonably satisfied that any "trophy birds" were taken in strict accordance with state and federal hunting laws. They cannot under any circumstances mount a protected bird, either for themselves or for someone else, unless state and federal permits are obtained. Such permits are so hard to come by that no one should bother applying unless he/she can present some extraordinary extenuating arguments. Of course, all of the strictures that apply to professional taxidermists also obtain in the case of would-be amateur bird stuffers.

Endangered Species are protected under the entirely separate federal Endangered Species Act (ESA). Many endangered species are also covered by the MBTA, but most endangered species prosecutions occur under the ESA, which carries higher penalties. Bald Eagles are additionally protected by the Bald Eagle Protection Act of 1940 and Golden Eagles were added in 1963.

Special permits may be issued at the discretion of the Secretary of the Interior in emergency situations or in cases not covered above which serve the interest of the birds involved, e.g., research projects.

EXEMPTIONS. Some special exemptions from the federal permit requirements noted above are as follows.

Indigenous Inhabitants (native Americans) of Canada and Alaska may take birds and their eggs "for their own nutritional and other essential needs" without permits. This activity is regulated in the United States by the Department of the Interior and by equivalent authorities in Canada.

Blackbirds, cowbirds, grackles, crows, and magpies may be controlled without federal permit when they seriously threaten trees, crops, livestock, or wildlife or when they are a nuisance (see PROBLEMS INVOLVING BIRDS). However, state permits may be required for such actions, and methods of control and disposition of the birds are under regulation.

Scaring or Herding pest species requires no permits, with the exception of eagles and other threatened or endangered species, which are protected from all molestation and harassment.

Ducks, Geese, and Swans. Most members of the family Anatidae may be imported with a permit from the U.S. Department of Agriculture—i.e., such transactions are exempt from federal bird protection laws. *Feathers* of legally hunted game birds (see above) can be put to such commercial uses as fishing flies, pillows, and mattresses, and feathers and skins of legally taken *game birds* (e.g., ones mounted by a taxidermist) can be owned or imported for *personal use* without a permit. *However,* it is illegal to buy, sell, or barter mounted specimens of such birds or to use their feathers for ornamentation.

Grandfather Clauses make it possible for persons who legally owned objects or substances before the passage of laws that forbid such owner-ship to continue to legally possess them. Therefore, birds, alive or dead, or parts thereof or their nests and eggs that were legally acquired prior to the date of the acts protecting them may be kept and transported (they must be marked, if shipped) by the owner. *However,* documentation of when they were acquired is mandatory and such goods cannot be imported, ex-ported, sold, or bartered without a federal permit. The offspring of live birds held under a grandfather clause are not exempt. Also, raptors ac-quired by falconers (including endangered species) before the enactment of federal regulations restricting their acquisition may be kept by their owners subject to the stipulations noted above.

PENALTIES. Most violations of the federal regulations described above are treated as misdemeanors punishable by a fine not exceeding $500 and/or imprisonment not longer than 6 months. Felony convictions involving the illegal taking and selling or bartering (or intent to do so) of protected birds is punishable by a maximum fine of $2,000 and/or 2 years in prison. Persons convicted of pursuing, molesting, disturbing, shooting, shooting at, wounding, poisoning, capturing, or killing a Bald or Golden Eagle are subject to a $5,000 fine and/or 1 year in prison for a first offense and $10,000 and/or 2 years in prison for subsequent offenses.

EXPANDED INTERPRETATION OF THE MBTA. A recent federal court case (Hill vs. Norton), decided in December 2001, may result in the pro-tections of the MBTA being applied to many of the nonnative bird species in the United States that are not now protected by the Act. This case ar-gued that the nonnative Mute Swan fit the definition of a migratory bird and should be protected by the MBTA. The definition of migratory bird differs between the four migratory bird treaties but the most restrictive definition is found in the treaty with Canada. The original 1916 treaty was amended with a 1995 Protocol, which defined migratory birds to include "Anatidae, or waterfowl (ducks, geese and swans)." A species' status as na-tive or indigenous is not referenced in the definition. Since the Mute Swan is indisputably in the family Anatidae, the court found that it is a "migra-tory bird" under the MBTA definition and is covered by the protections of the Act. However, the court noted that this "does not prevent the Secretary

from controlling any potential harmful effects caused by (locally invasive) mute swans."

For another summary of this subject, see Faanes et al. (1992) or go to http://www.npwrc.usgs.gov/resource/tools/birdlaws/birdlaws.htm.protect.

STATE LAW. The states have the primary responsibility to protect and regulate the take of *nonmigratory and nonnative bird species* that are not included on the MBTA regulations list. Native birds species that are not included on the MBTA regulations list, those that are considered nonmigratory, include all of the Galliforms (Wild Turkey and all grouse, quail, and ptarmigan). Most of these species may be hunted in accordance with regulations and licensing requirements established by each individual state. Nonnative species that have become established in North America but are not protected by the MBTA include such familiar species as the Rock Dove, European Starling, House Sparrow, Ringed-necked Pheasant, as well as other nonnatives such as European Tree Sparrow and various doves parrots, game birds and others. See EXOTIC SPECIES and INTRODUCED BIRDS.

The states may make laws that are more restrictive than the federal regulations but they cannot make laws that are less restrictive. As an example, a state may not lengthen a hunting season or increase a bag limit beyond what is provided by the federal regulations but a state may reduce the bag limit or close the season altogether for a particular species that may need more protection in an individual state.

A State Duck Stamp and a state hunting license is usually required in addition to federal licences to hunt migratory game birds.

Details of state laws can be found on websites of state wildlife agencies or on-line state law references.

INTERNATIONAL CONVENTIONS. The full security of migratory birds requires, of course, that they be legally protected in all countries in which they breed, winter, or visit during migration. Accordingly, the United States is a signatory of international treaties with Canada, Mexico, Japan, and the former USSR (including not only migratory birds themselves but also their environment!). In general, these treaties proclaim protection for species that migrate between the signatories, the major exception being cases in which such species are "injurious to agriculture and constitute plagues." It should be noted that we as yet have no treaties with any of the countries of Central or South America, where a large percentage of North American migrant birds winter.

CITES. The Convention on International Trade in Endangered Species of Wild Fauna and Flora is an international agreement between Governments. Its aim is to ensure that international trade in specimens of wild animals and plants does not threaten their survival (www.cites.org). This is one of the most broad-based conservation agreements in existence and the principal mechanism for protecting bird species (as well as

other animals and plants) that have a high commercial value as pets, collectibles, ornaments, clothing, medicinal remedies, and other human uses. The text of the convention was agreed to by representatives of 80 countries in Washington, DC in 1973 and put into force in 1975. The are now more than 150 "Parties" (nation states) that have agreed to be bound by the convention, which now lists 5,000 species of animals and 25,000 species of plants in its three "Appendices."

CITES is a voluntary Convention to which countries agree to adhere. It is legally binding on the signatory states or Parties to the Convention, which must adopt their own domestic legislation to ensure that the agreement is implemented in their country. The legislation must include the designation of a "Management Authority," which administers a licensing system for the import and export of species. It must also provide for a "Scientific Authority" to advise on the conservation status of species in the country in question and the potential effects of trade on these species.

CITES species are categorized in three "Appendices" according to their degree of vulnerability, starting with species that are threatened with extinction. The Management Authority can prohibit trade in a given species for its country or issue import or export permits according to CITES guidelines if it can be demonstrated that "the trade will not be detrimental to the survival of the species."

According to CITES, in the nearly 30 years that the Convention has been in force not a single species has gone extinct as the result of trade.

LAYING. The deposition of an egg or eggs; oviposition. The actual voiding of an egg from the end of the oviduct (vagina) is accomplished by wavelike (peristaltic) contractions of the uterine wall. In most birds, this "labor" takes from one to several minutes; at least some brood parasites (cuckoos), which must transact their business quickly to minimize detection, reputedly lay in a few seconds; at the other extreme, turkeys and geese are said to take 1–2 hours (Weidmann, rev. by Tullett in Campbell and Lack 1985–ORNITHOLOGY).

For variations in laying schedules and other related details, see EGG; EMBRYO; INCUBATION.

LAZULI (LAZZ-yoo-lye or LAZZ-yoo-lee) (Bunting). The word has the same Middle Eastern origins as "azure," connoting the blue of a clear sky, a fair description of the dominant color of an adult male Lazuli Bunting.

LBB/LBJ (also LGB, etc.) "Little Brown Bird" or "Little Brown Job." Small birds of obscure markings and drab coloration that are therefore difficult to identify. For the beginner birdwatcher, most of the sparrows are spoken of in frustration as LBBs, while fall warblers and most small flycatchers are referred to as Little Green (or Gray) Birds. The term may have been coined

during the tenure of Lyndon Baines Johnson, the late thirty-sixth president of the United States, who was often referred to by his initials. This gives LBJ a certain extra resonance for birders who were active in the 1960s and 1970s. LBB now dominates.

LEACH, William E., 1790–1836 (Leach's Storm-Petrel: *Oceanodrorna leucorhoa*). A world authority on the Crustacea and a broadly knowledgeable naturalist who revised the literature of his day on birds and insects as well as his specialty in his curatorial posts at the British Museum. Like many early naturalists, he began his career by taking a degree in medicine, but he never practiced. The storm-petrel was named by L. J. VIEILLOT, the French systematist.

LEADING LINE. A topographic feature, e.g., a coastline or mountain ridge, that causes migrants to follow the apparent path of least resistance. Circumstance dictates when a leading line is an aid or a hindrance. In the case of raptors following the Kittatinny Ridge (see HAWK MOUNTAIN) this is a useful, perhaps even necessary aid in successful completion of southward travel, whereas following some coastlines may lead migrants away from the most direct line of travel or even lead to them becoming lost. See MIGRATION; NAVIGATION.

LEAD POISONING. Fatal to large numbers of game birds annually in North America , especially certain species of dabbling ducks that swallow spent lead shot pellets as food or grit. Also a major contributor to fatality in scavenging birds of prey, e.g., California Condor and in Common Loons, that swallow fishing sinkers. Lead shot is now banned by federal law for the hunting of waterfowl (ducks, geese and swans), but it is still legal for other wetland game birds unless otherwise prohibited by state law. There is as yet little restriction on the use of lead sinkers by fishermen. Lead is fatally toxic in very small amounts and causes a lingering death from starvation. For more detail, see THREATS (OF HUMAN ORIGIN) TO BIRDLIFE, Lead Poisoning.

LEARNING. See INTELLIGENCE.

LE CONTE (luh-KONT), John, 1818–91 (Le Conte's Sparrow: *Ammodramus leconteii*). Son of a wealthy Georgia plantation owner who was a dedicated amateur scientist, John Le Conte took a degree in medicine and practiced briefly, but soon dedicated his life to the teaching of chemistry and physics, eventually becoming president of the University of California at Berkeley. He absorbed some of the family interest in natural history, but unlike his cousin, John L. Le Conte (see the following entry), did

not distinguish himself professionally in that field. His sparrow was named for him by AUDUBON.

LE CONTE, John Lawrence, 1825–83 (Le Conte's Thrasher: *Toxostoma lecontei*). Like his cousin John (no initial) Le Conte, after whom Audubon named a sparrow (see the preceding entry), John L. was wealthy, trained as a doctor of medicine, influenced by a scientifically inclined father, John E. Le Conte (a noted amateur zoologist and botanist), and forsook the medical profession to pursue other interests—in this case entomology. His scientific reputation rests mainly on his work with beetles and on the biogeographic theories that emerged from his studies of insects. He also published in the fields of geology, paleomammalogy, and ethnology and was the first biologist to map the faunal regions of the western United States. He served as the Chief Clerk of the U.S. Mint at Philadelphia under President Hayes. The desert thrasher that commemorates this Le Conte was named for him by yet another naturalist in his family, his cousin George N. LAWRENCE of goldfinch fame.

LECTOTYPE. When the author of a species (or other taxon) fails to designate a type specimen in his published description, one must be chosen subsequently from the original type series according to the rules of scientific nomenclature. Such a specimen is known as a lectotype. Compare HOLOTYPE; see NOMENCLATURE, Types.

LEG/FOOT. The awkward title of this entry reflects two facts: (1) that where the "foot" stops and the "leg" begins varies greatly among different kinds of animals, and (2) that for the most part the leg and the foot function as a unit, one being useless or nearly so without the other. Lest the reader be in doubt about the limb under discussion, it is that which begins at the top of the thigh and ends at the tip of the claws (or toenails).

    STRUCTURE. A fair notion of variation in leg/foot structure can be gained by comparing the human and avian versions. Using the human model as the standard, we find that (1) all but a few birds walk on their toes alone; (2) what birdwatchers call a bird's leg is more like its foot and ankle combined; (3) what we are likely to take for a bird's backward knee is in fact its heel; and (4) a great deal of what we call "leg" on ourselves is tucked away out of sight on most birds. See Figs. 27 and 35.

    Bones. Bone-by-bone details of the above comparison may be found under SKELETON. For present purposes, it is sufficient to consider a bird's leg as consisting of four main skeletal sections: (from top to bottom) the *femur,* the *tibiotarsus,* the *tarsometatarsus,* and the *digits* (toes). Most of the discussion below concerns the toes and the lower leg, or tarsometatarsus ("tarsus" for short).

    Muscles. Conspicuous fleshy muscles on a bird's leg are generally restricted to the upper bones (i.e., from the "drumstick" or *crus* up); these

may be very highly developed and capable of great sustained effort (see MUSCLES) in species that spend much of their time walking/running or swimming/diving (see below) and in climbing birds, which must hold themselves erect on the side of a tree or other surface. As expected, birds such as hummingbirds and nightjars, which use their legs little, show little muscular development there. The movements of the lower leg and toes are powered by the muscles via a series of specialized tendons.

Feathering. As noted, the thigh (femur) of all birds is tucked up next to the body, totally concealed under the feathers of the flanks, and only in the very longest-legged birds (Ostrich, cranes) do we ever get a glimpse of the knee in a live bird. The tibiotarsus is wholly or partially feathered in most species, but is "bare" almost up to the knee in herons, storks, flamingos, stilts, and other long-legged forms. The tarsometatarsus is "naked" in the great majority of birds, conspicuous North American exceptions being members of the grouse family, some hawks (Rough-legged and Ferruginous), the barn owls, true owls, swifts, and some swallows. Some of the grouse (ptarmigan), some swallows, and all of the true owls also have feathered toes.

Podotheca. The unfeathered, exposed parts of the avian leg (tarsus and toes in most cases) are covered by the *podotheca* (literally, "foot sheath"), which typically has a "horny" (fingernail-like) texture in land birds, a more pliable (leather-like) feel in many waterbirds. In most birds (all songbirds) the podotheca seems to be "laid down" in a series of overlapping scales, and legs/feet so covered are said to be *scutellate*; there are many different scutellation patterns, and those in which the feet are scaled but the tarsus smooth are said to be "booted." The tarsi of oystercatchers are *reticulate*, i.e., crisscrossed with a network of wrinkles, leaving a surface of raised polygons. Other birds, e.g., parrots, have feet and legs covered with little bumps; such legs/feet are termed *granulate* or *tuberculate*. Many species combine different types of podothecal structure on various parts of their legs/feet.

Claws. Except in the case of some albatrosses, birds' toes end in some form of claw or nail, a modified scale, the form of which is also highly variable consistent with its use (see below). Most perching birds have sharp, curved claws of moderate length. Bird claws, like human fingernails, grow continuously but are kept short by natural wear rather than by clipping or biting.

Spurs. A few birds, notably the turkeys and pheasants (as well as domestic chickens), have sharp, bony spurs that project from the rear of the tarsus and are covered (but not dulled) by the podotheca. These reach greatest development in males, are used in breeding combat with rivals, and are of course the weapons upon which COCKFIGHTING aficionados have "improved."

Heel Pads. Nestling kingfishers, woodpeckers, and members of a few other families hatch with horny, bumpy, or ridged structures covering the

rear of the "heel" joint. Nestling birds rest on their "heels" and the pads are shed when the young leave the nest.

Number and Position of Toes. The vast majority of birds have four toes; none has more; and only one, the Ostrich, has as few as two. In a number of nonpasserines, the first digit (hallux), which normally points rearward, has become much reduced in size and/or "elevated" on the tarsus above the level of the other toes through disuse. A few species (e.g., some albatrosses, plovers, most alcids, stilts, all oystercatchers, some flamingoes, some kingfishers, kittiwakes, Sanderling, and the three-toed woodpeckers in the genus *Picoides*) lack a hallux altogether and in others it is a barely discernible vestige.

Birds' toes are numbered and designated as in Figs. 1, 27, and 35. The arrangement of the toes tends to conform among broad categories of birdlife and is therefore of some significance as a taxonomic character. The principal toe arrangements are as follows.

Anisodactyl: Three toes (II–IV) pointing frontward and the hallux (I) pointing rearward. This is the most frequent pattern among birds in general and is universal among passerines.

Zygodactyl (or "yoke-footed"): Two toes (II and III) pointing forward and the other two (I and IV) pointing rearward. This is apparently an adaptation allowing for improved climbing and holding ability and is characteristic of woodpeckers (except three-toed), parrots (which climb around tree branches and often hold food with their feet), and cuckoos. Owls and the Osprey are also considered "zygodactyl" but are able to move their outer toe (IV) forward to the anisodactyl position.

Heterodactyl: Similar to zygodactyl but with toes III and IV pointing forward and I and II rearward, an arrangement unique to the trogons.

Syndactyl: Toes III and IV joined at the base, forming an unusually long "sole"; kingfishers.

Pamprodactyl: All four toes pointing forward; most swifts, which habitually cling to vertical surfaces and use their feet for little else.

Tridactyl: Sometimes used to describe birds that lack toe I (see above).

MODIFICATIONS AND USE. As with other parts of their anatomy, the many striking adaptations seen in the legs and feet of birds have evolved in conjunction with characteristic modes of behavior.

Fig. 17. *Specialized foot types* are adaptations suited to distinctive avian lifestyles. The ptarmigan grow "snowshoes" of stiff feathers on their feet during the fall, which allow them to cope more efficiently with their snowbound winter habitat. Cooper's Hawks and other accipiters have long toes and exceptionally long talons for seizing and killing prey—mostly other bird species. Grebes have legs set far back on their bodies for maximum (torpedo-like) propulsion during dives as well as uniquely lobed toes that spread into paddles on the rearward "power stroke" and then turn into narrow blades, slicing effortlessly through the water on the return stroke. The almost absurdly long, narrow, broadly splayed toes and long legs of the jacanas are perfectly suited to "lily trotting," i.e. padding securely over floating leaves of aquatic vegetation.

Willow Ptarmigan

Cooper's Hawk

Horned Grebe

Northern Jacana

Perching Feet. Most living species of birds have feet with a well-developed rearward-pointing hind toe (I) and are otherwise well adapted for holding firmly to a branch or other perch. The group containing most of these is in fact named for this characteristic—"perching birds," order Passeriformes. This does not mean that nonpasserines cannot perch effectively—most can; or that perching birds are all arboreal—many, e.g., longspurs, meadowlarks, are mainly terrestrial. Nevertheless, even the feet of the ground-loving pipits and larks are better suited to grasping a perch than are (for example) the feet of boobies, herons, sandpipers, and woodpeckers.

Long Legs are characteristic of birds that wade in relatively deep water (herons, storks, cranes, some sandpipers, etc.) and also of "cursorial" species for which walking and running, especially in tall grass are specialties. The Ostrich and the coursers are perhaps the world's champion long-legged runners. In North America, the long legs of the Crested Caracara, Northern Harrier, Wild Turkey, Upland Sandpiper, and Greater Roadrunner are related to terrestrial rather than wading habits. See also WALKING/RUNNING.

Webbed Feet enable many water birds to swim and dive faster and more efficiently by providing more surface area to "push" back the water. The webbing is part of the podotheca (see above) but appears as a fairly thick, leathery membrane spanning the space between the toes. This character has evolved separately in many families of birds only distantly related. The loons, albatrosses, shearwaters and petrels, storm-petrels, flamingoes, ducks, geese, and swans, jaegers, gulls, and skimmers have *palmate* feet, i.e., with webbing between the three forward-pointing toes. The tropicbirds, boobies and gannets, cormorants, anhingas, pelicans, and frigatebirds—which together make up the order Pelecaniformes—have webbing between all four toes (frigatebirds only at the base) and are known collectively as the *totipalmate* swimmers. The frigatebirds as well as some herons (see Fig. 35), storks, ibises, the Limpkin, plovers, and sandpipers, which have only partial webbing between any number of toes, are called *semipalmate(d)*.

Lobed (Lobate) Feet are another form of natural paddling adaptation and, as with webbing, occur in various "styles" and in diverse families. Perhaps the most "unconventional" of these is the grebe foot, with each toe a unified paddle ending with a flattened nail (see Fig. 17). Before bringing the foot forward from the paddle stroke, grebes' toes twist 90 degrees, allowing their thin lateral surface to knife through the water on the return stroke. Grebes' legs are also flattened laterally to minimize resistance when swimming and diving. These marvelous legs/feet are placed far back at the end of the body for maximum torpedo-like propulsion in the water. This makes them nearly useless on land, though several grebe species run erect on the water in one of their courtship rituals (see Fig. 17)

and at least one species (Eared) has been seen to perform this tiptoe race overland in an emergency.

Coots and phalaropes also have lobate toes, but the foot is not so fully transformed as in the grebes. The effect is rather as if full webs began to bridge the spaces between the toes but remained incomplete, and neither the claws nor the flexibility of the toes is strongly modified in these birds. See also SWIMMING/DIVING.

Long Toes/Claws. The toes of rails are somewhat elongated, giving added support in walking over the soft surface of their marshy habitat. The gallinules and moorhens of the same family have even longer toes, which permit them to pad about on a shaky floor of floating aquatic leaves such as pickerelweed or water lilies. The undisputed champions of lily-trotting adaptation, however, are the jacanas. To their long toes are appended long, straight claws, the rear one longer than the toe to which it is attached (see Fig. 17). These remarkable feet, together with their owners' light build and long legs, enable jacanas to step about on a bed of floating water lettuce as if it were the firmest ground.

Larks, pipits and wagtails, longspurs, snow buntings, and some other ground-dwelling passerines, which spend little or no time perching in trees, have moderately to very long hind claws. These may improve stability in moving rapidly over the earth.

The long rear claws of nuthatches and creepers are strongly curved, pointed, and sharp, giving stability and extra maneuverability in their characteristic foraging over tree trunks.

"Snowshoes" are another adaptation to traveling easily over a soft substrate. This adaptation is the extra fringe of stiffened feathers that ptarmigan acquire on the margins of their already feathered toes. Other grouse, whose feet are not feathered, grow a comb-like edging from the podotheca of the front toes. Both types of avian "snowshoes" allow grouse to travel over the top of soft snow in which they might otherwise flounder (see Fig. 17).

Talons is the name commonly used to designate the unusually long, sharp, strongly curved claws on raptorial feet—i.e., feet used by avian hunters to catch and kill live prey. In most cases, eagles, hawks, and owls execute their victims instantaneously upon seizing them (usually on the ground) by simply closing their powerful feet. This applies crushing pressure while the knife-like talons simultaneously pierce the prey's body. (Victims not killed by the talons are quickly dispatched by a bite to the base of the skull.) A thoughtful assessment of the feet of the Cooper's Hawk, shown in Fig. 17, inevitably yields the conclusion that these birds deal a very sudden death. Peregrines and other large falcons that kill birds on the wing knock their victims to eternity with a sharp blow from their large, heavy feet delivered at the climax of a stoop at 80 (or perhaps over 200) mph (see SPEED); they may also "rake" their prey with their long rear talon.

Digging/Scratching Feet. Gallinaceous birds, which live largely by scratching in the earth in search of seeds or insects, and the wide range of species—Burrowing Owl, Bank Swallow, kingfishers—which sometimes or invariably excavate their own nest burrows by digging, tend to have strong (though not necessarily large) feet and comparatively blunt, heavy claws.

Less Conspicuous Leg/Foot Modifications. Many bird species have special foot adaptations that are visible only on the closest inspection—not to mention those that require a millimeter rule or dissection to detect. In the former category are the spiny soles of the Osprey, an invaluable aid in holding slippery fish. Herons and nightjars have a small "comb" on the lower surface of the claw of their middle (III) toe, apparently a preening tool. Crossbills (see Fig. 3) have unusually muscular feet and stout claws for gripping pine cones firmly while they apply their specialized extracting tools (see FOOD/FEEDING).

Even in the hand, the feet of the Black-and-white Warbler seem to be those of a normal parulid with none of the obvious adaptations to a climbing lifestyle shown by woodpeckers or nuthatches. On dissection, however, Black-and-whites do show an unusually developed "clinging muscle."

How Come Their Feet Don't Freeze? Anyone who has seen ducks or gulls standing—apparently comfortably—on the ice has asked himself this question. In answering it, it should first be noted that sometimes birds' feet *do* freeze. Land birds (especially) occasionally lose a toe or an entire foot to exposure at below-zero temperatures. But waterbirds that winter in the Temperate Zone have the capacity to "automatically" reduce blood flow to their nether extremities as the temperature falls. There is also evidence (Irving and Krog 1956–INCUBATION) that such birds can lower the temperature of the blood flowing to unfeathered parts, which further minimizes heat loss (see TEMPERATURE, BODY). Finally, there is little fleshy muscle and relatively few nerve endings in a bird's foot, so that pain or other sensations are registered little if at all from the legs/feet. On the coldest days birds on the ice often sit on their feet.

Birds' feet can apparently withstand an ordeal by fire as well as ice. Norris-Elye (1945–TEMPERATURE, BODY) relates an account of Gray Jays that could stand atop a red-hot stove for at least eight seconds without evincing any discomfort.

For perching mechanism, see MUSCLES. See also WALKING/RUNNING; HOPPING; FOOD/FEEDING; CLIMBING; SWIMMING/DIVING.

LEK. Originally coined to describe the courtship arena of the Eurasian Black Grouse, the term is now used to describe any place where a number of male birds gather to perform display rituals. (The term is also used for the display behavior some mammals, e.g., walrus, fruit bats, and some

bovid ungulates.) In North America, lek-type "dancing grounds" are characteristic of the sage- and Sharp-tailed Grouse and the two species of
prairie chickens. In the other grouse species (except the ptarmigans) the
cocks display alone but may be heard by birds on adjacent display
grounds, an arrangement that has been termed an "exploded lek." As is
typical of lek performances, the males of these species affect highly stylized postures and gestures—spreading wing and tail feathers, inflating
colorful air sacs on the neck—accompanied by a concert of arresting
sounds. Lek behavior probably serves to establish hierarchy among males
of a population and to facilitate female mate choice. The quality of the
males "costume" and performance, both indicators of fitness, allows the
female spectataors to select the most promising mates (Davies 1991–
MATING SYSTEMS).

The Ruff (a largely Eurasian species of sandpiper now known to breed
in Alaska) is another bird famous for lek displays, performed by males
wearing strikingly individualized plumage "ruffs"; and bustards, and
some hummingbird, parrot, and passerine species also engage in their
own versions of lek behavior.

The word "lek" derives from the Swedish *leka,* which in certain contexts refers to "sex play."

See also DISPLAY; DOMINANCE.

LEUCISM (LOO-sizm). Abnormal paleness in the plumage of a bird resulting from the dilution of normal pigmentation (see COLOR AND PAT-
TERN). It is also called "imperfect albinism" and, like true albinism, may
in some cases be related to abnormal diet. Leucistic birds retain their
characteristic pattern but appear slightly or extremely "washed out." See
Fig 8; also ALBINISM; SCHIZOCHROISM; and references in the Bibliography under ALBINISM.

LEWIS, Meriwether, 1774–1809 (Lewis' Woodpecker: *Melanerpes lewis*).
Lewis' immortality resides, of course, not in his woodpecker, but in his
leadership with William CLARK of the heroic three-year exploration of an
overland route to the Pacific coast of the United States commissioned by
Thomas Jefferson. He was a Virginia aristocrat by birth, a soldier by training, but a gifted observer by nature and he recorded (as the President had
asked) an immense quantity of detail on the natural history, ethnology,
geography, and trade and settlement potential of the "new" lands he
traversed. The expedition's discoveries were published by Jefferson in a
presidential message (1806), and the journals of the explorers have been
published in several forms and editions, most recently in complete and
abridged editions edited by Gary E. Moulton. Several histories and novels
about this uniquely American adventure have also been published. Following his famous adventure, Lewis was appointed governor of the vast

Louisiana Territory, in which office—crazed by depression and opium—he committed suicide

L'HERMINIER (LAIR-min-yay), Felix-Louis, 1779–1833 (*Puffinus lherminieri*: Audubon's Shearwater). A French naturalist who did much of his work on the French colony of Guadelupe (Leeward Islands, West Indies). He developed seminal theories of taxonomy and nomenclature for which he was made Royal Naturalist by the government in Paris. Unaccountably (Gruson [1972–BIOGRAPHY] suggests snobbery), his ideas were largely ignored in England and America, to the detriment of the advancement of science in these countries. L'Herminier was also a practicing physician. He shares a shearwater with Audubon courtesy of fellow Frenchman and systematist R. P. Lesson. The German ornithologist F. H. O. Finsch later described this species *again* and named it after Audubon. By the rules of synonymy (see NOMENCLATURE, ZOOLOGICAL) the Latin name reverted to *P. lherminieri* when the duplication was discovered, but Audubon's name stuck in the English vernacular.

LICE. See ECTOPARASITE.

LIFE BIRD ("lifer"). A species of bird seen by a birdwatcher for the first time in his or her life. Certain ethical criteria may apply to adding a new species to one's life list. For example, some feel that honor requires one to find and identify one's own life birds, while others are content to check off species that have been found and identified for them.

In the heady atmosphere of big-time, competitive listing, where critical identifications must often be made, it is considered wise to have each "new bird" witnessed by a "competent observer."

Birding, the magazine of the American Birding Association, has published a number of lengthy discussions concerning what may be ethically counted and when. In the interest of protecting certain rare, shy, and nocturnal North American birds the ABA has seen fit to allow birders to count birds heard but unseen—though the organization has not extended this protection to exotic birds sought by globetrotting birders.

See also LISTING.

LIFE CYCLE. See REPRODUCTIVE SYSTEM; EGG; EMBRYO; INCUBATION; YOUNG, DEVELOPMENT OF; PARENTAL CARE; COURTSHIP; PAIR FORMATION; TERRITORY; AGE; MORTALITY.

LIFE LIST. The record—whether by simple check marks or richly annotated—of all the species of birds that a birdwatcher has seen during his or her life. A life list of substance (e.g., 600–700+ in North America; 4,500+ in international competition) carries a measure of prestige in listing circles

and is a means of access to birding fraternities. See LISTING; SIX HUN-
DRED CLUB.

LIFE ZONES. A system devised by C. H. Merriam in the 1890s as an attempt to correlate plant and animal distribution in North America with
latitudinal and attitudinal zones of temperature. Modern community/
biome classification systems include reference to water availability as
well as temperature, allowing most major vegetative communities to be
defined. When soil chemistry is taken into account such systems become
even more precise. Though Merriam's life zones have been superceded by
more sophisticated and accurate models, a basic knowledge of them is
still useful in reading pre-1960s biological literature.

Most of Merriam's zones encompass 7.2°F (4°C) of mean temperature
at midsummer, roughly equivalent to 400 miles of north–south distance
in North America and 2,500 vertical feet. From coldest to hottest (both in
descending latitude and in descending altitude) the life zones are Arctic-
Alpine, Hudsonian, Canadian, Transition (called Alleghenian east of the
100th meridian), Upper Austral (often called Carolinian east of the 100th
meridian and Upper Sonoran in the West), Lower Austral (and Lower
Sonoran), and Subtropical (including only southern Florida in North
America).

Compare BIOMES (mapped in Fig. 8); see DISTRIBUTION.

LIME. At least two meanings are connected with birdlife. First, accumulations of bird droppings at nest sites—especially colonial ones—are called
birdlime on account of their whitish color and chalky consistency (see
GUANO).

A more interesting "birdlime" is the sticky substance used for centuries and almost universally as a means of catching birds. This trick is
described by Aristotle (fourth century BC) and may have been used by
Chinese boys long before. The localities from which birdlime is known,
together with its raw constituents, include ancient Rome (Pliny says it
was made from mistletoe berries), Northern Europe (rotten holly bark),
Southern Europe (fig sap), Algeria (thistle sap), subsaharan Africa (fig sap
or *Euphorbia* "milk"), India (fig sap), Japan (holly and other bark), Polynesia (breadfruit sap), other Pacific islands (berries), and South America (a
variety of plants). The preparation process usually includes mortaring,
boiling, and/or chewing and/or mixing with olive or other oil. The African
Euphorbia recipe is said to be strong enough to hold a hornbill. Typically,
birdlime is spread on branches where birds are known to perch, or an artificial sticky tree is constructed and placed in a likely spot, sometimes using food or a caged bird of the desired species as bait. Or a glob of lime is
fixed to the end of a long, light pole and birds picked off their perches.

For other types of bird snares, see CAPTURE.

LIMPKIN. Standard English name for the only member of the family Aramidae (order Gruiformes). Sibley and Monroe (1993–SYSTEMATICS) place the species in its own tribe (Aramini) within the family Heliornithidae, which also contains the finfoots/sungrebe. The Limpkin is essentially restricted to the Neotropical region but reaches North America as a permanent resident throughout much of the Florida peninsula and adjacent Gulf coast.

The Limpkin might be described as a "crane-rail," being larger (25 inches) and longer-legged than any rail but shorter, more secretive, and more cryptically colored than any crane. Like the rails, it has a preference for nocturnal/crepuscular habits (especially in North America), but its call is a far-carrying cry like a crane's. It feeds almost exclusively on large "apple" snails, such as the ones favored by the Everglade Kite.

Limpkins nest in clumps of emergent marsh vegetation or in low trees or shrubs, making a loose, dish-shaped platform of Spanish moss *(Tillandsia usneoides),* vines, dead leaves, and the like. Their 4–8 eggs are buff to olive with reddish to dark brown blotches, smaller speckles, and paler subsurface markings.

The highly distinctive Limpkin call is a penetrating wail, reminiscent of howling alley cats or the mournful complaints of tortured souls. Limpkins also make some harsh guttural sounds, sometimes uttered in a marked rhythm. They call mainly between dusk and dawn.

The name is usually associated with the species' gait, but may also have originated in an indigenous South American language.

LINCOLN, Thomas, 1812–83 (Lincoln's Sparrow: *Melospiza lincolnii*). A gentle, retiring, well-to-do Maine farmer who as a young man accompanied Audubon on his Labrador expedition. Though he acquired no fame during his life, Lincoln seems to have been extraordinarily well-regarded by those who knew him. Describing the discovery of the "first" Lincoln's Sparrow, for example, Audubon wrote: "Chance placed my young companion, Thomas Lincoln, in a situation where he saw it alight within shot, and with his usual unerring aim, he cut short its career. On seizing it, I found it to be a species I had not seen; and supposing it to be new, I named it *Tom's Finch,* in honor of our friend Lincoln, who was a great favorite among us." Gruson (1972–BIOGRAPHY) notes that Lincoln also gave Audubon the dog that figured along with his master in the well-known portrait called "Old Woodsman."

LINNAEAN SOCIETY. One of the aristocrats of American bird clubs, the Linnaean Society of New York was founded in 1878 by 10 "amateurs," including John Burroughs, C. H. Merriam (of life zone fame; see above), and Eugene Bicknell (of thrush fame). The club holds twice-monthly meetings September through May at the American Museum of Natural History, fea-

turing both popular and technical lectures by authoritative guests. It also publishes a newsletter, offers weekly field trips, mainly in the New York City area, and sponsors a rare bird alert. For more information go to http://linnaeansociety.org.

LINNAEUS (luh-NEE-us or luh-NAY-us). Latinization of Linne, Karl von; see following entry.

LINNE, Karl von, 1707–78. Generally known by the Latinized form of his name: Linnaeus. The founder of the modern system of binomial nomenclature under which all plants and animals are now classified. The seminal work in the method is Linnaeus' *Systema Naturae,* first published in 1735, the 10th edition (1758) of which marks the starting point for the classification of all animals under the Linnaean system. Binomial nomenclature has been improved upon as the complex interrelationships of living things have emerged under increasingly sophisticated scientific study, but the elegant simplicity of Linnaeus' original idea remains (see NOMENCLATURE). He seems to have been a born plant lover and classifier. He was known as "the little botanist" as early as age eight. Though he became famous throughout the Western world at an early age, his entire career was spent in Swedish academia (mainly the University of Uppsala). He was educated as a physician and practiced briefly (and successfully) in Stockholm but returned to university shortly after the publication of his great work. His other major works include *Genera Plantarum* (1737), *Species Plantarum* (1753), as well as a *Flora* (1745) and *Fauna* (1746) of Sweden and two volumes of "observations" made on his botanizing expeditions around his native country. Linnaeus had no special interest in birds, but as the world's "head classifier," he received specimens from everywhere and named an enormous number of forms throughout the plant and animal kingdoms, including many birds. In spite of the countless additions and revisions since Linnaeus' death, a glance through a systematic checklist, such as the *AOU Checklist of North American Birds,* reveals that he has a lasting memorial in biological nomenclature.

LISTING. The competitive branch of birdwatching in which one competes against oneself and/or others for the greatest number of species seen in a given place and/or time. Some listers reinforce their interest by keeping detailed notes on phenological phenomena such as arrival and departure dates of migrant species near their homes or, among the more widely traveled, by recording faunal information for little-known localities. For most, however, sport and diversion are the chief attractions.

The AMERICAN BIRDING ASSOCIATION (ABA), sets official standards for validity of records and provides a forum for discussion of listing issues in its publication, *Birding.* The ABA also prints a tally of the longest state,

LISTING   470

provincial, North American, and international species lists, in an annual Supplement.

The excerpt from *Birding* reprinted below by permission of the ABA articulates, far better than any description, the "lure of the list."

Bird-listing is a much-discussed topic in the birding world, especially among ABA members. Some birders malign listing, some can take it or leave it, some are disgusted by it, and others are compulsive about it. Because I find myself in the latter category, I would like to take this opportunity to tell others how, in my opinion, listing enhances the sport of birding.

First, I will list the lists that I keep. For a lister, listing lists is really fun, and it is something I seldom get a chance to do. Here they are:

1. U.S. Life List (526)
2. Minnesota Life List (341)
3. Month Lists (2,468; average, 206/month)
4. County Lists (11,924 for 87 counties; average, 137)
5. Season Lists (Spring, 312; Summer, 274; Fall, 292; Winter, 160)
6. Breeding-Bird List (235)
7. Yard List (3 residences) (highest, 135)
8. Early Spring Dates
9. Average Spring Dates
10. Late Fall Dates
11. Average Fall Dates
12. Bell Ringers (birds seen in all months) (74)
13. January 1 List (98)
14. Day List (for each field trip) (highest, 177—May 22, 1976—Big Day)
15. Record Daily List by Month
16. Year List (since 1947) (highest, 296—1977)

Lists 2 through 16 refer to lists kept in the State of Minnesota, and Lists 1 through 13 are cumulative. All of these lists are self-explanatory, with the probable exception of 13. This is kind of a special list kept since 1949. It is a cumulative total of all species seen on January 1, the traditional day to take a field trip to start a new year list. The figures in parentheses are my personal species totals.

Possibly, the first question many people will ask is, "Why keep so many lists?" My first and best answer is that list-keeping is fun because it gives you a chance to compare one year with the next, one day with another day, one area with another, and on, and on, ad infinitum; secondly, lists give me (and others) a good picture of the present distribution of birds in the state. I believe that there need be no other justification for lists. Probably the list that has become the most fun for me is the County List. My goal, to see at least 100 species in each county, has been accomplished in 82 of the 87 counties of Minnesota, with my average for the 87 counties being 137 species. The

real fun of county listing is that it gets me into many different areas of the state, areas that probably would not be covered during regular birding trips. Some years ago I became somewhat tired of always going to the same place at the same time of year. County listing provided the means to break the routine and get into new unbirded areas. To further enhance county listing, I started a town list. This is a list of all the named places in the state. To get to each of these places you have to cover the county "like a blanket." There are 1,828 named places in Minnesota—so far I have been in all but 166 of them!

I have seen a number of birders become bored with seeing "the same old bird time after time." Although the thought of being bored by birds never occurred to me, one way in which I have escaped the possibility of boredom is by listing. Listing provides new challenges and an interest in seeing that "same old bird" in new areas and at different times of year.

—From Robert B. Janssen, "Listing: Minnesota Style," *Birding* (August 1979), 11 (4). See also Piatt (1973) and other titles in the bibliography.

A few stars in the listing galaxy deserve special mention. The source for the records noted below is the 2002 ABA List Report Supplement to *Birding*.

- Phoebe Snetsinger, who died on a birding trip to Madagascar, still holds the record for the highest number of species ever seen: 8,401. Her autobiography, *Birding on Borrowed Time*, was published by ABA in 2003. The only other person known to have broken the 8,000 barrier as of 2002 was Tom Gullick of Spain (8,195). Eleven people have topped 7,000.
- G. Stuart Keith of New York was the first person to have seen over half of the world avifauna in the 1970s and held this record for many years.
- Macklin Smith of Michigan is the current (2003) champ in the ABA Area (essentially the Continental United States and Canada): 862 of a possible 921; 26 others are over 800.
- Joseph W. Taylor of New York was the first person to see 700 species of birds in the ABA Area. This long-awaited *coup de liste* occurred on Attu Island in the Aleutians (Alaska) in the 1960s. The 700th species was the Grey-spotted Flycatcher *(Muscicapa griseisticta)*, a casual visitor from the Palearctic.
- Benton Basham of Tennessee appears to be the first person to have seen 800 species in North America (in the early 1990s), though this statistic proved suprisingly hard to nail down.
- Three dauntless birders apparently broke the 700-in-a-year barrier for North America in 1976: Paul DuMont of Virginia, Paul Sykes of Georgia, and Joe Taylor of New York—again, based on reliable but unofficial sources

- Kenn Kaufman, then just out of high school, broke the "Big Year" record in 1973, seeing 671 species between January 1 and December 31 in North America. His accomplishment is the more notable considering that he spent less than $1,000 total and did most of his traveling (69,000 miles) by thumb. (see Kaufman 1997).

Other totals by state, province, and various regions are recorded exhaustively in the annual Supplement to *Birding*, which now runs to 84 pages. See also BIRDWATCHING.

LISTSERVS. The birding world now has an extensive network of online of information and communication services, including BIRD CHAT GROUPS, special interest listservs (e.g., ones catering to hummingbird enthusiasts or scientists researching cavity nesting species), and RARE BIRD ALERTS. For an extensive listing of these services along with addresses and directions for logging on, go to the American Birding Association website: www.americanbirding.org.

LOCOMOTION. See FLIGHT; CLIMBING; HOPPING; WALKING/RUNNING; SWIMMING/DIVING.

LOGGERHEAD (Shrike, Kingbird). A loggerhead is a dunce (blockhead), but as a biological term the word seems to be used in the sense of bigheaded. Both the shrike and the kingbird (see Appendix II) have relatively, but not spectacularly, large heads, and the possibility of a lost folk connotation remains. Though the kingbird appears as a "casual winter vistor to southern Florida" in the *AOU Checklist*, 7th ed. (1998), all of these records are now subject to doubt (see Smith et al., 2000, *North American Birds* 54:235–240).

LONGEVITY. See AGE.

LONGSPUR. Standard English name in North America for 4 species of emberizine sparrow-buntings, all in the genus *Calcarius* (family Emberizidae order Passeriformes). All are birds of open country from high arctic barrens to grasslands of the Great Plains.

All but one of these sparrow-like birds breed and winter exclusively in North America. The exceptional Lapland Longspur, which ranges widely in the Holarctic, is known in British usage as the Lapland *Bunting*.

The name describes the elongated claw of the hind (I) toe, a feature that the longspurs have in common with other terrestrial songbirds, e.g., the larks.

For family characteristics, see SPARROW-BUNTING.

LONG-TAILED TITS. Standard English collective name for the 8 species of birds in the family Aegithalidae (order Passeriformes). For the single North American representative, see BUSHTIT.

LOON. Standard English name in North America for all members of the family Gaviidae, the sole family in the order Gaviiformes. There are 5 species of loons worldwide, all of which breed in North America.

Loons are moderately large (2–3 feet), slender, and elongate birds with narrow but powerful wings, long, sharp bills, very short but stiff tail feathers, and the three front toes webbed. They are strong swimmers, divers, and fliers, but extremely awkward on land, which they willingly visit only to nest. All loons of both sexes acquire a surpassingly handsome alternate ("breeding") plumage, which is replaced during the winter with a drab gray and white basic plumage.

These unmistakable water birds are denizens of frigid lakes, rivers, inlets, and wet tundra on their arctic and boreal breeding grounds, but all winter at sea, mainly along Temperate Zone coasts. They feed mainly on fish, but also take crustaceans, mollusks, sea worms, aquatic insects, and even a little plant matter—proportions of each depending on the abundance of local food sources. With the exception of the penguins, the loons hold the world record for deep dives—to 200 feet or more (see SWIMMING/DIVING).

The loons' flamboyant courtship rituals include both aerial displays and "water ballets," usually performed by pairs in unison (see DISPLAY).

The nests of loons may be no more than bare scrapes at the water's edge but in marshy situations or in shallow water a mound of wet vegetation may be pulled together with the bill; these heaps may be built up to considerable size if the water level rises. The 1–3 (usually 2) eggs are notably dark brown or olive with rather sparse black spots and speckles and a coarse surface texture (see Fig. 10). Young loons are transported on the backs of their parents during the first two to three weeks after hatching.

Loons are rather noisy birds, famous for their extended wailing or yodeling cries, which have been likened variously to demented laughter, the cries of banshees, or the quintessential "call of the wild." These calls are most typical of the breeding grounds, where they are heard at all times of day and night. All species also make various clucking or quacking sounds both during flight displays and in migration.

The loons are a Holarctic family. All 5 species breed in the Arctic and/or Subarctic; 1 (Red-throated) is circumpolar in distribution and 3 (Common, Arctic, and Pacific) regularly reach the Tropic of Cancer in winter.

The name is supposed by some to derive from Scottish and Scandinavian words meaning "lame," referring to the awkward hobbling gait of loons on land; a more vivid folk name based on this trait was "arsefoot," also applied to the grebes. Other authorities say the name comes from an

Old Norse word meaning "moan." Madmen are probably named for loons, not vice versa. In Britain, the standard English name for the members of this family is diver; since the group is Holarctic in distribution this is the source of some confusion, not to mention nomenclatural chauvinism (see NAMES, COLLOQUIAL).

LORE(S). The area between the base of the upper mandible and the eye. The Solitary Vireo has white lores; the Black-throated Gray Warbler has a diagnostic yellow *loral* spot. See Fig. 35.

LOUSE FLY. A parasitic fly of the family Hippoboscidae that lives on the bodies of birds and mammals. For details, see ECTOPARASITE.

LOXAHATCHEE National Wildlife Refuge. See FLORIDA.

LUCIFER (Hummingbird). The "light bringer," Satan's name as an archangel before his fall. With regard to the tiny, essentially Mexican hummingbird species, the name refers to the dazzling magenta gorget of the male.

LUCY Baird Hunter, 1848–1913 (Lucy's Warbler: *Vermivora luciae*). The daughter of Spencer Fullerton BAIRD, the eminent ornithologist who also named two other warblers for ladies of his acquaintance (see GRACE; VIRGINIA).

LUMPING (lumper). In an ornithological context, the practice of combining bird forms (especially subspecies) into larger taxonomic units (especially species). Taxonomists gain reputations as "splitters" or "lumpers" according to whether they perceive fine distinctions among closely related birds and classify them accordingly or, contrariwise, lump two or more apparently distinct forms into one.

Modern ornithology has been able to demonstrate that, in many cases, birds that seem superficially very different—e.g., "Oregon" and "Slate-colored" Juncos—are, in fact, well-marked racial variations of the same species (in this case Dark-eyed Junco [*Junco hyemalis*]), just as superficially very *similar* forms—e.g., Bicknell's and Gray-cheeked thrushes—may be biologically distinct.

For obvious reasons, instances of the former are not popular with those birdwatchers whose main pleasure comes from accumulating a long list of species (see LISTING). Some listers become so enraged by what they perceive as taxonomic larceny that they refuse to consider the scientific rationale for the decision.

LUTINO (loo-TEE-noh). A bird exhibiting a color aberration in which yellow pigmentation is abnormally apparent due to a lack of some other pig-

ment in the plumage. Used especially with reference to captive parrots in which the condition occurs routinely. See XANTHOCHROISM.

M

MACGILLIVRAY, William, 1796–1852 (MacGillivray's Warbler: *Oporornis tolmiei*). Like an uncanny percentage of early naturalists, the Scotsman MacGillivray began as a doctor of medicine (see BIOGRAPHY). He soon heeded his irresistible calling, however, and eventually became a distinguished curator and professor of natural history (universities of Edinburgh and Aberdeen and Royal College of Surgeons, Edinburgh). His interest was not confined to birds, and he wrote extensively on other matters related to his field. Audubon paid him (late and loathly) for writing a significant part of his *Ornithological Biographies*. Audubon's attempt to name a new warbler after MacGillivray was not entirely successful, for John TOWNSEND had already described the species and named it after his friend William TOLMIE. In the end both of these admirable Scotsmen were commemorated, one in Latin and one in English.

MACHIAS SEAL ISLAND (Maine/New Brunswick: claimed by both the United States and Canada). A 15-acre treeless island off the northeast coast of Maine, best known among North American birdwatchers as a reasonably accessible place to see and photograph breeding Atlantic Puffins. Leach's Storm-Petrels (in burrows by day, active and "songful" at night during the breeding season), Arctic Terns, and Razorbills also breed here; pelagics are often seen on the 1- to 2-hour boat trip out and back. Access is via private charter boat from Jonesport (shorter drive, longer boat trip) or Cutler (opposite), Maine; advance reservations recommended. Landing is tricky to impossible in some weather conditions; fog is frequent. Prime puffin time is mid-May to mid-August.

MADERA CANYON (Arizona). See SOUTHEASTERN ARIZONA.

MAGPIE. Standard English name for 13 members of the family Corvidae (order Passeriformes), 3 of which breed in North America. Most of the magpies are in 2 closely related genera of Asian distribution and one, the Australasian Magpie, is in a different tribe with butcherbirds, currawongs, and wood swallows. The typical magpies are large, garrulous jay-like birds with a long tails, brightly colored and/or boldly patterned plumage, and assertive natures.

Except for their proportions and bold plumage pattern, the Black-billed and Yellow-billed Magpies of North America are typical crows. They are birds of open country; are nearly omnivorous (especially with regard to animal foods); make bulky stick nests bound with mud; score high on avian-level IQ tests; have a large repertoire of mainly harsh calls and some skill at mimicry; pick up and hide found objects, including human possessions; and, in general, accommodate readily to the human presence. Our magpies also tend to nest in loose colonies and usually add a dome to their nests. They are known to pick ticks from the backs of wild and domestic animals and also feed at open wounds.

Until recently the Black-billed Magpies of Eurasia and North America—virtually identical in plumage—were considered to make up a single species. They have now been split into the Eurasian Magpie (*Pica pica*) and the Black-billed Magpie (*Pica hudsonia*). The former breeds throughout the Palearctic region and the latter exclusively in the American West from the Great Plains and southern Great Basin west to California and north to Alaska. The Yellow-billed Magpie (*Pica nuttalli*) is extremely local, breeding exclusively in the fertile valleys (mainly the Sacramento and San Joaquin) west of the Sierra Nevada in California. Its appearance and behavior are very similar to its black-billed congeners.

The "mag" of magpie is a shortened form of Margot and the name as a whole is therefore part of the same tradition that spawned several British bird names: Jack the Daw, Robin Redbreast, Maggie the Pie (or Maggoty Pie, still heard today in parts of England). The exact significance of "pie" is less clear. It was used historically in France to refer to the Black-billed Magpie, but the widely repeated notion that it may imitate some magpie call must be doubted, since no such call is commonly uttered. The more recent etymology of "pie" refers to the bird. The baked dish, being an assortment of odds and ends, was named after the magpies' habit of making such collections, and "pied," used in many English bird names (Old World species: Pied Wagtail, Pied Flycatcher), refers to the splotchy black and white plumage worn by magpies.

For additional family characteristics and references, see CROW; JAY.

MALAR (MAY-ler or MAY-lar) (region, stripe). In general anatomy refers to the cheek, specifically the zygomatic (cheek) bone. In birding parlance it has been used somewhat ambiguously to refer to markings between the cheek and the throat. Sibley (2000–IDENTIFICATION) has proposed a clarification based on the concept of "feather groups." In his formulation the side of a bird's head below the eye is divided into three feather groups clearly divided by visible "creases" or "seams": (1) the *auriculars,* the cheek or ear patch below and behind the ear; (2) the *malar* immediately below it, running from the base of the lower mandible along the jawline; and (3) the *throat.* Because "malar stripe" has often been used for a dark

stripe on the side of the throat that is not within the malar feather group, Sibley proposes abandoning this term and replacing it with "lateral throat stripe"—the "whisker" on Black-whiskered Vireo is an example. For implications for other lower face stripes, see MOUSTACHIAL.

MALHEUR National Wildlife Refuge (Oregon). Over 187,000 acres of flat, arid butte land and scrub (sage, greasewood) pocked with shallow saline lakes and rush beds in the Northern Great Basin region of southeastern Oregon. Malheur hosts excellent concentrations and variety of migrant waterbirds in spring (March and April) and fall (September and October) and a fine assortment of western breeding species. Noted especially for the Trumpeter Swan, Sandhill Crane, and Greater Sage-Grouse. Western Grebe, White Pelican, White-faced Ibis, Cinnamon Teal, Golden Eagle, Prairie Falcon, Long-billed Curlew, American Avocet, Wilson's Phalarope, California Gull, Say's Phoebe, Rock and Canyon Wrens, Sage Thrasher, and Yellow-headed Blackbird are also routine. Breeding species best found May through July. The refuge headquarters is situated on the south side of Malheur lake c. 32 miles southeast of Burns, Oregon.

See also BEAR RIVER National Wildlife Refuge.

MALLARD. Standard English name for a single widespread species of dabbling duck, *Anas platyrhynchos*. The name originally referred only to the male of the species, translated from Old French and Old English as "wild drake." For family characteristics, see DUCK.

MANDIBLE. In the narrowest technical usage, the lower jaw, paired with the upper jaw or maxilla. More commonly, however, both parts of the bill are referred to as the mandibles, upper and lower; e.g., the upper mandible of the Black Skimmer is strikingly shorter than the lower mandible. See BILL and Fig. 35.

MANGROVE. A distinctive type of tropical swamp forest consisting of an association of several species of trees with ovate, shiny, leathery, dark green leaves and smooth, light bark, supported by a remarkable structure of stilt roots, which give a mangrove "swamp" its characteristic gothic, haunted quality. Trees from several families are typically grouped collectively as "mangroves," though one species, *Rhizophora mangle,* may be designated as "*the* mangrove." Mangroves thrive in brackish water and are therefore characteristic of tidal river mouths. In North America this tropical formation occurs only in southern Florida, where it is the preferred habitat of the Mangrove Cuckoo as well as other south Florida specialties, such as White-crowned Pigeon, Gray Kingbird, and Black-whiskered Vireo. Mangroves are also inhabited by a great variety of water-associated birds, such as anhinga, herons, ibises, Belted Kingfisher,

certain raptors, and Prothonotary Warblers (winter and waterthrushes (winter); and (somewhat surprisingly) are a preferred breeding habitat of Prairie Warbler.

MANKIND AND BIRDLIFE. See AVICULTURE; BANDING; BIRDING EVENTS; BIRDWATCHING; COCKFIGHTING; CONSERVATION; DOMESTICATED BIRDS; EDIBILITY; FALCONRY; HUMAN CULTURE, BIRDS IN; HUNTING; ILLUSTRATION; IMAGINATION, BIRDS IN; LAWS PROTECTING BIRDLIFE; LISTING; THREATS (OF HUMAN ORIGIN) TO BIRDLIFE; ORNITHOLOGY; PROBLEMS INVOLVING BIRDS.

MANOMET Center for Conservation Science. See OBSERVATORY and WESTERN HEMISPHERE SHOREBIRD RESERVE NETWORK.

MANTLE. The feathers of the back, scapulars, and upper wing coverts; a topographical region sometimes distinctly colored or patterned. The differences in mantle color among large gulls are the object of much intense scrutiny by some field ornithologists. See also terms under FALCONRY.

MARKET GUNNING. Throughout the latter half of the nineteenth century and the early decades of the twentieth century, game was shot in great quantities, often by professional gunners, and shipped to city markets. Shorebirds and songbirds were taken as readily as the ducks and upland gallinaceous species we now think of as "game birds." The number of birds taken of all species was so enormous as to bring some species, especially of shorebirds, close to extinction. It was the principal factor in the extinction of the Passenger Pigeon—a bird whose population probably numbered in the billions at the time of Columbus—and has probably sealed the fate of the Eskimo Curlew (see EXTINCT BIRDS; ENDANGERED BIRDS).

MARKING (of live birds). (See Fig. 2.) Though it is often possible to differentiate birds on sight into age and sex groups by noting plumage and obvious size characters, individual birds within these large categories remain virtually anonymous—at least to the human eye. Therefore, in studying behavior or movements of particular birds, it is often essential to add distinguishing features artificially. For example, investigators trying to determine which of a number of nearby Herring Gull colonies contributed the most birds to a potentially hazardous roosting area at a coastal airport sprayed the breasts of the birds in question with a harmless dye, a different color for each colony. By observing the proportion of colors that appeared on the runways, it was possible to pinpoint where control measures would be most effective. Fish and wildlife agencies trying to differentiate the habits of migratory Canada geese (some popula-

tions of which are declining) from resident feral Canada Geese (whose populations have exploded to pest proportions in some places) have placed plastic neck collars on a sample of both types of geese. The collars are printed with a number code that can be read easily with binoculars or even with the naked eye in the case of the all too tame resident birds. If the results reported by birdwatchers and others show that the two kinds of geese tend to inhabit different localities, an expanded hunting season could be designed that would cull the numbers of the pest Canadas without taking birds out of the population of the declining population.

A number of marking methods have been developed and used with varying degrees of success. The dyeing of breasts or other parts is highly satisfactory so long as the paint or dye used does not mat or otherwise injure the plumage. The marking substance may be applied directly to captured birds; or the dye can be placed in such a way, e.g., near a nest site, that the bird in effect marks itself; or birds can be marked at a distance by squirt gun. Lightweight, colored plastic markers attached to wing or bill or circling the neck or leg serve the same purpose. By using several different colors and spraying different body parts or using different combinations of colored leg bands, a fairly high degree of individual recognition can be achieved. Adult female Least Sandpipers from Churchill, for example, might be marked with a single red band on their left leg, adult males with the same color on their right leg, juvenile females with a green band on their left leg, juvenile females from Cambridge Bay with a green band on the left leg and a yellow band on the right, etc. ·

All marking schemes are recorded at the Bird Banding Laboratory in Laurel, Maryland, so that no two investigators will use systems simultaneously that might be confused. Marking birds for any reason requires a federal permit. See LAWS PROTECTING BIRDS and BANDING for further detail.

MARSH. An open wetland with water shallow enough to support a more or less continuous dense stand of emergent herbaceous vegetation, especially cattails (*Typha*), rushes (Juncaceae), sedges (Cyperaceae), and/or grasses (Poaceae), but deep enough to inhibit the growth of woody plants and more terrestrial herbaceous species. The ground is typically saturated year round or in the case of SALT MARSH during high tides, and there may be intermittent shallow ponds and islands of higher ground with trees or shrubs. Marshes are open systems with some degree of flow, which delivers minerals and flushes organics and excessive acidity. Technical wetland classifications distinguish among a number of different freshwater marsh types based on water levels, soil chemistry, vegetation, and other factors. Marshes are sometimes imprecisely called "swamps," which by ecological definition are *wooded* wetlands.

A number of North American bird species breed in freshwater marshes, exclusively in some cases, and many others feed there regularly

without nesting. Among familiar "obligate" marsh breeders are Snail (Everglade) Kite (mainly rush beds), American and Least Bitterns, all native rails, Common and Purple Gallinules, American Coot, Common Snipe, Franklin's Gull, Forster's Tern, Black Tern, Marsh Wren, Red-winged, Tricolored, and Yellow-headed Blackbirds, and Swamp Sparrows.

MARTIN. Standard English name (including crag-martins and house-martins) for 31 species of swallows (family Hirundinidae; order Passeriformes). The name has imperfect taxonomic integrity (the species we call Bank Swallow is known as Sand Martin in Britain); however, all the species in the New World genus *Progne* are known as "martins." One of these, the Purple Martin *(P. subis)*, breeds continentwide in North America. Four or five other "martins" have been recorded as vagrants (see Appendix II).

The Purple Martin has been widely touted as an effective natural mosquito-control agent, but such claims are at best exaggerated. While the species is undeniably a voracious insectivore, it feeds mainly on dragonflies, beetles, butterflies, grasshoppers, small flies and wasps, and other insects that are abroad mainly in the heat of the day. Most martins have gone to roost by the time the bulk of the mosquito population has begun to fly in the cool of the evening and nighttime. Swifts, bats, and dragonflies are more effective mosquito eaters.

Because of the supposed effectiveness of Purple Martins as "skeeter eaters" as well as their inherent attractiveness, many people erect apartment-type martin houses to attract them (see BIRDHOUSE and Fig. 4). Native Americans may have started the practice by hanging dried gourds as nest sites to exploit the martin's mobbing behavior to run off crows from their fields. Modern martin houses if appropriately sited are frequently well occupied in spite of the fact, revealed in recent studies, that martins are not by nature truly colonial birds (see Bitterbaum and Brown, *Natural History* (1981), 90:64–69).

Choate and Paynter (1985–BIOGRAPHY) explains the origin of the Christian name Martin as a diminutive, viz., "little Mars," and speculates at length upon how the term came to be used for swifts as well as swallows. This is another case, like magpie or robin, of Christian names applied to familiar bird species.

For family characteristics, see SWALLOW.

MATING. Either the formation of a pair bond (see COURTSHIP; MATING SYSTEMS) or the act of copulation (see REPRODUCTIVE SYSTEM).

MATING SYSTEMS. A key aspect of the human fascination with birdlife is the apparent similarity of many of our mating rituals. Both birds and people engage in conspicuous displays of their physical charms, sing love songs, "bill and coo," hold dances, fight with rivals, and cheat on their

partners. Other animals do these things as well, of course, but birds seem to share the human penchant for theatricality so that their sexual behavior often seems to parody our own or in some cases to provide positive role models. One of the most comforting examples that many people cite from the natural world is that swans mate for life.

Peering beneath the humor and sentiment that adheres to these superficial comparisons, we find that all of these bizarre activities are grounded in the evolutionary imperative to immortalize our genes through our offspring. For birds at least this means successfully rearing as many young as possible. In addition, whatever rituals are devised to achieve this end are variously promoted or constrained by prevailing ecological realities such as food availability. These fundamental influences are readily seen by observing actual mating strategies practiced by birds.

Monogamy. While both males and females have a stake in reproducing their own genes, the two genders bring different skills to the task. Males can produce great quantities of potential offspring in the form of sperm, while the female reproductive system is designed to nurture the development of a small number of fertilized eggs. Once the eggs are laid and the chicks hatch, both parents have an incentive to expend time and energy assuring that their offspring reach maturity. For males a long-term monogamous relationship provides an exclusive source of eggs to fertilize over an extended period and a cooperative parental system that maximizes his offspring's chances of survival. He is also relieved of the time-consuming hassles involved in more adventurous mating practices (see below). Against these advantages males must weigh missed opportunities to mate with other females and increase their progeny through the broadcasting rather than the nurturing of their sperm. Females' genetic interests are also clearly served by a system in which males share domestic chores and defend territories containing an abundant food supply, and female birds are at pains to choose the healthiest, most competent possible males as their constant mates. But they may be tempted to improve the quality (rather than the quantity) of their descendants if they have the opportunity to copulate with a fitter male.

Given these familiar tensions, it is significant that over 90% of all bird species are essentially monogamous, a higher percentage than in any other class of organisms. While a few groups of birds—albatrosses, some of the largest raptors, pigeons, and, yes, swans as well as geese—do indeed mate for life, even these most faithful pairs occasionally separate and will typically find a new partner if the current one dies. And in many cases monogamy is maintained only through one breeding season and very often is less than perfect in the observance.

While monogamy is the prevailing system, the use of molecular markers to trace paternity increasingly reveals that both males and females of many "monogamous" species commonly engage in "extra-pair copulations"

(see Westneat et al. 1987). It is in the early period of the breeding cycle before the nearly full-time drudgery of feeding young begins that males may visit females in neighboring territories. And these forays are apparently successful in many cases; for example, up to 40% of the chicks in an Indigo Bunting nest may not be the progeny of the resident male (Westneat et al. 1987).

Polygyny (puh-LIJ-uh-nee) is the mating of a male with more than one female during a single breeding season. Only about 2% of bird species worldwide and 5% of North American songbirds (Gill 1995–ORNITHOLOGY) practice this variation routinely. It is most common in marsh and grassland birds, e.g., Marsh Wren, Red-winged Blackbird and Lark Bunting, and is apparently driven by dominant males' ability to hold the territories with the best resources (food and shelter). In such habitats females can rear more young even with reduced help from a shared mate than they could do with a full-time mate on a poor territory. Within such harems, the male bird has a favorite mate with whom he shares more parental duties, paying significantly less attention to secondary mates.

Polygyny also tends to evolve in situations in which males are relieved of parental chores, e.g., precocial species of shorebirds in which the young forage for their own food very soon after hatching, fruit-eating birds in which females can find food very close to the nest site, and brood parasites.

Polyandry is the mating of a female with more than one male during a single breeding season. It is a rare breeding system involving less than 1% of bird species worldwide. In its classic form, e.g., among the phalaropes, it amounts to a reversal of the usual sexual roles, with females being larger, more brightly colored, and the dominant partner in courtship and territorial defense and the males taking complete responsibility for incubating the eggs. Spotted Sandpiper also follows this pattern, with females freed from all parental duties and therefore able to mate with and provide clutches for up to four different males. Another form of polyandry—practiced by Harris's Hawks and Acorn Woodpeckers in North America—involves several males helping a single female with rearing responsibilities. There is as yet no consensus about the evolutionary origins of polyandry.

Polygynandry is another rare mating system in which both males and females have several mates. It is characteristic of the flightless ratite birds (the African Ostrich, Australian Emu, and South American rheas), the Neotropical tinamous, and in North America the subarctic-breeding Smith Longspur. In the tinamous and ratites, several females lay eggs in different nests tended by males, which incubate the mixed clutches.

Promiscuity. In about 6% of all bird species, including the grouse, hummingbirds, and certain shorebirds, males attract females with conspicuous displays and then mate with all that make themselves available. In a number of instances, e.g., our sage grouse and prairie chickens,

promiscuous mating takes place in so-called leks, communal arenas where numbers of males gather to show off prominent plumage or other features, such as colorful combs or air sacs, while performing ritualized "dances" (see Fig. 7). Females evaluate and mate with the fittest specimens among the performers with the result that a small minority of males—less than 10% in some sage grouse leks (Wiley 1974)—mate with the great majority of females. After the necessary copulation, the female goes her own way to lay her eggs and rear her young unassisted by a mate.

While it is convenient to separate different avian mating systems into discrete categories such as those above, it is probably more accurate to envision a continuum of viable reproductive options with each species and in many cases particular populations and individuals creating their own variations based on existing ecological conditions. Every model has its advantages and disadvantages for both males and females and each is constantly being tested for its effectiveness in moving each partner's genes into another generation.

See also COURTSHIP; DISPLAY; LEK.

MATURITY. The age at which an organism is capable of reproduction. In birds, this varies from as little as 5 weeks (*Coturnix* quail) to 9 (or possibly 12) years in some albatross species. Most small songbirds breed for the first time when just under a year old, and many other species attain sexual maturity near the end of their second year. There is also some variation within species, some individuals maturing a year earlier than others.

Plumage is often taken as an indication of maturity; birds in "adult" (definitive) plumage are said to be "mature"; those not fully in adult plumage are called "immature." In general, this is valid, but it should be borne in mind that some birds are capable of reproduction while still in subadult plumage, while others look like adults before they are sexually mature.

See also AGE.

MAURI, Ernesto, 1791–1836 (*Calidris mauri*: Western Sandpiper). An eminent Italian botanist (director of the Rome Botanical Gardens) and a friend of Charles Lucien BONAPARTE, who named this shorebird in a work that compared the birds of Rome with those of Philadelphia.

MAXILLA (mak-SILL-uh) (pl.: maxillae). The upper jaw. In the narrowest technical sense, the bill of a bird can be said to consist of a maxilla (upper mandible) and mandible (lower mandible), though normally both parts of the bill are called mandibles. See Fig. 35.

MCCOWN, John C., c. 1817–79 (McCown's Longspur: *Calcarius mccownii*). An army naturalist who collected in the West (mainly Texas) for the

Philadelphia Academy of Natural Sciences. He collected his longspur on its wintering grounds in Texas, and it was named for him by George N. LAWRENCE. McCown was from Tennessee and graduated from West Point; Gruson (1972–BIOGRAPHY) notes that when the Civil War broke out, he resigned his U.S. commission (captain) to fight for the South. He survived the war and died in Little Rock.

MCKAY, Charles L., ?–1883 (McKay's Bunting: *Plectrophenax hyperboreus*). A young soldier (U.S. Army Signal Service) sent to Alaska to collect specimens for the National Museum in addition to performing his official duties—in this case as the keeper of a weather station. He drowned on duty but was commemorated by RIDGWAY in the name of the species first called McKay's Snowflake.

M'DOUGALL, Patrick, c. 1770–c. 1817 (*Sterna dougallii*: Roseate Tern). Dr. M'Dougall is a shade of immortality. He is credited by the author of the species (George Montagu) with shooting the type specimen of the exquisite Roseate Tern. He *may* have been the Dr. M'Dougall who was involved in a fracas at the University of Glasgow Medical School in 1809. And this is all history remembers of him.

MEADOWLARK. Standard English name for 5 or 6 (depending on taxonomy) members of the New World blackbird family (Icteridae; order Passeriformes), all in the genus *Sturnella*. The sixth species, Lilian's Meadowlark of the Southwestern United States and Northwestern Mexico is recognized as a full species by Sibley and Monroe (1993), but is still treated as a subspecies of the Eastern Meadowlark by the *AOU Checklist*, 7th edition.

The only superficial hint that the meadowlarks are closely related to the blackbirds and orioles is their long, sharply pointed bill. Otherwise, they are almost quail-like in proportions, with a stout build, broad wings, a short tail, sturdy, fairly long legs, and large feet adapted to walking on the ground. Our species average 9–10 inches in length. They are cryptically patterned in brown and black above and brilliant yellow below. Though nearly identical in appearance, Eastern and Western Meadowlarks have proven to be well-differentiated species with distinct songs that normally do not interbreed where their ranges overlap (see Lanyon, *Auk* [1962], 79:183–207).

As their name correctly implies, the meadowlarks are birds of open, grassy habitats. Three-quarters of their diet consists of insect and other invertebrate food, which they pick from vegetation or probe for in the earth. They also eat grass seeds, including grain. One grackle-like trait is the occasional eating of road-kill carrion (Terres, *Auk* [1956], 73:289–90).

The song of the Western Meadowlark is a rich, bubbly fluting; that of the Eastern is less melodious—more "twangy." Song is the best character for separating the two species in the field.

The nest is a rather large structure made of coarse grasses and weed stems. Over the ground cup, the birds construct a canopy that is woven into the surrounding grass stems. The lining is of finer grasses and occasionally hair. As the birds come and go, a tunnel is often formed leading from the nest entrance into the dense surrounding grasses.

The 2–7 (usually 3–5) eggs are white, finely speckled or rather coarsely splotched with brownish, reddish, or purplish.

Like all other icterids, the meadowlarks are restricted to the New World. The Western Meadowlark reaches the edge of the boreal forest on the northern prairies of central Canada and the Eastern species (including *lillianae*) breeds as far south as northern South America. Between the two, their ranges broadly span North America from coast to coast with a considerable zone of overlap in the Midwest and Southwest.

Meadowlarks are not larks but were so named because of their lark-like preference for open country and their habit of singing exuberantly on the wing.

For characteristics of other icterids, see BLACKBIRD; COWBIRD; ORIOLE; GRACKLE; BOBOLINK. See also Fig. 14.

MEASUREMENTS (of birds). The comparison of external dimensions of a bird's body is often crucial in making taxonomic distinctions, and more general notions of size are key factors in field identification. It is important that measurements be taken according to a consistent method, and some basic bird measurements and the accepted ways of making them follow. Precise measurements are usually made with the aid of dividers or, in the case of eggs, calipers. In the field, bird banders use a "wing rule" to measure the unflattened wing chord (see below).

Overall Length. Best taken from a fresh (unskinned) specimen. It is laid on its back on a level surface with the bill pointing directly ahead and the tail directly behind. The specimen should be in a "relaxed" or "normal" state, i.e., the neck should be neither stretched nor compressed. Then a straight-line measurement is taken from the tip of the bill to the tip of the longest tail feather. Once a specimen is prepared for preservation in a collection (see BIRD SKIN), it shrinks, or it may be deformed in the skinning and stuffing process. Therefore, measurements of skins are, in general, less reliable than those taken from a fresh specimen.

In many species, lengths yielded by the above method will be greater than is apparent when a bird is standing or perched in its normal posture in life. To give a truer impression of the length of the living bird, some field guides (e.g., Robbins et al. 1966–FIELD GUIDE) have stated an average "natural" length, which may be considerably shorter than the "standard"

length described above. Since accurate field identification depends far more on relative size than absolute size, this measurement "correction" has little practical value.

Wingspan. With wings spread to their fullest *natural* expanse, a straight-line measurement is taken between the tips of the longest primaries with the bird lying on its back. It is not possible, of course, to take this dimension on a prepared skin.

Wing Length. The outer edge of the folded wing from the bend (carpal joint) to the tip of the longest primary. Since birds' wings have a slight natural camber, two measuring methods have been developed, one which calls for flattening the wing on a rule and the other measuring the unflattened wing, i.e., the chord. The latter is the method preferred by North American bird banders for measuring the wings of live birds.

Tail Length. One point of the dividers is placed between the two central rectrices where they emerge from the skin and the other point at the tip of the longest rectrix.

Bill Length. The upper mandible is measured with dividers from the tip to the base, i.e., the point at which it meets the skull. The bill base is feathered in many species and sometimes the measurement is made to the roots of the outermost frontal feathers. In birds that have a cere, the length from its outer (distal) edge to the bill tip is measured. Bills with long nostril openings are sometimes measured from the distal end of the opening to the tip. The type of bill measurement taken should be noted along with recorded dimensions. Note that bill dimensions are not the length of the culmen (except in perfectly straight-billed species), but rather the *chord* of the culmen.

Tarsal (Tarsometatarsus) Length. One point of the dividers is placed at the outside of (i.e., below or behind) the "heel/ankle" joint and the other at the distal end of the last tarsal scale before the toes on the upper surface of the tarsus—the measurement runs diagonally across the side of the tarsus.

Eggs. Length of the long axis is taken with calipers between the poles of the "pointed" ends. Width is measured at the point of greatest diameter.

See Figs. 1 and 35 for anatomical parts mentioned above. See Palmer (1962) or Godfrey (1986–STATE/PROVINCIAL BIRD BOOKS, Continental Avifaunas) for illustrations of how to take these measurements.

MELANISM (MELL-uh-nizm). Dark coloration due to unusually large deposition of the pigment melanin (see COLOR AND PATTERN). Regularly occurring "dark morphs" of various species, e.g., Rough-legged Hawk, are sometimes referred to as "melanistic." However, some authorities restrict the term to cases of abnormal excesses of melanin, whether of genetic origin or related to diet or disease. Melanism is recorded from a wide variety of species.

MEMORY. As in people, memory functions in birds are located in hippocampus (shaped like a seahorse) and related structures; this hippocampal complex rests along the center line on the top of the forebrain. Spatial memory is of critical importance to birds especially to migratory species and those that store food to be retrieved in times of scarcity. Specialists in food caching, especially woodpeckers, titmice, nuthatches, and corvids have enlarged hippocampi. Balda and Kamil (1989) have documented prodigious spatial memory in Clarke's Nutcracker, which caches pine seeds in up to 2,000 different locations to be retrieved as long as 9 months later. The birds use a system of specific landmarks to relocate their winter reserves. See also FOOD/FEEDING. Barnea and Nottebohm (cit.) have shown that chickadees grow new neurons in the hippocampus each fall and early winter, indicating that they need a burst of neuronal growth to memorize the locations of their stores.

MERGANSER (mer-GAN-zer, sometimes MER-gan-zer). Standard English name for 6 species of ducks (family Anatidae; order Anseriformes), which also includes the Smew. Three species of mergansers breed and winter in North America and a fourth occurs as a migrant in the Aleutians (Alaska) and as a very rare vagrant elsewhere. These distinctive ducks are placed in their own subfamily (Merginae) by some authorities but lumped with the sea ducks (Tribe Mergini) by most.

The mergansers are all handsome diving ducks with crested heads and long, cylindrical, serrate bills, adapted for catching and holding small, slippery fish. The Hooded Merganser (see Fig. 23) is a North American endemic; the other 2 resident species are widespread in the Holarctic region. All of them are migratory.

"Merganser" is a Latin compound meaning "diving goose." This relates to Goosander, the preferred British name for the Common Merganser, which averages an inch longer than a Brant.

For family characteristics, see DUCK.

MERLIN. Standard English name for a single species, *Falco columbarius* (family Falconidae; order Falconiformes), which breeds throughout the Holarctic region. The name has been used by some authors for a few other falcon species, e.g., the Red-headed "Merlin" (Falcon) of Africa and India. In North America the Merlin breeds continentwide in the boreal forest and has recently expanded its range southward; it largely winters in the southern and southwestern states (as well as South America). It is a splendidly agile hunter of small land birds and shorebirds.

The ornithological etymologists give little satisfaction on the derivation of "merlin." Not surprisingly, its present form evolved from falconry, but connections with the Arthurian magician are nowhere to be found. The Merlin was once widely known in North America as the Pigeon Hawk,

which is not implausible in terms of the species' feeding habits and corresponds to its Latin species name, *columbarius.*; it also looks something like a (sleek) pigeon in flight, especially the slate-mantled males.

For family characteristics, see FALCON.

METABOLISM. In the broadest sense, *all* of the physiological processes in any living organism, including digestion, reproduction, muscular activity, etc. (see DIGESTIVE SYSTEM; MUSCLES; etc.). Usually, however, metabolism has the more specific meaning of conversion of raw materials (nutriment in food) into the energy, which keeps an organism alive and all its systems functioning normally.

The metabolic process in the body of a mammal or bird is extremely complex, involving interaction with a variety of enzymes and all of the body's living tissue. Two basic types of metabolic reaction are recognized: one that uses energy to break down raw materials into substances that can in turn be converted into energy (anabolic) and another that actually releases the energy (catabolic); clearly, the functions of these two processes are intimately interdependent.

One of the major metabolic functions is the breakdown of fats and carbohydrates into heat energy for the maintenance of normal body temperature (see TEMPERATURE, BODY). Another fundamental metabolic sequence is conversion of carbohydrates into stored animal starch (glycogen), which, in turn, is converted as needed into a sugar (dextrose) that supplies energy for muscular and other activities.

Basal metabolism is the minimum of energy required to keep the body's basic (involuntary) functions operating, and is used in diagnosing the general health of an organism and as a bench mark for measuring metabolism under varying conditions. It is measured in calories per square meter of body surface or per gram of body weight or by amount of oxygen used per gram of body weight.

Metabolism is one of the limitations on the size of animals. Very small birds, such as hummingbirds, must metabolize food at a fantastic rate to supply their energy needs from such a limited "power and storage plant." They must also reduce metabolism to a minimum when food is not available, to keep from exhausting the limited resources of their tiny bodies (see TORPIDITY); they walk a metabolic tightrope, so to speak, and a bird smaller than the smallest hummingbird is probably not physiologically practical. Conversely, a bird the size of an Apatosaurus (formerly Brontosaurus), in spite of great capacity for energy production and storage, would probably be unable to manage its bulk effectively.

See also ENERGY; FAT; SIZE; TEMPERATURE, BODY.

MEW (Gull). "Sea mew" is an archaic British term for "sea gull," making "Mew Gull" redundant in one interpretation. However, "mew" undoubt-

edly echoes a generalized gull cry (particularly gulls heard at a distance or through a fog) and is thus analogous to "Screech Owl." The unusual, high-pitched call of the Mew Gull *(Larus canus)* is something like *kee-ah.*

MIGRATION (migrant, migratory). See Fig. 18. In the most general sense, any extended movement by an organism from one place to another. The phenomenon is strongly associated with birds, probably because bird migration is relatively conspicuous (more bird species migrate than do species of any other class of animals); many bird migrations are easily and frequently observed; and these migrations take place over virtually the entire surface of the earth.

The term is restricted here to regular, seasonal movements, thus excluding various forms of dispersal and activities such as traveling between feeding and roosting areas, which are sometimes referred to as migrations. See also DISPERSAL; FLIGHT; IRRUPTION/ERUPTION; NAVIGATION; NOMADISM.

Migration is arguably the most spectacular and intriguing aspect of bird behavior. In North America, it involves about 80% of the approximately 645 species of breeding birds; may be observed anywhere from the High Arctic to the tropics, from the Pacific Ocean to the Atlantic; and is accomplished in as many variations of timing, routes, and techniques as there are migratory species to practice them.

Almost everything we know about bird migration has been learned in the past 150 years, prior to which sophisticated men of science could theorize that swallows spent part of the year hibernating in the mud or on the moon without fear of contradiction. Modern techniques (see BANDING; RADAR; MOON WATCHING; TELEMETRY), the accumulation of basic data on arrivals and departures, and the present mobility of people, which allows us to observe birds on their summer and winter quarters and en route, are responsible for what we now know. Some of the new-found facts—high-altitude, nocturnal migration, for example—are scarcely more credible than the myths they supplant. Still, our knowledge of bird migration is far from comprehensive, and new insights are gained constantly by birdwatchers as well as professional ornithologists.

WHY BIRDS MIGRATE. The reasons for migration will always be subject to speculation and controversy. It seems obvious that the advantages gained through the evolution of migration have been great; otherwise, the many dangers and enormous expenditures of energy involved would not have proven worthwhile for so many species of birds. It is also clear on a more observable level that the vast majority of migrant birds worldwide are retreating, on one leg of their journey, from harsh climatic conditions that reduce or eliminate their available food supply. The mystery is why insect- or nectar-eating species don't simply remain where they can obtain food year-round instead of flying hundreds or thousands of miles twice a

year at great risk. Most authorities favor one of two general explanations. In considering both, it should be borne in mind that despite the broad scope of present-day migration, each species evolved its migratory pattern in its own way, not as part of a mass phenomenon. (1) One theory argues that about a half-million years ago during the last (Pleistocene) ice age, when a third of North America was covered by glaciers, birds dependent on a warm climate for food were forced into what are now tropical regions but retained an innate instinct to return to their original ranges and did so as the ice retreated. Since the predominant pattern of bird migration is north-south and largely involves flight from a cold climate to a warmer, this scheme is logical and is supported by a widespread pattern of well-documented behavior. However, critics point out that many types of birds that migrate today, including those apparently physically adapted for long flights, existed before the ice advanced; they also note that there are other migration patterns, e.g., east-west or within the ever-warm tropics, that cannot be explained by glaciation. (2) Another popular scenario is that present-day migrants that breed in North America originated in the tropics and expanded into northern habitats, where there was less competition for food and territory. From this perspective, the cold, Temperate Zone weather and consequent lack of appropriate food compel the annual return to (rather than retreat from) a species' place of origin. It is also possible that the range expansions took place when climate was more equable—the birds then evolved into new species better adapted to new latitudinal daylight regimes and the onset of the Pleistocene ice age forced these new species to take up migration back to ancestral lands during Boreal winter. See Fretwell and Keast in Keast and Morton (1980) for a good review of this question.

WHEN BIRDS MIGRATE

Season and Schedules. We justifiably associate bird migration with spring and fall, since peak numbers of many species pass through North America in April–May and September–October. However, significant migration takes place almost throughout the year, with perhaps least activity in January and June. Diversity in migration schedules is predicted by diversity in lifestyles. Many shorebirds and other tundra breeders time arrivals and departures to and from the Arctic to coincide with the brief period of midsummer insect activity; thus they may arrive as late as early June and depart by mid-July when their young are independent. Many arctic seabirds, on the other hand, which can find food as long as there is open water, arrive at breeding colonies as early as April, remain in the area until fall, and may not complete their relatively short migration to wintering grounds off the coasts of northern states until November or December.

The hordes of migrants arriving in the spring from tropical America begin to hit the Gulf coast and other southern borders beginning in late March and peaking in April; peaks in the northern states and Canada fol-

low a month later. These dates can be seen to coincide roughly with the increasing availability of insect food as the season advances. In general, the passage back to winter quarters takes place on a more leisurely and protracted schedule, with some leaving in midsummer and others not heading south until November—though most true Neotropical migrants are gone by mid-October.

Dates of arrival and departure vary among different populations of the same species: as a rule, northern populations arrive later both on breeding and on wintering grounds. Adult and immature birds of the same species may migrate on different schedules. In some instances, notably that of arctic shorebirds, adults depart as soon as the young are self-sufficient, with the latter following a month or so after. In most songbird species, adult and young usually migrate at about the same time, although some young birds precede the adults.

In contrast to the great variation in migration schedules among different *populations* of the same species, *individual* birds as a rule arrive and depart very punctually, though departures are less conspicuous. The literature abounds in instances of individual birds arriving at specific migration spots, nesting territories, or wintering grounds on the same date year after year.

The Time of Day at which specific birds choose to migrate differs as does the time of year. Birds of prey and other soaring birds, which take advantage of warm air currents rising from the earth (see FLIGHT) tend to move in greatest numbers from midmorning until late afternoon. Swallows and swifts, which feed on the wing, also travel by day. The majority of small songbirds migrate at night, which explains why their sudden annual disappearances have until recently seemed so mysterious. Many species of waterfowl move at any hour, apparently indifferent to the degree of light. And, obviously, nocturnal migrants such as warblers or shorebirds, which meet the dawn over deserts or water, must keep going regardless of the time of day.

How Birds Migrate

Locomotion. The great majority of bird migrants fly to their destinations, but some species of seabirds supplement flights by swimming significant distances. Turkeys are reputed to have undertaken extensive journeys on foot in times when their habitat was not severely broken up as it is today; modern populations of this species are essentially nonmigratory.

Direction. The usual course of bird migration over North America is roughly from north to south after the breeding season and the reverse on the return from the wintering area. There are a number of exceptions, however. (1) South-north: Several of "our" species of shearwaters and petrels breed on oceanic islands in the Southern Hemisphere during the northern winter and migrate to the North Atlantic or North Pacific during

nonbreeding periods. Juvenile birds of many species tend to wander extensively once self-sufficient, and a certain percentage of normally southward migrating birds will initially move northward (as well as to all other points of the compass) in this haphazard manner. More significantly, the young of some southern species, e.g., egrets and Bald Eagles, *habitually* move north shortly after quitting the nest, frequently as far as Canada. (2) East-west: White-winged Scoters that breed in central and northwestern Canada migrate both due east and due west to the coasts for the winter; some Midwestern breeding populations of Evening Grosbeaks (sometimes) move east to winter in New England; and a few pelagic species make east-west oceanic crossings, e.g., Cory's Shearwater (breeds eastern Atlantic and Mediterranean and migrates to northwestern Atlantic), Black-footed Albatross (breeds north-central and western Pacific islands and disperses to northeastern Pacific), and Sooty Tern (breeds Dry Tortugas and disperses to west coast of Africa). (3) Northeast-southwest: essentially Palearctic species (e.g., Red-necked Stint, Yellow Wagtail), which breed as far east as extreme northwestern Alaska follow the migration route of their Siberian populations to winter in southern Asia and/or Australasia. (4) Northwest-southeast: Blackpolls and other wood warblers whose breeding ranges extend well into western Canada follow an eastern migration route rather than heading directly south from their nesting grounds. One theory holds that these species evolved in the East, spreading to the West only fairly recently, and continue to follow their ancestral migration pattern; however, they are also following prevailing autumn wind directions. The eastern Canadian populations of Northern Wheatear also travel east in the fall toward their continent of origin before turning southward toward African winter quarters.

Of course, migrants frequently deviate from their intended directions because of environmental influences (see Effects of Weather, below).

Routes. Birds migrate over the entire face of the continent but, particularly in the case of daytime migrants, tend to follow topographical features such as mountain chains, river valleys, and coastlines. This tendency has given rise to the speculation that there are four major "flyways"—the Pacific, Central, Mississippi, and Atlantic—along which migration is concentrated. This concept has been a boon to those (e.g., the U.S. Fish and Wildlife Service) whose job it is to keep tabs on numbers of migratory waterfowl and other game species: abundance is much easier to assess if nearly all birds follow only a few unvarying routes. Unfortunately for the census takers, much recent evidence refutes the notion of flyways as a principal pattern of migration.

There are, however, four main flight plans by which birds reach Latin American wintering grounds once across the southern U.S. border: (1) directly into the peninsular extension of Mexico and Central America, (2) across the Gulf of Mexico from the Gulf states to southern Mexico,

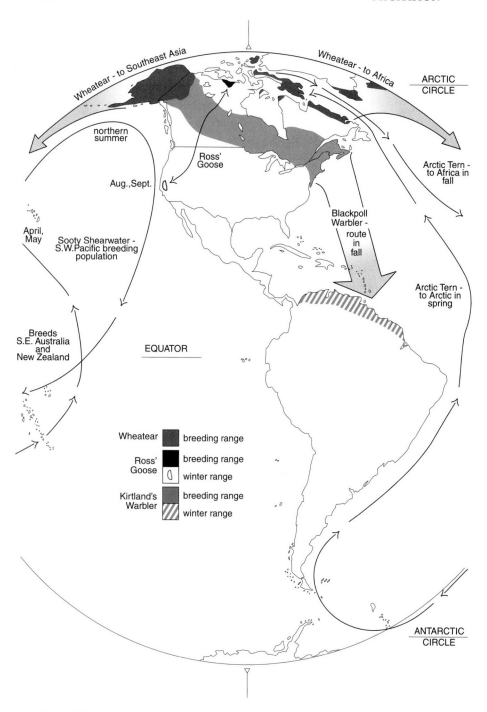

Fig. 18. *Migration routes.*

principally the Yucatán Peninsula, (3) island hopping from Florida across the Caribbean to South America, and (4) direct transatlantic flight from extreme northeastern Canada and the United States to South America. A great diversity of specific itineraries is included within these broad basic patterns.

Some migrants travel south by one route and north by another; others follow the same route in both directions. It seems that very few songbirds risk the southward passage over the Gulf of Mexico because of the less urgent nature of autumn migration, but most return northward across the Gulf. Several species with north/central breeding ranges (e.g., Western and Buff-breasted sandpipers, long-billed dowitcher, Connecticut Warbler) which are scarce or absent in spring in the east are regular fall migrants there.

Routes tend to be precisely followed and unvarying among individual birds and populations; however, different populations of widespread species may reach similar destinations by two or more different routes. Some pelagic birds with no fixed wintering area use less direct, less clearly defined routes, but wander in broad loops, in some cases taking more than a year to return to their breeding grounds but always doing so on schedule, sometimes even to the day.

Techniques by which routes are followed are discussed under NAVIGATION.

Manner of Flight. All nocturnal and most diurnal migrants propel themselves by the continual strenuous exertion of beating their wings. Tailwinds (see Effects of Weather, below) and flying in V formations (see Flocking, below) allow modest savings of energy, but most migrants must break their journeys regularly for food and rest. A few groups of birds have evolved methods of travel that are highly energy-efficient. Albatrosses and shearwaters are adapted for "sailing" long distances with little effort using wind currents (see FLIGHT), and species of pelicans, raptors, herons, storks, and cranes move largely by soaring high on updrafts of warm air currents called "thermals" (see Soaring under FLIGHT) and then drifting gradually and effortlessly in the direction of their destination. Some of the longest migratory journeys are accomplished using this method, the efficacy of which may be confirmed by a few observations indicating that soaring migrants seldom feed en route. Because thermals are not generated at night or over water, soaring birds migrate only by day and skirt large bodies of water (see Concentrations, below).

WHERE MIGRANTS GO. The winter destinations of birds vary widely among species and often among different populations of the same species. Overall, North American birds winter throughout the Western Hemisphere from the edge of northern pack ice to the Antarctic. A few species that breed in extreme northwestern Alaska winter in southern Asia and Australasia, and a few oceanic species also reach the Eastern Hemisphere in both oceans. A majority of migrant species winter between

the southern half of the United States and northern South America. Only about 25% of total species winters *exclusively* south of the U.S. border; i.e., the winter range of about 75% of migrant species is at least partially within North America. The winter range of about 20% of all North American migrants extends as far south as South America, though only about 5% winters *exclusively* on that continent. The majority of North American *species* that migrate to the Neotropics winter in Mexico, Central America, and the Caribbean Basin.

Winter ranges may be much more extensive than breeding ranges so that the northernmost wintering population of a given species may be hundreds, even thousands of miles away from the southernmost. Nesting Western Hemisphere Sanderlings, for example, are confined largely to the high arctic archipelago of Canada, but the species winters regularly in numbers from New England and the Pacific Northwest along Atlantic and Pacific coasts all the way to the southern tip of South America. Sanderlings tend to be comparable to or greater than breeding ranges in extent. On the other hand, many songbird species occupying vast breeding ranges that nearly span North America are constrained in winter to crowd into the southern isthmus of Middle America or a few Caribbean islands. Regardless of their extent, the wintering grounds of a particular species are usually well defined: virtually all Hudsonian Godwits winter in the southern third of South America; all Magnolia Warblers from southern Mexico through Panama. A few nonbreeding individuals often remain on the wintering grounds through the breeding season, just as stragglers occasionally remain north of the normal wintering range.

Banding has proven that individual birds of many species return to the same relatively restricted breeding *and* wintering areas year after year once adult patterns have been set; stops en route are also known to be precisely programmed in some species, and often coincide with the availability of a rich food source.

How Far? The world's longest migration route is that of the western arctic populations of the Arctic Tern, some members of which travel as far as 11,000 miles *each way* between breeding grounds and winter range near the Antarctic Circle (see Fig. 18). The American and Pacific Golden-Plovers, which fly 2,000–2,400 miles nonstop over the ocean from Alaska to mid-Pacific islands (Pacific) or from northeastern Canada to the West Indies (American), probably make the longest *uninterrupted* flights. Wilson's Storm-Petrel, which breeds on sub-Antarctic islands and approaches the Arctic Circle on its "wintering" grounds during the northern summer, holds the distance record for Southern Hemisphere breeders and for its order (the Procellariiformes); the Sooty Shearwater, which follows a similar itinerary, is a close second in both categories.

Few land-bird migrations approach these distances. However, Swainson's Hawk breeds as far north as central Alaska and winters almost exclusively on the Argentine pampas; both Barn and Cliff Swallows nest as far

north as the Subarctic and winter regularly south to central Argentina (the former reaching Tierra del Fuego with some frequency); and some Bobolinks commute between southern Canada and northern Argentina. (For distance in relation to time, see How Fast? below.)

Why the longest migration routes should have evolved is by no means clear. The notion occasionally advanced that Buff-breasted Sandpipers, for example, can find no suitable feeding habitat between their arctic breeding grounds and the Argentine grasslands where they winter is belied by their active and presumably successful exploitation of numerous open-country habitats during stopovers en route.

Excluding altitudinal migrants (see below), the *shortest* migrations are those of some northern seabirds, which move only as far south as the freezing of their marine habitat demands and birds that breed on the edge of the North Temperate Zone and must shift but a few hundred miles south to find adequate winter food supplies.

There is no correlation between species' physical capacities and the length of their migrations: many strong fliers are comparatively sedentary, while apparently feeble or hesitant fliers, such as rails, cover great distances. There is some correspondence, however, between the degree of latitude at which bird populations breed and the distances of their migrations. As one moves south in the North Temperate Zone, the percentage of long-distance migrants decreases and the percentage of nonmigratory species increases. Moreover, it has been proven that the northernmost breeding populations of many species winter the farthest south, leapfrogging the populations in between and traveling the maximum distance for their species. In such cases, the southernmost breeding populations often do not migrate at all.

Females of a few species have been shown to travel farther in migration than adult males of the same populations, and juvenile birds of at least some species tend to wander much farther afield in their first autumn than is normal for adults of their population. For example, of the small proportion of Northern Gannets that reach the Gulf of Mexico from their North Atlantic breeding grounds, the overwhelming majority are birds of the year. Juvenile Herring Gulls have a similar habit and travel even farther south. Such youthful wanderers do not always follow the route that is "normal" for their species (see Direction, above).

Finally, the extent of migration may vary within a single population (e.g., of Song Sparrows), with both migratory and nonmigratory individuals, as well as some birds that stay one year and go the next.

How Fast? "Cruising speeds" maintained during normal migratory flights are lower than maximum speeds attained by birds in chase situations or in aerial display. (For velocity records, see SPEED.) Generalizations supported by significant evidence include (1) waterbirds (including small sandpipers as well as larger, stronger fliers) migrate faster than

small songbirds; (2) long-distance migrants travel faster than those making shorter journeys; (3) migrant birds en route to their breeding grounds travel faster than they do when bound for winter quarters; (4) the average rate of travel increases as a migrant nears its final destination, because stops tend to be fewer; (5) speed increases with altitude; and (6) migrants tend to maintain a constant ground speed by exerting more or less effort in response to unfavorable or favorable winds, respectively.

Most migrating songbirds travel at airspeeds between 20 and 40 mph, larger species averaging faster than smaller. Species of ducks, pelagic birds, shorebirds, and falcons seem to average between 40 and 60 mph airspeed, but small shorebirds flying at high altitudes have been clocked at airspeeds exceeding 100 mph.

Duration of uninterrupted flight is a crucial factor in calculating overall rate of travel. Warblers and other small songbirds may average 30 miles per day during the first stages of their migration and increase to 200 or more as they approach their destinations. Likewise, migrants forced to stay aloft over long water crossings make better time overall than those able to land regularly. Homing experiments have produced rates of 250–300+ miles per day (for albatrosses, shearwaters, and petrels, which can, of course, rest periodically on the water); the Peregrine Falcon is known to be capable of at least 1,350 miles within 24 hours.

How High? In general: (1) Nocturnal migrants fly higher than diurnal migrants; in at least some cases the former gradually ascend and then descend during the course of a night's travel, reaching maximum altitude around the middle of the night. (2) Migrants tend to fly higher over land than over large expanses of water. (3) Perhaps obviously, migrants crossing high mountain ranges tend to fly at greater than average heights. The altitude record for a migrant bird is held by the Bar-headed Goose, flocks of which regularly cross the Himalayas flying at about 28,000 feet.

Nocturnal songbird migrants normally travel between 3,000 and 5,000 feet, but altitudes of between 8,000 and 10,000 feet are not unusual. Radar scans have picked up flocks (plausibly of long-distance, transoceanic migrants) as high as 21,000 feet. Clouds and other atmospheric conditions obviously affect the altitude at which birds can or prefer to migrate (see Effects of Weather, below).

At the opposite extreme, many daytime migrants fly well below 100 feet over land and especially over the sea; small, low-flying land birds sometimes barely clear the waves, and shearwaters regularly touch the surface with their wing tips.

Preparing to Migrate. Defining a bird's urge to migrate is akin to explaining various complex urges of our own, such as hunger. We recognize the feeling of hunger, we know it coincides with the body's need for food, and we realize, at least in some cases, that it is stimulated by some external source such as the smell of a freshly baked pie. But these

observations explain nothing about how the process works. The beginning of a bird's migratory urge is probably "external," e.g., a change in day length or temperature. This in turn triggers a physiological reaction, e.g., an "awakening" of the sexual glands in birds returning north in the spring. One well-documented symptom of the metabolic changes that occur in birds about to migrate is called "premigratory restlessness." As a species' characteristic departure time approaches, it becomes hyperactive and increasingly unable to rest during the night. The increased energy and the greater time in which to expend it are largely directed into a single activity—eating. The result is a prodigious accumulation of fat, the fuel supply for the great flight ahead.

It has been demonstrated, for example (Nisbet et al. 1963–FAT), that Blackpoll Warblers reach New England in September from their breeding grounds to the north and west and, after locating good feeding areas, gorge for several weeks until their weight reaches more than twice what it was on arrival (to 27 grams, up from 11–12 grams). On attaining this "signal" weight they take off as soon as weather conditions permit—typically following a cold front from the northwest—with enough "fuel" on them to fly up to 120 hours without stopping, more than enough to take them from New England to their wintering grounds in northern South America.

FLOCKING. Most migrant birds travel in groups, though individual songbird migrants are known to maintain considerable "flying room" around them and solitary migrants are not unusual. Migrant flocks may be composed of a single species, age, or sex, or a mixture of any or all of the three. Birds of different species that migrate together usually have similar migratory habits: manner of flight, speed, altitude, season, time of day, etc. Flocks of nocturnal migrants keep together by constant calling.

Advantages of flocking in migration include protection against predators, improved directional bearings due to consensus among experienced birds (particularly advantageous to juvenile birds), and, in the case of birds flying in V formation, energy conservation (see FLIGHT, V Formation).

Relatively little is known about the degree to which flocks remain together during the course of migration, on the wintering grounds, or through successive years. At least some species of anatids and cranes remain together in family groups from breeding grounds to wintering grounds and back to breeding grounds. Though the young birds usually form their immediate families during their first breeding season, they may still travel with the larger "extended family" group (see FLOCK).

EFFECTS OF WEATHER. Weather in the sense of climatic conditions is an essential element in the major theories on the origins of migration (see Why Birds Migrate, above).

Day-to-day weather conditions affect migrant birds much as they do traveling humans. Clouds, fog, and precipitation often result in poor visibility, greater expenditure of energy, and occasionally physical danger

(see Hazards, below). A clear atmosphere frees migrants from these negative factors, produces certain benefits, such as thermals for soaring birds (see How Birds Migrate, above, and Soaring under FLIGHT), and is often accompanied by favorable winds.

Wind is the most important single climatic element affecting bird migration. Recent analyses have shown that principal migration directions and routes coincide worldwide with prevailing directions of upper-level winds. It is reasonable to speculate that high-altitude migrants might evolve migration patterns that would coincide with consistent tailwinds. And this theory seems to be supported, for example, by the generally northwest-to-southeast direction of fall migration in North America and an absence of migrant concentrations in regions where winds blow consistently contrary to the course of migration. Further evidence of the influence of wind on migration appears in instances of reverse migration in which birds migrating with the prevailing wind will change their course when the wind does, even when this takes them in the opposite direction from their intended destination and exposes them to danger.

The northwest winds that accompany cold fronts in the fall are thought to act as a "green light" for birds that are "ready" to migrate.

See also WEATHER.

HAZARDS. When migrating, birds are more vulnerable due to lack of cover, the stresses and complexities of the long journey, and the vagaries of the weather. Traveling in the open, they are more susceptible than usual to predators. Merlins and Sharp-shinned Hawks, for example, rely on migrating smaller birds as food to maintain their own migratory energy levels.

It is well known that juvenile birds on their first migration are beset with problems. Some are led astray by confusing winds, others simply migrate in the wrong direction, while others find themselves far out to sea—where they perish. Both oceans become the final resting place for untold thousands of young migrants. While juveniles may be more vulnerable than adults, all are subject to climatic vagaries as well as physical imperfections and simple mistakes that can cause the death of millions of birds (see MORTALITY) or drive them thousands of miles off course. It is by such accidents that Black-and-white Warblers end up in the California desert and Fork-tailed Flycatchers on the coast of Maine, causing excitement among the birding community.

Of increasing concern to conservationists is harassment of coastal migrants, such as terns and shorebirds, which must rest and feed along certain beaches, mudflats, and marshes. The greatly increased recreational use of such places competes with the birds' need to make restorative stops. In some instances—e.g., the wasteful horseshoe crab fishery on Delaware Bay and elsewhere—we are depleting critical food supplies without which some of the most spectacular long-distance migrations

may be impossible. Other man-made hazards to migrant birds include lighthouses, skyscrapers, and communications towers, the lights of which attract nocturnal migrants, particularly in bad weather. Hundreds of birds frequently become disoriented by the light and injure or kill themselves against the structures as they fly about aimlessly (see THREATS (OF HUMAN ORIGIN) TO BIRDLIFE).

Birds are also vulnerable to toxic emissions that pollute the air along their migration routes.

CONCENTRATIONS. Nocturnal migrants tend to travel in fronts or "waves" that coincide with favorable/unfavorable weather patterns. This phenomenon often results in the arrival of a large number of birds of many species at favorable or opportune stopping points. Spectacular concentrations of migrants often occur as a result of bad weather, as when a "norte" meets a wave of migrants arriving on the U.S. Gulf coast from Mexico. When this happens, millions of exhausted birds concentrate on the first available landfall rather than dispersing northward as they normally would (see Gauthereaux and Moore in Able [1999]).

Concentrations also occur at the tips of certain peninsulas that lie in the path of a migration. Migrants following a coastline to the shortest crossing point between two shores "pile up" in the topographical cul-de-sac before they head out across the water (see POINT PELEE). A similar "funnel effect" can be expected where soaring migrants, which must avoid long water crossings, find a "bridge" or narrows between two large bodies of water (see CAPE MAY).

Soaring birds, particularly raptors, also concentrate along mountain ridges that parallel the migration route, where updrafts help keep the birds aloft (see HAWK MOUNTAIN).

VERTICAL MIGRATION. Many bird species that summer at high elevations move on a regular seasonal basis down to foothills or plains for the winter. Though they travel only a few thousand feet at most, these altitudinal migrants are responding to the same stimulus as the long-distance latitudinal migrants—namely, the need to retreat from a climate that cannot support them.

THE LITERATURE. The complexity and fascination of the migration phenomenon are reflected in the vast literature on the subject, much of it produced within the last 50 years. A brief treatment such as the above can only summarize richly detailed revelations, and the reader is urged to refer to the Bibliography, where some of the classic, most interesting and/or most readable works on migration are listed. For an excellent recent nontechnical summary see Able's (ed.) *Gatherings of Angels* (1999).

See also NAVIGATION.

MIMICRY. In a biological context, imitation in form, color, pattern, and/or behavior of one species by another to the advantage of the imita-

tor. So-called Batesian mimicry, in which a relatively uncommon species closely resembles a common but unpalatable or otherwise protected one and thereby gains security by disguise, is fairly common among insects but unknown in birds.

It has been suggested that the Zone-tailed Hawk has evolved to mimic the Turkey Vulture and thereby gains advantage over prey, which ignore vultures as harmless. (A similar claim has been made for the Common Black-Hawk and its look-alike, the Black Vulture.) There can be no question that the hawk strongly resembles the vulture in color, pattern, form, and distinctive manner of flight. But it has also been suggested that the similarity is attributable simply to parallel evolution of an aerodynamically sound "design" for a raptor that forages over an extensive area. For a discussion of the question, see Willis (*Condor,* 65:313); Willis (*Condor,* 68:104); Mueller (*Condor,* 74:221); and Zimmermann (*Condor,* 78:420).

For "mimicry" of habitat, see COLOR AND PATTERN, Concealment; for vocal mimicry, see SONG, Vocal Mimicry.

MIMIC THRUSH. A standard collective name for all 34 members of the family Mimidae (order Passeriformes), also known as the mockingbird or mockingthrush family. Sibley and Monroe (1993–SYSTEMATICS) place the group within its own tribe (Mimini) in the starling family (Sturnidae). The family includes the catbirds, mockingbirds, thrashers, and tremblers. Ten species of mimic thrushes breed in North America and two other species (Bahama and Blue Mockingbirds) have been recorded as vagrants (see Appendix II).

The mimic thrushes are medium-sized (8½–12 inches), mostly elongate songbirds, most of which have fairly long, narrow, decurved bills, pale (yellow, white, red) irises, relatively short, rounded wings, fairly long legs, and a long tail. A number of species are nearly uniform gray, brown, or black, while others are heavily streaked or spotted below.

The mimids are birds of brushy tangles, whether in the shrubby forest understory or sparse desert scrub. Many species inhabit open arid habitats. They forage largely on the ground in leaf litter, stony, dry riverbeds, and the like, feeding on small insects and other invertebrates as well as fruits and seeds. Some of the longer-billed thrashers probe into the soil for subterranean morsels. The butterfly-like flight of most mimics does not seem very efficient, and they are seldom seen to fly long distances, though several species are migratory.

The Northern Mockingbird is an extraordinarily talented vocal mimic, incorporating in its repertoire not only the songs of other birds but mechanical sounds as well, and in captivity readily imitates the human voice and other household noises (see SONG, Vocal Mimicry). Other members of the family also practice mimicry but none with the skill and enthusiasm of the Northern Mocker. Some mimids *never* imitate sounds,

but all have repetitive, elaborate "bubbly" songs sometimes punctuated with harsher chatterings and abrupt snaps and clucks.

The nests of this family are usually set fairly low in shrubs or small trees and hidden by dense vegetation; some species will nest on the ground. The nests may be basket-like, i.e., loosely woven of sticks, or made of finer materials and with a more compact shape, similar to the nests of many finches. The lining is of fine plant fibers, shredded bark, etc. Most species average 4–5 eggs (range: 2–7) but some average only 2–3. The eggs are pale to medium blue, immaculate or with fine or coarse reddish/brownish markings.

The mimic thrushes are a strictly New World family, ranging from southern Canada to the Patagonian desert (Argentina). Several of the North American species range continentwide, but there is an unusual variety of dry-country thrashers with local southwestern distributions.

See also MOCKINGBIRD; CATBIRD; THRASHER.

MIRROR (in wing). Occasionally used to refer (somewhat mysteriously) to the white spots in the black primary tips of many gull species. More rarely (but more plausibly) it is used as a synonym for speculum, the shiny area of feathers in the secondaries of many duck species. Compare WINDOW.

MIST NET. Now the most popular method of catching live birds for banding or marking, mist nets are made of very fine strands of black silk or nylon. They average between 30 and 40 feet in length and are available in various widths (3–7 feet) and mesh sizes. When hung between poles against a background of vegetation they are practically invisible, so that birds blunder into them and become harmlessly entangled.

In North America mist nets are available through biological suppliers, but only to licensed bird banders. For further details, see BANDING.

MITE. See FEATHER MITES; ECTOPARASITE.

MOBBING. See Fig. 19. The harassing of a predatory species, often by mixed flocks of smaller passerines. Perched owls and hawks are frequently victims of noisy groups of tits, nuthatches, warblers, wrens, and other species, which call at, fly at, and, rarely, even strike at the presumed threat. Grackles, jays, and other nest robbers are "mobbed" in flight by

Fig. 19. *"Mobbing"* of owls in their daytime roosts is a strong, innate defensive urge in many forest birds. This is why imitating or playing a tape of screech- or pygmy-owls will reliably lure any birds within earshot. Notice that one of the chickadees is engaged in feeding actions and the thrush is preening its breast, both "irrelevant" expressions of the birds' ambivalence about whether to flee from the predator or act aggressively toward it (see REDIRECTION).

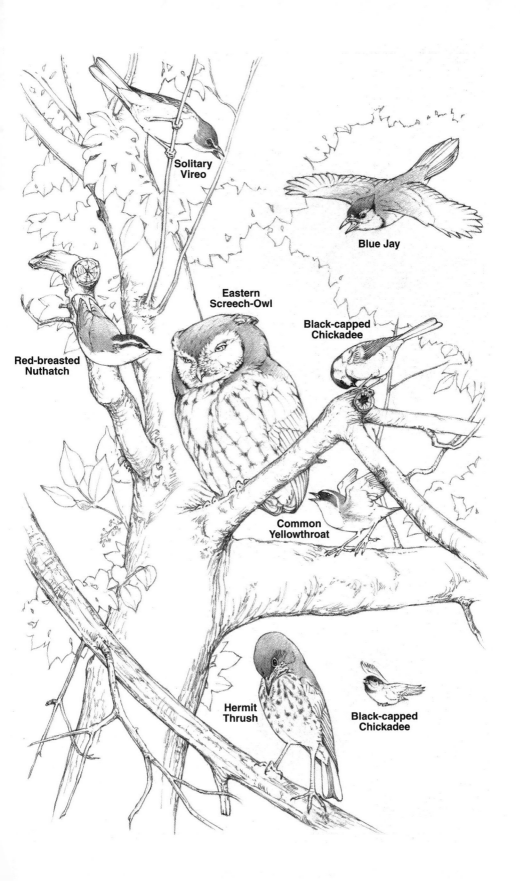

Solitary
Vireo

Blue Jay

Eastern
Screech-Owl

Black-capped
Chickadee

Red-breasted
Nuthatch

Common
Yellowthroat

Hermit
Thrush

Black-capped
Chickadee

tyrant flycatchers and other medium-sized species, and flocks of crows and jays harry owls and hawks in a similar manner. It seems clear that the activity is a collective response to a common danger (participants are known to cross territorial boundaries in joining such mobs), but whether the intention is to drive the enemy away or simply to alert the avian community to the threat is unclear. The degree of feverish displacement activities (feeding, preening) often evident among members of a mob suggests that their response is an ambivalent mixture of fear and aggression. See especially Curio (1978). There is also evidence (Knight and Temple 1988) that the identity of the predator affects the intensity of mobbing: mobbing seems to decrease as the size of the predator increases, for example, but a high degree of perceived threat tends to heighten the mobbing response.

It is, of course, the mobbing response that birders take advantage of when they imitate alarm calls (see PISHING) and owl "songs."

MOCKINGBIRD. Standard English name for 16 members of the family Mimidae or Sturnidae (order Passeriformes), most of them in the genus *Mimus*. The name is sometimes used as a collective to refer to the family as a whole (the mockingbirds). The Northern Mockingbird *(Mimus polyglottos)* is a common and widespread resident of the southern half of North America and northern Mexico. It is one of our best-known songbirds and among the most accomplished (and obsessive) vocal mimics in the world (see SONG). Along with several other "southern" species (e.g., Northern Cardinal, Tufted Titmouse), the Northern Mockingbird has extended its breeding range significantly northward in the last 50 years. The 1956 edition of Peterson's *Field Guide to the Birds* gives the northern limit of the main population of Northern Mockingbirds as Maryland, with "a few north to Massachusetts." By 1982 the species is a common resident of Massachusetts and breeds locally in Newfoundland (see DISTRIBUTION). The other species of mockingbirds are distributed in the Caribbean and Latin America. Two of these, the Bahama and Blue Mockingbirds, have been recorded in southern Florida and southern Texas respectively as vagrants (see Appendix II).

For general characteristics of the mockingbird family (which also includes the catbirds and thrashers), see MIMIC THRUSH.

MOLECULAR SYSTEMATICS. See SYSTEMATICS.

MOLT. The process by which a bird renews a part or all of its plumage, including the growth of new feathers (endysis) as well as the loss of the old (ecdysis). Sometimes, confusingly, "molt" is used to mean the shedding process only. Other types of plumage changes—such as those caused by feather wear—and the shedding of parts other than feathers are sometimes encompassed in a looser definition of the term (see Nonfeather Molt, below).

A bird's plumage is crucial to its survival. Its specific functions vary greatly from one type of bird to another, but for most it serves at least as insulation, protection, transportation, and identity. Plumage also wears out by normal friction (see ABRASION), is eaten by a variety of live-in pests (see ECTOPARASITE), and is vulnerable to accidental damage (see THREATS (OF HUMAN ORIGIN) TO BIRDLIFE). These facts of birdlife explain the need for periodic molting.

PHYSIOLOGY. Complex, variable, and incompletely understood, but based on the best current evidence, the following may be ventured. The shedding of most feathers seems to result from being pushed out of place by the growth of the incoming feather (see FEATHER), i.e., the old feather plays no active role in the molt. The exceptions are the cases (e.g., ducks, owls) in which all the wing or tail feathers fall out at once (see Order of Feather Loss, below).

It is the thyroid hormone thyroxin that stimulates the growth of new feathers and regulates the timing of molt. Thyroxin is therefore crucial to the process, and experiments have shown that its presence or absence (artificially controlled) can stimulate or obstruct the process in certain circumstances. However, it is the sexual glands (gonads) that apparently control molt overall. Secretion of the sexual hormones (which trigger thyroid and other reactions) is, in turn, influenced by environmental factors, such as amount of daylight and (especially in the tropics) rainfall.

FREQUENCY. Birds molt more frequently in their first year of life than in any subsequent year, due to the down and/or juvenal plumages, which are, of course, unique to young birds. In addition to these two relatively brief stages, a first-year bird will also undergo the usual adult molts into a winter plumage and (often) into a summer ("breeding") plumage the following spring (see Molt/Plumage Sequence, below). Thus, yearling birds, in many cases, molt their body feathers three times to an adult's twice. A few birds (kingfishers, woodpeckers, the odd passerine) are completely naked until the juvenal plumage grows in and so *skip* a molt in the first year; other species (e.g., petrels and owls) have two down coats and so *add* one.

All adult birds molt at least once annually, and most birds renew all of their flight feathers annually, though this may take place throughout the year rather than all at once, and some eagles and cranes molt wing feathers over a span of two years. Many species molt only once a year, following the breeding season, at which time they renew their entire plumage. But a significant number—especially those species that migrate long distances or are otherwise subject to heavy feather wear—undergo at least a partial molt *before* the breeding season as well.

Drake Oldsquaws, departing from the normal pattern of male ducks in the Northern Hemisphere (see Eclipse Plumage, below), have a distinctive winter plumage (October to April), a spring plumage through the end of June, followed by the "eclipse" stage. A complete renewal of all feathers

is achieved only after a full year's cycle, but most feathers are changed twice, and the longest scapular feathers are replaced three times in this species.

Ruffs (males) undergo three annual molts—a "supplemental" plumage intervenes in late winter between the basic (winter) and alternate ("breeding") plumages—and other species of sandpipers are suspected of doing likewise. *Passerina* buntings (e.g., Indigo Bunting) also have a supplemental molt. See Thompson (1991) and Rohwer et al. (1992).

Ptarmigan typically molt before the breeding season into their brown "summer" plumage, then begin a partial molt that leaves blotches of white amid the brown, and finally (in response to low temperature) change into their snow-white plumage. As many as four individual molts are perceived in this sequence by some authorities.

DATE AND DURATION. Timing of molt generally correlates with rhythms of the breeding cycle and therefore varies widely among species. Adults of some arctic-breeding shorebirds begin to molt into basic (winter) plumage as early as June before starting south in July, whereas double-brooded passerines in warmer climates may not begin this pre-basic ("post-breeding") molt until August or September. A similar-range applies to the pre-alternate molt, which can take place in February for early nesters or not be complete until May for arctic species.

The calendar for birds that breed in the Southern Hemisphere is, of course, reversed, and for some seabirds that skip a breeding season, molt may extend throughout the year. Given the many variations and the protracted nature of the process, it is clear that something is molting somewhere year round.

The dropping of any given feather is of course more or less instantaneous—even the simultaneous shedding of the flight feathers of the wing as in ducks usually takes only a matter of hours. It is the growth of the new feathers that takes time—how much time varying greatly among different species according to genetic characteristics, age, climate, and, of course, whether the molt is partial or complete. Individual primaries and tail feathers of House Sparrows can attain full growth in 19–23 days (Zeidler 1966), whereas those of the Eurasian Kestrel take 45 and 50 days (Welty 1988–ORNITHOLOGY). Flight feathers of ducks (dropped simultaneously) may not be functional for 3 weeks to a month, and swans can remain flightless for up to 7 weeks. Birds that lose feathers traumatically tend to replace them faster than they would in the course of a normal molt.

With certain exceptions (see Order of Feather Loss, below), birds lose feathers gradually rather than all at once, the span of a full molt running from the loss of the first "old" feather(s) until the last "new" one(s) is (are) fully grown. A complete molt in passerines as a rule is encompassed between the dropping of the first flight feather and the full growth of the last one. This period tends to be shorter in long-distance migrants than in sedentary birds. The pre-basic ("post-breeding") molt may take as little as

a month for some migrant songbirds, though the 49–56 days recorded for the Northern Wheatear (Williamson 1957) is probably closer to the average. By comparison, the nonmigratory House Sparrow averages 82 days to complete the same molt (Zeidler 1966). And as noted above, some raptors (and other birds) shed and regenerate some feathers continually and do not complete a cycle for about two years.

Natal down feathers are pushed out on the tips of the incoming juvenal feathers and fall off almost immediately. The scant down of songbird nestlings is lost within a few days of hatching. The precocial chicks of many waterbirds lose their heavy down coat more slowly and gradually and may retain vestiges of this first plumage for 6 weeks or more. The body feathers of the juvenal plumage are relatively transitory in passerines, in some cases yielding to the first basic (winter) plumage before the juvenal wing and tail feathers are fully grown. But in shorebirds, gulls, raptors, and other large nonpasserines it persists as a major plumage coat. In both cases flight feathers remain until the second complete molt.

Another molt variable is the time required to reach "adult" plumage. There is a measure of ambiguity here since some species achieve adult *plumage* before they are sexually mature, while others are ready to breed though still superficially subadult. However, many small perching birds acquire a "definitive" plumage within three months of hatching. Others (e.g., Rose-breasted Grosbeak) spend a year in a recognizable "immature" plumage. Adult plumages remain "imperfect" (i.e., subadult) for several years in many species, and not a few (e.g., gulls, gannets) pass through distinctive stages over 3, 4, or 5 years. It has been reported that some eagles do not attain a fully "definitive" plumage for 8–10 years, though 5 or 6 seems to be the norm.

Most migratory species complete their pre-basic molt before departing for winter quarters, but swallows and some hawks, falcons, and flycatchers delay the process until they reach their destination.

EXTENT. The molt of natal down (if any) is, of course, complete. The subsequent juvenal plumage may be shed completely in favor of the first basic (winter) plumage, but in many species the wing and tail feathers of this first coat of contour feathers are retained through the first year. If there is a spring molt, it, too, is usually partial, omitting the flight feathers. A number of so-called breeding plumages result from feather wear and some heightening of pigment rather than feather renewal. Sharp-tailed Sparrows and Bobolinks, in contrast, are known to undergo a complete molt into their spring plumage.

The molt that follows the breeding period in adults is complete in almost all birds, though it may be delayed (see under *Duration,* above). Long-term, continuous molting of flight feathers in certain eagles and the "eclipse" molt of ducks (see *Sequence,* below) are, of course, not consistent with a single, complete pre-basic molt.

The extent of molt has been tied, in the Phainopepla (Miller 1933), to the length of the breeding period. In a late-breeding, migratory population in California, young birds underwent an incomplete post-juvenal molt as compared to the complete molt in juvenals of an early-breeding, resident population of the same subspecies.

There is some evidence that molt is sexually dimorphic in some species. Nolan (1978), for example, notes an apparently more complete pre-alternate molt into spring plumage in male Prairie Warblers than in females.

MOLT/PLUMAGE SEQUENCE AND ITS TERMINOLOGY. See Fig. 20. Despite many variations in frequency, duration, and extent of molt, all birds change their feathers according to a regular sequence, which is highly predictable for any one species and is surprisingly consistent for all birdlife. To compare the differences, it is obviously necessary to have a standard terminology for referring to each distinctive plumage and the intervening molts. Early terminology that became traditional was proposed by Dwight (1900) on the basis of his studies in New York State. In 1959, Humphrey and Parkes proposed a new terminology intended to be more broadly applicable and to refine certain concepts. The basic differences in the two systems are these: (1) Dwight's terminology has a North Temperate Zone bias. What he calls "winter" plumage can with equal accuracy be called a "summer" plumage in the case of pelagic species that breed in the Southern Hemisphere during their summer and migrate to the Northern for our summer (their winter). Furthermore, molts of tropical species are usually correlated with wet and dry seasons, which are not completely analogous to our summer and winter. Humphrey and Parkes replaced "winter" with "basic" to refer to that plumage that is acquired annually in almost all birds by a complete molt regardless of season. The partial molt undergone annually by many species then produces an "alternate" plumage in the Humphrey-Parkes terminology. (2) Dwight ties his sequence to the breeding season, e.g., "first pre-nuptial molt," "first nuptial plumage." This makes it difficult to compare sequences of tropical species that breed more than once a year and pelagics and others that breed only every other year. Furthermore, many species are not yet ready to engage in nuptial activities in their first "nuptial" plumage. "Nuptial" also implies that breeding is the *reason* that alternate plumages evolved; while theories of sexual selection suggest that this may be so, it has not been clearly established. The term "alternate" accommodates these issues.

Humphrey and Parkes also suggested the following refinements: (1) All molts should be named according to the incoming plumage, e.g., "post-juvenal" becomes "first pre-basic. (2) A "plumage" is defined as only those feathers acquired in the preceding molt. Dwight's nuptial plumage includes all of a bird's feathers worn after the pre-nuptial molt; in the Humphrey-Parkes terminology this "plumage" would not include the flight feathers retained from the basic (winter) plumage. The broad use

of "plumage" to mean all the feathers currently worn is replaced in Humphrey-Parkes by "feather-coat." (3) Once the appearance of a bird's plumage has ceased to change with age it is called "definitive." This obviates the necessity of counting plumages after this point: a bird can be said to be in definitive basic plumage rather than its eighth (or eighteenth) winter plumage—unless, of course, its eighth basic (winter) plumage does show a change from the preceding.

The Humphrey-Parkes system has not been accepted universally (see Stresemann 1963 and Rohwer et al. 1992), but they are followed in most recent ornithological publications and field guides. The Dwight system is now little used, but prevails, of course, in works written before about 1970. In the summary of plumage sequences immediately below, the Humphrey-Parkes names are given first, but the Dwight names are noted in parentheses. In addition to Humprey-Parkes, it is customary (despite the anomalies noted above) to refer to plumages with seasonal designations, so that Dwight's "nuptial" plumage translates as "alternate plumage" in Humprey-Parkes and is commonly known as "spring" or "summer plumage." It is also common to hear (or read) "breeding plumage," though, of course, this makes the same evolutionary presumption as "nuptial."

Natal Down (Natal Down). Present to some degree in most birds; lacking in woodpeckers, kingfishers, some passerines; scant in cuckoos, trogons, hummingbirds, and most passerines (winter breeding crossbills exceptional); thick and virtually complete in hawks, owls, gallinaceous birds, and most waterbirds; some swifts are naked when hatched and acquire a heavy down covering; petrels and many owls have two successive down coats; hawks and eagles have two overlapping down coats of different textures.

Pre-juvenal Molt (Post-natal Molt). Always complete; down feathers attached to tips of juvenal feathers drop off soon after appearance of new feather.

Juvenal Plumage (Juvenal Plumage). First true contour feathers, but plumage appears "looser," softer, fluffier than following, and tail feathers are often distinctively shaped. A brief stage in passerines, with body feathers sometimes molting before flight feathers are fully grown; longer lasting in raptors, many waterbirds, etc.

First Pre-basic Molt (Post-juvenal Molt). May be complete but often flight feathers of juvenal plumage are retained.

First Basic Plumage (First Winter Plumage). May closely resemble adult winter plumage or be distinct in color and pattern; this and following plumages that are not "definitive" (see above) are often called "immature" plumages; worn at least through the first winter.

First Pre-alternate Molt (First Pre-nuptial Molt). Does not occur in all species; is usually partial (flight feathers retained) when does occur, but is complete at least in a few species.

First Alternate Plumage (First Nuptial Plumage). Also called "spring," "summer" or "breeding," plumage. Usually brighter than basic (winter) plumage, sometimes due to feather wear and/or fading rather than feather renewal (e.g., European Starling, Snow Bunting); some species acquire special features, e.g., plumes, "extra" patches of color; retained only through the breeding period; yearling birds of some species indistinguishable from adults in this plumage.

Second Pre-basic Molt (First Post-nuptial Molt). Almost invariably complete (some raptors and cranes prolong change of flight feathers over two years); migratory species usually complete before departure; some delay until wintering grounds.

Second Basic Plumage (Second Winter Plumage). Most species show no signs of "immature" plumage by this stage and their plumage can then be called "definitive basic" or "adult winter."

Subsequent molts and plumages follow the same timing and duration pattern as this second cycle, though the plumage patterns of a number of species (e.g., gulls) continue to change for 4 or 5 years and continue to be numbered accordingly. It is routine in field guides, for example, to find distinctive gull plumages labeled as "3rd winter," etc.

Eclipse Plumage. In most male ducks of the Northern Hemisphere the pre-alternate molt begins in the fall and is completed in the winter rather than occurring near the beginning of the breeding season as in most birds that undergo such a molt.

The basic ("winter") plumage in ducks, which is assumed during summer (after the eggs are laid), is, as in most birds, dull in comparison to the nuptial plumage, resembling, in fact, the relatively unchanging female plumage. Because of this dullness and the "premature" beginning of the pre-alternate molt, the basic plumage seems more like a brief effacing of the drakes' bright breeding plumage than the more usual long-term basic (winter) plumage. However, except for the timing and the fact that ducks drop all their wing and tail feathers simultaneously in the pre-basic (post-nuptial) molt, the term "eclipse" could be applied with equal accuracy to the basic (winter) plumage of the Scarlet Tanager. The latter simply lasts longer.

Exceptions are male Ruddy Ducks, which have a "normal" pre-alternate (pre-nuptial) molt in spring, and Oldsquaws, which have summer, winter, *and* eclipse plumages (see above).

ORDER OF FEATHER LOSS. Except for a slightly unkempt appearance or gaps in the wings of large birds in flight, the molting process seldom comes to our attention. This is because in the vast majority of species it occurs over a period of weeks or months in an overlapping and symmetrical order without sudden changes or conspicuous bare patches.

The order in which feathers are lost is part of a bird's genetic heritage and is so consistent for a given species or groups that it has been used as

a taxonomic character. However, a few generalities may be ventured regarding molt sequence.

A complete molt (usually the pre-basic) normally begins with the innermost (first) primaries of each wing (see Figs. 20 and 35); when these two feathers have dropped and the new first primaries are partially grown, the two second primaries are shed, and so on. In some cases, the first and seventh primaries are shed simultaneously and the molt proceeds outward from two (actually four) starting points. When about half the primaries are molted, the tertials begin to drop from the outermost (first) inward. The first (outermost) secondary falls after the loss of the third (last) tertial and is also succeeded inward. Clearly, the gradual, sequential, and symmetrical pattern of this molt is crucial in maintaining the ability to fly—which, in turn, is a small bird's greatest asset in avoiding predators.

The molt of the tail feathers follows a similar pattern. In most species, it begins with the central pair of rectrices and proceeds outward in opposite directions; in a few, the sequence is exactly the reverse; and in fewer still, an intermediate pair is the first to fall and the sequence proceeds both inward and outward. Woodpeckers and Brown Creepers, in which the tail molt proceeds outward, retain the two central feathers for support in perching until the other rectrices are well grown.

The molting of the body feathers begins during the wing molt and has been shown to follow a highly predictable progression in at least some species. Baird (1958) chronicles this progression in male Brown-headed Cowbirds undergoing their (incomplete) first pre-basic (post-juvenal) molt. He finds that the first area of body feathers to complete the molt sequence is the breast, followed by the nape, and that the underwing areas are completed last. Following the nape, the other head feathers of juvenal cowbirds are molted in the following order: throat, lores, crown, forehead, chin, malar area, auriculars, and orbital area. Except for the breast, the other regions of the body (back, belly, sides, flanks, rump) progress more or less simultaneously (though gradually). Baird further observed that within each body region feathers are lost and regained in a consistent direction, e.g., the nape feathers from the inside out (centrifugally); the lores from the outside in (centripetally); the back feathers from front to back and from the center toward the edges; and the belly feathers from front to back and from the edges toward the center. In general, the feathers at the periphery of the feather tracts are molted last, and in immature cowbirds the molt process often comes to an end before these last juvenal feathers are shed.

The sudden loss of many feathers at once in healthy birds is characteristic of only a few groups of birds. Loons, grebes, anhingas, flamingoes, ducks, geese, and swans, most rails, many alcids, and dippers lose their wing feathers simultaneously and so are rendered flightless for a period ranging from a few days (dippers) to 7 weeks (swans). Ducks, geese, and

swans also lose all their tail feathers at once during this molt, and smaller owls lose just their tail feathers in this precipitous manner.

The relative helplessness of ducks while flightless is a plausible factor in the evolution of the dull eclipse plumage, which "conceals" their normally conspicuous plumage from potential predators.

A few members of the crow family, e.g., Blue Jay, shed all head and neck feathers in a very short period, resulting in many queries to Audubon societies and on-line bird chat rooms about "bald" jays.

IRREGULAR AND ABNORMAL MOLTS. It should be clear from the preceding section that most birds seen lacking a tail or other feathers have lost them accidentally. Such losses regenerate within a few weeks rather than waiting for the next normal molting period. However, it has been demonstrated in some species that the replacement feathers are "subtracted," so to speak, from the upcoming molt and will not be shed again at that time. Thus, if one were to pluck a Scarlet Tanager in basic (winter) plumage, the red feathers of the upcoming alternate (breeding) plumage will come in, producing a splotchy effect. Birds have been made to delay or skip molts in laboratory experiments, but wild individuals whose plumage is "out of sync" with that of its fellows can be presumed to be suffering from a disease or other abnormality. For other irregularities of this kind, see PLUMAGE, Abnormal Variation.

NONFEATHER MOLT. As noted in the definition (above), molt is sometimes used broadly as a synonym for "shed." Thus, puffins and auklets in the genera *Cerorhinca* and *Aethia* and American White Pelicans, which acquire bill sheaths or ornaments prior to the breeding season, are said to "molt" them afterward. The term is also applied to the egg tooth and heel pads found in nestling birds. In defense of this usage the keratin acquisition and loss involved is presumably under similar physiological control and has similar genetic controls as feather molt.

MOLT MIGRATION. Certain bird species, e.g., loons, grebes, and waterfowl, which molt all their flight feathers simultaneously, routinely move to a well-defined "molting grounds" each year. This is typically an isolated area where presumably they gain added protection from predators during this period of extreme vulnerability.

MONOMOY National Wildlife Refuge (Massachusetts). A 10-mile-long sand spit (at present two separate islands) extending southward from the "elbow" of Cape Cod into Nantucket Sound. At times Monomoy has been accessible by foot (albeit wet foot) from the mainland, but its fragile form is subject to the whims of winter storms, and at present it must be reached by boat. Because it is out of reach for the casual beachgoer, Monomoy has remained a true coastal wilderness, combining unspoiled ocean beach, dunes, tidal flats, migrant-trapping copses of bayberry and beach plum,

Fig. 20. *Molt sequence.* The illustration shows the sequence in which feathers change during the molting cycle of a male Chestnut-sided Warbler: 1a—Juvenal Plumage acquired in a complete molt following natal down stage. 2b—First Basic (First Winter) Plumage; flight feathers of wing and tail retained from Juvenal plumage. 3c—First Alternate (First Summer or Breeding) Plumage; body plumage brighter, shows adult characteristics; flight feathers still retained. 4d—Second Basic (Second Winter) Plumage; a complete molt including flight feathers. 5e—Second/Definitive Alternate (Second Summer or Breeding) Plumage; full adult breeding plumage attained through molt of body feathers; flight feathers retained from Second Basic Plumage. The sequence then alternates annually between 4 and 5—Definitive Basic and Definitive Alternate Plumages. 6—Flight feathers of the wing are molted and replaced in an overlapping sequence to maximize flying ability. Primaries change from innermost outward; tertials change halfway through primary sequence from outermost to innermost (not shown) and after the last tertial falls the secondaries molt from outermost to innermost. 7—Tail feathers molt beginning with middle two and moving outward symmetrically in opposite directions. For more detail and variations, see MOLT and Fig. 15 (gulls).

freshwater "kettle" ponds, and—because of its seaward-jutting length—excellent vantage points for watching pelagic birds without risking sea-sickness. Virtually every species of bird ever recorded in Massachusetts has been seen on Monomoy, and it seems to harbor at least one avian rarity—arctic, western, tropical, or Eurasian—continually. The 2,700-acre refuge includes part of Morris Island (connected by bridge to the mainland at Chatham), where the management office is located. Unless you have boat-owning friends in the area, the best access to Monomoy is by private charter from Chatham.

MONOPHAGOUS (mo-NAH-fa-gus). Tolerant of only a single type of food. The Snail (Everglade) Kite, for example, apparently feeds on nothing but the large snails in the genus *Pomacea*. Needless to say, the fate of monophagous birds is closely linked with that of their preferred food. If "apple" snails disappear due to disease or draining of wetlands, Snail Kites may also be at risk.

MONOTYPIC. Referring to a taxonomic category that contains only a single representative of the category immediately below it. The loon family, Gaviidae, is monotypic since it contains only a single genus, *Gavia*. However, the genus *Gavia* is polytypic, since it contains 4 species. An example of a monotypic genus is *Dolichonyx*, which contains only the Bobolink *(D. oryzivorus)*, and the American Avocet, which has not been divided into subspecies, is a monotypic species. It is not possible to have a single subspecies; there must be either none or more than one.

MONTANE. Of the mountains; montane birds are those characteristic of elevations at least 1,000 feet (usually higher) above sea level. A montane region is generally determined by the presence of plant or animal life that is distinct from that of the lowlands. This transition takes place gradually, of course, with increase in elevation and consequent change in climate, and it varies from one highland region to another, so that some montane zones begin lower than others. The alpine zone above tree line is sometimes treated as distinct from the montane zone, immediately below.

MONTEREY (California). This region of coastal California, including the Monterey Peninsula, Pacific Grove, Point Lobos, and Big Sur immediately to the south, offers some of the best Pacific waterbirding at any season as well as excellent land-birding in adjacent pine/oak and redwood groves. The municipal pier in Monterey has been the starting point for many a fine pelagic trip; boats can be chartered at will, but local bird clubs run a number of trips a year at appreciably less cost to the individual (see Appendix VI for species timing). A few of the specialties of the greater Monterey region are (birds marked with an asterisk are best seen at sea):

Black-footed Albatross,* a variety of shearwaters* and storm-petrels,* Brandt's and Pelagic Cormorants, numbers of sea ducks, Black Oystercatcher, Black Turnstone, Wandering Tattler, Rock Sandpiper, Western, Glaucous-winged, and Thayer's Gulls, a variety of alcids,* Steller's and Scrub Jays, Chestnut-backed Chickadee, Pygmy Nuthatch, Varied Thrush (winter), Hutton's Vireo, Townsend's and Hermit Warblers, and Cassin's Finch (winter). Sea otters are common in coastal kelp beds, and the wintering hordes of monarch butterflies at Pacific Grove are another non-avian winter diversion.

MONTEZUMA, c. 1480–1520 (Montezuma, or Harlequin, Quail: *Cyrtonyx montezumae*). Chief of the Aztecs, who were the indigenous rulers of much of Mexico until their empire fell to Cortez and his conquistadors. Most of this quail's range lies in Mexico; it reaches the United States only in southernmost Arizona, New Mexico, and western Texas.

MOON WATCHING. A technique for studying certain aspects of nocturnal bird migration, made popular by Lowery and Newman (Newman 1952). The procedure for collecting the raw data is quite simple. In a typical instance an observer trains an ordinary 20× spotting telescope on the face of the moon, usually from two days before to two days after the full moon, when the maximum lunar surface is illuminated. Birds seen flying across the moon are recorded in terms of their numbers, the size of their image, the time of their passing, and their direction in relation to the moon face, e.g., "9 o'clock to 3 o'clock." If to this information the observer adds the elevation of the moon—obtained by fastening a protractor to the side of the scope—he or she can then calculate the real direction and number of birds passing on a mile front using a formula and table devised by Nisbet (1959).

Antedating the study of nocturnal migration by RADAR, moon watching yielded much new information on numbers of migrants, the importance of "flyways" (relatively slight), spatial density (individual migrating songbirds tend to maintain wide spacing rather than travel in compact flocks), and the influence of wind (relatively great), among other data.

See MIGRATION.

MOORHEN. Standard English name for 5 species of wetland birds all in the genus *Gallinula* (Family Rallidae; order Gruiformes). Closely related to the gallinules and coots, the moorhens are distributed worldwide except for the highest latitudes. The Common Moorhen, once known as Common Gallinule, is distributed through much of the Old World as well as the New. Its North American distribution is peculiar: widespread east of the Mississippi and from most of Mexico southward, but absent or local in the West. It also seems to have a different "personality" here than in at

least part of its European range: here a rather retiring marsh bird; there an almost sociable lawn forager in public parks. "Moor" in this context is used in the archaic sense of "marsh," rather than as a term for heathland.

MORPHOLOGY (morphological). In the strictest sense, morphology is form or the study thereof. However, in zoology, it is now widely applied to any structural aspect of an organism whether external or internal. For example, both the pattern of intestinal loops and the position of the toes in birds are known as "morphological taxonomic characters."

MORPH. Literally "form." In biology, a variation—among birds most conspicuous in plumage coloration—that occurs with some frequency *within a population of a species.* In general, the phenomenon is presumed to arise as an adaptation to an environmental condition and to confer some selective advantage. The red/gray color morphs of Ruffed Grouse, for example, are thought to match local vegetation and thus enhance concealment from predators. Some of the more readily recognized morphs among North American birds include the light, dark, and intermediate morphs of the Northern Fulmar; the white and "blue" morphs of the "Lesser" Snow Goose; the light and dark morphs of the Rough-legged, Ferruginous, Red-tailed, Swainson's, and Short-tailed Hawks; the red and gray morphs of the Ruffed Grouse and Screech and Flammulated Owls; the white and gray morphs of the Great Blue Heron; the white and red morphs of the Reddish Egret; the light and dark ("Cory's") morphs of the Least Bittern; the almost infinite variations in the alternate (nuptial) plumage of the male Ruff; the light, dark, and intermediate morphs of the jaegers and skuas (especially Parasitic and Pomarine); and the "ringed" or "bridled" and "plain" morphs of the Common Murre. This kind of variation should not be confused with "deeper" genetic distinctions between similar species (e.g., the sapsuckers), with consistent age, sex, or seasonal variations or with abnormal conditions such as albinism or melanism.

In the past "phase" was widely used as a synonym for morph, but this term has an implication of transience (e.g., the phases of the moon) and is being . . . phased out.

See also COLOR AND PATTERN; POLYMORPHISM; and Fig. 23.

MORTALITY. Sheltered as many of us now are from the majority of nature's deadliest ravages by recent discoveries in medicine and other technologies, we are inclined to be appalled at the comparatively huge mortality rates sustained by birds and other forms of animal life. It has been estimated, for example, that during the nestling stage, when vulnerability is generally greatest, the *average* mortality rate among passerine birds is about 50% (Nice 1957). Within this average there is enormous variation based on species biology, food supply, weather conditions in a

given season, and many other unpredictable factors obtaining only locally. But the average shows that for every circumstance in which 90% of
passerine nestlings survive, there exists another in which 90% perish. Nor
does maturity bring any great security. The toll that weather, predation,
and the "success" of our own species take on bird populations makes a
bird species' normal life span totally inconsistent with its expected
longevity in captivity (see AGE).

The many instances of awesomely vast "natural" mortalities of
birdlife now documented seem at first to encourage the notion that bird
populations must be invulnerable to any threats posed by human agency.
But natural mortalities are redressed by long-term counterbalances that
have been built into the rhythm of nature over eons. Species that are subject to heavy predation or that suffer great annual losses due to the many
hazards of long-distance migration, for example, tend to compensate for
the drain on their overall population with such biological characteristics
as large clutch size and number of broods, density within breeding
niches, broad total range, colonial nesting, etc. Thus, when 148,000 waterfowl succumb to hailstorms in Alberta over a 22-month period (Smith
and Webster 1955–WEATHER) or untold thousands of songbird migrants
are drowned in Lake Huron due to adverse weather conditions during
their crossing (Saunders 1907) or like numbers of Dovekies are stranded
ashore by fall gales and die of starvation or predation by gulls (Snyder
1960), the populations of the species involved recover fully and, as it were,
automatically. We may notice temporary population declines locally, as in
the well-documented decimation of the northeastern bluebird population during early-spring ice storms in 1940 or declines of Carolina Wrens
after very harsh winters in the northeast, e.g., in 1978–79, but we can confidently predict a rapid recovery from such natural cataclysms, unless,
like the California Condor, the species as a whole is reaching the end of its
tenure on the planet.

So integrated into the maintenance of population stability are such
normal mortality factors as weather and predation that, viewed objectively, they can be seen as beneficial influences that keep us from being
buried in warblers or Dovekies (see also POPULATION; PREDATION).

In sharp contrast to the ecological give-and-take that ultimately permits the harmonious coexistence of an unimaginable variety of organisms
are the occasional great upsets that devastate a wide range of organisms
on many fronts and thereby ultimately alter the whole system profoundly.
One good example of this sort of upset is a major ice age. Another is humanity's recent domination of the earth. The resiliency of bird populations is amply demonstrated in their ability to sustain multiple losses such
as those cited above, but within the last 300 years or so they have ceased to
be a match for our ubiquity and our still increasing efficiency in altering the planet's surface and atmosphere. With one invention alone—

firearms—coupled with the insatiable appetite of our burgeoning population, we accomplished in a few decades what previously was the reserved for "acts of God," namely the extinction of entire species (see EXTINCT BIRDS). Yet guns are now the least of our life-threatening inventions, and the ability of birds or anything else to "bounce back" from the cumulative effect of deforestation, oil spills, pesticides, radio towers, automobiles, acid rain, picture windows, domestic animals, thermo-nuclear weapons, etc., must be deeply doubted. (See THREATS (OF HUMAN ORIGIN) TO BIRDLIFE for statistics on some of these hazards.)

Having overwhelmed the natural balance, we rely on our alleged ability to balance the world ecosystem ourselves. Regarding the likelihood of this, the optimist points to our retreat from the wanton slaughter of egrets for hat decorations (see CONSERVATION), the cynic to our retreat from environmental protection policy in the face of minor reductions in the gluttonous living standard to which we in the West have recently become accustomed.

MOULT. The preferred spelling in Britain and Canada. See MOLT.

MOUNT LEMMON. See SOUTHEASTERN ARIZONA.

MOUSTACHIAL (muss-TASH-ul) (stripe). A light or dark stripe of varying length and thickness beginning above the gape and extending along the lower borders of the auriculars. A strong moustachial stripe is a good field mark for Clay-colored Sparrow. The term "submoustachial" has been used for a stripe below the moustachial running through the malar region or "feather group." For more detail on the somewhat ambiguous terminology describing the lower reaches of a bird's head see MALAR and Sibey (2000–IDENTIFICATION).

MURPHY, Robert Cushman, 1887–1973. One of the most prominent American ornithologists of the twentieth century. Murphy's reputation is inextricably bound to the seabird fauna of South America. Born in Brooklyn, he developed strong passions for both natural history and the nautical life while growing up on Long Island, interests that together formed the basis of his long career. His professional ornithological life began immediately following his graduation from high school when he helped Frank Chapman edit his forthcoming *Warblers of North America* at the American Museum of Natural History in New York City. After receiving his undergraduate degree at Brown University, Murphy at once set sail on the brig *Daisy* to circumnavigate South America on what was perhaps the last commercial whaling voyage ever under sail. From this experience came his classic journal *Logbook for Grace* (1947), kept for the new bride he had left at home, and the inspiration for his lifelong study of pelagic birds. His magnum opus on the subject is *Oceanic Birds of South America* (1936), a

two-volume work noted for its meticulous detail, finely written anecdotal text, and evocative illustrations by F. Lee Jaques. Though he never took a PhD, he eventually assumed the chairmanship of the department of ornithology at the American Museum, held his share of prestigious offices (e.g., president of the AOU, 1948–1950), and garnered the awards due our most distinguished ornithologists. He was an ardent conservationist. Writing *in memoriam,* Dean Amadon implies that Robert Cushman Murphy inspired affection as well as respect by achieving an admirable balance of character traits: he was meticulous without being fussy, ambitious but patient, well-to-do yet liberal.

MURRE (rhymes with "fur," not "cure"). Standard English name in North America for the 2 species of auks in the genus *Uria* (family Alcidae; order Charadriiformes), both of which breed and winter in North America.

Like all but a few species of alcids, the murres are birds of arctic and subarctic seas. They nest on narrow ledges on precipitous cliffs or rocky islets and spend the rest of their lives at sea. Both the Thick-billed Murre and the Common Murre inhabit the North Pacific as well as the North Atlantic Oceans.

According to Lockwood (1993–NAMES) "murre" is of Cornish origin and was at first applied to the Razorbill, referring to that species' low, guttural call. Standard English names in Britain for Common and Thick-billed Murres are Guillemot and Brünnich's Guillemot, respectively.

For family characteristics, see AUK.

MURRELET (MERR-lit). Standard English name for 7 species of auks (family Alcidae; order Charadriiformes) in 2 genera, all but one of which breed along the Pacific coasts of North America. With the possible exception of the Ancient and Japanese Murrelets, which acquire some modest head plumes in alternate plumage, the murrelets are plain of plumage and do indeed resemble small (under 10 inches) murres.

It is in their breeding habits that the murrelets distinguish themselves from the other auks. Xantus's and Craveri's Murrelets (and perhaps the Scripps's subspecies of the former, believed by some to be a distinct species) breed farther south than any other species of alcid—the latter species nesting on islands in the Gulf of California and ranging *north* for the winter. Kittlitz's Murrelet breeds above the tree line on mountaintops, some distance from the sea, laying its single egg on bare rock. Most remarkable of all are the Marbled and Long-billed Murrelets, which typically nest in trees. One Ancient Murrelet nest site 148 feet from the ground on a branch (near the trunk) of a Douglas fir was discovered by accident in 1974 south of San Francisco; a nest of the (recently "split") Long-billed Murrelet was found a mere 20 feet up in a larch tree in taiga near the Russian coastal city of Okhotsk.

For family characteristics, see AUK.

MUSCLES. In birds as in humans, muscles are the principal mechanisms by which the needs and desires of the body are transformed into action. There are three basic types of muscles: the *visceral* or *smooth* muscles, which control involuntary movement such as those of the internal organs; the *skeletal* muscles, which act in conjunction with the skeleton at the will of the brain; and the specialized *cardiac* muscles, which make up the greatest part of the heart. The skeletal muscles are the most familiar to us. They are the meat or flesh of a bird's body and on average make up about 50% of body weight.

Anyone who has eaten a chicken knows that these skeletal muscles come in two colors, one dark and one light. These are composed of different types of muscle fiber, which are fueled in different ways and function in different manners. The dark red fiber burns accumulated fat, using oxygen carried by the blood. The muscles thus fueled are capable of strenuous sustained activity, e.g., the wing muscles of strong fliers or the leg muscles of species that walk, run, or paddle. The paler fibers (white meat) are fueled by a carbohydrate (glycogen), which is stored in the liver of most animals; these provide quick bursts of power, which, however, cannot be sustained for long. There is a third type of muscle fiber intermediate between these two in both color and function.

There are 175 skeletal muscles, most of them paired symmetrically, one on each side of the body. They function in virtually all parts of the body, sometimes working in intricate combinations or performing subtle operations, but always on a fundamentally simple principle. Basically, they work by pulling and releasing or, more precisely, contracting and relaxing. The brain transmits an impulse through nerve fibers that are connected to muscle fibers. Given the appropriate signal, the center of the muscle contracts, pulling its extremities inward. The extremities end in strong, fibrous, inelastic *tendons,* which attach the muscles to a bone. These often pass over another bone or through a loop of tissue, so that when the tendons are pulled on by the contracting muscles, they haul on the bone to which they are attached in a manner strongly reminiscent of a rope and pulley. An excellent example of this is the way the wings are raised and lowered by the pectoral muscles (see below and Fig. 14).

To define all of the muscles of a bird and their functions and variations among different groups and to sort out the nomenclature and confusions that have plagued avian myology from its inception to the present would require a book larger than this one. However, a few muscular phenomena that are specialized in birds deserve mention.

Not surprisingly, the areas of complex or highly developed musculature in birds are the ones that play the most significant roles in their habits, e.g., the muscles of jaw, neck, wings, and legs. Abdominal muscles and those of the lower back are relatively little used by birds and therefore tend to be less prominent than in mammals.

Control of Body Feathers is achieved by muscles of the skin. These serve to streamline body contours for efficient aerodynamics (see FLIGHT); to "fluff" or raise feathers for preening and drying; to squeeze air from the body feathers to reduce buoyancy, as for the kind of "sinking" dive practiced by some grebes; and to erect and lower crests or other features used in display. Of course, some "motions" used in display, such as the erecting of fleshy wattles or inflating of air sacs, are achieved by engorging the tissue with blood or by respiratory action, rather than by muscle contraction.

Neck Muscles are unusually numerous and complex in birds with long, mobile necks, e.g., herons and anhingas. Birds that plunge from the air into the sea, e.g., gannets and pelicans, have unusually powerful neck muscles capable of absorbing shocks.

In this context of neck motions—many of which are forward or thrusting—it is interesting to reflect that *all* muscular actions are accomplished by "pulling" as described above and none by "pushing."

Jaw Muscles. *Adductors* are muscles that move things together, and those controlling the closing of a bird's bill are highly developed in finches, which must crush hard seeds. In some seed-eating species the equivalent of more than 100 pounds per square inch of pressure is applied to the crushing of hard fruit pits (see BILL).

The Breast (Pectoral) Muscles are the muscles that power flight. They are usually the most prominent of a bird's muscles and may account for up to a third of body weight (hummingbirds). They are securely anchored to the broad surface of the breastbone (sternum), pass through scapular and coracoidal bones, and pull the upper wing bone (humerus) up and down in a classic example of the rope-and-pulley action described above (see FLIGHT and Fig. 14).

The Hatching Muscle, attached to the back of the skull, begins to appear early in the development of the embryo and attains full growth in time to aid the young bird in pipping and emerging from the egg (see HATCHING). This specialized muscle disappears gradually after its function has been fulfilled.

Perching Ability. It was long supposed that as a bird flexed its "ankle" (tarsal) joints in perching, the tendons that pass down the leg and over this joint to the tips of the toes were "automatically" pulled, closing the toes like a clenched fist around the perch. This also provided a convenient explanation for how birds are able to cling to a perch while asleep. However, research and observation do not support this logical description and reveal in fact that the front toes do not need to be clenched tightly around the perch and the hind toe (hallux) need not necessarily even be in contact with the perch, much less lock around it (see Bock 1965). On the other hand, a locking mechanism does exist in the tendons of a bird's front toes to hold the toes in whatever position they assume when the bird perches.

Hundreds of tiny projections from the undersurface of the toe tendons catch firmly in corresponding ridges on the inner surface of the tendon sheaths when the weight of the bird presses down on the toe bones under which the tendons lie.

Formula Muscles. Late in the nineteenth century the anatomist A. H. Garrod discovered that certain muscles of the pelvis and legs varied extremely and consistently among categories of birds, one species having more than another, for example, or the same number in a different combination. This system has been refined by various workers (e.g., George and Berger 1966) as a method of classification and now uses up to 13 different muscles, lettered A, B, C, D, E, F, G, M, N, V, X, Y, and Am. The formula represented in the muscles of most passerines, for example, is ACEFMNXY, while that of the Chimney Swift, with scant musculature in the pelvic region, is simply AEN. For recent work on limb musculature as a guide to systematic relationships see the work of Robert Raikow.

MUSEUMS. For the public at large, the relationship between museums and birdlife is discovered in those high-ceilinged halls in which mounted bird specimens are displayed in glass cases. Such exhibits range in quality from dismal regiments of misshapen avian corpses, made anonymous by a combination of inept taxidermy and years of accumulated dust, to wonderfully vivid re-creations of habitat with birds mounted skillfully in lifelike postures and placed against evocative painted backgrounds, e.g., the famous dioramas at the American Museum of Natural History in New York City. At their best, museum displays are undoubtedly effective in educating visitors about the wonders of the world avifauna or their own local one and in fanning the enthusiasm of young naturalists. But the museum's greater purpose in the study of birdlife is housed beyond those signs that say "Employees Only," in the rooms filled with enormous cases, reeking of fumigants and a variety of other pungent odors, where the collections of scientific specimens are stored. In the largest and best-curated collections, tens of thousands of carefully prepared and meticulously labeled bird skins lie side by side in drawer after drawer, showing (ideally) a complete range of size and age, geographical, plumage, and other variations for each species and arranged in their proper taxonomic order. The uninitiated can be forgiven if they find the idea of these vast ornithological mortuaries unappealing on first encounter, but eventually they should understand that scientific collections are crucial to the study of phylogeny, evolution, plumage and molt, migration, anatomy, and other subjects that contribute to our understanding of living birds. Even the field guides, without which the increasingly popular sport of birdwatching would not exist, could not have been written or illustrated without the use of specimens. For a more specific discussion of the uses and "ethics" of museum collections, see BIRD SKIN; COLLECTING; and the Bibliography for this entry.

Now that the collecting of specimens is being severely restricted even in the remotest parts of the world, the great bird collections assembled over decades are an increasingly valuable, essentially nonrenewable scientific resource.

As of 1973, ten North American museums owned over 100,000 bird skins. Ranked in order of their specimen wealth, they are

American Museum of Natural History, New York City (900,000 skins)
National Museum, Smithsonian Institution, Washington, DC (400,000 skins)
Field Museum of Natural History, Chicago (300,000 skins)
Museum of Comparative Zoology, Harvard University, Cambridge, MA
    (300,000 skins)
University of Michigan Museum of Zoology, Ann Arbor (200,000 skins)
Academy of Natural Sciences, Philadelphia
Carnegie Museum, Pittsburgh
Louisiana State University
Museum of Vertebrate Zoology, University of California, Berkeley
Royal Ontario Museum, Ottawa

Of course, natural history museums also frequently contain collections of skeletons, specimens preserved in fluid, eggs, etc., in addition to bird skins, all of which fill the needs of particular branches of ornithological research.

For information about specific collections on-line, go to www.nmnh.si.edu/BIRDNET/ORNCOLL.

For a systematic listing by state of museum collections in North America with statistics on specimens (of all kinds) and the regional or taxonomic "bias" (if any) of each, see Banks et al. (1973).

MUSIC (birds in). See HUMAN CULTURE, BIRDS IN.

MUSKEG. A term that has been applied to a wide range of boreal/low arctic habitats from open boglands to "forested tundra." Some authorities resolve the ambiguity by describing as many as 5 different kinds of muskeg. A common element in most definitions is a degree of wetness, which in turn implies the presence of plants such as *Sphagnum* moss and cotton grass and other sedges, but spruces, scrub willows, and alders at borders or on islands of higher ground may also be considered characteristic of muskeg. In its open wetland incarnation, muskeg is typically frequented by a variety of duck and sandpiper species. Hawk Owl, Palm Warbler, and Rusty Blackbird are among the characteristic species of more wooded muskeg. See also TAIGA; TUNDRA; BOREAL; ARCTIC; SUBARCTIC.

MUSTACHE (stripe). See MOUSTACHIAL.

MYCOPLASMOSIS. A group of diseases caused by parasitic bacteria in the genus *Mycoplasma.* The agent of infection in a recent North American outbreak of conjunctivitis in House Finches. See DISEASE, Mycoplasmosis.

MYIARCHUS (my-AR-kuss). A New World genus containing 22 species of tyrant flycatchers (family Tyrannidae; order Passeriformes), 4 of which breed in North America. Two other species have been recorded as vagrants (see Appendix II). In birdwatching circles this genus name is used as a convenient collective term as in "an unidentified *Myiarchus* was reported from Mount Auburn cemetery."

Most *Myiarchus* are fairly large (8–9 inches), long-tailed, somewhat crested flycatchers. Most have olive backs and heads, some rufous in wings and tail, some yellow on the belly, and some gray on the throat. North American species are normally sorted out easily on the basis of range and habitat as well as comparatively obvious superficial differences. In the Neotropics, where the ranges of two or more very similar species frequently overlap, they are often best distinguished by voice. This problem also arises when vagrant *Myiarchus* appear in North America out of their normal range, including western Ash-throated Flycatchers that turn up with surprising frequency in the East in fall.

The *Myiarchus* are cavity nesters, an unusual preference among the tyrant flycatchers. For family characteristics, see TYRANT FLYCATCHER.

MYNA (mynah). Standard English name for about 22 species of Asian birds in the starling family (Sturnidae), 3 of which now occur in North America as introduced exotics. One of these is a popular cage bird, the Hill or Talking Mynah, *Gracula religiosa,* a few of which have been at large in southern Florida for some years, but have not (yet?) become established (see AVICULTURE; SONG, Vocal Mimicry). The Crested Mynah, *Acridotheres cristatellus,* of eastern Asia was introduced to the Vancouver region of British Columbia around the end of the nineteenth century and persists there foraging in farmland and dumps, but has not increased notably or expanded its range. The Common Myna (*Acridotheres tristis*), which is native to the Middle East through Southeast Asia, has been widely introduced in the Old World tropics and subtropics and establishes itself readily. A southern Florida population present since at least 1983 is growing and extending its range (see INTRODUCED BIRDS).

The name probably originates from Sanskrit via Hindi deriving from words that mean "delightful or joyful" or in verb form, "it bubbles."

For family characteristics, see STARLING.

MYTHICAL BIRDS. See IMAGINATION.

NAIL (of bill). The ducks, geese, and swans (family Anatidae) have a hard hooked tip on the upper mandible. This functions in the cropping of aquatic vegetation—or grass in the case of grazing geese—and is called the "nail" or, more technically, the unguis. Birds also have toenails, though they are usually called claws.

NAMES, COLLOQUIAL. People the world over give names to conspicuous birds or those that have some significant impact on their daily lives. Cultures—even so-called "primitive" ones that use birds extensively for food or adornment—tend to have a high degree of recognition at least of the useful bird species and invent names to differentiate them. These colloquial or local names almost always refer to some distinctive plumage, voice, or behavioral characteristic. In this regard, in fact, they are often more relevant and almost invariably more imaginative and pleasing than standardized vernacular (common) names (see NAMES, VERNACULAR).

Of course, the great majority of "official" or standard English names for North American species derive from colloquial stock, sometimes of ancient lineage. "Finch," for example, can be traced back at least 3,000 years to a similar word that echoes (quite recognizably) the call of the Eurasian Chaffinch; other, seemingly distinctive names, such as "Merlin" can be traced back only so far before disappearing in a tangle of linguistic roots. The American Robin would doubtless have been called Red-breasted Thrush or the like had it not reminded British colonists of the Robin Redbreast (European Robin) of their homeland. "Nuthatch" is only very slightly removed from the original colloquial name "nuthack," based on observed behavior. "Anhinga" and "caracara" come to us virtually unchanged from Tupi, a common language of the natives of the Amazon Basin.

Despite the fact that we have now constructed a reasonably standardized English nomenclature for our native (and other) avifauna(s), it should be remembered (probably with considerable gratitude) that the great majority of people have paid not the slightest attention. A few of us insist that this bird here is a "Common Nighthawk," but those who know it (in some ways at least) as well or better than most ornithologists do, know full well that it is a "bullbat," which, after all, is shorter and hardly less accurate than the "official" name.

The main objection raised against colloquial names, of course, is that they are confusing. One person's Black-bellied Plover is another's "gump" or "chucklehead" and still another's "too-lee-huk." But it is on Latin names that we depend for nomenclatural consistency (see NOMENCLATURE,

ZOOLOGICAL), and the terrible ambiguity exemplified above can usually be relieved with a little conversation. Furthermore, it is absurd to claim that standard vernacular names are especially apt. Golden and Blacksmith Plovers are just as "black-bellied" as *Pluvialis squatarola* yet, alas, no one had the imagination to call it "Silver Plover." The smorgasbord of regional flavors and the local humor contained in North American bird slang easily outweigh any fancied need to cleave rigidly to an ornithological Esperanto.

It is gladdening to think that someone out there still knows the Ruddy Duck as a biddy, blatherskite, butterball, blackjack, hobbler, broadbill, bluebill, daub duck, dipper, dapper, copper, bullneck, bumblebee buzzer, butter bowl, chunk duck, deaf duck, dinky, dip-tail diver, goddamn, goose teal, greaser, broadbill dipper, creek coot, pond coot, dumb bird, goose wigeon, stiff-tailed wigeon, wigeon coot, hardhead, toughhead, steelhead, sleepyhead, hardheaded broadbill, booby, murre, pintail, hickoryhead, leatherback, leather breeches, lightwood knot, little soldier, muskrat chick, noddy paddy, paddywhack, quill-tail coot, rook, spoonbill, gray teal, bumblebee coot, saltwater teal, shanty duck, shot pouch, spiketail, spatter, spoon-billed butterball, stiffy, stub-and-twist, water partridge, wiretail, and who knows what else. This is a mere 60-odd names; Terres (1980–BIRD) notes that there are at least 132 "common" names for the Northern Flicker.

Needless to say, it is impossible to give more than a sample of such names here. The names below were selected by the author for their general usage, their historical, anthropological, ornithological, or etymological interest, or because they made him laugh.

Bee-martin: Eastern Kingbird; though it is known to eat honeybees occasionally, this species eats many more insects (such as robber flies) that are injurious to bees.

Beetlehead: Hunter's name for the Black-bellied Plover.

Bluebill: Hunter's name for both species of scaup and, less frequently, for the Ruddy Duck. For other nicknames of the Ruddy Duck, see ABOVE.

Bogsucker: American Woodcock; refers to its characteristic probing for earthworms and other invertebrates, though this activity is seldom pursued in bogs and probably involves little or no sucking.

Bos'n (boatswain) bird: Seamen's name referring to the elongated central rectrices of the jaegers and tropicbirds, which are reminiscent of the notched ribbon of old-fashioned boatswain's caps and/or the bos'n's splicing tool, the marlinespike (see below). The name may also refer to the shrill calls of tropicbirds, not unlike the sound of the bos'n's whistle (Palmer 1962–ORNITHOLOGY).

Bullbat: Refers to the nighthawks, connoting a *large* bat and the crepuscular habits of these birds or to the lowing sound the bird makes in its display dive, which sounds like the bellow of a distant bovine paramour.

Burgomaster: Seamen's name for the Glaucous Gull, which tends to have a well-filled figure and a proprietary bearing.

Butcher bird: Northern and Loggerhead Shrikes, both of which kill large insects, small mammals, and birds and then hang the "meat" in the crotch of a branch or on a thorn.

Butterball: Hunter's name for the Bufflehead, referring to its chubby form and perhaps the presence of large quantities of fat in the fall.

Butterbill: "Coot" shooter's name for the Black Scoter, referring to the bright orange-yellow bill knob of the drake.

Buzzard: Popular name for the Black and Turkey Vultures; a corruption of the traditional British use of this name to refer to medium-sized, broad-winged raptors, mostly in the genus *Buteo.* For a comprehensive discussion of the corruption in usage of the names of day-flying raptors; see HAWK.

Calico plover: Hunter's name for the Ruddy Turnstone, referring to its multicolored breeding plumage.

Callithumpian duck: Long-tailed Duck (until recently Oldsquaw—see p. 585); a callithumpian band is an amateur musical group that characteristically produces an odd assortment of notes at random; the same may be said of flocks of Long-tailed Ducks.

Carey chicks: Storm-petrels; see Mother Carey's chickens, below.

Chaparral cock: Local name for the (Greater) Roadrunner. Though they belong to the cuckoo family, roadrunners do look and act rather like some gallinaceous birds—whence "cock." For a description of one of the southwestern habitats they frequent, see CHAPARRAL.

Chebec (chi-BEK): Least Flycatcher; a close literal rendering of this species' "song."

Chewink (chuh-WINK): Rufous-sided Towhee. "Chewink" and "towhee" (properly pronounced "tuh-WHEE") are both intended to resemble one of the calls of the species to which they refer.

Chucklehead: Hunter's name for the Black-bellied Plover.

Creaker or creaker pert: Hunter's name for the Pectoral Sandpiper, referring to call(s) often given when flushed.

Dabchick: Pied-billed Grebe.

Devil-downhead: Applied to all of the nuthatches, which frequently forage over tree trunks head downward; the "devil" is a little mysterious, as it is hard to imagine species that present a more benign temperament; perhaps "daredevil" is implied.

Diablotin (de-AH-blow-TAHN): Applied, in the Caribbean, to the Black-capped Petrel. See also CAHOW and GADFLY.

Doughbird or doebird: Though Thomas Nuttall and many shorebird shooters came to regard this name as generic for many of the larger, longer-billed sandpipers, it originally referred specifically to the Eskimo Curlew, and, as A. C. Bent (1929–ORNITHOLOGY) explains, the name was

spelled "doughbird," not "doebird," "for it was so fat when it reached us in the fall that its breast would often burst open when it fell to the ground, and the thick layer of fat was so soft that it felt like a ball of dough."

Dunk-a-doo: American Bittern; echoes its call.

Erne: An old Anglo-Saxon name for the White-tailed (Sea) Eagle, perpetuated in modern usage in the Scandinavian words for eagle (ørn or öre); well known to workers of crossword puzzles.

Fish hawk; less frequently, fish eagle: Widespread name for the Osprey, referring, of course, to its preferred prey.

Fool hen: Applied to several members of the grouse family, but especially to the Spruce and Blue Grouse, connoting fearlessness of man, *ergo* stupidity. From a behavioral, if not a taxonomic, point of view, a fool hen is a booby is a dodo.

Garefowl or gairfowl: A name once in wide usage for the Great Auk *(Pinguinus impennis).* According to Newton (1893–96–ORNITHOLOGY), it is either a corruption of a Gaelic name meaning "strong, stout bird with a spot" (referring to a large, white facial spot) or of a general Norse name for all of the alcids. Lockwood (1993) refers it to Old Norse and says it has the same root as the gyr of Gyrfalcon, implying a quality of excellence or the remarkable.

Goonybird: Seamen's name for the albatrosses, referring to their comical courtship antics.

Grasshopper hawk: Applied locally to the shrikes, which often prey on large insects.

Greenhead: A common hunter's name for the Mallard.

Greenlet: Widespread English name for the vireos before the turn of the century—the Philadelphia Vireo was then known as the Brotherly-love Greenlet. Now restricted to members of the Neotropical genus *Hylophilus,* none of which reaches North America.

Groundbird: Generalized name for sparrows and other ground-feeding, "nondescript" passerines.

Ground warbler: Common Yellowthroat, which habitually feeds and nests on or near the ground.

Grunter: Hunter's name for Wilson's Phalarope, referring to the call sometimes given when flushed.

Gump: Hunter's name for the Black-bellied Plover.

Hagdon, hagdown: Widely used seamen's name for shearwaters, especially the Greater Shearwater; the name is modified when used for other species, e.g., "black hagdon" for Sooty Shearwater. Lockwood (1993) says this name originated in the Isle of Man, but that its provenance is unknown.

Harrywicket: One of numerous names applied to the Northern Flicker, echoing its distinctive call.

Hell-diver: The smaller grebes, particularly the Pied-billed; grebes often seem to disappear when they dive and this name offers a superstitious opinion as to where they go.

Honker: Canada Goose.

Humility: Fanciful name for the Willet; like the current name, this echoes the species' call.

Ice bird: Seamen's name for both the Dovekie and the Razorbill, possibly referring to their habit (common to many birds of northern seas) of feeding at the edge of the pack ice or in the wake of icebergs, where upwellings of invertebrate food tend to occur.

Jiddy hawk: Seamen's name for the species of jaegers; this is a laundered version of a name that refers to jaegers' alleged habit of eating excrement expelled by terns and other birds that they harass. The Latin genus and family names of the jaegers (*Stercorarius,* Stercorariidae) also mean "eaters of excrement."

Linnet: Standard English name for a Eurasian finch *(Acanthis cannabina),* the males of which have a rosy breast and front; this explains the colloquial usage in North America referring to the House Finch and less frequently the Purple Finch.

Logcock: Pileated Woodpecker.

Lord and lady: Describes a *pair* of Harlequin Ducks.

Mackerel goose: Fishermen's name for the two species of seagoing phalaropes, Red and Northern; they are not geese, of course, and are now usually placed in the sandpiper family (Scolopacidae).

Mackerel gull: Widespread seamen's name for species of *Sterna* terns, especially Common, Arctic, and Roseate. These birds and Atlantic mackerel share a taste for small saltwater schooling fishes, such as lances and silversides, and therefore often occur in the same place at the same time.

Man-o'-war bird: A variant of "frigatebird," likewise referring to these birds' majestic "sailing" manner of flight.

Marlin: Hunter's name for the godwits, apparently referring to the resemblance between the upturned bills of these birds and a type of old-fashioned marlinespike that was similarly curved.

Marlinespike: Seamen's name for the Parasitic and Long-tailed Jaegers and the tropicbirds, referring to the resemblance between the elongated central rectrices of these species and the pointed metal rope-splicing tools.

Mollymauk or mollymoke (many other spellings): A widespread seamen's name that may have originally referred to the Northern Fulmar. Used loosely since for many tubenose species (order Procellariiformes), but in its strictest current usage refers specifically to the smaller species of albatrosses in the genus *Diomedea.*

Mope: Used for Pine Grosbeak in Newfoundland, referring to its quiet, "moping" demeanor and tameness.

Mosquito hawk: Local name for the nighthawks, from their habit of catching ("hawking") small insects on the wing.

Mother Carey's chickens: Seamen's name for the storm-petrels, particularly British, Wilson's and Leach's. Speculation that this widespread

nickname is associated with the Virgin Mary (i.e., *mater cara*) seems at odds with the usual superstitions about "Carey chicks," which describe them as tormented souls of lost sailors or cruel ship's officers or even avian demons keeping watch over the drowned. It is more likely a so-called "noa" name, i.e., a name used to avoid calling an evil spirit by its right name and thus attracting it.

Mud hen: Common Moorhen and several species of rails; refers, of course, to their preferred marshy habitat.

Mutton bird: Name for several medium-sized seabirds, especially the Slender-billed and Sooty Shearwaters, which breed in vast colonies in southeastern Australia (Slender-billed) and New Zealand (Sooty), where the chicks are "harvested" and sold commercially for food. The name comes from their flavor.

Nonpareil: Painted Bunting; literally (French), "without equal"; "uniquely splendid." As in many other instances, the less colorful female was ignored by the coiners of both this and the standard English name of this species.

Ouzel (OO-zul) (water ouzel): From an Old English word for the Eurasian Blackbird (*Turdus merula*). A popular British name for the Eurasian Dipper is water ouzel and this name is also used colloquially for the American Dipper. Though classified in their own families, dippers are closely related to the "true" (Turdine) thrushes and are thrush-like in general appearance.

Oxeye: Hunter's name for some of the "peeps," particularly the Semipalmated Sandpiper.

Peabody bird: White-throated Sparrow, one song of which is often verbalized by residents of the United States as "Old Sam Peabody-Peabody-Peabody"; Canadian ears hear "Oh, sweet Canada, Canada, Canada."

Peep: See entry in main text.

Prairie pigeon: Franklin's Gull, which breeds on the northern prairies of North America.

Preacher: Colloquial name for the Red-eyed Vireo, which is noted for its monotonous, endlessly repeated song.

Quailhead: Lark Sparrow, referring to the adults' boldly striped head.

Quandy: Hunter's name for a *female* goldeneye.

Quank: White-breasted Nuthatch, in imitation of its nasal calls; the Red-breasted Nuthatch is sometimes called "little quank."

Quawk: Popular nickname for the Black-crowned Night-Heron; an excellent literal rendering of this species' characteristic call.

Rain crow: Applied to the Black-billed and Yellow-billed Cuckoos, in the belief that the frequent calling of cuckoos is a reliable prediction of rain (see IMAGINATION, BIRDS IN).

Redbird: Popular name, particularly in the southern states, for the male Northern Cardinal; the discerning distinguish the Summer Tanager as the *summer* redbird.

Ricebird: Popular name for the Bobolink around the turn of the century, when migratory hordes of this species stopped to feed on southern rice and other grain crops en route to their South American wintering grounds in the fall. Many of the birds killed as crop pests were sold to restaurateurs, so that "Ricebirds" was once a common menu item (see EDIBILITY).

Robin snipe: Hunter's name for the Red Knot and the two species of dowitcher, referring to the red underparts of the alternate (breeding) plumage of these species.

Sawbill: Colloquial name for the mergansers, referring to their prominent bill serrations, useful in grasping slippery fish.

Scissorbill: Black Skimmer; see SKIMMER for a description of the unique bill adaptation of this family; also Fig. 3.

Sea hen: Seamen's name for the Great Skua.

Sea parrot: Seamen's name for the Common Puffin.

Sea pigeon: Seamen's name for the Black Guillemot; also applied to a wide variety of vaguely "dove-like" warm-water seabirds, e.g., tropicbirds, petrels, small gulls.

Sea swallow: Seamen's name for the species of *Sterna* terns with long, forked tails, e.g., Common, Arctic, and Roseate.

Shag: See entry in main text.

Shitepote or shitepoke: Laundered version of a name applied to several species of herons, especially the Green Heron and the Black-crowned Night-Heron, referring to their habit of defecating conspicuously when alarmed.

Skunkhead: Hunter's name for the drake Surf Scoter.

Smutty-nosed coot: Hunters of North Atlantic waterfowl call all of the scoters "coots." This variation refers to the fatty orange knob at the base of the bill of the male Black Scoter.

Snakebird: Describes the sinuosity of the Anhinga, which often swims with only its long, serpentine head and neck above the surface.

Snowflake: A once popular name for the Snow Bunting.

Solan goose: Colloquial and, of course, taxonomically misleading name for the Northern Gannet. "Solan" comes from the Old Norse name for gannet, *sula,* now the generic Latin name for the boobies. Lockwood (1993) says this literally meant "cleft stick" referring to the conspicuous black-tipped crossed wings of adult birds at rest. (?)

Sprig: Hunter's name for the Pintail.

Stib: Hunter's name for several of the larger "peeps," particularly the Dunlin and Sanderling.

Swamp angel: Wood and Hermit Thrushes and perhaps the Veery, referring to the "heavenly" songs of these species.

Teacher bird: Ovenbird (Parulidae), the loud and distinctive song of which sounds like a repetition of the word "teacher" strongly accented on the first syllable; song analysis shows that the phrases, in fact, begin with

the unemphasized syllable, so that the species "really" says *"erteach-erteach-erteach."*

Teeter-bob: Spotted Sandpiper; refers to its characteristic, nearly continual tail bobbing. Many variations, e.g., teeter-tail, teeter-peep, teeter-arse snipe, tip-up, tip-tail.

Thistlebird: An apt name for the American Goldfinch, deriving from its close association with thistle. Not only do adult goldfinches eat thistle seed; they feed their young on it and line their nest with thistle down. In some regions late-season nesting of this species follows the thistle bloom.

Throat-cut: Rose-breasted Grosbeak (male).

Thunderpump: American Bittern; refers to this species' distinctive call.

Tickle-arse: Seamen's name for the Black-legged Kittiwake; the name is a contraction of "tickle-your-arse-with-a-feather" and is inspired by the giggle-like calls of this northern gull.

Timberdoodle: American Woodcock.

Tinker: Seamen's name for the Razorbill.

Titlark: Name of British origin for the pipits.

Turr: Seamen's name for the species of murres.

Wamp: Hunter's name for species of eider, especially the Common Eider; the King Eider is sometimes called "wamp's cousin."

Water hen: American Coot.

Water witch: Pied-billed Grebe; probably refers to its habit of slowly submerging and apparently not resurfacing.

Wavy: Hunter's name for the Blue/Snow Goose.

Whalebird: Seamen's name for the two species of seagoing phalaropes, Red and Northern. These phalaropes, along with other pelagic birds, often feed in the oily slicks that surround whales feeding or traveling at the surface.

Whiptail: Seamen's name for the Long-tailed Jaeger in breeding plumage.

Whiskey Jack: Popular colloquial name for the Gray Jay; a corruption of an American Indian name ("wiskedjak," or the like) for a trickster god personified by this species.

Whistler: Hunter's name for the goldeneyes. The characteristic "whistling," produced by the birds' wings in flight, is probably discernible at least as far away as the color of the eye. See also WHISTLING-DUCK.

Whooper: Nickname for the Whooping Crane or, in Europe, for the Whooper Swan.

Wide-awake: Applied in the Caribbean to the Sooty Tern, in approximation of that species' call.

Wobble: Seamen's name for the Great Auk—describing its penguin-like gait? Not to be confused with "wobbla," the collective name in New England for the members of the family Parulidae, e.g., "a wobbla wave at Mount Awbun Cemetery."

Yellowhammer: Colloquial name for the yellow-shafted race of the Northern Flicker; also the standard English name for a species of Eurasian bunting that occurs virtually throughout the Palearctic region and has been successfully introduced in New Zealand but has never occurred naturally in North America.

NAMES, SCIENTIFIC. The widespread publication of standardized English bird names in field guides has for the most part relieved birdwatchers of the burden of learning the scientific names of the species they pursue. However, there are still many discrepancies and ambiguities in the use of common names (see NAMES, VERNACULAR), especially in the more remote parts of the world, where there is not enough of a birdwatching community to develop a popular consensus in the matter. Furthermore, there are occasions when the use of scientific nomenclature facilitates the discussion of a field problem, e.g., how to distinguish among the gray-headed *Oporornis* warblers or the characteristics of the longer-billed *hendersoni* race of the Short-billed Dowitcher. Also, if you find yourself birding in a part of the world where you don't speak the language, scientific names can provide a lingua franca. Finally, the ability to "translate" the names of some of the birds and other organism we identify adds yet another pleasure to birding.

The fear and loathing with which many people regard Latin and Greek words of which scientific names are composed is understandable. Few people today have had even a smattering of the classical languages, so that these name "are Greek" to most people. Then, too, as with other foreign languages, the rules of Latin pronunciation (though simple) are quite unlike those of English, creating an intimidating risk of making a fool of oneself in front of the more knowledgeable.

The only way to become acquainted with the meaning of scientific names is to learn a little Latin and Greek etymology. Fortunately, this does not require enrolling in a language school. Many technical names are simply descriptive, referring to color or size or number, and therefore certain roots appear over and over again: *atr-* is a Latin prefix meaning black, *gula* is Latin for throat; *cap-*, also Latin, refers to the head; thus *Spizella atrogularis* (Black-chinned Sparrow) and *Vireo atricapillus* (Black-capped Vireo). Not all technical names are straight descriptions. Many of the early namers *did* have thorough classical educations and gave free rein to their imaginations in their nomenclatural inventions. "Prairie-chicken" is a pleasant name, but it pales beside its Latin equivalent, *Tympanuchus,* which according to Coues (1903–COUES) refers to the kind of drum played during pagan bacchanals—a wonderful evocation of both the sound and the purpose of courtship dances of male prairie-chickens (see DISPLAY). For anyone interested in acquiring the rudiments of scientific Latin, Borror (1985) is highly recommended. For those who prefer to have

their Latin and Greek interpreted for them, Jobling (1991) is authoritative and comprehensive for scientific bird names; Choate and Paynter (1985) covers the North American avifauna readably.

Pronouncing scientific names is less straightforward than understanding them. There are, of course, rules, but when comprehensive they are rather extensive, some are downright perverse, and they vary from authority to authority and from country to country. The result is that while speaker A insists his Latin pronunciation impeccably follows *the* rules, speaker B pronounces things differently with equal self-confidence. The lack of a comfortable standard can be frustrating, but the more positive view is that if your pronunciation is logical, allows a listener to write down a fair approximation of what you have said, and agrees with local conventions, only a fussbudget would be so narrow-minded as to declare you "wrong." A set of rules is, of course, essential, if only to have a standard to depart from. The official authority on language conventions as applied to the scientific naming of animals is the International Code of Zoological Nomenclature (ICZN) (1985). Again, for a good, concise approach, see Borror (1985).

One obstacle that English speakers uniquely face in pronouncing technical names is that their vowel sounds are different not only from Latin but from all the modern languages that derive from Latin (Spanish, French, Italian) as well as most others, such as German. For example, a long "a" in English is pronounced as in "jay," while in all the other languages mentioned it is pronounced as in "swallow." And the Latin long "e" is "ay" not "ee." The greatest perversity of makers of Latin pronunciation rules for English speakers is to insist that we should say *Tringa* FLAY-vuh-peas (*flavipes*), when the rest of the world instinctively says FLAV-uh-pace.

NAMES, VERNACULAR OR COMMON. Standardized names by which bird species are known in the language of the country or countries where they occur; distinguished here both from scientific names in Latin and from colloquial names. The "purpose" of vernacular names falls somewhere between that of colloquial and technical names. On the one hand, many common names derive from colloquial usage (e.g., Bobolink); on the other, they are (at least in English) standardized by ornithologists, as are Latin names. They are not meant to reflect the continual process of taxonomic revision as are scientific names, but they are meant to be far more stable—thus much more useful—than the anything-goes usage of local names can ever be. (The function of technical naming is discussed under NOMENCLATURE, ZOOLOGICAL, and the problems inherent in inconsistency in naming life forms are discussed there and under NAMES, COLLOQUIAL. See also NAMES, SCIENTIFIC).

The etymology of generic names such as "sandpiper" and selected modifiers such as "Pectoral" as well as brief biographies for eponyms (e.g.

Bell's Vireo) are given in the main text. Modifiers such as "Hooded" and "Smooth-billed" are left for readers to work out on their own. This leaves a couple of categories of vernacular names that perhaps deserve passing mention. One contains species that seem have been willfully named for their least conspicuous traits. Ring-necked Duck with only the faintest hint of a neck ring and several more apt alternatives (Ring-*billed* Duck?) may be the most glaring example, but Red-bellied Woodpecker is close behind. But the two "Semipalmated's" and various "-eyed's" also pique one's curiosity. Are these modest attempts at taxonomic humor or perhaps just the myopia of museum-bound ornithologists? We are unlikely ever to know for sure.

The other bird names that are bound to strike today's birders as whimsical at best are those that seem to try to tie a species down to a particular place or habitat that now seems equivocal. Connecticut, Kentucky, Nashville, Tennessee, and Magnolia Warblers are prime examples. The place names were clearly intended as commemorative (of the place where the species first fell to the collector's gun) and we owe many of these to Alexander Wilson. Here he is explaining why a boreal Tennessee Warbler bears the name of a southern state: "This plain little bird has hitherto remained unknown. I first found it on the banks of the Cumberland River in the state of Tennessee, and suppose it to be rare." He further supposes that it is "most probably a native of a more southerly climate."

There are those inclined to be annoyed at these anomalous labels and would prefer (for example) that Magnolia Warbler be more "accurately" known as Black- and Yellow Warbler as Audubon called it. Others are content on having a rare encounter with a Connecticut Warbler in New England to be reminded of the days when the next bird one saw might be new to science.

Despite the efforts of ornithologists to standardize vernacular names, inconsistencies tend to remain when a single bird species occurs in two (or more) countries, each with its own cultural traditions and ornithological establishment. For example, members of the family Gaviidae have long been called "divers" in the standard vernacular nomenclature of the British Isles, while the preferred standard English name in North America has always been "loon." Since all the diver/loon species have a Holarctic distribution, some confusion is possible when an American talks to an Englishman about these birds. The converse problem also occurs in which two different regions inadvertently come up with the same name for two distinct species: the Black Duck of Australasia *(Anas superciliosa)* is not the same as the Black Duck of North America *(A. rubripes)*. In the case of cosmopolitan species, the ambiguity may be bewilderingly compounded. *Ardea alba* is variously known as Great Egret (in North America, where it was formerly called Common Egret and, before that, American Egret), Great White Egret (in Britain, where it was formerly known as Great

White Heron—not to be confused [!] with the white morph of the Great Blue Heron of the same name—and Large Egret), and White Egret (in Australia).

Such discrepancies in common names are clearly a bother, though perhaps not a major stumbling block to the progress of ornithology or birdwatching. Systematists and birders alike always have recourse to the Latin nomenclature for resolving ambiguities. Furthermore, the great majority of birdwatchers pursue only the members of their own avifauna, and most of the (admitted increasing number) who do bird abroad might prefer to say Black-throated Diver when in Scotland rather than be told by a committee on common bird names that they must learn to say it at home as well in preference to Arctic Loon. Nevertheless, there doubtless should be a work entitled *Standard Vernacular Names in English of the Birds of the World* that would publish the compromises of an international panel of interested ornithologists and give all the accepted synonyms of the common names decided on. It is a lacuna in the literature that should be filled regardless of whether an American birder can ever be persuaded to call a Dovekie a Little Auk. For the present, Monroe and Sibley's *A World Checklist of Birds* (1993) and Clements' *Birds of the World: A Checklist* (2000) do a more than adequate job of sorting out many of the worst muddles.

The vernacular-name ambiguities that most often befuddle North American birdwatchers are those in which there are different names for the same species in British and American usage. The species listed below are of regular occurrence in both the United Kingdom and North America.

American	*British*
Common Loon	Great Northern Diver
Arctic Loon	Black-throated Diver
Red-throated Loon	Red-throated Diver
Horned Grebe	Slavonian Grebe
Eared Grebe	Black-necked Grebe
Greater Shearwater	Great Shearwater
Great Cormorant	Cormorant
Brant	Brent Goose
Green-winged Teal	Teal
Greater Scaup	Scaup
Common Goldeneye	Goldeneye
Common Eider	Eider
Black Scoter	Common Scoter
White-winged Scoter	Velvet Scoter
Common Merganser	Goosander
Northern Harrier	Hen Harrier
Hawk (for buteos)	Buzzard (for buteos)
Willow Ptarmigan	Willow Grouse (and Red Grouse)

Rock Ptarmigan	Ptarmigan
Great Egret	Great White Egret
Black-crowned Night Heron	Night Heron
Black-bellied Plover	Grey Plover
Snowy Plover	Kentish Plover
Ruddy Turnstone	Turnstone
Red Phalarope	Grey Phalarope
Northern Phalarope	Red-necked Phalarope
Common Snipe	Snipe
Parasitic Jaeger	Arctic Skua
Pomarine Jaeger	Pomarine Skua
Long-tailed Jaeger	Long-tailed Skua
Mew Gull	Common Gull
Black-legged Kittiwake	Kittiwake
Common Murre	Guillemot
Thick-billed Murre	Brünnich's Guillemot
Dovekie	Little Auk
Atlantic Puffin	Puffin
Boreal Owl	Tengmalm's Owl
Horned Lark	Shore Lark
Barn Swallow	Swallow
Bank Swallow	Sand Martin
Common Raven	Raven
Chickadee (for most *Parus* species)	Tit (for most *Parus* species)
Winter Wren	Wren
Kinglets	Goldcrest, Firecrest
Bohemian Waxwing	Waxwing
Northern Shrike	Great Grey Shrike
Common Redpoll	Redpoll
Hoary Redpoll	Arctic Redpoll
Red Crossbill	Crossbill
White-winged Crossbill	Two-barred Crossbill
Lapland Longspur	Lapland Bunting

NARIS (NAY-riss or NAIR-iss) (pl.: nares [NAY-reez or NAIR-eez]). Technical term for NOSTRIL.

NATIONAL AUDUBON SOCIETY. Founded in 1905, this is one of the oldest and largest conservation organizations in the world, with 600,000 members, 500 chapters, 27 state offices and Audubon Centers and sanctuaries throughout the country. Its national Headquarters are at Audubon House, 700 Broadway, New York, NY 10003. The Society's mission is "to conserve and restore natural ecosystems focusing on birds and other wildlife for the benefit of humanity and the earth's biological diversity."

As of this writing (2003), National Audubon is focusing its attention on six major Conservation Campaigns:

- Conserving marine wildlife though a *Living Oceans* program
- Protecting and promoting growth of America's *National Wildlife Refuges*
- Protecting the *Upper Mississippi River*
- Restoration of *Florida's Everglades*
- Restoration of the *San Francisco Bay Area*
- Promoting a responsible *U.S. population policy*

The Society carries out its mission using a combination of strategies, including hands-on conservation programs, habitat protection, advocacy from the grassroots to the national level, and scientific research and education.

Publications. NAS publishes *Audubon,* a glossy quarterly magazine that includes natural history articles, photo essays, campaign updates, and many other features relating to bird conservation and national environmental issues. It also publishes the results of the annual Christmas Bird Count and an electronic periodical, *Audubon Bird Conservation Newsletter.*

For the history of the Audubon movement, see AUDUBON SOCIETIES and Graham (1990–CONSERVATION). For more on the National Audubon Society visit its website at www.audubon.org.

NATIONAL WILDLIFE REFUGE. A parcel of habitat—often including extensive wetlands—owned, protected, and managed by the U.S. Fish and Wildlife Service for the benefit of birds and other life-forms. The first federal refuge was Pelican Island, a rookery on the Indian River near the east coast of Florida, acquired in 1903 by executive order of Teddy Roosevelt. As of October 2002 there were 575 refuges (and wetland management districts), comprising over 93 million acres with at least one refuge in every state and U.S. Territory.

The ***Mission*** of the National Wildlife Refuge System is: *To administer a national network of lands and waters for the conservation, management and where appropriate, restoration of the fish, wildlife and plant resources and their habitats within the United States for the benefit of present and future generations of Americans.* Many refuges are strongly identified either with a particular species—the Aransas refuge encompasses most of the wintering range of the Whooping Crane—or as a regular stopping place for large concentrations of migrating water birds, as at the BEAR RIVER refuge at Great Salt Lake. Most refuges are actively managed to maintain or improve the habitat favored by the species under protection. For example, dikes may be constructed to increase the area of wetland available for resting ducks and to control water levels. Often blinds, boardwalks, and trails are maintained to encourage the public to enjoy the nation's wild

heritage, subject, of course, to access restrictions imposed for the welfare of protected species. On many refuges, waterfowl shooting and hunting of other game is permitted during a limited season.

The Canadian Wildlife Service operates a similar system of refuges with a strong legal mandate for bird conservation. The initial enabling legislation was the Migratory Bird Convention of 1917, which led to the establishment of Migratory Bird Sanctuaries. As of October 2002 there were 98 MBS's throughout Canada, comprising 11.3 hectares (27.9 million acres). In 1973 the Canadian Wildlife Act created a broader mandate to *conserve essential habitat for migratory birds and, if in the national interest and with the support of provinces, other wildlife species, especially endangered wildlife.* This led to the establishment of additional refuges called National Wildlife Areas, of which there are now (2002) 48, totaling 489,332 hectares (12.1 million acres).

For refuges of particular interest to birders, see the Bird Finding listing on pp. xxiv–xxv.

The October 2002 issue of *National Geographic* contains a comprehensive photo essay on the U.S. National Wildlife Refuges system with typically brilliant graphics.

A free list of National Wildlife Refuges, with their addresses and managers, is available from the main office of the U.S. Fish and Wildlife Service in Washington, DC, or from its website: http://refuges.fws.gov/.

More information on the Canadian refuge system can be found at www.cws-scf.ec.gc.ca/.

NATURAL SELECTION. The process, articulated by Charles Darwin in 1859, by which evolution proceeds. The theory of natural selection involves many complexities, but, in essence, it holds that inheritable traits that allow an individual organism to cope more successfully with its environment will increase the individual's "survivability," allowing it to produce more offspring with the same advantageous trait(s), thus ultimately perpetuating successful genetic changes. This is "survival of the fittest," although this phrase is often misapplied to the triumph of the "strong" over the "weak," e.g., predators that kill and eat life forms of which humans are fond. In fact, chickadees are also predators and every bit as "fit" as the Sharp-shinned Hawks that sometimes prey on them; the proof of their fitness in the Darwinian sense is their abundance. See SPECIATION.

NAVIGATION. Once science confirmed the astonishing fact that most of the birds of the North Temperate Zone travel hundreds or thousands of miles each year to more southerly wintering grounds (see MIGRATION), it was faced with the need to explain how that is possible. How does a bird with its apparently meager intelligence find its way to and from remote and restricted breeding and wintering areas? How does it know in which

direction to go? How does it maintain its course, particularly in the dark, when many migrants travel? How can it tell when it has arrived at the right place in the Central American rain forests or Caribbean highlands? Does it really know where "home" is, or does it just follow an innate "flight plan" blindly? Does it know where to go "instinctively" or must it learn by experience—or both?

The sensory processes that encompass these difficult "hows" have so far been only partially explained. What *has* been learned—almost entirely since 1940—is summarized below.

Experiments in Bird Navigation. The experiments that have been undertaken to determine the extent and nature of birds' navigational capabilities have generated some of the most interesting reading in the ornithological literature. Some of the best-known of these are noted here, and other classic and/or interesting studies and summaries are listed selectively in the Bibliography.

To begin to assess the accuracy, effectiveness, and extent of a bird's ability to return to where it "wants to be," a number of species have been banded and then transported not only away from breeding or wintering sites but also far out of their normal migration route. Manx Shearwaters, known to be long-distance pelagic migrants, have been taken from British breeding colonies and released on the east coast of North America (Mazzeo 1953) and at various points in southern and western Europe (Matthews 1953) and were found to return to their nest burrows with remarkable efficiency (12½ days for the Atlantic crossing) and little or no apparent hesitation. Mewaldt (1964) made similar tests on White-crowned and Golden-crowned Sparrows, which breed in northwestern North America (including Alaska) and winter in southern California. He trapped hundreds of birds on their wintering grounds and released them on the Gulf coast of Louisiana and the east coast of Maryland. A number of these birds were recaptured the following winter in California, presumably having returned to their breeding grounds in the interim.

Homing experiments with Feral Pigeons (e.g., Matthews 1963), a nonmigratory species, and with other "short-distance" migrants resulted in a higher percentage of disoriented birds and the conclusion that local landmarks are of great importance to the navigating skills of such birds as they near their destination. An experimental group of pigeons reached the general area of their destination near Boston without reference to landmarks but then used a conspicuous building to give them an accurate bearing on their home roost (Michener and Walcott 1967).

Kramer's experiments with starlings in Germany (1952) resulted in the first well-substantiated information on *how* birds find their way. During the period in spring when starlings normally migrate, he placed a bird reared in captivity in a structure from which only the sky was visible through the windows. He found (1) that when the sun was out, the bird

would flutter restlessly in the direction of its species' migratory destination at that time of year; (2) that if he changed the position of the sun with the use of mirrors, the starling would alter course accordingly and fly in the "wrong" direction; (3) that the bird remained on course through the sun's normal daily arc, i.e., that its orientation system compensated for this movement; and (4) that on overcast days when the sun's position was obscured, the bird was apparently disoriented.

The first experiments with nocturnal migrants (see Sauer [1957] and Sauer and Sauer [1960]), using species of Old World warblers (Sylviidae) reared in the lab and a planetarium where the stars in the night sky could be altered, yielded similar findings: (1) Exposed to a clear night sky during a migratory period, the warblers would orient correctly for the season. (2) When, for example, they were shown a fall sky in the spring under the planetarium ceiling, they would "follow the stars" in the "wrong" direction. (3) When the stars were invisible or when the sky of a nonmigratory season was displayed, the birds became disoriented.

The myriad experiments that have followed from these classic pioneering ones, as well as uncovering important "new" factors, have tended on the whole to (1) increase respect for the complexity of avian navigation; (2) confirm the importance of celestial guidance; and (3) reinforce a growing awareness that birds' extraordinary homing capability is achieved not by one area of the brain processing one type of information but by combining several kinds of information using several physiological faculties.

General Summary of Present Knowledge. There is experimental evidence to support the following facts and speculations:

- Many species of birds have been shown incontestably to perform spectacular "homing" feats involving great distances and radical dislocations.
- Navigational ability varies widely among different species of birds. At least some species that typically spend their whole lives within a limited area have comparatively simple "homing" abilities, which would seem to correspond to their limited needs; species that undertake long migrations have evolved more sophisticated techniques, and nocturnal and pelagic migrants, which normally must find their way without the aid of landmarks, probably have the most highly developed orientation abilities of all.
- The use of landmarks plays a significant role in homing for many birds. Species of limited range memorize key features of their neighborhood and can be taught to learn landmarks of a wider area. Birds deliberately disoriented (e.g., Griffin and Hock 1949) often wander at random, apparently searching for familiar places or "clues" such as a coastline that may bring them back into their familiar home range if followed. Birds that depend on the celestial

clues described below may follow coasts or mountain ranges (leading lines) when the sky is overcast.

- The sun is known to be a means of orientation in birds. Day-flying migrants unable to see the sun's position (as under a heavy overcast) become disoriented. Birds can also determine direction by referring to skylight polarization patterns at dawn and dusk rather than via direct reference to the sun itself (Able 1993, 1995).

- Birds have some form of "internal clock" that allows them to compensate for the sun's normal daily movement and keep a steady course.

- Birds' use of the sun apparently involves a form of bicoordinate navigation, perhaps making use of the discrepancy in the sun's azimuth between where they are and where they want to be. (Azimuth is an arc on the horizon measured clockwise from the north or south compass point to the point on the horizon intersected by a vertical circle passing through the center of a celestial body, e.g., the sun). Though it has yet to be conclusively demonstrated, birds may also be able to sense variations in the earth's magnetic field (see below) that occur in relation to latitude and longitude; this would in effect provide them with a grid map of the earth surface

- Nocturnal migrants depend partly on the stars for orientation. Experiments with caged migrants by the Sauers (1960) and by Emlen (1967) showed that birds presented with artificial "skies" for a given migratory season oriented in the appropriate direction; when the sky was reversed the birds changed course accordingly and when they sky was obscured they became disoriented. By selectively blocking out key stars such as the North Star and major constellations, Emlen showed that Indigo Buntings could use any one of several celestial patterns if other were obscured. Time compensation in relation to star movements does not appear to be as highly developed as it is in solar navigation, though it may be more refined in long-distance migrants that require a more complex set of directional clues.

- The direction of migration (north or south) is clearly influenced at least in some species by hormonal predisposition. By artificially altering day length for different groups of caged birds Emlen (1970) was able to stimulate physiological "readiness" to migrate north in one group and south in another. When he exposed the birds to the same false sky, the birds followed their hormonal drives rather than the available star map.

- It has been amply demonstrated that birds can sense and orient according to the earth's magnetic field. This has been shown in controlled experiments both by attaching magnets to birds, thereby disrupting the sensation produced by the earth's magnetism (Kee-

ton 1972), and by observing birds' reactions to an artificially created field similar in force to the earth's (Lancaster and Johnson 1976). Walcott et al. (1979) located a small structure between the brain and the skull in pigeons that contains magnetite and that is used to sense the earth's magnetic field for the purpose of orientation. Birds use their magnetic compass by detecting the direction of electromagnetic force and the dip angle of the lines of force. There is evidence that a bird's magnetic compass may be a fundamental innate navigational system that can function in the absence of observed cues such as the stars. For a summary of research on this use of the magnetic field, see especially Wiltschko and Wiltschko (1988).

- Some aspects of timing and course setting also appear to be innate. Captive birds exhibit migratory restlessness and other physical phenomena over the same time periods—sometimes several months— during which they would normally be migrating. And migrants reared in captivity make compass corrections in the laboratory that correspond to those their species typically makes along traditional travel routes.

- Navigational ability is also acquired from experience at least in some species. Perdeck's famous experiments (1958, 1967) proved that displaced adult European Starlings readily corrected course to reach their traditional wintering grounds while inexperienced juvenile birds from the same population seemed to know the direction they should follow but could not adjust their course when they were displaced. The implication is that while they are born with some basic instructions about which direction to go in and perhaps how far, juvenile birds of at least some species must learn the more detailed geography of their specific wintering areas.

- At least some birds use smell to find their own nest sites once they are, so to speak, in the neighborhood. This has been experimentally demonstrated in Leach's Storm-Petrels, which fly downwind of their colony on arrival to pick up and follow the scent of their particular nest burrow (Grubb 1974). This would seem to be especially practical for birds such as many seabirds that must find a tiny burrow among hundreds at night amidst acres of similar habitat; these birds are known to have an acute sense of smell, which they use to locate food as well as home. Pigeons may have a similar ability, but the experimental evidence is ambiguous.

- Migration routes of species and populations may change more often than we have previously supposed and the genetic programs that set a bird's course can apparently evolve rapidly to accommodate the new travel plan. In recent years some Blackcaps (a species of Old World warbler) from Germany began wintering in the British Isles rather than their "normal" wintering grounds in the western

Mediterranean and North Africa. The young of the British-wintering Blackcaps showed an innate tendency to head northwest rather than southwest in the fall (Berthold 1991).

- Several studies (e.g., Bellrose 1958) have demonstrated that some displaced birds have a tendency to orient decisively in the *wrong* direction (i.e., away from any conceivable "home"). Matthews (1961) terms this "nonsense orientation."
- Many factors in addition to the ones noted above may play a role in bird navigation. Theories linking avian orientation to perception of infrared light rays or the Coriolis force have been hotly debated. The possible influences of prevailing winds continue to be investigated, and most workers in the field concede the possibility of influences, or even avian faculties, as yet unimagined.

In summary, the sophisticated navigation systems used by birds clearly involve a *combination* of orientation aids beginning with innate physiological factors, such as magnetic orientation and hormonal rhythms, that dictate flight duration and the like and supplemented with a wide range of external cues, such as celestial bodies, landmarks, wind direction, odors, or other perceptions of which we are still unaware. It is also increasingly evident that there is great variation among different groups of birds in the mechanisms used. Far from dispelling our amazement that a supposedly "simple" creature with no instruction can routinely find its way between two highly specific "addresses" separated by thousands of miles, the research of the last 50 years serves rather to increase our wonder. Considering that to date our studies have explored this remarkable phenomenon among a mere handful of migratory species, it seems more than likely that many details of this intricate design remain to be filled in.

See also MIGRATION.

NEARCTIC REGION (nee-ARK-tik). One of the six major zoogeographic regions of the world. It includes all of North America south to an irregular line across Mexico that marks the northern limits of tropical rain forest. At the edges of the Nearctic, there are zones of overlap with adjacent regions in which the neighboring avifaunas are strongly represented. Western Alaska, for example, shares many species with the contiguous Palearctic region, and the southern borders of the Nearctic are crossed by many species of largely Neotropical distribution.

"Nearctic birds" include those that breed exclusively within the Nearctic region but winter in the Neotropics (e.g., most wood warblers) as well as those that range wholly in North America (e.g., Henslow's Sparrow). Compare NEOTROPICAL REGION; PALEARCTIC REGION; HOLARCTIC REGION; see also ZOOGEOGRAPHY; DISTRIBUTION; and Fig. 34.

NECTIVOROUS (nek-TIH-vor-us). Literally, nectar-eating. Nectivorous birds are those that feed largely on nectar from flowers or the juices of

fruits. The most highly specialized of nectivores are, of course, the hummingbirds, with powerful hovering flight and long bills adapted for probing the calyxes of blossoms as a principal feeding technique. The bills of orioles are also adapted for nectar feeding, as are those of some warblers—especially the Cape May with its tubular, slightly decurved bill and brush-tip tongue—and the Bananaquit. All of these birds also must seek a protein supplement of insects, which in many cases are easily found around the same flowers from which the birds are feeding on nectar. Many other birds, including woodpeckers, tanagers, and finches, occasionally feed on nectar.

NEOSPECIES. A modern species, i.e., one that has lived within the recent geological period, whose status as a species can be defined according to the usual biological criteria (see SPECIES; SPECIATION). Compare PALEOSPECIES.

NEOTROPICAL REGION (Neotropics). One of the six major zoogeographic regions of the world, each of which is distinguishable by broad floral and faunal characteristics. The northern boundary of the Neotropics is an irregular line across Mexico that marks the northern limits of tropical rain forest. The region encompasses everything south of this line in the New World, excepting American Antarctica, but including the islands of the West Indies, the islands of coastal Latin America, and the entire mainland of South America south of the Tropic of Capricorn. The political boundaries of North America largely coincide with the boundaries of the Nearctic region; however, many bird species that breed mainly in the Neotropics (and in tropical lowland habitats) reach the southernmost regions of the United States, e.g.: the Masked Duck, Short-tailed Hawk, Northern Jacana, White-tipped Dove, Mangrove Cuckoo, several hummingbird species, Elegant Trogon, Tropical Kingbird, Green Jay, and Black-headed Oriole, to name a few. See also NEARCTIC REGION; ZOOGEOGRAPHY; DISTRIBUTION; and Fig. 34.

NERVOUS SYSTEM. The function of any animal nervous system may be compared to an electrical network attached to a control center. In effect, it "turns on" all the bodily functions—senses, muscles, internal organs—and regulates and coordinates their activities, enabling most humans, for example, to think, breathe, hear, smell, walk, and chew gum all at the same time. The nerves, like wires, pick up sensations through the sensory organs and either induce an automatic reaction or transmit the signal to the brain or spinal cord, which processes the data and determines an appropriate response. This response is also transmitted by nerves and stimulates muscular action.

A bird's nervous system has the same major parts arranged in the same general pattern as that of other vertebrate animals, but with

numerous specific modifications that relate to a bird's unique manner of living.

Nervous systems are usually explained in terms of three "subsystems"—the *central nervous system* (brain and spinal cord), the *peripheral nervous system* (the main voluntary nerves controlling senses, movement, etc.), and the *autonomic nervous system* (the self-controlling or involuntary nerves that operate the heart, glands, blood flow, and other internal functions).

But these are all part of one unified system and are inextricably interconnected with the other systems. It may be easier, therefore, to understand its workings in terms of the major parts and their functions.

THE BRAIN. Despite the derogatory implications of "bird brain," birds have the largest brains in proportion to body weight of all animals except some mammals. As in humans, a bird's brain is divided into front, middle, and rear sections (the fore-, mid-, and hindbrains). The arrangement of these parts in a bird's skull is somewhat different from that in the skulls of other animals, and the presence and/or size of specific parts are indications of the physical and mental strengths and weaknesses of birds. Brains of different groups of birds vary in adaptation to specialized habits and in general development.

The Forebrain is largely taken up by two symmetrical lobes, the *cerebral hemispheres* or cerebrum, which is composed mainly of a mass of nerve cells called basal ganglia. Covering the cerebral hemispheres in humans is that gray, convoluted, and furrowed structure that most of us associate strongly with the physical appearance of the brain. This is the cerebral *cortex* or pallium and is responsible for man's learning capacity and intelligence. This structure is all but lacking in birds, at best reduced to a thin layer atop the cerebrum, and this vestigial cortex was long believed to imply great mental limitations in birds. Research has revealed, however, that as birds and mammals diverged from reptiles, the brains of both groups enlarged significantly but evolved different anatomical means of expanding intelligence. Replacing the mass of the cortex in birds is the *corpus striatum* composed mainly of the *hyperstriatum* and below it the *neostriatum*. The hyperstriatum is found only in birds and corresponds to the cortex in mammals as the powerhouse of intelligence. A bird's most sophisticated intellectual processes appear to be centered in the *Wulst,* an enlargement at the front of the hyperstriatum. As one would predict, the hyperstriatum is most highly developed in the smartest birds, e.g., members of the parrot and crow families (see INTELLIGENCE).

The forebrain as a whole acts as a command center, integrating sensory signals, applying learned abilities, and issuing instructions governing complex behaviors such as nest building and migratory strategies. Attached to the front of the cerebrum is the olfactory bulb or lobe (see SMELL). The rear part of the forebrain (diencephalon) consists in part of

the hypothalamus, which is important in the function of the endocrine as well as the nervous system. It regulates body temperature, involuntary sensations such as sleepiness, hunger, and thirst, and certain physical reactions to emotional stimulation. The hippocampal complex, critical to memory functions, rests atop the forebrain (see MEMORY).

The Midbrain of a bird consists essentially of the optic lobes, which are located on the sides of and below the cerebrum, rather than on top of it, as in most animals. Given the importance of sight to most birds, it is not surprising to find that they have large and prominent optic lobes; in species in which vision is less important, the lobes are smaller. (Some works include the cerebellum as part of the midbrain; see below).

The Rear of the Brain includes the cerebellum and the medulla oblongata. The cerebellum, located behind and below the cerebrum, is relatively large in birds—understandably, as it coordinates muscular activity, controls balance, and determines the quality of each movement, and is thus of prime importance in flight. The medulla oblongata may be thought of as an enlargement on the top of the spinal column. It functions in voice production, hearing, breathing, and circulation, among other things.

The Cranial Nerves attach in twelve pairs to all three regions of the brain. They are named and numbered (I–XII) exactly as in the human system and activate both senses and muscles in the head and neck: smell, eye functions (five of the cranial muscles are involved with vision and eye movement), hearing, taste, salivation, bill, tongue, neck, larynx, and syrinx.

SPINAL CORD AND NERVES. The spinal cord runs from the base of the brain to the last vertebra in a narrow canal down the center of the backbone. Pairs of spinal nerves, spaced along the length of the spinal cord, lead to and control the external muscles. The spinal cord is enlarged where the two great pairs of nerve networks (wing plexus and leg plexus) arise to control functions of those limbs. These two major spinal nerve centers vary in size and complexity, depending on the degree to which a species habitually uses its wings or legs. (For reaction of muscles to nerve impulses, see MUSCLES.)

Balance is controlled from the cerebellum through the spinal cord, but the spinal cord itself controls most of the motor activities of the body. This spinal independence from the brain is clearly inferred from the ability of a chicken to run around the barnyard for a short period after it has been decapitated.

INVOLUNTARY NERVES (AUTONOMIC NERVOUS SYSTEM). These nerves stimulate internal functions, such as circulation, digestion, and the secretion of hormones, over which animals have little voluntary control. There are two types of involuntary nerves, which work, as it were, *against* each other. The first type (sympathetic) stimulates those processes appropriate for activity or excitement, e.g., increasing pulse rate and adrenaline

secretion while shutting off digestion; the opposing (parasympathetic) does just the reverse. Both types are ultimately connected to the cranial or spinal nervous systems, which integrate their actions with the working of the entire system. They are regulated in part by the hypothalamus.

NEST (nesting). A broad term even when restricted to a zoological context, but most often refers to a place where eggs are laid and develop. Some bird's nests are no more than "a place," but many more are distinctive structures of intricate architecture.

FUNCTION. Since some species construct no enclosure whatever for their eggs, it can be argued that nests are not, strictly speaking, necessary. However, it is clear from their elaborate evolution and general prevalence that nests have aided survival by protecting eggs and young from weather and predation and perhaps by increasing the efficiency of the rearing process.

A single small family of birds, the Australasian megapodes, bury their eggs in warm earth or decaying vegetation, thereby relieving themselves of the duties of INCUBATION (though trading these for the perhaps only slightly less tedious "oven-tending." Grebes and a few other species of North American birds cover their eggs with dead plant material when they leave their nests temporarily, and it has been suggested that this, too, is a form of "carefree" incubation.

Cactus Wrens and Verdins, which build enclosed nests, and many hole nesters use their nests "off season" or in bad weather for night roosting and shelter. Nests may also provide hospitality for an astonishing variety of nonavian creatures. Small rodents frequently take over abandoned bird's nests and legions of invertebrates may be resident, especially while a nest is in use (see NEST FAUNA).

Aside from aesthetic pleasure, humans have found little use for bird's nests; however, see BIRD'S NEST SOUP.

PHYSIOLOGY. Like most other functions of avian life, the nesting urge is tied to a bird's hormonal cycles. The earliest manifestation of this urge—prospecting for a suitable site—coincides with the mating and copulation period and, at least in some species, nest building parallels the development of the fertilized ovum.

Hormonal triggers (mostly estrogens and androgens) are in turn set off by external phenomena such as temperature and precipitation, so that site selection, for example, may be prolonged due to bad weather.

NESTING BEHAVIOR

Site Selection. Once a pair of birds has mated, choosing a place to lay the eggs becomes a high priority. Either or both partners may undertake this responsibility, according to the habits of their species, but the female dominates the process in the majority of cases. Birds that return to old nest sites in successive years are, of course, relieved of this responsibility.

For some species, e.g., many colonial seabirds, choosing a site is mostly ritual, with the final selection apparently quite arbitrary. Most species, however, "shop around" for a while, a process that may include "fitting" the body into prospective tree forks or patches of ground. This prospecting period varies in length from species that seem to take the first site they see and immediately start construction, to tits and others that inspect sites year round. Specialized, relatively scarce sites, e.g., tree cavities, require more rigorous testing and prolonged searching than more commonplace ones, but for the majority of species site selection probably consumes a few days under optimal conditions.

Nest Building seems on superficial observation to be clear proof of a highly sophisticated avian brain. Any human who tries to make a good facsimile of a Baltimore Oriole's closely woven sack or a Cliff Swallow's gracefully sculptured pottery cell cannot but be impressed by these species' architectural and engineering skills. However, even given recent research that has generally upgraded our estimation of avian intelligence, we also need to recognize that individual birds are not inventing original works of art or specialized craftsmanship from scratch when they set out to make their first nest. It is evident that many nest-building skills are, as it were, "hard-wired" genetically. Through observation we know that birds (both of one species and different species) use a lot of stereotyped motions in building nests, and it has been shown experimentally that captive-reared birds can make decent facsimiles of finished nests without ever seeing one built. It is also true, however, that abnormal nests are not uncommon and that young birds are often less skilled engineers than their elders, so that some learning of the "practice makes perfect" kind must also occur. Furthermore, no bird can possibly be born knowing where particular lining material can be found. As with migration/navigation, this kind of "explanation" never seems to adequately account for the apparent discrepancy between a bird's limited intelligence (compared, at least, with that of humans) and the complexity of the nest-building process. It is perhaps not too inaccurate to say that a bird has something like an inherited mental program that shows it what the nest is supposed to look like at various stages of construction and that when one stage has been adequately completed, the bird gets a "sense of satisfaction" and has the urge to proceed, so to speak, to the next illustration in the mental plan.

The many individual tasks required in nest construction vary greatly among species because of different nesting habits (see below). Birds that live in the ground or in banks must expend time and energy in excavation, unless they colonize another species' hole. Many icterids are unusually skilled in weaving. Some swallows and swifts are expert masons. And, except for brood parasites, all passerines (as well as many nonpasserines) are natural masters of a variety of building and shaping skills. Ornithologists have defined a number of nest-building gestures, such as "tacking,"

"drawing," "looping," and "squatting," which are characteristic of many species. Gill (1995–ORNITHOLOGY, pp. 387–389) illustrates some basic techniques.

The effort that goes into nest construction also varies among species. Many species forgo the process altogether and simply lay their eggs on a bare surface or take over an abandoned nest without making alterations. Eagles and other members of their family that return each year to old nest sites apparently never lose the urge to build. In some species additions are perfunctory, but Bald Eagles add many new sticks each year, creating an enormous edifice over decades. Male wrens build a series of DUMMY NESTS, and species, such as rails, that nest low near water must continue or resume nest building if the water level rises. Furthermore, in many species these various labors are repeated once or more in a single season (see Nesting Pattern, below).

In some species, a young bird from a first brood will help in the construction of its parents' second nest of the season, a practice with apparent benefits to all concerned.

Nesting Pattern and Timing. Most birds build a new nest for each brood they rear, even when double- or triple-brooded, but less time and energy are expended each time in nest construction; gnatcatchers often transport old nest materials to a new nest site. The California Condor and a few species of long-distance pelagic migrants that breed in the Southern Hemisphere (e.g., Greater Shearwater) breed only every other year. But the former builds no nest of any kind and the latter usually reoccupy old burrows and make no obvious improvements, so that there is little or no nesting effort by either one in any case.

Whether a species is single- or multiple-brooded depends on both the inherent nature of the species and the climate in which it lives. Some species or families (e.g., wood warblers) tend to be single-brooded even in southern North America, where climate would permit a second or third brood. Most North American birds are single-brooded, but a significant percentage of passerines rear a second brood and a few (e.g., Mourning and other doves, some wrens, mimids, bluebirds, House Finch, and Song

Fig. 21. *Nesting habits* are wonderfully varied among different groups of birds. The examples illustrated are (clockwise from top left): stick platforms in an arboreal heronry; tree cavity excavated by woodpeckers; pendulous sack woven by some oriole species; the "standard" cup nest of most songbirds set on a wide branch, in a crotch, or on a level surface on a building; the cup suspended from a small fork typical of vireos; the clustered, flask-shaped "adobe" homes of Cliff Swallows; the tunnel and chamber excavated by kingfishers (shown "cut-away"); the floating platform of soggy aquatic plants favored by grebes; the ground burrow of a storm-petrel; the unlined scrape of a Least Tern; a swan's mound of plant material and debris; the spherical basket woven into rushes or cattails by male Marsh Wrens; and the massive heap of sticks (with central cup) piled up year after year by Golden Eagles and other diurnal birds of prey.

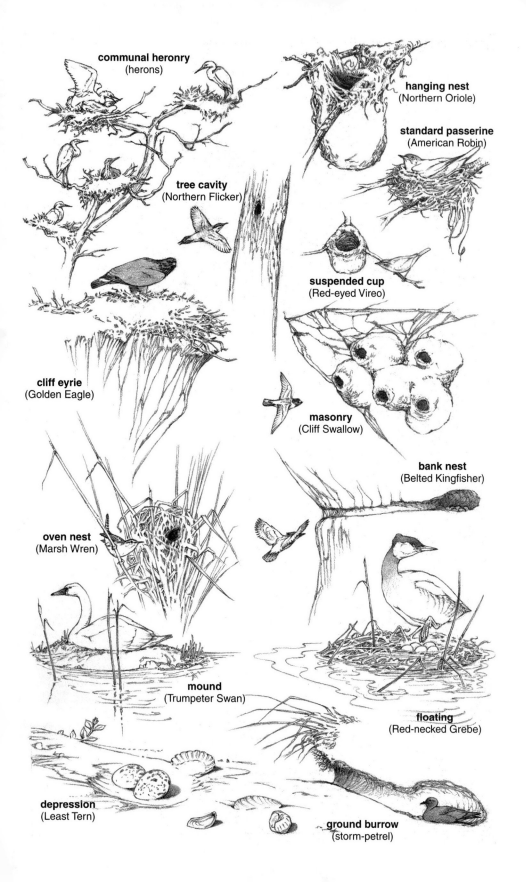

communal heronry
(herons)

hanging nest
(Northern Oriole)

standard passerine
(American Robin)

tree cavity
(Northern Flicker)

suspended cup
(Red-eyed Vireo)

cliff eyrie
(Golden Eagle)

masonry
(Cliff Swallow)

bank nest
(Belted Kingfisher)

oven nest
(Marsh Wren)

mound
(Trumpeter Swan)

floating
(Red-necked Grebe)

depression
(Least Tern)

ground burrow
(storm-petrel)

and Field Sparrows) are typically treble-brooded in the southern parts of their range. More than three broods is very exceptional, but the Common Ground-Dove, with a prolonged breeding season (February–November), is suspected of rearing up to four broods and the Inca Dove, on a similar schedule, is known to have reared five. None of these numbers include renesting due to parasitism or loss of eggs or young—not uncommon events in avian life.

The time required to build the nest is also highly variable. None is required, of course, for nestless species. Most passerines do the job in 3–9 days, though the period may be prolonged by cold or otherwise bad weather; this is especially true of Tree and some other swallows, which can take over a month to build as nest. As might be expected, nest construction, like the rest of the breeding cycle, is accelerated in the brief arctic summer, and the process tends to be prolonged in the warmer climate of southern areas. The complexity of the nest structure is also a factor: the long, pendulous sack of the Altamira Oriole may take 3 weeks or more; but, in general, birds are surprisingly efficient. A Bank Swallow, for example, can excavate a 2-foot tunnel nest in 5–6 days, though apparently ill-equipped for digging.

Sexual Roles. Site selection and nest building (as well as other nest activities; see INCUBATION and PARENTAL CARE) tend, on the whole, to be dominated by the female. On the other hand, males are rarely exempted entirely from these duties. Verner and Wilson (1969) determined that in 56% of North American passerines, males made some contribution to nest building. In most species they play only a minor or ritual role, but in others (e.g., gnatcatchers), males are very effective nest builders.

The Red Phalarope may be the only North American species in which the male alone is responsible for nest construction, although unmated male cormorants are known to build a nest, which is then rearranged by the female if and when she consents to mate. Among all hummingbirds; most tits, icterids, tanagers, and finches; and some flycatchers, swallows, vireos, and wood warblers, the female alone builds the nest. In most species nest building is shared in a variety of ways. Pairs of woodpeckers, waxwings, gnatcatchers, and some swallows divide responsibility equally; in Mourning and other dove species, the female builds while the male brings materials; among frigatebirds the reverse applies; in some cases the male will build certain parts of the nest and the female the rest; male Phainopeplas begin their nests and their mates finish them; male wrens of some species build a series of nest "shells" and the female selects one and lines it for occupation; however, in House Wrens the female does all the real work, with the male reduced to ineffective and ritualistic stick-carrying (Alworth and Scheiber 2000).

MATERIALS. In general, birds of a given species will use similar materials in making their nest; however, there is considerable variation, de-

pending on the availability of materials and individual "taste." Great Cormorant nests on offshore islands have a large component of seaweed, for example, while inland arboreal nests of the same species are made mainly of sticks with little or no seaweed. When horses were ubiquitous many species built with horsehair, a scarce material today, which has been replaced by plant fibers. Though the vast majority of nests are made with a small number of "basic" components—mostly plant material—in some cases held together with a binding substance (see below), a few species characteristically incorporate an "odd" item. Great Crested Flycatcher nests, for example, usually contain snakeskin—though not for protective purposes, as is sometimes supposed. Some species seem to like to "decorate" their nests with flowers or man-made materials, such as paper (Blue Jay), rags (Northern Mockingbird, American Robin), or yarn (Baltimore Oriole). Individual birds learn where certain materials can be found within their home range or territory and will return to the source consistently.

Materials commonly used for basic external nest structure include sticks, grasses, cattail, sedges (*Scirpus*, etc.), rushes (*Juncus*), seaweed, wet decaying aquatic plants, Spanish moss (*Tillandsia usneoides*), bark, foliose lichens, paper, string/yarn, "debris," and mud.

All passerines and many other species line their nests; some ground nesters (e.g., phalaropes, Savannah Sparrow) make no external nest but simply line a scrape or hollow in the earth. Lining is the last stage in the construction of complex nests and the materials used are much finer than those used in the "walls." Typical lining materials are leaves (dead or fresh), fine grasses, *Usnea* lichens, fungal fibers (mycelia), moss, plant down (thistle, milkweed, etc.), bark fibers, pine needles, contour feathers, down feathers (Anseriformes only), and animal hair/fur.

Some nests are loose and dry—the flimsy platform of sticks typical of most doves and pigeons are the ultimate in this mode. Other nests (e.g., orioles, vireos) are given shape and coherence by careful "sewing" or weaving techniques.

Many species solidify their nests with some form of binding material. This process varies widely in both extent and materials used. Some nests are pure "adobe" (e.g., Cliff Swallow; see below); the phoebes build largely of mud but with a larger proportion of plant material; American Robins "plaster" their interior walls with mud and then add a further lining of fine grasses; crows sometimes use small amounts of mud or animal dung; the excrement of nestlings adds to the solidity of the nest structure in some species; swifts (most species) are unique in cementing their nests with their own gluey saliva (see below); and hummingbirds, kinglets, and other small species use spider and caterpillar silk to bind the fine materials used in their diminutive nests.

Red-breasted Nuthatches daub pine sap around the entrance holes of their nest cavities, and Red-cockaded Woodpeckers create a copious flow

of resin around their nest holes by drilling tap holes in the surrounding bark. It is thought that these practices may afford protection from insects, snakes, and/or other nest pests.

NESTING LOCATIONS. Bird's nests are found in virtually every conceivable situation except in midair, on the surface of the sea (the legends of the halcyon to the contrary notwithstanding), and underwater. Placement ranges from 3 or more feet below the earth's surface (Burrowing Owl, some auks) to over 100 feet in trees (kinglets, Lewis's Woodpecker, Marbled Murrelet: 148 feet). The tops of our tallest trees, e.g., the sequoias, which often approach and occasionally exceed 300 feet, seem to be avoided by birds—or at least there are no data for these heights. Particular species tend to nest within a characteristic range of heights, which, however, may be quite broad and span two or more niches. Ground nesters never nest in treetops and treetop species do not nest on the ground, but some ground nesters will also build in low shrubs or the lower branches of trees and treetop species may descend to within a few feet of the ground. This variation may be seasonal and geographical as well as individual. Eastern Towhees and Song and Field Sparrows frequently build their first nest of the season on the ground and move up into the shrubbery for successive broods. Species, such as the Osprey, that use trees where they exist will nonetheless nest on the ground in barren country; they also use tall manmade structures—channel markers, jetties, silos, power poles, etc.—with such frequency that they almost seem to prefer them to trees.

Requirements as to the kind of situation in which the nest is built are also very generalized in many cases. Long-eared Owls will nest well up in trees (in abandoned raptor or squirrel nests), on the forest floor at the base of a tree, in scrubby growth, or even in open marshland or sand dunes. Some cavity nesters, e.g., the House Wren, will appropriate virtually any hole of the right size regardless of the substance in which it occurs (see Audubon's plate—Havell LXXXIII); the American Robin may prefer a tree branch but will not disdain a rock ledge, the eaves of a house, or even the ground under some circumstances. Many species have come to regard man-made structures as acceptable nest sites (see below) and a few—the Barn Swallow, phoebes, House Sparrow, Chimney Swift—have come to prefer them to what nature offers. Barn Swallows, House Sparrows, and wagtails have been recorded with some frequency nesting on ferries, following the craft on its daily rounds to brood their eggs and feed their young.

Some birds enhance nesting security—whether by design or chance—by nesting close to other, more aggressive bird species. For example, several species of songbirds have occasionally nested among the twiggy interstices of a raptor's nest, and birds nesting within tern or gull colonies doubtless derive some benefit from the latter's no-nonsense approach to

nest defense. A number of Neotropical bird species routinely nest near wasp or ant colonies, thereby deriving protection from predators without apparently incurring any risk to themselves; this technique is apparently not documented as yet for any North American species.

TYPES OF NESTS. Given the great diversity in bird forms, habitats, and habitat preferences, a comparable variety in nesting styles is hardly surprising. It is entirely appropriate that the tiny Calliope Hummingbird should build a nest measuring 1½ inches in diameter, ⅞-inch high, and weighing perhaps an ounce; equally so that a Bald Eagle's nest accumulated over decades should attain a diameter of 9 feet, a depth of 20 feet, and eventually weigh a ton or two.

The type of nest a species makes (or does not make) is less variable than the materials it uses or the location it chooses. However, many species (especially passerines) build similar structures. Basic types of North American bird's nests are categorized below. The categories are broad, i.e., a range of variation is represented within each type—all cup nests, for example, are not exactly the same. Other circumstances related to nesting (e.g., preference for man-made structures) are also categorized. Certain species, especially those with variable habits, will appear under more than one heading. Nest types are also noted briefly under bird group headings in the main text, e.g., GREBE.

1. *No nest* or at most a scrape with scant lining, in the open:
   Loons: also #3
   Northern Fulmar: usually cliffs
   Masked and Blue-footed Boobies: make circle of guano on ground; Masked also #7
   Vultures and California Condor: also #5 and #6; Black Vultures sometimes move eggs to new sites
   Gyrfalcon: also #13
   Prairie Falcon: also #13
   Peregrine Falcon
   Merlin: very variable
   Kestrels: make no modifications to cavity nests; thus consistent with other falcons
   Grouse family (Tetraonidae): sometimes form a nest hollow
   Pheasant/quail family (Phasianidae)
   Oystercatchers
   American Avocet
   Plovers: often sparsely lined
   Jaegers
   Most tern species
   Black Skimmer
   Some alcids: murres, Kittlitz's Murrelet (usually on cliffs or open ground)

Larger owls: many, however, also use cavities or old hawk nests

All nightjars: sometimes move eggs to new sites

2. *Lined scrape,* i.e., little or no external nest structure, but with a substantial lining:

Anseriformes: unique in lining their nests with down feathers plucked from the breast of the female, except for the whistling ducks and the stifftails; geese line with plant material as well as down; ducks line with down only (see also #6)

Sandpipers (Scolopacidae): lined with grasses and other dry plant material; depth of scrape variable but Sanderling exceptional in making true cup (see #9); Solitary Sandpiper also exceptional (see #13)

Some gulls: Sabine's, Ring-billed, Mew, and Ivory

Some sparrows: e.g., Savannah and Grasshopper make little more than a cup-shaped lining in a depression in the ground, i.e., midway between this category and #9

3. *Mounds* on open ground or in shallow water:

Loons: also #1

Grebes: also #4

Northern Gannet: largely seaweed

Pelicans: earth and debris

Cormorants: largely seaweed; Great and Neotropic also #7

Herons: in treeless country; most species usually #7; bitterns usually low in dense marsh vegetation

Roseate Spoonbill: rarely (see #7)

All ibises: mainly #7; but also on ground in dense marsh vegetation

Swans: large mounds of plant material, hollowed at top; down-lined; sometimes use muskrat houses

Whistling ducks: do not line with down; Black-bellied usually #6

Canvasback: also #4

Ruddy Duck: also #4; usually lacks down lining; known to use muskrat house

American Flamingo: low mud cylinders with hollow in top for egg

Bald Eagle: in treeless country; normally #7

Everglade Kite: occasionally; sticks with finer lining; primarily #7

Osprey: in treeless country; normally #7

Northern Harrier: sticks and reeds

Cranes: marsh-plant materials

Limpkin: in marshes; also #7

Gallinules and American Coot: in marsh vegetation

Some gulls: large species, Herring, etc., as well as Laughing and Kittiwake

Forster's Tern: sometimes #4 or on muskrat house

Black Tern: usually #4

Brown Noddy: occasionally; primarily #7

4. *Floating nests,* normally made of dead aquatic vegetation and anchored to living plants:

Grebes: sometimes #3; unlined

Tundra: occasionally; also #3; down-lined

Canvasback: occasionally; also #3; down-lined

Ruddy Duck: also #3; no down

Northern Jacana: loose, wet plant matter lying atop floating vegetation

Franklin's Gull

Forster's Tern: also #3

Black Tern: also #3, #13

5. *Ground holes,* including burrows, bank holes, and crevices in rocks. Some species, e.g., tubenoses, alcids, Burrowing Owl, kingfishers, and swallows, can dig their own holes, though many will also occupy sites that were dug by other members of their species or by different species.

Shearwaters and petrels: burrows or rock crevices of varying depths; scantily lined with debris

Tropicbirds: often in rock holes or crevices, unlined

Some ducks: tree-hole nesters (see #6) will occasionally use a hole in a bank or an old rabbit hole; down-lined

Some alcids: most auklets, Dovekie, Xantus's Murrelet, Razorbill, and guillemots usually prefer rock crevices with little or no lining; Rhinoceros Auklet, puflms, and Ancient Murrelet use burrows of varying depths, usually with linings

Burrowing Owl: usually in prairie dog or other mammal burrows; debris-lined

White-throated Swift: rock crevices, old Rough-winged Swallow holes (rarely); varied nest material glued with bird's saliva

Elegant Trogon: rarely; usually #6

Kingfishers: earth banks; unlined but rank with excrement and food remains

Bank and Rough-winged Swallows (will use old, dry drain pipes)

Juniper/Oak Titmouse: rarely in earthen bank; usually #6

Many wrens (e.g., House, Winter, Carolina, Bewick's): occupy almost any opening of the right proportions, including crevices in banks or rocks; generously lined; also #6, #8, #11, and #16

Canyon and Rock Wrens: often in rock cavity; cup-like construction

Mountain Bluebird: sometimes in rock crevices or earthen banks; lined, cup-like construction; also #6

Northern Wheatear: rocky crevices; loose, cup-like construction; rabbit burrows in Eurasia.

Townsend's Solitaire: sometimes in rocky crevice; cup-like construction (#8) with lining; also #6, #10

White Wagtail: sometimes in rock cavities or holes in earthen banks; very variable; lined, cup-like construction (#8)

American Pipit: sometimes in shallow bank or rock cavity; lined, cup-like construction (#9); also #10

European Starling: occasionally in rock crevice; very variable (see #6, #16, etc.); loose, messy cup

Lucy's Warbler: rarely in earthen bank; usually #6

Waterthrushes: sometimes in banks very near water

Rosy-finches: occasionally in hole or rock crevice; cup-like construction

6. *Tree holes,* whether natural cavities in rotted trees, stumps, and fallen logs or (frequently) abandoned woodpecker holes. In addition to the woodpeckers, only the tits, nuthatches, and trogons often do their own excavation. While it is possible to define species generally as "tree-hole nesters" or "ground-hole nesters," it should be noted that it is the hole—the fact that it is a cavity, its size and location—rather than the material in which it occurs, or has been dug, that is of prime importance to the prospective occupants. Thus, most of the species below feel equally at home in a woodpecker hole, natural tree crevice, or nest box and a number occasionally fit in category #5.

Vultures, the tree ducks, the owls, and the trogons leave their cavities unlined; the ducks add only down and most of the passerines construct some form of lined cup.

Tree holes are scarce in nature compared with other nest sites, with fewer sites than prospective occupants, at least in some areas. Therefore, the fact that woodpeckers construct new holes each year crucially affects populations of forest and other cavity-nesting species. It is also clear that "cleaning" forests of dead and rotting timber—once entrenched dogma among foresters—has a major detrimental impact on the diversity of these ecosystems.

In view of the normal scarcity and recently accelerated decline of tree holes, the setting of nest boxes (see BIRDHOUSE) is all the more worthwhile and likely to be successful.

Ducks: Black-bellied Whistling-, Wood, Bufflehead, goldeneyes, Hooded and Common Mergansers

Merlin: occasionally; very variable; see also #1, #13

American Kestrel

Most owls: frequently; see also #13

Elegant Trogon

Woodpeckers

Flycatchers: Sulphur-bellied, Great Crested, and Western (sometimes)

Tree and Violet-green (rarely Rough-winged) Swallows, Purple Martin

All tits

All nuthatches

Brown Creeper: lined cup in crevice under loose bark of tree trunk

Some wrens: House, Bewick's, Carolina, and Winter; but all widely variable; see also #5, #8, #10, #16

All bluebirds: see also #5, #16

European Starling and mynahs: also #5 (starling) and #16

Prothonotary Warbler

Lucy's Warbler: also #5

Brewer's Blackbird: rarely; usually #8

7. *Stick platforms* in trees or lower vegetation. Nonpasserine nests are lined sparsely if at all.

Red-footed (and sometimes Masked) Booby

Great and Neotropic Cormorants: both also build on the ground (#3) in coastal areas, the former more frequently

Anhinga: lined with fresh leaves and moss

Most herons: also under #3

Wood Stork

Roseate Spoonbill

All ibises: also on ground (#3)

Most eagles, hawks, and Osprey: a few nest on ground in open country (#3), Northern Harrier habitually; some (e.g., falcons) use other species' abandoned nests (#13); American Kestrel and Merlin often in tree cavities (#6); mostly line (except falcons)

Plain Chachalaca: sparsely lined with leaves

Limpkin: sometimes in low trees; mainly #3; loose plant materials rather than sticks

Brown Noddy: sparsely lined with debris

Pigeons and doves: usually loosely constructed and very frail

Yellow-billed Cuckoo: other cuckoos under #8

Large owls: sometimes take over old stick platform built by hawks

Note: The nests of the larger corvids (especially Northern Raven) often seem to be simply large platforms of sticks (and are sometimes taken over by hawks and owls) but are essentially large cup nests (#8).

8. *Cup nests,* the "classic" bird's nest, typically with a coarser outer wall and finer lining, sometimes cemented with mud or dung, and, unless otherwise noted, in trees or shrubs. Species that build ground cups, domed nests, suspended nests, or mud cups—all essentially variations of the cup—are excluded here and listed under #9, #10, #11, and #12.

Bonaparte's Gull: in northern spruce forests; sticks, lined with grasses, lichen, etc.

Cuckoos (except Yellow-billed; #7), anis, Roadrunner: loosely made

Hummingbirds: nests; variable fine materials (e.g., lichen flakes) bound with spider silk, caterpillar silk, and/or plant fibers

Most flycatchers: see also #6, #10, #11

Crows and jays: see also #7 (Note) and #12

Brown Creeper: behind tree bark, equivalent to #6?

Wrentit

Red-whiskered Bulbul

All mimic thrushes: occasionally on ground (#9)

Most thrushes

Gnatcatchers

Waxwings

Phainopepla

Shrikes

Many warblers: including most *Dendroica*s, Bachman's, Olive, MacGillivray's (near ground), Yellowthroat (low), Yellow-breasted Chat, Hooded Warbler, and American Redstart

Some blackbirds: Red-winged and Tricolored (see Note below); Rusty, Brewer's (usually, but variable), grackles (often low)

White-collared Seedeater

Fringillid finches; tundra breeders (e.g., Hoary Redpoll) also on ground (#9)

Tanagers

Cardinal-Grosbeaks (including *Passerina* buntings)

Brown and Abert's Towhees

Many sparrows: some (e.g., Field and Song) nest on ground for first brood

Note: Red-winged and Tricolored Blackbirds and Sharp-tailed, Seaside, and Swamp Sparrows, all of which habitually nest in marshland, usually "weave" cup nests onto standing cattail or sedges, well above water level. Chimney and Vaux's Swifts build half-cups of twigs cemented together with their saliva and fixed to the inside of a hollow tree, chimney, or other vertical interior surface.

9. *Ground cups,* similar to #8 but on the earth, in marshland, or on rock ledges:

Rails: in marshland; with grass canopy, so listed also under #10; also affinities with mound-type nests (#3) but cup well made and lined with finer material

Sanderling (most sandpipers under #2)

Black Swift: mosses, mud (no saliva), on wet ledges, usually near seeping water

Yellow-bellied Flycatcher: in moss clumps or tree roots; often somewhat elevated

Cordilleran and Pacific-Slope Flycatchers

Larks

Canyon Wren: on open ledges or shelves; also #5

Some thrushes: Hermit, Veery (sometimes), Townsend's Solitaire (also #5), and Bluethroat

White Wagtail (sometimes)

Yellow Wagtail

Pipits (American Pipit also #5)

Many warblers: all *Vermivora*s (except Bachman's and Lucy's), plus Black-and-white, Worm-eating, Blackpoll (rarely), Kirtland's, Palm (usually), Kentucky, Mourning, Connecticut, Red-faced, Wilson's, Canada, Painted Redstart, and waterthrushes (also #5)

Bobolink and Brewer's Blackbird (rarely)

Dickcissel

Green-tailed, Eastern and Spotted Towhees (also #8)

Emberizid Sparrows: most sparrows nest on the ground, but many will also place their cups in low shrubbery at least occasionally; in some species (e.g., Field and Song) the higher nests are characteristic of later broods; some grassland sparrows (e.g., Savannah) have rather rudimentary nests amounting to little more than a lined scrape (#2)

Longspurs

10. *Domed or enclosed nests,* usually with a well-lined internal cup and either arboreal or on the ground:

Great Kiskadee

Northern Beardless Tyrannulet

Magpies: canopy of twigs

Verdin: spherical; thorny twigs

American Dipper: made of moss; on ledge or bank near river

Winter Wren: in some form of cavity (#5 and #6)

Carolina Wren: dome may be lacking in hole nests (#5 and #6)

Cactus Wren: often in cactus or other thorny plant

Marsh Wren: supported among marsh vegetation (cattail, sedges, rushes); relatively high above shallow water

Sedge Wren: supported among marsh sedges or rush; generally lower, over drier ground than preceding

Arctic Warbler: ground

Ovenbird: ground; named for its nest

Common Yellowthroat: on or very near ground; sometimes partially canopied

Meadowlarks

House and Eurasian Tree Sparrows: lack dome in cavities (#5, #7, #16)

Olive Sparrow

Seaside Sparrow: in salt-marsh grass clumps; sometimes partially domed

Note: Among the rails, Common Gallinule, some sandpipers (e.g., Upland) and phalaropes, living grasses or other plants near the nest may be pulled over it to form a rough concealing canopy.

11. *Suspended nests,* i.e., attached to and hanging from a branch or other support; form varies from the long, pendulous bags made by some orioles to the cups which the vireos hang between forked branches.

Rose-throated Becard: globular mass; entrance near bottom

Acadian Flycatcher: partially suspended, usually with a long unkempt festoon

Bushtit (a penduline tit): a long bag; entrance at top

Kinglets: usually a deep, suspended cup

All vireos: cup suspended in fork

All orioles: Baltimore, Bullock's, Spot-breasted, and Altamira weave long, hanging bags attached to branch ends (entrance at top); the other species' nests are more cup-like and are hung from a variety of sites—Hooded Oriole, for example, sometimes "sews" the top of the nest to the underside of a palm frond.

Note: Tropical and Northern Parulas and Yellow-throated Warbler often suspend their cup-like nests in hanging festoons of *Usnea* lichen or Spanish moss in regions where these epiphytic plants are common.

12. *Mud nests,* not including earthen mounds, e.g., Pelicans (#3). Barn and Cave Swallows and Eastern and Black Phoebes make cups (or half-cups) by the accretion of mud pellets mixed with binding substances such as grass, hair, or feathers. Except that the structures are built "wet" rather than of dried bricks, the similarity to human "adobe" construction is striking. By far the most skillful of the North American "potter" birds is the Cliff Swallow, which assembles "pueblos" of graceful beehive-shaped nests beneath overhanging rock faces or eaves. The Cave Swallow also attaches its nest to a vertical surface (in caves and sinkholes) but makes only a half-cup.

The Black Swift, Blue and Steller's Jays, the magpies and crows, Clark's Nutcracker, American Robin, and Varied, Gray-cheeked and Bicknell's Thrushes typically use some mud and/or dung in their nests.

13. *Secondhand nesters.* Almost all tree-cavity nesters (#6) use old woodpecker nests. Indeed, most depend on them for maintaining their population, though other kinds of cavities may also be used and some non-woodpeckers are capable of hewing out their own. *These species are omitted from the following list* unless they *also* appropriate other nest types. (In the list below, birds whose nests are taken over by a given species appear in parentheses.) A few species not only use another species' nest but also avail themselves of free incubation service (see BROOD PARASITISM); these species are marked "P."

Anhinga (egret)

Many ducks, esp. Hooded Merganser, Ruddy Duck, bay ducks: often lay eggs in other species' nests, especially before their own nests are complete; in some cases such birds may not lay a clutch of their own and thus rate a full "P" (see also DUMP NEST)

Falcons (ravens, Rough-legged and other hawks)

Solitary Sandpiper (American Robin, Bohemian Waxwing, Rusty Blackbird, Eastern Kingbird, and other songbirds)

Forster's Tern (grebes; also muskrats) (see also #4)

Black Tern (grebes, coots) (usually #3 or #4)

Mourning Dove (in rare cases builds on top of old songbird nests)

Large owls (ravens, hawks)

Yellow-billed and Black-billed Cuckoos (P: occasionally—with other cuckoos, Gray Catbird, Wood Thrush, Yellow Warbler, Chipping Sparrow) (usually #7 or #8)

Ash-throated Flycatcher (Cactus Wren)

Violet-green Swallow (Cliff and Bank Swallows)

Rough-winged Swallow (kingfishers)

Bluebirds (Cliff and other swallows)

White Wagtail (other songbirds, Osprey—crevices among sticks)

Lucy's Warbler (Verdin)

Great-tailed Grackle (heron rookeries)

Brown-headed Cowbird (P: wide range of small to medium-sized species, esp. flycatchers, vireos, warblers, and finches)

Bronzed Cowbird (P: wide range of small to medium-sized species, esp. orioles but also ground doves, flycatchers, thrashers, wrens, warblers, and finches)

House Finch (many songbirds, including Cliff Swallow)

14. *Communal nesters,* i.e., species that use a single nest for the eggs of several (or many) pairs. Some ducks will deposit "extra" eggs in the nest of another duck of the same or different species (see DUMP NEST). Only the Groove-billed and Smooth-billed Anis and the Acorn Woodpecker are known to make a habit of communal nesting in North America. In all these species, both sexes and most or

all individuals in a communal group incubate. Record numbers of eggs in a single nest of the Smooth-billed Ani is 29; Groove-billed Ani, 15; Acorn Woodpecker, 10.

15. *Colonial nesters,* see COLONY.
16. *Nests in/on man-made structures,* excluding the rarest incidences and the use of nest boxes (see #6 for latter). Species which seem now to prefer man-made structures to "natural" ones are marked with an asterisk.

Leach's Storm-Petrel: walls, buildings
Osprey: telephone poles, etc.—see list above (*?)
Peregrine*
American Kestrel
Herring and other gulls: flat gravel rooftops in cities
Rock Dove*
Barn Owl
Common Nighthawk:
Chimney* and Vaux's Swifts
Phoebes*
Some swallows—Barn,* Cliff, Rough-winged (pipes, holes in dry-docked boats), and Purple Martin
Some wrens—House, Bewick's, Carolina, Canyon, even Winter—on an iron bridge! (Ellison, personal communication)
American Robin
White Wagtail: walls, pipes, buildings
European Starling and Crested Mynah
Common Grackle
House* and Eurasian Tree Sparrows
House Finch: often in hanging plant baskets and wreaths

FINDING AND IDENTIFYING NESTS. Not very long ago one could still mount an expedition to search for a North American bird's nest that no one had ever seen. The last vestige of this frontier passed into history on August 7, 1974, when the nest of the Marbled Murrelet was found—a small cup, made mainly of guano, laid improbably 148 feet up in a Douglas-fir in Big Basin State Park, Santa Cruz County, California. Another wet blanket on the ardor of the would-be nest seeker is the fact that the laws that prohibit the collection of most native birds also protect their nests and eggs (see LAWS PROTECTING BIRDLIFE).

These realities of the modern era do not, however, prevent the dedicated birdwatcher from both adding to our knowledge of birdlife and having fun with nests. Countless details of nest construction, site preferences, frequency of renesting, and the degree of variation shown by any given species remain to be recorded. Properly identified off-season nests can be used in confirming the presence of a particular species in breeding-bird atlas work—a popular concept that is entering its second generation in

some states even as new ones are started in many western states (see ATLAS, BREEDING BIRD).

Looking for nests in winter, when the absence of most leaves makes the beginner's efforts reasonably rewarding, can add a lot to a stroll through your neighborhood or a nearby wilderness. There are now a number of good field guides to help with identification, and most people over twelve will probably not be very disappointed at not being able to bring these treasures home.

Watching nesting activities "live" is also rewarding—once you've watched a Baltimore Oriole stitching its distinctive bag together, you may find yourself addicted to this benign form of voyeurism.

Caution must always be mentioned in this context, but common sense will guide most people who are taking the trouble to read this. Most birds will abandon their nest without a pang given what they regard as due cause, and some species are much more skittish than others. Birds are particularly liable to disturbance during the early phases of the cycle. Whole colonies of terns, for example, may abandon a site they've used for years for reasons that seem (to us at least) whimsical at best. On the other hand, most birds are quite tolerant of observation and once your presence has been found innocuous you can often count on being ignored.

If a bird flushes off eggs or stops feeding young at your approach, back off; you're too close, at least for the present. If you are the kind of person who wants to fondle, sniff, and eyeball each of life's new wonders, restrain yourself—at least where active nests are involved.

For nesting habits (including descriptions of nest and eggs) of particular families, see ALBATROSS; BOOBY; CORMORANT; etc.

See also EGG; INCUBATION; PARENTAL CARE; YOUNG, DEVELOPMENT; BIRDHOUSE; NEST FAUNA.

NEST BOX. See BIRDHOUSE.

NEST FAUNA. As Harold Oldroyd, the British fly specialist, has pointed out succinctly (1964–NEST): "The nests of birds are attractive to a variety of insects because they provide at the same time shelter, concealment, a supply of highly nutritious bird guano and the opportunity to attack the birds themselves." It should be added that invertebrate inhabitants of bird's nests are by no means restricted to insects. Ticks and mites are particularly well represented in terms of both species and numbers, and the boarders may even include an occasional moth larva.

Many of these creatures are harmful to the birds with which they cohabit (see ECTOPARASITE); other species, however, may actually be beneficial to their hosts by helping to clean the nest of feces and other organic debris and by eating or parasitizing the bird parasites. Some species have broadly defined habitats and regard a bird's nest as one of any number of

similar cozy niches where food is abundant, but a great many others are restricted exclusively to nests for at least part of their life cycle. In the case of flies, beetles, and moths, it is often the immature stages that are most active in and dependent on the nest, but adults may also be present. At least one species of louse fly (Hippoboscidae) overwinters in the nest as a pupa and hatches when the occupants return to renest.

As might be predicted, large, heavily constructed nests and those in crevices, holes, and nest boxes tend to have a richer, more numerous fauna than openwork nests of flimsy construction.

Adjectives such as "teeming" and "aswarm" barely do justice to the condition of some bird's nests. Hundreds of individual arthropods may be present in a given nest, especially with some species (e.g., Eastern Phoebe); the invertebrate species count can quickly run into the hundreds if a series of nests of different bird species are censused.

NESTLING. A young bird that is helpless at birth and therefore confined to the nest. Not, in the strictest sense, synonymous with CHICK. See also ALTRICIAL; PSILOPAEDIC; NIDICOLOUS; YOUNG, DEVELOPMENT OF.

NETS. See MIST NET; BANDING; CANNON NET; CAPTURE.

NEWBURYPORT/PLUM ISLAND (Massachusetts). An area on the north shore of Massachusetts that encompasses a harbor with vast mud flats (at the mouth of the Merrimack River), extensive salt marshes, freshwater marshes, diked impoundments, dunes with kettle-hole copses, and 9 miles of barrier beach. Most of Plum Island is preserved as the Parker River National Wildlife Refuge. A profitable birding area at any time of year but particularly so during migration, when over a hundred species can be found with relative ease in a day. That the area's diverse habitats are visited constantly by legions of faithful Massachusetts birders ensures that rarities such as Ross's Gull are regularly encountered and widely publicized.

NEWPORT BAY (California). Highly productive waterbirding locality on the coast of southern California about 40 miles south of Los Angeles. The mud flats, marshes, and inshore waters attract large numbers and a great variety of loons, grebes, herons, ducks, rails, shorebirds, gulls, and terns.

NEW WORLD. In a strict geographical sense, the landmasses of the Western Hemisphere of the earth. These consist principally of North and South America, but also include a corner of Siberia, New Zealand, part of Antarctica, and most of the smaller Pacific island groups. In the zoogeographic sense, "New World" is generally taken to mean only the Nearctic and Neotropical regions combined (see DISTRIBUTION). Thus, references to New World families of plants or animals (e.g., New World vultures,

Cathartidae; New World flycatchers, Tyrannidae) are equivalent to "American" families. The fauna and flora of Siberia, New Zealand, and much of Oceania are "Old World" in nature. See ZOOGEOGRAPHY. Compare OLD WORLD.

NICHE (nitch or neesh). In the ecological sense, the role an organism plays within the ecosystem; its interrelationship with all of the factors of its environment. Sometimes wrongly used in the sense of place or habitat. See DISTRIBUTION.

NICTITATING (NIK-tuh-TAY-ting) **MEMBRANE.** A kind of "third eyelid," which lies under the "main" eyelids on the inner, i.e., bill, side and is drawn obliquely or horizontally across the cornea to keep it moist and clean. Most birds blink with their nictitating membrane and close their main eyelids infrequently except when asleep. In birds active by day the membrane is transparent, whereas in owls and other nocturnal species it is translucent. In at least some waterbirds (e.g., loons, alcids) the nictitating membrane is modified with a transparent "window" to aid underwater vision. Reptiles, amphibians, and some mammals also have nictitating membranes. See VISION.

NIDICOLOUS (nye-DIK-uh-lus). The technical term for young birds that remain in the nest completely dependent on the parent birds for a period after hatching. Compare NIDIFUGOUS. See YOUNG, DEVELOPMENT OF.

NIDIFICATION (NID-ih-fih-KAY-shun). Technical term for nest building or, in a more general sense, the entire nesting process, including site, construction, clutch size, timing, etc. See NEST.

NIDIFUGOUS (nye-DIFF-yuh-gus). The technical term for young birds that leave the nest soon after hatching. Compare NIDICOLOUS. See also PRECOCIAL; PTILOPAEDIC; YOUNG, DEVELOPMENT OF.

NIGHTHAWK. Standard English name for the 3 species of nightjars in the genus *Chordeiles* (family Caprimulgidae; order Caprimulgiformes). The nighthawks are restricted to the New World and differ from other caprimulgids in several details of form and behavior: they have sharply pointed, rather than rounded wing tips; they lack rictal bristles; their calls consist of a nasal *peent* (Common Nighthawk) and a low trill (Lesser) rather than the resonant "articulate-sounding" songs common to other nightjars; they nest and roost on open ground, on flat gravel rooftops (Common), or on tree limbs (Lesser) rather than in forest leaf litter; and they habitually fly in broad daylight (as well as at dawn, at dusk, and after dark).

Nighthawks are somewhat falcon-like in form, "hawk" for insects, and hunt in the evening, but the name doubtless originated in the same way as "bullbat," another nickname for these birds, so that "nighthawk" is an apt example of popular rather than scientific taxonomy.

For family characteristics, see NIGHTJAR.

NIGHT-HERON. Standard English name for all 7 members of the tribe Nycticoracini (family Ardeidae; order Ciconiiformes), 2 of which, the Black-crowned and Yellow-crowned Night-Herons, breed in North America.

The night-herons are stocky birds with comparatively shorter necks and legs and stouter bills than the other members of their family. They roost communally in trees during the day, fly out to wetland habitats at dusk, and feed during the night—though the Yellow-crowned is less nocturnal in habit than the Black-crowned and both are often seen during the daytime, especially in cloudy weather. The Yellow-crowned Night-Heron is generally less common here than the Black-crowned, has a more tropical distribution in the New World (to which it is restricted), is less gregarious, and in the tropics shows a decided preference for mangroves. The Black-crowned Night-Heron is nearly cosmopolitan (absent from arctic and subarctic areas and Australasia).

For general physical characters and food preferences, see HERON.

NIGHTINGALE. A small drab thrush, *Luscinia megarhynchos,* of the southwestern Palearctic' famous for its plaintive song. Newton (1893–96–ORNITHOLOGY) points out that in romantic literature the species is always referred to as female and its notes interpreted as expressions of anguish, as if "leaning its breast upon a thorn." In reality, of course, the noctural serenades are performed by males. To North Americans who have never heard it, the charm of the song might be likened to that of the Hermit Thrush, though Nightingales are also capable of loud, rather raucous bubbling and chattering phrases that puts one more in mind of a mimic thrush. To the north and east *L. megarhynchos* is replaced by the very similar *L. Iuscinia,* the Thrush Nightingale or (in German) *Sprosser,* whose song is thought by some to rival "her sister's." Both sing during the day as well as at night. Nightingales reach North America only in reputation.

NIGHTJAR. Standard English collective name for the 78 members of the family Caprimulgidae (order Caprimulgiformes), most in the genus *Caprimulgus.* Eight species breed in North America and a ninth (Jungle Nightjar) has been recorded once as a vagrant in the Aleutians.

The nightjars range in size from 7¾ inches (Poor-will) to about a foot (Chuck-will's-widow). In general form they are strongly tapered from a large head and prominent breast to a long tail. The bill is tiny, but the gape is enormous (see Fig. 13), an adaptation to their habit of feeding on flying insects. This behavior may also explain the presence of long rictal bristles

in most species (see TOUCH). The wings are long and rounded or sharply pointed (nighthawks). The legs and feet are very small and weak, but the middle toe is longer than the others and bears a pectinate (comb-like) claw.

The nightjars are among the best examples of cryptic coloration in birds, their plumage pattern consisting of marvelously intricate vermiculations and irregular splotches in browns and grays, which blend beyond perception into leaf litter, branch, or pebbly ground. Most species have white "banner marks" on wings and/or tail.

They have large eyes, as befits their crepuscular/nocturnal habits, and in some species (genus *Caprimulgus*) these give off a brilliant red, orange, or pink "eyeshine" when caught in the beam of headlights or a flashlight.

The nightjars are almost totally insectivorous, taking large moths, beetles, flies, and wasps on the wing while coursing through the air with their huge mouths agape, or darting out from a sedentary position like a flycatcher. Nighthawks have especially large stomachs, which when opened have been found to contain prodigious numbers of insects, e.g., 1,800 winged ants or "a mass of living, glowing fireflies" (Forbush 1925–29–STATE BOOKS, Massachusetts). These birds probably consume more mosquitoes in a single night's feeding than the average Purple Martin does in a lifetime. Chuck-will's-widows have been known to swallow a small bird or bat on occasion.

The nightjars roost on the ground or in trees (Lesser Nighthawk) during the day and apparently are most active in the dim light before dawn and after dusk, except for the nighthawks, which habitually hunt in early morning and late afternoon as well as after dark. A western nightjar, the Poor-will, is the only bird species in which hibernation has been demonstrated (see TORPIDITY).

Caprimulgids make no nest, laying their eggs directly on the ground; and it has been reported that they occasionally transport their eggs and young from their original nest sites. Their (almost invariably) 2 eggs are white, pink, or buffy. Those of the Poor-will are usually unmarked; those of *Caprimulgus* spp. sparsely to densely marked with rather pale blotches; those of the nighthawks densely marked with dark and light brown and gray speckles.

Nightjars have highly distinctive voices, and the vernacular names of many species echo their "songs." As is true of the owls, the peculiar form, nocturnal habits, and weird cries of the nightjars have given rise to superstitious beliefs, the most tenacious and widespread of which is the fantastic notion that these birds suck milk from the teats of goats and cows, eventually causing the animals' death. (*Caprimulgus* is Latin for "goat milker," and "goatsucker" is another collective term for the family.)

The nightjars are distributed virtually worldwide (absent from arctic tundra and Patagonia) and throughout North America. All of our species are migratory.

The songs of most caprimulgids indubitably "jar" the stillness of the night; however, it is likely that the derivation of the name is more prosaic and echoes (rather imperfectly) the "churring" ("jarring") sound made by the common Eurasian Nightjar *(Caprimulgus europaeus)*.

NOCTURNAL. Active at night. Among birds, nocturnal habits vary greatly: there are species that are normally active only at night, e.g., many species of owls; those that are normally active both during the day and at night, e.g., many species of petrels and shearwaters; those that may be more active near dawn and dusk than during the dead of night (see CREPUSCULAR), e.g., species of nightjars; and those that, normally active by day (diurnal), undertake nocturnal migrations. Advantages of nocturnal habits include protective concealment and availability of prey that is not active by day.

NODDY. Standard English name for 3 species of terns in the genus *Anous* and a fourth species in the genus *Procelsterna* (family Laridae; order Charadriiformes). The Brown Noddy, cosmopolitan in tropical and subtropical oceans, breeds in the Dry Tortugas and the Black Noddy has summered (but not bred) there annually since 1960.

The noddies are almost perfect negative images of the usual tern pattern, being dark with white caps (rather than light with black caps) and with wedge-shaped rather than forked tails. They are pantropical pelagic terns that typically nest on coral or sandy islands.

"Noddy" is an archaic English word for a simpleton and is thus analogous to "booby," i.e., a bird too dumb to flee from club-wielding sailors.

For family characteristics, see TERN.

NOMADISM. Migrant birds normally move according to orthodox traveling schedules, flying between two highly specific localities, following a standard route, and arriving at and departing from stopping points and ultimate destinations on or near the same dates, year after year (see MIGRATION). Even individuals that stray from the usual migration plan of their species tend to show up in the same places at the same dates for as long as they survive. Certain species are forced to make more or less irregular migrations from their usual ranges due to a combination of high populations and low food supply (see IRRUPTION/ERUPTION), but even in these cases, the timing and the direction of travel are predictable to some degree.

In contrast, a few species seem to live according to no fixed schedule, breeding at different times and places and following no established routes. Such birds may be termed "nomadic." Their behavior is not totally haphazard, of course: they conform to given range limitations and biological strictures—a population of temperate zone nesters will never arrive

and attempt to breed on the arctic tundra. And nomadic behavior may be confined to a certain part of a species' annual cycle—many pelagic species apparently wander wide expanses of ocean according to where food is available when not breeding but return to specific nesting grounds on a regular schedule. Nomadic movements can usually be related to climatic factors and/or food supplies, their uniqueness lying in the fact that the birds that undertake them seem to react spontaneously rather than according to an inflexible behavior pattern. Further research may well show that nomadic birds are much more strictly "programmed" than they appear to be.

The phenomenon is pronounced in desert and tropical dry forest birds, especially so among the desert birds of Australia. In addition to pelagic species (e.g., Northern Fulmar, Great Skua), Cedar Waxwings, Dickcissels, crossbills, and Lawrence's Goldfinches are among the few North American avian nomads.

NOMENCLATURE, ZOOLOGICAL. The orderly naming of animal species and subspecies and of the higher taxonomic groupings in which they are placed.

The need for a consistent, universal, centrally governed system of naming life-forms as they are differentiated and described should be clear from several standpoints.

1. *Identity.* A unique animal without a unique name is like the philosopher's tree falling unnoticed in the forest—its very existence is in question. Naming something does not, of course, give it its identity, but if it has no name, it is difficult to consider it as an entity.

2. *Communication and consistency.* What North Americans call a Parasitic Jaeger, the British call an Arctic Skua; the same bird in Germany is a *Schmarotzerraubmöwe*; in Japan it is called *Kurotózoku-kamome* and this name is written in kanji characters that neither the average American nor the average German could read. However, in all of these countries ornithologists and well-informed birdwatchers would understand what species of bird was meant by *Stercorarius parasiticus*, a Latin species name that remains understandable the world over. Even if everyone in the world spoke English (or Italian or Russian), it would still be awkward to discuss different animal species intelligently using vernacular language. When Edward Howe Forbush wrote the *Birds of Massachusetts* (1925–29), he cited the following alternative names for the species then "officially" known as the Florida Gallinule: Gray Pond Hen, Meadow Hen, King Rail (!), and Red-billed Mud Hen. Doubtless this is but a small sample of the names by which this widespread species is called in North America alone. The standard English

name here is now Common Moorhen, but this has only been the case since 1983 when the AOU changed it (officially) from Common Gallinule. The same species has another list of colloquial labels in Britain, where it is also common and is now officially called Moorhen, though this name has been in place only since 1843, before which it was called (guess what?) Common Gallinule! Many of these names are both colorful and apt, but each identifies the species only to a limited number of people. The scientific name *Gallinula chloropus* was not the first Latin name given to this species and it may change again, but it has been stable since 1760 and if it does change in the future it will change according to the rules of a universal system and will therefore change for everyone simultaneously.

3. *Order.* Most American birdwatchers may be indifferent to the fact that there are over 8,000 species and over 25,000 subspecies of living birds that never visit this continent, but an ornithologist studying a particular family of birds needs to be aware of its members worldwide—there is only one exclusively North American bird family, the Peucedramidae, recently created to house the anomalous Olive Warbler. Just defining the subject matter would be a life's work were it not for a system for cataloguing scientifically described species and recording taxonomic changes as they occur. This is no trivial task. The 15 volumes of the *Checklist of the Birds of the World,* the first volume of which appeared in 1931, was a project that has outlived its original author, James Peters; it has been continued by a number of the world's foremost ornithologists and was not "completed" until 1986. The quotation marks signify that no such listing is ever truly complete—the early volumes of this *Checklist* were already being revised before the latest were published.

The basis for our present system of zoological nomenclature is the 10th edition of the *Systema Naturae Regnum Animale,* published in 1758. Its author, Karl von Linné (whose name, appropriately, is most familiar in its Latinized version, Carolus Linnaeus), was a Swedish botanist who gave us not only a nomenclature system but also a structure for classifying all life-forms. Linnaeus' original taxonomic hierarchy and its current, more sophisticated incarnation are given under SYSTEMATICS. The essence of his method of naming species remains unchanged and in the manner of most great ideas is ingeniously simple. All species are given two names: the second name identifies a species considered to be unique in nature; the first name assigns it—and perhaps other, similar species—to a genus. The process is therefore called the binomial ("double-name") system; it was expanded beginning in 1844 into a trinomial system to allow for the naming of races or subspecies—forms that, though recognizable, are not specifically distinct (see SPECIATION). The creation of the trinomial does

not alter the rules of the basic system. The placement of species in genera and in the higher categories is at the discretion of the "author" (i.e., the describer) of the species or of taxonomists who may later revise the classification on the basis of research into relationships among species, genera, families, etc. (The concept of the subspecies has always been controversial among evolutionary biologists. Even today there are many who dislike the necessarily arbitrary criteria used to describe subspecies, and many others who say, "if an organism deserves a taxonomic identity and name why not call it a species?")

The procedures that govern the use of world zoological nomenclature have expanded in proportion to our knowledge of the planet's life-forms. The ultimate authority in these matters is the *International Code of Zoological Nomenclature* (latest edition, 1985), published by the nomenclatural commission of the International Congress of Zoology. The code is the rulebook and standard for current usage of Linnaean principles; it is supplemented by the periodical *Bulletin of Zoological Nomenclature,* which reports recent rulings of the commission.

Precision being crucial to a useful nomenclatural system, the code sets guidelines on every facet of the subject, from the use of diphthongs (eschewed) to fine points of Latin grammar. Such details and the elaboration of technical phenomena such as "secondary homonyms" and "*nomina dubia*" seem impenetrable thickets of nomenclatural jargon to the layman, but their result is clarity, and they are crucial to the orderly and efficient study of animal life.

Though taxonomy would be impossible without nomenclature and nomenclature useless without taxonomy, it should be emphasized that the code governs only the *naming* of life-forms, not their classification, and that nomenclature, though it has become complex, is not a discipline unto itself but rather a tool of science.

Some basic nomenclatural considerations are given below; for further details see the Bibliography. Many nomenclature terms are defined under separate entries.

Priority. The first name properly published is the valid name for any taxon (taxonomic category, e.g., family, genus, species; pl.: taxa). The starting point is January 1, 1758, the year the 10th edition of Linnaeus' *Systema Naturae* was published.

It is not uncommon for a zoologist to describe and name what he considers a "new" species, which turns out eventually to be a race of a species previously named. In this case, the original name stands, though the second species name may be retained as the *subspecific* name if the race in question has not previously been described. Later published names are termed *junior synonyms.* It can sometimes be very important when consulting older bird books to know what the synonyms of a bird's name were in the past. For example, Bicknell's Thrush (*Catharus bicknelli*)

was until recently considered a subspecies of the Gray-cheeked Thrush (*Catharus minumus*) and designated with the trinomial, *Catharus minumus bicknelli*. But for an ornithologist to make sense of the historical record of the "new" species, he/she needs to know that Gray-cheeked Thrush is called *Hylocichla aliciae* and its subspecies *H.a. bicknelli* in earlier literature.

If two species originally assigned to two different genera are "lumped" together under one of them, the first-coined generic name is used. With a little imagination one can appreciate the potential complexities that arise in maintaining the rule of priority through a constant flood of taxonomic revision and the need for strict rules and periodical nomenclature publications becomes clear.

Uniqueness. All species and subspecies names must be unique within their genera; names of subgenera and higher taxa must be unique in the Animal Kingdom.

Authorship. The author of a species is the person who first publishes a scientific description of it. His or her name may appear after the species binomial, e.g., *Anas penelope* Linnaeus. If the species ends up in a different genus the author's name is put in parentheses, e.g., *Archilochus colubris* (Linnaeus) was originally *Trochilus colubris* Linnaeus. A proper name appearing after a *trinomial* is the author of the subspecies, and an author's name may also appear after a generic name standing alone, referring to the person who coined the *genus* name.

Application of the Code. The International Code of Zoological Nomenclature does not include taxa above superfamily essentially because these higher categories have been defined and used in such a variety of ways that it is impossible to formulate a set of rules that would apply to all cases.

Language. All names must be Latin or "Latinized." Many names are simply Latin nouns which apply to the form being named: *Hirundo*, the generic name for the Barn and other swallows, is the Latin word for swallow. Others are descriptive compounds: the genus of the Vermilion Flycatcher, *Pyrocephalus*, is Latinized Greek, meaning fire (pyro)—i.e., red—head (*cephalus*). Still others commemorate a person: *Sayornis* (Say's bird), *Dendroica graciae* (Grace's tree dweller); a few are words from other languages, which happen to have Latin-sounding endings, e.g., *Anhinga*, the Tupi Indian name for the Anhinga (*Anhinga anhinga*), or are simply made up at the whim of the author.

Appropriateness. That a scientific name be appropriate to the animal it labels is preferable but not necessary to the functioning of the system. The specific name of the Red-cockaded Woodpecker is *borealis,* implying that it is a northern species. The fact that it is endemic to *southeastern* North America and many species of woodpeckers range much farther north is of no nomenclatural significance. The usefulness of the name is its published association with the description of a unique species.

Conventions of Form. There are rules governing capitalization, typeface, standardized taxon endings, formation of subgroup names, parts of speech, and agreement of Latin endings for all taxa. Some of these are noted under the separate entries for each category: SPECIES; FAMILY; GENUS; etc.

Types. A mainstay of the present nomenclature system is that each name is associated with a "type." The concept enhances stability and consistency and is best explained by example. The "type" of a species or subspecies is a "type specimen," an actual preserved bird skin from which the species or race was described. Such specimens are so labeled and (barring loss) can be reexamined in museum collections. The "type" of a genus (or subgenus) is a "type species," the characteristic form from which the genus was described. Families are described from "type genera," etc. For more explicit definitions of the terms of the type concept, see GENOTYPE; HOLOTYPE; LECTOTYPE; MONOTYPIC; NOMINATE; PARALECTOTYPE; PARATYPE; POLYTYPIC; TOPOTYPE; TYPE GENUS; TYPE LOCALITY; TYPE SERIES; TYPE SPECIES; TYPE SPECIMEN; SYNTYPE. The use of "types" is a throwback to the Aristotelian academics of the late Gothic, Renaissance, and Enlightenment periods. Evolution with its requirement of variation in nature to eventually produce new species goes against this Platonic/ Aristotelian grain of "typical" examples of species, genera, etc. Still for the purposes of having good traceable names we will always need to know what the original species was that the author had in mind and what kind of material caused her/him to decide to propose a new species or genus.

See also TAXONOMY; SYSTEMATICS.

NOMINATE (NOM-ih-nit). When a taxon (e.g., family, genus, species) is subdivided into lower taxa, the subdivision that contains the type (see NOMENCLATURE, ZOOLOGICAL) repeats the name of the higher taxon and is known as the "nominate" subdivision (e.g., subfamily or subspecies). The concept is more easily explained by example than by definition. When the Common Nighthawk, *Chordeiles minor,* was divided into races or subspecies, the subspecies in which the original type specimen belongs had to be designated as the "nominate subspecies," and named *Chordeiles minor minor.* Likewise, when a family is subdivided into subfamilies, one subfamily (the one that contains the type of the family) must take its root from the family name and is called the nominate subfamily. For example, the so-called dabbling ducks are the nominate subfamily, Anatinae, of the family Anatidae, which also contains other subfamilies, such as the Anserinae (geese), and the Dendrocygninae (Whistling-Ducks), etc.

Note that the "nominate" concept has nothing to do with phylogeny or any characteristic of the form in question, but is purely a nomenclatural convention.

NORTH AMERICAN BIRD CONSERVATION INITIATIVE (NABCI). A coalition of government agencies, private organizations, academic institutions, and representatives of industry in Canada, the United States, and Mexico. To quote from its mission statement, "NABCI aims to ensure the long term health of North America's native bird populations by increasing the effectiveness of existing and new bird conservation initiatives, enhancing coordination among the initiatives, and fostering greater cooperation among the continent's three national governments and their people." Its approach to bird conservation is "regionally based, biologically driven, and landscape oriented." For more information, go to www.nabci.org.

See also AMERICAN BIRD CONSERVANCY; PARTNERS IN FLIGHT.

NORTH AMERICAN ORNITHOLOGICAL ATLAS COMMITTEE (NO-RAC). An organization created to facilitate the implementation of breeding bird atlases in the Americas. The membership consists of state atlas representatives, atlas editors and representatives of federal agencies involved in bird censusing. The committee sponsors a conference every 3–4 years. Its website is maintained through the American Birding Association site: www.americanbirding.org.

NORTHER (in Spanish: *norte*). For the average Texan or Mexican a norther simply means bad weather—cold, windy, and rainy. But for birdwatchers seeking spring migrants along the upper Texas coast (see ROCK-PORT; GALVESTON ISLAND; HIGH ISLAND), a well-placed norther can mean a bonanza. Land-bird migrants arriving in North America from their Neotropical wintering grounds across the Gulf of Mexico tend to continue their flight into the interior when they arrive over the United States with the prevailing southerly tail winds. But when a cold front hits the coast from the north at the same time the migrants are arriving from the south, millions of birds may be forced to seek shelter from strong contrary winds and heavy rain at their first landfall, e.g., the live oak copses at High Island and Rockport. There is perhaps a ghoulish element in birders enjoying events that kill thousands of birds at sea, but the phenomenon is a natural spectacle nonetheless. See Moore *in* Able 1999–MIGRATION.

NORTH TEMPERATE ZONE. That part of the earth north of the Tropic of Cancer and south of the Arctic Circle. It includes most of North America and Europe, much of Asia, and part of Greenland and Africa. Many bird species reside solely in the North Temperate Zone; many others migrate from the NTZ to the tropics for the winter; but only a few species—e.g., Swainson's Hawk, Arctic Tern, a number of shorebird species Barn Swal-

low, and Bobolink—migrate between the NTZ and the SOUTH TEMPER-
ATE ZONE.

NOSTRILS. As in humans, a bird's nostrils (technically called nares; sing.:
naris) are paired, external openings to the RESPIRATORY SYSTEM. They
open into passages in the skull that lead ultimately to the windpipe
(trachea).

Except for the kiwis of New Zealand, whose nostrils are located near
the tip of their long bills, birds' nostril openings are located near the base
of the upper mandible. In most cases they are relatively inconspicuous
slits or holes, but in some birds they are uniquely modified or accompanied by special appurtenances.

The most elaborate external nostril structure is that of the so-called
tubenoses, the oceanic birds of the order Procellariiformes. In shearwaters (family Procellariidae) and storm-petrels (family Hydrobatidae) the
base of the culmen consists of two tubes joined along their length like
the barrels of a tiny shotgun; in the albatrosses (family Diomedeidae) the
tubes are raised separately from the sides of the upper mandible. One explanation for these unusual bill/nostril modifications is that they direct
the flow of air over a structure within the nasal passages the purpose of
which is to sense slight changes in air currents produced over the sea surface, allowing tubenoses to navigate with great precision over waves and
swells even in the most turbulent weather. For another function of these
distinctive structures, see SALT GLAND.

Softer, less conspicuous nostril tubes are present in some nightjars.

At the other extreme are members of the order Pelecaniformes (pelicans, cormorants, boobies, anhingas), in most of which the nostril slits
are completely closed and obsolete in adulthood, though in some species
they are open at hatching. This adaptation presumably evolved in conjunction with these birds' underwater habits, a theory bolstered by the
fact that boobies and cormorants have "secondary nostrils" at the corners
of their mouths, which are closed "automatically" by a special flap when
the birds submerge.

In hawks and eagles, falcons, owls, and parrots the nostrils open
through a fleshy "saddle" at the base of the bill called a CERE. This structure may be feathered (parrots) or naked and brightly colored (falcons),
but its function is unclear. Pigeons, gallinaceous birds, and a few passerines (none in North America) have a fleshy flap or "operculum" that partly
occludes the nasal passages; its purpose too is debatable.

Corvids (crows, jays, etc.) and grouse have their nostril openings covered by a layer of feather-like bristles, and many flycatchers and other insectivorous birds have nasal bristles (see FEATHER) "screening" the nares.

The nostril openings in the *bone* (as opposed to the rhamphotheca or
bill sheath) of the upper mandible have been divided by taxonomists into

four major categories based on shape and internal structure and used to posit relationships among birds. See also SMELL.

NOUNS OF ASSEMBLAGE (or collective nouns). "Flock" is the collective noun that is most generally applied to birds and that is appropriate to any species or mixture thereof as long as there are more than two individuals; it is also the usual collective for sheep. Of course, many other general group nouns, e.g., "group," "bunch," "pack," "host," may also be used for birds, and a few terms relating specifically to birds are also in wide use, e.g., "flight" (of any birds in the air); "raft" (of ducks, usually sea or bay ducks); "kettle" (of soaring birds, e.g., hawks or storks, referring to the vortex shape flocks assume when riding thermals; see FLIGHT, Soaring, and Fig. 28); and skein (in flight) or gaggle (on land or water) of geese. A few other words, especially "brace" (two dead game birds) and "covey" (a family group of small game birds), are common hunter's terms.

Then there is a long (perhaps endless) list of fanciful, poetical, and/or comical nouns of assemblage, which are collected and sometimes coined by aficionados of avian togetherness. A sampling follows. Many of these were also originally sportsman's terms.

Bouquet or nye of pheasants	Ostentation of peacocks
Building of rooks	Pack of grouse
Cast of hawks	Paddling of ducks
Charm of finches	Parliament of owls
Clamor of rooks	Peep of chickens
Cluster of knots	Pitying of doves
Commotion or covert of coot	Rafter of turkeys
Congregation of plover	Richness of martins
Dissimulation of birds	Siege of herons
Dule of doves	Spring of teal
Exaltation of larks	Stand of flamingoes
Fall of woodcock	Strand of silky-flycatchers
Gulp of cormorants	Tiding of magpies
Murder of crows	Unkindness of ravens
Murmuration of starlings	Walk or wisp of snipe
Mustering of storks	Watch of nightingales

Another flock of collectives applies to bird colonies:

Rookery: originally (Eurasian) Rooks, now applied to any species of tree-nesting colonial birds

Heronry: herons, egrets, perhaps mixed with ibis, spoonbills, or other species

Shaggery: shags or cormorants

Cormorantry: cormorants or shags
Gullery: gulls
Loomery: alcids, especially murres

NUCHAL (NYEW-kl or NOO-kl). Referring to the back of the neck or nape. "Nucha" is a technical synonym for this region (see Fig. 35). The Band-tailed Pigeon has a narrow white nuchal collar.

NUMBERS. See ABUNDANCE; CENSUS; COUNTING; EVOLUTION OF BIRDLIFE; POPULATIION; SPECIES.

NUPTIAL (NUPP-shul). Referring to some aspect of the breeding cycle, e.g., nuptial plumage. However, see MOLT for problems with this usage in reference to plumage. See also DISPLAY.

NUTCRACKER. Standard English name for the 2 members of the genus *Nucifraga* (family Corvidae; order Passeriformes), 1 of which, Clark's Nutcracker, breeds in North America; the other is a Palearctic boreal/alpine species.

In general form and behavior, both nutcrackers resemble the other members of their family, the crows and jays. However, both have unusual plumage patterns, are essentially birds of coniferous alpine habitat, and show a strong feeding preference for pine seeds, which they pry out from between cone scales with their long, pointed bills. In the absence of their favorite food, they become typical corvine omnivores. They are obsessive food storers (see FOOD/FEEDING).

Clark's Nutcracker nests near the tree line in late winter when the temperature regularly drops below zero and heavy snowfalls are routine. Both nutcrackers are given to irregular winter IRRUPTIONS to the south and east of their normal range.

For family characteristics, see CROW; JAY.

NUTHATCH. Standard English name for all but one of the 25 members of the family Sittidae and for the family as a whole; 4 species breed in North America (and the New World as a whole). The exceptional species, Wall-creeper, occupies a subfamily of its own.

The nuthatches are small birds (4½–7 inches) with a highly distinctive shape—compact and tapered at both ends. The bill is narrow and sharp, somewhat elongated, and though straight, it gives the impression of jutting upward slightly from the horizontal. The wings are fairly long and pointed. The tail is short but broad. The legs are short and the toes are rather long with long, sharp, strongly decurved claws. Most nuthatches are blue-gray above with darker crowns and white to reddish buff below.

   The manner in which nuthatches feed is even more distinctive than their form: they scale the trunks of trees in short hops, moving with head pointed downward as readily as in the "normal" vertical ascent of woodpeckers or creepers. Some Old World nuthatches prefer rocks, but all our species are arboreal. They probe in bark crevices for insects and other invertebrate life-forms, but also like conifer and other seeds and readily take suet and peanut butter at feeders. Though capable of long distance movements, nuthatches are usually seen flying only in short, woodpecker-like undulations between tree trunks. They produce no elaborate songs, but may twitter softly and/or give abrupt, regular piping or nasal notes.

   Nuthatches construct cups of hair and delicate plant fibers in a tree cavity, the entrance to which is often thickly smeared with resin. The 4–12 eggs are white with fairly fine, dense to sparse reddish-brown speckles (see Fig. 10).

   The nuthatches are overwhelmingly Eurasian in distribution, with 14 species restricted to the Himalaya or southern Asia and only 4 species reaching the New World and only one (Pygmy) penetrating the Neotropics in the highlands of Mexico. At least one species of nuthatch occurs in every part of North America where there are trees, except the northernmost boreal forest and tropical palm areas. Only the northernmost populations of Red-breasted Nuthatch are regular migrants, though other populations are subject to seasonal irruptions. "Nuthatch" is a pleasing corruption of "nuthack," which refers to a characteristic practice of securing a nut in a niche and hammering it open with the bill; "nut jobber" is another variation that captures the rather comical comportment of these birds.

NUTTALL, Thomas, 1786–1859 (*Phalaenoptilus nuttallii*: Poor-will; formerly *Nuttallornis borealis*: Olive-sided Flycatcher). Born in Yorkshire, England, where he worked as a printer's apprentice until his emigration in 1808 to Philadelphia, then the "Athens" of American natural history, Nuttall was chiefly a botanist. He made extensive collecting expeditions alone and on foot across much of North America, especially in the South and West. He worked initially for Benjamin Barton of the University of Pennsylvania; took an ill-paid curatorial chair at Harvard for eleven years—a period in his life which he described as "vegetating with vegetation"; and accompanied the Philadelphia Academy of Natural Science Columbia River Expedition headed by John K. TOWNSEND. In 1842 he inherited an uncle's estate in England and returned there to live for the rest of his life. Nuttall's greatest works were botanical; however, he also produced an account of some of his travels, called *Journal of a Journey into the Arkansas Territory* (1821), and two small volumes that might qualify as the first field guide to North American birds (see FIELD GUIDE). Despite his botanical bent, his name is memorialized in that of the Nuttall *Ornithological* Club,

the oldest of its kind in North America and the progenitor of the American Ornithologists' Union (see next entry). His nightjar and flycatcher were named for him by Townsend, who also named a monotypic genus of fly-catchers for him. *Nuttallornis,* which once contained only the Olive-sided Flycatcher, has now been subsumed in *Contopus.*

NUTTALL ORNITHOLOGICAL CLUB. The most venerable of North American bird clubs. Founded in 1873, it gave rise, through the energies of its distinguished ornithological membership, to the AMERICAN OR-NITHOLOGISTS UNION in 1888. The "Nutt. Club" meets monthly during school term at the Agassiz Museum, Harvard University, and features speakers on avian subject matter. Dues and endowment finance bird re-search and a distinguished series of ornithological papers, published ir-regularly. All members are elected. No field trips. For a list of publications go to http://www.mcz.harvard.edu/Publications/nuttall.htm.

OBERHOLSER, Harry C., 1870–1963 (*Empidonax oberholseri*: Dusky Fly-catcher). Noted American ornithologist and, as a protégé of RIDGWAY, one of the last-surviving direct links to what Coues called the "Bairdian epoch" in American ornithology. It was a period of furious data collection and obsessive classifications, and it therefore seems fitting that Dr. Ober-holser was known as a walking ornithological data bank and one of the greatest "splitters" of all time. During his long life, much of which was spent in the U.S. Fish and Wildlife Service, he filled in many gaps in our knowledge of the native avifauna. He was an authority on the birds of Texas (see the Bibliography under STATE BOOKS–Texas).

OBSERVATORY. A bird observatory is a place set aside for the purpose of studying birdlife, especially migration. Typically, observatories are lo-cated on coastal points where both land bird and waterbird migration can be monitored. They run large-scale banding operations; are staffed by one or a few scientists and a host of enthusiastic, mostly young, volunteers; and periodically publish the results of their studies.

The progenitor of the modern bird observatory was Heinrich Gätke's bird-censusing program undertaken on the North Sea island of He-ligoland (Germany) in the mid-nineteenth century. In 1909, Gätke's pio-neering project was institutionalized as a major banding station, which trapped migrants by means of a wire contraption bearing the name of its

place of origin (see HELIGOLAND TRAP). The first British bird observatory was founded by R. M. Lockley in 1933 on the island of Skokolm, and today there are about 15 observatories in the British Isles and a number of others in northwestern Europe. There are now about 30 bird observatories in North America that identify themselves as such in 20 states and pro-

Fig. 22. *Birds of record.* The selection of avian record holders illustrated includes Bee Hummingbird (1; smallest living bird: 2¼ inches, ½₁₀ oz.); Ostrich (2; largest living bird; 8–9 feet tall, c. 350 lb; note hummingbird silhouette near eye for comparison); Teratornis (3; largest flying bird known to have lived, with a 25-foot wingspan and weighing c. 175 lb); Wandering Albatross (4; perhaps the greatest wingspan of a living bird at c. 13 feet); Trumpeter Swan (5; largest North American flying bird at 38 lb with an 8-foot wingspan; Eagle Owl and Least Pygmy Owl (6; great size range between members of the same bird family: 28¾–4¾ inches); Emperor Penguin (7; deepest dive: 265 meters/869 feet; possibly as deep as 1,585 feet); White-throated Needletail Swift (8; *possibly* the fastest flier at 106¼ mph; however, see SPEED); Common Tern (9; longest recorded distance flown in one direction: 16,150 miles from Finland to Australia). For additional records, see especially SIZE, SPEED.

vinces. Among the oldest and best known are the Point Reyes Bird Observatory, founded in 1965, on a headland just north of San Francisco, Cape May Bird Observatory under the auspices of the New Jersey Audubon Society, Long Point Bird Observatory on the north shore of Lake Erie in Ontario, Whitefish Point Bird Observatory on Lake Superior in Michigan, and Manomet Bird Observatory, now part of the Manomet Center for Conservation Science in Plymouth, Massachusetts. For a comprehensive listing of North American bird observatories and links to sites elsewhere in the world, go to www.nmnh.si.edu/BIRDNET/OBSERVATORY.

For an overview of bird observatories see Living Bird. (cit.). See also BANDING; MIGRATION.

OCEANIC BIRDS. See PELAGIC; ALBATROSS; SHEARWATER; PETREL; STORM-PETREL; TROPICBIRD; BOOBY; JAEGER; PHALAROPE; ALCID; CHUMMING; DISTRIBUTION.

ODOR

Aviculturist: I plugged my parrot's nares with cotton yesterday.
Ornithologist: Really? How does he smell?
Aviculturist: Terrible!

Not surprisingly, the body odors of birds have so far proven of little general (or even specialized) interest, and literature on the subject is scant. Nevertheless, a few broad comments may be ventured if for no other reason than to encourage pioneers into this ornithological frontier. It should be obvious that bird colonies or nest sites, where excrement and putrefying food matter are allowed to accumulate, may have a very insistent odor, offensive to humans in many cases. However, birds themselves may also have characteristic odors, ranging from stenches to fragrances. Black and Turkey Vultures at least part of the time carry the unpleasant smell of their preferred food, carrion. Great Horned Owls, which feed frequently on skunks, tend to acquire more than a hint of butyl mercaptan. Tubenoses have a very distinctive oily or musky odor, a mild version of the strong-smelling stomach oil that they are liable to vomit onto molesters. Alcids have a similar (but distinct) musky air. Most land birds are reputed to have little or no natural odor; however, to the writer's nose many shorebirds and passerines have a pleasant, almost floral (though not sweet) smell. Doug Pratt (1992) has pointed out that Hawaiian Honeycreepers have a very distinctive odor even when embalmed among the preservatives in museum trays. He offers the lack of this distinctive smell as one of his reasons for excluding the Poouli and members of the genus *Paroreomyza* from the family.

Banders sometimes notice various smells of our polluted environment (e.g., sulfur dioxide) in the plumage of nocturnal migrants, which have presumably arrived in their nets through city skies.

As a final proof that much work remains to be done in this field, I cite Robert Storer (in Campbell and Lack 1985–ORNITHOLOGY), who states that the bill plates of the Crested Auklet "give out an odor like that of tangerine oranges" (!). See also SMELL.

OIL, STOMACH. See STOMACH OIL.

OIL GLAND (oiling of feathers). A small, usually bilobed organ located beneath the rump at the base of the tail in most birds. It contains an oily substance that is secreted via a duct through an external opening at the surface of the skin. Though covered by the feathers of the upper tail coverts, the oil gland can usually be easily located by its nipple-like form and tends to be more prominent among aquatic birds. It is sometimes called the "uropygial (rump) gland" or the "preen gland."

Along with the tiny wax-secreting glands of the outer ear and the little-understood glands surrounding the anus, the oil gland is one of only three localized skin glands in birds—in marked contrast to the vast subcutaneous glandular system in humans.

Though a few birds (e.g., most ratites, some pigeons, and woodpeckers) lack preen glands and others have negligible, seemingly useless ones, most birds repeatedly touch the uropygium during PREENING. The bill apparently presses oil from the opening and then spreads it over the contour feathers with the normal preening gestures. Oiling usually follows bathing, and some species typically dip their bills in water before touching the oil gland. It therefore is generally supposed that water facilitates spreading the oil quickly and evenly before it "sets."

The "oil" itself is composed of fat, fatty acid, and wax. In some birds—notably the tubenoses—it has a strong musky odor (or worse) and it may be tinted at certain seasons in some gull, tern, and other species and applied to the breast to produce a pink or tawny nuptial "bloom."

The function of preen oil is still much debated. Logic strongly urges the theories that, applied to the feathers as a surface coating, preen oil aids insulation and waterproofing, a notion supported by the prominence of the gland on many waterbirds. But while some scientific corroboration of this has been obtained, other experiments indicate that the oil is at best inessential for this purpose in some species. The oil apparently lubricates the horny covering of the bill, minimizing flaking deterioration, and it doubtless also prevents the feathers from becoming brittle. The smell and color of the oil present in some birds seem to point to some recognition function. One investigator has shown that, when activated by the sun on the feathers, the oil produces vitamin D, which is absorbed through the skin. This may prevent rickets from developing in some birds—though not, it has been demonstrated, in all. One may speculate that the oil might also have an antibiotic or pesticidal function in preserving feathers, but such functions have not been documented.

The evidence increasingly tends to support the theory that the oil gland is an organ with more than one function, variable in its use among different kinds of birds.

OIL POLLUTION. See THREATS (OF HUMAN ORIGIN) TO BIRDLIFE.

OLDSQUAW. Formerly, the standard English name in North America for a single species of sea duck, *Clangula hyemalis,* with a nearly Holarctic distribution; per the Forty-second Supplement to the *AOU Checklist of North American Birds* (2000), the standard name for the species is now Long-tailed Duck, conforming to long-standing British usage. The change resulted from a petition from biologists of the U.S. Fish and Wildlife Service in Alaska, where this duck is declining. They were concerned that the name would be offensive to local Native Americans whose help they were seeking in their conservation efforts. The white-headed winter plumage especially of the drakes suggests a full head of white hair, hence "old"; doubtless the characteristic yodeling gabble of this gregarious species suggested "squaw," so that, in fact, the name manages to be ageist and sexist as well as racist. The AOU Committee on Classification and Nomenclature "declines to consider political correctness alone in changing longstanding English names of birds but is willing in this instance to adopt an alternative name that is use in much of the world." (*op. cit.*)

The Long-tailed Duck is notable for its unusual plumage sequence (see MOLT). It is also one of the fastest-flying ducks, with a recorded speed of up to 72 mph, and one of the deepest-diving birds (to 200 feet). For family characteristics, see DUCK.

OLD WORLD. The Eastern Hemisphere, including Europe, Africa, Asia, and Australia. In a number of cases used to distinguish groups of birds that have the same English names, e.g., Old World flycatchers (family Muscicapidae) vs. New World flycatchers (family Tyrannidae). The birdlife of the Old World is homogeneous in many respects and may be distinguished as a whole from the birdlife of the New World. See DISTRIBUTION; ZOOGEOGRAPHY. Compare NEW WORLD.

OLD WORLD FLYCATCHER. Standard English name for the tribe Muscicapini (Order Passeriformes), containing 117 species (Sibley and Monroe 1990–SYSTEMATICS). Formerly corresponded to the family Muscicapidae, which in its most conservative incarnation contained approximately 375 species, including many Old World "thrushes." In a still broader interpretation the family was enlarged to c. 1,250 species encompassing the turdid thrushes, Old World warblers, babblers, and other taxa.

Some Old World flycatchers superficially resemble New World (tyrant) flycatchers in plumage colors and patterns that run to earth tones and yellow, but many others are brilliantly colored and would probably suggest

bluebirds or thrushes more than "flycatchers" to a North American bird-watcher unfamiliar with the group.

No species of Old World flycatcher occurs regularly in North America; however, 6 species have occurred as accidental stragglers to Alaska (see Appendix II).

OLD WORLD SPARROW. Standard English collective name for the 36 members of the family Passeridae (order Passeriformes), which includes the petronias and snowfinches. Sibley and Monroe (1990–SYSTEMATICS) consider this group as a subfamily (Passerinae) of a larger Passeridae that also includes the wagtails and pipits, the accentors, the weavers, and the waxbills. As the family name indicates, this is an Old World family represented by only 2 introduced species in North America. It is not to be confused with the emberizid sparrows of North America (see SPARROW-BUNTING).

The Old World Sparrows are generally small birds (c. 4–8 inches), typically with rather drab plumage of browns and grays, though the snowfinches are often boldly patterned and the male Sudan Golden Sparrow is bright yellow and chestnut. Most passerids are birds of open habitat, often preferring extreme conditions such as deserts and alpine barrens. The snowfinches nest as high as 14,500 feet, making them among the most altitude-tolerant breeding birds in the world. Several species have come to prefer the environs of human habitation (see below).

The Old World sparrow with which North Americans are most (all too?) familiar is the House Sparrow, *Passer domesticus* (see INTRODUCED BIRDS for its North American history). It is a small (average 6 inches), rather stocky songbird with a moderately large head, conical seed-eating bill, short legs, and tail of medium length. On the whole, it is an unimposing little creature, though the optimists among us are often at pains to point out how handsome we would find the males if only the species weren't so damnably abundant.

The House Sparrow is arguably *the* wild bird of temperate zone cities—wilder than pigeons and far more integrated with town life than starlings. It thrives on potato-chip crumbs, spilled popcorn, and other detritus of the city streets and in suburbia finds crabgrass and other grass seeds and, of course, bird feeders very much to its taste. To its credit, it also consumes significant numbers of cutworms, aphids, Japanese beetles, and other insect pests.

The species rarely sings extended songs but cheeps ("cheerfully" to some ears) almost continually.

House Sparrows occasionally nest in tree cavities, but, as their name implies, they have come to prefer niches in human habitations and birdhouses. Notably undiscriminating in their choice of nesting material, they will use grass, cloth, paper, cotton, feathers, etc., in which to lay their 3–5

(exceptionally, 8) white or pale green, sparsely to densely marked eggs. Occasionally they will build a globular nest with a side entrance in conifers, tangled vegetation (e.g., ivy vines), or even an Osprey nest. After breeding, House Sparrows roost and feed in flocks—sometimes large ones.

From its native range in northern Eurasia the House Sparrow has been transported by man nearly worldwide. It is now present wherever enough dwellings are gathered to deserve the name "town," including communities on remote islands, such as the Falklands in the South Atlantic Ocean. Though House Sparrows are much less numerous here than in the days when horse droppings filled the streets with undigested seeds, they remain common and are often the bane of bird house and feeder proprietors. In the United Kingdom, however, their numbers have dwindled alarming due largely to hyperefficient agricultural practices.

The Eurasian Tree Sparrow belongs to the same genus (*Passer*) as the House Sparrow and resembles it in most aspects of appearance and behavior, replacing it as a city dweller where the latter is absent in Asia. In Western Europe it breeds in tree cavities and rocky crevices and prefers abandoned country houses to inhabited city ones. It was introduced in St. Louis, Missouri, in the 1870s, and has remained a local resident in eastern Missouri and neighboring Illinois.

For derivation of sparrow, see SPARROW.

OLD WORLD WARBLER. Formerly the standard English collective term for all (approximately 395) members of the family Sylviidae or subfamily Sylviinae (order Passeriformes), most which were indeed known as "warblers," though the family also traditionally included the Holarctic kinglets and the New World gnatcatchers. As a result of DNA-DNA hybridization analysis (Sibley and Ahlquist 1990–SYSTEMATICS; see SYSTEMATICS), an extensive revision of the taxonomy of these birds has been proposed with the leaf-warblers (Acrocephalinae), grass-warblers (Megalurinae) and *Sylvia* warblers (Sylvini) remaining in the Sylviidae (along with the laughingthrushes and babblers), the kinglets (Regulidae) and African warblers (Cisticolidae) occupying families of their own, and the gnatcatchers (Polioptilinae) placed in a family (Certhiidae) with the wrens and tree creepers; in this system, the name Old World warbler for a single taxon becomes obsolete. The 7th edition of the *AOU Checklist* (1998) recognizes a separate family for the kinglets, but otherwise retains the traditional structure of the Sylviidae including the gnatcatchers.

The Old World warblers (in the old sense) are generally small (3½–7½ inches), mainly rather dull in color and pattern (some striking exceptions) and in many ways represent the quintessential insectivorous songbird. They occupy virtually every habitat, including desert, tundra, marshes, and all major types of forest types.

The distribution of the family is nearly cosmopolitan, though it is very

poorly represented in North America and (if the gnatcatchers and gnatwrens are excluded) absent in South America as well as the remotest oceanic islands.

The one Old World warbler known as a "warbler" that breeds in North America is the Arctic Warbler, a typical member of the large genus *Phylloscopus*. Like most of its congeners, *P. borealis* is spectacularly drab and anonymous, with only a faint wing bar and narrow eye line emerging from the general greenish-brownish murk of its plumage. Except that there are far more of them, the *Phylloscopus* might be thought of by field ornithologists as the Palearctic's answer to EMPIDONAX flycatchers; where two or more species overlap in distribution, they are often distinguished mainly by song or by local experts.

The Arctic Warbler nests in arctic and subarctic conifers as well as in dwarf tundra birches and willows. It is mainly (if not exclusively) insectivorous. Its song, like that of many another leaf warbler, is a "buzzy trill," distinctive if you know all the similar songs. It builds a dome nest of mosses, grasses, and dead vines, lined with fine grass and with an entrance hole at one side. The 3–7 (usually 5–6) eggs are white and finely marked with reddish or brownish speckles.

The Arctic Warbler ranges across all of the northern Palearctic south of the barren lands and reaches the eastern extremity of its range in Alaska. The Alaskan population, like its Siberian counterpart winters in Southeast Asia.

Five additional species of Old World warblers (3 other *Phylloscopus* and 2 *Locustella*'s have occurred as casual visitors to Alaska and the West Coast; see Appendix II).

See also GNATCATCHER and KINGLET for details of these species.

OLFACTORY (awl-FAK-ter-ee) **SENSE.** See SMELL.

OMENS, BIRDS AS. See ORNITHOMANCY; IMAGINATION.

OMNIVOROUS (om-NIH-vuh-rus). Eating anything or at least any kind of normally edible substance. True omnivory is a very rare phenomenon in nature, as recent food web analyses have shown repeatedly, and the term usually refers to animals that habitually take both animal and plant food to some extent or to those that are not notably selective in their feeding preferences. Even birds such as gulls and corvid that exploit a wide range of food sources tend to prefer animal protein, and plant-eating corvids generally seek out large, high-protein items such as seeds and nuts.

Specific food preferences are described under family entries. See FOOD/FEEDING. Compare CARNIVOROUS; FRUGIVOROUS; GRAMINIVOROUS; GRANIVOROUS; HERBIVOROUS; INSECTIVOROUS; NECTIVOROUS; PISCIVOROUS.

ONTOGENY (on-TODGE-uh-nee). The development of an individual organism from its conception to its maturity; as compared, for example, with a species' development over time, or the history of animal evolution as a whole (phylogeny).

OOLOGY (oh-AHL-uh-jee). The study of bird's eggs, especially their superficial aspects: color, shape, size, number/clutch, etc., and variations thereof among different species and individuals. Once a very active branch of ornithology, recently much less so, as knowledge of the subject in the North Temperate Zone has approached the exhaustive and interest in external physical aspects of birdlife has diminished. See EGG; EGG COLLECTING.

OPORORNIS (OPP-er-OR-niss) (Warbler). A genus of wood warblers (family Parulidae) containing 4 species: Kentucky, Mourning, MacGillivray's, and Connecticut Warblers. The last three are very similar, particularly in juvenal plumage, and the genus name is frequently used among birdwatchers in speaking of these collectively or of an individual bird that cannot be identified to species: Q: "Did you get a look at it?" A: "Briefly; it was an *Oporornis* of some kind."

For family characteristics, see WOOD WARBLER.

OPTICAL EQUIPMENT. The current popularity of birdwatching would simply not exist were it not for the high quality of modern binoculars and telescopes. Less than a hundred years ago the amateur pursued his hobby with the aid of a shotgun and would have been mightily amused at anyone claiming to identify a Cape May Warbler on sight—that is, without examining it "in the hand." Good "glasses" have completely reversed our perspective. Today anyone attempting to point a shotgun barrel into the leafy domains of our feathered friends is likely to be throttled by birders with thousands of dollars' worth of Japanese or German optical devices hanging about their necks.

Compared to even the best "field glasses" of fifty years ago modern binoculars are marvels of scientific achievement. At their best they provide high magnification and bright, clear, broad images without distortion all delivered in a compact, lightweight form. Though the jewels of the binocular market command prodigious prices (see *Buying*, below), glasses that can fairly claim to embody the above qualities are affordable by almost everyone living in those countries where birdwatching is most popular (see BIRDWATCHING). Indeed, so many brands and models of binoculars are now on the market that neophytes are likely to feel intimidated when they arrive at the optics counter. To these and to anyone who wishes to know a little more about the precision instruments they carry so casually into the field, the following may be helpful.

TERMINOLOGY. A few basic optical terms, some of them bandied widely in birdwatching circles, are useful in any discussion of binoculars.

Power is the amount of magnification your binoculars provide. This is expressed in the first part of a numerical formula engraved somewhere on the body of your glasses, e.g., 7 × 35 or 10 × 40. 10 × means the binoculars magnify the image your eye sees ten times. Through them, a bird 500 feet away will appear to be only 50 feet away. Birders often ask, "What power are your glasses? Answer: "ten power" or "ten ×" or simply "tens." (More difficult to answer is the curious nonbirder's: "How far can you see with those?")

Ocular Lens. The lens you put your eye to, i.e., the "small end" of your binoculars or telescope is the ocular lens.

Objective Lens. The opposite lens, the "big end," is the objective lens. The second number in the formula described above is the diameter in millimeters of the objective lens. 10 × 40 binoculars have an objective lens measuring 40 mm across. This corresponds to your "field" (see below) and to relative brightness. It also relates to weight: the larger the objective lens, the heavier the binoculars.

Brightness is the amount of light admitted by your binoculars. This is governed both by power and by the diameter of the objective lens. The lower the power and the wider the objective lens, the greater the amount of light admitted. The pupil of the human eye closes to a diameter of about 2–3 mm in bright sunlight and opens to 6–7 mm in low light. Binoculars, too, have a pupil, which can be seen by holding your glasses about a foot away from your eyes and looking through the ocular lenses. The bright spot you see is called the "exit pupil" and is measured by dividing the objective lens diameter by the power. For 10 × 40s the diameter of the exit pupil is 4. Binoculars cannot, of course, supply any more light than your pupil can take in, but they may (often do) take in *less* light than your pupil can. At dusk or on a very dark day or when focused on a bird in deep shadow, your 10 × 40s will let in only "4 mm worth" of light, when your own pupils would be capable of admitting 6–7 mm worth. 7 × 50s, on the other hand, would admit as much light as your eyes, and therefore enable you to see what you were looking at better. The exit pupil for birding binoculars should be no less than 4 mm.

Field (of View) is, in effect, how big a picture you can see when you look through your "bins" or telescope. This is measured in the breadth of view at a standard distance, e.g., 122 meters at 1,000 meters or the degree of any circle on the earth's plane taken in by your binoculars from the center, e.g., your glasses might take in 8° of the horizon's total of 360°. Field tends to decrease as magnification increases. The greater the field, the easier it is to pick up small, moving objects, such as feeding warblers or distant, fast-moving shorebirds.

Coated Optics. Modern prism binoculars contain at least ten lens and prism surfaces through which light is transmitted to your eye. En route, a significant amount of light is reflected from these surfaces within the

binoculars and fails to reach your eye. This reflection is reduced by coating the surfaces with transparent chemicals, such as magnesium fluoride, to cut glare and make the image you see brighter and sharper. The coating accounts for the bluish, yellowish, greenish, or reddish tint your lenses show at some angles. In the best optics all of the surfaces have multiple coatings. However, beware of brightly colored lenses, which reduce light.

Alignment. For the images you see through each side of your binoculars to combine precisely into a single stereoscopic image, the optical axes must be parallel, i.e., vertical and horizontal lines should appear at exactly the same angle on both sides. Severe misalignment, caused, for example, by dropping your glasses, would be easy to recognize. But very often, slight misalignments occur with long use and may not be noticed unless they are looked for (see below). This can cause an indefinable discomfort due to the slight compensation your eyes must constantly make.

Roof-prism vs. Porro-prism Binoculars. A porro-prism binocular is the traditional model with off-set prisms and lenses; the roof-prism model looks like two parallel tubes with the prisms in line with each other. It costs more to produce good optical quality with the roof prism design, so that porro-prism glasses can deliver better optics at a lower price. However, the roof-prism model is more durable and many birders find their streamlined design easier to hold. Whether one of these models outperforms the other for brightness and clarity when binoculars of equal specifications and quality are compared is debated.

Field Glasses. Strictly speaking, field glasses are nonprismatic binoculars. Their magnification is achieved solely by the opposition of the ocular and objective lenses and is therefore relatively low—often about 5 × in portable-sized glasses. They also have a very narrow field by nature. To increase magnification and fields the lenses and the body of such binoculars must be enlarged and lengthened to a size that is too unwieldy for birdwatching. Beginning birdwatchers sometimes try to "make do" with some old field glasses they find in the attic or with "opera glasses," which are constructed the same way. Like other occupations, birdwatching requires adequate tools.

What to Call Them. "Binoculars" fits all occasions, of course; by the way it is perfectly correct to call what you have in your hands "a binocular," i.e., an optical instrument with two oculars, but, of course, no one does. Those wishing to add a layer of in-crowd savvy can consider "glasses" (pretty conservative), "bins" (striving for hip?), or even "nockies" (ridiculous or amusing/ironic).

THE RIGHT BINOCULARS FOR YOU. Leaving quality aside for the moment, it is important to choose binoculars that meet your personal needs and that you feel comfortable with. These factors vary with different birding styles and physical capabilities. Here are some points to consider in choosing binoculars that you will be happy with.

Power. Birders seldom use binoculars with a magnification less than 7 × or greater than 10 ×. Any less and the images of distant birds are not enlarged sufficiently; any greater and the field tends to become unduly restricted and the effect of vibration—which increases with power—may outweigh the benefit of the higher magnification. Experience and physical condition should be considered in choosing the proper power for you. Young, experienced field ornithologists often opt for the extra power of 10's, knowing they will have no trouble holding them steady or in adapting their eyes to the limitations of light and field that tend to accompany greater power. Novice and older birders tend to prefer 7's and 8's.

Suit Yourself. Is field identification or aesthetic enjoyment your main objective in watching birds? If you will be using your binoculars primarily to pick up field marks, high power may add to your capability. If you like to study birds for long periods at close range, magnification is not as crucial, but you want to be sure that your glasses transmit maximum light (see Brightness, above) and that you can focus on near objects. Many birders today are also keenly interested in butterflies, dragonflies, and other nonavian subjects so that close-focusing capability is a key factor in evaluating binoculars; high- and even mid-priced models should offer a focus distance inside 10 feet.

Wide-angle. There is a little knack to picking up small and/or moving birds in binoculars (see Using, below), and there is no doubt that it is easier to do using glasses with a *wider field*. Furthermore, people often feel uncomfortably restricted when looking through glasses with the narrowest of fields. On the other hand, the "wide angle" binoculars now available offer no particular advantage to birdwatchers and may in fact show the novice a bewildering panorama of leafage that makes it difficult to zero in on individual birds. Bottom-line: pick models with a standard field-of-view unless you have a clear reason for preferring a wide-angle model.

Central Focus. Unless you have a well-considered reason for buying binoculars that have individual focus adjustments on each eyepiece, select glasses with a central focusing device.

If you wear eyeglasses, be sure the binoculars you buy have appropriate eyepieces or ones that can be modified to meet your needs. Wearers of glasses need shallow rims on the ocular lens of their binoculars to be as close to their glasses as possible in order to have an adequate field of view. The term for this distance is "eye relief" and it is listed in binocular brand comparisons.

Weight. One of the major advantages of modern binoculars is their lightness, but there is still considerable variation in the weights of different styles and makes. How heavy your binoculars are affects how long and steadily you can hold them up to your eyes, and, though it may seem minimal at any given moment, there is a cumulative strain felt by many people from wearing binoculars hung around their necks all day. If you generally

fetch your binoculars from a kitchen shelf to look at a feeder, or bird mainly from the car with your bins on the seat next to you, weight may not be a major issue. But if you typically wear your binoculars around your neck for many hours, you may want to look into the various forms of neck straps and shoulder harnesses that distribute the weight more broadly.

Stabilizers. There are now binoculars available in which the image remains steady no matter how badly the boat is rocking. The feature is far from "must have" (as of 2003), but it's a technology to watch.

USING YOUR BINOCULARS. Looking through binoculars is a pretty straightforward business, but even veteran birders sometimes unwittingly reduce their pleasure and field competence by ignoring a few simple procedures and techniques.

Interpupillary Distance. Properly used, binoculars should always resolve a single image. Because the spacing between our eyes varies from person to person, binoculars are designed to be adjusted along their long axis to fit your particular "interpupillary distance." Bend your binoculars up or down as you look through them until the separate images in each ocular become one, and the margin of the image is circular, as if you were looking through a telescope. A calibrated scale, located between the eyepieces on most glasses, gives you a setting for your correct interpupillary distance. In some adults and many children, this distance is too narrow for many standard model binoculars and a special effort is needed to find a suitable product.

Focus Adjustment. Even center-focus binoculars have a separate adjustment for the right eye in order to accommodate any difference between your two eyes. To set your binoculars for focusing, close or cover your *right* eye and look through the left eyepiece only. Aim at a target in the middle distance, such as a printed sign, and turn the central focus wheel (or other device) until the image is perfectly sharp. Then close or cover the *left* eye and adjust the individual focus for your right eye. The focusing mechanism for the right eye is usually on the right eyepiece, but in some glasses it is located at the end of the bridge shaft opposite the central focus wheel. In either case the wheel is calibrated so that you can reset the right ocular without refocusing it every time. Once you have set your glasses for the difference between your eyes, the adjustment is maintained when you focus with the central focus wheel alone. With separate-focus binoculars, it is necessary to change the setting of both eyepieces every time you refocus. For birdwatchers, who refocus constantly, this system is not practical.

Eye on the Bird. It takes a little practice to find birds quickly in your binoculars. The trick is to fix the bird with your eyes and then bring your binoculars up—the same principle as keeping your eye on a baseball when you are trying to hit it. This sequence becomes second nature in no time.

Stability. It is essential that you be able to hold your binoculars steady, and this is made more difficult, of course, if your binoculars are

unduly heavy or of high power or if you are moving (e.g., standing on the deck of a ship) or you personally are shaking for whatever reason. The first rule of steadiness is: always hold your binoculars with both hands; one hand simply doesn't provide enough support, and, besides, it looks silly. The eyepieces should be braced gently but firmly against your eye sockets (or glasses). If you can't hold steady with your elbows raised, bring your elbows down and brace them against your sides. Leaning on a fixed surface such as your car roof is also helpful. Many European birdwatchers carry their binocular cases into the field with them and use them for stabilizing their glasses while scanning. The binoculars are placed on top of the case, which is held at the bottom. This allows the elbows to brace more comfortably at your sides and the case can be held and moved more steadily (for some reason) than the binoculars themselves.

Maintenance. A surprising number of birdwatchers let their lenses become encrusted with layers of grime and then complain that they can't see anything. At the opposite extreme, some birders carry expensive airbrushes or Windex into the field with them and spend more time polishing than watching birds. Keeping your glasses clean need not be a complex chore. The important thing to remember is that even the finest dust particles can scratch glass, so try to blow off surface dust before wiping. Try to shield your binoculars from excessive dirt and, after birding in sandy or dusty places, it is a good idea to give your glasses a thorough cleaning to prevent grit from clogging the main hinge and focusing wheels and dust from infiltrating the lens housings. While you're at it, check the leather strap periodically to be sure that it is not wearing thin at its points of attachment; more than one birder has pawed the air vainly as he watched his glasses hit the water or pavement after falling from around his neck.

Service. Most people soon forget that binoculars are precision optical instruments and treat them rather casually. Good (i.e., expensive) binoculars are built to withstand a lot of abuse, but if they are used regularly in the field they are bound to show the strain sooner or later. A common symptom of heavy use is misalignment, which you may sense or can check for (see below). Unfortunately, there is little you can do about this or more serious problems except take them to an expert. Even trying to oil your own glasses is courting disaster if your total optical expertise consists of "common sense." Ask birding friends about reliable and (relatively) inexpensive cleaning/repairing services in your area. Often the best solution with high-quality binoculars is to return them to the manufacturer for service. If you drop your binoculars in water, have them examined professionally *at once*. Rust, mold, and corrosion can cause irreparable harm.

BUYING BINOCULARS. There is no dearth of variety at the binocular counter these days. The problem is sorting out different styles, qualities,

and prices and going home with glasses that suit your needs. Here are some general guidelines and specific caveats.

Price may be the first criterion to check when buying binoculars. The highest quality binoculars made with birders in mind currently (2002) retail for over a thousand dollars. Conversely, you can buy a pair of binoculars for fifty dollars that will almost certainly fail you after slight use if not immediately. It is best to face the fact that there is really no such thing as "good, cheap" binoculars; they represent the kind of merchandise it is best to invest heavily in and keep for a long time. If your intent is the least bit serious, you should probably spend no less than $200. If you have a serious young naturalist in the house, do everyone a favor and buy her or him good binoculars; they easily repay the cost and headaches of repairing and discarding cheap ones.

Once you have found a pair of binoculars that seem to suit you, ask to take them outside and use them in natural light. Check off the following criteria in your head:

- Do they come with a warranty?
- Can they be serviced locally? Most glasses are foreign-made, and if the manufacturer is a small one, the nearest parts and repair center may be in Tokyo.
- Do the glasses feel comfortable in your hands?
- Are they too heavy? Hold them to your eyes for several minutes.
- Are they water*proof* or only water-resistant? This makes a big difference if you are unlucky enough to drop your bins in the water.
- Do they have some form of armoring to minimize damage during the inevitable bangs and drops?
- Shake them gently to see if anything is loose inside.
- Look through the objective lenses (big end) for dirt inside and scratches or other imperfections on the lens and prism surfaces you can see.
- Make sure the ocular and objective lenses are coated (see above) and ask if the other optical surfaces are. In the best glasses all are, and this badge of superiority is usually flaunted in the accompanying literature.
- Check how close you can focus and if distant forms are clear when you focus on infinity.

There are also more sophisticated tests you can make, which are especially useful for evaluating binoculars of obscure make and unknown quality. Most of them require a steady surface on which to place the binoculars while you look through them and straight, dark lines both vertical and horizontal (e.g., a telephone pole and a fence rail) on which to focus.

- *Alignment:* With the glasses on a steady surface focus on a vertical form in the middle distance. Look through each lens separately and

compare them by these criteria: When the vertical object is placed in the center of both lenses, it should stand at the same angle in both, i.e., be parallel; when the vertical is placed off to the side of the field or at the bottom, it should appear in the same place in both oculars. Now hold the glasses away from your eyes so that you can see the lens pupils through the ocular lenses and focus on a horizontal line; the line should be on the same plane in both lenses.

- *Distortion:* Start with the vertical object at the center of the field and move the steady surface slowly until the vertical is at the edge of the field. Near the edge, the vertical may appear slightly curved. In general, the greater the curve and the farther from the edge it is apparent, the poorer the optical quality of the binoculars.

- *Chromatism:* Focus on the dark vertical, and look for edges of any spectral color. There should be no chromatic edge when the vertical is at the center of the field in good glasses and perhaps a slight one at the edge of the field; in poor glasses the color will be visible at the center and broaden markedly toward the edge of the field.

- *Coma:* With the binoculars resting steadily focus on a starry sky, then compare the stars in the center of the field with those at the edge. The stars at the edge may appear less sharp than those in the center and perhaps misshapen, i.e., not perfectly round. The greater the "fuzziness" of the edge stars, the poorer the optical quality.

It may be difficult to perform this battery of tests at the mall. An alternative is to watch for optics demonstrations featuring a variety of products offered by your local nature center or at birding festivals. Manufacturers also sponsor such programs, which, of course, promotes the company's line. Once you know the brand and model you want, you can compare prices, which often differ significantly at different retail outlets. Good values can sometimes be had by buying used binoculars of known quality, but you should be aware that some elements, such as lens coating, deteriorate with age and cannot be economically restored.

TELESCOPES are crucial to effective and enjoyable waterbirding and raptor watching as when thousands of tiny distant forms must be scanned in search of the unusual species or for separating species of similar shorebirds or hawks. They also allow you to become practically intimate with less distant birds. Many of the basic rules cited above for choosing and using binoculars apply equally to telescopes. What you want is a modern, lightweight prism telescope, not an ancient, bronze spyglass that your seafaring great-uncle left you in his will (however, see Oddie [1980–BIRDWATCHING], p. 62). A few specific recommendations:

- Many telescopes are adapted for interchangeable lenses. Younger birders often prefer a 30× lens, but the best choice for all-purpose use is 20×. Power is too slight under 20, and over 30 the narrower

field and the distortion of distant images may be a bit of a trial (especially if you're over thirty).

- Zoom telescopes with excellent optical qualities are now available. if you want to pay the price (see below). A typical zoom range is 20 × –60×, and even the high end is useful under good conditions with the highest quality brands.

- Some scopes offer a choice between straight and angled eyepieces, and both styles have their ardent proponents. The advantage of the angled eyepiece is that you can look at subjects high in the air (e.g., a parrot perched atop a rainforest giant or a kettle of hawks) without standing on your head. Straight-lensers say they can "get on a bird" faster with this system because they don't have to adjust their "aim" for the angle.

- A good, new telescope can be purchased (2003 prices) for $300 or less. However, the cutting edge birding scopes (with eyepieces) are in the $800–$1500 range.

- A reliable tripod is nearly as important as the scope attached to it. It should combine lightness with stability. You want it to be easy to lug over your favorite dike or beach but not so light that it won't hold the scope in place in a stiff breeze (scopes are often at their most useful in very stiff coastal breezes). The legs and neck should be very easy to extend and retract and should not slip or stick unduly. Alas, tripods continue to be made to meet the needs of the photographer more than those of the birder. However, some new prototypes are in the works that feature fast and trouble-free handling.

There is a plethora of information on optics in birding journals and on line. See, for example, (http://betterviewdesired.com/) or www.binoculars101.com.

ORBITAL (OR-bih-tull) (region, ring). Referring to the region around the eye; an "orbital ring" is identical to an eye ring.

ORD, George, 1781–1866. A Philadelphia aristocrat and a bastion of that city's thriving community of early American naturalists, Ord is best remembered as Alexander WILSON's editor, biographer, and champion in the famous conflict with Audubon about who painted what, where, and when. He was also the author of a few North American bird species, e.g., Bonaparte's Gull. By most accounts, George Ord was a cold and difficult personality and a pretentious and high-handed editor with little respect for accuracy or the integrity of his author.

ORDER. The major taxonomic category between class and family: classes may be divided into subclasses and orders; orders into suborders and families (see SYSTEMATICS and Appendix I and V). An order may also be

defined as a grouping of phylogenetically related families. Two widely recognized ordinal breakdowns of the class Aves are that of Stresemann (1959–SYSTEMATICS), which proposes 51 orders of modern birds worldwide, and that of Wetmore (1960–SYSTEMATICS), which proposes only 27. The recent revisions by Sibley and Ahlquist (1990–SYSTEMATICS) propose 23 orders. As is customary for the present in North American ornithology, Wetmore is followed in this book. In this system, all ordinal names end in *-iformes.*

All 22 orders of birds that occur in North America are listed below in alphabetical order. For a "definition" of these—which and how many families and species they contain and their phylogenetic position–note the page number given after each order, which refers to Appendix I.

Anseriformes, p. 905
Apodiformes, p. 919
Caprimulgiformes, p. 918
Charadriiformes, p. 910
Ciconiiformes, p. 904
Columbiformes, p. 916
Coraciiformes, p. 920
Cuculiformes, p. 917
Falconiformes, p. 907
Galliformes, p. 901
Gaviiformes, p. 908
Gruiformes, p. 910
Passeriformes, p. 921
Pelecaniformes, p. 903
Phoenicopteriformes, p. 905
Piciformes, p. 920
Podicipediformes, p. 902
Procellariiformes, p. 902
Psittaciformes, p. 916
Strigiformes, p. 917
Trogoniformes, p. 920
See Appendix II

ORIGINS OF NORTH AMERICAN BIRDLIFE. See DISTRIBUTION, Origins of Birdlife.

ORIOLE (OR-ee-ole or OR-ee-yull). Standard English name for 24 members of the New World family Icteridae (order Passeriformes), all in the genus *Icterus*; and also for a similar number of species in the Old World family Oriolidae (order Passeriformes), all in the genus *Oriolus.* (See below for more on the nomenclatural ambiguity.) Of the *Icterus* orioles, seven species are

native, regular breeders in North America, an eighth (Streak-backed) is a rare visitor from Mexico and casual nester in Arizona, a ninth (Black-vented) has occurred along the Mexican border as a vagrant, and a tenth (Spot-breasted) has been introduced from the Neotropics to Florida (Appendix II).

The New World orioles range in size from the 7¼-inch Orchard Oriole to the 10-inch Altamira. They are generally slender birds with a sharply pointed bill of medium length, relatively long tail, and strong, perching legs. The adult male plumage of most species is a bold pastiche of brilliant orange or yellow, black, and white.

Most of our orioles feed primarily on insects, though they are also fond of fruit and adapted for sipping nectar from the corollas of flowers. Despite their bright colors, they are often inconspicuous, spending most of their time hidden beneath the leafy canopies of trees, especially during the breeding season. Their songs consist of loud, clear, rich whistles and warbles in phrases of varying length.

The American orioles are noted for their skillfully woven pendulous nests suspended from the forked end of a branch. Such nests are typical of Northern, Altamira, and Spot-breasted Orioles, but the nests of our other species are more cup-like than bag-like and may be "sewn" to the underside of yucca, palmetto, or other large leaves or surfaces (Hooded and Scott's). The weave is of long grasses, plant fibers, aerial roots, and sometimes string or yarn, and the lining typically consists of plant down, moss, fine plant fibers and grasses, hair, and/or feathers.

The 2–7 (usually 3–5) eggs are very pale blue (to almost white) with rather distinct purplish, reddish, or grayish spots or long scrawls.

The *Icterus* orioles are restricted to the New World and achieve greatest diversity in Middle America. In North America, orioles are essentially birds of deciduous forest and arid scrublands (acacia or pinyon/juniper). Most species winter in Latin America.

"Oriole" is widely purported to derive from a Latin root meaning "golden" and the Latin word *oriolus,* which referred specifically to the European oriolid oriole now called Golden Oriole *(Oriolus oriolus).* This redundancy of gold is entirely justified in the case of many of the Old World orioles, but no less so among the brilliant New World birds, which were, of course, named for their superficial similarity in color. Lockwood (1993–NAMES), however, says the name comes from the Old French *oriol* and imitates the distinctive flute notes of the Golden Oriole.

For other icterids, see BLACKBIRD; COWBIRD; GRACKLE; BOBOLINK; MEADOWLARK.

ORNITHICHNITE (OR-nih-THIK-nite). The fossilized footprint of a bird.

ORNITHOLITE (or-NITH-uh-lyte) A bird fossil. See EVOLUTION OF BIRDLIFE.

ORNITHOLOGICAL COUNCIL. A consortium of ornithological societies (see following entry) organized for the purpose of "linking the scientific community with public and private decision makers; providing timely information about birds to help ensure scientifically-based decisions, policies, and management actions; informing ornithologists of proposals and actions that affect the study of birds; and speaking for scientific ornithology on public issues." The Council also serves as a professional information source for funding and job opportunities in bird-related fields, specifically through its on-line service vehicle, BIRDNET. For more information, go to www.nmnh.si.edu/BIRDNET/OC/.

ORNITHOLOGICAL SOCIETIES OF NORTH AMERICA (OSNA). A service organization created in 1979 to facilitate the mailing of *Ornithological Newsletter*, the jointly produced publication of The American Ornithologists' Union, the Cooper Ornithological Society and the Wilson Ornithological Society. OSNA now serves this and other liaison functions for seven additional professional ornithological societies: The Association of Field Ornithologists, the Seccion Mexicana del Consejo Internacional para las Preservacion de las Aves (CIPAMEX), the Pacific Seabird Group, the Raptor Research Foundation, the Society of Canadian Ornithologists (Societe des Ornithologistes du Canada), the Society for the Conservation and Study of Carribbean Birds and the Waterbird Society. It publishes *The Flock*, a joint membership list of these organizations with contact information—*the* source for tracking down bird people.

For more information, go to: www.nmnh.si.edu/BIRDNET/OSNA.

ORNITHOLOGY (ornithologist). The scientific study of birdlife. Among recent trends in academia is the abandonment of taxon-specific biological professions in favor of fields such as ecology, genetics, physiology, or behavioral studies, except for those employed in the systematics of a particular group. Typically these days one is an Ecologist first with a capital "E" in Ecology and Evolutionary Biology Department and only secondarily an ornithologist with a decidedly small "o." Ornithologists employed outside the academic sphere, e.g., in wildlife management agencies of the government, though once mainly concerned with control of "nuisance birds" and management of game species, are increasingly involved in the conservation and management of "nongame," especially endangered species. It should also be noted that there is now a class of birdwatchers whose knowledge is so comprehensive as to compare favorably with the ornithologists of 50 years ago, though they may lack advanced degrees and make their living in other professions. Such individuals may with justification be called field ornithologists (see BIRDWATCHING).

Like all scientific disciplines, the study of birdlife has altered its focus and become more complex as succeeding generations of ornithologists

have added to the accumulation of knowledge about the class. Scholars of ancient Greece puzzled over the mysteries of flight and migration and made early attempts at scientific description and classification. From the eighteenth century to the early twentieth, and particularly after the publication of Linnaeus' seminal nomenclatural work, *Systema Naturae* (10th ed., 1758), most ornithological effort was concentrated in defining and ordering the world avifauna, a process that continues today. It has been said that birds are the best-known group of animals taxonomically, and therefore are frequently cited as examples in phylogenetic and evolutionary works. Other broad fields of scientific inquiry in which birds have played significant roles include animal movements (MIGRATION), communication (SONG), and behavioral ecology.

If we compare an issue of an ornithological journal such as *The Auk* from 1890 with one from 2002, we find that the emphasis on various aspects of birdlife has shifted drastically and our methods of studying them have taken leaps in sophistication to a degree that would be unimaginable to a nineteenth-century ornithologist. Whereas ornithologists of the nineteenth century still had their hands full describing species, subspecies, nests, eggs, distributions, and the like, the modern ornithologist has enough data and technique at his disposal to begin asking some of the more difficult questions of "how?" and "why?" True, new species of birds are still being discovered and described, but they tend to be found in the remotest regions and most difficult habitats of the planet, such as the mountaintop cloud forests of Peru. Taxonomic theory is beginning to depend heavily on factors such as biochemical analysis of DNA rather than on more superficial characteristics, which are more subject to adaptive modification and thus evolutionary convergence. Such techniques together with the rise of cladistic classification have reinvigorated the field of avian systematics, which was recently deemed a moribund pursuit (see SYSTEMATICS).

Rather than simply *describing* the details of a bird's life, modern bird students attempt to define a species' total role—how it affects other organisms and how they affect it—within its environment. Now that science has learned what route Blackpoll Warblers take to their wintering grounds it has proceeded to discover at least in part how they store energy for such stupendous journeys and what physiological modifications have evolved to aid the effort.

Given the size of the world avifauna, the number and complexity of the questions still unanswered, and the rate at which man is altering the natural laboratory, it is clear that ornithologists will not lack new challenges for the foreseeable future. Happily for the intellectually inclined, answering sophisticated inquiries tends to yield mainly additional even more complex questions.

The history of science is itself now a branch of knowledge, and the history of ornithology a well-grown twig. For summaries of the progress of

both world and North American bird study, see Coues (1903; obviously dated but fascinating), Stresemann (1975), Barrow (1998) and Davis and Jenkins (1995, 2000).

ORNITHOMANCY (OR-nih-tho-MAN-see). Magical prediction of the future by observing the behavior of birds. See IMAGINATION, BIRDS IN.

ORNITHOPHILOUS (OR-nih-THAH-fih-luss). A botanical term for plants that are distributed, germinated, or fertilized by birds. See POLLI-NATION; SEED DISPERSAL.

ORNITHOSIS (OR-nih-THO-siss). A bacterial disease of birds occasionally transmitted to people, especially those who keep birds for a living or as a hobby. See DISEASE.

OSCINES (OSS-seens; also OSS-synes, OSS-ins, or in Latin OSS-ih-neez). This was once the scientific name of the suborder containing the so-called songbirds, now replaced by Passeri. It is the largest suborder of the largest order of birds, namely the Passeriformes, or "perching birds." The only nonoscine perching birds in North America are the flycatchers (suborder Tyranni, aka suboscines). The division of passerines into oscines and suboscines is based on details of the structure of the syrinx, especially the number of muscles, associated with the production of complex song.

OSPREY (OSS-pray). Standard English name for a single, nearly cosmopolitan bird of prey *(Pandion haliaetus),* which occupies its own subfamily (Pandioninae) of the hawk family Accipitridae. Taxonomists have found that the Osprey has a number of anatomical features that indicate a sizable evolutionary gap between it and the hawks and eagles, which it otherwise resembles.

   In addition to the powerful, broad wings and heavy, hooked bill, traits it shares with other diurnal raptors, the Osprey is equipped with unusually long talons, a reversible fourth (outer) toe, and spines on the soles of its feet, all adaptations for grasping slippery, struggling fish. Ospreys feed almost exclusively on fish and are therefore typically found near water—especially large lakes, rivers, and bays.

   Because of their food preference, Ospreys suffered a severe decline during the 1960s from indiscriminate use of pesticides (especially DDT; see THREATS (OF HUMAN ORIGIN) TO BIRDLIFE), which washed from agricultural lands and sprayed trees into rivers and lakes and concentrated in the tissues of fish. With the banning of DDT in North America (1972) and a concerted effort by conservationists to provide nesting platforms, this exquisite raptor has made a spectacular recovery in many places.

The nesting habits of the Osprey are similar to those of its near relatives, the hawks and eagles. The nest is a large, bulky stick platform lined with finer plant material and set in the top of a tree (or utility pole), on a rock ledge, or on the ground where trees or poles are lacking; the site is never far from water. The 2–4 (usually 3) eggs are notably round (short subelliptical) and yellowish white, fairly to very heavily spotted and splotched with tan, reddish, and/or dark brown.

The most frequently heard Osprey call is a series of clear, almost musical piping notes.

The Osprey is migratory throughout most of its range and nearly cosmopolitan in total distribution; it occurs throughout North America, except for the barrens of the High Arctic.

"Osprey" is a unique ornithological word that, disappointingly, derives from a series of not very interesting errors and corruptions. Its root is *ossifraga,* or "bone breaker," a term most aptly applied to an Old World marrow-eating vulture, the Lammergeier, which resembles the Osprey not at all.

OSSIFICATION (of birds, skulls). The formation of bone. Like the skull of a human infant, that of a young bird is not fully hardened (ossified) at birth/hatching and becomes thicker with age. Bird banders unable to "age" a bird by plumage or other characters, can detect birds of the year by examining the skull. By wetting and parting the feathers on the top of the head behind the eyes, it is possible to see the skull through the transparent skin. If the top of the skull appears pink and transparent, only one layer of bone has formed, indicating that the bird is immature. If, on the other hand, it is whitish and spotted ("granulate"), the individual is an adult or an immature that is at least 4–6 months old. Different age classes can be determined by the shape and extent of the second "granulate" layer in a young bird's skull. The rate of skull ossification varies among different groups of birds, and this aging technique is used for the most part on passerine species.

The same test can be made—much more easily, in fact—while making a bird skin, when the cleaned skull can be held up to a light for a close inspection.

For another aging technique, see BURSA OF FABRICIUS.

OVENBIRD. Standard English name for a single species of wood warbler (Parulidae), *Seiurus aurocapillus.* Its nest is a domed construction of dead leaves and other plant materials. It has a side entrance and overall may be compared to the shape of a Dutch oven. The name "ovenbird" also applies to a large, exclusively Neotropical family of birds, the Furnariidae; many members of this family also build oven-like nests and are somberly colored, forest-haunting species like the North American Ovenbird, but they are not closely related. See WOOD WARBLER.

OVIPAROUS (oh-VIP-er-us). Characterizing animals that hatch from eggs outside the body of the female. All birds are oviparous, as are most reptiles, amphibians, fishes, and insects. Mammals, by contrast, are almost exclusively *viviparous*, i.e., bear live young, with the exception of 6 species in the order Monotremata, e.g., the duck-billed platypus, all endemic to Australia, Tasmania, and New Guinea.

OVIPOSITION (OH-vih-puh-ZISH-un). The act of laying an egg. See EGG.

OVULATION (OH-vyoo-LAY-shun or AHV-yoo-LAY-shun). Production of eggs (ova) in the ovary and/or discharge therefrom into the oviduct. See REPRODUCTIVE SYSTEM.

OWL. Standard English name for all of the approximately 155 members of the family Strigidae (order Strigiformes), 18 of which breed in North America; 3 other species have been recorded as accidental stragglers from Asia or the Neotropics.

Owls are small (5¾ inches) to moderately large (over 2 feet) birds of prey (see Fig. 22) . They mostly appear to be of stocky build, an impression enhanced by their large heads and extraordinarily soft plumage. Their eyes are large, often with yellow irises, and are placed in the front of their heads rather than on the sides as in most birds. The effect of a human expression is heightened by facial plumage forming a more or less round visage-like disk. Their bills are short with a strongly decurved upper mandible that normally completely covers the lower one and bears a basal cere largely concealed by feathers. Owls are typically long- and broad-winged and short-tailed (some exceptions); their legs and toes are densely feathered and end in long, sharp claws. The outer, i.e., fourth, toe is reversible, so that they can perch in either a zygodactyl or anisodactyl manner (see LEG/FOOT). Many species have "horns" or "ears," tufts of feathers at the front corners of the head that have no auditory function. In general, owls are somberly colored but heavily patterned with streaks, bars, and spots. "Red" (rufous) and gray (and sometimes intermediate) color morphs occur in a number of species.

Most owls hunt exclusively at night or during the twilight hours at dawn and dusk and are peculiarly adapted in several ways to suit this mode of living. Their eyes, in addition to being large, have high concentrations of light-gathering cells (rods) in the retina (see VISION). The ear openings of many species of owls are larger than is usual among birds and are located asymmetrically on the sides of the head, both adaptations to locating prey by sound in the dark (see HEARING). The forward webs (leading edge) of the flight feathers are serrated (i.e., the barbs are separated at the tips), which reduces noise from air passing over the feathers in flight, allowing a stealthy approach to prey.

Owls feed on a wide assortment of animal prey from insects and other invertebrates to birds, reptiles, amphibians, and even fish. Many species depend largely on small mammals, but the largest, most powerful species (e.g., Great Horned Owl) have no hesitation about attacking a skunk or a domestic cat. They swallow smaller prey and large chunks of larger prey whole and later regurgitate indigestible bones, fur, and feathers in a compact pellet. A few species of owls gather in winter roosts or at a source of abundant food, but they are mostly solitary.

Owls nest in tree (or cactus) cavities or nest boxes, abandoned hawk, eagle, or corvid nests, and (less usually) in buildings, on the ground, or in burrows. They lay 2–13 eggs (average 3–6 in most species) that are white or off white, glossy, and in many species almost round (short subelliptical; see Fig. 10).

The "songs" of the large owls are usually sonorous hoots or seemingly well-articulated phrases, e.g., the *"Who cooks for you-all"* of the Barred Owl. Smaller species tend to wail or toot.

Their human expressions, nocturnal habits, and variety of "unearthly" calls have made owls the most prominent of birds in myth, folklore, and superstition (see IMAGINATION, BIRDS IN). They are often thought to portend death.

Owls occur in all major biomes (except marine), though the majority are forest birds. They are present in some diversity on all the major landmasses of the world (except Antarctica) and tolerate the coldest and warmest, driest and wettest climates. This broad adaptability is evident in the overlapping distributions of North American owls, some of which are very widespread and others very local. Some species are migratory, while others are essentially sedentary, and several arctic species are given to moving south in large numbers during "flight years" when food is scarce within their normal range (see IRRUPTION/ERUPTION).

"Owl" is onomatopoeic and descends from the same Latin root as "ululate."

OWLING. Select a winter's night on which it is highly likely to be bitter cold with record-breaking wind chill. (If you live where winters are mild, aim for a night in the wet season when you are likely to encounter a constant downpour of monsoon proportions.) Wait until everyone has more or less settled in for the evening after a good dinner. (For best results this should be at the end of a brutal day of birding that started before dawn, listening for wintering rails.) Then say: "Let's go do some owling." Everyone will feign great enthusiasm lest they be accused of wimping out. Go to a heavily wooded trail where there are massive roots and gullies every five paces or so and walk in a minimum of one mile (more is better) to "the place where we've always had good luck in the past." Now stand for an incomprehensibly long time cupping your mittened hands behind your

frozen ears. You will hear nothing whatever except the wind howling in the conifers, but someone is sure to say: "There, there . . . did you hear that?"—to which no one will respond. Then play a recording of an owl call; start with either the species that's least likely in the habitat (e.g., a screech-owl deep in the forest) or the rarest species possible. If the guy (it will be a guy) with the tape deck doesn't play the tape after half an hour, you will be thinking, "Why doesn't he play the——ing tape!" But don't say this. Instead, say very affably as if it just occurred to you: "How about trying the tape." Another thing you can do to take your mind off your pain and boredom is to make owl calls yourself. Other members of the group will then join in making a hilarious variety of sounds, and this tends to relieve the collective tension. Now repeat all this several times until you begin to worry about hypothermia in your weakest participants. Then say: "Well, not a lot calling tonight" as if this is a perfectly reasonable outcome and head back, if possible taking a wrong turn or two en route. You will have heard nothing except a barking dog, which one of your party will insist was a Barred Owl ("I heard it, and I'm counting it!").

While this is by no means a fanciful description of "owling," the activity can actually be quite exciting in those instances in which there is at least one owl present. The author has personally witnessed an "owl prowl" in North America when 5 species were not only heard but also seen (in the good spotlight that normally no one remembers to bring). A tip for would-be owlers who value their sleep: Owls tend to be most vocal just after dark and just before dawn (which comes quite late in the northern winter). If you seize this option you can avoid the frostbite-at-midnight scenario described above. However, even if no owls are likely, owling is simply something that all *real* birders must do from time to time to prove their mettle. Also (according to a friend with a very long life list) the suffering associated with owling gains merit that pays off when the gods send rare birds in your direction: "You don't do enough owling," he says, "and I guarantee you you'll be in your bunk when that Short-tailed Albatross flies across the bow."

OYSTERCATCHER. Standard English name for all 6–8 members of the family Haematopodidae (order Charadriiformes), 2 of which breed in North America; a third species has occurred as a vagrant from Europe.

Oystercatchers are medium-sized (15–20 inches), blackish or blackish-and-white shorebirds with long, laterally compressed, red bills, red fleshy eye rings, and bright golden irises. Their legs are pink and moderately long and their feet are narrowly webbed at the bases of the three front toes; the hind toe (hallux) is lacking.

The unusual oystercatcher bill is specially adapted for penetrating the shells of bivalves and snipping their adductor muscle(s) (see BILL;

FOOD/FEEDING; and Fig. 3), but these shorebirds also eat crustaceans, limpets, sea urchins, and sea worms.

Oystercatchers make a shallow scrape on beaches, dunes, rocks, or in salt marshes, lining it sparsely if at all with bits of shell, pebbles, weeds, and other debris. In this they lay 2–4 (usually 3) yellowish-buff eggs, which may be finely and densely speckled or rather heavily but less densely, spotted with dark brown and lighter shades.

The commonest oystercatcher calls are sharp *kleep*'s or *wheep*'s, but lower, more melodious trills are also produced on occasion. The calls of our two species (American and American Black) are rather similar.

Oystercatchers are found along coastlines throughout most of the world (except high arctic regions), and some species also feed routinely in pastures well inland. The American Oystercatcher prefers marine sandy shores and mudflats, while the American Black Oystercatcher of the Pacific coast favors wave-washed rocks.

PAIR. In reference to birds, the word usually means two mated individuals, which normally, of course, are adults of the same species and different sexes.

PAIR FORMATION. An early stage in the breeding cycle, during which male and female birds of the same species establish an intimate bond that facilitates reproduction. The duration and nature of the bond vary greatly among different groups of birds.

Pair formation begins in some species before wintering flocks break up in the spring. For many, however, the bonding begins on the breeding ground after a female has been attracted to a male's territory by his singing. At first the male behaves aggressively toward his prospective mate, as he would toward other intruders of his species into his domain (see TERRITORY). The female responds initially by fleeing, but she returns shortly and then hangs around, making nonthreatening responses to the aggressive displays of the male. These attacks gradually give way to courtship displays, and soon it is the male that is hanging around (see COURTSHIP). The courtship rituals are highly characteristic for each species and therefore are safeguards against hybridization in addition to promoting the pair bond. Copulation may occur soon after pair

formation or there may be a chaste "engagement" lasting two weeks or more.

Through the use of molecular markers to trace paternity we now know that pair bonds are not as strong as previously supposed and that "extra pair" copulations and broods of mixed parentage are quite common in some species.

See also COURTSHIP; DISPLAY; LEK; MATING SYSTEMS; TERRITORY.

PALAEOSPECIES (PAY-lee-oh-SPEE-sheez). A species known only from fossil remains. Since the present definition of a species depends on the interrelationships of living animals, a palaeospecies has no biological basis. *Archaeopteryx lithographica* is perhaps the best-known avian palaeospecies. See EVOLUTION OF BIRDLIFE.

PALATABILITY. See EDIBILITY.

PALEARCTIC REGION (PAIL-ee-ARC-tik or PAL-ee-ARC-tik). The largest of the six major zoogeographic regions of the world. It includes all of Europe, Asia north of the Himalayas, and Africa to the southern edge of the Sahara. Iceland, Greenland, and western Alaska are transitional between the Palearctic and Nearctic regions. "Palearctic birds" include those that breed exclusively within the Palearctic region but winter in tropical Africa (e.g., most Old World warblers) as well as those relatively few species that range wholly in Europe, North Africa, or northern Asia (e.g., Crested Tit). Some of the western Alaskan species that are primarily Palearctic in distribution are Steller's Eider, Bar-tailed Godwit, White and Yellow Wagtails, Arctic Warbler, Bluethroat, and Gray-headed Chickadee (Siberian Tit). And many of the rarities that occur as casual visitors or vagrants to the west coast, especially western Alaska, are of Palearctic origin. Compare NEARCTIC REGION; HOLARCTIC REGION; see also ZOOGEOGRAPHY; DISTRIBUTION; and Fig. 34

PALLIUM (PAL-ee-yum). A little-used technical term equivalent to MANTLE.

PALMATE. Describes a bird's foot that is webbed between the three forward toes, characteristic of the majority of swimming birds. Compare TOTIPALMATE.

PANTING. Rapid breathing is a frequent method of dissipating excess body heat among birds. See TEMPERATURE, BODY, Cooling Off.

PARAKEET. Standard English name for about 80 members of the family Psittacidae (order Psittaciformes), one of which, the Carolina Parakeet,

was endemic to North America until its extirpation, completed in the early 1920s (see EXTINCT BIRDS). Three other species of Neotropical origin have established populations here following introduction, and a number of others have escaped from captivity and fly freely around several of our southern metropolises. Generally speaking, a parakeet is a small parrot with a relatively long tail, but there are exceptions, and the name has little taxonomic integrity. In Australasia, for example, the term is eschewed in favor of other names for small, long-tailed parrots, such as lorikeet and rosella. "Parakeet" (unmodified) is also used in the pet trade as a generic name for the Budgerigar. For family characteristics, see PARROT.

PARALECTOTYPE. When a particular specimen of a bird (or other animal) has been designated from a type series as a LECTOTYPE (as opposed to HOLOTYPE), the other specimens in the series are the paralectotypes. See NOMENCLATURE, ZOOLOGICAL, Types.

PARAPATRIC. Describes two or more species whose distributions are distinct, but contiguous. Used for example in describing "secondary contact" among divergent species. See SPECIATION.

PARASEMATIC (PAAR-uh-seh-MAT-ik). Refers to appearance or behavior that distracts the attention of a potential predator from a more vulnerable body part or individual (e.g., young bird) to a less vulnerable. Many insects have evolved cryptic forms or patterns that "trick" predators (often birds) into striking at a wing tip or leg under the impression that they are aiming for the head, thorax, or abdomen; the predator may end up with a piece of wing or even a leg, but the insect remains essentially unharmed and has time to escape. This kind of distraction is not so highly developed among birds; however, white rump patches and especially white outer tail feathers may be considered in this context (though not exclusively), and injury feigning, which distracts predators from eggs or young, may be considered parasematic behavior. The false eyespots on the back of the heads of the American Kestrel and the pygmy-owls may also buy some time for these species if they are attacked from behind. See COLOR AND PATTERN; DISPLAY.

PARASITISM. A parasite is an organism that lives with and obtains food from another organism called a "host." In the strictest sense of the term, the host derives no benefit from the relationship and suffers some degree of harm, though this is rarely life threatening. (For other types of relationships, see COMMENSALISM and SYMBIOSIS.) An *obligate* parasite is one that *must* live off another organism, as distinct from a *nonobligate* parasite, which can live parasitically or not. The best North American avian

examples of obligate parasites are our two native species of cowbirds. These are *brood parasites,* which make no nests of their own but invariably lay their eggs in the nests of other species, which rear the young blackbirds at the expense of their own brood. Some duck species are nonobligate parasites, occasionally laying one or more eggs in another bird's nest but also rearing broods in their own nests.

Nest parasitism, in which one species of bird takes over the nest of another by force for its own use, is rare in North America but is known to be practiced occasionally by Black-billed Magpies.

While parasitic birds are relatively uncommon, birds are hosts to an impressive variety of parasites, mainly invertebrates and microbes, for which see ECTOPARASITE; ENDOPARASITE; NEST FAUNA.

For parasitism practiced by birds on other birds, see also PIRACY (kleptoparasitism); BROOD PARASITISM.

PARATREPSIS (PAH-ruh-TREP-siss). A technical term encompassing all forms of distraction display. See DISPLAY.

PARATYPE. When a particular specimen of a bird (or other animal) has been designated from a type series as a HOLOTYPE of a species or subspecies, the other specimens in the series are the paratypes. See also PARALECTOTYPE; NOMENCLATURE, ZOOLOGICAL, Types.

PARENTAL CARE. The behavior of parent birds toward their young from hatching to independence. The usual criteria for independence in young birds are (1) the ability to fly and (2) the ability to find food for themselves. For care of eggs, see INCUBATION; for early stages of nest life apart from parental roles, see YOUNG, DEVELOPMENT OF.

DIVISION OF LABOR. Brooding of the young normally follows the same pattern of responsibility as incubation, whether shared or relegated to one parent only. Very often males are active in the feeding of young (see below), whether or not they share brooding. Sometimes they begin bringing food to the nest before the eggs are hatched. As the young grow, and they need less brooding and more feeding, the parental roles usually change accordingly. In the case of two consecutive broods the male may be left to "finish" the first family while the female lays the groundwork for the second.

Virtually all variations of shared responsibility (or lack of it) have been recorded, from all-male or all-female to "equal rights." In some species (e.g., Snow Bunting, Hudsonian Godwit) each parent takes responsibility for part of the brood. Roles have also been seen to vary among different pairs of the same species.

Young of the Common Eider, Sandwich Tern, and a few other species of colonial waterbirds are combined into a kind of avian nursery school or

CRÈCHE. Nestling anis are born and reared communally in a single nest by a number of pairs; all members of the commune, including both sexes, share incubation, brooding, and feeding of young, and the young of early broods often remain to help feed successive ones.

HELPERS. There are several species in which adult "helpers" of the same species regularly aid parents in feeding young. These helpers may be siblings ("retained offspring") of the current brood (as in Florida Scrub Jays) or may be unrelated (as in Mexican Jays). It is believed that sibling helpers gain experience and often inherit territories in or near the parent's home range. The reasons for helping nonrelatives are more complex, including acquisition of experience and the long-term benefits of moving up socially in the group. In Mexican Jays, nonsibling helpers have benefited by successful matings with the mother of the current brood. The helping phenomenon is more common in the tropics and subtropics than in the Temperate Zone, and notably widespread in Australia. In addition to the jay species mentioned, North American communal breeders include American Crow (retained offspring) and Acorn and Red-cockaded woodpeckers (extended family and unrelated helpers).

"Helping" by another species is always some form of misdirected behavior, and this may also be true in some cases of conspecific helping, but much communal breeding is of evolutionary significance. See Brown (1987) for a review of helping and communal breeding behavior.

HATCHING. Parent birds are aware when their eggs become "pipped," i.e., cracked from within by the mature embryo. At this point, the usual procedure of turning the eggs ceases, leaving the pipped side up. Parents may occasionally remove a piece of the cracked eggshell or dump the hatchling out of part of the shell once it is completely open, but for the most part, parent birds are passive during hatching.

RECOGNITION OF YOUNG. Colonial seabirds can discriminate their own young with remarkable acuity from among hundreds of apparently identical chicks, and usually reject importunate offspring of other pairs, though some gulls and terns will "adopt" stray wandering youngsters. In the communal confusion of a crowded colony, feeding the "right" chick has survival value. Songbirds and other species that tend their young in relative isolation do not "need" to do more than feed whatever asks to be fed in their nest. It is this lack of discrimination that permits brood parasitism practiced by cowbirds and others, and substitution experiments by humans have shown similar results. (For recognition of parents by young, see YOUNG, DEVELOPMENT OF.)

DISPOSING OF EGGSHELLS. Once they have served their purpose, eggshells become useless clutter in the nest and even a potential hazard to the delicate skin of naked nestlings. If they are simply jettisoned over the side, they advertise the presence of the nest. So most birds eat or carry used eggshells away from the nest. Ducks, geese, and swans and gallinaceous

birds, whose young abandon the nest within hours of hatching, simply leave the shells behind, but other "precocial" species, e.g., shorebirds, remove the shells in spite of an early departure. A few species (e.g., Northern Goshawk, cuckoos) simply leave the eggshells as part of the furniture of their nests.

In at least some species there seems to be a generalized "tidying" instinct that urges the disposal not only of eggshells but also of displaced nest material, fallen leaves, or any foreign object. The most obsessive housekeepers will, on occasion, even discard their own young to get rid of an unsightly band that has been attached to one of the nestling's legs.

DISPOSING OF NESTLING EXCREMENT. Nests occupied by young birds over a period of weeks have an obvious potential sanitation problem. Birds use three basic approaches in addressing it. (1) A few species, e.g., kingfishers and some woodpeckers (among other hole nesters), are content to wallow in their own wastes; despite the unwholesomeness we naturally attach to this "solution," it does not seem to affect the success of the species that practice it. (2) Most nonpasserine nestlings early develop the habit of defecating over the edge of the nest or from the entrance of the nest hole. (3) Adult passerines and some nonpasserines eat their young's excreta or carry it away for disposal. The latter is facilitated by the enclosure of the waste products in a gelatinous mass known as a fecal sac. Parental collection of feces usually occurs following the feeding of the nestlings. In some instances the young raise their tails and "present" the fecal sac to the parent bird, or the young birds may deposit feces conveniently at the edge of the nest.

There is a general tendency, as the nestlings mature, for parents to carry wastes away rather than consume them and also for zeal in nest sanitation to wane. By the end of the nestling period, therefore, the nests of many species—most obvious in finches—are coated with "lime" around their rims, though others are kept clean for the entire period.

BROODING. Keeping nestlings next to the brood patch and under the insulating feathers of the parent birds serves the same basic function as incubating the eggs, namely, the maintenance of adequate temperature for the developing organism. In addition to transferring their own body heat, adult birds also shield their young from precipitation and the direct rays of the sun. It is often imagined that brooding must be constant and that any disturbance causing a parent bird to leave nestlings uncovered will inevitably result in their premature demise. In fact, nestlings can withstand temperatures considerably lower than their "optimal" body temperature and, on balance, are probably in greater danger from overheating in the sun than from exposure to summer chills.

The brooding rhythm changes as nestlings acquire their juvenal plumage and become less helpless. For the first few days after hatching, the brooding parent leaves the nest only infrequently and adopts behavior consistent with concealing the nest contents. But as the young gain

more control over their body temperature, learn to react to signals of danger, and manifest their growing appetites, the parents spend more and more time finding and delivering food and do less and less brooding.

Environmental conditions affect the brooding rhythm. Birds in enclosed nests are less vulnerable to exposure than those in open ones and need not be covered by the parents as much. The brooding period may be lengthened by unseasonably cold or wet weather. And nestlings tend to be covered more continuously during the night than the day.

FEEDING

Degree of Dependence. So-called nidifugous young—those that leave the nest almost immediately after hatching—are soon able to find their own food with little or no preliminary "coaching" from their parents. The most independent of these, such as ducks and most shorebird chicks, follow their parents away from the nest but almost immediately begin testing the palatability of substances they encounter, apparently with no influence whatever from the parents. Parents of gallinaceous species typically pick up edible items and drop them, perhaps several times, while giving a feeding call; the chick at first picks up the items chosen by the parent but very soon begins foraging on its own. Loons, grebes, cranes, and members of the rail family at first procure food—usually in the presence of the young—and give it to them directly or lay it near them. Young diving birds may practice submerging within a few days but may not be able to catch their own food for up to 6 weeks (Common Loon).

Forming a link between these nidifugous young and the nidicolous, or nest-bound types are species such as the gulls, terns, and other colonial nesters whose chicks become fairly mobile soon after hatching and may wander about their colony, yet remain incapable of procuring their own food and must be fed entirely by the parents until fledged.

Normally, one or both parents of nidicolous species start feeding nestlings within a few hours of hatching; as noted, male birds may even begin bringing food before the eggs have hatched. Bad weather or other conditions unfavorable for finding food occasionally delay meals throughout the nesting period. Young passerines can usually withstand a day or so of starvation, while the young of some tubenoses have fat reserves on which they can survive for weeks.

Period. The total period of parental feeding in nidicolous species ranges from about a month for most passerines to 8 months or more in the case of some albatross species. Half—or much more—of this period takes place after the young have quit the nest. As the young birds become more competent physically, a gradual weaning process develops in which parents bring food less frequently. This promotes aggressiveness, which fuels the drive to find food rather than beg and wait for it. The point at which a young bird supplies all its own food is probably the best demarcation of independence from parental care, though parent-young encounters often evoke a begging response after this point.

Type of Food supplied to young may correspond to the usual adult diet or differ markedly. Many species that are largely fruit or seed eaters give their nestlings a protein-rich menu of insects and other invertebrates. The atypical waxwings, which nourish their young on a fruit diet, have proven to be poor hosts for cowbirds.

Mechanics. The transfer of food from adult birds to nestlings is a largely mechanical ritual involving the exchange of special "releaser" signals. Adult gulls, for example, will not feed their young unless they are stimulated by them to disgorge food. A Herring Gull may be "ready" to feed its chicks but unless it is pecked on the bill near its red spot, the food will remain in its gullet. Adult passerines are moved to feed by the sight of open gapes accentuated by prominent mouth corners (flanges) and (often) brightly colored and patterned mouth interiors, usually accompanied by a characteristic begging call. However, this response is very generalized, and at least some species will give food to almost anything that gapes and cheeps. If *nothing* gapes and cheeps at a parent bird holding food, the latter eventually departs with its catch or swallows it on the spot.

The actual transfer of food is accomplished in different ways by different kinds of birds. Most birds of prey deliver an entire carcass to the nest and tear off manageable bits of meat for the nestlings. As the latter mature, they learn to butcher the prey for themselves. Most passerines carry food in their bills and place it into the yawning gapes of their young. Nonpasserines and some passerines generally swallow the intended baby food and regurgitate it at the nest in one of three basic ways: (1) gulls, some herons, and others regurgitate into the nest or onto the ground beside the chick and allow it to pick up the food by itself; (2) some passerines disgorge into the nestlings' open mouths, and hummingbirds thrust their bills well down in the young birds' throats to "pump" in regurgitated food; (3) herons typically (though not exclusively) practice a kind of beak-to-beak regurgitation in which the young clasps the parent's bill in its own; in pigeons the adult clasps the young bird's bill in a variation on the same principle. The young of many seabirds (e.g., fulmars, gannets, pelicans, cormorants) and some wading birds (e.g., Roseate Spoonbill) reach into the open mouth or throat of the parent bird and pull or scoop out regurgitated or unregurgitated food.

With all of these methods, the consistency of the food offered becomes coarser as the nestlings mature, the youngest birds sometimes getting a nearly liquid (perhaps predigested) "formula."

Distribution. Generally, parents give food to the nestling that is most aggressive in begging for it. This bird is fed until its gullet is full and it can no longer make the swallowing contraction that stimulates the parent to continue to feed. Once a nestling is "full" its begging ceases and its siblings are then fed in turn. When responses are more or less equal, parent

birds may test the degree of hunger by placing the food and judging the swallowing reaction. When hatching is staggered, the oldest bird, if normal, will always get the first meal and the youngest remain unfed until its older siblings are sated; when food is scarce, the younger nestlings are thus "automatically" sacrificed ensuring the survival of the older. In some boobies, heron, and raptors deliberate siblicide by the older, stronger nestling is common.

Frequency. Up to a point, feeding increases with growth, i.e., in proportion to the needs of a growing bird, and then it drops off as the weaning process progresses. At the peak of their nutritive need, nidicolous nestlings may be fed as often as every 20–30 minutes during the day, with parent birds devoting almost all of their time and energy to foraging and delivery. By contrast, some young seabirds are accustomed to a single daily feeding or one meal every few days; at the end of the nesting period many species of tubenoses are abandoned altogether by their parents and left for weeks to survive on their accumulated fat until they can go to sea and find food for themselves.

Water and Grit. The bringing of pure water—i.e., other than what is contained in food—to nestlings has been recorded in only a very few instances (Eurasian White Storks, large birds that occupy open nests, and sandgrouse, which nest in very arid habitats).

Grit, necessary for digestion in some species, may also be supplied by parent birds.

DEFENSE. Parent birds defend their nests against predators by methods ranging from total passivity—simply covering the nest and remaining silent and motionless (characteristic of many passerines)—to savage aggressions, e.g., brooding Northern Goshawks. Between these extremes, parents protect their young by giving alarm calls, which signal them to scatter, take cover, and/or remain still; by "shepherding" (precocial) young to safety; by distracting the attention of potential predators away from the young and onto themselves; by frightening them by raising the feathers and screaming or hissing (see DISPLAY); and by "dive-bombing" or making threatening gestures without actual contact.

In colonies or forest communities, birds of the same or different species sometimes act in concert to sound an alarm and drive predators from the otherwise easy predation on nearly immobile nestlings (see FLOCK; MOBBING).

TRANSPORTATION. Species of loons, grebes, coots, swans, and ducks carry young nestlings on their backs or under their wings while swimming and in some cases even dive with them in this position. Picking up young birds in the bill is much less frequently seen (Virginia and Clapper Rails, ptarmigan) and seems to be a last-ditch rescue measure only. Reports and legends of many other species (e.g., nightjars) walking or even flying around with young tucked in various body crannies are not well substantiated.

TEACHING/URGING. Numerous parent/young interactions are sometimes interpreted from the human point of view as forms of rational communication—the parents "urging" the young to fly, for example, or "teaching" them to dive or preen. While parents of some precocial species (e.g., gallinaceous birds) certainly introduce their chicks to edible substances, the experimental evidence indicates that many basic skills, e.g., flying, feeding, the rudiments of song, are substantially innate. This is not to say that a great deal of refinement does not take place often requiring assistance from adult birds. For example, to develop a "perfect" song a young bird must hear and imitate an adult. Male birds increase their rate of song after their young have hatched to reinforce this necessary honing of skills.

PARIS BROTHERS (*Icterus parisorum:* Scott's Oriole). Obscure early-nineteenth-century French businessmen, based in Mexico, who sent numerous zoological specimens back to Paris. One of the latter, now known as Scott's Oriole, was named for the brothers (note the genitive plural) by Charles Lucien BONAPARTE.

PARKER RIVER NATIONAL WILDLIFE REFUGE. See NEWBURYPORT/ PLUM ISLAND.

PARROT. Standard English name for about 130 members of the family Psittacidae (order Psittaciformes), including the fig-parrots, Pygmy-parrots, tiger-parrots, king-parrots, and hanging parrots; also a collective term for the whole family, which comprises about 280 species, including macaws, cockatoos, lories, lorikeets, amazons, conures, rosellas, lovebirds, parakeets, and parrotlets. In the New World, parrots are generally larger species with shorter, blunt-tipped tails, and parakeets smaller with relatively long, graduated tails. The distinction has little taxonomic integrity, however, many small parrots being smaller than large parakeets. Except for escaped cage birds (see EXOTIC SPECIES), only 2 species of parrots are native to North America: the Carolina Parakeet, a North American endemic, which bred widely throughout the southeastern region of the continent and was extirpated by the 1920s at the latest (see EXTINCT BIRDS), and the Thick-billed Parrot, which visited the highland pine forests of southeastern Arizona and New Mexico sporadically until 1936 and is now decreasing alarmingly due to lumbering and other disturbances of its habitat in Mexico; reintroduction efforts in Arizona have so far proven unsuccessful (see ENDANGERED BIRDS).

Parrots vary in size from 3¾ inches to over 3 feet in length, one of the greatest size ranges within a family of birds. They come in a wide assortment of shapes and colors, with many brilliant green species, but also many with spectacular, multicolored plumage. They typically have short

bills with strongly decurved upper mandibles closed over a much shorter lower one; these are used not only in cracking hard nuts but also as an extra appendage for climbing around in trees. They have short legs and feet with toes I and IV pointing rearward and the others forward (zygodactyl). Most species feed primarily on fruits, nuts, and seeds and nest in unlined cavities, but there are many exceptions within this large family. Parrots are highly social and most species occur in flocks; the African Grey Parrot has demonstrated extraordinary mental ability (see INTELLIGENCE) and this may be prove to be more generally true within the family. The Carolina Parakeet and Thick-billed Parrot were/are tree-cavity nesters, the latter at least occasionally occupying abandoned holes of the nearly extinct Imperial Ivory-billed Woodpecker. Parrots typically lay 2–5 eggs, which are invariably white, but variable in shape.

The calls of parrots are typically harsh, shrill, rasping, or grating screeches, often given in chorus by flocks in flight. A few species are noted for their ability to mimic human speech (see SONG) and this, together with their brilliant plumage, makes them attractive as pets (see AVICULTURE).

Though there are several species of parrots that endure severe climates in the Southern Hemisphere, parrots achieve their greatest diversity in the tropics, and they occur in this zone throughout the world.

The supposed provenance of "parrot" is too vague and irrelevant to warrant repeating. To "parrot" now, of course, is to imitate or repeat.

PARTIAL MIGRANT. A species in which some members of a population leave the breeding area after nesting while others remain behind. Particularly prevalent in colder climates and as an age phenomenon. Young Herring Gulls and Blue Jays, for example, regularly wander much farther from their nesting area than adults of the same population. For other examples, see MIGRATION.

PARTNERS IN FLIGHT (PIF). Created in 1990, Partners in Flight was inspired by the evident decline of many species of Western Hemisphere landbirds, especially Neotropical migrants, the conservation of which was not being adequately addressed by existing treaties, government agencies, or nongovernmental conservation organizations. A driving insight was that conserving a group of living organisms as wide-ranging and diverse in their habits as migratory birds would inevitably require a conservation network spanning the Americas and involving as many of society's major stakeholders as possible. To quote from its mission statement, PIF is "a cooperative effort involving partnerships among federal, state, and local governments, philanthropic foundations, professional organizations, conservation groups, industry, the academic community, and private individuals." Its goal is "to focus resources on the improvement of monitoring and inventory, research, management and education involving

birds and their habitats." In addition to coordination, PIF's action agenda focuses on the development of Bird Conservation Plans (BCPs), a series of which is currently being completed for all of the continental United States. While it continues to concentrate on birds using terrestrial habitats, it works in parallel with other initiatives that focus on seabirds, waterfowl, and shorebirds.

PIF is organized in a hierarchy of committees and working groups, the upper tier of which includes National Committees, National Oversight Committees, Technical Working Groups, Regional Working Groups, State, Territory, and Physiographic Area Working Groups, and Regional Coordinators. A listing of PIF partners are collected in the *Bird Conservation Directory* maintained by the AMERICAN BIRD CONSERVANCY and project descriptions appear in ABC's magazine, *Bird Conservation.*

For more information, go to: www.partnersinflight.org. See also NORTH AMERICAN BIRD CONSERVATION INITIATIVE.

PARTRIDGE. Standard English name for about 40 members of the family Phasianidae (order Galliformes), which also includes the snowcocks, francolins and spurfowl, Old World quail, tragopans, jungle fowl, pheasants, peafowl, grouse (including ptarmigan and prairie-chickens), and turkeys. The wood-partridge belong to a separate family, the Odonophoridae or New World Quail. The name is applied rather promiscuously to several genera. In North America, the only species of partridge so-named is the introduced Gray Partridge, though most members of the genus *Alectoris,* to which the (introduced) Chukar belongs, are called partridges. Partridge is also a common nickname for the Ruffed Grouse.

Gruson (1972–BIOGRAPHY) traces the name back through the Latin *perdix* (*Perdix perdix* is the Latin name of the Gray Partridge) and the Greek *perdika,* which is derived from the verb meaning "to fart"—referring (thinks Gruson) to the flatulent sound made by the bird's wings when it flushes.

PARULA (PAA-ruh-luh or puh-ROO-luh). Standard English and Latin name for 2 rather similar species of wood warblers (family Parulidae; order Passeriformes). The Northern Parula (*Parula americana*) ranges throughout most of eastern North America; the Tropical Parula (*P. pitiayumi*) is a widespread Neotropical species that reaches the northernmost extent of its range in the lower Rio Grande Valley of Texas. Both parulas are notably small and colorful warblers and prefer to build their nests in pendulous masses of *Usnea* lichen (old-man's-beard) or Spanish moss *(Tillandsia usneoides).*

"Parula" is a diminutive form of *parus,* the Latin word for titmouse. Since "titmouse" itself means a "small, small bird," "parula" might be translated as "tiny bird," which is fair enough.

For family characteristics, see WOOD WARBLER.

PARVORDER. A taxonomic category between suborder and superfamily. See INFRAORDER for an example of its function.

PASSAGE. Widely used in Britain and parts of the former empire as a synonym for bird migration, e.g., the "fall passage." In this context a "passage migrant" is a species that migrates through a region but neither breeds nor winters there, i.e., a "transient." The Buff-breasted Sandpiper, for example, is a passage migrant in the United States.

PASSERES (PASS-uh-reez). One of Linnaeus' original ordinal names and an old synonym for the order now called the Passeriformes (perching birds); also used until recently as the name for the passerine suborder that comprises the songbirds or Oscines. The current name for this suborder is the Passeri.

PASSERI. The suborder comprising the songbirds or Oscines; see also preceding entry.

PASSERINE (PASS-er-ine, PASS-er-een or PASS-er-in). A perching bird; in its strictest sense referring to species belonging to the order Passeriformes. Sometimes used more loosely as "land bird," but this is imprecise: all passerines are land birds, but many land birds (e.g., raptors, gallinaceous birds, pigeons, cuckoos, owls, nightjars, swifts, hummingbirds, trogons, and woodpeckers) do not belong to the Passeriformes. Another near synonym is "songbird," but this term is more accurately used for the Passeri (Oscines), the largest suborder of the Passeriformes. In Europe, there are no passerines that are not oscines and one may call any passerine a songbird without fear of contradiction. In North America, however, the tyrant flycatchers (Tyrannidae) are perching birds (passerines) but not songbirds (oscines). These are sometimes referred to as "suboscine passerines." See Appendix I.

PATAGONIA (Arizona). See SOUTHEASTERN ARIZONA.

PATHOLOGY. See DISEASE.

PATRISTIC. Referring to resemblances among species or other taxa that can be attributed to a common origin rather than convergent evolution. The resemblance between gulls and jaegers is patristic; that between Dovekies and diving petrels is not. See also CLADISTICS; CONVERGENCE; GENOTYPE.

PAURAQUE (puh-RAH-kee). Standard English name for a single species of nightjar, *Nyctidromus albicollis*, which breeds from southern Texas to northern Argentina. The name apparently is a Spanish rendition of a

native Mexican word; it may have been intended originally to echo the species' call, but in its present form, it is not very close except for having three syllables. Another widespread Mexican name, *culejo* or *cuejo*, is a better "translation." For family characteristics, see NIGHTJAR.

PAWNEE NATIONAL GRASSLAND (Colorado). Approximately 775,000 acres of shortgrass prairie habitat in northeastern Colorado (between Greeley and Sterling), partly owned and administered by the National Forest Service. Bird specialties include Golden Eagle (mainly winter), Ferruginous and Swainson's Hawks, Prairie Falcon, Mountain Plover, Long-billed Curlew, Burrowing Owl, Sprague's Pipit, McCown's and Chestnut-collared Longspurs, Western Meadowlark, Say's Phoebe, and Brewer's Sparrow. Intermittent wet areas hold Franklin's Gulls and Forster's Terns and attract migrant waterfowl and shorebirds. Pronghorn Antelope, Coyotes, jackrabbits (two species), and Black-tailed Prairie Dogs also occur, and the wildflower show is spectacular from April to June, which is also the best period for seeing resident birds. December–January is the peak period for raptors.

PEACOCK. Vernacular name for the Indian Peafowl, *Pavo cristatus* (family Phasianidae). Familiar worldwide as a domesticated ornamental bird, the cock peafowl has been displaying its remarkable tail fan and metallic-blue body in gardens since before the birth of Christ. Though essentially a lowland forest species in its original range, it frequently forages in the open. It is still a common sight in fields and even along the roadsides in India, where even such highly edible life-forms are revered by the Hindu majority and go unmolested.

There are two other species of peacock: the very similar Green Peafowl *(Pavo muticus)*, which replaces *cristatus* in Asia, and the very rare, secretive African Peafowl *(Afropavo congensis)* of the central Congo. The Indian Peafowl is naturalized in a number of North America localities, especially in Southern California.

The feminine form of "peacock" is "peahen."

Anyone attracted to the notion that a peacock or two would add a charming touch to the garden should be made aware that their characteristic call may be likened to the amplified mating yowl of an alley cat.

PECK(ING) ORDER. A term deriving from the dominance hierarchy among flocks of domestic chickens, now broadly applied to such hierarchies among other social birds and even to human institutions, as the "pecking order" among the executives of a corporation. In the classic instance, the "head chicken" at the top of the peck order has established the right to peck where she chooses and to peck any other member of the flock unchallenged. The hen that is second in line dominates all but the

head chicken, and so forth, down to the most subordinate bird, which must submit to the will of the entire flock. See DOMINANCE.

PECTORAL (PEK-turr-ull) (Sandpiper). Pertaining to the breast, e.g., pectoral muscles. In the case of the sandpiper, referring to the heavy vertical barring that stops abruptly along the lower margin of the breast. Often shortened by the ornithologically hip to "pec": "Just had a flock of pecs."

PEEP. Originally a hunter's term for all of the small sandpipers, deriving from the high-pitched calls characteristic of several species. Now widely used by birdwatchers for the smallest, most "confusable" species of sandpipers in the genus *Calidris*—in North America: Semipalmated, Western, Least, White-rumped, and Baird's. Essentially synonymous with "stint," the standard English generic name for these birds in British usage.

PELAGIC (puh-LADGE-ik) (Cormorant, trip). Oceanic; of the open sea; more technically referring to the upper strata of deep waters beyond the influence of either the mainland or the bottom. Pelagic birds are those that prefer a marine habitat beyond the coastal zone and normally visit land only to breed. The most truly pelagic birds are the tubenoses (Procellariiformes)—the albatrosses, shearwaters, petrels, and storm-petrels—many of which spend their entire lives, except for breeding periods, hundreds of miles from any shore. Other birds that may correctly be called pelagic are the tropicbirds, phalaropes, jaegers (especially Long-tailed and Pomarine) and skuas, certain gulls (Sabine's), terns (Sooty, Bridled, and the noddies), and many of the alcids. Other species, such as the gannets and boobies and some gulls (e.g., the kittiwakes) and terns (e.g., Arctic), are at home in both coastal and deep waters. The Pelagic Cormorant, like the other marine members of its family, prefers the coastal zone and its standard English name is therefore something of a misnomer.

A "pelagic trip" is an outing by boat (often to offshore fishing banks) organized by a group of birdwatchers for the purpose of seeing "pelagics," i.e., oceanic birds.

PELICAN. Standard English name for all 8 members of the family Pelecanidae (order Pelecaniformes), 2 of which breed in North America. Sibley and Ahlquist (1990, 1993–SYSTEMATICS) place the Shoebill of Africa in its own subfamily of the pelicans.

Pelicans are very large (see below), peculiarly shaped waterbirds with heavy, bulky bodies, short, stout legs, long necks, and unusually adapted heads. The bill is very long and hooked at the tip with no external nostril openings (as in most Pelecaniformes). From near the end of the lower mandible to the base of the throat is suspended a great extensible sac of skin capable of holding at least 3 gallons of water—several times more

than "its belly can." This unique adaptation acts as a scoop that takes in fish and water together when the bird's head is underwater; when the pelican lifts its head from the surface, the water escapes from the corners of the gape, leaving the catch behind to be swallowed or stored temporarily in the esophagus. Pelicans waddle in an ungainly manner on land but are among the most graceful of birds in the air: riding air currents over coastal wave lines; soaring high over the ocean; migrating effortlessly on extended wings; and (in seagoing species) executing precision aerial dives into shoals of surface-feeding fish.

Most of the world's pelicans are white or whitish, often with black or dark wing tips and yellow-orange bills. One North American species, the American White Pelican, fits this pattern, whereas the other, the Brown Pelican, is handsomely patterned in deep chestnut, black, gray, white, and tawny.

Pelicans are among the world's largest birds, some species attaining a length of 6 feet (North American species, 4¼ to a little over 5 feet), a wingspan of 6–9 feet, and a weight of 10–17 pounds. The longest bill in the world belongs to the Great White Pelican of Eurasia (18½ inches) and the second longest to the American White Pelican (14½ inches). The Brown Pelican, once common along the Pacific, Gulf, and southeastern Atlantic coasts of the United States, has declined drastically as the result of indiscriminate use of pesticides. It has recovered well along the Gulf coast and in Florida but remains on the federal Endangered Species List elsewhere in the United States (see ENDANGERED BIRDS and THREATS (OF HUMAN ORIGIN) TO BIRDLIFE).

American pelicans are colonial. Their nests are shallow depressions or mounds of mud or debris on flat ground (White and Brown) or stick platforms in trees or bushes (Brown only). They lay 1–4 eggs, averaging 2 (White) and 3 (Brown); these are white with a chalky white outer coating that soon becomes stained in the nest.

Nestling pelicans are notably noisy, the adults much less so; the repertoire of both runs to grunts, groans, barks, and screams.

The pelicans are widespread as a family, absent only from the Arctic and Antarctic, most of South America, and waterless regions. One of the North American species (White) breeds on interior (often saline) lakes and winters in coastal shallows (California and Gulf coast); the other (Brown) breeds along the coasts and ranges into offshore waters.

"Pelican" is very close to the Greek word from which it comes and which refers appropriately to bill characters. Originally, however (cf. *The Birds* by Aristophanes), it described an ax-like tool and, by association, a woodpecker!

PELLET. A mass of indigestible matter—e.g., bones, fur, feathers, shell, stones, hard insect parts (legs, elytra), seed husks, rubber bands—formed in the stomachs of many (perhaps most) birds and eventually regurgi-

tated. The gray or brown, ovoid owl pellet, consisting of rodent bones embedded in clotted fur, is the most familiar of these "castings," but pellets are also produced by species of grebes, cormorants, vultures, hawks and eagles, herons, rails, shorebirds, gulls and terns, swifts, flycatchers, swallows, crows and jays, dippers, thrushes, catbirds, kinglets, wagtails, shrikes, and wood warblers. The larger pellets and those that accumulate at a roost or nest site are, of course, much better known than the tiny boluses ejected by songbirds and immediately lost in vegetation. Therefore, the list of species known to make pellets can be expected to increase with continued observation.

The details of pellet formation have been studied only recently. In owls, the indigestible materials are apparently separated from the softer food substances in the gizzard (see DIGESTIVE SYSTEM and Fig. 27) and the hard, sharp, and/or linear objects such as bones enclosed in a relatively smooth, rounded mass of fur or feathers. The finished pellet then travels up into the proventriculus, where it is held for a number of hours before being regurgitated. The entire process from ingestion to ejection of pellet takes from 9 to 16 hours in the few species studied, but the actual formation of the pellet may take only half as long. Though a pellet very often contains parts of several food items, it is likely that once it reaches the proventriculus, it must be disgorged before another meal can be swallowed. Thus, the stimulus for pellet regurgitation may be hunger, the sight of prey, or other feeding-related phenomena.

From the observer's point of view, the regurgitation process looks like some acute form of respiratory or digestive distress until the pellet emerges from the mouth and the bird settles itself in evident satisfaction.

On cursory inspection, the "pellet system" would seem to be simply a means of eliminating certain kinds of solid wastes by birds that swallow their food whole. However, experience in feeding sick or injured raptors has shown that the "roughage" of bone, fur, and feather is essential to the good health of these species. Pellet regurgitation may, for example, serve to clean the upper digestive tract.

Since pellets neatly collect bones, insect parts, and the like, often intact or in fragments large enough to be identified, they can yield valuable data on feeding habits when carefully dissected and analyzed.

From the birdwatcher's perspective, pellets are useful in locating roosting owls, especially when there is a snow cover.

PEN. A little-used term for the female of any species of swan.

PENDULINE TITS. Standard English generic name for 10 of the 12–13 species of birds in the family Remizidae (order Passeriformes), often considered a subfamily (Remizinae) of the "true" tits (family Paridae). Traditionally, the Verdin has been considered to be the sole North American representative of this family and is still so classified in the *AOU Checklist,*

7th edition (1998). However, Sibley and Ahlquist (1990, 1993–SYSTEM-ATICS) include this species in a subfamily with the gnatcatchers in a family (Certhiidae) that also contains the wrens and treecreepers. For characteristics, see VERDIN.

PENNA (pl.: pennae). Any feather in which the barbs unite (connected by the barbules) to form a continuous surface, i.e., the vane or web; as distinct from a "pluma" in which each barb branches separately from the rachis. See also SEMIPLUME; FEATHER; and Fig. 13.

PERCHING BIRDS. The species of the vast order Passeriformes. The observant reader will remark that all birds perch in one fashion or another. It should therefore be explained that the names (both Latin and English) refer to the characteristic foot structure of passerines, with three forward toes and one behind, which, like the human thumb and finger arrangement, is ideal for grasping (e.g., a perch). See PASSERINE.

PEREGRINE (PAIR-uh-grin) (Falcon). Standard English name for a single cosmopolitan bird of prey, *Falco peregrinus* (family Falconidae). Its speed, agility, and handsome plumage justify its reputation as one of the most majestic of all birds, which in turn explains its preferred status among falconers and the wide popular support for restoring the eastern North American populations decimated by DDT poisoning (see ENDANGERED BIRDS; THREATS (OF HUMAN ORIGIN) TO BIRDLIFE). The name means traveler or wanderer, referring to its long-distance migrations. See FALCON; FALCONRY; SPEED.

PEREGRINE FUND. Founded in 1970 at Cornell University by then professor Tom Cade, this seminal conservation organization was inspired by the apparently imminent extinction of the Peregrine Falcon largely as a result of pesticides in the food chain (See THREATS (OF HUMAN ORIGIN) TO BIRDLIFE). From the beginning the Fund's emphasis was on successfully rearing Peregrines (and eventually other raptor species) in captivity and then releasing them to reestablish self-sustaining populations in the wild. It is largely as a result of this effort that the Peregrine has now been removed from the federal endangered species list. In 1984 the Fund consolidated in operations at the World Center for Birds of Prey in Boise, Idaho. From these headquarters the organization uses the rearing and hacking techniques it has developed and refined for the conservation and restoration of threatened raptor species in more than 25 projects worldwide. For more details, go to http://www.peregrinefund.org/.

PERIODICALS, ORNITHOLOGICAL AND BIRDWATCHING. See the Bibliography under PERIODICALS for a listing of major ornithological journal and birdwatching publications.

PERMANENT RESIDENT. A somewhat problematic term referring to species or individual birds that both breed and winter in the same region, i.e., a nonmigratory species or population. The concept is a little more complex than might be assumed. Since there are Blue Jays year-round in New England, it seems fair to say that the Blue Jay as a species is a permanent resident there. However, only some Blue Jays reside permanently in the region, while others move south in the fall and return in the spring. Furthermore, the breeding success of Blue Jays during a given year and the abundance of acorns and other food sources affect how many individuals stay or depart. Residency patterns also vary greatly among different species and regions. Some woodpeckers and gallinaceous birds, for example, can justifiably be called permanent residents as *species,* so limited are their movements under normal circumstances. Certain "winter finches," e.g., redpolls, will reside year-round in an area as long as seed crops support the population, but will move south en masse when a food shortage develops (see IRRUPTION/ERUPTION). In general, as one moves south in North America the percentage of species that occur as permanent residents increases because of year-long availability of food. Thus, Eastern Bluebirds in the southeastern states tend to be nonmigratory and are joined in winter by migratory bluebirds from the northern states and Canada. (However, the bluebird's winter range has been moved northward gradually over the last three decades, so that the area of their "permanent residency" has expanded.)

One point of clarity is that individual birds that overwinter in their breeding area in defiance of the normal habit of their species, e.g., at a feeding station, are *not* properly called permanent residents.

Perhaps a key question is: What percentage of a species' summer population and breeding range must be occupied in a state/region before you call it a "permanent resident"?

PERSPIRATION. Birds do not perspire by means of sweat glands in the skin as do humans, but give off excess heat in the form of water vapor, mainly by panting. See TEMPERATURE, BODY, Cooling Off.

PESTS, BIRDS AS. See PROBLEMS INVOLVING BIRDS.

PETERSON, Roger Tory 1908–96. With the possible exception of John James Audubon, the man most closely associated in the public's mind with birds and, especially, their identification in the field. As with many life-long birdwatchers, Peterson's passion ignited early. Born in Jamestown, New York to Swedish immigrants who had fled from famine in their homeland, Peterson was fond of saying that he couldn't remember a time when he didn't watch birds. He was small ("the runt of the primary school clutch" he wrote), shy and bookish, and found comfort and a calling in the natural world and particularly its birdlife. Getting little encouragement from his

practical-minded family and open derision from his peers, Peterson found his first supporter and mentor in a seventh-grade teacher, Miss Blanche Hornbeck, whom he unfailingly credits in accounts of his amazing career for viewing his obsession sympathetically. The "pretty, red-headed" Miss Hornbeck organized a Junior Audubon Club and armed with some leaflets from the National Audubon Society and a copy of Chester Reed's pocket *Bird Guides* created a cell of young listers. As if being a birdwatcher wasn't bad enough, young Roger was also an artist (perhaps inheriting a creative instinct from his cabinetmaker father) and after an undistinguished academic career in high school—where he was always "in trouble up to my scrawny neck" for drawing birds in his notebooks and contradicting his teachers on their bird facts—he lit out for New York City and a career in commercial art. While studying at the Art Students' League and the National Academy of Design, he began attending meetings of the Linnaean Society at the American Museum of Natural History. There—along with many others, but especially seven keen young members of the Bronx County Bird Club—he fell under the personal spell and peerless tutelage of Ludlow Griscom, the father of modern birdwatching.

In defining the nature of his immense achievement Peterson was always at pains to point out that he did not invent the concept of "field marks" (Edward Howe Forbush may have introduced that idea), nor did he invent the reductionist approach to bird identification that focused on points of distinction (that was Griscom's genius). Rather what Peterson did—certainly better than anyone before him, and arguably at least as well as his many imitators—was to create a *system* of highly accessible painted images that showed at a glance how one species differed from another. The birds were intentionally depicted in a simple, almost diagrammatic, style and adorned with little arrows that pointed to the most useful field marks. The first edition of *A Field Guide to the Birds* was published by a risk-taking editor at Houghton Mifflin (Paul Brooks) in 1934 in the depths of the Great Depression, and, contrary to the expectations of many, soon became a best seller.

The success of the first field guide was, of course, just the beginning of a brilliant career that brought Peterson worldwide recognition not just as *the* bird man, but also as the preeminent interpreter of the natural world. Through a field guide series that now numbers over 60 titles and also as a lecturer, artist, photographer, and advocate for the natural world, Peterson was not only instrumental in introducing millions of people to the fascination of natural history, but also helped to build the powerful constituency on which the conservation of the natural world depends.

In addition to his published works, the legacy of Roger Tory Peterson is carried on at a thriving institute of natural history education that bears his name in Jamestown, New York (see http://www.rtpi.org).

See also FIELD GUIDE.

PETREL (PET-truhl). Standard English name for about 46 members of the family Procellariidae (order Procellariiformes), mainly in two genera: *Pterodroma* and *Procellaria,* not including the storm-petrels and diving-petrels. Two *Pterodromas*—Black-capped and Cook's Petrels—are regular visitors to North American waters and 6 other petrels are rare but occur annually or are casual visitors. For family characteristics, see SHEAR-WATER; see also GADFLY PETREL and STORM-PETREL; see the latter for the origin of the name.

PETTINGILL, Olin Sewall, 1907–2001. One of the most distinguished American ornithologists of the twentieth century, Pettingill was born in Belgrade, Maine. He earned his PhD at Cornell, where he was one of Arthur A. ALLEN's protégés along with other bird luminaries-to-be, such as Ludlow Griscom and George Miksch Sutton. He was an accomplished writer, lecturer, and filmmaker. In addition to his long teaching career at Carleton College (Minnesota) and the University of Michigan Biological Station, "Sewall" as he was known to friends, wrote a classic ornithology textbook that was first published in 1939 and had its fifth printing in 1985. In birding circles he is perhaps best known as the author of the first bird-finding books: *A Guide to Finding Birds East of the Mississippi* (1951) and its western counterpart (1953). He traveled widely to film wildlife, notably penguins and albatrosses in Antarctica, and contributed footage to Disney nature classics, such as "Nature's Half Acre" and "The Vanishing Prairie." He was Director of the Cornell Lab of Ornithology from 1960 to 1973 and served for many years on the board of the National Audubon Society.

PEWEE (PEE-wee). Standard English name for all but one of the 12 species of tyrant flycatchers in the genus *Contopus* (family Tyrannidae; order Passeriformes). Four species of Contopis flycatchers breed in North America, including the nonpewee, Olive-sided Flycatcher (*C. cooperi*).

   Pewees are exceedingly drab, rather small (6–72 inches) flycatchers of the forest and forest edge. Our Eastern and Western Wood-Pewees are virtually indistinguishable except by call and replace each other in eastern and western North America. They would seem to represent a classic case of recent (Pleistocene/ Pliocene) species divergence. Where these two forms now overlap in breeding range, they are not known to interbreed.

   "Pewee" is a fair imitation of the most frequently heard call of the Eastern Wood-Pewee.

   For family characteristics see TYRANT FLYCATCHER.

PHAINOPEPLA (FAY-noh-PEP-la). Standard English name for one of the 4 members of the Silky-flycatcher family (Ptilogonatidae; order Passeriformes) and the only one that breeds in North America. The Gray Silky-Flycatcher of Mexico and Guatemala has been recorded as an accidental

straggler to Texas and perhaps California (natural occurrence questioned). Sibley and Ahlquist (1990–SYSTEMATICS) put the silky-flycatchers in the family Bomycillidae together with the 3 waxwing species and the monotypic Palmchat.

The Phainopepla is a small (7¾ inches), slender songbird with "silky" plumage similar to that of the waxwings, to which it may be closely related. It has a prominent crest, a short, but moderately broad bill, broad, rounded wings, and a long tail. The sexes are dimorphic: the male glossy blue-black, the female dull olive-brown; both have large pale areas in the primary webs and red irises.

The Phainopepla is a bird of arid mesquite scrub, including cultivated lands. Like many other dry-country songbirds, it is likely to be found along streams, where it feeds mainly on berries (e.g., mistletoe and the fruits of the Peruvian pepper or mastic, *Schinus molle*); it also eats insects, frequently catching them on the wing. Phainopeplas tend to travel in small flocks except when nesting and their broad wings give them a distinctive "butterfly" flight.

The song is somewhat weak and "irresolute," often containing squeaks as well as pleasant liquid notes.

A typical nest site is the fork of a low tree (e.g., mesquite). The nest is a shallow cup of comparatively delicate construction—small twigs, stems, and leaves bound with spider silk and lined with down or hair. The 2–3 (rarely, 4) eggs are very pale gray to slightly pinkish with moderately dense black and paler subsurface spotting.

The Phainopepla occurs from central California, southern Utah, and western Texas and south with its habitat to the limits of the central plateau of Mexico. Northernmost populations move south after breeding and, like the waxwings, Phainopeplas are somewhat nomadic, probably moving according to food availability; a few stray birds have been recorded in eastern Canada and the New England coast.

Phainopepla (also the Latin name of the monotypic genus) is a classical Greek compound that translates prettily as "shining robe" (Choate and Paynter 1985–BIOGRAPHY).

PHALAROPE (FAL-uh-rope). Standard English name for 3 distinctive members of the sandpiper family (Scolopacidae; order Charadriiformes), all of which breed in North America.

Phalaropes are small (average 7¾ – 9¼ inches) sandpipers with lobed and partially webbed toes evolved for swimming. Two of the three species (Red and Red-necked Phalaropes) are highly pelagic in habit and spend most of the year resting and feeding in flocks on the ocean. Another notable trait of the phalaropes is their reversal of sexual attributes: females are larger and wear a more brilliant alternate (breeding) plumage, while the male incubates the eggs and tends the young after they hatch (see

MATING SYSTEMS). The phalaropes also share a unique feeding method. Whether at sea, in tidal pools or alkaline lakes, the birds spin rapidly in a tight circle, stirring up stirring up zooplankton in the water column, which they deftly pick up in quick stabbing motions as they turn. The seagoing species are often seen in the company of marine mammals—presumably benefiting from the small animal life churned up in their wake—and are widely known as "whalebirds" among seafarers.

The nests of phalaropes are shallow hollows on the ground lined with grasses and often built into a clump of grass with surrounding vegetation pulled over the top to form a canopy. The 4 (rarely, 3) eggs are off-white to brownish yellow or olive, covered rather densely (particularly at the large end) with well-defined dark brown speckles and splotches.

The phalaropes are not as songful on the breeding grounds as the sandpipers, but make occasional nasal wheezings, grunts, and quacks. The piping call note of the pelagic phalaropes is loud and sharp enough to be audible over the noise of wind, water, and ships' engines.

Red and Red-necked Phalaropes breed on arctic tundra (circumpolar) and winter at sea over most of the globe except Antarctic waters. Wilson's Phalarope is the landlubber of the family, nesting largely in northern prairie sloughs and wintering in Central and South America. It breeds exclusively in North America and has expanded its range dramatically eastward (as far as the Atlantic coast) in recent years.

"Phalarope" derives from a Greek compound meaning "coot-footed," referring to the lobed feet of phalaropes—miniature versions of those of the coots.

See references in the Bibliography under SHOREBIRD.

PHANERIC (fuh-NAIR-ik). Referring to conspicuous colors or patterns, e.g., in the plumage of birds, which serve to attract attention to, rather than conceal, their owners. The bright gorgets of male hummingbirds are examples of phaneric plumage. See COLOR AND PATTERN; DISPLAY.

PHASE. Once widely used to refer to morphological plumage variation within a population of birds, e.g., red and gray "phases" of the Eastern Screech Owl or the ringed "phase" of the Common Murre. It has been pointed out that the term seems to imply *transience* in the condition described, (e.g., the phases of the moon), which in polymorphic birds is not typically the case. The preferred term is now "morph"; see POLYMORPHISM.

PHEASANT. Standard English name for about 31 members of the family Phasianidae (order Galliformes), which also includes the snowcocks, francolins and spurfowl, partridges, Old World quail, tragopans, jungle fowl, peafowl, grouse (including ptarmigan and prairie-chickens), and

turkeys. One species, the Ring-necked (or Common) Pheasant *(Phasianus colchicus),* has been widely introduced in North America as a game bird. Most of these birds are bred in captivity for the express purpose of being shot and are restocked each year in areas where they cannot sustain their populations. Three races of the Ring-necked Pheasant range as natives across Eurasia from the Caucasus to Japan; the green race of Japan, which lacks a ring-neck and is sometimes considered a separate species, has also been locally introduced in the eastern United States.

Pheasants have short, rounded wings capable of propelling them almost vertically when flushed but not able to power sustained flight (see MUSCLES). Like most gallinaceous birds, pheasants feed largely on grains, seeds, and some fruit. They forage on the ground and roost in trees during the night.

Like the quail and other members of their family, pheasants make a shallow hollow on the ground in which to lay their large clutches of eggs. This nest is often concealed in ground vegetation and is sometimes sparsely lined with handy plant material. The 7–15 (usually 10–12) eggs are blue-gray to light or dark olive and unmarked. Hens not infrequently lay eggs in nests of other pheasants or other ground-nesting birds, such as ducks or woodcocks.

The pheasant "song" sung by males on territory and at other times is a harsh, abrupt, two-syllable crowing, similar in quality to the first part of a rooster's *cock-a-doodle-doo.* It is generally accompanied by a loud beating of the wings.

Pheasants are restricted to the Palearctic and Oriental regions and reach their greatest diversity in the Asian highlands. Because the male plumage of many species is spectacular, pheasants are popular with collectors and exotic pheasants are widely reared and sold as ornamental garden birds. "Pheasant" comes from a Greek word meaning "bird of the river Phaisos," which flows into the Black Sea from the Caucasus, where one race of the Ring-necked Pheasant is native.

See references in the Bibliography under GALLINACEOUS BIRDS.

PHENETIC (feh-NET-ik) **CLASSIFICATION.** The practice of pooling observable characters in a group of species and subjecting them to analysis using an objective mathematical technique to determine their overall statistical similarity. The end product is a tree diagram that groups species based on their overall similarity. It has been argued that such an objective approach will generate true phylogenies based on the overwhelming statistical signal obtained if enough characters are used in the analysis. Proponents of cladistic classification scoff at this, and point out that convergent and misinterpreted characters are so common that phenetic methods will often produce incorrect phylogenies. Despite these objections, most current computer programs used to determine phylogeny now use a hybrid

of cladistic character selection and weighting with phenetic statistical methods. See CLADISTICS; SYSTEMATICS.

PHENOLOGY (feh-NAHL-uh-jee). The study of visible changes that occur in plants and animals on a regular seasonal basis and in response to climate. Phenological information includes, for example, the arrival and departure dates of bird migrants in a given season, the duration of territorial singing in a given bird species; and the flowering dates of plant species.

PHENOTYPE (FEE-no-type). The sum of an organism's observable physical characteristics deriving from the interaction of its hereditary traits (its genotype) and the environmental influences upon it. Red and gray morph screech-owls from the same brood have a very similar, though not identical genotype (only identical twins and clones are exact genetic matches); but their phenotypes are distinct due to a different expression of the gene that controls plumage color.

PHILOPATRIC (noun: philopatry). Exhibiting faithfulness to a home territory. Young birds that stay in or return to their natal area in maturity are said to be philopatric; species may also be characterized as philopatric. See DISPERSAL; SPECIATION.

PHOEBE (FEE-bee). Standard English name for the 3 species of tyrant flycatchers in the genus *Sayornis* (family Tyrannidae; order Passeriformes), all of which breed in North America.

Phoebes are medium-sized (about 7 inches) flycatchers with relatively long tails, which they flick in a characteristic *downward* motion. They have distinctive nesting practices, preferring to build on a flat solid surface (usually with an overhang), such as a rock shelf, the eaves of a house, or a beam beneath a bridge. Eastern and Black Phoebes construct "adobe" cups of mud mixed with plant fibers. Phoebes often (but by no means exclusively) feed and nest near running water.

The name "phoebe" imitates the song of the Eastern Phoebe.

For family characteristics, see TYRANT FLYCATCHER.

PHOENIX (FEE-nix). Perhaps the best-known of legendary birds, famed for its splendid plumage, its beautiful song, and its association with fire and the sun. Its life history was set down by the Greek historian Herodotus (fifth century BC) and the Roman naturalist Pliny the Elder (first century AD), among others, and it was believed to be seen occasionally by travelers to the Middle East at least until the Middle Ages. Authorities differ on the details of Phoenix biology, but there is general agreement on its most spectacular characteristics: Only one Phoenix, always a male, inhabits the

earth at any given time, living for 500 or perhaps as long as 12,954 years. It ranges in Arabia and/or Egypt or perhaps in a paradise beyond the eastern horizon. At the end of its life, it builds a nest of aromatic vegetation, sings its surpassingly lovely song, enacts some kind of self-fertilization (details obscure), and sets its nest and itself on fire. (One legend says the fire is set by sparks thrown from the hooves of the horses of the sun god, who stops his chariot to listen to the Phoenix sing.) In the ashes of the nest is a white grub, which is ultimately transformed into the new Phoenix.

The most celebrated appearance of a Phoenix in recent times is that of Fawkes, the familiar of Professor Dumbledore in the Harry Potter saga by J. K. Rowling. Fawkes is apparently on a shorter life cycle than that described above, but in any case plays a critical role in at least two books of the series. Also, the core of Harry's wand is a Phoenix feather.

For other fabulous birds and some Phoenix taxonomy, see IMAGINATION, BIRDS IN.

PHOTOGRAPHY (aka "imaging" to encompass digital technology). Obviously no attempt can be made here to survey the vast topics of photographic equipment and technique—even as they relate to birds alone. However, an outline of some of the basic considerations involved in photographing birds may be possible.

While photographic technology has become immensely sophisticated, the basic challenge that makes bird photography attractive to so many remains quite simple. The earthbound cameraperson's aim is to capture a relatively large, clear, aesthetically appealing, and/or useful image of a living creature that is instinctually shy and tends to move (indeed, fly!) rapidly, frequently, and unpredictably into conditions (poor light, awkward position, beyond the horizon) that tend to thwart the photographer's intention.

In the early days of bird photography, the practitioner had little to offset these disadvantages except patience and luck. Today, however, the physical versatility and "intelligence" of camera equipment, the amount of literature on the subject, and the number of bird "imagers" out developing new techniques have all increased to such a degree that the bird is more likely to be inconvenienced than the photographer.

SOME BASIC RULES OF THUMB

- *Determine your objective (s).* If your dream is to display prints of your photographs in your home or a gallery or to publish your work in books or glossy magazines, you will probably want to invest in the best traditional single-lens reflex (SLR) cameras and glass lenses. But if you are mainly interested in taking record shots of rarities or sending images to friends on the Internet, your choice of equipment is likely to tilt toward the new spectrum of digital cameras.

- *Educate yourself.* Read up, take workshops, talk to bird photographers, try stuff out at the camera store before you invest.
- *Buy the best equipment you can afford.* This is perhaps especially true of telephoto lenses. The cost of the best equipment has always been and continues to be quite daunting, with single lenses going for thousands of dollars, but the rule stands.

EQUIPMENT. In bird photography the gadgets and features of greatest interest are those that help the photographer remedy the inherent challenges noted above. The only constraint on your freedom of choice in selecting accessories will be your bank account.

SLR Versus Digital. At present the image quality possible using traditional photographic cameras and lenses to produce color slides for projection or print work is superior to that of digital cameras, though this gap seems to be closing rapidly. Bird photographers using traditional equipment must resign themselves to hauling around large (to enormous) telephoto lenses and the cumbersome tripods necessary to hold them steady while photographing Dovekies in a gale. Digital still cameras are light, compact, and permit more spontaneity of movement; if a new state record pops up in front of you, you can just point and shoot. Manipulation and storage of images also deserve consideration. Digital images can be instantly viewed and erased if below the photographer's standards, whereas slides need to be developed and then (in all too many cases) tossed. Digital pictures can also be improved in a variety of ways using computer software. Though slides can be scanned, thus turning them into digital images, the digital camera and computer are, quite literally, made for each other. Digital cameras are even less tolerant of bashing and dowsing than sensitive SLR computer cameras.

SLR Camera Bodies. In the last 20 years the basic SLR camera has been transformed from a mechanical device to a small computer. Though oldtimers have many credible arguments about the advantages of the classic SLRs, the new cameras are unquestionably lighter, faster, "smarter," and more versatile than their ancestors. They can also be confusing—too many options "at your fingertips"—and may be less hardy under typical birding conditions (sandstorms, rain forest humidity). Desirable features in a modern camera body include:

- *Motor drive* allowing fast, trouble-free loading and rewinding and the ability to fire off many frames per second (expensive but indispensable for capturing the perfect flight shot).
- *Autofocus* with a sensor system that adjusts to moving subjects; this and the next feature must be combined with compatible automatic lenses.
- *Auto-exposure,* which adjust aperture and shutter speed (see below) to ambient conditions and preset image priorities (e.g., depth of field).

Manual options: While automatic features can be very convenient, there are some conditions in which you will want to use your own eyes and brain.

- *Built-in flash.*

Telephoto Lenses (for SLRs) are, of course, essential in getting a big image of a small, camera-shy subject. Unless a blind is used or very patient stalking contemplated, 400 mm is probably the smallest lens size practical for getting reasonably large images of small birds. Larger lenses are even more effective, of course—serious bird photographers routinely use 500- to 600-mm monsters—but weight and bulkiness increase with the degree of magnification and stability decreases, so that a tripod becomes essential and mobility is reduced.

Zoom lenses permit quick changes in magnification without changing lenses, and provide great flexibility not only in magnification but in overall composition. They are particularly handy in situations where the camera, the photographer, and the target are all in motion—as on pelagic trips.

At present (2003) the two most prominent rivals for the SLR nature photographer market are Canon and Nikon.

Digital Still Cameras (with zoom lenses) are highly portable, ideal for creating computer images and for displaying photos on the Web, and essential for "digi-scoping" (see below). So far, however, digital images cannot match the quality of the best film photos. Only a few digital cameras currently on the market are useful for bird photography. Ideally, these combine

- *Telephoto capability,* expressed as a zoom range of 14×, which translates as a magnification of 10× (as in binoculars) or the approximate equivalent of a 500-mm camera lens
- *Automatic and manual focus and exposure capability*
- *Image stabilization*
- *High resolution* (1024 × 768 or greater pixel array)
- *Ability to take teleconverters* (1.4× and 2×)
- *Built-in flash*

Digital Video Cameras (Camcorders) add action to your bird pictures, a dimension that can aid identification as well as enhance dramatic and aesthetic appeal. They can be used with interchangeable telephoto lenses and 1.4× and 2× teleconverters. As with SLR telephoto camera systems, a high-quality tripod and head are crucial for best results. Other desirable features for camcorders include

- *3-chip image sensors,* which provide good color and still image quality
- *Editing capability:* a direct port to your computer and editing software so that you can covert raw footage into art—or at least an entertaining scrapbook (Your viewers will approve.)
- *Manual focus option*
- *A large instant playback screen* (LCD: liquid crystal display)
- *A microphone windscreen*

Digi-scoping is the practice of taking a photo using a digital camera (still or video) through another optical device, usually a telescope. With practice this can yield some surprisingly good images and while most are far from great art they are often more than adequate to establish the identity of a rare bird. The technique is a hot topic on the birdnet at present (2003) and it is becoming commonplace for birders to digi-scope a good bird during a field trip just for fun. Expect rapid evolution.

Teleconverters (Extenders). In the never-ending quest for greater focal length (to cream that treetop warbler), a valuable and (relatively) inexpensive gizmo is the teleconverter. A 2× extender will double magnification so that your 400-mm lens becomes an 800-mm one; the other standard teleconverter enlarges the image by 1.4×. The downside is that with increased focal length you lose light: one f-stop (light intensity reduced by half) with the 1.4× extender and two stops with the 2×.

Extension Rings, Tubes, and Bellows are inserted between lens and camera body and are useful for getting closer to your subject than the normal focal length of your lens allows. They permit extreme close-ups and close stalking with a long telephoto lens.

Lens Aperture and Shutter Speed. The more light that can enter through the lens, the greater the photographer's ability to shoot moving subjects or those in low light or to increase image depth. (Shutter speed also determines how much light falls on the film and automatic cameras can balance these two factors for specific effects.) Lenses with low f-stops are preferable, and lenses with a low stop greater than 5.6 are not recommended for bird photography.

Tripods. With a big lens, a moving bird, and a high wind the last straw—guaranteeing a tragically "soft" photo—is a shaky hand; thus the need for a sturdy tripod. In addition to the right legs, you should also consider a high-quality "head" that adds maximum flexibility in aiming the camera as well as the all-important stability. The fact that the best recommended tripod and head combinations will set you back another $1,000+ is slightly sick-making, but experienced photographers insist it is worth it. With lighter gear and higher speed film, hand-holding is possible, and middle ground can be sought in the form of a gunstock-type mount. These may be purchased with fingertip focusing systems and cable-release triggers.

Flash enables the bird photographer to shoot in the worst of lighting conditions and to stop motion in his subjects, ensuring clarity of focus. An aesthetic drawback to flash pictures is that—with the exception of nocturnal subjects—they tend to have an artificial look with a brightly lit foreground and a background that is swallowed in darkness. The nature of the artifice is altered, but its presence no less obvious, when an artificial "sky" or other reflecting background is used.

Film. Discussing film with photographers is like talking wine with oenophiles: all have their own preferences and biases bordering on su-

perstition—perhaps another reason to go digital. The innocent neophyte should simply be aware that films come in different speeds and functions using different processes, and you should choose the right film for your purpose and your taste. Though fast film might seem an easy answer to stopping action and shooting in dim habitats, there is a general inverse relationship between high speed and bad color in film. High-speed film (especially (ASA1000 and above) is also vulnerable to damage by airport security scanners. Different film types are developed using different processes. Ectachrome processing can now be done quickly by local developers, while Kodachrome must be sent away, requiring more time. All film brands and types also have their own characteristics of tone or brightness, which are variously perceived by the viewer, and photographers inevitably develop favorites. An odd characteristic of some new film types is that they produce images that are more vivid than the real subjects and many photographers prefer this.

Blinds are essential for photographing nesting birds, both to ensure unselfconscious subjects and to prevent disrupting the nesting cycle. They are also valuable in getting close to moving subjects, such as shorebirds, which "spook" easily. Lightweight collapsible blinds are available commercially or they can easily be made with simple materials (designs can be found in most wildlife photography books). It is usually necessary to accustom birds to the presence of a blind over a period of a few days. For nesting birds the blind should be set up at some distance (10 feet is recommended for small birds) and left for a day, then moved up to shooting distance (no closer than 5 feet) and left again. If no disturbance is evident, the photographer can use the blind. If birds see someone enter a blind, they will often feel threatened by the human presence even if they cannot see into the blind. They can sometimes be deceived if two people enter the blind and one leaves.

USES OF BIRD PHOTOGRAPHY. In addition to the challenge, fun, and aesthetic enjoyment to be had from photographing birds, the modern camera is useful for scientific and educational purposes. Stop action allows analysis of flight and other movements normally too fast for the human eye to see. Aerial photos of flocks, roosts, and colonies are an invaluable tool in census work. Good photos have now largely obviated the need to take specimens of birds as occurrence records—even diagnostic details such as wing formulas can be photographed in birds taken from mist nets. Photographs used as text illustrations can be less expensive and (in some cases) more accurate than paintings or drawings. Display rituals and other avian activities can now be recorded with complete fidelity in color videos. And, of course, it is in no small measure due to nature photography that birds are now more widely appreciated than ever before.

AESTHETICS. Frame-filling subjects, in pleasing compositions, perfect focus, and brilliant color, were once the only goals to which bird photographers aspired. This aesthetic was enforced to a certain extent by clumsy, un-

sophisticated equipment that demanded a relatively stationary subject. Such bird portraits—often recording a nest tableau—are still taken, of course, and, with justification, widely appreciated. But the definition of a good photograph has been expanded. Action stills, for example, especially "wing shots," now draw praise even if not completely in sharp focus. Photographs showing a species in a characteristic habitat or exhibiting a typical behavioral trait (even if not "full frame") are deemed more interesting than the standard portrait or nest shot. And a quality of wildness in a photograph—as of a shy species painstakingly stalked—is more appealing than the tame indifference recorded in "setups." See, for example, the haunting portraits in William Burt's *Shadowbirds* (1994–RAIL).

For a list of links to websites see Carey et al. (2001–PHOTO); for a selection of recent books on bird and nature photography, see the bibliography; for a continuous window on this rapidly changing world, see *Outdoor Photographer* magazine.

PHOTOPERIODISM. The effect of light—especially length of day—on animal physiology and behavior. Stimulation of birds' reproductive systems in response to increased hours of daylight has been demonstrated repeatedly in the laboratory and on chicken farms. The phenomenon also plays a role (of debated importance) in the urge to migrate. Berthold (1993–MIGRATION), a confirmed genetic determinist, points out that *Zugunruhe* arises from an internal "circannual clock" in birds. See MIGRATION; NAVIGATION; and the Bibliography.

PHYLETIC (fye-LET-ik). Referring to evolutionary descent and relationship; phylogenetic. See PHYLOGENY; SYSTEMATICS.

PHYLOGENY (fye-LODGE-uh-nee) (less frequently, phylogenesis [fye-luh-JEN-ih-sis]). Evolutionary history as a whole or that of any given taxon (species, family, etc.) and therefore the relationships among these units and groupings. The framework of modern taxonomy consists of the attempt to place organisms in *phylogenetic* order—the order of their descent from common ancestors. Shearwaters are *phylogenetically* closer to the penguins than to the gulls, though they more resemble the latter. Placing the Yellow-breasted Chat in its proper family involves discovering its *phylogenetic* (or phyletic) relationships with other birds. See also SYSTEMATICS and Appendix I.

PHYLUM (FYE-lum) (pl.: phyla). The major taxonomic category between kingdom and class. The five kingdoms are each divided into phyla; the phyla into subphyla and classes. Depending on taxonomic interpretation, there are between 10 and 33 phyla in the animal kingdom. Birds (class Aves) belong in the phylum Chordata, which contains all vertebrates and other animals with nerve cords. See SYSTEMATICS.

PHYSIOLOGY. The study of the *functions* of living organisms as a whole and of their components. Bird physiology is treated here under the various systems (DIGESTIVE, REPRODUCTIVE, etc.), senses (VISION, SMELL, etc.), and specific organs (OIL GLAND, etc.).

PIGEON. Standard English name for about 135 members of the family Columbidae. The only other family in the order Columbiformes is the Raphidae, containing 3 recently extinct island species, the Dodo and 2 solitaires. Counting the DOVES, the family contains a total of about 313 species worldwide. Nine species of pigeons and doves, including the extinct Passenger Pigeon, are native to North America; 3 others, including the ubiquitous Feral Pigeon, have been "successfully" introduced (see INTRODUCED BIRDS); and 6 species have occurred as accidental stragglers (see Appendix II). Pigeons are generally larger than doves, with short, blunt rather than long, pointed tails, but the terms have little taxonomic integrity; our feral city columbid, for example, is widely known both as Rock Dove and as Feral or Common Pigeon.

Columbids vary in size from 6 to 30 inches (6½ to 14½ inches in North America). They are plump, small-headed, short-legged birds, usually somberly colored (though often with patches of iridescent feathers). Their bills are slender and short with a cere or operculum above the nostrils at the base.

Pigeons and doves feed largely on fruits and seeds, either in trees or on the ground. They are often gregarious while feeding, and a few species (notably the extinct Passenger Pigeon) nest in colonies. They are capable of drinking without raising their heads as most birds must, and they are unique in producing a secretion from the crop on which they "nurse" nestlings (see CROP MILK). Their vegetarian eating habits and plump form make them popular "table birds," and there is a season here on several species.

The Rock Dove nests on cliffs when thoroughly wild, but in its more familiar feral state prefers man-made structures: building ledges, eaves, etc. Native pigeons tend to nest fairly low in trees or shrubs (ground doves infrequently on the ground). The typical nest is a flimsy stick platform; several species occasionally use abandoned songbird nests. The usual columbid clutch consists of 2 glossy, white to buff eggs (see Fig. 10).

Pigeon/dove calls are invariably moans, coos, or hoots, some haunting, others mechanical and monotonous.

As a family, the pigeons and doves occur throughout the world except in arctic and antarctic extremes, and the native Mourning Dove occurs throughout North America south of the subarctic region. Most of our pigeons and doves are permanent residents, and even in the migratory species some populations are sedentary.

"Pigeon" is descended from the Latin *pipire,* "to peep," through the French *pilon,* a nestling bird.

PIGEON'S MILK. See CROP MILK.

PIGMENT. See COLOR AND PATTERN.

PILEATED (PILL-ee-ay-ted or PYE-lee-ay-ted) (Woodpecker). Crowned, capped, or crested, i.e., having feathers in a distinctive shape or color covering the pileum.

PILEUM (PILL-ee-yum or PYE-lee-yum). Technical term for crown; the top of the head between the forehead and the nape. See Fig. 35.

PINFEATHER. An early stage of feather growth in which only the feather sheath is apparent. See FEATHER.

PINION (pinioning). Sometimes used in a literary context to mean simply a bird's wing or a flight feather, but more specifically, it refers to the wrist and hand (carpals and phalanges) of a bird's wing, including the primary feathers. Pinioning involves severing this portion of one wing to *permanently* keep captive birds from flying. Not the same as CLIPPING.

PINTAIL. Standard English name for 4 species of ducks in the genus *Anas*. The pintails all have elongated tails to *some* degree. However, only drakes of the so-called blue-billed pintails and especially the Northern Pintail *(Anas acuta)* have the two greatly elongated central rectrices that evoke the English generic name. The latter is also the only pintail that occurs regularly (widespread) in North America; the White-cheeked Pintail has been recorded here as a vagrant from the Caribbean. Pintail is also a colloquial name for the Long-tailed Duck (formerly Oldsquaw). For family characteristics, see DUCK.

PINYON (or Piñon) (Jay). Spanish for "pine nut," the seed of the pinyon pines *(Pinus edulis* and *P. monophylla)*, which, along with juniper and yucca, characterize the arid slopes of the mountains of western North America (pinyon/juniper biome) between desert and forest zones. This is the breeding habitat of the Pinyon Jay, which, like the human inhabitants of the region, is fond of eating *piñones.*

PIPIT. Standard English name for 45 members of the family Motacillidae (order Passeriformes), which also includes the WAGTAILS and the (exclusively African) longclaws, for a family total of 65 species. Sibley and Ahlquist (1990, 1993–SYSTEMATICS) consider this taxon a subfamily (Motacillinae) in a family (Passeridae) that also includes the *Passer* sparrows and snowfinches, the accentorsthe weavers, and the waxbills. Except for the unique Golden Pipit of Africa, all pipits belong to the genus *Anthus.* Three species of pipits breed in North America, 1 occurs annually as a casual migrant in the western Aleutians, and 2 others have been recorded as vagrants in Alaska (see Appendix II).

The pipits are a rather homogeneous group of small (4½–7½ inches), drab, ground-feeding birds with slender, pointed bills of medium length, fairly long legs, and toes with an elongated hind claw in most cases. Pipits are typically tan, brown, or olive above with some degree of streaking on the breast and/or sides. Their tails are usually moderately long with white outer margins—the extent varying among species. Though a few species nest in trees, pipits are the quintessential open-country birds, thriving best in arctic barrens, deserts, and especially fields and paddies. They walk—rather than hop, as do most songbirds when on the ground— "pumping" their tails and stopping periodically to pick up worms, insects, snails, and other small invertebrates as well as weed seeds.

On their breeding grounds, pipits perform aerial song flights. The sound, which issues from as high as 500 feet in the air, may be quite melodious or not—e.g., the strange dry rattle or hiss of our Sprague's Pipit. On migration their presence is often evident from their distinctive flight calls.

Most pipits nest on the ground (sometimes in rock crevices), building cup nests of grasses, fiber, hair, and/or mosses. The 3–7 (usually 4–5) eggs are rather glossy and variable in color and markings, the ground color ranging from pale gray to pinkish, finely—but often very densely—speckled or lined. Many pipit species are highly migratory and the family is therefore distributed worldwide, including many remote oceanic islands. Our native pipits occur in open country (including arctic and alpine barrens) throughout the continent.

The name "pipit" imitates the flight call of the Meadow Pipit of Eurasia, which is very like that of our American Pipit.

PIRACY. Refers to the "stealing" of food from one bird by another, more technically known as kleptoparasitism. The practice has been recorded in many species, including a variety of songbirds. Some raptors and seabirds obtain a significant proportion of their diet by harassing other birds for food they have caught, but all avian pirates are fully capable of catching or finding their own food. Where Bald Eagles and Ospreys occur together the former will often pursue the latter until it drops the fish it has caught. Frigatebirds specialize in chasing boobies and other seabirds over tropical seas and will even strike a bird reluctant to give up its catch. The food item does not have to be visible; pelagic pirates are aware that a pursued bird will disgorge swallowed food to "lighten its load" and make a faster escape. The most skillful maritime pirates habitually catch regurgitated tidbits before they hit the water. Being among the most resourceful feeders, gulls have also mastered piratic techniques. In addition to chasing other birds, they have learned to accompany fishing Brown Pelicans (Laughing Gulls) or flocks of sea ducks (Herring Gulls), hoping to snatch a free meal when these divers resurface. Perhaps the most dedicated and certainly the most agile of the kleptoparasites are the jaegers and skuas

subfamily (Stercorariinae). The slightly built Long-tailed Jaeger is the least inclined to thievery. But the Great Skua has been seen to grab gannets by the wing and pull them into the sea and to try to push birds beneath the surface with its feet to force regurgitation. Parasitic and Pomarine Jaegers must be the chief bane of seagoing terns and gulls, but the sight of these consummate "aerobats" in pursuit of an uncooperative victim is one of the classic thrills of birdwatching.

For other details of avian piracy, including an account of a "four-way snatch," see Meinertzhagen (1959) and in Campbell and Lack (1985– PIRACY).

PISCIVOROUS (piss-SIV-er-us). Describes organisms that feed largely or exclusively on fish. Great Cormorant, Red-breasted Merganser, Osprey, and Belted Kingfisher are all piscivorous birds. See FOOD/FEEDING; SWIMMING/DIVING.

PISHING (or spishing). Onomatopoeia for an oral sound made by bird-watchers in the field in the hope of attracting birds or encouraging them to forsake the cover of vegetation. For an analysis of its effectiveness, see BIRD CALLS.

PLANTING FOR BIRDS. See BIRD FEEDING.

PLASTIC (plasticity). A plastic species is one that is highly variable over its range, i.e., one in which many regional subspecies can be distinguished. The Ruffed Grouse, with 10 subspecies recognized over its Canadian-Transition Zone distribution, is a notably plastic species, whereas the more widely ranging Pied-billed Grebe is thought to contain at most 2 North American races. Other native exemplars of avian plasticity are Canada Goose (11 North American subspecies), Rock Ptarmigan (11), Hairy Woodpecker (12), Horned Lark (20), Marsh Wren (10), Bewick's Wren (13), Winter Wren (12), Fox Sparrow (18), Song Sparrow (30), Dark-eyed Junco (12), Savannah Sparrow (12), Rufous-sided Towhee (13), Brown Towhee (10), Common Yellowthroat (11), Red-winged Blackbird (14), and Scrub Jay (11). Of course, opinion varies among taxonomists about the validity of some races, and the concept of subspecies as a whole has been questioned (See SPECIATION).

PLAY. Many young vertebrate animals are observed to be "playful," a behavior pattern usually associated with "practicing" or preparing for such adult activities as catching and killing of prey and dominance contests. Animal play in young or adults that does not have any clear behavioral context, i.e., play with no apparent "purpose," is sometimes explained as exercise or an innate honing of physical dexterity, both of which can be seen

as serving an individual's survival potential without implying that "lower" animals are capable of anything as intellectually sophisticated as frivolity.

Human beings, of course, have raised playing for fun to an art form, but it is impossible to detect with any certainty whether birds and other animals derive anything like the pleasure we get from recreation for its own sake. Certainly they appear to. Nestling birds are clearly not aware that they are "practicing" for adulthood when they spar energetically with nest mates or jump up and flap their wings as fledgling raptors often do. It is therefore not unreasonable to suppose that such activities yield some kind of gratification. Brown and Amadon (1968–HAWK) point out that hawks and eagles often soar with full crops and without enacting any particular courtship ritual, implying that fun rather than hunting or sexual activity is the motive for such flights. Fulmars accompanying ships habitually engage in aerobatics, using the air currents set up by the moving vessel; a favorite trick is to careen along the rails or waterline and then dart across the bow as closely as possible. Dolphins do this as well (not to mention young humans racing trains to a crossing), and it is difficult to relate this game, which fulmars play over and over again for hours, to any "practical" purpose other than staying with the ship (see FOLLOWING SHIPS)—which they could do with far less effort. Ravens and other members of the crow family perform particularly elaborate flight maneuvers, including barrel rolls and flying upside down and in complex synchronous patterns, and it may not be entirely fanciful to speculate that these and other birds spend their few "off-duty" moments simply enjoying themselves, whether or not the activity is "emotionally analogous" to human joy.

Another phenomenon related to the little-studied subject of avian emotions is ecstasy flights and certain types of atypical SONG.

PLAYBACK. Birders' jargon for taping the song of a bird and then playing it back. Hearing what it assumes is the song of a rival—singing a song that by definition is as good as its own—the duped territorial male typically appears to confront the interloper only to find a flock of birdwatchers with their binoculars and checklists poised. The technique is used most often with hard to see species such as rails and skulking passerines. Used to excess, playback can be a source of disturbance both to the breeding routines of birds and to the tranquility other birders.

PLOVER (rhymes with "lover," not "clover"). Standard English name for about 40 members of the family Charadriidae (order Charadriiformes). Narrowly defined, the plover family contains a total of 66 species, some of which are known as lapwings and dotterels. Sibley and Ahlquist (1990, 1993–SYSTEMATICS) propose a larger Charadriiadae of 88 species comprising the oystercatchers and the stilts and avocets as well as the plovers, which are reduced to a subfamily (Charadriinae). Twelve species of plovers breed in North America, including Eurasian Dotterel and Mongolian

Plover, which breed or have bred in northern and western Alaska; and 4 additional species have been recorded as rare stragglers (see Appendix II).

Plovers are small to rather large (6¼–16 inches), plump, compact shore-birds, with short, stubby bills, legs of moderate length, and somberly col-ored, but usually strikingly patterned, plumage. Many species have prominent breast bands, eye stripes, and wing stripes conspicuous in flight. The bill is typically swollen at the tip, the toes are generally unwebbed (par-tially webbed in some cases), and the hind toe (hallux) is minute or lacking.

Plovers move over mudflats, beaches, and ploughed fields in a char-acteristic run-and-stop motion, picking up small invertebrates and plant matter.

Their nest is a shallow scrape in sand, mud, or dry tundra, sometimes sparsely lined with plant debris. The 2–5 (usually 4) eggs are brownish yellow with distinct dark brown spots of variable density (see Fig. 10).

Most plover species have plaintive whistling cries, among the great wild sounds of the world.

Like the SANDPIPERS, the plovers were heavily shot until well into the present century and shipped to market by the wagonload (see CONSER-VATION). The populations of many species were severely reduced thereby, but with full protection they have recovered.

The plovers are distributed throughout the world from the High Arctic through the tropics to the Antarctic, and occur in all open-country habitats in North America. Some of the longest migration routes are un-dertaken by plover species, the American and Pacific Golden-Plovers, for example, traversing thousands of miles of open ocean from arctic Alaskan breeding grounds to winter quarters on islands of Oceania, Australia, and New Zealand.

"Plover" probably derives from the plaintive call, which for many species might be rendered as some version of "pluu." However, there is also a long-standing folk tradition associated with the Latin root, *pluv-*, referring to rain. Of the various legends figuring plovers as "rain birds," some are purely superstitious but others may contain some substance. Shorebird shooters along our east coast, for example, knew to expect flocks of golden-plovers to put down in coastal fields in the fall when there were onshore storms. And even today plover-starved inland birders know that the best time to check the local sod farm or airport is just after the passage of heavy rain-bearing fronts in the fall.

PLOWSHARE BONE. The pygostyle, a "tailbone" consisting of the fused vertebrae at the end of the backbone. It is named for its shape. See SKELETON and Fig. 27.

PLUMA (pl. plumae). Any feather in which the barbs branch separately from the rachis and are not united to form a vane as in a pennaceous feather (penna). See FEATHER and Fig. 13.

PLUMAGE. The collective term for all of the feathers that cover a bird's body; a technical synonym is "ptilosis." All birds eventually wear such a "feather coat," a characteristic that distinguishes them from all other classes of animal life.

PLUMAGE COMPOSITION. The individual feathers, which together constitute the plumage, vary greatly in both shape and structure. Only major structural variations are described below; many of the italicized specific terms are treated in somewhat greater detail elsewhere under headings of their own, and structural details are discussed at length under FEATHER. See also Fig. 13.

Almost all of the feathers normally visible on a bird, including the relatively large, stiff wing and tail feathers and the smaller, softer feathers that give a bird its smooth outline, are called the *contour feathers*. All of these have a *rachis* and in the great majority the *barbs* are closely "zippered" together to form a unified surface or *vane* on either side of the rachis. However, "plumaceous" contour feathers—with barbs unconnected—are also present in many species.

Beneath the contour feathers there is usually a layer of short, soft, vaneless feathers present in varying degrees and in different locations among different species. These are either *down* feathers or *semiplumes*. Down feathers may be no more than rachisless tufts of barbs, but they intergrade in structure with the slightly more rigid semiplumes, which (though vaneless) in turn intergrade with the softer, more plumaceous type of contour feathers. Down feathers are absent altogether in some species.

Fig. 23. *Plumage variations.* All species of birds exhibit some form of variation in the appearance of their plumage, but these differences are related to a number of phenomena. Populations of certain species exhibit color variations unrelated to sex, age, season, or speciation, a phenomenon known as *polymorphism*. Dark and light "morphs" of Rough-legged Hawks (1) and jaegers and the red and gray morphs of screech-owls are other examples, and a range of intermediate plumages often occurs. The variations presumably confer some selective advantage, such as cryptic concealment in different habitats. Plumage variations that characterize different *races* or *subsepcies* of the Dark-eyed Junco are so distinctive that the Oregon and white-winged forms (2) were once classified as separate species. Sexual *dimorphism* is the rule among ducks such as Hooded Mergansers (3); the male's striking plumage aids his nuptial display, while the femal's drab coloration helps conceal her while she is a "sitting duck" on the nest. Birds of tundra and snowfield, ptarmigan (4) undergo three molts each year. In winter both sexes are pure white or nearly so; in spring the male assumes a patchy breeding plumage that both is showy and mimics the thawing landscape while the hen becomes brown with a camouflage pattern of browns that match the ground where she nests; in late summer both sexes don another cryptic plumage. All ages and both sexes of Black Guillemots (5) are largely white in basic (winter) plumage and all acquire a mainly black alternate (breeding) plumage. Black-crowned Night-Heron plumage (6) is identical in adults, but juvenile birds are streaked and speckled in brown and white; juvenal and 1st basic (1st summer) plumages are distinctive in most birds, typically drabber than those of the adults.

See also COLOR AND PATTERN; DISPLAY; MOLT; PLUMAGE; POLYMORPHISM; and Figs. 15 and 20.

In addition to the contour feathers and the undercoat of down and semiplumes, there are *filoplumes,* long, narrow feathers, usually with a few barbs at the tip. These always grow with a contour feather and may be distributed over most of a bird's body, but are difficult to see, unless you know what to look for and have really good optics (or the bird in hand). In some freshly molted passerines, filoplumes are visible above the feathers of the nape.

Hardly recognizable as feathers are the *vibrissae,* stiff, hair-like feathers that appear as "eyelashes" in a few species of birds (e.g., Northern Harrier) but more often as *rictal* (or *nasal*) bristles around the top of the gape and over the nostrils, as in most flycatchers and nightjars (see Fig.13).

Finally, there are the strongly modified feathers known as *powder down.* These are evenly distributed under the contour feathers of most birds but in a few species they occur in concentrated patches; they give off a fine dust made up of minute scale-like particles of keratin, the purpose of which is imperfectly understood.

Contour feathers + down + semiplumes + filoplumes + vibrissae + powder down = plumage. (*Natal down,* as differentiated from the adult down referred to above, is described under DOWN.)

ARRANGEMENT OF FEATHERS. On casual inspection, a bird's body feathers seem to be evenly distributed, much in the way hair covers the human head. The reality, however, more resembles the head of the balding man who combs hair rooted in one place over a bare patch, for the body feathers (and attendant filoplumes) of all but a few species of birds (e.g., Ostrich, penguins; none North American) are rooted in discrete regions of the skin called *feather tracts* or *pterylae,* between which are open patches called *apteria.* The pattern made by the tracts, which varies consistently among different groups of birds and governs how the feathers are distributed, is called *pterylosis.* Typically, major tracts cover most of the head, throat, and neck; run down the center of the back in varying widths from neck to tail; surround the breast and belly; and cover the leading margins of the wings above and below and parts of the upper leg. The location and extent of the tracts obviously determine the location, extent, and number of the apteria. As noted, the overall pattern is highly variable among different types of birds; more information on comparative pterylosis, along with a more formal description of the feather tracts and apteria, will be found under FEATHER TRACTS.

Down feathers may occur within both the feather tracts *and* the apteria, i.e., more or less evenly over the body; *or* be restricted to the apteria; *or* be absent altogether. Semiplumes may also be present in the apteria and/or along the edges of the feather tracts. Put another way, the apteria may be bare or covered thinly or thickly with down and semiplumes.

Normally, of course, the contour feathers lie over the apteria, so that, unlike most bald human pates, a bird's bare patches are effectively con-

cealed. For the arrangement of the contour feathers of WING and TAIL, see under those entries.

NUMBER OF CONTOUR FEATHERS. There are relatively few data on feather numbers (due in part, no doubt, to the tedious nature of the research), but a few basic tendencies have been established. As one would expect, small birds have fewer feathers than very large birds. The fewest contour feathers yet recorded is 940 for the Ruby-throated Hummingbird (Wetmore 1936); the highest, 25,216 for the Tundra Swan (Ammann 1937). The numbers for passerines studied to date range between about 1,000 and almost 5,000, but, excluding a few extremes, the normal range seems to be between 1,500 and 3,000.

Feathers are not distributed in equal numbers over a bird's body. The abundantly feathered swan cited above had 80% of its feathers concentrated on its head and very long neck. Small birds tend to have more feathers per square inch and in proportion to their body weight than large birds (Hutt and Ball 1938). This is consistent with the fact that smaller birds lose heat more rapidly and require more insulation. At least some species that must endure cold winters have up to 112% more feathers during that season (Staebler 1941).

PLUMAGE VARIATIONS. Most of a bird's color and pattern and much of its form and "personality" are realized in its plumage, but plumage characteristics are not static. They vary enormously from species to species in accordance with specialized lifestyles; moreover, the plumage of individual birds can vary by sex, age, season, feeding habits, and a wide range of abnormalities. The pattern of normal change is "programmed" genetically in a given species, but the change itself is often triggered by hormonal activity (see MOLT and Figs. 20 and 23).

Functional Variation. Many details of a bird's plumage reflect its manner of living:

- Most waterbirds have comparatively dense feathering with thick undercoats of down for added insulation.
- The flight feathers of migratory populations are often longer than those of sedentary populations of the same species—a variation that can extend to migratory vs. sedentary *age classes* (e.g., Red-tailed Hawk).
- Ptarmigan, which spend much of their life foraging in snow, have heavily feathered legs and feet (see Fig. 17).
- The cryptic plumage of nightjars, which nest and roost on the ground, has evolved to camouflage them from potential predators.
- The stiff, spiny-tipped tails of woodpeckers and swifts have adapted to support the bodies of their owners as they cling to a vertical surface (see Fig. 30).
- The tails of many fly-catching species are unusually long and seem to aid aerial agility (see Fig. 30).

- Many other plumage characteristics aid recognition and sexual display. These may be patches of bright color (e.g., the iridescent plumage of many hummingbirds) or accouterments such as the distinctive central rectrices of adult jaegers or the peculiar facial plumes of many alcids.
- Plumage "flashes" or "banner marks," such as the flicker's white rump or the wing patches of a White-winged Dove, may serve to distract potential predators momentarily and divert their "aim" to less vulnerable parts of the body.
- Wing or tail feathers (e.g., of the American Woodcock and Common Snipe) may be so shaped as to produce a sound used in courtship or territorial display.

Sexual Differences. Male and female birds of the same species may have strikingly different plumages. The difference may be permanent in adults (e.g., Northern Cardinal) or become accentuated during the breeding season (e.g., American Goldfinch). The plumages of many shorebirds, raptors, swifts, and other birds do not differ sexually; however, in those species that do show a difference, it is almost invariably the female that exhibits the duller plumage, perhaps to make her less conspicuous while nesting. In North America, the only exceptions to this "rule" are the phalaropes, in which the males are the less vividly colored and patterned and also incubate the eggs and perform other tasks usually relegated to female birds; the Spotted Sandpiper, in which females are more heavily and distinctly spotted than males (and which also practices the phalaropean reversal of gender roles; and the Belted Kingfisher, in which the female has a rusty chest band that the male lacks. See also DIMORPHISM.

Seasonal Differences. The acquisition of an alternate (breeding) plumage (see MOLT) is most striking in males (with above-noted exceptions) but may also occur in females. It may be only a minor change, e.g., the "cleaner" look of American Robins due to feather wear (see ABRASION), or a spectacular total transformation, e.g., the Common Loon or Scarlet Tanager. In sexually dimorphic species, the male often assumes a duller plumage resembling the female's in the pre-basic (post-nuptial) molt, e.g., Indigo Bunting. Seasonal plumages may also be adaptations to habitat, e.g., the white plumages of the ptarmigan, which become browner in the warmer months when their habitat is less likely to be snow-covered.

Age Differences. All birds go through some degree of plumage change as they mature (see MOLT). In species that hatch with a full, often strikingly patterned covering of natal down, the first plumage change is a total metamorphosis into a full coat of contour feathers. This juvenal plumage may resemble that of one or both of the parents (e.g., Blue Jay); or resemble that of neither parent—whether the adults are sexually dimorphic (e.g., frigatebirds) or not (Purple Gallinule). With the first pre-basic (post-juvenal) molt some species attain a "definitive" plumage, i.e., one indistinguishable from that of an adult of their species. But in many species the

first basic (first winter) plumage is distinct from both the juvenal and the definitive adult plumages. In some sexually dimorphic species (e.g., Rose-breasted Grosbeak), the tendency to revert to a duller plumage after breeding diminishes with age; i.e., the older a male becomes, the less of his bright coloration he loses in the post-nuptial molt. Behavioral ecologists have debated the possible adaptive value of this "delayed plumage maturation," speculating, for example, that it might serve as a "warning" to females of the wearer's inexperience or preserve younger males from predation in their first nesting season as they acquire experience. For the full range of hypotheses, see Rohwer et al. (1980, 1988), Procter-Gray and Holmes (1981), Lyon and Montgomerie (1986), Enstrom (1992a, b), and Woods (1999).

Streaking and spotting, typical of many juvenal plumages, tends to disappear or diminish with age, regardless of sex (e.g., Cedar Waxwing, Fig. 33). In a very few instances, juvenile birds have *brighter* plumage than adults of either sex. This occurs, for example, in young Downy and Hairy Woodpeckers, which have more extensive red areas on the crown than either parent until their first pre-basic (post-juvenal) molt.

Racial Differences and Morphs. Geographical races of species tend to differ consistently in certain adaptive plumage characteristics. Western races of the Fox Sparrow, for example, are dark brown and generally unstreaked above, in striking contrast to their bright rufous and boldly streaked eastern counterparts (see SPECIATION; GLOGER'S RULE; ALLEN'S RULE; KELSO'S RULE). Permanent plumage differences may also occur among individuals of the same population of a single race, e.g., the dark, light, and intermediate morphs in the jaegers and some raptors, the gray/red variations of the Screech Owl, and the "ringed" and "plain" forms of the Common Murre. See MORPH; POLYMORPHISM.

Externally Caused Differences. Diet is responsible for some plumage coloration, e.g., the bright salmon pink of the American Flamingo. When the plants or animals containing these pigments are not consumed regularly, the color fades. Such color loss occurs infrequently in the wild but is fairly common among captive birds.

"Blooms," such as the pink suffusions that appear on the breasts of Roseate Terns and Franklin's Gulls in the breeding season, may be produced by a special secretion of the oil gland and applied, like makeup, to the breast. The substance fades in the sun and air and the source presumably "dries up" during the nonbreeding season. The source of warm "peachy" breast color the Common Merganser in breeding condition is apparently something of a mystery; it has been seen to fade quickly after death.

Examples of plumage variations that are purely adventitious are the "rusting" of the white head and neck of Snow Geese acquired by feeding in water or mud stained with iron ore and the earth tones acquired by woodpeckers from their roost holes and nest cavities. See also COLOR AND PATTERN.

Abnormal Variation. The plumage of hybrids often combines the characteristics of both parents or even produces "original," perhaps atavistic, colors and patterns (see HYBRIDIZATION).

A disruption in the endocrine system caused by injury or disease can produce "cock-plumaged" females (see SEX, CHANGE OF) and, more rarely, "hen-plumaged" males. Another kind of sexual ambiguity, gynandromorphism, produces individuals with typical male plumage on one side of the body and typical female plumage on the other.

Genetic aberrations can produce hairy-looking plumage due to an absence of barbicels in the contour feathers (accompanies some cases of albinism); weak wing and tail feathers, which break off at the base when the affected bird tries to fly; and wing and tail feathers in which the rachis extends beyond the vane tip, giving an effect similar to the (normal) tail of a Chimney Swift.

For other color abnormalities, see ALBINISM; MELANISM; LEUCISM; SCHIZOCHROISM; ERYTHRISM; XANTHOCHROISM.

CARE OF PLUMAGE. A bird's feathers become dirty, are eaten by feather mites and other pests (see ECTOPARASITE), and lose oils essential for insulation and waterproofing. To stay healthy, therefore, birds must constantly maintain their plumage by a combination of preventative and corrective measures, such as PREENING; ANTING; BATHING; DUSTING; SUNNING; SCRATCHING.

USE. If we ask what benefits a bird derives from its feathers, the first answer likely to occur to us is: the ability to fly. Aerodynamically, plumage is the ideal body covering: it is light; it can be streamlined by compressing the body feathers to minimize drag; and the wing and tail feathers are flexible enough to allow high maneuverability yet stiff enough to use wind power for lift and motion (see FLIGHT).

Control of body temperature, especially heat, may be an even more important function of plumage. The semiplume and down "underwear" provides insulation next to the skin, and the overlapping contour feathers can be "fluffed" to trap a maximum of warm air and "closed" to insulate swimming birds from cold water (see TEMPERATURE, BODY). Embryonic temperature and that of naked nestlings are also maintained by the natural insulation of parental plumage in addition to the "direct heat" applied through the brood patch. "Slippery" semiplumes and down may also serve as an "anti-friction" mechanism around the bases of wings and legs.

Plumage colors and patterns play essential roles in recognition, display, and protection against predators (see COLOR AND PATTERN, Concealment; and DISPLAY).

Female ducks, geese, and swans line their nests with down feathers plucked from their breasts, and some songbirds use "found" feathers both for lining and for decoration.

Feathers also serve as a binding material in the pellets regurgitated by bird-eating raptors, and grebes eat their own feathers to serve a similar digestive function.

PLUME HUNTERS. Men who shot birds, especially certain species of herons, in order to sell their nuptial plumes to milliners and other purveyors of feather fashions. A thriving occupation well into the twentieth century before it was outlawed. See CONSERVATION for a more detailed account.

PLUM ISLAND (Massachusetts). See NEWBURYPORT.

PLUMULE (or plumula; pl.: plumulae). An individual down feather. See FEATHER; DOWN; and Fig. 13.

PNEUMATIZATION (NOO-muh-tih-ZAY-shun) **OF BONE.** The remarkable process by which the bones of birds are hollowed and filled with air sacs connected to the respiratory system. See SKELETON.

POCHARD (POACH-erd or POTCH-erd or POKE-erd or POCK-erd). A generic name for the bay ducks (in North America synonymous with the genus *Aythya*). The Common Pochard of Eurasia, which looks like a hybrid between our Canvasback and Redhead (pochards both), is recorded annually as a casual visitor to Alaska. According to Lockwood (1993–NAMES), the name comes from an East Anglian duck hunter's characterization of the Common Pochard's habit of "poking" at the water as it feeds. He further notes that the American Wigeon has also been called "poker" colloquially for this habit. The problem with this analysis is that bay ducks are diving ducks, which seldom "poke," unlike the dabbling ducks (such as wigeon), which do this habitually. A more interesting theory is that the name originated with the French "pocharde," meaning drunkard and referring to the red "faces" of both the Common Pochard and the Eurasian Wigeon—from which the American Wigeon picked up the name.

PODOTHECA (POD-uh-THEE-kuh). The leathery or horny "hide" that covers unfeathered parts of a bird's leg and foot; on close inspection it is seen to be textured in arrangements of plates or scales, which vary among different groups of birds. See LEG/FOOT.

POIKILOTHERMAL (POY-kill-oh-THUR-mul) (also poikilothermic or poikilothermous). "Cold-blooded"; i.e., with body temperature fluctuating with that of the environment rather than being under physiological control. All animals except mammals, birds, certain reptiles (e.g., croco-

diles), and some large fish (e.g., tuna) are "poikilotherms," and the young of bird species that are born naked are, in fact, "cold-blooded" until at least partially fledged. Opposite of HOMOIOTHERMAL. See TEMPERATURE, BODY.

POINT PELEE National Park (Ontario). A tiny (6 square miles) peninsula jutting south into Lake Erie, 35 miles east of Windsor, Ontario/Detroit, Michigan; famed for the spectacular concentrations of migrant birds during both the spring and the fall passage. The park also encompasses substantial samples of deciduous woodland, marsh, and, of course, shore and open water, so that on a good day during a migratory wave, seeing over a hundred species of birds at Point Pelee is practically routine. Migration peaks are mid-May and mid-September (see Appendix VI for extended period). For more detail, see Tom Hince's *A Birder's Guide to Point Pelee* in the ABA/Lane series (1999) or go to the Friends of Point Pelee website at http://www.wincom.net/~fopp/.

POINT REYES. See OBSERVATORY.

POISON. For lead poisoning, pesticides, etc., see THREATS (OF HUMAN ORIGIN) TO BIRDLIFE; for "food poisoning," e.g., salmonellosis and botulism, see DISEASE.

POLE TRAP. A steel spring-jaw trap fixed to the top of a pole and set where birds of prey are likely to perch. This was once a very popular method of killing "chicken hawks" and other species deemed (usually mistakenly) to be a threat to poultry or livestock. The use of pole traps is now illegal, and all North American raptors are protected by Federal law. See LAWS PROTECTING BIRDLIFE.

POLITICS, BIRDS IN. At least one famous North American instance. During the investigation by the House Committee on Un-American Activities of former State Department official Alger Hiss in 1948 as an alleged Communist subversive, it was crucial to establish the veracity of the testimony of Whittaker Chambers, himself a former Communist of questionable character. Chambers claimed intimate association with Hiss and, among many other corroborating details, noted that Hiss was an enthusiastic birdwatcher and had once been excited at having seen a Prothonotary Warbler along the Potomac River. By feigning casual good-fellowship in subsequent interrogation, Richard Nixon and U.S. Representative John McDowell (R.-Pa.), also a birdwatcher, elicited from Hiss a confirmation of his encounter with the species and excitement over it. "Beautiful yellow head," Alger Hiss exclaimed, "a gorgeous bird." He was ultimately convicted on two counts of perjury and sentenced to ten years in jail.

POLLEX. The first digit, or "thumb," of a bird's hand. See SKELETON, Bones of the Wing, and Fig. 27.

POLLINATION. Pollination by birds is most prevalent in tropical regions, where a relatively wide range of bird species sip nectar and take insects from the many flowers with deep corollas. In North America, hummingbirds are by far the most effective avian pollinators, though other insectivorous/nectivorous species, e.g., warblers and orioles, doubtless make some contribution to plant reproduction here. While it may be said that the combined effect of all bird pollinators is relatively insignificant compared to the role played by bats, insects, and the wind, the phenomenon is nonetheless crucial to those species of plants that depend on avian pollinators.

In the southwestern United States, where hummingbirds are nearly ubiquitous, it is not unusual to see hummers with yellow faces. Visiting birdwatchers unable to find a yellow-headed species in their field guides may be told by locals that they have been seeing "pollinated hummingbirds."

POLYANDRY (PAH-lee-AN-dree). The mating of a female with more than one male during a single breeding season. See MATING SYSTEMS.

POLYGAMY (puh-LIG-uh-mee). A member of one sex mating with two or more members of the opposite sex; encompasses polyandry, polygyny, and polygynandry. See MATING SYSTEMS.

POLYGYNANDRY (puh-LIDGE-uh-NAN-dree). A rare mating system in which both males and females have several mates, e.g., Ostriches. See MATING SYSTEMS.

POLYGYNY (puh-LIDGE-uh-nee). The mating of a male with more than one female during a single breeding season. See MATING SYSTEMS.

POLYMORPHISM. The occurrence of two or more stable forms—often called "morphs" or (in older literature) "phases"—existing *within a single population of a species.* The most familiar form of polymorphism in birds appears in plumage variation, e.g., the white and "blue" morphs of the Snow Goose. The fact that variation is constant in a polymorphic species does not mean that the different morphs always occur in equal numbers or equal proportions throughout the geographical range of the species; rather, the opposite tends to be the case. The "purpose" of polymorphism seems to be to allow a species to "choose" by natural selection the morph that carries the advantage in a particular habitat or climate. Thus, gray phases of the Ruffed Grouse apparently survive better in coniferous forest, because they are less conspicuous to predators in that habitat,

whereas the red morphs survive better in deciduous forest for the same reason (Gullion and Marshall 1968). Gray Eastern Screech-Owls seem to have greater tolerances for cold than red ones and therefore predominate in harsher climates (Mosher and Henny 1976). In other species, e.g., the White-throated Sparrow, survivability seems to have little to do with the perpetuation of polymorphism.

Polymorphism is more prevalent in some groups of birds than in others, notably in petrels, herons, geese, buteos, falcons, owls, and jaegers (see MORPH for a more detailed list of species). It may be lifelong (e.g., Rough-legged Hawk; see Fig.23) or predominate in a particular age group (dark immature Long-tailed Jaegers, white Mute Swan cygnets). Or it can arise from diet as in the orange-tailed morph of the Cedar Waxwing. In many cases (e.g., Northern Fulmar) there is a spectrum of variation between the darkest and lightest individuals.

The term may also be used to describe the same kind of regularly occurring differences in size, egg coloration or pattern, or even functions, such as clutch size. When only two distinct morphs occur—as with the bridled and plain Common Murres—it is not incorrect to refer to the species in question as "dimorphic." However, that term is widely used to describe sexual, racial, seasonal, and age differences that do *not* exemplify true polymorphism. Even cases in which "many morphs" occur within the same species are not always polymorphic in the strict genetic sense, e.g., the zone of secondary hybridization where "red-shafted" and "yellow-shafted" races of the Common Flicker meet and produce an assortment of hybrids; or the large number of distinct racial variations of the Song Sparrow continentwide; or aberrant populations of a particular species that perpetuate some form of mutation such as albinism in many variations. None of these are genetically permanent variations within a single population.

See Fig. 23.

POLYTYPIC (PAHL-ee-TIPP-ik). A taxonomic category that contains two or more representatives of the category immediately below it. A polytypic family contains two or more genera; a polytypic genus contains more than one species; etc. Compare MONOTYPIC.

POMARINE (POH-muh-reen) (formerly Pomatorhine) (Jaeger). Literally, "flap-nosed," referring to the cere-like "saddle" unique to the bills of all skuas and jaegers and not peculiar to the one species. The flap overlaps the ridge of the upper mandible from the base to just beyond the end of the nostrils, which it overlaps. See NOSTRILS.

POOR-WILL. Standard English name for a species of nightjar, *Phalaenoptilus nuttallii,* which breeds from southwestern Canada to central Mexico. The name is a literal approximation of its call. Two other nightjar species (genus *Otophanes*) of Mexico and northern Central America have

"poor-will" in their names, but "poor-will" is not a good "translation" of the call of either. See NIGHTJAR.

Phalaenoptilus is the only bird in the world known to "hibernate," reducing its body temperature to c. 40°F for 2–3 months; see TORPIDITY.

POPULATION. The total number of individuals in a given area. The term can be used to describe all of the individuals that occupy a particular plot of habitat at a particular time, e.g., the breeding-bird population of a specific pine/oak woodland; or to refer to all the living members of a species, e.g., the world population of Brown Creepers. The study of *population dynamics* asks how, why, and to what degree populations change, and what factors are involved in limiting such changes and maintaining a balance among populations of different organisms.

Answering these questions requires first of all that we accurately count and recount the number of birds in a population over an extended period of time—a tedious chore that has yet to be facilitated by any sophisticated labor-saving device. Once the statistics are gathered, the student of populations must evaluate the myriad variables—food availability, predation, disease, weather, habitat destruction, etc.—that may affect the stability of the community of birds in question.

Because of these difficulties, irrefutable conclusions about specific problems in population dynamics are still rare in the literature. However, a few facts have been established, theories abound, and many intriguing examples of population changes have been recorded.

- A stable population implies a birth rate in balance with the death rate.
- Birds tend to have as many young as prevailing conditions, such as the length of season, will allow and do not significantly control their population by manipulating their own birth rates. Birds do, however, seem capable of manipulating the sex ratio of their offspring under certain conditions, see Komdeur et al. (1997).
- Birds sustain an enormous death rate, particularly as juveniles. The yearly death rate of *adult* passerines is between 40 and 60% or more, but the percentage of *eggs* that reach full adulthood averages is only about 12%, on the basis of available information (see also AGE).
- Food availability seems to exercise great influence on population stability. Birds are known to (1) time breeding to coincide with maximum food availability; (2) stagger egg laying (many raptors and large waterbirds), so that the younger birds are "automatically sacrificed" when food is scarce; (3) suffer greater mortalities in years or seasons of food shortage due to droughts or other environmental factors; (4) leave areas where food is scarce in proportion to populations (e.g., northern raptors, finches, waxwings); and (5) become more aggressive when feeding in flocks in times of food scarcity.

- Though predation and disease may also be important influences on populations, solid documentation of their effects is difficult to collect and is therefore very thin so far.

A confirmative example for disease is the recent outbreak of conjunctivitis the House Finch, which resulted in a well-documented population decline (Hartup and Bickal 2001–DISEASE).

- Most population changes seem to be "unpredictable," but a few (e.g., Ruffed Grouse) have been thoroughly studied and proven to occur in regular cycles.

Introduced species are good material for population studies. After the European Starling became successfully established in North America, it went through a period of alarming increase, but its population now seems to have peaked and Christmas Bird Count data indicate an actual decline over the last few decades. This pattern is common among introduced animals and implies that that initially alien organisms can "run wild" in an ecosystem in which they are not "naturally" controlled but that such controls eventually evolve. Introduced species can also be expected to influence populations of native species with which they compete for food and nesting sites (see INTRODUCED BIRDS).

To form a notion of the difficulties inherent in studying bird populations, try to determine exactly how many individuals of a given species visit your feeder regularly. Many people suppose that they are host to a single flock of a dozen chickadees when, in fact, they are helping to support several times that many, visiting in alternating shifts. This is virtually impossible to notice unless the birds are artificially marked or individual plumage characters can be discerned. See DISTRIBUTION; TERRITORY; COLONY; ABUNDANCE; AGE; CENSUS. See also the relationship of populations to SPECIATION.

Many interesting studies have been done in this field; see the Bibliography.

PORTLANDICA. In the broadest sense refers to a distinctive subadult plumage of any tern in the genus *Sterna*. The term's usual context, however, is the problem of recognizing Common and Arctic Terns encountered in this plumage and distinguishing between the two.

Portlandica terns are immature birds (1–2 years old), most of which remain in the Southern Hemisphere wintering area of their species until they are old enough to breed. Exceptional individuals occasionally return prematurely to their natal areas with adult birds, where they often confuse Northern Hemisphere birdwatchers unfamiliar with the plumage.

Historically, portlandica-plumaged birds have occurred rarely in the Northern Hemisphere, the name deriving from *Sterna portlandica*, the binomial coined by British ornithologists who mistook an individual of this kind for a new species. But in recent decades, there have been occasional,

inexplicable occurrences of large numbers of such birds. Numerous notes on portlandica have been published in *British Birds* since 1969.

POULT (pollt). A young domestic fowl, especially a turkey.

POULTRY. Domestic fowl, especially chickens, turkeys, guinea fowl, pheasants, and, in the very broadest usage, ducks and geese.

POWDER DOWN. A modified type of body feather that disintegrates at the tip into a fine dust made up of scale-like particles. These feathers occur in most birds and may be dispersed evenly among the body feathers, but in a few groups (e.g., herons) they occur in well-developed patches. The powder gives a bloom to the plumage and may play a role in cleaning and/or waterproofing the feathers.

PRAIRIE. A broadly inclusive term of French origin used in North America to describe treeless, often "rolling," grassy plains such as once covered much of the continent from the Mississippi Valley to the Rocky Mountains and from the boreal forests of Canada to the deserts of Texas. In addition to grasses, prairies nurture many other characteristic plant species, often including many legumes. More restricted botanical communities are recognized under such names as "tallgrass" prairie. Sadly, these unique plant and animal communities have today largely been replaced by farmland and suburban sprawl and exist in a pristine condition only in a few preserved patches (see *National Geographic,* Vol. 157, No. 1, January 1980, for a map of remnant spots of tallgrass prairie and a glimpse of its former glory).

In central Eurasia, land with the above characteristics is usually called "steppe."

Typical North American "prairie birds" (excluding many waterbirds typical of prairie marshes) are Swainson's Hawk, Greater and Lesser Prairie-Chickens, Sandhill Crane, Mountain Plover, Marbled Godwit, Franklin's Gull, Burrowing Owl, Sprague's Pipit, meadowlarks, Lark Bunting, and McCown's and Chestnut-collared Longspurs.

Prairie Warblers are birds of second-growth and other shrublands and therefore are found in true prairies even less frequently than Connecticut Warblers are found in Connecticut.

PRAIRIE-CHICKEN. Standard English name for 2 species of grouse in the genus *Tyrnpanuchus* (family Tetraonidae; order Galliformes), both of which are endemic to North America. The prairie-chickens (Greater and Lesser) are famed for the elaborate courtship "dances" performed by males in spring (see DISPLAY; LEK.). The dance is accompanied by an indescribably haunting sound and the inflation of colorful air sacs in the neck.

The prairie-chickens have declined as a result of the development of their habitat—which is correctly identified in their name. The eastern race of the Greater Prairie-Chicken, known as the Heath Hen, became extinct in 1932 and another race is currently on the brink (see ENDANGERED BIRDS).

For general family characteristics, see GROUSE.

PRECOCIAL (pree-KO-shul). Describes young birds that are relatively well-developed at hatching. Typically, precocial young have a thick coat of natal down (ptilopaedic), leave the nest soon after hatching (nidifugous), and feed themselves at an early stage. Contrast with ALTRICIAL. See YOUNG, DEVELOPMENT OF.

PREDATION (predator, predacious). The killing and eating of one animal by another (excluding parasites). The word "predator" is often used to refer to hawks, eagles, and falcons, owls, and shrikes, i.e., birds that habitually take warm-blooded prey; but it is no less accurate to refer to herons as predacious on fish or flycatchers as predatory on insects.

Though it is one of the most pervasive, ineluctable facts of life on this planet, predation has strong negative connotations for many people. It suggests a common perception of the world ecosystem as a realm of chaotic cruelty—"nature red in tooth and claw"—where certain "vicious" animals (e.g., wolves, bears, big cats, raptorial birds) prey "mercilessly" on a majority of "gentle creatures" (e.g., mice, antelopes, chickadees). This view reflects a tendency among people with little knowledge of animal life or ecology to project human emotions and motives onto other species. This anthropomorphism is highly selective. The little songbirds whose "murder" by hawks some find deplorable are themselves predatory, the difference being that we have a hard time feeling sorry for the invertebrate prey of titmice and warblers. The falcon that attacks the "gentle" heron is a brute beast, but the heron is welcome to stab all the cold, slimy (i.e., in-human) fish and frogs it likes without being damned as a predator. Of course, we humans are the ultimate predators, the only species that deliberately rears other animals for the express purpose of killing and eating them and the only one to kill for fun. Neither these practices nor the kills of wild predators need be condemned, but rather viewed in their proper context as a balancing element in a biological system that generates an unimaginable mass of matter through continual growth—matter that must be consumed as fast as it is produced if the ecosystem is to remain in equilibrium and a healthy diversity of organisms is to survive.

Specific effects of predation—both good and bad—are often exaggerated. For example, Golden Eagles have been persecuted on the ground that they are a serious threat to livestock, especially sheep, whereas, in fact, these eagles feed mainly on rabbits. Equally erroneous is the notion that predation by Purple Martins can be an effective means of mosquito control.

On the other hand, H. Hartley (in Campbell and Lack 1985–ORNITHOLOGY) notes the existence of a mathematical model showing that predation of sick individuals in a disease-ridden population can actually result in an increase in the predated population. He also notes the role of predation in the evolution of cryptic coloration and adaptive behaviors in prey species.

The relatively few data that exist seem to indicate that the impact of insectivorous birds feeding on outbreaks of pest insects or of hawks and owls on "explosions" of rodents is normally quite small, though greater, of course, in proportion to the concentration of predators. In years when northern raptors, e.g., Snowy and Short-eared Owls and Rough-legged Hawks, are particularly abundant on their wintering grounds, rodent populations there presumably suffer a greater mortality rate from predation.

For types of prey, see FOOD/FEEDING; for predatory in the sense of one species stealing food from another, see PIRACY.

PREEN GLAND. See OIL GLAND; PREENING.

PREENING. The cleaning, manipulation, and arrangement of individual feathers of a bird's plumage using the bill; in the broadest sense, it includes the application of oil from the "preen gland" (see OIL GLAND).

In the course of normal activities, a bird's plumage becomes dirty, wet, matted with old preen oil, and infested with parasites, and the barbs of individual feathers become separated. All are potentially hazardous to the health and well-being of a bird (see PLUMAGE, Uses), and preening is the innate activity—performed regularly and frequently—by which these conditions are rectified.

The basic preening action involves grasping an individual feather at its base and "nibbling" along its length to the tip or simply drawing the bill along the feather in a single, less meticulous action. This reattaches separated barbs, removes water and dirt, and in some instances applies oil. During preening, birds often come upon ectoparasites, which they usually seize and eat. The process involves all parts of the plumage and requires birds to assume an amusing variety of contorted postures (see, for example, the European Starling in Fig. 24 and the Hermit Thrush in Fig. 19). Swimming birds that preen while sitting on the surface execute what is known as a "rolling preen," in which they turn over on their side while floating with one leg in the air and preen their belly with their bill, apparently in perfect comfort.

The one area of the body which birds cannot reach with their own bill is the head. This is "preened" by SCRATCHING, by rubbing with the wing, or with the assistance of another bird (see ALLOPREENING).

Birds often engage in prolonged preening sessions during which—barring disturbance—the whole plumage is tended to, virtually feather by feather. A complete preening operation of this kind often follows other plumage-maintenance activities, such as BATHING, DUSTING, or ANTING,

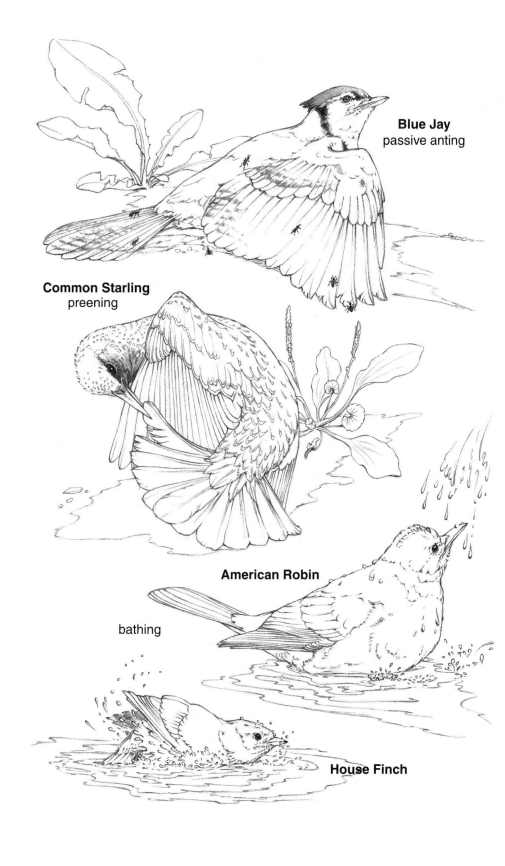

Blue Jay
passive anting

Common Starling
preening

American Robin

bathing

House Finch

and the body feathers are typically "fluffed" for easy access. Birds also may be seen to make preening gestures at any time while in the midst of some other activity, e.g., feeding or simply out of nervousness (see REDIRECTION).

PRIBILOF ISLANDS (Alaska). See ALASKA

PRIMARIES. The flight feathers (remiges), which are attached to the bones of the "hand" (manus). All flying birds have between 9 and 12 primaries and the number tends to be the same within groupings of closely related birds. The primaries are numbered from the innermost to the outermost. Perching (passerine) birds have 10 primaries but in some songbird (oscine) families the 10th (outermost) is greatly reduced, in which case it is known as the remicle. These families, including swallows, pipits, wood warblers, icterids, tanagers, and fringillid finches, and parts of other families are sometimes called 9-primaried songbirds. See WING and Figs. 1, 20, and 35.

PROBLEMS INVOLVING BIRDS. This entry attempts to summarize the main instances in which birdlife causes problems for people, whether as serious threats, e.g., to health or agriculture, or as minor annoyances. Solutions to the problems are noted briefly when known.

It should be emphasized at the outset that on balance birds are far more beneficial to human endeavor than they are detrimental. Birds' greatest crime against humanity, the eating of grain and fruit crops, for example, is easily outweighed by the service birds perform in controlling numbers of insects and other nonavian pests that menace agriculture. Furthermore, studies of the feeding habits of birds reveal that it is not possible to distinguish "good" birds from "bad" birds on the basis of their relationship with people, since birds tend to combine traits that serve our interests with those that are competitive with our purposes. Generally beloved American Robins, for example, often plague blueberry and other fruit crops, while the largely noxious European Starling eats a great many Japanese beetle grubs. Most "bird problems" in North America are local and temporary in nature, though they may recur in succeeding years. Therefore, stopgap solutions usually suffice.

Though birds may be annoying on occasion, it is worth remembering that (1) they have no *intention* to cause problems, but are simply following instinctive behavior patterns that happen to run afoul of our best laid plans, and (2) with a few exceptions they are protected to a great extent by both state and federal law (see LAWS). Whether out of intelligent understanding or enlightened self-interest, then, it is wise to seek humane solutions to problems involving birds (see LAWS PROTECTING BIRDLIFE).

Fig. 24. *Plumage maintenance.* It is essential for a bird's well being that it keep its feathers clean and free of parasites.

Agricultural Pests. Eighty percent of North American crop damage by birds is attributable to songbirds, especially blackbirds, starlings, and crows. By comparison, damage done by seed-eating ducks, geese, doves, and cranes is of little significance (unless, of course, it is *your* crop that has been attacked). Those who have never seen the hordes of Red-winged Blackbirds, grackles, cowbirds, and starlings that winter in the southeastern states (200 million in the Gulf states alone) should not underestimate the impact of these birds on rice crops and feedlot grains. In other regions, vineyard and orchard owners can suffer serious economic consequences as a result of migrating or dispersing robins, starlings, and other fruit-eaters. *Solution:* There are no universal solutions. The ages-old answer to avian crop pests has been to scare them away—with scarecrows, strips of tinfoil that move, gleam, and rustle in the wind, and automatic "guns" that go off at irregular intervals. The fact that large farms and vineyards sometimes employ airplanes to chase off bird flocks is a measure of the cost of the potential damage. The problem with any "unmanned" scarecrow device is that birds learn with surprising rapidity that they are not in any danger no matter how loud, bright, menacing, or irregular the effect. Recordings of the problem species' own alarm or distress calls have been shown to have a longer "scare life," but even these are eventually perceived as innocuous. Periodic chasing to maintain a continuing sense of danger in the birds is still essential in dealing with this problem. Practically speaking, all such cases require their own unique solutions, in many instances involving a combination of techniques. An intelligent citizen confronted with a potential problem should begin by considering the possibility of "exclusion" of pest birds (obviating the necessity for further action), move on, if necessary to harassment (as described above), and resort to attempts at "radical removal" only in the most extreme instances and in strict compliance with bird protection laws. Consultation with local agricultural extension services and environmental law enforcement agencies is a wise staring point in such cases lest the "solution" prove worse than the perceived problem.

Large Roosts. Congregations of birds near residential areas usually involve starlings, species of blackbirds, crows, and vultures. Aside from the relatively trivial nuisances of noise and unsightly droppings, the fear of disease is sometimes aroused. Histoplasmosis, a fungus that thrives in piles of bird droppings and can affect humans who inhale the spores (see DISEASE), is the only significant potential health hazard connected with roosts and can be contracted only through close contact with the droppings. There have also been instances of large roosts posing threats to aircraft landing and taking off nearby. *Solution:* Harassment of the birds, especially when they first select the roost site, is often effective in forcing them to choose another location where the conflict with human activity is minimal. Unfortunately, starlings have become particularly fond of city structures as night roosts and are therefore likely to move from one urban

site to another. A more drastic solution involves altering the roosting habitat of the birds so that it no longer suits their purpose. A grove of trees, for example, might be thinned, thus eliminating the togetherness potential that roosting birds require.

In the late winter of 1975, the U.S. Army undertook the control of a large blackbird roost near Fort Campbell, Kentucky, by spraying the roosting birds with a detergent-like chemical from the air. The "avian stressing agent" used (Tergitol) dissolves the oil in birds' plumage (see OIL GLAND; PREENING) that normally prevents them from becoming "soaked to the skin" and that is essential for maintaining proper insulation in cold and wet weather. When the temperature drops near freezing, sprayed birds die of exposure. In Kentucky, 500,000 blackbirds succumbed to this technique. This action was opposed (unsuccessfully) by conservation and humane organizations—not because they oppose radical control of pest species in all circumstances, but because (1) the Kentucky roost was about to disband naturally, since the birds were within days of departing on their northward migration; (2) the ambient temperature was not low enough on the proposed spraying date to kill the birds quickly, making the humaneness of the operation questionable; and (3) the method inevitably leaves a significant number of birds disabled but not dead, another humanitarian concern.

Feral Pigeon Nests/Roosts. Though Feral Pigeons don't usually roost communally in groups containing millions of birds as do starlings and blackbirds, they are very fond of colonizing niches of buildings, where they foul the architecture and present some (slight) risk of disease (chlamydiosis, histoplasmosis: see DISEASE). Their abundance in cities and towns is commensurate with the presence of food sources such as open dumpsters, as well as the density and enthusiasm of the local pigeon feeders, pigeon breeders, and/or pigeon racers. Pigeons are not native to North America and, aside from providing sustenance for a few urban-dwelling Peregrines, have few redeeming attributes in their feral incarnation. (Their cliff-dwelling Rock Dove ancestor in its native habitat by contrast is at least as handsome as the next wild columbid). *Note:* Some of the following solutions may also apply to gulls and other species as well as pigeons. *Solutions:* Pigeons are not protected by law and may be controlled at the discretion of the law-abiding citizen. Regrettably, they are indifferent to owl replicas and are highly shoo-resistant, and stronger measures are usually called for. The best solution, of course, is prevention undertaken while the nest site is inactive.

If the birds are nesting on a ledge, an effective strategy is to eliminate the flat surface by adding strip of sheet metal at an angle of about 60%; be sure to block the ends so birds can't nest inside. Metal strips with spikes affixed (called Nixalite or porcupine wire) can be installed where the birds roost or nest, but this is relatively expensive, nearly as unsightly as the pigeons, and may have to be maintained because the birds sometimes pile twigs and litter on the spines and then nest on top. Caustic substances

that irritate birds' feet marketed under brand names such as Roost-No-Mor, Flyaway, and 4-the-Birds are *not* recommended.

Pigeons using rafters are best excluded by installing a false ceiling of netting or screening; the mesh size should be no larger than 1 inch and must be tightly and completely sealed lest you create ideal conditions for the untidy nests of that other urban alien, the House Sparrow.

For balconies the best dodge is to enclose them with screening; if this is forbidden by the rules of your condo or apartment building, affixing plastic or Mylar streamers about 12 inches apart so that they flutter in the wind near the nest site discourages colonization.

For pigeons trapped indoors, see below.

As noted, the health risks associated with pigeon nests and roosts is slight. However, nests near ventilation systems and air conditioners should be removed promptly and any cleanup operation is best left to professionals, who can be contacted through your local department of public health.

Reminder: Shooting, poisoning, or trapping and transporting your feathered problems are variously impractical, illegal, unethical, and/or dangerous.

For pigeons at bird feeders, see BIRD FEEDING; for lost racing pigeons, see BIRD BANDING.

Canada Geese. In the Northeast and other regions where Canada Geese were once exclusively migrant visitors, they have become abundant full time residents. The causes of this change were mainly the release of captive birds in the 1930s when the practice of using live decoys for hunting was outlawed and winter feeding by people. Because they are grazers, geese in large flocks have become a nuisance on golf courses and residential lawns and when large numbers congregate on small bodies of water they may affect water quality.

Solutions

- *Stop feeding.* If waterfowl are fed at a local duck pond, their populations are able to grow and remain abnormally high. There is no need to feed waterfowl even in winter and they will disperse to find food in the wild if artificial feeding is discontinued.

- *Habitat modification.* One reason geese favor lawns is that they are fond of bluegrasses (*Poa,* spp.), which are common turf grasses. Planting a different, unpalatable ground cover such as English Ivy or Pachysandra will inhibit grazing. They also favor expanses of grass where they have a broad view and can take of and land easily, and they want easy access to a nearby water body. Strategic placement of hedges, other shrubbery, tall grass, or fencing between lawn and water will cut off access, especially in spring and summer when the geese are tending flightless chicks or when adults are in wing molt and unable to fly themselves.

- *Scare tactics* can work, but they usually need to be modified frequently because the birds quickly realize that the "scaregeese" don't pose any real threat. The most effective devices are flags, streamers, balloons, or other light, conspicuous objects that move actively in the wind; these should be placed at intervals over the grazing areas. Dogs can be trained to chase geese away without harming them. Loud noises usually have only a short-term effect and may, of course, be unpopular with the neighbors; in fact, there are often local ordinances prohibiting this tactic.
- *Repellents* for waterfowl that can be sprayed on lawns have been developed but as of 2003 none had been registered by the Environmental Protection Agency and their effect on human health and non-target species is not completely known.

Hazards to Aircraft. Flocks of small birds or single large birds have been implicated in fatal airplane crashes either by clogging jet engines or by damaging the hull as a result of impact at high speed. A bird the size of a large gull, goose, or vulture hitting an aircraft traveling at 400–600 mph can penetrate windshields, wings, tail, or fuselage, causing the pilot to lose control of the plane. The worst such accident in history was the crash of an Eastern Airlines Electra jet in Boston on October 4, 1960. A flock of starlings en route to their airport roost were sucked into the jet engines, causing immediate failure in one and loss of power in another two, resulting in a loss of control. Sixty-two of the 72 people on board were killed. Bird-aircraft collisions are very infrequent (Drury [1966] says 1–3 instances in 10,000 takeoffs and landings) and usually innocuous. However, the costs of a single mishap can, of course, be very high. *Solutions:* At least some jet engines are now so designed as to inhibit the ingestion of birds. Design and construction have also been tested for "bird resistance" and some modifications made accordingly. Airports now actively discourage the presence of birds by employing loudspeaker trucks or other harassing techniques to clear runways periodically of roosting gulls and the like. A few airports have employed falconers to clear their runways by flying falcons at flocks of roosting birds. Concerted efforts to alter airport habitat to make it less attractive to potential troublemakers and/or to discourage breeding colonies in the immediate vicinity are now standard operating procedures at all major airports. This process can be complicated by the fact that some airports provide ideal nesting habitat for rare grassland bird species or for concentrations of migratory waterbirds and wintering raptors.

Predation on Livestock and Game Animals. Golden Eagles and Common Ravens are known to take sheep or other small stock animals (usually young and/or weak individuals) as well as deer or antelope *on rare occasions.* Ducks, grouse, pheasants, and quail are among the many game birds that Northern Goshawks and other large hawks and owls prey upon. Free-range chicken yards may be raided on occasion by Cooper's

Hawks and Great Horned Owls, very rarely by other diurnal or nocturnal raptors. It can now be stated on the basis of much accumulated data and without a hint of sentimental bias that (1) the amount of damage done to livestock and/or game by bird predators is insignificant and amply compensated by these birds' roles in controlling potential pests such as rodents and rabbits; and (2) the vengeful "control" methods practiced by farmers, ranchers, and others based on prejudice have been vastly out of proportion to the actual threat and a great disservice to the wildlife fauna of North America. Terres (1980–BIRD) notes that *at least* 20,000 eagles were shot (mostly from small airplanes) in the southwestern United States between 1940 and 1962, when full protection was accorded. The fact that most of these birds were killed for "sport" masquerading as predator control makes it all the more contemptible.

Fish hatchery managers and fish farmers complain with justification that cormorants, herons, and fish-eating ducks (especially Common Mergansers) sometimes eat significant numbers of fingerlings. Populations of freshwater sport fish have been depleted by large cormorant colonies on rare occasions, but the prejudice of commercial marine fishermen against cormorants has been shown to be unjustified, as these birds eat mostly small "trash fish." *Solutions:* Covered fish tanks and ponds. Harassment or removal of predators caught in the act. Jail sentences and stiff fines for killing protected birds.

Raptors at Feeders. Sharp-shinned and Cooper's Hawks, Northern Shrikes, and even Northern Goshawks occasionally exploit bird feeders as reliable feeding grounds, reacting to the localized abundance of food in much the same way as the small birds that are attracted to your feeder. There is no danger that your chickadee or junco populations will be decimated, and the larger hawks may also provide squirrel and rat control if you have those problems. Predators are far rarer in nature than the species they feed on and are fully protected by law. They kill to live, without emotion, quickly and with admirable agility. *Solutions:* Tolerance or, failing this, stop feeding.

Birds and Windows. During the breeding season, male birds defending their territories often catch sight of themselves in reflective surfaces such as windows, doorknobs, car hubcaps, and the like, and thinking their own image to be a rival, attack the reflective surface in a vain attempt to chase the perceived intruder away. Though rarely fatal, this behavior may damage the defender's bill, causes unnecessary stress, and wastes time that would be better spent tending to more fruitful parental duties. *Solutions:* The phenomenon will cease as the breeding season wanes, but if it is seriously bothersome the reflection can be temporarily eliminated by covering the *outside* of the window with a nonreflective material. A medium-weight plastic painters drop cloth—readily available at hardware stores—attached to the top of the window, eliminates the reflection and scares birds with its fluttering motion, yet allows light to pass through. For single brooded birds

in the northern half of the continent, this is largely a spring phenomenon, but can extend to later in the year where the breeding season is longer.

Particularly in migration, birds often crash into large windows. They are notably susceptible to situations in which they can look through a room to habitat on the other side or when the window mirrors the vegetation in *front* of it. Large picture windows, especially ones near feeders, are also more than usually hazardous. Normally, of course, this situation does more harm to the birds involved than to the windows, though large birds (hawks, grouse) may crack or shatter panes. Depending on their flight speed, the birds may only stun themselves momentarily or—not infrequently—they may be killed by the impact. *Solutions:* Many stores that sell nature products stock cutout silhouettes of hawks or falcons that can be stuck on the offending windows; these inhibit birds from flying in that direction. Some stores stock a thin, wide netting that does not substantially mar the view and can be hung in such a way as to prevent birds from reaching the window. Otherwise, any technique that corrects the impression that glass is air or reduces its reflective characteristics, e.g., curtains, streamers, tape, wax, will also solve the problem.

Birds Indoors. Starlings, Chimney Swifts, and (with surprising frequency) Wood Ducks sometimes enter chimneys while prospecting for roosting or nesting sites. Once inside they may find themselves with no place to perch and too little maneuvering space to execute the necessary vertical exit flight. Such birds often arrive in a panic in the living room. As anyone who has had this happen can attest, a frantic starling can knock over an amazing number of objects in a very short time. *Solution:* Keep birds (as well as other uninvited visitors, e.g., raccoons) out of the chimney in the first place by covering it with ¾-inch to 1-inch galvanized wire mesh. If a bird beats you to the chimney, keep in mind that the bird doesn't want to be in your house any more than you want it to be there. Therefore, your goal should be to show your guest the easiest escape route. Accordingly, open the nearest door or large window that leads to the outside and at the same time close or curtain off other windows and doors leading to other parts of the house. *Do not* be afraid of the bird; it has little capacity and no desire whatever to do you any harm. *Do not* chase the bird around with a broom or a butterfly net; this will only cause the bird to panic and to fly into your most precious knickknacks and confuse its perception of the best exit.

House-eating Woodpeckers. Homeowners are justifiably annoyed when they find woodpeckers chipping away at their dearly purchased (or deeply mortgaged) real estate. This is not an uncommon complaint, especially in the fall (mid-September through November in the Northeast), and usually involves Downy Woodpeckers, which seem to prefer shingles (especially cedar ones) to clapboards and to be particularly destructive of the facing below gutters and at the corners of buildings. Interrogations of affected homeowners reveal that the woodpeckers are not feeding on

carpenter ants or other house-inhabiting insects, nor are they drilling where insect-like sounds might be emitted by electrical wirings of the like. Their actual motive seems to be the construction roosting holes. This fits well with the season, the preference for tree-like coverings, and the sheltered locations chosen. And there are now a few accounts of birds actually completing and occupying such a house cavity. Often—unfortunately for all concerned—when the woodpeckers find they cannot get through the house's tar paper or other obstruction, they try another location—and extend the damage. *Solutions:* Harass the offending bird—scare it off, spray it with a hose. If repeated often enough, this will eventually discourage it in many cases. Temporarily placing a sheet of plywood or heavy plastic over the favored area has also proven effective. The above solutions also work (sometimes) in discouraging courting woodpeckers hammering out nuptial messages at dawn on a hollow drainpipe or other metal amplifiers near your bedroom window. Techniques that have *not* worked include plastic owls, rubber snakes, and painting or spraying the affected area with a supposed anti-woodpecker substance.

Attacks by Birds. Some species of birds defend their nests with unusual ferocity. Terns nesting on swimming beaches will "dive-bomb" you in an intimidating but usually harmless manner if you come too near. Northern Mockingbirds, Barn Swallows, and, rarely, other songbirds will menace people (more frequently dogs and cats) that they perceive as threatening to their eggs or young. Defensive behavior is characteristic of a short segment of the breeding cycle and the best solution is to steer clear of the birds' territory if possible or tolerate the mild nuisance for a few weeks.

One notable exception to the above generalizations is the Northern Goshawk, which defends a circle of several hundred feet around its treetop nest with such ferocity that an unsuspecting human wandering too close at the wrong time could be seriously injured. Because goshawks generally prefer to nest in remote areas far from human habitation, the problem seldom arises, but campers or owners of country cottages arriving in the midst of the breeding season (late spring to early summer is the danger period in most cases) occasionally find their site already occupied and fiercely defended. *Solutions:* Goshawks are among our most magnificent birds of prey and, while they seem to be increasing locally in recent years, they are by no means common. In normal circumstances, seeing a goshawk is a rare treat. Therefore, annoying though it is to be attacked, especially on your home turf, it should be remembered that these birds are not vermin or household pests to be disposed of at will. Goshawks are protected by law, and a special dispensation is required before they can be "controlled." Furthermore, amateur attempts to deal with the goshawk problem often end in a hospital visit for the would-be "controller." In view of these considerations, the best way to deal with usurping goshawks is to (1) stay away during the two or three weeks of the

current breeding season, (2) remove the nest when the danger period is past (large raptors tend to reuse old nests), and (3) establish your presence the following year before the birds have taken possession of the site for the new season. If you feel that a more immediate solution is essential, the aid of a local falconer or other expert in handling raptors should be enlisted if possible. He or she could arrange for the removal of the nest in a manner that would serve the best interests of all concerned, once the proper permits have been issued.

Those tempted by the "no bird's going to push me around—where's my shotgun?" approach should remember that the hasty disposal of a goshawk may well create a far greater hassle than dealing with the situation rationally and humanely.

Maybe *You're* the Problem. Nature centers and animal welfare organizations that offer free advice to the public receive a significant number of calls from people who in effect are complaining about the intrusion of nature into our increasingly controlled, human-oriented environment. That Northern Mockingbirds often sing during warm, moonlit nights, for example, seems to be a nuisance rather than a delight to a lot of people; they want to know how to get rid of the noisy pest: "Can't you kill it or trap it or something?" they shout at the poor nature center volunteer. It is difficult to be sympathetic to this point of view in an era when a more legitimate complaint is that machine-made noise shuts out birdsong in many places and that animal life is generally less evident as a result of the human fondness for pavement and the multifarious pollutants that we have released, sprayed, poured, and buried during the recent past.

It is possible to argue that people living in North America today have a better opportunity to enjoy the exquisite complexities of the natural world than anyone ever has or will. We rarely have to fear the wilderness and its inhabitants as threatening to our well-being. Most of us have the leisure to explore and study the natural aspects of our extraordinary planet, aided by a wealth of illustrated books that describe species of plants, birds, mammals, insects, etc. And we have not yet committed ourselves to the necessity of living in "controlled atmospheres" underground or in space. It is pitiful, then, that so many people regard the other animals with which they share space as a menace rather than a rare luxury.

If you have a "bird problem" that is not discussed above, take a minute to consider (1) whether it is really a problem and (2) whether the solution might be found in a slight reassessment of your values rather than a massive disruption in the life of a fellow earthling.

PROCRYPTIC. Blending with the natural background; disguised so as to be ignored by potential predators (compare ANTICRYPTIC). The nightjars, bitterns, and rails are notable for their procryptic plumage among North American birds. See also COLOR AND PATTERN, Concealment.

PROLACTIN (pro-LAK-tin). A hormone secreted by the pituitary gland (see ENDOCRINE SYSTEM) that controls the onset of broodiness and the development of a brood patch, and affects various forms of sexual behavior; also stimulates production of CROP MILK.

PROMISCUITY. See MATING SYSTEMS.

PRONUNCIATION. For treatment of pronunciation of English terms in this book, see p.xxvi. See also NAMES, SCIENTIFIC.

PROTECTION OF BIRDS. See LAWS PROTECTING BIRDLIFE; CONSERVATION.

PROTHONOTARY (pruh-THON-uh-tair-ee or PROH-thuh-NOH-tuh-ree) (Warbler). The chief clerk or notary of the English court system and in some U.S. state courts. Also one of seven members of the College of Prothonotaries Apostolic of the Catholic Church, who concern themselves with recording canonizations, signing papal bulls, and other clerical responsibilities. The robe of an English prothonotary includes a saffron yellow cowl and therefore is an apt metaphor for the brilliant golden head and breast plumage of *Protonotaria citrea.*

PROVENTRICULUS (PRO-ven-TRIK-yuh-luss). The first (uppermost) of two enlargements in a bird's digestive tract, which together function like the human stomach. See DIGESTIVE SYSTEM and Fig. 27.

PROXIMAL (PROCKS-ih-mul). Nearest to the main body. The term is little used in ornithology, and then is generally synonymous with BASAL. For example, the proximal (or basal) portion of a drake King Eider's wing is largely white. Opposite of DISTAL.

PSILOPAEDIC (SYE-low-PEE-dik). Naked when hatched, completely lacking in natal down or with only a few tufts on the head and back. See PTILOPAEDIC; ALTRICAL; YOUNG, DEVELOPMENT OF.

PSITTACOSIS (SIT-uh-COH-siss). Parrot fever. A bacterial disease of birds of the parrot family, which in rare instances is transmitted to humans; a parrot-restricted form of ornithosis (chlamydiosis). See DISEASE.

PTARMIGAN (TAR-muh-gun). Standard English name for 3 species of grouse in the genus *Lagopus* (family Phasianidae; order Galliformes), all of which breed in North America and one of which (White-tailed Ptarmigan) is endemic.

Ptarmigan are birds of the arctic and subarctic regions, including the arctic-alpine zones of high mountains. They are noted for a sequence of

cryptic plumages that are molted to match their habitat: as the tundra turns from variegated brown to snow white, so do the ptarmigan. The Rock Ptarmigan is among the few birds to remain in the High Arctic during the winter, when it survives by feeding on seeds in places that the wind has swept clear of snow or by digging through the snow crust with its sharp claws. These birds are a staple and favorite food of the Innuit people, and the Red Grouse, a subspecies of Willow Ptarmigan confined to the heather moorlands of the United Kingdom, is the favorite quarry of shooting parties in the Scottish highlands.

Choate and Paynter (1985–NAMES) surmise that ptarmigan springs from a Gaelic word, *tarmachan*, which they say means "mountaineer" or "white game" (?); Lockwood (1993–NAMES), always the champion of onomatopoeia, says that tarmachan means "croaker" and imitates the call of the Red Grouse. The superfluous "p" was an error in classical scholarship (many Greek words with "t" sounds begin "pt") committed in 1684 and repeated ever since.

For general family characteristics, see GROUSE.

PTERODACTYL (TAIR-uh-DAK-tull). Any member of an ancient order (Pterosauria) of prehistoric (Jurassic and Cretaceous) flying *reptiles*. Pteranodon, familiar to most young dinosaur enthusiasts, was one of these.

PTERYLA (TERR-ih-luh) (pl.: pterylae). Technical term for FEATHER TRACTS.

PTERYLOSIS (tair-ih-LOH-siss). Plumage; the distribution and arrangement of feathers over the body. Except in the Ostrich, penguins, and two other small groups of birds (none of which occur in North America), the body feathers all arise from a pattern of tracts, technically known as pterylae. See FEATHER TRACTS; PLUMAGE.

PTILOPAEDIC (TYE-low-PEE-dik). Covered with down when hatched. See PSILOPAEDIC; PRECOCIAL; YOUNG, DEVELOPMENT OF.

PTILOPODY (tih-LOP-uh-dee). A technical term meaning feathered toes and legs, as is characteristic, for example, of the ptarmigan; see Fig. 17 and LEG/FOOT.

PTILOSIS (tuh-LOW-sis). Technical term for plumage; all the feathers of a bird's body. See PLUMAGE.

PUBLICATIONS, ORNITHOLOGICAL AND BIRDWATCHING. See the bibliography under PERIODICALS.

PUFFIN. Standard English name for 3 species of auks with white, "clownlike" faces and large, laterally compressed bills that acquire highly colored

"sheaths" in alternate (breeding) plumage (see BILL). All three puffins (Common, Horned, and Tufted) belong to the genus *Fratercula* (family Alcidae; order Charadriiformes). All breed and winter in North America.

The puffins all nest in burrows, which they excavate in the usually shallow soil of sea islands or remote coasts; they winter at sea. The Common Puffin inhabits the North Atlantic and is replaced by the Horned and Tufted Puffins in the North Pacific.

According to Lockwood (1993–NAMES), "puffin" was originally the commercial fowlers' name for the notably fat (i.e., "puffy") chicks of (Manx) shearwaters in the British Isles, the salted carcasses of which were prized food items. The word eventually came to refer shearwaters in general and this usage is preserved in the genus name *Puffinus*. The name was broadened again to refer to the alcids that had their nest burrows near those of the shearwaters, but it was not until the nineteenth century that puffin became the accepted common name for these auks.

For family characteristics, see AUK.

PULLET. A young domestic hen; in the strictest sense, one under a year old.

PULLUS (POOL-us). A young bird from the time of hatching until it is more or less independent of its parents.

PYGMY-OWL. Standard English collective name for the 24 species of small (about 7 inches), mainly diurnal and crepuscular owls in the genus *Glaucidium* (family Strigidae; order Strigiformes), 2 of which, the Ferruginous Pygmy-Owl and the Northern Pygmy-Owl, are resident in western North America.

To most birdwatchers, these little owls are irresistible, though they are widely shunned as omens of death in Latin America. They can often be readily attracted by imitating their staccato tooting, which, in turn, often attracts a "mob" of small songbird species (see Fig. 19).

For family characteristics, see OWL.

PYGOSTYLE (PYE-guh-style). A "tailbone" consisting of the fused vertebrae at the end of a bird's backbone; the plowshare bone. See SKELETON and Fig. 27.

PYRRHULOXIA (peer-uh-LOCKS-ee-uh). Standard English name for a single species of large, crested finch, *Cardinalis sinuatus* (family Cardinalidae; order Passeriformes). It breeds in arid scrublands from southern Arizona and Texas south to central Mexico. The name is a somewhat muddy classical compound, which refers to the red in the plumage and the curved, somewhat parrot-like mandibles; something like "crooked-billed cardinal" may have been intended. See CARDINAL-GROSBEAK.

QUAIL. Standard English name for a variety of gallinaceous birds now divided between two families. The 13 species of Old World Quail (including the bush-quail) belong the family Phasianidae along with the snowcocks, francolins and spurfowl, partridges, tragopans, jungle fowl, peafowl, grouse (including ptarmigan and prairie-chickens), and turkeys. The 31 species of New World quail (including the wood-quail and wood-partridges) now reside in the family Odontophoridae; both families are in the order Galliformes. No species of Old World quail is native to North America, though the Common Quail of Eurasia has been domesticated here for its meat and eggs. This account describes the New World quail.

Six species of quail are native to North America north of the Mexican border; most of these are restricted to the West and Southwest, with only one species, the Northern Bobwhite, occupying most of the continent east of the Mississippi and south of the coniferous forest zone. Quail are medium-sized (8¾–11 inches), squat, ground-hunting, largely herbivorous birds (seeds, fruit, some insects) that prefer open woodland or scrub habitats often in mountains or desert. They are somberly colored on the whole but strikingly patterned, and all have distinctive, loud whistled calls. Most are decorated with improbable head plumes.

Quail make a shallow scrape on the ground, often concealed under a bush or other cover. This nest may be unlined or contain fragments picked from nearby plants. The eggs are characteristically numerous (to 28 in a single clutch; 8–15 average) and very variable in color and pattern among different species: white to dark buff; immaculate, finely speckled or heavily splotched with buff, reddish, or dark brown.

Quail vocalizations comprise a great variety of distinctive, penetrating whistles and "well-articulated" phrases (e.g., *bob white*) as well as low "conversational" cluckings and sharp, abrupt alarm calls. Males of some species have characteristic breeding "songs," and a few species are known to engage in DUETTING.

"Quail" originated with a distinctive call of the Eurasian *Coturnix* quail, but catches the effect of the sounds made by the American species.

See references in the Bibliography under GALLINACEOUS BIRDS.

QUILL. In the vernacular, an entire long feather, such as a primary or tail feather, the former used in colonial times and earlier as a pen. In respect to the technical anatomy of a feather, it may refer to the stiff, but light, central "spine" (calamus and rachis together), i.e., the "shaft," or to the calamus alone. See FEATHER and Fig. 13.

RACE. An "unofficial" alternative term for subspecies. The subspecies *Seiurus noveboracensis notabilis* is known in English as the Grinnell's race of the Northern Waterthrush. A nuance of this term is that it hints at *geographical* variation among species. See NOMENCLATURE.

RACHIS (RAY-kiss). The stiff central spine of a feather from the point where the vane begins to the tip (distal end), i.e., excluding the calamus. See FEATHER and Fig. 13.

RADAR. The development of increasingly powerful and sophisticated radar technology beginning during the Second World War (1940) has greatly advanced our knowledge of specific details of nocturnal migration, which were once undetectable.

Essentially, radar (RAdio Detection and Ranging) involves sending into the air very high-frequency radio waves that reflect off the surface of any object they encounter. The returning images are collected by large (e.g., 28-inch diameter) parabolic dish antennas and projected onto a viewing screen.

Radar was developed, of course, to detect enemy aircraft at long range and at night, but even in the earliest days, an unexpected type of "echo" was picked up. These "angels," as radar technicians named them, were eventually proven to be migrating birds.

Using this system to detect high-flying nocturnal migrants (see MIGRATION), ornithologists have been able to observe and count for the first time the number of birds involved in migratory movements (far greater than previously suspected); to detect specific directions and routes taken (often more varied than imagined); and to obtain accurate data on timing, speed, elevation, and correlation with weather patterns. It is even possible to identify species using characteristic "echo signatures." When combined with ground observation of migrants in the daytime, radar information allows a close monitoring of migratory activity.

The history of migration study using radar—for example, Gauthreaux's long-term pioneering research on trans-Gulf migration—is an
exciting one to read because of the scope of the phenomenon and the
continual succession of unexpected revelations. And anyone who has an
opportunity to watch a radar screen fill up with the illuminated "shadows"
of small birds on a night of heavy migration can experience one of the
great benign miracles of modern technology; it is now possible to do this
on-line!

For key works on radar studies of bird migration see the bibliography.
For a good short summary of radar technology and its use in bird studies
as well as a listing of websites relevant to "birding radar" see Larsen
(2000–TECHNOLOGY FOR BIRDERS). See also TELEMETRY.

RADIATION. In the context of bird distribution, used to describe the
movement over time of species, families, etc., out from the regions in
which they originally evolved; or the shorter-term range expansions such
as the recent conspicuous movement of certain southern species, e.g., the
Northern Cardinal, north of previously defined breeding limits.

Adaptive radiation is a concept of evolution describing how a
grouping of closely related but highly diverse organisms diverges
markedly from a common ancestor by adapting to particular modes of
life. The family Icteridae, which includes oropendolas, orioles, cowbirds,
meadowlarks, Bobolink, a number of blackbird types, is a good example.
Compare with CONVERGENCE; see also DISPERSAL; DISTRIBUTION;
SPECIATION.

RAIL. Standard English name for about 62 members of the family Rallidae
(order Gruiformes), including the forest-rails and wood-rails. Also, the
generic term for all 143 members of the family, including crakes, flufftails,
moorhens, gallinules, swamphens, and coots. Nine members of the rail
family breed in North America, and 4 other species have been recorded as
accidental stragglers (see Appendix II).

Rails range in size from 5½ to 20 inches (6 to 15½ inches in North
America). Their legs are moderately long—adapted to wading in shallow
water—but not very long, as in the herons and cranes. Their toes are unwebbed, but are peculiarly lobed in the coots. They may have relatively
long, slender bills or shorter, stubby ones, and their bodies are typically
compressed laterally ("skinny as a rail"), apparently an adaptation to
walking amid dense marshland vegetation (see illustration, Terres, 1980–
BIRD, p. 757).

Though there are many upland and forest species, rails are the quintessential secretive marshland birds. They are usually somberly and cryptically colored, frequently of crepuscular habits, and walk deliberately
while foraging along muddy marshland edges. They are also adept swimmers, and though loath to fly any great distance when flushed, many

species undertake long-distance migrations. Like their near relatives the cranes, rails eat almost anything of the right size—animal or vegetable—that comes their way.

The nests of rails, coots, and gallinules are piles of marsh vegetation, in some species shaped into a rather neat, deep cup. They are placed on clumps of emergent marsh plants or in shallow water and may be built up as rising water levels demand. Typically, surrounding vegetation is pulled over the top of the nest to form a dome or canopy. Common Moorhens lay from 2 to 21 eggs, but 8–10 is more usual in this family. They are off white, buffy, pinkish, or olive and generally rather sparsely spotted and speckled with reddish or dark brown and paler subsurface markings.

Rails call mainly between dusk and dawn, making a wide variety of whinnies, clicks, cackles, and pumping sounds often more suggestive of frogs or insects than birds. Because rails are so secretive by nature, their presence is often revealed first by their vocalizations. If you have never stood by a marsh before dawn during the breeding season and listened to the wails, moans, and lunatic laughter with which these birds express their territorial jealousies and sexual longings, you have missed one of nature's strangest delights.

Like many other bird names, "rail" is supposed to derive from the birds' cries, specifically from *raelare,* a Latin verb meaning "to scrape," a good description of one call of several North American rails. Lockwood (1993–NAMES) notes that the modern French version *râle* refers to the death rattle.

See also COOT; CRAKE; GALLINULE; MOORHEN.

RAMSEY CANYON (Arizona). See SOUTHEASTERN ARIZONA.

RAMUS (RAY-muss) (pl.: rami). Literally, a "branch." One of the two lateral halves of the lower mandible; or the barb of a feather. See BILL; FEATHER.

RANGE. The geographical area normally occupied by a given organism or group of organisms beyond which they are normally absent. In migratory species well-defined breeding and wintering ranges are discernible as well as a total or "gross" range including the area over which a particular species migrates. Ranges are normally described or mapped in terms of geographical extremities; however, most species are restricted to habitats within their broader range, so that no range is uniformly occupied. No two species occupy exactly the same range. For specifics such as disjunct ranges, cosmopolitan ranges, etc., see DISTRIBUTION.

RAPTOR. Generally refers to the hawks, eagles, falcons, and their relatives (except for the vultures) and the owls. However, see discussion under BIRD OF PREY, which is essentially synonymous.

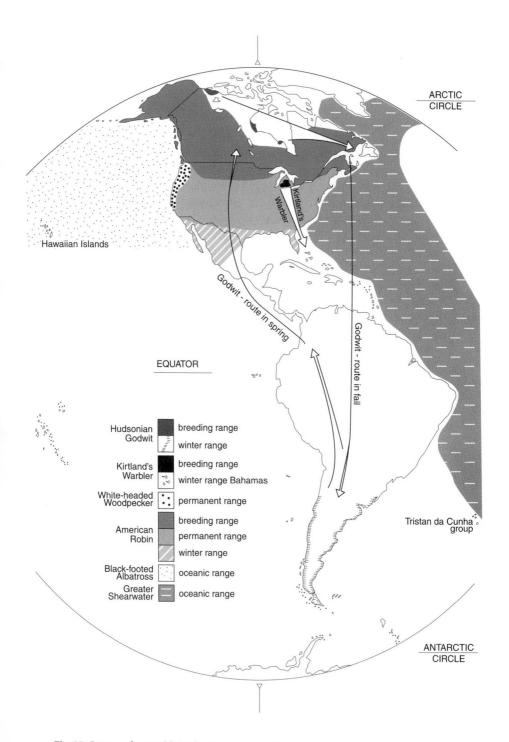

Fig. 25. *Ranges* of several "North American" species.

RARA AVIS (RARE-uh AY-vis or [Latin] RAH-ruh AH-wiss). Latin for "rare bird." Typically used metaphorically to describe a highly unusual person or creature, and therefore as applicable in some cases to birdwatchers as to birds.

RARE BIRD ALERTS. Also known as Bird Hot Lines. A recorded telephone message, available at any hour of the day or night, providing an up-to-date account of what birds—especially rarities—have recently been reported in a particular area. In the case of "super rarities," explicit directions to the bird's last known perching place may be given. Initiated by the Massachusetts Audubon Society in November 1954 as the VOICE OF AUDUBON, the service is now available in almost every state and province in the United States and Canada; New York, California, and Texas have more than 10 different hot lines each. A similar service is also widely available through Internet listservs. There are also national services, including the National Rare Bird Alert (NARBA), operated as a nonprofit service by the Houston Audubon Society with income going to support the organization's nature sanctuaries (www.narba.org), and the National Birding Hotline Cooperative. The "style" of the hotline messages varies according to the needs and tastes of a given birding community, and calling a few of these numbers around the continent is a great way to sample the diversity of the birder's world. For an extensive listing of North American Rare Bird Alerts with contact information, visit the American Birding Association website: www.americanbirding.org. See also BIRDCHAT GROUPS and LISTSERVS.

RATITE (RAT-ite). Flightless birds that lack a keel down the center of the breastbone (see SKELETON), including among living species the Ostrich, rheas, cassowaries, Emu, and kiwis. These were once lumped into a single family (Ratidae) but are now placed (Sibley and Ahlquist 1990– SYSTEMATICS) in four families in the Order Struthioniformes. There are no ratites living in North America except in zoos. See Cracraft, 1974, Phylogeny and evolution of ratite birds, *Ibis* 115:494–521.

RAVEN. Standard English name for 10 members of the crow family (Corvidae; order Passeriformes), 2 of which breed in North America. Ravens are larger members of the genus *Corvus,* which also includes the crows.

The Northern Raven is the largest songbird in the world, if we exempt the lyrebirds, some birds of paradise, and other long-tailed species. It ranges throughout the Arctic and mountainous regions of the Holarctic and is one of the few animals that habitually endures the arctic winter; it also penetrates the Neotropics in the highlands. Its size, blackness, and apparent intelligence have made the raven an object of superstition, an

embodiment of deity, and/or a literary metaphor almost universally (see IMAGINATION, BIRDS IN; HUMAN CULTURE, BIRDS IN). The crow-sized Chihuahuan Raven is a bird of the arid lands of the Southwest. The general habits of ravens are typical of their genus, for which see CROW.

"Raven" descends from the Anglo-Saxon word *hraetn,* which referred to the Common Raven and was meant to imitate its characteristic croaking call.

RAZORBILL. Standard English name for a single species of auk, *Alca torda* (family Alcidae; order Charadriiformes), the sole member of its genus. The Razorbill breeds on remote coasts and islands of the northern North Atlantic and adjacent subarctic and low arctic seas, and winters offshore. The name is an exaggerated description of the laterally flattened, knife-like bill. For family description, see AUK.

RECORDING OF BIRD SOUNDS. The history of recording birdsong parallels the development of sound-recording devices beginning near the end of the last century (1877). Like human song, that of birds was initially captured on wax cylinders and disks, which were supplanted by wire recorders and film media and finally our present highly sophisticated systems using magnetic tape and optical disks (CDs). The earliest-known birdsong recordings are of cage birds in Europe (late 1880s) and soon afterward (1898) a record of a captive Brown Thrasher was being played before a congress of the American Ornithologists' Union.

The recording of wild birdsong in North America owes much to the efforts of the fascinating Albert Rich Brand, a successful businessman who began recording songs with fanatical zeal in his forties and by the time of his death in 1940 had collected the songs of over 300 North American species. This collection provided the beginning of the natural sounds library at the CORNELL LAB OF ORNITHOLOGY, which remains the most comprehensive in the world.

The modern scientific birdsong technician goes into the field with high-fidelity tape recorders or comparable digital recording devices capable of picking up the full range of avian sounds, including those inaudible to the human ear (see HEARING). Her microphone is fixed at the center of a parabolic reflector, a gently and uniformly curving metal disk a yard or more in diameter. This allows her to "concentrate" a bird's song from as far away as several hundred feet under ideal conditions and to exclude many extraneous noises; elongated "shotgun" mikes are also used to "zero in" on a particular singer.

Since we cannot hear certain bird sounds, either because they are uttered too rapidly or at a frequency beyond our perception, recordings are sometimes made into "sonograms," which look like cardiograms and represent in effect a written record of a given sound. With these, variations

within and between species can be compared and can provide clues to phylogeny and the nature of song development. Sonograms are also useful in understanding the "cultural" transmission of song and tracking the movements of birds within populations by distinguishing their "accents."

The songs of all North American bird species are now on tape and most of them are available to the public on tape cassettes and CDs. The cutting edge of sound recording now involves capturing song variations and calls and the illusive voices of the world's most reclusive species. Much of this work is still being done by "professional amateurs."

Birdwatchers have long since discovered that recordings, especially songs taped "on location" can be very effective in arousing secretive birds. Nothing outrages a singing male bird more than playing his own voice back to him within his own territory, and in many cases he will appear immediately to challenge the presumed intruder. It is particularly useful for seeing such species as owls, rails, and reclusive forest or brush birds, whose secretive habits are thought by some competitive birders to give such species an unfair advantage. Owl calls—especially those of the small screech/scops (*Otis*) and pygmy (*Glaucidium*) owls—are also played to evoke a "mobbing" response and bring in a variety of songbirds for close inspection. Alas, in a few instances the tyranny of the list has resulted in the disruption of breeding activities when insensitive birders have plagued rare species nonstop at their nests and recordings are now banned at many refuges.

See the Bibliography for more on technique and a selected listing of available tapes and CDs of North American birds.

RECTRICES (REK-truh-seez or rek-TRY-zeez) (sing.: rectrix). The main feathers of the tail not including the coverts (see Fig. 35); usually more or less long and stiff (the grebes are notable exceptions) and serving the functions of steering, balance, and maneuvering in flight. They are paired and overlap fanwise, with the central rectrices topmost. Most species have 12 rectrices, but a few typically have 20 or more. See TAIL.

REDHEAD. Standard English name for a single species of bay duck, *Aythya americana,* which breeds exclusively in North America. The name, of course, refers to the rufous head of the drake. See DUCK; POCHARD.

REDIRECTION. A term frequently encountered in behavioral literature, referring to an action substituted for a more appropriate one in a situation calling for a definite response but involving some ambiguity. For example, chickadees and other species mobbing an owl (see Fig. 19) often glean and peck at branches or preen, "redirecting" the hostility meant for the predator into substitute modes of behavior.

REDPOLL. Standard English name for 2 species of cardueline finches (family Fringillidae; order Passeriformes), both of which have a circumpolar arctic breeding distribution. In North America, redpolls remain largely in the Arctic and Boreal zones, even in winter, but like other "winter finches" are subject to periodic "irruptions," during which they appear in large numbers and range as far south as southern South Carolina (Common Redpoll).

The "poll" is the crown of the head (to take a poll is to count heads); both male and female redpolls have red polls.

For general family characteristics, see FRINGILLID FINCHES.

REDSTART. Standard English name for 12 species of wood warblers in the genera *Setophaga* and *Myioborus* (family Parulidae; order Passeriformes), 2 of which breed in North America; also the standard English name for 15 species of small Old World chats (family Muscicapidae; order Passeriformes), all but 4 in the genus *Phoenicurus*.

"Start" is cognate with the Old English word *steort*, meaning tail, and the Old World redstarts do indeed have red (bright rufous) tails, which they bob and "shiver" conspicuously and habitually. The American Redstart was named by association after the Old World species because of the characteristic fanning of its red (orange) marked tail, despite the fact that it is a wood warbler and not closely related to the chat redstarts. The other tail-fanning wood warblers—e.g., the Painted Redstart—were in turn named for their relative despite the fact that none have any red in the tail. Alden and Gooders (1981–BIRD FINDING) have suggested the name "whitestart" for all of the *Myioborus* warblers.

For family characteristics, see WOOD WARBLER.

REEVE. The female RUFF; a usage similar to the familiar gander and goose, though referring to one species only. Lockwood (1993–BIOGRAPHY) and others believe that "reeve" preceded "ruff" as the species name, pointing out that it is an old English term for an overseer or bailiff. This fits with the male's breeding-plumage "ruff," which might be seen as a "coat of office," and with the apparently aggressive male courtship displays, which also inspired the Latin generic and specific names, *Philomachus pugnax*, or "combative war-lover."

REFUGE. In the broadest sense, similar to "sanctuary" or "reserve," i.e., a parcel of land set aside for the protection of birds and other wildlife. However, the word is strongly associated with the NATIONAL WILDLIFE REFUGE system administered by the Fish and Wildlife Service of the U.S. Department of the Interior and consequently carries a connotation of extensive wetland habitat preserved and managed for the benefit of migratory waterfowl and the conservation of endangered species. See also SANCTUARY.

RELEASER. A behaviorists' term for a sound, gesture, or plumage character that signals another bird that a particular action—fighting, courting, feeding, etc.—is appropriate. The red spot on a Herring Gull's bill "releases" nestling gulls' urge to peck at it, which in turn "releases" the adult's urge to regurgitate food. Such sequences of stimulus and response are innate and immutable and therefore essential to the basic routines of a bird's life. See also FIXED ACTION PATTERN; INTELLIGENCE.

RELICT (RELL-ikt or ruh-LIKT). Refers to a population of birds or other organisms contained within a limited range and isolated from other populations of that species or from any similar form. The word also implies that such a population is "left behind" from a once wider distribution.

The Caspian Tern ranges nearly worldwide, but today breeds largely in local "relict" populations, which presumably were more continuous in prehistory. In North America, for example, it nests in widely scattered colonies on Great Slave Lake, NWT; in Labrador; on the Great Lakes; at the mouth of the St. Lawrence; and along southeastern coasts. See DISTRIBUTION.

RELIGION, BIRDS IN. In Islam, Judaism, and Christianity, man is seen as a superior being made in the image of the one true God. Birds and other animals are therefore traditionally held in rather low esteem—at best thought to have been created for man's benefit, at worst deemed "unclean" (some 20 proscribed species are noted in Leviticus and Deuteronomy). In this light it is perhaps not surprising that in Islamic, Judaic, and Christian countries, birds have been recklessly destroyed for food and sport though conservation efforts have stemmed some of the excesses in the most prosperous and educated societies. By contrast, the Hindu and Buddhist traditions espouse reverence for all life and consider human life simply a part (and a very transitory one) of a living whole. As a result of this less anthropocentric tradition, wild birds in India sometimes exist unmolested alongside burgeoning cities and villages, many of whose people are in need of edible protein but will not sacrifice the life of a fellow creature to get it. Certain birds, e.g., cranes, are objects of particular reverence throughout most of Asia. The Hindu-Buddhist tradition holds that we pass through a series of lives, in each of which we learn something of value to guide us ultimately to the blissful nonexistence called Nirvana in Sanskrit. For example, a soul might pass through one life as a falconer, the next as a falcon, and the next as a teal, each experience adding a measure of enlightenment. Alas, birds are still in serious trouble in much of Asia due to the need of the continent's enormous human population for the same resources the birds require to survive.

Of the more than 400 bird species known in modern Israel, fewer than 40 are identifiable in the Bible (see Shulov in Campbell and Lack [1985—ORNITHOLOGY] for an analysis). However, the Old Testament contains numerous passages in which birds play prominent roles for dra-

matic effect. They are the first animals mentioned in the description of the creation (Genesis, Chapter 1) and "fowl of the air" fly commonly throughout the first book of Moses. Noah sends a raven, a kingfisher, and a dove to look for the land that would signal the subsiding of the waters and God's wrath. The last returned with an olive branch from the top of Mount Ararat. An English tradition says that the (Eurasian) kingfisher flew high into the sky, thus acquiring its blue back, and too near the sun, thus "scorching" its breast, and for its foolishness Noah made it stay out on the roof of the ark and catch its food from the water.

Other bird species, while not specifically mentioned in the Bible, have come to be symbolic of certain biblical themes and often appear as such in religious painting: the Eurasian Goldfinch, because of its association with thistle (= thorns), came to stand for the Passion of Christ; doves represent purity as well as peace and are therefore often depicted in the company of the Virgin; the dove also is representative of the "Holy Ghost" or "Spirit" and thus was sent by "the Father" to inseminate the Virgin with "the Son"; the eagle is a symbol of the Resurrection as well as the personal sign of St. John the evangelist; the pelican is sometimes associated with Christ because of the erroneous notion that it can feed its young with blood from its own breast. A number of species, e.g., the Barn Swallow, have traditionally been credited with trying to ease Christ's suffering by pulling thorns from the Crown or nails from the Cross, drawing blood from their own breasts in the process; and the peculiar mandibles of the crossbills have also been attributed to the pulling of crucifixion nails.

REMEX (REM-eks or REE-mecks) (pl.: remiges). One of the flight feathers of a bird's wing: primary or secondary. See WING and Fig. 35.

REMICLE (REM-uh-cl). A small feather attached to the second phalanx of the second digit of the wing (see SKELETON, Bones of the Wing, and Figs. 1 and 27). It occurs in a wide spectrum of families (passerine and nonpasserine) and is generally believed to be a vestigial outermost (10th, 11th, or 12th) primary. So inconspicuous is it in small songbirds that the many species of songbirds in which it makes a 10th primary are known as 9-primaried oscines.

An alternative explanation of the remicle's origin is that it was a covert for the wing claw of ancestral forms.

REMIGES (REM-ih-jeez or REM-ih-jiz). Plural of REMEX.

REPRODUCTIVE ISOLATION. The condition of being unable to interbreed with another organism because of some physical or behavioral incompatibility. As a hypothetical example, a bird species that normally forms pairs in March would probably be reproductively isolated from one that did so in May, whatever their similarities; incompatible genital

structure that makes copulation physically impossible would also enforce reproductive isolation. This is not to be confused with the situation in which species are prevented from interbreeding by *spatial* isolation, e.g., total discontinuity of range. See SPECIATION.

REPRODUCTIVE SYSTEM. See Fig. 26. In animals that reproduce sexually, the essence of the process is the uniting of a cell (spermatozoon) from the male parent and a cell (ovum) from the female parent to form a single third cell (zygote). The resulting fertilized ovum contains the genetic material of both parents and will, if all goes well, develop into a unique individual. In humans and most other mammals, the embryo develops within the body of the female; all birds and most reptiles, however, lay a hard-shelled egg almost immediately following fertilization, so that embryonic development takes place outside the female's body.

Perhaps the most notable structural differences between the avian and mammalian reproductive systems are (1) the virtual lack of external sexual organs in birds and (2) the prodigious change that birds' internal reproductive organs undergo during the breeding cycle. (The sexual organs of birds may truly be called private parts; the ones on the inside are difficult to find during most of the year, and there is nothing significant to conceal on the outside.) A key advantage of this system is that the "baggage" of the sexual organs is greatly reduced while it is not needed, thus making flight less "expensive."

Male Reproductive Organs. The testes are a pair of glands (in birds they are attached to the abdominal wall and lie near the top of the kidneys) in which the sperm cells are produced. A bird's testes are usually roughly egg-shaped and, unlike the main female reproductive organs, are both functional, though one may be larger than the other. The sperm cells develop within the mass of tiny tubules that make up the interior of each testis. When mature, they travel along a tube (one from each testis) called the deferent duct (vas deferens) to the cloaca, from which ejaculation (as well as urination and defecation) takes place. The ejaculatory duct, which is simply the cloacal end of the deferent duct, is made of erectile tissue,

Fig. 26. *Reproduction.* These herons demonstrate the rather awkward (at least by human standards) position most birds assume in copulation. The female must raise her tail and twist her lower abdomen acutely to one side to present her cloacal opening to the male above. The "cloacal kiss" that passes for intercourse among most birds is essentially performed sideways and at right angles. In many smaller species, the male actually stands on the back of the female during copulation, a procedure known as "treading." The "disected" urogential systems show the male system "off-season," with the testes only partially enlarged (upper left); the same system in breeding condition (upper right), with greatly enlarged testes and deferent duct; and a female system in an early stage of ovulation. The inactive female system would show no egg mass whatever at the ovary and the right oviduct little larger than the normally useless left one shown. In full breeding condition, however, some of the eggs and the oviduct itself become 3–4 times the size illustrated. The figure also shows the main elements of the urinary system (see EXCRETORY SYSTEM).

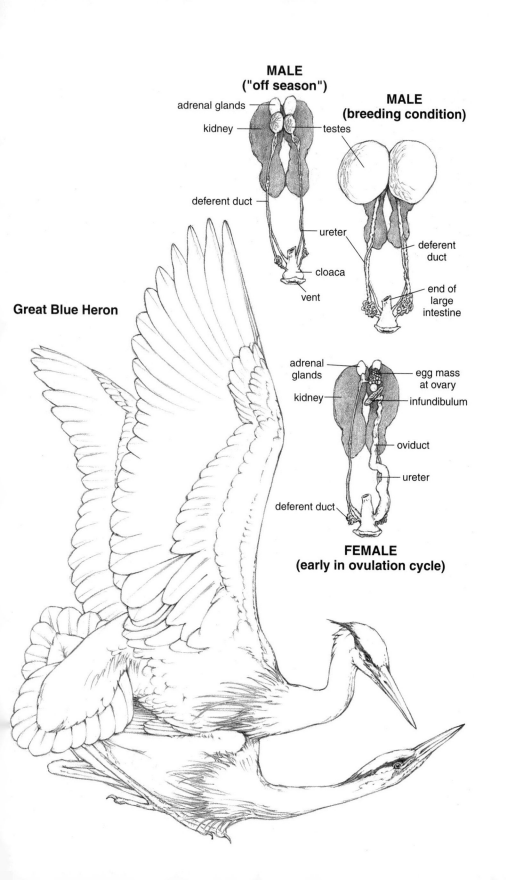

**MALE
("off season")**

adrenal glands
kidney
testes
deferent duct
ureter
cloaca
vent

**MALE
(breeding condition)**

deferent duct
end of large intestine

Great Blue Heron

adrenal glands
kidney
egg mass at ovary
infundibulum
oviduct
ureter
deferent duct

**FEMALE
(early in ovulation cycle)**

but only a few orders of birds have a prominent penis, and this remains within the cloaca until copulation (see below).

During the breeding season the testes of birds increase in size by hundreds or even thousands of times and the deferent ducts may quadruple in length, becoming heavily coiled and with a much greater diameter. In most land birds this enlargement of the ducts makes an external bulge in the lower abdomen, the cloacal protuberance; this is the birds' only claim to an external genital character, and it is sometimes used by banders and others to determine the sex of species in which this is impossible on the basis of plumage. Because the bulge fills with semen, which may cool somewhat in its partially external sac, the structure has been compared to the semen storage sacs (seminal vesicles) and scrotums of mammals, but this does not seem otherwise justified by either structure or function.

Female Reproductive Organs. Like the testes, a bird's ovaries are reproductive glands attached to the abdominal wall and situated near the top of the kidneys. Except in certain hawks, only the left ovary functions in birds; the right ovary ceases to develop in an early stage and degenerates. In about half of female accipiters, harriers, and falcons, both ovaries develop but are only rarely are both capable of ovulation. If ova do mature on the right, they continue development in the left oviduct (see also SEX, CHANGE OF). The ovary produces thousands of ova (female germ cells) of which only a few reach maturity. From the ovary, an ovum falls into the enlarged mouth (infundibulum) of the oviduct, a tube that ends, like the male's deferent duct, at the cloaca. There are four major sections of the oviduct, the first three of which contribute significantly to the production of a finished bird's egg. The ovum, essentially the egg yolk, is fertilized by the sperm cells in the uppermost part of the oviduct, called the magnum. Following fertilization the ovum travels through the magnum, which makes up about half the entire length of the oviduct. Mucous glands lining the magnum secrete several layers of egg white (albumen) around the yolk, which then passes into the narrower isthmus. In the isthmus two shell membranes are secreted: an inner one to enclose the nearly liquid yolk and albumen and an outer one to adhere to the shell-to-be. Beyond the isthmus is the wider shell gland, which occupies the same position in the female bird's oviduct as the uterus does in the human female's genital tract, and is often so named. But though the amnion (see EGG) is homologous in mammals and birds (as well as reptiles), this comparison is not exact. After the shell, including its distinctive coloration, is added, the egg is ready to be laid. However, below the shell gland is a final short segment of the oviduct, a "vagina," constricted above and below by a ring-like closing (sphincter) muscle. In domestic hens at least, the walls of the uterus invert through this last section of oviduct into the cloaca, so that the egg is laid, as it were, from the "uterus." The whole process from the time the ovum enters the oviduct to laying takes only about twenty-four hours. See also EGG, Formation and Structure.

Copulation and Fertilization. The striking development of the reproductive organs which characterizes the onset of breeding condition in
birds is triggered by hormonal secretion of the pituitary gland. Once the
ova have been released from the ovary into the oviduct of the female and
the male's sperm cells are mature, the stage is set for copulation. From the
human point of view, the avian sex act is both bizarre and, well, anticli-
mactic. The male stands on the female's back; she lifts her tail; they both
force their cloacas inside out and the semen is transferred in a kind of anal
kiss (Fig. 26). As may be imagined, it is difficult to observe the precise internal details of the procedure, but it may be that part of the male's inverted
cloaca is actually inserted into the female's oviduct for ejaculation. A few
groups of birds (Ostrich, kiwis, most waterfowl, some gallinaceous birds,
and at least one songbird) have evolved a penis of sorts. The ostrich's "intromittent organ" is red and 8 inches long, and the phallus of the stiff-tailed
ducks is heavily "ornamented." In most birds, however, the male member
may be described as a sac of erectile tissue that is thrust out or retracted in
a manner that has been compared (Newton 1893–96–ORNITHOLOGY) to
reversing the finger of a glove. Females of the better endowed males possess a rudimentary clitoris. An explanation for the additional equipment in
waterfowl is that it facilitates transfer of sperm in the water.

Bird semen is similar to human semen in color and consistency and
though, of course, the quantity transferred in a single ejaculation is far
less in birds than in humans, the concentration of spermatozoa may be
many times greater—up to 3 billion per ejaculation as compared with the
human average of 300–500 million.

Once in the oviduct the sperm cells "swim" toward the upper end,
where the ova await fertilization. The journey takes between one and three
days. Sperm from a single copulation may remain alive in the oviduct and
continue to fertilize ova for up to a month, though in general the percentage
of fertile eggs laid decreases sharply by the third week. The female's ability
to store sperm from different copulations (e.g., in polyandrous species) is
the subject of much recent research under the rubric of "sperm competition;" see, for example, Birkhead and Møller (1992) and Oring et al. (1992).

RESERVE. A parcel of land set aside (reserved) for birds and/or other animals or plants with restrictions placed on use or disturbance by people.
More often used in the Old World than in North America, where "sanctuary," "wildlife refuge" and "reservation" are in wider usage. See SANC-
TUARY; NATIONAL WILDLIFE REFUGE.

RESIDENT. In the broadest sense, a species that either nests or winters in
a given area, e.g., Marbled Godwits are common winter residents along the
coast of southern California; the Hooded Warbler is a common summer
resident throughout much of eastern North America. Sometimes the term
is used unmodified to mean summer resident, e.g., the House Wren may be

said to be resident in Massachusetts, though it does not normally winter there; but Lapland Longspurs, though winter residents of most of the northern United States, are never referred to simply as resident in that region. In the narrowest sense the term is synonymous with PERMANENT RESIDENT; this, given the other usages, is likely to be misunderstood.

RESPIRATORY SYSTEM. For birds as for mammals, the breathing apparatus is mainly a system for exchanging oxygen for carbon dioxide in the bloodstream, and is enclosed and protected by the rib cage. However, the avian respiratory system differs in a number of significant details from the human system and serves some additional functions, some of which are still imperfectly understood.

Air Routes. Except for gannets, boobies, and cormorants, which have closed external nostrils and must take air into the mouth through the sides of the bill, birds inhale and exhale through openings at the base of the bill, the nares or nostrils. In a few groups these nasal openings are peculiarly modified; a small closable flap (*operculum*) keeps some aquatic birds from inhaling water and may keep out pollen in species that feed in flowers (see NOSTRILS; also CERE). Then the air passes through the mouth cavity into the pharynx. As in humans, this is the throat passage connecting the mouth with both the gullet (esophagus) and the windpipe (trachea). The entrance to the windpipe is a slit called the glottis; birds lack an epiglottis, the one-way flap of cartilage that normally prevents food from going down the human windpipe. At the top of the windpipe is a structure called the larynx, which holds the vocal cords in mammals but is not the voice-producing organ in birds. This function is performed by the SYRINX, a mechanism unique to birds. It, too, is a modification of the windpipe and is located at its lower end, where it divides into two main bronchi. The main bronchial tubes enter the lungs, where they divide and redivide into secondary and tertiary bronchi and finally into a fine network of air capillaries, which intermeshes with the capillary network carrying blood laden with carbon dioxide (see CIRCULATORY SYSTEM). The bronchi exchange oxygen for carbon dioxide and carry the latter back to the nostrils to be exhaled into the atmosphere. In the human system, the finest of the bronchial tubes (bronchioles) end up in tiny air sacs called alveoli. But birds' bronchi are interconnected and the passage of air is continuous in one direction.

The lungs of birds are comparatively small, usually taking up less than half the proportion of space in the body that mammalian lungs occupy; however, their tissue is much denser and their *weight* is equivalent to that of similar size (weight). In addition birds have a unique system of balloon-like extensions of the lungs, called simply air sacs.

Air Sacs are directly connected to the primary and secondary bronchi and fill most of the extra space left between organs and muscles in a bird's body cavity, amounting to about 20% of the total space. In the majority of

bird species nine main air sacs are located symmetrically: (1) along the upper spinal column (cervical), (2) between the shoulder blades (interclavicular), (3) in the upper chest cavity (anterior thoracic), (4) in the lower chest cavity (posterior thoracic), and (5) in the belly (abdominal). The abdominal, thoracic, and in some cases the cervical sacs occur in pairs; the single interclavicular sac spans the space between the shoulder blades; and the cervical sac, though usually unpaired, branches in some species into a pair of sacs (median clavicular) partway along its length. Left and right members of the paired sacs may be of different shapes and are sometimes numbered separately, so that birds may be said to have 4–5 main air sacs on the average or 8–9; as many as 12 or more (storks, shorebirds). These main sacs extend into the remotest crannies of the body, reaching under the skin in a few cases and, most remarkably, entering into the bones of many species (see PNEUMATIZATION OF BONE).

The principal functions of the air sacs are
- To facilitate an optimally efficient, continuous movement of air in one direction through the lungs
- To provide the large amount of oxygen needed by birds, especially in flight
- To dissipate excess heat created from the exertion of flight by water vaporization from the air-sac surfaces
- To act as cushions for vulnerable internal organs
- To provide a striking inflatable display device as seen in the neck pouches of frigatebirds and prairie chickens

It has also been observed that birds that are constantly airborne seem to have more or bigger sacs than more earthbound species and that birds that must make deep and long dives tend to have fewer and smaller sacs. The capacity of the sacs is not great enough to allow a hot-air balloon effect, but the intrusion of air sacs into hollowed leg and wing bones must improve buoyancy in both air and water. Whether birds can use the sacs as "spare air tanks" when diving is debated.

Breathing Rate and Rhythm. Birds normally breathe much faster than human beings, but the rates of both vary similarly for reasons of physical and emotional stress. In general, smaller birds breathe faster than larger ones, and torpid birds breathe much more slowly than normal (see TORPIDITY). The average human respiration rate is 11–12 breaths per minute; small birds average over 100 per minute but with a wider range (50–200) among different species. Very large birds and torpid ones may take fewer than 10 breaths per minute.

Some birds were once thought to breathe and flap their wings in a synchronized rhythm, leading to speculation that the two functions might interconnected in all species. We now know, however, that—though certain muscles are shared between lungs and wings—flapping and breathing are independently controlled by the central nervous system.

RETROMIGRATION. A term coined to describe the migratory movement of birds that are misled into taking a course divergent from—even opposite to—their normal direction as the result of following a coastline or other topographical feature or "leading line." Not to be confused with reverse migration (see MIGRATION; LEADING LINE).

RHAMPHOTHECA (RAM-fo-THEE-ka). The horny sheaths covering the bones of the bill, i.e., the part of the bill we normally see and refer to when we note the color or texture. The upper and lower sheaths may be referred to separately as the rhinotheca and the gnathotheca, respectively. See BILL.

RHOMBOID SINUS. A cavity in the lower spinal cord containing a gelatinous substance, nerve fibers, and glycogen. It is unique to birds, but its function is poorly understood (see NERVOUS SYSTEM).

RICTAL (bristles). The "rictus" is the mouth opening, the gape. Rictal bristles in birds are hair-like feathers that project over the gape from above. They are present in many insectivorous species and are most conspicuous in some nightjars and flycatchers. See FEATHER and Fig. 13.

RIDGWAY, Robert, 1850–1929 (*Caprimulgus ridgwayi*: Buff-collared Nightjar). One of the young men whom Spencer BAIRD sent West to collect birds in the latter half of the nineteenth century, Ridgway began as a shy, ill-educated boy artist-naturalist from Illinois and ended as a shy ornithologist at the top of his profession: Curator of Ornithology at the U.S. National Museum in Washington, president of the AOU, and author of a large scientific oeuvre. The bulk of his achievement was accomplished at his desk, but he accompanied the survey expedition to Utah, Nevada, and Wyoming in the late 1860s, the Harriman Expedition to Alaska in 1899, and made early exploratory forays to Central America (Costa Rica) in 1904 and 1908. He described a number of "new" North American bird species and many others from Mexico. His multivolume opus *Birds of North and Middle America,* 1901–1950 (completed by Herbert Friedmann), a "descriptive catalogue" containing keys and detailed descriptions of all taxa (including subspecies) of the birds of North America, Mexico, Central America, the West Indies, and the Galápagos, remains authoritative. Ridgway was also the author of the single-volume *Manual of North American Birds* (Philadelphia, 1887), consisting mainly of keys and technical drawings "for determining the character of any given specimen" of North American bird species or subspecies. Ridway along with Coues was a major early proponent of describing subspecies and using trinomial scientific names.

RINGING. The preferred British term for BANDING.

RING SPECIES. A species that varies over a more or less circular range to such a degree that at the point where the divergent forms rejoin (through subsequent range expansion) they are no longer inclined to interbreed. Visualize an imaginary species (with a circular range) that is gray at due north, becomes progressively darker in geographical races to the west and south, and progressively paler as it ranges to the east and south; when the races overlap in the south they have become so different (one black, one white) as in effect to be two separate species though originating as one. This is an oversimplification, but it illustrates the general concept.

The distribution of Herring Gulls today forms a continuous ring around the Holarctic and consists of a number of intergrading racial variations. It is thought that many of the variations on the Herring Gull "theme" that now exist—e.g., Iceland Gull, Western Gull, etc.—evolved when parts of a similar ring were isolated during the Pleistocene glacial advance. See Mayr (1963–SPECIATION) for a fuller account and illustration of this phenomenon.

RIO GRANDE VALLEY (Texas). Literally, of course, the valley cut by the Rio Grande from its source in the San Juan Mountains of Colorado to its mouth at the Gulf of Mexico. In Texas, however, *the* Valley is the lower Rio Grande Valley, beginning somewhere south of San Antonio. This corresponds fairly well to the birdwatcher's Rio Grande Valley, which connotes an avifauna typical of the arid mesquite scrublands of northern Mexico that extend north of the national boundary. Among the Tex-Mex species that fire the imaginations of birders visiting the Valley for the first time are Least Grebe, Neotropic Cormorant, Black-bellied Whistling Duck, Hook-billed Kite, White-tailed Hawk, Plain Chachalaca, Red-billed Pigeon, White-tipped Dove, Pauraque, Buff-bellied Hummingbird, Ringed and Green Kingfishers, Golden-fronted Woodpecker, Brown Crested Flycatcher, Great Kiskadee, Green and Brown Jays, Tamaulipas Crow, Long-billed Thrasher, Tropical Parula, Rufous-capped Warbler, Black-headed and Altamira Orioles, White-collared Seedeater, and Olive Sparrow plus the possibility of finding a Crimson-collared Grosbeak or other vagrant from south of the border.

Several specific localities in the Valley are *de rigueur* as birding stops, among them Santa Ana National Wildlife Refuge, Brownsville, Bentsen-Rio Grande State Park, and Falcon Dam.

For details see Lockwood et al. (1999–BIRD FINDING, Texas).

For birding highlights of the *upper* Rio Grande Valley in Texas, see BIG BEND.

ROADRUNNER. Standard English name for 2 very similar species of large ground cuckoos (family Cuculidae; order Cuculiformes), 1 of which breeds in North America.

Roadrunners are large (about 2 feet), long-tailed, crested, brown-striped terrestrial birds that live in open, arid country (to nearly 9,000 feet in the tropics) and feed on a wide assortment of large invertebrates (e.g., beetles, caterpillars, tarantulas), small vertebrates (e.g., rodents, lizards, rattlesnakes, and nestling birds), as well as some fruits, seeds, and bird's eggs. They fly well, but prefer to flee predators and chase their prey on foot. They are very agile and have attained running speeds of at least 15 mph.

Roadrunners nest in low trees, shrubs, and cactus clumps; rarely on the ground. They fashion a well-made cup of sticks lined with finer plant material, leaves, feathers, and "decorative" debris, e.g., shed snakeskin. The eggs are white or off white and unmarked and usually number 3–6, though larger clutches have been recorded—possibly resulting from contributions from more than one female.

The roadrunners' vocal repertoire is quite extensive and contains an assortment of whining and crowing noises as well as cuckoo-type staccato hoots and clucks.

Roadrunners are a New World phenomenon. The North American Greater Roadrunner resides in the deserts and dry scrublands of the Southwest; it is nonmigratory.

See references in the Bibliography under CUCKOO.

ROBIN. Standard English name used by itself or in combination for about 125 species worldwide, especially the Papuan robins (family Petroicidae) and a wide variety of chats (family Muscipacidae), including the European Robin, whose plump form and/or red breast inspired the ornithological repetition of its name almost worldwide. It is also the prototype for the American Robin and a few other (Neotropical) thrushes in the genus *Turdus*. Most of these species are called simply thrushes and some consistency-minded nomenclators would like to see Clay-colored Robin (for example) become Clay-colored Thrush. This fate will never befall the American Robin *(Turdus migratorius),* arguably the most familiar and best-loved songbird of North America. It has entered enthusiastically with humankind into the pursuit of the American dream—pulling worms from suburban lawns, nesting near us in shade trees and eaves, and serving as chief herald of the beginning and end of our summer days. Though we have at times responded ungratefully by spraying deadly insecticides into the American Robin's arboreal habitat in the vain hope of ridding ourselves of insect pests (see THREATS (OF HUMAN ORIGIN) TO BIRDLIFE), our more sensitive children spend untold hours yearly rescuing nests, eggs, and young of this species from the dangers of life in general and suburbia in particular. When their efforts fail, the ensuing funerary rites are frequently elaborate and affecting.

The original "Robin Redbreast" *(Erithacus rubecula)* is a widespread Palearctic species named in England in the tradition of "Jenny Wren" (to

whom in folk tradition Robin is said to be married) "Jack the Daw," and "Mag the Pie." English colonists, seeing the American red-breasted thrush, which both looked and behaved somewhat like the friend of their birthplace, transferred the name along with their affection.

For general characteristics of the Turdidae, see THRUSH.

ROC (originally Rukh). A gigantic bird of Arabic legend, said to be able to carry off elephants in its talons. In the Western world, it is best known from the second and fifth voyages of Sinbad in *A Thousand and One Nights*. In the phylogeny of myth, the Roc is closely related to other avian giants such as the Anka (Arabia), Simurgh (Persia), and Phoenix (classical legend). It was thought to nest on an island in the Indian Ocean and eventually became identified with the Elephant Bird of Madagascar *(Aepyornis titan)*, which, though flightless, was the heaviest bird we know of and laid eggs with a capacity of two gallons (see SIZE). The enormous fronds of the *Raphia (Sagus)* palm of Madagascar were passed off (on the Great Khan among others) as feathers of the Roc. Compare PHOENIX and see IMAGINATION, BIRDS IN.

ROCKPORT (Texas). A small town and famous birding area on the Texas coast north of Corpus Christi; many individual bits of habitat, including ponds, marshes, beaches, and live oak copses, have contributed to Rockport's reputation, originally created by a local bird lady, Connie Hagar. The copses are flooded at times with exhausted northern land bird migrants returning over the Gulf in spring, and the wetlands contain at one season or another a majority of the water-bird species of North America. In addition, Rockport is handy to Whooping Cranes in winter and marks the northern boundary for some Rio Grande Valley species (e.g., Least Grebe, White-tailed Hawk).

ROCKY MOUNTAIN NATIONAL PARK (Colorado). 416 square miles of unspoiled American highland habitat between 7,500 and 14,259 feet (65 peaks over 10,000 feet), including deciduous woodland (aspen, willow) open ponderosa pine woods, dense spruce and fir forest, stunted "wind timber" above 10,000 feet, alpine meadows and tundra (both with unique and spectacular floral displays peaking in June and July), snowfields, icy tarns, and swift, rocky streams. The park was decared a Biosphere reserve in 1976 and nearly 90% of it is managed as wilderness. Avian specialties are boreal and western montane species, such as Northern Goshawk, Golden Eagle, Prairie Falcon, Blue Grouse, White-tailed Ptarmigan, Black Swift, Broad-tailed and Rufous Hummingbirds, Williamson's Sapsucker, Northern Three-toed Woodpecker, Hammond's, Dusky, Western, and Olive-sided Flycatchers, Violet-green Swallow, Gray and Steller's Jays, Clark's Nutcracker, Mountain Chickadee, American Dipper, Rock Wren, Mountain Bluebird,

Townsend's Solitaire, MacGillivray's Warbler, Western Tanager, Cassin's Finch, Pine Grosbeak, rosy-finches, and Lincoln's Sparrow.

Mammals of note include mule deer, elk, moose, and bighorn sheep.

The peak of birdsong in the mountains is around mid-June and the road to the tundra area is usually not open until the beginning of that month. Wildflower spectacles continue from late June to September; tourists peak in high summer.

Access on U.S. Highway 34 is via Loveland and Estes Park from the east and Granby from the southwest.

For other western mountain birding, see YELLOWSTONE; YOSEMITE.

RODENT-RUN. A form of distraction display in which parent birds crouch low to the ground and dash away from their nest hoping to draw the attention of a potential predator. In some cases (e.g., shorebirds) the ruse (aka "rat-trick") is accompanied rodent-like squeaking. There is some danger, of course, that the trickster will be caught, but usually the bird is able to escape using a technique unavailable to rodents: flight. See DISPLAY.

ROOKERY. Originally referring to the communal nesting colonies of the European crow called the Rook. Now expanded in usage to other tree-nesting colonial species, e.g., a heron or water-bird rookery, and occasionally even to colonies of ground nesters, e.g., pelicans.

ROOST (roosting). A place where birds congregate to rest or sleep, by day or (usually) night, in trees, on water, or on the ground. Roosts are primarily a protective strategy against predators, but they also serve as loci for the exchange of information (e.g., the location of the best feeding areas), as a means of keeping warm, and as a comfort zone where birds can find relief from environmental stresses.

Some roosts are stupendously large—European Starlings and blackbird species regularly gather by the millions in dense roosts in the southeastern states (see PROBLEMS INVOLVING BIRDS)—but it is also correct to speak of a single bird "roosting for the night." Roost sites often become part of a population's habitual behavior pattern, some sites being known to have existed for over 100 years and to attract birds from feeding areas as far as 30 miles away (European Starlings).

Some birds, e.g., herons, may roost in the same place where they nest, following the breeding season; however, a clear distinction exists between "roost" and terms such as "colony," "rookery," and "heronry," all of which are used for breeding as opposed to resting.

"Roosting" is frequently used to mean "sleeping," but, as noted, the two words are not synonymous; for sleeping behavior see SLEEP.

For more detail on the roosting phenomenon, see especially Ward and Zahavi (1973) and other references in the Bibliography.

ROSEFINCH. Standard English name for 18 of the 21 species of cardueline finches (family Fringillidae; order Passeriformes) in the genus *Carpodacus* plus one Asian species in the monotypic genus *Uragus* (Long-tailed Rosefinch). The exceptional species are the three resident American rosefinches: Purple Finch, Cassin's Finch, and House Finch.

Carpodacus is a fairly homogeneous genus, with males ranging in color from pink to scarlet to slightly purplish, the streaky females and juveniles usually lacking any trace of rose.

They range throughout the Palearctic region south of the Arctic in coniferous and deciduous woodland, desert, and montane barrens; two of the North American species reach the Neotropics (Mexico) in the highlands. A fourth species the Common Rosefinch of Eurasia is a casual visitor to Alaska.

Not to be confused with ROSY-FINCH. For general family characteristics, see CARDUELINE FINCHES.

ROSS, Bernard Rogan, 1827–74 (Ross's Goose: *Anser rossii*). Born in England, and a lifelong naturalist, Ross became head trader for the Hudson's Bay Company. This gave him the opportunity to collect the type specimen of his goose (named for him by John CASSIN) near Great Slave Lake, NWT, in 1861. For the Ross of gull fame, see the following entry.

ROSS, Sir James Clark, 1800–62 (Ross's Gull: *Rhodostethia rosea*). Great British naval explorer of the Arctic and Antarctic who sailed with Booth and Parry as a young man and commanded the *Endeavor* expedition to look for John Franklin. No more fitting avian memorial to an explorer of polar seas can be imagined than the high arctic gull that bears Ross's name. For the Ross of goose fame, see the preceding entry.

ROSTRUM. Technical term for the bill; it is also the Latin word for "bill" and is combined in the scientific names of many species with distinctive bills, e.g., *Rostrhamus,* literally "hooked bill," is the genus of the Everglade Kite.

ROSY-FINCH. Standard English name for 4 species of cardueline finches (family Fringillidae; order Passeriformes) all in the genus *Leucosticte*; the 2 other members of this genus are known as mountain-finches. The taxonomy of this genus has been much disputed. Several distinctive populations of rosy-finches are isolated on alpine peaks where they have no breeding contact with other forms, so that their degree of biological differentiation was never tested until recently (see SPECIATION), and many authorities once believed that all of the North American rosy-finches (Gray-crowned, Brown-capped, and Black) constituted a single variable species. With the advent molecular analysis, these species are now authoritatively deemed to be distinct and a three-way split may be in the offing for Gray-crowned.

Whatever their taxonomic status, the rosy-finches are fascinating birds, among the few songbirds adapted to the harsh conditions of the alpine barrens above tree line on our highest mountains. They generally arrive on still-snowy peaks by early April. Their bulky nest of grasses, sphagnum moss, and stems, lined with finer plant fibers, fur, hair, and feathers, is tucked under rocks on talus slopes or into crevices or on ledges of cliff walls. They feed (themselves and nestlings) almost exclusively on seeds, for which they forage in alpine meadows, at the edge of the snowfields, and along the shores of frigid tarns. In winter, some populations descend to the plains, but others remain above 6,000 feet, where large roosts have been recorded, individual birds huddling in rock crevices or abandoned Cliff Swallow nests to conserve heat. The rosy-finches also breed on rocky arctic barrens at sea level (Alaska).

Rosy-finches are found in alpine and arctic regions only in the eastern Palearctic and western Nearctic regions; their migrations are almost exclusively altitudinal. In North America they are confined to the highest western mountains (and adjacent plains) and the Arctic.

Male birds in breeding plumage are subtly handsome with distinct patterns of rose on wings, belly, and rump, but this color is less evident or absent in females, during other seasons, and at different ages. The name mountain-finch used for the 2 Himalayan species of *Leucosticte* is perhaps more apt and avoids confusion with the ROSEFINCHES (*Carpodacus* spp.).

For general family characteristics, see CARDUELINE FINCHES.

ROUNDUP. A birdwatching event in which a given area is covered as thoroughly as possible by teams of birders. For most participants, a roundup is a dawn-to-dusk affair, though some of the "hard core" can usually be counted on to start earlier and go out after dinner for night birds. There is no limitation on number of participants or area covered. Traditionally, there is an evening gathering to compare notes and combine the team lists into a total count. See also BIRDING EVENTS.

RUFF. Standard English name for the male of a single species of medium-sized sandpiper, *Philomachus pugnax*. The name is also used for the species as a whole; however, females are often distinguished as "reeves." In spring migration, this species now occurs regularly in small numbers almost wherever concentrations of shorebirds occur in North America—inland as well as along both coasts—and recently has nested nesting in northwestern Alaska. There are also records from South America and Australia/New Zealand.

The provenance of this name is a kind of etymological chicken-egg quandary. A natural assumption is that this species was named for the frilly collars popular among both men and women in the sixteenth and seventeenth centuries and referring to the spectacular varicolored "ruff"

of colorful feathers that adorns the male sandpiper's head and neck in breeding plumage. But Newton (1893–96–ORNITHOLOGY) opines that the human neck adornments may have been named for the bird! See also REEVE.

For family characteristics, see SANDPIPER.

RUFOUS (ROO-fuss) (Hummingbird, -capped Warbler, -crowned Sparrow, -winged Sparrow). Ideally, the bright orangy-brown exhibited by adult male Rufous Hummingbirds, but often generalized as any shade of reddish brown. The crown of a Rufous-crowned Sparrow, for example, is different from either the hummingbird's shade or the cap of a Rufous-capped Warbler.

RUMP. The area between the end of the lower back and the base of the tail. A "rump patch" of contrasting color is cited as a good field mark, especially in flight, for various bird species, e.g., Northern Flicker (white), Yellow-rumped Warbler. A "rump patch" may include the upper tail coverts but extends beyond them onto the back. See TOPOGRAPHY.

RUNNING. See WALKING.

SABINE, Sir Edward, 1788–1883 (Sabine's Gull: *Xema sabini*). English general, physicist, and astronomer, veteran of the War of 1812, and member of the Ross and Parry expeditions to the Arctic (1818 and 1819). An early authority on the earth's magnetic field and its use in navigation. His gull was named for him by Joseph Sabine, Sir Edward's younger brother naturalist.

Birders sometimes say SAY-byne's Gull and other variations are also heard. On good authority, however, Sir Edward pronounced his name SABB-un.

SAGE (i.e., sagebrush). A dominant shrub (*Artemesia tridentata;* family Compositae) of a distinctive type of cool desert that occurs at higher elevations than the low, hot scrub deserts in the western mountain states of North America; also known as "shrub-steppe." It is the preferred breeding habitat of four bird species, which are named for it: Greater

Sage-Grouse *(Centrocercus urophasianus)*, Gunnison Sage-Grouse *(Centrocercus minimus)*, Sage Thrasher *(Oreoscoptes montanus)*, and Sage Sparrow *(Amphispiza belli)*. The breeding ranges of the grouse and the thrasher, like the occurrence of sagebrush, are restricted to North America; the sparrow also breeds in lower desert scrub as far south as northern Baja California.

The leaves, buds, and shoots of sagebrush are an enormously nutritious food source on which the Sage Grouse depends almost entirely during the winter months.

See BIOME; DISTRIBUTION; and Figs. 8 and 9.

SALMONELLOSIS. A common bacterial "food poison," which infects a wide variety of animals, including birds as well as people. See DISEASE.

SALT GLAND. Humans must void excess salt in urine via the kidneys. Flushing the salt from our system requires fresh water, which explains why drinking seawater is counterproductive to castaways dying of thirst. It has been demonstrated that the capacity of birds' kidneys to deal with excess salt is even poorer than our own, and yet seabirds frequently drink quantities of their preferred habitat with no ill effects.

The solution to this apparent paradox was revealed in experiments performed on the so-called nasal gland—since renamed the salt gland (Schmidt-Nielsen et al. 1959). This paired, linear structure lies in grooves in the skull over and/or in front of the eyeholes (orbits) and is connected to the nasal openings by a duct. The salt is transferred from the bloodstream to the glands and is then secreted in a highly concentrated solution via the ducts and nostrils. The tubenoses (order Procellariiformes) "fire" the salt solution through their double-barreled nostrils, but in most seabirds the colorless liquid dribbles along the bill and drops off the tip. This accounts for the frequent head shaking seen in oceanic birds and perhaps the perpetual drop adorning the bill tips of such birds at sea. Not surprisingly, seabirds have been shown to possess the most well-developed salt glands, but ducks and other waterbirds that inhabit interior salt lakes also have them (Cooch 1964).

SALT MARSH. A coastal wetland habitat, regularly flooded at high tide, dominated by species of *Spartina* grass and containing other salt-loving plants, such as glassworts (*Salicornia* spp.), sea lavender (*Limonium nashii*), and marsh elder (*Iva frutescence*). It is the near-exclusive habitat of Seaside Sparrow (*Ammospiza maritima*), Saltmarsh Sharp-tailed Sparrow *(Ammodramus caudacutus)*, and coastal populations of Nelson's Sharp-tailed Sparrow (*Ammospiza nelsoni*) and Clapper Rail. Salt marshes also harbor a wide variety of other bird species, including wading birds, shorebirds, and raptors attracted by the availability of abundant fish and

invertebrate food sources. A similar habitat (lacking endemic bird species) occurs along the edges of alkaline lakes in the interior.

SALTON SEA (California). A large lake in the southern California desert (southeast of Palm Springs) formed early in this century by a combination of hydrological experimentation and natural flooding. This oasis is home to tens of thousands of wintering waterfowl and shorebirds as well as interesting land birds attracted to the (relatively) lush vegetation. In fall "Mexican" vagrants such as the Blue-footed Booby often stray northward from the Gulf of California, and rarities of all kinds are sought—and frequently found—by local birders during spring and fall migration. A profitable birding area at any season; *very* hot in summer.

SANCTUARY. A parcel of land of any size where human use is restricted for the benefit of birds and other organisms. The term is very general, orininally implying a place where birds could take *refuge* (a frequent synonym) from hunting. It does not carry any implications of management policy. Some sanctuaries are little more than public parks with restricted vehicle access, while others may be visited only by obtaining a written permit. Some contain rare organisms; others are simply green spaces or resting areas for migrant birds. See the Bibliography for listings of specific sanctuaries and other conservation lands. See also NATIONAL WILDLIFE REFUGE.

SANDERLING. Standard English name for a single species of sandpiper, *Calidris alba* (family Scolopacidae; order Charadriiformes). The breeding distribution of the Sanderling is circumpolar arctic, and since they regularly winter as far south as the southern antipodes, they are among the most cosmopolitan of birds. They are among the few birds to breed exclusively in the stony barrens of the High Arctic, and while the migration of some individuals is among the longest of any bird species, others winter farther north (e.g., coast of New England) than almost any other shorebird. Though in many ways the quintessential sandpiper familiar to beachgoers the world over, the Sanderling is something of an anomaly. It is unique in the sandpiper family in lacking a hind toe (hallux), and its nesting habits are also atypical (see NEST; INCUBATION). The name may be a corruption of an Icelandic name translatable as "sand wagtail" or simply a vernacular evocation of its preferred feeding habitat away from the breeding grounds—the wave edge of sandy beaches. For family characteristics, see SANDPIPER.

SANDHILL (Crane). Sandhill Cranes normally nest and forage in marshland, prairie, or tundra habitats; however, in migration across interior North America some populations rest and feed in many of the extensive areas of dunes commonly called "sandhill country" by Midwesterners.

SANDPIPER. Standard English name for 23 members of the family Scolopacidae (order Charadriiformes) as well as a name for the family as a whole. The sandpiper family contains a total of 87 species, including the CURLEWS, DOWITCHERS, DUNLIN, GODWITS, KNOTS, PHALAROPES, SANDERLING, SNIPES, STINTS, SURFBIRD, TATTLERS, TURNSTONES, WILLET, WOODCOCKS, and YELLOWLEGS, in addition to the species that are named "sandpipers."

Members of the sandpiper family come in a wide assortment of shapes and sizes (6 inches to 2 feet) with great variation in leg length and bill length and shape. They are mostly somberly colored in earth tones, usually marked in cryptic patterns of lines, spots, and "scales." Legs are sometimes brightly colored and the toes are unwebbed or partially webbed; all except the Sanderling retain the hind toe (hallux).

Sandpipers feed on a wide variety of plant and animal food from berries of arctic plants (e.g., *Empetrum nigrum,* an abundant arctic ground cover widely known as "curlewberry") to large sea worms pulled from mudflats by the long probing bills of the godwits. Many smaller, shorter-billed species dab on surf-washed beaches, picking up tidbits too small to identify even with binoculars.

The nests of sandpipers are usually shallow scrapes in the open or concealed in ground vegetation and typically lined fairly heavily with moss, lichens, leaves, and the like. The Solitary Sandpiper nests in a tree in an abandoned songbird's nest. The Sanderling makes an unusually deep, tidy cup. The 3–6 (usually 4) eggs are very variable in color and markings among different species: pale yellow-buff, yellow-olive, brownish yellow, or greenish; sparsely or densely marked with dark brown, reddish, or purple—usually rather distinct—speckles and/or splotches.

On the breeding grounds many sandpiper species utter extended trills and warbles, comparable to those of wood warblers, finches, or larks. Snatches of these songs are sometimes heard on migration, but most bird-watchers who have not visited the Arctic are familiar only with the shorter calls, which range in quality from abrupt, staccato chirps or pipings (peeps) to strident yelps (yellowlegs) and pleasing, mellifluous yodels (curlews).

The shorebirds are distributed worldwide (several cosmopolitan species) and a significant proportion breed in the Arctic and undertake long migrations to tropical wintering grounds or pass through the tropics en route to antipodean winter quarters (see, for example, the Hudsonian Godwit route, Fig. 25). They occur in virtually all water-edge situations as well as upland habitats such as shortgrass prairies and cultivated fields.

Sandpiper and other shorebird populations in North America had been decimated by market gunners by late in the nineteenth century (see CONSERVATION; EXTINCT BIRDS; EDIBILITY). Most species have made good recoveries with full protection, but the Eskimo Curlew (see ENDANGERED BIRDS) may have been shot beyond its ability to recover.

In the narrowest sense "sandpiper" is used to refer only to the smaller species in the genus *Calidris* , sometimes called "peeps"; see also STINT.

Only a few sandpipers prefer sandy habitats, but most do utter characteristic piping notes.

SANDWICH (Tern). *Sterna sandvicensis* was named for the English town in Kent where the type specimen was collected in the eighteenth century and not for the famous earl, known to us for his islands and lunchtime staple.

SANIBEL ISLAND. See FLORIDA.

SANITATION (of nest). See NEST.

SANTA ANA National Wildlife Refuge (Texas). See RIO GRANDE VALLEY.

SAPSUCKER. Standard English name for the 4 species of woodpeckers in the genus *Sphyrapicus* (family Picidae; order Piciformes), all of which breed and winter (in part) in North America.

The sapsuckers differ from other woodpeckers in their highly specialized method of feeding. They drill lines (horizontal or vertical) of round or square holes in a wide variety of woody plants (conifers as well as broadleaf species) and lick the sap that accumulates, using the brush-like modification on the tip of their extensible tongue. They also eat the green inner bark (cambium) and a wide variety of insects. Many species of hummingbirds, songbirds, as well as other woodpeckers have learned to visit fresh sapsucker holes, both for the accumulated sap and the insects that it attracts (see Foster and Tate 1966–FOOD/FEEDING Erlich and Daily 1988–FOOD/FEEDING). For family characteristics, see WOODPECKER.

SAPSUCKER WOODS (New York). A patch of deciduous woodland not far from the campus of Cornell University in Ithaca. Famed not so much for its birdlife, which is typical of upstate New York—Ruffed Grouse, American Woodcock, Pileated Woodpecker, Great Horned Owl, Brown Creeper, Black-throated Green Warbler, etc. (in addition to the Yellow-bellied Sapsucker)—as for the Cornell ornithologists—Arthur A. Allen, Frank Chapman, Albert Brand, and the consummate bird portraitist Louis Agassiz Fuertes—with whom it is closely associated. See also CORNELL LAB OF ORNITHOLOGY.

SAVANNA(H) (Sparrow). The ecological term originated in the tropics and has been used in various specific contexts (especially South America and Africa) to describe relatively flat or "rolling" areas with rank grasses and scattered shrubs or low trees with or without marked seasonal rainfall

and sometimes bridging forest and pure grassland. The origins and life spans of savannas are disputed by plant ecologists, but they are often relatively stable plant associations maintained by poor soil and in some cases limited rainfall. Some present day tropical savannas appear to have resulted from the clearing and cultivation of forests by indigenous peoples hundreds of years ago.

The Savannah Sparrow prefers open, usually grassy country and scattered scrubs under which to nest, usually near water (salt or fresh). Its name, however, has nothing to do with habitat, but refers to Savannah, Georgia, where Alexander Wilson first noted this species. Its range is continentwide.

SAY, Thomas, 1787–1834 (*Sayornis phoebe*: Eastern Phoebe; *S. nigricans*: Black Phoebe; and *S. saya*: Say's Phoebe). Perhaps the most brilliant and most broadly knowledgeable of the early Philadelphia naturalists. Say's main interests and contributions were in entomology and conchology (mollusk shells). However, his general expertise was exercised as professor of natural history at the University of Pennsylvania; as expedition zoologist in the West; and as editor of Charles Lucien BONAPARTE's *American Ornithology*. Collecting excursions took him all over the United States and into parts of Mexico; on one of these to the Rockies, the Black Phoebe was first collected and became the type for the genus that was eventually named for Say by Bonaparte. Say's Phoebe had already been described by Bonaparte as *Muscicapa saya,* and when the taxonomy of the flycatchers was revised, Say became the only man to be binomially commemorated in the name of a species of North American bird; the addition of the eponymous vernacular name confers a further distinction.

SCANSORIAL (skan-SOR-ee-yul). Specially adapted for climbing. Woodpeckers, Brown Creeper, nuthatches, and Black-and-white Warbler are examples of scansorial North American birds. See CLIMBING.

SCAPULARS (SKAP-yuh-lerz). Prominent feathers along the margins of the back (i.e., above the shoulders), which also overlap the lesser coverts and tertials. They provide a smooth transition of plumage from the feathers of the upper wing surface to those of the back. Known in birder coolspeak as the "scaps." See Fig. 35.

SCAPUS (SKAY-pus). A little-used term for the stiff tapering shaft of a contour feather, i.e., the CALAMUS and RACHIS combined. See also FEATHER.

SCAUP (skawp). Standard English name for 2 species of the so-called BAY DUCKS in the genus *Aythya.* The Greater and Lesser Scaups are difficult to

distinguish in the field except under the most favorable circumstances. However, the habits of the two species are more distinctive than their respective plumages. The Greater breeds largely in marshy tundra above tree line and winters along the seacoasts of the continent. The Lesser prefers muskeg ponds and lakes below the tree line ranging into prairie marshes; it tends to winter farther south than its congener and is then more characteristic of inland bodies and sheltered coastal waters.

"Scaup" comes from "skalp," an old British term for the beds of mud and grasses on which mussels grow. Mussels and other shellfish are preferred foods of these ducks on coastal wintering grounds. Both species are aptly called "bluebills" by hunters. For family characteristics, see DUCK.

SCHIZOCHROISM (SKIZ-oh-CROH-izm). An abnormal lack of one of a bird's normal plumage pigments (see COLOR AND PATTERN), resulting in an oddly colored individual (e.g., birds normally green turning blue in the absence of yellow) or an unusually pale individual (recorded in alcids and other species). See also LEUCISM; ALBINISM.

SCLATER (SKLAY-ter), Philip L., 1829–1913 (*Parus sclateri*: Mexican Chickadee). Eminent British ornithologist (a founder of the British Ornithologists' Union and secretary of the Zoological Society of London) who traveled in North America but whose main contribution to our ornithology was as the describer and author of many species and subspecies. See also under ZOOGEOGRAPHY.

SCLEROTIC (skleh-ROT-ik) or **SCLERAL** (SKLAIR-ul) **RING.** A circle of overlapping bony plates in the eyes of birds, reptiles, and certain fishes; it helps to stabilize the eye during focusing. See VISION.

SCOTER. Standard English name for 3 species of sea ducks, in the genus *Melanitta* (family Anatidae; order Anseriformes), all of which occur in North America.

The scoters are large black diving ducks that breed on arctic tundra and subarctic muskeg and winter along both coasts—to Baja California in the West.

On their wintering grounds the scoters eat prodigious numbers of mussels and other shellfish, which are pulverized by the powerful muscles of their gizzards. Shellfishermen accuse these birds of competition for more valuable species such as oysters and scallops, but these have proven not to be very significant items of the scoter diet. "Coots," as hunters of sea ducks call scoters, migrate to their wintering grounds in long lines and are shot for sport—especially on the east coast of North America—during this fall passage. Their flesh is not generally esteemed; however, see recipe under EDIBILITY. On shoals such as those off Cape

Cod, Massachusetts, scoters winter in great rafts consisting of hundreds of thousands of birds; such concentrations are particularly vulnerable to oil spills (see THREATS (OF HUMAN ORIGIN) TO BIRDLIFE).

The Surf Scoter is a North American endemic; the Black and White-winged (including the "Velvet") also range throughout most of the Holarctic region.

One speculation on the origin of "scoter" is that it is derived from "coot" owing to the superficial resemblance between these common members of the rail family and the black sea ducks. However, Lockwood (1993–NAMES) thinks it is a printer's or manuscript copier's error from "sooter" referring to the sooty color of the drakes.

SCOTT, General Winfield, 1786–1866 (Scott's Oriole: *Icterus parisorum*). Hero of the War of 1812 and Mexican War, a brave and intelligent soldier, famed for his talents as a peacemaker. Sometimes called the greatest American general between Washington and Lee, Scott was also known as "Old Fuss and Feathers" because of his personal vanity and an obsessive punctilio. He was a national political figure during his entire career, but failed (rather badly) as the Whig candidate for President in 1852, running against Franklin Pierce. Lucien Bonaparte gave the general his ornithological distinction.

SCRAPE. The most rudimentary nest form, a mere depression in sand or earth scraped out by the feet of the parent birds, unlined or lined with a few bits of shell or pebbles, or scraps of plant material. The Least Tern, Black Skimmer, and several of the *Charadrius* plovers make this kind of nest along the coast; most grouse species make scrapes in their appropriate habitats. See NEST and Fig. 21.

SCRATCHING (of head with foot). One of birds' basic, innate behavior patterns, often practiced or attempted within hours of hatching. It is often, as in humans, a straightforward response to an itch. But since birds cannot reach the head with their main preening tool, the bill, scratching also serves to control lice and other ECTOPARASITES, to clean and straighten the feathers, and to spread preen oil in this region (see PREENING).

There are two stereotyped head-scratching methods: direct and indirect. *Direct* scratchers raise their foot directly to the head below the wing, i.e., without requiring any adjustment in the position of the wing. *Indirect* scratchers extend the wing downward and extend the leg *over the wing base* to reach the head. Most (though not all) passerines scratch indirectly. Most birds overall—including those considered more primitive—are direct scratchers. There is much controversy over which scratching method is "better" (i.e., easier to perform, more efficient) and how much variation exists in scratching technique among different orders, families, genera,

and even individual birds. It is widely held that one method or the other is fairly consistent among the larger taxonomic groupings and that the character is therefore of some use in confirming phylogenetic relationships.

See Nice and Schantz, *Auk* (1959), 76:339–42.

SCREECH-OWL. See Fig. 19. Standard English name for 16 of the c. 46 species of small, nocturnal owls in the genus *Otus* (family Strigidae; order Strigiformes), 4 of which breed in North America. The term is used only for New World species, Old World *Otus* being called "scops" owls. Both terms are used as collectives for the genus.

On the whole, *Otus* owls do more wailing, hooting, and whistling than screeching.

SCUTELLATE (SKYOO-teh-late). Scaly; referring, for example, to the overlapping horny plates covering the legs and feet of many species of birds; see LEG/FOOT.

SEABIRD. In the broadest sense, any bird species that habitually frequents the ocean. However, often used in a more restrictive sense to refer to pelagic birds, i.e., those characteristic of offshore waters, e.g., the tubenoses, gannets and boobies, jaegers, two phalaropes, and some gulls, terns, and alcids. This narrower definition excludes such essentially coastal seabirds as SEA DUCKS and cormorants.

SEA DUCK. Collective name for ducks belonging to the tribe Mergini (where these are distinguished from other "true ducks"), including the eiders, scoters, goldeneyes, Bufflehead, Oldsquaw, Harlequin Duck, and mergansers. All of these ducks live primarily at sea—largely coastally or over shoals—when not on their breeding grounds.

For further description, see DUCK; EIDER; SCOTER; etc.

SEAGULL. A colloquial name for any species of gull, including those that breed inland. Many people think it is the definitive name for the commonest gull of their region, but no *birder* worthy of the name ever uses the term.

SEAWATCHING. A form of relatively stationary birdwatching typically at a coastal point where large numbers of waterbirds of more than routine interest can be expected to pass at certain seasons and under particular weather conditions. (Lakewatching is similar, though typically requires more patience.) One difference between seawatching and that other birding subcategory, hawkwatching, is that the latter is best done on a fine spring or fall day in some majestic scenic location such as a mountaintop or an escarpment above a river valley. On a promising seawatching day, by

contrast, the weather is likely to be spectacularly foul—gale force winds howling and sheets of sleet streaming directly into your face and telescope. It is true that the sea can take on a dramatic appearance during such events, but it is often obscured by some form of precipitation. The bad weather has the effect of pushing bird species that normally shun the sight of land (e.g. shearwaters, jaegers, phalaropes) into viewing range, and if onshore winds coincide with migration, spectacular movements of loons, sea ducks, and alcids, often laced with rarities, sometimes pass well within binocular range. In another common seawatching scenario, the weather is quite good but the birds are scarce to absent; this requires a different kind of endurance.

The propensity to seawatch appears to be a reliable genetic marker that neatly divides the birding community. On one side are those (present author included) for whom there is no greater pleasure (a couple of exceptions) than to repose near the coast in the teeth of a cyclone watching masses of Razorbills passing through foggy oculars and keeping a sharp lookout for the Long-tailed Jaeger or Bridled Tern that is bound to show up if you stick it out a little longer. The other subspecies is exemplified by Bill Oddie, who calls seawatching "*the* most tedious of all pursuits" (including cricket!) and devotes an entire chapter of a book to excoriating the activity and its practitioners: "The confident expert will pick out dots beyond the normal range of human vision and tick them off as rare petrels or shearwaters." Etc. (Oddie 1980–BIRDWATCHING).

Even if you were born seawatch-negative, you should endure the experience at least once, if for no other reason than to gain merit for the bestowal of future rarities (see OWLING).

There is also, of course, scientific seawatching for the purpose of gathering data on migratory species, for which see CENSUS.

SECONDARIES. The flight feathers (remiges) that are attached to the "forearm" (ulna), less frequently referred to as the "cubitals." The number of secondaries is much more widely variable than that of the primaries and is apparently proportional to attachment space, i.e., the length of the ulna: hummingbirds have as few as 6, while some albatross species have more than 30; most passerines have 9. The secondaries are numbered from the outermost (i.e., that nearest the innermost primary) to the innermost (that nearest the body). The three innermost secondaries are also distinguished as the TERTIALS; see also WING and Figs. 20, 27, and 35.

SEDENTARY. May be used in the same sense as "permanent resident," i.e., referring to a bird species that does not migrate.

SEED DISPERSAL. The majority of birds at least occasionally play some role in plant dispersal by carrying seeds from one place and depositing them in another. Obviously, birds that feed most heavily on fruits and seeds

are the most effective dispersers, and long-distance migrants may distribute seeds over hundreds or even thousands of miles. The briefest consideration of some of the ways in which birds transport seeds shows the resourcefulness of plant adaptation and the "interconnectedness" of organisms.

- Some plants, e.g., jewelweeds (*Impatiens* spp.), have "explosive" seed pods that scatter their contents when touched by foraging birds and other animals.
- Seed-eating birds scatter seeds from dry pods in a local area simply by landing on a plant and shaking it while feeding.
- Many frugivorous birds remove and swallow only the fleshy outer part of a fruit, letting the seed fall to the ground.
- A number of plants have sticky, fuzzy, or barbed seeds that cling to plumage (and fur) and may thereby be transported considerable distances.
- Seeds or other reproducing parts of plants that grow in or near water readily adhere to the plumage and/or legs and feet of ducks, shorebirds, and other aquatic species and then float or brush off in another pond or marsh.
- Jays, nutcrackers, etc., bury acorns and other nuts, sometimes far from their place of origin.
- Some hard seeds are regurgitated hours after being eaten, following the digestion of the soft part of the fruit (see PELLET).
- Many seeds pass through a bird's digestive tract unharmed and land in suitable habitat many miles from the parent plant. Some seeds actually require the action of strong digestive acids to germinate properly.
- Raptors that kill seed/fruit-eating animals may determine the ultimate destination of the contents of their prey's digestive tract.
- Some plant features such as brightly colored fruits and sticky seeds may have evolved specifically to "encourage" dispersal by birds and other animals, either externally or internally.

SEEDEATER. In the broadest sense, a descriptive term for members of various bird families, especially the Emberizidae, Cardinalidae, Fringillidae, and Passeridae, that feed on seeds. Also the standard English name for about 17 species of African cardueline finches (Fringillidae) in the genus *Serinus* and for the 32 members of the New World genus *Sporophila* (family Emberizidae; order Passeriformes).

One member of the essentially Neotropical *Sporophila* seedeaters, the White-collared Seedeater, is a rare resident of the lower Rio Grande Valley of Texas.

All *Sporophila* species are noted for their distinctive short, deep, conical bills. White-collared Seedeaters feed on grass and weed seeds up to about 5,000 feet in the tropics.

For family characteristics, see EMBERIZID.

SEMIPALMATED (Plover, Sandpiper). Having partial webbing between the front toes. The Willet (*Catoptrophorus semipalmatus*) bears this characteristic along with the Semipalmated Plover, the Semipalmated Sandpiper, and other species.

SEMIPLUME (also semipluma; pl. semiplumae). A type of feather intermediate between adult down feathers and contour feathers, i.e., they have a well-developed rachis (longer than the longest barb) but little or no cohesive vane owing to the lack of barbules (see Fig. 13). Semiplumes typically occur at the margins of feather tracts/apteria and—like down—apparently function mainly as insulation. See PLUMAGE for other plausible functions. See also FEATHER for comparison with other feather types.

SEMISPECIES. A term coined by Mayr (1942–systematics) to refer to forms that are obviously closely related but totally isolated geographically. Since the two (or more) populations never meet under natural circumstances, it is impossible to judge by the usual criterion of interbreeding whether they consist of fully distinct species or subspecies. See also SUPERSPECIES; SPECIATION.

SENSES. See HEARING; NAVIGATION; SMELL; TASTE; CIRCADIAN RHYTHM; TOUCH; VISION.

SET (of eggs). Same as CLUTCH.

SETOSE (SEE-tohs). Having bristles, which in birds are modified feathers. See FEATHER; RICTAL.

SEX. See REPRODUCTIVE SYSTEM; COPULATION; DIMORPHISM; HOMOSEXUALITY.

SEX, CHANGE OF. The sexual glands (gonads) of bird embryos in early stages have the potential to develop into either testes (male organs) or ovaries (female organs). Vestiges of potential testes are retained in mature females, and in rare instances, when the left ovary (the only one that normally develops in most birds) is damaged or diseased, a healthy testis may develop on the right. The bird may then become a fully functional male with the plumage and behavioral characteristics of that gender. This is a rare phenomenon and would, of course, go unnoticed in most cases in wild birds; the known instances are recorded in domestic hens and pigeons. See REPRODUCTIVE SYSTEM.

SEXUAL DIMORPHISM. See DIMORPHISM and Figure 23

SEXUAL SELECTION. A mode of evolution first articulated by Charles Darwin. Noting that many male birds have striking plumage characteristics or songs or behavioral displays, he theorized that these features—absent in the females—had evolved as the result of competition between males and selection by the females of the "winners." If the biggest, prettiest, most extroverted males are preferred by the females, their genes would survive better than those of lesser males, and mutations that enhanced the attractive qualities would also be favored, making for ever more striking effects. The concept also encompasses male fitness, with larger or otherwise better endowed males able to defeat rivals and capture the best territories, thus proving their superiority and attracting more or "better" females. The theory has inspired much fascinating research (see examples in the Bibliography), which has shown, for example, (1) that females of some species do indeed prefer the males with the longer tails or the ones that do the most elaborate displays, (2) that the reproductive success of males in species where competition for females is evident is more variable than that of females, and (3) that some male plumage characteristics really do signal more fit individuals. See also DISPLAY; COURTSHIP; PAIR FORMATION.

SHAFT. The stiff central spine of a contour feather, i.e., the calamus and rachis together. A little-used synonym is scapus. See FEATHER and Fig. 13.

SHAG. An alternative standard name for cormorants, applied to 14 species, all but one residents of the south temperate south temperate coasts and islands. This distinction without a difference doubtless owes its origin to the two resident British species, one known originally simply as Shag (*Phalacrocorax. aristotelis*) and the other with equal majesty as Cormorant (*P. carbo*). In North America the standard English name for all birds in this family is cormorant; however, Atlantic fishermen often refer to all species indiscriminately as shags.

"Shag" refers to the tuft of feathers adorning the head of the European Shag, but this is not a reliable way of telling the cormorants called shags from the shags called cormorants. See also CORMORANT.

SHEARWATER. Standard English name for 21 species (all but 2 in the genus *Puffinus*) of the family Procellariidae (which also includes the PETRELS and FULMARS) and used here to designate the family as a whole. Of the 23 species recorded in North American waters, only 1 (Northern Fulmar) regularly breeds; 6 are vagrants and the remaining 16 are rare to abundant seasonal visitors (see Appendixes I and II).

The shearwaters and petrels comprise a varied segment of the order Procellariiformes—the tubenoses. They vary considerably in size (10 inches to 3 feet worldwide), though species that visit North America are in

the middle range (12–20 inches). They are patterned in shades of black, white, gray, and brown, sometimes relieved by a touch of yellow or pink on bill and/or feet. They have relatively short (stubby or slender), hooked bills, with nostril tubes situated on the top of the bill at its base (see SALT GLAND; NOSTRILS). The front three toes are webbed and the hind toe (hallux) is vestigial. All species are awkward on land, where they must waddle on their tarsi rather than walk erect. The shearwaters and fulmars are graceful fliers adapted, like the albatrosses, to soar on ocean wind currents (see FLIGHT, Dynamic Soaring, and Fig. 32). Gadfly and other, smaller petrels, however, may fly in a more erratic, jerky manner. Many species profit from the refuse of offshore fishing operations. When molested, shearwaters will often vomit forth whatever is in their gullet, along with a musky STOMACH OIL, which effectively repulses most would-be captors.

The skill with which shearwaters can sail at the very edge of the waves even in the roughest weather is one of the wonders of birdlife and one of the joys of birdwatching. On a calm day, when the sea is glassy, it is often possible to see that shearwaters do indeed "shear" the surface with their wing tips from time to time. It is thought that their ability to maneuver so accurately is assisted in great measure by their elaborate nostril modifications (see NOSTRILS).

Like the storm-petrels, these tubenoses are colonial nesters that dig their own burrows, take over abandoned ones, or simply occupy crevices on rocky slopes. The chamber may be thinly or heavily lined with plant material and normally contains a single immaculate white egg.

On a calm day at sea, where shearwaters are gathered in flocks they can be heard to utter various squawks, grunts, cackles, and even "buzzes." Bizarre nocturnal wailing and moaning are characteristic sounds at breeding colonies.

The shearwaters and petrels range over all the oceans of the world, but are most diverse and abundant in colder waters, where marine life is especially prolific—particularly around Antarctica.

The majority of our shearwaters and petrels are nonbreeding summer visitors to North American waters and nest in the Southern Hemisphere during the northern winter. The Northern Fulmar, which breeds in the Arctic in both the Atlantic and the Pacific, Audubon's Shearwater, which breeds in the Bahamas, The Black-vented Shearwater, which breeds off Baja California, and the Manx Shearwater, which breeds mainly in the northeastern Atlantic (also Newfoundland since 1977 and 1 nest record in Massachusetts in 1973), are the exceptions.

For the derivation of "shearwater," see above.

SHOREBIRD. A vernacular term essentially encompassing the families Scolopacidae (woodcocks, snipes, sandpipers, and phalaropes) and Chara-

driidae (oystercatchers, avocets, stilts and plovers). The perspicacious reader will not fail to notice that many undisputable "birds of the shore," e.g., gulls, terns, ducks, are not "shorebirds," while many "shorebirds," e.g., Upland Sandpiper, woodcock, and snipe, are not, for the most part, "birds of the shore." To further confuse the matter, the British collective term for these birds is "waders," which North Americans tend to associate with herons and storks.

SHOVELER. Standard English name for 4 species of dabbling ducks worldwide, all of which have distinctive long bills broadened at the tip. One species, the Northern Shoveler, *Anas clypeata,* occurs throughout most of North America (as well as the Old World). The name, of course, refers to the shape of the bill, which, however, is used not as a shovel but rather as a strainer (see FOOD/FEEDING). For family characteristics, see DUCK.

SHRIKE. Standard English name for most of the approximately 30 members of the family Laniidae (order Passeriformes), as well as the collective term for the family as a whole. Two species—Northern and Loggerhead Shrikes—breed in North America, and a third Asian species, Brown Shrike, has been recorded as an accidental straggler to Alaska, California, and Nova Scotia.

Shrikes are medium-sized songbirds (6¼–14½ inches) with short, heavy, strongly hooked bills; proportionately large heads; strong, rounded wings; long tails; and powerful legs, feet, and claws. Their overall shape is somewhat accipiter-like. Shrikes are usually boldly patterned with dark facial markings, wings, and tail, contrasting with pale underparts and white "flashes" on wings and tail. Dominant colors are black, white, gray, and brown.

The shrikes are the only songbirds that prey habitually on vertebrate animals. They are birds of open country and forest edge and tend to seek prominent perches where they can scan for their prey, which also includes large insects and crustaceans. Both of our species of "butcher birds" practice the famous shrike habit of hanging "meat" on thorns or in narrow crotches, sometimes returning to the mummified remains as long as months afterward.

Loggerhead and Northern Shrikes are usually silent, except for a few harsh calls, but both have true songs, which are often likened to those of the mockingbirds, with sweet, melodic phrases interspersed with harsh chatters and squeaks as well as mimicry of other birds.

The cup nest has a bulky exterior of sticks and stems lined with fine plant fibers, plant down, hair, and feathers. It may be placed in the crotch of a low, dense, thorny shrub or high (over 50 feet) in a tree. The 5–9 (usually 4–7) eggs are white or off white, densely marked with comparatively pale, brownish and grayish blotches and speckles.

Shrikes occur throughout North America, Europe, Asia, and Africa, are absent in Australia and New Zealand, and reach only the edge of the Neotropics at the southern end of the high central plateau of Mexico. The superficially similar African bush-shrikes once placed in this family are now classified in the Corvidae (crows and allies). Together, the distributions of our two shrikes cover all of North America except the most barren, treeless parts of the Arctic, the breeding range of the more southerly Loggerhead picking up roughly where that of the Northern leaves off. The Northern Shrike also occurs widely in the Palearctic, where its English name is Great Grey Shrike. Both of our shrikes are migratory from the northernmost parts of their range. The Loggerhead Shrike has undergone a recent precipitous decline with the migratory population (it was once known as Migrant Shrike) close to extinction.

The notion that shrikes were so named because they "shriek" is not very satisfactory because they don't, but there is some evidence of early confusion with the Eurasian Jay, which is similarly proportioned, quite predatory, and shrieks a lot.

SIBLEY, Charles G., 1917–98. Research ornithologist and biology professor whose scientific work focused mainly on geographic variation, speciation, interspecific hybridization in wild bird populations and most notably biochemical and molecular studies of proteins and DNA as they relate to phylogenetic relationships and classification. Professor Sibley's most famous work (with Jon Ahlquist, Burt Monroe, and others) was the development of the theory and practice of DNA-DNA hybridization as a means of determining the evolutionary "distance" between bird species (see SYSTEMATICS, Biochemical and Molecular Analysis). Sibley received his PhD in Zoology at Berkeley and passed his professional career in academia, including professorships at the University of Kansas, Cornell, and Yale, where he was also Curator of Birds at the Peabody Museum of Natural History. He published 132 titles of which more than half relate to molecular systematics and evolution. Two of his four books, *Phylogeny and Classification of Birds* (1990; with Jon Ahlquist) and *Distribution and Taxonomy of Birds of the World* (1990; with Burt Monroe), summarize what is often characterized as a major contribution to avian systematics that has revolutionized our understanding of bird taxonomy. For a popular summary of Sibley's work (including critiques), see Saltzman (1993–SYSTEMATICS).

SIBLICIDE. In an avian context, the killing of one nest mate by another, typically to avoid sharing food, thus enhancing prospects for survival. For an example, see PARENTAL CARE.

SIBLING SPECIES. Species that are very closely related but that do not normally interbreed where their ranges overlap. Eastern and Western

Meadowlarks exemplify the phenomenon in North America. See also SU-PERSPECIES; REPRODUCTIVE ISOLATION.

SIGHT. See VISION.

SIGHT RECORD. The occurrence of a bird species in a given locality corroborated only by one or more eyewitnesses and perhaps their notes and sketches made at the scene; sightings not confirmed by a specimen, photograph, or tape recording. See VERIFICATION OF RECORDS.

SIGN STIMULUS. A phenomenon, usually visual (e.g., an action, shape, or color), to which birds (or other animals) can be expected to respond predictably. Such stimuli may be so broad as to elicit a mistaken response—flocks of ducks or other birds sometimes "spook" at the passing shadow of a Great Blue Heron, which they mistake for the threatening presence of an eagle. Or, as in many forms of recognition among members of the same species, they may be too subtle to be perceived by human senses.

SILKY-FLYCATCHER. Standard English collective name for the 4 species of birds in the family Ptilogonatidae (order Passeriformes); Sibley and Ahlquist (1990–SYSTEMATICS) place these with the waxings in the family Bombycilidae. Three species of silky-flycatchers breed exclusively in the highlands of Mexico and Central America, and one of these, Gray Silky-flycatcher, has been recorded as a vagrant in Texas and California (though the natural occurrence of the California birds is questionable). For the single species that breeds in North America and family characteristics, see PHAINOPEPLA. See also WAXWING.

SINGING. See SONG.

SISKIN. Standard English name for 19 species of small cardueline finches (family Fringillidae; order Passeriformes), 16 in the genus *Carduelis* and 3 in the genus *Serinus*. One species, the Pine Siskin (*Carduelis pinus*), breeds throughout most of the boreal and montane coniferous forest of North America; it also winters mainly in the Nearctic region, though wandering as far south as Guatemala in "irruption" years.

The Pine Siskin feeds mainly on small, soft seeds and insects, as befits its narrow, sharply pointed bill. It often nests in loose colonies and in flight years may remain south of its normal summer range to breed. The Eurasian Siskin (*Carduelis spinus*) has been recorded as a vagrant in Alaska and has also occurred in a numbers of localities in the Northeast, though the natural occurrence of these birds has been questioned since they are still popular cage birds.

"Siskin" was first applied to the Eurasian Siskin, one of whose calls may be rendered as *tsyzing*. According to Lockwood (1993–NAMES), the

onomatopoeic name came to English from a Slavonic language via German as an artifact of the cage bird trade.

For general family characteristics, see FRINGILLID FINCHES.

SIX HUNDRED CLUB. Once an elite organization open only to those members of the bird-listing fraternity who had seen 600 or more species in North America in accordance with the guidelines articulated by the American Birding Association. According to the 2002 ABA List Report, more than 750 birders have now listed 600 or more species in the ABA Area (over 300 have seen 700 or more and 26 have broken the 800 barrier), and passing the 600 mark can no longer be considered the mark of an elite. Neither a 700 nor an 800 Club has been formally established.

SIZE (including length, weight, and wingspan) See Fig. 22. Birds as a class exhibit an enormous variation in the several size criteria, the more so if we consider the gigantic extinct birds, known from fossil skeletons. Before noting some of the extremes, a few generalizations about size in birds:

- Many more very large bird forms existed in earlier geological epochs than have occurred in recent times. Like some of the largest mammals, some bird giants may have perished as a result of the Pleistocene ice age, but the extinction of huge modern birds, such as the Elephant Bird of Madagascar and the moas of New Zealand, was related to the ascendancy of humanity rather than to unfavorable climatic changes (see, for example, Worthy and Holdaway 2003–EVOLUTION OF BIRDLIFE). See Extremes of Size, below; also DIATRYMA; TERATORNIS; EVOLUTION OF BIRDLIFE.
- Bird species (and other "warm-blooded" animals) tend to be larger in overall body size in the northern parts of their range than in the southern (Allen's rule). This is probably related to the fact that the ratio of surface area to mass or volume decreases as size increases, so that proportionally less heat is lost from larger bodies.
- Sexual differences in size tend to be slight among the great majority of bird species. When sexual dimorphism in size does occur, however, it is the male that is slightly larger in the majority of cases (noticeable in many gallinaceous birds). However, female hawks, eagles, etc., and falcons (order Falconiformes) are conspicuously larger than their mates in many species as are females of many shorebirds—perhaps a precursor to polyandry?
- There is some evolutionary correlation between size of predator and size of prey: Northern Goshawks hunt grouse; Sharp-shinned Hawks prey on small land birds.
- There is some correlation between size (body weight) and flying ability. The heaviest birds are flightless, and the largest of flying birds (albatrosses, condors) have extreme wing adaptations (see FLIGHT).

- There are also limitations to smallness. Hummingbirds can store very little energy in their tiny, but comparatively heavy, vertebrate bodies and must therefore feed almost constantly (or become torpid) to maintain basic metabolism. A hummingbird any smaller than the smallest species (see below) could probably not eat enough to meet the energy needed to feed.

EXTREMES OF SIZE. It should be noted here that disparities in records and opinions of various sources still lend a broad margin of ambiguity to many of these "records."

The Largest Bird Known to Have Lived. The Giant Moa (*Diornis maximus*) of New Zealand, a wingless ratite that stood as high as 13 feet with neck extended and weighed over 500 pounds, is the *tallest* known bird, while the Elephant Bird of Madagascar (*Aepyornis titan*), which stood a mere 9–10 feet tall but probably weighed over 950 pounds, is the *heaviest* known.

The Largest Living Bird is the African Ostrich (*Struthio camelus*), some of which stand 8–9 feet tall and weigh at least 345 pounds. Other living ratites, e.g., cassowaries, Emu and rheas, are also far from petite.

The Largest Flying Bird Known to Have Lived. A recently discovered species of prehistoric condor in the genus TERATORNIS had a wingspan of 25 feet (see Fig. 22) and is thought to have weighed about 175 pounds.

The Largest Living Flying Birds are species of bustards, pelicans, swans, and condors. The Kori Bustard of Africa weighs up to at least 40 pounds, and Mute and Trumpeter Swans equal or exceed this weight (the ability of an alleged 49.5-pound Mute Swan to become airborne has been officially doubted, however [McWhirter 1980]). In North America, the Trumpeter Swan may be the largest native bird overall, males attaining weights of up to 38 pounds, a length of 6 feet, and a wingspan exceeding 8 feet.

Birds with Greatest Wingspan. See above for the largest flying bird known to science. Among living species, the Marabou Stork of Africa may have the greatest wingspan—to 12 feet (Fisher and Peterson 1964–BIRD), though 9 feet is more usual for this species. Wandering and Royal Albatrosses, on the other hand, *average* wingspans of over 10 feet and some individuals may achieve a 13-foot span (11 feet 4 inches confirmed for Wandering). The native California Condor has a wingspan of up to 9 feet 7 inches (Koford 1953–ENDANGERED BIRDS), which exceeds that of even our regularly occurring Black-footed Albatross (7–7½ feet), and with a weight of up to 31 pounds, the condor has a reasonable claim to be the largest flying bird in the world.

The Smallest Living Birds. The Bee Hummingbird (*Mellisuga helenae*), endemic to Cuba and the Isle of Pines, is generally acknowledged to be the smallest living bird, males measuring 2¼ inches from bill tip to tail end. The Calliope Hummingbird is the smallest North American bird at 3¼ inches. Both of these species weigh about 1/10 of an ounce (3 grams).

For other mensural figures, see BILL; EGG; for standards of calculation, see MEASUREMENTS.

See also SEXUAL DIMORPHISM.

SKELETON. See Fig. 27. In the broadest sense, the skeleton of a bird
serves the same basic functions as it does in all the other animals that
possess one: it is a more or less rigid frame to which the muscles are attached and in which the softer, more delicate organs of the body are supported and protected. In its overall design and the structure of many of its
parts, however, the bird skeleton is unique, and most of its singular features are related to the ability to fly. Not surprisingly, lightness and a flexible but unified framework have been the principal skeletal adaptations
to flight. Many bones present in earthbound animals are absent altogether in birds or have become fused into less cumbersome units. In addition, the larger bones of most strong-flying species are essentially
hollow (see Pneumatization, below), lightening the load still further without sacrificing strength. The major specializations of the avian skeleton
are summarized as below.

Skull. The bones of the cranium are thin and closely fused. Eye
sockets are very large, separated by only a thin partition of bone. There are
no teeth (present only in some fossil species, e.g., *Archaeopteryx* and *Hesperornis*). Palate bones are narrow in most cases, so that mouth and nasal
cavities are not completely separated as in mammals and the formation
of these bones has been used as a taxonomic character. A flexible jaw
mechanism allows a wider gape. Development of tongue bones (hyoids)
is unique, allowing exceptional mobility in some cases (see WOOD-
PECKER; HUMMINGBIRD; TONGUE).

Vertebrae. The neck (*cervical*) vertebrae are relatively numerous and
variable (13–25; mammals invariably 7), allowing great flexibility. By contrast many *spinal* vertebrae are fused, making the backbone relatively immobile but strongly supportive. The number of vertebrae below the neck
and the pattern of fusion vary widely among families, species, and even individual birds. Some groups (e.g., falcons, cranes, pigeons) have a series of
2–5 bones in the upper back (dorsal vertebrae) fused into an *os dorsale* or
notarium. This is followed by one or a few "free" (i.e., unfused) vertebrae,
which in turn link with the *synsacrum*. This structure is present in all birds
and consists of 10–23 fused vertebrae, which in most cases are also fused to
the *ilium* (see Pelvic Girdle, below). Below the synsacrum are 4–9 (usually
6–7) free tail or *caudal* vertebrae and finally a structure of fused vertebrae
called the *pygostyle*. This structure is shaped somewhat like the cutting
blade of a plow and therefore is sometimes called the plowshare bone.

The Sternum, or breastbone, is uniquely modified in all birds (except
the ratites) with a more or less pronounced *keel* to which the flight muscles

Fig. 27. *Digestive system and skeleton.*

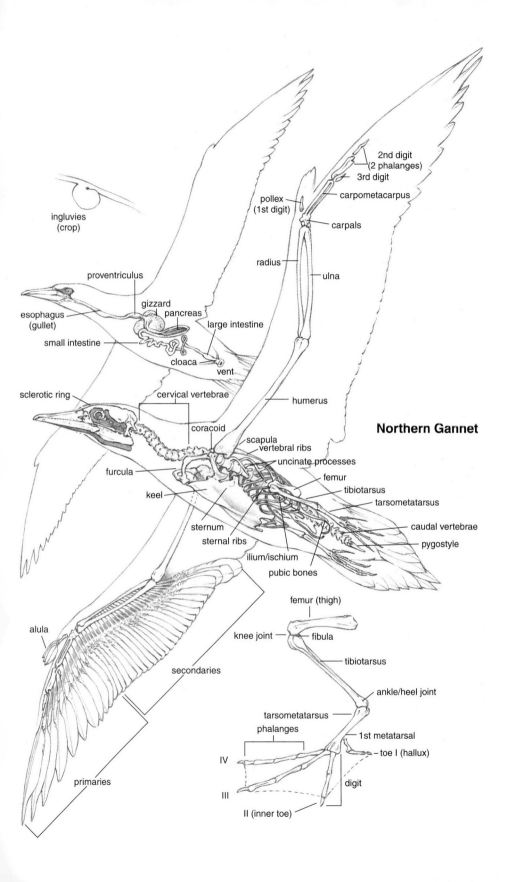

ingluvies
(crop)

2nd digit
(2 phalanges)
3rd digit
carpometacarpus
pollex
(1st digit)
carpals
radius
ulna

proventriculus
gizzard
pancreas
large intestine
esophagus
(gullet)
small intestine
cloaca
vent

Northern Gannet

sclerotic ring
cervical vertebrae
humerus
coracoid
scapula
vertebral ribs
uncinate processes
furcula
femur
keel
tibiotarsus
tarsometatarsus
sternum
caudal vertebrae
sternal ribs
pygostyle
ilium/ischium
pubic bones

femur (thigh)
knee joint
fibula
tibiotarsus
alula
ankle/heel joint
secondaries
tarsometatarsus
phalanges
1st metatarsal
toe I (hallux)
IV
digit
primaries
III
II (inner toe)

are attached. In general, strong fliers have broader sternums and deeper keels than weak fliers. This includes hummingbirds, which have deeper keels relative to body size than any other birds.

Ribs. Each of the middle ribs has a bony extension called an *uncinate* (i.e., hooked) *process,* which is attached to the rib behind; the structure is nearly unique to birds and gives the rib cage (which is also anchored to the backbone and the breastbone) extra unity and strength.

The Pectoral or Shoulder Girdle is also a modification for structural strength and unity, consisting of three interconnected pairs of bones that support the wings: the long shoulder blades (*scapulae*) are anchored by ligaments to the rib cage; the *coracoids,* the largest bones of the girdle, connect the front of the scapulae with the breastbone (*sternum*) on both sides; and the *wishbone* or *furcula,* consisting of two fused collarbones (clavicles), is attached to the upper ends of the coracoids and provides extra support in front. The upper arm (humerus) of the wing rests at the point of maximum support where these three paired structures join. At this same juncture is located the *triosseum canal,* the "pulley" through which the "rope"—the tendon of the supracoracoideus muscle—passes and attaches to the base of the humerus, allowing the wing to be "hoisted" in flight (see MUSCLES; FLIGHT; and Fig. 14).

The Pelvic or Hip Girdle consists of a plate not unlike the sternum in general shape but made up of three fused bones (*ilium, ischium,* and *pubis*). This plate is anchored firmly along the major fused part of the backbone (synsacrum). It bears the socket of the upper leg bone (femur) and, like the sternum, provides a broad surface for the attachment of important muscles, in this case those of the legs. In addition to support, it is a kind of shock absorber for the "landing gear." The conjunction of the femur and the pelvic girdle is specially modified to enable some birds to stand comfortably on one leg.

The Bones of the Wing conform very closely to the bones of the human arm, at least down as far as the wrist. The bone of the upper arm (*humerus*) is the strongest bone of the arm/wing and, together with the appropriate muscles, bears the main burden of moving it. Its heavy appearance is belied by its essentially hollow interior in most species (see Pneumatization, below). In some long-winged birds (e.g., the Northern Gannet in Fig. 27) a series of long feathers (sometimes called tertials or tertiaries) are attached to the humerus. Beyond the humerus come the bones of the forearm (*radius* and *ulna*), also rather similar to the corresponding human structure. The ulna bears the secondary feathers. Starting at the bend of the wing the modifications of bird wing and human arm diverge strikingly. Where humans have 27 bones in the wrist and hand, birds make do with 7–9. The human wrist is an agglomeration of 8 bones (*carpals*) and is followed by 5 hand bones (*metacarpals*); these in turn are attached to 5 digits, each consisting of 3 finger bones (*phalanges*), except for the thumb, which has only 2.

A bird has only 2 distinct wrist bones. The other wrist bones and all of the hand bones are fused into a "double" bone called the *carpometacarpus*. At the base of the carpometacarpus is attached the avian "thumb" (first or "alular" digit or *pollex*), which usually consists of 1 phalanx, rarely, 2 (loons, some geese). At the end of the carpometacarpus, two more digits are attached: the larger consists of either 2 or 3 phalanges; the smaller invariably has only 1. The bird's hand bones (except the two tiny carpals) hold the primary feathers and the "thumb" holds the alula (see Fig. 27).

The Bones of the Leg. At first glance the leg of a bird seems more like a human leg than a wing seems like an arm. Particularly on a long-legged bird such as a heron, we can see clearly what appears to be a thigh ending in a prominent knee followed by a very plausible shin, ankle, and foot with toes. Except for the toes, this is a thorough misreading of the anatomy of a bird's leg. The real thigh bone (*femur*) is short and stout and rests close to the body under the feathers and skin, where it is hidden from view unless you are making a bird skin or carving a roast. The femur ends at the knee joint, which is also normally buried under the feathers of the belly. The first exposed part of a bird's leg corresponds to our shin or lower leg and, like it, is made up largely of two bones (*tibia* and *fibula*), which are partly fused. Thus the conspicuous knob that we at first take for a bird's knee is really its ankle (or heel) joint and bends in the opposite direction from the knee. A bird's ankle bones (*tarsals*), like those of the wrist, are reduced in number and strongly modified. Some of them are fused with the lower end of the tibia, so that this bone is properly called the *tibiotarsus*. Other ankle bones are fused with bones of the foot (*metatarsals*) to make what looks to be a shin but in reality is more like the human instep and is properly called the *tarsometatarsus*. To ensure confusion, this precise term is often shortened to *metatarsus* or, in birding jargon, simply *tarsus* (see Fig. 35).

The tibiotarsus (the leg bone above the ankle) is feathered in most birds though bare in many long-legged species such as herons and shorebirds. The rest of the leg is naked in most species, but a few hawks have feathered "tarsi," and owls and some grouse have feathered tarsi and toes (see Fig. 17).

Most birds, then, stand and walk on the balls of their feet and their toes, of which, with a few exceptions, there are four. The "little toe" (fifth digit) is missing and the "big toe" (first digit or *hallux*) usually points rearward, leaving three toes in front (for other arrangements, see LEG/FOOT). In many species the hallux is thumb-like in that it is crucial for grasping perches or prey; in others, it is much reduced in size and functionless; and in a very few cases (e.g., the plovers) it has disappeared altogether. All of the toes bear claws, which, like the toes themselves, may be greatly modified in accordance with the habits of different species (see LEG/FOOT).

Pneumatization. As noted above, one striking skeletal adaptation to flight is the evolution of "hollow" bones—particularly well developed in

large, strong fliers, in which the weight-saving advantages are obvious. The process by which the phenomenon occurs is called pneumatization (i.e., filling with air). It is a function of the respiratory system and indisputably one of the most astonishing "miracles" of animal evolution.

Late in the incubation period, air sacs connected to the ear and nasal cavities and the lungs (see RESPIRATORY SYSTEM) invade the bones of the embryo by way of natural openings such as those through which veins pass. At this point, possibly due to the release of certain hormones, part of the bone core "dissolves," allowing the air sac to penetrate the entire core and leaving only a tracery of thin, interlocking bony struts to retain internal strength. The process may continue up to two years after hatching and occurs in varying degrees among different species of birds. It is usually best developed in the bones of the upper arm (humerus), thigh (femur), ribs, and vertebrae, but in some birds the process extends to the skull and "fingers." For reasons that seem obvious in some cases but remain obscure in others, pneumatization is less prevalent in many deep-diving birds (e.g., loons), in fast-flying birds (e.g., shorebirds), and in parts of the body that must withstand unusual stresses (e.g., the heads of woodpeckers).

SKIMMER. Standard English name for all 3 members of the subfamily Rynchopinae (family Laridae, order Charadriiformes); or, following Sibley and Ahlquist (1990–SYSTEMATICS), the tribe Rhynchopini (family Laridae, order Ciconiiformes), all of which belong to a single genus, *Rynchops*. One species, the Black Skimmer, breeds in North America.

Skimmers are peculiar-looking water birds whose closest relatives are the gulls and terns. They have long powerful wings attached to a comparatively short body; their legs are short (tern-like) with partial webbing between the front three toes. The Black Skimmer is about 18 inches long. All species are dark above, white below, with yellow or red legs and mandible bases. The most distinctive skimmer characteristic is the bill, which is deep but compressed laterally to knife-like thinness with the lower mandible extending a quarter of its length beyond the upper. See FOOD/FEEDING; and Fig. 3 for a description and illustration of the use of this apparatus.

Like most terns, skimmers are colonial and lay their eggs in an unlined, shallow scrape. The 2–5 eggs are white to buff and boldly splotched with blackish-brown and paler (grayish) subsurface markings and some smaller speckles.

Skimmers make a very distinctive, low *kaup* and *aur,* reminiscent of a dog's bark and frequently heard in the still air of dawn and dusk, when they prefer to feed.

Skimmers are essentially tropical birds (New World, Africa, Asia) and frequent quiet bays, estuaries, and river mouths where they can feed most

effectively. The single North American species breeds only along the Atlantic and Gulf coasts, reaching as far north as Massachusetts; some populations winter along the Gulf.

SKIN. The bodies of birds, like those of other vertebrates, are encased in skin. Except at the dinner table, this feature of a bird's anatomy is inconspicuous because of the thick layers of feathers that are rooted in it and that cover it almost completely. Even those features that are usually unfeathered—bill, legs, and feet—have a horny or leathery covering over the true skin, so that we normally see bird skin only in those species that have bare face patches or adornments such as wattles, combs, pouches, and fleshy eye rings.

The skin of both birds and humans consists of upper and lower layers (epidermis and dermis), but bird skin is a less complex organ than human skin. It lacks self-lubricating glands; it cannot perspire and therefore plays only a minor part in controlling body temperature. It is also probably less sensitive to touch than human skin.

However, it is capable of "blushing," at least in some species. As in humans, this phenomenon is associated with emotional excitement and results from blood rushing to vessels at the skin's surface. It accounts, in part, for the transitory brightening of legs, bills, and colored areas on the faces of many heron species during the breeding season. See also BIRD SKIN; TOUCH; COLOR AND PATTERN; TEMPERATURE, BODY.

SKUA (SKEW-uh). Standard English name for 5 members of the genus *Stercorarius* (until recently distinguished in their own genus, *Catharacta*) (subfamily Stercorariinae, family Laridae, order Charadriiformes; or, following Sibley and Ahlquist [1990–SYSTEMATICS], the tribe Stercorariini, family Laridae, order Ciconiiformes), and frequently used as a collective name for the skua/jaeger subfamily/tribe. In British usage, the other 3 members of the genus *Stercorarius,* known in North America as jaegers are also called skuas. Two species of "*Catharacta*" skuas are visitors to North American waters: the Great Skua, which breeds mainly on islands of the northwestern Atlantic, and the South Polar Skua, which nests in Antarctica; another Southern Hemisphere species, Brown Skua may also occur but has yet to be confirmed.

The skuas are large, plump, brown, aggressive pelagic predators and "pirates," which in general habits greatly resemble the other members of their family, the jaegers.

"Skua" arrived in English via Faeroe Islands (where the Great Skua breeds) and echos the species' gull-like cry.

For general family characteristics, see JAEGER.

SKULL. See SKELETON.

SKYLARK. Standard English name for 3 of the 4 members of the lark genus *Alauda* (family Alaudidae; order Passeriformes). The Eurasian Skylark (*Alauda arvensis*) is one of the Western world's best-known songbirds, and inspired one of the best poems on an avian theme in English literature, Shelley's *To a Skylark* (see HUMAN CULTURE, BIRDS IN). The species has been widely introduced wherever the English have settled, which accounts for its presence on Vancouver Island, British Columbia, where it was introduced in the first decade of this century. It has since spread to the adjacent San Juan Islands, Washington. The species has also occurred as a natural vagrant to Alaska and California.

Its name derives from its song flight, a characteristic of most members of its family.

For other family characteristics, see LARK.

SLEEP. As with most other animals, including humans, birds pause at intervals during their daily routines and become inactive. Such resting periods do not always involve the relatively deep dormancy of sleep—birds are often seen to sit motionless at midday with their eyes open. And birds are also known to "nap," i.e., close their eyes and sleep for a matter of minutes in the midst of feeding or other activities. However, it is with the more or less prolonged, regular periods of true sleep that this entry is concerned.

There is much variation in sleeping behavior, not only among different species but among individuals of the same species. Many of the sleeping styles that have been recorded are adaptations to two fundamental survival requirements: the need to keep warm and the need to remain secure from predators—to which animals are particularly vulnerable when not fully alert.

Posture. One of the most widespread misconceptions about birds is that they sleep with their heads under their wings. In fact, the commonest sleeping posture, especially among songbirds, is with the head turned and resting on the back and the bill tucked under the feathers of the shoulder (scapulars). Not all birds sleep in this position, however, and even species that normally do, sometimes don't. Members of some groups, e.g., grebes, storks, doves, *never* sleep this way, but adopt the second most frequent posture—with the back of the head retracted and apparently resting on the shoulders and the bill pointing forward. Swifts, woodpeckers, and Brown Creepers sleep as they perch, clinging to a vertical surface.

Whether on the ground or grasping a branch, land birds normally squat down over their legs and feet while sleeping. Many waterbirds will do this as well, but will also stand erect with their bills tucked in. A great many species, including songbirds, habitually sleep standing or perching with one foot while the other is tucked up into the plumage, and it has been shown (Berger 1968) that at least some species shift, flex, and alter-

nate the perching/standing foot frequently. Fluffing the feathers to retain maximum body heat is also characteristic of sleeping birds.

It has long been believed and widely repeated that perching birds are held fast to their sleeping perches by the "automatic" action of the flexor tendons of the legs and feet. The theory was that the more a bird relaxed, closing its heel joint as it squatted, the stronger the pull on the tendon, which passes across this joint and runs to the toes. This was supposed to pull the toes together in an immovable grasp on the branch. It has been demonstrated, however, that in at least some songbirds the rear toe is not flexed and in fact does not even touch the perch.

Nestling birds simply close their eyes and sleep as they are, perhaps resting their heads on nest mates; there is evidence that they are not capable of assuming an adult sleeping posture for two weeks or more after hatching.

Where Birds Sleep. Birds tend to sleep in the same habitat they prefer when awake and in a way that enhances their security. Many waterbirds sleep sitting on or standing in their native element or on predator-free islands. Horned Larks and many quail, partridge, and sparrow species sleep on the ground. Cavity nesters tend to sleep in their trees, chimneys, nest boxes, etc. The Common Swift of Eurasia vindicates its reputation as the most aerial of birds by sleeping on the wing (also in cavities). It is no accident that the majority of bird species—including pheasants, and other nonarboreal species—prefer to sleep in trees or dense shrubbery, where they are out of reach of those predators that cannot climb and are warned by vibration long before more agile carnivores can reach them. Species such as some swallows and blackbirds that roost in emergent aquatic vegetation, such as cattails, are doubly protected.

Some birds require more structured sleeping accommodations. These may use their nests of the year to sleep in during the off-season, or use cup nests or cavities abandoned by other species, or in a few cases (Cactus Wren, some woodpeckers) build separate "dormitory" nests near the ones in which they rear their young.

In many cases sleeping habits change with the seasons. Territorial birds usually sleep on their territories (including in their nests) during the breeding season. Thereafter, some species remain solitary in their sleeping habits, but roost in many different sites (especially on migration), while others sleep communally (see below) and return to the same sites year after year. Woodpeckers sometimes excavate new sleeping cavities in the fall instead of roosting in their breeding-season holes. Ruffed Grouse, which usually prefer the cover of dense conifers, sometimes burrow into the snow to sleep, and begin their excavation by diving into a snow bank from the air, a tactic also used to escape hungry Northern Goshawks.

Communal Sleeping Roosts. Birds that are gregarious in their nesting habits (e.g., herons, ibises, gulls and terns, swifts) or feeding habits (e.g.,

shorebirds, starlings, blackbirds) or both (crows) often sleep together in large (sometimes gigantic) aggregations. Such roosts may contain a single species only but more frequently are mixed, and single winter roosts in the southeastern states consisting of four blackbird species and starlings may contain a million or more birds. The chief benefit of sleeping in this manner would appear to be defensive, since the slightest disturbance in any quarter of the roost inevitably sends the entire assembly into a noisy panic.

Other (mainly passerine) birds huddle together in crevices or cavities to sleep on winter nights. Swifts, tits, nuthatches, tree creepers, and other birds known to congregate in this manner are not typically gregarious (or only mildly so); this and the fact that all are also known to sleep individually suggest that the principal motivation for this kind of roost is heat conservation. Coveys of some quail and partridge species huddle in a similar way, but on the ground and in the open, and they compensate for their apparent vulnerability by clustering in a circle with all heads pointed outward, so that the birds can make an instantaneous escape, each in a different direction (see Audubon's plate: Havell LXXVI).

The occasional communal sleeping arrangements of eagles, vultures, Rough-legged Hawks, Northern Harriers (on the ground), Long-and Short-eared Owls, Wood Ducks, and nighthawks (sometimes large, all male roosts) are not as easily explained as the above examples. None of these species is typically gregarious, none huddles for warmth, and all are less vulnerable to predation than many noncommunal sleepers. In at least some cases, local abundance, combined with a favorable roosting site and the proximity of a reliable food supply, may suffice to explain propinquity. Or perhaps there is an additional incentive such as information exchange (see Ward and Zahlavi 1973–ROOST).

When and How Long Birds Sleep. In general, the sleeping rhythms of birds correlate with their feeding habits. Species that are active throughout the hours of daylight (most birds) tend to sleep relatively soundly and uninterruptedly through the night.

Nocturnal species such as owls and nightjars follow the opposite rhythm. Shorebirds and other waterbirds whose feeding habits are often governed by the tides sleep accordingly. One frequently sees large flocks of sandpipers sleeping on the upper beach at midday when high water covers the flats, and since most feed by "feeling" for prey with their bills, they easily adapt to being active at night when the tide is favorable. Food preferences and requirements and feeding methods also affect sleeping schedules. At least a few insectivorous species may "sleep in" until the air temperature is warm enough to activate their preferred prey. Arctic species that are normally diurnal must feed in darkness or near darkness in the northern fall and winter to get enough food to sustain them. And birds that soar in search of food (vultures, hawks and eagles, etc.) need thermals gen-

erated by the sun's rays to hunt effectively (see FLIGHT) and therefore tend to leave their roosts later and return earlier than most other birds.

The sleeping/feeding rhythms of birds are not static schedules but change according to environmental factors. The same arctic species that must feed in darkness in the winter could be active constantly in the northern summer with twenty-four hours of daylight. Yet they do have regular sleeping periods—though these tend to be shorter or more sporadic than their winter sleeps. As noted, many waterbirds feed and roost with the tides.

These examples raise the question of how birds know when they are supposed to do what. There is some good evidence that specific light intensities trigger the urge to wake or roost in many species. Many songbirds do not become active at the same hour each morning but alter their schedule according to the sun's. On cloudy days, songbird activity is conspicuously diminished, and heavy overcast often brings normally crepuscular/nocturnal night-herons out to feed. As we have seen, however, this model would not work for arctic species, nor does it explain sensitivity to tidal changes.

Experiments have shown that at least some birds have an "internal clock" that guides their behavior (at least temporarily) in the absence of all normal environmental stimuli (see CIRCADIAN RHYTHM; NAVIGATION). The question warrants much more study.

For more on birds asleep, see especially Skutch's monograph of that title (1993); see also ROOST.

SMELL. Fishermen and birders have known for ages that rancid cod livers or the like spread on the sea at a favorable place and season can rapidly attract flocks of seabirds from beyond the horizon and have assumed that they must be attracted by the smell. On the other hand, John James Audubon, once proved (at least to *his* satisfaction) that Turkey Vultures found his painting of an eviscerated sheep more attractive than a genuine "ripe" carcass that he had hidden nearby.

As the avian sense of smell became a matter of scientific investigation, ornithologists initially tended to correlate birds' ability to detect odor with the size of their olfactory bulb relative to that of the forebrain. The not-illogical assumption was that birds with big olfactory bulbs— notably kiwis, grebes, tube-nosed seabirds, New World vultures, rails and nightjars—were accomplished smellers and species with negligible smelling apparatus, e.g., songbirds, had little or no ability with this sense. In the 1980s, however, a range of experiments testing neurological responses to strong odors and the ability of various birds to find food or nest sites when the olfactory apparatus was deliberately impaired or a variety of smelly clues were provided have altered that assumption. We now know, for example, that

- The avian olfactory apparatus is in the same league with that of reptiles and mammals and that some birds can outperform these other classes in certain smelling tests. Storm-petrels for example can detect the gaseous emanations of krill from as far away as 25 km (Hutchinson and Wenzel 1980).
- The olfactory bulb correlation was not wrong, just insufficient, and the birds that were assumed on this basis to have "good noses" (see above) actually do. The converse is not true, however, and it is now assumed that small songbirds with apparently weak equipment use smell routinely as a detection device.
- Birds that have been proven to have a good sense of smell fall into some logical categories, e.g., birds that must search for food that is not readily visible over a wide area (seabirds, vultures), birds that must find food or nest sites in the dark or in dense habitats (kiwis, tubenoses, rails, nightjars) and species with special requirements that are detectable by smell (honeyguides and beeswax).
- At least some male ducks are attracted to sexual odors given off by females in the breeding season.
- In some instances smell is of prime importance in locating nest sites, e.g., storm-petrel burrows that must be located at night in dense forest. This homing function may also be more important that we thought in at least some land birds, e.g., pigeons.
- Birds can discriminate among plant as well as animals smells and use this ability to choose appropriate food items and nesting materials.

While there remains a consensus that for most birds, vision and hearing are more important than smell in living their lives successfully, it is now apparent that for some "guilds" the precise detection of odors is critical and that, overall, birds smell a lot better than we thought.

For how birds smell to humans, see ODOR.

SMITH, Gideon B., 1793–1867 (Smith's Longspur: *Calcarius pictus*). According to Gruson (1972–BIOGRAPHY), Smith was an early authority on the propagation of silkworms in the United States, a friend of Audubon's, and one of the many doctors prominent in the annals of American ornithology (see BAIRD; BIOGRAPHY). His medical career was marred by expulsion from the Baltimore Medical Society for "unprofessional conduct," but Gruson was unable to discover the reason for his disgrace.

SMOKE/FIRE (birds' reaction to). It is well documented that forest fires drive a great variety of organisms from their burning habitat, thereby exposing them to predation. It is also known that certain insects (e.g., some species of long-horned beetles (family Cerambycidae) are attracted to smoke, especially that generated by pine-woods blazes. Both the flight and the attraction phenomena are at times exploited for food by kites and other insectivorous birds, which catch and eat their prey on the wing.

Birds are also known to use smoke and even burning twigs or live flames in a way that resembles anting, i.e., to derive some sort of heat stimulation and possibly to help control ectoparasites. This playing with fire has led to more than one case of accidental arson. See ANTING.

It is not inconceivable that one of the above phenomena helped inspire the legend of the PHOENIX.

SNIPE. Standard English name for 19 members of the subfamily Scolopacinae (family Scolopacidae; order Charadriiformes or Ciconiiformes), which also includes the woodcocks. One species, the Common Snipe, breeds in North America and two others have occurred as accidental stragglers (see Appendix II).

Snipe are long-billed "shorebirds" of marshes, bogs (where they often breed), swamps, and muddy banks and fields. They are cryptically colored—often overlooked until flushed—and sometimes gather in groups traditionally known as "wisps." They probe for earthworms but also pick small insects and other invertebrates as well as plant matter from the surface of the ground. At dawn, at dusk, on moonlit nights and overcast days during the breeding season, male snipe perform a courtship flight consisting of a relatively direct ascent to as high as 300 feet and a zigzagging return to earth. On the descent the wings are folded, but the tail is spread wide and the outermost pair of rectrices moved beyond the penultimate pair, leaving a space at the outer ends (base) of the fan. Air rushing across these two last feathers makes them vibrate, which, in interaction with the flow of air over the wings, produces an eerie tremulous whistle called "winnowing" or "bleating."

There is a hunting season on Common Snipe, which test marksmen by their erratic zigzag flight when flushed.

The Common Snipe is nearly cosmopolitan in distribution (absent from Australasia) and in North America breeds from the Arctic to the northern United States and winters in most of the remainder of the continent as well as farther south.

"Snipe" derives from ancient Germanic roots referring to the elongate bill. In the days of the shorebird gunners many sandpiper species were known as "snipe" (e.g., "robin snipe" for dowitchers) and the root is retained in the many Swedish sandpiper names which end in -*snäppa.*

For family characteristics, see SANDPIPER; references in the Bibliography under SHOREBIRD.

SNOWCOCK. Standard English name for 5 species of large Eurasian partridges in the genus *Tetraogallus,* all of which inhabit high-altitude (above tree line) habitats from the Caucasus to the Himalayas. A population of the Himalayan Snowcock (*Tetraogallus himalayensis*) has been established as a game bird in the Ruby Mountains of Nevada.

SOARING. Sustained flight without wing flapping and therefore aided by some form of air movement such as thermals or updrafts. Pelicans, anhingas, storks, cranes, vultures, hawks, eagles, falcons, and gulls are among the bird groups that soar habitually in search of food or as a method of long distance migration. See FLIGHT; WING; MIGRATION; and Figs. 28 and 32.

SOCIAL PHENOMENA. See FLOCK; COLONY; ROOST; COMMENSALISM; DISPLAY; FOOD/FEEDING; MOBBING; MIGRATION; NEST.

SOCIETIES, ORNITHOLOGICAL. See ORNITHOLOGICAL SOCIETIES OF NORTH AMERICA.

SOFT PARTS. Exposed, unfeathered parts of a bird's body, including the bill, legs and feet, fleshy eye rings, facial skin, combs, wattles, and iris. In some species, soft-part colors can change rapidly—becoming more intense during courtship or the breeding season, fading to a subtler hue during the rest of the year. At any season, soft-part colors fade after death and therefore must be noted on the labels of museum specimens. The name is not very apt, since, excepting the skeleton, many of the "soft" parts are in fact among the hardest parts of the bird's body. Soft-part colors are sometimes useful field marks for identifying bird species.

SOFTWARE. Many identification and bird-finding guides, full-scale ornithologies (e.g., *The Complete Birds of the Western Palearctic,* Snow and Perrins, eds., 1999) as well as various forms of listing programs are now available on CD-ROM or other software. The most comprehensive projects incorporate hundreds of painting and photographs, video clips, recordings of songs and calls, as well as text on a disk or two. These products are listed by any good dealers in products for birders, e.g., ABA Sales.

SOLITAIRE. Standard English name for 11 species of thrushes in the genus *Myadestes* and 3 others in *Entomodestes* and *Cichlopsis* (family Turdidae or, following Sibley and Ahlquist [1990–SYSTEMATICS], subfamily Turdinae, family Muscicapidae; order Passeriformes). One species, the Townsend's Solitaire, breeds and winters in North America.

Solitaires are notably short-billed, long-tailed, somberly colored, arboreal thrushes. They feed mainly on insects—sometimes "flycatching"

Fig. 28. *Thermal soaring.* Many hawks, such as these soaring Red-tails, as well as other broad-winged birds (e.g., pelicans, storks, and cranes) gain almost effortless lift by seeking out ascending "bubbles" of hot air called thermals, which rise in a widening cone from the sun-warmed earth. Once they have gained the desired height in a swirling "kettle" formation, the birds leave the air mass and drift gradually in the direction they wish to follow. For a more detailed description of this technique, see FLIGHT.

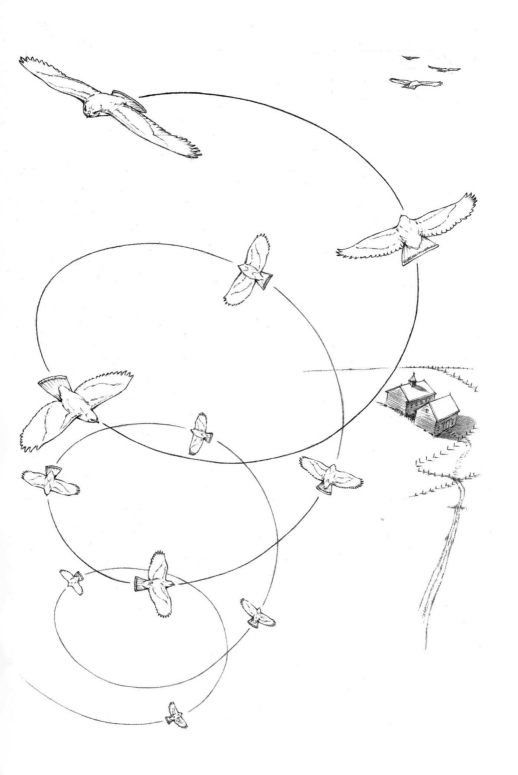

on the wing—and berries, but often sit with uncanny stillness in the shadows, all but invisible, though in plain view.

The solitaires are noted songsters, some of them uttering ethereal, ventriloquial, harmonic pipings that seem to ascend and descend the musical scale simultaneously. The song of the Townsend's Solitaire is neither preeminent nor untypical and is sometimes delivered in a song flight.

Our native solitaire nests in the coniferous forests (or sometimes above the tree line) of the western mountains, especially where there are rocky slopes. It descends to cedar canyons in the winter. The nest is a loose, rather messy cup made of coarse grasses, twigs, stems, and pine needles, lined with moss and finer plant fibers. It is placed in a tree stump, among roots, in an earthen niche, on a bank, or in a rock crevice—often highly inaccessible to human investigators.

The 3–5 (usually 4) eggs are white or pale blue, green, yellowish, or pinkish and densely speckled, splotched, and/or scrawled with brownish, purplish, reddish, and/or grayish.

The solitaires are essentially confined to the New World, and Townsend's is the only mainland species that is not of exclusively Neotropical distribution. It occurs along the western cordillera from Alaska to northern Mexico and east to Colorado and western Texas. Surprisingly, three species of *Myadestes* (that are not called solitaires) occur in the Hawaiian Islands; a fourth is now extinct.

"Solitaire" refers to the somewhat reclusive, solitary habits of these birds. The name is also applied to two species of flightless, turkey-sized, pigeon-like birds belonging to the same family as the Dodo (Raphidae; order Columbiformes). Like their more famous relative, these solitaires were endemic to small islands in the Indian Ocean and became extinct shortly after their first contact with people.

See references in the Bibliography under THRUSH.

SONG. Including all types of vocalizations made by birds, as well as mechanical or "instrumental" sounds produced by bill, feathers, or other body parts.

To the human sensibility, birdsong is mainly a source of aesthetic delight. It is a major component of our general concept of "nature"; it may even have given rise to our realization—not reliable in all cases—that we too can sing. For a very few people it has also provided a challenge, a biological mystery to be solved through patient observation and comparison. With the help of sophisticated technology, such as sound spectography, which allows us to see as well as hear sounds, many of the fundamental questions about birdsong have been answered and are summarized below. Many more await further investigation.

From a bird's perspective, of course, the sounds it makes have an altogether different significance. They are practical means of communication and expression, which for most species are as necessary for survival

as visual signals, such as distinctive color, pattern, and physical gesture. Bird sounds also help fill the "communications gap" left by most birds' less acute senses of smell, taste, and touch.

It is not surprising then that bird sounds are by now highly evolved. Although sound plays an important role in the lives of many insects, amphibians, and mammals, only human speech and perhaps the vocalizations of some cetaceans surpass bird sounds for vocal subtlety and complexity.

Not that all birds rely to the same degree on making and perceiving noises. The American vultures have no syrinx and storks lack crucial syrinx muscles (see How Birds Sing, below); therefore, except for the rare hiss or croak, members of these families live in silence. The auks, cormorants, and some other seabirds tend to be vocally reserved, though many tubenoses are given to weird nocturnal arias during the breeding season. Nevertheless, the vast majority of bird species rely to some extent on sounds that they produce, and versatility in this regard is by no means restricted to the suborder Oscines, the so-called songbirds.

In North America, this large grouping includes all of the perching birds (the order Passeriformes) except the flycatchers and our single becard. The Oscines are technically distinguished by their relatively numerous and intricately arranged syrinx muscles. This anatomical complexity, however, is not always reflected in the sounds produced. True, some of our finest songsters, e.g., the Hermit Thrush, belong to the Oscines, but so do the crows and jays. Conversely, virtuosi among the shorebirds, owls, and nightjars are not even in the same order as the "official" songbirds.

HOW BIRDS SING. Regardless of how the singers are labeled, virtually all vocal bird sounds are produced in an organ called the syrinx, which is unique to birds. The human voice is produced in the larynx, a modification of the upper part of the windpipe (trachea), which holds the vocal cords. In birds, the upper part of the trachea is also called the larynx but it contains no vocal cords and does not produce sound. In a few species the syrinx is located at the lower end of the trachea just above where the bronchi divide (an arrangement found only in suboscine species of the American tropics—none of which occurs in North America); or it is a paired structure, in effect two syringes, one modifying the top of each of the two bronchi (cuckoos, nightjars, and some owls); or, as is the case in the majority of birds, it involves both the trachea and the bronchi at their juncture. The syrinx can therefore be thought of structurally as a second larynx, lacking in humans, or functionally as the uniquely avian organ analogous to the human voice box (larynx).

Attached to the syrinx are pairs of muscles that control the quality of sound production. The songbirds (Oscines) have a maximum complement of syringeal muscles, up to 8 or 9 pairs (depending on which authority is counting), whereas most other birds make do with 1 or 2 pairs. Within the syrinx are elastic membranes that can be stretched and relaxed

both by air pressure and by the workings of the syringeal muscles. The membranes can also be manipulated within the air passages of the bronchi to regulate the amount of air passing through. When air is forced through the syrinx from the lungs, the membranes are made to vibrate, producing a sound in the way that a blade of grass held between the thumbs will "whine" if air is blown across it. The sound can be modified (1) by stretching or loosening the membranes (for higher and lower pitch); (2) by making them vibrate slowly or rapidly (for tonal qualities); (3) by altering the direction of the air passage (for loudness or softness); and (4) by stopping and starting air flow (for rhythm).

It will be noticed that birdsong, unlike human speech, is not inflected much (if at all) by resonating in nasal, mouth, or throat cavities. This is dramatized by the ability of many species to sing full, rich songs with their mouths full or their bills closed.

Perhaps the most remarkable feature of a bird's voice is the ability to sing through both bronchi simultaneously or separately. This twin voice is responsible for the harmonic sounds present in most songs and can also produce two distinct themes at the same time, giving songs like the Veery's their unearthly quality.

As with a wind instrument, the versatility of the syrinx depends on the diversity of means and combinations by which the state of the membrane and air passage can be modified. Therefore, there is a general correlation between the complexity of the syringeal muscles—which in effect "play" the syrinx with greater or lesser virtuosity—and the complexity of a bird's "music." In many cases vocal ability is more real than apparent—the negligible *stlick* of a Henslow's Sparrow does scant justice to the evolution of its syrinx. On the other hand, splendid sounds such as the Common Loon's wail or the trumpeting of cranes can be produced on comparatively simple instruments. It must be admitted, however, that the truly fabulous songsters—the thrushes, wrens, and some larks, icterids, and wood warblers—owe their renown to the Stradivarian subtlety of their vocal anatomy.

Cranes and swans have greatly elongated tracheas, which loop down into specially adapted hollows in the breastbone (sternum). Traditionally these have been supposed to function in voice production and have been likened to the tubes of instruments such as the trombone, but recent evidence (Greenewalt 1968) makes such theories dubious.

For production of nonvocal sounds, see below.

How Birds Acquire Their Songs. The answer to whether birds *inherit* their characteristic repertoire of sounds or *learn* them through imitation and practice appears to be: *both*. Early experiments involving birds hatched and reared in total isolation from any contact with their species have shown that with the passage of time these birds not only know as many songs and calls as their normal counterparts and know when to sing

them but also—at least to the ears of the experimenters—give them the same intonations heard in wild birds (Sauer 1954). Subsequent experiments on different species, however, indicate that young birds hatch knowing a sort of generalized song but must listen to adult birds singing it "correctly," and then imitate them, before they perfect their vocal technique. Such birds deprived of this learning experience may stick with the simple "baby song" or they may invent the missing elements and end up with a full, complex song, which, however, does not conform closely to the characteristic song of their species. If they are exposed when young to the song of a different species they may "adopt" its song or use elements of it to devise an original composition. How to make particular call notes (see definitions of song vs. call below) may be more firmly fixed genetically at hatching, yet untutored individuals may not understand in what circumstances they should be used and must learn this from experience, i.e., by hearing other birds use them in the appropriate situation.

Given the different results obtained from experiments and the great diversity birds exhibit in other forms of behavior, it seems probable that the proportional influence of nature and nurture in song development varies significantly from species to species.

Passerines typically make "begging" sounds within the first couple of days after hatching, and the first generalized singing may begin as early as the 13th day in some species, but not for 8 weeks in others (see Nice 1943–PARENTAL CARE; Thorpe 1961). Young male Song Sparrows appear to advance gradually—during a period when they are exposed to the adult song of their species—from a nondescript warble to shorter phrases to a recognizable adult song. Males singing on territory their first spring may begin with a rather crude rendition, but improve noticeably as they listen to and conform with the songs of neighboring males. At least in some species, the entire vocal repertoire is completely acquired and "fixed" within the first year. Once this happens birds seem to have an infallible vocal memory and can, for example, reproduce their territorial songs precisely after a winter of silence or even if deafened.

Much important work has been published in recently on song development and learning, including neurobiological aspects; see especially Marler (1981, 1983), and Nottebohm and Kroodsma (1991).

WHY BIRDS SING. As a class, birds are perhaps the most vocal of animals. The majority of species have an elaborate vocabulary equaled by only a few gregarious mammals and conspicuously surpassed only by ourselves. Not long ago it would have seemed pointless to ask *why* birds sing. But since Darwin the inquisitive have been schooled to realize that the presence of such a conspicuous trait in many successful species must imply significant "reproductive advantage" since elaborate song seems to figure significantly in mate choice, sexual selection, and competition among males. That there must be advantages in making loud noises is

further urged by very apparent disadvantages. What better way, after all, to attract the attention of predators than to sing a lengthy song over and over from a prominent perch? As we shall see, some birdsongs seem to be purely expressive, serving no obvious function other than the expenditure of "emotional" energy, but overall the sounds made by birds confer the same broad advantage as human speech—the ability to efficiently communicate a wide range of essential information, all of which contributes to the "survivability" of an individual bird and its species.

Bird sounds, like other languages, take a variety of distinctive forms, which in many cases imply a particular usage. The major forms of vocalizations and their functions are as follows.

Song. Anyone who has paid any attention to the sounds birds make is aware of two broad categories of vocalization. The one we call "song" typically contains a series of different notes uttered in a cohesive sequence so that they form a characteristic phrase with a recognizable rhythm and "tune" like a line of music. Some songs, such as the abrupt *chebec* of the Least Flycatcher, don't fit this description very well but are still defined as songs because of their function.

Most of the birdsongs we hear are those of male birds advertising their presence on their territories to prospective mates and to potential rivals of their own sex and species (see PAIR FORMATION; TERRITORY). Neighboring males may engage in singing contests to establish their invisible boundary lines. They may "escalate" their song battles by adding aggressive motifs, but they almost always come to terms vocally without resorting to physical violence. Wandering males are also warned efficiently when they trespass on occupied territory. This territorial song usually continues through the breeding cycle and seems to cement the pair bond after mating. When a similar (or identical) song is sung by a male to communicate with its mate and serves no aggressive or advertising functions, it is sometimes distinguished as a "signal song."

Another type of song, usually very distinct in phrasing from the territorial/signal song, seems to be unrelated to the breeding cycle, but rather to be pure release of energy of the kind that Shelley attributed to his skylark. "Emotional-release songs" of this kind have been recorded for many passerine species. They usually happen at random; they may be accompanied by an "ecstasy flight" (not to be confused with territorial song flights characteristic of many open-country species); in some species (e.g., several tyrannid flycatchers), they are likely to be performed at twilight; but they may also be given at night during migration or on the wintering ground. They often contain many improvised elements. The function of this category of song is unclear. But even sober scientists, who eschew anthropomorphism by profession, acknowledge its expressive quality and have even suggested that it contains a germ of artistic invention (!).

In certain circumstances, birds also sing extraordinarily softly. This form of song may be simply a *sotto voce* rendition of the territorial song ("whisper song") or be completely distinct. The different variations are often lumped together as "subsongs" or "secondary songs" and are often lower in pitch and more extended as well as lower in volume than ordinary songs. Adult birds sometimes sing a whisper song in bad weather or during the heat of the day. The early warblings and hesitant imitations of adult songs sung by young birds (see above) and weak territorial songs sung by males that have yet to attain full gonadal development in spring are also categorized as subsongs.

Calls are typically brief, as befits their function of conveying immediate information within the routine activities of a bird's daily life. They consist of single "call notes," such as the familiar *snap* of the Common Yellowthroat, or a short phrase—rarely more than 5 notes—such as the *klew-klew-klew* of a Greater Yellowlegs.

There is a great variation among species in richness of call vocabulary. All birds are capable of producing some kind of call, if only a hiss or grunt elicited under the direst stress. Many species (e.g., grebes, herons) have no true song as defined above, but produce a fair diversity of calls, especially on the breeding grounds. The precise import of each of these sounds has not been defined for many species, but some of them clearly serve a function not unlike that of signal songs. Songbirds are the most articulate, with more than 20 distinct vocalizations recorded for several species.

The distinction between a long call (the bugling call of a Herring Gull) and a short song (Kiskadee) is best defined by function. Among the commonest functions of calls are defense, warning, distress, begging (by nestlings), flock cohesion (e.g., on migration), identification of a food source (e.g., in foraging birds), gathering (e.g., by parents of precocial broods), and comfort. Within these broad categories there may be two or more distinct calls appropriate to slightly different situations. For example, a number of bird species give a soft, hard-to-place "seeping" call that alerts nearby birds to a passing hawk without drawing attention to the caller's location. The same species, however, may utter a loud scold to warn of a perched owl or cat and rally birds in the vicinity to "mob" it (see Fig. 19).

Certain calls may be used exclusively by birds of a certain age or sex, or in highly specific situations (e.g., for maintaining contact within a migratory flock), or, like the hawk or mobbing call, they may be used and recognized among many different species.

Though experience may be required to learn the precise "etiquette" of using some specific calls, the ability and inclination to make and respond to most calls is innate. This helps to explain the instantaneous response to an alarm call given among a flock of birds feeding in the open. Blackbirds and starlings, for example, are frequently seen to rise as if linked to a single nervous system, close into tight formation, and dodge erratically in

unison even when no apparent threat exists, as if to be safe rather than sorry (see FLOCK).

WHEN AND HOW OFTEN BIRDS SING

Season. Whereas calls tend to be uttered "as needed," song is under the influence of the hormonal rhythms of the breeding cycle and therefore has a pronounced seasonality. In most species, full male territorial song begins shortly (rarely immediately) after arrival on the breeding ground, wanes briefly during the mating period, picks up again after copulation, drops off during incubation, then picks up again immediately after the young hatch continuing through their "sensitive" period, and finally stops altogether as a bird's reproductive system enters its dormant phase in late summer/early fall. Of course, there are departures in many cases from this basic pattern. Snow Buntings and Brown Thrashers, for example, apparently stop singing altogether after mating is established, whereas a number of species show undiminished enthusiasm throughout the breeding cycle.

A few species—e.g., Northern Mockingbird, Carolina Wren, Northern Cardinal—sing regularly throughout the year, especially in the southern parts of their ranges. This is true of many species that stay on their breeding territories year round. Partial, muted, and/or infrequent songs are given by some males (1) after the pre-basic (post-nuptial) molt, (2) on migration, and (3) on the breeding grounds before the territorial drive has reached full throttle.

Time of Day. The "dawn chorus" of birdsong is familiar to anyone who is awake that early or who reads romantic poetry. The hour around sunrise on a clear morning during the breeding season is likely to contain the voices of all the resident species of a given locality. In some cases dawn songs are given more rapidly and/or frequently than normal, which adds a sense of extra enthusiasm to the performance.

There is a close correlation between when birds start and stop singing and the light level. This varies from species to species and according to weather conditions (see below).

There is also a "dusk chorus" during which birds are generally more songful than at midday, though less spectacularly so than at sunrise. A number of species have a distinctive "evening song." Many thrushes sing such variations beginning after sunset and continuing into darkness; tyrant flycatchers and swallows have a special predawn song; and, as already noted, some species of flycatchers add an exuberant song flight to their evensong that is not normally performed at other times of day.

Night singing is characteristic of most owls and nightjars, and again there is often a notable intensification of effort near dawn and dusk. The American Woodcock is a crepuscular songster—the males beginning their nuptial ritual well after sunset but continuing till midnight only when the moon provides enough light to trigger their urge to perform and resuming

in predawn hours. A few day singers regularly sing at night as well—the famous nightingale is supreme in this category. Its North American counterpart is the Northern Mockingbird (though in the modern suburb its efforts are probably more likely to be associated with insomnia than with romance). Night singing is also typical of other mimids, and marsh and grassland sparrows (Emberizidae) and Marsh and Sedge Wrens. Occasionally during the breeding season, other species will give out with a nighttime "emotional song" (see above) that bears little or no resemblance to their day songs. Thoreau's mysterious "nightsinger" turned out to be an Ovenbird demonstrating this phenomenon.

Weather. Because they reduce light levels, clouds obscuring the sun tend to retard and diminish the dawn chorus and hasten the end of evening songs. However, they also ameliorate the heat of midday, when many birds seek shade and stop singing or murmur a whisper song. A cloudy day, then, tends to have a more even level of song throughout.

Wind and precipitation can shut off birdsong completely if heavy enough, but there is considerable tolerance for low levels of both. There are a few recorded instances of very specific responses to particular weather conditions. Tinbergen (1939) recorded that male Snow Buntings stop singing as soon as snow begins to fall, and he interpreted this behavior as a response to the possibility that the birds' food source would soon be covered, a signal that they should therefore stop singing and start feeding. By contrast, spring snowstorms often stimulate song in recently arrived migrants, which apparently sing as a redirected activity (see REDIRECTION).

Number of Songs. The Red-eyed Vireo, with its short phrase uttered seemingly without pause through the day, appears to hold the North American record for most songs sung per unit of time: 22,197 in 10 hours (de Kiriline 1954). Other such patiently gathered statistics indicate that the norm for passerine species may be closer to 1,000–2,500 songs per day. Birds involved in disputes over territorial boundaries sing more frequently than more "secure" members of the same species and unmated birds sing more frequently than mated ones. Therefore, there is individual variation in number of songs sung per day as well as the obvious variations caused by weather and the breeding rhythms.

WHERE BIRDS SING. Territorial songs must, of course, be heard over a sizable range to attract a mate and warn off trespassers, and audibility is affected not only by the volume and carrying quality of the song but also by the location of the singer. In most species, males choose several conspicuous singing perches within their territories from which they habitually broadcast their message. These may be the tops of high trees, shrubs, rocks, or telephone poles, depending on the habitat of the species. Some species that nest in tundra or other types of flat, open country (e.g., many sandpipers, most longspurs, Horned Lark) compensate for the lack of

good song posts by singing from the air; these territorial song flights are performed as regularly as their earthbound counterparts and are not to be confused with "ecstasy songs" described above.

Not all birds sing from a conspicuous open perch. Some arboreal species (e.g., vireos, tanagers), birds of the forest floor (e.g., Ovenbird), and those that favor dense cover (e.g., wrens, Mourning Warbler) often remain within their preferred habitat while singing, but their songs tend to be notably loud and/or carrying. Thrushes, which may sing either from an open perch or from deep within the forest, have a wide volume range and may adjust it to suit their location.

Regardless of whence territorial song issues, there appears to be a rough correlation between its range and the average territory size of the species singing—i.e., a song emanating from the center of a territory tends to be audible roughly to the boundaries of the territory and no farther. It follows that birds with smaller/larger territories should have quieter/louder songs (or vice versa), and while there is some evidence that this tends to be so, the great variations in territory size and song volume among different individuals and differences in habitat structure and resulting acoustics often obscure the validity of this generalization.

Another tendency that appeals to human logic is that males usually sing at some distance from their nest. However, males of a few species (e.g., Warbling Vireo, Black-headed Grosbeak) have been observed giving a full song while sitting on the nest—a practice that is hard to rationalize in terms of survival value.

VARIATION IN SONG. Even excluding the few bird sounds that the human ear cannot discern (see HEARING), the variety of utterances of which birds as a class are capable is sufficiently impressive. Consider for a moment the range in pitch, volume, meter, tune, harmonics, and length represented by the Common Loon's wail, the various honkings of geese and quackings of ducks, the scream of an eagle, the cluckings of gallinaceous birds, the "pumping" of the American Bittern, the trumpeting of cranes, the clattering of rails, the pipings of shorebirds, the hootings of owls and doves, the explosive name-calling of nightjars, the twitterings of swifts and hummingbirds, the staccato exclamations of woodpeckers, and the apparently infinite assortment of lisps, buzzes, chirps, tweets, and warbles by which passerines express themselves. Like other characteristics, these vocal variations have evolved according to adaptation and selection pressure over eons (see NATURAL SELECTION), but it should not be assumed that the course of vocal evolution is always in the direction of greater complexity. It is true that the relatively "recent" songbirds have the most highly developed vocal organs (see How Birds Sing, above), but many nonsongbirds with relatively simple vocal instruments nevertheless make elaborate sounds, just as there are songbirds that are practically songless in spite of their highly evolved "voice box."

Extent of vocal repertoire is another obvious variation among different species. We have already seen that some species are normally mute or nearly so, while a vocabulary of more than 20 distinct songs and calls is probably not unusual among songbirds. Many of the sounds made by the more articulate species are very similar or used relatively infrequently in situations that humans seldom observe. Therefore, only the student of a species' life history or of birdsong is likely to become aware of the full scope of a species' vocal capabilities. Even skilled and experienced bird-watchers may distinguish only a single call for many species or, in the case of songbirds, one territorial song and one frequently used call. Many wood warblers have two or more distinct territorial songs that are sung by all males of the species; typically an "accented" song is sung during the intense period of defending a territory and attracting a mate and is replaced with a more rambling, unaccented song after a domestic routine has been established. Within genera and families, there tends to be much divergence in song pattern, which no doubt aids recognition and reproductive isolation in closely related forms. There are also cases of convergence of songs between two unrelated species. Thus, the Warbling Vireo sounds more like a Purple Finch than like any other North American member of its own family.

Different geographical races often sing distinctive variations of the basic song of their species—one often hears birdwatchers from out of state say, "That doesn't sound like *our* Song Sparrow"—and it is not unusual to detect different "dialects" even among different populations of a single race. The difference between "song races" can be so great that members of one race do not recognize and respond to some calls made by the other.

The degree to which a different race alters or expands its vocal repertoire sometimes depends on other species with which it coexists. If it does not have to distinguish itself by song from other closely related species, it may evolve a range of musical variations, some of which may resemble by chance the song of a related species; but if a near relative with a similar song occupies the same range, it may be obliged to give a very typical, "conservative" rendition of its species' song as a reinforcement of reproductive isolation.

In contrast to males of different races or populations, males within a single population tend to sing very much like their neighbors and indeed imitate each other in defending their territories; young birds establishing new territories generally fall in with the local dialect.

Despite this tendency toward similarity of song among the members of a population, sensitive recording devices and spectrographic analysis have revealed that relatively subtle *individual variations* of the "basic" song seem to be more the rule than the exception. A single male bird may sing more than 50 versions of his territorial song (Borror 1961); he may

share *some* of these variations with other males of the same population; he will tend to sing some versions more frequently than others; and his offspring will not inherit his variations.

On the whole, individual variations are seldom obvious enough to attract the attention of the casual listener. However, those who listen habitually to the songs of common species in their yard may notice a change in phrasing or the absence of one or more striking "motifs" as generations of singers succeed each other.

The fact that individual birds routinely invent new versions of the basic song patterns they inherit raises some provocative questions about learning, creativity, and language, the more so in the case of "talented" vocal mimics (see below).

Female Song. Among female birds as a whole, the singing of a full (i.e., territorial-type) song is unusual and it has even been demonstrated that there is some causal relationship between sex hormones and the development of the syrinx. Females that *do* sing tend to do so much less frequently than the males and only in specific situations.

It is now clear, however, that female song is by no means rare. It is practiced in some form by species of thrushes, mimids , dippers, wrens, orioles, tanagers, finches, and the Wrentit, and in a few species (e.g., Northern Cardinal, Rose-breasted Grosbeak, several thrushes) the female's song is equal to her mate's in complexity and intensity.

As might be expected, female Northern Phalaropes (and perhaps the other two species) give a display "song" on the breeding grounds, while the male's vocal repertoire is restricted to terse calls.

Multiple Vocalizations. A few bird species habitually sing duets, either giving the same phrases simultaneously or alternating *different* phrases in such close synchronization that the effect is of a single "antiphonal song." Duetting seems to be commonest among species living in dense habitats (e.g., many tropical wrens) and may be a means of reinforcing pair bonds in birds that often lose sight of each other in thick vegetation. Only a few North American bird species are known to sing duets, among them the Northern Bobwhite, California and Gambel's Quail, Carolina Wren, Red-winged Blackbird, and Brown-headed Cowbird (see Brackbill 1961; Stokes and Williams 1968). See also DUETTING.

Family groups of Plain Chachalacas engage in cackling choruses, especially at dawn and dusk. Voice quality varies in this species according to age and sex (Delacour and Amadon 1973–GALLINACEOUS BIRDS), and when mature males and females and young birds "sing" together, a distinct (though unpredictable) antiphonal rhythm emerges.

Some species of swifts that nest in colonies engage in communal flights accompanied by intermittent bursts of simultaneous twittering.

Roosts of starlings, blackbirds, and other communal species often produce a high level of noise, especially when individuals are flying in and

settling down for the night, but whether we are hearing an intentional "concert" or simply the accumulation of many individual calls is hard to judge. On the other hand, it seems clear that the chorus of calls produced by migrating flocks results from individuals contributing to flock cohesion.

The territorial song of a single male sometimes "sets off" neighboring males; in colonial species, e.g., gulls, this may result in a choral effect.

VOCAL MIMICRY. As we have seen, many birds "perfect" their species' song by imitating their parents or other adult birds of their own kind and are also capable of improvising individual song variations. This kind of learning and ability reaches its greatest avian development in the so-called vocal mimics—birds that can (and habitually do) reproduce the sounds made by other birds and animals, including human speech, and even the "inanimate" sounds of the modern world. The phenomenon in its several variations has long been a rich source of fanciful speculation; its biological "hows" and "whys" come much less readily, however, and are still far from completely understood.

Forms of Vocal Mimicry. Two types of vocal mimicry can be distinguished fairly sharply on a circumstantial basis. The first type consists of "natural" mimics such as the Northern Mockingbird and the European Starling. Such species use imitated sounds along with motifs characteristic of their species to create a unique individual song, the functions of which are analogous (with some differences; see Why, below) to normal territorial songs. This type of mimic may incorporate train whistles or other nonbird sounds and can, if kept in captivity, imitate human speech, but normally has significant nonimitative components in its song as well. The composition and virtuosity of these songs varies widely among individuals and to some extent among different geographical populations.

The other type of avian mimics are the "talking birds." Certain members of the parrot family and the Hill (or Talking) Mynah (*Gracula religiosa*) are in such wide demand as pets because of their imitative talent that their populations are subject to significant pressure. Unlike the first type of mimic, talking birds *never* (as far as is known) use their mimetic faculty in the wild.

Blue Jays are known to imitate the calls of hawks and crows in the wild, though these are not incorporated into any kind of song; and other corvids, e.g., ravens, crows, and magpies, readily learn to talk in captivity.

The ability and/or inclination to mimic varies widely among species. Northern Mockingbirds, for example, are much more versatile and enthusiastic imitators than the other North American representatives of their family. One mocker may appropriate 30 or more different sounds from other birds as well as ones from other sources; and it has been suggested (Borror 1964) that northern mockers use more mimicry in their songs than southern.

Among talking birds, the Gray Parrot (*Psittacus erithacus*) of Africa, the Yellow-headed Amazon (*Amazona ochrocephalus*) of Middle America, and the little Budgerigar (*Melopsittacus undulates*) of Australia are widely known as superior mimics, while many other psittacids show little or no such ability. The Hill Mynah, which can not only repeat human words but also give a very accurate rendering of a person's particular inflections and tone of voice, is probably supreme in this category. Many other mynahs and starlings and at least some crows exhibit some degree of imitative proficiency in captivity, though only a few (e.g., the European Starling) use this ability in the wild. It should be noted here that the cruel practice of "splitting the tongues" of captive birds to enhance their speaking ability does nothing to achieve this end (see How Birds Sing, above) and in fact will cause the pet's death.

How. A great many, if not all, songbirds show some skill in vocal mimicry in their ability to learn the nuances of their species' song (see How Birds Acquire Their Songs, above). Moreover, a number of species that we do not normally think of as mimics have been heard to sing notes or phrases of other birds in subsongs, which, however, are dropped when they sing their full territorial songs. In rare instances (Thomas 1943; Short 1966) wild birds not known as vocal mimics have learned to sing the songs of a different species (in the same family) in place of their own song. Taken as a whole, these records begin to suggest that the ability and inclination to imitate sounds is widely developed in birds, albeit in varying degrees. If we add the well-documented fact that many birds routinely "compose" individual song variations based on motifs in their species' basic song, it is only a short jump to mockingbirds, which use imitation of other sounds *and* innovative composition together to make up their characteristic song type. Another example of "social induction" of song is potentially "outnumbered" Blue-winged and Golden-winged Warblers singing each other's songs where their territories come in contact.

The best of the "natural" mimics have the greatest possible number of syringeal muscles (8–9 pairs), so that their physical ability to reproduce a wide variety of bird sounds does not seem very surprising.

The imitation of human speech, however, is a different matter. Our ability to produce a wide range of vowel sounds is attributable to the ample resonating chambers of our throat, mouth, and nose; and our tongue, teeth, and other mouth structures give us considerable versatility in producing consonants. Birds, by contrast, seem to have few of these speech-producing modifications, and even animals, such as the great apes, which seem far better equipped in this department, never utter anything that resembles a word.

Some talking birds resolve this problem in part by "faking it," i.e., using changes in pitch to simulate the variations of vowel and consonant sounds. In addition, human vocal coaches can often hear their bird say

the things they have taught them with much greater clarity than an impartial auditor. These two factors in combination explain why "Budgie" says "Good morning, gorgeous," as clear as a bell to Aunt Lulu while all you can hear is a jumble of psittacine squawks and gargles. Nevertheless, Hill Mynahs and other species can reproduce human speech with extraordinary fidelity, emitting vowels and consonants that are unmistakable even under audiospectrographic analysis. Exactly how they do this with their limited equipment is still poorly understood.

Why. Since many of the favorite talking birds never mimic any sounds in the wild and begin imitating speech only when confined in close contact with humans and away from their own species, it would seem that "talking" may be a form of social adjustment. Parrots are known to "pine" and die if deprived of association with their fellows, and talking may be a way of creating a necessary attachment to their captors. Once this is accepted, it is easy to understand apparently intelligent uses of language, such as speaking to people they "like," saying, "Come back here!" when you leave the room, and making other apt or amusing comments.

The explanation for "natural" mimicry is not so apparent. If anything, the inherent random quality seems to diminish some of the functions of territorial song. It has been suggested (Marshall 1950) that many mimics live in dense habitats and, in effect, need more sound for attraction and defense to compensate for less visibility; but does a bird need to mimic other species to sing loud and/or long? Perhaps a more plausible theory (Thorpe 1961) is that mimicry gives an edge in developing highly individual sounds that would help in *individual* recognition and thus reinforcement of pair bonds in dense habitats. What then of the open–country mimics? Baylis in Kroodsma and Miller (1982) suggests that mimics are responding to territorial rivals of different species and attempt to protect their resources by creating an "array" of apparent defenders—the so-called beau geste hypothesis. Perhaps the best explanations of the mimetic impulse is that it a form of showing off to a prospective mate or to put it in the jargon of behavioral ecology a "demonstration of fitness." The most talented Northern Mockingbird males can imitate at least 150 sounds and do so mainly in the context of attracting and keeping mates (including in the midst of the reproductive act!). And the largest repertoires seem to translate into the greatest mating and reproductive success (Derrickson and Breitwisch 1992).

Finally, it should be mentioned that at least one appreciative listener has advanced the attractive theory that some mimics imitate sounds for "positive self-reinforcement"—that is, in essence, for fun.

NONVOCAL SOUNDS. The syrinx is not the only sound-producing mechanism available to birds. Even species such as the vultures and storks, which essentially lack a syringeal sound system, nevertheless can produce a few rudimentary sounds from the throat. The American Bittern,

NONVOCAL SOUNDS

Species	Sound	Function
Black-footed Albatross	Bill snapping by individuals and "billing" by pairs	Courtship
Red-throated Loon	"Rushing train" noise made by wings when gliding down	Courtship flight
Grebes, several species	Bill "fencing"	Courtship
Great (and other) Cormorants	"Gurgles" and other sounds made by vibration of throat pouch	Courtship
Magnificent Frigatebird	Bill clacking, perhaps using inflated throat pouch as a resonator	Male on nest; part of courtship (?)
Herons: most North American species	Bill snapping and/or mutual "billing"; Great Blue makes (nonvocal?) gurgling	Courtship
American Bittern	"Swallows air" and releases, making 2- to 3-note "pumping" or "stake-driving" sound	Territorial "song" (?)
Wood Stork	Hissing ("fizzing"); bill nibbling and clacking; loud wing "whoosh" in flight, esp. on downswoop	Nest ritual; courtship; incidental
White Ibis	Bill snapping	Courtship
Waterfowl: many species, esp. swans, whistling ducks, and goldeneyes ("whistlers")	Whistling noise from air through wings in flight; variable in pitch and volume; also foot splashing	Courtship
Ruddy Duck	"Bubbling" and other water sounds and perhaps clucking notes produced with aid of tracheal air sac	Courtship

NONVOCAL SOUNDS (continued)

Species	Sound	Function
American vultures	Hisses, grunts, cooing, etc., from throat and mouth	Alarm, threat, etc.
Spruce Grouse	Wing "whirring"	Courtship
Ruffed Grouse	"Drumming" sound made by wings beating rapidly over (but not touching) breast	Courtship, but heard year-round
Prairie chickens, and Sage, Sharp-tailed, and Spruce Grouse	Weird cooing, plopping, and booming sounds made with the aid of esophagus and air-sac system	Courtship: male lek display
Many gallinaceous species, e.g., pheasant	Notable, explosive whir or whistle on takeoff.	Surprise predators (?); incidental
Some rails	Esophageal (?) "pumping" sounds similar to American Bitterns' (see above)	Territorial "song" (?)
Pectoral (and other?) sandpiper species	"Booming" not unlike prairie chickens' made by pumping air in and out of esophagus	Courtship
American Woodcock	Soft twittering made by passage of air through modified outer 3 primaries	Made during ascent in males' territorial/courtship flight
Common Snipe	Stiffened outer pair of tail feathers held at right angle to body in steep descent; air passing over wings causes these feathers to vibrate, producing an intermittent, tremulous "winnowing" or "bleating" sound	Territorial/courtship flight

NONVOCAL SOUNDS *(continued)*

Species	Sound	Function
Auks, some species	Bill "fencing"	Nest ritual
Pigeons and doves, most species	Generally noisy flight	Incidental
Columba pigeons, including Common Pigeon	Wing clapping: explosive sound made by carpal area of wings meeting over back; bill sounds also recorded	Takeoff (predator surprise?); also part of courtship ritual
Greater Roadrunner	"Rattles" mandibles	Courtship (?)
Most owls	Bill snapping	Defense/threat
Long- and Short-eared Owls	Clap carpal joint of wings *below* body	Courtship flight and nest defense
Nightjars (known in Chuck-will's-widow and Poor-will)	Wing clapping	Courtship/territorial display
Common Nighthawk	"Blooming," like blowing over mouth of empty bottle, caused by air rushing through wings on sharp upswing	Courtship (?)
Hummingbirds (in general)	Clearly audible hum or whirring noise made by rapidly beating wings in normal flight	Incidental
Broad-tailed Hummingbird	Two outer primary tips of male modified to produce trill/rattle in flight	Courtship/territorial display
Rufous and Allen's Hummingbirds	Wing buzz or whine; Allen's modifies with tail bobbing and makes ripping noise at climax of courtship flight	Courtship

NONVOCAL SOUNDS *(continued)*

Species	Sound	Function
Most woodpeckers	Drumming noises with bill	Incidental while feeding but also using hollow logs, metal surfaces, or other "sounding boards" in courtship
Some species of waxwings, thrushes, crows, and finches	Various bill noises	Mostly associated with nest rituals
Many (most?) insectivorous birds	Bill snapping	Incidental while feeding

many grouse species, and Pectoral Sandpiper make their unique hooting sound by forcing air in and out of their inflating esophagus, greatly enhancing the distance over which these eerie sounds can be heard. Bills become percussion instruments when snapped or hit against each other; and the sounds made by air passing through feathers in different ways are wonderfully diverse (see, for example, WOODCOCK and SNIPE). Of course, some sounds made by birds are purely incidental. The whoosh made by the flapping of the wings of large birds and the audible snapping shut of a flycatcher's bill when it is feeding are simply by-products of routine behavior. But some wing and bill noises, as well as many other specialized sounds, have evolved—either in part or totally—as functional sounds, most often in association with courtship rituals.

North American species that produce significant nonvocal sounds are listed on pp. 744–747 along with the sounds they produce and their function.

LEARNING BIRDSONGS. All field guides make a heroic effort to teach the novice birdwatcher what various species sound like. Three methods are widely favored: (1) The rendering into words (or at least syllables) the sound of a song or call. Except for the "talking birds" (see Vocal Mimicry, above), birds are generally inept at forming vowels and consonants and this "verbalization" technique is therefore doomed to more or less fanciful approximation. Once you know what a Chestnut-sided Warbler sounds like, you may or may not be willing to concede that it "says" "I wish to see Miss Beecher." But it is extremely difficult to apply "Skip-teer Rea-cheer-for You, Cheet-weigh get-yuWhip . . . ReeChee-raYeer-chWoo" or the like (Spot-breasted Wren; Davis 1972) to a bird with whose song you are unfamiliar. (2) Only slightly more helpful are attempts to *explain* what a bird sounds like: a thin, nasal, but "airy" trill or rattle ending in four melodious but eerie notes. This may be compared to the song of another species with which the novice is, of course, also unfamiliar. (3) Finally there is the "sonogram," which shows us indubitably what a birdsong *looks* like—even parts of it that are inaudible to the human ear. Except for bird-minded audiospectrographers, however, no one has yet been able to apply these fascinating, meticulously graphed runes to learning what birds *sound* like.

In fairness, all of these methods become more useful as the novice bird listener gains some experience—even a sonogram will help you confirm that the insect-type trill you have just heard is more likely to originate in a Prairie Warbler than a Barred Owl.

Excellent tapes and CDs including all North American birdsongs (with variations in some cases) are now available (see the Bibliography under RECORDING OF BIRD SOUNDS for a list of titles) and are invaluable aids to learning songs. However, by far the best method of acquiring this arcane expertise is to search out the singer of every song you don't recog-

nize. The effort will help fix the sound in your memory, and you will have eliminated at least one machine from your effort to make contact with nature.

The wealth of literature on birdsong befits the intricacy and fascination of the subject. Some of the classic, most interesting, and/or most readable books and papers are listed in the Bibliography.

SONGBIRD. Widely used English name for the Passeri (Oscines), the largest suborder of the Passeriformes, or "perching birds." All North American perching birds except for the tyrant flycatchers and the Rose-throated Becard are "songbirds."

SONOGRAM (or audiospectrogram). Written reproduction of birdsong (or other sounds) made by a stylus that transfers the complex patterns of pitch and frequency from a recording to a moving belt of graph paper. The result is an interrupted series of smudges that purport to show what bird-song sounds like; in reality they show what birdsong *looks* like and are of limited value for field use except for audiospectrographers and a few birdwatcher-musicians. See, however, J. C. Beaver, "Sonograms as Aids in Bird Identification," *American Birds* (1976), 30:899. For other methods of learning birdsongs, see SONG.

SORA. Standard English name for a single species of short-billed rail, *Porzana carolina,* which breeds exclusively in North America. Short-billed rails in this and other genera are for the most part called "crakes." The name is a mystery; possibly of Native American origin. See RAIL; CRAKE.

SOUTHEASTERN ARIZONA. In birders' terms, the highlands from Tucson south, including the Santa Catalina, Santa Rita, Huachuca, and Chiricahua Mountains and the intervening arid lowlands. An impressive variety of "Mexican" bird species reach the northernmost extent of their range in this region (including adjacent New Mexico) and occur nowhere else in North America, except in southwestern Texas (see BIG BEND), where, however, they are generally much less common and less easily found. Among these specialties are Zone-tailed, Gray, and Common Black Hawks, Montezuma Quail, Flammulated and Whiskered Screech-Owls, Magnificent, Blue-throated, Violet-crowned, White-eared, and Broad-billed Hummingbirds, Elegant Trogon, Arizona Woodpecker, Rose-throated Be-card, Sulphur-bellied Flycatcher, Thick-billed Kingbird, Dusky-capped Flycatcher, Northern Beardless-Tyrannulet, Greater Pewee, Mexican Jay, Mexican Chickadee, Bridled Titmouse, Brown-throated Wren, Olive and Red-faced Warblers, Painted Redstart, Yellow-eyed Junco, and Rufous-winged and Five-striped Sparrows. In addition to these "highlights,"

southeastern Arizona has a fine variety of other "western" birds, an abundant and cooperative avifauna generally, and a vastly interesting flora and fauna apart from birds, and enjoys a superb climate and some of the most pleasing landscapes in North America.

A number of place names come readily to the lips of birders who visit the region, among them *Mount Lemmon:* 9,185-foot peak of the Catalinas with a paved road traversing four life zones to the top; *Madera Canyon* in the Santa Ritas: trogon, hummers, and other pine-oak birds; *Patagonia:* a small town about 15 miles north of the Mexican border and the region of excellent roadside birding surrounding it; Patagonia is also the "address" of The Nature Conservancy's Sonoita Creek Sanctuary: a fine patch of arid scrub and gallery woodland, which contains most of the lowland bird specialties of the region along with a great many others; *Ramsey Canyon* in the Huachucas: best known for The Nature Conservancy's Mile Hi Ranch, where dozens of hummingbird feeders are maintained for the benefit of hundreds of hummingbirds and visitors; *Cave Creek Canyon* in the Chiricahuas: home of the American Museum's Southwest Research Station and a locality from which virtually all of the southeastern Arizona specialties (desert and montane) can be seen within a 5-mile radius.

See Taylor (1995–BIRD FINDING).

SOUTH TEMPERATE ZONE. That part of the earth south of the Tropic of Capricorn and north of the Antarctic Circle. It includes the southern half of South America, the southern tip of Africa, the southern half of Australia, and all of New Zealand. A small percentage of the bird species that breed in the STZ migrate north to the tropics for the southern winter; of these only a few pelagic species, e.g., the Greater Shearwater, Wilson's Storm-Petrel, regularly reach the NORTH TEMPERATE ZONE.

SPARROW. Standard English name for a broad assortment of "finches" in at least two families. Twenty-three species of OLD WORLD SPARROWS—including the House Sparrow (*Passer domesticus)* together with the Petronias and Snowfinches, make up the family Passeridae (or, following Sibley and Ahlquist [1990–SYSTEMATICS], the subfamily Passerinae). It is also applied to about 60 species of generally drab New World finches in the family Emberizidae or subfamily Emberizinae, family Fringillidae).

The New World sparrows are analogous in many ways to the Old World emberizine buntings and their general characteristics are considered under SPARROW-BUNTINGS. For a sorting out of the complex nomenclature and taxonomy of the "finches," see FINCH.

The New World sparrows are mostly birds of open habitats—tundra, desert, grassland, and shrubby savanna—but a number of species are forest birds and several prefer fresh or salt marshes.

They achieve their greatest diversity in North America and a number of species are endemic to the Nearctic region. Several species range conti-

nentwide, and most are migratory, but the majority also winter at least partially in North America.

"Sparrow" comes initially from the Indo-European word *sper,* meaning "flutter," thence to German and then Old English *spearwa,* meaning any small (fluttering) bird.

SPARROW-BUNTING (and allies). Collective name of convenience for the family Emberizidae as defined by the *AOU Checklist,* 7th edition (1998), to include the grassquits, seedeaters, West Indian bullfinches, flowerpiercers, brush-finches, towhees, New World sparrows, juncos, longspurs, Old World buntings, and a variety of other "finches." In this classification system there are 60 North American species, including 11 rare or accidental visitors. Alternatively "sparrow-buntings" may be used (following Sibley and Ahlquist 1990–SYSTEMATICS) to refer to the tribe Emberizini (subfamily Emberizinae, family Fringillidae), comprising 157 species worldwide (57 including 8 vagrants in North America) and including only the towhees, New World sparrows, juncos, Old World buntings, longspurs, and Lark, Snow and McKay's Buntings.

For an account of the complex taxonomy and nomenclature of these and other "finches," see FINCH.

North American sparrow-buntings, like other "finches," have conical bills adapted for crushing seeds, but these never reach the massive proportions seen in some of the CARDINAL-GROSBEAKS and FRINGILLID FINCHES and in some cases (e.g., Seaside Sparrow) they are relatively long and slender. The birds vary widely in size (4½–9½ inches) and form, and while many are boldly patterned and even highly colored (e.g., Eastern Towhee), they never exhibit the brilliant reds and blues that appear in the plumage of the cardinal-grosbeaks or cardueline finches.

Most emberizine finches are ground and bush birds, hopping and scratching energetically in leaf litter, grass, or bare soil or foraging in low shrubbery for food, though a few species favor dense underbrush, wooded edges, or the forest floor. The mainstay in the diet of most of these finches is seeds, but all species at least supplement their vegetarian regimen with a significant proportion of insects and other invertebrate food. Fruit is also a regular food item of many species, and the large towhees even take small salamanders, lizards, and snakes. The Seaside and Sharp-tailed Sparrows feed *primarily* on invertebrates, including many aquatic forms such as amphipods and crabs, and this departure from typical sparrow behavior probably explains their notably long, narrow bills.

Many open-country sparrow-buntings nest exclusively on the ground, and even those that favor shrubland or woodland rarely nest higher than 5 feet (exceptional Song and White-crowned Sparrow nests placed 25 and 35 feet in trees, respectively, have been recorded). The emberizine nest is usually the typical songbird cup, made loosely or compactly of small sticks, coarse grasses, bark strips, dead leaves, and the like

and lined with hair, fur, fine plant fibers and/or down, and occasionally some feathers. A number of ground nesters (Savannah Sparrow, Lark Sparrow, juncos, Chestnut-collared Longspur) make a shallow hollow in the earth and line it or fill it with a frail, rudimentary cup. Sharp-tailed Sparrows weave a semi-dome structure around the stems of emergent sedges or rushes.

The sparrow-buntings lay between 2 and 8 eggs per clutch, the average for most species being 3–5 or fewer. The eggs vary by species from pale white to light blue/green and from immaculate to densely speckled or prominently blotched or scrawled with reddish/brownish or purplish/blackish.

Some emberizines have fairly musical songs with a strong cadence and bell-like quality; others utter barely perceptible insectile buzzes and clicks.

The sparrow-buntings achieve their greatest diversity in the Holarctic region, but also occur in South America, Africa, and southern Asia. They are absent (except for introduced members of European species) from Australasia. In North America, this subfamily breeds from the high Arctic to the subtropical extremities of southern Texas and Florida. Many species range continentwide; the great majority are migratory but winter largely (or wholly) in North America and in the main move no farther south than the central plateau of Mexico.

For name derivations, see SPARROW; BUNTING.

SPECIATION (spee-she-AY-shun or spee-see-AY-shun). The process by which new life forms evolve from those already in existence. More specifically, the separation of a population of organisms into two or more distinct populations that eventually become unable to interbreed.

All plants and animals—including birds and humans—have always been, and continue to be, ever-changing. The "opportunity" to change is offered by the regular occurrence of gene mutation, which is controlled, according to its survival value (or lack of it), by NATURAL SELECTION. In a reproductively integrated population of a species any advantageous mutation that arises in an individual tends to be acquired in time through interbreeding by the whole population. In this case, the species in question changes in character over time but it remains a single entity made up of like individuals (phyletic evolution). However, if two or more populations of a species become separated from one another, the characteristics of each begin to change in their own unique ways, and because the isolated populations no longer have the opportunity to interbreed, new mutations cannot be shared. Differences between separate populations may begin as barely discernible tendencies, e.g., a greater number of slightly paler, longer-billed individuals in one population than in another. If the tendencies continue in different directions, the populations will become

readily recognizable races or subspecies—one long-billed and pale, the other short-billed and dark—but would still interbreed freely and successfully if the populations were reunited. As the populations continue to "grow apart," however, their "willingness" and ability to interbreed continue to decline, and when the sharing of genetic traits becomes impossible (or at least highly unlikely), the populations have evolved into distinct species. Though this process is called speciation, it begins, as we see, with individual variation and does not stop with the evolution of a new species. Each new species has the potential for continued divergence, and because much additional variation is possible, indeed, inevitable the process can continue up the phylogenetic ladder. The same "system" that produced that slightly paler, longer-billed individual was also responsible, as it were, for making birds from dinosaurs.

How FAST? Needless to say, speciation takes time. *Archaeopteryx* did not go to bed a reptile and wake up a bird. A traditional view of deep biological change (evolution) is that it takes place very gradually over eons, but some theorists (notably Stephen Jay Gould and Niles Eldridge 1972) have suggested that it can occur in (relatively) quick adaptive bursts, interspersed with long periods during which the organism in question remains stable genetically, a concept known as "punctuated equilibrium."

Of course, fundamental and complex changes, e.g., skeletal modifications or the transformation of scales into feathers, are long-term processes. But relatively superficial, yet conspicuous adaptive changes, e.g., in color and size, can be noticed within a few decades or less. House Sparrows, for example, which were first introduced into North America around 1850, have already evolved distinctive forms in response to different ecological influences in their transcontinental, arctic-to-tropics distribution.

How POPULATIONS BECOME ISOLATED. The geographical isolation (allopatry) of animal populations usually occurs in one of two ways: (1) through the colonization of oceanic islands or (2) through the separation of populations due to habitat fragmentation. A few specific phenomena can be mentioned:

Continental Drift. The separation of the continents from seabed expansion began with the breakup of the supercontinent Pangaea beginning around 200 million years ago, well before the appearance of the first birds about 150 million years ago. But early birds had evolved before the great southern continent Gondwanaland had split into what are now South America, Africa, and Australia. This could explain the presence of large flightless birds—rheas, ostriches and emus—descended from a common Gondwanaland ancestor—as distinct endemic species on their respective continents. Continental drift also set the stage for the evolution of our present biogeographic regions with their distinctive avifaunas (see DISTRIBUTION).

Oceanic Islands. The great majority of the world's oceanic islands are volcanic in origin. This means that they emerged from the sea as the result of volcanic eruptions—another effect of seabed expansion associated with continental drift—and began their existence above the waves as biological blank slates. Research has shown that new islands are rapidly colonized by a variety of life-forms. Some of these, e.g., highly migratory colonial seabirds, are well adapted for discovering and establishing themselves on such unoccupied real estate. Others, including most land birds, arrive as wind-blown waifs from mainland populations. Of course, the majority of such vagrants fail to survive, but those that manage to establish a breeding population have taken the first step in the evolution of new species and perhaps an entire endemic avifauna. This scenario in various stages of development is evident to some degree in all of the world's remote marine archipelagos, but has its most spectacular expression in tropical island groups, such as the Galapagos, the West Indies, or the Hawaiian Islands, where adaptive radiation has had time to create a spectrum of new species from the pioneer stock.

Glaciers moving southward across the landmasses of the Northern Hemisphere split continents and fragmented habitats into temporarily isolated regions. For example, transcontinental forests in North America have been divided by ice masses during multiple past glacial periods, allowing bird (and other organisms) to take separate genetic courses. This is one explanation for why it is now practical to have eastern and western field guides and why many songbirds, e.g. Eastern and Western Bluebirds, have similar yet distinctive counterparts on either side of the continent. For a hypothetical diagram of this process, see Fig. 29). However, Klicka and Zink (1997) have shown that *recent* ice ages are unlikely to have had a major influence on avian speciation in North America.

Alpine Islands. Climbing a mountain resembles traveling to higher latitudes, with the climate becoming colder as one goes up and the habitat changing accordingly. On the highest peaks this creates, in effect, an arctic island in the sky to which characteristic species are confined by their habitat preferences. We can speculate that our Black and Brown-capped Rosy Finches were part of a widespread tundra inhabiting species during a colder climatic period. As the climate warmed and boreal habitat types moved up the mountainsides, populations of finches became isolated in islands of tundra on high peaks in the Rockies and evolved into distinct—though obviously still closely related—species.

Ecological and Topographic Fragmentation. Many species are dependent on the characteristics of the habitat in which they have evolved. Climate shifts can change the distribution of habitats; for example, during a dry era an extensive area of humid forest might be reduced to isolated patches of such forest amidst a distinct dry forest type. These populations of humid forest birds, confined by their habitat preference and separated

from their former siblings and cousins, must now follow their own evolutionary course, in time, perhaps, becoming new species. Similarly, a major shift in the course of a river might isolate populations of forest birds that have instinctive inhibitions about crossing extensive stretches of water.

THE WAYS OF CHANGE. Geographic isolation provides a physical opportunity for speciation, but biological change proceeds through a number of specific mechanisms.

Genetic Influence. The character traits of birds as a whole seem to have a medium to high degrees of "heritability," i.e., the degree to which variation in such traits is controlled by the genes rather than by environmental influences. This means that bird species are susceptible to genetic changes over long periods through natural selection. However, they are also significantly prone to short-term changes as the result of environmental factors. The degree of heritability varies among bird species.

The degree of genetic variation among populations of similar bird species has been found to vary significantly in relation to distribution and climatic factors. Black-capped Chickadees throughout North America have a virtually identical (mitochondrial DNA) genotype, indicating constriction of genetic change during the last glacial interval and then a rapid expansion with little opportunity for divergence following the retreat of the ice. By contrast the genotype of the southern Carolina Chickadee, whose genetic history was not interrupted, shows significant variation (Gill et al. 1995–ORNITHOLOGY).

Adaptive Changes occur as the result of environmental pressures and opportunities, and some changes can take place quite rapidly. A severe drought in the Galapagos Islands in 1976–77 drastically reduced the seed crop and favored individual ground finches (*Geospiza fortis*) with large bills capable of cracking the most prevalent remaining seeds, which were large and hard. Natural selection pressure was so strong under these harsh conditions that the average bill size of a population of finches on Daphne Island increased dramatically in just 2–3 generations (Boag and Grant 1981). The situation reversed itself when the smaller seeds became available again and smaller bills were more useful.

Adaptive radiation describes the response to the evolutionary opportunity afforded a population that arrives in a place—ideally an isolated island—where many ecological niches are vacant. As members of the early generations of the new fauna explore the possibilities of an environment with little or no competition, physical or behavioral traits that increase survival are favored and exaggerated by natural selection until they reach an optimal range. The host of confusingly similar finches and mockingbirds on the Galapagos Islands presumably represents one stage in the gradual differentiation of species, while the 14 highly distinctive species of vangas of Madagascar seem to have diverged much farther from the

founding helmet shrike stock. One of these measures under 5 inches and looks and acts like a nuthatch, another is more than twice as big and probes tree holes for food with a long sickle-shaped bill, and yet another seems to be on its way to becoming a hornbill; several still look pretty much like helmet shrikes but have sorted themselves out into different habitat types from desert to rain forest. Faced with a museum tray of vanga specimens few observers would guess how closely they are related.

The term radiation can be applied to particular characteristics of a related group—e.g., the bills of Hawaiian Honeycreepers—as well as to species.

Mate Selection. Early in life, birds learn to recognize members of their own species (see INTELLIGENCE, Imprinting) and this serves to reinforce appropriate mate selection and therefore maintain the integrity of the species as a whole. However, this phenomenon ("positive assortative mating") may also apply within populations of species and lead to the evolution of distinct forms. If individuals consistently pair preferentially with members of the population with which they share small distinctions, these may become reinforced by additional characters until the two elements of the population only rarely exchange genes with each other. Sexual selection greatly reinforces this effect. The nearly identical (to people) Clark's and Western Grebes, until recently considered a single species, were seen to sort themselves out in this way and were eventually proved to be genetically distinct (Storer and Nuechterlein 1992).

Cultural Speciation. Individual birds are capable of learning new tricks, such as tool use, that help them, for example, to exploit additional food sources (see INTELLIGENCE), and such breakthroughs can be transmitted culturally through a population. Pairing with these brainier birds in the population should confer a significant selective advantage on the resulting offspring (smart is sexy!). Similarly, birds that develop louder or more elaborate songs, perhaps initially out of intense competition for mates, demonstrate a high degree of fitness that is attractive to prospective mates. If "smart" and "talented" birds mate assortatively, this amounts to a behavioral or cultural path to speciation (see Wyles et al. 1983).

Population Size. Speciation tends to be a relatively slow process within large, reproductively integrated breeding populations (demes) because adaptive changes get modulated within the large gene pool. Conversely, small populations are more likely to be swept off relatively rapidly in new evolutionary directions by chance mutations. Such smaller, genetically dynamic populations can be initiated in a variety of ways, e.g., pioneer populations breaking away from larger colonies, the accidental colonization of a relatively depauperate biota (e.g., the radiation scenarios described above), or even human-assisted introduction into a new breeding area, e.g., the House Sparrow example given above. Rapid, small-population evolution can also occur when a new dominant male of

a lek species successfully woos a high percentage of the available females (see MATING SYSTEMS).

Dispersal of young birds from the place where they were born to their own breeding sites is the means by which a given population expands. The degree to which juveniles prefer to stick close to home (philopatry) as opposed to venturing far afield varies among different species and between sexes of the same species. This affects the potential for speciation in several ways. The most adventurous dispersers are the most likely to found new populations with their inherent potential for rapid change and they also have increased opportunities for "outbreeding." Young birds that are very closely attached to their natal areas are more susceptible to inbreeding but also promote small population size. The largest effective breeding populations belong to species in which juvenile dispersal extends the boundaries of the population to its maximum extent; as noted above these larger populations are genetically more stable.

Geographic Variation and Subspecies. It is well-known that the appearance of many bird species varies—sometimes dramatically—in different parts of their range. The Song Sparrow may be our champion "diverger," with about 30 recognized "races" within its transcontinental distribution, but about a third of all North American bird species have one or more distinctive geographical variations. Ecological adaptation clearly plays a role in promoting many such divergent forms. For example, populations of many bird species tend to be smaller and paler in hot, dry habitats and larger and darker in cool, humid ones (see ALLEN'S, BERGMANN'S, GLOGER'S, and KELSO'S RULES). But the relative importance of genetics versus environmental influences remains poorly defined. In a classic experiment (James 1983–BERGMANN'S RULE), eggs of Red-winged Blackbirds from a northern population were transferred to the nests of a southern population with distinct differences in wing length and bill shape—features that might be assumed to be genetically controlled. As they matured however, the nestlings developed the distinctive physical features of their adoptive rather than their biological parents.

Species with broad ranges may evolve in different directions toward the extremities of their range, while maintaining genetic continuity. In rare instances the extreme ends of the range meet and the differentially evolved "races" fail to recognize each other as the same species and are unable to interbreed. Such instances are called "ring-species" and present the conundrum of two species contained in a single, genetically integrated population.

In an effort to impose some order on evolving species and provide consistent names for geographical variants, taxonomists have traditionally divided species into subspecies or "races." Since speciation often produces a continuum of forms (e.g., gradations from darker to lighter plumage; see CLINE) rather than distinct entities, a rule was established

that characters meriting subspecific distinction must be present in 75% of a population before it can be described as a geographic race. As our knowledge of variation within and among populations has increased however, the concept of the subspecies turns out to be a poor match for biological reality (see Mayr 1982–SUBSPECIES).

Secondary Contact. Just as populations of a species may become isolated as the result of various factors (see above), so long-separated bird populations are sometimes reunited as glaciers melt, rivers alter their courses, habitat changes, and the two populations expand and reconnect. What happens next varies depending on how far the related forms have evolved away from each other. If isolating mechanisms evolved during the separation are highly developed—the related forms may, for example, have developed different songs, plumage, courtship rituals, and/or feeding habits—then the related forms may not recognize even the possibility of interbreeding, though they share a close common ancestry. Or initial attempts at hybridization may result in infertile eggs or sterile offspring due to genetic incompatibility. In other words in this scenario the separation into two distinctive species is complete. If such species have maintained similar ecological niches they may end up living as noncompetitive neighbors (parapatric distribution) or they may overlap in distribution and coexist defensively in well-defined territories. If the species in question have diverged ecologically while separated, they may slip into separate niches when they reunite. For example, the breeding ranges of two or three species of the closely related flycatchers in the genus *Empidonax* overlap almost everywhere in North America, yet they have largely sorted themselves into distinct habitats so that competition is minimized and hybrids are unknown.

At the opposite extreme, forms reunited after a relatively brief separation with little opportunity for change might interbreed with abandon, so that both populations would merge into one. Genetically, the new hybrid population would, of course, be different from the species that existed before the populations were separated, but it would once again represent a single species. It has been suggested (Short 1965–HYBRIDIZATION) that the Gilded Flicker is such a "recombined" species (however, see Moore et al. 1991), and the recent reuniting of Blue-winged and Golden-winged Warblers seems to be resulting in the genetic conquest of the latter by the former.

Many cases fall between the two extremes. If hybrids produced by the union of related forms turn out to be inferior to the "pure" forms on either side of the family, the hybrid form will be "selected out" and the distinct forms will remain intact even though their ranges overlap and they continue to interbreed occasionally; Rose-breasted and Black-headed Grosbeaks seem to represent such a case in North America (Rising 1983). Sometimes there is a stable zone of overlap in which nearly all birds are

hybrids with clear boundaries between the pure forms on either side. These are either population "sinks," graveyards, in effect, for the less fit hybrids, or they may develop in localities where ecological conditions favor the hybrid form over either of the parent species. The classic North American example of this model is that of the "yellow-shafted" (eastern) and "red-shafted" (western) races of the Northern Flicker (Moore and Buchanan 1985). See also the cases of Baltimore and Bullock's Orioles and Myrtle and Audubon's Warblers described under SYSTEMATICS.

Human beings are compulsive organizers obsessed with defining things and putting them in categories (see SYSTEMATICS). As such we are naturally inclined to think of a species as a distinct and immutable entity. A mockingbird should be a mockingbird, not some amorphous "form" subject to the whims of environmental circumstance. But counterintuitive though it may be within our short life spans, nature is not so much a collection of objects (species), but a process (speciation or evolution) in which birds and other organisms are transitory manifestations rather than final products. We are just beginning to understand the mechanisms by which this all-encompassing phenomenon creates and re-creates the natural world.

See also DISTRIBUTION; HYBRIDIZATION; SPECIES; SYSTEMATICS.

SPECIES (sing. and pl.) (SPEE-shees or SPEE-sees). In Ernst Mayr's classic definition, biological species (1970), are "groups of interbreeding natural populations that are reproductively isolated from other such groups." For example, while all Hermit Thrushes can interbreed with each other, they cannot normally do so with Swainson's Thrushes even though these two species are closely related. By comparison the Oregon and Slate-colored populations of the Dark-eyed Junco, though their plumage characteristic are highly distinctive, interbreed freely where their ranges overlap (see Fig. 23). While in one sense species are ever-changing via the processes of genetic mutation and natural selection (see SPECIATION), they represent separate lines of evolution and tend to remain relatively stable and identifiable over long periods of time in most cases.

Because it can be defined biologically, the species is the fundamental unit of taxonomy (see SYSTEMATICS). All other taxonomic categories are artificial groupings defined (and continually redefined) by human beings to classify related groupings of species. A genus, for example, is an aggregation of what taxonomists believe to be phylogenetically closely related species.

For systematists, a drawback to the biological species concept is that in many cases the capacity for interbreeding among closely related forms cannot be tested. How do we know that the Golden-cheeked Warbler is not just a dark form of the Black-throated Green Warbler since their breeding ranges are widely separated and they have no opportunity to

test the strength of their presumed reproductive isolation. Or, conversely, how do we know that the Ipswich Sparrow—isolated during the breeding season on Sable Island, Nova Scotia from its nearest relatives—is not a full species, incapable of interbreeding with other forms of Savannah Sparrow? To resolve such cases taxonomists have proposed the "phylogenetic species." This concept seeks to identify the smallest possible population or assemblage of populations that bear a unique set of common characteristics, regardless of whether such populations interbreed with similar ones. In this formulation all 18 forms of the Fox Sparrow that have been described as races or subspecies (and perhaps a number of additional ones) would be considered species. This approach is compatible with the emergence of CLADISTICS as the prevailing mode of biological classification and with our increasing ability to make biochemical distinctions among organisms because it facilitates the construction of lineages from common ancestry. The main problem with interbreeding as a defining criterion for species is that it is a "retained" ancestral trait—not a good cladistic character for defining a new form. Furthermore, evolution does not proceed by tidy tree-like branching; there are now several examples of "paraphyletic" species arising from within broadly distributed ancestors (e.g., Chihuahuan Raven from Common Raven).

In the context of birdwatching, the adoption of phylogenetic species would certainly add a new level of challenge for listers, though it is daunting to contemplate the arguments that would inevitably ensure about the field marks of the new "species" and whether one had actually seen them. We would need a new generation of bird books with titles such as *A Field Guide to the Horned Larks of North America.*

In the vernacular, "species" is often used to mean simply a "kind" of animal, but this usage can create confusion about the nature of the organism in question. Great Blue and Great White Herons are indisputably different "kinds" of birds, but in the context of biological species they are actually two different color forms of the same "kind" (species).

The latest authoritative tally of the number of bird species alive today is that of Monroe and Sibley (1993–CHECKLIST), which lists 9,702 species in 145 families and 23 orders. Needless to say, this total is subject to other taxonomic interpretations, but it is worth noting that this represents an increase of a thousand or more species from preceding world bird lists. This is not because that many new bird species—of which perhaps less than 100 remain undescribed—have been discovered, but because modern classification techniques favor the splitting of existing species.

About 672 bird species breed in North America (north of the Mexican border), about 66 more occur here regularly but do not breed, and about 175 species have been reliably recorded as rare visitors from other avifaunas. All species of regular occurrence in North America are listed in phylogenetic order in Appendix I. Casual and accidental species are listed in Appendix II.

In modern biological nomenclature, a species is designated by a binomial—two Latin (or "Latinized") names, a generic name followed by a specific name, e.g., *Somateria spectabilis,* the species name for the King Eider (see NOMENCLATURE).

The abbreviations "sp." (sing.) and "spp." (plural) are sometimes used for "species" when species identity is unknown or when one wishes to refer collectively to some or all species in a higher category. For example, "Peep sp." or "*Calidris* sp." refers to one or more unidentified shorebirds of a single species; "*Calidris* spp." indicates that more than one species is involved. The total number of a raft of scoters containing all three species might be expressed as "Scoters, spp.—500."

SPECIFIC. In a biological context, refers (specifically) to a species. For example: "It was decided that the form should be elevated from subspecific to specific level."

SPECIMEN (of a bird). Usually, the preserved skin of a bird, stored in a museum collection and vital to the pursuit of numerous ornithological objectives, including, for example, comparison of forms for taxonomic purposes and the making of accurate illustrations for field guides. In matters of critical determination, whether in the field or the lab, birders and ornithologists alike were once heard to discuss the desirability of collecting or examining "specimens," though conservation and humanitarian concerns together with the modern ability to obtain high-quality photographs with relative ease has made this an increasingly rare practice. See BIRD SKIN.

Occasionally whole birds (not just their skins) are preserved in fluid (when continued reference to internal structures is wanted) or freeze-dried. These too, of course, are "specimens."

SPECULUM (SPEK-yuh-lum). A patch of contrasting color on the wing, especially that on the upper surface of the secondary feathers of dabbling ducks. See WING.

SPEED. Somewhat surprisingly, the maximum speed that birds are capable of attaining in flight is the subject of considerable controversy. In normal, traveling flight most birds proceed at between 20 and 50 miles per hour, but are generally capable of higher speeds at least for short distances, as when they are being chased by a predator. Racing pigeons and the Red-breasted Merganser have been reliably clocked at air speeds of 80 mph, and doubtless many other species have a similar capacity.

The characteristics shared by the fastest-flying birds are powerful flight (pectoral) muscles (see Fig. 14), streamlined bodies, flat wings (i.e., little camber), a high aspect ratio, and no slots (see FLIGHT). The ultimate "high-speed" wings are those of the swifts—with very long primaries and

very short secondaries—but falcons, many shorebirds, hummingbirds, and swallows share most if not all of these characteristics to some degree.

There are "reports" that the fastest birds may at times attain speeds reaching or exceeding 200 mph; however, such speeds have never been recorded in a controlled scientific procedure. Many velocity records come from pilots who check their speedometers as their planes are passed by birds. Some alleged and confirmed speed records are as follows.

Fastest Bird Worldwide (flapping flight). This record *may* belong to the White-throated Needle-tailed Swift (*Hirundapus caudacutus*), an Asian species, whose speed has been reliably clocked at 106.25 mph; the same species is also said to reach 219.5 mph (ground speed), but the method of recording this statistic has been called into question. A species of swiftlet, tracked with Doppler radar as it entered its nesting cave was doing 111 kph. See also SWIFT.

Fastest North American Bird. The speed record for flapping flight here *might* belong to the White-throated Swift, which has been "estimated" to attain 200 mph. If true, of course, it *could* beat out its relative above. Dunlins have been clocked from a plane (McCabe 1942) at "not less than 110 mph." The Peregrine Falcon in a stoop has long been credited with a speed of at least 175 mph and possibly over 200 mph by several pilots. However, experimenters who recently attached small air speedometers to this species were unable to confirm a diving speed over 82 mph.

Fastest Running Birds. The Ostrich holds the world record, which is at least 44 mph and may well reach 50 or 60 mph. In North America the Wild Turkey may attain 30 mph for short periods and frequently travels on foot at 15 mph. Cottam et al. (1942) give speeds of 15 mph for the Greater Roadrunner and up to 21 mph for the Common Pheasant.

Fastest Swimming Bird. The Gentoo Penguin has been timed underwater at 22.3 mph (McWhirter 1980–SIZE).

SPISHING. See PISHING; BIRD CALLS.

SPLITTING (splitter). In an ornithological context, the practice of separating bird forms (especially species) into smaller taxonomic units (especially subspecies). The taxonomist who performs this kind of dissection is known as a "splitter." The splitter is the bird listers' champion, because, in effect, s/he adds species to the avifauna. Compare LUMPING. With the advent of molecular analysis, the trend is distinctly toward splitting.

SPOONBILL. Standard English name for all 6 members of the subfamily Plataleinae (family Threskiornithidae; order Ciconiiformes); Sibley and Ahlquist (1990–SYSTEMATICS) abolish the subfamily and simply lump the spoonbills with the ibses in the Threskiornithidae. One species, the Roseate Spoonbill, breeds in North America.

The most notable of spoonbill characteristics is, of course, their peculiar spatulate bill, which is really more a sensory device than a spoon. The inside of the broad, flattened tip is lined with sensitized tissue that feels small food items as the birds swing their partially opened bills through shallow, murky water. When small prey such as insect larvae, shrimps, or shellfish are encountered the "spoon" snaps shut on them.

All spoonbills except the New World species are largely white. The unique roseate plumage of our species put its owners' existence in peril during the days of the plume trade (see CONSERVATION).

Like their near relatives the ibises, spoonbills are colonial nesters and make a platform of sticks in low trees (e.g., mangroves) or shrubs or (less usually) rush beds or on the ground. They often occupy mixed "rookeries" with herons, ibises, etc. The 2–4 eggs are whitish with both fine speckles and larger splotches of light reddish brown, the latter concentrated near the large end.

Spoonbills are generally silent but make low grunts and clucks when alarmed or at the nest site.

The small, local North American spoonbill populations in Florida and Texas are now fairly stable or on the increase; the species also occurs throughout the New World tropics.

SPORT (bird-related). See BIRDWATCHING; COCKFIGHTING; FALCONRY; HUNTING; LISTING.

SPRAGUE (sprayg), Isaac, 1811–95 (Spague's Pipit: *Anthus spragueii*). Prominent nineteenth-century illustrator from Massachusetts. His chief fame (aside from the pipit) lies in his fine drawings for Asa Gray's *Botanical Textbook*. He was a friend of Audubon, who was the author of Sprague's Pipit.

SPURS (on wings and legs). See WING; LEG/FOOT.

SQUAB. In the broadest sense, any nestling bird without down or feathers; more specifically, a nestling pigeon, sometimes cooked and eaten as a delicacy.

STARLING. Standard English name for about 90 of the 114 members of the family Sturnidae (order Passeriformes), which also includes the mynas and oxpeckers. Sibley and Ahlquist (1990) divide the family into two tribes, adding the "mimic thrushes" (Mimini) to the groups noted. Four exotic sturnids are currently established in North America.

Worldwide, the starlings and mynas range in length between 7 and 17 inches; the European Starling measures 8½ inches. Most starlings and mynas are sturdy-looking compact birds with sharp, straight, or slightly

curved bills of moderate length, short tails (with a few exceptions), and strong legs and feet. Many of the African starlings have spectacular glossy, iridescent plumage as adults, and the striking plumage of European Starling would probably be more often admired here were its wearer not alien, abundant, and occasionally noisome.

Many starlings roost and feed in flocks, sometimes very large ones (see PROBLEMS INVOLVING BIRDS). They often feed in fruiting trees, but are equally at ease walking (not hopping) on the ground, probing for beetle grubs and picking up other invertebrates and seeds. The European Starling and the Common and Crested Mynas are well known for their fondness for garbage dumps, stockyards, and cultivated fields, and all three are attracted to man-made urban structures (bridges, office buildings) as roosts. Starling songs tend to be raucous and rather chaotic, though with some musical notes or phrases, and many species, including ours, add motifs learned from other birds. Mynas, of course, are famed as talking birds. The Hill Myna is arguably the world's most talented avian mimic (see SONG), and captive European Starlings readily pick up human sounds.

Starlings are mostly cavity nesters and will occupy rock crevices, holes in earthen banks, and niches in houses as well as tree cavities. One of the reasons our introduced starlings are considered banes rather than blessings is that they are too successful in competing with "nicer" native species such as bluebirds for nest sites. By contrast, in parts of rural Europe, where the European Starling is indigenous and not inordinately prolific, birdhouses are erected specifically to attract them. The nest cavity typically contains an untidy lining of coarse plant materials as well as paper and other debris. Mynas lay 6–7 (usually 4–5) eggs, starlings 4–9 (usually 5–7). In both cases the eggs are pale to darker greenish blue.

The starling family is native to Europe, Asia, Africa, New Guinea, northern Australia, and much of Oceania and achieves its greatest diversity in Africa and Asia. The introduced European Starling is well established continentwide in North America, and 3 species of exotic mynas, have established local footholds: a population of Crested Mynas (*Acridotheres cristatellus*) established near Vancouver, British Columbia around 1897 is now in decline; a few escaped Hill Mynas (*Gracula religiosa*) may breed in Florida and California; and the Common Myna (*Acridotheres tristis*) of southern Asia, which has successfully colonized parts of Africa, Australia, and various Pacific islands, appears to be increasing rapidly in southern Florida. See INTRODUCED BIRDS).

Recognizable forms of the name "starling" appear in Old English, originally a diminutive referring to the young "stare" (European Starling); this in turn derives from the Latin "sturnus," also referring to the European Starling and now the genus name for 16 species of starlings. The notion that "starling" refers to the fact that the European species is somewhat

star-shaped in flight or that its winter plumage spots look like little stars is appealing but erroneous.

STATE/PROVINCIAL BIRDS. The "official" bird species of a given political unit, proclaimed or voted into law in most cases. The North American roster of honored species is as follows:

United States (National Bird: Bald Eagle)

Alabama: Northern Flicker
Alaska: Willow Ptarmigan
Arizona: Cactus Wren
Arkansas: Northern Mockingbird
California: California Quail
Colorado: Lark Bunting
Connecticut: American Robin
Delaware: Blue Hen (chicken)
District of Columbia: Wood Thrush
Florida: Northern Mockingbird
Georgia: Brown Thrasher
Hawaii: Nene (Hawaiian Goose)
Idaho: Mountain Bluebird
Illinois: Northern Cardinal
Indiana: Northern Cardinal
Iowa: American Goldfinch
Kansas: Western Meadowlark
Kentucky: Northern Cardinal
Louisiana: Brown Pelican
Maine: Black-capped Chickadee
Maryland: Baltimore Oriole
Massachusetts: Black-capped
  Chickadee
Michigan: American Robin
Minnesota: Common Loon
Mississippi: Northern Mockingbird
Missouri: Eastern Bluebird
New Jersey: American Goldfinch

New Mexico: Greater Roadrunner
New York: Eastern Bluebird
Montana: Western Meadowlark
Nebraska: Western Meadowlark
Nevada: Mountain Bluebird
New Hampshire: Purple Finch
North Carolina: Northern Cardinal
North Dakota: Western Meadow-
  lark
Ohio: Northern Cardinal
Oklahoma: Scissor-tailed Fly-
  catcher
Oregon: Western Meadowlark
Pennsylvania: Ruffed Grouse
Rhode Island: Rhode Island Red
  (chicken)
South Carolina: Carolina Wren
South Dakota: Ring-necked
  Pheasant
Tennessee: Northern Mockingbird
Texas: Northern Mockingbird
Utah: California Gull
Vermont: Hermit Thrush
Virginia: Northern Cardinal
Washington: American Goldfinch
West Virginia: Northern Cardinal
Wisconsin: American Robin
Wyoming: Western Meadowlark

Score: Northern Cardinal, 7; Western Meadowlark, 6; Northern Mockingbird, 5.

In 1982 the U.S. Postal Service issued a block of 50 stamps commemorating the state birds and state flowers.

Canada did not begin to designate provincial birds until the 1980s. It is interesting to compare the two lists. The U.S. birds are almost all pretty

garden songbirds with no birds of prey or corvids represented. Modern Canadians clearly have a very different view of what constitutes a proper avian emblem.

Alberta: Great Horned Owl
British Colombia: two species—
  Steller's Jay and Varied Thrush
Manitoba: Great Gray Owl
New Brunswick: Black-capped
  Chickadee
Newfoundland: Atlantic Puffin
Northwest Territories: Gyrfalcon

Nova Scotia: Osprey
Nunavut: None designated as yet
Ontario: Common Loon
Prince Edward Island: Blue Jay
Quebec: Snowy Owl
Saskatchewan: Sharp-tailed
  Grouse
Yukon: Common Raven

STATE/PROVINCIAL BOOKS. See the Bibliography under this heading for major works on the avifauna of North American states and provinces, with illustrators noted where exceptional.

STELLER, Georg Wilhelm, 1709–46 (Steller's Eider: *Polysticta stelleri*; Steller's Sea-Eagle: *Haliaetus pelagicus*; Steller's Jay: *Cyanocitta stelleri*). A doctor-naturalist (see BIOGRAPHY), Steller was born in Germany and spent much of his short life chronicling the natural history of Siberia/ Alaska. He was a member of the Bering expedition of 1740–42 and his extensive fieldwork and writings on the flora and fauna of the northeastern Palearctic easily merit his present nomenclatural prominence. He died appropriately (though apparently despondently) in Siberia. For a fuller biography, see Sutton and Sutton, *Natural History* (1956), 65:485–91.

STERNUM. The breastbone. See SKELETON and Fig. 27.

STIFFTAIL DUCK. Collective name for all members of the subfamily Oxyurinae or the tribe Oxyurini (family Anatidae; order Anseriformes). There are 9 species of "stifftails" worldwide, 2 of which, the Ruddy Duck and Masked Duck, breed in North America. The former is a lake and pond species widespread in the New World south of the Arctic, and the latter is a secretive marsh species largely confined to the American tropics but just reaching the United States as a rare breeder in southern Florida and Texas.

The name refers to the long tail, characteristic of most members of the group; it is often held erect and plays a part in courtship rituals (see DISPLAY).

STILT. Standard English name for 6 members of the family Recurvirostridae (order Charadriiformes), which also includes 4 species of avocets; Sibley and Ahlquist (1990–SYSTEMATICS) place these birds in a tribe

(Recurvirostrini) within a subfamily (Recurvirostrinae) that appends the oystercatchers within a family (Charadriidae) that adds the plovers. One species, the Black-necked Stilt, breeds in North America.

Stilts are tall (av. 14 inches), gracefully elongated black-and-white shorebirds with bright pink legs and a long, thin, slightly upturned bill. They wade (and sometimes swim) in shallow water, feeding on small vertebrates (fish, frogs) and large invertebrates (shrimp, insects) as well as some plant matter. They usually feed in flocks.

They nest colonially in a short-grass marsh or in the open, making a shallow depression in mud or sand, sparsely or fairly heavily lined with plant debris. The nest is typically placed near or even in shallow water and in the latter case additional "walls" are added. The 3–5 (usually 4) eggs are brownish yellow, rather heavily marked with prominent dark brown spots.

The frequently uttered stilt call consists of sharp, loud, piping notes: *pep* or *ip.*

The stilts are most prevalent throughout the warmer regions of the world but range well into the Temperate Zone, e.g., to southern Oregon and Delaware in North America. Northern populations are migratory.

"Stilt," of course, refers to these birds' extraordinary legs.

STINT. Standard English name in Britain and its former empire for the smaller sandpipers in the genus *Calidris.* As a collective term, essentially synonymous with "peep."

STOMACH. See DIGESTIVE SYSTEM.

STOMACH OIL. A fatty, usually pinkish liquid produced in the stomachs (proventriculi) of the tubenosed birds (order Procellariiformes). The substance is apparently similar to the oils found in the heads and stomachs of some whales and dolphins and, when cooled, hardens to a waxy consistency like that of ambergris or spermaceti. It has a strong, distinctive (some say "foul") musky odor, and is used in self-defense by nestlings and adults, which expel it violently from mouth and nostrils onto would-be molesters. The plumage of albatrosses, shearwaters, petrels, and their allies usually smells strongly of musk, and while the oil secreted from the uropygial gland (see OIL GLAND) is also strong-smelling, it has been suggested that stomach oil, too, may be applied to the feathers (see PREEN-ING). It may also aid in the metabolic production of fresh water in the bodies of the strictly oceanic tubenoses.

STOOP. The characteristic dive of some species of falcons onto their prey from above. It was once widely stated with authority that Peregrine Falcons attained speeds of up to 180 mph (passing an airplane diving at

175 mph) and even to 275 mph! (Brown and Amadon 1968–HAWK). But recent attempts to confirm such velocities, using air speedometers attached to stooping birds, have been unable to prove speeds in excess of 82 mph (see SPEED). Because large birds (e.g., Great Blue Heron, Red-tailed Hawk) have been seen killed instantaneously on impact by a stooping Peregrine, it has long been surmised that death is effected by a blow from the falcon's large, powerful feet. Recent evidence indicates that a raking action by the long claw of the hind toe may also play a role.

STORAGE OF FOOD. See FOOD/FEEDING.

STORK. Standard English name for 14 members of the family Ciconiidae (order Ciconiiformes), of which 1 species, the Wood Stork, breeds in North America; another, Neotropical species, the Jabiru, has occurred as a vagrant in Texas. Traditionally the Ciconiiformes has been a relatively small order, comprising the heron, ibis, and stork families. Based on a variety of analyses, the *AOU Checklist*, 7th edition (1998) moved the New World Vultures (family Cathartidae) from the Falconiformes to the Ciconiiformes, adding 7 species to the order. In a much more comprehensive taxonomic reorganization based on DNA-DNA hybridization studies, Sibley and Ahlquist (1990–SYSTEMATICS) have proposed a greatly expanded Ciconiifomes that subsumes the Gaviiformes (loons), the Podicipediformes (grebes), the Procellariiformes (tubenoses), the Pelecaniformes (boobies, cormorants, pelicans, and allies), the Charadriiformes (shorebirds, gulls, auks, and allies), and the Falconiformes (hawks, eagles, falcons, and allies) as well as the taxa already noted. In this new arrangement, which also suggests new evolutionary relationships, the storks and New World vultures occupy a place between the pelicans and the frigatebirds (see Appendix III).

Storks are among the largest waterbirds (30–60 inches), with long necks, legs, and bills and short tails, characters that sometimes lead to confusion with HERONS and CRANES. The three front toes are webbed at the bases and their bills are massive and among the longest in the world (to 13½ inches).

Many of the world's storks are at home in dry uplands, including tilled fields, where they feed on a wide range of small vertebrates and large insects. The Wood Stork is equally catholic in its diet (it will gladly swallow a young alligator, though it prefers fish), but is by preference a waterbird and often wades up to its belly, "feeling" with its bill below the surface. The species is typically gregarious in both its feeding and nesting habits. The sight of black-and-white Wood Storks soaring over a broad wetland is one of the great sights of the warmer parts of the New World, though becoming a rare one in North America.

Our native stork typically builds its stick platform in trees rooted in water, e.g., cypresses and mangroves. It lines the nest with finer twigs and leaves, and lays 3–4 (rarely, 5) off-white, unmarked eggs.

Storks are usually silent and, in fact, are ill-equipped vocally, capable only of hissing when alarmed or disturbed. According to Palmer (1962– ORNITHOLOGY), the young also make "goose-like" calls. Adults not infrequently snap their great bills loudly and make an impressive "whooshing" sound as they flap overhead.

The Wood Stork once bred across the southern border of the United States from California to the east coast and north to Tennessee. More recently its U.S. population dwindled drastically, due to the draining of its habitat and other factors, and colonies survived only in Florida. Though it has recovered somewhat in the Gulf states (nests in Texas, Louisiana, and Georgia) and continues to hold its own in Florida, the species continues to be listed as Endangered under federal law (see ENDANGERED BIRDS).

"Stork" as a name for these distinctive birds—especially the White Stork of Europe—has an ancient lineage. It is cognate with the German "storch" meaning "stick," plausibly referring to the birds' long legs or to the characteristic erect and rigid form and postures of storks. Lockwood (1993–NAMES) notes that a secondary meaning of *storch* is penis, which may explain the fanciful notion of storks delivering babies.

For the short-legged American storks, see VULTURE.

STORM-PETREL. Standard English name for all 21 members of the family Hydrobatidae (order Procellariiformes); Sibley and Ahlquist (1990– SYSTEMATICS) reduce this taxon to a subfamily of the family Procellariidae (order Ciconiiformes). Four species of storm-petrels breed in North America; 3 more occur as regular visitors to our offshore waters in either the Atlantic or the Pacific, and yet another 3 are rare or casual visitors (see Appendix II).

The storm-petrels are small (5½–10 inches), usually sooty-black, pelagic birds with short, slender, hooked bills, tubular nostrils located above at the bill base, and rather long, slender legs, which they characteristically dangle in the water while hovering. The front three toes are webbed (the webbing yellow in one of our species) and the hind toe (hallux) is vestigial. On land, they hobble awkwardly on their tarsi, rather than walking erect.

Storm-petrels are seldom seen from land but are often common on offshore fishing banks, where they flit over the waves like swallows, butterflies, or bats. In rough weather, they seem to survive by giving themselves up to the will of the winds. Seafarers traditionally regard these Mother Carey's chickens (or Carey chicks) as the souls of the drowned and as omens of ill fortune or bad weather. Like other tubenoses, storm-petrels have a musky odor and are able to confer it on molesters by vomiting forth a strong-smelling STOMACH OIL similar to the head oil of sperm whales. Some species habitually follow ships, others never do.

The storm-petrels nest colonially in rock crevices (including walls) or in ground burrows abandoned by other animals or dug by themselves (see

Fig. 21). The site is lined in some cases with bits of plant material; the single egg is white and sometimes has a "wreath" of fine blackish or reddish speckles at the larger end.

The voices of the Carey chicks are seldom heard at sea except on calm nights near breeding colonies. However, most species have a great repertoire of twitters, chirps, wails, gasps, whistles, etc., and sometimes give extended weird "songs" on the breeding grounds, all of which enhances their reputation as demons.

The family ranges over all the oceans of the world, but shows greatest diversity and abundance in colder waters with upwellings where marine food sources are most prolific.

"Petrel" is commonly associated with St. Peter's attempt to walk on the lake of Gennesaret (Sea of Galilee) (Matthew 14), referring to the characteristic storm-petrel habit of dangling its feet in the water as it forages over the surface. Lockwood (1993–NAMES) affirms the association with water walking, but says that the original form of the name was "pitteral" as in "pitter-patter" of tiny feet. For Mother Carey's Chickens, see NAMES, COLLOQUIAL.

STRUTTING GROUNDS. The open sagebrush plains used for courtship display by the Sage Grouse. Like the prairie-chickens, male Sage Grouse gather in spring, sometimes in hundreds, to perform a dawn prenuptial ritual involving a characteristic "dance" with accompanying sounds. See also BOOMING; LEK; DISPLAY.

STUDY SKIN. A specimen of an animal, especially a bird or mammal, prepared in such a manner as to be easily stored in a museum collection. Bird skins that are mounted in lifelike poses by taxidermists are not study skins. See also BIRD SKIN.

SUBADULT. Not fully mature. Commonly used to describe an intermediate *plumage* that immediately precedes that of a fully adult bird. For example, the immature male American Redstart in the fall and winter closely resembles a female (of any age), but by spring—following a prealternate (pre-nuptial) molt—it has acquired a blotchy black-and-olive-brown plumage that readily identifies it as a male. It will not assume the fully adult black-and-orange plumage until its next molt at the end of the summer. Species such as the Herring Gull (see Fig. 15) and Northern Gannet pass through a similar sequence of plumage changes, but the process takes three or more years to complete, and the result is a bewildering array of motley variations made even more confusing by feather wear. In referring to such "long sequence" species, birdwatchers frequently call birds in the earlier plumages (i.e., those that more resemble juveniles than adults) immatures and the later ones subadults. Birds in

subadult plumage may be fully mature in terms of their reproductive behavior and capability. See also MATURITY; MOLT.

SUBARCTIC. The region south of the arctic isotherm in which the mean temperature does not exceed 10°C for more than *four* months in summer and does not rise above 0°C during the coldest month. In this definition, the Subarctic roughly coincides with the combined Hudsonian and Canadian life zones (in Merriam's dated scheme) and with the coniferous forest biome. It is the region of the boreal forest, also called the taiga. For birds typical of the North American Subarctic, see BOREAL; compare ARCTIC; see also TAIGA; MUSKEG.

SUBCLASS. Secondary taxonomic category between CLASS and ORDER. Formerly, birds have been divided into three subclasses: the Sauriurae—toothed, reptile-like birds represented by a single species, *Archaeopteryx lithographica;* the Odontoholcae—diving birds with teeth set in grooves in the jaws (e.g., HESPERORNIS); and Ornithurae—all modern (untoothed) birds, fossil and recent. Wetmore (1960–SYSTEMATICS) placed all known birds (fossil and recent) in a single subclass, Neornithes (usually referred to as the "true birds"), with the single exception of *ARCHAEOPTERYX*, which alone occupies a second subclass, Archaeornithes. For the most recent arrangement of subclasses following Feduccia (1999–EVOLUTION), see Appendix IV. For basic taxonomic structure see SYSTEMATICS.

SUBGENUS. Secondary taxonomic category sometimes interposed between GENUS and SPECIES typically to define cohesive groupings within larger genera. For example, *Cerchneis* has sometimes been recognized as a subgenus encompassing the kestrels under the genus *Falco.* See SYSTEMATICS.

SUBFAMILY. Secondary taxonomic category between FAMILY and GENUS or between family and TRIBE when the latter category is used. In zoological nomenclature subfamily names invariably end in *-inae.* For example, the Polyborinae is the subfamily in which the caracaras are distinguished within the family Falconidae, containing the falcons and caracaras (see SYSTEMATICS). For "definitions" of all North American subfamilies, see Appendix I.

SUBORDER. Secondary taxonomic category between ORDER and FAMILY. In zoological nomenclature, subordinal names take the appropriate Latin plural ending rather than bearing a fixed ending in all cases. The widely followed taxonomy of Wetmore (1960–SYSTEMATICS) defined 22 suborders of birds worldwide, while the recent, more complex system of Sibley and Ahlquist recognizes but 4. For basic taxonomic structure see SYSTEMATICS and Appendix I.

SUBOSCINE. Refers to perching birds (order Passeriformes) that are not songbirds (i.e., not members of the suborder Paseri (Oscines). These birds are collectively called suboscine passerines or simply suboscines. In North America there is only one suboscine family, the Tyrannidae (tyrant flycatchers). For pronunciation, see OSCINES.

SUBSONG. A song that differs from the main characteristic song of a species; typically softer, of generally lower frequency, often longer, and with a different pattern. See SONG and compare especially the "whisper song" described in that entry.

SUBSPECIES (sing. and pl.). A population of a species in which individuals show the same structurally definable variation from other populations of the same species. The breeding areas of subspecies or "races" of the same species are normally separated geographically and represent early stages in the process of speciation. No matter how distinctive in appearance, races of the same species are presumed to be able to interbreed freely if given the opportunity. Failure to do so would indicate that effective isolating mechanisms had evolved, thereby defining the forms in question as distinct species (however, see RING SPECIES). Often, species vary gradually over a wide geographical range (see CLINE); in such cases racial boundaries cannot be sharply defined and subspecies must be described on the basis of averages in size, coloration, song dialect, etc., or combinations of these characters. It should be clear from this example that the subspecies is an invention of taxonomists and not a natural biological entity. The term allows for description and discussion of variation within species.

By biological convention, characters meriting subspecific distinction must be present in 75% of a given population before it can be described as racially distinct.

In modern biological nomenclature, a subspecies is designated by a "trinomial," a name consisting of the species designation (genus plus specific name) modified by a third name which identifies the race. For example, *Catoptrophorus semipalmatus* designates the species known in English as the Willet; *Catoptrophorus semipalmatus semipalmatus* is the subspecies known as the Eastern Willet, which breeds along most of the Atlantic and Gulf coasts from Nova Scotia to southern Texas; and *C. s. inornatus* describes the paler, longer-legged Western Willet, which occupies a geographically isolated breeding range in the western interior of the continent. Some species are subject to much racial variation—11 North American subspecies of the Rock Ptarmigan have been recognized—while other species, e.g., the Ring-billed Gull, do not vary enough superficially to warrant the description of any subspecies, despite a wide distribution consisting of several discrete populations—*which may bear significant—though invisible—genetic distinctiveness.*

With the advent of molecular analysis, the utility of the subspecies as a tool of avian systematics has been increasingly questioned. As of the 6th edition, the *AOU Check-list of North American Birds* ceased to include subspecies, though recent field guides include ever better detail on racial variations. For a comprehensive listing of the subspecies of North American birds, see the *AOU Check-list,* 5th ed. (1957). See also Phillips (1986, 1991–CHECKLIST) and Pyle (1997–IDENTIFICATION), who also treat subspecies.

See also SPECIES; SPECIATION; SYSTEMATICS and Appendix I.

SUMMER RESIDENT. A species that breeds in a given area but spends the winter elsewhere. Obviously, the use of the term in reference to a given species varies geographically, i.e., the Palm Warbler is a summer resident throughout much of Canada but not in the central United States, where it occurs only as a migrant, or in the southeastern United States, where it winters. All North American breeding birds are summer residents *somewhere* on the continent. Compare next entry.

SUMMER VISITOR (or visitant). A species that regularly spends the summer months (variable with respect to global position) in a given area but breeds elsewhere. Wilson's Storm-Petrel, which breeds during the Southern Hemisphere summer (our winter) in Anarctica, is also a summer visitor to the North Atlantic during the southern winter. Compare preceeding entry.

SUNNING. Many species of birds are known to assume "peculiar" postures, spreading and fluffing their feathers to expose their plumage to the light and/or heat of the sun. Though the behavior is sometimes observed on cool days, a number of witnesses record that the assumption of a sunning posture seems to be triggered when a bird suddenly experiences a rise in heat (and light?) intensity.

Sunning behavior varies among species and apparently also according to the sun's intensity. Among songbirds, a typical posture involves squatting on the ground at a right angle or facing away from the sun with wings drooped or outspread, tail fanned, and body feathers (especially those of the head and tail) erected, i.e., fluffed (not unlike the anting jay in Fig. 24). In this position the bird's head, neck, mantle, rump, and the upper surfaces of wings and tail receive the full impact of the sun's rays. Another posture, assumed by some swallows, pigeons, and others, is to roll over on one side, raise the wing, and expose the undersurface to the sun. Many waterbirds simply stand with their backs to the sun, perhaps with their wings drooped or necks stretched. Especially when the heat is most intense, sunning birds frequently open their bills and pant. As in water bathing and dusting, birds often have favorite sunning spots to which they return regularly.

While sunning, birds often seem to go into a kind of trance, allowing people to approach much more closely than normal. The bizarre posture

and behavior strongly suggest to the human observer that sunning birds are injured—or perhaps suffering from sunstroke!

The main theories that have been advanced to date to explain sunbathing in birds are (1) that exposure to heat and light activates ECTOPARA-SITES such as bird lice and perhaps drives them from areas of the body that the bird has most trouble reaching and/or to areas where they can be captured most easily in the bill; (2) that the sun's ultraviolet rays release vitamin D from the preen oil, which in turn is ingested by the bird in the preening that typically follows a sunbath; (3) that the sun dries and fluffs the feathers by evaporating moisture and oils from the plumage (as may be true of DUSTING), thus maintaining good insulation; (4) that birds may be able to increase energy reserves by absorbing solar radiation directly through the skin (Storer et al. 1975); (5) that it feels good, especially when molting causes skin irritations; and, of course, (6) some optimal combination of 1–5.

For a book-length treatise on this subject, see Simmons (1986).

For related behavior, see BATHING; PREENING; DUSTING; ANTING; OIL GLAND.

SUPERCILIUM (superciliary line or stripe). An area of (usually pale) feathers on the side of the head above the eye; the eye *brow.* This may be distinguished from an eye-line or eye-stripe, which in the strictest sense runs "through" the eye or behind it following the upper margins of the auriculars (ear coverts). However, the terms are frequently confused. See Figs. 1 and 35.

SUPERFAMILY. A secondary taxonomic category between SUBORDER and FAMILY. In zoological nomenclature names of superfamilies end in *-oidea.* In the Sibley and Ahlquist taxonomy (1990–SYSTEMATICS), the superfamily is used extensively within the order Ciconiiformes to distinguish or group families under suborders infraorders and parvorders. For basic taxonomic structure see SYSTEMATICS.

SUPERORDER. Secondary taxonomic category between SUBCLASS and ORDER. Wetmore (1960–SYSTEMATICS) recognized four superorders of birds: the Odontognathae, containing only the extinct order Hesperornithiformes (see HESPERORNIS); the Ichthyornithes, containing only the Ichthyonithiformes (see ICHTHYORNIS), also extinct; the Impennes, containing only the penguins (order Sphenisciformes); and the Neognathae, containing all other birds, recent and fossil. For the most recent arrangement of superorders following Feduccia (1999–EVOLUTION), see Appendix III. For basic taxonomic structure see SYSTEMATICS.

SUPERSPECIES. A taxonomic concept referring to groups of distinct species that are presumed to have evolved relatively recently from a common ancestor and that occupy distinct (often separate) ranges and/or ecological niches. For example, the so-called Black-throated Green Warbler

group—including the Black-throated Green, Townsend's, Golden-cheeked, Hermit, and Black-throated Gray Warblers (see Fig. 29)—conforms to the definition of a superspecies. The term is not an "official" nomenclatural category as is the species or subspecies, but as a grouping of species, it applies below subgenus. For basic taxonomic structure see SYSTEMATICS.

Fig. 29. *Superspecies.* The five wood warblers shown (clockwise from upper right: Townsend's, Black-throated Green, Golden-cheeked, Black-throated Gray, and Hermit) are often cited collectively as a classic *superspecies*, i.e., a closely related group of species that have diverged relatively recently from a common ancestor. In a classic paper, Mengel (1964–SPECIATION) postulated that an early Black-throated Green ancestor native to a southeastern deciduous forest expanded into the transcontinental coniferous forest created during the Pleistocene glacial advances; subsequent advances isolated several populations of the original species in the West (e.g., on coniferous mountaintop "islands," allowing new species to evolve (see SPECIATION). With the advent of molecular analysis of species relationships, it now appears that this process took much longer than Mengel thought, beginning millions of years before the late Pleistocene (Klicka and Zink 1997–SPECIATION) and that Black-throated Gray is the "basal branch" from which the other modern species evolved (Bermingham et al. 1992–SPECIATION).

SUPRASPECIFIC. Referring to any taxonomic category higher than a species, e.g., genus, family, order, etc.

SURFBIRD. Standard English name for a single species of shorebird, *Aphriza virgata* (order Charadriiformes). The taxonomic position of the unique Surfbird with its stubby bill and turnstone-like build and behavior has been much debated. Sibley and Ahlquist (1990–SYSTEMATICS) place it in the sandpiper subfamily Tringinae (family Scolopacidae) between the dowitchers and the knots.

Surfbirds are short-legged, gray shorebirds (speckled in summer, rather uniform in winter) with plover-like bills. They are almost exclusively birds of the rocks, both on their breeding grounds, where they nest in alpine fell-fields, and in winter, when they seldom stray from wave-washed coastal rocks. They are known to eat many insects on the breeding grounds and seemingly prefer mussels on the coast.

Palmer in Stout (1967–SHOREBIRD) notes their defensive habit of "sitting tight" on their nest until almost stepped on and then flying in the face of the intruder—a behavioral trait he supposes may have evolved due to frequent disturbance by White (Dall) Sheep (*Ovis dalli*).

Surfbirds are known to breed only in Alaska and the Yukon; they winter along the Pacific coast all the way to Tierra del Fuego.

SWAINSON, William, 1789–1855 (Swainson's Hawk: *Buteo swainsoni*; Swainson's Thrush: *Catharus ustulatus*; Swainson's Warbler: *Limnothlypis swainsonii*). A brilliant and prolific English writer-artist-naturalist who was dogged by misfortune for much of his life. His collecting trip to Brazil in 1816–17 was stymied by a revolution; he was seldom able to make ends meet despite his great effort and achievements; and he swam all his life against the increasingly prevailing current of Linnaean classification, preferring a long-forgotten alternative called the Quinary System (Gruson 1972–BIOGRAPHY). Hoping to make a new start, he emigrated to New Zealand, only to lose his precious collections en route. Audubon named his warbler, Bonaparte his hawk.

SWALLOW. Standard English name for 52 of 89 members of the family Hirundinidae (order Passeriformes), which they share with the MARTINS. Eight species of swallows and martins breed in North America, and 6 others have occurred as vagrants (see Appendix II).

Swallows are small (5 inches) to medium-sized (to 9 inches) songbirds with short, flattened bills, wide gapes, long wings, and short legs. The three forward-pointing toes are partially fused at the base. Many species are brightly colored, often with glossy metallic green or blue backs.

Swallows are adapted for catching insects on the wing and are therefore among the most graceful and agile birds in the world. Unlike the

swifts, with which they share their food preference, swallows are capable of perching horizontally in the normal songbird manner.

Many swallows (Cliff, Cave, Bank, and the martins in North America) nest colonially. Some (e.g., Barn, Cliff, and Cave) make "adobe" cups or vase-like structures from pellets of mud mixed with plant fibers (see NEST and Fig. 21) and affix them to cliff faces, cave walls, or buildings, while others are cavity nesters that use old woodpecker holes, dry pipes, or bird boxes, or excavate burrows in earthen banks (Bank Swallow). Inside the mud cup or cavity, there is a loose cup of plant material, lined with feathers, fine grasses, hair, and the like. The eggs number 3–8 (average 4–5) in most species. They are white and unmarked in all but the "adobe" species; the latter's eggs are sparsely to densely speckled and spotted with varying shades of brown and gray.

Most swallow species make pleasant, liquid chirping sounds or twitters. Northern Rough-winged and Bank Swallows are at the drier, buzzier end of this range.

The swallows are among the most thoroughly cosmopolitan of bird families. They range from the Arctic throughout the tropics to the subantarctic islands and are absent only from the most barren tundra and desolate ocean islands. Several species undertake long transoceanic migrations, and the Alaskan populations of the Barn Swallow undertake perhaps the greatest such journey of any native passerine—7,000 miles one way to Argentine wintering grounds. Certain swallow species are among the first migrants to return to the Temperate Zone in the spring and therefore have long been considered heralds of that season. All but 2 North American swallow species breed continentwide; all are migratory and only the southernmost populations of a few species winter here.

"Swallow" derives from an early Germanic word meaning "cleft stick" (*fide* Lockwood 1993–NAMES) referring to the forked "swallow-tail" of the Barn Swallow. The earliest forms of the name were also applied to the fork-tailed (*Apus*) swifts, but the European swallows without such tails were called martins; this distinction was abandoned in naming of hirundines elsewhere in the world. See also MARTIN.

SWAMP. As an ecological term refers to a variety of *wooded* wetland habitats in which the ground is inundated for at least part of the year. The wettest of such habitats cannot support trees and are dominated by emergent shrubs (shrub swamp). Swamp forest may be dominated by a variety of tree species (e.g., Red Maple, cypress, mangrove), depending on climate, soil chemistry, and other factors. Characteristic birds of wooded swamps include Wood Duck, Green Heron, Barred Owl, Veery, Northern Waterthrush and Prothonotary, and Swainson's Warblers, among other species. Though often called swamps in popular usage, marshes have deeper water, cannot support woody growth, are dominated by emergent

herbs (e.g., cattail) and/or grasses, and attract different bird species, e.g., rails and bitterns. Reflecting this confusion, the Swamp Sparrow prefers marshes. See also MARSH.

SWAN. Standard English name for all 7 members of the subfamily Cygninae (family Anatidae; order Anseriformes), of which 2 (Tundra and Trumpeter) breed regularly in North America. The Eurasian Whooper Swan has bred once in westernmost Alaska, occurred as a vagrant, and established itself locally after having escaped from captivity. The exotic Mute Swan, also native to Eurasia, is now well established along the coast of North America from southern New England to Virgina and locally in the Great Lakes.

Swans are among the largest living birds (see SIZE). All of our species are wholly white except for "soft parts" and are distinguished by bill characteristics and posture. Like most other members of their family, swans have a broad, flat bill with a terminal "nail" and sieve-like lamellae along the internal edges; the front three toes are webbed. The characteristic long neck of swans is an adaptation for feeding on bottom vegetation in the shallows of lakes, ponds, and estuaries. Swans are among the world's most graceful and splendid wild creatures and have always captured people's imaginations, e.g., the Leda myth (see IMAGINATION, BIRDS IN), Tchaikovsky's ballet *Swan Lake,* and Yeats's "The Wild Swans at Coole."

They have also long been popular game birds, and the Trumpeter Swan was shot to the brink of extinction in the nineteenth century for its feathers (see CONSERVATION) and flesh. There is still a hunting season on the Whistling Swan. Populations of Mute Swans have reached pest proportions in some areas where they scour ponds of aquatic vegetation sometimes to the exclusion of native waterfowl.

For nests, swans construct large piles of vegetation on the bank or in the shallows of a lake, pond, or river (see Fig. 21). They occasionally use the ready-made piles of muskrat lodges, and Whistling Swans sometimes make floating nests. Females line their nests sparsely with down from their breasts and lay 2–12 (usually 5–7) white to yellowish, unmarked eggs (Mute Swan, pale gray, blue, or green).

Mute Swans generally live up to their name, though they can hiss impressively when disturbed. Whistling Swans make a melodious bugling, often heard in chorus from a flock in the air. Trumpeter Swans give a distinctive, deep, disyllabic honking call. See also SWAN SONG.

The swans are birds of the Temperate Zone and are mostly distributed in the Holarctic region, though there is a single Australian species (the Black Swan, popular as an ornamental here) and 2 in southern South America.

The word "swan" comes to us unchanged from Old English.

SWAN SONG. Debate about the nature—or very existence—of a unique "song" uttered by some swan species with their last breath has raged at least since classical times. Plato did not doubt that swans sang in their last

hour but argued that this was simply a final affirmation of their cheerful, musical disposition—a description that few present-day swan watchers would recognize. Other commentators have contended that the swan song is as mythical as the lustful cygnine that ravished Leda.

There can be no doubt that swans are capable of a variety of vocalizations—most notably "bugling" or "trumpeting" notes, possibly facilitated by their unusually long, coiled tracheas—but also muted "conversational" sounds and, especially in the Tundra Swan, pleasing, musical tones; pairs of this species are known to engage in prolonged "duets" with the two sexes taking different parts. Delacour (1954–WATERFOWL) opines that the swan song is simply (unpoetically) the expulsion of air from the trachea of a shot swan as it plummets to earth, but there are several authoritative accounts of an extended, melodious, but rarely heard call made by Tundra Swans, sometimes (but not always) during their death agony. The waterfowl expert A. H. Hochbaum (1955–BIRDWATCHING) records what he calls a departure song—a soft, beautiful series of notes uttered before takeoff—and this description agrees well with the account of the nineteenth-century naturalist D. G. Elliot, who recorded a similar "song" from a Whistling Swan he brought down out of the North Carolina sky.

In vernacular usage, the swan song is a metaphor for a last earthly act, usually a creative one, e.g., a poet's last sonnet or an actor's last role. Even a politician's last speech may be so described by the broad-minded.

SWIFT. Standard English name for most of the 99 members of the family Apodidae (order Apodiformes), 4 of which breed in North America. Five other species have been recorded as vagrants (see Appendix II).

Some swifts measure as little as 3½ inches in length, but North Americans may be surprised to learn that others reach 9½ inches (larger than a robin). Swifts have very small bills and wide gapes, like the nightjars, which have similar feeding habits (see below). Their wings are very long and pointed, most of the length extending from the "wrist" (bend of the wing), giving the swifts a characteristic fluttering flight. The spinetailed swifts (subfamily Chaeturinae), to which our 2 commonest species belong, have very short tails, the rachises of which extend beyond the vanes at the tips. This series of rigid spines that forms the end of the tail acts as a prop when the birds perch on vertical surfaces (see Fig. 30). Even the longer-tailed species have a generally fusiform body shape and suggest "flying cigars."

The feet of swifts are very small (one of the few obvious characters they share with their order mates, the hummingbirds) and strongly modified for clinging—the only kind of perching that swifts do. All four toes are directed forward (pamprodactyl) and bear long, strong, hooked claws. Most swifts (all in North America) are somberly plumaged in white, black, grays, and browns.

Swifts are the most aerial of birds, capable of fast, agile, and high-altitude flight. They feed exclusively on airborne invertebrates (mainly

insects and "ballooning" spiders), which are carried in surprising numbers thousands of feet into the air. Many of the routine activities of everyday life that most birds perform on the ground—e.g., bathing, drinking, gathering nesting material—swifts can accomplish in flight; they routine spend the night on the wing and are the only birds known to copulate while airborne.

Swifts often feed in flocks and nest colonially, placing cup or half-cup nests on cliff faces, inside hollow trees, or in chimneys. Many species glue their nest materials together with their sticky saliva (see BIRD'S NEST SOUP) and affix the structure to vertical surfaces by the same method.

Black Swifts lay but a single egg, other North American species 3–7 (usually 4–5). All are white to pale yellowish and unmarked.

Because of their dependence on live, airborne prey, swifts are vulnerable to cold or wet spells during which insects are not flying. Both adults and nestlings of at least some species respond to such emergencies by assuming a temporary state of dormancy (see TORPIDITY) in which bodily functions are "shut down" almost completely, thus requiring little sustenance.

The songs and calls of swifts are typically high-pitched, often metallic or bell-like twitters, chatters, or shrill screeches with occasional single sharp chips. Many swifts engage in communal flight displays in which the flock breaks into a choral tintinnabulation that can be quite earsplitting at close range or when reverberating from the walls of a narrow gorge.

Swifts are distributed worldwide (absent from the coldest northern and southern extremes and some oceanic islands). In North America, swifts are absent from tundra, boreal forest, and central plains (except in migration). Except for the White-throated Swift, which is a permanent resident in parts of the Southwest, all of our species are long-distance migrants.

The name "swift" refers to the obvious, though the swiftness of these birds is controversial. It has been "alleged" that the greatest natural flight speed in nature is that of the White-throated Needle-tailed Swift (*Hirundapus caudacutus*) at 219.5 mph (other allegers say a mere 170 kph). However, Rayner (in Campbell and Lack 1985–ORNITHOLOGY) contends that swifts are actually "among the slowest of birds." Nevertheless, in del Hoyo et al. (1992–ORNITHOLOGY) points out that swifts' unusually long primaries and very short secondaries can create a very powerful forward and downward force, and species of swiftlets (*Collocalia*) have timed using Doppler radar at 111 kph. Anyone who has witnessed needle-tailed swifts or, say, White-throated Swift at close range when they are in a hurry can confirm that they seem to be going wicked fast—just *how* fast apparently still needs further study (Chantler 1999) (see SPEED). Swifts, like owls and nightjars, have been widely associated with the devil and seen as omens of ill-fortune.

SWIMMING/DIVING. Over 20% (about 150 species) of the regularly occurring North American avifauna habitually swim and/or dive. However, not all swimming birds dive, nor do all divers swim. And, of course, there

are numerous waterbird species (e.g., plovers, herons) that seldom do either (see below, however).

Evolution has wrought an impressive number of avian variations and combinations with these two forms of behavior. The loons, grebes, some tubenoses, cormorants, anhingas, coots, alcids, and about 60% of native duck species are highly adept at both swimming and diving from the surface. The albatrosses, shearwaters, storm-petrels, White Pelican, gulls, swans, geese, dabbling (surface-feeding) ducks, and phalaropes swim as a way of life, but in most cases dive only infrequently and near the surface, if at all. Most tubenoses and gulls will force themselves a few feet beneath the surface to attack a school of fish. The nondiving anatids normally "tip up" in a kind of halfhearted dive to pluck bottom vegetation, but they will also submerge completely (though briefly), especially when ice or rough or deep water makes tipping up ineffective, and they will also dive to escape a Peregrine or other predator.

Tropicbirds, Manx Shearwater (occasionally), boobies and gannets, Brown Pelican, most terns, Osprey, and all our native kingfishers plunge from the air into the water after fish. This technique varies from the gannets, which may begin their plunge from over 100 feet in the air and pursue fish to moderate depths once submerged, to the kingfishers, which often hover only a relatively few feet above the water and barely penetrate the surface on their splashdowns. Among this group of divers, Brown Pelicans swim habitually, the Osprey and kingfishers not at all, and the others sit on the water relatively infrequently or for short periods only.

Though adapted most conspicuously for walking and wading, the flamingoes, rails, and most shorebirds swim well. Some have partially webbed toes, and a few species (e.g., yellowlegs, Stilt Sandpiper) swim routinely while feeding. Avocets and stilts not only swim well but also dive expertly. Even herons will "swim" on occasion: Great Blue Herons have been seen to alight on the open sea (briefly), presumably to rest.

The only truly aquatic songbirds are the dippers, which, however, behave uniquely in the water. Their feet are not webbed and they more "drift" or "ride" than "paddle" when traveling on a surface current. Though they swim or "fly" using their wings underwater, their actual feeding behavior largely involves *walking* on the bottom (see DIPPER).

The swimming ability of other passerine birds is decidedly limited. They have a certain natural buoyancy due to the air trapped in their plumage and body cavity (see RESPIRATORY SYSTEM) and are usually capable of flapping a short distance to shore if accidentally dunked. But their feathers rapidly become waterlogged and drag them down, and many thousands of exhausted migrants perish by drowning in the ocean in spring and especially in fall (see MIGRATION, Hazards).

PHYSICAL ADAPTATIONS

- A bird's source of locomotion when swimming at the surface is its legs and feet and these are strongly modified in all true swimming/

diving birds. The most frequent swimming modification is, of course, webbing between the toes, but phalaropes and coots have scalloped lobes along the margins of each toe, and in the grebes, each toe is a flat, mobile paddle which can be "feathered" like oars when in use (see LEG/FOOT and Fig. 17).

- The feet of waterbirds that don't swim are often clues to behavior. Though frigatebirds belong to the same order as the pelicans and boobies (Pelecaniformes), which have webbing between all four toes, the former have relatively tiny, only partially webbed feet, reflecting the fact that they are essentially aerial birds that don't swim and that perch awkwardly.

- When progressing normally at the surface, swimming birds paddle with alternating strokes, one foot pushing the water behind as the other returns forward. However, birds that use foot power while diving (see below) push with both feet at once. Most swimming birds also have laterally flattened legs to allow minimum drag when paddling. The "engines" that permit this kind of paddling locomotion are appropriately enlarged thigh muscles.

- Wings modified for diving are not common among birds, since most adaptations of these limbs are related to flight. The most striking exception to this rule is the penguins, whose forelimbs have become flippers—useless for flying in air, but perfectly adapted for "flying" underwater. Of all birds, penguins are by far the most at home in the water. They are as agile as any marine mammal (or more so) and can swim underwater faster than some birds can fly (Gentoo Penguins more than 22 mph). Among North American birds only the alcids have wings that seem strongly adapted for use underwater. Though fully feathered and capable of flight in living species, these appendages are notably narrow and flipper-like when extended.

- Birds that both swim and dive habitually should ideally be both buoyant and have a high specific gravity. This seemingly contradictory condition is achieved in most swimmers/divers by a combination of anatomical specialization and behavior. Birds' body cavities are lined with a system of air sacs that fill the spaces between the other organs and can be inflated and deflated, as the lungs are, by inhaling and exhaling (see RESPIRATORY SYSTEM). These air sacs even penetrate many bones (see SKELETON, Pneumatization), so that even a bird's skeleton is partially air-filled. The buoyancy thus achieved is, of course, an advantage in flight and, when combined with the air-trapping capacity of the plumage, also makes birds natural floaters. In addition, most swimming/diving birds have particularly large oil glands, from which they continually coat their feathers, making them waterproof—sealing in the trapped air and preventing them from becoming waterlogged while active in their preferred habitat. We take it for granted that water "naturally" rolls

off a duck's back and the same can be said of loons, grebes, gulls, and most other water-inhabiting species.

When it comes to diving, buoyancy becomes a liability, working against a bird's efforts to penetrate water, which becomes ever denser with increasing depth. Species that plunge into the water from the air depend partly on gravity to counteract their natural "floatability," and those that dive from the surface and pursue prey once submerged push themselves under, using their legs and feet. More subtle is the ability of many waterbirds to compress their plumage, squeezing the trapped air out and raising their specific gravity. It is this trick that permits the grebes to sink like a submarine, apparently without exerting any effort. The plumage of cormorants and anhingas is relatively porous and fills with water readily; this makes for efficient diving but also explains the amount of time these birds spend drying out with their wings spread (see also SUNNING). In preparing for a dive, birds also expel air from their air sacs, further reducing buoyancy. Loons and other birds that dive often and deep also tend to have heavier—i.e., less pneumatized—bones.

- Anyone who has watched a gannet plummet headfirst into the sea from high in the air is likely to wonder how the impact can be sustained time after time without resulting in a broken neck or at least a bad headache. In its practical way, evolution has given gannets unusually powerful neck muscles, a thickened and strongly supported skull, and air sacs lying under the skin of the head, which act as a kind of padded crash helmet.

- If diving birds expel air from their respiratory systems before submerging, where is their oxygen supply contained? Answer: In the red pigment of red blood corpuscles (oxyhemoglobin), which are more numerous in divers than in other types of birds. In a dive, the flow of oxygenated blood can be regulated so that the brain and the rest of the nervous system continue to receive oxygen from the blood, which is being supplied temporarily at a much slower rate to muscular tissue.

- The eyes of diving birds are modified to see prey accurately underwater (see VISION).

- The nostril openings of pelicans, cormorants, and gannets and boobies are either closed at birth or become so by adulthood and breathing is done through openings at the corners of the gape (see NOSTRILS); this is probably an adaptation to underwater habits.

DIVING "STYLES." The beginning of a standard "surface dive"—i.e., one that starts from a sitting position on the water—is a strong push forward—sometimes almost a leap upward—followed by a downward bowing of the neck and back, so that the bird breaks the surface in an arc, striking it almost vertically. Loons, grebes, and anhingas sometimes perform a sinking dive by "squeezing" the air from their body feathers and emptying their air sacs (see above). The "plungers" use gravity instead of muscle

power to penetrate the water surface, but hit the water and "recover" in a variety of ways. The terns and kingfishers, which take fish from near the surface, make shallow splashdowns and return to the air with a shake (and sometimes a fish) almost at once. Tropicbirds as well as the terns and kingfishers often hover before plunging, and kingfishers frequently dive from fixed perches. Ospreys hit first with their feet, extended at the last moment by their long legs to grasp the unsuspecting fish. Their weight and the momentum of the dive may submerge them completely, but only momentarily, after which they too regain the air. Brown Pelicans and the gannets and boobies enter the water bill-first with neck extended and often from considerable heights (gannets from more than 100 feet at times).

The pelicans fold their wings and push them far back just before entry; their great mass prevents them from submerging very deeply and they almost immediately bounce back to the surface (see BILL). The gannets and boobies fold their wings tightly as they begin their dives and then open them slightly just before impact. Palmer (1962–ORNITHOLOGY) notes that Northern Gannets rotate slightly during their descent and also that the greater their starting altitude, the steeper is their angle of entry. Members of this family (Sulidae) also sometimes dive from the surface. Though they hit the water with great force, pursue fish underwater, and may stay submerged for up to 40 seconds, most of their dives (whether from the surface or from "on high") are short and relatively shallow (to 6 feet or less).

Birds also use a variety of techniques in underwater swimming. Loons and grebes have legs set at the extreme tail end of their bodies and propel themselves with maximum efficiency torpedo-like through the water, wings tightly folded and neck extended. By contrast, the alcids use their feet little, if at all, when submerged but rather use their wings as penguins do to "fly" at relatively high speed underwater.

The gannets and boobies, cormorants and anhingas, and diving ducks use *mainly* their feet for propulsion underwater but also use their wings to varying degrees and in various ways. The ducks may use their wings to steer with to some extent. The White-winged Scoter is known to dive with wing tips crossed over its tail, its "wrist" joints protruding, and its long alulas extended.

DEPTH AND DURATION OF DIVES. The farther down a bird dives, the harder and slower the going, and therefore there is some correlation between the depth of a dive and its duration. However, long dives are not necessarily deep dives: one Western Grebe submerged for 63 seconds in 5½ feet of water (Palmer 1962–GREBE).

The majority of diving birds are not deep or long divers; most species rarely exceed 10 feet or stay under more than 10–20 seconds. Even the champion deep divers, such as the loons, grebes, sea ducks, and alcids, rarely approach their full diving potential. The record-holding Common Loon (see below) *usually* dives to a depth not exceeding 35 feet and takes less than a minute (sometimes much less) to resurface. Also, birds under

duress (e.g., chased or shot) will typically stay submerged much longer than normal.

World's Record Dive. The Emperor Penguin can reach at least 534 meters (1,752 feet) below the surface and stay under for at least 16 minutes (Kooyman and Kooyman 1995).

North American Record Dives. The Common Loon and Long-tailed Duck are tied for the deepest-diver record, both having been trapped in fishing nets at depths of 180–225 feet and perhaps slightly deeper. Though their average dives are much shorter (see above), these birds are apparently little taxed by dives lasting 3 minutes and the loon has survived forcible submersion for 15 minutes. Except for the penguin record noted above, these are also world records.

SYMBIOSIS (sim-be-OH-sis). In the broadest sense, any association between two different organisms, including parasitism, commensalism, etc. In the narrower usage, a symbiotic relationship is one in which both partners derive benefit for which the preferred term is now *mutualism*. For examples relating to birds, see COMMENSALISM; BROOD PARASITISM; ECTOPARASITE; MUTUALISM, PIRACY.

SYMBOLIC BIRDS. See IMAGINATION, BIRDS IN.

SYMPATRIC (sim-PAT-rik). Referring to closely related species or subspecies whose geographical ranges overlap. Sympatry is often cited in questions of speciation. For example, in Texas and Louisiana where the Great-tailed and Boat-tailed Grackles are sympatric, they do not normally interbreed. Converse of ALLOPATRIC. See SPECIATION.

SYNONYMS. In a taxonomic context, two or more names for the same species or other taxon. Synonyms are created, for example, when a species is mistakenly redescribed by an author under the impression that he is dealing with a new species. In such cases, the law of priority holds that the first name is the valid one and the new synonym is discarded. Synonyms are also created by taxonomic revision. The original Latin name given to the White-rumped Sandpiper was *Tringa fuscicollis,* thus placing it in a genus with nearly all of the other sandpipers, including, for example, the yellowlegs. More recently the smaller sandpipers were "split" into several different genera, e.g., *Erolia, Ereuntes,* and *Calidris,* at which time the White-rumped became *Erolia fuscicollis.* In 1976, the AOU Committee on Taxonomy and Nomenclature ruled that most of the small sandpipers (including the three genera noted above) should be "lumped" into a single one. As the earliest name used for these birds, *Calidris* was the generic name of choice and the White-rumped Sandpiper became, and remains today, *Calidris fuscicollis.* All of these Latin name variations are "synonyms."

SYNTYPE (SIN-type). When the author of a species designates a type series as the criterion for his original description but does not designate a particular type specimen, all of the specimens in the series are called "syntypes." See NOMENCLATURE, ZOOLOGICAL, Types.

SYRINX (SEER-inks) (pl.: syringes [suh-RIN-jeez]). The organ of voice production unique to birds; a bird's "voice box." It is located either (1) near the lower end of the windpipe (trachea); (2) over the junction of the trachea and the fork of the bronchi (most birds); or (3) as a paired organ, one syrinx on each of the two bronchi. In general, species with the most highly evolved syringes produce the most complex sounds. Birds also have a larynx, the voice box of humans (and other mammals). It is located above the syrinx but is little developed and is not involved (or only marginally so) in voice production. The syrinx is sometimes referred to as the lower of a bird's two larynges: For more detail on the structure and function of the syrinx, see SONG.

SYSTEMATICS. In modern biology the study, description, and orderly arrangement of life-forms based on evolutionary relationships. Frequently used interchangeably with "taxonomy," though in the strictest sense the latter refers only to classification.

There is a Chinese saying that "the beginning of wisdom is calling things by their right name." In biological systematics affixing the "right name" implies far more than a simple label. Rather it is a process, involving (1) the discovery of an organism's evolutionary relationships—its phylogeny: from which other species is it descended and which are its descendants? (2) organizing related organisms in a coherent classification system (taxonomy), and (3) defining biological entities (species) and giving them names that distinguish them from all others (see NOMENCLATURE, ZOOLOGICAL). Of course, naming things has been around since the dawn of language. And organizing names to reflect evolutionary truth has preoccupied biologists for centuries and continues to present fascinating challenges.

HISTORY OF AVIAN SYSTEMATICS. People have classified birds (and other organisms) from earliest times. The oldest classifications tend to be utilitarian—which species are good to eat, have usable parts, are dangerous or possess supernatural powers. Aristotle (384–322 BC) devised a system that categorized birds largely by behavioral traits—swimming birds, singing birds, birds of the fields—and, of course, we still place birds of disparate origins in such categories when we speak of "seabirds" or "marsh birds" or "birds of prey." This system was used with modifications until the late seventeenth century, when physical features such as the shape of bill or type of foot began to be compared. With the publication of Darwin's *Origin of Species* (1859), it became logical to try to arrange living things according to the sequence of their evolution. It also became evi-

dent that birds that appear quite different (consider the sandpiper family) might still be closely related—early inklings of the concept of *adaptive radiation*—or conversely that relatively unrelated birds might have evolved a similar type of foot (e.g., albatrosses and gulls)—now known to be a result of *adaptive convergence.* By the end of the nineteenth century taxonomists were looking for structural characters in plants and animals that reliably indicated evolutionary relationships rather than adaptive features, not always an easy distinction to make. The most recent breakthroughs in systematics appeared in the 1970s with (1) the advent of *cladistic analysis,* a new way of assessing relationships between species based on distinguishing shared traits recently derived from a common ancestor from primitive characters (see below); and (2) a leap in biochemical technology allowing ornithologists to use characteristics at the molecular level for constructing avian genealogies (see below).

The birth of modern classification systems dates from 1735, when a Swedish botanist, Karl von LINNÉ (Carolus Linnaeus), proposed a hierarchical system of grouping and naming life forms. All names were to be in Latin, the language of science, and his original categories were

Classis
Ordo
Genus
Species
Varietas

Each species was referred to by a binomial name consisting of the genus and species.

Linnaeus's system has been expanded and refined to reflect the enormous growth in our knowledge of biodiversity and its evolution, but his basic taxonomic structure still forms the skeleton, as it were, of modern systematics. An example of the traditional taxonomic hierarchy as used, for example, in the latest edition of the *AOU Checklist of North American Birds* (1998) is given below, using a single species as an example. Primary categories are in boldface.

Kingdom: Animalia (all multicellular animals, as distinguished from plants, fungi, protists, and bacteria; see KINGDOM)

Phylum: Chordata (animals with a hollow dorsal nerve cord)

Subphylum: Vertebrata (animals with a well-developed brain encased in a bony skull and, in all living vertebrates, a segmented vertebral column)

Class: Aves (Birds)

Subclass: Neornithes (True Birds, including some but not all fossil species)

Superorder: Neognathae (Typical Birds, including most living species as well as some fossil forms)

Order: Falconiformes (Diurnal Birds of Prey, including ospreys, kites, hawks, eagles, Old World vultures, secretarybirds, falcons, and caracaras)

Suborder: Falcones (Caracaras and Falcons)

Superfamily: Falconoidea (an obsolete taxon that once combined the falcon and carararas and the secretarybirds)

Family: Falconidae (Falcons, Laughing Falcons and Caracaras)

Subfamily: Falconinae (True Falcons and Laughing Falcons)

Tribe: Falconini (True Falcons)

Genus: *Falco*

Subgenus: *Cerchneis* (an obsolete grouping of kestrels and other falcons within the genus)

(Superspecies: not applicable here but sometimes used to distinguish a group of closely related species within a given genus)

Species: *F. sparverius* (American Kestrel)

Subspecies: *F. s. paulus* ("Florida" Kestrel)

The recent innovations in biochemical determinants of phylogenetic relationships pioneered by Sibley and Ahlquist (1990–SYSTEMATICS) attempt, so to speak, to measure the evolutionary distance between species and higher taxa. This has resulted in a revised taxonomy in which additional categories are required to accurately reflect the "spacial" relationships among these groups and also in many cases a radical revision of the traditional phylogeny with which ornithologists and birdwatchers are familiar. To give some sense of the magnitude of difference between the two systems, here is American Kestrel again as classified in the Sibley system:

Kingdom: Animalia (Animals)

Phylum: Chordata (Chordates)

Class: Aves (Birds)

Subclass: Neornithes (True Birds)

Infraclass: Neoaves (All modern birds except Ratites)

Parvclass: Passerae (All modern birds except ratites, gallinaceous birds, ducks and geese, woodpeckers and relatives, hornbills, kingfishers and relatives, and mousebirds)

Superorder: Passerimorphae (All modern birds excluding the above and the cuckoos, parrots, swifts, hummingbirds, owls, and nightjars)

Order: Ciconiiformes (includes not only the diurnal raptors, but also the shorebirds and relatives, gull and terns, alcids, grebes, cormorants and boobies, herons and relatives, pelicans, storks and New World vultures, penguins, loons, and tubenoses)

Suborder: Ciconii (all of the Order except the shorebirds and relatives, the gulls and terns, and the alcids)

Infraorder: Falconides (Diurnal Birds of Prey)

Parvorder: Falconida (Caracaras and Falcons)

Family: Falconidae (Caracaras and Falcons)

Genus: Falco

Species: *Falco sparverius*

For further discussion of the use of the categories and the naming process, see NOMENCLATURE, ZOOLOGICAL. See also entries for taxonomic categories: ORDER; FAMILY; etc.

The first authoritative classification of the world avifauna was published by the Anglo-German zoologist Hans Friedrich Gadow in 1862. Other major works of this scope building on Gadow's foundation include the taxonomies of Stresemann (1927–34), Mayr and Amadon (1951) Wetmore (1960), and Storer (1971), and the monumental *Checklist of the Birds of the World* by James Peters et al. (1931–86), which filled 15 volumes and took 55 years to complete. The latest addition to these painstakingly constructed lists is Sibley and Monroe's *Distribution and Taxonomy of Birds of the World* (1990) and its *Supplement* (1993) based on Sibley and Ahlquist's *Phylogeny and Classification of Birds* (1990). As noted these works did not simply add incrementally to an existing framework, but expounded a new methodology for defining phylogenetic relationships and gave fresh inspiration to an area of inquiry that had seemed to be reaching a dead end.

THE CLASSIFICATION PROCESS. Creating a biological taxonomy is a little like doing the kind of crossword puzzle in which you must figure out where the words fit as well as discover their definitions. A taxon's identity depends on its position relative to other taxa—and vice versa. Playing this game with living organisms is especially challenging because the units involved are not discrete entities but continually evolving forms that

occupy virtually every possible position in relation to their nearest relatives from very close to quite distant. A key starting point is the species, the only objectively real or natural category in the taxonomic hierarchy. A biological species is a population (or multiple populations) of interbreeding organisms that seldom if ever interbreeds with any other such group (see SPECIES and SPECIATION). All the other categories both above and below are groupings (or subsets) of species defined subjectively by the taxonomist's theories about which species are closely related to each other. Such theories are based on real anatomical, behavioral, or other criteria (see Taxonomic Characters, below), but interpreting such evidence to show relationships between organisms is an exercise of human intellect that does not correspond to any fixed natural structure. Nature has created an inconceivably complex fabric, and systematics is a way of trying to understand it by cutting it up into what seem to be differentiable parts and giving them names.

Given the species as a starting point, our goal as would-be taxonomists is clear: figure out what all the species are and group them into categories reflecting relationships—similar species go into genera, a bunch of like genera become a family, etc. We are apt to underestimate this task. As we glance through a field guide of North American birds, things seem to be sorted out much as we would have done it had we been asked—drab, fat-billed birds over with the sparrows; a brightly colored, fast-moving, slender-billed bird must be a wood warbler; the Wrentit doesn't look like anything in particular—give it a family of its own. In fact, this common sense approach is not very different from the actual practice of the earliest scientific classifiers—and, furthermore, in quite a lot of cases and up to a point, it works. In many instances the most sophisticated modern techniques for defining genetic relationships have simply confirmed the educated guesses of eighteenth-century naturalists. No one, after all, would be likely to classify any of the world's four species of flamingos anywhere but among its fellows, and few, looking around at other possible relationships, would hesitate to give the flamingos at least a family of their own. It might take more time to be sure that the grebes are not just funny-looking ducks or loons or gallinules, but once you had made a general survey of avian feet, you would probably conclude that all grebes were much more like each other than like any other birds.

Alas, common sense takes one only so far and is often an illusion. To begin to understand the challenge of biological systematics, imagine yourself as Catesby or Audubon looking at North American birds for the first time with only your eye and your intuition to help you decide what is a species and what is not. Would you have recognized all the plumages of a Yellow Warbler (age, sex, and season) as variations within a single species or would you have called them three different species as Audubon did (Havell Plates XXV, LXV, and XCV)? How about the light, dark, intermediate, regional, and age variations of the Red-tailed Hawk? Would you

have guessed that the large, pale Ipswich Sparrow, which breeds only on Sable Island, Nova Scotia, was a race of the same species as the small, dark Labrador Savannah Sparrow? Having learned this lesson, would you have been sure that the Western Bluebird was not just a geographical color variation of the Eastern Bluebird? How many *Empidonax* flycatcher species would you allow if museum specimens of all the North American species were laid before you? Three? Six? There are eleven, two of which were "split" within the last decade. And Brewster's Warbler—a highly distinctive species in the same genus as the Golden-winged and Blue-winged Warblers? Wrong again—a hybrid between the two! Though aided by new technologies, such problems of species differentiation (see DIMORPHISM; POLYMORPHISM; GEOGRAPHICAL VARIATION; SIBLING SPECIES; HYBRIDIZATION) remain to be resolved in many cases, especially in the world's less studied avifaunas.

In addition, there is the problem of determining the relationships between families and the other larger groupings of birds. It is all very well to recognize that a flamingo is a flamingo, but what exactly *is* a flamingo as defined by its nearest relatives. It's long legs and neck suggest heron or stork relatives, but its bill with its tooth-like serrations and large tongue and its webbed feet are decidedly goose-like, and its feeding and nesting habits resemble those of certain shorebirds. This is an example of the dual conundrum that constantly confronts the biological classifier: Many species superficially resemble many other species to which they are not closely related—e.g., shearwaters and gulls, herons and storks, swifts and swallows—while others bear little obvious resemblance to their close relatives—New World vultures and storks, swifts and hummingbirds, tanagers and (Emberizine) sparrows.

These puzzles arise largely from two phenomena of evolution, adaptive convergence and adaptive radiation. In the former, birds (and other organisms) of different lineages tend to evolve the same traits as adaptations to specialized lifestyles. A clear example is the general similarity that has evolved between the auks (and especially the extinct Great Auk) of the northern oceans and the penguins of the similarly cold, nutrient-rich southern seas (see Fig. 6). Auks are closely related to gulls and penguins to petrels—they belong to different Orders or Suborders (depending on the taxonomic system), yet both have evolved short swimming wings (to the point of flightlessness), a torpedo-like shape, black-and-white countershading, a preference for fish and marine arthropods as food, and many other traits that make for a successful existence in diving seabirds. As the name implies, adaptive radiation (or divergence) is an evolutionary force in the opposite direction. It "encourages" a single species to evolve into multiple—sometimes strikingly different—forms to exploit unoccupied ecological niches. This is well illustrated among the members of the American blackbird family (Icteridae): the Bobolink has developed the appearance and habitat and food preferences common to sparrows and many other

seedeaters; orioles, on the other hand, are more like tanagers or warblers in these respects; grackles look and behave rather like crows; the meadowlarks are also icterids, despite their name, but do indeed look and act like larks or pipits. And none of these groups of species resembles any of the others.

How then is a taxonomist to distinguish the deeper clues to ancestry from relatively recent adaptive changes?

TAXONOMIC CHARACTERS. Systematists struggling with this quandary have identified a variety of traits that have proven reliable in defining a bird's true relatives. Of course, even anatomical structures and behavioral quirks can be adaptive, so the best evidence of relationships between taxa is the conjunction of several different types of character. Some of the most useful categories are as follows.

Structural (Morphological) Characters have, of course, been used since the earliest attempts at classification and still provide crucial insights. Modern taxonomy has tried to identify "conservative" aspects of an animal's anatomy, i.e., those that are not as subject to adaptive changes as external features, such as general bill shape or leg length, which are notably "responsive" to selective pressures. Some of the parts of a bird's anatomy that are most frequently analyzed are

- Shape of the breastbone, and whether or not it has a keel
- Number of neck vertebrae
- Shape of the nostril opening in the bill and whether open or closed
- Form of the bony palate of the mouth
- Structure of the columella, the single bone in the bird's middle ear
- Form and number of jaw, wing, and thigh muscles (see MUSCLES, Formula Muscles)
- Form and internal structure of the syrinx
- Number, symmetry, and pattern of the carotid arteries
- Pattern in which the small intestine is coiled
- Form of scaling on the legs
- Number and position of toes
- Pattern in which the feathers grow from the skin (see FEATHER TRACTS)
- Color patterns of downy chicks
- Presence or absence of a tuft of feathers on the oil gland

Behavioral Characters providing clues to avian lineages include

- Nest construction—supported by biological phylogeny in the swallows (Winkler and Sheldon 1993)
- Nature of the mating system
- Type of courtship display
- Song patterns
- Care of young (e.g., whether both parents brood and/or feed)

Habitat and Distribution may reveal distinctions not exhibited by dead specimens or internal structure. In addition to song these factors

provide clues to relationships between superficially very similar forms, such as the meadowlarks, *Empidonax* flycatchers, and the southwestern thrashers. The separate wintering ranges of similar forms such as Gray-cheeked and Bicknell's Thrushes are also examples.

Biochemical Analysis of various body substances has provided not merely new taxonomic characters but entirely new ways of evaluating relationships among taxa. While the new methods have often confirmed phylogenetic suppositions based on morphological characters, they have also produced many revelations and surprises. By comparing patterns produced by subjecting egg-white proteins to an electric current (electrophoresis), Sibley and others (1968, 1973) were able to reposition a number of avian oddities (e.g., Wrenthrush and Hoatzin of the Neotropics) on the evolutionary tree. In the 1980s, enzymes called allozymes from adult birds replaced egg-white proteins as the most promising medium for showing well-marked genetic patterns and were used to determine species affinities in adult wood warblers and Emberizine sparrows (Barrowclough and Corbin 1978; Zink and Avise 1990; Lovette and Bermingham 2002–SPECIATION).

The biochemical technique that has produced the most radical proposed rearrangements of the avian evolutionary map to date is DNA-DNA hybridization pioneered by Sibley and Ahlquist (1990–SYSTEMATICS). In essence, the technique involves separating under high temperature the characteristic double strands of the DNA molecule of a given species and allowing one to form a hybrid molecule with a strand from a different species. The closer the relationship between the two species, the more stable the bond and the more heat required to separate the strands. A control melting temperature is set at the point required to separate two recombined strands from the same species and this is compared to the amount of heat required to separate strands from different species. The resulting discrepancy represents the genetic "distance" between the two. When this analysis is performed on a series of closely related species, a genealogical tree can be constructed based on the relative distances between forms. This technique has not only confirmed phylogenetic realignments suggested by more traditional taxonomic characters—such as that New World (Cathartid) vultures are short-legged storks rather than skin-head eagles—but also drastically revised the presumed order of evolutionary descent. As shown in the Sibley-model phylogeny above, falcons—once in an order containing only other day-flying birds of prey—are now included in a much larger order, which begins with sandgrouse and ends with storm-petrels; in the line of descent just above the former Falconiformes are the alcids and immediately below, the grebes.

The Sibley-Ahlquist phylogeny should not be seen as the new Truth vanquishing a discredited earlier vision. It is rather a hypothesis—a bold one—supported by some proofs. Both its experimental design and the

analysis of the data have been criticized by colleagues, which is how science proceeds. There is no question, however, that increasingly sophisticated methods of DNA analysis have opened a new path of biological systematics that will provide immense opportunities for new research as well as fresh insights into evolutionary relationships for decades to come.

CLADISTIC ANALYSIS. If comparative studies of DNA have given us an important new source of taxonomic characters, the emergence of cladistic analysis shows a similarly important new way to organize such traits. Rather than placing species and larger taxa along branches of a theoretical evolutionary tree, the cladistic approach focuses on defining relationships among taxa based on the distribution of shared characters derived from a common ancestor. The method builds classifications by seeking the next closest relationship or "sister group," thus moving outward from well-founded relationships rather than creating a hypothetical primitive ancestry as a hierarchy into which all taxa must be slotted. Its greatest advantage is that it is a universally applicable and essentially objective technique. While some aspects of the approach continue to be debated, cladistics is now the prevailing methodology among systematists. For additional details, see CLADISTICS.

OF TAXONOMISTS AND BIRDWATCHERS. Birdwatchers sometimes complain about what they perceive as arbitrary and irrational changes in the taxonomic status of species, especially when two or more species are "lumped" and the effect is to shorten one's lifelist. In fact, changes to authoritative taxonomies such as the *AOU Checklist of North American Birds* are now invariably based on scientific studies documenting the evolutionary relationships between the forms in question. These cases, which typically occur at the species/subspecies level, remind us that contrary to the impression given by field guides, species are not immutable objects like works of art, but living organisms that—through adaptive pressures and natural selection—change over time.

Excellent cases in point are the recent taxonomic sagas of the Yellow-rumped Warbler complex and the Baltimore/Bullock's Orioles. These are only two of many species groups that were split into eastern and western populations in times past. Klicka and Zink (1997–SPECIATION) give a molecular clock-based estimate that the orioles were separated about 2.35 million years ago (prior to any glaciations) in the late Pliocene, while the split of Yellow-rumped Warbler complex was more likely of glacial origin about 300,000 years ago. Since that time the warbler and oriole populations have reunited, providing the best possible test of whether the divided forms have become full biological species no longer able to interbreed readily with each other or whether the degree of evolutionary change was more superficial. If we simply look at plumage—especially that of adult males—the answer seems clear. Even a beginning birdwatcher would have no trouble distinguishing male Myrtle from Audubon's Warblers or male Baltimore from Bullock's Orioles (though the identification

of females and especially immatures is a different story). However, as described above, plumage patterns are poor indicators of evolutionary distance, and ornithologists studying these birds in the areas where the similar forms overlapped concluded that based on the degree of hybridization, the species pairs should be lumped: Myrtle and Audubon's Warbler were now "mere" subspecies of the Yellow-rumped Warbler, and the two orioles were subsumed under the admittedly uninspired name, Northern Oriole.

These and other lumpings codified by the American Ornithologists Union's Committee on Classification and Nomenclature in the 6th (1983) edition of the *AOU Checklist* caused widespread indignation that made national news. This came not just from listers annoyed at seeing their capital diminished, but also from the bird-loving general public who—especially in the case of the orioles (and especially in the city of Baltimore and the state of Maryland)—was dismayed that the anonymous experts apparently could not tell the difference between these distinctive "species" and that a favorite songbird must consequently lose its famous name. The irony is that with these taxonomic revisions, nothing was lost—the warblers, orioles, and other birds did not become less distinctive, nor were the familiar names banished, but merely reapplied to the appropriate subspecies. To the contrary, there was a notable *gain*—in our knowledge of the phylogeny these birds at a transitional stage of their evolution.

As it happens the story ends happily for oriole lovers, even those who prefer tradition to biology: subsequent studies on overlapping Baltimore/Bullock's populations convinced the taxonomic arbiters of the AOU that, though these forms do interbreed freely in a few areas, they are reproductively isolated in others and all factors considered they are, as it were, more different than they are alike. (Indeed, based on molecular phylogeny, they are not even each other's closest relatives among the orioles [*fide* Omland et al. 1999].) Lord Baltimore has returned to the field guides. Listers can also take heart, because with the advent of molecular systematics, cladistics and a lively debate about the definition of a species, systematics is emphatically in a "splitting" mode, and the world's bird list is growing. (For the relevant citations for the above species, see the species accounts in the *AOU Checklist,* 7th edition, 1998.) See also SPECIATION.

SO, WHAT *IS* A FLAMINGO? Lest the reader think that the mysteries of bird taxonomy have been reduced to a simple matter of grinding up some avian tissue and subjecting it to molecular analysis, it is worth noting that despite more than a century of scrutiny the taxonomic place of the flamingos is just as obvious and just as ambiguous as ever. In 1893, Gadow classified them as a suborder under the storks (Ciconiiformes). Storer (1971) gave them an order of their own (Phoenicopteriformes) between the storks and the ducks. Noting that flamingos have peculiar leg muscles similar to those of the Australian Stilt, Olson and Feduccia (1980) proposed that the former are actually a family in the shorebird order (Charadriiformes). A

superficial glance at the revolutionary Monroe-Sibley checklist (1993) suggests that these distinctive birds are back where they started—in a suborder of the Ciconiformes. However Monroe-Sibley's stork order is very different from Gadow's and includes the shorebirds (not to mention the hawks)—but not the ducks. Far from falling silent as the great taxonomist Stresemann once predicted (1959), systematists have never been more articulate.

TAIGA (tye-GAH or TYE-guh). Subarctic coniferous forest such as is typical of most of Siberia and most of Canada south of the tundra. In North America it consists largely of black and white spruce (*Picea mariana* and *P. glauca*), balsam fir (*Abies balsamea*), tamarack (*Larix laricina*), and jack pine (*Pinus banksiana*) and is typically interspersed with lakes, bogs (muskeg), and bare outcroppings of rock. It is essentially synonymous with "boreal forest." For characteristic birds, see BOREAL.

TAIL. Like many of man's primate ancestors, the earliest birds, such as *Archaeopteryx*, had long, bony tails. This reptilian appendage has long since ceased to be part of avian anatomy, however, and when we speak of the tail of a modern bird, we usually mean a more or less elongated group of feathers extending rearward from the end of its body. Birds that lack these feathers by accident or have very short ones by nature are likely to be labeled "tailless." This is not quite accurate, however, for the tail feathers are embedded in skin covering muscles that govern tail movements. The muscles in turn are anchored to the plowshare bone (pygostyle) at the end of the backbone and the series (usually 6) of unfused vertebrae that precede it. Speaking precisely then, a bird's tail is all of these—bones, muscle, skin, and feathers—beginning at an imaginary circle drawn from the end of the rump down through the vent and back up to the rump on the other side and ending at the tips of the longest tail feathers.

Fig. 30. *Specialized tails* are adapted to suit particular forms of bird behavior. The greatly elongated rectrices of the Scissor-tailed Flycatcher aid the quick stops and turns crucial to the life style of an insectivorous "aerobat." The broad fan of the Red-tailed Hawk is likewise essential as a "rudder," but also provides an extra "lifting" surface for this soaring species (see FLIGHT and Fig. 28). By contrast, the tail of the Chimney Swift is of scant use in flight but serves as an indispensable prop or brace in the swifts' characteristic vertical clinging posture—the only form of perching these birds do.

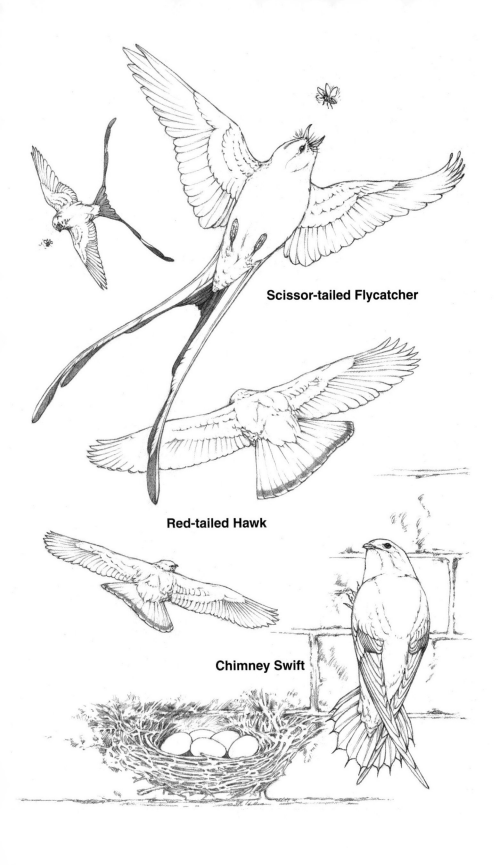

Scissor-tailed Flycatcher

Red-tailed Hawk

Chimney Swift

Arrangement of Tail Feathers. The main "flight" feathers of the tail are known collectively as the *rectrices*. In most birds these take the form of a fan made up of pairs of closely overlapping feathers: the outer pair is overlapped by the pair immediately inside and so on until the innermost pairs meet at the center of the tail, usually overlapping each other completely, giving the illusion of a single central feather. The number of rectrices varies among different species from 8 (e.g., anis) up to 32 (a species of snipe) but most birds have a total of 12. The number is not necessarily consistent within families or even within genera.

Overlapping the bases of the rectrices from above are the greater upper tail coverts (the number varies: one covert per rectrix, or less, or more); lesser upper tail coverts overlap the greaters and merge indistinguishably into the feathers of the rump. The undertail coverts follow a similar arrangement on the underside of the tail but in a less well-defined pattern.

Use. Many water birds (e.g., grebes, loons, most auks, rails) have scarcely any visible tail feathers and have little use for them. Many of these birds use their feet both in the air and while diving to replace the tail's function as a rudder. Soaring birds (e.g., vultures, buteos, eagles) tend to have very broad tails, which, when fully "fanned," become almost an extension of the wing. This extra surface increases "lift" and the "slots" between wing and tail aid stability (see FLIGHT). When the tail is lowered against the wind, it serves as a brake. And when it is twisted horizontally, it acts as the main turning mechanism or rudder. Most birds also depend on their tails for balance—the awkwardness of a tailless bird in flight or perching on a phone wire is obvious. Woodpeckers, swifts, and creepers have the tips of the tail feathers pointed and stiffened to brace their bodies as they cling or climb vertically. Finally, the shape, color, pattern, movement, and even musical capacity of the tail feathers are all used in various forms of display.

Shape. The shape the rectrices take as a unit depends on their length and how they are arranged. If a long outermost pair graduates to a short central pair, the result is a deep fork such as the Barn Swallow's. The opposite pattern (short outer graduating to long inner) produces the wedge (cuneiform) shape of the tails of gannets and Mourning Doves. Most birds' tails are between these two extremes of shape, varying from forked (Scissor-tailed Flycatcher, Fig. 30) to notched (Red Crossbill, Fig. 3) to squared (Red-tailed Hawk, Fig. 28) to rounded (Herring Gull, Fig. 15). A number of grassland birds—Grasshopper, Henslow's, Le Conte's, Sharp-tailed, and Seaside Sparrows and Bobolinks—have comparatively short, pointed tails with sharp individual rectrices. A few species (tropicbirds, jaegers, male Northern Pintails, and Long-tailed Ducks) have greatly elongated or modified central rectrices; these seem to function mainly in recognition or display rather than as flying aids.

Length. In many instances there is a strong correlation between aerobatic agility and tail length. Accipiters, jaegers, falcons, harriers, and

many flycatchers would be unable to execute their characteristic split-second stops and turns were it not for long tails under powerful muscular control. Long, *forked* tails (terns, Swallow-tailed Kite, Barn Swallow, Scissor-tailed Flycatcher) seem to permit particularly graceful maneuvers without sacrificing speed. While the most versatile fliers all have at least moderately long tails, the converse—that birds with long tails are all aerial masters—is not true. Chachalacas, cuckoos, and thrashers, all of which have long, "loose-jointed" tails, are birds of trees and dense shrubbery and spend little time on the wing except during migration, when endurance, not agility, is required. Magpies, wagtails, and grackles feed mostly on the ground and make relatively little use of their long tails in flight maneuvers.

The evolution of the Anhinga's long tail is interesting to contemplate, since swimming, diving, and soaring birds tend to have comparatively (or very) short tails. The species does cock and spread the tail during courtship rituals; in addition, perhaps it counterbalances the species' extraordinarily long neck.

Position and Gesture. Most birds at rest hold their tails in roughly the same plane as their backs—which may be parallel or perpendicular to the ground depending on the bird's posture. However, some ducks, some alcids, rails, dippers, and wrens "cock" their tails more vertically even in repose. The tails of woodpeckers and treecreepers, because of their function as props, are normally cocked downward (i.e., inward against the tree trunk), and the Bushtit, tits, and Verdin flex their tails toward the belly for equilibrium when they hang from branches.

Almost constant tail movements are common among many passerines, e.g., flycatchers, thrushes, thrashers, and warblers, and the exact nature of the gesture (whether flicked up or down and in what sequence) is a clue to field identification of some of the difficult *Empidonax* flycatchers. Most tail wagging is vertical, but anis, mimic thrushes, and a few other species have extremely mobile tails, which they habitually move through nearly all points of the compass.

The Spotted Sandpiper, wagtails and pipits, Kirtland's and Palm Warblers, Ovenbird, and the waterthrushes "pump" their tails and, to varying degrees, the whole of their hindquarters, almost without interruption. This motion is distinct from the more abrupt bobbing or "teetering" of dippers and many shorebirds (especially *Tringa* spp.), but no clear-cut explanation of its function has yet emerged. It has often been noted that many bobbing or wagging species frequent watery habitats.

Tail cocking is a common gesture of the courtship displays of many species and its effect is heightened in some cases by special tail features (e.g., the elongated central rectrices of male Long-tailed Ducks and Northern Pintails) or by beautifully patterned and colored tails, which are fanned to show them off (e.g., Wild Turkey, Ruffed and Sage Grouse, Killdeer). Tail fanning is not a common habit among North American

songbirds, the conspicuous exceptions being the American and Painted Redstarts, both of which keep their boldly patterned tails (and wings) spread while catching insects in the air, scolding potential predators, courting, or simply foraging.

TALKING BIRDS. See SONG, Vocal Mimicry.

TALON. In the broadest sense, the claw of any animal. Usually, however, talons refer to the relatively long, sharp claws of birds of prey. See LEG/FOOT and Fig. 17.

TAMENESS. Like other "wild" animals, birds are generally wary of close contact with human beings, yet the degree to which some species or individual birds will tolerate our company is by no means uniform, and cases of extraordinary tameness are common in the literature. In many cases it is clear that birds sometimes relinquish much of their wariness not from any desire for intimate contact with people themselves, but rather because human society makes food and shelter available either inadvertently (cleaning fish) or by design (birdhouses). Yet there are numerous other instances of both fear and tameness in birds that cannot be explained as learned behavior and that therefore seem to have some genetic basis. So many phenomena have been cited under the heading of "tameness," and so little effort made so far to relate one to another, that it seems best simply to list some of the more conspicuous facts in the matter.

- Birds that are wary of humans *per se* often overcome their seemingly innate fear when compensation in the form of food or nesting sites is available. There are innumerable examples: gulls coming on board fishing boats; gulls, crows, and other birds following on the heels of a plowman; Barn Swallows, phoebes, robins, wrens, and others nesting over a much-used doorway or inside someone's porch; Gray Jays raiding campers' rations; and, of course, the enthusiastic response of many species to being fed store-bought seeds and other "bird food."
- Certain families and species of birds seem to be "naturally" tamer than others and need no training by or experience with humans in the matter. Many seabirds, grouse, owls, shorebirds, corvids, tits, kinglets, waxwings, and "winter finches" seem not to recognize a human being as a threat and are thought variously to be "friendly," "bold," or "stupid" by the objects of their trust.
- Many of the species and individuals in the preceding groups breed in remote areas of the world where their contact with humans can be presumed to be limited. The birds (and other animals) of the Galápagos and other remote oceanic islands are notably fearless. The species of grouse, owls, jays, waxwings, and finches that have

the greatest reputation for tameness breed largely in remote boreal forests, many shorebirds in a vast wilderness of uninhabited tundra.

- There are numerous cases of apparently inexplicable geographical variation in tameness within a single species or among like ones. American birdwatchers are always struck by the reclusiveness of many woodland birds (e.g., woodpeckers) in the British Isles as compared with the United States—where persecution of songbirds has if anything been far greater than Britain's in recent times—or with other parts of Eurasia, where ancient traditions of trapping songbirds for food are still intact.
- There is much variation in wariness among individuals of a species: not all Pine Grosbeaks may be closely approached; American Robins breeding in forested areas are likely to be shyer than their suburban counterparts.
- It has been demonstrated that organisms tend to have an innate negative response to sizes, shapes, and movements that correspond to those of their natural predators. Some species may be genetically "programmed" to respond in this way to humans, whereas others may have to learn this fear. In this connection it is interesting to note that birds that are very wary of a person on foot are often not nearly so wary when approached in a car or on horseback.
- To the extent that this can be fairly judged, some individual birds seem to "enjoy" human company over and above the practical benefits (food) they derive therefrom. There are numerous records of birds in captivity being petted and ultimately seeking out their captor and "begging" to be stroked. This may be referable to some birds' urge to preen other birds and be preened (see ALLOPREENING).
- The "tameness" of birds that stay on their nests and allow themselves to be touched or that attack a human being who trespasses on breeding territory is probably best interpreted as defensive behavior, which represents a distinctly different response to the human presence than the other reactions discussed here.
- The "tameness" of birds that become imprinted by a human at hatching (see INTELLIGENCE) should probably also be considered as a separate phenomenon, due to its abnormality.

TAMIAMI TRAIL. See FLORIDA.

TANAGER (TAN-uh-jur). Standard English name for most of the approximately 250 members of the family Thraupidae (order Passeriformes). Sibley and Ahlquist (1990–SYSTEMATICS) treat the tanagers as a tribe (Thraupini) within the subfamily Emberizinae and family Fringillidae; in addition to the "traditional" tanagers, euphonias, conebills, honeycreepers, and flowerpiercers, this tribe includes a variety of finches and seedeaters. Four species

of tanagers are native to North America, and 2 have been recorded with some frequency as vagrants.

Though a few tanagers are as small as 3 inches and others as long as feet, most species, including all North American ones, measure 6–8 inches. They are well-proportioned songbirds with long, conical bills, usually with a slight hook and a "tooth" (i.e., a single serration) along the cutting edge of the upper mandible. Their legs are relatively short. Some drab tanagers exist, and in many species (including native North American ones) females and juvenal and basic (winter) plumage males are less than spectacular. But overall this mainly tropical family can be said to contain a better than average share of the surpassing splendor of birddom. Our native tanagers display only the red/yellow end of the spectrum; still, for sheer "dazzle" few birds can compete with a male Scarlet Tanager in nuptial plumage.

Tanagers are mainly arboreal birds that feed on a wide variety of insects, other invertebrates (spiders, snails), and fruit, especially berries.

Some tanagers have extended, warbling songs, others raspy, squeaky ones; our native species all have songs popularly described as "robin-like," but with more of a "burr," i.e., hoarser.

The nests of North American tanagers are typically fairly shallow cups of twigs, stems, coarser grasses, sometimes moss, lined with finer grasses, plant fibers, and/or hair. The 3–5 (usually 4) eggs are pale blue to greenish and finely to fairly coarsely marked with brown and/or reddish and/or lavender.

The tanager family is restricted to the New World and achieves exuberant diversity in the Neotropics, especially in South America. In North America, the native tanager species are largely segregated in northeastern (to midwestern) deciduous forest (Scarlet); southern deciduous and mixed forest, continentwide (Summer); western conifers and aspen (Western); and southwestern montane pine/oak (Hepatic). All but the Hepatic winter exclusively in the Neotropics, except for laggard Western Tanagers that try to survive at Temperate Zone feeders.

Like many tropical bird names, "tanager" comes to us via Portuguese (or Spanish) from Tupi, a common language of the natives of the Amazon Basin. It may have referred originally to any small, brightly colored bird.

TARGET SPECIES. An avian specialty of a given locality at which bird listers take particularly careful aim. It is both natural and intelligent, of course, to study and hope to see birds endemic to a limited region to be visited. However, to some, the term has an unfortunate acquisitive ring, as when some birders speak of "getting" some rarity; it seems to imply that the target species exists chiefly to fill a space on a list.

TARSOMETATARSUS (pl. tarsometatarsi). The bone of a bird's leg between the ankle and the toes; a fusion of tarsal and metatarsal bones. See LEG/FOOT; SKELETON; and Fig. 27.

TARSUS (pl. tarsi). The part of a bird's leg between the ankle and the toes. See SKELETON; and Fig. 35.

TASTE. From a human perspective, taste is a sophisticated sensation blending the four basic elements—salty, sour, bitter, sweet—in various strengths combined with a much broader range of perceptions received through our sense of smell. The main organs of taste in all vertebrate animals are collections of cells—the taste buds—that send and receive signals to and from the brain via aggregations of nerve fibers. Human taste buds are located mainly on the tongue—where they are readily visible to the naked eye—and in the wall of the pharynx (upper throat).

The taste sense in birds is much simpler structurally, with an average of only 30–70 inconspicuous taste buds (humans have about 9,000) located mainly in the throat and the softer areas of the palate, and usually only a few in the relatively soft back of the tongue; taste buds have also been detected in the bill edges of some species. Among the exceptional aspects of the large fleshy tongues of parrots is the presence of some 400 taste buds.

The physiology of taste is not completely understood in humans and is little studied in birds. Individual human nerve fibers transmitting taste sensations respond differently to salt, bitter, sour, and sweet—each sensing only one or two (and none responding directly to sweet stimuli)—and there is a great range of taste acuity and values among people. This information doubtless plays a role in taste tests on birds in which some are found to have little or no response to bitter or sweet, while sour seems to be readily detected in small amounts, and food or water to which salt has been added may be preferred to the unaltered substance. Since most birds seem to have a limited sense of smell, and since the avian mouth and upper throat hold food only briefly during normal feeding in most birds (in marked contrast to humans; see DIGESTIVE SYSTEM), it is reasonable to assume that taste holds little of the subtle gratification for birds that it does for us. However, it may play a significant role in discriminating appropriate from inappropriate foods. It appears that birds feeding at winter roosts of monarch butterflies in the central Mexican highlands may learn to detect the presence or absence of toxic cardiac glycosides by making quick "taste tests" on the insects' wings. This kind of discrimination is apparently rather limited, however, and no one has yet found a harmless substance that, for example, will make grain taste bad to flocks of blackbirds.

For how birds taste in another sense, see EDIBILITY. See also SMELL; TONGUE; FOOD/FEEDING.

TATTLER. Standard English name for the 2 species of sandpipers in the genus *Heteroscelus* (family Scolopacidae; order Charadriiformes); Sibley and Ahlquist (1990–SYSTEMATICS) put the tattlers in the large sandpiper genus *Tringa*). The Wandering Tattler, breeds in Alaska and winters along

the coast of southern California (as well as widely over the Pacific). The Gray-tailed Tattler, occurs as an uncommon to rare migrant in Alaska.

Tattlers have gray upperparts with heavily barred underparts in alternate (breeding) plumage. They frequent swift rocky streams on their breeding grounds and wave-washed rocks in their coastal winter quarters. Like other stream-haunting birds, tattlers habitually and constantly "pump" their tails.

The name refers to their clear, loud call notes.

For family characteristics, see SANDPIPER.

TAUTONYM (TAW-tuh-nim). A Latin binomial in which the generic and specific names are the same. *Nycticorax nycticorax* (Black-crowned Night-Heron) is an example of tautonymy.

TAVERNER (TAV-er-ner), Percy A., 1875–1947. Perhaps Canada's best-known ornithological figure, Taverner was for most of his life ornithologist-zoologist-curator of the National Museum of Canada. His chief interests and achievements were not in taxonomy. Rather, he excelled as a "popularizer" of nature (especially birds), as a "museum builder," and as an instigator of scientific and conservation efforts. He published a number of comprehensive works on the avifauna of Canada—e.g., *Birds of Canada* (Toronto, 1947)—which were unique in North America for their time in being profusely illustrated in color.

Taverner was noted for his sense of humor and was an enthusiastic contributor to the facetious edition of *The Auk,* known as *The Auklet.*

TAXIDERMY. The craft or skill of skinning and then mounting birds and other animals in lifelike poses. Stuffed exhibits of virtually any species of bird were once popular either as parlor decorations or sport trophies. Mail-order courses in taxidermy, showing how to mount clocks in the bellies of owls as well as more practical techniques, were once highly popular with adolescent boys. It is now illegal to make or own stuffed specimens of protected birds without a federal permit (see LAWS PROTECTING BIRDLIFE), and avian application of the taxidermist's art is now largely confined to game birds and museum exhibitions. See also BIRD SKIN.

TAXON, pl. taxa. Generic (and in the plural collective) term for any taxonomic unit or units. Referring to a form the taxonomic status of which is uncertain, one might say, "I'm not familiar with that taxon." Or referring to a trait characteristic of different groupings of birds: "Lek behavior occurs in several taxa."

TAXONOMY (tax-ON-uh-mee). In biology, the classification and arrangement of life-forms based on their similarities and differences. Modern systems of taxonomy are based on phylogeny; i.e., life-forms are theoreti-

cally grouped in the order of descent from common ancestors, oldest forms coming first, most recently evolved, last. Any classification structure is inextricably dependent on a formal system of names by which individual organisms or groups thereof can be labeled once they have been distinguished (see NOMENCLATURE, ZOOLOGICAL). In the strictest sense, taxonomy refers solely to classification, though it is often used interchangeably with systematics, a broader concept that includes the study of evolutionary relationships as well as the classification systems derived from them. For discussion of this important subject see SYSTEMATICS.

TEAL. Standard English name for about 17 species of small dabbling ducks mostly in the genus *Anas,* of which 3 breed in North America. Three other species (including the Garganey, usually thought of as a teal, and the Falcated "Teal") have occurred as migrants or vagrants in Alaska and elsewhere. The word has no taxonomic significance, but only a general implication of small size. The relatively large Falcated "Teal" is now officially relabeled as the Falcated Duck. "Teal" originated as a name for the (Eurasian) Green-winged Teal; Lockwood (1993–NAMES) says it refers to "a chuckling sound heard from the birds while feeding"(?). For family characteristics, see DUCK.

TECHNOLOGY FOR BIRDERS. A hundred years ago the only technology a "birder" needed to master was the operation and maintenance of a shotgun and some basic taxidermy techniques. Fifty years ago birding technology was even simpler. With the advent of post-World War II optics, all the equipment a cutting edge birder was expected to carry was a pair of binoculars and—if sufficiently serious and affluent—a telescope. In the last twenty years, however, the birding world, like the rest of the world, has gone high tech. It may be slightly alarming to technophobes and birders of a certain age, but the bird dude who rocks today is plugged in to columns such as *The Wired Birder* (Larsen 2000), and many bird clubs have at least one "robo-birder" on whose body hang the accoutrements of an ornithologically oriented media complex.

An emerging benefit of a technologically savvy birding community is that science has become less daunting and more user-friendly, and through computer-based citizen science programs such as the Cornell Lab's *E-Bird,* nonacademic field observers are able and keen to contribute to bird research and conservation projects. For many people, of course, birding serves as a refuge from the information overload, electronic static, and gadgetry of the modern world, and they are finding it increasingly difficult to visit the most popular birding spots without encountering small armies of birdfinders communicating noisily on CD-radios or duping the avifauna with instant playbacks. While most of us may agree that technology is a net benefit to society, one of the challenges of the twenty-first century will surely be how to keep Nature from being swallowed up into The Matrix.

This entry does not aspire to comprehensive descriptions of all birding related technologies. Rather it gives brief definitions of major relevant categories and sources of further information, including cross-references to longer entries in the present volume.

THE INFORMATION FLYWAY. As in nearly all other human endeavors, most if not all of the birding information that you once had to gather from an assortment of print and electronic sources can now be collected by spending a few minutes in front of your computer screen. Continuous weather information, including radar images, is available from the National Oceanic and Atmospheric Administration/National Weather Service websites (www.nws.noaa.gov) as well as commercial sites such as Weather Underground (www.wunderground.com). And local information is also available on such bird-relevant data as tides, sea conditions, and sunrise/sunset. As for the birds themselves the American Birding Association maintains a listing of North American rare bird alerts and bird chat rooms on their website (www.americanbirding.org), and a National Rare Bird Alert is accessible at www.narba.org.

RECORD KEEPING. Though some of us have been slow to give up the tactile pleasure of journal and pen (see FIELD NOTES), many (most?) birders now keep records of what they see (sometimes accompanied by digital images—see below) on computers. Several software packages are available that allow the user to keep her life list in order in various scales (world, state, yard, etc.) and formats or you can create your own using spreadsheet and database programs such as Microsoft Excel or Microsoft Access. With the advent of Palm Pilots, it is easy to record numbers of birds seen in the field, locality by locality anywhere in the world.

IMAGING. Until quite recently capturing high-quality images of birds involved the use of very expensive photographic equipment by someone skilled and experienced in matters of light and motion and gifted with oceanic patience. The fruits of these expensive labors were typically seen either in exhibitions or publications of printed photographs, slide shows, or cinematic "film safaris." The expensive part of bird "imaging" hasn't changed that much—though indisputably more people are obtaining better and better images for less and less money than ever before—but the advent and rapid development of video, digital, and computer technology in combination with advances in traditional optical technology has revolutionized the way we make and use pictures of birds. If you are mainly interested in the artistic end of the spectrum, i.e., creating aesthetically fine images of publication or exhibition quality, you will want to school yourself in the latest advances in 35-mm single-lens reflex (SLR) camera technology for the production of color transparencies (slides). If your primary focus is recording bird sightings or sharing images of birding trips via computer, then you will want to get up to speed in the new world of digital photography, including techniques such as "digi-

scoping." For some basic rules of thumb and useful popular references, see PHOTOGRAPHY.

WEB CAMS are "simply" cameras attached to computers connected to web sites so that anyone who wants to can look at any pictures you care to display. What can currently be viewed using this technology on the World Wide Web is hopefully way beyond your imagination, but the birding version of it is so far fairly straightforward and innocent. Many conservation organizations and government wildlife agencies have set up web cams on nesting sites of spectacular birds, especially raptors, as a way of getting the public interested in their work. And increasingly individual birders with a knack for computer technology have set up web cams (trained on their backyard feeder for example) as part of their personal web site. Basically what you need is a camera (digital still or video), a dedicated computer, a connection between the two (cable or wireless) and the software to upload the camera images to the web server. Techno-savvy folks who describe this process say it's "fairly simple," but also use a lot of terms like "ftp" (you know, file transfer protocol), so *caveat camtor.* For an excellent introduction to the subject see Larsen (2000), which provides many additional references and sample web sites. If you want to see what (still) web cam is like right now, you could try http://birds.cornell.edu/birdhouse/nestboxcam/.

RECORDING AND PLAYBACK. Increasing sophistication in recording systems now makes it possible to extend the scientific scope of recording technology, for example, by allowing researchers to census high-flying nocturnal migrants by taping their calls with ultrasensitive sound-gathering devices. And portable CD players are now being used to call out that skulking Wrentit with maximum efficiency. For a summary of the state of the recording arts and sciences, see RECORDING OF BIRD SOUNDS.

FIELD COMMUNICATIONS. Various forms of radio communication devices are used by birders in the field to inform each other about the whereabouts of rarities, organize searches, and deal with emergencies as well as for casual birdbanter.

CB (Citizen's Band) radios have been used for years, especially by bird clubs traveling in caravans of vehicles. Participants purchase radios and (exterior mount) antennae for their vehicles, and birders in a given region will typically designate one of the 40 available channels over which to communicate. Like truckers and other CB enthusiasts, birders often adopt catchy "monikers" to identify themselves. Despite the term, "portable" CBs are rather cumbersome to haul around while birding on foot but they have a relative broad range (up to a 5-mile radius)—subject to local topography.

FRS (Family Radio Service) units are smaller and lighter than CBs and get less interference because they operate on the FM rather than the AM band. The FCC prohibits vehicle-mounted units, so they can be used only as handsets. These radios have 14 channels that are subdivided into 38

"privacy codes," so that 532 connection options are theoretically available. FRS units have about a 2-mile range.

GMRS (General Mobile Radio Service) units are more powerful versions of FRSs, but they are also bulkier, more expensive, and require a permit from the FCC, so their birding application seems limited so far.

Good quality sets of all of these radio systems can be purchased for under $200. with recommended options such as "squelch control" (essential for CBs), but without bells and whistles such as headsets and lapel mikes.

Cell Phones appear to be less than ideal for birder communications at this point. Coverage is spotty in remote areas, the cost can be prohibitive, and the role of cell towers in bird mortality is a concern.

Note that many wildlife sanctuaries and wildlife refuges impose limits on the use of electronic devices and that American Birding Association rules prohibit the use of radios for Big Days (see BIRDING EVENTS).

For a detailed summary of communications systems, including pertinent web sites, see Larsen (2000).

Location and Mapping. Often developed for military or business uses, new technologies in these realms have rapidly become essential tools for bird research and conservation and will soon be standard operating equipment for birders.

GPS (Global Positioning System) uses multiple satellite signals collected by a receiver on the ground to locate objects on the earth's surface within the diameter of a meter or less. Palm-sized computerized units now make it possible (for example) to record nest locations or territories in remote areas, eliminating the need for cumbersome surveying equipment, greatly improving accuracy and permitting easy entry into a larger database. Census points, transects, and plots—e.g., for Breeding Bird Surveys, Christmas Counts, etc.—are now marked as a matter of routine using GPS. In the not very distant future GPS units will be standard dashboard features, and birders looking for a Mountain Plover in a vast prairie or a feeder rarity in an unfamiliar city will simply enter the coordinates reported by the last observer or the street address and then follow the directions on the screen. Wilderness birders can now carry compact GPS units—with thermometer, barometer, altimeter, or other features included, depending on their budget—eliminating much of the anxiety of leaving the trail to chase that probable Three-toed Woodpecker drumming.

GIS (Geographic Information System). Though GIS is widely used simply to make beautiful and informative maps, e.g., of refuge trail systems, its greatest utility is as a powerful analytical tool—with many applications in bird conservation. The system can be visualized as a series of data layers that can be entered into a computer as appropriately formatted statistics or an existing graphic representation. These might include an aerial photograph of a mosaic of habitats, the GPS coordinates (see above) of the nest localities of a rare bird species, and the lot lines of

all the properties in the mapped area. Once the layers have been justified to conform to the same format, the three elements can be analyzed in relation to each other and readily reveal which areas of habitat are most important to protect for the conservation of the species and which property owners must be involved if it is desirable to acquire this habitat. If additional rare species are involved, the maps of their territories can be added as additional layers and the places where the territories of two or more rare species overlap can be identified as "hotspots" with conservation priority. For a graphic demonstration of how a GIS system works in practice, visit the BioMap section of the Massachusetts Natural Heritage Program's web site www.state.ma.us/dfwele/dfw/nhesp/nhbiofind.htm.

For a detailed overview of many aspects of birding technology see David Larsen's excellent series, The Wired Birder in the *Bird Observer* (Vols. 28–30, 2000–2002) and the "Tools of the Trade" column of *Birding*.

For technology used in bird research, see also RADAR and TELEMETRY; for binoculars and telescopes see OPTICAL EQUIPMENT.

TECTRIX (pl. tectrices). An individual feather of wing or tail coverts; in the plural, equivalent to "coverts."

TEETH. No modern birds have any ("scarce as hens' teeth"), and with the notable exceptions of some early fossil forms, toothless jaws are among the major departures in the evolution of birdlife away from reptilian ancestry. The earliest-known bird, *ARCHAEOPTERYX,* had individual teeth set in sockets in the jawbones, and a later fossil species, *HESPERORNIS,* had teeth set in grooves. The latter was once held to be one of an entire superorder of toothed birds (Odontognathae), which lived during the Cretaceous Period (see EVOLUTION OF BIRDLIFE).

A number of modern birds have tooth-*like* bill modifications, e.g., the serrations of mergansers' bills, which help them grasp and manipulate slippery fish, and the "tomial tooth" of the falcons' bills (see Fig. 1). Though these "bill teeth" may serve some of the same purposes as true "jaw teeth," the two structures are not homologous.

See also EGG TOOTH.

TELEMETRY. The technology that allows the automatic transmission of information from remote sources by radio signal or other means. Among the inherent problems of bird research and conservation is that most birds easily elude humans trying to study them either by simply flying rapidly away—sometimes very far away—or by retreating into impenetrable habitats. Starting in the 1960s we began to improve our ability to track birds by developing compact radio circuits light enough (no more than 3–5% of the subject's body weight) to be carried by at least some birds. Radio tracking has by now proven its value in numerous applications. For example, it helps us locate the nesting or wintering areas of

long-distance migrants in vast wilderness areas such as arctic tundra, tropical rain forest, or the open ocean, and it has also permitted us to eavesdrop, as it were, on the home life of rails and other species that do much of their behaving in dense habitats and/or in the dark. Various tiny sensing devices can be rigged by ingenious telemeters to perceive and record how birds are spending their time (sleeping, feeding, etc.). The technology already exists (in many cases developed for military purposes) to conduct more sophisticated tracking on smaller birds using micro-transmitters: Imagine being able to have a detailed record of a warbler's activities (including such factors as altitude and temperature) as it makes its way from some boreal vastness to a neotropical wintering ground and back again. One problem with this and even the tracking devices already in use is that they range from very to prohibitively expensive. This will probably change in time. Another issue relating to radio track is the subject's well-being. Some of the more clumsy transmitter packs have been shown to reduce a bird's ability or desire to feed or to make it more vulnerable to predators, and harming individual animals even with a rationale of helping to save their species is increasingly unacceptable in developed societies.

For a concise overview of basic transmitter design and some of the potential technical problems see Amlaner (RADIO TRACKING AND BIO-TELEMETRY) in Campbell and Lack (1985–ORNITHOLOGY).

The term "biotelemetry" refers to the remote monitoring of an organism's *physiological functions* using telemetry technology.

See also RADAR.

TEMPERATURE, BODY. Birds, like people and other mammals, are "warm-blooded", i.e., capable of maintaining a relatively constant body temperature by means of their own heating and cooling systems, rather than depending on external heat sources as, for example, do most reptiles. Three major differences between the avian heating system and our own stand out: (1) all birds have higher normal body temperatures than we do; (2) the body temperatures of birds normally fluctuate during the day to a greater degree than do ours; and (3) birds lack our principal cooling mechanism, the ability to sweat.

Range and Rhythm. The normal body temperature of all species of birds falls between 100 and 112°F, with small perching birds generally at the higher end of the range. The temperature of an individual bird may fluctuate a few degrees in either direction in response to various stimuli in its normal daily routine, such as physical activity, emotional stress, eating, a rise in air temperature, and the reverse of all these. It has also been demonstrated that there is a usual daily rhythm to these variations in body temperature. The lowest temperatures in most species have been recorded while they were roosting or sitting on the nest during the cool of

midnight; their temperature rises and peaks coincident with a peak of avian activity and atmospheric heat around midday and then declines again. As one might guess, the rhythm is more or less reversed in nocturnal birds.

Body temperature does not fluctuate in relation to climate; birds of the Arctic and the tropics have similar normal temperatures, though their respective adaptations to temperature control may vary.

Making Heat. Like mammals, birds produce heat by transforming nutrients and stored fats into energy; therefore, keeping warm is directly dependent on taking in sufficient food.

In extreme cold, birds must eat constantly to produce at least as much heat as they lose, and those that perish in subzero temperatures may thus be said, with equal truth, to die of the cold or of starvation. Larger birds have an advantage in this respect, since the ratio of their body surface to total volume is less than that of smaller species. They therefore have less area from which heat can escape and do not have to eat as much in proportion to their weight as do smaller birds (see BERG-MANN'S RULE).

Keeping Warm. As anyone who lives north of the 40th parallel knows, good insulation is the key to staying warm.

Seabirds, in particular, rely to some extent on a layer of fat below the skin to retain body warmth, but by far the most important insulator for all birds is their feathers. The several types of body feathers (see FEATHER) are layered and overlapped in such a way as to trap and stabilize a layer of air next to the body and greatly slow the outward radiation of body heat. These feathers are under muscular control and can be raised to increase the air space and amount of insulation. This explains the familiar cold-weather sight of birds "fluffing out" their feathers.

The oil with which birds coat their feathers when preening helps create a surface shield that protects the inner layer of insulation against wind and water. Birds inhabiting cold regions often have notably deep and thick coverings of feathers and may exhibit behavioral traits such as huddling together in communal roosts, sleeping in caves or tree cavities, or burrowing into the snow (ptarmigan) to stay warm.

Inasmuch as temperature is controlled to a great extent by the feathers, young birds that are born naked cannot maintain a steady body temperature. Such "psilopaedic" species are essentially "cold-blooded" at birth, and therefore dependent on the parent birds to keep them warm enough or shaded from the sun. Passerine nestlings gain significant control of their own heating plant within their first week but are not in full command until fledged. Species born with a covering of down are less dependent on parental warmth and rapidly become thermally self-sufficient.

Heat loss from unfeathered parts of the body such as legs and feet can be reduced by slowing circulation selectively to these extremities—in

some instances to just above freezing. Conversely, a temperature increase may be achieved by "shivering," which produces heat from muscular activity.

Perhaps the ultimate in metabolic control is practiced by a few species (e.g., swifts, nightjar, hummingbirds) that can "shut down" almost completely during cool periods and lapse into a state similar to hibernation (see TORPIDITY).

Cooling Off. Lacking sweat glands in the skin, birds must avoid overheating by other means. To some degree their air-conditioning system is simply the reverse of their heating system. Instead of "fluffing" feathers to increase insulation, for example, they compress their plumage to retain as little body heat as possible. Or they can increase circulation to unfeathered parts to give off more heat rather than reduce circulation to retain it.

Many Temperate Zone species molt into a thinner plumage for the summer or achieve one gradually by normal feather loss and/or wear. Birds also adapt their *behavior* to the air temperature, often seeking rest and shade during the hottest part of the day.

Though they cannot perspire, birds do vaporize water in the lungs and internal air sacs (see RESPIRATORY SYSTEM) and release it by panting. Another cooling device is known in ornithological jargon as "gular flutter." The skin of the throat is quivered rapidly while the blood flow to the region is increased, thus letting off internal heat. This practice is especially prominent in birds with fleshy throat pouches, e.g., cormorants, frigatebirds, pelicans, and boobies. A good place to witness either or both of these phenomena is at a seabird colony at midday when parent birds must sit on their nests and endure the full force of the sun while protecting their eggs or young from it.

By human standards, practicality has always characterized the species of American vultures far better than fastidiousness. Their method of cooling off is consistent with their reputation—they defecate on their feet. Species of storks—now known to be closely related to the New World vultures—also practice this untidy method of evaporative cooling.

See also ENERGY; METABOLISM; DESERT.

TERATORNIS (TAIR-uh-TOR-nis); teratorn. A fossil genus of enormous vultures that lived during the Pleistocene Epoch and are known from skeletal remains recovered from the famous natural asphalt pools at Rancho La Brea, California, and elsewhere. A recently discovered teratorn species had a wingspan of 25 feet and probably weighed about 175 pounds; it is therefore the largest known flying bird (see Fig. 22). See EVOLUTION OF BIRDLIFE.

TERN. Standard English name for almost all (approximately 44) members of the subfamily Sterninae (family Laridae [gulls and terns]; order Charadriiformes); Sibley and Ahlquist (1990–SYSTEMATICS) consider the terns

to be a tribe (Sternini within the subfamily Larinae within a larger Laridae that includes the jaegers, skimmers, and alcids). Four tern species are called by the name NODDY. Fourteen species of terns breed in North America. In addition, Bridled Tern is a regular visitor to offshore waters, especially in the Southeast and after tropical storms; Black Noddy occurs as an annual summer visitor to the Dry Tortugas, Florida, and 3 other species have occurred as vagrants from Eurasian or the Neotropics (see Appendix II).

Terns are slender, graceful water birds with long wings; short neck and legs; slender, pointed bill; and the front three toes fully webbed. They range in length from 8 inches (Least) to nearly 2 feet (Caspian). Many species have crested heads and most have notched or deeply forked tails. The plumage of the majority of tern species is gray above and white below with a black cap in alternate (nuptial) plumage. But there are a number of exceptions, some of which (the noddies) are almost perfect "negatives" of the usual tern coloration, being *dark* below with a *white* cap and a *wedge-shaped* rather than forked tail. Many species of terns have bright red or yellow bills and/or legs.

In general, terns feed by diving on fish and other surface-swimming organisms from the air. Unlike their near relatives the gulls, they are picky eaters, often preferring particular types of fish and never taking plant food or refuse. Most species are primarily inhabitants of the coastal zone; however, there are several highly pelagic tropical species (Sooty, noddies) and others (Black, Forster's) that also breed on freshwater marshes of the interior. The Gull-billed Tern feeds by coursing over marshes, where it catches insects on the wing and picks up small invertebrates and even small frogs or lizards from the ground—a notable exception to the aerial-diving habit of most terns.

Terns usually nest in densely populated colonies near water, often on sandy beaches. Most species lay their eggs in a shallow scrape, either unlined or sparsely lined with some pebbles, shells, or other handy debris. Black and Forster's Terns nest on floating mats of accumulated marsh vegetation anchored to emergent plants, on marshy ground among reeds or rushes, or on abandoned muskrat lodges or the abandoned nests of other waterbirds (e.g., grebes). The Brown Noddy builds a stick or seaweed platform on low trees, shrubs, cacti, rocks, or on the ground, often with coral, shells, and other debris as lining. Royal, Sooty, and Noddy Terns typically lay only a single egg; 2 or 3 are usual for most species, but as many as 5 have been recorded for a few. The color and markings are very variable, even within a species: white, pale pink, buff, or olive with sparse or dense speckles and/or splotches in reddish, purplish, or dark brown.

Most terns are very vocal, typical sounds being drawn-out nasal cries and sharp, staccato pipings.

The terns are distributed worldwide from the Arctic to the Antarctic and over most landmasses where there are wetlands, as well as over the

oceans. Several species of terns (Gull-billed, Caspian, Sandwich) are cosmopolitan in distribution, and one population of Arctic Terns makes one of the longest migrations of any bird species—22,000 miles or more round trip from its breeding grounds in high arctic Canada to the Antarctic via the coasts of Africa and South America (see Fig. 18).

"Tern" comes from very similar words in Old Norse and Swedish referring specifically to these birds and roughly echoing their cries.

TERRITORY (territoriality). In the broadest sense, simply a defended area, but usually implies distribution of available habitat among members of the same species. Though its importance as a zoological phenomenon was pointed out only fairly recently (Howard 1920), territoriality is common in the animal kingdom, with many examples among mammals, fish, insects, etc., as well as birds. The behavior patterns associated with territory (see below) are conspicuous among many species of birds, but the territorial urge is apparently lacking in some species (e.g., the sharp-tailed sparrow) and not very evident in others. The form that territoriality takes, the purposes that it serves, and the strength or weakness with which it is enforced are extremely variable among different species and individuals.

DIFFERENT KINDS OF TERRITORIES. Four basic types of breeding territories are now widely recognized:

1. A relatively large area (see Size of Territory, below) in which a pair of birds court, mate, feed, and rear their young. This is the commonest form of territoriality and is practiced by a wide variety of passerine species, e.g., the wood warblers.

2. Another type of territory is much like the preceding except that the adult birds leave the territory to do most of their feeding and food finding for their young. Many shorebirds and at least a few passerines (e.g., the Red-winged Blackbird) follow this pattern. There is much intergradation between this kind of territory and the first-described, and some authorities believe that few if any species restrict themselves entirely to their own territory while searching for food during the breeding season.

3. A very restricted area that barely extends beyond the actual nest site. Most easily observed among colonial seabirds (e.g., gannets, murres) and herons, but also characteristic of a few solitary nesters (e.g., the Mourning Dove). In this case it is hard to distinguish defense of territory from defense of "person," mate, eggs, or young.

4. A relatively small area used only for the courtship ritual and mating, but not for nesting or (except casually) for feeding. This is exemplified by male grouse and hummingbirds, which perform "dances" in arenas called LEKS (see also DISPLAY) or flights from conspicuous perches. The courtship area is not defended and the nest site of the female is not considered a breeding territory.

Nonbreeding territories include: defended feeding areas outside the breeding territory; night roosts, which are defended in some cases; and winter territories, which may or may not correspond closely to the breeding territory (see below).

SIZE OF TERRITORY. The amount of defended breeding territory varies widely not only among different species but among members of the same species. In the densest seabird colonies the distance from one nest to another is equivalent to the reach of the nestlings, and the total territory of a pair can therefore be measured in square inches. Many birds of prey, by contrast, vigilantly defend a square mile or more, and have more or less exclusive hunting rights for their own species over much more of the landscape (see HOME RANGE). The territories of most passerines are measured in acres, but, again, the variation is great: some American Robins are content with (or must settle for) as little as a tenth of an acre, while some Blackcapped Chickadees patrol more than 17 acres.

Perhaps the most fundamental variation among species is dictated by innate behavior patterns: cliff-nesting kittiwakes never claim more than their foothold of ledge, while Song Sparrows, given their preference, will energetically defend an acre or more.

Birds that maintain the first type of territory described above must, of course, have enough habitat to supply an adequate amount of the right kind of food for themselves and their young. In general, though, such species are apt to defend more than the minimum space needed to survive. It has been observed that species breeding on islands, where space is limited, tend to have much smaller territories than the same species breeding on the mainland. Accidents of topography on the mainland (e.g., water, geological formations) can also leave "islands" of habitat, which may be sufficient as territories even though they measure smaller than the average for the species in question. The "personality" of individual birds is another influence on size of territory. More aggressive proprietors tend to claim larger areas than meeker members of their own species and may annex part of a neighbor's territory by winning boundary disputes.

It is sometimes stated that size of territory is roughly proportional to species size: the bigger the bird, the bigger the territory. Many examples can be found to support this notion, e.g., House Wren vs. Peregrine Falcon, but these discrepancies in territorial size have more to do with food preferences and species characteristics than size, and exceptions to the proposed rule are numerous. Many large birds, for example, are colonial nesters with far smaller breeding territories than the average wood warbler, though, of course, their feeding ranges are much wider (see HOME RANGE). Even among passerines, however, size correlation does not hold: the territory of the Red-eyed Vireo averages five times as large as the American Robin's.

The difficulty of measuring territorial space adds to the difficulty of making such comparisons, because territories have volume as well as

linear dimensions. The ground-nesting Ovenbird has no occasion to repel rivals in the forest canopy above it, where a Scarlet Tanager's territory starts and ends.

TERRITORIAL BEHAVIOR. The duties of establishing and maintaining a territory largely fall to the male of the species. (As in other matters involving avian gender roles, the phalaropes are exceptional.) Females may participate to a limited degree in territorial rituals, but on the whole they play a backup position and consent to the males' initiatives. (Feminists will appreciate the female Eurasian Blackbird in England, which refused to be courted within the boundaries set by her mate, forcing him to alter his invisible fences.) When females do participate in territorial defense, they concentrate on members of their own gender.

Males of some species arrive back on their breeding grounds several days ahead of the females; in other species both sexes arrive at the same time. In some cases, males remain silent for a brief time after arrival and wander around the general area without "acting territorial." Males in flocks will stay together during this period until the territorial urge turns their flocking companions into rivals and they begin singing and defending their own parcels of habitat.

A male attempting to establish a territory for the first time begins with an innate recognition of the proper habitat for its species. This ensures, for example, that pipits don't end up colonizing cliff faces and that puffins eschew cattail marshes. In addition to its general aspect, a prospective territory may have to include certain specific features, such as a conspicuous song perch or, in the case of colonial species, the presence of other birds. A newcomer prospecting for a territory in an area where its species is already common will be driven from most of the likely sites by males whose land titles are established from previous seasons' occupations. If the young male finds an unoccupied territory at all in this situation, it is likely to be less favorable than those of its older neighbors. But there is strong evidence that many young males simply do without. When 81% of territorial male birds on a 40-acre plot of Maine forest were systematically "removed" in two successive years (Stewart and Aldrich 1951; Hensley and Cope 1951), replacement males filled the vacancies with revealing alacrity in both years.

Most "land" birds (including owls) announce their dominion over their territory by uttering their characteristic (often surprisingly loud) song from a conspicuous perch. Open-country species, such as the Horned Lark, that lack permanent perches broadcast their claim while hovering high in the air. It has been shown in at least a few instances that the range of a species song corresponds roughly to its normal territory size.

Display of bright plumage or other distinctive characteristics is also essential for holding territory in some species. For example, some male Red-winged Blackbirds, deprived of their red "epaulets" experimentally,

quickly lost their credibility as landowners. Display *postures* are also part of the territorial apparatus of some species (see Fig. 7).

A few species (e.g., among the corvids and hawks) maintain their territories simply by being in residence, without any elaborate song or display activities.

Once a male has declared his sovereignty over a territory, he must defend its borders against potential usurpers *of his own species*. Different species using different "niches" in the same habitat are usually ignored, but similar species may evoke at least some defensive reaction from territorial males. (And, of course, predators recognized as threats to eggs or young are also harassed, though the urge here is not territorial—see MOB-BING; FLOCK.) Territorial boundaries may be marked by particular trees or other features prominent to the human eye, but often there is simply an intangible line perceivable only by the defenders of adjacent lots. If an ambitious neighbor or wandering landless male trespasses, he is likely to be met by the owner with feathers erected in indignation and issuing a characteristic vocal threat. If "words" do not suffice, the defender may chase the intruder off his territory and may even attack physically (see AGGRESSION), though this is usually unnecessary. Birds have an innate sense of territorial rights and it has often been shown that when a defending male chases an interloper onto the latter's side of the fence, the roles automatically reverse: the former interloper becomes the righteous chaser, and the former defender, the submissive chasee. Ornithologists disagree on whether the aggressive defending urge or the instinct to avoid conflict is more important in maintaining territories.

Not that the outcome of territorial disputes is always inevitable. The strength of the aggressive urge varies among different individuals of the same species, and, as noted, weaker males are known to yield acreage to stronger neighbors. There is also a kind of seniority system, enforced by an increase of aggressiveness in males as they age, so that, as in our own society, it is often the successful old birds who hold the best and biggest sites.

The passion for territorial defense is at its height between the males' arrival and the hatching of the eggs. After this point, aggressive urges usually cool somewhat; border incidents become less frequent, less prolonged, and less apoplectic. The male's protective instincts often shift focus from the territory to mate and young; in some species, family and not territory is apparently the object of male defenses from the beginning of the breeding cycle.

PURPOSES OF TERRITORIALITY. Territorial instincts are so elaborate, well developed, and widespread that we must assume they confer significant advantages on the practitioners. A number of *possible* functions suggest themselves very readily and behaviorists have offered many subtler ones. However, the phenomenon includes so many variables and intangibles that it is difficult to collect meaningful data, much less come to

definitive conclusions. Some of the most widely articulated speculations about why territoriality evolved follow. It is reasonable to suppose that territoriality has a combination of advantages and that the combination differs from species to species.

Distribution of Birdlife. Experiments (cited above) strongly suggest that, at least in some habitats, there are many more prospecting males than available territories. In this context, territoriality seems to provide a kind of natural "spacing," which prevents overcrowding and the food and other shortages that it might cause. It also forces younger males to accept less desirable habitat, so that the ecosystem runs, so to speak, at peak capacity.

Familiarity. Returning to the same territory year after year, birds inevitably learn the best alternatives for feeding, gathering nesting material, and escaping from predators. These small efficiencies doubtless add up to significant survival value.

Self-sufficiency. It was once widely assumed that a territory was analogous to a family farm and provided all the necessities of life for a family of birds. But observations now suggest that few if any species rely *completely* on the resources (food, nesting material, cover, etc.) of their territories.

Reservation of Specialized Nest Sites. Isolated cliffside eyries favored by certain raptors and holes in banks or trees are in shorter supply than other sites. "Single-family" occupancy is obviously essential in these cases and there is probably an advantage to the species in having such scarce housing "reserved" by older, successful individuals.

Mating Efficiency. The territorial songs of males also serve to attract females of the species. The courtship and mating rituals can proceed inside the territory without interference from other individuals of the species. The relationship between males and females (pair bond) is reinforced year after year, so that time which might be spent searching for new mates in new locations can be applied to the breeding cycle. Young males prospecting for unoccupied territory are, in effect, ushered to any available territory by the rapid aggressive responses of defending males.

Protection. Widely spaced nests and individuals are harder for predators to find. Even cryptically colored ground nesters, such as Whip-poor-wills, would be much more vulnerable to trial-and-error hunting by predators if they were more densely distributed. Colonial nesters mount a collective defense of their territories, which helps offset their conspicuousness.

It is also logical to suppose that wide spacing might lower incidence of disease, but as yet there is no evidence that this is a factor in territoriality.

Social Interaction. Notably gregarious species (e.g., parrots) have been known to despair and die if deprived of the company of their kind. It has been suggested that the interaction among holders of neighboring territories may provide essential social stimulation.

WINTER TERRITORIES. Certain species that winter in the same area where they nest continue to defend their territory throughout the year, though much less vigorously than in the breeding season; male and female Northern Mockingbirds each defend their own separate winter territories. It has also been established (see, for example, Schwartz 1964) that many long-distance migrant species defend territories on their tropical wintering grounds.

During the breeding season you can readily test the territorial defenses of birds in your neighborhood with a few simple props. A mirror or other reflective surface placed where a territorial male is likely to notice his own image will provoke paroxysms of rage in mockingbirds, robins, cardinals, and many other species. In fact, shiny windowpanes and hubcaps provoke many such performances each spring, usually to the perplexity of the home or car owner (see PROBLEMS INVOLVING BIRDS for what to do). A similar response can be obtained with a paper "dummy" of a breeding-plumage male—it need not be a particularly good likeness as long as the right colors and patterns are prominent. A tape recording of a breeding song is also effective, particularly if you can arrange to play back the male's own song. If you present your mirror, model, or tape in different locations and observe the response (active or passive) of a particular male, you can establish the border lines of his territory. Such experiments should, of course, be performed with the welfare of the bird in mind. Too much disturbance can disrupt a pair's essential breeding activities.

See also SONG; DISPLAY; COURTSHIP; PAIR FORMATION; AGGRESSION.

TERTIALS (TURR-shuls) (also tertiaries [TURR-shee-air-eez]). Alternative name for the three innermost secondary feathers of the wing (see Fig. 35) in certain groups (e.g., ducks) these feathers are often shaped, colored, and molted differently from the other secondaries but they are attached to the same bone (ulna) and in some groups are indistinguishable. In another usage, the long, covert-like feathers that are attached to the humerus and fill the space between the secondaries and the body of some long-winged birds; see, for example, the Northern Gannet in Fig. 27.

THAYER, John Eliot, 1862–1933 (Thayer's Gull: *Larus thayeri*). According to his eulogizer, G. M. Mathews, John Thayer was "amply supplied by inheritance with this world's goods" and after graduating from Harvard largely gave himself over to the occupation of "gentleman farmer." He was generously supportive of his alma mater and (due to a strong interest in natural history) especially of its Museum of Comparative Zoology. He financed expeditions to Latin America, China, Siberia, and Alaska and was an active collector of bird skins and eggs. He built a museum near his home in Lancaster, Massachusetts, to house these and other treasures,

but later donated them—28,000 skins, 15,000 eggs, including many rarities—to the MCZ.

Thayer nomenclature fame has been buffeted by the changeable winds of taxonomic theory. His gull was first described as a new species in 1915, then reclassified as a race of the Herring Gull then restored once again to full species rank.

THERMALS. "Bubbles" of warm air rising from the heated surface of the earth. For relation to birdlife, see FLIGHT, Thermal Soaring.

THERMOREGULATION. See TEMPERATURE, BODY.

THRASHER. Standard English name for 14 species of "mimic thrushes" or "mimids" (family Mimidae; order Passeriformes), all but four of them in the genus *Toxostoma*. Sibley and Ahlquist consider this group a tribe (Mimini) of the family Sturnidae, which includes the starlings and mynas. Seven species of thrashers breed in western (mainly southwestern) North America and one additional species (Brown Thrasher) is widespread east of the Mississippi.

As a group, the thrashers have shown particular resourcefulness in exploiting the ecological niches of arid habitats—witness the assortment of pale (desert-colored) forms of the American Southwest. For other characteristics of the family (including the catbirds and mockingbirds), see MIMIC THRUSH.

Disappointingly, "thrasher" is simply a variant of "thrush"; thrashers do not "thrash"—despite long, mobile tails—nor do they "thresh"—despite the scythe-like bills of some species.

THREAT. See DISPLAY.

THREATS (OF HUMAN ORIGIN) TO BIRDLIFE. With the exception of major climatic and tectonic events—hurricanes, volcanic eruptions, earthquakes—it has been a long time since we could claim that humankind was locked in an equal life-or-death struggle with nature. In fact, long after nature surrendered to our tools, machines, master plans, and fecundity, we continued to "conquer" her—if not out of necessity precisely, then for profit and pleasure. The rightness of this urge to exploit the biosphere was bolstered by the notion, popular in Western religions, that the earth was created for our benefit.

By the late nineteenth century the expiration of several bird species (see EXTINCT BIRDS) and the impending man-induced doom of a number of others made it clear to a few people that men with guns represented a mortal threat to wildlife. In the first half of the twentieth century this small band of "conservationists" managed to convince the public at large that nature itself was at risk, that this was a bad thing, and that legislation

should be passed to rigidly restrict the killing of animals. Today in North America the major threat to wildlife is no longer the clear, direct one of men killing animals, but the rather more insidious and ill-defined one of a sophisticated technology working beyond our control, killing organisms pervasively, but gradually, indirectly, in ways we didn't predict and in many cases still don't understand. "Conservationists" have become "environmentalists," having realized that the new dangers threaten ourselves as well as other animals.

With this brief historical perspective, consider the following man-made threats to birdlife.

Overharvest. Shooting for the game markets as well as for sport in the late nineteenth and early twentieth century is generally credited with the extinction of the Passenger Pigeon and the Heath Hen and the mortal decline of the Eskimo Curlew. It also drastically reduced the numbers of many other native shorebirds and upland game birds before effective conservation laws were passed. The Great Auk was hunted to extinction for its eggs, meat, and feathers, and populations of Great, Snowy, and Reddish Egrets and Roseate Spoonbills were drastically reduced by plume hunters between about 1875 and 1900 (see EXTINCT BIRDS; ENDANGERED BIRDS; AUDUBON SOCIETIES; CONSERVATION). Game and conservation laws now restrict hunting: to certain species of birds (chiefly the ducks, geese, grouse, pheasants, quail, rails, doves, and crows); to certain clearly defined seasons; to a limited number of birds; and to licensed hunters using approved methods (see LAWS PROTECTING BIRDLIFE for further details). In North America responsible hunters now consider themselves conservationists and support research on and propagation of game species and protection, management, and restoration of their habitat.

The last vestige of large-scale legal wildlife harvest on the planet is commercial fishing, and at present (2002) 70% of the world's major fisheries are on the brink of depletion. In addition to its general degradation of ocean ecosystems, this industry has a direct impact on marine bird populations, for example, albatrosses hooked on Pacific long lines.

Habitat Destruction. This is the single greatest threat to wildlife on the planet. It occurs in direct proportion to population growth and development, though it takes many forms: draining and filling of wetlands for highway and mall construction, destroying prairie lands for agriculture, clearing of forest for lumber and house lots. It was a major factor in the decline of the Whooping Crane and Everglade Kite and the extinction or impending extinction of Ivory-billed Woodpecker, Bachman's Warbler, and Dusky Seaside Sparrow. It is particularly threatening to species with highly restrictive habitat preferences: prairie-chickens need shortgrass prairie; Red-cockaded Woodpeckers depend on diseased long leaf pine trees; Golden-cheeked Warblers require stands of mature juniper; Seaside Sparrows exist exclusively in salt marshes; Spotted Owls and Marbled Murrelets nest only in old growth Douglas fir forest; California Gnatcatchers

live only in coastal sage scrub. Without these specific habitat requirements, the bird species that depend on them are doomed.

There has been considerable public sympathy recently for the preservation of unique habitats in North America, as people have recognized their intrinsic beauty as well as their value in maintaining biological diversity. This is commendable, but it should not be allowed to mask the fact that habitat destruction elsewhere in the world—e.g., the chopping of tropical rain forest at the rate of about a football field per *second* as of 1989 (Wilson 1992–CONSERVATION)—is of more than just local concern. Wood Thrushes and Hooded Warblers, which breed in North America, winter almost exclusively in Middle American rain forests. Furthermore, it has been argued that the survival of tropical forests is crucial to such fundamental matters as the planet's oxygen supply, its climate, and its genetic diversity—about 50% of the world's species of plant and animal life occur exclusively in tropical rain forest, a habitat covering only about 6% of the earth's surface.

Habitat Fragmentation. Many bird species require relatively large tracts of undisturbed forest in which to reproduce successfully. When we divide extensive contiguous areas of forest with roads and invade them with residential development, we expose species requiring the security of the forest interior to predators, both wild and domesticated, that share our taste for more open habitats—raccoons, skunks, foxes, house cats, crows, jays, grackles—and to the brood parasite, Brown-headed Cowbird.

Fig. 31. *Extinct, endangered, and recovering species.* All of the birds pictured here are or have been on one side or the other of the ultimate brink—that of extinction. The spectacular Carolina Parakeet (2), once abundant, has been gone unequivocally for nearly a century, the victim of "pest management." The Ivory-billed Woodpecker (1) has been surpassingly rare for decades and is presumed extinct by many, though tantalizing reports continue to issue from Louisiana and Cuba. Whooping Cranes (3) have made a slow recovery from a low of 15 birds in 1941–42; with strict protection and careful management, including the creation of new populations, they seem to be holding their own but still number in the low hundreds and remain vulnerable to various catastrophes. The graceful Roseate Tern (4) is Threatened throughout the Western Hemisphere and its North American populations are considered Endangered; it is vulnerable to all forms marine polution from oil spills to PCBs and it is trapped for its edible protein on its wintering grounds. Though always restricted to a narrow breeding range along adjacent coasts of arctic Siberia and Alaska, the Spectacled Eider (5) fared well enough until the 1970s when it began a precipitous decline, losing 96% of its breeding population by 1996; the cause is probably a combination of factors—all of human origin. The Coastal California Gnatcatcher (6) is a Threatened subspecies confined to a narrow belt of coastal sage scrub; briefly a symbol of cooperation between developers and conservationists, it now appears to be losing its battle with unrelenting greed. On a happier note, the Bald Eagle (7)—once nearly extinct in many parts of its range due to the indiscriminate use of DDT and other pesticides— has recovered so well due to legal intervention and reintroduction programs that it was recently removed from the Endangered Species List.

For full biographies of these and other rare, threatened and extirpated birds see EN-DANGERED BIRDS and EXTINCT BIRDS; see also THREATS (OF HUMAN ORIGIN) TO BIRDLIFE.

Pesticides and Other Chemical Poisons. The indiscriminate use of highly toxic chemicals to control insect pests stands as one of the chief follies of the modern era. Those who continue to urge heavy reliance on nonspecific, highly toxic, persistent pesticides argue that they are the most effective and efficient means of controlling pest insects, such as mosquitoes, caterpillars, and leaf beetles. Opponents reply that such pesticides

- Are insufficiently specific, killing "good" insects as well as "bad" along with other insect-controlling organisms such as birds, amphibians, etc., and potentially destabilizing entire ecosystems, making them highly vulnerable to unpredictable new problems (even relatively "specific" agents such as BT (*Bacillus thuringensis*) kill many kinds of nontarget flies, a huge order of insects on which many bird and other species depend).
- Are difficult to control in application, especially when sprayed from airplanes and carried by winds away from target areas.
- Are highly persistent and mobile both in soil, whence they are washed into bodies of water, and in animal tissue, where they accumulate and increase in concentration as they are passed up a food chain (see below) (pesticide residues have been detected in the tissue of humans living in.the remotest reaches of the earth); though many popular agents now have short half-lives in the environment, their breakdown by-products are often not carefully investigated.
- Are often applied carelessly and without sufficient warrant, as when thousands of acres are sprayed in a knee-jerk, sometimes politically motivated reaction to an outbreak of eastern equine encephalitis or West Nile virus, in a futile attempt to kill the adult mosquitoes that bear the disease, instead of requiring and enforcing measures such as the inoculation of horses, which would help stem the disease in mid-cycle.
- Exacerbate the problem since their effect is short term; insect populations readily produce resistant generations, which in turn require the use of even deadlier pesticides or heavier applications of the original one.

DDT (dichlorodiphenyltrichloroethane), once considered a miracle chemical essential to man's struggle against crop pests and disease vectors, has been shown to have been the principal cause of the precipitous decline of a number of bird species in North America and Europe during the 1960s and early 1970s as well as being implicated in human health problems. DDT washed by rain from uplands into lakes and rivers became highly concentrated in the tissues of large fish. Bird species, especially the Brown Pelican, Bald Eagle, and Osprey, feeding heavily on these, accumulated still higher concentrations—enough in some cases to kill the birds outright. A more insidious effect of the pesticide was to create an imbalance in the ratios of two nutrients, magnesium and phosphate, that are laid down in trace quantities in developing eggshells. The effect was to

inhibit the ability to produce calcium for eggshells. Affected females laid thin-shelled eggs, which could not survive incubation, or even eggs with no shells at all. Peregrine Falcons feeding on fish-eating ducks and insectivorous birds also fell prey to the DDT miracle. The decline in populations of the four species mentioned above during years of maximum DDT use was dramatic, as has been the recovery of some populations since the ban on DDT in 1972.

Because of the persistence of DDT, we may continue to discover more subtle but no less pernicious side effects of its indiscriminate use for a long time to come. And DDT is only one of many toxic chemicals that were ladled freely into the environment, the effects of which, in many cases, we are just beginning to discover. Among those proven dangerous are aldrin, dieldrin, endrin, toxaphene, BHC (benzene hexachloride), HCB (hexachlorobenzene), heptachlor epoxide, and PCBs (polychlorinated biphenyls). Chemical companies, of course, have not abandoned the quest for profitable poisons simply because some have been banned. Indeed, one drawback to DDT from the commercial point of view was that it was very cheap to produce. As a result of the ban, chemical companies were able to sell off their supplies to developing countries that lack strong toxics laws and then develop more profitable (i.e., more expensive) pesticides for domestic use.

The public now tends to believe that Rachel Carson solved the pesticide problem and that whatever the booming landscape industry sprays onto suburban lawns must be "green" and cleverly engineered to kill only "bad" things. In fact, thousands of birds are sickened and killed by such treatments and the government regulations and testing requirements for these substances are alarmingly lax.

Lead Poisoning. One of the oldest and most pervasive man-made threats to waterbirds is lead, especially pellets from shotgun cartridges, the inevitable remains of the thousands of rounds of ammunition spent during the hunting season. Fatal lead poisoning has been recorded in a wide range of gallinaceous birds and waterfowl, which ingest the shot along with other grit. Loons have been found to suffer high mortalities caused by the ingestion of lead fishing sinkers; and raptors are often killed by shot ingested when feeding on wasted game. Lead can also be picked up in many other ways, including residues from automobile pollution, in ambient air pollution, and as pesticide residues persisting in agricultural habitats, especially orchards. But particularly susceptible are those species of dabbling ducks that feed largely on the hard, round seeds of aquatic plants to which shot pellets bear a strong resemblance. Terres (1980–BIRD) notes the case of 110,000 Mallards succumbing to lead poisoning *on a single occasion* in Illinois, and Bellrose (1964) estimates that waterfowl deaths from this source may have accounted for 2–3% of North American populations.

Lead toxins enter the bloodstream of their victims via the stomach and intestinal walls after being pulverized from the shot pellets in the

gizzard (see DIGESTIVE SYSTEM). Effects include liver and kidney damage and paralysis of the muscles of the digestive tract. Lead also effects the central nervous system and many of its symptoms can be attributed to brain damage. Within a few days affected birds develop diarrhea and begin to lose their appetite; they soon become pathetically weak and unable to function normally but may take three weeks or more to die of starvation. A single lead pellet is sufficient to cause death in some instances, but dead ducks found in heavily hunted areas normally contain 10–40 times this number.

Fortunately, the use of lead shot in hunting ducks, geese, and swans is now banned by federal law, though the ban does not apply to all hunted waterbirds (e.g., cranes and rails), and, of course, tons of lead shot remain in wetland sediments. Lead sinkers are regulated in only a few states.

Oil Spills. It does not require much imagination to understand that petroleum, seawater, and swimming birds do not mix well. Loons, grebes, tubenoses, sea ducks, alcids, and other oceangoing species that are caught in the thick phlegm of an oil spill quickly become hopelessly mired, totally unable to function, and thus doomed to a slow death by starvation, exposure, and poison. Even birds with apparently negligible oil stains may be dangerously liable to total loss of body heat because the oil creates a gap in the insulation system that maintains a bird's body temperature on the cold ocean. Ingestion of oil can also kill—postmortem examinations of some alcids found dead on beaches with no oil at all on their plumage have revealed lung and intestinal tissue clotted and destroyed by oil.

In recent years, conservationists have had all too many opportunities to experiment with techniques of cleaning oiled birds. After a major oil spill, hundreds of thousands of dead and dying seabirds wash up on our beaches—probably a small fraction of those that perish offshore. And in spite of improved cleaning methods, the survival rate among oiled birds is very low.

The millions of tons of oil that we have put into the oceans was not all spilled by accident. Much of it results from the deliberate flushing of tanks and oily bilges at sea. In the winter of 1956, a year in which no major oil spills were reported, 7,500 fatally oiled seabirds washed up on the beaches of Nantucket Island (Massachusetts) alone. This form of pollution has been "limited" by international convention, but no one suggests that the practice has been effectively curtailed. Think of this the next time you get "tar" on your feet at the beach.

In the panic to exploit native oil resources here, some are willing to risk the living resources of offshore fishing banks and Arctic wilderness for a problematical and very limited return of petroleum. In these instances large concentrations of whales, caribou, seabirds, shorebirds, and all the other organisms that live atop oil-bearing rock are being wagered against the possibility of finding enough oil to meet the energy needs of the United States for a matter of weeks or months.

It is still common for people to sigh in relief when a euphoric news-caster reports that the latest oil spill is being blown or carried "out to sea" away from bathing beaches. We still know very little about the long-range effects of oil on the marine environment, but we do know that when the oil sinks to the bottom of the ocean, it has a devastating and long-term ef-fect on benthic (bottom-dwelling) organisms.

Companion Animals. The dogs, cats, rats, pigs, goats, and other ani-mals that have followed the spread of Western civilization around the world pose serious threats to wildlife. Their arrival has been particularly devastating among endemic island species such as the Laysan Island Rail, which, due to the absence of predators on its native island, had lost the ability to fly. However, any burrow-nesting or ground-nesting bird is po-tentially threatened by these animals. Pigs, for example, were a factor in the decline of the Bermuda Petrel or Cahow *(Pterodroma cahow)* and rats often menace petrel, tern, and alcid colonies. Suburban neighborhoods, which may support several dogs and/or cats per household, are treach-erous breeding areas for songbirds. For more detail on the especially se-vere threat to birdlife posed by free-ranging cats, see CATS.

Man-made Structures. Skyscrapers, power-generating windmills, and television towers represent hazards to low-flying migrants and other birds. Especially on foggy nights, the bright lights of city buildings may at-tract thousands of birds, which become disoriented, unable to find their way out of the maze of reflecting glass, and often kill themselves by flying into windows in their panic. Mortalities at television towers, ceilometers, and the like are the result of birds migrating at night under low ceilings being attracted and baffled by the lights and striking the towers and guy wires. Johnston and Haines (1957) record two particularly disastrous nights in early October 1954 during which over 100,000 migrant birds were killed in only 25 localities sampled from New York to Georgia. Picture windows also exact their toll—although the number of birds killed at any given window is small, the aggregate is undoubtedly enormous (see Klem 1990; Dunn 1993). A reasonable estimate of birds killed annually in North America by encounters with buildings, picture windows, and TV towers begins in the millions. Golden Eagles, Mute Swans, Red-tailed Hawks, and other large birds are often killed or fatally injured by flying into or being electrocuted by high-tension power lines; raptors also strike the blades of windmills in power-generation "farms."

Automobiles. In the 1960s it was estimated that about 2.5 million birds were killed annually in collisions with automobiles in *Britain*. The number of birds killed on North America's much more extensive network of highways must be staggering.

Sharing the Beaches. Several species of sand plovers and terns that nest in what might be called the "beach blanket zone" of heavily used beaches have experienced precipitous declines in recent decades and in many cases are listed as Threatened or Endangered in the Federal

Endangered Species Act. In studying the causes of these declines, many contributing factors have emerged, all of them of human origin. Colonial Terns, for example, can be quite sensitive to disturbance of their breeding areas either by people or by various predators such as skunks, raccoons, and crows, which, in many cases, arrive on the beaches via nearby suburban developments where they thrive. In some instances the terns will abandon the colony altogether and not renest, thus losing a generation from their population. The erection of predator "exclosures" and seasonal wardening programs can be effective in minimizing disturbance but they require constant, ongoing vigilance.

It has been conclusively demonstrated that the decline the Federally Threatened Piping Plover, is the result of unregulated Off-Road Vehicle traffic in their breeding areas. The vehicles create tire ruts in the sand that act as death traps when plover chicks fall into them and are crushed by the next vehicle that comes along. In places where conservation organizations working in concert with government agencies have been able to impose strict regulations prohibiting beach driving during nesting season plover breeding success has improved dramatically. Other aspects of the barrier beach ecosystem, e.g., tiger beetle and rare plant populations and even the geomorphology of the beach itself have been found to benefit once the odd notion of driving cars on beaches has been abandoned. Placing restrictions on where people can drive is not popular, of course, and in some beach recreation areas where bird conservation measures are in effect, it is not unusual to see bumper stickers with slogans such as, "Piping Plovers—taste like chicken."

Beaches also serve as haven for many species of shorebird migrants that need relatively undisturbed areas to rest and feed at key points during their long journeys between arctic breeding grounds and wintering grounds as far away as Tierra del Fuego. Increased development of beach real estate and public demand for recreational access have made such quiet refuges scarce along the coasts of North America. After decades of confrontation, it has become clear that by following a few simple guidelines people and birds can share beach habitat compatibly. There is also a growing consensus among beachgoers as well as environmentalists that driving motorized vehicles on barrier beaches is an idea that should be consigned to the dustbin of history.

Invasive Exotics. Alien bird species brought to North America for reasons ranging from the wildly frivolous to the well-intentioned and pseudo-scientific have at times threatened populations of native birds. For accounts of such detrimental effects caused by House Sparrows, European Starlings, and other resident aliens, see INTRODUCED BIRDS. A more insidious threat is that from invasive plant species such as Phragmites, Purple Loosestrife, European Buckthorn, Garlic Mustard, and others. The objection to these plants is not that they are of foreign origin,

but rather that they alter the structure and composition of wetland and upland habitats, making them unusable by native species and reducing their overall biodiversity. A striking instance is that of our native marsh bird community, including species such as Pied-billed Grebe, bitterns, rails, and Common Moorhen, many of which are becoming scarce due to wetland degradation caused in significant measure by invasive exotic plants. Eradication of these plants once they are established has proven to be labor intensive, expensive, and sometimes impossible.

Threatening the Whole. As noted earlier, the most alarming of today's man-made threats to birdlife are more subtle but also more far-reaching than the simple destructiveness of men shooting birds. One reason so many people have recently become interested in the welfare of the world's wildlife is that our own fate is inextricably involved with that of our fellow organisms (see, especially, Ehrlich and Ehrlich 1981–EXTINCT BIRDS; Wilson 1992–CONSERVATION). We may survive "frail" species such as the Bachman's Warbler or the blue whale, but other creatures, such as the cockroach, have already demonstrated greater staying powers than our own.

Listed above are a few of the many threats to the environment that we have posed quite recently. They are ones that relate particularly to birdlife and in ways that have been clearly documented. Many others, such as air pollution, acid precipitation, disposal of chemical and nuclear wastes and the release of greehouse gasses leading to global climate change—both alone and in combination—gnaw inexorably away at the abundance and diversity of earthly life. This self-inflicted corrosion afflicts not only our physical well-being but also what we alone have the ability to appreciate—the overall quality of life.

It has long been traditional among coal miners to take a caged canary down into the shaft with them. When the canary falls off its perch—killed by lethal fumes—it's time to get out. If we wake up one morning to find birds falling off their perches, it will be too late to correct earlier miscalculations. And, of course, there is nowhere else to go

See also CONSERVATION; MORTALITY.

THRUSH. Standard English name for about 140 members of the family Turdidae (order Passeriformes), including combined forms such as ground-thrush and nightingale-thrush and also used to refer to the family as a whole. Sibley and Ahlquist (1990–SYSTEMATICS) consider this group to be a subfamily (Turdinae) in the large family Muscicapidae, which separates the chats and Old World flycatchers into another tribe (Muscicapini). Fifteen species of thrushes breed in North America, and another 13 species have been recorded as rare visitors or vagrants from Eurasia or the Neotropics (see Appendix II).

Thrush species go by a wide variety of names besides the familial one, e.g., robins, bluebirds, solitaires, wheatears, nightingales, chats, and

redstarts, as well as by a variety of one-species names such as Veery. Some of these standard English names refer reliably to specific genera or sub-families, but others are used ambiguously. The thrushes are such a het-erogeneous group that it is difficult to make familywide generalizations about either their form or their behavior, even among the comparatively few North American species. They range in size between 4½ and 13 inches (5¾–10 inches in North America). Their bills are usually short to medium-length and may be narrow or fairly heavy. Their wings, tails, and legs may be short to fairly long. Many species are somberly colored in browns and grays and/or finely spotted and streaked, but many others are brilliantly colored and boldly patterned. Despite the variations, however, there is a generalized "thrush shape," which closely corresponds to the generalized "songbird shape," i.e., the image many people would make if asked to draw a bird. And members of other families are frequently described as "thrush-like."

Thrushes occupy all land habitats, from barren, stony tundra (Northern Wheatear) to rain forest (Varied Thrush), though there are no true desert thrushes in North America and the family shows a bias here for woodland and woodland edge (including farmland and suburbs). All our thrushes prefer insects, worms, and other invertebrates when the climate makes them available, but are also fond of fruits and readily shift to them when convenient or necessary.

Virtually all thrushes have pleasing, melodious songs, and some (the nightingale comes inevitably to mind) are among the world's preeminent avian virtuosi. The cheerful warbling of the American Robin may be the most familiar birdsong in North America, and the caroling of several of our forest thrushes (especially the Wood and Hermit Thrushes and the Veery) ranks with the finest in the world.

Most thrush nests epitomize the common notion of a bird's nest, i.e., a rather neat cup of woven sticks and grasses, lined with finer plant fibers. Many species use mud as a kind of interior wall between the stick shell and the inner lining. Most species place their nests in a crotch or on a branch near the trunk of a tree, but others nest on the ground, in rock crevices, or in tree cavities (see NEST). Bluebirds readily occupy bird-houses, and American Robins will build on a properly placed nest "shelf" (see BIRDHOUSE). Elsewhere in the world, thrushes lay white eggs, but in North America, all are blue (pale to moderately dark); those of some species are immaculate, others are finely to heavily speckled or splotched (see Fig. 10).

The distribution of the thrush family approaches the truly cos-mopolitan; native species are absent only from New Zealand (where, however, two Eurasian thrush species have been introduced) and some islands of Oceania. The North American species occupy virtually the whole of the continent at one season or another, and several species breed from coast to coast. All of these are migratory in at least part of their

range and several are long-distance migrants—see especially the Northern Wheatear routes mapped in Fig. 18.

"Thrush" is of ancient—though not very interesting—provenance. Its oldest known antecedents may have referred to birds in general (Greek), and in earliest English apparently referred specifically to the Mistle Thrush.

See also BLUEBIRD; BLUETHROAT; NIGHTINGALE; ROBIN; SOLI-TAIRE; VEERY; WHEATEAR.

THUNDERBIRD. A bird deity recognized widely among native North American tribes; the guardian of fire, war spirit, and protector of mankind. Thunderbird figures appear in many Amerind rituals, and the power of the image even inspired the American auto industry to name a car after this bird spirit. For a further description in context, see IMAGINATION.

TIBIOTARSUS (pl. tibiotarsi). With the fibula, the leg bones of a bird between the knee and ankle; a fusion of the tibia with some of the tarsal bones. See LEG / FOOT; SKELETON; and Fig. 27.

TICK. A check mark. Used (mainly by British birders) in referring to birds added to their life (and other) lists. Particularly rare or spectacular birds are sometimes said to be "good ticks." Oddie (1995–BIRDWATCHING) also describes "megaticks" (very good ticks) and a term unprintable here for the ultimate very good megatick. Also, in a (somewhat derogatory) personal context: "ticker" (or "tick hunter"), and a joyous exclamation upon seeing a "new" species: "Tick!" All of these are little used in North America. See LISTING; BIRDWATCHING; CHECK; TWITCHER.

Also, of course, a noisome arachnid pest that locks its jaws into the flesh of birdwatchers (and others) whose business takes them into rank grasses and shrubbery during the summer months. For avian context see ECTOPARASITE.

TIME SENSE. See CIRCADIAN RHYTHM; NAVIGATION.

TIT (titmouse). Standard English name for most of the 53 members of the family Paridae (order Passeriformes) and a collective term for the family as a whole. Sibley and Ahlquist (1990–SYSTEMATICS) include the 12 species of penduline-tits as a subfamily (Remizidae) of the Paridae, but keep the long-tailed tits in their own family (Aegithalidae); the single North American representatives of the latter groups, see VERDIN and BUSHTIT. In North America, tits with crests are called "titmice" and those with dark caps and "bibs" that lack crests are called "chickadees." Eleven species of chickadees and titmice breed in North America.

Except for the Sultan Tit of Asia, which is 8 inches long, tits are all small birds (average 5 inches) with short, sharp bills (a fairly deep base in some species), short, but strong legs, and (in North American species)

moderately long tails. Tits are highly active birds of forests and their edges and often forage with flocks of their own or mixed species. They feed mainly on small insects and other invertebrates, but also eat fruits and seeds, particularly in winter. They tend to be among the first birds to discover a newly erected feeding station.

The tits' preferred nest site is a tree cavity, which chickadees usually excavate for themselves in rotten wood. Old woodpecker holes, dry pipes, and bird boxes are also acceptable. Within the cavity, most tits lay down a thick base of moss, on top of which they place a cup of fine plant fibers, down, fur, hair, and/or feathers. The 4–13 (average 6–8) eggs are white to slightly yellowish and either unmarked (Mountain Chickadee, Bridled Titmouse) or finely speckled with reddish or dark brown over the whole surface or in a "wreath" at the large end.

Many tits have two distinct call types, one that includes a variety of buzzy and tinkling sounds and another consisting of a series of clear, whistled notes. In several species one of the first type sounds something like *chick-a-dee-dee.*

Tits are essentially birds of Temperate Zone forests (including tropical highlands). They are widely distributed in the Holarctic region, absent from most of the Neotropics, Madagascar, Australia, and Polynesia. In North America they are absent only from treeless regions, e.g., arctic tundra and desert (however, see VERDIN).

"Tit" connotes anything small, and the "mouse" of "titmouse" is from an Anglo-Saxon word, *mase,* which referred to any small bird. Choate and Paynter (1985–BIOGRAPHY) points out that "titmouses" rather than "titmice" should be the correct plural of "titmouse"—another good reason to dispense with the "mouse" and hang on to the "tit."

TITMOUSE. See TIT.

TITYRA (tuh-TYE-ruh). Standard English name for 3 species of Neotropical passerine birds considered by the *AOU Checklist,* 7th edition (1998) to be of uncertain taxonomic status but closely allied to the tyrant flycatchers (family Tyrannidae) and the cotingas (family Cotingidae). Sibley and Ahlquist (1990–SYSTEMATICS) include them along with the becards in a separate tribe (Tityrini) and subfamily (Tityrinae) within the Tyrannidae. There is one record for the Masked Tityra form the lower Rio Grande Valley of Texas. See BECARD; COTINGA; TYRANT FLYCATCHER.

TOLMIE, William, 1812–86 (*Oporornis tolmiei:* MacGillivray's Warbler). A Scottish physician who immigrated to Canada when he was twenty, eventually becoming the head of the Hudson's Bay Company. He was the first person to conquer Mount Rainier. He owes his ornithological immortality to a meeting with John TOWNSEND in British Columbia in 1836.

TOMIUM (TOH-mee-yum) (pl. tomia). The cutting edge of both mandibles of the bill.

TONGUE. In birds as in humans, the tongue is a muscular organ attached
to the floor of the mouth. The human tongue is a fleshy member supported by a single hyoid (U-shaped) bone. It is crucial to our manipulation of food, our highly developed sense of taste, and the articulation of
our speech. By contrast, the avian tongue is usually tough (cartilaginous)
in texture, especially toward the tip, and the hyoid apparatus has evolved
into a series of small narrow bones, most of them paired, which in some
species is prodigiously elongated (see below). Birds' tongues come in a
great variety of sizes and shapes. In pelecaniform species (pelicans, boobies, cormorants, etc.), ibises, and storks, it is reduced to a vestige, while
ducks, flamingoes, parrots, and many finches have comparatively large
and even fleshy tongues. In general, the shape of birds' tongues conforms
to the shape of the bills that enclose them and accordingly are subject to
great variation: long and thin, short and wide, spoon-shaped or globular,
rounded to nearly rectangular.

The tongue modifications that appear most frequently (but by no
means universally) among different forms of birdlife are (1) surface spines
or barbs, which are directed back toward the throat and probably aid the
movement of food in that direction, and (2) barbed edges (e.g., woodpeckers) and/or split tips (e.g., tits, hummingbirds, nuthatches, crows),
which facilitate the picking up or prizing out of food items.

Most birds apparently do not have a sophisticated sense of taste nor
do their tongues play a role in voice production. Thus it is in manipulating
food that human and avian tongues have most in common, and in this we
are vastly outdone by many bird species in complexity of structure and
versatility.

Many birds have great concentrations of tactile sensors on the tips of
their tongues (see TOUCH), perhaps a heritage from their reptilian ancestors, which, like modern reptiles, used their tongues routinely as "feelers."
Birds do not "wag" their tongues like snakes and lizards, but some doubtless find food and judge its suitability by touch, and the Australian Mallee
Fowl may gauge the temperature of its peculiar "nest" with its tongue (see
INCUBATION).

A few "famous" bird tongues deserve special emphasis.

Woodpecker tongues tend to be unusually long and extensible. Their
hyoid apparatus is elaborated into long, flexible pairs of branchial bones or
"horns" that extend from near the base of the tongue around the back of the
skull and find their ultimate attachment (in some species) inside the nostril
openings of the bill. Extensibility is apparently achieved by the ability of the
hyoid mechanism to "fold up" accordion style. Along with sensitive tissue,
the tongue tops of woodpeckers are fixed with backward-projecting barbs

and a sticky saliva. Thus equipped, woodpeckers can probe deep into holes, locate insect prey, and extract it with great efficiency.

The longest tongues of the bird world (in proportion to body size) are probably those of the peculiar Old World woodpeckers called wrynecks, whose apparatus measures more than half its owner's total body length. The Common Flicker, a ground-loving, ant-eating woodpecker, may have the longest tongue (proportionate to body size) of any North American bird, measuring over 5 inches from the tip to the end of the hyoid horns anchored at the back of the skull. The tongues of the sapsuckers are not particularly long, but are covered with fine bristles, which soak up sap by capillary action.

Hummingbird tongues are also long and extensible by means of a hyoid system like that of the woodpeckers. In addition, the tongues of most hummers are deeply split at the tip, bilaterally grooved, and capable of being furled into a tube. This last feature led observers to believe that hummingbirds sucked nectar from flowers as if drinking through a straw, but it has since been demonstrated (Weymouth et al. 1964) that this is not the case; the liquid is drawn onto the tongue (probably by capillary action), then the tongue is returned to the mouth and the nectar is swallowed in the usual manner. Some hummers also have fringes on the tongue tips that aid in gleaning insects from vegetation or picking them from the corollas of flowers.

Flamingo tongues are fat and fleshy with serrated edges and bear numerous small, soft protuberances (papillae). This unusual organ is used in conjunction with the lamellae of the bill to sieve minute food items from mud (see BILL; FLAMINGO). The tongues of surface-feeding ducks (especially the shovelers), which also have lamellate bills, are also large and papillate. The serrations on the tongue edges of grazing geese are used in conjunction with the bill to hold and break off vegetation.

Many seed-eating finches have large (fat) tongues with which they manipulate seeds or fruits so that they may be "husked" inside the bill (see BILL for description). Crossbill tongues are thick and bear a cutting "tool" at the tip with which they detach conifer seeds once the cone scales have been separated (see FOOD/FEEDING and Fig. 3).

The notably large, thick, mobile tongues of parrots may play a part in the ability of some species to produce "articulate" sounds (see SONG).

TOOL USE. See INTELLIGENCE.

TOOTH. See TEETH; EGG TOOTH.

TOPOGRAPHY. In zoology, the delineation and identification of the external features and areas of the body surface of a bird or other animal. See topographic diagrams, Figs. 1 and 35.

TOPOTYPE. A specimen collected at the same place where the original type specimen or type series was taken. See NOMENCLATURE, ZOOLOGICAL, Types.

TORPIDITY. A slowing down or reduction in bodily function usually as a reaction to cold or stress or as a technique for conserving energy.

Torpidity in birds has been reported in three closely related families: the hummingbirds, the swifts, and the nightjars (and, in one instance, a species of swallow). In all cases, body temperature is greatly reduced, breathing and heartbeat become negligible, and the birds can be handled without arousing them.

Because of their small size and extremely high metabolism when active, most hummingbird species can barely sustain themselves overnight without feeding. To reduce energy requirements, some species of hummingbirds become dormant each night and return to normal at daylight, when they can resume feeding.

Flocks of White-throated Swifts of the western mountains are known to roost in rock crevices in a torpid state during periods of cold weather when insect food is unavailable. This survival technique is also practiced by swift nestlings, which become torpid during the night in times of food scarcity.

The longest known period of torpidity—amounting to hibernation— is endured by the Poorwill, which is known to "sleep" for nearly three months in rock crevices in the American Southwest. As with the swifts, the Poorwill's torpidity coincides with cold weather and the consequent lack of insect food. Its temperature drops to 40°F below normal and it survives on stored fat. Though this is the only species of bird found hibernating in the wild so far, torpidity has been observed in other species of nightjars in captivity. See also TEMPERATURE, BODY.

TOTIPALMATE (TOH-tuh-PAHL-mate). Describes a bird's foot that is webbed between all four toes, thus bringing the fourth (usually hind) toe forward. Characteristic of the Pelecaniformes (pelicans, boobies, gannets, tropicbirds, frigatebirds, cormorants, and anhingas)—the "totipalmate swimmers."

TOUCH. Much remains to be learned about the extent to which birds feel pressure, pain, vibration, and variations in temperature. Present assumptions about tactile sensations are based on physiological evidence such as concentrations of nerve endings in the skin, bill, feet, and elsewhere and observations of behavior that implies a sense of touch.

Nerve endings in the bill tips of shorebirds that probe deep in the mud for invertebrates, which they cannot see, are reasonably supposed to help locate food by touch, as are those in the tongues of woodpeckers and

at the base of rictal bristles. Concentrations of presumed tactile receptors in the bills of ducks may serve to sort food by texture.

Apparently unique to birds are two bodies of encapsulated nerve endings, called Herbst's and Grandry's corpuscles, which are located in the lower skin layer (dermis) at various points in the body. Since they do not lie at the surface, they may be responsible for birds' observed sensitivity to vibrations and changes in atmospheric pressure. The ability of barnyard fowl or cage birds to "predict" earthquakes, presumably by feeling vibrations not perceptible to people, has often been observed; and it is suspected that birds may be able to "feel" weather changes approaching in their migration path.

We infer from watching gulls and ducks standing on the ice that their feet are either insensitive to cold or that the tactile receivers in these extremities can be "turned off" when necessary. We are probably justified in concluding, when we see a bird scratch an area beneath feathers that it cannot see, e.g., on its face, that it is reacting to the attacks of an ectoparasite or other felt stimulus.

TOWHEE (TOE-ee; however, see below). Standard English name for 7 species of large New World emberizine finches (family Emberizidae or Fringillidae; order Passeriformes), all in the genus *Pipilo*. Six of the towhees breed in North America.

In addition to being relatively large, towhees are notably long tailed and typically forage in underbrush and leaf litter in forests or scrublands. Several species are colorful, boldly patterned birds.

The towhees eat a great many insects (even some small vertebrates, e.g., lizards) as well as seeds and fruit.

The name derives from the nasal, whistled call of the Eastern Towhee, and if intended to echo the bird, should properly be pronounced too-WHEE.

For family characteristics, see FINCH.

TOWNSEND, John Kirk, 1809–51 (Townsend's Solitaire: *Myadestes townsendi*; Townsend's Warbler: *Dendroica townsendi*). Well-to-do and well-educated son of a Quaker family and a member of the flourishing natural history establishment in Philadelphia in the early 1800s. He is chiefly remembered for his expedition to the Pacific Northwest, on which he was accompanied by Thomas NUTTALL. The trip resulted in the discovery and collection of several "new" North American bird species. Townsend was fated to be a contemporary of Audubon, whose *Birds of America* overshadowed a similar comprehensive work attempted by Townsend but never completed. He abandoned natural history for dentistry in 1845 but apparently failed at this and a number of other things before his early demise. Not to be confused with Charles W. Townsend, a prolific (amateur) ornithologist, author of *Birds of Essex County, Massa-*

chusetts, and a number of the "biographies" in BENT's *Life Histories of North American Birds* series. For a fuller biography of J. K. Townsend, see Stone, Cassinia (1903), 7:1–5.

TOXIC CHEMICALS. For effects on birds, see THREATS (OF HUMAN ORIGIN) TO BIRDLIFE.

TRAILL, Thomas S., 1781–1862 (*Empidonax traillii:* Willow Flycatcher). A doctor-zoologist (see BIOGRAPHY), Traill was a professor of medical jurisprudence and a light of the cultural and intellectual life of Liverpool, England, and Edinburgh, Scotland, where he was born and died. The obscure flycatcher that once bore Traill's name in English as well as Latin was named by Audubon, whose cause Traill championed in Britain. The species was subsequently split into two obscure flycatchers, now called Willow and Alder.

TRANSIENT. A species (or population) that migrates through a given area but neither breeds nor winters there. Obviously, the use of the term in reference to a particular species varies geographically; i.e., the Palm Warbler is a transient in most of the east-central United States but not in the eastern boreal zone of Canada, where it breeds, or in Florida, where it winters.

TRAPPING (of birds). See HELIGOLAND TRAP; CANNON NET; BANDING; LIME; and POLE TRAP for specific trapping methods. A brief discussion of bird catching in general is given under CAPTURE.

TRASH BIRD. In some (very hard-core) birding circles, applied to any abundant species regardless of its beauty, grace, or charm, sometimes with the express purpose of infuriating a more sensitive element of the birdwatching community. Typical usage as follows:

> *Novice birder (first trip to Texas):* "Oh, I just think that little Vermilion Flycatcher is the most *bee-oo-tee-ful* bird I've ever seen.
> *Veteran birder (trying to "get" 300 species in 24 hours):* "Forget the trash birds and listen for the Botteri's Sparrow that's supposed to be here."

TREAD. "Treading" refers to the male bird's action in copulation, based on the fact that in many cases he stands on the back of the female. See REPRODUCTIVE SYSTEM; COPULATION.

TREE-CREEPER. Standard English collective name for the 6 members of the family Certhiidae (order Passeriformes), 1 of which breeds in North America. Sibley and Ahlquist (1990–SYSTEMATICS) expand this family to include the wrens, gnatcatchers, and verdin and confine the genus *Certhia*

to its own tribe (Certhiini). The name "creeper" is used alone or in combination to refer to many species in a wide range of families, e.g., wallcreeper (Sittidae), woodcreeper (Dendrocolaptidae), and Australian treecreeper (Climacteridae), while "tree-creeper" is used as the standard English generic name for all species in the genus *Certhia*, except in North America, where the species *Certhia americana* is called Brown Creeper. Vernacular nomenclature might be well served by calling this species American Tree-creeper as suggested by Monroe and Sibley (1993–CHECKLIST).

Tree-creepers are small (4½–5 inches), delicately built birds, colored and patterned cryptically to resemble the surface of a rough-textured tree trunk above and white or off-white below. The bill is fairly long, narrow, and decurved; the legs are slender with long toes and sharp, strongly decurved claws; and the longish tail has stiff, pointed woodpecker-like rectrices which act as a prop as the bird climbs.

Unlike the nuthatches, tree-creepers are exclusively vertical climbers, often following a spiral course upward from the base of a tree and then flying down to the base of another. They are essentially forest birds but will also glean walls and buildings. Their food preferences run to small insects, spiders, and other animal matter—e.g., insect eggs prized from crevices—but they also eat seeds occasionally and take suet at feeders.

Most tree-creepers, including the North American one, have a pleasingly clear, sweet, high-pitched melodious song, and thin lisping or piping calls.

The Brown Creeper stuffs its loose cup nest behind a section of loose bark on a tree trunk (rarely among rocks). The construction is of moss, small sticks, and grass and the lining is typically of feathers and soft plant down. The 3–9 (usually 6) eggs are white with fine reddish-brownish speckling at the "blunt" end.

The distribution of tree-creepers is mainly Holarctic, though they reach the Neotropics (Central America), India, and Africa, mainly in the highlands. The Brown Creeper breeds from southwestern Alaska to Nicaragua and occurs at some season throughout most wooded areas of North America south of the boreal forest.

TREE-DUCK. Once the standard English generic name for members of the genus *Dendrocygna*, only a few of which nest and/or roost regularly in trees. WHISTLING-DUCK is now the standard collective name for these birds. See also DUCK.

TRIBE. Taxonomic category between SUBFAMILY and GENUS. In zoological nomenclature, tribal names invariably end in -*ini*. The tribe is a tertiary category below subfamily. For example the ducks and geese are classified into subfamilies (varying with taxonomic opinion), which are then subdivided into tribes (e.g., Mergini: sea ducks). See TAXONOMY.

TRINOMIAL. A three-word scientific name, the third word of which designates the subspecies of a plant or animal. The binomial *Dendroica petechia* designates the *species* of the Yellow Warbler as a whole. The several races or *subspecies* of the Yellow Warbler each bear a trinomial, e.g., *Dendroica petechia rubignosa,* the Alaskan Yellow Warbler.

TRITURATION (TRICH-ur-AY-shun). Crushing or grinding into fine particles. Used to describe the muscular action of a bird's gizzard, which pulverizes hard seeds, mollusk shells, etc. See DIGESTIVE SYSTEM.

TROGON (TROH-gun). Standard English name for most of the 39 members of the family Trogonidae, the sole family in the order Trogoniformes (5 species of large Neotropical trogons are called quetzals). One species of trogon, the Elegant, breeds in North America, and one other (Eared Trogon) has occurred as a vagrant (see Appendix II).

Though in many respects they exemplify quintessential "tropical birds," trogons are unique in appearance. They are medium-sized (9–12 inches), very colorful, usually with iridescent metallic (often green) upperparts, a brilliant red or yellow belly, a conspicuously barred or spotted undertail pattern, and a brightly colored fleshy eye ring. The bill is short but rather broad and deep, the nostrils heavily bristled, the feet extraordinarily small, and the tail long and (in most cases) abruptly squared at the end. They are the only birds to have toes I and II turned backward, III and IV frontward (heterodactyl).

The trogons are fruit-eating forest birds capable of sitting with uncanny stillness while croaking in a ventriloquial manner and screwing up their courage to launch an attack on an unsuspecting berry. They vary their diet occasionally with insects or even small reptiles or amphibians.

Many trogons excavate their own nest cavities in rotten tree trunks or wasp nests, but the Elegant (Coppery-tailed) prefers to occupy natural tree cavities (exceptionally, holes in earthen banks) or abandoned woodpecker holes, which it lines sparsely (if at all) with a little plant down, grass, and/or other debris. The 3–4 (rarely, 2) eggs are white or pale blue.

Trogon calls consist of short or long series of hoots, croaks, or clucks; our native species typically gives 4–6 notes in the second category.

Trogons are pantropical (except for Australia and Oceania), though they range well into the Temperate Zone on tropical mountains. The single North American representative reaches the northernmost limit of its extensive Mexican and Central American range in the pine/oak zone of the highlands of southeastern Arizona and New Mexico from which most individuals depart in the winter. In the tropics trogons are nonmigratory.

"Trogon" is Greek for "the gnawer," an odd characterization probably meant to refer to the way they hollow out their nest cavities.

TROPICBIRD. Standard English name for all 3 members of the family Phaethontidae (order Pelecaniformes; or per Sibley and Ahlquist [1990–SYSTEMATICS] order Ciconiiformes), 2 of which—White-tailed and Red-billed—occur annually in North America, mainly in offshore waters. The third species is a rare visitor mainly to the deep waters off California. None of the tropicbirds is resident here, though the White-tailed Tropicbird (*Phaethon lepturus*) breeds in Bermuda.

Tropicbirds are graceful, largely white seabirds with yellow or orange bills and greatly elongated central tail feathers (rectrices), a feature that contributes to their ethereal bearing. They are 15–18 inches long excluding the elongated tail feathers, which contribute an additional foot and a half or more. Like the other Pelecaniformes, tropicbirds have webs between all four toes. Their legs are very short and on land they hobble along on their tarsi rather than walk upright as do the pelicans and boobies. Tropicbirds sail high over tropical seas looking for shoals of fish or squid, which they hover over and then dive into. They are partially migratory.

All three species are loosely colonial and lay their eggs in an unlined natural cavity or crevice in rock, an abandoned (or pirated) petrel burrow, or a hollow on the ground amidst vegetation. They lay only a single egg, which is very variable in color and markings: white to reddish brown with darker spots and blotches of yellowish to dark red-brown or purple.

Unlike most members of their order, tropicbirds are rather noisy, making a variety of loud, shrill screams, rattles, and clicks. A rasping call given at sea, *clik-et-clik-et,* gave rise to the nickname "bos'n bird" according to Palmer (1962–ORNITHOLOGY).

The name is an apt reflection of their pantropical distribution.

TROUPIAL (TROO-pee-yul). The first-named (*Icterus icterus*) and largest of the New World orioles. It has been suggested that the icterid orioles of the New World be called troupials to avoid confusion with the oriolid orioles of the Old World; or that the term be used collectively to refer to *all* members of the family Icteridae, i.e., blackbirds, cowbirds, meadowlarks, etc. The name is of French derivation and refers to flocking, which, though typical of many American blackbirds as well as most of the caciques and oropendolas of Latin America, is not characteristic of most icterid orioles including the Troupial.

TUBENOSES. Standard English name for the order Procellariiformes, which includes the albatrosses, shearwaters, petrels, and storm-petrels. For further reference to this bill structure and other characteristics of this order, see SALT GLAND; NOSTRILS.

TUBERCULOSIS. See DISEASE.

TUNDRA. Treeless barrens characteristic of arctic regions between the permanent glacier zone and the tree line. When poorly drained, as it is in vast areas underlain by permafrost, it is swampy, but in upland areas it is dry and "turfy." Botanically it is characteristically made up of a great abundance and variety of mosses and lichens, as well as grasses and sedges (particularly in wetter areas), many species of uniquely arctic flowers, low-growing shrubs of the heath family (Ericaceae), and small sprawling "trees," mostly willows and birches, which in sheltered localities may reach the proportions of small bushes. In North America, virtually all land between the Arctic Circle and the north polar sea ice is tundra and it accounts for perhaps half of the landscape north of the 60th parallel. Below 60° N, it occurs in western Alaska, northern Québec, and a narrow strip along the western shore of Hudson Bay to below 55° N. A similar condition prevails on the highest peaks of the Rockies and other high mountains and is often called "alpine tundra." In general, tundra regions are frozen solid with a relatively thin snow cover for at least nine months of the year, but they spring into riotous life during the height of summer.

Tundra birdlife is characterized by many waterbird species, especially loons, ducks, the majority of North American shorebird species, jaegers, a few gulls, and Arctic Tern; other typical species include the ptarmigans, Snowy Owl, Northern Raven, Smith's and Lapland Longspurs, and Snow Bunting. Where cliffside nest sites are available, Peregrine Falcon, Gyrfalcon, Rough-legged Hawk, and Golden Eagle often occur, and where the vegetation reaches shrub proportions, a few other hardy passerines, such as Harris's Sparrow and Hoary Redpoll, can be expected.

See also ARCTIC and the Bibliography under same.

TURKEY. Standard English name for the only 2 members of the New World subfamily Meleagridinae (family Phasianidae order Galliformes); Sibley and Ahlquist (1990–SYSTEMATICS) do not recognize the subfamily. Both turkeys are large birds, standing to 4 feet tall with neck stretched normally. They have a bare, colored, carunculated head, neck wattles, spurs on the tarsus, and gorgeous iridescent plumage including a magnificent tail fan.

Turkeys fly well, but, like other gallinaceous birds, do so only in short bursts, usually when alarmed. They are birds of the forest and forest edge, foraging in flocks at a stately pace, scratching in leaf litter for grain, nuts, and other seeds, picking fresh fruits and buds, and nabbing the occasional invertebrate. Turkeys roost for the night in trees.

The nest is a shallow depression on the ground, scantily lined with handy plant material. The 8–12 eggs (up to 20 recorded) are white to pale buff or yellowish and densely but rather finely speckled and spotted with reddish or darker brown.

The voice of the Wild Turkey cock has changed little with domestication; "gobble-gobble" does not begin to do it justice.

The Wild Turkey (*Meleagris gallopavo*), once resident throughout most of North America south of the coniferous forest zone, was reduced to remnant populations due largely to its appeal as a game and table bird. Ironically, the turkey's popularity with sportsmen has also been its salvation, for it has been artificially reestablished in many states by fish and game agencies at the urging of turkey shooters. The Wild Turkey is a magnificent American species that has made its mark in the history of the Republic: the Pilgrim Fathers gave thanks to it (and with it); Benjamin Franklin nominated it as the national bird; and it has become a staple of the American poultry industry.

Opinions vary about the relationship (if any) between turkey, the bird, and Turkey, the country. Gruson (1972–BIOGRAPHY) says that it is a Tartar word (meaning "brave") used in the sixteenth century to refer both to part of Asia Minor but also very generally, to any form of exotica. There is some evidence that guinea fowl were the original avian "turkeys," so named because they were imported from Africa to Europe via Turkey or simply because of the connection with Ottoman exoticism. When an even more bizarre fowl arrived in Europe from America, it captured the misnomer. In Turkey on the other hand turkeys are called *Hindi*, implying (incorrectly of course) that they came from another exotic place—India!

For Thanksgiving-type turkeys see DOMESTICATED BIRDS. See also references in the Bibliography under GALLINACEOUS BIRDS.

TURNSTONE. Standard English name for the 2 distinctive sandpipers in the genus *Arenaria* (family Scolopacidae; order Charadriiformes or Ciconiiformes); The *AOU Checklist*, 7th edition (1998) gives these birds their own tribe (Arenariini), while Sibley and Ahlquist (1990–SYSTEMATICS) include them in the sandpiper subfamily Tringinae. Both turnstones breed in North America.

Turnstones are medium-sized (9½ inches), strikingly patterned shorebirds with somewhat wedge-like, slightly upturned bills, which they use to turn over small rocks and debris in search of anything edible; sometimes these birds will join forces to flip a stone too heavy or too securely embedded for one. They are by no means restricted to this manner of feeding, however, and in fact appear to be among the most resourceful of shorebirds: digging with bill and feet in sand for buried eggs of marine invertebrates, taking maggots from putrefying seal carcasses, rooting vigorously in piles of rotting seaweed and other beach detritus; they are even known to take bread crumbs from people's hands (Palmer in Stout [1967–SHOREBIRD]). Their strong, stout bills are used for breaking into mollusk shells and eggshells of nesting birds as well as for turning. Like other shorebirds, they readily eat fruit on their breeding grounds. Their manner of walking is similar to the step-and-stop movement characteristic of plovers.

The Black Turnstone is almost exclusively a bird of wave-washed rocks (except when nesting), and though the Ruddy Turnstone is also inclined to prefer this habitat, it is much more tolerant of sandy beaches, mudflats, and even marsh pools.

Black Turnstones breed only in coastal Alaska and the northwestern Yukon and winter at least as far south as the coast of Sinaloa, Mexico. The Ruddy Turnstone is one of the few shorebirds (along with the Red Knot and Sanderling) to nest on the stony barrens of northernmost Greenland. Its breeding distribution is circumpolar arctic and it migrates or winters over most of the rest of the world, to as far south as Tierra del Fuego and New Zealand.

For family characteristics, see SANDPIPER.

TURTLE DOVE. Standard English name for some of the doves in the Old World genus *Streptopelia,* including *the* (Eurasian) Turtle Dove, *S. turtur. Turtur* is the Latin word for "turtle" and echoes the gentle, purring call of this species. Three species of *Streptopelia* doves have been introduced into North America: the Barbary or Ringed Turtle-Dove, *S. "risoria,"* an aviary-bred form of the African Collared-Dove, *S. roseogrisea,* is not well-suited to life in the wild and is weakly established in a few cities along the southern border of the United States; the Spotted Dove, *S. chinensis,* a widespread Asian species seems content to inhabit the suburbs of Los Angeles and Orange counties, California; and the most recent arrival, Eurasian Collared-Dove (*S. decaocto*) arrived in southern Florida in the late 1970s from the Bahamas and is speading rapidly to the North and west.

TWITCHER. British equivalent of "lister," i.e., one whose chief interest in birds is checking them off on lists (in British "getting ticks"). According to Bill Oddie (1980–BIRDWATCHING), the term derives from such birders' emotional state over the prospect of seeing a good bird: "He is so wracked with nervous anticipation (that he might see it) or trepidation (that he might miss it) that he literally twitches with the excitement of it all." See also TICK; BIRDWATCHING; LISTING.

TYPE GENUS. A genus of birds or other animals designated by the author as the basis for his description of a new family, superfamily, subfamily, or tribe. If a type genus is not published by an author, one is subsequently designated. See NOMENCLATURE, ZOOLOGICAL, Types.

TYPE LOCALITY. Ideally, the exact place where the type specimen of a bird or other animal species was collected. If a type locality is not designated by an author when he publishes the description of a species (as was the case in many early species descriptions), one is chosen and published by a later authority. See NOMENCLATURE, ZOOLOGICAL, Types.

TYPE SERIES. Two or more specimens of a bird or other animal from which a type specimen is selected as the basis for the description of a new species or subspecies. See NOMENCLATURE, ZOOLOGICAL, Types.

TYPE SPECIES. A species designated by an author as the basis for his description of a new genus (or subgenus). If a type species is not published by an author, one is subsequently designated. See TYPE SPECIMEN; NOMENCLATURE, ZOOLOGICAL, Types.

TYPE SPECIMEN. An actual specimen of a bird (or other animal), usually in the form of a museum "study skin," to which the scientific description of a species or subspecies (both in the case of a nominate subspecies) refers in the "type" system. See NOMENCLATURE, Types; also HOLOTYPE; LECTOTYPE; SYNTYPE; PARATYPE; TYPE SERIES.

TYRANNULET (tuh-RAN-yuh-let). Standard English generic name for many species of tiny flycatchers of several genera in the family Tyrannidae (tyrant flycatchers; see following entry). The only tyrannulet to reach North America from the Neotropics is the Northern Beardless-Tyrannulet (*Camptostoma imberbe*), which breeds from southernmost Texas and Arizona to northwestern Costa Rica.; it is called the Beardless Flycatcher in North America.

TYRANT FLYCATCHER. Standard English collective name for approximately 340 members of the family Tyrannidae (order Passeriformes), 35 of which breed in North America; 9 other species have occurred as vagrants from further south (see Appendix II). Sibley and Ahlquist (1990– SYSTEMATICS) have included the cotingas (including tityras and becards) and the manakins—both retained as distinct families in the *AOU Checklist,* 7th edition (1998)—as subfamilies within the Tyrannidae; with these additions the species count for the family reaches 539 species.

The tyrant flycatchers are such a varied group that few characters apply to all the species. They range in size from 3 to 16 inches (4½ to 10 inches in North America). Most have relatively large heads and tails of medium length (some moderately long to very long). Larger species tend to have broad, heavy, hooked bills (all species show some degree of hook at the tip). The great majority have well-developed rictal bristles (absent in the Northern Beardless-Tyrannulet). The legs and feet of all North American species are relatively small and weak. The coloration of most species is drab—combinations of grays, browns, and olives. But some species have brilliant yellow breasts; the kingbirds have brilliant orange or red crown patches (usually concealed) and some *Myiarchus* and the Great Kiskadee have areas of bright rufous in wings and tail. The male of one North American species is vivid vermilion. Many species have conspicuous wing bars and eye rings.

As their name implies, tyrant flycatchers tend to be active, often aggressive birds, many of which habitually sit in conspicuous perches and sally into midair after flying insects or to chase potential nest robbers, such as crows and jays. They are usually solitary. They feed mainly on insects, but all species take some fruit and a few are primarily frugivorous.

Tyrannids typically build cup nests, usually in a tree in the open, but in some species in cavities (*Myiarchus*) or on buildings or rock ledges (phoebes); a few (e.g., Kiskadee) build enclosed nests. The eggs are white to buff-yellow, immaculate, finely speckled/streaked, boldly streaked, or spotted with dark brown, reddish, and/or grayish.

The calls of tyrant flycatchers are distinctive but unmusical, usually short, often harsh and abrupt.

The tyrant flycatchers are an exclusively New World family, which achieves its greatest diversity in the Neotropical region, where it undoubtedly evolved. In North America, they inhabit all major biomes except arctic tundra; a few species range continentwide.

See also BECARD; COTINGA; EMPIDONAX; KINGBIRD; MYIARCHUS; OLD WORLD FLYCATCHER; PEWEE; PHOEBE; TITYRA; TYRANNULET.

U

UNCINATE (UN-sin-et) **PROCESS.** A bony projection from a rib, linking by means of a tendon to the rib behind; present only in birds and a few reptiles. See SKELETON and Fig. 27.

UNDERPARTS. Strictly interpreted, synonymous with "ventrum," i.e., everything below a lateral midline including, for example, the underside of the tail. However, normally used to describe general pattern or coloration of the throat, breast, belly, and undertail coverts—or the greater part thereof. The Yellow-breasted Chat may be said to have bright yellow underparts even though the lower belly and vent are white.

UNGUIS (UNG-gwis). Technical term for the bill NAIL present in the ducks, geese, and swans.

UPPERPARTS. Strictly interpreted, synonymous with "dorsum," i.e., everything above a lateral midline, including, for example, the forehead. However, normally used to describe general pattern or coloration of the head, back, wings, rump, and tail—or the greater part thereof. The Red-eyed

Vireo may be described as having olive-green upperparts even though it has a gray crown.

URINARY SYSTEM. See EXCRETORY SYSTEM.

UROPYGIUM (YOOR-uh-PIDGE-ee-yum). Technical term for a bird's rump, where the uropygial, i.e., oil or preen, gland is located. See OIL GLAND.

VAGRANT, VAGRANCY. In an ornithological context, these terms refer to birds that occur outside their normal range; as a term of abundance (or lack thereof) it is essentially synonymous with "accidental." It is possible to define several different patterns of vagrancy, e.g., (1) weather-related instances in which tropical birds are carried north by hurricanes or Eurasian species to our Northern shores by seasonal gales; (2) the wanderings of inexperienced or "defective" juvenal birds that fail to follow their genetically prescribed migration routes; and (3) the rare but regular occurrence of individuals that are in effect pushing the limits of their dispersal instincts. Veit (2000) has demonstrated that there is a strong correlation between population growth within limited sectors of a species' normal breeding range and the subsequent occurrence of that species as a vagrant hundreds or thousands of miles beyond its usual dispersal boundaries. Especially interesting is his suggestion that at least some vagrants may be more likely to originate from remote localities where there has been high reproductive success in the previous breeding season than from much closer breeding areas where productivity was low or unexceptional. Defined in this way, vagrants are not "accidental" at all, but rather the extreme "tail" of a species' characteristic dispersal tendency. Because the dispersal of young birds to their eventual breeding sites is a key determinant of a species' population structure, and because populations founded by colonists of remote origins are prone to rapid evolution (see SPECIATION), the nature of such "normal vagrancy" takes on a heightened evolutionary significance.

Of course, to many birdwatchers a vagrant is more or less synonymous with a "good tick," with the remoteness of its origins positively correlated with its "quality." For a listing of verified vagrants (in the broad sense) that have occurred in North America, see Appendix II.

For related topics, see CAPTIVIT;, DISPERSAL; EXOTIC SPECIES; IN-
TRODUCED BIRDS; IRRUPTION; VERIFICATION OF RECORDS; WEATHER.

VANE. The flat, relatively soft area of a feather extending outward on both
sides from the central shaft (rachis). The vane is also called the web (inner
and outer) or the vexillum and is made up of a series of interlocking barbs.
See FEATHER and Fig. 13.

VARIETY. In botany, a taxonomic category below subspecies, but in zoology refers to individuals within a population that differ from the norm;
also used more loosely for any variation within a species.

VAUX (vawks), William S., 1811–82 (Vaux's Swift: *Chaetura vauxi*). A pillar
of the hyperactive natural history community of Philadelphia in the nineteenth century. His specialties were archaeology and mineralogy, not
birds; his commemorator was William TOWNSEND.

VASCULAR SYSTEM. See CIRCULATORY SYSTEM.

VEERY. Standard English name for a single species of thrush, *Catharus
fuscescens,* family Turdidae (AOU) or Muscicapidae (Sibley and Monroe),
that breeds exclusively in North America, typically occupying moist deciduous and coniferous woodlands nearly continentwide. The name gives
a feeble suggestion of the species' inimitable, ethereal song. For family
characteristics, see THRUSH.

VENT. A single anal opening (cloacal aperture) through which pass solid
and liquid wastes as well as the products of the reproductive system.
Characteristic of birds, as well as reptiles, amphibians, most fishes, and a
few Australasian egg-laying mammals (Order Monotremata), e.g. the duck-
billed platypus. Also an acronym for Victor Emmanuel Nature Tours (see
BIRDING TOURS).

VENTRAL. Lower or under, as: the "ventral surface" of an animal's body;
in birds, "ventral surface" is synonymous with "underparts." Opposite of
DORSAL.

VENTRICULUS (ven-TRIK-yuh-luss). The second of two enlargements
in a bird's digestive tract, which together function like the human
stomach; it could also be described as the lower of a bird's two stomachs.
Also called the GIZZARD. See DIGESTIVE SYSTEM and Fig. 27.

VERDIN. Standard English name for a single species, *Auriparus flavi-
ceps,* classified by the AOU (1998) as the sole North American member of
the penduline tit family (Remizidae) and by Sibley and Ahlquist (1990–

SYSTEMATICS) with the gnatcatchers in the subfamily Polioptilinae (family Certhiidae), order Passeriformes.

The Verdin is a small bird (4½ inches) with a short, pointed (tit-like) bill. In its generally grayish plumage and active, often gregarious feeding behavior, it resembles the "true" tits, but the yellow head and chestnut "shoulder" patch of the adults distinguish it from any other North American bird species.

Verdins are birds of arid *Acacia* scrub, through which they forage, probing bark and twigs and gleaning leaves for insects, as well as taking berries when available. The species apparently never bathes or drinks and gets all necessary moisture from its food.

Its song is a series of loud, clear, whistled notes, which carry well through the still desert atmosphere, and it also gives a number of buzzy calls, which also recall the tits.

The Verdin nest is placed from 2 to 20 feet (usually about 5 feet) up in a cactus or thorny desert shrub and consists of a ball of thorny twigs with a side entrance, lined with spider silk, grasses, leaves, feathers, and plant down. In addition to its usual function, the nest is used as a night and winter roost.

The 3–6 (usually 4) eggs are pale blue or greenish blue, finely marked around the larger end with reddish speckles.

The Verdin is resident in desert or semidesert habitats from southern California to western Texas south through Baja California and to central Mexico. It is endemic to this range and nonmigratory. The other penduline tits occur in Eurasia and Africa.

The provenance of "verdin" is obscure, but it is a colloquial French name for the Eurasian bunting called the Yellowhammer (*Emberiza citrinella*), males of which, like *Auriparus,* have bright yellow heads.

VERIFICATION OF RECORDS. Not very long ago, the only satisfactory means of verifying the occurrence of a particular bird in a particular place was to shoot the bird, prepare it as a specimen, label it, and preserve it in a museum drawer for future reference. Photographs and well-documented sight records by reliable observers are now widely accepted as proof of the occurrence of rare species, but it should be noted that in many cases subspecific determination is impossible from a photograph and still requires a bird "in the hand." Of course, anyone wishing to falsify such a record could easily do so using a bogus photograph or specimen. Hoaxes of this kind have been perpetrated (see, for example, the fascinating cases of the "Hastings Rarities," *British Birds* [1962]), but the crime is such an absurd one that it evokes more amusement than indignation.

Since the advent of good optical equipment and the resulting improvement in our ability to identify birds by sight, it has been recognized that there should be a system for evaluating "sight records," i.e., those for which no cor-

roborating specimen or photograph could be obtained. Such a standard became all the more necessary with the exponential increase in the number of competent (and incompetent) field observers and with the increasing prohibitions, both legal and moral, against shooting birds in most places.

The following are the main criteria that have evolved over the years for the consideration of sight records.

1. A record that is within some parameter of plausibility. A novice may be heard to explain his report of a nonmigratory Andean endemic in his backyard in Texas by saying: "Well, birds fly, don't they?" The fact is that, without in any way belittling birds' well-documented capacity for long-distance travel, a James' Flamingo in El Paso is either an escape or a mistake; criteria for assessing possible escapes are discussed under CAPTIVITY.

2. The competence and reputation of the observer. Field identification is an acquired skill; the more accomplished the observer, the more credible his records, especially if he is known to be "reliable." It may surpass the imagination of the uninitiated to contemplate an adult human being getting any satisfaction out of "fudging" the identification of a bird, but unfortunately the phenomenon is by no means rare, even among birders of known competence.

3. Corroboration from other witnesses. The more competence and reliability present, the better, especially since two people with impeccable credentials in field identification have been known to stand side by side, look at the same bird, and call it a different species; and as Bill Oddie (1980–BIRDWATCHING) has noted, even with "groups largely concerned with ticking off rare birds, the temptation to see something good can be so great that mass hysteria is quite common."

4. Previous experience with the species in question as well as the species it might be confused with. If you have studied birds in both Australia and North America, your record of a Sharp-tailed Sandpiper in New Jersey is more credible.

5. Field notes and sketches. In this useful documentation technique, British birders have always been far more diligent their American counterparts. Even the most distinguished British field ornithologist would not expect to have his record of a rare bird considered for acceptance without submitting detailed notes—preferably with a sketch indicating the basis for his identification and *made on the spot without reference to guides.* Alas, the field notebook remains a rarity in North America.

6. An evaluation committee to pass judgment on all of the above. Fortunately, in the last 20 years with the enormous increase in birders and sight records, such avian records committees meet regularly in many states.

For a take-no-prisoners account of how bird records are made, fabricated, and verified, see Oddie (1980–BIRDWATCHING), especially chapters 4, 5, and 6.

See also BIRDWATCHING.

VERMILION (Flycatcher). A vivid red hue on the yellow rather than the blue side of the spectrum, i.e., tending toward orange. Not very different from scarlet. Only the *adult male* Vermilion Flycatcher is largely brilliant red.

VERREAUX (vair-OH), Jules Pierre, 1807–73 (*Leptotila verreauxi:* White-tipped Dove). A widely traveled French naturalist who, along with his brother, established in Paris the Maison Verreaux, "one of the greatest, if not the greatest emporium of natural history the world has ever seen" (quoted by Gruson 1972–BIOGRAPHY). As a youth Verreaux studied with Baron Cuvier, collected an impressive number of specimens during his peregrinations, and applied himself seriously to taxonomic work in Paris. He seems never to have traveled in the Americas. The largely Neotropical dove was named by a fellow French naturalist, Charles Lucien BONAPARTE.

VESPER (Sparrow). Latin for evening. In the tradition of Western Christian Churches Vespers is a service held at this time of day, called "Evensong" in the Anglican church. Of the Vesper Sparrow the Reverend J. H. Langille writes in *Our Birds and Their Haunts:* "It is heard to the best advantage when the rosy hues of sundown are tinting the road, the rocks, and all the higher lights of the evening landscape. Then an innumerable company of these poets of the plain unadorned pastures . . . swell into the finest chorus, while most other birds are gradually subsiding into silence." Alas, the "innumerable company" of this species has dwindled alarmingly in many places due to loss of habitat.

VEXILLUM (VEK-sill-um). Synonymous with "web" or "vane" of a feather. See FEATHER and Fig. 13.

V FORMATION. A distinctive flock configuration in flight, characteristic of certain large waterbirds, e.g., cormorants, pelicans, cranes, ducks, geese, and swans and sometimes gulls. Birds flying in V formation (except for the leader) gain additional lift by flying in the "slipstream" of the bird in front. See FLIGHT.

VIBRISSA (vih-BRISS-uh) (pl. vibrissae). A bristle; in birds such bristles are modified feathers that occur around the gape, nostrils, and eyes. See FEATHER; RICTAL; and Fig. 13.

VICARIANCE (vy-CARRY-ence). In zoology describes the natural separation of a population of organisms by a geographical barrier, such as a

glacier, mountain range, or water body that results in the evolution of distinct forms or species. For example, the Black-throated Green complex of wood warbler species (see Fig. 29) is assumed to have evolved in this fashion, though the details are still under scrutiny (e.g., see Bermingham et al. [1992–SPECIATION]).

VIEILLOT (VYEH-yoh), Louis Jean Pierre, 1748–1831. Master taxonomist of France, whose influence on the study of North American birdlife is abundantly recorded throughout its technical nomenclature. He named 26 genera and 32 species of North American birds, a remarkable percentage of which have not been altered by taxonomic revision, attesting to the acuity of Vieillot's perception. In an obituary, Lesson called him the "dean of ornithologists," but the details of his life are little known. His ornithological career began in the then French colony of Santo Domingo (Hispaniola) but he fled to the United States from a revolution on the island. He spent a number of years studying the U.S. avifauna and produced (in French) an early (1807) work on the birds of North America. He also published an illustrated volume on beautiful tropical birds (*Oiseaux Dorés*), an ornithology of France, and a book on mammals. His life was apparently a constant struggle to survive, and Lesson notes that he died "on the brink of poverty."

VIREO (VEER-ee-oh). Standard English name for about 31 of the 52 members of the family Vireonidae (order Passeriformes) and the collective term for the family as a whole, which also includes the peppershrikes, shrike-vireos, and greenlets. Fourteen species of vireos breed in North America and 2 others have been recorded as rare visitors (see Appendix II). Once classified near the wood warblers, the vireos have now been shown (e.g., Sibley and Ahlquist 1982) to be more closely related to the shrikes.

The vireos are all small (4–6½ inches) songbirds, typically with a rather heavy, hooked bill, large head, and moderately short tail. They are generally dull-plumaged (olives, grays, browns), but some have patches of bright yellow and a few have white, yellow, or red irises. They are arboreal birds of woodland and scrub, where they actively (though more sluggishly than wood warblers) glean foliage for insects and other small invertebrate food. They are also known to take small vertebrates (e.g., small lizards) and regularly eat berries.

Most vireo songs are abrupt, distinctive, whistled phrases, but some are more extended and "warbling."

The nests of all vireos are cups suspended from forks of narrow branches. They tend to be tidy structures, woven of grasses, fibers, and hair and bound with spider silk. The site may be as low as 2 feet in dense shrubbery or 60 feet up in a tall tree. Eggs normally number 3–5 (rarely, 2) and are either immaculate white or sparsely marked with dark brown or black spots. The vireo family is restricted to the New World and reaches its

greatest diversity in the Neotropics. In North America, vireos are distributed from the subarctic to the subtropics. All but one species (Hutton's)
are migratory at least from the northern parts of their breeding range, and
most winter in the tropics.

Aristotle apparently used the Latin word *vireo,* from the verb *virere,*
"to be green," to refer to the Eurasian Greenfinch. The name was next
used by VIEILLOT as the Latin genus for the birds presently called vireos.
This is fair enough, as most vireos are as green as greenfinches, i.e., not
very.

VIREO. Visual Resources for Ornithology. Established in 1979 at the Philadelphia Academy of Natural Resources, *VIREO* now curates "the world's
most comprehensive collection of bird photographs. The collection currently contains 111,000 images, which it makes available as reasonable
cost to scientists and the general public. For more on this invaluable resource, a catalogue of images and terms, go to vireo@acnatsci.org.

VIRGINIA Anderson (Virginia's Warbler: *Vermivora virginiae*). Spencer
BAIRD named this warbler for the wife of the army surgeon who sent him
the specimen of this dry-country species. Dr. William Wallace Anderson
collected his wife's warbler near Fort Burgwyn, New Mexico, c. 1858. For
other army doctors who played a significant role in American ornithology—a small army of their own—see BIOGRAPHY and Hume (1942–
BIOGRAPHY).

VISION. The vertebrate eye is a very complex organ about which much
remains to be learned. This entry is restricted to some conspicuous pecu-
liarities of the avian eye and its function in comparison with the human
eye. However, a rudimentary description of how vision works for both
men and birds will be useful in understanding some of the details
described.

The eye of vertebrate animals is a modified sphere, most of which is
concealed from view within the eye sockets (orbits) of the skull. Covering
the surface of the part of the eye through which we see is a layered transparent membrane called the *cornea.* Beneath the cornea is a (usually)
round, colored membrane, the *iris,* with a hole in the middle, the *pupil.*
The iris is made up of muscle fibers which control the size of the pupil and
thus the amount of light allowed into the eye. Beneath the iris is an ovoid
lens, behind which is a clear gelatinous mass, the *vitreous* (glass-like) *body*
or *humor,* which takes up the greatest part of the eye's interior. Lining the
back wall of the eye is a layered membrane of nerve fibers (formed by
the expansion of the optic nerve) called the *retina.* The eye is connected to
the brain by the optic nerve, and its movements are controlled by a complex of external muscles.

Light rays entering the eye are refracted (bent) by the cornea and again by the lens, which also focuses the incoming image. The image passes through the vitreous body (with little or no further refraction) and is projected upside down on the sensitive retina. One layer of the retina is made up of perceptor cells, called rods and cones because of their shape. The rods are effective in perceiving low levels of light, as in night vision; the cones permit perception of detail and color in high levels of light. Cones are distributed relatively sparsely over the retina except in depressions (usually one to each eye, but see below) called *foveae*, where fine cones are closely concentrated to perceive the sharpest details of an image.

THE AVIAN EYE IN GENERAL. Before offering generalities, it should first be noted that there is an enormous variation among eyes of different kinds of birds, so that the eye of a Dickcissel is as different from the eye of a goshawk as either is from the eye of an owl or a human. Nevertheless, it is broadly accurate to say that birds have proportionately very large eyes and acute vision and depend on this sense more than any other.

Though we normally see only a small portion of them, a bird's eyes take up far more room than any other part of its head; certain large predators have eyes as large as or larger than ours; and it has been stated that the Ostrich's eyes (diameter 2 inches) may be the largest of all terrestrial vertebrates. Another oft-quoted measure of avian eye size is that the eyes frequently outweigh the brain.

There is much disagreement about various types of visual competence (resolution, light sensitivity, focusing, etc.) in birds as compared with humans. There is no doubt, however, that *some* birds "see better" than we do—how much better is disputed—and that some have specialized powers—highly developed night vision, good accommodation underwater—which we lack. It may also be true that many passerine species in a general sense see less well than we do. Some details are discussed below.

Birds require sight to find food, to orient themselves when traveling, and to perform basic functions, such as landing and flying between trees rather than into them. Other senses may assist these actions but cannot compensate for blindness. A bird that has lost both eyes is doomed, though there are cases of apparently healthy birds surviving with just one.

ABILITY TO DISTINGUISH DETAIL, technically called visual acuity or "resolving power," is best developed in birds (e.g., flycatchers and hawks) that must be able to see very small (or distant) moving objects. Birds with high acuity tend to have relatively large eyes with flat lenses at a greater distance from the retina—a combination that allows the projection of a larger image—and a very high concentration of cones in the foveae. It is widely published and repeated that the most keen-eyed day-flying raptors have resolving power *eight* times greater than that of a human, but

this now known to be an exaggeration. By comparing the number of cones in the foveae of raptors (about 1 million per sq mm) with the human concentration (a mere 200,000 per sq mm), some authorities deduce that the disparity is "only" ×5; but the most widely accepted estimate contends (on a different basis) that ×2 or ×3 is more like it. If you try to imagine seeing twice or three times "as well"—i.e., acutely—as you now do, the visual competence of hawks and their relatives remains sufficiently impressive even by the most conservative standards. In fact, it is probably the most highly developed eyesight that exists.

The range of visual acuity in other types of birds ranges from significantly (perhaps ×2 to ×3) poorer than ours to measurably—but not dramatically—better.

LIGHT-GATHERING ABILITY, or visual sensitivity, makes it possible to see well when very little light is present. It is most highly evolved in owls but is present to a significant degree (i.e., greater than in humans) in a great many birds. The eyes of owls are large and elongated (tubular) with comparatively wide corneal and lens surfaces, allowing a maximum amount of light to reach the retina. As would be expected, the concentration of light-sensitive rods is very high; cones are proportionately few, which means that owls have low visual acuity compared to day-flying raptors. (Rods and cones tend to be present in inverse proportions.)

Contrary to what is sometimes supposed, owls cannot see prey in total darkness and at least some species depend heavily on sound as well as sight. It is also a mistake to believe that nocturnal owls are "blind," or nearly so, during the day simply because they are inactive; the visual acuity, at least of some species, is better than ours, night or day.

Night vision in birds, though in general superior to humans', usually takes longer to "turn on"—perhaps an hour or more as compared to about 10 minutes for us.

Birds that make deep dives (e.g., loons) have increased rods for finding prey in nearly sunless depths.

FOCUSING, or "accommodation," is the ability to retain a sharp image at varying distances or under changing refractory conditions. It is mainly achieved by muscular action on the lens, stretching it flatter for seeing into the distance, making it more convex for examining the foreground. In birds, unlike mammals, the cornea also bends to aid focusing. A wide range of accommodation and the ability to focus rapidly are of special importance to fast-flying birds and particularly to those that make fast dives from the air to catch prey. Species such as cormorants, which make long dives underwater, must be able to focus through water was well as air. Birds with such special needs may have a focal range five times that of humans, but the capacity of more sedentary land birds may be less than or about equal to ours.

The chief factors that allow exceptional powers of accommodation in birds are (1) high development in the muscle apparatus (ciliary body),

which controls the shape of the lens; (2) a very soft lens; and (3) a ring of small overlapping bones, the scleral ossicles (sclerotic ring), which stabilizes the eyeball while the lens is being pushed and squeezed.

Terns, which dive on fish from the air, cannot focus underwater and must rely on a "preset" aim. Penguins, by contrast, see well *only* in the water, where their eyes have evolved to follow fast-swimming fish.

SIZE OF FIELD AND DEPTH AND DISTANCE PERCEPTION. How much of the surrounding visible sphere one sees at a given time, the sense of three dimensionality, and judgment of relative distances depend on where the eyes are placed in the head, the extent to which they can be moved, and the ability (or lack of it) to turn the neck.

Human eyes are located close together in the front of the head. We therefore command a relatively narrow total field without moving the eyes or turning the neck. This field is significantly enlarged if we turn the neck without moving the rest of the body, but it is still by no means total. Because we receive a slightly different image in each eye, and the two images are combined by the brain (binocular vision), we readily perceive the depth as well as the length and width of objects (stereoscopic vision) and can tell how far away things are and the degree to which they get closer as we approach them. The field of binocular vision is, of course, always narrower than the total field, but the ratio of one to the other varies among different animals according to eye placement and other factors.

The eyes of owls are placed like humans' and have similar field (110° total; 70° binocular) and depth and distance perception. The fact that their eyes are rigidly fixed in their sockets is compensated for by an extraordinarily mobile neck. (This is true to a lesser extent of most birds.) The eyes of day-flying raptors are set somewhat more to the sides, so that their total field is wider (about 250°), but their binocular field is reduced to 35° to 50°. The eyes of most birds, however, are placed almost opposite each other on either side of the head. This gives them an enormous total field (up to 340°) but a very narrow binocular field (as low as 6° with an average of about 20° to 25°). Most birds, then, see most things with only one eye and have little depth perception. This may explain why ground-feeding birds will often cock their heads sideways—to see if that is really a seed or just a yellow spot on the ground—and why shorebirds (and others) turn one eye to the sky to appraise the threat posed by a form passing over, rather than cock their necks backward as we would do. It may also explain why some birds bob their heads when a potential threat approaches—to get a quick double-angle fix on an object in order to gauge its form and distance.

No discussion of visual field is complete without mentioning the woodcocks and the bitterns. The large eyes of the former are so set in the skull that, except for small "blind spots" directly in front and behind, their visual field is nearly total, even including the area directly above them; this may be an adaptation for perceiving danger from above by birds that

spend much of their time focusing on the ground. The eyes of bitterns, on the other hand, are angled downward when the head is horizontal—so that they can see food on the ground without cocking or nodding the head—and forward when the head is upraised in their characteristic cryptic "freeze" posture. If you think this is easy, try looking someone in the face while your nose is pointed to the ceiling.

SEEING COLOR. Day-flying birds apparently have a significant richer experience of color than we do. We deduce this from their sensitivity to the near ultraviolet spectrum, the presence of large numbers of cones containing visual pigments and of colored oil droplets within the cones. These range from yellow to red and seem to act as filters, shutting out some of the blue/violet values and increasing sensitivity to yellow/red; it is interesting in this context to note the high percentage of avian display features that are yellow/red. The droplets may also help to cut glare and increase contrast, but there remains much to learn about their function.

Because color is perceived by the cones, nocturnal birds, which have relatively few, are believed to be color-blind.

The speculation that owls can perceive infrared light and thus "see" the heat generated by their prey in the "dark" is unproven.

IRIS COLOR AND EYESHINE. Birds, of course, have no eye whites as do humans, and eye color (exclusive of external eye rings) is that of the iris. In most birds the iris is dark brown or black, but a significant number of species have colored eyes. In some cases this color is sexually dimorphic—males having the brighter color—and bright eye color is usually characteristic of adult birds and may heighten during the breeding season. The function of iris color is undetermined but it may play a part in display.

"Eyeshine" is a brilliant red or yellow (more rarely white or pale green) reflection emanating from the eyes of nightjars and other nocturnal birds and mammals when a light hits them at a certain angle. This is produced by a thin iridescent membrane behind the retina called a tapetum (ta-PEE-tum), which shines through the colored but translucent surface of the retina.

OTHER FEATURES unique to or conspicuous in the avian eye deserve brief mention.

The Nictitating Membrane lies under the main eyelids of all birds and moves across the cornea at an angle from the lower inside of the eyeball (near the bill) to the upper outside. It is transparent in most birds (exceptions among nocturnal species) and used for regularly moistening the eye and perhaps for protection in the same way that we use our outer eyelids when we blink. (Birds rarely close their eyelids except to sleep.) The nictitating membrane of some diving birds is modified to aid accommodation underwater. It has been suggested that the transparent membrane may act as a "windshield" for birds in flight.

Frogs, all reptiles, and some mammals also have nictitating membranes.

The Pecten is a membranous organ that takes up considerable space within the avian eye and is unique to birds. Filled with blood vessels, it is attached to the optic nerve and extends out into the vitreous body. It has an elaborate pleated structure that has been compared in appearance to a radiator. A great many theories have been advanced as to its function, the most plausible having to do with supplying sustenance to the retina, which unlike that of mammals does not have its own network of blood vessels. Other aspects of the pecten's function remain to be discovered.

Pupil Dilation in most animals is an involuntary function performed by the nervous system in conjunction with the iris muscles in response to the amount of light available. The pupils of birds open and close in a rapid and complex manner, but not particularly in response to light changes, and it has been suspected, but not proved, that the pupils of birds may be under voluntary control.

VISITOR (visitant). A species that does not breed in a given place and (in the strictest sense) occurs on an *irregular* basis, i.e., complementary to RESIDENT. See SUMMER VISITOR; WINTER VISITOR.

VOCALIZATION. See SONG.

VOICE OF AUDUBON. The first automated telephone answering service to give details of recent bird occurrences. It was begun by the Massachusetts Audubon Society in November 1954. The original "voice" was that of Ruth Emery, a pillar of the venerable Massachusetts birding establishment. It has always been traditional for the Voice of Audubon to relay reports of common as well as rare birds, thereby conveying, however sketchily, the avian state of the state to callers. Some RARE BIRD ALERTS ignore the "trash birds" and concentrate on giving specific directions for finding rarities and up-to-the-minute accounts of their whereabouts.

VOLANT (VOH-lunt). Capable of flight. A bird, like a bat or bee, is a volant organism; also, rarely, rather poetically, "in flight," "on the wing."

VULTURE. Standard English name for 5 of the 7 members of the family Cathartidae (order Ciconiiformes); the two largest members of this family are called CONDORS. The cathartids are the New World vultures, closely related to the storks and confined in distribution to the Americas. They are not to be confused with the Old World vultures, which belong to the family Accipitridae (order Falconiformes) along with the hawks and eagles, and are restricted to the Old World. Two species of cathartid vultures (Black and Turkey) breed in North America in addition to the California

Condor. There is a detailed old record of the Neotropical King Vulture by the distinguished botanist William BARTRAM from southern Florida in 1774–75, but the report has not been deemed convincing by the AOU.

The New World vultures are large birds (2 to nearly 4 feet in length), the California Condor having the greatest wingspan (to 9½ feet) of any North American land bird (see SIZE). They have broad as well as long wings adapted for slow soaring over wide areas in search of their preferred food, carrion. Their heads are unfeathered, a trait that doubtless evolved from their habit of probing with their heads into the greasy, decomposing entrails of carcasses. Except for the Black Vulture, members of this family have fairly heavy bills for tearing flesh, but all have weak feet unsuitable for grasping prey. In addition to carrion, garbage, and offal, vultures will occasionally take weak (i.e., young or injured) live animals, some fruit, and in rare cases will kill a healthy small animal. It has been proven that Turkey Vultures do find at least some of their food by scent (see SMELL), though other cathartids are less talented in this regard. Though many people regard these birds as unsavory, such scavengers do yeomanly service as unpaid garbage men.

Brown and Amadon (1968–HAWK) opine that the Black Vulture probably has the largest total population of any bird of prey in the Western Hemisphere.

Vultures sometimes nest in small, loose groupings. They make no nest but lay their eggs in a cave, rock crevice, hollow tree trunk, stump, or on the ground under the cover of vegetation. The eggs may be moved within the general nesting area. Black and Turkey Vultures lay 2 (rarely, 1 or 3), off-white, yellowish, buff, gray, or greenish eggs, sparsely to rather densely marked with reddish or dark brown speckles and splotches. The California Condor lays a single white to pale green/blue egg—the largest of any North American bird.

Vocal apparatus is almost totally lacking in the vultures, and it is therefore unsurprising that they are normally silent and only rarely utter faint hisses, grunts, and barks—usually when alarmed.

As a family the vultures range nearly throughout the Nearctic and Neotropical regions (excepting the highest latitudes) and over almost all biomes. The northern distribution of the Turkey Vulture stops roughly at the southern edge of the boreal forest zone; the Black Vulture's center of abundance here is more to the south and east.

The name was taken from the distantly related Old World vultures, which our species resemble in general form and habits. The word derives from the Latin infinitive *vellere*, "to tear," and the noun *vultur*, which referred to the accipitrid vultures of Europe. The colloquial name "buzzard" widely used for these birds in North America is a corrupt usage and properly refers to the broad-winged, day-flying raptors in the genus *Buteo* and related species.

WADERS. In North America, a little-used word referring collectively to long-legged wading birds such as herons, ibises, storks, etc. In Britain and throughout the rest of the English-speaking world, the standard term for "shorebirds."

WAGTAIL. Standard English name for 12 members of the family Motacillidae (order Passeriformes), all but one in the genus *Motacilla*. Sibley and Ahlquist (1990–SYSTEMATICS) classify the wagtails as a subfamily (Motacillinae) of the family Passeridae, which also includes the Old World sparrows, accentors, weavers, and waxbills. The wagtail taxon also includes the pipits and the African longclaws. The wagtails are essentially an Old World group, but 3 species breed in western Alaska, and two others occur there as rare visitors (see Appendixes I and II).

The wagtails are implausibly slender, graceful, ground-haunting birds, their elongate form accentuated by their characteristic energetic tail wagging. Our species range between 6½ and 7½ inches in length. As with other terrestrial birds, their legs are relatively long and sturdy. Adult males of most species are strikingly colored and/or patterned.

The wagtails forage methodically on the ground, typically in open country and mainly for insect food, but also for other small invertebrates (e.g., snails) and fruit.

Wagtail songs, often given on the wing up to several hundred feet above the ground, are generally buzzy or twittery; more often heard are their sharp call notes.

White and Black-backed Wagtails are comfortable in a wide range of breeding habitats and nest sites. They will build in grass clumps in dunes, cultivated fields, rock crevices, walls, niches in buildings, dry pipes, abandoned nests of other bird species, even crevices in an inhabited Osprey nest. The Yellow Wagtail is more particular, preferring a ground site on tundra or grassland, sometimes nestled in shrub roots or under a bank. All species usually nest near water.

The 3–7 (usually 5–6) eggs are off white (buff, bluish, or grayish), densely and finely speckled with gray or brown (White and Black-backed Wagtail) or buff-brown (Yellow Wagtail).

The North American wagtail populations winter mainly in Southeast Asia. For other facts of distribution, see above. See also PIPIT.

WALKING/RUNNING. The usual manner of locomotion for non-passerine birds on the ground.

Many waterbirds that are superbly adapted for moving efficiently in the water are extremely awkward when called upon to move on land, as they are during the nesting season. Loons and grebes, with their short legs placed far to the rear, cannot walk on their toes as most birds do (see SKELETON) but must push themselves along on their bellies, giving the impression of having had some injury to their legs.

The shearwaters and large petrels (Procellariidae) and the storm-petrels (Hydrobatidae) must also, as it were, crawl along on their "ankles" when going to and from their nesting burrows, and the upright waddle of the alcids is only slightly more graceful and effective. Primarily aerial birds are also poorly equipped for terrestrial movement. Most hawks, eagles, and falcons manage little more than a slow waddle, though vultures, the Crested Caracara, and a few others have long legs and walk habitually and easily. The legs and feet of swifts and hummingbirds are practically nonexistent (hence the name of their order, Apodiformes, which denotes footlessness) and they are capable only of clinging and grasping, respectively.

Other nonpasserine families with strikingly deficient ambulatory capacity are the tropicbirds, frigatebirds, anhingas, cuckoos (except the roadrunners), owls (except the Burrowing and Barn), nightjars, trogons, and kingfishers. The remaining species walk adequately (some, e.g., pelicans, boobies, and swans, barely so) to skillfully.

The gallinaceous birds (chachalacas, turkeys, grouse, quail, and pheasants), the rails, and the roadrunners should perhaps be singled out as species that often prefer to walk (or run) from danger rather than fly. These and the long-legged waders (storks, herons, ibises, and cranes), the shorebirds, and most of the doves also walk a great deal while feeding.

Most passerines hop rather than walk (see HOPPING); however, there are the following noteworthy exceptions: most corvids (jays do both), the Horned Lark, pipits and wagtails, starlings, the ground-haunting icterids (meadowlarks, grackles, etc.), and the Savannah Sparrow.

Though many birds run, either from danger or in the course of feeding (e.g., the Snowy Egret, yellowlegs), only one species can be referred to with any conviction as a "running bird." The Greater Roadrunner has been clocked at speeds of up to 15 mph and uses this talent rather than flight to catch fast-moving prey such as small rodents and reptiles.

The physiology of avian walking is quite different from that of humans. To maintain our balance when one foot is off the ground, we use muscle contractions from the hip to shift our center of gravity over one leg or the other. Birds keep their balance by rotating their lower leg inward at

the knee to place their foot under their centerline. This motion is easily seen in the "pigeon-toed" waddle of an oncoming goose.

Many birds that walk habitually—especially the gallinaceous birds and doves—accompany their strides with a pronounced, synchronous back-and-forth head-bobbing motion that allows the head to remain effectively motionless for most of the time that the bird is moving and thus allows it to see food and predators more effectively while walking. The plovers may achieve the same end with their characteristic run-and-stop locomotion.

See also LEG/FOOT; HOPPING.

WARBLER. See OLD WORLD WARBLER (family Sylviidae) and WOOD WARBLER (family Parulidae).

WATER BIRD. A term of convenience, without taxonomic or other scientific significance, for birds that habitually frequent fresh or salt water, including many species, e.g., certain shorebirds, that feed at the water's edge but never (or rarely) wade, swim, or dive. It excludes certain water-haunting species: the Osprey, kingfishers, dippers, and waterthrushes are not generally called "waterbirds," though they are more closely associated with aquatic habitats than some species that are so called. The waterbird families represented in North America are the loons, grebes, albatrosses, shearwaters, storm-petrels, tropicbirds, pelicans, frigatebirds, gannets and boobies, cormorants, anhingas, ducks, geese, and swans, herons, storks (many largely terrestrial), ibises and spoonbills, flamingoes, cranes, Limpkin, rails, oystercatchers, stilts and avocets, plovers (several largely terrestrial), sandpipers, phalaropes, jaegers, gulls and terns, skimmers, and auks.

See also SEABIRD; PELAGIC; SWIMMING/DIVING; LAND BIRD.

WATERFOWL. In North America, the ducks, geese, and swans collectively; the members of the family Anatidae. Used both more and less specifically elsewhere in the English-speaking world. Compare WILDFOWL; WATERBIRD.

WATERTHRUSH. Standard English name for 2 of the 3 members of the wood warbler genus *Seiurus* (family Parulidae; order Passeriformes). Despite their, phylogeny, the waterthrushes are named aptly enough. They frequent watery habitats, particularly forest streams and rivers, and their coloration and preference for shady situations suggest the true thrushes.

Like other birds that frequent running-water habitats, the waterthrushes bob their tails continuously. The "reason" behind this characteristic is imperfectly understood, but it may enhance the cryptic effect of the waterthrushes against the changing pattern of moving water.

For family characteristics, see WOOD WARBLER.

WATTLE. Any of a variety of fleshy or leathery, unfeathered, usually wrinkled or warty processes on the head of a bird (or reptile). These are often brightly colored, particularly during courtship rituals (see DISPLAY). Though the red patch on the face of the cock Ring-necked Pheasant may be referred to as a wattle, the word often implies a pendulous quality, e.g., the dangling folds of skin that hang from the throat and neck of the Wild Turkey. Few North American birds have wattles, but the phenomenon is characteristic of certain groups in other avifaunas, e.g., the Australasian wattlebirds.

WAVE. A birdwatching term that refers to an abundance of migrant land birds of many species putting down in a particular locality. Since bird migration tends to coincide with the passage of weather fronts, the metaphor is not inappropriate. At favorable localities and under the right weather conditions, a "warbler wave" can be a truly spectacular event, particularly in spring, with thousands of birds in brilliant plumage and stunning variety all vying for tree space or even "littering the ground." See also FALLOUT.

WAXBILL. Collective name for about 156 species of small finches in the family Estrildidae, and generic name for members of the genus *Estrilda*. These are mainly birds of Africa, southern Asia, and Australasia, with no native representatives in the New World. Many of them are brightly colored and therefore highly "collectible"- a misfortune for the rarer species (see CAPTIVITY). The only rationale for this entry is that escapes of one member of the family, Scaly-breasted (or Nutmeg) Mannikin (*Lonchura punctulata*; aka Spice finch and Spotted Munia!), have established small populations in California and Florida. Other "petshop waxbills," e.g., the Java Sparrow (*Padda oryzivora*), also skip out on their keepers regularly, and sometimes turn up at feeders.

WAXWING. See Fig. 33. Standard English name for 3 members of the family Bombycillidae (order Passeriformes), all in the genus *Bombycilla*. The waxwings are sometimes classified as a family unto themselves (AOU,1998) or as part of a broader taxon; Sibley and Ahlquist (1990– SYSTEMATICS) include them as one of three tribes (Bombycillini) in a family that also encompasses the Neotropical silky-flycatchers and the Palmchat of Hispaniola. Two species of waxwings breed in North America.

The waxwings are all rather similar in appearance, with a smooth, elegant form; short, fairly thick bill; crested head; and short legs with two of the forward-pointing toes (III and IV) joined at the base. The wings are fairly long and pointed, the tail of medium length with a squared end. The basic plumage coloration is soft browns and grays highlighted with areas of red, yellow, and/or white.

Waxwings typically feed and travel in flocks when not nesting. They are mainly (and voraciously) frugivorous (berries, crab apples) but are highly competent "flycatchers" during the warmer seasons and feed their young exclusively on insects. The most commonly heard sound waxwings make is a high, thin, almost whispering monotone.

Waxwing nests are cups made from twigs, grasses, fruticose lichens, etc., and lined with pine needles, fine fibers, and/or plant down. The site is usually 5 feet or more up in a tree. The 3–5 (rarely, 6) eggs are pale bluish gray with sparse to moderately heavy "ink spots" as well as paler subsurface spots.

The waxwings breed throughout the northern Holarctic region. The Bohemian Waxwing is an almost cosmopolitan resident of boreal forest/taiga; the Cedar Waxwing replaces it to the south (in North America only) and winters as far as northern South America. Waxwings are somewhat nomadic; one can expect Cedar Waxwings to appear unexpectedly at any season, and Bohemian Waxwings are given to irregular "irruptions" south of the Subarctic. These movements are at least partially related to food availability (see IRRUPTION/ERUPTION; NOMADISM).

"Waxwing" refers to the brightly colored (red or yellow) waxy secretions produced at the tips of the secondary feathers and to a lesser extent on the tail tip. What function these peculiar decorations serve, if any, is unknown.

WEATHER. In the broadest sense of climatic conditions, weather has been one of the formative influences of the planet, profoundly affecting EVOLUTION, DISTRIBUTION, ABUNDANCE, and species diversity, not only of birdlife but of the entire world biota. However, this entry concentrates on the immediate effects of present-day weather conditions on various aspects of birdlife.

Outright Destruction. Severe weather conditions not infrequently kill birds directly. Hailstorms have been responsible for the deaths of vast numbers of birds, for example: more than 1,000 Sandhill Cranes in 30 minutes (Merrill 1961), 148,000 waterfowl in Alberta over a 2½-month period (Smith and Webster 1955), and 2 California Condors (Rett 1938). Lightning is known to have dispatched flying birds (Zimmer 1951). Freezing rain or mist occasionally traps prairie-chickens under the snow, where they habitually roost on winter nights (Linsay 1967). Tornadoes can destroy up to 96% of breeding-bird populations locally (McClure 1945). And, of course, sudden or unseasonable shifts in temperature, wind, or precipitation often fatally complicate bird migration or breeding success (see below).

Effect on Food Supply. Many kinds of insects, especially flying forms (e.g., odonata, diptera, hymenoptera) that make up a significant part of the diet of flycatchers, warblers, and other insectivores, cannot survive

below certain temperatures and are inactive below others. Their availability as food is also greatly reduced by strong winds or heavy precipitation. Unseasonable cold or drought can also adversely affect supplies of
plant foods such as nectar, fruits, and seeds. Heavy snow cover may make
it difficult or impossible for ground-feeding birds (e.g., gallinaceous
species, doves, sparrows) to reach their food supply. And the freezing of
water cuts off usual food sources for such birds as herons, rails, and many
species of waterfowl. Many of these effects in turn influence bird movements (see below).

Effect on Breeding Success. Nesting is often timed to coincide with
the availability of a food source necessary for nourishing young (see
NEST). In unusually cold seasons, reduced food supplies may result in a
smaller percentage of young birds surviving. This is especially true in the
short summers of the Arctic, when breeding shorebirds and other species
depend on a few weeks of warm weather during which insect food is
abundant. Less usually, cold and wet weather can be the proximate cause
of bird deaths (see, for example, Stewart 1972).

Effect on Bird Movements. In many instances, bird migrants take advantage of beneficial weather conditions. Major migration routes tend to
coincide closely with patterns of favorable upper-level winds that both
guide migrants and help them conserve energy. Conversely, contrary
winds or severe storms may drive birds far from their normal range or migratory course and sometimes cause "wrecks" involving the deaths of
many thousands of birds (see MORTALITY). Migrants dependent on favorable winds for guidance are known to follow winds blowing in the
"wrong" direction to their doom (see MIGRATION). Clouds obscuring the
sky can also cause disorientation in migrants dependent on celestial NAV-
IGATION, and fog or low ceiling is usually implicated in the deaths of
small migrants that are attracted to or blunder into radio towers or illuminated office buildings. Bagg (1967) has plausibly demonstrated how
exceptionally cold weather in western Europe coinciding with broad
transatlantic depressions apparently carries Northern Lapwings to the
Newfoundland/St. Lawrence region, but seldom farther south. Arrival
times of migrants in northern areas coincide with the onset of mean
temperatures at which insect food becomes available in life-sustaining
quantity.

The effect of weather on fluctuations in crops such as conifer seeds
indirectly influences the irregular movements of certain birds, e.g., winter
finches (see IRRUPTION/ERUPTION).

Effect on Flight. Because of specialized physical adaptations, large
seabirds such as albatrosses are dependent to a great extent on wind to
travel over their marine habitat (see FLIGHT, Dynamic Soaring). Hawks,
vultures, storks, and other birds that depend on soaring to find food
and migrate require thermals, which are best generated on sunny days

(see FLIGHT, Thermal Soaring); such birds are at a severe disadvantage in dark, cold, rainy weather. As implied above, small birds and weak fliers (e.g., Dovekies) occasionally find themselves at the mercy of severe windstorms.

Effect on Birdwatching. It is well known that some of the best bird-watching takes place in the worst of weather conditions. Onshore gales along the coast routinely drive large numbers of pelagic species within easy "scoping" distance. Along the Gulf coast of Texas, birders are alert to storms (see NORTHER) that force exhausted land-bird migrants to seek the first available refuge after making the long flight across the Gulf of Mexico in the spring. At times, incredible numbers of migrants crowd a few stands of live oaks or even "crash" on coastal roads and dunes, unable to proceed inconspicuously inland as they would do under favorable conditions.

Days on which the sun's rays penetrate a thin, low overcast may be the ideal hawk-watching conditions, providing enough ground-warming heat to create thermals (see above) but not enough to permit the birds to disappear into the firmament; a uniform cloud cover also makes it easier to locate groups of migrating raptors.

Because of the above-mentioned effect on insect life, rain can put a damper on watching warblers and other insectivorous species. But far worse is wind, which above a certain velocity can reduce song and activity almost to zero.

Feeder attendance becomes frantic before storms and is usually much improved when a snowfall covers other food sources.

For further details of the relationship between weather and birdlife, see MIGRATION; MORTALITY. For general treatments of the relationship between birds and weather, see especially Elkins (1983), Moss (1995), and Larsen (2001; includes weather websites).

WEAVER (Weaverbird, Weaver Finch). Standard English name for about 77 members of the family Ploceidae (order Passeriformes), including the buffalo-weavers, sparrow-weavers, and other hyphenated weavers; Sibley and Ahlquist (1990–SYSTEMATICS) place the weavers, widowbirds and related "finches" as a subfamily (Ploceinae) under a larger family that also includes the Old World sparrows, accentors, wagtails and pipits, wax-bills, and whydahs. One species of weaver, the Orange Bishop, native to central Africa, has established a small breeding population in southern California.

For the House and Eurasian Tree Sparrows, sometimes described as "weaver finches," see OLD WORLD SPARROWS.

WEB. An alternative name for the vane or vexillum of a feather, as, for ex-ample, "the inner or outer webs of the primaries." Also the flexible skin

connecting the toes in various groups of waterbirds. See FEATHER; LEG/FOOT; and Figs. 13 and 35.

For birding on the World Wide Web see TECHNOLOGY FOR BIRDERS; LISTSERVS; RARE BIRD ALERTS, etc.

WEIGHT. See SIZE.

WESTERN HEMISPHERE SHOREBIRD RESERVE NETWORK (WHSRN). To quote from its website, "WHSRN is a voluntary consortium of over 240 organizations and agencies across the Americas, working together to protect and manage wetlands, grasslands and coastal areas to benefit shorebirds." Founded in 1986, WHSRN is directed out of the Manomet Center for Conservation science in Manomet, Massachusetts and (as of 2003) provides technical, educational, and support services to 54 sites in 7 countries with new sites added annually. The voluntary reserve system now contains more than 20 million acres. For more detail, go to http://www.whsrn.org.

WETMORE, Alexander, 1886–1978. Arguably the most versatile and prolific of all American ornithologists, Alexander Wetmore began modestly enough as a boy naturalist from North Freedom, Wisconsin. But he soon showed the promise of a distinguished future by publishing his first ornithological paper (on Red-headed Woodpecker behavior) at the age of thirteen. After earning a BA at the University of Kansas, he went to Washington, DC, where he naturally fell in with Robert RIDGWAY and his circle of eminent zoologists at the National Museum. Wetmore took his PhD at Georgetown University and four years after (1924) was appointed Assistant Secretary of the Smithsonian Institution, head of the National Museum. Like other ornithologists of his stature, Wetmore presided over a number of professional organizations (president of the American Ornithologists' Union, 1926–29) and received his share of awards. But the real measure of his career is his bibliography, which includes authoritative papers on avian physiology, pathology, behavior, distribution, migration, taxonomy, and paleontology (155 titles on the last subject alone). He also wrote the text for several popular bird books published by the National Geographic Society (see the Bibliography under BIRD), but his magnum opus in book form is his four-volume *Birds of the Republic of Panama* (Smithsonian Misc. Coll. No. 150), for which he displayed his considerable skill as a field man and on which he was working at the time of his sudden death at the age of ninety-two. See also the Bibliography under EVOLUTION OF BIRDLIFE and SYSTEMATICS.

WHEATEAR. Standard English name for about 22 species of small thrushes in the genus *Oenanthe* (family Turdidae; Order Passeriformes); Sibley and Ahlquist (1990–SYSTEMATICS) classify the wheatears, Old

World redstarts, and similar forms in a separate tribe (Saxicolini—Old World chats) within the large Old World family Muscicapidae. Only one species, the Northern Wheatear, *Oenanthe oenanthe,* occurs in North America. It seems to have reached the eastern Canadian Arctic (at least as far west as the Boothia Peninsula) from the east via Greenland—and Alaska from the eastern Palearctic. The eastern North American population follows the European population south to Africa in the winter; the Alaskan population winters in southern Asia. The species also occurs frequently as a vagrant south of its North American breeding range.

One explanation of the curious name makes a case for the species' fondness for wheat, but wheatears are largely insectivorous, and while they occasionally eat fruits and seeds, their fondness for wheat grains would hardly stand out as characteristic. In fact, the name refers to the strikingly white rump of the Northern Wheatear and all its congeners. It derives from the Middle English "whiters" meaning "white arse."

For family characteristics, see THRUSH.

WHIFFLING. In an avian context, describes the fast, relative steep descent of birds using a side-to-side motion ("side slipping"); seen frequently in waterfowl and gulls dropping onto a body of water, beach or other resting area.

WHIMBREL (WIM-brul). Standard English name for a single species of CURLEW, *Numenius phaeopus* (family Scolopacidae; order Charadriiformes), which has a Holarctic breeding range and winters in most of the other regions of the world. For general characteristics of the family, see SANDPIPER. The North American subspecies, *N. p. hudsonicus* is sometimes distinguished as Hudsonian Curlew.

The name supposedly derives from a "wimper-like" call, which may refer to one of its breeding "songs" but is a poor description of the species' usual call, a staccato, slightly plaintive piping.

WHIP-POOR-WILL. Standard English name for a single species of nightjar, *Caprimulgus vociferus,* which breeds from central and eastern Canada south to the highlands of Honduras. The name is an approximation of its call.

The Buff-collared Nightjar, *Caprimulgus ridgwayi,* which just reaches North America in southwestern Arizona and New Mexico, was once known as Ridgway's Whip-poor-will, despite the fact that its call does not sound at all like "whip-poor-will."

For family characteristics, see NIGHTJAR.

WHISTLING-DUCK. Standard English name for 8 members of the family Anatidae (order Anseriformes), all belonging to the genus *Dendrocygna* comprised by their own subfamily (Dendrocygninae); Sibley and Ahlquist

(1990–SYSTEMATICS) give these distinctive ducks their own family, the Dendrocygnidae, in which they also include the White-backed Duck of Africa. Two species of whistling-ducks breed in North America.

The New World members of the group were once called "tree-ducks" (the scientific genus and family names might be translated as "tree swan"), and while this is a misnomer in the majority of cases, one of our species, the Black-bellied Tree-Duck, does nest in tree cavities up to 30 feet from the ground and in the American tropics can be seen perching atop giant ceibas of 100 or more feet. Unlike almost all other anatids, the whistling-ducks do not line their nests with down—or with anything else.

Whistling-ducks are long-necked and long-legged, which gives them a somewhat goose-like appearance, and they also share some behavioral traits with the geese. They are essentially (but not exclusively) a tropical group and are migratory (sometimes erratic) in the northern extremities of their range. They are named for their high-pitched, piping calls.

WHITE-WINGED GULL. A birdwatchers collective term for large, white-headed gulls that have little or no black in the tips of the primaries as adults. The term—strictly one of convenience—embraces the Glaucous, Iceland, Glaucous-winged, and Thayer's Gulls, but not the smaller Ivory Gull, the whitest-winged of all.

WHITNEY, Josiah Dwight, 1819–96 (*Micrathene whitneyi*: Elf Owl). A prominent geologist (founder of the Harvard School of Mines) and early worker on the U.S. Geological Surveys.

WIGEON (WIDGE-n) (formerly spelled widgeon). Standard English name for 3 species of dabbling ducks in the genus *Anas;* family Anatidae; order Anseriformes). One of these, the American Wigeon (*A. americana*), aka Baldpate, breeds exclusively in North America and ranges nearly through-out the continent. Another species, the Eurasian Wigeon (*A. penelope*), ranges throughout the Palearctic region. It occurs as a migrant, winter vis-itor or vagrant in small numbers across North America, but breeding has never been verified here.

According to Lockwood (1993–NAMES) wigeon reaches us via Old French from the Latin *vipio*—not a bad rendition of the drakes' pleasant, high-pitched, piping call.

For family characteristics, see DUCK.

WILDFOWL. The preferred British collective term for the ducks, geese, and swans; little used in North America, where WATERFOWL is the pre-ferred synonym.

WILLET. Standard English name for a single species of long-legged sand-piper, *Catoptrophorus semipalmatus*, which breeds exclusively in North

America along inland lakes and in east coast salt marshes; it winters along all of our southern coasts and south to Peru and Brazil. A nondescript shorebird at rest, the Willet gains a measure of glamour in flight when it spreads its boldly patterned black-and-white wings. The species' characteristic cry is often rendered as "bill-will-willet." For family characteristics, see SANDPIPER.

WILLIAMSON, Robert Stockton, 1824–82 (Williamson's Sapsucker: *Sphyrapicus thyroideus*). West Point graduate, "military engineer," distinguished Civil War veteran, and participant in surveying the railway route to the Pacific (see BAIRD). The woodpecker that bears his name was so designated by one of his junior officers, one Dr. Newbury, yet another of the legion of ornithological "surgeons" of nineteenth-century North America (see BIOGRAPHY).

WILSON, Alexander, 1766–1813 (Wilson's Storm-Petrel: *Oceanites oceanicus;* Wilson's Plover: *Charadrius wilsonia;* Wilson's Phalarope: *Steganopus tricolor;* Wilson's Warbler: *Wilsonia pusilla*). Perhaps even more deserving than CATESBY or AUDUBON of the title "father of American ornithology." Wilson produced the first comprehensive, systematic, illustrated account of North American birdlife, and the greatest natural history publication to its time in America. His *American Ornithology* in nine volumes was produced between 1808 and 1814, the last two volumes being published posthumously and the final one written by Wilson's friend, patron, and editor, George ORD. The work includes drawings of 320 individual birds in 76 plates, which amount, according to current taxonomy, to about 279 species. Wilson's accomplishment is all the more impressive given his humble beginnings as the son of a weaver in Paisley, Scotland, the interruption of his education at the age of thirteen, his struggles to survive as a surveyor and teacher in Pennsylvania; and his complete ignorance of science and drawing prior to undertaking the writing and illustration of his *Ornithology.* As with Audubon, some clue to his success may be found in his personality. He was a romantic poet in the tradition of Robert Burns and, as he said of himself in a letter to his future engraver, Alexander Lawson of Philadelphia, "long accustomed to the building of Airy Castles and brain Windmills." He was also possessed of strong convictions, which got him jailed in Scotland for writing political poetry in support of mill workers—probably largely responsible for his emigration to America. His personal stubbornness and intolerance of criticism made him a touchy friend but were probably crucial to the completion of his life's work. He was also fortunate in attracting the support of William BARTRAM, prominent botanist and sometime ornithologist of the day; of the famous painter and curator Charles Willson Peale; of Samuel E. Bradford, his employer as editor of *Ree's New Cyclopedia,* who eventually published *American Ornithology;* and of George Ord, the wealthy and influential naturalist of

Philadelphia, who championed Wilson's work, acted as his editor, wrote the final volume after Wilson's death, and defended his reputation against Audubon's inferences of ornithological plagiarism.

The famous rivalry between the two artist-naturalists arose (mainly after Wilson's death) from Audubon's assertion that Wilson's "Smallheaded Flycatcher" was copied from his own drawing of 1808. Ironically, the controversy centered on an anonymous immature-warbler-like form which no one has seen (or recognized) since Audubon and/or Wilson encountered it. In defending his protégé's scruples, Ord pointed out with undeniable accuracy that a number of Audubon's portraits bear a striking likeness to ones of Wilson. Why Audubon, an infinitely superior draftsman, should have been tempted to copy Wilson is mysterious, but the resemblance between his Bald Eagle (Havell XXXI), his Mississippi Kite (Havell CXVII), and his Red-winged Blackbirds (Havell LXVII) and the indisputably prior drawings by Wilson of these species is beyond coincidence. Wilson died of dysentery and/or tuberculosis.

WILSON ORNITHOLOGICAL SOCIETY. A nonprofit organization that promotes the scientific study of birdlife. It was founded in 1902 under its present name, which commemorates Alexander WILSON, one of the several "fathers of American ornithology." Originally a midwestern group, the WOS now has a national, indeed international membership. The society publishes a quarterly journal, *The Wilson Bulletin*, containing scientific papers, bird notes of more general interest, book reviews, etc. Membership is open to the public by subscription. See the Bibliography under PE-RIODICALS for current address or contact through BIRDNET at: www. nmnh.si.edu/BIRDNET/.

WINDOW (in wing). A pale, translucent area at the base of the primaries. Such a "window" is, for example, a good field mark for immature Red-shouldered Hawks.

For the relationship between birds and real windows, see PROBLEMS INVOLVING BIRDS; THREATS (OF HUMAN ORIGIN) TO BIRDLIFE.

WING. In birds, the front legs or arms modified for flight. By comparison, insect wings evolved from the upper sides of the thorax and have no direct relationship with the limbs. Bat wings, like those of birds, are modified forelimbs but are characterized by great elongation of the bones of the hand and an elastic membrane of skin that stretches not only between the fingers and arm but along the sides of the body and hind legs. The structure of bird wings is restricted to the front limbs, and the bones of the hand, rather than being extended and elaborated, are drastically reduced and/or fused.

BASIC STRUCTURE. See Fig. 27. The wing skeleton consists of an upper arm bone (humerus), two parallel bones (ulna and radius), which make up the forearm, and a wrist/hand arrangement, which, as noted, is

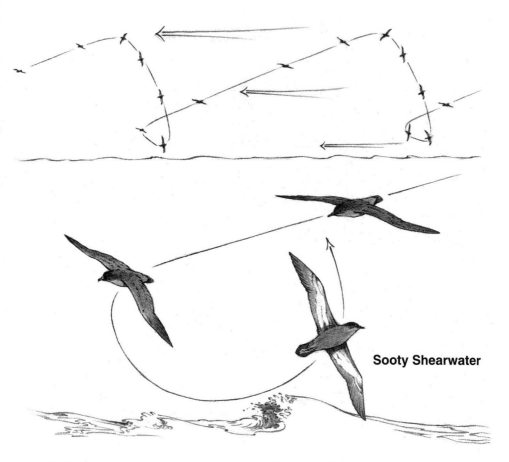

Fig. 32. *Dynamic soaring.* Many of the larger seabirds with high *aspect ratios* travel almost effortlessly over their oceanic habitat by letting the wind hurl them into the air and then gliding gradually back to sea level, aided by decreasing wind speed over the water as they descend. For a more detailed description of this and similar techniques, see FLIGHT, *Dynamic Soaring.*

greatly modified. (For a more detailed analysis of these bones, see SKELETON, Bones of the Wing.) The wing muscles attached to the bones are analogous to human arm muscles (see MUSCLES) but, of course, strongly modified for flight. Over bone and muscle lies a covering of skin (*ala membrana*) out of which grow the wing feathers.

PLUMAGE. See Figs. 1 and 35. The plumage of the wing consists of distinguishable series of feathers that overlap closely and neatly from front to back and inside to outside.

The Flight Feathers, or remiges, consist of the *primaries* and *secondaries.* The primaries are all attached to the bones of the "hand" and vary consistently in number among different groups of birds between 9 and 12,

including the sometimes tiny last primary, or remicle. They are usually numbered from the inside outward toward the wing tip, though another system reverses this (!). The secondaries (or cubitals) are more numerous and variable in number depending on the length of the "forearm": hummingbirds have as few as 6, most passerines have only 9, whereas albatrosses may have over 30. They are usually numbered from the bend of the wing inward toward the body. All of the secondaries are attached to the ulna. The innermost secondaries, which in certain groups (notably ducks) are differently shaped and colored and may molt in a different sequence, are often called the *tertials* or *tertiaries*. (See TERTIALS for another use of the term.)

All flight feathers overlap in continuous sequence, the innermost secondary covering part of its immediate neighbor (on the upper surface) and so on to the last primary.

The Alula is a group of relatively short feathers attached to the "thumb" bone (pollex). These vary in number from 2 to 7 (usually 3 to 4) and serve as a stabilizing mechanism in flight and underwater for some diving birds.

The Coverts are small contour feathers that overlap the bases of the flight feathers and then each other, covering the entire surface of the forewing both above (*upper wing coverts*) and below (*lower wing coverts* or wing lining). The rows of coverts are subdivided and named. Thus, the largest coverts, which cover the bases of the primaries, are called the *greater primary coverts,* those that overlap the gpc's are called the *median primary coverts,* which in turn may be overlapped by the *lesser primary coverts.* The coverts of the secondaries have a similar sequence and names (*greater secondary coverts,* etc.). The rows of coverts on the undersurface of the wing are less distinctly differentiable but follow the same pattern. Covering the lesser coverts (both primary and secondary) are the *marginal coverts,* which cover the entire forward inner corner of the wing, from shoulder to beyond the bend and merging indistinguishably with the lesser coverts above and below.

Each quill of the alula has a covert feather at its base.

The Scapulars are "shoulder feathers," which overlap the base of the wing and the tertials.

The Axillaries, or axillars, are the (usually elongated) feathers covering the armpit, i.e., the area between the base of the underwing and the body.

USE. See Fig. 14. Wings have evolved primarily as adaptations for flight (for details of function, see FLIGHT), though in a few cases the ability to fly has been lost in the evolution of completely terrestrial habits (e.g., Ostrich) or aquatic ones (penguins). However, birds also put their wings to a number of secondary uses. Wing surfaces are often brightly colored and patterned (e.g., Willet) or their shape modified (e.g., the elongated, curled secondaries of cranes) for use in courtship displays; and a number of sounds (the explosive wing clapping of pigeons, the "drum-

ming" of Ruffed Grouse) are also produced by the wings as part of a display ritual (see SONG, Nonvocal Sounds).

The wings are also used for fighting, and some species (only the Northern Jacana in North America) have sharp spurs at the bend of the wing, turning this seemingly innocent member into a deadly weapon. Some diving birds, notably the auks and some sea ducks, propel or steer themselves underwater with their wings rather than folding them and relying only on the paddle power of their feet as do other divers, such as the loons (see SWIMMING/DIVING).

VARIATION. One has only to think of the wings of hummingbirds, albatrosses, condors, falcons, and owls to realize that the evolutionary variations that have been wrought on the "alar theme" are numerous and highly specialized.

The function of different wing shapes is discussed under FLIGHT.

WING BAR(S) (wing patch). One or (often) two contrasting (almost always paler) lines running across a bird's folded wing (see Fig. 1). This effect, cited with great frequency as a mark of identification, results from pale tips of the greater and middle (median) covert feathers. Generally used quite specifically and *not* synonymous with "wing patch," in which most or all of the greater coverts are pale or white (e.g., adult male Magnolia Warbler), or WING STRIPE.

WING FORMULA. A method of recognizing certain hard-to-identify bird species by noting the comparative length of the primary feathers and the presence or absence of emargination. Needless to say, use of this technique requires either a live bird taken from a mist net or a museum specimen. In North America, wing formulas are consistently useful in determining species of *Empidonax* flycatchers as well as some immature warbler species (e.g., MacGillivray's, Mourning, and Connecticut). Wing formula is reliable as long as the feathers measured are full-grown and unworn.

WINGSPAN. The distance between the tips of a bird's extended wings. See SIZE; MEASUREMENTS.

WING STRIPE. Normally refers to a pale (usually white) margin running along the base of the primaries and secondaries of the wing and sometimes including the edges of the greater coverts. Often very inconspicuous on a bird at rest but striking when the wing is unfolded in flight. The presence or absence of a wing stripe is cited frequently as a field mark, especially among the sandpipers and plovers. Compare WING BAR.

WINTER FINCHES. Usually applied to certain cardueline seedeaters that breed in the boreal forest and move south in large numbers during winters when their populations are high, the cone crop is poor, or both.

"Classic" winter finches include the Evening Grosbeak, Pine Grosbeak, the redpolls, Pine Siskin, and the crossbills. Juncos, longspurs, and other emberizine seedeaters that arrive on their wintering grounds on a somewhat more regular schedule are not usually included under the term. All winter finches visit feeding stations, some more regularly than others.

WINTERING GROUNDS (or winter quarters). The place where a given species or individual spends the winter. In North America, a majority of bird species move south from their breeding grounds during the colder months of the year, though the tendency becomes less pronounced as one moves south into zones of milder winters. In general, ranges of species and territories of individuals are as well defined in their winter quarters as during the breeding season (see MIGRATION; DISTRIBUTION; TERRITORY). Birds that live at high elevations (e.g., rosy-finches) may descend to foothills or lowlands for the winter instead of migrating south; some, while moving south out of their breeding range, remain in the North Temperate Zone (e.g., Tree Sparrow); some populations remain in the same locality the year round even in regions of extreme cold and heavy snow (e.g., Black-capped Chickadee); and some have fluctuating winter ranges as food availability dictates (e.g., Pine Siskin and other "winter finches").

WINTER PLUMAGE. The plumage acquired in the first pre-basic (post-juvenal) molt and thereafter in successive pre-basic (post-nuptial) molts; on the whole, synonymous with "basic" plumage. The winter plumage is less colorful in many species than the "breeding" or "nuptial" or "alternate" plumage. See MOLT.

WINTER RESIDENT. A species that regularly spends the winter in a given area but breeds elsewhere. Usage varies, of course, geographically: Harris's Sparrow is a winter resident in parts of Texas, a SUMMER RESIDENT in parts of arctic Canada, and a TRANSIENT or VAGRANT elsewhere. The term might also be used in the same sense as "summer resident" to describe those few species (e.g., Red Crossbill, Mourning Dove) that sometimes nest during the winter months. Compare WINTER VISITOR.

WINTER VISITOR (or visitant). A species that is present on an irregular basis in a given area only during the winter. Usage varies, of course, geographically: Common Redpolls are winter visitors throughout much of the northern United States but SUMMER RESIDENTS in parts of arctic and subarctic Canada and Alaska and TRANSIENTS or VAGRANTS elsewhere in North America. Because it implies irregularity, "winter visitor" is usually applied to irruptive species and those at the edge of their wintering ranges, i.e., as a term complementary to WINTER RESIDENT.

It is possible for a species to be both a summer resident and a winter visitor in a given area. For example, Northern Goshawks breed in New England, but more northerly populations may also be present in winter during flight years (see IRRUPTION).

WIREBIRDS. Species that characteristically perch on telephone, fence, and other roadside wires: American Kestrel, Belted Kingfisher, swallows, many flycatchers, magpies, shrikes, Northern Mockingbird, bluebirds, Common Starling, meadowlarks, blackbirds, and many open-country finches are typical wirebirds. Watching wires for such species is a helpful diversion for a birdwatcher driving cross-country.

WISHBONE. The fused clavicles or collarbones characteristic of birds; the furcula; the merrythought (British). See SKELETON and Fig. 27.

WOLLWEBER (Christian names and dates unknown) (Bridled Titmouse: *Parus wollweberi*). A little-known collector who sent specimens—including the one that immortalizes him—from Mexico back to his native Germany. Nothing of his biography has survived (Gruson calls him "a traveler"). His tit was named by Charles Lucien BONAPARTE.

WOODCOCK. Standard English name for 6 members of the subfamily Scolopacinae; family Scolopacidae; order Charadriiformes (AOU 1998) or Ciconiiformes (Sibley and Monroe 1990), which also includes the snipes. One species, the American Woodcock (*Scolopax minor*), breeds in North America and another, the Eurasian Woodcock (*S. rusticola*), has occurred here as an accidental straggler (see Appendix II).

Woodcocks are chubby "shorebirds" with long bills, short legs and tail, and rounded wings. They inhabit the edges of wet wooded areas (e.g., alder and red maple swamps), though seldom mature forest. They are largely nocturnal and are usually encountered near dawn and dusk, when they emerge to court and feed, and remain inactive and concealed by their cryptically patterned plumage by day. They feed almost exclusively on earthworms, for which they "feel" in soft earth and mud with their long, sensitive, probing bill. The large, protruding eyes of woodcocks are set rather high in the skull and are centered on either side, so that except for small "blind spots" directly in front and behind, their visual field is nearly total, even including the area directly above them.

A requirement of the American Woodcock's breeding territory is the proximity of an open field, where the males come to perform their courtship flight during a couple of months in spring. Emerging from cover just before dark, the male first sits in the open and utters a distinctive buzzy *peent* at regular intervals. Periodically he takes to the air, making a staccato whistling sound, which results from air passing through "slots" of

the peculiarly narrowed outer primary feathers. He flies in widening spirals, rising 100–200 feet from the earth, and then circles at the highest point, uttering an almost songbird-like chirping-twittering sound. In the first part of his descent, he makes yet another type of mechanical chirping sounds in a series of precipitous zigzags. Back at his ground station, he resumes his *peent*-ing. This performance continues until after dark (more prolonged on moonlit nights) and is repeated before dawn.

The American Woodcock was once far more abundant than it is at present, especially in fall migration, when 1,000 birds might be shot in a day's hunting. Overshooting reduced their numbers drastically by the early twentieth century, but with hunting restrictions (seasons, bag limits) they are once more fairly common throughout their range. However, they have never regained their former abundance and are especially vulnerable to pesticides (see THREATS (OF HUMAN ORIGIN) TO BIRDLIFE) that accumulate in the tissue of their preferred food and to loss of their specialized habitat requirements.

The American Woodcock is endemic to North America and largely restricted to the eastern half of the country. It breeds into southeastern Canada and winters to the tip of the Florida peninsula.

For family characteristics, see SANDPIPER; see also references in the Bibliography under SHOREBIRD.

WOODPECKER. Standard English name for most of the approximately 216 members of the family Picidae (order Piciformes), of which 23 (including the sapsuckers and the probably extinct Ivory-billed Woodpecker) breed in North America. Two other species have occurred as vagrants to northwestern Alaska.

Worldwide, woodpeckers range in size from 3½ inches to nearly 2 feet (6¾ to 16½ inches in North America). Most species have a dominant plumage pattern of black (or brown) and white, usually highlighted by bright splashes of red or yellow; a few species are largely metallic green. Not a few species are crested. The typical woodpecker form and behavior are highly distinctive and familiar to everyone. And most of the specific characteristics of the family are adaptations to the birds' mode of living, consisting in most cases of climbing trees and "drilling" and probing for insects or sap. The bill is hard, straight, and chisel-shaped. The skull is specially reinforced to withstand continual shocks and vibrations. The unusually long, mobile tongues of most species can be extended to an extraordinary degree into drilled holes to extract wood-boring insects; this ability is effected by a unique elongation of a set of special small bones and muscles in the skull known as the hyoid apparatus (see TONGUE). The tongues of woodpeckers also have barbed tips with sticky secretions, facilitating the extraction of their prey or, in the case of sapsuckers, brush tips for soaking up tree juices. The neck muscles are unusually strong. The legs are short and the feet are "yoke-toed" (zygodactyl), with toes I and IV

pointing to rearward and II and III forward (some species with only one rear toe). The claws are notably long, decurved, and pointed to maintain a firm grip on vertical surfaces. The tail is usually wedge-shaped and the tail feathers are very stiff and pointed, acting as a prop and stabilizer in climbing.

Woodpeckers are primarily arboreal and insectivorous, though several species (e.g., the flickers) are primarily ground feeders (ants) and the sapsuckers show the preference that their name implies. Insectivorous species usually also eat a significant amount of fruit, nuts, bark, and/or other plant matter. Most species are solitary in behavior, but the Acorn Woodpecker nests, roosts, and often feeds in groups.

All woodpeckers nest in unlined tree cavities (less usually in earthen banks or termite nests) that they excavate. Typically, they construct a new site each year, and abandoned woodpecker holes are the chief source of sites for other cavity-nesting birds (see NEST). Woodpecker eggs are white, glossy in most species, and the average clutch is 3–5 (extremes: 1–14).

Woodpecker calls are loud, often staccato, metallic or "laughing," and are supplemented in the breeding season by courtship "drumming" with the bill on hollow trees or otherwise resounding surfaces (see DRUM-MING for details)

Woodpeckers are distributed throughout the world with the notable exceptions of Madagascar, Australia, New Zealand, and Oceania. In North America, several species occur wherever there are trees or tree cacti (i.e., absent from arctic tundra) and some species are very widespread; most are essentially nonmigratory; the three-toed woodpeckers are given to periodic IRRUPTIONS.

WOOD WARBLER. Standard English collective name for about 115 species of New World songbirds traditionally defining the family Parulidae (order Passeriformes); Sibley and Ahlquist (1990–SYSTEMATICS) consider this taxon to a trbie (Parulini) in the subfamily Emberizinae; family Fringillidae. Individual species of wood warblers are called simply warblers (e.g., Yellow Warbler) and thus may be confused with the superficially similar OLD WORLD WARBLERS (e.g., Arctic Warbler), which belong to the family Sylviidae. A total of 52 species of wood warblers (including the probably extinct Bachman's Warbler) breed in North America, and another 5 have occurred as vagrants from the Neotropics.

Excluding the 7½-inch Yellow-breasted Chat, the wood warblers are all small (4¼–6 inches), well-proportioned songbirds, typically with a moderately short, slender, pointed bill and tail of medium length. Many species are brilliantly colored (yellow predominates, but blue, orange, and red also occur) and/or boldly patterned with black and white. A few species forage largely on the ground, but most are arboreal and actively glean leaves, limbs, and trunks for insects and other invertebrate prey.

Parulids are also fond of nectar, sap (including pine pitch), and berries, and those that regularly winter in temperate climates (e.g., Pine and Yellow-rumped Warblers) will eat seeds and suet at feeding stations. Wood warbler songs are highly distinctive and immensely variable, ranging from rich melodies to nearly inaudible lisps and trills reminiscent of cricket or cicada sounds. Many parulid "chips" are also distinctive.

Nests of wood warblers are small cups (sometimes domed: Ovenbird, Common Yellowthroat), which in most species are neat and compact, made with fine grasses, plant down, and spider silk, but may also be more bulky and loose, made with twigs, stems, bark, and dead leaves. The lining is usually of fine grasses, plant fibers, hair, moss, and plant down. Most wood warblers build in shrubs or trees, but some are habitual ground nesters. Two North American species (Prothonotary and Lucy's) are cavity nesters, and the parulas build in pendant festoons of *Usnea* lichen or Spanish moss (*Tillandsia usneoides*). Eggs number 3–8, but clutches of most species average 4–5. Eggs may have a white, gray, pale blue, or green ground color and be immaculate to heavily speckled or blotched in reddish or brownish.

The wood warbler family is confined to the New World, with about an equal number of species breeding in the Nearctic and Neotropical regions. They occur in all major biomes, occupying a great variety of specific breeding niches, and range from the Arctic to the South Temperate Zone of Argentina. All North American wood warblers are migratory (at least in part of their range) and the great majority winter exclusively in the tropics.

One of the great, uniquely American, birdwatching experiences is a spring "warbler wave" when hundreds—occasionally thousands—of wood warblers of many species, all clad in gorgeous nuptial plumage, descend from their nocturnal migration to rest and feed in favorable areas (see WAVE; HIGH ISLAND; NORTHER; MIGRATION).

Relatively few warblers warble, a practice much more typical of the FINCH family.

For the warblers of the family Sylviidae, see OLD WORLD WARBLER.

WORLD SERIES OF BIRDING. See BIRDING EVENTS.

WORMS, PARASITIC. See ENDOPARASITE.

WRECK. When migration coincides with strong onshore winds, the result may be "wrecks" of pelagic birds. The term is of British origin, implies large numbers of birds incapacitated on land, and is therefore most usually applied to alcids, which require a watery "runway" to become airborne. Dovekies are particularly susceptible to these conditions and are often blown far inland, sometimes by the thousands. Many such casualties fall prey to cars, cats, penguin-loving humans, and starvation. For a vivid account of a Dovekie wreck, see Snyder (1960–MORTALITY).

WREN. Standard English name for all 74 members of the family Troglodytidae (order Passeriformes) and for the family as a whole; Sibley and Ahlquist treat this group as a subfamily (Troglodytinae) under the family Certhiidae in which they also include the tree-creepers and gnat-catchers. Nine species of wrens breed in North America.

The basic wren form is a familiar one to North Americans: generally small (4–6 inches; Cactus Wren to 8½ inches); brown above, paler below; compact shape; wings short and rounded; tail long or short but characteristically "cocked up." The wrens' preference for dense shrubbery, their active feeding habits, and their "bubbly," often rather long and chaotic songs are also widely known. They feed mainly on insects and other invertebrates, but larger species are known to take small lizards and the like and they readily take to fruit in cold seasons.

Wrens frequently build rather large, loose, domed nests in trees, shrubs, cacti, or cattails, but they also often nest in tree and rock cavities, rodent holes and birdhouses, where they may omit the superfluous dome. The lining may be of feathers, hair, plant fiber or down, and other soft materials. Male wrens of some species build a series of DUMMY NESTS, one of which the female selects and lines. House Wrens are famous for nesting in unusual man-made localities, such as hats, cans, teapots, and shoes, and they will also use abandoned nests of swallows and other bird species. Wren eggs are variable: white to brown; immaculate to heavily marbled with reddish-brown speckles.

The wrens are generally supposed to have evolved in North America and spread southward into the Neotropics, where they currently attain their greatest diversity. Only one species, the Winter Wren, ever reached the Old World, where, however, it is widespread; it is presumed to have spread via the now submerged land bridge across the Bering Strait, and it is currently the only North American wren species to reach as far north as Alaska. Several other North American wrens range widely on the continent but only a few reach southern Canada.

The name "wren" comes to us essentially unchanged from the Anglo-Saxon and similar words in old Scandinavian languages that (*fide* Lockwood 1993–NAMES) referred to the distinctive little tail of the Winter Wren. Oddly, the wren is the villain of a number of Celtic and Christian legends in which it betrayed Irish Soldiers to their Norse adversaries and also Saint Stephen, the first Christian martyr. As a result these tiny songsters were ruthlessly hunted by "wrenboys" (mummers) as part of traditional St. Stephen's Day (December 26) festivals and their bodies nailed to poles carried in the processions.

WRENTIT. Standard English name for a unique North American songbird classified in the *AOU Checklist* (1998) in the babbler family (Timaliidae; order Passeriformes) and by Sibley and Ahlquist (1990–SYSTEMATICS) as

the sole member of its own tribe (Chamaeini), closely allied to the babblers within the family Sylviidae.

Like a number of babblers, the Wrentit has what North Americans and Europeans think of as wren-like characteristics: a thin, sharp bill; short, rounded wings; a long, "cocked-up" tail; generally brown coloration; a loud, clear, trilled song; and a fondness for dense, brushy habitat. As with wrens, tits, and many other small passerines, Wrentits feed largely on insects and other invertebrates when they are available but switch readily to fruit and other plant matter in cold weather.

Wrentits nest in dense shrubbery, building a shallow, compact cup of twigs, bark, dead leaves, grasses, etc., bound with spider silk, lined with fine fibers (including hair), and decorated with bits of lichen. The 3–5 (usually 4) eggs are unmarked and greenish blue.

The species is strongly associated with the coastal chaparral scrub west of the Sierra Nevada in California and in northern Baja California, but it also occupies other types of brush north to western Oregon. It is nonmigratory. The name, of course, reflects the taxonomic confusion that long surrounded the Wrentit.

WRIGHT, Charles, 1811–85 (*Empidonax wrightii:* Gray Flycatcher). Wellborn, self-taught botanist and consummate plant collector, whose work in Texas was published by Asa Gray as *Plantae Wrightianae.* He also collected in the Pacific Northwest, Japan, China, and Africa. He was briefly curator of the herbarium at Harvard. While in the West, Wright also collected a few birds and sent them to Spencer BAIRD, who named one for him.

XANTHOCHROISM (ZAN-thoh-CROW-izm). An abnormal dominance of yellow coloration in the absence of normal amounts of darker pigments. The condition is seen only rarely in wild birds but occurs regularly among cage birds, especially parrots. Both red and green portions of some plumages are apt to turn yellow as a result of a deficiency in diet. Birds in this condition are called "lutinos" in avicultural jargon. A few presumed xanthochroistic birds, e.g., all yellow Evening Grosbeaks, have been recorded in the wild.

XANTUS (ZAN-toose), John, 1825–94 (Xantus's Murrelet: *Endomychura hypoleuca*). A Hungarian lawyer, soldier, impostor, and, after emigration

to the United States, a jack-of-all-trades, including naturalist-collector. Considering his lack of credentials, his resumé bespeaks no small intelligence and/or a persuasive personality, for he managed to win the confidence of Spencer BAIRD; became (briefly) a U.S. consul in Mexico; posed as a captain in the Navy; and ended respectably as the director of the Zoological Garden of Budapest (see Gruson 1972–BIOGRAPHY, for further details). On a trip to Baja California, Xantus collected the southernmost-ranging alcid, described it, and, given his style, was probably at least influential in choosing its name.

XEROPHILOUS (zer-OFF-uh-luss). Literally, loving dryness. In reference to birds and other organisms, it describes a preference for arid habitats, especially deserts. Le Conte's Thrasher is a North American example of a xerophilous species.

YELLOWLEGS. Standard English name for 2 of the 15 species of long-legged sandpipers in the genus *Tringa*. Greater and Lesser Yellowlegs breed only in North America and generally nest in low arctic and subarctic muskeg habitat. They are common migrants on both coasts, and some populations winter on marshes, flats, and interior wetlands along the southern shores of the continent. Other populations reach the southern tip of South America. Their loud, piping calls are among the most distinctive of American shorebird notes.

For a discussion of intermediate forms, see Sill (1988).

For family characteristics, see SANDPIPER.

YELLOWSTONE National Park (mainly Wyoming). Famous worldwide for its spectacular scenery, Old Faithful Geyser (and 10,000 other hot springs, large mammals (Grizzly Bear, American Bison, Elk), and hordes of summer tourists, Yellowstone is both the oldest (est. 1872) and the largest (3,468 square miles) of U.S. national parks (excepting the great Alaskan ones). It is also an excellent place to see a wide range of the breeding-bird specialties of the western highlands as well as northern forest species, e.g., Trumpeter Swan, Golden Eagle, Blue Grouse, Sandhill Crane, Williamson's Sapsucker, Hammond's and Cordilleran Flycatchers, Violet-green Swallow, Gray and Steller's Jays, Black-billed Magpie, Clark's Nutcracker, Mountain Chickadee, American Dipper, Mountain Bluebird,

Townsend's Solitaire, Bohemian Waxwing (winter), Townsend's and MacGillivray's Warblers, Western Tanager, Cassin's Finch, rosy-finches, and Green-tailed Towhee. Accommodations are available year round; be sure to make reservations (including camping) during the peak season, Memorial Day to Labor Day. For more detail go to http://www.nps.gov/yel/.

YELLOWTHROAT. Standard English name for 9 species of wood warblers (family Parulidae), all in the genus *Geothlypis*. One of these, the Common Yellowthroat, is one of the most familiar of North American songbirds and breeds across the entire continent and south to southern Mexico. All yellowthroats in all plumages have yellow throats.

For family characteristics, see WOOD WARBLER.

YOLK. In birds, a yellow or orange mass of protein and fat granules produced by the ovary, enclosed in a thin, transparent membrane. After passage through a bird's oviduct, it is surrounded by a clear gelatinous substance (the albumen) and a hard eggshell. The yolk is the "food" that sustains the embryo until hatching. See EGG; EMBRYO; REPRODUCTIVE SYSTEM.

YOLK SAC. A membranous pouch containing the egg yolk and connected by a tube (the yolk stalk) to the underside of the embryos of fishes, reptiles, and birds. The yolk is largely consumed by the embryo during the incubation period. Just before hatching, the yolk sac is forced by muscular contraction inside the abdomen of the embryo. Thus, all birds are born with an internal yolk sac, which, however, disappears within the first week after hatching. Humans and other mammals have a similar structure, but it contains no yolk.

See EMBRYO and Fig. 11.

YOSEMITE National Park (California). One of the venerable jewels in the crown of the U.S. national park system and the best possible refutation of the generally reliable ornithological maxim that the best birding is always to be found in garbage dumps and sewer beds. The park contains almost 750,000 of the Sierra Nevada's most spectacular acres, beginning at an elevation of about 4,000 feet on the floor of the Yosemite Valley and climaxing in an array of alpine peaks, eight of them exceeding 10,000 feet, the two highest over 13,000. To the public at large, Yosemite is probably best known for its spectacular rock formations such as Half Dome, El Capitan, and Cathedral Spires; waterfalls such as the 1,430-foot Upper Yosemite; Mirror Lake; multicolored alpine meadows; and groves of giant sequoias. To the birdwatcher interested in highland bird species of the American West, however, it offers a wide range of habitats from the

dipper-infested rapids of the Merced River to the rocky edges of the snow-fields preferred by Gray-crowned Rosy-Finches. In between there are both coniferous and deciduous woodlands holding specialties such as Blue Grouse, Band-tailed Pigeon, Great Gray Owl, Northern Pygmy-Owl, Black Swift, White-headed Woodpecker, Williamson's Sapsucker, Cordilleran Flycatcher, Steller's Jay, Clark's Nutcracker, Canyon Wren, Mountain Blue-bird, Townsend's Solitaire, Western Tanager, and Black-headed Grosbeak. Overhead look for Golden Eagle, White-throated Swift, and Violet-green Swallow.

The park is easily reached by following State Highway 140 about 70 miles east from Merced. Early summer offers the appealing combination of breeding-bird activity and less than peak tourist activity.

For more detail see Oliver Scott's *A Birder's Guide to Wyoming* in the ABA/Lane series and the Yosemite website at http://www.nps.gov/yos/. For other western mountain birding, see ROCKY MOUNTAIN; YELLOWSTONE.

YOUNG, DEVELOPMENT OF. Details of a bird's maturation from the time it is hatched until it becomes functionally independent of its parents, i.e., can fly and/or find its own food.

It is natural and convenient to consider the development of young birds beginning with the moment they leave the egg. When we do this we find that birds at hatching divide into two main types: (I) those that are essentially helpless and totally dependent on their parents (altricial) and (II) those that are relatively well developed and able to fend for themselves to some degree (precocial). In addition, there are two fairly distinct "subtypes," types III and IV, that are a little less helpless than type I and a little less independent than type II, respectively. In one sense, these differences at hatching are more apparent than real, for, in general, those birds that emerge helpless from the egg have a markedly shorter incubation period than those that emerge more or less ready to face the world. In other words, some birds hatch sooner and develop longer in the nest, whereas others hatch later and spend little or no time in the nest, having developed longer in the egg. Many factors influence incubation and post-hatching development time, but among comparable species development follows a generally similar schedule and the time from *laying* to independence is likely to match fairly well even though the time from *hatching* to independence is very different.

Before proceeding to a schematic comparison of the main development patterns just described, here are a few more generalities about the development of young birds.

- Birds grow rapidly in early stages, at the end of which they cease to grow. Most birds attain adult proportions and size well before independence and are only slightly short of adult weight when ready to fend for themselves. Many people used to the mammalian (espe-

5-day-old nestling
naked at hatching

17 days
juvenal plumage

Cedar Waxwing

immature
1st basic
(winter) plumage

adult

immature
1st basic
(winter) plumage

Laughing Gull
chick
hatchling to 5 days

adult
basic
(winter) plumage

adult
alternate (breeding) plumage

Laughing Gull

cially the human) growth pattern will say, when faced for the first time with an adult kinglet or other diminutive species: "How sweet, is it a baby?"

- Larger species generally have longer development periods than smaller.
- Birds with "safe" nesting habits, e.g., hole nesters, develop at a slower rate than more vulnerable forms such as ground nesters.
- In defiance of the above "rule" by which altricial species have shorter "egg lives" and precocial species shorter "nest lives," some groups (see especially type III below) have both long incubation periods and long stretches of post-hatching dependency. The Black-footed Albatross, for example, remains in the egg for more than 2 months, yet does not become independent for 5 months or more *after hatching.*

The following is a schematic comparison of the major aspects of the basic development patterns of young birds. For convenience, the North American avifauna is divided into four "types" of development, though, as noted above, types III and IV are probably more accurately regarded as "subtypes" of I and II, respectively. The data included have been gleaned from a variety of sources, which are listed in the Bibliography. For thorough day-by-day accounts of development, see, especially, Nice (1943, 1962).

Description of Types

Type I—Typical Altricial: Helpless and therefore confined to the nest (nidicolous) and dependent on parents for an extended period after hatching; essentially naked, i.e., lacking down except perhaps for a small amount on the back and head (psilopaedic); typical of the following families (listed by order) of North American birds: *Pelecaniformes* (acquire a down coat after hatching)—pelicans, frigatebirds, boobies and gannets, cormorants, and anhingas (tropicbirds are born with down, see type III); *Columbiformes*—pigeons and doves; *Cuculiformes*—cuckoos, anis, and roadrunners; *Apodiformes*—swifts (some acquire down after hatching) and hummingbirds; *Trogoniformes*—trogons; *Coraciiformes*—kingfishers; *Piciformes*—woodpeckers; and *Passeriformes*—c. 25 families of "perching birds," flycatchers through finches.

Type II—Typical Precocial: Mobile and ready to leave the nest soon after hatching (nidifugous); clothed in a (usually thick) coat of down

Fig. 33. *Growth and plumage development.* The young of songbirds, such as the Cedar Waxwing, are *altricial* (helpless for a period after hatching); *nidicolous* (confined to the nest during the helpless period); and *psilopaedic* (naked with scant down at hatching). The young of some other bird families (e.g., ducks, rails, sandpipers) are *precocial* (able to walk and look for their own food almost immediately); *nidifugous* (leave the nest soon after hatching); and *ptilopaedic* (covered in a thick coat of natal down). Laughing (and other) Gull chicks are *semi-precocial,* because although they are downy and able to move about almost immediately, they stay near the nest and depend on their parents to feed them for a period of weeks after hatching.

DEVELOPMENT OF YOUNG

	Type I	Type II	Type III	Type IV
1. Incubation Period	25–55 days (Pelecaniformes); 11–19 all others; most passerines 11–16.	17–37 days; most 3–4 weeks. Loons, grebes, anatids, gallinaceous birds, cranes, rails, and shorebirds.	Variable: 41–65 days (tubenoses); 17–32 (herons); 38–42 (vultures and condors); 21–34 (owls).	20–30 days (gulls, terns, skimmers, and alcids); 19–20 (nightjars).
2. Condition at Hatching	Naked or minimal down dorsally; eyes closed (open within 3–5 days); helplessly confined to nest; large head and belly, small wings and legs; skin usually pinkish; prominent whitish or yellowish mouth corners (rictal flanges); bill, legs, and mouth lining often brightly colored/patterned; raises head and "gapes" almost immediately.	Down-covered; eyes open; mobile immediately or nearly so; proportions more like adult except for small wings; no rictal flanges; bill, leg, and mouth color usually dark; unable to lift head at first.	Superficially like II, but confined to nest and dependent on parents for extended period; petrels and owls have eyes closed at hatching, unlike most of type III.	Like II, but stays in or near the nest and is tended by parents in spite of early mobility.
3. Plumage Growth	First adult feathers "sprout" within first 4 days (passerines), especially on wings and back; full growth of feathers more or less coincides with leaving the nest.	First adult feathers "sprout" within first 5–6 days, especially on wings and tail; in swimming birds, feathers on ventral surfaces appear first (1–3 weeks); head and pelvic	Most if not all tubenoses have 2 coats of nestling down; in some cases the second is paler and curlier than the first. Fulmars begin to show juvenal plumage at 4–5 weeks, but albatrosses	Gulls and terns lose most down for juvenal plumage before fully grown, but species which take longer to mature can still appear largely downy after 3 weeks or more and not be fully fledged for 7.

DEVELOPMENT OF YOUNG *(continued)*

	Type I	Type II	Type III	Type IV
		regions often last to lose down; timing/sequence variable among groups—e.g., ducks, geese, etc., retain down longer than most.	take much longer and this plumage is not fully developed until 5 or 6 months (Palmer 1962– ORNITHOLOGY). Most owls and at least some diurnal raptors also have 2 down coats, but the juvenal plumage develops rapidly in the nest within 3 weeks (small hawks and owls) to 23 *months* (large owls, condors), depending on the species. Heron down is generally thinner than typical precocials' and molts into juvenal plumage within first third of nest life, or about 2 weeks.	
4. Body Temperature Control	Lacking at hatching but developed rapidly and acquired essentially by midpoint of nest life, i.e., well before adult feather coat is complete.	Partially developed at hatching because of down, but continued development slower than in type I and not complete for about a month after hatching.	Generally as in type II.	Generally as in type II.

DEVELOPMENT OF YOUNG *(continued)*

	Type I	*Type II*	*Type III*	*Type IV*
5. Motor Activities	Very limited at first; within few days grips floor of nest tightly; by middle of nest life begins to yawn, stretch, preen, etc.	Well developed from start and practiced within hours of hatching.	Similar to type I.	Similar to type II, but nevertheless remains in or near the next for long period dependent on parental feeding.
6. Vocalization	May not call immediately but begins "begging" sounds within first 2–3 days; capable of "distress calls" by midpoint of nest life but may not utter first "adult" calls until near independence.	Often begins to call *before* hatching; "brood call" continues throughout "family period." Other distinctive calls rapidly developed include alarm, begging (if fed by parents), distress (when molested), threat (mostly in sibling rivalry), and "contentment" (while being brooded).	Generally as in type I.	Generally as in type I.
7. Leaves the Nest	As early as 7–8 days for vulnerable ground nesters (e.g., Ovenbird, Mourning Warbler); later for more secure cavity nesters, such as woodpeckers (20–30	As soon as down dries (a few hours) or within the first day (24 hours).	In tubenose species that have open nest sites (e.g., Black-footed Albatross), young birds begin to wander from the nest area at about 2–3 months,	Gull and tern chicks usually wander from the nest site within a few days of hatching, but remain within the parental territory. The young of Royal

DEVELOPMENT OF YOUNG *(continued)*

Type I	*Type II*	*Type III*	*Type IV*

days), kingfishers (30–38 days). In more secure nesters, the leaving of the nest is often simultaneous with first flight, but ground nesters may vacate before able to fly. The majority of passerine species leave the nest in 10 days to 2 weeks, but there are many exceptions, e.g., most corvids don't leave for 3 or more weeks, likewise the two large grackles and some wrens.

but are coaxed back into the nest territory for feeding by parents. However, this wandering precedes independence by several months (see number 8 and number 10). Burrow-nesting tubenoses (e.g., Greater Shearwater, Leach's Storm-Petrel) emerge in the evening or at night for a few days before first flight but reenter the burrow during the day. After first flight, they may return to the nest site but not reenter the burrow. In herons, departure generally coincides with first flight, but young birds may climb around on the nest tree (usually returning to the nest) for as much as a week before first flight. In the Wood Stork and many hawks, eagles, etc., leaving coincides with first flight, but

and Sandwich Terns form groups (crèches) within 2–3 days (Royal) or in 2nd week (Sandwich) where they continue to be fed by their own parents; first flight does not occur until much later (see number 8). The young of many alcid species go to sea several weeks *before* first flight, either alone or with parents, which continue to feed them. Young nightjars may be moved by the parents from the nest site in response to danger; they also may wander on their own almost immediately, but remain close enough to be located by parents for feeding.

DEVELOPMENT OF YOUNG *(continued)*

	Type I	Type II	Type III	Type IV
8. First Flight	Very variable among "types," families, and even species; ranges from 8 days (wood warblers) to 190 (frigatebirds); the Pelecaniformal take between 1 and 3 months to fly; kingfishers and crows may take more than a month; most passerines fly between the 2nd and 3rd weeks after hatching.	Fairly consistent at family level; range great, from gallinaceous birds—some can fly as early as 7 days after hatching and all are normally airborne in less than 3 weeks—to swans, which may not fly until their 108th day; loons fly at 70–80 days; Anseriformes (except swans) anywhere between 35 and 77; cranes 60–70. Arctic breeding sandpipers may fly within	Black-browed Albatross at 5–6 months; Leach's Storm-Petrel 2–2½ months. Herons 3 (Green) to 5 (larger species) weeks; Wood Stork 7–8 weeks; American Flamingo 10–11 weeks. Small falcons 2–3 weeks; eagles about 2 months; Black and Turkey Vultures 10–11 weeks; California Condor about 5 months. Owls 3 weeks to 2 months, generally with larger species taking longer.	Gulls 5–7 weeks; terns about a month; alcids 5–6 weeks; nightjars 3–4 weeks.
			in some species, young return to the nest for a period of up to 3 weeks to roost for the night and be fed. Most nestling owls may climb out of nests and onto adjacent branches well before they are able to fly (1 to several weeks).	

DEVELOPMENT OF YOUNG *(continued)*

	Type I	Type II	Type III	Type IV
		2 weeks, while plovers of more southern distribution can take as long as 40 days.		
9. Finds Own Food	Begins tentatively soon after leaving the nest (see number 7) and continues as parent begins "weaning" until young is self-sufficient; about a month for passerines, but possibly more than a year for frigatebirds.	As soon as departure from nest (see number 7) or with some parental guidance within a few days of hatching for most precocial species, but loons and grebes may continue to be fed by their parents for 6 weeks or more, though they are active and follow their parents from the beginning.	Tubenoses begin to find own food only after having flown to sea; this follows a period of starvation and weight loss (in many species) after abandonment by parents. Most heron young fly to feeding grounds with adults as soon as able. Hawks and eagles learn to tear up prey by end of nestling period and learn gradually to kill for a period of weeks after, while still being fed by parents. Owls also depend on parental feeding while learning to hunt for themselves.	Gulls and terns begin fishing (or scavenging) for themselves soon after their first flights; alcids begin diving for food soon after they leave the nest site, i.e., *before* they can fly in many cases. Nightjars' self-sufficiency in catching insects follows shortly after first flight.

DEVELOPMENT OF YOUNG *(continued)*

	Type I	Type II	Type III	Type IV
10. Full Independence from Parents	In about a month for most passerines; much longer for Pelecaniformes: gannets and cormorants become independent in 3–4 months, and frigate birds may be partially fed by parents for more than a year after hatching (Palmer 1962–ORNITHOLOGY).	Variable. There is a tendency in several groups of precocial birds for the young to remain with the parents after they are functionally independent (i.e., can fly and feed themselves). Geese and crane families are known to remain together in migration and winter quarters and not split up until the return to the breeding grounds the following spring. Young Red-throated Loons may be abandoned on nest ponds by parents before they can fly and then rejoin them on salt water when able (Palmer 1962–ORNITHOLOGY). At least some arctic breeding shorebirds	Many tubenoses are abandoned by their parents weeks before they are fledged or can find food for themselves; they live on large fat reserves, complete fledging, and are ultimately forced to fly to sea to avoid starvation. In herons, hawks, and owls, feeding by parents continues after first flight and departure from the nest; full independence may exist within a few weeks (some herons and hawks), but many are dependent for 6 weeks or more and California Condor young are fed by their parents for more than a year after hatching.	Independence in gulls and terns closely follows ability to fly and find food; alcids may be fed briefly on the ocean during their early flightless period but soon learn feeding techniques and become functionally self-sufficient. Nightjars also gain independence more or less simultaneously with ability to fly and find food.

DEVELOPMENT OF YOUNG (continued)

	Type I	Type II	Type III	Type IV
		abandon young before they can fly and migrate south, leaving the young to follow with their peers a month or more later.	Tubenoses are exceptional in reaching a weight which *exceeds* that of the parents well before fully fledged; these large fat stores help see the chicks through the period of parental abandonment, which usually occurs weeks before independence, and may also serve as a hedge against bad weather when parents are unable to obtain food or return to the nest. Most other type III species generally similar to type II.	Generally similar to type II.
11. Weight Pattern	In majority of passerines, weight is 6–8% that of adult female at hatching; rises very rapidly to 50–80% of adult female's weight t departure from the nest; then rises more gradually until near adult weight at independence. Weight may decline slightly during "weaning" (Nice 1943–YOUNG, DEVELOPMENT OF).	Less at hatching than type I; 1–6% of adult female weight as compared to 6–8%. Precocials drop in weight slightly just after hatching when learning to feed themselves, as altricials do just after they leave the nest. But precocials are still 30–40% short of adult weight when able to fly.		

feathers (ptilopaedic); typical of the following North American families: *Gaviiformes*—loons; *Podicipediformes*—grebes; *Anseriformes*—swans, geese, and ducks; *Galliformes*—chachalacas, turkeys, grouse, quail, pheasants, and partridge; *Gruiformes*—cranes, Limpkin, rails, gallinules, and coots; and *Charadriiformes* (in part)—oystercatchers, avocets and stilts, plovers, sandpipers, woodcock, snipe, and phalaropes.

Type III—Semi-altricial: Like type I, i.e., helpless, but clothed in heavy down (ptilopaedic); typical of the following North American families: *Procellariiformes*—albatrosses, shearwaters, petrels, and storm-petrels; *Pelecaniformes* (in part)—tropicbirds only; *Ciconiiformes*—herons, storks, ibises and spoonbills, and flamingoes; *Falconiformes*—vultures, hawks and eagles, and falcons; and *Strigiformes*—owls (including the Barn Owl).

Type IV—Semi-precocial: Like type II, but remain in nest to be cared for by parent for an extended period (nidicolous) in spite of ability to move; typical of the following North American families: *Charadriiformes* (in part)—gulls, terns, skimmers, and alcids; and *Caprimulgiformes*—nightjars.

See also the excellent ecological overview of avian development and growth in O'Connor's *The Growth and Development of Birds* (1984).

ZÉNAIDE (zeh-NED). Princess Zénaide Charlotte Julie Bonaparte (White-winged Dove: *Zenaida asiatica*; Mourning Dove: *Zenaidura macroura*). Charles Lucien Bonaparte named two genera of doves after his wife, who was also his cousin.

ZOOGEOGRAPHY. The study of the distribution of animal species over the surface of the earth. Put simply, the zoogeographer asks how a given species has come to occur where it presently does and what factors keep it there. Such judgments involve broad, long-term phenomena, such as continental drift, the uplifting of mountains, changes in the level of the seas, and animal evolution.

The concept of zoogeographic regions or realms was articulated by the eminent British ornithologist Philip L. SCLATER in 1851. The notion was elaborated and refined by Alfred Wallace in 1857 into the system of the six major areas we recognize today: Nearctic, Neotropical, Palearctic,

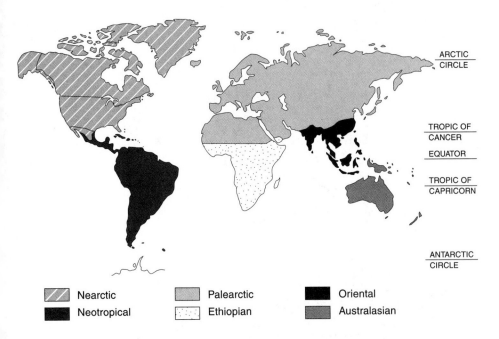

Nearctic	Palearctic	Oriental
Neotropical	Ethiopian	Australasian

Fig. 34. *Zoogeographic regions of the world.* The Nearctic and Palearctic regions together make up the Holarctic region. Madagascar, Oceania, Antarctica, and the marine environment are usually considered apart from the six major regions. See DISTRIBUTION.

Ethiopian, Oriental, and Australasian. (See NEARCTIC, NEOTROPICAL, and PALEARCTIC for descriptions; see Fig. 34 for boundaries.) Subregions have been proposed for a number of isolated landmasses and island groups, such as Madagascar and New Zealand.

There are, of course, broad transition zones between regions, and the regions are not meant to indicate strict range limitations. Virtually all migrating species range across two zoogeographic regions, and many wide-ranging species occur normally in three or more. The numerous discrepancies and exceptions that are inevitable in such a broad concept have led to criticism of the theory as a whole, but it clearly embodies enough general truth to be at least useful for basic reference.

North America lies entirely within the Nearctic region but has many species in common with the Palearctic and Neotropical regions and particularly strong influences from these regions in western Alaska and along the Mexican border, respectively. See DISTRIBUTION.

ZOOLOGY. The study of animal life or the science that derives therefrom; a subdivision of biology (plant and animal life); divided into specialized branches, such as ornithology, the study of birdlife.

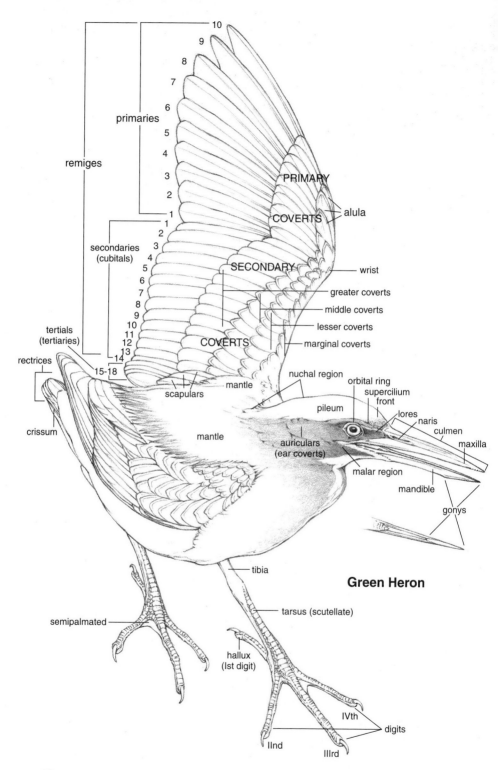

Fig. 35. *Typography of a bird.* Most technical terms; for field terms see Fig. 1.

ZOOME. A major worldwide community of animals; the animal component of a biome; animals characteristic of rain forests make up the rain forest zoome. See also BIOME; DISTRIBUTION.

ZOONOSIS (ZOH-uh-NOH-siss). Any disease that is transmitted from animals to man, e.g., rabies. Certain bird diseases are zoonotic. See DISEASE.

ZUGUNRUHE (TSOO-gun-ROO-uh). A German term meaning, literally, "travel urge." Applied by ornithologists to the restlessness exhibited by birds immediately before they begin to migrate.

ZYGODACTYL (ZYE-goh-DAK-tull). Describes the form of a bird's foot when the first and fourth toes point to rearward and the second and third forward. Among North American species, cuckoos and woodpeckers have typical zygodactyl feet; the feet of owls and the Osprey are considered zygodaclyl though their outer toes can be moved to either the forward or backward position. For other foot types, see LEG/FOOT; also SKELETON, Bones of the Leg.

Checklist of North American Birds

The list that follows contains several "layers" of information:

1. It includes all species of birds known to occur regularly in North America, as the continent is defined on p. xvii. These fall into two broad categories: species that breed here and those that occur regularly during part of the year but breed elsewhere. The latter species are marked "(visitor)"; those not so marked can be assumed to breed here. The meaning of the term "regular" applied to the occurrence of bird species is not always clear. The goal here has been to include all species that can reasonably be counted as integral parts of the North American avifauna and to exclude those that occur here only sporadically or unpredictably, even though the latter may have been recorded many times. Put another way, this list closely corresponds to the *ABA Checklist* (6th edition) Codes 1–3 and with a very few exceptions (e.g., certain irregular breeders) relegates Code 4 ("Casual") and Code 5 ("Accidental") species to Appendix II.

With the recent increase in competent observers combing the avifaunal peripheries of the continent—especially western Alaska and the Mexican border—many species formerly thought to occur only irregularly as vagrants are now being encountered on an annual basis or nearly so. In addition to "transforming" some species from vagrants into regular visitors, this demonstrates that a few species, e.g., Red-footed Booby, may occur annually—probably a fair criterion for inclusion in the avifauna—but not be *seen* so often. In categorizing such cases, I have been guided by the record and knowledge of the species in question, but will not claim that a few of the judgments made are anything but subjective. Also included in Appendix I are well-established introduced species (e.g., European or Common Starling), extinct species (e.g., Passenger Pigeon), and species that have been of regular occurrence in North America but are now rarely recorded (e.g., White-tailed Eagle). For a summary of records for casual and accidental species (Codes 4 and 5), see the *ABA Checklist*, 6th edition (2002).

2. The list can also be used to learn the "definition" of particular taxa (orders, suborders, families, subfamilies, genera, and species), i.e., their relationship to other taxonomic groupings and their size both worldwide and in North America. The numbers following the major taxa signify as follows:

Orders (names ending in –iformes): The number of *families* an order contains worldwide/in North America follows the ordinal names. The

third order listed, Procellariiformes, contains 4 families worldwide, 3 of which occur regularly in North America.

Suborders: (names ending in –ae, –i, or –es): No numerical breakdown given.

Superfamilies: (names ending in –oidea): Only a few of these; no numerical breakdown given.

Families (names ending in –idae): The number both of *genera* and of *species* a family contains worldwide/in North America follows the familial names. The third family listed, Diomedeidae, contains 4 genera worldwide, 1 of which occurs regularly in North America. It also contains 14 species worldwide, 3 of which occur regularly in North America.

Subfamilies: (names ending in –inae): No numerical breakdown given.

Tribes: (names ending in –ini): No numerical breakdown given.

Genera (names with initial capitals and italic): The number of species a genus contains worldwide/in North America follows the generic names. The fourth genus listed, *Podiceps,* contains 9 species worldwide, 3 of which occur regularly in North America.

Species names consist of the genus name plus the species name; the species in a given genus are listed under the genus name using only the first initial of the genus name. Though the use of subspecies has been questioned by some authorities, the number of those that were included in the *AOU Check-list of North American Birds,* 5th edition (1957) are included here following the specific name as a general indication of the species variability and of its potentially distinguishable "races." The Northern Fulmar, *F. glacialis,* has been divided into 3 subspecies in North America. When only a single race of a polytypic species occurs regularly in North America the species name is followed by "(1 N.A.)." Species followed by "(1)" are monotypic (worldwide).

Any taxon (order, family, genus, or species) followed by "(1)" is monotypic, i.e., it contains only one immediately subordinate taxonomic unit, except for monotypic species, which contain no subordinate units (subspecies). The first order listed, **Gaviiformes** (1), contains only a single family, the **Gaviidae** (1), which in turn contains only a single genus, *Gavia.* The genus of the California Condor, *Gymnogyps* (1), contains only a single species, *G. californianus* (1), which is also monotypic.

Definitions of taxonomic categories—CLASS, SUBCLASS, ORDER, etc.—including their significance in avian taxonomy, appear as entries in the main text. Definitions of bird groupings also have entries of their own under their English names: TUBENOSE, ALBATROSS, FULMAR, etc. Definitions of specific Latin taxa, Procellariiformes, Diomedeidae, Diomedea, etc., are defined only here in Appendix I. For the convenience of readers wishing to look up a particular Latin order, suborder, or family, these are listed alphabetically under ORDER, SUBORDER, and FAMILY along with the numbers of the pages on which they appear in Appendix I.

3. With the advent and increasing sophistication of molecular analysis in phylogenetic studies, bird systematics is undergoing an exciting period of rapid revision and counter-revision. I have tried to make rational use of the current diversity of taxonomic opinion in Appendixes I and III. The phylogenetic order, breakdown of taxa, and scientific and standard English nomenclature in Appendix I follows the *AOU Check-list of North American Birds,* 7th edition (1998) as being the most reputable source for our region of the planet. However, in giving the *number of genera and species worldwide,* I have followed Monroe and Sibley's *A World Checklist of Birds* (1993) as representing the most vivid modern view of the shape of the world avifauna. While this combination creates some discrepancies, they are surprisingly few at the genus and species level. Nevertheless, because of the wide range of taxonomic opinion, the larger numbers used should be taken as approximations based on conservative sources. In addition, Appendix III gives the Sibley/Ahlquist/ Monroe phylogeny down to the subfamily level for comparison. These lists are not intended to express any taxonomic opinion, but rather to lay some of the prevailing ones before the reader. For more on this general topic, see SYSTEMATICS.

Appendix I lists 21 orders, 75 families, 266 genera, and 747 species of birds that occur regularly (as defined above) in North America (as defined on p. xvii). Appendix II lists an additional 6 families and 175 species that have occurred here as casual visitors or vagrants. Any disparity between these totals and others that have been published are readily explained by the differences in taxonomic opinion discussed above and by legitimate differences of opinion about the status of some species in North America. The reader would do well to append the adverb "approximately" to all such broad numerical summaries.

Class AVES: All birds, living and extinct
Living orders: 23–28/21
Living families: 145–170/75
Living (and recently extinct) species (per Monroe and Sibley 1993): 9,702/747 (regular)

ORDER
  SUBORDER
    SUPERFAMILY
    FAMILY
     SUBFAMILY
      TRIBE
       Genus
        Species

GAVIIFORMES: Loons (1)
    GAVIIDAE: Loons (1). Species: 5/5
       Gavia (5/5)

G. stellata, Red-throated Loon (1)
G. arctica, Arctic Loon (1)
G. pacifica, Pacific Loon (1)
G. immer, Common Loon (1)
G. adamsii, Yellow-billed Loon (1)

PODICIPEDIFORMES: Grebes (1)

PODICIPEDIDAE: Grebes. Genera: 6/4; species: 22/7

Tachybaptus (5/1)
T. dominicus, Least Grebe (1 N.A.)
Podilymbus (2/1)
P. podiceps, Pied-billed Grebe (1 N.A.)
Podiceps (9/3)
P. auritus, Horned Grebe (1 N.A.)
P. grisegena, Red-necked Grebe (1 N.A.)
P. nigricollis, Eared Grebe (1 N.A.)
Aechmophorus (1)
A. occidentalis, Western Grebe (1)
A. clarkii, Clark's Grebe (1)

PROCELLARIIFORMES: Tubenoses—Albatrosses, Shearwaters & Petrels, Storm-Petrels, and Diving Petrels. Families: 4/3

DIOMEDEIDAE: Albatrosses. Genera: 2/1; species: 14/3

Phoebastria: (?/3)
P. immutabilis, Laysan Albatross (1) (visitor)
P. nigripes, Black-footed Albatross (1) (visitor)
P. albatrus, Short-tailed Albatross (1) (visitor)

PROCELLARIIDAE: Shearwaters & Petrels. Genera: 13/4; species: 79/17

Fulmarus: Fulmars (2/1)
F. glacialis, Northern Fulmar (3)
Pterodroma: Gadfly Petrels (35/6)
P. arminjoniana, Herald Petrel (rare visitor)
P. ultima, Murphy's Petrel (rare visitor)
P. inexpectata, Mottled Petrel (1) (rare visitor)
P. hasitata, Black-capped Petrel (1 N.A.) (visitor)
P. cookii, Cook's Petrel (visitor)
P. feae, Madeira, Fea'/Zino's Petrel (aka Cape Verde/ Madeira Petrel) (rare visitor)
Calonectris: (2/1)
C. diomedea, Cory's Shearwater (1 N.A.) (visitor)
Puffinus: Shearwaters (19/9)
P. creatopus, Pink-footed Shearwater (1) (visitor)
P. carneipes, Pale-footed (Flesh-footed) Shearwater (1) (visitor)
P. gravis, Greater Shearwater (1) (visitor)

P. bulleri, Buller's Shearwater (1) (visitor)

P. griseus, Sooty Shearwater (1) (visitor)

P. tenuirostris, Short-tailed Shearwater (1) (visitor)

P. puffinus, Manx Shearwater (1 N.A.) (mainly visitor; breeds Newfoundland and once in Massachusetts)

P. opisthomelas, Black-vented Shearwater (1) (visitor)

P. lherminieri, Audubon's Shearwater (1 N.A.) (visitor; breeds in Bermudas)

HYDROBATIDAE: Storm-Petrels. Genera: 7/2; species: 21/7

Oceanites (2/1)

O. oceanicus, Wilson's Storm-Petrel (1 N.A.) (visitor)

Oceandroma (12/4)

O. furcata, Fork-tailed Storm-Petrel (2)

O. leucorhoa, Leach's Storm-Petrel (2)

O. homochroa, Ashy Storm-Petrel (1)

O. castro, Band-rumped Storm-Petrel (1) (visitor)

O. melania, Black Storm-Petrel (1)

O. microsoma, Least Storm-Petrel (1) (visitor)

PELECANIFORMES: Tropicbirds, Frigatebirds, Cormorants, Darters, Boobies & Gannets, and Pelicans. Families: 6/6

PHAETHONTES: Tropicbirds

PHAETHONTIDAE: Tropicbirds (1). Species 3/2

Phaethon (3/2)

P. lepturus, White-tailed Tropicbird (1 N.A.) (rare visitor)

P. aethereus, Red-billed Tropicbird (1) (rare visitor)

PELECANI: Boobies & Gannets, Pelicans, Cormorants, and Darters

SULIDAE: Gannets and Boobies. Genera 2/2; species: 9/3

Sula (9/2)

S. dactylatra, Masked Booby (rare visitor)

S. leucogaster, Brown Booby (1 N.A.) (rare visitor)

Morus (3/1)

M. bassanus, Northern Gannet (1)

PELECANIDAE: Pelicans. Genera: 2/1; species 9/2

Pelecanus (6/2)

P. erythrorhynchos, American White Pelican (1)

P. occidentalis, Brown Pelican (2)

PHALACROCORACIDAE: Cormorants (1). Species: 37/6

Phalacrocorax (29/6)

P. penicillatus, Brandt's Cormorant (1)

P. olivaceus, Neotropic Cormorant (1 N.A.)

P. auritus, Double-crested Cormorant (4)

P. carbo, Great Cormorant (1 N.A.)

P. urile, Red-faced Cormorant (1)

P. pelagicus, Pelagic Cormorant (2)

ANHINGIDAE: Darters (1). Species: 4/1
> *Anhinga* (1–4/1)
>> *A. anhinga,* Anhinga (1 N.A.)

FREGATAE
FREGATIDAE: Frigatebirds (1). Species: 5/1
> *Fregata* (5/1)
>> *F. magnificens,* Magnificent Frigatebird (1)

CICONIIFORMES: Herons, Ibises & Spoonbills, Storks, and American Vultures. Families: 5–6/4

> ***ARDEAE:*** Herons and Bitterns
> ARDEIDAE: Herons and Bitterns. Genera: 21/8; species: 65/12
>> Botaurini: Bitterns
>>> *Botaurus* (4/1)
>>>> *B. lentiginosus,* American Bittern (1)
>>> *Ixobrychus* (8/1)
>>>> *I. exilis,* Least Bittern (2)
>> Ardeini: Typical Herons
>>> *Ardea* (11/2)
>>>> *A. herodias,* Great Blue Heron (3, incl. Great White Heron)
>>>> *A. alba,* Great Egret (1 N.A.)
>>> *Egretta* (12/5)
>>>> *E. thula,* Snowy Egret (2)
>>>> *E. caerulea,* Little Blue Heron (1)
>>>> *E. tricolor,* Tricolored Heron (1 N.A.)
>>>> *E. rufescens,* Reddish Egret (2)
>>> *Bubulcus* (1)
>>>> *B. ibis,* Cattle Egret (1 N.A.)
>>> *Butoroides* (3/1)
>>>> *B. virescens,* Green Heron (2)
>> Nycticoracini: Night Herons
>>> *Nycticorax* (2/1)
>>>> *N. nycticorax,* Black-crowned Night Heron (1 N.A.)
>>> *Nyctanassa* (1)
>>>> *N. violacea,* Yellow-crowned Night Heron (1 N.A.)

> ***THRESKIORNITHES:*** Ibises & Spoonbills
> THRESKIORNITHIDAE: Ibises and Spoonbills. Genera: 14/3; species: 28–30/4
>> *THRESKIORNITHINAE:* Ibises
>>> *Eudocimus* (2/1)
>>>> *E. albus,* White Ibis (1)
>>> *Plegadis* (3/1)
>>>> *P. falcinellus,* Glossy Ibis (1 N.A.)
>>>> *P. chihi,* White-faced Ibis (1)
>> *PLATALEINAE:* Spoonbills

Ajaia (1)
    A. ajaja, Roseate Spoonbill (1)
CICONIAE: Storks and American Vultures
    CICONIIDAE: Storks. Genera: 6/1; species: 19/1
        MYCTERIINI: Wood Storks
            Mycteria (4/1)
                M. americana, Wood Stork (Ibis) (1)
    CATHARTIDAE: American Vultures. Genera: 5/3; species: 7/3
            Coragyps (1)
                C. atratus, Black Vulture (1)
            Cathartes (3/1)
                C. aura, Turkey Vulture (3)
            Gymnogyps (1)
                G. californianus, California Condor (1)
PHOENICOPTERIFORMES: Flamingos (1)
    PHOENICOPTERIDAE: Flamingos (1). Species: 5/1
            Phoenicopterus (5/1)
                P. ruber, Greater (American) Flamingo (1 N.A.) (visitor)
ANSERIFORMES: Swans, Geese & Ducks, and Screamers. Families: 2–4/1
    ANSERES: Swans, Geese, and Ducks
        ANATIDAE: Whistling-Ducks, Geese, Swans, and Ducks. Genera: 43/20; species: 157/52 (incl. 1 introduced and 1 extinct)
        DENDROCYGNINAE: Whistling-Ducks, etc.
            DENDROCYGINI: Whistling-Ducks
            Dendrocygna (8/2)
                D. autumnalis, Black-bellied Whistling-Duck (1)
                D. bicolor, Fulvous Whistling-Duck (1 N.A.)
        ANSERINAE: Geese and Swans
            ANSERINI: True Geese
            Anser (9/5)
                A. fabalis, Bean Goose (1 or 2) (rare visitor)
                A. albifrons, Greater White-fronted Goose (3)
            Chen
                C. canagicus, Emperor Goose (1)
                C. caerulescens, Snow Goose (2)
                C. rossii, Ross's Goose (1)
            Branta (5/2)
                B. canadensis, Canada Goose (11)
                A. bernicula, Brant (2, incl. nigricans, Black Brant)
            CYGNINI: Swans
            Cygnus (6/4)
                C. olor, Mute Swan (1) (introduced; invasive)
                C. buccinator, Trumpeter Swan
                C. columbianus, Tundra Swan (1 N.A.)

C. cygnus, Whooper Swan (1) (rare visitor and introduced; potentially invasive)

ANATINAE: True Ducks

  ANATINI: Surface-feeding Ducks

    Aix (2/1)

      A. sponsa, Wood Duck (1)

    Anas: (42/12)

      A. strepera, Gadwall (1 + another extinct race)

      A. penelope, Eurasian Wigeon (1) (numerous records annually, but breeding not proven)

      A. americana, American Wigeon (1)

      A. rubripes, American Black Duck (1)

      A. platyrhynchos (incl. diazi), Mallard (incl. Mexican Duck—once regarded as separate species) (2)

      A. fulvigula, Mottled Duck (2)

      A. discors, Blue-winged Teal (1)

      A. cyanoptera, Cinnamon Teal (1 N.A.)

      A. clypeata, Northern Shoveler (1)

      A. acuta, Pintail (1 N.A.)

      A. querquedula, Garganey (1) (rare visitor)

      A. crecca, Green-winged Teal (2)

  AYTHYINI: Pochards, Bay Ducks, etc.

    Aythya: (12/7)

      A. valisineria, Canvasback (1)

      A. americana, Redhead (1)

      A. ferina, Common Pochard (1) (rare visitor)

      A. collaris, Ring-necked Duck (1)

      A. fuligula, Tufted Duck (1) (rare visitor)

      A. mania, Greater Scaup (1 N.A.)

      A. affinis, Lesser Scaup (1)

  MERGINI: Sea Ducks and Mergansers

    Polysticta (1)

      P. stelleri, Steller's Eider (1)

    Somateria: Eiders (3/3)

      S. fischeri, Spectacled Eider (1)

      S. spectabilis, King Eider (1)

      S. mollissima, Common Eider (4)

    Histrionicus (1)

      H. histrionicus, Harlequin Duck (1)

    Camptorhynchus (1)

      C. labradorius, Labrador Duck (1) (extinct)

    Melanitta: Scoters (3/3)

      M. perspicillata, Surf Scoter (1)

      M. fusca, White-winged Scoter (1 N.A.)

M. nigra, Black Scoter (1 N.A.)

Clangula (1)

   C. hyemalis, Long-tailed Duck (1)

Bucephala: Goldeneye (3/3)

   B. albeola, Bufflehead (1)

   B. clangula, Common Goldeneye (1 N.A.)

   B. islandica, Barrow's Goldeneye (1)

Mergellus (1)

   M. albellus, Smew (1) (rare visitor)

Lophodytes (1)

   L. cucullatus, Hooded Merganser (1)

Mergus: Mergansers (5/2)

   M. merganser, Common Merganser (1 N.A.)

   M. serrator, Red-breasted Merganser (1 N.A.)

OXYURINI: Stifftail Ducks

Nomonyx

   N. dominicus, Masked Duck (1) (rare visitor and sporadic breeder)

Oxyua (7/1)

   O. jamaicensis, Ruddy Duck (1 N.A.)

FALCONIFORMES: Diurnal Birds of Prey Families: 4/3

  ACCIPITRES: Osprey, Hawks & Eagles, etc.

    ACCIPITRIDAE: Osprey and Hawks & Eagles. Genera: 66/14; species: 238/25

     PANDIONINAE: Osprey

      Pandion (1)

       P. haliaetus, Osprey (1 N.A.)

     ACCIPITRINAE: Kites, Eagles, Hawks, and Harriers

      Chondohierax (1)

       C. uncinatus, Hook-billed Kite (1 N.A.) (rare resident S. Texas)

      Elanoides (1)

       E. forficatus, American Swallow-tailed Kite (1 N.A.)

      Elanus (4/1)

       E. leucurus, White-tailed Kite (1 N.A.)

      Rostrhamus (2/1)

       R. sociabilis, Snail (Everglade) Kite (1 N.A.)

      Ictinia (2/1)

       I. mississippiensis, Mississippi Kite (1)

      Haliaeetus (8/2)

       H. leucocephalus, Bald Eagle (2)

       H. albicilla, White-tailed Eagle (1) (rare visitor; has bred in Aleutians)

      Circus: Harriers (13/1)

    C cyaneus, Northern Harrier (1 N.A.)

   Accipiter (49/3)

    A. striatus, Sharp-shinned Hawk (3)

    A. cooperii, Cooper's Hawk (1)

    A. gentilis, Northern Goshawk (2)

   Asturina (1)

    A. nitida, Gray Hawk (1 N.A.)

   Buteogallus (5/1)

    A. anthracinus, Common Black Hawk (1 N.A.)

   Parabuteo (1)

    P. unicinctus, Harris' Hawk (2)

   Buteo (27/9)

    B. lineatus, Red-shouldered Hawk (5)

    B. platypterus, Broad-winged Hawk (1 N.A.)

    B. brachyurus, Short-tailed Hawk (1 N.A.)

    B. swainsoni, Swainson's Hawk (1)

    B. albicaudatus, White-tailed Hawk (1 N.A.)

    B. albonotatus, Zone-tailed Hawk (1)

    B. jamaicensis, Red-tailed Hawk (7)

    B. regalis, Ferruginous Hawk (1)

    B. lagopus, Rough-legged Hawk (1 or 2 N.A.)

   Aquila (9/1)

    A. chrysaetos, Golden Eagle (1 N.A.)

 FALCONES: Caracaras and Falcons

  FALCONIDAE: Caracaras and Falcons. Genera: 10/2; species; 63/7

   CARACARINAE: Caracaras

    Caracara (1–3)

     C. cheriway, Crested Caracara (1)

   FALCONINAE: True Falcons, etc.

    Falconini: True Falcons

     Falco (38/6)

      F. sparverius, American Kestrel (2)

      F. columbarius, Merlin (3)

      F. femoralis, Aplomado Falcon (1 N.A.) (formerly resident in Southwest, then extirpated; reintroduction in progress)

      F. rusticolus, Gyrfalcon (2)

      F. peregrinus, Peregrine Falcon (3)

      F. mexicanus, Prairie Falcon (1)

GALLIFORMES: Gallinaceous Birds. Families: 3 or 5 (with cracids and megapodes included)/4 (incl. cracids)

  Cracoidea (Superfamily): Gallinaceous Birds—Megapodes, Guans & allies, Partridges & Pheasants, Grouse & allies, Turkeys, and Old World Quail

CRACIDAE: Currassows, Guans, and Chachalacas. Genera: 11/1; species: 50/1

    Ortalis (12/1)

        O. vetula, Plain Chachalaca (1 N.A.)

PHASIANIDAE: Partridges & Pheasants; Grouse & allies, and Turkeys. Genera: 44/11 (incl. 4 introduced); species: 176/16 (incl. 4 introduced)

  PHASIANINAE: Partridges and Pheasants

    Alectoris (7/1)

        A. chukar, Chukar Partridge (many races; now interbred) (widely introduced; established in the West)

    Tetraogallus (5/1)

        T. himalayensis (introduced and established in Nevada)

    Perdix (3/1)

        P. perdix, Gray Partridge (1 N.A.) (widely introduced and established)

    Phasianus (1)

        P. colchicus, Ring-necked Pheasant (hybrids of several races) (widely introduced and established)

  TETRAONINAE: Grouse, Ptarmigan, and Prairie Chickens

    Bonasa (3/1)

        B. umbellus, Ruffed Grouse (10)

    Centrocercus (2)

        C. urophasianus, Greater Sage-Grouse

        C. minimus, Gunnison Sage-Grouse

    Falcipennis (1)

        F. canadensis, Spruce Grouse (5)

    Lagopus: Ptarmigan (3/3)

        L. lagopus, Willow Ptarmigan (7)

        L. mutus, Rock Ptarmigan (11; 7 in Aleutians)

        L. leucurus, White-tailed Ptarmigan (5)

    Dendragapus (2/1)

        D. obscurus, Blue Grouse (8)

    Tympanuchus: Prairie Chicken (3/3)

        T. phasianellus, Sharp-tailed Grouse (6)

        T. cupido, Greater Prairie Chicken (2 + 1 extinct)

        T. pallidicinctus, Lesser Prairie Chicken (1)

  MELEAGRIDINAE: Turkeys. Genera: 2/1; species: 2/1

    Meleagris (1)

        M. gallopavo, Wild Turkey (4)

ODONTOPHORIDAE: New World Quail. Genera: 9/4; species: 31/6.

    Oreotyx (1)

        O. pictus, Mountain Quail

    Callipepla (4/3)

        C. squamata, Scaled Quail (2)

        C. californicus, California Quail (7)

        C. gambelii, Gambel's Quail (3)

      Colinus (3/1)

        C. virginianus, Northern Bobwhite (4 + 1 extinct, Arizona)

      Cyrtonyx (2/1)

        C. montezumae, Montezuma Quail (1 N.A.)

GRUIFORMES: Mesites & Monias, Bustard Quail & Hemipodes, Collared Hemipodes, Cranes, Limpkin, Trumpeters, Rails (incl. Gallinules and Coots), Sungrebes, Kagu, Sunbittern, Seriemas, and Bustards; Button-quails sometimes included. Families: 9–12/3.

    RALLIDAE: Rails & Gallinules and Coots. Genera: 34/7; species: 143 (several recently extinct)/9

      Coturnicops (3/1)

        C. noveboracensis, Yellow Rail (1 N.A.)

      Laterallus (9/1)

        L. jamaicensis, Black Rail (2)

      Rallus (9/3)

        R. longirostris, Clapper Rail (8)

        R. elegans, King Rail (1 N.A.)

        R. limicola, Virginia Rail (1 N.A.)

      Porzana (16, incl. 3 extinct/1)

        P. carolina, Sora (1)

      Porphyrula (5/1)

        P. martinica, Purple Gallinule (1)

      Gallinula (9, incl. 1 extinct/1)

        G. chloropus, Common Moorhen (1 N.A.)

      Fulica (11/1)

        F. americana, American Coot (1 N.A.)

    ARAMIDAE: Limpkin (1), Species: 1/1

      Aramus (1)

        A. guarauna, Limpkin (1 N.A.)

    GRUIDAIE: Cranes and Crowned Cranes. Genera: 2/1; species: 15/2

      GRUINAE: Typical Cranes

      Grus (10/2)

        G. canadensis, Sandhill Crane (3)

        G. americana, Whooping Crane (1)

CHARADRIIFORMES: Sandgrouse, Seedsnipes, Plains-wanderer, Sand-pipers & Phalaropes, Painted Snipes, Jacanas, Sheathbills, Magellanic Plover, Thick-knees, Oystercatchers, Avocets & Stilts, Plovers, Coursers, Pratincoles & Crab Plover, Skuas & Jaegers, Skimmers, Gulls & Terns, and Auks. Families: 12–18.

CHARADRII: Thick-knees, Plovers, Oystercatchers, Avocets & Stilts, and allies

    CHARADRIIDAE: Plovers and Lapwings. Genera: 11–16/2; species: 55/11

      CHARADRIINAE: Plovers

        Pluvialis (4/2)

          P. squatarola, Black-bellied Plover (1)

          P. dominica, American Golden Plover (1)

        Charadrius (30/9)

          C. mongolus, Mongolian Plover (1 N.A.) (rare visitor; rare breeder in Alaska)

          C. alexandrinus, Snowy Plover (2)

          C. wilsonia, Wilson's Plover (1 N.A.)

          C. hiaticula, Common Ringed Plover (1 N.A.)

          C. semipalmatus, Semipalmated Plover (1)

          C. melodus, Piping Plover (2)

          C. vociferns, Killdeer (1 N.A.)

          C. montanus, Mountain Plover (1)

          C. morinellus, Eurasian Dotterel (1)

    HAEMATOPODIDAE: Oystercatchers (1). Species: 11, incl. 1 extinct/2

        Haematopus (11/2)

          H. palliatus, American Oystercatcher (1 N.A.)

          H. bachmani, Black Oystercatcher (1)

    RECURVIROSTRIDAE: Stilts, Avocets, and Ibisbill. Genera: 4/2; species: 7/2

        Himantopus (5/1)

          H. mexicanus, Black-necked Stilt (1 N.A.)

        Recurvirostra (4/1)

          R. americana, American Avocet (1)

SCOLOPACI: Jacanas, Painted Snipes, Sandpipers & Phalaropes, Coursers, Pratincoles & Crab Plover, Skuas & Jaegers, Gulls, Terns & Skimmers, and Auks.

    JACANIDAE: Jacanas. Genera: 6/1; species: 8/1

        Jacana (2/1)

          J. spinosa, Northern Jacana (1 N.A.) (breeds irregularly S. Texas)

    SCOLOPACIDAE: Sandpipers and Phalaropes. Genera: 21/17; species: 88/51

      *SCOLOPACINAE:*Sandpipers and allies

        TRINGINI: Tringine Sandpipers

          Tringa (10–15/6)

            T. nebularia, Common Creenshank (1) (migrant W. Alaska)

            T. melanoleuca, Greater Yellowlegs (1)

T. flavipes, Lesser Yellowlegs (1)
T. erythropus, Spotted Redshank (1) (migrant W. Alaska)
T. glareola, Wood Sandpiper (1)
T. solitaria, Solitary Sandpiper (2)
Catoptrophorus (1)
  C. semipalmatus, Willet (2)
Heteroscelus: Tattlers (2/2)
  H. incanus, Wandering Tattler (1)
  H. brevipes, Grey-tailed Tattler (1) (migrant W. Alaska)
Actitis (2/2)
  A. hypoleucos, Common Sandpiper (1) (migrant W. Alaska)
  A. macularia, Spotted Sandpiper (1)
Xenus (1)
  X. cinereus, Terek Sandpiper (visitor to Alaska)
Numeniini: Curlews
  Bartramia (1)
    B. longicauda, Upland Sandpiper (1)
  Numenius: Curlews (8/4)
    N. borealis, Eskimo curlew (1) (extinct?)
    N. phaeopus, Whimbrel (2)
    N. tahitiensis, Bristle-thighed Curlew (1)
    N. americanus, Long-billed Curlew (2)
Limosini: Godwits
  Limosa: Godwits (4/3)
    L. limosa, Black-tailed Godwit (1)
    L. haemastica, Hudsonian Godwit (1)
    L. lapponica, Bar-tailed Godwit (2)
    L. fedoa, Marbled Godwit (1)
Arenariini: Turnstones
  Arenaria (2/2)
    A. interpres, Ruddy Turnstone (2)
    A. melanocephala, Black Turnstone (1)
Calidrini: Calidridine Sandpipers
  Aphriza (1)
    A. virgata, Surfbird (1)
  Calidris: Stints (18–19/18)
    C. canutus, Red Knot (2)
    C. alba, Sanderling (1)
    C. pusilla, Semipalmated Sandpiper (1)
    C. mauri, Western Sandpiper (1)
    C. ruficollis, Red-necked Stint (1)
    C. minuta, Little Stint (rare visitor and migrant)
    C. temminckii, Temminck's Stint (1) (migrant W. Alaska)

C. subminuta, Long-toed Stint (1) (migrant W. Alaska)

C. minutilla, Least Sandpiper (1)

C. fuscicollis, White-rumped Sandpiper (1)

C. bairdii, Baird's Sandpiper (1)

C. melanotos, Pectoral Sandpiper (1)

C. acuminata, Sharp-tailed Sandpiper (1) (migrant W. Alaska; may breed)

C. maritima, Purple Sandpiper (1)

C. ptilocnemis, Rock Sandpiper (3)

C. alpina, Dunlin (1 N.A.)

C. ferruginea, Curlew Sandpiper (1) (breeds very locally, Alaska; rare visitor elsewhere)

C. himantopus, Stilt Sandpiper (1)

Tryngites (1)

T. subruficollis, Buff-breasted Sandpiper (1)

Philomachus (1)

P. pugnax, Ruff (1) (has bred NW Alaska)

LIMNODROMINI: Dowitchers

Limnodromus (3/2)

L griseus, Short-billed Dowitcher (3)

L. scolopaceus, Long-billed Dowitcher (1)

GALLINAGINI: Snipes

Gallinago (15/1)

G. gallinago, Common Snipe (1 N.A.)

SCOLOPACINI: Woodcocks

Scolopax (6/1)

S. minor, American Woodcock (1)

PHALAROPODINAE

Phalaropus (3/3)

P. tricolor, Wilson's Phalarope (1)

P. lobatus, Red-necked (Northern) Phalarope (1)

P. fulicarius, Red Phalarope (1)

LARIDAE: Skuas & Jaegers, Gulls & Terns, and Skimmers. Genera: 11/11; species: 103/46

STERCORARIINAE: Skuas and Jaegers

Catharacta: Skuas (5/2)

C. skua, Great Skua (rare visitor)

C. maccormicki, South Polar Skua

Stercorarius: Jaegers (3/3)

S. pomarinus, Pomarine Jaeger (1)

S. parasiticus, Parasitic Jaeger (1)

S. longicaudus, Long-tailed Jaeger (1)

LARINAE: Gulls

Larus (44/19)

L. atricilla, Laughing Gull (1)

L. pipixcan, Franklin's Gull (1)

L. minutus, Little Gull (1) (rare breeder and visitor)

*L. ridibundus,*Black-headed Gull (1 N.A.)

L. philadelphia, Bonaparte's Gull (1)

L. heermanni, Heermann's Gull (1) (visitor, breeds off Baja, California)

L. canus, Mew Gull (1 N.A.)

L. delawarensis, Ring-billed Gull (1)

L. californicus, California Gull (1)

L. argentatus, Herring Gull (1 N.A.)

L. thayeri, Thayer's Gull (1) (formerly lumped with argentatus)

L. glaucoides, Iceland Gull (2)

L. fuscus, Lesser Black-backed Gull (1) (frequent visitor)

L. schistisagus, Slaty-backed Gull (1) (visitor to Alaska; bred once)

L. livens, Yellow-footed Gull (1) (visitor; formerly lumped with next species)

L. occidentalis, Western Gull (3)

L. glaucescens, Glaucous-winged Gull (1)

L. hyperboreus, Glaucous Gull (2)

L. marinus, Great Black-backed Gull (1)

Xema

X. sabini, Sabine's Gull (2)

Rissa

R. tridactyla, Black-legged Kittiwake (2)

R. brevirostris, Red-legged Kittiwake (1)

Rhodostethia (1)

R. rosea, Ross' Gull (1)

Pagophila (1)

P. eburnea, Ivory Gull (1)

STERNINAE: Terns

Sterna (32/12)

S. nilotica, Gull-billed Tern (2)

S. caspia, Caspian Tern (1)

S. maximus, Royal Tern (1 N.A.)

S. elegans, Elegant Tern (1)

S. sandvicensis, Sandwich Tern (1 N.A.)

S. dougallii, Roseate Tern (1 N.A.)

S. hirundo, Common Tern (1 N.A.)

S. paradisaea, Arctic Tern (1)

S. forsteri, Forster's Tern (1)

S. albifrons, Least Tern (3)

S. aleutica, Aleutian Tern (1)

S. *anaethetus,* Bridled Tern (visitor)
S. *fuscata,* Sooty Tern (1 N.A.)
Chlidonias (3/1)
C. *niger,* Black Tern (1 N.A.)
Anous: Noddies (3/2)
A. *stolidus,* Brown Noddy (1 N.A.)
A. *minutus,* Black Noddy (summers in Dry Tortugas, Fla.)
RYNCHOPINAE: Skimmers (1) Species: 3/1
Rynchops
R. *niger,* Black Skimmer (1 N.A.)
ALCIDAE: Auks, Genera: 12/12; species: 23/21 (incl. 1 extinct)
ALCINI: Dovekies, Murres, and Auks
Alle (1)
A. *alle,* Dovekie (1)
Uria (2/2)
U. *lomvia,* Thick-billed Murre (2)
U. *aalge,* Common Murre (3)
Alca (1)
A. *torda,* Razorbill (1 N.A.)
Pinguinus (1)
P. *impennis,* Great Auk (1) (extinct)
CEPHINI: Guillemots
Cepphus (3–4/2)
C. *grille,* Black Guillemot (3)
C. *columba,* Pigeon Guillemot (2)
BRACHYRAMPHINI: Brachyramphine Murrelets
Brachyramphus (3/2)
B. *marmoratus,* Marbled Murrelet (1 N.A.)
B. *brevirostris,* Kittlitz's Murrelet (1)
SYNTHLIBORAMPHINI: Synthlioramphine Murrelets
Synthliboramphus (4/3)
S. *hypoleucus,* Xantus' Murrelet (1)
S. *craveri,* Craveri's Murrelet (1) (rare visitor)
S. *antiquus,* Ancient Murrelet (1)
AETHIINI: Auklets
Ptychoramphus (1)
P. *aleuticus,* Cassin's Auklet (1 N.A.)
Aethia (4/4)
A. *psittacula,* Parakeet Auklet (1)
A. *pusilla,* Least Auklet (1)
A. *pygmaea,* Whiskered Auklet (1)
A. *cristatella,* Crested Auklet (1)
FRATERCULINI
Cerorhinca (1)
C. *monocerata,* Rhinoceros Auklet (1)

Fratercula (3/3)

F. arctica, Atlantic Puffin (1 N.A.)

F. corniculata, Horned Puffin (1)

F. cirrhata, Tufted Puffin (1)

COLUMBIFORMES: Dodo & Solitaires (extinct), and Pigeons & Doves. Families: 2/1

COLUMBIDAE: Pigeons & Doves. Genera: 40/6; species: 313/14 (incl. 4 introduced and 1 extinct)

Columba (54/4 incl. 1 introduced)

C. livia, Rock Dove (feral pigeon) (1) (introduced; widely established and domesticated)

C. leucocephala, White-crowned Pigeon (1)

C. flavirostris, Red-billed Pigeon (1 N.A.)

C. fasciata, Band-tailed Pigeon (2)

Streptopelia (15/3, all introduced)

S. decaocto, Eurasian Collared-Dove (introduced; spreading rapidly northward and westward from S. Florida)

S. chinensis, Spotted Dove (1 N.A.) (introduced)

S. "risoria," Ringed Turtle-Dove or Barbary Dove (introduced; feral aviary-bred stock derived from *S. roseogrisea* of Africa)

Zenaida (6/2)

Z. asiatica, White-winged Dove (2)

Z. macroura, Mourning Dove (2)

Ectopistes (1)

E. migratorius, Passenger Pigeon (1) (extinct)

Columbina (9/3)

C. inca, Inca Dove (1)

C. passerina, Common Ground-Dove (2)

C. talpacoti, Ruddy Ground-Dove

Leptotila (11/1)

L. verreauxi, White-tipped Dove (1 N.A.)

PSITTACIFORMES: Parrots (1)

PSITTACIDAE: Parrots, Parakeets, and Macaws, Genera: 80/7; species: 360/7 (1 native extinct, many introduced (c. 5 established), 1 native no longer occurs)

PLATYCERCINAE: Australian Parakeets

Melopsittacus

M. undulatus, Budgerigar (escape; locally established)

PSITTACINAE: Typical Parrots

Myiopsitta (1)

M. monachus, Monk Parakeet (1 N.A.) (introduce; locally established)

Conuropsis (1)
   C. carolinensis, Carolina Parakeet (2) (extinct)
Aratinga
   A. holochlora, Green Parakeet (introduced; locally estab-
   lished; may also occur as a vagrant to S. Texas)
Rhynchopsitta (2/1)
   R. pachyrhyncha, Thick-billed Parrot (1) (formerly a spo-
   radic visitor to Arizona/New Mexico; recent reintroduc-
   tions apparently failed)
Brotogeris
   B. versicolurus, White-winged Parakeet (introduced; lo-
   cally established)
Amazona
   A. viridigenalis, Red-crowned Parrot (introduced; locally
   established; may also occur as a vagrant to S. Texas)
Other exotic parrots, escaped from captivity, fly free and occasionally
nest, especially in S. Florida; see EXOTIC SPECIES.
CUCULIFORMES: Cuckoos & Allies. Families: 2–6/1–4 (the subfamilies
listed below have been proposed for full family status, based on molecular
analysis)
   CUCULIDAE: Cuckoos, Roadrunners, and Anis. Genera: 30/4;
   species: 143/7
      CUCULINAE: Old World Cuckoos
         Cuculus (14/1)
         C. canorus, Common Cuckoo (rare migrant in W. Alaska)
      COCCYZINAE: New World Cuckoos
         Coccyzus (9/3)
            C. erythropthalmus, Black-billed Cuckoo (1)
            C. americanus, Yellow-billed Cuckoo (2)
            C. minor, Mangrove Cuckoo (1 N.A.)
      NEOMORPHINAE: Ground Cuckoos and Roadrunners
         Geococcyx: Roadrunners (2/1)
            G. californianus, Greater Roadrunner (1)
      CROTOPHAGINAE: Anis
         Crotophaga (3/2)
            C. ani, Smooth-billed Ani (1)
            C. sulcirostris, Groove-billed Ani (1 N.A.)
STRIGIFORMES: Owls—Barn Owls and Typical Owls. Families: 2/2 (Some
authorities included the nightjars and allies in this order.)
   TYTONIDAE: Barn Owls. Genera: 2/1; species: 17/1
         Tyto (15/1)
            T. alba, Common Barn Owl (1 N.A.)
   STRIGIDAE: Typical Owls. Genera: 23/10; species: 156/18
         Otus: Scops-Owls & Screech-Owls (46/4)

       O. flammeolus, Flammulated Owl (1 N.A.)
       O. kennicottii, Western Screech-Owl (1)
       O. asio, Eastern Screech-Owl (15)
       O. trichopsis, Whiskered Screech-Owl (1 N.A.)
    Bubo (15/1)
       B. virginianus, Great Horned Owl (9)
    Nyctea (1)
       N. scandiaca, Snowy Owl (1)
    Surnia (1)
       S. ulula, Northern Hawk Owl
    Glaucidium: Pygmy-Owls (24/2)
       G. gnoma, Northern Pygmy Owl (4)
       G. brasilianum, Ferruginous Pygmy Owl (1 N.A.)
    Micrathene (1)
       M. whitneyi, Elf Owl (2)
    Athene (3–4)
       A. cunicularia, Burrowing Owl (2)
    Strix (18/3)
       S. occidentalis, Spotted Owl (3)
       S. varia, Barred Owl (3)
       S. nebulosa, Great Gray Owl (1 N.A.)
    Asio (7/2)
       A. otus, Long-eared Owl (2)
       A. flammeus, Short-eared Owl (1 N.A.)
    Aegolius (3/2)
       A. funereus, Boreal Owl (1 N.A.)
       A. acadicus, Northern Saw-whet Owl (2)

CAPRIMULGIFORMES: Owlet-Nightjars, Frogmouths, Oilbird, Potoos, Eared-Nightjars, Nighthawks, and Goatsuckers. Families: 7/1
    CAPRIMULGIDAE: Nightjars. Genera: 14/4; species: 79/8
       CHORDEILINAE: Nighthawks
          Chordeiles (5/3)
             C. acutipennis, Lesser Nighthawk (1 N.A.)
             C. minor, Common Nighthawk (8)
             C. gundlachii, Antillean Nighthawk (1) (breeds in Florida Keys)
       CAPRIMULGINAE
          Nyctidromus (1)
             N. alibicollis, Common Pauraque (1 N.A.)
          Phalaenoptilus (1)
             P. nuttallii, Common Poor-will (4)
          Caprimulgus (55/3)
             C. carolinensis, Chuck-will's-widow (1)
             C. vociferus, Whip-poor-will (2)

C. ridgwayi, Buff-collared Nightjar (1 N.A.) (rare resident
S. Arizona)

APODIFORMES: Swifts, Treeswifts, and Hummingbirds. Families: 3/2
(Some authorities give the hummingbirds their own order: Trochiliformes)

APODIDAE: Swifts. Genera: 18/3; species: 99/4

CYPSELOIDINAE: Cypseloidine Swifts

Cypseloides (±8/1)

C. niger, Black Swift (1 N.A.)

CHAETURINAE: Chaeturine Swifts

Chaetura (±21/2)

C. pelagica, Chimney Swift (1)

C. vauxi, Vaux's Swift (2)

APODINAE: Apodine Swifts

Aeronautes (2/1)

A. saxatalis, White-throated Swift (2)

TROCHILIDAE: Hummingbirds. Genera: 108/10; species: 322/16

TROCHILINAE: Typical Hummingbirds

Cynanthus (2/1)

C. latirostris, Broad-billed Hummingbird (1 N.A.)

Hylocharis (8/1)

H. leucotis, White-eared Hummingbird (1 N.A.) (visitor to
SW; may breed)

Amazilia (30/3)

A. beryllina, Berylline Hummingbird (1) (rare visitor
to SW)

A. yucatanensis, Buff-bellied Hummingbird (1 N.A.)

A. violiceps, Violet-crowned Hummingbird (1 N.A.)

Lampornis (6/1)

L. clemenciae, Blue-throated Hummingbird (2)

Eugenes (1)

E. fulgens, Magnificent Hummingbird (1 N.A.)

Calothorax (2/1)

C. lucifer, Lucifer Hummingbird (1)

Archilochus (2/2)

A. colubris, Ruby-throated Hummingbird (1)

A. alexandri, Black-chinned Hummingbird (1)

Calypte (2/2)

C. anna, Anna's Hummingbird (1)

C. costae, Costa's Hummingbird (1)

Stellula (1)

S. calliope, Calliope Hummingbird (1)

Selasphorus (6/3)

S. platycercus, Broad-tailed Hummingbird (1 N.A.)

S. rufus, Rufous Hummingbird (1)

S. sasin, Allen's Hummingbird (2)
TROGONIFORMES: Trogons (1)
   TROGONIDAE: Trogons, Genera: 6/1; species: 39/1
     Trogon (16/1)
      T. elegans, Elegant Trogon (1 N.A.)
CORACIIFORMES: Rollers, Ground-Rollers, Cuckoo-Roller, Motmots, Todies, Kingfishers, and Bee-eaters. Families: 9/1
  ALCEDINES: Todies, Motmots, and Kingfishers
   Alcedinoidea (Superfamily): Kingfishers
    ALCEDINIDAE: Kingfishers. Genera: 18/2; species: 95/3
     CERYLINAE: Typical Kingfishers (Some authorities divide the Alcedinidae into 3 families and raise this subfamily to family rank.)
      Ceryle (5/2)
       C. torquata, Ringed Kingfisher (1 N.A.)
       C. alcyon, Belted Kingfisher (2)
      Chloroceryle (4/1)
       C. americana, Green Kingfisher (2)
PICIFORMES: Puffbirds, Jacamars, Woodpeckers, Barbets, and Toucans. Families: 6/1 (Some authorities include the honey guides and put the jacamars and puffbirds in orders of their own).
   PICIDAE: Wrynecks, Piculets, and Woodpeckers. Genera: 28/6; species: 216/23 (incl. 1 nearly or actually extinct)
   PICINAE: Woodpeckers
    Melanerpes (22/6)
     M. lewis, Lewis' Woodpecker (1)
     M. erythrocephalus, Red-headed Woodpecker (2)
     M. formicivorus, Acorn Woodpecker (2)
     M. uropygialis, Gila Woodpecker (2)
     M. aurifrons, Golden-fronted Woodpecker (2)
     M. carolinus, Red-bellied Woodpecker (4)
    Sphyrapicus: Sapsuckers (4/4)
     S. thyroideus, Williamson's Sapsucker (2)
     S. varius, Yellow-bellied Sapsucker (?)
     S. nuchalis, Red-naped Sapsucker (1)
     S. ruber, Red-breasted Sapsucker (2?)
    Picoides (11/9)
     P. scalaris, Ladder-backed Woodpecker (2)
     P. nuttallii, Nuttall's Woodpecker (1)
     P. pubescens, Downy Woodpecker (7)
     P. villosus, Hairy Woodpecker (12)
     P. stricklandi (incl. *arizonae*), Strickland's (or Arizona) Woodpecker (1 N.A.)
     P. borealis, Red-cockaded Woodpecker (2)
     P. albolarvatus, White-headed Woodpecker (2)
     P. tridactylus, Three-toed Woodpecker (2)

P. arcticus, Black-backed Woodpecker (1)

Colaptes: Flickers (9/2)

C. *auratus* (incl. *cafer*), Northern Flicker (incl. Yellow-shafted and Red-shafted, and Gilded)

C. *chrysoides,* Gilded Flicker (1)

Dryocopus (7/1)

D. *pileatus,* Pileated Woodpecker (4)

Campephilus (11/1)

C. *principalis,* Ivory-billed Woodpecker (1 N.A.) (extinct?)

PASSERIFORMES: Passerine or Perching Birds. Families: 46–62/c.30

TYRANNI: Suboscines: Ovenbirds, Woodcreepers, Antbirds, Antthrushes & Antpittas, Tapaculos, Tyrant Flycatchers, Cotingas, Manakins, and Sharpbills.

Tyranoidea (Superfamily): Tyrant Flycatchers, Cotingas, Manakins, and Sharpbills

TYRANNIDAE: Tyrant Flycatchers. Genera: c.107/10; species: c.417/35 (incl. becards)

ELAENIINAE: Tyrannulets, Elaenias, etc.

Camptostoma (2/1)

C. *imberbe,* Northern Beardless-Tyrannulet (2)

FLUVICOLINAE: Fluvicoline Flycatchers

Contopus (12/4)

C. *cooperi,* Olive-sided Flycatcher (1)

C. *pertinax,* Greater Pewee (1 N.A.)

C. *sordidulus,* Western Wood-Pewee (2)

C. *virens,* Eastern Wood-Pewee (1)

Empidonax (15/11)

E. *flaviventris,* Yellow-bellied Flycatcher (1)

E. *virescens,* Acadian Flycatcher (1)

E. *alnorum,* Alder Flycatcher (1)

E. *traillii,* Willow Flycatcher (1)

E. *minimus,* Least Flycatcher (1)

E. *hammondii,* Hammond's Flycatcher (1)

E. *wrightii,* Gray Flycatcher (1)

E. *oberholseri,* Dusky Flycatcher (1)

E. *difficilis,* Pacific Slope Flycatcher (1) (lumped until recently with the following species as Western Flycatcher)

E. *occidentalis,* Cordilleran Flycatcher (1) (lumped until recently with the preceding species as Western Flycatcher)

E. *fulvifrons,* Buff-breasted Flycatcher (1 N.A.)

Sayornis: Phoebes (3/3)

S. *nigricans,* Black Phoebe (1 N.A.)

S. *phoebe,* Eastern Phoebe (1)

S. *saya,* Say's Phoebe (3)

Pyrocephalus (1)

P. rubinus, Vermilion Flycatcher (2)

TYRANNINAE: Tyrannine Flycatchers

Myiarchus (22/4)

M. tuberculifer, Dusky-capped Flycatcher (1 N.A.)

M. cinerascens, Ash-throated Flycatcher (1 N.A.)

M. crinitus, Great Crested Flycatcher (2)

M. tyrannulus, Brown Crested Flycatcher (2)

Pitangus (1–2/1)

P. sulphuratus, Great Kiskadee (1 N.A.)

Myiodynastes (5/1)

M. luteiventris, Sulphur-bellied Flycatcher (1 N.A.)

Tyrannus (13/8)

T. melancholicus, Tropical Kingbird (1 N.A.)

T. couchii, Couch's Kingbird (1)

T. vociferans, Cassin's Kingbird (1 N.A.)

T. crassirostris, Thick-billed Kingbird (1 N.A.)

T. verticalis, Western Kingbird (1)

T. tyrannus, Eastern Kingbird (1)

T. dominicensis, Gray Kingbird (1 N.A.)

T. forficatus, Scissor-tailed Flycatcher (1)

Pachyramphus (16/1) (Once classified with the Cotinga, the relationships of this genus within the Superfamily Tyranoidea is deemed uncertain by the AOU (1998); the ABA places it at the end of the Tyrant Flycatchers.)

P. aglaiae, Rose-throated Becard (2)

PASSERI: Oscines or Songbirds

LANIIDAE: Shrikes. Genera: 3/1; species 30/2 (If Old World bushshrikes and allies are included, 27 genera and 107 species are added to this family.)

Lanius (26/2)

L. ludovicianus, Loggerhead Shrike (7)

L. excubitor, Northern Shrike (2)

VIREONIDAE: Vireos, Greenlets, Shrike-Vireos, and Peppershrikes. Genera: 4/1; species: 52/14

Vireo (31/14)

V. griseus, White-eyed Vireo (4)

V. bellii, Bell's Vireo (4)

V. atricapillus, Black-capped Vireo (1)

V. vicinior, Gray Vireo (1)

V. flavifrons, Yellow-throated Vireo (1)

V. plumbeus, Plumbeous Vireo (1) (This and the following two forms were until recently considered races of a single species, Solitary Vireo.)

V. cassini, Cassin's Vireo

V. solitarius, Blue-headed Vireo (2)

V. huttoni, Hutton's Vireo (4)

V. gilvus, Warbling Vireo (3)

V. philadelphicus, Philadelphia Vireo (1)

V. olivaceus, Red-eyed Vireo (2)

V. flavoviridis, Yellow-green Vireo (rare breeder in S. Texas)

V. altiloquus, Black-whiskered Vireo (1 N.A.)

CORVIDAE: Crows, Ravens, Magpies, and Jays. Genera: 25/8; species: 118/18

Perisoreus (3/1)

P. canadensis, Gray Jay

Cyanocitta (2/2)

C. cristata, Blue Jay (4)

C. stelleri, Steller's Jay (6)

Cyanocorax (16–17/2)

C. yncas, Green Jay (1 N.A.)

C. morio, Brown Jay (1 N.A.) (rare, local resident S. Texas)

Aphelocoma (5/4)

A. coerulescens, Florida Scrub-Jay (10)

A. insularis, Island Scrub-Jay (1)

A. californica, Western Scrub-Jay

A. ultramarina, Mexican Jay (2)

Gymnorhinus (1)

G. cyanocephalus, Pinyon Jay (1)

Nucifraga: Nutcrackers (2/1)

N. columbiana, Clark's Nutcracker (1)

Pica: Magpies (3/2)

P. pica (*hudsonia*), Black-billed Magpie (1 N.A.) (There is now a consensus that this species is distinct from the Eurasian Magpie [*P. pica*] and is properly called *P. hudsonia.*)

P. nuttalli, Yellow-billed Magpie (1)

Corvus: Crows and Ravens (43/6)

C. brachyrhynchos, American Crow (4)

C. caurinus, Northwestern Crow (1)

C. imparatus, Tamaulipas Crow (1 N.A.) (visitor to S. Texas)

C. ossifragus, Fish Crow (1)

C. cryptoleucus, Chihuahuan Raven (1)

C. corax, Common Raven

ALAUDIDAE: Larks. Genera: 19/2 (incl. 1 introduced); species: 91/2 (incl. 1 introduced)

Alauda (4/1)

A. arvensis, Eurasian Skylark (1 N.A.) (introduced and established resident Vancouver Island, British Columbia, and vicinity; migrant in W. Alaska)

    Eremophila (2/1)

     E. alpestris, Horned Lark (20)

  HIRUNDINIDAE: Swallows. Genera: 14/6; species: 89/8

  HIRUNDININAE: Typical Swallows

    Progne: Martins (5/1)

     P. subis, Purple Martin (2)

    Tachycineta (8/2)

     T. bicolor, Tree Swallow (1)

     T. thalassina, Violet-green Swallow (1 N.A.)

    Stelgidopteryx (4/1)

     S. serripennis, Northern Rough-winged Swallow (2)

    Riparia (4/1)

     R. riparia, Bank Swallow (1 N.A.)

    Petrochelidon (Hirundo) (10/2)

     P. pyrrhonota, Cliff Swallow (4)

     P. fulva, Cave Swallow (1 N.A.)

    Hirundo (39/1–3)

     H. rustica, Barn Swallow (1 N.A.)

PARIDAE: Tits (Titmice and Chickadees). Genera: 3–5/2; species: 53/11 (Some authorities lump the next two families in this one).

    Poecile (?/7)

     P. carolinensis, Carolina Chickadee (5)

     P. atricapillus, Black-capped Chickadee (9)

     P. gambeli, Mountain Chickadee (5)

     P. sclateri, Mexican Chickadee (1 N.A.)

     P. rufescens, Chestnut-backed Chickadee (3)

     P. hudsonicus, Boreal Chickadee (5)

     P. cinctus, Gray-headed Chickadee (1 N.A.)

    Baelophus (4/4)

     B. wollweberi, Bridled Titmouse (1 N.A.)

     B. inornatus, Oak Titmouse (This and the next species were once lumped into a single species, Plain Titmouse with 8 subspecies.)

     B. ridgwayi, Juniper Titmouse

     B. bicolor (incl. *atricristatus*), Tufted Titmouse (5, incl. "Black-crested" Titmouse)

REMIZIDAE: Penduline Tits and Verdins. Genera: 4/1; species: 12/1

    Auriparus (1)

     A. flaviceps, Verdin (2); this species belongs with the gnatcatchers according to some authorities.

AEGITHALIDAE: Long-tailed Tits and Bushtits. Genera: 3/1; species: 8/1

    Psaltriparus (1)

P. minimus (incl. *melanotis*), Bushtit (6, incl. "Black-eared" Bushtit)

SITTIDAE: Nuthatches and Wallcreeper. Genera: 2–4/1; species: 25/4

   SITTINAE: Nuthatches

      Sitta (24/4)

         S. canadensis, Red-breasted Nuthatch (1)

         S. carolinensis, White-breasted Nuthatch (6)

         S. pygmaea, Pygmy Nuthatch (4)

         S. pusilla, Brown-headed Nuthatch (2)

CERTHIIDAE: Creepers (or Treecreepers). Genera: 2/1; species: 7/1 (Some authorities include the wrens and gnatcatchers in this family).

   CERTHIINAE: Northern Creepers

      Certhia (5/1)

         C. americana, Brown Creeper (7)

TROGLODYTIDAE: Wrens. Genera: 17/7; species: 75/9

      Campylorhynchus (13/1)

         C. brunneicapillus, Cactus Wren (1 N.A.)

      Salpinctes (1/1)

         S. obsoletus, Rock Wren (1 N.A.)

      Catherpes (1/1)

         C. mexicanus, Canyon Wren (2)

      Thryothorus (27/1)

         T. ludovicianus, Carolina Wren (3)

      Thryomanes (2/1)

         T. bewickii, Bewick's Wren (13)

      Troglodytes (8/2)

         T. aedon, House Wren (4)

         T. troglodytes, Winter Wren (12)

      Cistothorus (4/2)

         C. platensis, Sedge Wren (1 N.A.)

         C. palustris, Marsh Wren (10)

CINCLIDAE: Dippers (1). Species: 5/1

      Cinclus (5/1)

         C. mexicanus, American Dipper (1 N.A.)

PYCNONOTIDAE: Bulbuls. Genera: 21/1; species: 138/1 (introduced)

      Pycnonotus (40/1)

         O. jocosus, Red-whiskered Bulbul (introduced and established in S. Florida)

REGULIDAE: Kinglets (1). Species: 6/2

      Regulus: Kinglets (5–6/2)

         R. satrapa, Golden-crowned Kinglet (4)

         R. calendula, Ruby-crowned Kinglet (4) (constitutes a Subgenus: *Corthylio*)

SYLVIIDAE: Old World Warblers and Gnatcatchers. Genera: 37/2; species: 247/3 (excludes so-called African warblers often included in this family.) (This is a much-debated taxon with molecular studies suggesting inclusion of Australian wrens, and all babblers and parrotbills and omission of Sylviine warblers.)

   SYLVIINAE: Old World Warblers

      Phylloscopus (46/1)

         P. borealis, Arctic Warbler (1 N.A.) (At least 6 other species of Old World warblers have occurred as rare visitors in the West—see Appendix II.)

   POLIOPTILINAE: Gnatcatchers and Gnatwrens. Genera: 3–4/1; species: 14–15/2–3 (There is molecular evidence that this group should be classified with the wrens and creepers rather than with the Old World Warblers.)

      Polioptila (11/4)

         P. caerulea, Blue-gray Gnatcatcher (2)

         P. californica, California Gnatcatcher (1?)

         P. melanura, Black-tailed Gnatcatcher (3–4)

         P. nigriceps, Black-capped Gnatcatcher (1) (rare breeder S. Arizona)

MUSCICAPIDAE: Old World Flycatchers (see Appendix II for occurrence of this family in North America)

TURDIDAE: Thrushes. (Considered a subfamily of the Muscicapidae by some authorities.) Genera: 51/8; species: 335/18; includes Old World chats, but not Old World Flycatchers.

      Luscinia (11/2)

         L. calliope, Siberian Rubythroat (rare migrant in W. Alaska)

         L. svecicus, Bluethroat (1 N.A.)

      Oenanthe: Wheatears (22/1)

         O. oenanthe, Northern Wheatear (2)

      Sialia: Bluebirds (3/3)

         S. sialis, Eastern Bluebird (4)

         S. mexicana, Western Bluebird (2)

         S. currucoides, Mountain Bluebird (1)

      Myadestes: Solitaires (13, incl. 1 extinct/1)

         M. townsendi, Townsend's Solitaire (1 N.A.)

      Catharus (11–12/5)

         C. fuscescens, Veery (3)

         C. minimus, Gray-cheeked Thrush (1)

         C. bicknelli, Bicknell's Thrush (1)

         C. ustulatus, Swainson's Thrush (4)

         C. guttatus, Hermit Thrush (8)

      Hylocichia (1)

H. mustelina, Wood Thrush (1)

Turdus (66, incl. 1 extinct/4)

   T. obscurus, Eye-browed Thrush (rare migrant in W. Alaska)

   T. grayi, Clay-colored Robin (rare breeder S. Texas)

   T. rufopalliatus, Rufous-backed Robin (rare visitor in SW)

   T. migratorius, American Robin (5)

Ixoreus (1/1)

   I. naevius, Varied Thrush (2)

TIMALIIDAE: Babblers. Genera: 55/1; species: 315/1. The traditional babbler taxa are placed by some authorities in the Sylviidae on the basis of molecular studies.

Chamaea (1)

   C. fasciata, Wrentit (5)

MIMIDAE: Mockingbirds and Thrashers. Genera: 11/4; species: 34/10

Dumetella (1)

   D. carolinensis, Gray Catbird (1)

Mimus: Mockingbirds (9/1)

   M. polyglottos, Northern Mockingbird (2)

Oreoscoptes (1)

   O. montanus, Sage Thrasher (1)

Toxostoma: Thrashers (10/7)

   T. rufum, Brown Thrasher (2)

   T. longirostre, Long-billed Thrasher (1 N.A.)

   T. bendirei, Bendire's Thrasher (1)

   T. curvirostre, Curve-billed Thrasher (3)

   T. redivivum, California Thrasher (2)

   T. dorsale, Crissal Thrasher (2)

   T. lecontei, Le Conte's Thrasher (1 N.A.)

STURNIDAE: Starlings and Mynas. Genera: 27/2 (introduced); species: 114/2 (introduced)

Sturnus (16/1)

   S. vulgaris, European Starling (1 N.A.) (introduced)

Acridotheres (7/2)

   A. tristis, Common Myna (1 N.A.) (introduced; established in S. Florida)

   A. cristatellus, Crested Myna (1 N.A.) (introduced; established near Vancouver, British Columbia)

PRUNELLIDAE: Accentors (see Appendix II)

MOTACILLIDAE: Wagtails and Pipits. Genera: 5/2; species: 65/7. Considered a subfamily of the Passeridae (Old World Sparrows) by some authorities, on the basis of molecular analysis.

Motacilla: Wagtails (11/3)

   M. flava, Yellow Wagtail (1 N.A.)

M. alba, White Wagtail (1 N.A.)

M. lugens, Black-backed Wagtail (1) (rare migrant in W. Alaska);

Anthus: Pipits (45/4)

A. hodgsoni, Olive-backed Pipit (1) (rare migrant in W. Alaska)

A. cervinus, Red-throated Pipit (1) (breeds locally in W. Alaska)

A. rubescens, American Pipit (1?)

A. spragueii, Sprague's Pipit (1)

BOMBYCILLIDAE: Waxwings. (1) Species: 3/2

Bombycilla (3/2)

B. garrulus, Bohemian Waxwing (1 N.A.)

B. cedrorum, Cedar Waxwing (1)

PTILOGONATIDAE: Silky Flycatchers. Placed in the preceding family by some authorities. Genera: 3/1; species: 4/1

Phainopepla (1)

P. nitens, Phainopepla (2)

PEUDRAMIDAE: Olive Warbler (1)

Peudramus (1)

P. taeniatus, Olive Warbler

PARULIDAE: Wood Warblers Genera: 25/15; species: 115/51. Considered part of the family Emberizidae or Fringillidae by some authorities.

Vermivora (9/9, incl. 1 extinct)

V. bachmanii, Bachman's Warbler (1) (extinct)

V. pinus, Blue-winged Warbler (1)

V. chrysoptera, Golden-winged Warbler (1)

V. peregrina, Tennessee Warbler (1)

V. celata, Orange-crowned Warbler (4)

V. ruficapilla, Nashville Warbler (2)

V. virginiae, Virginia's Warbler (1)

V. crissalis, Colima Warbler (1)

V. luciae, Lucy's Warbler (1)

Parula (4/2)

P. americana, Northern Parula (1)

P. pitiayumi, Tropical Parula (1 N.A.) (breeds very locally S. Texas)

Dendroica (27/21)

D. petechia, Yellow Warbler (6)

D. pensylvanica, Chestnut-sided Warbler (1)

D. magnolia, Magnolia Warbler (1)

D. tigrina, Cape May Warbler (1)

D. caerulescens, Black-throated Blue Warbler

D. coronata, Yellow-rumped Warbler (4, incl. Myrtle and Audubon's subspecies)
D. nigrescens, Black-throated Gray Warbler (1)
D. chrysoparia, Golden-cheeked Warbler (1)
D. virens, Black-throated Green Warbler (2)
D. townsendi, Townsend's Warbler (1)
D. occidentalis, Hermit Warbler (1)
D. fusca, Blackburnian Warbler (1)
D. dominica, Yellow-throated Warbler (3)
D. graciae, Grace's Warbler (1 N.A.)
D. pinus, Pine Warbler (2)
D. kirtlandii, Kirtland's Warbler (1)
D. discolor, Prairie Warbler (2)
D. palmarum, Palm Warbler (2)
D. castanea, Bay-breasted Warbler (1)
D. striata, Blackpoll Warbler (1)
D. cerulea, Cerulean Warbler (1)
Mniotilta (1)
M. varia, Black-and-white Warbler (1)
Setophaga (1)
S. ruticilla, American Redstart (2)
Protonotaria (1)
P. citrea, Prothonotary Warbler
Helmitheros (1)
H. vermivorus, Worm-eating Warbler (1)
Limnothlypis (1)
L. swainsonii, Swainson's Warbler (1)
Seiurus (3/3)
S. aurocapillus, Ovenbird (3)
S. noveboracensis, Northern Waterthrush (3)
S. motacilla, Louisiana Waterthrush (1)
Oporornis (4/4)
O. formosa, Kentucky Warbler (1)
O. agilis, Connecticut Warbler (1)
O. philadelphia, Mourning Warbler (1)
O. tolmiei, MacGillivray's Warbler (2)
Geothlypis: Yellowthroats (9/1)
G. trichas, Common Yellowthroat (11)
Wilsonia (3/3)
W. citrina, Hooded Warbler (1)
W. pusilla, Wilson's Warbler (3)
W. canadensis, Canada Warbler (1)
Cardellina (1)
C. rubrifrons, Red-faced Warbler (1)

Myioborus (12/1)

   M. pictus, Painted Redstart (1 N.A.)

Icteria (1)

   I. virens, Yellow-breasted Chat (2)

THRAUPIDAE: Tanagers. Genera: 63/1; species: 252/4. (Included by some authorities in the family Emberizidae or Fringillidae.)

   Piranga (9/4)

      P. flava, Hepatic Tanager (2)

      P. rubra, Summer Tanager (2)

      P. olivacea, Scarlet Tanager (1)

      P. ludoviciana, Western Tanager (1)

EMBERIZIDAE: Seedeaters, Longspurs, Snow Bunting(s), Lark Bunting, Old World Buntings, New World Sparrows, Juncos, and Towhees. Genera: 74/18; species: 318/51. (Included by some authorities in a much larger Emberizine concept including the wood warblers, tanagers, cardinal-grosbeaks and New World blackbirds and orioles.)

   Sporophila: Seedeaters (32/1)

      S. torqueola, White-collared Seedeater (1 N.A.) (rare and local breeder in S. Texas)

   Arremonops (4/1)

      A. rufivirgatus, Olive Sparrow (1 N.A.)

   Pipilo: Towhees (8/7)

      P. chlorurus, Green-tailed Towhee (1)

      P. macualatus, Spotted Towhee (1)

      P. erythrophthalmus, Eastern Towhee (12)

      P. albicollis, White-throated Towhee (1)

      P. fuscus, Canyon Towhee (1)

      P. crissalis, California Towhee (1)

      P. aberti, Abert's Towhee (2)

   Aimophila (14/6)

      A. carpalis, Rufous-winged Sparrow (1 N.A.)

      A. cassinii, Cassin's Sparrow (1)

      A. aestivalis, Bachman's Sparrow (3)

      A. botterii, Botteri's Sparrow (2)

      A. ruficeps, Rufous-crowned Sparrow (6)

      A. quinquestriata, Five-striped Sparrow (1 N.A.)

   Spizella (7–8/6)

      S. arborea, American Tree Sparrow (2)

      S. passerina, Chipping Sparrow (3)

      S. pallida, Clay-colored Sparrow (1)

      S. breweri, Brewer's Sparrow (2)

      S. pusilla, Field Sparrow (2 N.A.)

      S. atrogularis, Black-chinned Sparrow (3)

Pooecetes (1)
　P. gramineus, Vesper Sparrow (3)
Chondestes (1)
　C. grammacus, Lark Sparrow (2)
Amphispiza (2/2)
　A. bilineata, Black-throated Sparrow (3)
　A. belli, Sage Sparrow (4)
Calamospiza (1)
　C. melanocorys, Lark Bunting (1)
Passerculus
　P. sandwichensis, Savannah Sparrow (12, incl. "Ipswich"
　Sparrow)
Ammodramus (9/7)
　A. savannarum, Grasshopper Sparrow (5)
　A. bairdii, Baird's Sparrow (1)
　A. henslowii, Henslow's Sparrow (2)
　A. lecontei, Le Conte's Sparrow (1)
　A. nelsoni, Nelson's Sharp-tailed Sparrow (2?)
　A. caudacutus, Salt Marsh Sharp-tailed Sparrow (2?)
　A. maritimus, Seaside Sparrow (9, incl. the extinct Dusky
　Seaside Sparrow)
Passerella (1)
　P. iliaca, Fox Sparrow (18)
Melospiza (3/3)
　M. melodia, Song Sparrow (30)
　M. lincolnii, Lincoln's Sparrow (3)
　M. georgiana, Swamp Sparrow (3)
Zonotrichia (5/4)
　Z. albicollis, White-throated Sparrow (1)
　Z. querula, Harris' Sparrow (1)
　Z. leucophrys, White-crowned Sparrow (5)
　Z. atricapilla, Golden-crowned Sparrow (1)
Junco: Juncos (4/2)
　J. hyemalis, Dark-eyed Junco (12, incl. "Slate-colored,"
　"White-winged," "Gray-headed," and "Oregon" Juncos)
　J. phaeonotus, Yellow-eyed Junco (1 N.A.)
Calcarius: Longspurs (4/4)
　C. mccownii, McCown's Longspur (1)
　C. lapponicus, Lapland Longspur (2)
　C. pictus, Smith's Longspur (1)
　C. ornatus, Chestnut-collared Longspur (1)
Emberiza (34/1)
　E. rustica, Rustic Bunting (1 N.A.) (migrant in W. Alaska)
Plectrophenax (2/2)

P. *nivalis,* Snow Bunting (2)

P. *hyperboreus,* McKay's Bunting (1)

CARDINALIDAE: Cardinal-Grosbeaks: Saltators, plus certain cardinals, grosbeaks & buntings, and Dickcissel) (genera: 13/5; species: 42/10)

Cardinalis (3/2)

C. *cardinalis,* Northern Cardinal (5)

C. *sinatus,* Pyrrhuloxia (2)

Pheucticus (5/2)

P. *ludovicianus,* Rose-breasted Grosbeak (1)

P. *melanocephalus,* Black-headed Grosbeak (2)

Guiraca (1)

G. *caerulea,* Blue Grosbeak (3)

Passerina (6/4)

P. *amoena,* Lazuli Bunting (1)

P. *cyanea,* Indigo Bunting (1)

P. *versicolor,* Varied Bunting (2)

P. *ciris,* Painted Bunting (2)

Spiza (1)

S. *americana,* Dickcissel (1)

ICTERIDAE: Bobolink, Blackbirds, Meadowlarks and New World Orioles. Genera: 26/8; species: 97/23

Dolichonyx (1)

D. *oryzivorus.* Bobolink (1)

Agelaius (10/2)

A. *phoeniceus,* Red-winged Blackbird (14)

A. *tricolor,* Tricolored Blackbird (1)

Sturnella: Meadowlarks (6/2)

S. *magna,* Eastern Meadowlark (4)

S. *neglecta,* Western Meadowlark (2)

Xanthocephalus (1)

X. *xanthocephalus,* Yellow-headed Blackbird (1)

Euphagus (2/2)

E. *carolinus,* Rusty Blackbird (2)

E. *cyanocephalus,* Brewer's Blackbird (1)

Quiscalus: Grackles (7, incl. 1 extinct/3)

Q. *quiscula,* Common Grackle (3)

Q. *major,* Boat-tailed Grackle (2)

Q. *mexicanus,* Great-tailed Grackle (3)

Molothrus: Cowbirds (5/3)

M. *bonariensis* (1 N.A.) (established recently in S. Florida and expanding to North and West)

M. *aeneus,* Bronzed Cowbird (2)

M. *ater,* Brown-headed Cowbird (3)

Icterus: New World Orioles (25/9)

    I. spurius, Orchard Oriole (1 N.A.)

    I. cucullatus, Hooded Oriole (4)

    I. pustulatus, Steak-backed Oriole (2 N.A.) (rare breeder in Arizona)

    I. pectoralis, Spot-breasted Oriole (1 N.A.) (introduced and established in S. Florida)

    I. gularis, Altamira (Lichtenstein's) Oriole (1)

    I. graduacauda, Audubon's Oriole (1 N.A.)

    I. galbula, Baltimore Oriole (1)

    I. bullockii, Bullock's Oriole (1)

    I. parisorum, Scott's Oriole (1)

FRINGILLIDAE: Fringilline and Cardueline Finches. Genera: 21/7; species: 140/17 (Some authorities suggest a much larger Fringillid concept encompassing the Emberizid finches, wood warblers, tanagers, cardinal-grosbeaks, and New World blackbirds and orioles.)

FRINGILLINAE: Fringilline Finches

    Fringilla (3/1)

    F. montifringilla, Brambling (1 N.A.) (migrant in W. Alaska)

CARDUELINAE: Cardueline Finches: Rosy-Finches, Rosefinches, Crossbills, Redpolls, Siskins, Goldfinches, and Grosbeaks.

    Leucosticte: Rosy Finches (6/3)

        L. tephrocotis, Gray-crowned Rosy-Finch (?)

        L. atrata, Black Rosy-Finch (1)

        L. australis, Brown-capped Rosy-Finch (1)

    Pinicola (2/1)

    P. enucleator, Pine Grosbeak

    Carpodacus: Rosefinches (21/3)

        C. purpureus, Purple Finch (3)

        C. cassinii, Cassin's Finch (1)

        C. mexicanus, House Finch (3)

    Loxia: Crossbills (4–12/2–10)

        L. curvirostra, Red Crossbill (9 or more full species are now thought to exist within this traditional taxon)

        L. leucoptera, White-winged Crossbill (1 N.A.)

    Carduelis: Redpolls, Siskins and Goldfinches (31/6)

        C. flammea, Common Redpoll (3)

        C. hornemanni, Hoary Redpoll (2)

        C. pinus, Pine Siskin (1 N.A.)

        C. psaltria, Lesser Goldfinch (2)

        C. lawrencei, Lawrence's Goldfinch (1)

        C. tristis, American Goldfinch (4)

Coccothraustes (3/1)

    C. vespertinus, Evening Grosbeak (3)

PLOCEIDAE: See WEAVER in main text.

PASSERIDAE: Old World Sparrows. Genera: 4/1 (introduced); species: 36/2 (introduced). Some authorities suggest a larger Passeridae encompassing the wagtails & pipits, accentors, weavers, estrildine finches, and whydahs.

    Passer: Old World Sparrows (15/2)

        P. domesticus, House Sparrow (1 N.A.) (introduced, widely established)

        P. montanus, Eurasian Tree Sparrow (1 N.A.) (introduced in St. Louis, Missouri, and also established in neighboring states, but not widespread)

ESTRILIDIDAE: See WAXBILL in main text.

APPENDIX II

Checklist of Casual
and Accidental Species

The following table contains 175 species that occur only rarely in North America as defined on p. xvii. It conforms closely (but not exactly) to Codes 4 and 5 of the *ABA Checklist*, 6th edition (2002). It therefore combines *Casual* species, defined by ABA as "not recorded annually, but with 6 or more total records—including 3 or more in the past 30 years—reflecting some pattern of occurrence" and *Accidental* species, "species recorded 5 or fewer times, or fewer than 3 records in the past 30 years." A few species that are included in the latest *AOU Check-list* (1998), but not in the ABA list are included here for information, with no implied judgment about their validity. Abbreviated accounts of species native distribution and record of occurrence in North America appear in the second and third columns. The months in the third column represent the dates of occurrence.

For a detailed account of these rarities, including exact date, locality and verification information, and literature citations, see the *ABA Checklist*, 6th edition (2002).

Symbols and abbreviations. The symbol > separates breeding grounds from wintering grounds, e.g., Siberia > S. Asia = breeds in Siberia, winters in southern Asia. State names follow standard U.S. Postal Service abbreviations. Other abbreviations are as follows: BC, British Columbia; Is., Island; LAB, Labrador; MAN, Manitoba; NF, Newfoundland; NS, Nova Scotia; ON, Ontario; PQ, Province of Quebec; rec, record.

Species	Native Distribution	Occurrence
Yellow-nosed Albatross *Thalassarche chlororhynchos*	Southern Hemisphere oceans	Mainly Atlantic coast; also Gulf of Mexico (May–Aug)
Shy Albatross *Thalassarche cauta*	Southern Hemisphere oceans	c. 8 recs: WA, OR, CA (Jul–Jan)
Black-browed Albatross *Thalsaasrche melanophris*	Southern Hemisphere oceans	c. 20 Atlantic Coast reports, few confirmed (May–Sep)
Light-mantled Albatross *Phoebetria palpebrata*	Southern Hemisphere oceans	1 rec: CA (Jul) (photo); in AOU (1998); rejected by ABA as possibly ship-assisted
Wandering Albatross *Diomedea exulans*	Southern Hemisphere oceans	1 rec: CA (Jul) (photo)
Bermuda Petrel *Pterodroma cahow*	Bermuda	12+ confirmed recs: off Carolinas; also OR (May–Jun)
Stejneger's Petrel *Pterodroma longirostris*	Juan Fernandez Is. (Chile > N. Pacific)	6 recs: CA (Jul–Nov); also TX!
Bulwer's Petrel *Bulweria bulwerii*	Widespread in warm oceans	1 rec: NC; 1 rec: CA; 1 rec: OR (Jul–Aug)
Streaked Shearwater *Calonectris leucomelas*	NW Pacific	8 recs: CA (Aug–Oct)
Wedge-tailed Shearwater *Puffinus pacificus*	Widespread in warm oceans	7 recs: WA, OR, CA (Mar–Oct)
Little Shearwater *Puffinus assimilis*	Widespread in warm oceans	2 old recs: SC, NS
White-faced Storm Petrel *Pelagodroma marina*	Widespread in warm oceans	c. 50 recs: Canada south; mainly mid-Atlantic (May–Oct)
European Storm-Petrel *Hydrobates pelagicus*	NE Atlantic and W. Mediterranean > S. Africa	1 rec: Sable Island, NS (Aug)
Wedge-rumped Storm Petrel *Oceanodroma tethys*	E. Pacific; Galapagos > Chile	6+ recs: CA (Jul–Jan)
Red-tailed Tropicbird *Phaethon rubricauda*	Tropical Pacific and Indian oceans	c. 18 pelagic recs: CA; 1 rec: BC (Jul–Jan)
Blue-footed Booby *Sula nebouxii*	E. Pacific, Baja > Peru	Numerous W. coast recs; also inland, incl. NV, TX! (mainly Jun–Sep)
Red-footed Booby *Sula sula*	Widespread in warm oceans	c. regular at Dry Tortugas, FL; also off SC, TX, CA

Species	Native Distribution	Occurrence
Great Frigatebird *Fregata minor*	Widespread in warm oceans	3 recs: CA, OK!
Lesser Frigatebird *Fregata ariel*	Widespread in tropical oceans	1 rec: ME! (Jul)
Yellow Bittern *Ixobrychus sinensis*	E. Asia > Solomon Is.	1 rec: Aleutians (May)
Chinese Egret *Egretta eulophotes*	NE Asia > N. Borneo	1 rec: Aleutians (Jun)
Little Egret *Egretta garzetta*	Widespread E. Hemisphere; now breeds Barbados	30+ recs: NF–VA; also Aleutians (Apr–Jul)
Western Reef-Heron *Egretta gularis*	W. Atlantic–W. India	1 rec: Nantucket (Apr–Sep); also West Indies
Chinese Pond-Heron *Ardeloa bacchus*	E. Asia	1 rec: Pribilofs (Aug)
Scarlet Ibis *Eudocimus ruber*	N. South America	Several old and recent recs, but status doubtful dueto possible escapes
Jabiru *Jabiru mycteria*	Mexico–South America	8+ recs: TX; 1 rec: OK (Jul–Oct)
Pink-footed Goose *Anser brachyrhynchus*	Arctic Atlantic > NW Europe	c. 15 recs: mainly NF, PQ; also New England, PA, DE
Lesser White-fronted Goose *Anser erythropus*	N. Eurasia > southward	1 rec: Aleutians; also BC, ND, OH, PA, DE, but escapes suspected
Barnacle Goose *Branta leucopsis*	Old World Arctic > NW Europe	E. Canada, NE U.S.; many escapes, but some convincing recs
Falcated Duck *Anas falcata*	NE Asia > SE Asia	c. 15 recs: mainly Aleutians, Pribilofs
Spot-billed Duck *Anas poecilorhyncha*	S. and E. Asia	5 recs: Aleutians; 1 rec: Kodiak Island (Apr–May, Sep–Nov)
White-cheeked Pintail *Anas bahamensis*	Caribbean and South America	Many presumed escapes from E. North America, CA, NV; at least some winter in FL recs presumed valid
Baikal Teal *Anas formosa*	E. Siberia > E. Africa	10+ recs: N. and W. Alaska; also BC, WA, OR, CA; eastern recs possibly escapes
Steller's Sea-Eagle *Haaliaeetus pelagicus*	NE Russia > Japan	7+ recs: AK (May–Oct)

Species	Native Distribution	Occurrence
Crane Hawk *Geranospiza caerulescens*	Mexico–South America	1 rec: TX (Dec–Apr)
Roadside Hawk *Buteo magnirostris*	Mexico–South America	4 confirmed recs: TX (Dec–Apr)
Collared Forest-Falcon *Micrastur semitorquatus*	Mexico–South America	1 rec: TX (Jan–Feb)
Eurasian Kestrel *Falco tinnunculus*	Widespread Old World	9 recs: W. AK, BC, WA, NS, MA, NJ (year-round)
Eurasian Hobby *Falco subbuteo*	Eurasia > Africa and India	10 recs: W. AK; also WA and at sea off NF (spring and fall)
Corn Crake *Crex crex*	N. Eurasia > Africa	c. 20 recs: E. coast (mainly late fall)
Paint-billed Crake *Neocrex erythrops*	W. Panama–S. America	2 recs: TX, VA (Dec–Feb)
Spotted Rail *Pardirallus maculatus*	Greater Antilles + Central Mexico–S. America	2 recs: TX, PA (Aug–Nov)
Eurasian Coot *Fulica atra*	Widespread in Old World	5 recs: 2 LAB, 1 NF, 1 PQ, 1 AK (Nov–Dec)
Common Crane *Grus grus*	Eurasia > S. Europe– SE Asia	c. 15 recs: mainly W. and midwest U.S. and Canada (Mar–Dec)
Double-striped Thick-knee *Burhinus bistriatus*	Mexico–South America	1 valid rec: TX (Dec)
Northern Lapwing *Vanellus vanellus*	Eurasia > S. Europe– SE Asia	2 major flights, winters of 1927 and 1966; 30 other recs: mainly E. Canada and NE U.S.
European Golden-Plover *Pluvialis apricaria*	Greenland–Central Siberia > Europe and N. Africa	Many spring invasions in NE Canada (Apr–May); also MA, DE, AK
Collared Plover *Charadrius collaris*	Mexico–South America	1 rec: TX (May)
Little Ringed Plover *Charadrius dubius*	Widespread in Old World	3 recs: W. Aleutians
Eurasian Oystercatcher *Haematopus ostralegus*	Widespread in Old World	2 recs: NF (Apr–May)
Black-winged Stilt *Himantopus himantopus*	Widespread in Old World	1 rec: Aleutians (May–Jun)
Marsh Sandpiper *Tringa stagnatilis*	Widespread in Old World	2 recs: Aleutians (Aug–Sep)

Species	Native Distribution	Occurrence
Common Redshank *Tringa totanus*	Widespread in Old World	An invasion in NF, Apr–May 1995
Green Sandpiper *Tringa ochropus*	Widespread in Old World	7 recs: W. Aleutians; 1 rec: Gambell (May–Jun)
Little Curlew *Numenius minutus*	NE Siberian > New Guinea and Australia	6 recs: AK, WA, CA (May–Jun, Aug–Oct)
Far Eastern Curlew *Numernius madagas- cariensis*	NE Asia > Borneo and Australasia	21 recs: Aleutians, Pribilofs (May–Jul); 1 rec: Vancouver (Sep)
Slender-billed Curlew *Numenius tenuirostris*	Very local Central Siberia > S. Europe and N. Africa	1 rec: ON (fall, c. 1925)
Eurasian Curlew *Numenius arquata*	Widespread in Old World	7 recs: Nunavut, NS, NF, MA (Mar); NY (Sep–Mar)
Great Knot *Calidris tenuirostris*	NE Asia > India and Australasia	c. 16 recs: W. and N. AK (May–Jun); 1 rec: OR (Sep)
Spoonbill Sandpiper *Eurynorhynchus pygmaeus*	Very local NE Siberia > S. Asia	6 recs: N. and W. AK; sight recs: Al berta (May–Aug)
Broad-billed Sandpiper *Limnicola falcinellus*	Scandinavia–Siberia– > Africa–Australasia	5 recs: Aleutians; 1 rec: NY; 1 rec: MA (Aug–Sep)
Jack Snipe *Lymnocryptes minimus*	Scandinavia–Siberia > Africa–Australasia	4 recs: AK, CA, LAB (Sep–Dec)
Pin-tailed Snipe *Gallinago stenura*	Central and E. Siberia > India–SE Asia	2 confirmed recs: Attu, Aleutians (May)
Eurasian Woodcock *Scolopax rusticola*	Eurasia > S. Europe–SE Asia	Many early recs: NF, NJ, PA, OH, VA, AL; last rec (sight): NJ, 1956 (Nov–Mar)
Oriental Pratincole *Glareola maldivarum*	S. and E. Asia > Australasia	2 recs: W. AK
Black-tailed Gull *Larus crassirostris*	NE Asia > Taiwan	12+ recs: AK, c. 12 recs: E. coast: NF, NS, RI, NY, NJ, MD, VA; also BC, CA, MAN, TX; spring–fall
Yellow-legged Gull *Larus cachinnans*	E. Atlantic–Central Asia > Persian Gulf and India	Numerous recent recs: NF; also DC, MD, VA, NC (Oct–Mar)
Kelp Gull *Larus dominicanus*	S. temperate coasts and oceans	Recs: LA, TX; reports from IN, MD (year-round)
Large-billed Tern *Phaetusa simplex*	South America	3 recs: IL, OH, NJ (May–Jul)

Species	Native Distribution	Occurrence
White-winged Tern *Chlidonias leucopterus*	E. Europe–E. Siberia and China > Old World tropics	Numerous recs, esp. Atlantic coast: NB, PQ, MA, NY, NJ, DE, VA, NC, GA; also ON, VT, IN, WI, MAN, CA, AK; has nest PQ, NY (mainly May–Aug, Nov)
Whiskered Tern *Chlidonias niger*	Widespread in Old World	2 recs: NJ (Apr–Aug)
Long-billed Murrelet *Brachyramphus perdix*	NE Siberia and Japan > Central coast Japan	c. 36 confirmed recent recs: E. and W. coasts and interior (peaks Jul–Aug, Oct–Dec)
Scaly-naped Pigeon *Columba squamosa*	West Indies	2 recs: Key West, FL (May, Oct)
Oriental Turtle-Dove *Streptopelia orientalis*	E. Eurasia > southward	5 recs: N. and W. AK; also Vancouver
Zenaida Dove *Zenaida aurita*	West Indies and Yucatan	2 confirmed recs: FL Keys; also sight recs
Key West Quail-Dove *Geotrygon chrysia*	Bahamas and Greater Antilles	Hist. breed Key West? c. 15 recs: FL, since 1964 (mainly Oct–Jun)
Ruddy Quail-Dove *Geotrygon montana*	Mexico–South America and West Indies	6 recs: S. FL; 1 rec: TX (Dec–May)
Oriental Cuckoo *Cuculus saturatus*	C. Russia east and SE Asia > S. Asia and Australasia	10 recs: W. AK (May–Sep)
Oriental Scops-Owl *Otus sunia*	Widespread Asia	2 recs: Aleutians (Jun)
Mottled Owl *Ciccaba virgata*	Mexico and South America	1 rec: S. TX (Feb)
Stygian Owl *Asio stygius*	Mexico, South America, and West Indies	2 recs: S. TX (Dec)
Jungle Nightjar *Caprimulgus indicus*	Widespread E. Eurasia > SE Asia	1 rec: Aleutians (May)
White-collared Swift *Streptoprocne zonaris*	Mexico, West Indies, and South America	8 recs: TX, LA, FL, MI (Sep–May)
White-throated Needletail *Hirundapus caudacutus*	NE Asia + Himalayas > New Guinea	4 recs: W. Aleutians (May)
Common Swift *Apus apus*	Widespread Eurasia > S. Africa	3 recs: 2 Pribilofs, 2 St. Pierre-et-Miquelon (Jun)
Fork-tailed Swift *Apus pacificus*	Widespread N. Asia > SE Asia and Australia	c. 15 recs: mainly from Aleutians, Pribilofs (May–Sep)

Species	Native Distribution	Occurrence
Antillean Palm-Swift *Tachornis phoenicobia*	Greater Antilles	2 recs: Key West, FL (Jul–Aug)
Green Violet-ear *Colibri thalassinus*	Mexico–South America	48 recs: 30 TX; also MS, NC, MI, ON, AL (Apr–Dec)
Green-breasted Mango *Anthracothorax prevostii*	Mexico–Panama	12 recs: TX; 1 rec: NC (year-round)
Xantus's Hummingbird *Hylocharis xantusii*	Baja California	3 recs: CA, BC; c. resident birds, 1 nesting unsuccessfully
Cinnamon Hummingbird *Amazilia rutila*	Mexico–Costa Rica	2 recs: AZ, NM (Jul, Sep)
Plain-capped Starthroat *Heliomaster constantii*	Mexico–Costa Rica	20+ recs in AZ since 1969
Bahama Woodstar *Calliphlox evelynae*	Bahamas	4 confirmed recs: S. FL (year-round)
Bumblebee Hummingbird *Atthis heloisa*	Mexico (highlands)	1 old rec of 2 birds: SE AZ, Jul 1896
Eared Trogon *Euptilotis neoxenus*	Mexico (highlands)	24+ recs from AZ since 1977, incl. at tempted nestings (year-round)
Eurasian Hoopoe *Upupa epops*	Widespread in the Old World	1 rec: AK (Sep)
Eurasian Wryneck *Jynx torquilla*	Widespread Eurasia > N. Africa–SE Asia	1 rec: AK (Sep)
Great Spotted Woodpecker *Dendrocopos major*	Widespread Eurasia	Several recs: W. Aleutians (May, Sep–Nov)
Greenish Elaenia *Myiopagis viridicata*	Mexico–South America	1 rec: High Island, TX (May)
Caribbean Elaenia *Elaenia martinica*	West Indies	1 rec: FL; not accepted by AOU
Tufted Flycatcher *Mitreopanes phaeocercus*	Mexico–South America	2 recs: TX (Nov–Jan, Apr)
Nutting's Flycatcher *Myiarchus nuttingi*	Mexico–Costa Rica	3 confirmed recs: AZ, CA (Nov–Mar, Jul)
La Sagra's Flycatcher *Myiarchus sagrae*	West Indies	c. 25 recs from S. FL since 1982 (Oct–May); also AL
Piratic Flycatcher *Legatus leucophaius*	Mexico–South America	4 recs: 1 NM, 2 TX; 1 FL (Sep–Mar)

Species	Native Distribution	Occurrence
Variegated Flycatcher *Empidonomus varius*	South America	3 recs: ME, TN, ON (May, Oct–Nov)
Loggerhead Kingbird *Tyrannus caudifasciatus*	West Indies	Recs noted by AOU (1998), considered inconclusive by ABA
Fork-tailed Flycatcher *Tyrannus savanna*	Mexico–South America	Nearly annual and year-round; mainly E. and central U.S. and Canada; also AL, ID, WA, CA
Masked Tityra *Tityra semifasciata*	Mexico–South America	1 rec: S. TX (Feb–Mar)
Brown Shrike *Lanius cristatus*	Widespread N. Asia > S. Asia	8 recs: 5 AK, 2 CA, 1 NS (Jun–Dec)
Thick-billed Vireo *Vireo crassirostris*	West Indies	5 confirmed recs: S. FL (Apr–May, Sep–Oct)
Yucatan Vireo *Vireo magister*	Yucatan, Belize, and adjacent islands	1 rec: TX (Apr–May)
Eurasian Jackdaw *Corvus monedula*	Widespread Eurasia	Scattered recs from NE U.S. and Canada since 1982, possibly ship-assisted; nest attempts (year-round)
Cuban Martin *Progne cryptoleuca*	Cuba > South America?	1 confirmed rec: Key West, FL, May 1875; also other doubtful recs
Gray-breasted Martin *Progne chalybea*	Mexico–South America	2 old recs: TX (Apr–May)
Southern Martin *Progne elegans*	South America	1 rec: Key West, FL, Aug 1890
Brown-chested Martin *Progne tapera*	South America	2 confirmed recs: MA, NJ (Jun, Nov)
Bahama Swallow *Tachycineta cyaneoviridis*	Bahamas	c. 9 confirmed recs: S. FL (Mar–Aug)
Common House Martin *Delichon urbica*	Widespread > Old World tropics	7 recs: 6 AK, 1 St. Pierre, SPM (May–Aug)
Middendorff's Grasshopper-Warbl. *Locustella ochotensis*	NE Asia > Philippines	7 recs: N. and W. AK (Jun–Sep)
Lanceolated Warbler *Locustella lanceolata*	N. Eurasia > S. Asia	3 recs: 2 Aleutians, 1 CA (Jun–Jul, Sep)
Wood Warbler *Phylloscopus sibilatrix*	NW Europe > S. Africa	1 rec: Aleutians (Oct)

Species	Native Distribution	Occurrence
Dusky Warbler Warbler *Phylloscopus fuscatus*	Central Siberia and N. Asia > S. Asia	8 recs: AK; 9 recs: CA (spring, Sep–Nov)
Yellow-browed Warbler *Phylloscopus inornatus*	Siberia and N. Asia > S. Asia	1 rec: Gambell Island, AK (Sep)
Narcissus Flycatcher *Ficedula narcissina*	NE Asia > Philippines	2 recs: Aleutians (May)
Mugimaki Flycatcher *Ficedula mugimaki*	NE Asia > Philippines and SE Asia	1 controversial Aleutian rec based on fuzzy photo, but accepted by ABA and AOU (May)
Red-breasted Flycatcher *Ficedula parva*	Widespread N. Eurasia > S. Asia	c. 15 recs from W. Aleutians since 1977 (Jun)
Siberian Flycatcher *Muscicapa sibirica*	Central Siberia–N. SE Asia > S. Asia	6 recs: W. Aleutians; 1 rec: Pribilofs (May–Jun, Sep)
Gray-spotted Flycatcher *Muscicapa griseisticta*	NE Asia > Philippines– New Guinea	Numerous recs: mainly from W. Aleutians (early Jun)
Asian Brown Flycatcher *Muscicapa dauurica*	Widespread Asia	2 recs: AK: Attu and Gambell Island (May, Jun)
Siberian Blue Robin *Luscinia cyanae*	NE Eurasia > S. Asia	1 rec: Aleutians (Attu) (May)
Red-flanked Bluetail *Tarsiger cyanurus*	Widespread Eurasia > SE Asia	10 recs: N. and W. AK (May–Jun); also CA (Nov)
Common Stonechat *Saxicola torquata*	Widespread in Old World	5+ recs: AK; 1 rec: NB (Apr–Jun, Sep–Oct)
Orange-billed Nightingale-Thrush *Catharus aurantiirostris*	Mexico–N. South America	1 rec: S. TX (Apr)
Eurasian Blackbird *Turdus merula*	Widespread N. Eurasia > SE Asia	3 recs: NF, PQ, ON, the last 2 sus- pected of being escaped cage birds
Dusky Thrush *Turdus naumanni*	Central–E. Siberia > Japan and S. China	c. 20 AK recs since 1967; also Yukon, BC (mainly May–Jun; also Sep–Nov, Jan–Mar)
Fieldfare *Turdus pilaris*	Greenland–Central Siberia > Europe, N. Africa, and Middle East	Many recs from northeast: Nunavut, NF, NB, PQ, ON, MA, NY, CT, MN, DE; also AK (mainly Nov–Mar)
Redwing *Turdus iliaca*	Widespread N. Eurasia > N Africa–Transcaspia	10 recs: mainly NF; also NS, NB, PQ, NY (mainly Nov–Mar)

Species	Native Distribution	Occurrence
White-throated Robin *Turdus assimilis*	Mexico–N. South America	3 recs: S. TX (5 indiv.) (Feb–Apr)
Aztec Thrush *Ridgwayia pinicola*	Mexico (local, highlands)	c. 50 recs since 1977: mainly SE AZ; also TX (mainly Jul–Sep; also Jan, May)
Bahama Mockingbird *Mimus gundlachii*	Mainly Bahamas and Jamaica	15 recs in S. FL since 1973 (Apr–Jun, Aug [1 rec])
Blue Mockingbird *Melanotis caerulescens*	Mexico	Several recs: S. AZ, NM, TX; suspicion of escaped cage birds in some cases
Siberain Accentor *Prunella montanella*	Siberia > N Asia	12+ recs: N. and W. AK (Mar–Apr, fall); also BC, WA, ID
Citrine Wagtail *Motacilla citreola*	Siberia to Central Asia and Tibet > S. Asia	1 rec: MS! Jan–Feb, 1992
Gray Wagtail *Motacilla cinerea*	Widespread Eurasia > Eurasia–Old World tropics	17+ recs: W. and N. AK, mainly the Aleutians; 1 rec: CA (mainly May–Jun, Jan) +2 Oct
Tree Pipit *Anthus trivialis*	Widespread N. Eurasia > trop. Africa–India	2 recs: AK (Jun)
Pechora Pipit *Anthus gustavi*	N. Siberia > Philippines, Borneo, and Indonesia	c. 15 recs: AK, all but 1 from Attu (May–Jun)
Gray Silky-flycatcher *Ptilogonys cinereus*	Mexico and Guatemala	2 recs: S. and W. TX; 4 recs: CA, considered possible escapes (Oct–Mar)
Crescent-chested Warbler *Paula superciliosa*	Mexico	4 recs: SE AZ; sight rec: W. TX (Sep–Jun)
Gray-crowned Yellowthroat *Geothlypis trichas*	Mexico	Once resident in S. TX, but only 6 confirmed recs since 1930 (Feb–Jul)
Slate-throated Redstart *Myioborus miniatus*	Mexico–South America	8 recs: S. TX, NM, AZ (Mar–Jun, Aug)
Fan-tailed Warbler *Euthlypis lachrymosa*	NW Mexico	7 recs: SE AZ (May–Sep [mainly spring])
Golden-crowned Warbler *Basileuterus culicivorus*	Mexico–South America	11 confirmed recs: S. TX (Oct–Apr [mainly winter])
Rufous-capped Warbler *Basileuterus rufifrons*	Mexico–South America	16 confirmed recs from TX since 1973; 10 recs: SE AZ, where attempted nesting (year-round)
Bananaquit *Coereba flaveola*	West Indies and Mexico–South America	Many recs: S. FL (Sep–May [mainly Jan–Mar])

Species	Native Distribution	Occurrence
Flame-colored Tanager *Piranga bidentata*	Mexico–Panama	12+ recs: SE AZ; 2 recs: TX; has nested with Western and Hepatic Tanagers (Apr–Jul)
Western Spindalis *Spindalis zena*	West Indies	c. 560 good recs from S. FL since 1957 (year-round except Jul [mainly Apr–May, Dec])
Yellow-faced Grassquit *Tiaris olivacea*	West Indies and Mexico–South America	5 recs: S. FL; 1 rec: S. TX (Jan–Jul)
Black-faced Grassquit *Tiaris bicolor*	West Indies and South America	7 recs: S. FL (Oct–Jul)
Worthen's Sparrow *Spizella wortheni*	Very local, N. Mexico; possibly former resident in SW U.S.	1 rec: NM, Jun 16, 1884 (type specimen!)
Pine Bunting *Emberiza leucocephalos*	Siberia and N. China > Central Asia	2 recs: AK (Attu) (Oct–Nov)
Little Bunting *Emberiza pusilla*	N. Scandinavia and Siberia > Central Asia, N. India, and China	7 recs: W. and N. AK; 2 recs: CA (Aug–Oct)
Yellow-throated Bunting *Emberiza elegans*	China, Korea, and Japan > to Central China, Taiwan, and Burma	1 rec: Aleutians (Attu), May 25, 1998
Yellow-breasted Bunting *Emberiza aureola*	Widespread N. Eurasia > S. Asia	4 recs: AK: 3 Attu, 1 Gambell (May–Jun)
Gray Bunting *Emberiza variabilis*	Very local, NE Asia > Japan	2 recs: Aleutians (May)
Pallas's Bunting *Emberiza pallasi*	N. Siberia and Mongolia > mainly E. China and Japan	3 recs: AK (May–Jun)
Reed Bunting *Emberiza schoeniclus*	Widespread Eurasia > Old World Temperate Zone	6 recs: W. Aleutians
Crimson-collared Grosbeak *Rhodothraupis celaeno*	NE Mexico	8 confirmed recs: S. TX (6 from winter of 1987–88); also 1 (Jun–Jul)
Yellow Grosbeak *Pheuticus chrysopeplus*	W. Mexico and Guatemala	13 recs from SE AZ since 1971 (all but 1 Jun–Jul)
Blue Bunting *Cyanocompsa parellina*	Mexico–Nicaragua	21 confirmed recs from TX since 1980; 1 rec: LA (Oct–Apr)
Tawny-shouldered Blackbird *Agelais humeralis*	Cuba and Haiti	1 old rec: Key West, FL, Feb 27, 1936; also unconfirmed sight recs

Species	Native Distribution	Occurrence
Black-vented Oriole *Icterus wagleri*	Mexico–Nicaragua	2 recs: TX; 1 rec: AZ (Apr–Oct)
Common Chaffinch *Fringilla coelebs*	Widespread Eurasia > S. Eurasia and Middle East	Numerous northeast recs (Sep–May), some/most? probably valid; S. and W. recs more likely to be escapes
Common Rosefinch *Carpodacus erythrinus*	Widespread Eurasia > S. Asia	Many AK recs since 1974, mainly Aleutians, Pribilofs, Gambell (mainly May–Jun; also Aug–Sep [2])
Eurasian Siskin *Carduelis spinus*	Widespread N. Eurasia > to N. Africa	1 confirmed AK rec (Attu, May 1993); also many north-east recs, most suspected to be escaped cage birds
Oriental Greenfinch *Carduelis sinica*	E. Asia > southward	17 Aleutian recs since 1976; 1 rec: Pribilofs (May–Jun, Aug–Sep)
Eurasian Bullfinch *Pyrrhula pyrrhula*	Widespread Eurasia > S. Europe and temp. Asia	20 recs: AK (year-round)
Hawfinch *Coccothraustes coccothraustes*	Widespread Eurasia > southward	c 20 recs: AK, mainly Aleutians, Gambell, Pribilofs (May–Jun, Nov)

Alternative Phylogeny of North American Bird Families

(following Sibley and Monroe 1990, 1993 SYSTEMATICS)

Order CRACIFORMES
    Family Craciadae—Chachalacas
Order GALLIFORMES
    Family Phasianidae—Grouse, Turkeys, Pheasants, etc.
    Family Odontophoridae—New World Quails
Order ANSERIFORMES
    Family Dendrocygnidae—Whistling-Ducks
    Family Anatidae
      Subfamily Oxyurinae—Stiff-tailed Ducks
      Subfamily Cygninae—Swans
      Subfamily Anatinae
        Tribe Anserini—Geese
        Tribe Anatini—Typical Ducks
Order PICIFORMES
    Family Picidae—Woodpeckers
Order TROGONIFORMES
    Family Trogonidae—Trogons
Order CORACIIFORMES
    Family Cerylidae—American Kingfishers
Order CUCULIFORMES
    Family Coccyzidae—American Cuckoos
    Family Crotophagidae
      Tribe Crotophagini—Anis
Order PSITTACIFORMES
    Family Psittacidae—Parrots
Order APODIFORMES
    Family Apodidae—Typical Swifts
Order TROCHILIFORMES
    Family Trochilidae
      Subfamily Trochilinae—Typical Hummingbirds

Order STRIGIFORMES
    Family Tytonidae—Barn Owls
    Family Strigidae—Typical Owls
    Family Caprimulgidae
       Subfamily Chordeilinae—Nighthawks
       Subfamily Caprimulginae—Nightjars
Order COLUMBIFORMES
    Family Columbidae—Pigeons and Doves
 Order GRUIFORMES
    Family Gruidae
      Subfamily Gruinae—Typical Cranes
    Family Heliornithidae
        Tribe Aramini—Limpkin
    Family Rallidae—Rails, Gallinules and Coots
Order CICONIIFORMES
  Suborder CHARADRII
    Family Scolopacidae
       Subfamily Scolopacinae—Woodcock and Snipe
       Subfamily Tringinae—Sandpipers and Phalaropes
    Family Jacanidae—Jacanas
    Family Charadriidae
       Subfamily Recurvirostrinae
         Tribe Haematopodini—Oystercatchers
         Tribe Recurvirostrini—Avocets and Stilts
       Subfamily Charadrinae—Plovers and Lapwings
    Family Laridae
       Subfamily Larinae
         Tribe Stercorariini—Skuas and Jaegers
         Tribe Rhyncopini—Skimmers
         Tribe Larini—Gulls
         Tribe Sternini—Terns
       Subfamily Alcinae—Auks
  Suborder CICONII
    Family Accipitridae
       Subfamily Pandioninae—Osprey
       Subfamily Accipitrinae—Hawks and Eagles
    Family Falconidae—Caracaras and Falcons
    Family Podicipedidae—Grebes
    Family Phaethontidae—Tropicbirds
    Family Sulidae—Boobies and Gannets
    Family Anhingidae—Darters
    Family Phalacrocoracidae—Cormorants
    Family Ardeidae—Herons
    Family Phoenicopteridae—Flamingos

Family Threskiornithidae—Ibises and Spoonbills
Family Pelicanidae
   Subfamily Pelecaninae—Pelicans
Family Ciconiidae
   Subfamily Cathartinae—American Vultures
   Subfamily Ciconiinae—Storks
Family Fregatidae—Frigatebirds
Family Gaviidae—Loons
Family Procellariidae
   Subfamily Procellariinae—Petrels and Shearwaters
   Subfamily Diomedeinae—Albatrosses
   Subfamily Hydrobatinae—Storm-Petrels
Order PASSERIFORMES
  Suborder TYRANNI
   Family Tyrannidae
    Subfamily Pipromorphinae—Mionectine Flycatchers, Pygmy-Tyrants, and Tody-Tyrants
    Subfamily Tyranninae—Tyrant Flycatchers
    Subfamily Tityrinae
     Tribe Tityrini—Becards and Tityras
  Suborder PASSERI
   Family Laniidae—True Shrikes
   Family Vireonidae—Vireos and allies
   Family Corvidae
    Subfamily Corvinae
     Tribe Corvini—Crows, Jays, Magpies, etc.
   Family Bombycillidae
     Tribe Ptilogonatini—Silky Flycatchers
     Tribe Bombycillini—Waxwings
   Family Cinclidae—Dippers
   Family Muscicapidae
    Subfamily Turdinae—True Thrushes
    Subfamily Muscicapinae
     Tribe Muscicapini—Old World Flycatchers
     Tribe Saxicolini—Chats
   Family Sturnidae
     Tribe Sturnini—Starlings and Mynas
     Tribe Mimini—Mockingbirds and Thrushes
   Family Sittidae
    Subfamily Sittinae—Nuthatches
   Family Certhiidae
    Subfamily Certhiinae
     Tribe Certhiini—Northern Creepers
    Subfamily Troglodytinae—Wrens

Subfamily Polioptilinae—Gnatcatchers and Verdin
Family Paridae
  Subfamily Parinae—Titmice
Family Aegithalidae—Bushtits
Family Hirundinidae
  Subfamily Hirundininae—Swallows
Family Regulidae—Kinglets
Family Pycnonotidae—Bulbuls
Family Sylviidae
  Subfamily Acrocephalinae—Old World Warblers
  Subfamily Sylviinae
    Tribe Chamaeini—Wrentit
    Tribe Sylviini—*Sylvia* Warblers
Family Alaudidae—Larks
Family Passeridae
  Subfamily Passerinae—Passer Sparrows and Snowfinches
  Subfamily Motacillinae—Wagtails and Pipits
  Subfamily Prunellinae—Accentors
  Subfamily Ploceinae—Weavers and Bishops
Family Fringillidae
  Subfamily Fringillinae
    Tribe Fringillini—Chaffinch and Brambling
    Tribe Carduelini—Cardueline Finches
  Subfamily Emberizidae
    Tribe Emberizini—Emberizine Finches
    Tribe Parulini—Wood Warblers
    Tribe Thraupini—Tanagers, Neotropical Honeycreepers, Seed-
    eaters, and Flowerpiercers
    Tribe Cardinalini—Cardinal-Grosbeaks
    Tribe Icterini—New World Blackbirds

APPENDIX IV

Classification of Major Categories of Extinct Birds

(after Feduccia 1999–EVOLUTION OF BIRDLIFE)

Class Aves (Birds)
   Subclass Sauriurae ("lizard birds")
      Infraclass Archaeornithes ("ancient birds")
         Order Archaeopterygiformes
           Genus *Archaeopteryx* (Upper Jurassic, Germany)
         Order Confusiusornithiformes
           Genus *Confusiusornis* (Upper Jurassic, China)
      Infraclass Enantiornithes ("opposite birds")
         Order Sinornithoformes
           Genus *Sinornis* (Lower Cretaceous, China)
         Order Cathayornithiformes
           Genus *Cathayornis* (Lower Cretaceous, China)
         Order Iberomesornithiformes
           Genus *Iberomesornis,* etc. (Lower Cretaceous, Spain)
         Order Gobiterigyformes
           Genus *Gobiteryx,* etc. (Upper Cretaceous, Mongolia)
         Order Alexornithiformes
           Genus *Alexornis,* (Upper Cretaceous, Baja California)
         Order Enantiornithiformes
           Genus *Enantiornis,* etc. (Lower to Upper Cretaceous worldwide)
         Order Patagopterygiformes
           Genus *Patagopteryx,* Upper Cretaceous, Argentina)
   Subclass Ornithurae (all modern birds)
      Infraclass Odontornithes aka Odontoholcae ("toothed birds")
         Order Hesperionithiformes
           Genus *Baptornis* (Lower to Upper Cretaceous; probably worldwide)
           Genus *Hesperiornis* (Lower to Upper Cretaceous; probably worldwide)
      Infraclass Neornithes "recent birds"/True Birds aka Carinata ("keeled ones"); Lower Cretaceous to present.
         Superorder Ambiortimorphae

Order Abiortiformes

Genus *Ambiortus,* (Lower Cretaceous, Mongolia)

Order Icthyornithiformes

Genus *Icthyornis,* etc. (Upper Cretaceous, possibly world-wide)

Order Apatornithiformes

Genus *Apatornis* (Upper Cretaceous, North America)

Superorder Incertae Sedis

Order Gansuiformes

Genus *Gansus* (Lower Cretaceous, China)

Order Chaoyangiaformes

Genus *Chaoyangia* (Lower Cretaceous)

Superorder Paleognathae (Paleocene to present; includes living Ratites and Tinamous)

Order Lithornithiformes

Genus: *Lithornis,* etc. (Paleocene to Eocene, Europe and North America)

Order Remiornithiformes

Genus *Remiornis* (Upper Paleocene, France)

Superorder Neognathae (Upper Cretaceous to present; includes all Typical Birds living today)

Order Charadriiformes

Genus *Graclavus,* etc. the "transitional shorebirds" (Upper Cretaceous to Paleocene)

Order Gastornithiformes (or Diatrymiformes)

Genus *Diatryma,* etc. (Paleocene to Eocene, Europe and North America)

Order Sandcoliiformes

Genus *Sandcolius,* etc. Middle Eocene, Wyoming

APPENDIX V

Exotic Species

The list below contains nonnative species that have been seen in the wild in North America but are not generally regarded as fully naturalized or as having arrived here on their own as vagrants from their native ranges (noted in parentheses). Most are feral cage birds that have escaped from aviaries or pet owners. Many of the parrots on the list have bred at least once outside of captivity, but (with a couple of exceptions, noted below) are not considered "countable" members of the North American avifauna by the American Birding Association. For naturalized nonnative species, see Appendix I; for naturally occurring vagrants, see Appendix II. A few ambiguous cases appear in more than one list.

Scarlet Ibis, *Eudocimus ruber* (South America)
Black-necked Swan, *Cygnus melanocoryphus* (South America)
Black Swan, *Cygnus atratus* (Australia)
Swan (Chinese) Goose, *Anser cygnoides* (northern Asia)
Bar-headed Goose, *Anser indicus* (central Asia-India)
Ruddy Shelduck, *Tadorna ferruginea* (Eurasia and Africa)
Egyptian Goose, *Alopochen aegyptiacus* (Africa)
Mandarin Duck, *Aix galericulata* (northern Asia)
Black Francolin, *Francolinus francolinus* (Africa, W. Asia)
Red-legged Partridge, *Alectoris rufa* (Eurasia)
Common Peafowl, *Pavo cristatus* (S. Asia)
Golden Pheasant, *Chrysolophus pictus* (central China)
Helmeted Guineafowl, *Numida meleagris* (Africa)
Purple Swamphen, *Porphyrio porphyrio* (Old World)
Gray-necked Wood Rail, *Aramides cajanea* (Latin America)
Southern Lapwing, *Vanellus chilensis* (South America)
Sulphur-crested Cockatoo, *Cacatua galerita* (Australasia)
Cockatiel, *Nymphicus hollandicus* (Australia)
Budgerigar, *Melopsittacus undulatus* (Australia); included in the *ABA Checklist*, 6th edition (2002)
Rosy- (or Peach-) faced Lovebird, *Agapornis roseicollis* (SW Africa)
Masked Lovebird, *Agapornis personatus* (E. -C. Africa)
Rose-ringed Parakeet, *Psittacula krameri* (India and Africa)
Blossom-headed Parakeet, *Psittacula roseata* (southern Asia)
Chestnut-fronted Macaw, *Ara severa* (South America)
Blue-crowned Parakeet, *Aratinga acuticaudata* (South America)

Green Parakeet, *Aratinga holochlora* (Middle America; may occur natu-
rally in S. Texas included in the *ABA Checklist,* 6th edition, [2002])
Mitred Parakeet, *Aratinga mitrata* (Andes)
Red-masked Parakeet, *Aratinga erythrogenys* (W. South America)
Hispaniolan Parakeet, *Aratinga chloroptera* (Hispaniola)
Orange-fronted Parakeet, *Aratinga canicularis* (Middle America)
Dusky-headed Parakeet, *Aratinga weddellii* (South America)
Black-hooded (Nanday) Parakeet, *Nandayus nenday* (South America)
White-winged Parakeet, *Brotogeris versicolurus* (South America; included
in the *ABA Checklist,* 6th edition, 2002)
Yellow-chevroned Parakeet, *Brotogeris chiriri* (South America)
Orange-chinned Parakeet, *Brotogeris jugularis* (Latin America)
Hispaniola Parrot, *Amazona ventralis* (Hispaniola)
White-fronted Parrot, *Amazona albifrons* (Mexico and Central America)
Yellow-lored Parrot, *Amazona xantholora* (Yucatan, Cozumel Is., and Belize)
Red-crowned Parrot, *Amazona viridigenalis* (Mexico; may occur naturally
in S. Texas)
Lilac-crowned Parrot, *Amazona finschi* (W. Mexico)
Red-lored Parrot, *Amazona autumnalis* (Mexico to N. South America)
Blue-fronted Parrot, *Amazona aestiva* (South America)
Yellow-headed Parrot, *Amazona oratrix* (Mexico and Central America)
Yellow-naped Parrot, *Amazona auropalliata* (Central America)
Yellow-crowned Parrot, *Amazona ochrocephala* (Central and South
America)
Orange-winged Parrot, *Amazona amazonica* (South America)
Mealy Parrot, *Amazona farinosa* (Mexico to South America)
Ringed Turtle-Dove, *Streptopelia roseogrisea "risoria"* (Domesticated in
N. Africa)
Hill (Talking) Mynah, *Gracula religiosa* (Asia)
Orange Bishop, *Euplectes franciscanus* (Africa)
Java Sparrow, *Padda oryzivora* (Malaysia)
Common Waxbill, *Estrilda astrild* (Africa)
Spotted Munia (Nutmeg Mannikin), *Lonchura punctulata* (southern Asia)
Chestnut Munia, *Lonchura malacca* (southern Asia)
Troupial, *Icterus icterus* (South America)
Red-crested (Brazilian) Cardinal, *Paroaria coronata* (South America)
Yellow-fronted Canary, *Serinus mozambicus* (Africa) and captive-bred ca-
nary varieties)
European Goldfinch, *Carduelis carduelis* (Eurasia)

Birdwatcher's Calendar

Timing is very important in planning excursions to see particular bird species or avian events. The westerner wishing to experience an eastern warbler wave will be disappointed if he plans a visit to New England in April. Likewise New Englanders hoping to find a Colima Warbler at Big Bend may be disappointed if they arrive before the birds start singing. These and other temporal aspects of bird finding are addressed in the schedule below. It lists birding dates in three ways: by event (mainly migrations)—e.g., when best to see shorebird migrants on the Great Plains; by locality—e.g., when the greatest variety of species is to be found in Churchill; and by species—e.g., the period during which Kirtland's Warbler is singing on territory and thus is most easily located. Of course, the three categories overlap in numerous instances.

Fortunately, birding adventures cannot be planned with absolute precision. No one can predict on which days the best "waves" will hit the Texas coast in spring; you may arrive at the very peak of the puffin season at Machias Seal Island only to find that the birds are invisible behind a dense fog bank. "Fortunately" because without a strong element of chance the sport of birding would, like viewing historical monuments or visiting the zoo, lack the special piquancy of *la chasse*.

For locality information, see BIRD FINDING and the various specific locality entries listed on pp. xxiv–xxv.

PASSERINE MIGRATION (spring and fall). In general, the autumn passage of land birds tends to be more protracted than the spring. It involves greater numbers of individuals due to the addition of the young birds of the year, and it tends to contain a greater variety of species with a higher proportion of extralimital rarities in many localities (for the reason, see MIGRATION). Waves of warblers and other songbirds result from parallel patterns of weather fronts and migration that prevail only over eastern North America, and consequently waves do not occur regularly west of the foothills of the Rockies. Note: The dates given for migration periods are intended to encompass the time of greatest activity, not the much longer span between the arrival of the earliest migratory species and the departure of the latest.

Maritimes/New England: Late April to early June, with biggest waves usually between May 10 and June 1; most warblers, thrushes, etc., mid-August to mid-October; sparrows and other late migrants through early November, peaking in October.

Cape May (New Jersey): See under Localities, below.

Central South (North Carolina/Tennessee): Late March through early May; second week in September to early November.

Southern Florida: Late March to early May (peaks April); mid-September to early November.

Point Pelee (Ontario): See under Localities, below.

Gulf Coast (Texas/Louisiana): Spring migration much more spectacular than fall, especially when cold fronts from the north put down migrant flocks arriving from across Gulf of Mexico; first wave usually occurs late March; southern specialties (e.g., Swainson's Warbler) peak before April 15; greatest movement and best chance of waves between mid-April and first week in May; fall passage September to October.

Great Plains (Kansas/Nebraska): Spring passage more concentrated, spectacular; fall more diffuse. Scattered copses in prairie regions often harbor large concentrations of migrants. Second week in April to third week in May; late August to early November (main peaks September to October).

Central Rockies (Colorado): Spring peaks usually late April to early May; waves regular only in eastern foothills, but late snowstorms sometimes force down large numbers of migrants locally in mountains; eastern rarities and concentrations sometimes to late May; fall passage early September to early November.

Southern Arizona: Diffuse and unspectacular, without waves. Main movements April to May and August to September; note that many resident "Mexican" specialties do not arrive until mid-May or later.

Washington State: Generally unspectacular compared to East, without waves. Peaks mid-April to early June and mid-August to early October.

California: North-south migration generally diffuse and protracted, without waves. Bulk of passerines pass early April to mid-May and late August to early November. Much altitudinal movement of both highland species retreating from winter weather or returning to breeding areas and migrant wanderers. Concentrations may be encountered in foothills.

SHOREBIRD MIGRATION. Spring peaks generally parallel those of land-bird migration, but fall passage even more protracted than that of passerines, with first adult shorebirds returning from arctic breeding grounds only weeks after the last of the spring stragglers have moved north. Many species winter in part along southern coasts. Migratory concentrations of shorebirds occur continentwide.

New England/Maritimes: Late April through May and early July to early November with spectacular concentration of many common species in August and greatest species variety in September and early October.

Gulf Coast: Late March to early May (best numbers and variety in late March and April); August through October (best numbers and variety in September); many species overwinter.

Great Plains (Kansas/Nebraska): Late April to June 1 and early August to early October.

Central Rockies (Colorado): April to late May (peak late April to early May); late July to early October (peak August to September).

Washington State: Late April to June 1; fall passage peaks between late July and mid-September.

California Coast: Many species resident from mid-August to early May along southern coast; transients peak April to early May and late July through October.

WATERFOWL MIGRATION. The majority of North American swans, geese, and ducks breed in the northern half of the continent (many reaching the Arctic) and winter in the southern half. Some species migrate only far enough south to find open water (fresh or salt); others continue until they reach southern extremities of the United States or beyond. Peaks of waterfowl movements occur in early spring and late fall.

New England: Late March to late April and late September to mid-November. Most North American sea ducks species winter along the coast.

Great Plains (Kansas/Nebraska): Early March to mid-April and mid-October to early December (or earlier, depending on date of freeze-up).

Washington State: Late March to late April and mid-September to mid-November. Most North American sea and bay duck species winter along the coast.

Southern Half of United States: Most North American freshwater species are winter residents, many continentwide; some restricted to east, west, of Gulf coast.

HAWK MIGRATION. Peak numbers of hawks tend to pass earlier in the spring than the peaks of passerine or shorebird migrations. Thermal soarers (including cranes and pelicans as well as diurnal raptors) concentrate along mountain ridges, coastlines, land bridges, and other places offering favorable air conditions (see MIGRATION; FLIGHT). These conditions are not always present in a given locality in both spring and fall, and some hawk-watching points are therefore good only at one season or the other. The most spectacular movements often occur on only a few days during a season, and these events can never be precisely predicted. as with passerine migration, raptor passage seems to be more dispersed (therefore, less spectacular) in the West, but good new localities continue to be discovered and the spectacle has "improved" with better coverage.

For thorough accounts of North America hawk-watching areas, go to the Hawk Migration Association of North America's website: www.hmana.org.

New England/Great Lakes: Late March to mid-May (peaks in late April); September through mid-November (peak numbers mid to late-September).

Derby Hill (New York): Perhaps the most spectacular spring (peak in April) flight in the Northeast.

Hawk Mountain (Pennsylvania): See under Localities, below.

Cape May (New Jersey): See under Localities, below.

Florida Keys: Good to excellent flights recorded for Key West in October.

Rio Grande Valley: Peak numbers of Broad-winged and Swainson's Hawks late March to early April and September to October (much less spectacular). Because of the valley's generally flat terrain, movements are seen at many points over a wide front, but coastal concentrations occur from the Aransas area to the north, especially in the fall.

Utah (especially Wellsville Mountain near Logan): September to late October.

Pacific Northwest (British Columbia/Washington/Oregon): September to mid-October.

California (especially Mount Diablo and Mount Tamalpais [Point Diablo] near San Francisco): Mid-September to late October; spring flights are less impressive.

COASTAL WATERBIRD MIGRATION. This is essentially a phenomenon of coastal regions in the fall when large concentrations of loons, grebes, gannets, cormorants, sea ducks, pelagic gulls, and alcids stream southward to offshore or inshore wintering grounds. Since the winter ranges of most of these species are largely northerly, the number of birds involved diminishes to the south. The northward return of these birds in the spring tends to be more protracted and diffuse and thus far less spectacular in most places; however, see below. The phenomenon tends to be most rewarding when onshore gales push migrating birds toward the coast. Under these conditions, tubenoses, jaegers, and other pelagic species are often seen. Birders unaware of the joys of trying to distinguish species of loons or alcids while staring into the teeth of an ocean gale (see HARD CORE) are missing one of the great thrills of their sport; for details see SEA WATCHING.

Localities where this type of migration has traditionally been observed include southeastern Nova Scotia; several offshore islands in the Gulf of Maine; a few points along the Massachusetts coast (Rockport, Manomet, various localities on Cape Cod); Montauk Point, New York; Cape May, New Jersey; Cape Hatteras, North Carolina; Cape Flattery, Washington; and Point Reyes, California. In all of these places peaks for most species occur in October and November. An exception to the generality about the superiority of the fall coastal migration, St. Lawrence Island, Alaska, witnesses an excellent northward movement of the area's unique waterfowl and alcid species in May and early June—conveniently coinciding with the best period for finding Palearctic migrants and vagrants there.

PELAGIC BIRDS. Most tubenoses in North American waters are summer visitors from the Southern Hemisphere. Many of these species

arrive in early spring, but only far offshore (e.g., the spectacular concentrations of Greater Shearwaters present on the Grand Banks by May); however, they become more prevalent on the inner shoals in late summer and fall, when they are joined by arctic-breeding jaegers and phalaropes. Occurrence fluctuates radically with changes in the abundance and location of marine food sources.

North Atlantic: Outer banks (e.g., Grand and Georges) have good to great numbers of northbound pelagics (residents and visitors) late April to early June; inner shoals better in late summer (July on) and fall (through October; best variety in September). Alcids mid-November through early April.

Gulf Stream: Warm-water pelagic birding from the east coast has become popular in recent decades, due in part to the possibility of finding a few pelagic species "available nowhere else in North America." Though large concentrations do occur, it is in or near the Gulf Stream that North American birders have the best chance of seeing tropical visitors such as tropicbirds, boobies, various rare gadfly (*Pterodroma*) petrels, Audubon's Shearwater, and Bridled Terns. Seasonal bird distribution in these areas is still poorly understood, but pelagic trips off Florida and Cape Hatteras seem to have the best overall luck from midsummer to fall. If you can take the swell, you may have better than average variety in the Gulf Stream after southerly gales.

Washington State: Offshore birding can be very good at all seasons, but winter weather seldom allows access. Boats generally available late April through early October (hundreds of thousands of Sooty Shearwaters late August through September), and this coincides with the best birding, but heavy swells often prevail even in summer.

Southern California: Best numbers and variety mid-August through October; winter for alcids and Northern Fulmar. As in other areas, highly unpredictable.

VAGRANTS. Young birds tend to wander beyond their "normal" ranges after fledging, and many birds of the year lose their way while undertaking long-distance migrations (see VAGRANT). Migrants and seabirds are particularly vulnerable to strong winds and other unfavorable weather conditions. All of these phenomena have a recognizable seasonality and are most regular in certain localities.

Western North American Vagrants in the East: Late September through winter. Western vagrants of several species are routine in small numbers where migrants "pile up" on the east coast; some of these show up at feeding stations as the season progresses.

Eastern North American Vagrants in the West: Localities such as the Tijuana River valley, Death Valley (California), and other areas characterized by general barrenness relieved occasionally by isolated copses of vegetation where lost eastern forest species are forced to congregate are most

productive during migration in April and May; coastal areas (Farallon Islands, Monterey) are better in fall. Number and variety of vagrants fluctuate greatly from year to year.

Palearctic Vagrants in Alaska: Spring best overall, especially mid-May to mid-June. Fall more protracted, August to November, with shorebirds, warblers, and thrushes better earlier, finches and gulls later. The western Aleutians are more within Siberian-Asian migration patterns than North American-Neotropical ones, and many species once thought of as Palearctic vagrants are now known to be regular during the above periods. See Appendixes I and II.

West Indian Vagrants in Florida: Most prevalent August through November.

Neotropical Vagrants Along Mexican Border: Many occur in midsummer, though the intense heat of this season may discourage tenderfoot northern birders; summer rains cool things off in southern Arizona beginning in July; also fall and winter. Mexicans are very fond of keeping the more colorful or songful of their native species as cage birds; these can escape at any season.

LOCALITIES. Like the birding hot spots or regions described in the main text (see pp. xxiv–xxv), those listed alphabetically below are not necessarily the best in North America (though all are excellent); rather they are among the best *known.*

Alaska: See under Aleutian/Pribilof Bird Colonies and High Arctic, below, and under Vagrants, Palearctic, above. See also ALASKA.

Aleutian/Pribilof Bird Colonies: Activity best mid-May through August; many species resident in Alaskan waters year-round.

Arizona: Good year-round, but many resident specialties of the southern mountains do not arrive until mid-May and Mexican visitors tend to appear in July and August; April and early May are good for migrants, winter lingerers, and ideal weather. June is the hottest month, with summer rains beginning in July.

Cape May (New Jersey): Early August (Tree Swallows) to early December; passerines peak late September to early October; hawks early September to mid-November (peak numbers and variety around mid-October). Spring (late April to May) is not as varied or spectacular, but can be very exciting nonetheless.

Churchill (Manitoba): Earliest migrants (e.g., Snow Buntings) arrive late April; waterfowl begin to appear in numbers with first melts in late May; prime birding time is first two weeks in June, when bulk of high arctic migrants pass through, all resident species are in, and mosquitoes have not yet emerged in full force; unpredictable weather before June 15 sometimes makes for spectacular concentrations of "grounded" migrants. Adult shorebirds take off as early as mid-July and all ages are mostly gone by mid-August; passerine and waterfowl migration mid-August through

September. Wildflowers best late June and July. Polar bears begin to gather in mid-September and depart in November when Hudson Bay freezes over; though translocated wanderers can appear out of season.

Dry Tortugas (Florida): A few Sooty and Noddy Terns arrive in March, most not until mid-April, and Black Noddies and boobies (up to three species) best after mid-May; good through early September. See also FLORIDA.

Everglades (Florida): Most waterbirds and Snail Kite are present during the main tourist season, December 15 to April 15, and many (including the kite) are permanent residents. For seasonably specialties, see under Florida Keys, below; for migrants, see under Passerine Migration, above. See also FLORIDA.

Florida Keys: Most summer resident specialties present late March to September; see other Florida listings under Dry Tortugas and Everglades and under Passerine Migration, above. See also FLORIDA.

Hawk Mountain (Pennsylvania): First movement (Bald Eagle, Osprey) by late August; peak numbers mid to late September (usually around the 20th); best variety mid-October to mid-November.

High Arctic: Local conditions very variable, but, in general, mid-June to August 1 is peak time for resident specialties (many of which begin to head south around July 15) and for the often spectacular arctic wildflower display. In wet tundra areas mosquitoes often become a serious hindrance after mid to late June. For Alaska, see also under Vagrants and Aleutian/Pribilof Bird Colonies, above.

Northeastern Seabird Colonies (Bonaventure Island, Machias Seal Island, etc.): Birds arriving in most cases by late April, but mid-May to mid-August best for seeing birds onshore as well as offshore; other pelagic birding in adjacent waters improves in July.

Point Pelee (Ontario): Late April to early June (big waves usually mid-May); fall peaks in mid-September. See also PT. PELEE.

Rio Grande Valley (Texas): Good year-round, but some resident specialties do not arrive in Big Bend until May and Neotropical vagrants best in summer and fall. Midsummer temperatures often in excess of 100°F. April to May perhaps best all around for first visit; see also under Passerine Migration (Gulf Coast), above, and under Species, below. See also BIG BEND and RIO GRANDE VALLEY.

Rocky Mountains: June through early August for resident highland specialties (song best to early July); wildflowers best in June and July. See also under Passerine Migration and Shorebird Migration, above.

Southern California: Good birding and weather year-round. April to early May best for migrants and winter lingerers (April) and therefore perhaps best all around for first visit, since most specialties are permanent residents; August to November for fall vagrants; midsummer is the dullest season and many forested areas closed due to fire hazard.

Southern Florida: Mid-May best for seeing as many Florida special-ties as possible; however, see other Florida localities in this section, above, under Passerine Migration, above and under FLORIDA.

SPECIES. Virtually all bird species—even permanent residents—are more readily found at certain times of the year than at others. Those listed below are very local "target species" whose behavior or movements do not, however, fit within the schedules of migration or localities given above. Birders visiting Texas to see the spectacular coastal migration and the summer resident specialties, for example, will probably want to plan an itinerary that takes in the Whooping Cranes as Aransas National Wildlife Refuge before they depart in early April.

White-tailed Tropicbird (Bermuda): Resident mid-March through Oc-tober; birds disperse to sea in winter; may be absent for days at a time during cold spells in March and April; best seen inshore 8 a.m. to noon.

Sage Grouse: Displaying mainly March through early May.

Greater Prairie Chicken: Displaying March to May (April best) in Col-orado; December to May (early spring best) in Texas.

Lesser Prairie Chicken: Displaying March to May (April best).

Whooping Crane: On breeding grounds in Wood Buffalo National Park (Northwest Territories) from late April–early May until October; winter on Aransas National Wildlife Refuge near Rockport, Texas, from late October until early April.

Ross Gull: Irregular (sometimes impressive) passage of this species at Point Barrow, Alaska, in late September and October; Ivory Gulls have also occurred in this region at the same time. When breeding at Churchill, Manitoba, Ross' Gulls present continuously late June to early August.

Boreal Owl: Found with notable regularity in Toronto region in March.

Elegant Trogon: Most readily seen May through August; most vocal in May; a few (silent) birds remain through winter. For localities, see SOUTHEASTERN ARIZONA.

Colima Warbler: Singing late April to early June on Boot Springs Trail. See BIG BEND.

Golden-cheeked Warbler and Black-capped Vireo: Warbler present early March to late July; males sing mid-March to late June. Vireo arrives slightly later and does not depart until August (stragglers to September). See EDWARDS PLATEAU.

Kirtland's Warbler: Singing mid-May to mid-July. For localities, see ENDANGERED BIRDS.

BIBLIOGRAPHY

NOTE: *For comprehensive treatment of individual bird species and accompanying bibliographies, see Poole et al. (1992–*ORNITHOLOGY*). For species information on-line, see especially NatureServe Explorer at http://www.natureserve.org/explorer.*

ABNORMALITY

Buckley, P. A. 1973. Plumage aberrancies. *Am. Birds* 27:585.
Ellegren, H., Lindgren, G., Primmer, C. R., and Møller, A. P. 1997. Fitness loss and germline mutations in barn swallows breeding in Chernobyl. *Nature* 389:593–6.
Michener, H. 1936. Abnormalities in birds. *Condor* 38:102–9.
Nickell, W. P. 1965. Adaptive behavior under handicaps of several species of Michigan birds. *Wilson Bull.* 77:396–400.
Pomeroy, D. E. 1962. Birds with abnormal bills. *Br. Birds* 55:49–72.

ABUNDANCE

Aldrich, J. W., and Robbins, C. S. 1970. Changing abundance of migratory birds in North America. In *The Avifauna of Northern Latin America*, H. K. and J. H. Buechner, eds. Washington, DC.
Meanley, B., and Webb, J. S. 1965. Nationwide population estimates of blackbirds and starlings. *Atlantic Naturalist* 20:189–91.
Merikallio, E. 1958. *Finnish Birds, Their Distribution and Numbers.* Fauna Fennica no. 5. Helsinki.
Newton, I., ed. 1989. *Lifetime Reproduction in Birds.* New York.
Price, J., Droege, S., and Price, A. 1995. *The Summer Atlas of North American Birds.* London: Academic Press.
Ralph, C. J., and Scott, J. M., eds. 1981. *Estimating Numbers of Terrestrial Birds.* Studies in Avian Biology No. 6. Lawrence, KS: Cooper Ornithological Society.
Root, T. 1988. *Atlas of Wintering North American Birds: An Analysis of Christmas Bird Count Data.* Chicago: The University of Chicago Press.
See also Peterjohn (1994) and Robbins et al. (1986) under BREEDING BIRD SURVEY.

AGE

Bergstrom, E. A. 1956. Extreme old age in birds. *Bird-Banding* 27:128–9.
Fisher, H. L. 1975. Longevity of the Laysan albatross, *Diomedea immutabilis. Bird-Banding* 46:1–6.
Klimkiewicz, M. K. 2000. Longevity Records of North American Birds. Version 2000.1 Patuxent Wildlife Research Center, Bird Banding Laboratory, Laurel, MD. (See also sequence of papers by Clapp et al. and Klimkiewicz et al. in *J. Field Ornithol.* 1982–89.)
Rydzewski, W. 1962. Longevity of ringed birds. *Ring* 3:147–52.
Schumacher, D. M. 1964. Ages of some captive wild birds. *Condor* 66:309.
Tickell, W.L.N. 1968. *The Biology of the* Great *Albatrosses,* Diomedea exulans *and* D. epomophora. Am. Geophys. Union Antarc. Res. Ser., 12:1–55.

AGGRESSION

Andrew, R. J. 1957. Influence of hunger on aggressive behavior in certain buntings of the genus *Emberiza. Physiol. Zool.* 30:177–85.

Cottrille, B. D. 1950. Death of a Horned Lark in territorial combat. *Wilson Bull.* 62:134–5.

Dilger, W. C. 1956. Hostile behavior and reproductive isolating mechanisms in the thrush genera *Catharus* and *Hylocichla. Auk* 73:313–53.

Kilham, L. 1961. Aggressiveness of migrant Myrtle Warbler toward woodpeckers and other birds. *Auk* 78:261.

Mock, D. W. 1984. Infanticide, siblicide, and avian nestling mortality. In *Infanticide: Comparative and Evolutionary Perspectives,* G. Hausfater and S. Hrdy, eds. New York: Aldine, pp. 3–30.

ALBATROSS

Tickell, W.L.N. 2001. *Albatrosses.* New Haven, CT:
See also under SEABIRDS.

ALBINISM

Deane, R. 1876, 1878, 1879. Albinism and melanism among North American birds. *Bull. Nuttall Ornithol. Club,* Vols. 2, 3, and 5.

Gross, A. O. 1965. The incidence of albinism in North American birds. *Bird-Banding* 36:67–71.

Nero, R. W. 1954. Plumage aberrations of the Red-wing *(Agelaius phoeniceus). Auk* 71:137–55.

Sage, B. L. 1962. Albinism and melanism in birds. *Br. Birds* 55:201–22.

ALLEN'S RULE

James, F. C. 1983. Environmental component of morphological differentiation in birds. *Science* 221:184–6.

ALLOPREENING

Harrison, C.J.O. 1965. Allopreening as agonistic behavior. *Behavior* 24:161–209.

ALTITUDE

Black, C. P., and Tenney, S. M. 1980. Oxygen transport during progressive hypoxia in high-altitude and sea-level waterfowl. *Respir. Physiol.* 39:217–39.

Carpenter, F. L. 1975. Bird hematocrits: Effects of high altitude and strength of flight. *Comp. Biochem. Physiol.* 50A:415–7.

Eastwood, E., and Rider, G. C. 1965. Some radar measurements of the altitude of bird flight. *Br. Birds* 58:393–426.

Footman, T., ed. 2001. *Guinness World Records 2001.* New York, London, etc.

Jessen, T. H., Weber, R. E., Fermi, G., Tame, J., and Braunitzer, G. 1991. Adaptation of bird hemoglobins to high altitudes: Demonstration of molecular mechanisms by protein engineering. *Proc. Natl. Acad. Sci. USA* 88:6519–22.

Laybourne, R. C. 1974. Collision between a vulture and an aircraft at an altitude of 37,000 feet. *Wilson Bull.* 86:461–62.

Oberthür, W., Godova-Zimmerman, J., and Braunitzer, G. 1982. Hämoglobine, XLII. Das Hämoglobine der Streifengars (*Anser indicus*). Primärstructur und Physiologie der Amtung, Systematik und Evolution. *Hoppe-Seyler's Z. Physiol. Chem.* 363:581–90.

Swan, L. W. 1970. Goose of the Himalayas. *Nat. Hist.* 70:68–75.

Tucker, V. A. 1968. Respiratory physiology of House Sparrows in relation to high altitude flight. *J. Exp. Biol.* 48:55–66.

AMERICAN ORNITHOLOGISTS UNION (AOU)

Barrow, M. V., Jr. 1998. *A Passion for Birds: American Ornithology After Audubon.* Princeton, NJ.

ANI

Bolen, E. G. 1974. Factors affecting feeding rates of anis. *Auk* 70:26–30.

Rand, A. L. 1953. A note on the foraging behavior of Groove-billed Anis. *Bull. Texas Ornithol. Soc.* 7:8.

ANTING

Mayfield, H. 1966. Fire in birds' nests. *Wilson Bull.* 78:234–5.

Potter, E. F. 1970. Anting in wild birds, its frequency and probable purpose. *Auk* 87:692–713.

Potter, E. F., and Hauser, D. C. 1974. Relationship of anting and sunbathing to molting in wild birds. *Auk* 91:537–63.

Terres, J. K. 1962. Anting behavior of a Wood Thrush with a snail. *Wilson Bull.* 74:187.

Whitaker, L. M. 1957. A resume of anting, with particular reference to a captive Orchard Oriole. *Wilson Bull.* 69:195–262.

ARCTIC

Karplus, M. 1952. Bird activity in the continuous daylight of arctic summer. *Ecology* 33:129–34.

Salomonsen, F. 1972. Zoogeographical and ecological problems in arctic birds. *Proc. (XVth) Internatl. Ornithol. Congr.,* Leiden.

Snyder, L. L. 1957. *Arctic Birds of Canada.* Toronto.

ATLAS, BREEDING-BIRD

Andrle, R. F., and Carroll, J. R. 1988. *The Atlas of Breeding Birds in New York State.* Ithaca, NY: Cornell University Press.

Bevier, L. R. 1994. *The Atlas of Breeding Birds of Connecticut.* Hartford, CT: Department of Environmental Protection.

Brauning, D. W. 1992. *Atlas of Breeding Birds in Pennsylvania.* Pittsburgh, PA: University of Pittsburgh Press.

Buckelew, A. R., Jr., and Hall, G. A. 1994. *The West Virginia Breeding Bird Atlas.* Pittsburgh.

Busby, W. H. and Zimmerman, J. L. 2001. *Kansas Breeding Bird Atlas.* University Press of Kansas.

Castrale, J. S., Hopkins, E. M., and Keller, C. E. 1998. *Atlas of Breeding Birds of Indiana.* Indiana DNR.

Davis, W. E., Jr. 1997. Breeding bird atlases. *Birding* 29:194–205.

Erskine, A. J. 1992. *Atlas of Breeding Birds of the Maratime Provinces.* Chelsea Green.

Gauthier, J., and Aubry, Y., eds. 1996. *The Breeding Birds of Quebec: Atlas of the Breeding Birds of Southern Quebec.* Canadian Wildlife Service.

Gibbons, D. W., et al. 1993. *The New Atlas of Breeding Birds in Britain and Ireland: 1988–1991.* London.

Jackson, L. S., et al. 1996. *The Iowa Breeding Bird Atlas.* Des Moines.

Jacobs, B., and Wilson, J. D. 1997. Missouri Breeding Bird Atlas: 1986–1992. Jefferson City.

Kingery, H. E., ed. 1998. *Colorado Breeding Bird Atlas.* Denver.

Laughlin, S. B., and Kibbe, D. P., eds. (1985). *The Atlas of Breeding Birds of Vermont.* Hanover, NH: University Press of New England.

Mollhoff, W. J. 2001. *The Nebraska Breeding Bird Atlas:* 1984–89. Nebraska Game and Parks Commission.

Nicholson, C. P. 1997. *Atlas of the Breeding Birds of Tennessee.* Tennessee Ornithological Society.

North American Ornithological Atlas Committee (NORAC). 1990. *Handbook for Atlasing American Breeding Birds.* On-line at www.americanbirds.org/norac.

Palmer-Ball, B., Jr. 1996. *The Kentucky Breeding Bird Atlas.* University Press of Kentucky.

Peterson, R. A. 1995. *South Dakota Breeding Bird Atlas.* South Dakota Ornithologists' Union.

Petersen, W. R. and Meserve, R. W., eds. 2004. *Massachusetts Breeding Bird Atlas.* Lincoln, MA: Massachusetts Audubon Society.

Price, J., Droege, S., and Price, A. 1995. *The Summer Atlas of North American Birds.* London: Academic Press.

Robbins, C. S., and Blom, E.A.T. 1996. *Atlas of the Breeding Birds of Maryland and the District of Columbia.* Pittsburgh, PA: University of Pittsburgh Press.

Semenchuk, G. P. 1992. *The Atlas of Breeding Birds of Alberta.* Federation of Alberta Naturalists.

Root, T. 1988. *Atlas of Wintering North American Birds: An Analysis of Christmas Bird Count Data.* Chicago: The University of Chicago Press.

Sharrock, J.T.R. comp. 1976. *The Atlas of Breeding Birds in Britain and Ireland.* Berkhamsted, England.

Wiedenfeld, D. A., and Swan, M. M. 2000. *Louisiana Breeding Bird Atlas.* Baton Rouge.

AUDUBON

Audubon, J. J. 1831–39 (several subsequent editions). *Ornithological Biography: or an Account of the Habits of the Birds of the United States of America, Accompanied by Descriptions of the Objects Represented in the Work Entitled the Birds of America, and Interspersed with Delineations of American Scenery and Manners.* 5 vols. Edinburgh.

Audubon, M., ed. 1897. *Audubon and His Journals* (with notes by Elliott Coues). Reprinted New York, 1960. (Great historical interest.)

———— 1966. *The Original Water-color Paintings by John James Audubon for The Birds of America.* Intro. by M. B. Davidson. 2 vols. New York. (Reproductions of Audubon's actual paintings in 2 large volumes.)

———— 2000. *Birds of America.* New York: Welcome Rain. (Inexpensive edition with decent plates.)

Low, S. 1988. *An Index and Guide to Audubon's Birds of America.* New York: Abbeville Press.

Peterson, R.T., ed. 2003. *Audubon's Birds of America: The Audubon Society's Baby Elephant Folio*. New York: Abbeville Press.
Steiner, B. 2003. *Audubon Art Prints: A Collector's Guide to Every Edition*. University of Southern California.
Tyler, R., and Tyler, R. C. 1993. *Audubon's Great National Work: The Royal Octavo Edition of the Birds of America*. Austin, TX.

AUK

Gaston, A. J. and Jones, I. L. 1998. *The Auks:Alcidae*. Oxford, UK.
Lockley, R. M. 1953. *Puffins*. New York.
Tuck, L. M. 1961. *The Murres: Their Distribution, Populations, and Biology*. Canadian Wildlife Serv. Ser. no. 1. Ottawa.
See also references under SEABIRD.

AVICULTURE

See under CAPTIVITY, BIRDS IN.

BAIRD

Baird, S. F., Cassin J., and Lawrence, G. N. 1859. *The Birds of North America*. Philadelphia.
Baird, S. F., Brewer, T. M., and Ridgway, R. 1874 and 1884. *A History of North American Birds*. (Land Birds and Water Birds, 5 vols.) Boston.
Rivinius, E. F., and Youssef, E. M. 1992. *Spencer Baird of the Smithsonian*. Washington, DC: Smithsonian Institution Press.

BANDING

Bub, H. 1991. *Bird Trapping and Bird Banding: A Handbook For Trapping Methods All Over the World*. Ithaca, NY.
Dill, H. H., and Thornsberry, W. H. 1950. A cannon-projected net trap for capturing waterfowl. *J. Wildlife Management* 14:132–7.
MacPherson, H. A. 1897. *History of Fowling: An Account of Devices for Capturing Wild Birds*. Edinburgh.
Thompson, M. C., and DeLong, R. L. 1967. The use of cannon and rocket-projected nets for trapping shorebirds. *Bird-Banding* 38:214–8.
For bird banding history and how-to, see web sites in BANDING entry.

BATHING

Dow, D. D. 1971 Avian bathing behaviour. *West. Aust. Nat.* 11:184–6.
Slessers, M. 1970. Bathing behavior of land birds. *Auk* 87:91–9.

BECARD

Lanyon, S. M. 1985. Molecular perspective on higher-level relationships in the Tyrannidae (Aves). *Syst. Zool.* 34:404–18.

Prum, R. O., and Lanyon, W. E. 1989. Monophyly and phylogeny of the *Schiffornis* group (Tyrannoidea). *Condor* 91:444–61.

BENT

Taber, W. 1955. In memoriam: Arthur Cleveland Bent. *Auk* 72:332–9.

BERGMANN'S RULE

James, F. C. 1983. Environmental component of morphological differentiation in birds. *Science* 221:184–6.
Kendeigh, S. C. 1969. Tolerance of cold and Bergmann's rule. *Auk* 86:13–25.

BIOGRAPHY

Choate, E. A., and R. A. Paynter. 1985. *The Dictionary of Bird Names.* Boston.
Gruson, E. S. 1972. *Words for Birds.* New York.
Hanley, W. 1977. *Natural History in America from Mark Catesby to Rachel Carson.* New York.
Hume, E. E. 1942. *Ornithologists of the United States Army Medical Corps.* Baltimore.
Palmer, T. S., et al. 1954. *Biographies of Members of the American Ornithologists' Union.* Washington, DC.
Welker, R. H. 1955. *Birds and Men.* Cambridge, MA.

BIOLOGY

Mayr, E. 1997. *This Is Biology: The Science of the Living World.* Cambridge, MA: Harvard University Press.

BIOME

Barbour, M. G., and Billings, W. D., Eds. 1988. *North American Terrestrial Vegetation.* Cambridge, UK: Cambridge University Press.

BIRD

Amadon, D. 1966. *Birds Around the World: A Geographical Look at Evolution and Birds.* New York.
Austin, O. L., Jr., and Singer, A. 1971. *Families of Birds.* New York.
Campbell, B., and Lack, E. 1985. A *Dictionary of Birds.* Vermillion, SD.
Fisher, J. 1954. *A History of Birds.* Boston.
Fisher, J., and Peterson, R. T. 1964. *The World of Birds.* New York.
Peterson, R. T. 1977. *The Birds.* Morristown, NJ.
Terres, J. K. 1980. *The Audubon Society Encyclopedia of North American Birds.* New York.
Wetmore, A., et al. 1937. *The Book of Birds.* Washington, DC. (Illustr. by Allan Brooks.)
See also under BIRDWATCHING and ORNITHOLOGY for general references.

BIRD CALLS

Tucker, J. 1978. Swishing and squeaking. *Birding* 10:83–7.

BIRD FEEDING

Barber, M. A., and Griggs, J. 2000. *The Feeder Watchers' Guide to Bird Feeding.* New York (sponored by the Cornell Lab).

Dunn, E. H., and Tessaglia-Hymes, D. L. 1999. *Birds at Your Feeder.* New York.

Geis, A. D. 1980. *Relative Attractiveness of Different Foods at Wild Bird Feeders.* U.S. Fish and Wildlife Serv. Spec. Sci. Rept. C Wildlife, no. 233. Washington, DC.

Harrison, G. H. 1988. *The Backyard Bird Watcher.* New York.

Stokes, D. W. and Stokes, L. Q. 1987. *The Bird Feeder Book.* Boston.

———1991. *The Bird Gardening Book.* Boston.

BIRD FINDING

Guides to regions of North America and to states and provinces are listed alphabetically below by place name. Many of these guides are in the excellent series pioneered by Jim Lane and now edited and published by the American Birding Association. Guides for localities below the state/provincial level are now so numerous that it is impractical to list them all here.

For "wired" bird finding, see RARE BIRD ALERT, *and visit the ABA website (www.americanbirding.org) for compilations of hot lines and listservs.*

North America

Alden, P. C., and Gooders, J. 1981. *Finding Birds Around the World.* Boston. (14 North American localities.)

Cooper, J. A. 1995. *Birdfinder: A Birder's Guide to Planning North American Trips.* ABA, Colorado Springs

Heintzelman, D. S. 1979. *A Guide to Hawk Watching in North America.* University Park, PA. See also HAWKWATCHING for "hawk-finding" web site.

Lehman, P. E., comp., 2002. *A Birder's Guide to Metropolitan Areas of North America.* **ABA,** Colorado Springs.

Pettingill, O. S., Jr. 1977. *A Guide to Bird Finding East of the Mississippi,* 2nd ed. Boston; 1980. *A Guide to Bird Finding West of the Mississippi,* 2nd ed. Boston. (Dated but still useful for "the big picture.")

Stirling, D., and Woodford, J. 1975. *Where to Go Bird Watching in Canada.* Saanichton, BC.

Zimmer, K. J. 2000. *Birding in the American West: A Handbook.* Ithaca, NY: Cornell University Press.

Alabama

Porter, J. F., Jr., ed. 2001. *A Birder's Guide to Alabama.* University of Alabama Press.

Vaughan, R. 1994. *Birder's Guide to Alabama and Mississippi* Houston.

Alaska

West, G. C. *A Birder's Guide to Alaska.* 2002. **ABA**, Colorado Springs.

Arizona

Taylor, R. C. 1995. *A Birder's Guide to Southeastern Arizona.* **ABA**, Colorado Springs.

Arkansas

White, M. 1995. *A Birder's Guide to Arkansas.* **ABA**, Colorado Springs.

British Columbia

Aitchison, C. J., ed. 2001. *The Birder's Guide to Vancouver and the Lower Mainland.* Vancouver Natural History Society, Vancouver.

California
Kemper, J. 1999. *Birding Northern California.* Guilford, CT.
Schram, B. 1998. *A Birder's Guide to Southern California.* **ABA,** Colorado Springs.

Colorado
Holt, H. R. 1997. *A Birder's Guide to Colorado.* **ABA,** Colorado Springs.

Connecticut
Devive, B., and D. G. Smith. 1996. *Connecticut Birding Guide.* Thomson-Shora.
Rosgen, D., and G. Billings. 1996. *Finding Birds in Connecticut.* Vancouver, BC.

District of Columbia
Wilds, C. 1992. *Finding Birds in the National Capital Area.* Washington, DC.

Florida
Pranty, B. 1996. *A Birder's Guide to Florida.* **ABA,** Colorado Springs.

Georgia
Beaton, G. 2000. *Birding Georgia.* Guilford, CT.

Illinois
Carpenter, L., and J. Greenberg 1999. *A Birder's Guide to the Chicago Region.*
    DeKalb, IL.
De Vore, S. 2000. *Birding Illinois.* Guilford, CT.

Kansas
Zimmerman, J. L., and S. T. Patti. 1988. *A Guide to Bird Finding in Kansas and
    Western Missouri.* Lawrence, KS.

Maine
Pierson, E. C., Pierson, J. E., and Vickery, P. D. 1996. *A Birder's Guide to Maine.*
    Campden.

Manitoba
Chartier, B. 1994. *A Birder's Guide to Churchill.* **ABA,** Colorado Springs.
Manitoba Naturalists Society. 1988. *Birder's Guide to Southeastern Manitoba.*

Massachusetts
Bird Observer. 1994. *A Birder's Guide to Eastern Massachusetts.*

Minnesota
Eckert, K. 2002. *A Birder's Guide to Minnesota,* 4th ed. Williams.
Strangis, J. M. 1996. *Birding Minnesota.* Guilford, CT.

Mississippi
Vaughan, R. 1994. *Birder's Guide to Alabama and Mississippi.* Houston.

Missouri
Palmer K., and Palmer, B., eds. 2001. *A Guide to Birding in Missouri.* Audubon So-
    ciety of Missouri.

Montana
McEneaney, T. 1993. *Birding Montana.* Guilford, CT.

Nevada
Titus, C. K. 1991. *Southern Nevada Birds: A Seekers Guide.* Redrock Audubon Society.

New Brunswick
Burrows, R. 1992. *Birding in Atlantic Canada: Acadia.* Jespersen Press.

Newfoundland
Burrows, R. 1989. *Birding in Atlantic Canada. Newfoundland.* Jespersen Press.

New Hampshire
Delorey, A. 1996. *A Birder's Guide to New Hampshire.* **ABA,** Colorado Springs.

New Jersey
Boyle, W. J., Jr. 2002. *A Guide to Bird Finding in New Jersey.* Camden, NJ.

New Mexico
Parmeter, J., Neville, B., and Emkaus, D. 2002. *New Mexico Birdfinding Guide,* 3rd ed. New Mexico Ornithological Society.

New York
Drennan, S. R. 1981. *Where to Find Birds in New York State.* Syracuse.
Fowle, M. T., and Kerlinger, P. 2001. *The New York City Audubon Society Guide to Finding Birds in the Metropolitan Area.* Ithaca.

North Carolina
Fussel, J. L., III. 1994. *A Birder's Guide to Coastal North Carolina.* Chapel Hill.

Nova Scotia
Cohrs, J. S., ed. 1991. *Birding Nova Scotia.* Nova Scotia Bird Society.

Ohio
Thompson, T. 1994. *Birding in Ohio,* (2nd ed.) Bloomington.

Ontario
Goodwin, C. E. 1995. *A Bird-Finding Guide to Ontario.* University of Toronto Press, Toronto.

Pennsylvania
Ford, P. 1995. *Birder's Guide to Pennsylvania.* Houston.

Texas
Holt, H. 1993. *A Birder's Guide to the Texas Coast.* **ABA,** Colorado Springs.
Lockwood, M., Paton, J., Zimmer, B., and McKinney, W. B. 1999. *A Birder's Guide to the Rio Grande Valley of Texas.* **ABA,** Colorado Springs.

Utah
McIvor, D. E. 1998. *Birding Utah.* Guilford, CT.

Virginia
Johnston, D. W. 1997. *A Birder's Guide to Virginia.* **ABA,** Colorado Springs.
Simpson, M. B., Jr. 1992. *Birds of the Blue Ridge Mountains.* Chapel Hill.

Washington
Morse, B. 2001. *A Birder's Guide to Coastal Washington.* R. W. Morse.
Wahl, T. R., and Paulson, D. R. 1991. *A Guide to Bird Finding in Washington.* Seattle Audubon Society, Seattle.

West Virginia
Bullard, J. W., ed. 1999. *Birding Guide to West Virginia.* Brooks Bird Club.

Wyoming
Scott, O. K. 1993. *A Birder's Guide to Wyoming.* **ABA,** Colorado Springs.

BIRDHOUSE

Jackson, J. A., and Tate, J. Jr., 1974. An analysis of nest box use by Purple Martins House Sparrows and Starlings in eastern North America. *Wilson Bull,* 86:435–45.
Kale, H. W., II. 1968. The relationship of Purple Martins to mosquito control. *Auk* 85:654–61.

MacNeil, D. 1979. *The Birdhouse Book.* Seattle.
Pushel, B. 1981. The bluebird house that Bauldry built. *Birding* 13:14–5.
Semel, B., Sherman, P. W., and Byers, S. M. 1988. Effects of brood parasitism and nest-box placement on Wood Duck breeding ecology. *Condor* 90:920–30.
Stokes, D. W., and L. Q. Stokes. 1990. *The Bird House Book.* Boston.

BIRDING EVENTS

Gill, F. B., and LeBaron, G. S., eds. 2000. *American Birds: One-hundredth Christmas Bird Count:* National Audubon Society. (A collection of articles on various aspects of the CBC on its centennial.)
Peterson, R. T. 1955. The Christmas count. *Audubon* 57:52–3, 64–5.
Root, T. 1988. *Atlas of Wintering North American Birds: An Analysis of Christmas Bird Count Data.* Chicago: The University of Chicago Press.

BIRD SKIN

Anderson, R. M. 1965. *Methods of Collecting and Preserving Animals.* Natl. Mus. Can. Bull. no 69. Biol. Ser. no. 18.
Coues, E. 1890. Field ornithology. Part I of *Key to North American Birds,* rev. ed., p. 28.
Johnson, N. K., Zink, R. M., Barrowclough, G. F., and Marten, J. A. 1984. Suggested techniques for modern avian systematics. *Wilson Bull.* 96:543–60.
Longmore, N. W., and Boles, W. E. 1990. A method of combined skin-fluid specimen preparation. *Auk* 107:788–9.

BIRDWATCHING

Allen, R. P. 1957. *On the Trail of Vanishing Birds.* New York.
Brandt, H. 1940. *Texas Bird Adventures.* Cleveland, OH.
Butcher, G. 1996. 1994 ABA membership survey (review). *Winging It.*
Chapman, F. M. 1933. *Autobiography of a Birdlover.* New York.
Connor, J. 1991. *Season at the Point: The Birds and Birders of Cape May.* New York: The Atlantic Monthly Press.
Cordell, H. K., and Herbert, N. G. 2002. The popularity of birding is still growing. *Birding.* Feb. 2002.
Cordell, H. K., Herbert, N. G., et al. 1999. The growing popularity of birding in the United States. *Birding* 31:168–176.
Dunne, P. 1986. *Tales of a Low-Rent Birder.* New Brunswick, NJ: Rutgers University Press.
Dunne, P. 1992. *The Feather Quest: A North American Birder's Year.* New York: Dutton.
Dunne, P. 2003. *Pete Dunne on Birdwatching.* Boston.
Eubanks, T., Kerlinger, P., and Payne, R. H. 1993. High Island, Texas: A case study in avitourism. *Birding* 25:415–20.
Fisher, J. 1951. *Watching Birds,* rev. ed. Harmondsworth, England. (Classic)
Hickey, J. J. 1943. *A Guide to Birdwatching.* New York. (Classic)
Hochbaum, H. A. 1955. *Travels and Traditions of Waterfowl.* Minneapolis.
Hudson, W. H. 1918. *Far Away and Long Ago.* New York. (Classic)
Huxley, J. S. 1934. *Bird-watching and Bird Behavior.* London.
Kaufman, K. 1997. *Kingbird Highway: The Story of a Natural Obsession That Got a Little Out of Hand.* Boston: Houghton Mifflin.

Kerlinger, P., and Wiedner, D. 1990. Economics of birding: A national survey of active birders. *Am. Birds* 44:209–213.

Kim, et al. 1998. Economic impact of a birding festival. *Festival Management and Event Tourism* 5:51–8.

Matthiessen, P. 1973. *The Wind Birds.* New York.

Matthiessen, P. 2001. *Travels with Cranes.* (Illustrated by Robert Bateman). New York.

Murphy, R. C. 1947. *Logbook for Grace.* New York. (Classic)

Nice, M. M. 1939. *The Watcher at the Nest.* New York.

Oddie, B. 1980. *Bill Oddie's Little Black Bird Book.* London.

Peterson, R. T. 1948. *Birds Over America.* New York. (Classic)

———, ed. 1957. *The Bird Watcher's Anthology.* New York. (Classic)

Peterson, R. T., and Fisher, J. 1955. *Wild America.* Boston. (Classic)

Richards, A. J. 1980. *The Birdwatcher's A–Z.* London.

Scott, P., and Fisher, J. 1954. *A Thousand Geese.* Boston. (Classic)

Snetsinger, P. 2003. *Birding on Borrowed Time.* Colorado Springs.

Stokes, D. N., and L. Q. Stokes 1979–89. *A Guide to Bird Behavior,* Vols. 1–3. Boston.

United States Department of the Interior. 1993. *The 1991 National Survey of Fishing, Hunting and Wildlife-Associated Recreation.* U.S. Fish and Wildlife Service, Washington, DC.

Wauer, R. H. 1991. Profile of an ABA birder. *Birding* 2 3:146–54.

BLACKBIRD (ICTERIDAE)

Jaramillo, A., and P. Burke. 1999. *New World Blackbirds: The Icterids.* Princeton, NJ.

Lanyon, W. E. 1957. *The Comparative Biology of the Meadowlarks* (Sturnella) *in Wisconsin.* Nuttall Ornithol. Club Publ. no. 1. Cambridge, MA.

Orians, G. H. 1961. The ecology of blackbird (*Agelaius*) social systems. *Ecol. Monogr.* 31:285–312.

BLUEBIRD

Sauer, J. R., and Droege, S. 1990. Recent population trends of the Eastern Bluebird. *Wilson Bull.* 102:239–52.

Stokes, D. W., and L. Q. Stokes. 1991. *The Bluebird Book.* Boston.

BOOBY

Kepler, C. B. 1969. *Breeding Biology of the Blue-footed Booby.* Nuttall Ornithol. Club Publ. no. 8.

Nelson, J. B. 1970. The relationship between behavior and ecology in the Sulidae with reference to other seabirds. *Oceanogr. Marine Biol.,* 8:501–74.

———. 1978. *The Gannet.* Vermillion, SD.

See also references under SEABIRD.

BREEDING BIRD SURVEY

Peterjohn, B. 1994. The North American Breeding Bird Survey. *Birding* 26(6):386–98.

Robbins, C. S., Bystrak, D., et al. 1986. *The Breeding Bird Survey: Its First Fifteen Years, 1965–1979.* Washington, DC.

BREEDING SEASON

Crick, H.Q.P., Dudley, C., Glue, D. E., and Thomson, D. L. 1997. UK birds are laying eggs earlier. *Nature* 388:526.

Kuroda, N. 1960. Notes on the breeding season in the Tubinares (Aves). *Jpn. Zool.* 12:449–64.

Orians, G. H. 1960. Autumnal breeding in the Tricolored Blackbird. *Auk* 77:379–98.

Thomas, C. D., and Lennon, J. J. 1999. Birds extend their ranges northwards. *Nature* 399:213.

BREWSTER

Brewster, W. 1906. *Birds of the Cambridge Region.* Memoirs of the Nuttall Ornith. Club no. 4. Cambridge, MA.

———. 1936. *October Farm.* Cambridge, MA. (Classic)

BROOD PARASITISM

Davies, N. 2000. *Cuckoos, Cowbirds and Other Cheats.* New York.

Friedmann, H. 1930. Social parasitism in birds. *Smithsonian Rep.* 1929, pp. 385–95.

———. 1964. The history of our knowledge of avian brood parasitism. *Centaurus* 10:282–304.

Many other titles on brood parasitism by the same author, especially 1948, 1955, 1960, and under COWBIRD.

Gibbs, H. L., Sorenson, M. D., Marchetti, K., Brooke, M.D.L., Davies, N. B., and Nakamura, H. 2000. Genetic evidence for female host-specific races of the common cuckoo. *Nature* 407:183–6.

Hamilton, W. J., III, and Orians, G. H. 1965. Evolution of brood parasitism in altricial birds. *Condor* 67:361–82.

Keith, L. B. 1961. Parasitic egg laying by ducks. *Auk* 78:93.

Lanyon, S. M. 1992. Interspecific brood parasitism in blackbirds (Icterinae): A phylogenetic perspective. *Science* 255:77–79.

Marchetti, K., Nakamura, H., and Gibbs, H. L. 1998. Host-race formation in the common cuckoo. *Science* 282:471–2.

Nolan, V., Jr., and Thompson, C. F. 1975. The occurrence and significance of anomalous reproductive activities in two North American non-parasitic cuckoos *Coccyzus,* spp. *Ibis* 117:496–503.

Post, W., and Wiley, J. W. 1977. Reproductive interactions of the Shiny Cowbird and the Yellow-shouldered Blackbird. *Condor* 79:176–84.

Rothstein, S. I., and Robinson, S. K., eds. 1998. *Parasitic Birds and Their Hosts: Studies in Coevolution.* Oxford, UK: Oxford University Press.

Smith, N. G. 1968. The advantage of being parasitized. *Nature* 219:690–4.

Weller, M. W. 1959. Parasitic egg laying in the Redhead (*Aythya americana)* and other North American Anatidae. *Ecol. Monogr.* 29:333–65.

———. 1968. The breeding biology of the parasitic Black-headed Duck. *Living Bird,* 7th annual, pp. 169–207.

See also under COWBIRD.

BUNTING

Klicka, J., Fry, A. J., et al. 2001. A cytochrome-*b* perspective on *Passerina* bunting relationships. *Auk* 118:611–23.

BURSA OF FABRICIUS

Glick, B. 2000. Immunophysiology. In *Sturkie's Avian Physiology,* G. C. Whittow, ed., New York, pp.657–70.
Gower, C. 1939. The use of the bursa of Fabricius as an indication of age in game birds. Trans. (4th) N. Am. *Wildlife* Conf, pp. 426–30.

BUSHTIT

Sheldon, F. H., and Gill, F. B. 1996. A reconsideration of songbird phylogeny with emphasis on the evolution of titmice and their sylvioid relatives. *Syst. Biol.* 45:473–95.

CANNIBALISM

Ingram, C. 1959. The importance of juvenile cannibalism in the breeding biology of certain birds of prey. *Auk* 76:218–26.
Mock, D. W. 1984. Infanticide, siblicide, and avian nestling mortality. In *Infanticide: Comparative and Evolutionary Perspectives,* G. Hausfater and S. Hrdy, eds. New York, pp. 3–30.
Mock, D. W., and Parker, G. A. 1997. *The Evolution of Sibling Rivalry.* Oxford, UK: Oxford University Press.
Parsons, L. 1971. Cannibalism in Herring Gulls. *Br. Birds,* 64:528–37.

CAPE MAY

Connor, J. 1991. *Season at the Point: The Birds and Birders of Cape May.* New York: The Atlantic Monthly Press.
Sibley, D. A. 1993. *The Birds of Cape May.* Cape May, NJ: Cape May Bird Observatory, New Jersey Audubon Society.
Stone, W. 1937. *Bird Studies at Old Cape May.* 2 vols. *Proc. Delaware Valley Ornithol. Club.* Philadelphia. (Classic)

CAPTIVITY, BIRDS IN

Bessinger, S. R., Snyder, N.F.R., Derrickson, S. R., James, F. C. and Lanyon, S. M. 1991. International trade in live, exotic birds creates a vast movement that must be halted. *Auk* 108:982–4.
Nilsson, G. 1980. *The Bird Business: A Study of the Importation of Birds into the United States.* Washington, DC.
Nilsson, G. 1990. *Importation of Birds into the United States in 1986–1988.* Washington, DC.
Rutgers, A., and Norris, K. A. 1970. *Encyclopedia of Aviculture.* London. (All birds known to be kept by humans, treated by family.)

CARACARA

Dove, C. J., and Banks, R. C. 1999. A taxonomic study of Crested Caracaras (Falconidae). *Wilson Bull.* 111:330–9.

CARDINAL-GROSBEAK

Klicka, J., Fry, A. J., Zink, R. M., and Thompson, C. W. 2001. A cytochrome *b* perspective on *Passerina* bunting relationships. *Auk* 118:611–23.
Tamplin, J. W., Demastes, J. W., et al. 1993. Biochemical and morphometric relationships among some members of the Cardinalidae. *Wilson Bull.* 105:93–113.

CATESBY

Catesby, M. 1731–43 (Appendix 1748). *The Natural History of Carolina, Florida, and the Bahama Islands, Containing the Figures of Birds, Beasts, Fishes, Serpents, Insects, and Plants.* 2 vols. London.
See also in Hanley (1977–BIOGRAPHY).

CENSUS

Dobinson, H. M. 1976. *Bird Count: A Practical Guide to Bird Surveys.* New York.
Mikol, S. A. 1980. *Guidelines for Using Transects to Sample Non-Game Bird Populations.* Rept. of Office of Biological Services, U.S. Fish and Wildlife Service. Washington, DC.
Ralph, C. J., and Scott, J. M., eds. 1981. *Estimating Numbers of Terrestrial Birds.* Studies in Avian Biology No. 6. Lawrence, KS: Cooper Ornithological Society.
See also under ATLAS and BREEDING BIRD.

CHACHALACA

Delacour, J., and Amadon, D. 1973. *Curassows and Related Birds.* New York.

CHAPMAN

Chapman, F. M. 1930. *Handbook* of *Birds* of *Eastern North America.* New York.
———. 1933. *Autobiography of a Birdlover.* New York.

CHECKLIST

American Birding Association. 2002 *A.B.A. Checklist: Birds of Continental United States and Canada,* 6th ed. Colorado Springs.
American Ornithologists' Union. 1983. *Check-list of North American Birds.* Washington, DC: American Ornithologists' Union.
American Ornithologists' Union. 1998. *Check-list of North American Birds.* Washington, DC: American Ornithologists' Union.
American Ornithologist's Union. 2000. Forty-second supplement to the American Ornithologist's Union *Check-list of North American Birds. Auk* 117:847–58.
Clements, J. F. 2000. *Birds of the World: A Checklist.* Temecula, CA: Ibis.
Howard, R., and Moore, A. 1991. *A Complete Checklist of the Birds of the World,* (3rd ed.) San Diego.
Kessel, B., and Gibson, D. D. 1978. Studies and distribution of Alaskan birds. *Studies in Avian Biology,* no. 1. Cooper Ornithol. Soc. Berkeley.
Monroe, B. L., Jr., and Sibley, C. G. 1993. *A World Checklist of Birds.* New Haven, CT.
Peters, J. L., et al. 1931–86. *Checklist of Birds of the World.* Cambridge, MA.
Phillips, A. R. 1986. *The Known Birds of North and Middle America, Part I.* Denver, CO: Published by the author.

Phillips, A. R. 1991. *The Known Birds of North and Middle America, Part II.* Denver, CO: A. R. Phillips.
Sibley, C. G., and Monroe, B. L., Jr. 1990. *Distribution and Taxonomy of the Birds of the World* and *Supplement,* 1993. New Haven, CT: Yale University Press.
NOTE: A wide range of state and regional bird checklists in various formats are available through the American Birding Association and other organizations that specialize in birding supplies. Listing software is also widely available in a number of formats.

CHRISTMAS COUNT

See under BIRDING EVENTS.

CIRCADIAN RHYTHM

Gwinner, E. 1975. Circadian and circannual rhythms in birds. In *Avian Biology,* Vol. 4, D. S. Farner et al. eds. New York.
Gwinner, E., and Hau, M. 2000. The pineal gland, circadian rhythms, and photoperiodism. In *Sturkie's Avian Physiology,* G. C. Whittow, ed., New York, pp. 557–68.
Meier, A. H., and Russo, A. C. 1985. Circadian organization of the avian annual cycle. *Curr. Ornithol.* 2:303–43.
See also under PHOTOPERIODISM.

CIRCULATORY SYSTEM

Jones, D. R., and Johansen, K. 1972. The blood vascular system of birds. In *Avian Biology,* Vol. 2, D. S. Farner et al., eds. 2. New York.
Odum, E. P. 1941. Variations in the heart rate of birds: A study in physiological ecology. *Ecol. Monogr.* 3:299–326.
Smith, F. H., West, N. H., et al. 2000. The cardiovascular system. In *Sturkie's Avian Physiology,* G. C. Whittow, ed. New York, pp. 141–231.

CLIMBING

Spring, L. W. 1965. Climbing and pecking adaptations in some North American woodpeckers. *Condor* 67:457–88.

COLLECTING

Barrow, M.V.J. 1998. *A Passion for Birds: American Ornithology After Audubon.* Princeton, NJ.
Mearns, B., and Mearns, R. 1998. *The Bird Collectors.* New York: Academic Press.

COLONY

Brown, C. R., and Brown, M. B. 1996. *Coloniality in the Cliff Swallow: The Effect of Group Size on Social Behavior.* Chicago: University of Chicago Press.
Horn, H. S. 1968. The adaptive significance of colonial nesting in the Brewer's Blackbird (*Euphagus cyanocephalus*). *Ecology* 49:682–94.
Siegel-Causey, D., and Kharitonov, S. P. 1990. The evolution of coloniality. *Curr. Ornithol.* 7:285–330.

Ward, P., and Zahavi, A. 1973. The importance of certain assemblages of birds as 'information centres' for food-finding. *Ibis* 115:517–34.

COLOR AND PATTERN

Armstrong, E. A. 1951. The nature and function of animal mimesis. *Bull. Anim. Behav.* 9:46–58.

Averill, C. K. 1923. Black wing tips. *Condor* 25:57–9.

Bennett, A.T.D., Cuthill, I. C., Partridge, J. C., and Maier, E. J. 1996. Ultraviolet vision and mate choice in zebra finches. *Nature* 380:433–5.

Burtt, E. H., Jr., ed.1979. *The Behavioral Significance of Color.* New York.

Burtt, E. H., Jr. 1986. *An Analysis of Physical, Physiological, and Optical Aspects of Avian Coloration with Emphasis on Wood-warblers.* Washington, DC: American Ornithologists' Union.

Butcher, G. S., and Rohwer, S. 1989. The evolution of conspicuous and distinctive coloration for communication in birds. *Curr. Ornithol.* 6:51–108.

Dumbacher, J. P., Beehler, B. M., Spande, T. F., Garraffo, H. M., and Daly, J. W. 1992. Homobatrachotoxin in the genus *Pitohui*: Chemical defense in birds? *Science* 258:799–801.

Ficken, R. W., Matthiae, P. E., and Herwich, R. 1971. Eyemarks in vertebrates: Aids to vision. *Science* 173:936–9.

Finger, E., and Burkhardt, D. 1994. Biological aspects of bird colouration and avian colour vision including ultraviolet range. *Vision Res.* 34:1509–14.

Gower, C. 1936. The cause of blue color as found in the bluebird *(Sialia sialis)* and the Blue Jay *(Cyanositta cristata). Auk* 53:178–85.

Greene, E., Lyon, B. E., Muehter, V. R., Ratcliffe, L., Oliver, S. J., and Boag, P. T. 2000. Disruptive sexual selection for plumage coloration in a passerine bird. *Nature* 407:1000–3.

Hudon, J., and Brush, A. H. 1989. Probable dietary basis of a color variant of the Cedar Waxwing. *J. Field Ornithol.* 60:361–8.

Jablonski, P. G. 1999. A rare predator exploits prey escape behavior: The role of tail-fanning and plumage contrast in foraging of the Painted Redstart *(Mioborus pictus). Behav. Ecol.* 10:7–14.

Prum, R. O. 1999. The anatomy and physics of avian structural colours. In *Proceedings of the XXIInd International ornithological Congress,* N. J. Adams and R. H. Slotow, eds. Johannesburg.

Prum, R. O., Morrison, R. L., and Ten Eyck, G. R. 1994. Structural color production by constructive reflection from ordered collagen arrays in a bird *(Philepitta catanea*: Eurylaimidae). *J. of Morphol.* 222:61–72.

Savalli, U. M. 1995. The evolution of bird coloration and plumage elaboration. *Current Ornithology.* D. M. Power, ed. New York: Plenum Press, pp. 141–90.

Smithe, F. B. 1975–85. *Naturalist's Color Guide, Parts I, II and III.* New York: The American Museum of Natural History.

Sumner, F. B. 1934. Does "protective coloration" protect? Results of some experiments with fishes and birds. *Proc. Natl. Acad. Sci. USA* 20:559–64.

Thayer, G. H. 1918. *Concealing-coloration in the Animal Kingdom.* New York. (Classic)

CONSERVATION

American Ornithologists' Union. 1975. Report of the American Ornithologists' Union Committee on Conservation, 1974–75. *Auk* (Supplement), 92:1B–16B.

Askins, R. A. 2002. *Restoring North America's Birds.*New Haven, CT.

Buchheister, C. W., and Graham, F., Jr. 1973. From the swamps and back: A con-
cise and candid history of the Audubon movement. *Audubon,* 75:4–43.
Doak, D. 1989. Spotted Owls and old growth logging in the Pacific Northwest.
Conserv. Biol. 3:389–96.
Doughty, R. W. 1975. *Feather Fashions and Bird Preservation: A Study in Nature
Protection.* Berkeley, CA.
Faaborg, J. 2002. *Saving Migrant Birds.* Austin, TX.
Graham, F., Jr. 1990. *The Audubon Ark.* New York.
Henderson, C. L. 1988. Non-game bird conservation. *Curr. Ornithol.* 5:297–312.
Jackson, J. A. 1986. Biopolitics, management of Federal Lands and the conserva-
tion of the Red-cockaded Woodpecker. *Am. Birds* 40:1162–8.
Matthiessen, P. 1958. *Wildlife in America.* New York.
Moors, P. J. 1985. *Conservation of Island Birds.* Cambridge, UK.
Office of Migratory Bird Management. 1990. *Conservation of Avian Diversity in
North America.* Washington, DC.
Pearson, T. G. 1933. Fifty years of bird protection in the United States. In AOU,
Fifty Years Progress of American Ornithology: 1883–1933. Lancaster, PA.
Terborgh, J. 1989. *Where Have All the Birds Gone? Essays on the Biology and Con-
servation of Birds That Migrate to the American Tropics.* Princeton, NJ.
Wilson, E. O. 1992. *The Diversity of Life.* Cambridge, MA,

COTINGA

Prum, R. O., and Lanyon, W. E. 1989. Monophyly and phylogeny of the *Schiffornis*
group (Tyrannoidea). *Condor* 91:444–61.

COUES

Coues, E. 1874. *Birds of the Northwest: A Handbook of Ornithology.* Washington,
DC.
———. 1884 and 1903. *Key to North American Birds.* Boston.
Cutright, P. R., and Brodhead, M. J. 1980. *Elliott Coues: Naturalist and Frontier
Historian.* New York.

COURTSHIP

Lack, D. 1940. Courtship feeding in birds. *Auk* 57:169–78.

COWBIRD

Byers, G. W. 1950. Black-and-white warbler's nest with eight cowbird eggs. *Wilson
Bull.* 62:136–68.
Friedmann, H. 1929. *The Cowbirds.* Springfield, IL.
———. 1963. Host Relations of the *Parasitic Cowbirds.* U.S. Natl. Mus. Bull. no.
233. Washington, DC.
———. 1971. Further information on the host relations of the parasitic cowbirds.
Auk 88:239–55.
Hann, H. W. 1946. The cowbird at the nest. *Wilson Bull.* 53:209–21.
Lowther, P. E. 1993. Brown-headed Cowbird (*Molothrus ater*). In *Birds of North
America,* A. Poole and F. Gill, eds. Philadelphia, PA and Washington, DC:
Academy of Natural Sciences & American Ornithologist's Union, p. 24.
Nice, M. M. 1949. The laying rhythm of cowbirds. *Wilson Bull.* 61:231–4.
See also under BROOD PARASITISM.

CRANE

McMillan, J. L. 1988. The conservation of North American cranes. *Am. Birds* 42:1212–21.

Matthiessen, P. 2001. *Travels with Cranes.* (Illustrated by Robert Bateman). New York.

Walkinshaw, L. 1973. *Cranes of the World.* New York.

CROSSBILL

Benkman, C. W. 1992. White-winged Crossbill *(Loxia leucoptera).* Pp. 20 in *The Birds of North America.* A. Poole, P. Stettenheim, and F. Gill, eds. Philadelphia, PA and Washington, DC: Academy of Natural Sciences & American Ornithologists' Union.

Groth, J. G. 1993. Evolutionary differentiation in morphology, vocalizations, and allozymes among nomadic sibling species in the North American Red Crossbill complex. *Univ. Calif. Publ. Zool.* 127:1–143.

CROW

Amadon, D. 1944. The genera of the Corvidae and their relationships. *Am. Mus. Novit.* no. 1215:1–21.

Angell, T. 1978. *Ravens, Crows, Magpies and Jays.* Seattle.

Goodwin, G. G. 1976. *Crows of the World.* Ithaca, NY.

Heinrich, B. 2000. *Mind of the Raven.* New York: Cliff Street Books.

Linsdale, J. M. 1937. *The Natural History of the Magpies.* Pacific Coast Avifauna no. 25. Cooper Ornithol. Soc., Berkeley, CA.

Madge, S., and Burn, H. 1994. *Crows and Jays.* Boston.

CUCKOO

Davies, N. 2000. *Cuckoos, Cowbirds and Other Cheats.* New York.

See also under BROOD PARASITISM.

DIGESTIVE SYSTEM

Denbow, D. M. 2000. Gastrointestinal anatomy and physiology. In *Sturkie's Avian Physiology,* G. C. Whittow, ed. New York, pp. 299–325.

Grajal, A., Strahl, S. D., Parra, R., Dominguez, M. G., and Neher, A. 1989. Foregut fermentation in the Hoatzin, a neotropical leaf-eating bird. *Science* 245:1236–38.

McBee, R. H., and West, G. C. 1969. Caecal fermentation in the Willow Ptarmigan. *Condor* 71:54–8.

McLelland, J. 1981. Digestive system. In *Form and Function in Birds,* Vol. 1, A. S. King and J. McLelland, eds. New York, pp. 68–181.

Place, A. R. 1991. The avian digestive system—an optimally designed plug-flow chemical reactor with recycle? In *Acta XX International Ornithological Congress,* B. D. Ball, ed. Wellington, NZ, pp. 913–9.

DIMORPHISM

Amadon, D. 1959. The significance of sexual differences in size among birds. *Proc. Am. Philos. Soc.* 103:531–6.

Reynolds, R. T. 1972. Sexual dimorphism in accipiter hawks: A new hypothesis. *Condor* 74:191–7.

Sibley, C. G. 1957. The evolutionary and taxonomic significance of sexual dimorphism and hybridization in birds. *Condor* 59:166–91.

Snyder, N.F.R., and Wiley, J. W. 1976. Sexual size dimorphism in hawks and owls of North America. *Ornithol. Monogr.* no. 20.

Storer, R. W. 1966. Sexual dimorphism and food habits in three North American accipiters. *Auk* 83:423–36.

DIPPER

Backus, G. J. 1959. Observations in the life history of the dipper in Montana. *Auk* 76:90–207.

Brewer, D. 2001. *Wrens, Dippers and Thrashers.* New Haven, CT.

Goodge, W. R. 1959. Locomotion and other behavior of the dipper. *Condor* 61:4–17.

———. 1960. Adaptations for amphibious vision in the dipper *(Cinclus mexicanus). J. Morphol.* 107:79–92.

DISEASE

Arnall, L., and Keymer, I. F. 1975. *Bird Diseases.* Neptune City, NJ. (Abundantly illustrated.)

Davis, J. W., Anderson, R. C., Karstad, L., and Trainer, D. O., eds. 1971. *Infectious and Parasitic Diseases of Wild Birds.* Ames, IA.

Friend, M., McLean, R. G., et al. 2001. Disease emergence in birds: Challenges for the twenty-first century. *Auk* 118:290–303.

Hartup, B. K., Bickal, J. M., et al. 2001. Dynamics of conjunctivitis and *Mycoplasma gallisepticum* infections in House Finches. *Auk* 118:327–33.

Jennings, A. R. 1985. Disease. In *A Dictionary of Birds,* B. Campbell and E. Lack, eds. Vermillion, SD.

Lanciotti, R. S., Roerhing, J. T., et al. 1999. Origin of the West Nile virus responsible for an outbreak of encephalitis in the northeastern United States. *Science* 286:2333–37.

Steele, K. E., Linn, M. J., et al. 2000. Pathology of fatal West Nile virus infections in native and exotic birds during the 1999 outbreak in New York City, New York. *Vet. Pathol.* 37:208–24.

Worth, C. B., Hamparian, J., and Rake, G. 1957. A serological survey of ornithosis in bird banders. *Bird-Banding* 28:92–7.

DISPERSAL

Paradis, E., Baillie, S. R., et al. 1998. Patterns of natal and breeding dispersal in birds. *J. Anim. Ecol.* 67:518–36.

DISPLAY

Darwin, C. 1874. *The Descent of Man and Selection in Relation to Sex.* London.

Lank, D. B., and Dale, J. 2001. Visual signals for individual identification: The silent "song" of Ruffs. *Auk* 118:759–65.

Morris, D. 1956. The feather postures of birds and the problem of the origin of social signals. *Behavior* 9:75–113.

Snow, D. W. 1976. *The Web of Adaptation: Bird Studies in the American Tropics.* New York: Quadrangle, N.Y. Times Books.

DISTRIBUTION

Barbour, M. G. and Billings, W. D., eds. 2000. *North American Terrestrial Vegetation.* 2nd ed. Cambridge, UK.

Berger, A. J. 1954. Association and seasonal succession in the use of nest sites. *Condor* 56:164–65.

Bowen, V. T., and Nicholls, G. D. 1968. An egret observed on St. Paul's rocks, equatorial Atlantic. *Auk* 85:130–1.

Bradley, N. L., Leopold, A. C., et al. 1999. Phenological changes reflect climate change in Wisconsin. *Proc. Natl. Acad. Sci. USA* 96:9701–4.

Cody, M. L., ed. 1985. *Habitat Selection in Birds.* New York: Academic Press.

Cracraft, J. 1973. Continental drift, paleoclimatology, and the evolution and biogeography of birds. *J. Zool. London* 169:455–545.

Crosby, G. T. 1972. Spread of the Cattle Egret in the Western Hemisphere. *Bird-Banding* 43:205–12.

Darlington, P. J. Jr., 1957. *Zoogeography: The Geographic Distribution of Animals.* New York. (Classic)

Daubenmire, R. F. 1938. Merriam's life zones of North America. *Quart. Rev. Biol.* 13:327–32.

Hengeveld, R. 1990. *Dynamic Biogeography.* Cambridge, UK: Cambridge University Press.

Holdridge, L. R. 1947. Determination of world plant formations from simple climatic data. *Science* 105:367–8.

Hutchinson, G. E. 1957. Concluding remarks. *Cold Spring Harbor Symp. Quant. Biol.* 22:415–27.

Johnstone, D. W. 1971. Niche relationships among some deciduous forest flycatchers. *Auk* 88:796–804.

Klopfer, P. H., and MacArthur, R. H. 1960. Niche size and faunal diversity. *Am. Nat.* 94:293–300.

Lack, D. 1971. *Ecological Isolation in Birds.* Cambridge, MA.

MacArthur, R. H. 1959. On the breeding distribution of North American migrant birds. *Auk* 76:318–25.

———. 1968. *The Theory of the Niche: Population Biology and Evolution.* Syracuse, NY.

———. 1971. Patterns of terrestrial bird communities. In *Avian Biology,* Vol. 1, D. S. Farner et al., eds. New York.

———. 1972. *Geographical Ecology.* New York: Harper & Row. Reprinted by Princeton University Press.

MacArthur, R. H., and Wilson, E. O. 1967. *The Theory of Island Biogeography.* Princeton, NJ: Princeton University Press.

Mayr, E., and Short, L. L. 1970. *Species Taxa of North American Birds: A Contribution to Comparative Systematics.* Cambridge, MA: Nuttall Ornithological Club.

Merriam, C. H. 1894. Laws of temperature control of the geographical distribution of terrestrial animals and plants. *National Geographic Magazine* 6:229–38.

Milstead, W. W. 1972. Toward a quantification of the ecological niche. *Am. Midland-Nat.* 87:346–54.

Myers, A. A., and Giller, P. S., eds. 1988. *Analytical Biogeography: An Integrated Approach to the Study of Animal and Plant Distributions.* New York: Chapman & Hall.

Pitelka, F. A. 1941. Distribution of birds in relation to major biotic communities. *Am. Midland-Nat.* 25:113–37.

Price, J., Droege, S., and Price, A. 1995. *The Summer Atlas of North American Birds*. London.
Ricklefs, R. E. 1966. The temporal component of diversity among species of birds. *Evolution* 20:235–42.
Root, T. 1988. *Atlas of Wintering North American Birds: An Analysis of Christmas Bird Count Data*. Chicago: The University of Chicago Press.
Thomas, C. D., and Lennon, J. J. 1999. Birds extend their ranges northwards. *Nature* 399:213.
Udvardy, M.D.F. 1958. Ecological and distributional analysis of North American birds. *Condor* 60:50–66.
Wiens, J. A. 1989. *The Ecology of Bird Communities,* Vol. 2: *Processes and Variations*. Cambridge: Cambridge University Press.
See also some references under SPECIATION.

DOMESTICATED BIRDS

Jull, M. A. 1927. Races of domestic fowl. *National Geographic Magazine,* 51:379–452.
Schorger, A. W. 1966. *The Wild Turkey: Its History and Domestication*. Norman, OK.
Zeuner, F. E. 1963. *History* of *Domesticated Animals*. London.

DOVE

See under PIGEON.

DRUMMING

Ellison, W. G. 1992. Different drummers: Identifying the rhythms of northeastern woodpeckers. *Birding* 24:350–55.

DUMP NEST

Semel, B., Sherman, P. W., and Byers, S. M. 1988. Effects of brood parasitism and nest-box placement on Wood Duck breeding ecology. *Condor* 90:920–30.
Weller, M. W. 1959. Parasitic egg laying in the Redhead (*Aythya americana*) and other North American Anatidae. *Ecol. Monogr.* 29:333–65.
Wiens, J. A. 1971. "Egg-dumping" by the Grasshopper Sparrow in a Savannah Sparrow nest. *Auk* 88:185–6.

DUSTING

Healy, W. M., and Thomas, J. W. 1973. Effects of dusting in plumage of Japanese Quail. *Wilson Bull.* 85:442–8.
Simmons, K.E.L. 1985. Comfort Behaviour. In *A Dictionary of Birds*, B. Campbell and E. Lack, eds. Buteo Books, Vermillion, SD.

ECTOPARASITE

Boyd, E. M. 1951. The external parasites of birds: A review. *Wilson Bull.* 63:363–9.
Burtt, E. H., Jr. 1999. Think small. *Auk* 116:878–81.

Burtt, E. H., Jr., and Ichida, J. M. 1999. Occurrence of feather-degrading bacilli in the plumage of birds. *Auk* 116:364–72.

Dumbacher, J. P. 1999. Evolution of toxicity in pitohuis, I: Effects of homobatrachotoxin on chewing lice (Order Phtiriraptera). *Auk* 116:957–63.

Malcolmson, R. O. 1960. Mallophaga from birds of North America. *Wilson Bull.* 72:182–97.

EDIBILITY

Cott, H. B. 1946. The edibility of birds. *Proc. Zool. Soc. London* 116:371–524.

———. 1951 and 1954. The palatability of the eggs of birds. *Proc. Zool. Soc. London,* 121:1–41 and 124:335–463.

Dumbacher, J. P., Beehler, B. M., et al. 1992. Homobatrachotoxin in the genus *Pitohui*: Chemical defense in birds? *Science* 258(30 October 1992): 799–801.

Dumbacher, J. P., Spande, T. F., et al. 2000. Batrachotoxin alkaloids from passerine birds: A second toxic bird genus (*Ifrita kowaldi*) from New Guinea. *Proc. Natl. Acad. Sci. USA* 97:12970–5.

Garland, J. E. 1978. *Boston's North Shore.* Boston.

EGG

Baicich, P. J., and Harrison, C.J.O. 1997. *A Guide to the Nests, Eggs, and Nestlings of North American Birds.* New York: Academic Press.

Cody, M. L. 1966. A general theory of clutch size. *Evolution* 20:174–84.

Crowell, K. L., and Rothstein, S. I. 1981. Clutch sizes and breeding strategies among Bermudan and North American passerines. *Ibis* 123:42.

Lack, D. 1947–48. The significance of clutch size. *Ibis* 89:302–52 and 90:25–45.

———. 1958. The significance of the colour in turdine eggs. *Ibis* 100:145–66.

Preston, F. W. 1969. Shapes of birds' eggs: extant North American families. *Auk* 86:246–64.

Ricklefs, R. E. 1980. Variation in clutch size among passerine birds: Ashmole's hypothesis. *Auk* 97:38–49.

Romanoff, A. L., and Romanoff, A. J. 1949. *The Avian Egg.* New York.

Taylor, T. G. 1970. How an eggshell is made. *Scientific American,* 222:88–95.

For field guides, see NEST.

EMBRYO

Romanoff, A. L. 1960. *The Avian Embryo.* New York.

EMPIDONAX

Whitney, B., and Kaufman, K. 1985–87. The *Empidonax* challenge, Parts I–V. *Birding* 17–19.

ENDANGERED BIRDS

Agey, H. N., and Heinzmann, G. M. 1971. The Ivory-billed Woodpecker found in central Florida. *Florida Nat.* 44:46–7, 64.

Bodsworth, F. 1995. *Last of the Curlews.* Washington, DC: Counterpoint; Second edition with new epilogue by the author, and a new foreword and afterword.

Collar, N. J. and Andrew, P. 1988. *Birds to Watch: The ICBP Annotated Checklist of Threatened Birds of the World.* Cambridge, UK: International Council for Bird Preservation.

Collar, N. J., L. P., Gonzaga, et al. 1992. *Threatened Birds of the Americas.* Cambridge, UK: International Council for Bird Preservation.

Conner, R. N., Rudolph, D. C., et al. 2001. *The Red-cockaded Woodpecker: Surviving in a Fire-maintained Ecosystem.* Austin, TX: University of Texas Press.

Ehrlich, P. R., et al. 1992. Birds in Jeopardy: *The Imperiled and Extinct Birds of the United States and Canada, Including Hawaii and Puerto Rico.* Stanford.

Hagar, J. A., and Anderson, K. S. 1977. Sight record of Eskimo Curlew (*Numenius borealis*) on west coast of James Bay, Canada. *Am. Birds* 31:135–6.

Halliday, J. 1978. *Vanishing Birds.* New York.

Harwood, M. 1981. Kirtland's Warbler—a born loser? *Audubon* 83:99–111.

Hickey, J. J., ed. 1969. *Peregrine Falcon Populations: Their Biology and Decline.* Madison, WI.

Faanes, C. A., and Senner, S. E.. 1991. Status and conservation of the Eskimo Curlew. *Am. Birds* 45:237–239.

Layne, J. N. 1985. Audubon's Caracara. *Fla. Wildlife* 3940–2.

McNulty, F. 1966. *The Whooping Crane: The Bird That Defies Extinction.* New York.

NatureServe. 2003. NatureServe Explorer: An on-line encyclopedia of life [web application]. Version 1.8 NatureServe, Arlington, Virginia. Available http://www.natureserve.org/explorer.

Nesbitt, S., and Folk, M. J. 2000. Reintroduction of the Whooping Crane in Florida. *North American Birds* 54:248.

Snyder, N.F.R., et al. 1994. Thick-billed parrot releases in Arizona *Condor* 96:845–62.

Snyder, N. and Snyder, H. 2000. *The California Condor: A Saga of Natural History and Conservation.* New York.

Stattersfield, A. J., and Capper, D. R., eds. 2001. *Threatened Birds of the World: The Official Source for Birds on the IUCN Red List.* Barcelona: Birdlife International and Lynx Edicions.

Stieglitz, W. O., and Thompson, R. L. 1967. *Status and Life History of the Everglade Kite in the United States.* Bureau of Sport Fisheries and Wildlife, Spec. Sci. Rept.CWildlife, no. 109. Washington, DC.

Sykes, P. W., Jr., 1976. The Everglade Kite. In *Inventory of Rare and Endangered Biota of Florida*, J. N. Layne, ed. Gainesville, FL.

Tanner, J. T. 1942. *The Ivory-billed Woodpecker.* Natl. Audubon Soc. Res. Rept. no. 1. New York.

Thomas, et al. 1993. Viability assessments and management considerations for species associated with old-growth forest of the Pacific Northwest. Research Report of the Scientific Analysis Team. U.S. Forest Service, Washington, DC. 530 pp.

U.S. Fish and Wildlife Service. 1986. *Whooping Crane Recovery Plan.* Albuquerque.

Woolfenden, G. E., and Fitzpatrick, J. W. 1996. Florida Scrub Jay *(Aphelocoma coerulescens).* In A. Poole and F. Gill, eds. *The Birds of North America*, no. 228. Philadelphia and Washington, DC.

ENDOCRINE SYSTEM

Carsia, R. V., and Harvey, S., Dacke, C. G., Hazelwood, R. L., McNabb, F.M.A., and Scanes, C. G. 2000. In *Sturkie's Avian Physiology*, G. C. Whittow, ed. New York, pp. 437–568.

Whittow, G. C., ed. 2000. *Sturkie's Avian Physiology.* New York.

Wingfield, J. C. 1991. Mating systems and hormone-behavior interactions. In *Acta XX Congressus Internationalis Ornithologicus,* B. D. Ball, ed. Wellington, NZ: Ornithological Congress Trust Board. 4:2055–62.

Wingfield, J. C., Schwabl, H., et al. 1990. Endocrine mechanisms of migration. In *Bird Migration,* E. Gwinner, ed. Berlin: Spriner-Verlag, pp. 232–256.

ENERGY

Blem, C. R. 1990. Avian energy storage. In *Current Ornithology,* D. M. Power, ed. New York: Plenum. 7:59–114.

Blem, C. R. 2000. Energy balance. In *Sturkie's Avian Physiology,* G. C. Whittow, ed. New York: Academic Press, 327–41.

Calder, W. A., and King, J. R. 1974. Thermal and caloric relations of birds. *Avian Biol.* 4:259–413.

Gannes, L. Z. 2001. Comparative fuel use of migrating passerines: Effects of fat stores, migration distance, and diet. *Auk* 118(3):665–77.

Holmes, R. T. and Sawyer, R. H. 1975. Oxygen consumption in relation to ambient temperature in five species of forest-dwelling thrushes (*Hylocichla* and *Catharus*). *Comp. Biochem. Physiol.* 50A:527–31.

Kvist, A., Lindstrom, A., et al. 2001. Carrying large fuel loads during sustained flight is cheaper than expected. *Nature* 413:730–2.

Paynter, R. A., ed. 1974. *Avian Energetics.* Nuttall Ornithol. Club Pub. no. 15. Cambridge, MA.

ERYTHRISM

Greenlaw, J. S. 1973. An erythristic specimen of the Rufous-sided Towhee. *Auk* 90:428–29.

ESCAPES

Bolen, E. G. 1971. Some views on exotic waterfowl. *Wilson Bull.* 83:430–4.

Ryan, R. 1972. A guide to North American waterfowl escapes. *Birding* 4:159–60.

———. 1974. European escapes in northeastern U.S. *Birding* 6:3–4.

———. 1976. Escapes, exotics and accidentals. *Birding* 8:223–8.

ETHOLOGY

Dilger, W. C. 1962. Methods and objectives of ethology. *Living Bird,* 1st annual, pp. 83–92.

Ficken, R. W., and Ficken, M. S. 1966. A review of some aspects of avian field ethology. *Auk* 83:637–61.

Lorenz, K. 1962. *King Solomon's Ring.* New York. (Classic)

Tinbergen, N. 1953. *The Herring Gull's World: A Study* of *the Social Behavior* of *Birds.* New York. (Classic)

———. 1969. Ethology. in *Scientific Thought 1900–1960.* R. Harre, ed., Oxford, UK. (Reprinted in *The Animal in Its World,* vol. 2, 1973. Cambridge, MA.)

ETIQUETTE FOR BIRDWATCHERS

Balch, L. G. 1981. Birding ethics. *Birding* 13:171–3.

Tucker, J. A. 1981. Slob birders (editorial). *Birding* 13:112.
Wauer, R. 1974. Moral obligations of birders. *Birding* 6:227–9.

EVOLUTION OF BIRDLIFE

Andors, V. A. 1991. Paleobiology and relationships of the giant ground-bird *Diatryma* (Aves: Gastornithiformes). *Proceedings of the Twentieth International Ornithological Congress,* 563–71.
Brodkorb, P. 1960. How many species of birds have existed? *Bull. Florida State Mus.* 5:41–53.
Chatterjee, S. 1997. *The Rise of Birds: 225 Million Years of Evolution.* Baltimore.
Cooper, A., and Penny, D. 1997. Mass survival of birds across the Cretaceous-Tertiary boundary: Molecular evidence. *Science* 275:1109–13.
de Beer, G. 1954. *Archaeopteryx lithographica.* London.
Feduccia, A. 1999. *The Origin and Evolution of Birds.* New Haven, CT.
Gould, S. 1985. A clock of evolution. *Nat. Hist.* 94(4):12–25.
Janzen, D. H. 1995. Who survived the Cretaceous? *Science* 268:785.
Marsh, O. C. 1880. *Odontornithes: A Monograph of the Extinct Toothed Birds of North America.* Washington, DC.
Martin, L. D. 1983. The origin and early radiation of birds. In *Perspectives in Ornithology.* A. H. Brush and G. A. Clark, Jr., eds. 291–328, Cambridge.
Mindell, D. P., ed. 1997. *Avian Molecular Evolution and Systematics.* New York: Academic Press.
Nopsca, F. 1923. On the origin of flight in birds. *Proc. Zool. Soc. London,* pp. 223–36.
Olson, S. L. 1985. The fossil record of birds. *Avian Biol.* 5:79–238.
Osborn, H. F. 1900. Reconsideration of the evidence for a common dinosauravian stem in the Permian. *Am. Nat.,* 34:777–99.
Ostrum, J. H. 1974. *Archaeoptery* and the origin of bird flight. *Quart. Rev. Biol.* 49:27–47.
Padian, I., ed. 1986. The Origin of Birds and the Evolution of Flight. *Memoirs of the California Academy of Sciences,* No. 8.
Parkes, K. C. 1966. Speculations on the origins of feathers. *Living Bird,* 5th annual, pp. 77–87.
Stock, C. 1961. *Rancho La Brea: A Record of Pleistocene Life in California.* Los Angeles County Mus., Sci. Ser. no. 20.
Worthy, T. H., and Holdaway, R. N. 2003. *The Lost World of the Moa: Prehistoric life of New Zealand.* Bloomington, IN.
Xu, X., Zhou, Z.-H., et al. 2001. Branched integumental structures in *Sinornithosaurus* and the origin of feathers. *Nature* 410:200–3.

EXCRETORY SYSTEM

Goldstein, D. L., and Skadhauge, E. 2000. Renal and extrarenal regulation of body fluid composition. In *Sturkie's Avian Physiology,* G. C. Whittow, ed. New York, Academic Press, pp. 265–97.

EXOTIC SPECIES

Nilsson, G. 1990. *Importation of Birds into the United States in 1986–1988.* Washington, DC.
Owre, O. T. 1973. A consideration of the exotic avifauna of southeastern Florida. *Wilson Bull.* 85:491–500.

Ryan, R. 1979. Established exotics in the ABA area. *Birding* 11:116–21, 164–6, 244–5.

Trimm, W. 1972. The Monk Parakeet. *Conservationist* 26:4–5.

See also references under ESCAPES and INTRODUCED BIRDS.

EXTINCT BIRDS

Avise, J. C., and Nelson, W. S. 1988. Molecular genetic relationships of the extinct Dusky Seaside Sparrow. *Science* 243:646–8.

Bass, K. H. 1979. I'on Swamp revisited: A 1979 update. *Birding* 11:275.

Bucher, E. H. 1992. The causes of extinction of the Passenger Pigeon. *Curr. Ornithol.* 9:1–36.

Ehrlich, P., and Ehrlich, A. 1981. *Extinction.* New York.

Gross, A. O. 1928. The Heath Hen. *Memo. Boston Soc. Nat. Hist.* 6:491–588.

Nicholson, D. J. 1948. Escaped paroquets found breeding in Florida. *Auk* 65:139.

Pimm, S. L., Jones, H. L., and Diamond, J. 1988. On the risk of extinction. *Am. Nat.* 132:757–85.

Remsen, J. V., Jr. 1986. Was Bachman's Warbler a bamboo specialist? *Auk* 103:216–9.

Schorger, A. W. 1973. *The Passenger Pigeon.* Norman, OK.

Shuler, J. 1977. Bachman's phantom warbler and Bachman's Warbler habitat. *Birding* 9:245–54.

Stevenson, H. M. 1972. A recent history of Bachman's Warbler. *Wilson Bull.* 84:344–47.

Temple, S. A. 1986. The problem of avian extinctions. *Curr. Ornithol.* 3:453–85.

Wilson, E. O. 1992. *The Diversity of Life.* Cambridge, MA: Harvard University Press.

EYE

See under VISION.

FALCON

Brown, L., and Amadon, D. 1968. *Eagles, Hawks, and Falcons of the World,* Vol. 2. New York, pp. 727–856.

Cade, T. J. 1960. Ecology of the Peregrine and Gyrfalcon populations in Alaska. *Univ. Calif. Publ. Zool.,* 63:151–290.

———. 1982. *The Falcons of the World.* Ithaca, NY: Cornell University Press.

See also Hickey (1969—ENDANGERED BIRDS).

FALCONRY

Beebe, F. L. 1984. *Falconry Manual.* Blaine, WA.

Ford, E. 1998. *Falconry: Art and Practice.* New York.

Fuertes, L. A. 1920. Falconry, the sport of kings. *National Geographic Magazine,* 38:429–60.

Glasier, P. 1998. *Falconry and Hawking,* 3rd ed. New York.

Hall, T. 2003. *Falconry Basics,* Swan Hill.

Weaver, M. A. 2002. *Pakistan: In the Shadow of Jihad and Afghanistan.* (Chapter titled "Hunting with the Sheiks," first published in the *New Yorker* of December 14, 1992.) New York.
White, T. H. 1951. *The Goshawk.* New York.

FAT

Helms, C. W., and Drury, W. H., Jr. 1960. Winter and migratory weight and fat: Field studies of some North American buntings. *Bird-Banding* 31:1–40.
King, J. R. 1972. Adaptive periodic fat storage by birds. *Proc. (XVth) Internatl. Ornith. Congr.,* Leiden, pp. 200–17.
Nisbet, L.C.T., Drury, W. H., Jr., and Baird, J. 1963. Weight-loss during migration: Parts I and II (Blackpoll Warbler, *Dendroica striata*). *Bird-Banding* 34:107–59.

FEATHER

Brush, A. H. 1993. The evolution of feathers: a novel approach. *Avian Biol.* 9:121–62.
Clark, G. A., Jr. and de Cruz, J. B. 1989. Functional interpretation of protruding filoplumes in oscines. *Condor* 91:962–5.
Lederer, R. J. 1972. The role of avian rictal bristles. *Wilson Bull.* 84:193–7.
Prum, R. O. 1999. Development and evolutionary origin of feathers. *J. Exp. Zool. Mol. Dev. Evol.* 285:291–306.
Stettenheim, P. 1973. The bristles of birds. *Living Bird,* 12th annual, pp. 201–34.
For origins of feathers, see references under EVOLUTION OF BIRDLIFE. See also PLUMAGE.

FIELD GUIDE

Includes selected guides to birds of adjacent regions.
Beaman, M., and Madge, S. 1998. *The Handbook of Bird Identification for Europe and the Western Palearctic.* Princeton, NJ.
Bull, J., and Farrand, J., Jr. 1977. *The Audubon Society Field Guide to North American Birds: Eastern Region.* New York. (Photos)
Flieg, G. M., and Sander, A. 2000. *Birds of the West Indies.* Curtis Books.
Groggs, J. L. 1997. *All the Birds of North America.* London.
Hoffmann. R. 1902. *A Guide to the Birds of New England and Eastern New York.* Boston.
Hoffmann, R. 1927. *Birds of the Pacific States.* Boston.
Howell, S.N.G., and Webb, S. 1995. *A Guide to Birds of Mexico and Northern Central America.* Oxford, UK.
Jonsson, L. 1992. *Birds of Europe with North Africa and the Middle East.* Princeton, NJ.
Kaufman, K. 1990. *A Field Guide to Advanced Birding: Birding Challenges and How to Approach Them.* Boston: Houghton Mifflin.
Kaufman, K. 2000. *Birds of North America.* Boston.
Mullarney, K., Zetterström, D., Svensson, L., and Grant, P. J. 2002. *The Complete Guide to the Birds of Europe.* Princeton, NJ.
National Geographic Society. 2002 *Field Guide to the Birds of North America.* Washington, DC.
Nuttall, T. 1832–34. *A Manual of Ornithology of the United States and Canada,* Vols. 1 and 2. Boston.
Peterson, R. T. 1947. *A Field Guide to the Birds* (Eastern North America). Boston. (Classic edition)

———. 1960. *A Field Guide to the Birds of Texas and Adjacent States.* Boston.

———. 1990. *Western Birds.* Boston.

———. 2002. *Birds of Eastern and central North America,* 5th ed. Boston.

Peterson, R. T., and Chalif, E. 1973. *A Field Guide to Mexican Birds.* Boston. (Classic)

Peterson, R. T., Mountfort, G., and Hollom, P.A.D. 1993. *A Field Guide to the Birds of Britain and Europe,* 5th ed. Boston. (Classic)

Pough, R. H. 1949. *Audubon Land Bird Guide.* New York. (Classic)

———. 1951. *Audubon Water Bird Guide* New York. (Classic)

———. 1957. *Audubon Western Bird Guide.* New York. (Classic)

Raffaele, H., Wiley, J., Garrido, O., Keith, A., and Raffaele, J. 1998. *A Guide to the Birds of the West Indies.* Princeton, NJ.

Robbins, C. S., Bruun, B., and Zim, H. 1966. *Birds of North America: A Guide to Field Identification.* New York.

Sibley, D. A. 2000. *The Sibley Guide to Birds.* New York.

Sibley, D. A. 2003. *The Sibley Field Guide to Birds of Eastern North America.* New York.

Sibley, D. A. 2003. *The Sibley Guide to Birds of Western North America.* New York.

Stokes, D. W., and Stokes, L. Q. 1996. *Stokes Field Guide to Birds: Eastern Region.* Boston. (photos)

Stokes, D. W., and Stokes, L. Q. 1996. *Stokes Field Guide to Birds: Western Region.* Boston. (photos)

Svensson, L., Mullarney, K., et al. 1999. *Birds of Europe.* Princeton, NJ.

For monographic guides, see under taxonomic headings: ALBATROSS, GALLINA-CEOUS BIRDS, WOOD WARBLER, etc. See also references under IDENTIFICATION.

NOTE: many field guides are now available on CD-ROM, incorporating recordings and video clips as well as text and illustrations; carried by all good dealers in birding products.

FLAMINGO

Allen, R. P. 1956. *The Flamingoes: Their Life History and Survival* Natl. Audubon Soc. Res. Rept. no. 5. New York.

Hagey, L. R., et al. 1990. B-phocacholic acid in bile; biochemical evidence that the flamingo is related to an ancient goose. *Condor* 92:593–7.

FLASH MARKS

Jablonski, P. G. 1999. A rare predator exploits prey escape behavior: The role of tail-fanning and plumage contrast in foraging of the Painted Redstart *(Myioborus pictus). Behav. Ecol.* 10:7–14.

FLIGHT

Alexander, R. M. 1992. *Exploring Biomechanics.* New York.

Butler, P. J., and Bishop, C. M. 2000. Flight. *Sturkie's Avian Physiology,* G. C. Whittow, ed. New York, pp. 391–435.

Cone, C. D., Jr. 1962. Thermal soaring of birds. *Am. Scientist* 50:180–209.

Heppner, F. H. 1974. Avian flight formations. *Bird-Banding* 45:160–9.

Kerlinger, P. 1989. *Flight Strategies of Migrating Hawks.* Chicago: The University of Chicago Press.

Pennycuick, C. J. 1989. *Bird Flight Performance.* Oxford, UK.

Poole, E. L. 1938. Weights and wing areas in North American birds. *Auk* 55:511–7.

Rayner, J.M.V. 1988. Form and function in avian flight. *Curr. Ornithol.* 5:1–66.
Ruppell, G. 1977. *Bird Flight.* New York.
Tucker, V. A., and Schmidt-Koenig, K. 1977. Flight speeds of birds in relation to energetics and wind directions. *Auk* 88:97–108.
Weimerskirch, H., Martin, J., et al. 2001. Energy saving in flight formation. *Nature* 413:697–8.
Woodcock, A. H. 1942. Soaring over the open sea. *Scientific Monthly,* 55:226–32.

FLIGHTLESSNESS

Atkinson, I. A. E. and Millener, P. R. 1991. An ornithological glimpse into New Zealand's pre-human past. In *Acta XX Congressus Internationalis Ornithologici,* B. D. Bell, R. O. Cossee, J. E. C. Flux, et al., eds. Wellington, New Zealand, Ornithological Congress Trust Board. 1:129–92.
Olson, S. L. 1973. Evolution of the rails of the South Atlantic islands (Aves: Rallidae). *Smithsonian Contributions to Zoology* No. 152.

FLOCK

Allee, W. C. 1936. Analytical studies of group behavior in birds. *Wilson Bull.* 48:145–51.
Barnard, C. J. and Thompson, D.B.A. 1985. *Gulls and Plovers: The Ecology and Behaviour of Mixed-Species Feeding Groups.* New York.
Caraco, T., Martindale, S., et al. 1980. Avian flocking in the presence of a predator. *Nature* 285:400–1.
Emlen, J. T., Jr. 1952. Flocking behavior in birds. *Auk* 69:160–70.
Hamilton, W. D. 1971. Geometry for the selfish herd. *J. Theoret. Biol.* 31:295–311.
Meyerriecks, A. J. 1957. "Bunching" reactions of Cedar Waxwings to attacks of a Cooper's Hawk. *Wilson Bull.* 69:184.
Nichols, J. T. 1931. Notes on the flocking of shorebirds. *Auk* 48:181–5.

FLYCATCHER

Hamblin, B. 1994. *Tyrant Flycatchers of North America in Action.* (Video Tape)
Lanyon, S. M. 1985. Molecular perspective on higher-level relationships in the Tyrannidae (Aves). *Syst. Zool.* 34:404–18.
Prum, R. O., and Lanyon, W. E. 1989. Monophyly and phylogeny of the *Schiffornis* group (Tyrannoidea). *Condor* 91:444–61.

FOOD CHAIN/WEB

Lindeman, R. L. 1942. The trophic-dynamic aspect of ecology. *Ecology* 23: 399–418.

FOOD/FEEDING

Baldwin, W. P. 1946. Clam catches oystercatcher. *Auk* 63:589.
Barnard, C. J. and Thompson, D. B. A. 1985. *Gulls and Plovers: The Ecology and Behaviour of Mixed-Species Feeding Groups.* New York: Columbia University Press.
Beecher, W. J. 1951. Adaptations for food-getting in the American blackbirds. *Auk* 68:411–40.

Brower, L. P., and Brower, J.V.Z. 1964. Birds, butterflies and plant poisons, a study in ecological chemistry. *Zoologica New York.* 49:137–59.

Cottam, C. 1939. *Food Habits of North American Diving Ducks.* U.S. Dept. Agric. Tech. Bull. no. 643. Washington, DC.

Cottam, C., and Uhler, F. M. 1937. *Birds in Relation to Fishes.* U.S. Dept. Agric. Wildlife Res. and Management Leaflet no. BS–83. Washington, DC.

Cottam, C., Williams, C. S., and Sooter, C. A. 1942. Cooperative feeding of White Pelicans. *Auk* 59:444–5.

Dickson, J. G., et al., eds. 1979. *The Role of Insectivorous Birds in Forest Ecosystems.* New York.

Dusi, R. L. 1968. "Ploughing" for fish by the Greater Yellowlegs. *Wilson Bull.* 80:491–2.

Erlich, P. R. and Daily, G. C. 1988. Red-naped sapsuckers feeding at willows: possible keystone herbivores. *Am. Birds* 42:357–65.

Evenden, F. G., Jr. 1943. Food-washing habit of the Dipper. *Condor* 45:120.

Fitzpatrick, J. W. 1980. Foraging behavior of Neotropical tyrant flycatchers. *Condor* 82:43–57.

Foster, W. L., and Tate, J., Jr. 1966. The activities and co-actions of animals at sapsucker trees. *Living Bird,* 5th annual, pp. 87–113.

Heppleston, P. B. 1971. Feeding techniques of the oystercatcher. *Bird Study* 18:15–20.

Heppner, F. H. 1965. Sensory mechanisms and environmental clues used by the American Robin in locating earthworms. *Condor* 67:247–56.

Källender, H., and Smith, H. G. 1900. Food storage in birds: an evolutionary perspective. *Curr. Ornithol.* 7:147–208.

Lang, H. 1924. *Ampullarius* and *Rostrhamus* at Georgetown, British Guiana. *Nautilus* 37:73–77.

MacRoberts, M. H. 1975. Food storage and winter territory in Red-headed Woodpeckers in northwestern Louisiana. *Auk* 92:382–5.

Meyerriecks, A. J. 1959. Foot-stirring feeding behavior in herons. *Wilson Bull.* 71:153–8.

———. 1966. Additional observations on "foot-stirring" feeding behavior in herons. *Auk* 83:471–2.

Moffit, J., and Cottam, C. 1941. *The Eel-grass Blight and Its Effect on Brant.* U.S. Fish and Wildlife Service Leaflet, 204:1–26.

Morrison, M. L., Ralph, C. J., et al., eds. 1990. *Avian Foraging: Theory, Methodology, and Applications.* Studies in Avian Biology No. 13.

Nice, M. M., and Nice, C. 1950. The appetite of a Black-and-white Warbler. *Wilson Bull.* 62:94–5.

Place, A. R., and Stiles, E. W. 1992. Living off the wax of the land: Bayberries and yellow-rumped warblers. *Auk* 109:334–45.

Richardson, F. 1942. Adaptive modifications for tree-trunk foraging in birds. *Univ. Calif. Publ. Zool.* 46:317–68.

Sherry, D. F. 1989. Food storing in the Paridae. *Wilson Bull.* 101:289–93.

Smith, S. M. 1971. The relationship of grazing cattle to foraging rates in anis. *Auk* 88:876–80.

Snyder, N.F.R., and Snyder, J. A. 1969. A comparative study of mollusk predation by Limpkins, Everglade Kites, and Boat-tailed Grackles. *Living Bird,* 8th annual, pp. 177–223.

Sperry, C. C. 1940. *Food Habits of a Group of Shorebirds: Woodcock, Snipe, Knot and Dowitcher.* U.S. Dept. Agric., Bur. Biol. Surv. Wildlife Res. Bull. no. 1. Washington, DC.

Tomback, D. F. 1980. How nutcrackers find their seed stores. *Condor* 82:10–9.

Turner, R.R.A. 1964. Social feeding in birds. *Behavior* 24:1–46.

Werner, T. K. and Sherry, T. W. 1987. Behavioral feeding specialization in *Pinaroloxias inornata,* the 'Darwin's finch' of Cocos Island, Costa Rica. *Proc. Natl. Acad. Sci. USA* 84:5506–10.

Wetmore, A. 1920. A peculiar feeding habit of grebes. *Condor* 22:18–20.

FOREST

Kricher, J. 1993. *Peterson Field Guides: Rocky Mountain and Southwest Forests.* Boston.

———. 1998. *Peterson Field Guides: Eastern Forests.* Boston.

———. 1998. *Peterson Field Guides: California and Pacific Northwest Forests.* Boston.

FRAGMENTATION

Wiens, J. A. 1989. *The Ecology of Bird Communities,* Vol. 2: *Processes and Variations.* Cambridge, UK: Cambridge University Press.

See also THREATS (OF HUMAN ORIGIN) TO BIRDLIFE.

G

GADFLY PETREL

Bretagnolle, V. 1995. Systematics of the Soft-plumaged petrel *Pterodroma mollis* (Procellariidae): New Insights from the study of vocalizations. *Ibis* 137: 207–18.

GALLINACEOUS BIRDS

Beebe, N. 1918–22. *A Monograph of the Pheasants.* 4 vols. London. (Classic)

Delacour, J. 1951. *The Pheasants of the World.* New York. (2nd ed., 1977, Hindhead, UK.)

Delacour, J., and Amadon, D. 1973. Chachalacas. In *Curassows and Related Birds.* New York.

Edminster, F. C., et al. 1947. *The Ruffed Grouse: Its Life Story, Ecology and Management.* New York.

Johnsgard, P. A. 1973. *Grouse and Quails of North America.* Lincoln, NE.

Johnsgard, P. A. 1999. *The Pheasants of the World, Biology and Natural History.* Washington, DC.

Madge, S., and McGowan, P. 2002. *Pheasants, Partridges and Grouse.* Princeton, NJ.

Schorger, A. W. 1966. *The Wild Turkey: Its History and Domestication.* Norman, OK.

GENERAL REFERENCE

See under ORNITHOLOGY.

GENETICS

Avise, J. C., and Nelson, W. S. 1988. Molecular genetic relationships of the extinct Dusky Seaside Sparrow. *Science* 243:646–8.

Cooke, F., and Buckley, P. A., eds. 1987. *Avian Genetics: A Population and Ecological Approach.* New York: Academic Press.

Grant, P. R., and Grant, B. R. 1997. Genetics and the origin of species. *Proc. Natl. Acad. Sci. USA* 94:7768–75.

GREBE

Storer, R. W. 1963. Courtship and mating behavior and the phylogeny of the grebes. *Proc. (Xlllth) Internatl. Ornith. Congr., Ithaca, NY, 1962*, pp. 562–9.
See also Wetmore (1920–FOOD/FEEDING).

GRISCOM

Davis, W. E. 1994. *Dean of the Birdwatchers: A Biography of Ludlow Griscom.* Washington, DC.
Griscom, L. 1945. *Modern Bird Study.* Cambridge, MA. (Historical interest)
Griscom, L., and Snyder, D. E. 1955. *The Birds of Massachusetts.* Salem, MA.
Griscom, L., and Sprunt, A., Jr., eds. 1957. *The Warblers of North America.* New York. Reprinted 1979.

GRIT

Jenkinson, M. A., and Mengel, R. M. 1970. Ingestion of stones by goatsuckers (Caprimulgidae). *Condor* 72:236–37.
McCann, L. J. 1961. Grit as an ecological factor. *Am. Midland-Nat.* 65:187–92.

GUILD

Wiens, J. A. 1989. *The Ecology of Bird Communities,* Vol. 1: *Foundations and Patterns.* Cambridge, UK.

GULL

Dunn, J. (narrator). 1997 and 1999. *Large Gulls of North America* and *Small Gulls of North America.* (Video Tape) Peregrine Productions.
Dwight, J., Jr. 1925. The gulls (Laridae) of the world: Their plumages, moults, variations, relationships, distribution. *Bull. Am. Mus. Nat. Hist.* 3, art. III, 63–401.
Grant, P. J. 1986. *Gulls a Guide to Identification.* Vermillion, SD: Buteo Books (reprinted in 1997 by Academic Press, New York).
Nikula, B. 1993. Rare, little known, and declining North American breeders: Common Black-headed Gull. *Birding* 25:55–60.
Olsen, K. M. and Larsson, H. 2003. *Gulls:Of Europe, Asia and North America.* Princeton, NJ.
Tinbergen, N. 1960. Comparative studies of the behavior of gulls (Laridae). *Behavior* 15:1–70.
Vickery, P. D. 1977. Northeast maritime region. *Am. Birds,* 31:1112.
See also references under SEABIRD.

GYNANDROMORPHISM

Brodkorb, P. 1935. A Sparrow Hawk gynandromorph. *Auk* 52:183–4.
Laybourne, R. C. 1967. Bilateral gynandrism in an Evening Grosbeak. Auk 84:267–72.

ℋ

HARRIER

Rice, W. R. 1982. Acoustical location of prey by the Marsh Hawk: Adaptation to concealed prey. *Auk* 99:403–13.
Simmons, R. E. 2000. *Harriers of the World.* Oxford, UK.

HATCH

Fisher, H. I. 1958. The "hatching muscle" in the chick. *Auk* 75:391–9.
Skutch, A. F. 1952. On the hour of laying and hatching of birds' eggs. *Ibis* 94:49–61.

HAWK

Bosakowski, T., and Smith, D. G. 2002. *Raptors of the Pacific Northwest.* Portland, OR.
Brown, L. 1976. *Birds of Prey.* New York.
Brown, L., and Amadon, D. 1968. *Eagles, Hawks, and Falcons of the World,* 2 vols. New York.
Clark, W. S., and Wheeler, B. K. 1999. *A Photographic Guide to North American Raptors.* Princeton, NJ.
———. 2001. *Hawks of North America* (Peterson Field Guide), Boston.
Dunne, P. 1995. *The Wind Masters: the Lives of North American Birds of Prey.* Boston.
Dunne, P., Keller, D., and Kochenbocher, R. 1984. *Hawk-watch—A Guide for Beginners.* Cape May, NJ.
Dunne, P., Sibley, D., et al. 1988. *Hawks in Flight: The Flight Identification of North American Migrant Raptors.* Boston.
Ferguson-Lees, J., and Christie, D. A. 2001. *Raptors: Birds of Prey of the World.* Boston.
Kerlinger, P. 1989. *Flight Strategies of Migrating Hawks.* Chicago: The University of Chicago Press.
Newton, I. 1979. *Population Ecology of Raptors.* Vermillion, SD.
Walton, R. K., and Dodge, G. 1998. *Hawk-Watch: A Video Guide to Eastern Raptors.*
See also under FALCON and HARRIER.

HAWK MOUNTAIN

Bildstein, K. L. 1999. Racing with the sun: The forced migration of the Broad-winged Hawk. In *Gatherings of Angels: Migrating Birds and Their Ecology.* K. P. Able, ed. Ithaca, NY: Cornell University Press: 79–102.
Broun, M. 1949. *Hawks Aloft: The Story of Hawk Mountain.* New York.
Harwood, M. 1973. *A View from Hawk Mountain.* New York.

HAWKWATCHING

See under HAWK.

HEARING

Dooling, R. J. 1982. Auditory perception in birds. In *Acoustic Communication in Birds,* Vol. 1, D. E. Kroodsma and E. H. Miller, eds. New York, pp. 95–130.

Kreithen, M. L., and Quine, D. B. 1979. Infrasound detection by the homing pigeon. *J. Comp. Physiol. A* 129:1–4.

Necker, R. 2000. The avian ear and hearing. In *Sturkie's Avian Physiology.* G. C. Whittow, ed. New York, pp. 21–38.

Payne, R. S. 1962. How the Barn Owl locates prey by hearing. *Living Bird,* 1st annual, pp. 150–59.

Rice, W. R. 1982. Acoustical location of prey by the Marsh Hawk: Adaptation to concealed prey. *Auk* 99:403–13.

Thorpe, W. H. 1963. Antiphonal singing in birds as evidence for avian auditory reaction time. *Nature* 197:774–6.

HERON

Hancock, J. 2000. *Herons of North America.* New York.

Hancock, J., and Elliott, H. 1978. *The Herons of the World.* New York.

Male, M., and Fieth, J. 1999. *Watching Waders: A Video Guide to the Waders of North America.* (Not shorebirds)

Meyerriecks, A. J. 1960. *Comparative Breeding Behavior of Four Species of North American Herons.* Nuttall Ornithol. Club Publ. no. 2. Cambridge, MA.

HIGH ISLAND

Moore, F. R. 1999. Neotropical migrants and the Gulf of Mexico: The cheniers of Louisiana and stopover ecology. *Gatherings of Angels: Migrating Birds and Their Ecology,* K. P. Able, ed. Ithaca, NY. pp. 51–62.

HOMOSEXUALITY

Brackbill, H. 1941. Possible homosexual mating of the Rock Dove. *Auk* 58:581.

Conover, M. R., Miller, D. E., and Hunt, G. L., Jr. 1979. Female-female pairs and other unusual reproductive associations in Ring-billed and California Gulls. *Auk* 96:6–9.

Hunt, G. L., Jr., Wingfield, J. C., Newman, A., and Farner, D. S. 1980. Sex ratios of Western Gulls on Santa Barbara Island, California. *Auk* 97:473–9.

Starkey, E. E. 1972. A case of interspecific homosexuality in geese. *Auk* 89:456–7.

HUMAN CULTURE, BIRDS IN

Clark, Sir K. 1977. *Animals and Men: Their Relationship as Reflected in Western Art.* New York.

Friedmann, H. 1946. *The Symbolic Goldfinch: Its History and Significance in European Devotional Art.* Washington, DC.

Gelkie, A. 1916. *The Birds of Shakespeare.* Glasgow.

Howes, F. S. 1964. Music, birds in. In A *New Dictionary of Birds,* A. L. Thomson, ed. New York

Massingham, H. J., ed. c. 1922. *Poems About Birds from the Middle Ages to the Present Day.* New York.

Welker, R. H. 1955. *Birds and Men.* Cambridge, MA.

See also many references in the text of this entry.

HUMMINGBIRD

Dunn, J., Williamson, S., and Vanderpoel, J. 2002. *Hummingbirds of North America.* (Video Tape). Peregrine Productions.

Greenewalt, C. H. 1960. *Hummingbirds.* New York.
Howell, S.N.G. 2002. *Hummingbirds of North America.* New York.
Skutch, A. F. 1973. *The Life of the Hummingbird.* New York.
Tyrrell, R.A., and Tyrrell, E. Q. 1985. *Hummingbirds: Their Life and Behavior.* New York.
Williamson, S. L. 2002. *Hummingbirds of North America* (Peterson Field Guide). Boston.

HYBRIDIZATION

Banks, R. C., and Johnson, N. K. 1961. A review of North American hybrid hummingbirds. *Condor* 63:3–27.
Cockrum, E. L. 1952. A checklist and bibliography of hybrid birds of North America north of Mexico. *Wilson Bull.* 64:140–59.
Davis, I., and Webster, F. S. 1970. An intergeneric hybrid flycatcher *(Tyrannus X Muscivora). Condor* 72:37–42.
Dickerman, R. W. 1961. Hybrids among the fringillid genera *Junco, Zonotrichia,* and *Melospiza. Auk* 78:627–32.
Gill, F. B. 1980. Historical aspects of hybridization between Blue-winged and Golden-winged Warblers. *Auk* 97:1–18.
Grant, P. R. and Grant, B. R. 1992. Hybridization in bird species. *Science* 256:193–7.
Gray, A. P. 1958. *Bird Hybrids.* Tech. Communication no. 13. Commonwealth Agricultural Bureaux. London.
Short, L. L., Jr. 1963. Hybridization of the wood warblers *Vermivora pinus* and *Vermivora chrysoptera. Proc. (XIIIth) Internatl. Ornithol. Congr., Ithaca, NY,* pp. 147–60.
———. 1965. Hybridization of the flickers *(Colaptes)* of North America. *Bull. Am. Mus. Nat. Hist.* 129:307–428.
Sibley, C. G. 1957. The evolutionary and taxonomic significance of sexual dimorphism and hybridization in birds. *Condor* 59:166–91.
———. 1958. Hybrids of and with North American Anatidae. *Proc. (Xth) Internatl. Ornithol. Congr., Rouen, France,* pp. 327–55.
Sibley, C. G., and Short, L. L., Jr. 1959. Hybridization in the buntings *(Passerina)* in the Great Plains. *Auk* 76:443–63.

IDENTIFICATION

Beaman, M., and Madge, S. 1998. *The Handbook of Bird Identification for Europe and the Western Palearctic.* Princeton, NJ.
Grant, P. J., and Mullarney, K. 1989. *The New Approach to Identification.* Ashford, UK.
Griscom, L. 1976. The historical development of sight recognition. *Birding* 8:86–90.
Kaufman, K. 1990. *A Field Guide to Advanced Birding: Birding Challenges and How To Approach Them.* Boston: Houghton Mifflin.
Prater, A. J., Marchant, J. H., and Vuorinen, J. 1976. *Guide to the Identification and Ageing of Holarctic Waders.* London.
Pyle, P. 1997. *Identification Guide to North American Birds,* Part I: *Columbidae to Ploceidae.* Bolinas, CA.
Sibley, D. A. 2000. What is the malar? *Birding* 32:448–51.
Svensson, L. 1994. Jizz versus tertial fringes. *Birding* 26:52–3.
Whitney, B., and Kaufman, K. 1985–87. The *Empidonax* challenge, Parts I–V. *Birding* 17–9.
See also under FIELD GUIDE and specific groups, e.g., HAWKS; SHOREBIRDS; etc.

ILLUSTRATION

Audubon, J. J. 1966. *The Original Water-color Paintings by John James Audubon for the Birds of America.* Intro. by M. B. Davidson. 2 vols. New York.

Bateman, R. 2002. *Birds.* New York. (His other collections contain many bird images.)

Brynildson, I., And Hagge, W. 1990 *Birds in Art, The Masters.* Wausau and New York.

Catesby, M. 1731–43 (Appendix 1748). *The Natural History of Carolina, Florida, and the Bahama Islands, Containing the Figures of Birds, Beasts, Fishes, Serpents Insects, and Plants,* 2 vols. London. (Illustr. by the author)

Eckelberry, D. R. 1963. Birds in art and illustration. *Living Bird,* 2nd annual, pp. 69–82.

Fuertes, L. A. 1930. *Album of Abyssinian Birds and Mammals.* Chicago: Field Museum of Natural History. (32 plates)

Hammond, N. 1986. *Twentieth Century Wildlife Artists.* New York.

———. *Modern Wildlife Painting.* New Haven, CT.

Harris, H. 1926. Examples of recent American bird art. *Condor* 28:191–206.

Hill, M. 1987. *Bruno Liljefors: The Peerless Eye.* New York.

Jackson, C. E. 1999. Dictionary of Bird Artists of the World. Suffolk, UK.

Jaques, F. P. 1973. *Francis Lee Jaques: Artist of the Wilderness World.* New York.

Jonsson, L. 2002. *Birds and Light: The Art of Lars Jonsson.* London.
Though he has published numerous books in his native Sweden, Jonsson (arguably the greatest living artist of the natural world) is known here mainly for his field guides (see especially Jonsson 1992–**FIELD GUIDE**). However, see also Leahy et al. below.

Lansdowne, J. F., and Livingston, J. A. 1966. *Birds of the Northern Forest.* Boston.

———. 1968. *Birds of the Eastern Forest:* I. Boston.
Also three other titles in this series: *Eastern Forest II, Northern Forest,* and *Pacific Coast.*

Leahy, C., Mitchell, J., and Conuel, T. 1996. *The Nature of Massachusetts* (illustrated by Lars Jonsson). Reading, MA.

Leigh Yawkey Woodson Art Museum. *Birds in Art Exhibition.* Annual catalogues since 1994.

Leslie, C. W. 1995. *Nature Drawing: A Tool for Learning,* Chapter 7: Birds, pp. 130–57). Dubuque, IA. (Examples of many artists' work in black and white, bibliography; also "how to.")

Marsham, F. G., ed. 1971. *Louis Agassiz Fuertes and the Singular Beauty of Birds.* New York.

Mengel, R. M. 1980. Beauty and the beast: Natural history and art. *Living Bird.* 18th annual, pp. 27–70.

National Geographic Magazine.
Many early issues included fine examples of bird illustration before the advent of color photography; see especially the series on North American birds (July 1932–August 1937) with illustrations by Allan Brooks.

Norelli, M. R. 1975. *American Wildlife Painting.* New York.

Ott, R. 1998. *Alaska's Copper River Delta.* Seattle. (Illustrated by some of the world's best nature artists through Artists for Nature.)

Pasquier, R. F., and J. Farrand, Jr. 1991. *Masterpieces of Bird Art: 700 Years of Ornithological Illustration.* New York.

Peterson, R. T. 1942. Bird painting in America. *Audubon* 44:166–76.

Sutton, G. M. 1962. Is bird-art art? *Living Bird,* 1st annual, pp. 73–8.
Many examples of Sutton's fine watercolor and scratchboard illustrations are scattered profusely throughout popular and technical bird literature of the twentieth century, including many titles under the artist's name.

Tunnicliffe, C. F. 1979. *A Sketchbook of Birds.* New York.

For other examples of bird illustration, see references under FIELD GUIDE; STATE/PROVINCIAL BOOKS; and taxonomic groups, e.g., HAWKS; SHOREBIRDS; etc .

IMAGINATION, BIRDS IN

Armstrong, E. A. 1958. *The Folklore of Birds*. London.
Caduto, M. J., and Bruchac, J. 1991. *Keepers of the Animals: Native American Stories and Wildlife Activities for Children*. Golden, CO.
Coffin, T., and Cohen, H. 1966. *Folklore in America*. New York.
Ingersoll, E. 1923. *Birds in Legend, Fable and Folklore*. New York.
Kreithen, M. L., and Keeton, W. T. 1974. Detection of changes in atmospheric pressure by the homing pigeon, *Columba livia*. *J. Comp. Physiol.* 89:73–82.
Wakefield, J. 1964. *The Strange World of Birds*. Philadelphia.
White, T. H., trans. 1954. *The Book of Beasts: A Latin Bestiary of the 12th Century*.

INCUBATION

Drent, R. 1975. Incubation. In *Avian Biology*, D. S. Farner et al., eds. Vol. 5. New York.
Frith, H. J. 1956. Breeding habits in the family Megapodiidae. *Ibis* 98:620–40.
Irving, L., and Krog, J. 1956. Temperature during the development of birds in arctic nests. *Physiol. Zool.* 29:195–205.
Kendeigh, S. C. 1963. New ways of measuring the incubation period of birds. *Auk* 80:453–61.
Nice, M. M. 1954. Problems of incubation periods in North American birds. *Condor* 56:173–97.
Parmelee, D. F. 1970. Breeding behavior of the Sanderling in the Canadian High Arctic. *Living Bird*, 9th annual, pp. 97–146.
Ricklefs, R. E. 1993. Sibling competition, hatching asynchrony, incubation period and life span in altricial birds. *Curr. Ornithol.* 11:199–276.
Skutch, A. F. 1957. The incubation patterns of birds. *Ibis* 99:69–93.
———. 1962. The constancy of incubation. *Wilson Bull.* 74:115–52.
Tazawa, H., and Whittow, G. C. 2000. Incubation physiology. *Sturkie's Avian Physiology*. New York, pp. 617–34.
Verner, J., and Willson, M. F. 1969. Mating systems, sexual dimorphism, and the role of male North American passerine birds in the nesting cycle. *Ornithol. Monogr.* No. 9.

INTELLIGENCE

Alcock, J. 1970. The origins of tool-using by Egyptian Vultures, *Neophron percnopterus*. *Ibis* 112:542.
Barnea, A., and Nottebohm, F. 1994. Seasonal recruitment of hippocampal neurons in adult free-ranging black-capped Chickadees. *Proc. Natl. Acad. Sci. USA* 91:11217–21.
———. 1996. Recruitment and replacement of hippocampal neurons in young and adult chickadees: An addition to the theory of hippocampal learning. *Proc. Natl. Acad. Sci. USA* 93:714–8.
Brower, L. P., Alpert, B. S., et al. 1970. Observational learning in the feeding behavior of Blue Jays (*Cyanocitta cristata cristata* Oberholser, Fam. Corvidae). *Am. Zool.* 10:475–6.
Heinrich, B. 2000. *Mind of the Raven*. New York.
Hess, E. H. 1964. Imprinting in birds. *Science* 146:1128–39.

Jones, T. B., and Kamil, A. C. 1973. Tool-making and tool-using in the Northern Blue Jay. *Science* 180:1076–7.

Kamil, A. C. 1985. The evolution of higher learning abilities in birds. In *Proceedings XVIII Internatinal Ornithological Congress*. V. D. ªlyicheve and V. M. Gavrilov, eds. Moscow: Academy of Sciences of the USSR, pp. 109–19.

———. 1988. A synthetic approach to the study of animal intelligence. In *Nebraska Symposium on Motivation*, Vol. 35: *Comparative Perspectives in Modern Psychology*, D. W. Leger, ed. Lincoln, NE: University of Nebraska Press, pp. 257–308.

Kamil, A. C., and Jones, J. E. 1997. The seed-storing corvid Clark's nutcracker learns geometric relationships among landmarks. *Nature* 390:276–9.

Morse, D. H. 1968. The use of tools by Brown-headed Nuthatches. *Wilson Bull.* 80:220–4.

Pepperburg, I. M. 1987. Acquisition of the same/different concept by an African Grey parrot (*Psittacus erithacus*): Learning with respect to categories color, shape, and material. *Anim. Learning and Behav.* 15:423–32.

———. 1988. Comprehension of "absence" by an African Grey Parrot: Learning with respect to questions of same/different. *J. Exp. Anal. Behav.* 50:553–64.

———. 1991. Learning to communicate: The effects of social interaction. *Perspect. Ethol.* 9:119–64.

———. 1992. Proficient performance of a conjunctive, recursive task by an African Gray Parrot (*Psittacus erithacus*). *J. Comp. Etho.* 106:295–305.

Tinbergen, N. 1951. *The Study of Instinct*, Oxford, UK.

Vander Wall, S. B. 1982. An experimental analysis of cache recovery in Clark's Nutcracker. *Anim. Behav.* 30:74–84

INTRODUCED BIRDS

Chapman, F. M. 1925. The European Starling as an American citizen. *Nat. Hist.* (Reprinted April 1980, number, 89:60–65.)

Elliott, J. J., and Arbib, R. S., Jr. 1953. Origin and status of the House Finch in the eastern United States. *Auk* 70:31–7.

Hengeveld, R. 1993. What to do about the North American invasion by the collared-dove. *J. Field Ornithol.* 64:477–89.

Kinkead, E. 1978. In numbers too great to count. *The New Yorker*, May 22, "Profiles," pp. 40–88. (House Sparrow)

Long, J. L. 1981. *Introduced Birds of the World*. London.

Phillips, J. C. 1928. *Wild Birds Introduced or Transplanted in North America*. U.S. Dept. Agric. Tech. Bull. no. 61. Washington, DC.

Robbins, C. S. 1973. Introduction, spread, and present abundance of the House Sparrows in North America. In *A Symposium of the House Sparrow* (Passer domesticus) *and European Tree Sparrow* (P. montanus) *in North America*. Amer. Ornithol. Union. Monogr. no. 14.

Romagosa, C. M., and McEneaney, T. 1999. Eurasian Collared-Dove in North America and the Caribbean. *North Am. Birds* 53:348–53.

Stott, K., Jr. 1959. The Starling arrives in San Diego, California. *Condor* 61:373.

Weisbrod, A. R., and Stevens, W. F. 1974. The Skylark in Washington. *Auk* 91:832–5.

IRRUPTION/ERUPTION

Baird, J. 1964. The irruptive phenomenon. *Audubon Field Notes*, 17:6–8.

Bock, C. E., and Lepthien, L. W. 1972. Winter eruptions of Red-breasted Nuthatches in North America. *Am. Birds* 26: 558–561.

————. 1976. Synchronous eruptions of boreal seed-eating birds. *Am. Nat.* 110:559–71.

Davis, D. E. 1974. Emigration of Northern Shrikes, 1959–1970. *Auk* 91:821–5.

Davis, J., and William, L. 1964. The 1961 irruption of the Clark's Nutcracker in California. *Wilson Bull.* 76:10–8.

Hochachka, W. M., Wells, J. V., et al. 1999. Irruptive migration of Common Redpolls. *Condor* 101:195–204.

Koenig, W. D. 2001. Synchrony and periodicity of eruptions by boreal birds. *Condor* 103:725–35.

Koenig, W. D. and Knops, J. M. H. 2001. Seed-crop size and eruptions of North American boreal seed-eating birds. *J. Anim. Ecol.* 70:609–20.

Mueller, H. B., Berger, D. D., and Allez, G. 1977. The periodic invasions of Goshawks. *Auk* 94:652–63.

Shelford, V. E. 1945. The relation of Snowy Owl migration to the abundance of the collared lemming. *Auk* 62:592–6.

Widrlechner, M. P. and Dragula, S. K. 1984. Relation of cone-crop size to irruptions of four seed-eating birds in California. *Am. Birds* 38:840–6.

JACANA

Emlen, S. T., et al. 1989. Experimental induction of infanticide in female Wattled Jacanas. *Auk* 106:1–7.

JAEGER

Maher, W. J. 1974. *Ecology of Pomarine, Parasitic and Long-tailed Jaegers in Northern Alaska.* Pacific Coast Avifauna no. 37. Cooper Ornith. Soc. Los Angeles.

O'Donald, P. 1983. *The Arctic Skua: A Study of the Ecology and Evolution of a Seabird.* Cambridge, UK.

Olsen, K. M., and Larsson, H. 1997. *Skuas and Jaegers: A Guide to the Skuas and Jaegers of the World.* New Haven, CT: Yale University Press.

See also references under SEABIRD.

JAY

See under CROW.

KINGFISHER

Forshaw, J. M., and Cooper, W. J. 1980–85. *Kingfishers and Related Birds,*Vols. I and II. Sydney. (A stupendously beautiful and expensive set published in a limited edition of 1000 copies.)

Fry, C. H. 1980. The evolutionary biology of kingfishers (Alcedinidae). *Living Bird,* 18th annual, pp. 113–60.

Fry, C. H. and Fry, K. 1992. *Kingfishers, Bee-eaters and Rollers.* Princeton, NJ.

LARK

Meinertzhagen, R. 1951. Review of the Alaudidae. *Proc. Zool. Soc. Lond.* 121, 81:132.

LAWS PROTECTING BIRDLIFE

Bean, M. 1983. *The Evolution of Natural Wildlife Law.* Urbana, IL.
Faanes, C. H., Vaughn, C., Jr., and Andrews, J. M. 1992. Birders and U.S. Federal Laws. *Birding* 24:299–302.

LAYING

Skutch, A. F. 1952. On the hour of laying and hatching of birds' eggs. *Ibis* 94:49–61.

LEG/FOOT

Bock, W. J., and Miller, W. D. 1959. The scansorial foot of the woodpeckers, with comments on the evolution of perching and climbing feet in birds. *Am. Mus. Novit.*, no. 1931:1–45.
Delacour, J. 1951. The significance of the number of toes in some woodpeckers and kingfishers. *Auk* 68:49–51.

LEK

Crawford, J. A., and Bolen, E. G. 1975. Spring lek activity of the Lesser Prairie Chicken in West Texas. *Auk* 92:808–10.
Shepard, J. M. 1975. Factors influencing female choice in the lek mating system of the Ruff. *Living Bird,* 14th annual, pp. 87–111.

LINNE

Blunt, W. 1971. *The Compleat Naturalist, A Life of Linnaeus.* New York.

LISTING

American Birding Association Supplement: *List Summary and Big Day Summary.* published annually.
Emerson, G. 1940. The lure of the list. *Bird-Lore*, 42:37–39. Reprinted in Peterson (1957–BIRDWATCHING).
Kaufman, K. 1997. *Kingbird Highway: The Story of a Natural Obsession That Got a Little Out of Hand.* Boston.
Piatt, J. 1973. *Adventures in Birding: Confessions of a Lister.* New York.
Short, L. L., Jr. 1970. Bird-listing and the field observer. *Calif. Birds,* 1:143–55.
Snetsinger, P. 2003. *Birding on Borrowed Time.* Colorado Springs.
Vardeman, J. 1980. *Call Collect, Ask for Birdman.* New York.
NOTE: Several forms of listing software are now available from any good dealer in birding products.

LOON

Hutchinson, A. 1998. *Just Loons.* (comprehensive natural history of all species). Minocqua, WI.

M

MAGPIE

See under CROW.

MARKING

Marion, W. R., and Shamis, J. D. 1977. An annotated bibliography of bird marking techniques. *Bird-Banding* 48:42–61.

MATING SYSTEMS

Briskie, J. V. 1993. Smith's Longspur (*Calcarius pictus*) In *The Birds of North America*, no. 34. A. Poole and F. Gill, eds. Philadelphia and Washington, DC.

Davies, N. B. 1991. Mating systems. *Behavioural Ecology: An Evolutionary Approach*, J. R. Krebs and N. B. Davies, eds. Oxford, UK, pp. 263–94.

Haartman, L. von. 1951. Successive polygamy. *Behavior* 3:256–74.

Jenni, D. A. 1974. Evolution of polyandry in birds. *Am. Zool.* 14:129–44.

Oring, L. W., and Knudson, M. L. 1972. Monogamy and polyandry in the Spotted Sandpiper. *Living Bird*, 11th annual, pp. 59–73.

———. 1982. Avian mating systems. *Avian Biol.* 6:1–91.

———. 1986. Avian polyandry. *Current Ornithol.* 3:309–51.

Rimmer, C. C., McFarland, K. P., et al. 2001. Bicknell's Thrush (*Catharus bicknelli*). *The Birds of North America*, no. 592. A. Poole and F. Gill, eds. Philadelphia and Washington, DC.

Verner, J. 1964. Evolution of polygamy in the Long-billed Marsh Wren. *Evolution* 18:252–61.

Verner, J., and Willson, M. F. 1966. The influence of habitats in mating systems of North American passerine birds. *Ecology* 47:143–47.

———. 1969. Mating systems, sexual dimorphism, and the role of male North American passerine birds in the nesting cycle. *Ornithological Monographs*, No. 9.

Westneat, D. F., et al. 1987. The use of genetic markers to estimate the frequency of successful alternative tactics. *Behav. Ecol. Sociobiol.* 21:35–45.

Wiley, R. H. 1974. Evolution of social organization and life history patterns among grouse (Aves: Tetraonidae). *Q. Rev. Biol.* 49:201–227.

Zimmermann, J. L. 1966. Polygamy in the Dickcissel. *Auk* 83:534–46.

MEASUREMENTS

Palmer, R. S., ed. 1962. *Handbook of North American Birds*, Vol. 1. New York.

MELANISM

Gross, A. O. 1965. Melanism in North American birds. *Bird-Banding* 36:240–2.

Sage, B. L. 1962. Albinism and melanism in birds. *Br. Birds* 55:201–22.

MEMORY

Balda, R. P., and Kamil, A. C. 1989. A comparative study of cache recovery by three corvid species. *Anim. Behav.* 38:486–495.

MIGRATION

Able, K. P. 1970. A radar study of the altitude of nocturnal passerine migration. *Bird-Banding* 41:282–90.

———, ed. 1999. *Gatherings of Angels: Migrating Birds and Their Ecology.* Ithaca, NY.

Alerstam, T. 1990. *Bird Migration.* Cambridge, UK.

Austin, O. L., Jr. 1928. Migration routes of the Arctic Tern *(Sterna paradisoea). Bull. Northeastern Bird-Banding Assoc.* 4:121–5.

Baird, J., and Nisbet, I. C. T. 1959. Observations of diurnal migration in the Narragansett Bay area of Rhode Island in fall 1958. *Bird-Banding* 30:171–81.

Bellrose, F. C., Jr. 1971. The distribution of nocturnal migrants in the air space. *Auk* 88:397–424.

Berthold, P. 1993. *Bird Migration: A General Survey.* Oxford, UK.

Cox, G.W. 1985. The evolution of avian migration systems between temperate and tropical regions of the New World. *Am. Nat.* 126:451–74.

De Graaf, R., and Rappole, J. 1995. *Neotropical Migratory Birds: Natural History, Distribution & Population Change.* Ithaca, NY.

Dixon, K. L., and Gilbert, J. D. 1964. Altitudinal migration in the Mountain Chickadee. *Condor* 66:61–4.

Dorst, J. 1962. *The Migrations of Birds.* Boston. (Classic)

Dunn, E. H., and Nol, E. 1980. Age-related migratory behavior of warblers. *J. Field Ornithol.* 51:254–69.

Gannes, L. Z. 2001. Comparative fuel use of migrating passerines: Effects of fat stores, migration distance, and diet. *Auk* 118(3):665–77.

Gauthereaux, S. A., Jr., 1982. The ecology and evolution of avian migration systems. *Avian Biol.* 6:93–168.

Gwinner, E., ed. 1990. *Bird Migration.* Berlin.

Hamilton, W. J., III. 1962. Bobolink migratory pathways and their experimental analysis under night skies. *Auk* 79:208–33.

Keast, A., and Morton, E., eds. 1980. *Migrant Birds in the Neotropics: Ecology, Behavior, Distribution and Conservation.* Washington, DC.

Kerlinger, P. 1989. *Flight Strategies of Migrating Hawks.* Chicago: The University of Chicago Press.

———. 1999. *How Birds Migrate.* Mechanicsburg, PA.

Kerlinger, P., and Moore, F. R. 1989. Atmospheric structure and avian migration. *Curr. Ornithol.* 6:109–42.

Lack, D. 1960a. The height of bird migration. *Br. Birds* 53:5–10.

———. 1960b. The influence of weather on passerine migration: A review. *Auk* 77:171–209.

Lincoln, F. C. 1945. *The Waterfowl Flyways of North America.* U.S. Dept. Agric. Circ. no. 342. Washington, DC.

Lowery, G. H., Jr., and Newman, R. J. 1966. A continent-wide view of bird migration on four nights in October. *Auk* 83:547–86.

Nickell, W. P. 1968. Return of northern migrants to tropical winter quarters and banded birds recovered in the United States. *Bird-Banding* 39:107–16.

Nisbet, I.C.T. 1959. Calculation of flight directions of birds observed crossing the face of the moon. *Wilson Bull.* 71:237–43.

Snow, D. W., and Snow, B. K. 1960. Northern Waterthrush returning to same winter quarters in successive winters. *Auk* 77:351–2.

Weidensaul, S. 1999. *Living on the Wind: Across the Hemisphere with Migratory Birds.* North Point.

Williams, T. C., and Williams, J. M. 1978. An oceanic mass migration of land birds. *Scientific American* 239:166–76.

Wingfield, J. C., Schwabl, H., et al. 1990. Endocrine mechanisms of migration. In *Bird Migration*. Berlin, pp. 232–56.

Wolfson, A. 1959. The role of light and darkness in regulation of the spring migration and reproductive cycles of birds. In *Photoperiodism and Related Phenomena in Plants and Animals*. Amer. Assoc. Adv. Sci. Publ., no. 55:679–716. Washington, DC.

See also references under NAVIGATION.

MIMIC THRUSH

Engels, W. L. 1940. Structural adaptations in thrashers (Mimidae: genus *Toxostoma)* with comments on interspecific relationships. *Univ. Calif. Publ. Zool.* 42:341–400.

MOBBING

Altmann, S. A. 1956. Avian mobbing behavior and predator recognition. *Condor* 58:241–53.

Curio, E. 1978. The adaptive significance of avian mobbing. *Z. f. Tierpsychol.* 48:175–202.

Knight, R. L. and Temple, S. A. 1988. Nest-defense behavior in the Red-winged Blackbird. *Condor* 90:193–200.

MOLT

Amadon, D. 1966. Avian plumages and molts. *Condor* 68:263–78.

Baird, J. 1958. Post-juvenal molt of male Brown-headed Cowbirds. *Bird-Banding* 29:224–8.

Dwight, J., Jr. 1900. The sequence of plumages and moults of the passerine birds of New York. *Ann. N.Y. Acad. Sci.* 13:73:360.

Hahn, T. P., Swingle, J., et al. 1992. Adjustments of the prebasic molt schedule in birds. *Ornis Scand.* 23:314–421.

Host, P. 1942. Effect of light on the molts and sequences of plumage in the Willow Ptarmigan. *Auk* 59:388.

Humphrey, P. S., and Parkes, K. C. 1959. An approach to the study of molts and molting. *Auk* 76:1–31.

Jenni, L., and Winkler, R. 1994. *Moult and Ageing of European Passerines*. New York.

Mayr, E., and Mayr, M. 1954. The tail molt of small owls. *Auk* 71:172–78.

Miller, A. H. 1933. Postjuvenal molt and the appearance of sexual characters of plumage in *Phainopepla nitens. Univ. Calif. Publ. Zool.*, 38:425–46.

Nolan, V. 1978. *The Ecology and Behavior of the Prairie Warbler* Dendroica discolor. Lawrence, KS.

Palmer, R. S. 1972. Patterns of molting. In *Avian Biology*, Vol. 2, D. S. Farner et al., eds. New York.

Payne, R. B. 1972. Mechanisms and control of molt. In *Avian Biology*, Vol. 2, D. S. Farner et al., eds. New York.

Potter, E. F., and Howser, D. C. 1974. Relationship of anting and sunbathing to molting in wild birds. *Auk* 91:537–63.

Rohwer, S., Thompson, C. W., et al. 1992. Clarifying the Humphrey-Parkes plumage terminology. *Condor* 94:297–300.

Stresemann, E. 1963. Taxonomic significance of wing molt. *Proc. (Xlllth) Internatl. Ornithol. Congr., Ithaca, N.Y.*, 1962, pp. 171–5.

Thompson, C. W. 1991. The sequence of molts and plumages in Painted Buntings and implications for theories of delayed plumage maturation. *Condor* 93:209–235

Watson, G. E. 1963. The mechanism of feather replacement during natural molt. *Auk* 80:486–95.

Williamson, K. 1957. The annual post-nuptial moult in the Wheatear, *Oenanthe oenanthe*. *Bird-Banding* 28:129–35.

Zeidler, K. 1966. Untersuchungen uber Flogelbefiederung und Mauser des Haussperlings, *Passer domesticus. J. Ornithol.* 107:113–53.

MOON WATCHING

Newman, R. J. 1952. *Studying Nocturnal Bird Migration by Means of the Moon.* Special Publ. Mus. Zool. Louisiana State Univ., Baton Rouge.

Nisbet, I.C.T. 1959. Calculation of flight directions of birds observed crossing the face of the moon. *Wilson Bull.* 71:237–43.

MORTALITY

Fay, L. D., Kaufmann, O. W., and Ryel, L. A. 1965. *Mass Mortality of Waterbirds in Lake Michigan,* 1963–64. Univ. Mich. Mus. Zool. Misc. Publ. no. 13, Ann Arbor.

Lincoln, F. S. 1931. Some causes of mortality among birds. *Auk* 48:538–46.

Nice, M. M. 1957. Nesting success in altricial birds. *Auk* 74:305–21.

Saunders, W. E. 1907. A migration disaster in western Ontario. *Auk* 24:108–10.

Snyder, D. E. 1960. Dovekie flights and wrecks. *Bull. Mass. Audubon Soc.,* 44:3.

MUSCLES

Berger, A. J. 1960. The musculature. In *Biology and Comparative Physiology of Birds,* Vol. 1, A. J. Marshall, ed. New York.

Bock, W. J. 1965. Analysis of the avian perching mechanism. *Am. Zool.* 5:251.

George, J. C., and Berger, A. J. 1966. *Avian Myology.* New York.

Hudson, G. E. 1957. Studies on the muscles of the pelvic appendage in birds. *Am. Midland-Nat.* 18:1–108.

Owre, O. T. 1967. *Adaptations for Locomotion and Feeding in the Anhinga and the Double-crested Cormorant.* Am. Ornithol. Union Monogr. no. 6.

Raikow, R. J. 1978. Appendicular myology and relationships of the New World nine-primaried oscines (Aves:Psasseriformes). *Bull. Carnegie Mus. Nat. Hist. No. 7.*

MUSEUMS

Banks, R. C., Clench, M. H., and Barlow, J. C. 1973. Bird collections in the United States and Canada. *Auk* 90:136–70. Addenda and corrigenda: *Auk* 93:126–9.

Parkes, K. C. 1963. The contribution of museum collections to knowledge of the living bird. *Living Bird,* 2nd annual, pp. 121–30.

Van Tyne, J. 1952. Principles and practices in collecting and taxonomic work. *Auk* 60:27–33.

$\mathcal{N}$

NAMES, COLLOQUIAL/SCIENTIFIC/VERNACULAR

Borror, D. J. 1985. *Dictionary of Word Roots and Combining Forms.* New York.

Choate, E. A., and Paynter, R. A. 1985. *The Dictionary of Bird Names.* Boston.

Eisenmann, E., and Poor, H. H. 1946. Suggested principles of vernacular nomenclature. *Wilson Bull.* 58:100–15.

Forbush, E. H. 1925–29. *Birds of Massachusetts and Other New England States.* 3 vols. Boston.

Gruson, E. S. 1972. *Words for Birds.* New York.

Jaeger, E. C. 1955. *A Source Book of Biological Names and Terms,* 3rd ed. Springfield, IL.

———. 1960. *The Biologists' Handbook of Pronunciations.* Springfield, IL.

Jobling, J. A. 1991. *A Dictionary of Scientific Bird Names.* Oxford, UK: Oxford University Press.

Kortright, F. H. 1943. *The Ducks, Geese and Swans of North America.* Washington, DC.

Lockwood, W. B. 1993. *The Oxford Dictionary of British Bird Names.* Oxford, UK.

McAfee, W. L. 1955. Folk names of Georgia birds. *Oriole* 20:1–14.

———. 1955–56. Folk names of Florida birds. *Florida Nat.* 28:35–7, 64, 83–7, 91; 29:25–8.

———. 1955–56. Folk names of New England birds. *Bull. MA. Audubon Soc.* 39:307–16, 375–9, 441–6; 40:17–22, 79–84, 127–30, 253–6.

Newton, A. 1893–96. *A Dictionary of Birds.* London.

Skutch, A. F. 1950. On the naming of birds. *Wilson Bull.* 62:95–9.

Staloff, C., and Willoughby, H. 1981. Call them as you see them—but pronounce their names correctly. *Birding* 13:96–8.

Trumbull, G. 1888. *Names and Portraits of Birds Which Interest Gunners with Description in Language Understanded of the People.* New York.

See also under NOMENCLATURE, ZOOLOGICAL.

NAVIGATION

Able, K. P. 1993. Orientation cues used by migratory birds: a review of cue-conflict experiments. *Trends Ecol.* 8:367–71.

———. 1995. Orientation and navigation: a perspective on fifty years of research. *Condor* 97:592–604.

———. 1996. The debate over olfactory navigation by homing pigeons. *J. Exp. Biol.* 199:121–4.

———. 1998. A sense of magnetism. *Birding* 30:314–21.

Able, K. P., and Dillon, P. M. 1977. Sun compass orientation in a nocturnal migrant, the White-throated Sparrow. *Condor* 79:393–95.

Bellrose, F. C., Jr. 1958. Celestial navigation by wild Mallards. *Bird-Banding* 29:75–90.

———. 1972. Possible steps in the evolutionary development of bird navigation. In *Animal Orientation and Bird Navigation.* National Aeronautics and Space Administration. NASA SP-261, pp. 223–57.

Berthold, P., ed. 1991. *Orientation in Birds.* Basel.

Emlen, S. T. 1967. Migratory orientation in the Indigo Bunting, *Passerina cyanea,* Part 1: Evidence for use of celestial cues; Part II: Mechanism of celestial orientation. *Auk* 84:309–42, 463–89.

———. 1970. Celestial rotation: Its importance in the development of migratory orientation. *Science* 170:1198–201.

———. 1975. The stellar-orientation system of a migratory bird. *Scientific American.* 233:102–11.

Griffin, D. R. 1969. The physiology and geophysics of bird navigation. *Quart. Rev. Biol.* 44:255–76.

———. 1973. Oriented bird migration in or between opaque cloud layers. *Proc. Am. Philos. Soc.* 117:117–41.

Griffin, D. R., and Hock, R. J. 1949. Airplane observations of homing birds. *Ecology* 30:176–98.

Grub, T. C., Jr. 1974. Olfactory navigation to the nesting burrow by Leach's Petrel (*Oceanodroma leucorrhoa*). *Anim. Behav.* 22:192–202.

Keeton, W. T. 1972. *Effects of Magnets on Pigeon Homing.* National Aeronautics and Space Administration. NASA SP-262, pp. 579–94.

Kramer, G. 1952. Experiments on bird orientation. *Ibis* 94:265–85.

Lancaster, D. A., and Johnson, J. R. 1976. Birds navigate by magnetic field. *Cornell Lab. Ornithol. Newsletter* no. 82:5.

Matthews, G.V.T. 1953. Navigation in the Manx Shearwater. *J. Exp. Biol.* 30:370–96.

———. 1961. "Nonsense" navigation in the Mallard *(Anas platyrhynchos)* and its relation to experiments in bird navigation. *Ibis* 103a:211–20.

———. 1963. The orientation of pigeons as affected by learning of landmarks and by the distance of displacement. *Anim. Behav.* 11:310–17.

———. 1968 *Bird Navigation.* London.

Mazzeo, R. 1953. Homing of the Manx Shearwater. *Auk* 70:200–1.

Mewaldt, L. R. 1964. California sparrows return from displacement to Maryland. *Science* 146:941–2.

Michener, M. C., and Walcott, C. 1967. Homing of single pigeons–Analysis of tracks. *J. Exp. Biol.* 47:99–131.

Papi, F. 1991. Olfactory navigation. *Orientation in Birds,* P. Berthold, ed. Basel, pp. 52–85.

Papi, F., and Wallraff, H. G., eds. 1982. *Avian Navigation.* Berlin.

Perdeck, A. C. 1958. Two types of orientation in migrating Starlings, *Sturnus vulgaris,* and Chaffinches, *Fringilla coelebs,* as revealed by displacement experiments. *Ardea* 46:1–37.

———. 1967. Orientation of Starlings after displacement to Spain. *Ardea* 55:194–202.

Ralph, C. J., and Mewaldt, L. R. 1976. Homing success in wintering sparrows. *Auk* 93:1–14.

Sauer, E. G. F. 1957. Die Sterneorientierung nächtlich ziehender Grasmücken *(Sylvia atricapilla, borin, curruca). Z. f. Tierpsych* 14:29–70.

Sauer, F., and Sauer, E. 1960. Orientation of nocturnal bird migrants by the stars. *Proc. (Xllth) InternatL Ornith. Congr., Helsinki, 1958,* pp. 645–8.

Schmidt-Koenig, K. 1960. The sun-azimuth compass: One factor in the orientation of homing pigeons. *Science* 131:826–7.

Tatum, J. B. 1980. The effect of the Coriolis force on the flight of a bird. *Auk* 97:99–117.

Walcott, C., Gould, J. L., and Kirsctvink, J. L. 1979. Pigeons have magnets. *Science* 205:1027.

Wiltschko, R., and Wiltschko, W. 1988. *Magnetic orientation in birds. Curr. Ornithol.* 5:67–121.

NEOTROPICAL REGION

Buckley, P. A., Foster, M. S., Morton, E. S., Ridgely, R. S., and Buckley, F. G., eds. 1985. *Neotropical Ornithology.* Ornithological Monographs No. 36. Washington, DC: American Ornithologists' Union.

Hagan, J. M., III, and Johnston, D. W., eds. 1992. *Ecology and Conservation of Neotropical Migrant Landbirds.* Washington, DC.

Keast, A., and Morton, E., eds. 1980. *Migrant Birds in the Neotropics: Ecology, Be-havior, Distribution and Conservation.* Washington, DC.
Kricher, J. 1999. *A Neotropical Companion.* Princeton, NJ.

NERVOUS SYSTEM

Bennett, T. 1974. The peripheral and autonomic nervous systems. In *Avian Bi-ology,* Vol. 4, D. S. Farner et al., eds. New York.
Cobb, S. 1960. Observations on the comparative anatomy of the avian brain. *Per-spect. Biol. Med.* 3:383–408.
Hartwig, H.-G. 1993. The central nervous system in birds: A study of functional morphology. *Avian Biol.* 9:1–119.
Pearson, R. 1972. *The Avian Brain.* New York.
Portmann, A., and Stingelin, W. H. 1961. The central nervous system. In *Biology and Comparative Physiology of Birds,* Vol. 2, A. J. Marshall, ed. New York.
Stettner, L. J., and Matyniak, K. A. 1968. The brain of birds. *Scientific American,* 218:64–76.
See also under INTELLIGENCE.

NEST

Alworth, T., and Scheiber, I.B.R. 2000. Nest building in House Wrens (*Troglodytes aedon*): A reexamination of male and female roles. *J. Field Ornithol,* 71: 409–14.
Baicich, P. J., and Harrison, C.J.O. 1997. *A Guide to the Nests, Eggs, and Nestlings of North American Birds.* New York: Academic Press.
Beer, J. R., Frenzel, L. D., and Hansen, N. 1956. Minimum space requirements of some nesting passerine birds. *Wilson Bull.* 68:200–9.
Berger, A. J. 1968. Clutch size, incubation period, and nesting period of the Amer-ican Goldfinch. *Auk* 85:494–8.
Clark, L., and Mason, J. R. 1985. Use of nest material as insecticidal and anti-pathogenic agents by the European Starling. *Oecologia Berlin* 67:169–176.
Collias, N. E. 1964. The evolution of nests and nest building in birds. *Am. Zool.,* 4:175–90.
Collias, N. E., and Collias, E. C. 1984. *Nest Building and Bird Behavior.* Princeton, NJ.
Cruickshank, A. D. 1956. Nesting heights of some woodland warblers in Maine. *Wilson Bull.* 68:157.
Grubb, T. C., Jr. 1970. Burrow digging techniques of Leach's Petrel. *Auk* 87:587–8.
Harrison, C. 1978. *A Field Guide to the Nests, Eggs and Nestlings of North American Birds.* London.
———. 1979. *A Field Guide to Western Birds' Nests.* Boston.
Harrison, H. H. 1975. *A Field Guide to Birds' Nests.* Boston.
Holcomb, L. C., and Twist, G. 1968. Ecological factors affecting nest building in Red-winged Blackbirds. *Bird-Banding* 39:14–22.
Kendeigh, S. C. 1945. Nesting behavior of wood warblers. *Wilson Bull.* 57:499–513.
Nickell, W. P. 1944. Studies of habitats, locations, and structural materials of nests of the Robin. *Jack Pine Warbler* 22:48–64.
———. 1958. Variations in engineering features of the nests of several species of birds in relation to nest sites and nesting materials. *Butler Univ. Bot. Stud.* 13:121–40.
Oldroyd, H. 1964. *The Natural History of Flies.* New York.
Swennen, C. 1968. Nest protection of eider ducks and shovellers by means of faeces. *Ardea* 56:248–58.

Verner, J., and Willson, M. F. 1969. Mating systems, sexual dimorphism, and the role of male North American passerine birds in the nesting cycle. *Ornithological Monographs, No. 9.*

NICHE

Wiens, J. A. 1989. *The Ecology of Bird Communities,* Vol. 1: *Foundations and Patterns.* Cambridge, UK.

NIGHTJAR

Clere, N. 1998. *Nightjars: A Guide to the Nightjars, Frogmouths, Potoos, Oilbirds, and Owllet-Nightjars of the World.* New Haven, CT.
Ganier, A. F. 1964. The alleged transportation of its eggs and young by the Chuck-will's-widow. *Wilson Bull.* 76:19–27.
Holyoak, D. 2001. *Nightjars and Their Allies.* Oxford, UK.
Kilham, L. 1957. Egg-carrying by the Whip-poor-will. *Wilson Bull.* 69:113.

NOMENCLATURE

Coble, M. F. 1954. *Introduction to Ornithological Nomenclature.* Los Angeles.
International Commission on Zoological Nomenclature. 1985. *International Code of Zoological Nomenclature.* London.
See also NAMES, COLLOQUIAL/SCIENTIFIC/VERNACULAR.

NUTHATCH

Harrap, S. 1995. *Chickadees, Tits, Nuthatchers, and Treecreepers.* Princeton, NJ.
Norris, R. A. 1958. Comparative biosystematics and life history of the nuthatches *Sitta pygmaea* and *Sitta pusilla. Univ. Calif. Pub. Zool.* 56:119–300.

ODOR

Pratt, H. D. 1992. Is the Poo-uli a Hawaiian Honeycreeper (Drepanidinae)? *Condor* 94:172–80

OIL GLAND

Elder, W. H. 1954. The oil gland of birds. *Wilson Bull.* 66:6–31.

OLD WORLD WARBLER

Baker, K. 1997. *Warblers of Europe, Asia and North Africa.* Princeton, NJ.
Shirihai, H., Gargallo, G., and Helbig, A. J. 2001. *Sylvia Warblers.* Princeton, NJ.

OPTICAL EQUIPMENT

See entry in text for on-line sources.

ORNITHOLOGY

Includes general works on birdlife as well as ornithology texts.

Attenborough, D. 1998. *The Life of Birds.* Princeton, NJ.

Barrow, M.V.J. 1998. *A Passion for Birds: American Ornithology after Audubon.* Princeton, NJ: Princeton University Press.

Bent, A. C. Life histories of North American Birds. *U.S. Nat. Mus. Bull.* Various nos. A classic and monumental work, still eminently useful and accurate but now supplanted as the first reference for North American bird species by the *Birds of North America* (Poole, et al., eds.—see below).

Campbell, B. and Lack, E., eds. 1985. *A Dictionary of Birds.* Buteo Book, Vermillion, SD. ("Must-have" reference)

Coues, E. 1903. Historical preface and general ornithology. In *Key to North American Birds,* 5th ed. Boston. (Historical interest and vivid prose)

Cramp, S., et al., eds. 1977–1994. *Handbook of the Birds of Europe, the Middle East and North Africa:The Birds of the Western Palearctic,*Vols. 1–9. Oxford, UK.

Davis, W. E., Jr., and Jenkins, J. J. 1995, 2000. *Contributions to the History of North American Ornithology,* Vols. I & II. Cambridge, MA.

del Hoyo, J., Elliott, A., and Sargatal, J. 1992–1996. *Handbook of the Birds of the World.* (8 volumes as of 2003). Barcelona. (Indispensible)

Farner, D. S., King, J. R., and Parkes, K. C., eds. 1971–75. *Avian Biology.* 5 vols. New York.

Gill, F. B. 1995. *Ornithology.* New York: WH Freeman. (The current American ornithology "bible")

Griscom, L. 1945. *Modern Bird Study.* Cambridge, MA. (Historical interest)

Kaufmann, K. 1996. *Lives of North American Birds.* Boston.

King, A. S., and McLelland, J., eds. 1980–88. *Birds,* Vols. 1–4. London.

Marshall, A. J., ed. 1960–61. *Biology and Comparative Physiology of Birds,* 2 vols. New York.

Newton, A. 1893–96. A *Dictionary of Birds.* London.

Palmer, R. S. 1962, 1976. *Handbook of North American Birds,* Vols. 1–3. New Haven, CT.

Page, J., and Morgan, E. S. 1989. *Lords of the Air.* Washington, DC.

Pasquier, R. F. 1977. *Watching Birds: An Introduction to Ornithology.* Boston. (Dated but still a useful and very readable introduction to field ornithology)

Perrins, C. M., and Middleton, A.L.A. 1985. *The Encylopedia of Birds.* New York.

Pettingill, O. S., Jr. 1970. *Ornithology in Laboratory and Field,* 4th ed. Minneapolis.

———. 1985. *Ornithology in Laboratory and Field,* 5th ed. Minneapolis.

Poole, A., Stettenheim, P., and Gill, F., eds. 1992. *The Birds of North America, Life Histories for the 21st Century* Philadelphia and Washington, DC. (Indispensible current references for all North American bird species; see BIRDS OF NORTH AMERICA entry in text.)

Proctor, N. S., and Lynch, P. J. 1993. *Manual of Ornithology: Avian Structure and Function.* New Haven, CT.

Ridgway, R., and Friedmann, H. 1901–50. *Birds of North and Middle America.* U.S. Natl. Mus. Bulls. Washington, DC.

Sibley, D. A. 2001. *The Sibley Guide to Bird Life & Behavior.* New York.

Snow, D. W., and Perrins, C. M. 1998. *The Birds of the Western Palearctic: Concise Edition.* 2 Vols. Oxford, UK.

Stresemann, E. 1975. *Ornithology: From Aristotle to the Present* Cambridge, MA.

Sturkie, P. D., ed. 2000. *Avian Physiology,* 5th ed. New York.

Terres, J. K. 1980. *The Audubon Society Encyclopedia of North American Birds.* New York.

Van Tyne, J., and Berger, A. J. 1976. *Fundamentals of Ornithology*, 2nd ed. New York.
Webster, R. E. 1993. Building a birder's library. *Birding* 25:10–45.
Welty, J. C. 1988. *The Life of Birds*, 4th ed. Philadelphia.
Whittow, G. C., ed. 2000. *Sturkie's Avian Physiology*. New York.
Wiens, J. A.. 1989. *The Ecology of Bird Communities*, 2 vols. Cambridge, UK.
Wilson, B. W., ed. 1980. *Birds: Readings from Scientific American*. San Francisco.
    (Contains many of the *Scientific American* articles cited elsewhere in the Bibliography.)
See also references under BIRD.
NOTE: Many faunal works, some incorporating recordings and video clips as well as full text and illustrations are now available on CD-ROM.

OWL

Bosakowski, T., and Smith, D. G. 2002. *Raptors of the Pacific Northwest*. Portland, OR.
Burton, J. A., ed. 1973. *Owls of the World*. New York.
Clark, R. J., Smith, D. G, and Kelso, L. H. 1978. *Working Bibliography of Owls of the World with Summaries of Current Taxonomy and Distributional Status*. Natl. Wildlife Fed. Tech. Ser. no. 1. Washington, DC.
Eckert, A. E., and Karalus, K. E. 1974. *The Owls of North America*. New York.
Johnsgard, P. A. 1997. *North American Owls: Biology and Natural History*. Washington, DC.
König, C., Weick, F., and Becking, J.-H. 1999. *Owls: A Guide to the Owls of the World*. New Haven, CT.
Pyle, P., and Able, K. P., eds. 1997. Flight Feather Molt Patterns and Age in North American Owls. *ABA Monographs in Field Ornithology*. Colorado Springs.

PARENTAL CARE

Brown, J. L. 1987. *Helping and Communal Breeding in Birds: Ecology and Evolution*. Princeton, NJ.
Eisner, E. 1960. The relationship of hormones to the reproductive behavior of birds, referring especially to parental behavior: A review. *J. Anim. Behav.* 8:155–79.
Johnsgard, P. A., and Kear, J. 1968. A review of parental caring of young by waterfowl. *Living Bird*, 7th annual, pp. 89–102.
Kendeigh, S. C. 1952. *Parental Care and Its Evolution in Birds*. Urbana, IL.
Nice, M. M. 1937 and 1943. *Studies in the Life History of the Song Sparrow*, Parts 1 and 2. Trans. Linn. Soc. New York, nos. 4 and 6.
Silver, R., ed. 1977. *Parental Behavior in Birds*. Stroudsburg, PA.
Skutch, A. F. 1935. Helpers at the nest. *Auk* 52:157–69.
———. 1976. *Parent Birds and Their Young*. Austin, TX.
Verner, J., and Willson, M. F. 1969. Mating systems, sexual dimorphism, and the role of male North American passerine birds in the nesting cycle. *Ornithological Monographs*, No. 9.

PARROT

Forshaw, J. M. 1973. *Parrots of the World* New York. (Large format; brilliantly illustr. by W. T. Cooper.)

Juniper, T., and Parr, M. 1998. *Parrots: A Guide to Parrots of the World*. New
    Haven, CT.

PARTRIDGE

See under GALLINACEOUS BIRDS.

PELLET

Chitty, D. 1938. A laboratory study of pellet formation in Short-eared Owls, *Asio
    flammeus. Proc. Zool. Soc. London* 108 (series A):267–87.
Grimm, R. J., and Whitehouse, W. M. 1963. Pellet formation of a Great Horned
    Owl: A roentgenographic study. *Auk* 80:301–6.
Marti, C. D. 1973. Food consumption and pellet formation rates in four owl
    species. *Wilson Bull.* 85:178–81.
Storer, R. W. 1961. Observations of pellet casting by Horned and Pied-billed
    Grebes. *Auk* 78:90.
Tucker, B. W. 1944. The ejection of pellets by passerine and other birds. *Br. Birds*,
    38:50–52.

PERIODICALS

*The following ornithological journals or birdwatching magazines contain articles
of continentwide or international interest. They are listed alphabetically by title.*
American Birds. See *North American Birds*, below.
The Auk. Quarterly journal of the American Ornithologists' Union. Membership/
    subscription information through the Ornithological Societies of North
    America at http://www.nmnh.si.edu/BIRDNET/OSNA.
Birders' World. Popular glossy bimonthly with articles on every conceivable as-
    pect of birds and birding. To subscribe, go to www.birdersworld.com.
Birding. Bimonthly glossy magazine of the American Birding Association. For
    membership/subscription information go to www.americanbirding.org.
Birding Business. P.O. Box 1440, Land O'Lakes FL 34639;
    www.birdwatchamerica.com. Check out this glossy magazine to get a sense
    of the economic impact of birding.
Bird Study. Journal of the British Trust for Ornithology. Focuses on Western Eu-
    rope but includes many papers of broader interest; "caters to the profes-
    sional and the serious amateur . . . eschewing the frankly popular and the
    esoteric alike." Published 3 times a year; to subscribe, go to
    sue.starling@bto.org or BTO, The Nunnery, Thetford, Norfolk, UK IP24 2PU.
The Birdwatcher's Digest. Highly popular monthly magazine and on-line resource.
    P.O. Box 110, Marietta, OH 45750, or http://www.birdwatchersdigest.com.
British Birds (monthly). Published by BB200, Ltd., a trust established for the ben-
    efit of British ornithology. http://www.britishbirds.co.uk.. (Features on iden-
    tification and other topics of universal interest)
The Condor. Quarterly journal of the Cooper Ornithological Society. Membership/
    subscription information through the Ornithological Societies of North
    America at http://www.nmnh.si.edu/BIRDNET/OSNA.
Conservation Directory. Published annually by the National Wildlife Federation.
    Invaluable directory to major wildlife related organizations and agencies.
Hawk Migration Studies. Semiannual journal of the Hawk Migration Association
    of North America. HMANA also publishes conference Proceedings. For
    membership information go to www.hmana.org.

The Journal of Field Ornithology (formerly *Bird-Banding*). Quarterly journal of the Association of Field Ornithologists. Membership/subscription information through the Ornithological Societies of North America at http://www.nmnh.si.edu/BIRDNET/OSNA.

The Journal of Raptor Research (quarterly; treating all aspects of raptor biology). For information, go to http://www.nmnh.si.edu/BIRDNET/OSNA.

The Living Bird. Quarterly, glossy, award-winning magazine published by the Cornell Lab of Ornithology; bridges the worlds of academic ornithology and birding. From 1962 to the early 1980s published as a more scholarly annual.

Marine Ornithology. Peer-reviewed journal, published bia-annually by a global partnership of seabird societies. For information, go to www.marineornithology.org.

North American Birds. Birdwatchers' "journal of record," this publication originated in the National Audubon Society's Bird Lore, first issued in 1899 by the American Museum of Natural History and purchased by the National Audubon Society in 1935 . NAS continued to publish it as *Audubon Field Notes and American Birds* until 2000, when most of its contents were adopted by the AMERICAN BIRDING ASSOCIATION under the present title. It is issued quarterly with a mission to "provide a complete overview of the changing panorama of North America's birdlife, including outstanding records range extensions and contractions, population dynamics, and changes in migration patterns or seasonal occurrence." It is organized as four seasonal summaries comprising 27 regional reports, listing and analyzing bird records for the quarter. For subscription information, go to the ABA website: www.americanbirding.org. The record of the annual CHRISTMAS BIRD COUNT, formerly part of *Field Notes,* continues to be published by the National Audubon Society.

Pacific Seabirds (spring and fall). Pacific Seabird Group (also publishes technical publications and symposia proceedings. For a listing go to http://www.nmnh.si.edu/BIRDNET/OSNA.

El Pitirre. Peer-reviewed journal of the Caribbean Ornithological Society. For information, go to http://www.nmnh.si.edu/BIRDNET/OSNA.

RSPB Birds. Popular glossy quarterly with articles of general interest to all bird-watchers. Membership/subscription information at http://www.rspb.org.uk.

Waterbird Society Bulletin. A print journal until 1997; now published exclusively on-line. For information, go to http://www.nmnh.si.edu/BIRDNET/OSNA.

The Wilson Bulletin (quarterly). Membership/subscription information through the Ornithological Societies of North America at http://www.nmnh.si.edu/BIRDNET/OSNA.

Winging It. Monthly newsletter of the American Birding Association. For membership information, go to www.americanbirding.org.

NOTE: Most (if not all) states and provinces have at least one birding magazine and/or ornithological journal. Many of these are venerable publications that publish articles of general interest or continentwide significance. Contacts for these periodicals change frequently and it is therefore impractical to try to give them here. However, if you go on the internet and simply type in (for example) "Kentucky Birds," you are very likely to find any bird-oriented publications produced in that state/province.

Of course, many professional journals and popular magazines that focus on ecology, natural history, and conservation—e.g., *Conservation Biology, Natural History, National Geographic*—often contain interesting articles on birdlife pertinent to North America. Again, the internet now provides the most convenient vehicle for finding recent articles and searching of back issues.

PHAINOPEPLA

Crouch, J. E. 1943. Distribution and habitat relationship of Phainopepla. *Auk* 60:319–33.
Sibley, C. G. 1973. The relationships of the silky-flycatchers. *Auk* 90:394–410.

PHEASANT

See under GALLINACEOUS BIRDS.

PHOTOGRAPHY

Carey, S., et al. 2001. Bird imaging for art and documentation. *Bird Observer* 29:293–300.
Gallagher, T. 1994. *Wild Bird Photography.* Guilford, CT.
Morris, A. 1998. *The Art of Bird Photography: The Complete Guide to Professional Techniques.* New York.
Rohrbach, J. B. 1997. *A Passion for Birds: Eliot Porter's Photography.* Fort Worth, TX.

PHOTOPERIODISM

Bartholomew, G. A., Jr. 1949. The effect of light intensity and day length on reproduetion in the English Sparrow. *Bull. Mus. Comp. Zool.* 101:433–77.
Bissonnette, T. H. 1937. Photoperiodicity in birds. *Wilson Bull.* 64:197–220.
Karplus, M. 1952. Bird activity in the continuous daylight of arctic summer. *Ecology* 33:129–34.
Wolfson, A. 1959. The role of light and darkness in regulation of the spring migration and reproductive cycles of birds. In *Photoperiodism and Related Phenomena in Plants and Animals.* Amer. Assoc. Adv. Sci. Publ. no. 55:679–716. Washington, DC.
See also CIRCADIAN RHYTHM.

PIGEON

Gibbs, D, E. Barnes and J. Cox. 2001. *Pigeons and Doves: A Guide to the Pigeons and Doves of the World.* New Haven, CT.
Goodwin, D. 1970. *Pigeons and Doves of the World.* New York.
Levi, W. M. 1977. *The Pigeon.* Sumter, SC. (An exhaustive work on the domesticated Common Pigeon, *Columba livia,* in all its forms, abundantly illustrated.)

PIPIT

Alström, P., and Mild, K. 2002. *Pipits and Wagtails.* Princeton, NJ.

PIRACY

Meinertzhagen, R. 1959. *Pirates and Predators: The Piratical and Predatory Habits of Birds.* London. See also Meinertzhagen's "Piracy" entry in *A New Dictionary of Birds,* A. L. Thomson, ed. New York, 1964.
Van Tyne, J. 1946. Starling and Brown Thrasher stealing food from Robins. *Wilson Bull.* 58:185.

PLAY

Ficken, M. S. 1977. Avian play. *Auk* 94:573–82.
Kilham, L. 1974. Play in Hairy, Downy, and other Woodpeckers. *Wilson Bull.* 86:35–42.

PLUMAGE

Ammann, G. A. 1937. Number of contour feathers of *Cygnus* and *Xanthocephalus*. *Auk* 54:201–2.
Ashmole, N. P., Dorward, D. F., and Stonehouse, B. 1961. Numbering of primaries. *Ibis* 103a:297–8.
Brodkorb, P. 1949. The number of feathers in some birds. *Quart. J. Fla. Acad. Sci.* 12:241–5.
Buckley, P. A. 1973. Plumage aberrancies. *Am. Birds* 27:585.
Burtt, E. H., Jr. 1999. Think small. *Auk* 116:878–81.
Burtt, E. H., Jr., and Ichida, J. M. 1999. Occurrence of feather-degrading bacilli in the plumage of birds. *Auk* 116:364–72.
Clark, G. A., Jr., and deCruz, J. B. 1989. Functional interpretation of protruding filoplumes in in oscines. *Condor* 91:962–5.
Enstrom, D. A. 1992. Breeding season communication hypotheses for delayed plumage maturation in passerines: Tests in the Orchard Oriole, *Icterus spurius*. *Anim. Behav.* 43:463–72.
Enstrom, D. A. 1992. Delayed plumage maturation in the Orchard Oriole (*Icterus spurius*): Tests of winter adaptation hypotheses. *Behav. Ecol. Sociobiol.* 30: 35–42.
Fabricius, E. 1959. What makes plumage waterproof? *Report of the Wildfowl Trust,* 10:105–13.
Humphrey, P. S., and Parkes, K. C. 1959. An approach to the study of molts and plumages. *Auk* 76:1–31.
Hutt, F. B., and Ball, L. 1938. Number of feathers and body size in passerine birds. *Auk* 55:651–7.
Lyon, B. E., and Montgomerie, R. D. 1986. Delayed plumage maturation in passerine birds: Reliable signaling by subordinate males. *Evolution* 40:605–15.
Markus, M. B. 1965. The number of feathers on birds. *Ibis* 107:394.
Proctor-Gray, E., and Holmes, R. T. 1981. Adaptive significance of delayed attainment of plumage in male American Redstarts: Tests of two hypotheses. *Evolution* 35:742–51.
Rohwer, S., and Butcher, G. S. 1988. Winter versus summer explanations of delayed plumage maturation in temperate passerine birds. *Am. Nat.* 131:556–72.
Rohwer, S., Fretwell, S. D., et al. 1980. Delayed maturation in passerine plumages and the deceptive acquisition of resources. *Am. Nat.* 115:400–37.
Staebler, A. E. 1941. The number of feathers in the English Sparrow. *Wilson Bull.* 53:126–7.
Stresemann, E. 1963. Variations in the number of primaries. *Condor* 65:444–59.
Wetherbee, D. K. 1957. Natal plumages and downy pteryloses of passerine birds of North America. *Bull. Am. Mus. Nat. Hist.* 113:339–436.
Wetmore, A. 1936. The number of contour feathers in passeriform and related birds. *Auk* 53:159–69.
Woods, P. 1999. Delayed plumage maturation in orioles: Taking after the old lady. *Birding* 31(5):416–20

For other references, see under MOLT; ALBINISM; COLOR AND PATTERN.

POLLINATION

Pickens, A. L. 1929. Bird pollination problems in California. *Condor* 31:229–32.

POLYMORPHISM

Gullion, G. W., and Marshall, W. H. 1968. Survival of Ruffed Grouse in a northern forest. *Living Bird,* 7th annual, pp. 117–67.
Huxley, J. S. 1955. Morphism in birds. *Proc. (XIth) Internatl. Ornithol. Congr., Basel and Stuttgart,* pp. 309–27.
Mosher, J. A., and Henny, C. J. 1976. Thermal adaptiveness of plumage color in Screech Owls. *Auk* 93:614–9.

POPULATION

Baker, J. A., and Brooks, R. J. 1981. Distribution patterns of raptors in relation to density of meadow voles. *Condor* 83:42–7.
Dunning, J. B., Jr., and Brown, J. H. 1982. Summer rainfall and winter sparrow densities: A test of the food limitation hypothesis. *Auk* 99:123–9.
Haartman, L. von. 1971. Population dynamics. In *Avian Biology,* Vol. 1, D. S. Famer et al., eds. New York.
Komdeur, J., Daan, S., et al. 1997. Extreme adaptive modification in sex ratio of the Seychelles warbler's eggs. *Nature* 385:522–5.
Lack, D. 1954. *The Natural Regulation of Animal Numbers.* Oxford, UK.
———. 1966. *Population Studies of Birds.* London.
MacArthur, R. H. 1958. Population ecology of some warblers of northeastern coniferous forests. *Ecology* 39:599–619.
Skutch, A. F. 1967. Adaptive limitation of the reproductive rate of birds. *Ibis* 109:579–99.
Watson, A., ed. 1970. *Animal Populations in Relation to Their Food Resources.* Oxford, UK.
Wynne-Edwards, V. C. 1959. The control of population density through social behavior. *Ibis* 101:436–41.
See also references under TERRITORY.

PROBLEMS INVOLVING BIRDS

Anderson, T. E. 1969. Identifying, evaluating, and controlling wildlife damage. In *Wildlife Management Techniques,* R. H. Giles, Jr., ed. Washington, DC.
Beale, F.E.L. 1897. *Some Common Birds in Their Relation to Agriculture.* U.S. Dept. Agric. Farmer's Bull. no. 9. Washington, DC. (Historical interest)
Besser, J. F., et al. 1968. Costs of wintering Starlings and Red-winged Blackbirds at feedlots. *J. Wildlife Management* 32:179–80.
Dennis, J. B. 1963. Preventing bird damage. *Proc. Southeastern Wood Pole Conf., Univ. of Florida, Gainesville,* pp. 89–93.
Drury, W. H., Jr. 1966. Birds at airports. In *Birds in Our Lives,* A. Stefferud and A. L. Nelson, eds. Washington, DC.
Graham, F., Jr. 1976. Blackbirds: A problem that won't go away. *Audubon* 78:118–25.
Hadidian, J., Hodge, G. R., and Grandy, J. W., eds. (Humane Society of the U.S.) 1997. *The Humane Approach to Living with Wildlife.* Golden, CO.
Jackson, J. A. 1976. Blackbirds, scare tactics and irresponsible legislation. *Wilson Bull.* 88:159–60.

Landau, D., and Stump, S. (California Center for Wildlife). 1994. *Living with Wildlife.* San Francisco.

Mott, D. F. 1980. Dispersing blackbirds and starlings from objectionable roost sites. *Proc. Ninth Vertebr. Pest Conf, Fresno, Calif.*, J. P. Clark, ed. pp. 38–42.

Murton, R. K., and Wright, E. N., eds. 1968. *The Problems of Birds as Pests.* New York.

Williams, C. S., and Neff, J. A. 1966. Scaring makes a difference. In *Birds in Our Lives*, A. Stefferud and A. L. Nelson, eds. Washington, DC.

RADAR

Eastwood, E. 1967. *Radar Ornithology.* London.

Gauthreaux, S. A., Jr. 1971. A radar and direct visual study of passerine spring migration in southern Louisiana. *Auk* 88:343–65.

———. 1972. Behavioral responses of migrating birds to daylight and darkness: A radar and direct visual study. *Wilson Bull.* 84:136–48.

———. 1992. The use of weather radar to monitor long-term patterns of trans-Gulf migration in spring. In *Ecology and Conservation of Neotropical Migrant Landbirds*, J. M. Hagan III and D.W. Johnson, eds. Washington. DC, pp. 96–100.

———. 1999. Neotropical migrants and the Gulf of Mexico: the view from aloft. In *Gatherings of Angels: Migrating Birds and Their Ecology*, K. P. Able, ed. Ithaca, NY: pp. 47–9.

Nisbet, I.C.T. 1963. Measurements with radar of the height of nocturnal migration over Cape Cod, Massachusetts. *Bird-Banding* 34:57–67.

Schnell, G. H. 1965. Recording the flight speed of birds by Doppler radar. *Living Bird*, 4th annual, pp. 79–87.

RADIATION

Bedard, J. 1969. Adaptive radiation in the alcids. *Ibis* 3:189–98.

Storer, R. W. 1971. Adaptive radiation in birds. In *Avian Biology*, Vol. 1, D. S. Farner et al., eds. New York.

RAIL

Burt, W. 1994. *Shadowbirds, A Quest for Rails.* New York.

Ripley, S. D. 1977. *Rails of the World: A Monograph of the Family Rallidae.* Boston. (Large format; handsomely illustrated by J. F. Landsdowne)

Taylor, B. 1998. *Rails: A Guide to the Rails, Crakes, and Coots of the World.* New Haven, CT.

RECORDING OF BIRD SOUNDS

Boswall, J., and Couzens, D. 1982. Fifty years of bird sound publication in North America: 1931–1981. *Am. Birds* 36(6):924–43.

Davis, L. I. 1971. Birding with sound. *Birding* 3:123–50.

Davis, T. 1974 and 1978. Cassette tape recorders. *Birding* 6:166–8; 10:185–92.

———. 1979. Microphones and headphones for bird-recording. *Birding* 11:240–3.

Gulledge, J. L. 1976. Recording bird sounds. *Living Bird*, 15th annual, pp. 183–203.

Kellogg, P. P. 1962. Bird-sound studies at Cornell. *Living Bird*, 1st annual, pp. 37–48.

King, B. 1980. The magic wand ("shotgun" microphone). *Birding* 12:10–8.

Margoschis, R. 1977. *Recording Natural History Sounds.* Barnett, UK.
Sinderson, S. W., Jr. 1975. Making your own parabolic reflector for sound
    recording. *Birding* 7:1–3.

Tapes and CDs.
Colver, K. J. 1994. *Songbirds of the Southwest Canyon Country.*(Cassette or CD)
———. 1995. *Songbirds of Yosemite and the Sierra Nevadas.* (Cassette or CD)
———. 1996. *Songbirds of Yellowstone and the High Rockies.*(Cassette or CD)
———. 1999. *Stokes Field Guide to Bird Song (Western).* 4 cassettes or 4 CDs)
Elliott, L. 1997. *Stokes Field Guide to Bird Song (Eastern).* (3 cassettes or 3 CDs)
Keller, G.A. 1997. *Bird Songs of Florida.* (Cassette or CD)
———. 2000. *Bird Songs of the Lower Rio Grande Valley and Southwestern
    Texas.* (CD)
———. 2001. *Bird Songs of Southeastern Arizona and Sonora Mexico.* (2 CDs)
National Geographic Society/Cornell Lab of Ornithology. 1985. *Guide to Bird
    Songs.* (1 CD)
Neville, J. 1999. *Bird Songs of Canada's West Coast.* (CD)
Peterson, R. T. 1999. W*estern Bird Songs* (Peterson Field Guides) (2 cassettes or 1
    CD; keyed to field guide; Boston)
———. 2002 *Eastern/Central Bird Songs* (Peterson Field Guides) (2 cassettes or 1
    CD; keyed to field guide; Boston)
Peyton, L. J. 1999. *Bird Songs of Alaska.* Cornell Lab of Ornithology. (2 CDs)
Righter, R., and G. A. Keller. 1999. *Bird Songs of the Rocky Mountain States and
    Provinces.* (3 CDs; Cornell Lab of Ornithology)
Walton, R. K., and Lawsen, R.W. 1999. W*estern Birding by Ear.* (Peterson Field
    Guides) (3 cassettes or 3 CDs with booklet; Boston)
———. 2002. *Eastern/Central Birding by Ear.* (Peterson Field Guides) (3 cassettes
    or 3 CDs with booklet; Boston)
———. 2002. *Eastern/Central More Birding by Ear.* (Peterson Field Guides) (3 cas-
    settes or 3 CDs with booklet; Boston)

RELIGION, BIRDS IN

Shulov, A. 1985. Bible, Birds of the. In *A Dictionary of Birds,* Campbell and Lack,
    eds. Vermillion, SD.

REPRODUCTIVE SYSTEM

Birkhead, T. R., and Møller, A. P. 1992. *Sperm Competition in Birds.* New York: Aca-
    demic Press.
Briskie, J. V. 1998. Avian genitalia. *Auk* 115:826–8.
Briskie, J. V., and Montgomerie, R. 1997. Sexual selection and the intromittent
    organ of birds. *J. Avian Biol.* 28:73–86.
Fitzpatrick, F. L. 1930. Bilateral ovaries in Cooper's Hawk. *Anat. Rec.* 46:381–3.
Johnson, A. L. 2000. Reproduction in the female. *Sturkie's Avian Physiology,* G. C.
    Whitlow, ed. New York, pp. 569–96.
Kirby, J. D., and Froman, D. P. 2000. Reproduction in male birds. *Sturkie's Avian
    Physiology,* G. C. Whittow, ed. New York, pp. 597–615.
Lofts, B., and Murton, R. K. 1973. Reproduction in birds. In *Avian Biology,* Vol. 3,
    D. S. Farner et al., eds. New York.
McCracken, K. G. 2000. The 20-cm spiny penis of the Argentine Lake Duck
    (*Oxyura vittata*). *Auk* 820–5.

Oring, L. W, Fleischer, R. C., Reed, J. M., and Marsden, K. E. 1992. Cuckoldry through stored sperm in the sequentially polyandrous Spotted Sandpiper. *Nature* 359:631–3.

Witschi, E. 1935. Origin of asymmetry in the reproductive system of birds. *Am. J. Anat.* 56:119–41.

———. 1935. Seasonal sex characters in birds and their hormonal control. *Wilson Bull.* 47:177–88.

Wolfson, A. 1954. Notes on the cloacal protuberance, seminal vesicles and a possible copulatory organ in male passerine birds. *Bull. Chicago Acad. Sci.* 10:1–23.

———. 1960. The ejaculate and the nature of coition in some passerine birds. *Ibis* 102:124–5.

RESPIRATORY SYSTEM

Berger, M., Hart, J. S., and Roy, O. Z. 1970. Respiration, oxygen consumption, and heart rate in some birds during rest and flight. *Zeit. Vergleich Physiol.,* 66:201–14.

Berger, M., Roy, O. X., and Hart, J. S. 1970. The co-ordination between respiration and wing beats in birds. *Zeit. Vergleich Physiol.* 66:190–200.

Lasiewski, R. C. 1972. Respiratory function in birds. In *Avian Biology,* Vol. 2, D. S. Farmer et al., eds. New York.

Salt, G. W., and Zeuthen, E. 1960. The respiratory system. In *Biology and Comparative Physiology of Birds,* Vol. 1, A. J. Marshall, ed. New York.

Schmidt-Nielson, K. 1971. How birds breathe. *Scientific American,* 225:72–9.

Sheid, P. 1982. Respiration and control of breathing. *Avian Biol.* 6:406–53.

RIDGWAY

Ridgway, R. 1895. *Manual of North American Birds,* 2nd ed. Washington, DC.

Ridgway, R., and Friedmann, H. 1901–50. *Birds of North and Middle America.* U.S. Natl. Mus. Bulls. Washington, DC.

See also under BAIRD.

ROOST

Caccamise, L. M., Reed, L. M., Romanowski, J., and Stouffer, P. C. 1997. Roosting behavior and territoriality in American Crows. *Auk* 116:836–41.

Kacelnik, A. 1979. Studies of foraging behaviour and time budgeting in Great Tits *(Parus major).* D. Phil. thesis, Univ. of Oxford.

Smith, S. M. 1972. The roosting aggregations of Bushtits in response to cold temperatures. *Condor* 74:478–9.

Swinebroad, J. 1964. Nocturnal roosts of migrating shorebirds. *Wilson Bull.* 76:155–9.

Ward, P., and Zahavi, A. 1973. The importance of certain assemblages of birds as 'information centers' for food finding. *Ibis* 115:517–34.

SALT GLAND

Cooch, F. G. 1964. A preliminary study of the survival value of a functional salt gland in prairie Anatidae. *Auk* 81:380–93.

Schmidt-Nielson, K. 1959. Salt glands. *Scientific American.* 200:109–16. See also in Schmidt-Nielson. 1983. *Animal Physiology: Adaptation and Environment.* Cambridge, UK.

SEABIRD

Bourne, W.R.P. 1963. A review of oceanic studies of the biology of seabirds. *Proc. (Xlllth) Internatl. Ornith. Congr., Ithaca, N.Y., 1962,* pp. 831–54.
Enticott, J., and Tipling, D. 1997. *Seabirds of the World.* Stackpole.
Fisher, J., and Lockley, R. M. 1954. *Sea-birds.* Boston. (Classic)
Harrison, P. 1983. *Seabirds: An Identification Guide.* Boston, Houghton Mifflin.
———. 1997. *Seabirds of the World: A Photographic Guide.* Princeton, NJ.
Murphy, R. C. 1936. *Oceanic Birds of South America,* 2 vols. New York. (Classic)
Stallcup, R. 1990. *Ocean Birds of the Nearshore Pacific.* Point Reyes Bird Observatory.
See also references under seabird families: ALBATROSS; SHEARWATER; STORM-PETREL; etc.

SHEARWATER

Fisher, J. 1952. *The Fulmar.* London. (Classic)
Lockley, R. M. 1942. *Shearwaters.* London. (Classic)
See also references under SEABIRD.

SHOREBIRD

Drury, W. H. 1961. The breeding biology of shorebirds on Bylot Island, Northwest Territories, Canada. *Auk* 78:176–219.
Gibson, D. 1977. First North American nest and eggs of the Ruff. *Western Birds,* 18:25–6.
Hamilton, R. B. 1975. Comparative behavior of the American Avocet and the Black-necked Stilt (Recurvirostridae). *Ornithol. Monogr.,* no. 17.
Harrington, B. 1996. *The Flight of the Red Knot.* Norton.
Hayman, P., Marchant, J., et al. 1986. *Shorebirds: An Identification Guide to the Waders of the World.* Boston.
Hohn, E. O. 1969. The phalarope. *Scientific American,* 220:104–9, 111.
Johnsgard, P. A. 1981. *The Plovers, Sandpipers and Snipes of the World.* Lincoln, NE.
Paulson, D. 1993. *Shorebirds of the Pacific Northwest.* Vancouver.
Stout, G. D., ed. 1967. *The Shorebirds of North America.* New York. (Large format with fine paintings by Robert Verity Clem, text by Peter Matthiesson, and species accounts by Ralph Palmer.)
Tuck, L. M. 1972. *The Snipes: A Study of the Genus* Capella. Canadian Wildlife Serv. Monogr. Ser. no. 5. Ottawa.
Walton, R. K. and Dodge, G. 1998. *Shorebirds: A Guide to Shorebirds of Eastern North America.* (Video Tape) Brown Bag Productions.

SHRIKE

Harris, T. 2000. *Shrikes and Bush-Shrikes.* Princeton, NJ.
Lefranc, N. 1997. *Shrikes: A Guide to the Shrikes of the World.* New Haven, CT.
Miller, A. H. 1931. Systematic revision and natural history of the American shrikes *(Lanius). Univ. Calif Publ. Zool.,* 38:11–242.

Smith, S. M. 1972. The ontogeny of impaling behavior in the Loggerhead Shrike. *Behaviour* 42:232–47.

SIBLEY

Salzman, E. 1993. Understanding Sibley's classification of birds. *Birding* 25:446–455.

SIZE

Footman, T. ed. 2000. *Guinness World Records 2001*. New York.
Kendeigh, S. C. 1970. Energy requirements for existence in relation to size of bird. *Condor* 72:60–5.
———. 1972. Energy control of size limits in birds. *Am. Nat.,* 106:79–88.
Koford, C. B. 1953. *The California Condor.* Natl. Audubon Soc. Rept. no. 4. New York.
McWhirter, N., et al., eds. 1980. *Guinness Book of World Records.* New York.

SKIMMER

Zusi, R. L. 1962. Structural adaptations of the head and neck in the Black Skimmer. *Linnaeus Publ. Nuttall Ornith. Club* no. 3. Cambridge, MA.
See also references under SEABIRD and TERN.

SKIN

Lucas, A. M., and Stettenheim, P. R. 1972. *Avian Anatomy: Integument.* Washington, DC: U.S. Government Printing Office.
Rawles, M. E. 1960. The integumentary system. In *Biology and Comparative Physiology of Birds*, Vol. 1, A. J. Marshall, ed. New York.
Stettenheim, P. 1972. The integument of birds. In *Avian Biology,* Vol. 2, D. S. Farner et al., eds. New York.

SLEEP

Berger, A. J. 1968. Behavior of hand-raised Kirtland's Warblers. *Living Bird,* 7th annual, pp. 103–16.
Goodman, I. J. 1979. The study of sleep in birds. In *Birds: Brain and Behavior,* I. J. Goodman and M. W. Schein, eds. New York.
Skutch, A. 1993. *Birds Asleep.* Austin: Univ. of Texas Press.
See also references under ROOST.

SMELL

Audubon, J. J. 1826. Account of the habits of the Turkey Buzzard, *Vultor aura,* particularly with the view of exploding the opinion generally entertained of its extraordinary power of smelling. *Edinb. New Philos. J.,* 2:172–84.
Bang, B. G. 1971. Functional anatomy of the olfactory system in 23 orders of birds. *Acta Anat.* Suppl., 58:1–76.
Bang, B. G., and Cobb, S. 1968. The size of the olfactory bulb in 108 species of birds. *Auk* 85:55–61.
Clark, L., and Shah, P. S. 1992. Information content of prey odor plumes: What do foraging Leach's Storm-Petrels know? In *Chemical signals in Vertebrates,* Vol. 6, Doty and Meuller-Schwarze, eds. New York, pp. 231–238.

Clark, L., Avilova, K. V., and Bean, N. J. 1992. Odor thresholds in passerines. *Comp. Biochem.Physiol.* 104A:305–12.

Grubb, T. C., Jr. 1972. Smell and foraging in shearwaters and petrels. *Nature* 237:404–5.

———. 1974. Olfactory navigation to the nesting burrow in Leach's Storm-Petrel. *Anim. Behav.* 22:192–202.

Healy, S., and Guilford, T. 1990. Olfactory bulb size and nocturnality in birds. *Evolution* 44:339–46.

Henton, W. W., Smith, J. C., and Tucker, D. 1966. Odor discrimination in pigeons. *Science* 153:1138–9.

Hutchinson, L. V., and Wenzel, B. M. 1980. Olfactory Guidance in foraging by Procellariiformes. *Condor* 82:314–9.

Stager, K. E. 1964. The role of olfaction in food location by the Turkey Vulture (*Cathartes aura*). *Contr. in Science,* no. 81, Los Angeles County Museum.

Waldvogel, J. A. 1989. Olfaction orientation by birds. *Curr. Ornithol.* 6:269–322.

Wenzel, B. M. 1973. Chemoreception. *Avian Biol.* 3:389–415.

SONG

Ames, P. L. 1971. *The Morphology of the Syrinx in Passerine Birds.* Peabody Mus. Nat. Hist. Bull. no. 37.

Borror, D. J. 1961. Intraspecific variation in passerine bird songs. *Wilson Bull.* 73:57–78.

———. 1964. Songs of the thrushes (Turdidae), wrens (Troglodytidae) and mockingbirds (Mimidae) of eastern North America. *Ohio J. Sci.,* 64:195–207.

Borror, D. J., and Reese, C. R. 1956. Vocal gymnastics in Wood Thrush songs. *Ohio J. Sci.,* 56:177–82.

Brackbill, H. 1961. Duetting in Brown-headed Cowbirds. *Auk* 78:97.

Chapin, J. P. 1922. The function of the esophagus in the bittern's booming sound. *Auk* 39:196–202.

Davis, L. I. 1972. *A Field Guide to the Birds of Mexico and Central America.* Austin, TX.

de Kiriline, L. 1954. The voluble singer of the treetops. *Audubon* 56:109–11.

Derrickson, K.C., and Breitwisch, R. 1992 Northern Mockingbird. In *The Birds of North America,* A. Poole, P. Stettenheim and F. Gill, eds). Philadelphia: Academy of Nat. Science, and Washington, DC: AOU.

Farabaugh, S. M. 1982. The ecological and social significance of duetting. In *Acoustic Communication in Birds,* D. E. Kroodsma and E. H. Miller, eds. New York, pp. 85–124.

Frings, H., and Frings, M. 1959. The language of crows. *Scientific American,* 201:119–31.

Greenewalt, C. H. 1968. *Bird Song: Acoustics and Physiology.* Washington, DC.

Hartshorne, C. 1973. *Born to Sing: An Interpretation and Wold Survey of Bird Song.* Bloomington, IN.

Kellogg, P. P., and Hutchinson, C. M. 1964. The solar eclipse and birdsong. *Living Bird,* 3rd annual, pp. 185–92.

Kroodsma, D. E., and Konishi, M. 1991. A suboscine bird (Eastern Phoebe, *Sayornis phoebe*) develops normal song without auditory feedback. *Anim. Behav.* 42:477–487.

Kroodsma, D. E., and Miller, E. H., eds.1982. *Acoustic Communication in Birds.* New York.

Kroodsma, D. E., and Pickert, R. 1980. Environmentally dependent sensitive periods for avian vocal learning. *Nature* 288:477–9.

Lanyon, W. E., and Tavolga, W. N., eds. 1960. *Animal Sounds and Communication.* Amer. Inst. Biol. Sci. Publ. no. 7. Washington, DC.

Leopold, A., and Eynon, A. E. 1961. Avian daybreak and evening song in relation to time and light intensity. *Condor* 63:209–93.

Marler, P. 1981. Birdsong: The acquisition of a learned motor skill. *Trends Neurosci.* 4:88–94.

———. 1983. Some ethological implications for neuroethology: The ontogeny of birdsong. *Advances in Vertebrate Neuroethology,* J. P. Ewert, R. R. Caprianica, and D. J. Ingle, eds. New York., pp. 21–52.

Marshall, A. J. 1950. The function of vocal mimicry in birds. *Emu* 50:5–16.

Mathews, F. S. 1904. *Field Book of Wild Birds and Their Music.* New York. (Transpositions of birdsongs into traditional musical notation)

Mowrer, O. H. 1950. The psychology of talking birds: A contribution to language and personality theory. In *Learning Theory and Personality Dynamics,* O. H. Mowrer, ed. New York.

Nice, M. M. 1937 and 1943. *Studies in the Life History of the Sparrow,* Parts 1 and 2. Trans. Linn. Soc. New York, nos. 4 and 6.

Nottebohm, F. 1972. The origins of vocal learning. *Am. Nat.* 106:116–40.

———. 1975. Vocal behavior in birds. *Avian Biol.* 5:287–332.

Payne, R. B. 1973. Behavior, mimetic songs and song dialects, and relationships of the parasitic indigobirds (vidua) of Africa. *Ornithol. Monogr.* No. 11.

Perrone, M., Jr. 1980. Factors affecting the incidence of distress calls in passerines. *Wilson Bull.* 92:404–8.

Sauer, F. 1954. Die Entwicklung der Läutausserungen vom Ei ab schalldicht gehaltener Dorngrasmücken *(Sylvia c. communis)* im Vergleich mit später Isolierten und mit wildebenden Artgenossen. *Z. f. Tierpsychol.* 11:10–93.

Saunders, A. A. 1947. The seasons of birdsong: The beginning of song in spring. *Auk* 64:97–107.

———. 1948. The seasons of birdsong: The cessation of song after the nesting season. *Auk* 65:19–30.

Short, L. L. 1966. Field Sparrow sings Chipping Sparrow song. *Auk* 83:665.

Spector, D. A. 1992. Wood warbler song systems: A review of paruline singing behaviors. *Curr. Ornithol.* 9:199–238.

Stokes, A. W., and Williams, H. W. 1968. Antiphonal calling in quail. *Auk* 85:83–9.

Thielcke, G. 1969. Geographic variations in bird vocalizations. In *Bird Vocalizations: Their Relation to Current Problems in Biology and Psychology,* R. A. Hinde, ed. Cambridge, UK.

———. 1972. Duetting and antiphonal song in birds: Its extent and significance. *Behavior,* Suppl. 18 (187 pp.). See also *Auk* 90:451–3 (1973).

Thomas, E. S. 1943. A wren singing the songs of both Bewick's and House Wren. *Wilson Bull.* 55:192–3.

Thomson, W. L. and Pilcher, P. M. 1958. The nature and characteristics of subsong. *Br. Birds* 51:509–13.

Thorpe, W. H. 1961. *Bird Song.* London. (Classic)

Tinbergen, N. 1939. *The Behavior of the Snow Bunting in the Spring.* Trans. Linn. Soc. New York, no. 5.

For a listing of birdsong tapes and CD's, see RECORDING OF BIRD SOUNDS.

SPARROW-BUNTING

Beadle, D. D., and Rising, J. D. 2001. *Sparrows of the US and Canada: A Photographic Guide.* New York.

Byers, C. Olsson, U., and Cursion, J. 1995. *Buntings and Sparrows: A Guide to the Buntings and North American Sparrows.* Northumberland, UK.

Clement, P. 1993. *Finches and Sparrows: An Identification Guide.* Princeton, NJ.
Hamblin, B. 1993. *Sparrows and Other Members of the Finch Family in Action.* (Video tape)
Rising, J. D. 1996. *A Guide to the Identification and Natural History of the Sparrows of the United States and Canada.* New York.

SPECIATION

Bermingham, E., et al. 1992. Vicariance biogeography in the Pleistocene and speciation in North American wood warblers: A test of Mengel's model. *Proc. Natl. Acad. Sci. USA* 89:6624–8.
Boag, P. T., and Grant, P. R. 1981. Intense natural selection in a population of Darwin's Finches (Geospizinae) in the Galapagos. *Science* 214:82–85.
Diamond, J. M. 1974. Colonization of exploded volcanic islands by birds: The supertramp strategy. *Science* 184:803–6.
———. 1980. Species turnover in island bird communities. In *Acta XVII International Ornithological Congress,* R. Nöhring, ed. Berlin, pp. 777–782.
Dilger, W. C. 1956. Hostile behavior and reproductive isolating mechanisms in the thrush genera *Catharus* and *Hylocichla. Auk* 73:313–53.
Gould, S. J., and Eldridge, N. 1972. Punctuated Equilibria: An alternative to phyletic gradualism. In *Models in Paleobiology,* T.J.M. Schopf, ed. San Francisco.
Grant, P. R. 1999. *Ecology and Evolution of Darwin's Finches.* Princeton, NJ.
Grant, P. R., and Grant, B. R. 1997. Genetics and the origin of species. *Proc. Natl. Acad. Sci. USA* 94:7768–75.
Hubbard, J. P. 1969. The relationship and evolution of the *Dendroica coronata* complex. *Auk* 86:393–432.
———. 1973. Avian evolution in the aridlands of North America. *Living Bird,* 12th annual, pp. 155–96.
Klicka, J. A., and Zink, R. M. 1997. The importance of recent ice ages in speciation. A failed paradigm. *Science* 277:1666–9.
Lovette, I. J. and Bermingham, E. 2002. What is a wood warbler? Molecular characterization of a monophyletic Parulidae. *Auk* 119:695–714.
MacArthur, R. H., and MacArthur, J. W. 1961. On bird species diversity. *Ecology* 42:594–8.
Mayr, E. 1942. *Systematics and the Origin of Species.* New York.
———. 1963. *Animal Species and Evolution.* Cambridge, MA.
Mayr, E., and O'Hara, R. J. 1986. The biogeographic evidence supporting the Pleistocene refuge hypothesis. *Evolution.* 40:55–67.
Mengel, R. M. 1964. The probable history of species formation in some northern wood warblers (Parulidae). *Living Bird,* 3rd annual, p. 943.
———. 1970. The North American central plains as an isolating agent in bird speciation. In *Pleistocene and Recent Environments of the Central Great Plains,* W. Dort, Jr., and J. K. Jones, Jr. eds. Lawrence, KS.
Moore, W. S., and Buchanan, D. B. 1985. Stability of the Northern Flicker hybrid zone. *Evolution* 39:135–51.
Moore, W. S. and Price, J. T. 1993. Nature of selection in the Northern Flicker hybrid zone and its implications for speciation theory. *Hybrid Zones and the Evolutionary Process,* R. G. Harrison, ed. Oxford, pp. 196–225.
Moore, W. S., Graham, J. H., et al. 1991. Geographic variation of mitochondrial DNA in the Northern Flicker (*Colaptes auratus*). *Mole. Biol. Evol.* 8:327–44.

Omland, K. E., Lanyon, S. M., and Fritz, S. J. 1999. A molecular phylogeny of the New World orioles (*Icterus*): The importance of dense taxon sampling. *Mol. Phylogenet. Evol.* 12:224–39.

Ricklefs, R. E. and Schluter, D. 1994. *Species Diversity and Communities.* Chicago.

Rising, J. D. 1983. The Great Plains hybrid zones. *Curr. Ornithol.* 1:131–57.

Smith, N. G. 1966. *Evolution of Some Arctic Gulls* (Larus): *An Experimental Study of Isolating Mechanisms.* Am. Ornithol. Union Monogr. no. 4. Washington, DC.

Storer, R. W., and Nuechterlein, G. L. 1992. Western and Clark's Grebes. In *The Birds of North America,* No. 26. (A. Poole, P. Stettenheim, and F. Gill, eds. Philadelphia.

Wiens, J. A. 1989. *The Ecology of Bird Communities,* Vol. 1: *Foundations and Patterns.* Cambridge, UK: Cambridge University Press.

Winkler, D.W., and Sheldon , F. C. 1993. Evolution of nest construction in swallows (Hirundinidae): A molecular phylogenetic perspective. *Proc. Natl. Acad. Sci. USA* 90:5705–7

Wyles, J. S., Kunkel, J. G., and Wilson, A. C. 1983. Birds, behavior and anatomical evolution. *Proc. Natl. Acad. Sci USA* 80:4394–7.

See also references under DISTRIBUTION.

SPEED

Broun, M., and Goodwin, B. V. 1943. Flight speeds of hawks and crows. *Auk* 60:486–92.

Cooke, M. T. 1937. *Flight Speed of Birds.* U.S. Dept. Agric. Circ. no. 428. Washington, DC.

Cottam, C., Williams, C. S., and Sooter, C. A. 1942. Flight and running speeds of birds. *Wilson Bull.* 54:121–31.

Davis, R. A. 1971. Flight speed of Arctic and Red-throated Loons. *Auk* 88:169.

Footman, T., ed. 2001. *Guinness World Records 2001.* New York.

Hayes, S. P., Jr. 1929. Speed of flying hummingbirds. *Auk* 46:116.

McCabe, T. T. 1942. Types of shorebird flight. *Auk* 59:110–1.

Pearson, O. P. 1961. Flight speed of some small birds. *Condor* 63:506–7.

Thompson, M. C. 1961. The flight speed of a Red-breasted Merganser. *Condor* 63:265.

See also Schnell (1965–RADAR).

STARLING

Feare, C. and Craig, A. 1999. *Starlings and Mynas.* Princeton, NJ.

See also references under INTRODUCED BIRDS and PROBLEMS INVOLVING BIRDS.

STATE/PROVINCIAL BOOKS

Listed in alphabetical order by state or province. Many of these books are especially valuable for their fine illustrations and detailed natural history. Most are long out of print, and some are rare.

Alabama

Imhof, T. A. 1962. *Alabama Birds.* Birmingham. (Illustr. by Richard A. Parks and David C. Hulse.)

Alaska

Armstrong, R. H. 1980. *A Guide to the Birds of Alaska.* Anchorage.

Brandt, H. 1943. *Alaska Bird Trails.* Cleveland. (Illustr. by Allan Brooks and E. R. Kalmbach.)

Gabrielson, I. N., and Lincoln, F. C. 1959. *The Birds of Alaska.* Harrisburg, PA.

Alberta

Salt, W. R., and Wilk, A. L. 1966. *The Birds of Alberta,* 2nd rev. ed. Gov't of Alberta, Edmonton.

Arizona

Brandt, H. 1951. *Arizona and Its Birdlife.* Cleveland. (Illustr. by Allan Brooks, Roger Tory Peterson, Terrence Shortt, and George M. Sutton.)

Phillips, A., Marshall, J., and Monson, G. 1964. *The Birds of Arizona.* Tucson. (Illustr. by George M. Sutton and photos by Eliot Porter.)

California

Grinnell, J., and Miller, A. H. 1944. *The Distribution of the Birds of California.* Pacific Coast Avifauna no. 27. Cooper Ornithol. Club. Berkeley.

Small, A. 1974. *The Birds of California.* New York.

Colorado

Bailey, A. M., and Niedrach, R. J. 1965. *Birds of Colorado,* 2 vols. Denver. (Illustr. by 23 artists, including D. Eckelberry, Roger Tory Peterson, and Peter Scott, plus many full-page photos.)

Florida

Sprunt, A., Jr. 1954. *Florida Bird Life.* New York. (Illustr. by F. Lee Jaques and John Henry Dick.)

Georgia

Burleigh, T. D. 1958. *Georgia Birds.* Norman, OK. (Illustr. by George M. Sutton.)

Kentucky

Mengel, R. M. 1965. *The Birds of Kentucky.* Am. Ornithol. Union. Ornith. Monogr. no. 3. (Illustr. by the author.)

Louisiana

Lowery, G. H., Jr. 1974. *Louisiana Birds.* Baton Rouge. (Illustr. by Robert E. Tucker.)

Maine

Palmer, R. S. 1949. *Maine Birds.* Bull. Mus. Comp. Zool. 102:1–656.

Maryland and the District of Columbia

Stewart, R. E., and Robbins, C. S. 1958. *Birds of Maryland and the District of Columbia.* N. Amer. Fauna no. 62:1–401. U.S. Fish and Wildlife Service. Washington, DC.

Massachusetts

Forbush, E. H. 1925–29. *Birds of Massachusetts and Other New England States,* 3 vols. Boston. (Illustr. by Louis Agassiz Fuertes and Allan Brooks.)

Michigan

Wood, N. A. 1951. *The Birds of Michigan.* Univ. Mich. Mus. Zool. Misc. Publ. no. 75.

Minnesota

Roberts, T. A. 1932. *The Birds of Minnesota.* Minneapolis. (Illustr. by George M. Sutton, Walter Weber, F. Lee Jaques, and Louis Agassiz Fuertes; plates also published separately as *Bird Portraits in Color,* Minneapolis, 1960.)

Nevada

Linsdale, J. M. 1936. *The Birds of Nevada.* Pacific Coast Avifauna no. 23. Cooper
Ornithol. Club. Berkeley. (Also: Supplement 1951, *Condor* 53:228–49.)

New Brunswick

Squires, W. A. 1952. *The Birds of New Brunswick.* N.B. Mus. Monogr. Ser. no. 4.

Newfoundland-Labrador

Montevecchi, W. A., and Tuck, L. M. 1987. *Newfoundland Birds: Exploitation,
Study, Conservation.* Cambridge, MA.

Peters, H. S., and Burleigh, T. D. 1951. *Birds of Newfoundland.* Boston. (Illustr. by
Roger Tory Peterson.)

Todd, W.E.C. 1963. *Birds of the Labrador Peninsula and Adjacent Areas.* Toronto.
(Illustr. by George M. Sutton.)

New Mexico

Bailey, F. M. 1928. *Birds of New Mexico.* Albuquerque. (Illustr. by Allan Brooks and
Louis Agassiz Fuertes.)

New York (State)

Bull, J. 1974. *Birds of New York State.* Garden City, NY. (Illustr. by Don Eckelberry,
A. E. Gilbert, Roger Tory Peterson, Arthur Singer, Guy Tudor, and others.)

Eaton, E. H. 1909 and 1914. *Birds of New York.* New York State Mus. Memoir no.
12. 2 vols. (Illustr. by Louis Agassiz Fuertes.)

New York City

Bull, J. 1964. *Birds of the New York Area.* New York.

North Carolina

Pearson, T. J., Brimley, C. S., and Brimley, H. H. 1942. *Birds of North Carolina* (and
revision by D. L. Wray and H. T. Davis, 1959). N.C. Dept. Agric. Raleigh. (1959
edition illustr. by Roger Tory Peterson—field guide plates—and by Bruce
Horsfall.)

Nova Scotia

Tufts, R. W. 1961. *The Birds of Nova Scotia.* Halifax. (Illustr. by John Crosby, John
Henry Dick, and Roger Tory Peterson.)

Oklahoma

Sutton, G. M. 1967. *Oklahoma Birds.* Norman, OK. (Illustr. by the author.)

Oregon

Gabrielson, J. N., and Jewett, S. G. 1940. *Birds of Oregon.* Corvallis, OR.

Pennsylvania

Todd, W.E.C. 1940. *Birds of Western Pennsylvania.* Pittsburgh. (Illustr. by George
M. Sutton.)

South Carolina

Sprunt, A., Jr., and Chamberlain, E. B. 1949. *South Carolina Bird Life.* Columbia,
SC. (Illustr. by F. Lee Jaques, Roger Tory Peterson, and John Henry Dick.)

South Dakota

Over, W. H., and Thomas, C. S. 1946. *Birds of South Dakota.* Rev. ed. Univ. S.D.
Mus. Nat. Hist. Study no. 1.

Texas

Oberholser, H. C., and Kinkead, E. B., Jr., eds. 1974. *The Bird Life of Texas,* 2 vols.
Austin. (Illustr. by Louis Agassiz Fuertes.)

Washington
Aldrich, J. W., Jewett, S. G., Shaw, W. T., and Taylor, W. D. 1953. *Birds of Washington State*. Seattle.

Wisconsin
Gromme, O. J. (artist). 1963 and 1974. *Birds of Wisconsin*. (Plates only.) Madison.

Continental Avifaunas
Godfrey W. E. 1986. *The Birds of Canada*, rev. ed., Ottawa: National Museums of Canada.
Pearson. T. G., ed. in chief. 1937. *Birds of America*. Garden City, NY. (Illustr. by Louis Agassiz Fuertes.)
Reilly, E. M., Jr., and Pettingill, O. S., Jr., eds. 1968. *The Audubon Illustrated Handbook of American Birds*. New York.

Pacific Northwest
Rogers, I. E. 1974. *Shorebirds and Predators-Birds of the Pacific Northwest* (British Columbia, Washington, northern Oregon) Vol. 1. Vancouver. (Despite the title, covers loons through owls.)
See also ATLAS, BREEDING BIRD; BIRD FINDING; and ILLUSTRATION.

STOMACH OIL

Dennis, R. 1970. The oiling of large raptors by Fulmars. *Scot. Birds* 6:198–9.
Sweenen, C. 1974. Observations on the effects of the ejection of stomach oil by the Fulmar, *Fulmarus glacialis*, on other birds. *Ardea* 62:111–7.

STORK

Kahl, M. P. 1971. Social behavior and taxonomic relationships of the storks. *Living Bird*, 10th annual, pp. 151–70.

SUBSPECIES

American Ornithologists' Union. 1957 *A.O.U. Checklist of North American Birds*, 5th ed. (The last edition to include subspecies.)
Gill, F. B. 1982. Might there be a resurrection of the subspecies? *Auk* 99:598–9.
Mayr, E. 1982. Of what use are subspecies. *Auk* 99:593–5.
Phillips, A. R. 1986. *The Known Birds of North and Middle America, Part I*. Denver, CO: Published by the author.
———. 1991. *The Known Birds of North and Middle America*, Part II. Denver, CO: AR Phillips.
Pyle, P. 1997. *Identification Guide to North American Birds*, Part I: *Columbidae to Ploceidae*. Bolinas, CA: Slate Creek Press.

SUNNING

Barlow, J. D., Klass, E. E., and Lenz, J. L. 1963. Sunning of Bank Swallows and Cliff Swallows. *Condor* 65:438–40.
Cade, T. J. 1973. Sunbathing as a thermoregulatory aid in birds. *Condor* 75:106–8.
Hauser, D. C. 1957. Some observations on sun-bathing in birds. *Wilson Bull.* 69:78–90.

Hennemann, W. W. 1982. Energetics and spread-winged behavior of Anhingas in Florida. *Condor* 84:91–6.

Potter, E. F., and Hauser, D. C. 1974. Relationship of anting and sunbathing to molting in wild birds. *Auk* 91:537–63.

Simmons, K.E.L. 1986. *The Sunning Behavior of Birds: A Guide for Ornithologists.* Bristol, UK: British Ornithological Club.

Storer, R. W., Siegfried, W. R., and Kinahan, J. 1975. Sunbathing in grebes. *Living Bird,* 14th annual, pp. 45–56.

SWALLOW

Doughty, R., and Fergus, R. 2002. *The Purple Martin.* Austin, TX.

Turner, A. 1989. *A Handbook to the Swallows and Martins of the World.* London.

SWIFT

Chantler, P. Family Apodidae (Swifts), p. 390 in del Hoyo, J., Elliott, A., and Sargatal, J. eds. 1999. *Handbook of the Birds of the World.* Vol. 5. Barcelona.

Lack, D. 1956. *Swifts in a Tower.* London. (Eurasian Swift, *Apus apus*; classic)

SWIMMING/DIVING

Brooks, A. 1945. The underwater actions of diving ducks. *Auk* 6Z:517–23.

Chase, R. M. 1926. Crow alighting in the water. *Auk,* 43:237.

Dow, D. D. 1964. Diving times of wintering waterbirds. *Auk* 81:556–8.

Footman, T., ed. 2001. *Guinness World Records 2001.* New York.

Heard, W. R. 1960. A record of swimming in Bobwhites. *Wilson Bull.* 72:201.

Heintzelman, D. S., and Newberry, C. J. 1963. Some waterfowl diving times. *Wilson Bull.* 76:291.

Kelso, J. E. H. 1926. Diving and swimming activities displayed by Limnicolae. *Auk* 43:92–3.

Kooyman, G. L., Kooyman, T. G. 1995. Diving behavior of the emperor penguins nurturing chicks at Coulman Island, Antarctica *Condor* 97:536–49.

Merrell, T. R., Jr. 1970. A swimming Bald Eagle. *Wilson Bull.* 82:220.

Prange, H. D., and Schmidt-Nielsen, K. 1970. The metabolic cost of swimming in ducks. *J. Exp. Biol.,* 53:763–77.

Schorger, A. W. 1947. The deep diving of the loon and Oldsquaw and its mechanism. *Wilson Bull.* 59:151–9.

Speich, S., and Speich, M. A. 1972. Floating and swimming in passerines. *Calif. Birds* 3:65–68.

Storer, R. W. 1960. Evolution in the diving birds. *Proc. (Xllth) Internatl. Ornithol. Congr., Helsinki,* 1958, pp. 694–707.

Townsend, C. W. 1909. The use of the wings and feet of diving birds. *Auk* 24:234–48.

SYSTEMATICS

Avise, J. C. 1994. *Molecular Markers, Natural History and Evolution.* New York.

Barrowclough, G. F., and Corbin, K. W. 1978. Genetic variation and differentiation in the Parulidae. *Auk* 691–702.

Berger, A. J. 1959. Leg-muscle formulae and systematics. *Wilson Bull.* 71:93–4.

Blackwelder, R. E. 1967. *Taxonomy: A Text and Reference Book.* New York.

Cooke, F., and P. A. Buckley, eds. 1987. *Avian Genetics: A Population and Ecological Approach.* New York.

Gill, F. B., and F. H. Sheldon. The birds reclassified. *Science* 252:1003–5.

Hillis, D. M., Moritz, C., et al., eds. 1996. *Molecular Systematics.* Sunderland, MA.

Klicka, J., Johnson, K. P., et al. 2000. New World nine-primaried oscine relationships: Constructing a mitochondrial DNA framework. Auk 117:321–36.

Lewontin, R. C. and Hubby, J. L. 1966. A molecular approach to the study of genic heterozygosity in natural populations, II: Amount of variation and degree of heterozygosity in natural populations of *Drosophila pseudoobscura. Genetics* 54:595–609.

Mayr, E. 1942. *Systematics and the Origin of Species.* New York.

———, ed. 1957. *The Species Problem: A Symposium.* Am. Assoc. Adv. Sci. Publ. no. 50. Washington, DC.

Mayr, E., and Amadon, D. 951. A classification of Recent birds. *Am Mus. Novit.* 1496:1–42.

Mayr, E. and Ashcock, P. D. 1991. *Principles of Systematic Zoology.* 2nd ed., New York.

Mindell, D. P., ed. 1997. *Avian Molecular Evolution and Systematics.* New York.

Olson, S. L., and Feduccia, A. 1980. Relationships and evolution of flamingos. *Smithson. Contrib. Zool.* No. 316.

Omland, K. E., Lanyon, S. M., et al. 1999. A molecular phylogeny of the New World Orioles (*Icterus*): The importance of dense taxon sampling. *Mol. Phylogenet. Evol.* 12:224–239.

Payne, R. B. 1986. Bird songs and avian systematics. *Curr. Ornithol.* 3:87–126.

Phillips, A. R. 1986. *The Known Birds of North and Middle America,* Part I. Denver, CO: Published by the author.

———. 1991. *The Known Birds of North and Middle America,* Part II. Denver, CO: A. R. Phillips.

Salzman, E. 1993. Understanding Sibley's classification of birds. *Birding.* 25:446–55.

Selander, R. K. 1971. Systematics and speciation in birds. In *Avian Biology,* Vol. 1, D. S. Farner et al., eds. New York.

Sibley, C. G. 1960. The electrophoretic patterns of avian egg-white proteins as taxonomic characters. *Ibis* 102:215–85.

———. The relationships of the "wren-thrush," *Zeledonia coronata* Ridgway. *Postilla* No. 25.

———. 1970. *A Comparative Study of the Egg-white Proteins of Passerine Birds.* Peabody Mus. Nat. Hist. Bull. no. 32. New Haven, CT.

———. 1997. Proteins and DNA in systematic biology. *Trends in Biochem. Sci.* 22(9):364–7.

Sibley, C. G., and Ahlquist, J. E. 1973. The relationships of the Hoatzin. *Auk* 90:1–13.

Sibley, C. G. and Ahlquist, J. E. 1990. *Phylogeny and Classification of Birds: A Study in Molecular Evolution.* New Haven, CT: Yale University Press.

Sibley, C. G., and Monroe, B. L., Jr. 1990. *Distribution and Taxonomy of the Birds of the World* and *Supplement* (1993). New Haven, CT: Yale University Press.

Storer, R. W. 1969. What is a tanager? *Living Bird,* 8th annual, pp. 127–36.

———. Classification of birds. *Avian Biol.* 1:1–18.

Stresemann, E. 1927–1934. Aves, pp. 729–853. In *Handbush Zoologie,* Vol. VII B. Berlin.

———. 1950. The development of theories which have affected the taxonomy of birds. *Ibis* 92:123–31.

———. 1959. The status of avian systematics and its unsolved problems. *Auk* 76:269–80.

———. 1963. Taxonomic significance of wing molt. *Proc. (Xlllth) Internatl. Ornithol. Congr., Ithaca, NY,* 1962, pp. 171–5.

Wetmore, A. 1960. A classification for the birds of the world. *Smithsonian Misc. Coll.,* 139:1–37.

Winkler, D. W., and Sheldon, F. H. 1993. Evolution of nest construction in swallows (Hirundinidae): A molecularphylogenetic perspective. *Proc. Natl. Acad. Sci. USA* 90:5705–7.

Zink, R. M., and Avise, J. C. 1990. Patterns of mitochondrial DNA and allozyme evolution in the avian genus *Ammodramus. Syst. Zool.* 39:148–161.

TAMENESS

Huxley, J. S. 1947. Notes on the problem of geographical differences in the tameness of birds. *Ibis* 89:539–52. (Subsequent *Ibis* volumes carry responsive notes: 90:312–5; 91:108–10; 356–58, 528.)

Ivor, H. R. 1944. Birds' fear of man. *Auk* 61:203–11.

TANAGER

Morton, L., and Isler, P. R. 1999. *The Tanagers.* London.

Storer, R. W. 1969. What is a tanager? *Living Bird,* 8th annual, pp. 127–36.

TASTE

Duncan, C. J. 1960. Preference tests and the sense of taste in the feral pigeon *(Columba livia). Anim. Behav.* 8:54–60.

Wenzel, B.M. 1973. Chemoreception. *Avian Biol.* 3:389–415.

TAXONOMY

See under SYSTEMATICS.

TECHNOLOGY

Larsen, D. 2000–2002. The wired birder, *Bird Observer,* vols. 28–30.

TEMPERATURE, BODY

Bartholomew, G. A., and Dawson, W. R. 1954. Temperature regulation in young pelicans, herons and gulls. *Ecology* 35:466.

Bartholomew, G. A., Lasiewski, R. C., and Crawford, E. C., Jr. 1968. Patterns of panting and gular flutter in cormorants, pelicans, owls, and doves. *Condor* 70:31–4.

Dawson, W. R., and Whittow, G. C. 2000. Regulation of body temperature, *Sturkie's Avian Physiology,* G. C. Whittow, ed. New York, pp. 343–90.

Hatch, D. E. 1970. Energy conserving and heat dissipating mechanisms of the Turkey Vulture. *Auk* 87:111–24.

Kahl, M. P., Jr. 1963. Thermoregulation in the Wood Stork with special reference to the role of the legs. *Physiol. Zool.* 36:141–51.

Nickell, W. P. 1964. The effects of probable frostbite on the feet of Mourning Doves wintering in southern Michigan. *Auk* 81:56.

Norris-Elye, L.S.T. 1945. Heat insulation in the tarsi and toes of birds. *Auk* 62:455.

Ricklefs, R. E., and Hainsworth, F. R. 1969. Temperature regulation in nestling Cactus Wrens: The nest environment. *Condor* 71:32–7.

TERN

Olsen, K. M., and Larsson, H. 1995. *Terns of Europe and North America*. Princeton, NJ: Princeton University Press.
Wilds, C., and DiCostanzo, J. 2003 *A Guide to the Terns and Skimmers of the World*. New Haven, CT.
See also references under SEABIRD.

TERRITORY

Brown, J. L. 1969. Territorial behavior and population regulation in birds: A review and re-evaluation. *Wilson Bull*. 81:293–329.
Buckley, P. A. and Buckley, F. G. 1977. Hexagonal packing of Royal Tern nests. *Auk* 94:36–43.
Condee, R. W. 1970. The winter territories of Tufted Titmice. *Wilson Bull*. 82:177–83.
Emlen, J. T., Jr. 1973. Territorial aggression in wintering warblers at Bahama agave blossoms. *Wilson Bull*. 85:71–4.
Hensley, M. M., and Cope, J. B. 1951. Further data on removal and repopulation of the breeding birds in a spruce-fir community. *Auk* 68:483–93.
Howard, H. E. 1920. *Territory in Birdlife*. London. (Classic)
MacQueen, P. M. 1950. Territory and song in the Least Flycatcher. *Wilson Bull*. 62:194–205.
Nice, M. M. 1941. The role of territory in bird life. *Am. Midland–Nat*. 26:441–87.
Schoener, T. W. 1968. Sizes of feeding territories among birds. *Ecology* 49:123–41.
Schwartz, P. 1964. The Northern Waterthrush in Venezuela. *Living Bird*, 3rd annual, pp. 169–84.
Stewart, R. E., and Aldrich, J. W. 1951. Removal and repopulation of breeding birds in a spruce-fir forest community. *Auk* 68:471–82.
Tinbergen, N. 1957. The functions of territory. *Bird Study* 4:14–27.
Woolfenden, G. E., and Fitzpatrick, J. W. 1978. The inheritance of territory in group-breeding of birds. *Bio-Science* 28:104–8.

THRASHER

Brewer, D. 2001. *Wrens, Dippers and Thrashers*. New Haven, CT.

THREATS (OF HUMAN ORIGIN) TO BIRDLIFE

Ames, P. L., and Mersereau, G. S. 1964. Some factors in the decline of the Osprey. *Auk* 81:174–85.
Banks, R. C. 1979. *Human-related Mortality of Birds in the United States*. U.S. Fish and Wildlife Serv., Spec. Sci. Rept.—Wildlife, no. 215. Washington, DC.
Bellrose, F. C. 1964. Spent shot and lead poisoning. In *Waterfowl Tomorrow*, J. P. Linduska and A. L. Nelson, eds. Washington, DC.
Bourne, W. R. P. 1970. Special review, after the *Torrey Canyon* (oil spill) disaster. *Ibis* 112:120–5.
Cade, T. J., Lincer, J. L., White, C. M., Roseneau, D. G., and Schwartz, L. E. 1971. DDE residues and eggshell changes in Alaskan falcons and hawks. *Science* 172:955–7.
Carson, R. 1962. *Silent Spring*. Boston.
Cochran, W. W., and Graber, R. R. 1958. Attraction of nocturnal migrants by lights on a television tower. *Wilson Bull*. 70:378–80.
Cornwall, G., and Hochbaum, H. A. 1971. Collisions with wires—a source of anatid mortality. *Wilson Bull*. 83:305–6.

Cott, H. B. 1953–54. The exploitation of wild birds for their eggs. *Ibis* 95:409–49 643–75; 96:129–49.

Dunn, E. 1993. Bird mortality from striking residential windows in winter. *J. Field Ornithol.* 64:302–9.

Grier, J. W. 1982. Ban of DDT and subsequent recovery of reproduction in Bald Eagles. *Science.* 218:1232–35.

Hickey, J. J., and Anderson, D. W. 1968. Chlorinated hydrocarbons and eggshell changes in raptorial and fish-eating birds. *Science* 162:271–3.

Hodson, N. L., and Snow, D. W. 1965. The road deaths inquiry, 1960–61. *Bird Study* 12:90–9.

Johnston, D. W., and Haines, T. P. 1957. Analysis of mass bird mortality in October 1954. *Auk* 74:447–58.

Klem, D., Jr. 1990. Collisions between birds and windows: mortality and prevention. *J. Field Ornithol.* 61:120–8.

Moskoff, W. 2000. The impact of oil spills on birds: Looking back at the *Exxon Valdez. Birding* 32(1):44–9.

Risebrough, R.W. 1986. Pesticides and bird populations. *Curr. Ornithol.* 3:397–427.

Stewart, P. A. 1973. Electrocution of birds by an electric fence. *Wilson Bull.* 85:476–7.

Stoddard, H. L., and Norris, R. A. 1967. *Bird Casualties at a Leon County, Florida, TV Tower: An Eleven-Year Study.* Tall Timbers Res. Sta. Bull. no. 8. Tallahassee, FL.

Temple, S. A. 1972. Chlorinated hydrocarbon residues and reproductive success in eastern North American Merlins. *Condor* 74:105–6.

Tull, C. E., et al. 1972. Mortality of Thick-billed Murres in the West Greenland salmon fishery. *Nature* 237:42–4.

Wetmore, A. 1919. *Lead Poisoning in Waterfowl.* U.S. Dept. Agric. Bull. no. 793. Washington, DC.

THRUSH

Clement, P., Hathway, R., Wilczur, J., and Byers, C. 2000. *Thrushes.* Northumberland, UK.

TIT

Dixon, K. L. 1961. Habitat distribution and niche relationship in North American species of *Parus.* In *Vertebrate Speciation.* Austin, TX.

Harrap, S. 1995. *Chickadees, Tits, Nurthatches and Treecreepers.* Princeton, NJ.

Hartley, P.H.T. 1953. An ecological study of the feeding habits of the English titmice. *J. Anim. Ecol.* 22:261–88.

Smith, S.M. 1991. *The Black-capped Chickadee.* Ithaca, NY.

TONGUE

Gardner, L. L. 1927. On the tongues of birds. *Ibis* ser. 12:185–96.

Weymouth, R. D., Lasiewski, R. C., and Berger, A. J. 1964. The tongue apparatus in hummingbirds. *Acta Anal.* 58:252–70.

TORPIDITY

Bartholomew, G. A., Howell, T. R., and Cade, T. J. 1957. Torpidity in the White-throated Swift, Anna's Hummingbird, and the Poor-will. *Condor* 59:145–55; 61:180–5.

Bartholomew, G. A., Hudson, J. W., and Howell, T. R. 1962. Body temperature, oxygen consumption, evaporative water loss, and heart rate in the Poor-will. *Condor* 64:117–25.

Lasiewski, R. C., and Thomson, A. J. 1966. Field observation of torpidity in the Violet-green Swallow. *Condor* 68:102–3.

Pearson, O. P. 1960. Torpidity in birds. *Bull. Mus. Comp. Zool.* 124:93–103.

TOUCH

Necker, R. 2000. The somatosensory system. *Sturkie's Avian Physiology.* G. C. Whittow, ed. New York, pp. 57–69.

Schaeffer, F. S. 1973. Tactile bristles of Saw-whet Owl are sensitive to touch. *Bird-Banding* 44:125.

TREECREEPER

Harrap, S. 1995. *Chickadees, Tits, Nurthatches and Treecreepers.* Princeton, NJ.

TROGON

Jonsgard, P. A. 2000. *Trogons and Quetzals of the World.* Washington, DC.

TURKEY

Eaton, S. W. 1992. Wild Turkey (*Meleagris gallopavo*). In *Birds of North America*, A. Poole, P. Stettenheim, and F. Gill, eds. Philadelphia, PA and Washington, DC: Academy of Natural Sciences & American Ornithologists' Union.

TYRANT FLYCATCHER

Smith, W. J. 1966. *Communications and Relationships the genus* Tyrannus. Nuttall Ornithol. Club Publ. no. 6. Cambridge, MA.

VAGRANT, VAGRANCY

Veit, R. R. 1990. Do vagrant birds in Massachusetts reflect population growth and dispersal rather than weather patterns? *Bird Observer* 18:86–91.

———. 2000. Vagrants as the expanding fringe of a growing population. *Auk* 117:242–6.

VIDEO

See titles under bird groups e.g., SHOREBIRDS.

VIREO

Sibley, C. G., and Ahlquist, J. E. 1982. The relationship of the vireos (Vireoninae) as indicated by DNA-DNA hybridization. *Wilson Bull.* 94:114–28.

VISION

Bennett, A.T.D., Cuthill, I. C., et al. 1996. Ultraviolet vision and mate choice in zebra finches. *Nature* 380:433–5.

Donner, K. O. 1951. The visual acuity of some passerine birds. *Acta. Zool. Fennica* 66:1–40.

Finger, E., and Burkhardt, D. 1994. Biological aspects of bird colouration and avian colour vision including ultraviolet range. *Vision Res.* 34:1509–14.

Goodge, W. R. 1960. Adaptations for amphibious vision in the Dipper (*Cinclus mexicanus*). *J. Morphol.* 107:79–92.

Hocking, B., and Mitchell, B. L. 1961. Owl vision. *Ibis* 103a:284–8.

Miller, R. S., and Miller, R. E. 1971. Feeding activity and color preference of Ruby-throated Hummingbird. *Condor* 73:309–13.

Shaler, R. 1972. An eagle's eye: Quality of the retinal image. *Science* 176:920–2.

Sillman, A. J. 1973. Avian vision. In *Avian Biology,* Vol. 3, D. S. Farner et al., eds. New York.

Van Rossem, A. J. 1927. Eye shine in birds, with notes on the feeding habits of some goatsuckers. *Condor* 29:25–8.

Walls, G. L. 1942. *The Vertebrate Eye and Its Adaptive Radiation.* Cranbrook Inst. Sci. Bull. no. 19. Bloomfield Hills, MI. (Classic)

Ziegler, H. P., and H.-J. Bischof, eds. 1993. *Vision, Brain and Behavior in Birds.* Cambridge, MA.

VULTURE

Brown, L., and Amadon, D. 1968. *Eagles, Hawks and Falcons of the World,* Vol. 1. New York.

Snyder, N., and H. Snyder. 2000. *The California Condor.* New York.

WARBLER

See WOOD WARBLER, OLD WORLD WARBLER.

WATERFOWL

Bellrose, F. C. 1976. *The Ducks, Geese and Swans of North America.* Harrisburg, PA.

Delacour, J. 1954–64. *Waterfowl of the World,* 4 vols. London. (Illustr. by Peter Scott.)

Delacour, J., and Mayr, E. 1945–46. The family Anatidae. *Wilson Bull.* 57:3–55; 58:104–10.

Johnsgard, P. A. 1968. *Waterfowl: Their Biology and Natural History.* Lincoln, NE.

———. 1975. *Waterfowl of North America.* Bloomington, IN.

———. 1978. *Ducks, Geese and Swans of the World* Lincoln, NE.

Livezy, B. C. 1991. A phylogenetic analysis and classification of recent dabbling ducks (Tribe Anatini) based on comparative morphology. *Auk* 108:471–507.

———. 1995. A phylogenetic analysis of the whistling and White-backed ducks (Anatidae: Dendrocygninae) using morphological characters. *Ann. Carnegie Mus.* 64:65–97.

———. 1995. Phylogeney and comparative ecology of stiff-tailed ducks (Anatidae: Oxyurini). *Wilson Bull.* 107:214–34.

———. 1995. Phylogeny and evolutionary ecology of modern seaducks (Anatidae: Mergini). *Condor* 97:233–55.

———. 1996. A phylogenetic analysis of modern pochards (Anatidae: Aythyini).
    Auk 113:74–93.
———. 1996. A phylogenetic analysis of geese and swans (Anseriformes:
    Anserinae), including selected fossil species. *Syst. Biol.* 45:415–50.
Madge, S., and H. Burn. 1988. *Waterfowl: Identification Guide to the Ducks, Geese,
    and Swans of the World.* Boston.
Todd, F. S. 1997. *Handbook of Waterfowl Identification.* Austin, TX.
Wilmore, S. B. 1974. *Swans of the World.* New York.

WAXWING

Putnam, L. S. 1949. The life history of the Cedar Waxwing. *Wilson Bull.* 61:141–82.

WEATHER

Bagg, A. M. 1967. Factors affecting the occurrence of the Eurasian Lapwing in
    eastern North America. *Living Bird,* 6th annual, pp. 87–121.
Elkins, N. 1983. *Weather and Bird Behaviour.* Watford, UK.
Kreithen, M. L. and Keeton, W. T. 1974. Detection of changes in atmospheric pres-
    sure by the homing pigeon, *Columba livia. J. Comp. Physiol.* 89:73–82.
Lack, D. 1960. The influence of weather on passerine migration: A review. *Auk*
    77:171–209.
Larsen, D. M. 2001. The wired birder: birding weather. *Bird Observer,* 29:455–8.
    (Includes weather websites)
Linsay, G. 1967. Prairie Chickens died under crusted snow. *Passenger Pigeon* 29:25–8.
McClure, H. E. 1945. Effects of a tornado on birdlife. *Auk* 62:414–8.
Merrill, G. W. 1961. Loss of 1,000 Lesser Sandhill Cranes. *Auk* 78:641–2. (No-
    vember 10, 1960)
Moss, S. 1995. *Birds and Weather: A Birdwatcher's Guide.* Middlesex, UK.
Rett, E. Z. 1938. Hailstorm fatal to California Condors. *Condor* 40:255.
Richardson, W. J. 1978. Timing and amount of bird migration in relation to
    weather: A review. *Oikos* 30:224–272
Smith, A. G., and Webster, H. R. 1955. Effects of hail storms on waterfowl popula-
    tion in Alberta, Canada—1953. *J. Wildlife Management,* 19:368–74.
Stewart, P. A. 1972. Mortality of Purple Martins from adverse weather. *Condor*
    74:480.
Veit, R. R. 1990. Do vagrant birds in Massachusetts reflect population growth and
    dispersal rather than weather patterns? *Bird Observer* 18:86–91.
Zimmer, J. T. 1951. Birds and lightning. *Nat. Hist.* 60:143.

WILSON

Burns, F. L. 1908–10. Alexander Wilson. *Wilson Bull.* 20:1–18, 63–79, 130–45,
    165–85; 21:16–35, 132–51, 165–86; and 22:79–96.
Plate, R. 1966. *Alexander Wilson: Wanderer in the Wilderness.* New York.
Wilson, A. 1808–14. *American Ornithology, or the Natural History of the Birds of
    the United States,* 9 vols. Philadelphia. (A number of more recent editions in
    fewer volumes.)

WOODPECKER

Burt, W. H. 1930. Adaptive modifications in the woodpeckers. *Univ. Calif. Publ.
    Zool.* 3:455–524.

Ellison, W. G. 1992. Different drummers: Identifying the rhythms of northeastern woodpeckers. *Birding* 24:350–5.
Lawrence, L. de K. 1967. *A Comparative Life History Study of Four Species of Woodpeckers.* Am. Ornithol. Union Ornith. Monogr. no. 5.

WOOD WARBLER

Curson, J. 1994. *Warblers of the Americas: An Identification Guide.* Boston.
Dunn, J. L., and Garrett, K. 1997. *Warblers of North America.* (Peterson Field Guide) Boston.
Ficken, M. S., and Ficken, R. F. 1962. The comparative ethology of wood warblers: A review. *Living Bird,* 1st annual, pp. 103–22.
Griscom, L., and Sprunt, A., Jr., eds. 1957. *The Warblers of North America.* New York. Reprinted 1979.
Kendeigh, S. C. 1945. Nesting behavior of wood warblers. *Wilson Bull.* 57:499–513.
Male, M., and Fieth, J. 1996. *Watching Warblers: A Video Guide to the Warblers of Eastern North America.*
Mengel, R. M. 1964. The probable history of species formation in some northern wood warblers (Parulidae). *Living Bird,* 3rd annual, p. 943.
Morse, D. H. 1989. *American Warblers.* Cambridge, MA.

WREN

Brewer, D. 2001. *Wrens, Dippers and Thrashers.* New Haven, CT.

XANTHOCHROISM

Harrison, C.J.O. 1966. Alleged xanthochroism in bird plumages. *Bird-Banding* 37:121.
Saunders, A. A. 1958. A yellow mutant of the Evening Grosbeak. *Auk* 75:101.

YELLOWLEGS

Sill, B., Sill, C., and Sill, J. 1988. *A Field Guide to Little-known and Seldom-seen Birds of North America.* Atlanta.

YOUNG, DEVELOPMENT OF

Mock, D. W. 1984. Infanticide, siblicide, and avian nestling mortality. In *Infanticide: Comparative and Evolutionary Perspectives.* G. Hausfater and S. Hrdy, eds. New York: Aldine, pp. 3–30.
Mock, D. W., and Parker, G. A. 1997. *The Evolution of Sibling Rivalry.* Oxford, UK: Oxford University Press.
Nice, M. M. 1943. *Studies in the Life History of the Song Sparrow,* Parts 1 and 2. Trans. Linn. Soc. New York, nos. 4 and 6.
———. 1962. *Development of Behavior in Precocial Birds.* Trans. Linn. Soc. New York, no. 8.
O'Connor, R. J. 1984. *The Growth and Development of Birds.* New York.
Rabinowitch, V. E. 1968. The role of experience in the development of food preferences in gull chicks. *Anim. Behav.* 16:425–8.
Ricklefs, R.E. 1983. Avian postnatal development. *Avian Biol.* 1–83.

ZOOGEOGRAPHY

Darlington, P. J., Jr. 1957. *Zoogeography: The Geographic Distribution of Animals.*
    New York.
Udvardy, M.D.F. 1969. *Dynamic Zoogeography.* New York.
Vuilleumier, F. 1975. Zoogeography. In *Avian Biology,* Vol. 5, D. S. Farner et al., eds.
    New York.
See also references under DISTRIBUTION.